CRIMINAL LAW

CRIMINAL LAW

Mark Thomas

Hall and Stott Publishing Ltd
27 Witney Close
Saltford
BS31 3DX

British Library Cataloguing in Publication Data
Data available

ISBN 978 1 916243 13 2

Typeset by Style Photosetting Ltd, Mayfield, East Sussex

PREFACE

It is amazing to think that three years ago, I was asked by Hall and Stott to produce a criminal law textbook. Whilst the text is only in its second edition, I am ever so humbled by the fantastic feedback it has received. This text continues to be constructed in a manner I feel will act in the most beneficial manner for its readers. It begins with a discussion of general principles of the criminal law before then proceeding into a detailed review of the most common subjects to feature on a criminal law syllabus, including the major fatal and non-fatal offences against the person and offences against property. Each chapter is designed to introduce readers to the subject matter under consideration and provide a detailed account of the applicable rules before then proceeding to evaluate and comment upon the state of the law. Each chapter features examples to assist readers in applying the law to factual scenarios and a helpful summary of how such rules apply in practice. Each chapter ends with a review of the law as it stands, two examination-style questions for readers to test their understanding, and a list of further reading to allow readers to consolidate their study.

The text is also accompanied by a companion website (www.hscriminallaw.co.uk) which features an online chapter dedicated to answering questions in criminal law, a glossary of legal terminology and an updates section which features new statutory, case law and academic developments in the criminal law. Since the first edition, readers will have experienced a multitude of updates, ranging from case notes, legislation updates and academic commentary. Readers can also follow me @MThomas_CrimLaw on Twitter for regular updates.

The new edition of this text has been fully updated to reflect the current state of the criminal law. Since 2018, the law has been faced with a number of new and fascinating developments. To give one example, in April 2020, we learnt that the case of *Ivey v Genting Casinos* (which was a new and ground breaking development for the 1st edition of this text) has now been approved by the criminal courts with no uncertainty or confusion (*R v Barton; R v Booth* [2020] EWCA Crim 575). Since the last edition, society has also been faced with a new threat; and the coronavirus pandemic continues to sweep the globe. Commentary on how the criminal law has adapted to take account of COVID-19 related offences is a further addition included in this already fully packed textbook. To ensure that the book retains an element of practical and contextual focus, the book has been updated to take account of the changes made to the Crown Court Compendium (updated July 2020).

I hope that this textbook continues to act as an authoritative and up-to-date source of information, and detail, for those dealing with the criminal law.

The law is generally stated as at 6 June 2020, although account has been taken of some later developments as at 2 August 2020.

Mark Thomas
Nottingham Law School, Nottingham Trent University

CONTENTS

PART III OFFENCES AGAINST PROPERTY

TABLE OF CASES

A

B

C

D

E

N

O

P

R

U

V

W

Y

TABLE OF LEGISLATION

Page numbers in **bold** refer to statutory extracts

Statutory instruments

Codes

EU Legislation

International Legislation

France

Germany

Hong Kong

New Zealand

Youth Justice [illegible] 1999 [illegible]
s [illegible]
[illegible] and Criminal [illegible]
s 16 [illegible] 653

Youth Justice and Criminal Evidence Act 1999
s 24 [illegible]
s 41 [illegible]
s 41(3) [illegible]
[illegible]

Statutory Instruments
Criminal Procedure Rules 2015 (SI 2015/1490) [illegible]
r 10.2 [illegible]
Health Protection (Coronavirus, Restrictions) (England) Regulations 2020 (SI 2020/350)
reg 6 [illegible]
[illegible] Order [illegible] (SI [illegible])

Codes
Code for Crown Prosecutors
s [illegible]
Code of Practice on the Detention and [illegible]
[illegible]
s [illegible]
[illegible] 1999 [illegible]
s [illegible]
s [illegible]
s [illegible]

EU Legislation
Treaty of [illegible]

[illegible] Convention [illegible]
Article [illegible]
Art [illegible]
Art [illegible]
Article [illegible]
Article [illegible]
Article [illegible]
Article [illegible]
Article [illegible]
Article [illegible]
Article [illegible]
Article 7 [illegible]
Article 9, 10 [illegible]
Article 9, 10 [illegible]
Article 10 [illegible]
Rome Statute (1998) [illegible]
United States Constitution
Article XIV [illegible]

France
[illegible]
Article [illegible]

Germany
Penal Code
Article [illegible]

Hong Kong
Hong Kong [illegible]
[illegible]

New Zealand
New Zealand [illegible] Act [illegible]

ABBREVIATIONS

AAA 1861	Accessories and Abettors Act 1861
ABH	actual bodily harm
CAA [1968, 1995]	Criminal Appeal Act
CAA 1981	Criminal Attempts Act 1981
CADA 1998	Crime and Disorder Act 1998
CAJA 2009	Coroners and Justice Act 2009
CCA 2013	Crime and Courts Act 2013
CCRC	Criminal Cases Review Commission
CDA 1971	Criminal Damage Act 1971
CJA [1925, 1967, 1972, 1978, 1988, 1991, 1993, 2003]	Criminal Justice Act
CJIA 2008	Criminal Justice and Immigration Act 2008
CMCHA 2007	Corporate Manslaughter and Corporate Homicide Act 2007
CLA [1967, 1977]	Criminal Law Act
CPIA 1964	Criminal Procedure (Insanity) Act 1964
CPS	Crown Prosecution Service
ECHR	European Convention on Human Rights
ECtHR	European Court of Human Rights
FA 2006	Fraud Act 2006
GBH	grievous bodily harm
HA 1957	Homicide Act 1957
HRA 1998	Human Rights Act 1998
IA 1938	Infanticide Act 1938
LASPO 2012	Legal Aid, Sentencing and Punishment of Offenders Act 2012
MCA 1980	Magistrates' Courts Act 1980
MCA 2005	Mental Capacity Act 2005
OAPA 1861	Offences Against the Person Act 1861
SA 1961	Suicide Act 1961
SCA 2007	Serious Crime Act 2007
SOA [1956, 1976, 1993, 2003]	Sexual Offences Act
TA [1968, 1978]	Theft Act

chapter 1 Introduction to the Criminal Law

study points

After reading this chapter, you will be able to understand:

- what is meant by the study of the 'criminal law'
- how substantive criminal law differs from procedural or evidential law
- the definition of crime, and whether such definition is possible
- the principles and values that underpin the criminal law, and the functions of the criminal law
- the sources of the criminal law
- the process of the criminal justice system
- the basic principles of criminal liability.

1.1 Introduction

Welcome to the criminal law!

In this text, we shall be taking an expedition through the criminal law of England and Wales. The criminal law is a vast and diverse subject and arguably one of the most popular foundations of a law degree. I often explain to my own students that the criminal law is 'real life', in that it is easy to identify situations where the criminal law is involved in some way. This may be compared with other areas of law, such as equity and trusts, which, although essential to an understanding of law, does not fix itself quite so easily in the minds of students.

In this text, you will learn about the core features of the substantive criminal law. We shall explore the necessary elements for a criminal offence to exist, the participants involved in the criminal process and the main criminal offences covered on an undergraduate criminal law syllabus.

1.2 The purpose of this text

This text has been written to provide you with a clear and accurate account of the *substantive* criminal law in England and Wales. It is worth pausing here to consider why we refer in this book to the law of 'England and Wales' and not the 'United Kingdom'. England is a constituent part of the 'United Kingdom of Great Britain and Northern Ireland', alongside Wales, Scotland and Northern Ireland. However, as a result of different traditions and devolution over the years, the legal system of the UK has diverged. Legally speaking, the UK is divided into three 'constituent' countries, each of which is subject to the laws of the UK; however, each constituent country possesses devolved powers allowing it to legislate in particular areas. This text concerns only the law of England and Wales and does not deal with Scots law or the law of Northern Ireland.

1.2.1 'Substantive criminal law'

The term 'substantive criminal law' is used here to distinguish it from the wider concept of the criminal law, incorporating criminal procedure and the law of evidence. Substantive criminal law refers to the criminal offences that exist in our legal system and the elements that must exist in order for an individual to be liable for those offences. The term 'liability' will feature throughout this text and simply refers to the legal obligations or responsibilities that may arise against a particular individual. In the context of the criminal law specifically, 'liability' means 'responsibility for illegal behaviour that causes harm or damage to someone or something' (*Cambridge Business English Dictionary* (CUP, 2011)).

We can helpfully distinguish the substantive criminal law from other areas by observing the following table.

Table 1.1 Distinguishing the substantive criminal law

Term	Explanation
Substantive criminal law	The law relating to the manner in which criminal offences are defined and the elements of the offence necessary in order for an individual to be found liable.
Criminal procedure	The law relating to court structure and the progression of a criminal case through the criminal justice system, including the investigation of the crime by the police, the prosecution of offenders and criminal appeals. Criminal procedure also includes sentencing and the principles behind sentencing powers.
Criminal evidence	The law relating to the material that may be produced at trial in order to prove, or disprove, a particular issue in a criminal offence. The law of evidence is often referred to as 'adjectival' in nature.
Criminal justice	Criminal justice refers to the theory behind the criminal law in terms of its operation and its rationale. Criminal justice also includes a concept known as 'restorative justice' which is concerned with bringing those harmed by crime and those responsible for the harm into communication, enabling everyone affected by a particular incident to play a part in repairing the harm and finding a positive way forward.
Criminology	Criminology refers to the socio-legal study of why crime is committed, the reasons behind the commission of crime by certain individuals or groups of individuals and how legal policy may be implemented to prevent the commission of offences. A number of 'strands' of criminology exist, for example penology (the study of punishment of crime and prison management) and 'deviance' (the study of actions that violate social norms).

An example may assist you in understanding the focus of this book.

example

Jack and Jill go up the hill to fetch a pail of water. Jill pushes Jack down the hill and he is injured as a result (he breaks his crown).

In this very simple scenario, our concern is whether Jill, through her actions in pushing Jack down the hill, is criminally liable for an offence. That is the focus of the substantive law. In order to determine Jill's liability, we would have to establish:

- what kind or 'category' of offence Jill may be liable for;
- what the elements of that offence are and whether Jill satisfies those elements; and
- whether Jill has a potential defence to the charge against her.

Although a simple factual scenario, a number of questions should hopefully spring to mind. For example:

- Did Jill intend to push Jack *down the hill* or did she just intend to push him to the floor?
- Did Jill intend to push Jack at all or were her actions an accident?
- What level of harm did Jack suffer? Was he seriously hurt or just bruised?
- Did the pail of water fall down with Jack, and did that cause him any harm that would not have been caused had he not held the pail of water?

These questions, although abstract in nature, are essential for assessing the true extent of Jill's liability and the direction the criminal law will take in relation to her activities.

As a result, we are not concerned, for example, with:

- how it might be proved that Jill pushed Jack down the hill, eg through the testimony of an eye witness – a matter for the law of evidence;
- how Jill will be charged, prosecuted and sentenced for the offence in question – a matter for criminal procedure and sentencing;
- why Jill pushed Jack down the hill – a matter for the study of criminology.

Although our concern is with the substantive law, the remainder of this chapter will explain a number of key concepts that will help you to understand the wider context and dynamism of the criminal law in England and Wales.

The chapter will conclude with an overview of the three key components to establishing the criminal liability of an individual. This will then provide us with a comfortable transition into a more detailed appreciation of the substantive criminal law.

1.3 Defining crime

It is worth noting immediately that there is no 'universal' definition of a crime. What constitutes a crime in one country may not constitute a crime in another. For example, in Iran, homosexual relations are illegal and punishable in some cases by death. In England and Wales, homosexual acts were illegal prior to the Sexual Offences Act 1967. In this respect, it is also relevant to note that whether particular conduct amounts to a criminal offence will vary and change as time progresses. By way of another example, prior to the Suicide Act 1961, the act of suicide was a criminal offence. Where an individual failed in such an attempt, they would be liable to a criminal conviction, with the penalty ranging between a fine and imprisonment. Historically, where an individual succeeded in taking their own life, their belongings would be surrendered to the Crown. By way of a final example at this stage, prior to the ground-breaking case of *R v R (Rape: Marital Exemption)* [1992] 1 AC 599, it was not considered unlawful for a man to rape his wife.

These examples, however, do not actually tell us how we can define 'crime'. They merely provide examples of what amounts, or has amounted, to a criminal offence. For the most part, academics agree that the starting point in defining a crime is the attitude adopted by the state in relation to certain conduct. For instance, Farmer ('Definitions of Crime' in Cane and Conaghan (eds), *The New Oxford Companion to Law* (OUP, 2008)), contends:

> It is now widely accepted that crime is a category created by law—that is, a law that most actions are criminal because there is a law that declares them to be so—so this must be the starting point for any definition.

In *Board of Trade v Owen* [1957] AC 602, Lord Tucker in the House of Lords concluded that a crime could be defined as

> an unlawful act or default which is an offence against the public, and renders the person guilty of the act or default liable to legal punishment.

This definition, unfortunately, offers no assistance as to why certain conduct is considered 'criminal'. According to Farmer, modern definitions of crime fall under two headings:

- the moral definition; and
- the procedural definition.

Farmer explains the moral definition as

> based on the claim that there is (or should be) some intrinsic quality that is shared by all acts criminalized by the state. This quality was originally sought in the acts themselves—that all crimes were in an important sense moral wrongs, or *mala in se*—and that the law merely recognized this wrongful quality.

It can be explained then, by this definition, that certain conduct or actions are considered crimes in order to recognise public wrongs as violations of the rights and duties owed to the whole community. This view accords with that of Hart ('The Aims of the Criminal Law' (1958) 23 L & CP 401) who considered that a crime is 'conduct which … will incur a formal and solemn pronouncement of the moral condemnation of the community'.

The procedural definition is favoured by other writers such as Williams ('The Definition of Crime' (1955) 8 CLP 107), who defined a crime as

> An act capable of being followed by criminal proceedings having a criminal outcome, and a proceeding or its outcome is criminal if it has certain characteristics which mark it as criminal. ... Criminal law is that branch of law which deals with conduct … by prosecution in the criminal courts.

Albeit a rather circular term (a crime is a crime if it is a crime), this definition accords with the modern practicalities of the criminal law as providing a rigid and detailed structure for the operation of charging and punishing the commission of criminal offences (see below at **1.7**).

1.4 The need for the criminal law?

In speaking of the 'need' for the criminal law, we are essentially considering the justifications for the imposition of criminal liability. In addition, we are concerned with the respective 'functions' of the criminal law in its operation. By way of overview, the 'Report on Homosexual Offences and Prostitution' (1957) (Cmnd 247) (the 'Wolfenden Report') considered the purpose of the criminal law to be

> to preserve public order and decency, to protect the citizen from what is offensive or injurious, and to provide sufficient safeguards against exploitation and

> corruption of others, particularly those who are especially vulnerable ... It is not ... the function of the law to intervene in the private lives of citizens, or to seek to enforce any particular pattern of behaviour, further than is necessary to carry out the purposes we have outlined.

1.4.1 Functions of the criminal law

The functions (or 'purposes') of the criminal law are many and varied. Some commentators rank certain functions above others, whilst other commentators argue that the functions act in conjunction to provide for a consistent and clear approach. Understanding these functions is often helpful when critically analysing the state of the criminal law and observing whether the substantive law achieves, or fails to achieve, one of its functions. Some of the main functions of the law can be listed as follows:

- protection of individual rights and liberties;
- maintenance of public order;
- enforcement of legal rules and orders;
- the conferral of obligations;
- the regulation of human behaviour and relationships; and
- punishment of behaviour contrary to legal rules and orders.

1.4.2 An 'overuse' of the criminal law?

Ashworth ('Is the Criminal Law a Lost Cause?' (2000) 116 LQR 225) questions the extent to which the criminal law operates in today's legal structure. With reference to the lack of real comprehension as to the number of criminal offences in existence and the ambiguity as to the creation of new criminal offences, Ashworth contends that the criminal law may be a lost cause. See Chalmers and Leverick, 'Tracking the Creation of Criminal Offences' [2013] Crim LR 543 for an interesting discussion of the number of offences alleged to have been created by the Labour Government between 1997 and 2006 (suggested to be 3,023).

1.5 Principles of criminal law

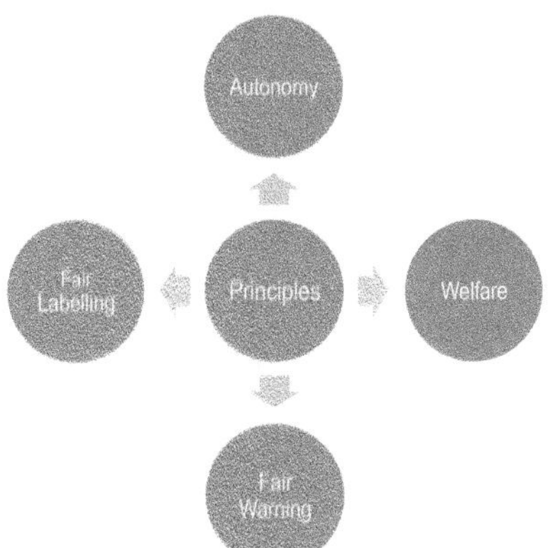

Figure 1.1 The principles of the criminal law

A number of principles or 'ideals' that underpin the operation of the substantive criminal law have been identified over the long history of our common law system. The principles, similar to the concept of the Rule of Law, are essentially the 'aims' or 'models' of behaviour and attitude expected of the criminal law.

The four key principles are identified in **Figure 1.1** and explained below at **1.5.1–1.5.4**.

For a more detailed account of the four principles, see Horder, *Ashworth's Principles of Criminal Law*, 9th edn (OUP, 2019).

1.5.1 Principle of 'fair warning'

This principle reflects the idea that the law should be communicated in a clear and accessible manner to the public. Given that England and Wales has a common law legal system, it has long been advocated that, in order to give true effect to this principle, the criminal law should be codified, as in civil law systems. Robinson ('A Functional Analysis of Criminal Law' (1994) 88 Nw UL Rev 857) is of the view that multiple codes are required in order to promote this principle. Robinson advocates the use of a code written in simple language explaining to the public what they can and cannot do (a 'rule articulation' code) and codes that are used for the administration and enforcement of law (a 'liability assessment' code).

The principle of fair warning is essential to understanding how an offence should be defined. References to undefined or ambiguous terms in a statute, for example, would be contrary to the principle of fair warning. By way of example, the term 'dishonesty' used in the Theft Act 1968 has not been afforded a statutory definition, despite its dominating presence in the law. The common law has had to step in to provide such a definition, but it is necessary, for the promotion of this principle, that the definition is clear, accessible and informs the general public of what they cannot do (ie what is dishonest and, as such, what they cannot do which is dishonest).

1.5.2 Principle of 'fair labelling'

Horder (*Ashworth's Principles of Criminal Law*, 9th edn (OUP, 2019)) states that the concern of fair labelling is as follows:

> ... to see that widely felt distinctions between kinds of offences and degrees of wrongdoing are respected and signalled by the law, and that offences are subdivided and labelled so as to represent fairly the nature and magnitude of the law-breaking.

In essence, there must be an accurate and visible link between the label (ie the name of the offence) and the conduct criminalised. The fairness of labelling is relevant for two main reasons:

- It promotes the fair warning principle in that people who understand the label associated with the offence will inevitably understand the offence and what they can and cannot do.
- It promotes transparency and objectivity in the criminal justice system by stigmatising individuals with an accurate label (eg a rapist or a murderer).

The key in this discussion, however, is on the concept of *fair* labelling. One of the biggest criticisms of the law of murder is the fact that an individual may be guilty of murder where they kill but did not intend to kill; rather, they intended to cause serious harm. Is it appropriate, or 'fair', to label these individuals as murderers in circumstances where they lacked the actual intention to kill? The label must fit the crime.

1.5.3 Principle of 'welfare'

The idea behind this principle is that the law acts in a quasi-paternalistic way by ensuring that society is protected from harm. This involves harm to individuals and harm to property. The concept of welfare, however, depends on the perception one adopts. From the standpoint of a victim, the welfare principle ought to be designed to ensure that the victim is protected from interference by another (linked closely with the autonomy principle), and in circumstances where an interference has occurred, the legal system is designed to promote the conviction of the offender. At the same time, the welfare principle must ensure that those alleged to have committed offences are appropriately safeguarded through ensuring proper procedures are adopted, a fair trial is in place and any sentence passed, should there be one, is reflective of the offence committed. The difficulty here is finding that appropriate balance between conflicting interests and understanding the circumstances where the interests come into play.

1.5.4 Principle of 'autonomy'

The last principle is that of autonomy. The idea behind autonomy is that an individual is subject to little restraint with minimal interference from another person. Autonomy is often linked with self-determination and integrity in the sense that no undue influence, pressure or interference should be made. Naturally, of course, the criminal law is designed to restrict the manner in which we can act – therefore interfering with our autonomy. In this respect, any interference with autonomy should be kept to a minimum as over-criminalisation is likely to interfere with this sacred principle.

1.6 Sources of criminal law

Throughout this textbook, references will be made to a multitude of legal authority stemming from both domestic and international sources. Before it is possible for you to get to grips with these sources of law, it is first necessary identify the basis, use and relevance of the authority in England and Wales. Being able to identify the relevant source of law is key when answering questions in criminal law.

1.6.1 Common law

For many years, the common law acted as the driving force for legitimising and providing authority for legal principles. The common law has developed over hundreds of years from the judgments and decisions of the judiciary in the senior appellate courts. Through the operation of case precedent and the principle of *stare decisis* ('let the decision stand'), England and Wales has operated, and continues to operate, as a common law system. Although many rules and principles have now been codified in legislative provisions, the common law continues to act alongside and fortify legislation in major areas of the criminal law. One important example of this is the law of murder, which continues to this day to operate as a common law offence defined, and interpreted, by judicial decision making. In addition, as part of their role, the judiciary are responsible for interpreting and giving effect to legislative provisions – such interpretations add to the common law and the judicial law-making system that we have today.

1.6.2 Legislation

The term 'legislation' is used, and preferred here, over the term 'statute' to refer to any law, primary or secondary, created by Parliament. Although the majority of criminal legislation is set out in statute, ie Acts of Parliament, a number of provisions continue to operate by other forms of legislation, such as byelaws (a form of delegated legislation). Unfortunately, there is no 'catalogue' of legislation for the criminal law. Many offences are contained within statutes which, for the most part, do not concern the criminal law. For example, the Companies Act 2006 creates a number of statutory criminal offences.

1.6.2.1 Case law and legislation

Although the starting point in any case is to consider the wording of the statute that creates the offence, if there is one, this is merely the first step. In order to properly understand legislation, one needs to appreciate how the courts interpret such legislation. For example, s 18 of the Offences Against the Person Act (OAPA) 1861 prescribes the offence of maliciously causing grievous bodily harm with intent. Without an appreciation of the meaning of such words as 'maliciously', 'causing' and 'bodily harm', one cannot truly understand the circumstances in which the offence applies. In this respect, case law is as important, if not arguably more important, than its legislative counterpart. Indeed, the Law Commission in a 1992 Consultation Paper, 'Legislating the Criminal Code: Offences against the Person and General Principles' (Law Com No 122, 1992) noted that some of the most important offences under the OAPA 1861 'have become in effect common law crimes, the context of which is determined by case-law and not by statute'.

For a discussion of the principles of statutory interpretation, see Sanson, *Statutory Interpretation*, 2nd edn (OUP, 2016).

1.6.3 International influences

Although the English legal system is distinct and admired across the world, it cannot of course be said to be perfect. Nor can it be said that the English legal system operates in a vacuum without any influence or information from other international states and organisations. This section will briefly consider international influences on the criminal law.

1.6.3.1 European Union

The origins of the EU, as we know it, can be located in the Treaty establishing the European Economic Community (EEC) 1957 (Treaty of Rome), signed by six founding states. This was the Treaty that set the foundations that the EU is built upon today. The UK joined the EEC in 1973 following the enactment of the European Communities Act (ECA) 1972.

The EU is built on three pillars and its role was traditionally understood as regulating trade and commercial matters in Member States. Criminal law matters have remained, largely, a matter for the Member States to decide for themselves. In this respect, it can be said that, traditionally, the EU lacked the competency to legislate in criminal law matters – this would explain the lack of consistency or uniformity across EU Member States in such matters as the age of criminal responsibility (see **Chapter 7**) and the age of consent to sexual conduct (see **Chapter 10**). In more recent years, however, EU law has been seen to have some impact on the domestic criminal law in the context of trafficking offences and European arrest warrants.

Ultimately, however, English and Welsh criminal law remains largely a matter of national regulation. As a result of the European Union Referendum Act 2015, a national referendum as to whether the UK should leave the EU was held on 23 June 2016. By a narrow margin, the vote to leave was successful and the UK is now in the process of formally removing itself from the EU. The future influence of EU law generally remains largely unknown; however, it is certain that the domestic criminal law will for the most part go untouched.

1.6.3.2 European Convention on Human Rights (ECHR)

The ECHR was drawn up by the Council of Europe, a body set up after the end of the Second World War. The Council (which is entirely distinct from the EU) was established to prevent any repetition of the atrocities that had occurred during the war and the period leading up to it. The ECHR was signed in Rome in 1950, ratified by the UK in 1951 and came into force in 1953. From 1966 onwards, citizens of the UK had the right to petition the ECtHR (which sits in Strasbourg) where there was an alleged breach of human rights.

The ECHR was transposed (ie incorporated) into national law by the Human Rights Act 1998, which came into effect on 2 October 2000. Prior to the incorporation of the ECHR in domestic law, there was no opportunity for citizens to enforce their Convention rights in the domestic courts, meaning that individual petition directly to the ECtHR was the only way to seek a remedy for alleged breaches.

Convention rights

Unlike domestic legislation or the common law, which sets out the offences that an individual may commit and the defences they may equally plead to a charge, the ECHR sets out a number of 'Convention rights' that apply to all natural persons. **Table 1.2** lists these rights and considers examples of their application in the criminal law.

Table 1.2 Convention rights under the ECHR

Article	Application
Article 2: Right to life	All persons are granted the right to life and the protection of such right by the state. In cases where a defendant kills another in self-defence, the law has to be interpreted in light of Article 2.
Article 3: Prohibition of torture	All persons are granted the freedom from torture and other inhuman and degrading treatment. Whether the chastisement of children (by parents or those responsible for children (eg teachers in schools)) falls within the prohibition in Article 3 has long been the subject of argument. Torture is a criminal offence under s 134 of the Criminal Justice Act 1988.
Article 4: Prohibition of slavery	All persons are granted the freedom from slavery and other forms of forced labour. Slavery is now criminalised under s 1 of the Modern Slavery Act 2015, which is particularly relevant in the context of human trafficking and sexual exploitation.
Article 5: Right to liberty	All persons are granted the right to liberty and security. Article 5 is particularly relevant in terms of pre-trial imprisonment and detention pending trial and is also relevant regarding the state's obligations to those found to be legally insane.
Article 6: Right to a fair trial	All persons are granted the right to a fair trial and to have their case heard and decided by an impartial tribunal. This right grants the presumption of innocence to a defendant and enforces obligations on the prosecution to prove the case against the defendant.
Article 7: Prohibition on retrospective law	All persons are granted the freedom from retrospective application of laws. Article 7 also requires sufficient clarity and consistency in the law and a minimised allowance of discretion.
Article 8: Right to private life	All persons are granted the right to private and family life. This right means that the life of an individual cannot be interfered with by another. Such rights include the right to privacy and the protection of personal information.

Article	Application
Article 9: Freedom of thought, conscience and religion	All persons are granted the freedom from other persons interfering with their thought or religion. Specific offences have been created to reflect the freedom of religion, eg aggravated offences based on religion or belief.
Article 10: Freedom of expression	All persons are granted the freedom of speech and the freedom to express themselves in a particular way. This right must be balanced against the right to privacy in Article 8.
Article 11: Freedom of assembly and association	All persons are granted the freedom to assemble. Article 11 is particularly relevant where the defendant is liable for a public order offence involving the assembly of more than one person (eg riot).
Article 12: Right to family life	Further to Article 8, all persons are granted the right to family life. One debate focuses on whether unmarried couples should be treated differently under the law to married couples.
Article 13: Right to an effective remedy	All persons have the right to an effective remedy where an individual's rights have been breached. Under s 8 of the HRA 1998, a court may grant such relief or remedy as it considers just and appropriate where it finds that an act by a public authority is unlawful.
Article 14: Right to non-discrimination	All persons have the right not to be discriminated against in terms of their Convention rights.

By s 6 of the HRA 1998, it is unlawful for 'public authorities' to violate any Convention right or act in a way that is incompatible with a Convention right. 'Public authority' includes courts and tribunals and private individuals and organisations performing public functions (s 6(3)(b)) but does not include either House of Parliament (s 6(3)).

Obligation on the courts

Section 2 of the 1998 Act provides that judges must take into account the jurisprudence of the ECtHR when determining an issue arising in connection with a Convention right. This is the relevance of the ECHR to domestic law. In addition to their obligations under s 2, s 3 of the HRA 1998 also provides that judges must interpret national legislation 'so far as is possible' in line with the Convention. In circumstances where the legislation cannot be interpreted in line with the Convention, domestic courts must make a declaration of incompatibility (HRA 1998, s 4). The effect of this declaration is not to make the law invalid but to require Parliament to consider the need for reform (see *AG's Reference (No 4 of 2002)* [2005] 1 AC 264).

1.6.3.3 International law

According to the website of the United Nations (<www.un.org>), international law 'defines the legal responsibilities of States in their conduct with each other, and their treatment of individuals within State boundaries'. International law sets rules and policies that govern relations between international states and their citizens.

Beginning with a membership of 51, the United Nations, amongst other bodies, is responsible for addressing the needs of 193 Member States. According to Article 2, para 1 of the UN Charter, international law is 'based on the principle of the sovereign equality of all its Members'. Each Member State is thus considered equal and not subject to any form of supranational authority without the consent of the Member State concerned.

International law can be considered as relevant to the domestic criminal law in two respects:

- *International criminal offences:* The Rome Statute 1998 had the effect of creating the International Criminal Court (ICC) and defining core international criminal offences, such as genocide, war crimes and crimes against humanity. These crimes were incorporated into domestic law by the International Criminal Court Act 2001. These offences are not considered in any further detail in this text, but for a full treatment, you may wish to consult, for example, Guilfoyle, *International Criminal Law* (OUP, 2016).
- *Influence on domestic law:* Given that the majority of offences lack any international sphere (eg a battery is unlikely to have any international implications), domestic law rarely integrates with international law and conventions. However, certain offences, for example fraud and blackmail, can be committed on such a large scale that their relevance moves towards the international remit.

1.6.3.4 The law of other jurisdictions

The criminal law is territorial in nature, meaning that it applies, for the most part, in England and Wales. However, law from such jurisdictions as Canada, New Zealand, Australia, and the USA may be relevant when considering our own law in comparison. On many occasions, the Supreme Court, in determining a matter of interpretation, will turn to the law of another state to understand how a term has been defined there. In this respect, the law of other jurisdictions (not to be confused with our concept of 'international law' above) is a useful and potentially persuasive aid to the interpretation of our own law. On a more academic level, law from other jurisdictions is vital in evaluating the law and identifying the strong (and equally weak) points in our own legal system.

1.6.4 Reform

The substantive criminal law is continuously under review as a result of judicial interpretation, Parliamentary reform and academic commentary. Such detailed review means that the criminal law is far from being a static subject; rather, it can best be described as a dynamic and cumulative body of rules influenced by a social and political backdrop. Throughout this text, references will be made to the 'reform' of a particular area of law. Such content will allow us to delve deeper into the substantive law and evaluate its effectiveness. In order to do so, however, we first need to be able to comprehend the different bodies responsible for reviewing and reforming the criminal law.

1.6.4.1 Law Commission

The Law Commission was set up in 1965 following the enactment of the Law Commissions Act (LCA) 1965 for the purpose of 'promoting the reform of the law' (LCA 1965, s 1(1)). The Commission is headed by a Chairman (at the time of writing, Sir Nicholas Green) and four Commissioners, including Professor Penney Lewis, who is the Commissioner for criminal law. The Commission is an independent body, though it is sponsored by the Ministry of Justice. The aim of the Law Commission is to ensure that the law is:

- fair;
- modern;
- simple; and

- cost effective.

The work of the Law Commission in reforming the criminal law has been pre-eminent for a number of years (and has effectively superseded the work of the Criminal Law Revision Committee (CLRC)). The Commission will produce a consultation paper before then publishing a full report, with the potential inclusion of a draft Bill. Many reports have been successfully adopted by the government of the day (see, for example, 'Assisting and Encouraging Crime' (Law Com No 131, 2006) which was implemented by the Serious Crime Act 2007). These reports are useful for providing detailed summaries of the law as it stands, the problems with the law and the proposals for reform. Other reports have not been accepted by the government (eg 'Intoxication and Criminal Liability' (Law Com No 314, 2009)).

1.6.4.2 Draft Criminal Code

Many countries, mostly civil law countries, have a Criminal Code, which sets out the definitions for all criminal offences, defences and procedures. These Codes are comprehensive in nature. The Law Commission, for many years, has proposed the adoption of a Criminal Code for England and Wales. In 1989, the Law Commission proposed a draft Criminal Code ('Criminal Code for England and Wales' (Law Com No 177, 1989)) which would have codified the majority of the existing laws on the general principles of criminal liability and specific offences against the person, property and those relating to public order. The Code lays out the fundamental rules of the criminal law and provides detailed definitions, explanations and circumstances to aid in the understanding of the criminal law.

Bennion ('Codification of the Criminal Law – Part 2: The Technique of Codification' [1986] Crim LR 105) took the view that the proposed reform was over-generalised and incomplete. Particularly, Bennion was critical of the simplified nature of the Code, expressing that 'you do not simplify by oversimplifying'. Ashworth ('Codification of the Criminal Law – Part 3: The Draft Code, complicity and the inchoate offences' [1986] Crim LR 303) furthers this view, contending that an oversimplified version of the Code would have provided judges with too much discretion.

Where relevant in this text, we shall be referring to key proposals made in the draft Code. At the time of writing, Parliament is yet to adopt the Code, and it is unlikely that the Code will ever be adopted, which Child and Ormerod (*Smith, Hogan, & Ormerod's Essentials of Criminal Law*, 3rd edn (OUP, 2019)) consider to be 'regrettable'. The Law Commission's response to this is to produce so-called 'mini-codes' that deal with specific areas of legal reform.

1.6.4.3 Judicial law making

It is essential to open this section by explaining that the role of judges and the courts is not to make law – it is to interpret law. Prior to the decision in *Knuller v DPP* [1973] AC 435, the appellate courts were understood as holding a power to create new criminal offences. In *Knuller*, however, the House of Lords renounced this power on the basis that any such changes should be made by Parliament.

Despite the decision in *Knuller*, many examples exist of the appellate courts exercising law-making powers. For instance, in *R v R (Rape: Marital Exemption)* [1992] 1 AC 599, the House of Lords took it upon itself to rule that non-consensual sexual intercourse within marriage should no longer be exempt from criminal liability. In essence, the House of Lords created a new offence of marital rape. I prefer to view *R v R* as more of a reflection of the gradual development of the common law. Indeed, this was the view taken by the ECtHR in *CR v UK* [1996] 1 FLR 434 upon a referral of *R v R*. The Court was of the view that, although Article 7 of the ECHR restricts and prevents the operation of retrospective laws, it does not prevent the evolution of the common law.

With the implementation of the Human Rights Act 1998, judicial law-making powers must now be read in accordance with their international obligations of consistency. As a result of the inherent change it was about to face, the House of Lords in *C v DPP* [1996] AC 1 gave the following guidance to judges (per Lord Lowry):

> (1) If the solution is doubtful, the judges should beware of imposing their own remedy. (2) Caution should prevail if Parliament has rejected opportunities of clearing up a known difficulty or has legislated while leaving the difficulty untouched. (3) Disputed matters of social policy are less suitable areas for judicial interventions than purely legal problems. (4) Fundamental legal doctrines should not lightly be set aside. (5) Judges should not make change unless they can achieve finality and certainty.

1.7 Criminal procedure, evidence and sentencing: an overview

As discussed earlier, the substantive criminal law is concerned with the definition and categorisation of offences; it concerns what features or elements must be present in a given case for a person to be 'liable' for a criminal offence. It is, however, naïve to believe that the substantive criminal law operates to the exclusion of other areas of criminal justice. The following section considers briefly some of the fundamental principles that shape the criminal justice system as we know it today. You are advised to consult a textbook on English legal system for a broader discussion (see, for example, Thomas and McGourlay, *English Legal System Concentrate*, 2nd edn (OUP, 2020)).

1.7.1 Criminal procedure

Criminal procedure refers to the manner in which an individual, charged with an offence, proceeds through the criminal justice system. The rules governing this procedure are set out in the Criminal Procedure Rules (Crim PR) (available at <www.justice.gov.uk>).

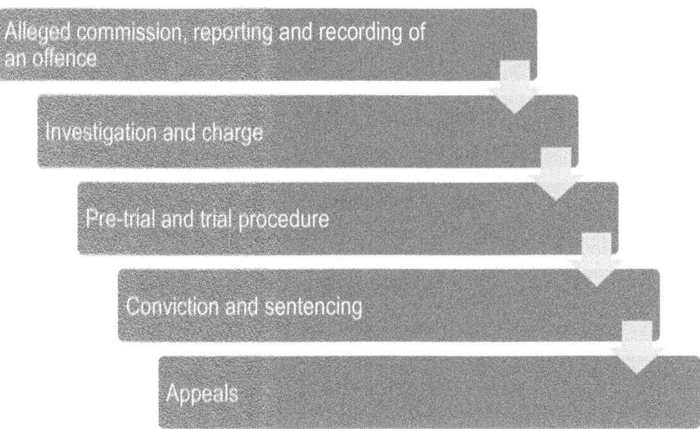

Figure 1.2 Process of the criminal justice system

For our purposes, we shall focus on classification of offences and sentencing, as these considerations will feature when discussing the substantive criminal offences.

1.7.1.1 Charge

Following the alleged commission of the offence and any investigation thereafter, if there is sufficient evidence against the individual suspected of committing the offence, that individual will be 'charged'. The decision to charge a suspect rests, largely, with the CPS. In order for a suspect to be charged, the 'Full Code Test' must be satisfied. The Full Code Test is provided under section 4 of the Code for Crown Prosecutors and is set out in two parts. The Code states that the individual or body considering a charge must be satisfied that:

(a) there is sufficient evidence to provide for a realistic prospect of conviction (known as the *evidential stage*); and
(b) it is in the public interest to prosecute (known as the *public interest stage*).

If the relevant officer is content that the Full Code Test has been met, he or she may proceed to charge the suspect with an offence. See the fascinating case of *SXH v CPS* [2017] UKSC 30 in which the Supreme Court had to consider whether it was a breach of Article 8 of the ECHR (right to private life) to prosecute an individual for a criminal offence.

1.7.1.2 Classification of offences

In charging an individual with an offence, it is essential to understand how criminal offences are classified in England and Wales. Such classification is generally provided by the statute creating the offence by way of the description of the nature of the penalty on conviction. Three types of classification can be identified:

(a) *Summary-only offences:* These are the least serious of the three classes of offences and are triable only in the magistrates' court.
(b) *Either-way offences:* Either-way offences may be tried either in the magistrates' court or in the Crown Court. Where an either-way offence is tried in the magistrates' court, it is tried as a summary offence, and where tried in the Crown Court, it is tried as an indictable offence.
(c) *Indictable-only offences:* These are the most serious of the three classes of offences and are triable only in the Crown Court with a jury.

Examples of such offences are provided in **Table 1.3**.

Table 1.3 Understanding the classification of offences

Type of offence	Court in which it will be heard	Examples and maximum sentence
Summary-only	magistrates' court	Common assault – 6 months
Either-way	magistrates' court/Crown Court	ABH – 6 months (summary); 5 years (indictment) Theft – 6 months (summary); 7 years (indictment)
Indictable-only	Crown Court	Murder – Life Rape – Life

1.7.1.3 Conviction and sentencing

Following trial, whether in the magistrates' court or the Crown Court, it will then be the responsibility of the jury or magistrates to return their verdict. Should the verdict be one of not guilty, the defendant is acquitted and is free to go. Should the verdict be one of guilty, the defendant is convicted and sentence must be passed.

For the principles of sentencing and the types of sentences available to the courts, see **1.7.3**.

1.7.2 Evidence

The law of evidence refers to the materials which may be produced in open court to prove that the defendant has, or has not, committed the offence in question. Although in theory (ie in the substantive law), a defendant may appear to be liable for a criminal offence, whether such liability is proven in practice will ultimately depend on the evidence available, the use of that evidence and how the arbiters of fact treat that particular evidence. For a thorough account of the law of evidence, see Doak, McGourlay and Thomas, *Evidence: Law and Context*, 5th edn (Routledge, 2018).

1.7.2.1 Principles of evidence

The rules of evidence are predicated on a number of core principles that apply to most forms of evidence. These core principles are detailed in **Table 1.4**.

Table 1.4 Core principles of evidence

Core principle	Explanation
Admissibility	The admissibility of evidence is a matter for the arbiter of law, ie the judge or magistrates. In *R v Terry* [1996] 2 SCR 207 (Canada) it was held that evidence will be admissible if: (a) it is relevant; (b) such that a jury, properly warned about any defects it might have, could place some weight on it; and (c) it is not excluded by any rule of law.
Relevance	The relevance of evidence is also a matter to be determined by the arbiter of law. According to Lord Simon in *DPP v Kilbourne* [1973] AC 729, evidence is relevant if 'it is logically probative or disprobative of some matter which requires proof'. This essentially means that if the evidence goes to prove or disprove a particular matter in issue between the parties, it is considered as being relevant.
Weight	The weight of the evidence is a matter for the arbiters of fact; it is their role to determine how much weight they wish to afford to a particular piece of evidence. Like relevance, weight is a question of degree and ultimately depends on how the arbiters of fact view the usefulness of the evidence. At one end of the spectrum, the evidence may be of little probative value, being so weak that it is described as 'insufficient evidence', whereas, at the other end, it may be virtually conclusive of the facts in issue that it is described as '*prima facie* evidence'.

The use of these principles ultimately depends upon the matter which is sought to be proven/disproven. In this respect, there are two matters that are relevant to the law of evidence:

(a) *Facts in issue:* These are the facts that are at the centre of a criminal trial and refer to the issue being contested between the parties. In a crime where the defendant pleads not guilty on account that he did not commit the offence, every element of that offence therefore becomes a fact in issue – ie whether the defendant committed each element is in contention. In a similar vein, where a defendant pleads not guilty on account of one element of an offence (eg that a complainant did consent to sexual intercourse), then the only fact in issue relevant to this case is whether the complainant consented or not. Every other issue, ie whether there has been an act of sexual intercourse, is therefore irrelevant.

(b) *Collateral facts:* These are facts that do not form part of the facts in issue. These facts are relevant in terms of the reliability of witnesses and the evidence produced. Counsel will often cross-examine a witness regarding their evidence in an attempt to discredit them, eg by suggesting that they are mistaken or, potentially, lying.

1.7.2.2 Types of evidence

There are a number of different forms of evidence that may be admitted in a criminal trial that go towards proving a fact in issue or collateral fact. These forms can be divided into a number of different categories:

Table 1.5 Types of evidence (explained)

Type of evidence	Explanation
Direct	This refers to evidence that is 'first hand', meaning that the witness who is communicating the evidence, either orally at trial (known as 'live evidence') or through a witness statement, witnessed the event personally. The witness may have evidence that relates to what they saw, heard, felt, smelt or tasted (ie their five senses). Such evidence is the most important and persuasive. An example could be that Jack saw Jill in an alleyway committing a murder.
Indirect	More often referred to as 'hearsay' evidence, this is admitted evidence that is not a direct testimony of what the witness saw or heard; rather, hearsay evidence concerns information that the witness was informed of by another. An example could be that Jack was told by Andy that he saw Jill in the alleyway where the murder was committed on the night of the murder, and Jack relays this information to the court because Andy is unable to do so for some reason.
Documentary	This refers to any evidence that is not produced in open court by live testimony. Such matters as witness statements, police interview records, CCTV recordings, etc all amount to documentary evidence. An example could be that the nightclub which is next to the alleyway has a CCTV recording of the alleyway showing Jill committing the offence.
Circumstantial	This refers to evidence that is neither direct nor hearsay, but rather goes to prove, by inference, a particular fact in issue. The focus on such evidence, therefore, is on the inference that may be drawn by the presence of such evidence. An example could be that Jack saw Jill running from the alleyway where the murder was committed.
Real	This refers to the physical objects relevant to the criminal offence, eg a knife or a gun. Such evidence is useful but only where it is used or considered alongside other evidence. An example could be that the police recover a knife from the alleyway where the murder was committed, Jack says that he saw Jill with the knife and it is discovered that Jill's fingerprints are on the knife.
Expert	This refers to the evidence given by an expert in relation to a matter that requires clarification or detailed knowledge in that area. An expert may be required to explain how a gun works, or whether the defendant is suffering from insanity, etc. An example could be that expert evidence is admitted to explain the presence of Jill's fingerprints on the knife.

1.7.2.3 Burden and standard of proof

Burden of proof

In criminal cases, the fundamental principle is that the prosecution bears the burden of proving that the defendant committed the offence in question. This fundamental principle is known as the 'golden rule' and was emphasised by the House of Lords in *Woolmington v DPP* [1935] AC 462, where Viscount Sankey famously stated:

> Throughout the web of English criminal law one golden thread is always to be seen, that it is the duty of the prosecution to prove the prisoner's guilt.

This principle is reinforced by Article 6(2) of the ECHR which prescribes that an individual is to be considered innocent until proven guilty. There are, however, exceptions to the principle that the prosecution bears the burden of proof. Before we consider these, however, it is first necessary to explain what burdens of proof exist. Two burdens of proof exist, namely:

- the legal (persuasive) burden; and
- the evidential burden.

The legal burden, also known as the 'persuasive' burden, is the obligation placed on a party to prove a fact in issue (see **1.7.2.1**). In the majority of cases, the prosecution bears the burden of proving the legal burden, ie it has the burden of proving all of the facts necessary to establish the defendant's guilt. This is so even if this involves proving negative elements; for example, in a case of rape, the prosecution bears the burden of proving that sexual activity took place (a positive element) and that the complainant did not consent (a negative element) (*R v Horn* (1912) 7 Cr App R 200). Whether the legal burden is discharged is a matter of fact for the arbiters of fact.

The legal burden can be compared with the evidential burden, which is merely an obligation on a party to adduce sufficient evidence to raise a fact in issue, ie to make an issue live. Such examples may be the need to raise sufficient evidence of the existence of a defence, such as self-defence. Whether the evidential burden is discharged is a matter of law for the judge. Where the evidential burden has been discharged, the judge can place the evidence before the arbiters of fact who can use it in determining whether the legal burden has been discharged.

As explained above, the golden rule (or 'thread' as it is also known) is that in all criminal proceedings, the prosecution bears the legal burden of proof. This is, however, subject to a number of exceptions which Doak, McGourlay and Thomas, *Evidence: Law and Context*, 5th edn (Routledge, 2018) argue have 'tarnished' the golden thread. These exceptions are more likely to concern the requirement to prove the existence of a defence, as opposed to disproving an element of an offence. The ways in which such exceptions come about are detailed briefly in **Table 1.6**.

Table 1.6 Tarnishing the golden thread

Exceptions to the golden rule	Explanation
Common law	The only common law rule which reverses the burden of proof involves the defence of insanity, where the defendant bears the burden of proving that the defence exists (*M'Naghten's Case* (1843) 10 Cl & Fin 200).

Exceptions to the golden rule	Explanation
Statute (express)	In many cases, legislation will stipulate quite clearly that there is a reverse burden and the defence must prove certain circumstances to be in existence in order to make use of an available defence. For example, s 2(2) of the Homicide Act 1957 provides that the defendant must prove the defence of diminished responsibility.
Statute (implied)	In other cases, the legislation will not prescribe that a reverse burden exists, but, as a result of s 101 of the Magistrates' Courts Act 1980, where the defendant intends to rely on any 'exception, exemption, proviso, excuse or qualification' in the statute, it is his obligation to prove such exception. This rule only applies to cases tried in the magistrates' court but the common law has extended the principle to cases tried in the Crown Court also (*R v Edwards* [1975] QB 27).

These reverse burdens are controversial given the potential effect they may have on a defendant's right to a fair trial. It is contended that such reverse burdens do not affect a defendant's right to a fair trial as they affect only the requirement to prove the existence of a defence and not to disprove an element of the offence. The presumption of innocence remains intact by requiring the prosecution to prove that an offence took place; it is only fair that the defence bears a limited burden of proving the existence of a defence. In circumstances where the reverse burden appears to require the defendant to disprove an element of the offence, the courts have been quick to 'read down' the provision under s 3(1) of the HRA 1998, such that it merely imposes an evidential burden. This was evident in the case of *R v Lambert* [2001] UKHL 37 concerning a charge of possession of drugs.

In *AG's Reference (No 4 of 2002)* [2005] 1 AC 264, the House of Lords held that in order for a reverse burden of proof to be legitimate, there must be compelling reasons justifying why it is fair and reasonable to deny the accused person the protected right under the ECHR. See Dennis, 'Reverse Onuses and the Presumption of Innocence' [2005] Crim LR 901 for a discussion of the lawfulness of such reverse burdens.

Standard of proof

In criminal cases, the standard of proof refers to the level or degree of proof that must be established. Two standards of proof exist, namely:

- the criminal standard: 'beyond a reasonable doubt'; and
- the civil standard: 'on the balance of probabilities'.

The criminal standard is expressed as a requirement to satisfy the burden of proof 'beyond a reasonable doubt'. This standard is quite often expressed as 'a', 'all' or 'any' reasonable doubt and has been defined by Lord Denning in *Miller v Minister of Pensions* [1947] 2 All ER 372 as follows:

> It need not reach certainty, but it must carry a high degree of probability. Proof beyond reasonable doubt does not mean proof beyond a shadow of a doubt. The law would fail to protect the community if it admitted of fanciful possibilities to deflect the course of justice. If the evidence is so strong against a man as to leave only a remote possibility in his favour which can be dismissed with the sentence, 'of course it is possible but not in the least probable', the case is proved beyond reasonable doubt but nothing short of that will suffice.

This criminal standard applies in all criminal trials, whether before magistrates or on indictment before a jury, and if there is a reasonable doubt created by the evidence adduced either by the prosecution or by the defence, the prosecution has not made out its case and the burden is not satisfied. The criminal standard has also been expressed over the years in terms of 'so that the jury are "sure"' (*R v Majid* [2009] EWCA Crim 2563). In *R v Folley* [2013] EWCA Crim 396, the Court of Appeal expressed these two terms as synonymous with each other.

The civil standard is expressed as a requirement to satisfy the burden of proof 'on the balance of probabilities'. Lord Denning offered a definition of this term, also in the *Miller* case, as: 'If the evidence is such that the tribunal may say "we think it is more probable than not" the burden is discharged, but if the probabilities are equal it is not.' In a similar vein, the Court of Appeal in *R v Carr-Briant* [1943] KB 607 reasoned that the burden of proof will be discharged where the arbiters of fact conclude that it is 'more likely than not' that the fact existed.

The correct 'use' of the standard of proof depends on the party who bears the particular burden of proof. This is detailed in **Table 1.7**.

Table 1.7 The appropriate standard of proof

Where the burden is on the ...	The standard is...
Prosecution	'Beyond a reasonable doubt'
Defence	'On the balance of probabilities'

1.7.3 Sentencing

The law on sentencing in criminal cases is detailed and complex. Textbooks, both academic and practitioner, are available solely dealing with the topic of sentencing. This section is aimed at giving you a brief overview of sentencing powers, the rationale for sentencing and the procedure involved.

1.7.3.1 Purposes of sentencing

Sentencing is best described as the manner in which the court deals with an offender who has been convicted of an offence. As a starting point, the 'purposes' of sentencing can be identified by reference to s 142(1) of the CJA 2003, which provides:

> Any court dealing with an offender in respect of his offence must have regard to the following purposes of sentencing—
> (a) the punishment of offenders,
> (b) the reduction of crime (including its reduction by deterrence),
> (c) the reform and rehabilitation of offenders,
> (d) the protection of the public, and
> (e) the making of reparation by offenders to persons affected by their offences.

It is worth noting at this stage that s 142(1) is applicable only to adult offenders. The law treats youth offenders in a different respect. By s 142A(3), the courts must take into account all of the purposes listed above with the exception of (b) 'the reduction of crime', and in addition must have regard to the 'principal aim' of the youth justice system, namely 'to prevent offending and re-offending' (Crime and Disorder Act 1998, s 37(1)). Furthermore, the welfare of the offender must be taken into account (Children and Young Persons Act 1933, s 44).

1.7.3.2 Sentencing Council

Established in April 2010 to replace and amalgamate the roles of the Sentencing Advisory Panel and the Sentencing Guidelines Council, the Sentencing Council for England and Wales is an independent body designed to create and issue guidelines on sentencing which courts must follow. See Part IV, Chapter 1 of the Coroners and Justice Act (CAJA) 2009.

As part of its role, the Council is responsible for:

- developing sentencing guidelines and monitoring their use;
- assessing the impact of guidelines on sentencing practice; and
- promoting awareness amongst the public regarding the realities of sentencing and publishing information regarding sentencing practice in the magistrates' court and the Crown Court.

In constructing these guidelines, the Council is required, by s 120(11) of the CAJA 2009, to have regard to:

(a) the sentences imposed by courts in England and Wales for offences;
(b) the need to promote consistency in sentencing;
(c) the impact of sentencing decisions on victims of offences;
(d) the need to promote public confidence in the criminal justice system;
(e) the cost of different sentences and their relative effectiveness in preventing re-offending;
(f) the results of the monitoring carried out under section 128.

Further, by s 121 of the CAJA 2009, the Guidelines must be designed in such a way that they include the following information.

Table 1.8 Structure of the Sentencing Council Guidelines

Source	The Guidelines should ...
s 121(2)	Describe the different categories of case involving the commission of the offence which illustrate in general terms the varying degrees of seriousness with which the offence may be committed.
s 121(4)(a)	Specify the range of sentences ('the offence range') which, in the opinion of the Council, it may be appropriate for a court to impose on an offender convicted of that offence.
s 121(5)	Specify the sentencing starting point in the offence range.
s 121(6)(a)	List any aggravating or mitigating factors which, by virtue of any enactment or other rule of law, the court is required to take into account when considering the seriousness of the offence and any other aggravating or mitigating factors which the Council considers are relevant to such a consideration.

These guidelines, although 'definitive', are not absolute in that they allow for the discretion of judges. By s 125(1) of the CAJA 2009, every judge in sentencing an offender must follow any sentencing guidelines that are relevant to the offender's case 'unless the court is satisfied that it would be contrary to the interests of justice to do so'.

1.7.3.3 Sentencing powers

Sentencing, generally, can take one of two forms (or both):

- custodial; and
- non-custodial.

The sentencing powers of both the magistrates' court and the Crown Court are detailed in **Table 1.9**. It should be noted that these powers are ultimately affected by a number of factors, including the statutory maximum for the offence, the court in which the offender is sentenced, the age of the defendant and the plea of the defendant.

Table 1.9 Sentencing powers

Sentencing power	magistrates' court	Crown Court
Custodial	• maximum 6 months (for a single summary offence); • maximum 6 months (for multiple summary offences); or • maximum 12 months (for multiple either-way offences).	No maximum except statutory maximum.
Non-custodial	Fine: Maximum £5,000 Community order (maximum 3 years), for example: • unpaid work; • curfew requirement; and • electronic monitoring requirement. Discharge: This is when the court decides that punishment would not be appropriate for this particular defendant. There are two types of discharge: (a) Absolute discharge – no further action is taken, although the offender will receive a criminal record. (b) Conditional discharge – no further action is taken, although the offender will receive a criminal record. Action may be taken where the individual commits a further offence within a period of time set by the court.	Fine: Unlimited

1.8 Nature of criminal liability

'Actus non facit reum nisi mens sit rea.'

Interpreted by Lord Hailsham LC in *Haughton v Smith* [1975] AC 476 as meaning '[a]n act does not make a man guilty of a crime, unless his mind be also guilty', this Latin maxim is the cornerstone of English criminal law.

Lord Hailsham LC went on to state that 'It is thus not the *actus* which is *reus* but the man and his mind respectively.' In basic form it means that in order for a defendant to be *reus* (Latin for 'guilty') of a criminal offence, they must complete an 'act' and also have the 'intention' to commit the act. Evil thoughts or bad intentions, therefore, are not sufficient to impose liability on an individual. They may, however, be used as evidence against him should he act on such thoughts.

The maxim does not tell the whole story though. There are certain offences where the need for a 'guilty mind' is unnecessary. These are generally known as 'strict liability' offences and often concern minor offences or offences that are regulatory in nature. We shall consider strict liability in greater detail in **Chapter 3**.

For the majority of crimes, there are three key elements that must be satisfied before a defendant can be liable for an offence. These are:

- *actus reus*;
- *mens rea*;
- no defence.

Figure 1.3 Elements of a criminal offence

Where a defendant is charged with a criminal offence and has pleaded not guilty, the prosecution is obligated to prove (beyond a reasonable doubt) that the defendant satisfied each element of the offence in question. This will involve proof of the *actus reus, mens rea* and a lack of defence. Failure to prove one of these elements (or a sub-element therein) will mean that the defendant is 'not guilty' or 'not liable' for the offence in question.

We shall now consider each of these elements in brief detail before then developing these key concepts in their respective chapters.

in practice

The difference between 'liability' and 'guilt' is important. It is often expressed that if an individual is 'liable' for an offence, they are also 'guilty' of that offence. However, this is a misnomer. Whether an individual is liable is a question of both fact and law, observing the circumstances of the case. The police will identify an individual as 'liable' for an offence when charging them with such. The Crown Prosecution Service will identify an individual as 'liable' for an offence when it proceeds with the prosecution. However, neither of these parties will identify the 'guilt' of that individual; guilt (if contested) is to be determined by the arbiters of fact at trial (whether they be the jury or the magistrates). For the purposes of this text, therefore, we shall be referring only to whether an individual is 'liable' for a criminal offence (and you are advised to do the same in your own criminal work) – whether they are 'guilty' of that offence or not is out of our hands.

1.8.1 *Actus reus*

Rather loosely used to describe the 'guilty act', the *actus reus* (plural: *actus rei*) of an offence is often the physical element of a crime requiring the defendant to perform a certain act or engage in certain conduct in order to commit a criminal offence. The word 'act', however, is far too narrow a concept to be applicable in all circumstances.

Refer back to our example of Jack and Jill at **1.2.1,** where Jill pushes Jack down the hill. Jill's conduct of pushing Jack is an 'act', and thus the *actus reus,* or one element of the *actus reus,* for a potential offence against Jack may have been satisfied. Suppose, however, that Jack were to fall and asked Jill to help him to prevent him tumbling down the hill. Should Jill refuse to help, she has not performed an 'act'. Rather, Jill has failed to act, also known as an omission.

Whether the failure to act will result in criminal charges being brought against Jill is a matter dependent on the circumstances. However, what can be made clear at this moment is that to define the *actus reus* as a 'guilty act' fails to account for the other circumstances and surrounding facts that may play a part in a criminal offence. As a result, therefore, it is more appropriate to use the term 'guilty conduct and circumstances' instead. An even broader definition of the *actus reus* is provided by Ormerod and Laird (*Smith, Hogan, & Ormerod's Criminal Law*, 15th edn (OUP, 2018)) who comment that it includes 'all the elements in the definition of the crime except D's mental element'.

The following can be characterised as potentially amounting to the *actus reus* of a particular crime:

- acts;
- conduct;
- omissions;
- consequences;
- surrounding circumstances; and
- state of affairs.

When dealing with criminal offences in Parts II and III of this text, it will be made clear what form of *actus reus* we are concerned with. For the most part, we are concerned with what can helpfully be described as the 'three Cs'.

We can examine the three Cs in more detail now:

Table 1.10 Detailing the three Cs

Word	Explanation
Conduct	Represents any acts or omissions required by the defendant in order to commit the respective *actus reus* of the offence. For example, the offence of theft requires an 'appropriation'.
Circumstances	Represents any surrounding factual circumstances or matters that must be present for the offence to take place. For example, the offence of theft requires property to 'belong to another'.
Consequences	Represents the requirements for an end result to occur in order for an offence to be committed. Many offences do not require it. For example, the offence of theft does not require the actual property to be stolen; a mere intention to steal is sufficient.

Certain offences may involve numerous different elements. As a quick example, take the offence of burglary. Burglary is a statutory offence contained within s 9 of the Theft Act (TA) 1968. Burglary is divided into two forms, contained in s 9(1)(a) and 9(1)(b) respectively. For our example, we shall consider s 9(1)(b), which concerns the circumstances where 'having entered any building or part of a building as a trespasser, the defendant steals or attempts to steal anything in the building or that part of it or inflicts or attempts to inflict on any person therein any grievous bodily harm'.

Table 1.11 demonstrates the individual elements of the *actus reus* of a s 9(1)(b) burglary. This is but one example of many that will arise throughout this text. There may be offences which do not contain all of the 'three Cs', for example rape does not require the existence of an 'end result' or 'consequence'. Rape requires the intentional penetration of the vagina, anus or mouth of another person with a penis (conduct) and such conduct must be done without consent and without a reasonable belief in consent (circumstance). Further examples are provided in **Chapter 2**.

Table 1.11 Elements of the offence of burglary

Elements of burglary	Form of *actus reus*
Entry	Act/conduct
Building or part of a building	Surrounding circumstance
As a trespasser	Surrounding circumstance
Commits or attempts to commit theft or GBH	Act/conduct and consequence

1.8.2 *Mens rea*

Rather loosely used to describe the 'guilty mind', the *mens rea* of an offence is the mental element of a crime, often requiring a defendant to intend the end result. Intention alone, however, does not satisfactorily encompass the spectrum of the *mens rea*. The first point to note is that the *mens rea*, like the *actus reus*, is unique to each particular crime. This was made clear by Lord Hailsham, in *DPP v Morgan* [1976] AC 182, who stated that '[t]he beginning of wisdom in all the "*mens rea*" cases ... is ... that "*mens rea*" means a number of quite different things in relation to different crimes'.

Take, for example, the *mentes reae* (plural of *mens rea*) of murder and common assault. Murder requires the intention to kill or cause grievous bodily harm (GBH), whereas the offence of common assault requires the intention to cause the apprehension of unlawful physical force or be reckless as to the thought of such apprehension occurring. As can be seen, both offences are unique in what is required to satisfy the mental element of the crime. The distinction between the two offences arises as a result of their classification as 'specific' and 'basic' intent offences, which we shall consider in **Chapter 3**.

Despite this, however, there are a number of concepts on which the mental element of a criminal offence is based; these are:

- intention;
- foreseeability;
- recklessness; and
- negligence.

We shall deal with each of these concepts in greater detail in **Chapter 3** alongside the requirement of contemporaneity (or coincidence) of the *actus reus* and *mens rea*.

Importantly, as made clear above, there are offences that do not require any form of *mens rea* or fault. These offences are known as 'strict liability offences' and shall also be dealt with in **Chapter 3**. In summary, a defendant may be liable for a criminal offence simply by satisfying the *actus reus* without any corresponding *mens rea*. We shall also look at the term 'absolute liability' in **Chapter 2** and compare that with strict liability.

1.8.3 No defence

The final element required for a defendant to be liable for an offence is the lack of a 'defence'.

in practice

When defence counsel first reads the papers regarding the alleged offence committed by their client, they will consider primarily whether the defendant has actually committed any offence, before then considering the potential defences that may be raised. The same applies to the study of criminal law and a simple exercise will always keep this process in mind: before there can be a *defence*, there has to be an *offence*.

Defences operate with different requirements, outcomes and burdens. With some defences, the defendant remains liable for a less serious offence, whereas, with other defences, the defendant escapes liability completely. Further, some defences impose the legal burden of proof on the defendant, whereas others merely impose an evidential burden of proof (see above at **1.7.2.3**).

Table 1.12 demonstrates these distinctions with examples, and we shall consider these in greater depth in **Chapter 7** when we consider defences.

Table 1.12 Distinguishing defences

Type of defence	Outcome	Example
'Complete'	Defendant is rendered 'not guilty'	Self-defence
'Partial'	Defendant's offence may be 'reduced' to a less severe offence	Intoxication
'Special'	Reduces a potential murder conviction to a conviction of voluntary manslaughter	Diminished responsibility

A point of interest that we shall return to in **Chapter 7** is whether defences form part of the definition of a crime (ie the constituent elements) or whether they are outside the definition, operating independently. Williams (*Criminal Law: The General Part* (Steven & Son, 1961)) takes the former view and argues that defences are not a separate element of liability as they simply form part of the *actus reus.* Kadish ('The Decline of Innocence' (1968) 26 Camb Law Journal 273), on the other hand, argues that there must be an absence of a defence (as a distinct element) given that the *mens rea* requires an element of blameworthiness. The latter view is also adopted by Lanham ('Larsonneur Revisited' [1976] Crim LR 276).

In respect of this argument, one would have to distinguish between those defences which are justificatory in nature, those defences which provide the defendant with an excuse for his crime, and those which negate an element of the offence. For example, intoxication is not a defence *per se* but rather is a denial of the *mens rea* of an offence (*R v Heard* [2008] QB 43). This is because intoxication acts to demonstrate that the defendant could not have formed the necessary *mens rea* for the offence, eg intention, because he was intoxicated. As a result, the 'defence' of intoxication is better understood as an element of an offence (in that it extinguishes *mens rea*), rather than as a distinct defence to a crime. This can be compared to self-defence (also known as private defence) which, if successful, amounts to a justification for the defendant's actions. This is because the defendant, through self-defence, is not claiming that he lacked the necessary mental element. Rather, he is seeking to 'justify' why he acted in such a manner. In this respect, we can say that self-defence, unlike intoxication, is a true defence. It is therefore a separate and distinct element which removes the already established liability from the defendant. At the same time, however, one could argue that the effect of self-defence is to make the defendant's conduct 'lawful'. The offence of battery, for example, requires the 'unlawful application of physical force'. If the defendant's conduct of acting in self-defence makes his conduct lawful, that would mean that self-defence was an element of the offence, and not a defence. Further discussion of this argument is made in **Chapter 8**.

To help with this distinction, let us look at three examples involving Jack and Jill with slightly different facts:

(1) Jill stabs Jack in the chest, and Jack dies as a result. Jill possesses the *actus reus* of murder and intended to kill Jack. Jill is liable for murder.

(2) Jill stabs Jack in the chest, and Jack dies as a result. Jill was intoxicated and claims that she had no idea what she was doing. Jill possesses the *actus reus* of murder but, as a result of her intoxication, may not have had the intention to kill or harm Jack. Jill may not liable for murder.

(3) Jill stabs Jack in the chest, and Jack dies as a result. Jill acted in defence of herself when Jack came home intoxicated and began to attack her. Jill feared for her life and stabbed Jack. Jill possesses the *actus reus* of murder, and the *mens rea*, given her intention to cause GBH to Jack (to stop him). Jill is liable for murder unless she was acting in defence of herself and her conduct is considered reasonable and necessary in the circumstances. Jill may therefore not be liable for murder.

It is these three components (*actus reus*, *mens rea* and defences) that shall form the bulk of our discussion in Part I of this text. In Part II, we shall consider how these principles apply to specific offences against the person, and in Part III how they apply to specific offences against property.

in practice

The prosecution must prove all elements of an offence in order for a defendant to be liable. By 'prove', we simply mean that the prosecution must convince the magistrate or jury that each element of the offence has been made out from the evidence to the appropriate standard (ie beyond reasonable doubt). Take the offence of assault occasioning actual bodily harm. Whilst the prosecution may succeed in proving that the defendant committed an assault, if it fails to prove that the victim actually suffered harm (eg the prosecution fails to ask the victim whether they suffered injury/harm), then the offence has not been proven. It is essential, therefore, to maintain a practical focus and be aware of what actually must exist in order for a defendant to be 'liable'.

1.9 Further reading

Ashworth, 'Is the Criminal Law a Lost Cause?' (2000) 116 LQR 225.

Ashworth, 'Punishment, Compensation and the State' (1986) 6(1) OJLS 86

Ashworth, and Blake, 'The Presumption of Innocence in English Criminal Law' [1996] Crim LR 306.

Ashworth, *Sentencing and Criminal Justice* (6th edn, 2015).

Baker, 'The European Union's "Area of Freedom, Security and (Criminal) Justice" Ten Years On' [2009] Crim LR 833.

Bingham, 'A Criminal Code: Must We Wait Forever?' [1999] Crim LR 694.

Chalmers and Leverick, 'Fair Labeling and Criminal Law' (2008) 71 MLR 217.

Ferguson, 'Codifying Criminal Law: The Scots and English Draft Codes Compared' [2004] Crim LR 105.

Gardner, 'Reiterating the Criminal Code' (1992) 55 MLR 839.

Glazebrook, 'Should We Have a Law of Attempted Crime?' (1969) 85 LQR 27.

Hare, 'A Compelling Case for the Code' (1993) 56 MLR 74.

Hirsch and Roberts, 'Legislating Sentencing Principles: The Provisions of the Criminal Justice Act 2003 Relating to Sentencing Purposes and the Role of Previous Convictions' [2004] Crim LR 639.

Husak, 'The Criminal Law as Last Resort' (2004) 24(2) OJLS 207.

Lamond, 'What Is a Crime?' (2007) 27 OJLS 609.

Murphy, 'The Principle of Legality in Criminal Law under the European Convention on Human Rights' (2010) EHRLR 192.

Roberts, 'Taking the Burden of Proof Seriously' [1995] Crim LR 783.

Smith, 'The Human Rights Act and the Criminal Lawyer: The Constitutional Context' [1999] Crim LR 25.

Stevenson and Harris, 'Simplification (of the Criminal Law) as an Emerging Human Rights Imperative' (2010) 74 J Crim L 516.
Williams, 'The Definition of a Crime' (1955) 13 CLJ 107.

- The criminal law refers to the study of criminal liability.
- Liability simply refers to the requirements that need to exist in order for a person to be guilty of a criminal offence.
- The criminal law functions to protect society, enforce rules and punish rule-breakers.
- The criminal law is built on a number of principles, including autonomy and welfare.
- Substantive criminal law must be distinguished from procedural law and evidential law.
- The elements of any offence are made up of the *actus reus*, *mens rea* and a lack of defence.

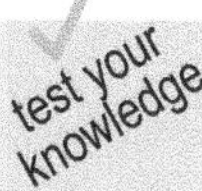

Essay

'The criminal law is designed to promote individual autonomy and fair warning. In its present state, it fails in its task'.'

Critically consider this statement in light of the so-called 'principles' of criminal law.

chapter 2

Actus Reus: The External Element of Crime

After reading this chapter, you will be able to understand:

- what elements are required to form criminal liability
- the term *actus reus* and explain how it applies in criminal cases
- the circumstances when a failure to act (or omission) may result in criminal liability
- the operation of causation in criminal law
- the principle that the defendant must 'take his victims as he finds them'
- how to critique the law of *actus reus* with reference to reasoned and thoughtful arguments.

2.1 Introduction to *actus reus*

As you will now know, from **Chapter 1**, the *actus reus* (plural: *actus rei*) is a legal term describing the external elements of a criminal offence (ie anything that is not the *mens rea*). It is concerned not only with the acts and conduct of the defendant, but also with certain surrounding circumstances and end results. Although the *actus reus* can be characterised as such, this does not mean that the *actus reus* is standardised. Each criminal offence bears with it a separate and distinct *actus reus*. Of course, this does not mean that a particular act or conduct on the part of the defendant can fulfil the *actus reus* of one crime but not the other. This ultimately depends on the circumstances or result that follows.

Suppose Jack shoots Jill. Should Jill survive, Jack is likely to have part of the *actus reus* for grievous bodily harm (GBH). Should Jill die, Jack has the same part of the *actus reus* for murder. The point is that the defendant's behaviour can be characterised as the same in both cases, but the offence charged against the defendant will ultimately depend on the consequence of the defendant's actions.

2.1.1 Finding the *actus reus*

We find the *actus reus* and know what the *actus reus* of an offence is by observing the common law and statute.

Table 2.1 Finding the actus reus

Example of offence	Type of offence	Where can the *actus reus* be found?
Murder	Common law	The definition long cited is that of Sir Edward Coke CJ who defined murder as the 'unlawful killing of a human being under the Queen's peace with malice aforethought, express or implied'. The *actus reus* in that definition includes: • unlawful killing; • of a human being; • under the Queen's peace.

Example of offence	Type of offence	Where can the *actus reus* be found?
Theft	Statutory	The definition is provided in s 1 of the Theft Act 1968 as the dishonest appropriation of property belonging to another with the intention of permanently depriving the other of it. The *actus reus* in that definition includes • appropriation; • of property; • belonging to another.

There are, of course, certain offences that do not fall neatly into these categories. Take, for example, the offence of common assault.

According to *DPP v Taylor; DPP v Little* [1992] QB 645, common assault is a 'statutory offence'. This means that when charged with an offence, the defendant would be charged 'contrary' to s 39 of the Criminal Justice Act (CJA) 1988. However, s 39 does not provide a definition of assault; rather it simply provides:

> Common assault and battery shall be summary offences and a person guilty of either of them shall be liable to a fine not exceeding level 5 on the standard scale, to imprisonment for a term not exceeding six months, or to both.

One must therefore turn to the common law to find the *actus reus* of an assault. According to Goff LJ in *Collins v Wilcock* [1984] 3 All ER 374, common assault can be defined as 'an act which causes another person to apprehend the infliction of immediate, unlawful force on his person'. The *actus reus* of common assault is therefore:

- an act;
- which causes another to;
- apprehend the infliction of immediate, unlawful force.

We shall consider each of these offences separately in the forthcoming chapters; however, it remains helpful to use these offences as examples. It is essential that you understand where we find the *actus reus* of a certain offence, and this will be detailed clearly in Parts II and III of this text.

2.1.2 Identifying the 'three Cs'

As we identified in **Chapter 1**, the *actus reus* can be composed not simply of a defendant's acts or conduct, but also of certain surrounding circumstances and consequences. These elements work together to create the necessary external elements of an offence (see Robinson and Grall, 'Element Analysis in Defining Criminal Liability: The Model Penal Code and Beyond' (1983) 35 Stan L Rev 681). For a detailed account of what each of the 'three Cs' means, please refer back to **Chapter 1**.

Using the above example in relation to common assault, the following elements of the *actus reus* can be identified.

Table 2.2 Identifying the 'three Cs' in assault

***Actus reus* element**	**Three Cs**
An act	Conduct
Which causes another person	Circumstances
To apprehend the infliction of immediate, unlawful force	Consequences

It is essential that these key elements are identified at an early stage to satisfy the requirement for the *actus reus* of the offence. Not all offences will include the three Cs; for example, conduct-only crimes (see **2.3.1**) require no consequence to exist. Take the offence of theft, for example.

Table 2.3 Identifying the 'three Cs' in theft

***Actus reus* element**	**Three Cs**
Appropriation	Conduct
Of property	Circumstances
Belonging to another	Circumstances

As you will see in **Chapter 11**, there is no requirement for there to be a 'stealing' in the ordinary sense of the word for the offence of theft to exist. The defendant must possess an intention to permanently deprive the individual of their property (a part of the *mens rea* of the offence), but there is no requirement in the *actus reus* for the individual to actually be deprived of the property.

The remainder of the chapter will now go on to consider the meaning of *actus reus*, its extent and specific applications of the principle.

2.1.3 'Guilty thoughts'

'Guilty thoughts' alone cannot amount to a criminal offence. A person may often think about committing a criminal offence; indeed, a person could even intend to commit a criminal offence. However, without the presence of *actus reus*, no offence is committed. The *actus reus* may require the individual to undertake a rather simplistic act to satisfy the elements of the offence (eg for the offence of theft, an individual may be liable in circumstances where they simply touch another person's property, so long as they did so with the dishonest intention to permanently deprive). However, there must be some sort of criminal conduct (see the 'three Cs' above). In summary, the law does not punish mere guilty thoughts; there must be a practical application of those guilty thoughts in order to be liable for an offence (*R v Deller* (1952) 36 Cr App R 184).

2.1.4 *Actus reus* committed by a third party

An interesting question to pose at this early stage is whether a defendant can be liable in circumstances where the *actus reus* of an offence is committed by a third party. Ordinarily, the answer would be 'no'; the defendant is required to satisfy the elements of the offence from his own conduct. However, there are a number of circumstances where the acts of another can form the basis of liability against the defendant. For example, an employer may be liable through the principle of vicarious liability for the conduct of their employee (see **Chapter 6**). Likewise, if a defendant causes the *actus reus* to be committed by an innocent third party (such as a child or an insane person), the defendant himself will be liable through the doctrine of innocent agency (see **Chapter 4**). For the majority of this text, we shall focus on the circumstances where the defendant has the relevant *actus reus*.

2.2 Defining the *actus reus*

From the above, you should have noticed that the meaning of *actus reus* is a hotly contested matter, with academics and the courts disagreeing over the appropriate terms to be used in a given case. Two statements deserve mention.

Lord Simon in *DPP for Northern Ireland v Lynch* [1975] AC 653 commented in his dissenting judgment that *actus reus* and *mens rea*

> have, however, justified themselves by their usefulness; and I shall myself employ them in their traditional senses—namely actus reus to mean such conduct as constitutes a crime if the mental element involved in the definition of the crime is also present (or, more shortly, conduct prohibited by law); and mens rea to mean such mental element, over and above volition, as is involved in the definition of the crime.

The most commonly cited judicial position is that of Lord Diplock in *R v Miller* [1983] 2 AC 161, who recounted that

> it would I think be conducive to clarity of analysis of the ingredients of a crime that is created by statute... if we were to avoid bad Latin and instead to think and speak... about the conduct of the accused and his state of mind at the time of that conduct, instead of speaking of *actus reus* and *mens rea.*

The Law Commission's draft Criminal Code of 1989 (Law Com No 177, 1989) followed the statement of Lord Diplock and advised the use of the term 'external elements' in place of *actus reus* and 'fault element' in place of *mens rea*. The Criminal Code was not, however, implemented.

Despite these criticisms, the author takes the view that such a debate is unproductive, and instead it should be accepted that the term is now used simply as a form of 'shorthand' for lawyers. Probably the best exposition of this point was provided by Perkins ('A Rationale of Mens Rea' (1939) 52 Harv LR 905), who argued:

> Some years ago the *mens rea* doctrine was criticised on the ground that the Latin phrase is 'misleading'. If the words '*mens rea*' were to be regarded as self-explanatory they would be open to this objection, but they are to be considered merely as a convenient label attached to any psychical fact sufficient for criminal guilt ... This includes a field too complex for any brief self-explanatory phrase, and since it is important to have some sort of dialectic shorthand to express the idea, this time-honoured label will do as well as any.

As a result, the terms *actus reus* and *mens rea* shall be retained for use in this text.

2.3 Conduct and result crimes

Criminal offences can, rather helpfully, be divided into two types:

- conduct crimes; and
- result crimes.

The distinction between these two types of crimes is essential when one has to consider causation. Causation is an element of the *actus reus* of an offence and requires the arbiters of fact to be sure that the defendant 'caused' the end result. Note those last two words, however – end result.

In brief, conduct crimes require no proof of causation (ie no proof of the 'consequences' element); whereas result crimes do require such proof. It is always necessary to identify the elements of an offence in order to be certain as to what the defendant must 'do' in order to be liable for an offence. It is an essential classification.

2.3.1 Conduct crimes

Conduct crimes are offences where the defendant's conduct is prohibited (unlawful) regardless of the end result. Another way of explaining this is to say that the consequences, if any, of the defendant's behaviour are irrelevant to his liability. Examples of conduct crimes include:

- perjury;
- theft; and
- rape.

As stated above, there is no need to prove causation when considering a conduct crime given that the end result brought about by the defendant is irrelevant to his liability. For example, in a case of theft, it is irrelevant in theory as to whether an individual has actually managed to steal an item from a supermarket. All that is required is that he appropriates such property with the dishonest intention to steal. In practice, of course, the police are unlikely to arrest and the CPS unlikely to charge an individual unless the item was actually stolen; however, there need be no proof of such causation when considering conduct-only crimes.

By way of a second example, consider the offence of perjury, contrary to s 1(1) of the Perjury Act 1911. Section 1(1) provides:

> If any person lawfully sworn as a witness or as an interpreter in a judicial proceeding wilfully makes a statement material in that proceeding, which he *knows to be false or does not believe to be true*, he shall be guilty of perjury. (emphasis added)

It is irrelevant whether the evidence actually turns out to be true, so long as the defendant believes it to be untrue. This is because the end result (ie whether the statement is actually untrue) is irrelevant; the conduct (ie the making of the statement) is the essential ingredient for the offence.

2.3.2 Result crimes

Result crimes are offences where the defendant's conduct has caused or resulted in certain specified consequences. Examples of result crimes include:

- murder;
- grievous bodily harm (GBH); and
- common assault.

In these cases, there must be proof that the defendant 'caused' the end result. For example, the offence of murder requires an 'unlawful killing of a human being'. In the case of murder, many students incorrectly state that causation is satisfied where the victim 'dies'. As will be discussed in **Chapter 8**, this is inappropriate, given that everyone must die at some point in their lives. As a result, therefore, the true causation element required for murder is that death has been 'accelerated' as a result of the defendant's conduct (*R v Dyson* [1908] 2 KB 454, per Lord Alverstone CJ).

For example, should Jill stab Jack to death, the stabbing is the conduct. The acceleration of the death of Jack is the result or consequence of that conduct. It must be proven, therefore, that Jill caused the death of Jack. In this example, it may appear obvious that Jill has caused Jack's death. However, consider these alternative facts:

- Jill had only stabbed Jack in the arm. As a result, Jack fell backwards, hit his head on a rock and died. Would Jill still be the cause of death?
- Jack, on being taken to the hospital, was involved in a car crash and died. Would Jill still be the cause of death?

Causation can be a difficult topic for students to grasp and will be considered below at **2.7.**

2.4 Voluntary and positive conduct

The majority of criminal offences require acts or omissions on the part of the defendant. Such acts or omissions must ordinarily be willed or 'voluntary' and often require a positive act from the defendant. Although absolute liability (see below at **2.5**) need not involve a positive or voluntary act on the part of the accused, it still requires the accused to have done something, or more accurately, 'be somewhere'.

We shall now consider both of these concepts.

2.4.1 Voluntary and involuntary conduct

It is first necessary to distinguish between voluntary conduct and positive acts. It is common for many textbooks to place positive acts in the same category as voluntary conduct. To do so, however, is inaccurate. An act may be voluntary without it being a positive act. For example, Jack may voluntarily decide to starve Jill. One may argue that this would amount to a positive act as Jack has voluntarily and intentionally withheld food from Jill. On the other hand, one may argue that this is a failure to act (an omission), as Jack has not given Jill food when he may be under a specific duty to do so. This distinction is drawn upon at **2.4.2.1,** and it is important that you bear this distinction in mind as you read the next few sections of this chapter.

2.4.1.1 Voluntary conduct

Voluntary conduct is self-explanatory as where the defendant acts voluntarily in a free and willed manner. As with our example above, Jill stabs Jack. Simply, Jill has voluntarily stabbed Jack. Take another example:

example

Jill dares Jack to jump from a third storey window onto a neighbour's car. Jack does so and damages the windscreen.

This is a voluntary act by Jack. Regardless of the dare from Jill, his conduct remains free and willed and he is likely to be liable for criminal damage.

2.4.1.2 Involuntary conduct

Involuntary conduct, on the other hand, can best be understood not as anything *done by* the defendant, but rather as something that *happens to* the defendant. If a person has acted involuntarily, he is generally not guilty of an offence. Horder (*Ashworth's Principles of Criminal Law*, 9th edn (OUP, 2019)) usefully summarises this principle by stating that, 'It is not merely a denial of fault ... It is more a denial of authorship.'

example

Jill dared Jack to jump from the window; however, he was too scared to do so. Jill then pushed Jack from the window, and Jack fell on top of the car, damaging the windscreen.

In this example, Jack has been physically compelled by Jill, and his conduct is involuntary given that he had no control over his actions. In such a case, Jack will not be liable for criminal damage but Jill may be.

Charge:
Murder

Case progression:
Crown Court – Guilty

Northern Ireland Court of Criminal Appeal – Conviction upheld

House of Lords – Conviction upheld

Point of law:
Defences of insanity and automatism

In *Bratty v AG for Northern Ireland* [1963] AC 386, the defendant strangled a woman whilst giving her a lift in his car and claimed that at the time of the incident he was not conscious of his actions.

The House of Lords was confronted with the question as to whether a defendant could raise the defence of automatism (where the body acts without control from the mind) to a case of murder. The decision focuses on the distinction between insanity and automatism, a matter we shall return to in **Chapter 7**; however, for present purposes, it is useful to cite the comment made by Lord Denning in relation to voluntary conduct. In particular, his Lordship stated:

> The requirement that [the act of the accused] should be a voluntary act is essential … in every criminal case. No act is punishable if it is done involuntarily.

The most cited example of involuntary conduct is that given by Lord Goddard CJ and Pearson J in *Hill v Baxter* [1958] 1 QB 277. Their Lordships gave the example (and it was *only* an example despite the belief of many that *Hill v Baxter* actually concerned a case involving a swarm of bees) of a man charged with dangerous driving. His driving would be involuntary if he was suddenly stung by a swarm of bees. Under these circumstances, their Lordships held that the *actus reus* of the offence would not be voluntary given that the defendant would be acting in a state of 'automatism' (see **Chapter 7**) and thus would not be liable for dangerous driving.

Generally, therefore, involuntary conduct will not result in a criminal offence being committed. Note, however, that there are circumstances, known as cases of 'situational liability', where voluntary/involuntary conduct on the part of the defendant is irrelevant. This is dealt with at **2.5.**

2.4.1.3 Distinguishing between the two

From the above examples, you may feel that the distinction between voluntary and involuntary conduct is quite straightforward. However, consider this third example and see if the distinction is as easy to make.

example

Jill dares Jack to jump from the window onto the car below. Jack is too scared to do so and refuses. Jill then threatens Jack with violence should he not jump. As a result of the threat, Jack jumps and damages the car below.

On one view, Jack is liable as his conduct was willed and voluntary as he jumped from the window; he was not pushed or thrown. On a second view, Jack is not liable as he was forced from the window in fear of his safety. The answer is that Jack's conduct remains voluntary. Although forced to jump from the window as a result of the threat, Jack's actions are still conscious, willed and rational. He may be able to rely on a defence to a crime, such as duress, but his actions are still deemed, until duress is proven, to be voluntary despite the threat or coercion. See **Chapter 7** for a discussion of the law of duress.

A second example may assist your understanding further.

example

Jill threatens to push Andy off a wall should Jack not go and steal an item of jewellery for her. Jack does so.

In this case, Jack's conduct remains voluntary despite the threat to Andy. You may consider this to be wrong given that Jack has, essentially, no choice: he either complies with Jill's threat or Andy is hurt. However, despite the threat, his conduct remains free, willed and voluntary. Again, he may be able to rely on a defence to any crime committed, but his conduct would remain voluntary. In summary (see **Table 2.4**), it is essential that you do not confuse physical compulsion with involuntary conduct.

Table 2.4 Voluntary or involuntary conduct

Example	Voluntary	Involuntary
Being thrown from a window		X
Jumping from a window as a result of a threat to oneself or another	X	
Damaging property after suffering an allergic reaction to a bee sting whilst behind the wheel of a car		X
Being pushed into a person's garden, damaging their fence		X
Being dared to 'garden-hop' (running through other peoples' gardens) and accidentally damaging a fence in doing so	X	

2.4.2 Positive acts

A positive act is an action taken by the defendant in relation to specific conduct. For example, the acts of stabbing another and stealing a bottle of whisky from a supermarket are positive acts. Both of these examples show a circumstance where the positive act is 'direct', in that the defendant has physically and personally undertaken such conduct.

Positive acts, however, can also be indirect. See, for example, the case of *DPP v K (a minor)* [1990] 1 All ER 331, where a schoolboy placed acid that he had taken from the science lab into a hand-drier in the boys' toilets. The victim, another pupil, used the hand-drier and was scarred by the acid. The Divisional Court held that the application of force need not be direct, but may also be indirect.

A second example is that of *R v Martin* (1881) 8 QBD 54. In this case, the defendant, upon placing an iron bar across the exit of a theatre and turning out the lights to that stairwell exit, shouted 'fire', which resulted in the injury of several people. The defendant was charged with inflicting GBH contrary to s 2 of the Offences Against the Person Act 1861, which the defendant argued could not be committed by an indirect act. The Court for Crown Cases Reserved ruled that an indirect application of force was sufficient to establish liability for GBH. There was no requirement for 'face-to-face' contact.

2.4.2.1 Distinguishing positive acts from voluntary conduct

At **2.4**, it was made clear that one must distinguish positive acts from voluntary conduct. Although the two concepts go hand-in-hand, they must be considered separately to account for their position in the criminal law.

To help with this idea, consider the case of *R v Savage; DPP v Parmenter* [1991] 3 WLR 914 (particularly, the facts of *R v Savage*).

case example

Charge:
Inflicting GBH
(OAPA 1861, s 20)

Case progression:
Crown Court – Guilty

Court of Appeal – Appeal allowed but replaced with charge of ABH

House of Lords – Conviction upheld

Point of law:
Requirement of *mens rea* to cause ABH

In *R v Savage; DPP v Parmenter* [1991] 3 WLR 914, the defendant threw a glass of beer over her husband's ex-girlfriend. The glass slipped from the defendant's hand and resulted in cuts to the wrist of the victim when the glass smashed. The defendant professed that she never intended to throw the glass; she merely intended to humiliate the victim by throwing the beer. The defendant was convicted of inflicting GBH in the Crown Court.

On appeal, the House of Lords was faced with the question as to whether the defendant was required to intend to throw the glass in order to be liable.

Lord Ackner reasoned that:

> the physical harm which the defendant intended or foresaw might result to some person need only be of a minor character for him to be guilty and it is unnecessary for the Crown to show that he intended or foresaw that his unlawful act might cause physical harm of the gravity described in s 20, ie either wounding or grievous bodily harm.

We shall return to this question in a later chapter, but, for present purposes, this case demonstrates, *inter alia*, that the defendant positively threw the glass at the victim but the act itself was not voluntary given that the glass, allegedly, slipped from her hand. Intention or foreseeability is not the question at this stage; rather, we are simply concerned with whether her act was voluntary. Another useful example of this can be seen in *R v Malcherek; R v Steel* [1981] 2 All ER 422 in relation to the switching off of a life support machine. This is a voluntary act, but is it a positive act? This is considered below.

In general, an act must be both voluntary and positive, although, as we shall see below, a positive act is not required in all circumstances and a failure to act may be sufficient.

2.5 State of affairs cases ('situational liability')

It was stated above that, in general, a defendant can only be liable where his conduct is 'voluntary'. It was noted, however, that there is one key exception to this rule, namely in state of affairs cases. Such cases have also been defined as 'status offences' and 'cases of situational liability' (Glazebrook, 'Situational Liability' in Glazebrook (ed), *Reshaping the Criminal Law* (Sweet & Maxwell, 1978)).

Referring back to the 'three Cs' listed above, state of affairs cases involve offences where the only requirement is for the existence of surrounding circumstances. Further, there is no requirement for the existence of *mens rea* so long as the circumstances can be proven. These offences are referred to as offences of 'absolute liability' (see **Chapter 3** for the distinction between 'strict' and 'absolute' liability).

In absolute liability cases, the defendant is 'being' rather than 'doing' a particular act. For example, an individual is liable for drink driving contrary to s 4(2) of the Road Traffic Act 1988 where they are '*being* in charge of a motor vehicle on a road or other public place while unfit to drive through drink or drugs' (see *Richardson v DPP* [2019] EWHC 428 (Admin) for a recent example of this offence). All that needs to be proven by the prosecution is that the defendant was in charge of the vehicle whilst unfit to be so. They may possess no *mens rea* for the offence, nor do they act voluntarily, but they are liable for an offence. Other examples may include '*being* in possession' of a controlled substance (Misuse of Drugs Act 1971) or '*having* an offensive weapon' in a public place (Prevention of Crime Act 1953). In this regard, it is the state of affairs that the defendant finds himself in which is criminalised.

Importantly, all situational liability offences are statutory based and can thus be readily identified. In *R v Robinson-Pierre* [2013] EWCA Crim 2396, Pitchford LJ in the Court of Appeal noted that

> the supremacy of Parliament embraces the power to create 'state of affairs' offences in which no causative link between the prohibited state of affairs and the defendant need be established. The legal issue is not, in our view, whether in principle such offences can be created but whether in any particular enactment Parliament intended to create one.

Thus, any offence creating a state of affairs case must be clear as to its intention. In that case, the statutory intention was not clear in relation to offences under the Dangerous Dogs Act 1991, s 3(1) and (4).

The following cases will make this area much clearer (whether you agree with the outcome or not is a different matter).

case example

Charge:
Landing in the UK without permission (Aliens Restriction (Amendment) Act 1919, s 10)

Case progression:
Assize Court– Guilty

Court of Criminal Appeal – Conviction upheld

Point of law:
Physical compulsion to commit an offence

In *R v Larsonneur* (1933) 24 Cr App R 74, the defendant, a French citizen, visited the UK for the purpose of entering into a marriage of convenience. The police prevented the marriage and she was ordered to leave and not re-enter the country. Instead of returning to France, the defendant travelled to Ireland. Whilst in Ireland, she was deported and was returned to the UK. The defendant was charged with and convicted of 'being found in the United Kingdom' in breach of the original order excluding her.

On appeal, the defendant claimed that her actions were involuntary. The Court of Criminal Appeal concluded that the fact that she had been returned to the UK under physical compulsion was 'perfectly immaterial' (per Hewart CJ). All that mattered was that she was *found* in the UK on the occasion in question.

Another example is the case of *Winzar v Chief Constable of Kent* (1983) *The Times*, 28 March 1983.

case example

Charge:
Being found drunk on a public highway (Licensing Act 1872, s 12)

Case progression:
Magistrates' court – Guilty

Divisional Court– Guilty

Point of law:
Physical compulsion to commit an offence

In *Winzar v Chief Constable of Kent* (1983) *The Times*, 28 March 1983, the defendant had been found drunk in a hospital and was asked to leave. He refused, whereupon the police were called. An officer forcibly removed him to his patrol car, which was parked on the highway outside, and charged him with 'being found' drunk there. The defendant was convicted in the magistrates' court.

Upholding his conviction, Goff LJ pointed out that a distinction would otherwise have to be drawn between a drunk who leaves a restaurant when asked to do so and one who is forcibly ejected after refusing to leave. His Lordship provides:

> Suppose a person was found as being drunk in a restaurant or a place of that kind and was asked to leave. If he was asked to leave, he would walk out of the door of the restaurant and would be in a public place or in a highway of his own volition. He would be there of his own volition because he had responded to a request. However, if a man in a restaurant made a thorough nuisance of himself, was asked to leave, objected and was ejected, in those circumstances, he would not be in a public place of his own volition because he would have been put there either by a gentleman on the door of the restaurant, or by a police officer, who might have been called to deal with the man in question. It would be nonsense if one were to say that the man who responded to the plea to leave could be said to be found drunk in a public place or in a highway, whereas the man who had been compelled to leave could not.

The focus is on the defendant 'being' in a particular place, as opposed to 'doing' a particular act. In *Larsonneur*, the defendant was found 'being' in the UK; and in *Winzar*, the defendant was found 'being' intoxicated on a highway. It is irrelevant that both defendants were compelled to be in those locations and that neither were necessarily at fault. A useful summation of this area of law is that defendants are simply in the 'wrong place at the wrong time'. Both cases are subject to considerable criticism on the ground that to criminalise an individual for 'being' rather than 'doing' is contrary to the general principle of *actus reus* – ie there must be a guilty act or conduct. Lanham ('*Larsonneur* Revisited' [1976] Crim LR 276), however, finds favour with the decisions above. Particularly in relation to *Larsonneur*, Lanham states:

> If Miss Larsonneur had been dragged kicking and screaming from France into the United Kingdom by kidnappers and the same judgment had been given by the Court of Criminal Appeal, the defence of unforeseeable compulsion would truly have been excluded and the case would be the worst blot on the pages of the modern criminal law. But she wasn't and it wasn't and it isn't.

2.6 Omissions

For some crimes, the *actus reus* may not be an act but, rather, a failure to act in circumstances where there is a duty to do so. JF Stephen, in his *Digest of the Criminal Law*, 3rd edn (Clowes and Sons, 1887), explained that generally there is no 'Good Samaritan law' as an omission will not usually result in criminal liability. JF Stephen gives the following famous example:

> A sees B drowning and is able to save him by holding out his hand. A abstains from doing so in order that B may be drowned, and B is drowned. A has committed no offence.

In this case, although A may have failed to save B, he did no positive act to cause B's death. In general, therefore, there can ordinarily be no liability for a failure (or omission) to act unless the law specifically imposes such a duty upon a particular person.

2.6.1 The position in other jurisdictions and conflicting views

In some jurisdictions, such as France and Germany, an individual would *always* be under a duty to act in what have become known as 'easy rescue' situations (French Penal Code: Article 63; German Penal Code: Article 323c). Easy rescue situations are those where the defendant can save another individual without placing himself in danger. English law, however, does not recognise such 'easy rescue' situations.

2.6.1.1 The 'social responsibility' view

Ashworth ('The Scope of Liability for Omissions' (1989) 105 LQR 424) argues that where the rescue of the victim would not pose a danger to the defendant, then liability should always be imposed for a failure to act, even where there is no pre-existing duty to act. Ashworth labels this as a 'social responsibility' on the part of citizens. You may find this approach sensible and worth investing in. Indeed, Cobb ('Compulsory Care Giving: Some Thoughts on Relational Feminism, the Ethics of Care and Omission Liability' (2008) 39 Cam LR 11) argues that a general 'citizenship duty' which would focus on a mandated reasonable action to prevent harm to one's fellow citizens would be 'fairer, clearer and simpler'. See also Ashworth and Steiner, 'Criminal Omissions and Public Duties: The French Experience' (1990) 10 LS 152.

This approach, however, is not short of difficulties, with two prominent questions needing to be answered:

(1) Who decides when intervening would or would not pose a danger?
(2) Is the test for such a decision subjective (looking at what the individual thought at the time) or objective (looking at what the reasonable man would do in that situation)?

2.6.1.2 The 'conventional' view

In addition to those two questions, Williams ('Criminal Omissions – The Conventional View' (1991) 107 LQR 86) counters Ashworth's arguments by defending 'individualism' and making a key moral distinction between 'killing and letting die'. Williams conforms to the conventional view that there is no social responsibility placed on a stranger to act and save another, and criminal law resources ought to be focused on those individuals who actively seek to harm, through positive actions, another. With a lack of 'fair warning' to citizens as to how far their duty extends, Williams contends that the conventional view ought to be maintained.

2.6.2 Classifying omissions

Fletcher in his text, *Rethinking Criminal Law* (Little Brown, 1978) distinguishes two forms of liability for omissions:

- 'breach of duty to act'; and
- 'commission by omission'.

According to Fletcher, where liability may be imposed for breach of a statutory obligation to act, this is known as a 'breach of duty to act'. Specifically, this relates to conduct crimes where there is no requirement for the incidence of harm to be proved.

The second type relates to result crimes which Fletcher labels 'commission by omission'. This is where liability is imposed 'for failing to intervene, when necessary, to prevent the occurrence of a serious harm such as death or the destruction of property'.

This classification is useful and provides a strong starting point for omission liability. However, you will find that the law of omissions is generally classified now as determinative on the facts of the particular case. For example, we do not speak of a general 'breach of a duty to act' but, rather, of a breach of a contractual duty to act (see *R v Pittwood* (1902) 19 TLR 37 below). Likewise, we do not speak of a general 'commission by omission', but, rather, we look towards specific established duties such as those created by relationship or dependency. Fletcher's classification remains helpful in a given case; however, it is the author's contention that omissions require no general classification and instead the focus should be on the specific facts of the case at hand.

2.6.3 Imposition of a duty

It will be useful at this stage to return to the example given by Stephen J and adapt the facts to observe whether the requirement of A to save B is changed.

Table 2.5 Adapting Stephen J's facts

Facts: What if …	**Is there a legal duty?**
B was a child?	
A was B's parent or legal guardian?	
A was B's teacher out on a school field trip?	
A was a qualified lifeguard at a swimming pool?	
A could not swim and was scared of water?	

These are all excellent questions to ask and naturally lead us on to the circumstances when a failure to act may result in criminal liability. Once we have considered the law on omissions, come back to this table and consider whether an obligation exists.

There are several established circumstances where there is a duty to act. These duties to act are often imposed by statute, by a legal contract/voluntary agreement or by a relationship. Quite simply, if there is no such duty, there can be no liability for an omission (though see below at **2.6.4.7** for a discussion of extending the duties).

Before we proceed to the established duties, it is essential that we first make clear that there are several requirements for a failure to act to give rise to criminal liability:

(a) the defendant's offence must be capable of commission by omission;
(b) the defendant must have a legally recognised duty to act; and
(c) the defendant must have unreasonably failed to act on that duty.

The above list is quite self-explanatory, but it will be useful to delve into the conditions in greater detail.

2.6.3.1 Capable of commission

First, there are some crimes that are not capable of being committed by an omission. For example, the offences of robbery and burglary require the use of force or fear of force and entry into a building or part of a building respectively. Naturally, neither of these conditions can be met by a failure to act; thus the offences cannot be committed by omission. In addition, as the name suggests, unlawful act manslaughter cannot be committed by omission (*R v Lowe* [1973] QB 702). Further, inchoate offences cannot be committed by omission (see **Chapter 5**). A notorious example often cited is that of *R v Ahmad* (1986) 52 P & CR 346 which concerned a landlord who was charged with having done 'acts calculated to interfere with [the victim's] peace and comfort' contrary to the Protection from Eviction Act 1977. In that case, the landlord had merely failed to carry out renovations to the victim's house and this left the property uninhabitable (thus interfering with their peace and comfort). The Court of Appeal considered such a failure to amount to an omission, and not an act, and therefore the defendant could not be liable for an offence requiring him to 'do acts'.

An example of an offence that can be committed by a failure to act is murder, which has long been held to be able to be committed by an omission (*R v Gibbins and Proctor* (1918) 13 Cr App R 134). Ultimately, deciding whether an offence is capable of commission by omission is a matter of interpretation and such interpretation must be done on a case-by-case basis.

Table 2.6 Offences and omissions

Offences capable of commission by omission	Offences incapable of commission by omission
Murder	Theft and robbery
Gross negligence manslaughter	Unlawful act manslaughter
Actual bodily harm	Burglary
Grievous bodily harm	Rape; assault by penetration; sexual assault
Criminal damage	Certain offences of fraud

There are certain offences for which the law is unsure as to whether an omission can satisfy liability. Take, for example, the offence of common assault. At present, there is no judgment which provides that common assault may only be satisfied by an 'act'. Indeed, Smith ('Liability for Omissions in Criminal Law' (1984) 4 LS 88) argues that the need for an act in such circumstances is 'unnecessary'. In **Chapter 9**, we consider the cases of *Fagan v Metropolitan Police Commissioner* [1969] 1 QB 439 and *DPP v Santana-Bermudez* [2004] Crim LR 471 which may shed some light on this issue or give rise to further problems.

2.6.3.2 Legally recognised duty to act

The second factor is that the defendant must have a legal duty to act. There are two concepts here that need to be considered: what do we mean by 'legal' duty, and is there a distinction between a duty 'to act' and a duty 'of care'?

Legal duty

We are concerned with a recognised duty to act on the part of the individual, not merely a moral obligation or duty they may consider that they have. This principle is essential to distinguish those individuals whose failure to act is worthy of criminal repercussions and those who are clearly not deserving of such a criminal label. Whilst most individuals would baulk at the idea of a passer-by ignoring a child drowning in a lake, the criminal law is not concerned with such moral dilemmas. Instead, the law aims to pinpoint liability on those individuals where a specific and identifiable duty can be found, and not simply on an individual who chooses, as is their right, to walk by a drowning child with no relationship to, responsibility for, or association with, that child.

Duty to act, not duty of care

The second point to note is not to confuse a legal duty to 'act' with a duty of 'care'. The former is the requirement to establish omission liability; the latter is a tort law concept which bears use in terms of gross negligence manslaughter. In order to establish liability for gross negligence manslaughter, it must be proved that the defendant owed a duty of care to the victim. In circumstances where the defendant is charged with gross negligence manslaughter, and he does not perform a positive act (ie his liability is omission-based), the prosecution would not only have to establish a duty of care but would also have to establish a duty to act. We discuss this in more detail in **Chapter 7**.

The established duties to act are detailed below at **2.6.4** and are generally concerned with duties that exist as a result of a familiar relationship, assumed responsibility or other association.

2.6.3.3 Unreasonable failure to act

The third factor is that the defendant unreasonably failed to act on that duty. Should a defendant do what ordinary people would consider reasonable in the circumstances, he will not be liable for his failure to act. This question essentially asks whether the defendant breached his duty to act and whether that breach was unreasonable in the circumstances.

example

Jill is drowning in a lake. Jack reaches in to try to save her but cannot get to her. Jack is unable to swim himself, so he cannot jump in to save Jill. Instead Jack calls for assistance.

This scenario is a good example of how one should consider the question of reasonableness. In the circumstances where Jack is unable to swim, his failure to act (ie jumping into the water himself) would not be considered so unreasonable that he is liable for an offence. This is so on account that Jack is liable to do more harm than good if he himself cannot swim. In particular, there is a risk that Jack could exacerbate the circumstances for Jill and put himself in danger at the same time. His reasonable refusal is, further, strengthened by his reasonable act of calling for assistance. Had Jack not called for assistance, it is plausible that, overall, he might be considered as having acted unreasonably. Reasonableness is considered by the arbiters of fact.

It is important to emphasise that even if these three elements are satisfied, the prosecution must still prove that the defendant's omission caused the end result and the defendant possessed the necessary *mens rea*. In that regard, if the end result would have occurred anyway (ie there was no factual causation), then the defendant cannot be liable (though some other offence may be available).

We shall now consider the established duties to act.

2.6.4 The established duties

Below are detailed explanations of the current established duties to act in England and Wales. A failure to act in these circumstances may result in criminal liability. Note here the word 'may'. The conditions for liability listed above (**2.6.3**) must be met. No liability will arise where a defendant fails to act in such circumstances, unless that failure to act is considered unreasonable.

2.6.4.1 Official duty

Where a person has an official duty to act, for example a member of the emergency services, their omissions can give rise to criminal liability. For example, in *R v Dytham* [1979] QB 722, the defendant, a uniformed police officer, whilst on duty (though shortly to go off duty), stood aside and watched as a man was beaten to death outside a nightclub. He then left the scene, without calling for assistance or summoning an ambulance. The defendant was charged with and convicted of wilful misconduct in public office. On appeal, Lord Widgery CJ commented:

> The allegation made was not of mere non-feasance but of deliberate failure and wilful neglect. This involves an element of culpability which is not restricted to corruption or dishonesty but which must be of such a degree that the misconduct impugned is calculated to injure the public interest so as to call for condemnation and punishment.

There is a possibility that Dytham could have faced prosecution for manslaughter if it could have been proven that his inaction contributed to the victim's death. However, there was no clear evidence in that case which showed that the defendant could have saved the victim, even if he tried. Indeed, Hogan ('Omissions and the Duty Myth' in Smith (ed), *Criminal Law Essays in Honour of JC Smith* (Butterworths, 1987)) argues that it would be inappropriate to punish a defendant like Dytham for the consequences of his omission given that he did not actually *cause* such consequences. In particular, Hogan states that 'public officers who neglect without reasonable cause to perform the obligations of their offices may be convicted of an offence but the offence lies in the neglect and the office holder does not become a party to the harm he might have prevented'. Whether Dytham could have been convicted of manslaughter is now a moot point; however, it is worth considering this matter in case a similar situation arises in a problem-based question.

Should a case similar to *Dytham* arise today, the defendant may also be liable for the new offence of corrupt or improper exercise of police powers contrary to s 26 of the Criminal Justice and Courts Act 2015.

2.6.4.2 A duty imposed by statute

There are many statutory provisions (mostly regulatory) which specifically impose duties on particular persons to act in certain ways and which impose criminal sanctions for failing to act. Such liability is often referred to as 'direct liability'. Road traffic law provides many examples of this, including *failing* to provide a specimen of breath when required to do so (Road Traffic Act (RTA) 1988, s 7(6)) and *failing* to provide the name and address of a person involved in a road traffic accident (RTA 1988, s 170). A useful guide when considering duties imposed by statute is to check the wording of the offence.

We shall take two more examples to prove this point. Section 24A of the Theft Act 1968 provides that it is an offence if a person should dishonestly *fail* to take such steps as are reasonable in the circumstances to secure that any wrongful credit to an account held by him is cancelled. In addition, s 5 of the Domestic Violence, Crimes and Victims Act 2004 creates an offence of failing to protect a child or vulnerable adult from a risk of death or serious physical harm by a person who lives with them or has frequent contact with them (see *R v Khan* [2009] EWCA Crim 2).

All four examples above refer to a 'failure' to act in a certain capacity. Although there are other duties imposed by statute that do not include the word 'failure' (for example, s 19 of the Terrorism Act 2000 and s 84 of the Companies Act 2006 use the phrases 'does not disclose' and 'fails to comply' respectively), the statutes are clear in their wording that there is a duty to act, and an omission will result in criminal liability.

2.6.4.3 Contractual obligations

Ordinarily, a contractual obligation exists only between those individuals party to the contract (often referred to as being *inter se*). In this regard, the law of contract is often distanced from the reach of criminal law. However, it has been understood that a failure to fulfil contractual obligations, that is likely to endanger lives, can lead to criminal liability. The classic example of this can be seen in *R v Pittwood* (1902) 19 TLR 37. The defendant was employed to operate a level-crossing on a railway but omitted to close the crossing gates when a train was signalled. A cart was crossing when a train struck it and killed one of the carters. The defendant was charged with and convicted of gross negligence manslaughter. As you may have learned in the law of torts, there is often a difficult divide to be made between contractual and tortious breaches. Pittwood was likely in breach of contract by failing to close to gate; however, the victim was not a party to the contract (the contract was between the defendant and his employers), and thus no claim could be founded there. More accurately, the defendant's liability can be found in the tortious duty of care to the users of the crossing, whom he was paid to protect in his duty and whose lives may be endangered should he fail to perform his duty. For a more recent application of the principle in *Pittwood*, see *R v Yaqoob* [2005] EWCA Crim 1269 where a taxi manager was liable for failing to have the tyres of a minibus checked as part of the vehicle's MOT resulting in a fatal accident involving that vehicle.

Importantly, the issue here is whether an individual has failed to perform their contractual obligation. Should an individual perform such an obligation but the victim suffers regardless, it will become harder to establish that individual's liability. Take the following example:

example

Jack is a lifeguard at the local swimming pool. Jack notices that Jill is struggling to swim and appears to be drowning. Jack dives into the pool without hesitation to save her. Unfortunately, despite his best efforts, Jack is unable to save Jill from downing.

In this instance, Jack cannot be said to have failed to act – he dived into the pool to save Jill. His contractual obligation will require him to protect the safety of pool users. Whilst Jack has failed to save Jill, he has appeared to make every effort to do so and has not omitted in his contractual duties. In that regard, Jack may not be liable for the death of Jill.

A debate that is open for interpretation is whether the duty to act imposed on emergency service providers, such as the police, paramedics and the fire service, would more accurately fall under this heading. Indeed, each of these services act under an official duty; however, such duty cannot exist without a contract of employment. On that basis, it is questionable whether the duty on emergency services personnel would be more apt under this heading given their contractual obligation or whether the duty remains one of official duty. Such point remains moot as, in practice, a failure to act will be found in certain circumstances, but it is still helpful to attempt to categorise such individuals and find the potential basis for their duty to act.

2.6.4.4 Duty by relationship

One of the most common and cited examples of the duty to act is in the circumstances where a duty arises as a result of a relationship between the defendant and the victim. Known as 'derivative liability', where a bond exists between two individuals such that they are in a close or special relationship with one another, the law may impose a duty on either individual to act. In practical terms, the closer the relationship between the pair, the more likely the law is to impose a duty to act on one for the other.

Examples of common duties by relationship include:

- parent and child;
- spouses; and
- doctor and patient.

As shall be questioned below, however, the extent of relationships may well vary with certain classes of individual being responsible for others. Indeed, the law in this area has developed on a case by case basis and may not always appear to be consistent or coherent. **Table 2.7** provides an overview of these duties.

Table 2.7 Duty established by special relationship

Duty	Examples
Parent and child	Section 1 of the Children and Young Persons Act 1933 provides: 'A parent or any other person over the age of 16 years who has responsibility for a child under that age may incur liability for any wilful neglect of that child that was likely to cause unnecessary suffering or injury to health.' This includes a failure to provide adequate food, clothing, medical care, etc. See *R v Lowe* [1973] QB 702 for an example of an upheld conviction under this statute.
	In *R v Gibbins and Proctor* (1918) 13 Cr App R 134, the defendants deliberately starved the victim, Nelly (D1's daughter; D2 being the girlfriend of D1), who died as a result. Both defendants were convicted of murder. D1 owed the victim a duty as a parent, and D2 owed a duty by voluntarily assuming parental responsibility for the victim (in that she received money for purpose of buying food but failed to do so). It remains unclear how far this relationship ground may extend and whether an obligation is owed by a child to their parent.
Spouses	In *R v Hood* [2003] EWCA Crim 2772, the defendant failed to summon help for his wife who had fallen three weeks earlier, due to her poor health and condition, and suffered broken bones. She died as a result and the defendant was charged with gross negligence manslaughter due to his failure to act in circumstances where there was a familial duty to act. (Note that the defendant's appeal was against sentence and not conviction.) In the older case of *R v Smith* [1979] Crim LR 251, the Court of Appeal held that a duty to act between spouses existed upon a voluntary assumption of care and not simply because they are married.
Doctor and patient	A doctor owes a duty to their patient to act to preserve life. Such is detailed in the Hippocratic Oath sworn by doctors. They have a duty to act in the best interests of their patient. Can a doctor therefore kill a patient if it is in the patient's best interests? According to Lord Goff in *Airedale NHS Trust v Bland* [1993] AC 789, a doctor will be liable for murder or manslaughter where his positive act brings about the death of the patient. However, an omission on the part of a doctor (ie the withdrawal of treatment where it is in the best interests of the patient) may be lawful. See below at **2.6.6**.

At the start of this section, it was stated that this is one of the most cited examples of liability arising out of a failure to act. However, there remains relatively little case law on such relationships. The question before us is exactly how far this duty will extend.

Based on the idea of a special relationship, would you say that the following owe a duty of care to their counterpart:

- unmarried couples;
- siblings;
- extended family (uncles and aunts);
- students or friends cohabiting together;
- parent and child over the age of 18?

Using the authorities before us, it appears unlikely that any of the above situations would justify imposing a duty to act (see cases such as *R v Shepherd* (1862) Le & Ca 147 and *R v Sinclair* (1998) (unreported) 21 August, CA). It is for this reason that Child and Ormerod (*Smith, Hogan, & Ormerod's Essentials of Criminal Law*, 3rd edn (OUP, 2019)) argue that the better and 'more justifiable' way to proceed is to focus on 'dependence' as opposed to special relationships. Let us use an example to assist our understanding here.

example

Jack and Jill are law students sharing a flat at university. Jack locks himself in his bedroom refusing to eat or drink. It is later discovered that Jack has died from starvation.

A number of questions arise from this scenario, including:

- Is Jill under a duty to ensure that Jack is safe?
- If Jill tries to offer Jack food and drink, does she then assume responsibility for Jack?
- Is there a point where Jack becomes dependent on Jill (ie how much dependence is required) and does Jack or Jill have to be aware of this? (see Ashworth, 'Manslaughter by Omission and the Rule of Law' [2015] Crim LR 563)

Put yourself in Jill's shoes. Would you:

- contact the police;
- speak to a member of staff at the university;
- try to contact a member of Jack's family?

These are the sorts of questions you will have to consider when assessing the potential liability of individuals. Remember, the law here is judge-made and therefore has the opportunity to develop. An interesting case that considers these questions is *R v Ruffell* [2003] EWCA Crim 122, where the defendant and victim had both self-administered drugs. The victim showed signs of overdose and collapsed. The defendant first attempted to revive the victim before then leaving him outside his house and asking his mother to collect him. The victim died as a result of hypothermia and opiate intoxication and the defendant was charged with gross negligence manslaughter. Whilst the appeal was made against sentence, the Court of Appeal took the opportunity to affirm the reasoning of the trial judge who concluded that:

> the deceased was a guest of the appellant in the appellant's family home and that he was a friend ... and that he had taken upon himself the duty of trying to revive him after what had happened.

HHJ Fawcus would explain on appeal that '[w]hat followed, of course, was putting the deceased outside, and that clearly gave rise to the situation in which the jury could consider whether there had been a breach of that duty'.

Had the defendant not attempted to resuscitate the victim, would he be liable? Although he did invite him into his home, he did not voluntarily assume care, nor was there necessarily a dangerous situation created by the defendant exclusively. This case demonstrates the difficult boundaries that are often drawn and require extensive thought and critique throughout your studies. See also *R v Barrass* [2011] EWCA Crim 2629, in which the defendant owed a duty to act in relation to his elderly sister for whom he cared for a failure to summon medical help (though note that the defendant pleaded guilty and this case is better observed as one of dependency rather than relationship). In *R v Evans* [2009] EWCA Crim 650, a half-sister was not considered as holding a duty to act by relationship (though see **2.6.4.6**).

2.6.4.5 Duty by assumption of care (voluntary undertakings)

A duty to act may also be established where the defendant voluntarily undertakes to care for another who is unable to care for himself. He may be unable to care for himself as a result of age, illness or other infirmity. As made clear above, a parent has no legal duty to care for a child who has reached the age of 18 and is 'entirely emancipated' (*R v Shepherd* (1862) Le & Ca 147). However, should that child become ill and thus dependent on his parents, there may well be a voluntary assumption of care by the parents in given circumstances requiring them to act (*R v Chattaway* (1922) 17 Cr App R 7).

Here, a duty may either be express or implied (see Mead, 'Contracting into Crime: A Theory of Criminal Omissions' (1991) 11 OJLS 147).

Express duty

An example of an express duty can be seen in the case of *R v Nicholls* (1874) 13 Cox CC 75, where the defendant agreed to assume care of the victim, her granddaughter, upon the passing of the victim's mother. The victim was neglected and died as a result. The defendant was charged with and convicted of gross negligence manslaughter as a result of her failure to care for the victim with an express agreement to do so. Brett J directed the jury as follows:

> If a grown up person chooses to undertake the charge of a human creature, helpless either from infancy, simplicity, lunacy, or other infirmity, he is bound to execute that charge without (at all events) wicked negligence, and if a person who has chosen to take charge of a helpless creature lets it die by wicked negligence, that person is guilty of manslaughter.

Nicholls did not owe a duty simply because she was the victim's grandmother; instead, the duty arose due to the assumption of care.

Implied duty

An example of an implied duty can be seen in the case of *R v Instan* [1893] 1 QB 450. In this case, the defendant lived with the victim, her aunt, who was taken ill (prior to her death no one but Instan had any knowledge of her aunt's condition). The victim became bed-bound and was unable to care for herself or call for help. The defendant failed to provide the victim with food or call for medical assistance, but was comfortable in continuing to care for herself (she was happy to eat her aunt's food). The defendant was convicted of gross negligence manslaughter as a result of the implicit duty of care she held in the given circumstances. Lord Coleridge CJ in the Court for Crown Cases Reserved explained that:

> It would not be correct to say that every moral obligation involves a legal duty; but every legal duty is founded on a moral obligation. A legal common law duty is nothing else than the enforcing by law of that which is a moral obligation without legal enforcement. There can be no question in this case that it was the clear duty of the prisoner to impart to the deceased so much as was necessary to sustain life of the food which she from time to time took in, and which was paid for by the deceased's own money for the purpose of the maintenance of herself and the prisoner; it was only through the instrumentality of the prisoner that the deceased could get the food. There was, therefore, a common law duty imposed upon the prisoner which she did not discharge.
>
> ... The prisoner was under a moral obligation to the deceased from which arose a legal duty towards her; that legal duty the prisoner has wilfully and deliberately left unperformed, with the consequence that there has been an acceleration of the death of the deceased owing to the non-performance of that legal duty.

As you can identify from the passage of Lord Coleridge CJ, the precise nature of the duty to act imposed on Instan was not expressly categorised. For example, Hawkins J questioned whether an obligation existed by way of implied contract. However, Lord Coleridge CJ, who provided the judgment of the Court, did not identify the nature of the duty to act; his Lordship merely affirmed that a legal obligation to act in this case existed. In that regard, *Instan* may be characterised as a case involving an implied voluntary undertaking of responsibility or one of implied contract.

The principle of *Instan* was applied in the most cited of omissions cases: *R v Stone; R v Dobinson* [1977] QB 354.

case example

Charge:
Gross negligence manslaughter

Case progression:
Crown Court – Guilty

Court of Appeal – Conviction upheld

Point of law:
Duty to act after assuming responsibility

In *R v Stone; R v Dobinson* [1977] QB 354, the victim (Fanny) suffered from anorexia and came to live with her brother (Stone) and his mistress (Dobinson). The victim was, at first, able to care for herself; however, her condition quickly deteriorated to the extent that she became bed-bound. The victim required urgent medical assistance which was not summoned and she died as a result of the lack of care received. The defendants were charged with and convicted of gross negligence manslaughter as a result of their failure to care for the victim upon the assumption of her care when she first came to live with them.

The Court of Appeal upheld their convictions on the basis that the pair had voluntarily assumed responsibility over the wellbeing of the victim and as such owed a duty of care to her which, if breached (as it was), was capable of amounting to a crime.

Lord Justice Lane explained the duty to act on Stone and Dobinson as follows:

> Whether Fanny was a lodger or not she was a blood relation of the appellant Stone; she was occupying a room in his house; the appellant Dobinson had undertaken the duty of trying to wash her, of taking such food to her as she required. There was ample evidence that each appellant was aware of the poor condition she was in ...

> This was not a situation analogous to the drowning stranger. They did make efforts to care. They tried to get a doctor; they tried to discover the previous doctor. The appellant Dobinson helped with the washing and the provision of food. All these matters were put before the jury in terms which we find it impossible to fault. The jury were entitled to find that the duty had been assumed. They were entitled to conclude that once Fanny became helplessly infirm … the appellants were, in the circumstances, obliged either to summon help or else to care for Fanny themselves.

This case is often viewed as harsh in nature. Both defendants were of low intelligence and struggled to care for themselves (Stone being partially deaf and almost entirely blind, and Dobinson being described as 'ineffectual and inadequate'). *Stone and Dobinson* demonstrates a wide extension of the test set in *Instan*, given that a duty was held to be owed by the defendants even in circumstances where it was burdensome, difficult or onerous to perform. Williams ('Criminal Omissions—The Conventional View' [1991] 107 LQR) described such a decision as a demonstration of 'judicial cruelty' given the characteristics of the defendants. Further, what is not clear from *Stone and Dobinson* is whether the defendants would have remained liable had they simply ignored the victim and not attempted to care for her. I would submit that they would have been liable given that the victim still came to live with the defendants. Although she was able to care for herself at first, the defendants would have assumed a duty as a result of taking Fanny into their home.

2.6.4.6 Duty by creation of a dangerous situation

Also known as the 'doctrine of supervening fault', the final circumstance where a duty to act may exist arises where the defendant sets in motion a dangerous chain of events and then fails to correct it. The defendant is required in such circumstances to take reasonable steps to avert the danger, and a failure to do so may result in criminal liability for the consequences that follow.

The classic authority on this point is that of *R v Miller* [1983] 2 AC 161.

case example

Charge:
Arson (Criminal Damage Act 1971, s 1(3))

Case progression:
Crown Court – Guilty

Court of Appeal – Conviction upheld

House of Lords – Conviction upheld

Point of law:
Creation of a dangerous situation and a duty to avert danger

In *R v Miller* [1983] 2 AC 161, the defendant was 'sleeping rough' in a building and fell asleep on a mattress whilst smoking a cigarette. He awoke to find the mattress smouldering but, instead of calling for help, he simply moved into the adjoining room and fell asleep again. As a result, a fire started and spread throughout the building causing extensive damage. The defendant was charged with and convicted of arson in the Crown Court.

The House of Lords upheld his conviction (affirming the decision of the Court of Appeal) on the basis that the defendant created a dangerous situation which he was under a duty to put right.

Above, it was mentioned that the defendant must take reasonable steps in the circumstances to avert the danger he has created. In this case, what did the law expect the defendant to do? Ultimately that would depend on the circumstances:

- If the fire was a raging inferno, the law would not have expected the defendant to attempt to extinguish it himself. However, the law would expect him to call for help.
- If the fire was small and containable, the law might reasonably expect the defendant to attempt to extinguish it. If such was not possible, the reasonable man would call for emergency assistance.

This discussion led to Lord Diplock, in the House of Lords, commenting:

> I see no rational ground for excluding from conduct capable of giving rise to criminal liability conduct which consists of failing to take measures that *lie within one's power* to counteract a danger that *one has oneself created*, if at the time of such conduct one's state of mind is such as constitutes a necessary ingredient of the offence. (emphasis added)

His Lordship followed this by reasoning that:

> I cannot see any good reason why, so far as liability under criminal law is concerned, it should matter at what point of time before the resultant damage is complete *a person becomes aware* that he has done a physical act which, whether or not he appreciated that it would at the time when he did it, *does in fact create a risk* that property of another will be damaged; provided that, at the moment of awareness, it lies within his power to take steps, either himself or by calling for the assistance of the fire brigade if this be necessary, to prevent or minimise the damage to the property at risk. (emphasis added)

Following *Miller*, the questions to be asked in this regard were:

(a) Did the defendant create a dangerous situation?
(b) Did the defendant realise that he has created this dangerous situation?

If the answer to both questions is 'yes', the defendant is under a duty to act to rectify the situation within his power. A failure to do will be a criminally liable omission.

Miller was subsequently applied by the trial judge in the trial at first instance of *R v Khan and Khan* [1998] Crim LR 830 and was fully endorsed by the Law Commission in its draft Criminal Code (Law Com No 177, 1989) at clause 23. However, the Court of Appeal quashed the convictions of Khan and Khan and the draft Code has not been brought into force.

A point of difficulty arose in the law as a result of the case of *R (Lewin) v DPP* [2002] EWHC 1049 (Admin), where the Divisional Court held that the defendant owed the victim no duty of care in leaving his intoxicated friend in a car during extremely hot weather conditions. Such an omission led to the victim's death. This decision did not, necessarily, conflict with the decision in *Miller* given that there was no evidence to suggest that the defendant knew that such a risk of death was possible. Whether *Lewin* would now be decided in the same way is questionable as a result of the decision in *R v Evans* [2009] EWCA Crim 650.

case example

Charge:
Gross negligence manslaughter

Case progression:
Crown Court – Guilty

Court of Appeal – Conviction upheld

Point of law:
Creation of a dangerous situation and a duty to avert danger

In *R v Evans* [2009] EWCA Crim 650, the defendant, the half-sister of the victim, supplied the victim with heroin which she self-administered. The victim reacted badly to the drug and collapsed. The defendant failed to summon help out of fear of prosecution for supplying the drug and the victim died. The defendant was charged with gross negligence manslaughter as a result of her failure to act in contacting the emergency services.

The conviction was upheld by the Court of Appeal on the basis that the defendant had contributed to the dangerous situation through her failure to seek help or support for the victim. The dangerous situation had already been created by another through the supply of drugs; the defendant had contributed to that situation by failing to summon help. Lord Judge CJ ruled:

> [F]or the purposes of gross negligence manslaughter, when a person has *created or contributed* to the creation of a state of affairs which he *knows, or ought reasonably to know*, has become life threatening, a consequent duty on him to act by taking reasonable steps to save the other's life will normally arise. (emphasis added)

As with *Miller*, the duty arose in this case as a result of the creation of, or contribution to, a dangerous situation. In supplying the drugs to the victim, Evans had set in motion a dangerous chain of events for which she was under a duty to avert, ie by calling for help. By failing to call for help or seek assistance, the defendant's conviction for manslaughter was upheld.

One should notice immediately that the phraseology used by Lord Judge CJ in *Evans* differs to some extent from that of Lord Diplock in *Miller*. The first is identified in **Table 2.8.**

Table 2.8 Miller and Evans

R v Miller	***R v Evans***
Defendant is liable if he 'does in fact create a risk'.	Defendant is liable if he 'created or contributed to' a dangerous situation.

From this variation in words, *Evans* has been criticised by the likes of Baker ('Omissions liability for homicide offences: reconciling *R v Kennedy* with *R v Evans*' [2010] J Crim L 310), who argues that *Evans* has stretched the *Miller* principle to circumstances where the defendant 'simply contributed to, rather than created, the dangerous situation'. Likewise, Ashworth ('Manslaughter by Omission and the Rule of Law' [2015] Crim LR 563) argues that:

> Lord Judge's extension of the *Miller* principle dilutes it to too great a degree, not least because 'all kinds of background acts of facilitation' could now be found to support a duty sufficient for manslaughter liability, expanding both the potential ambit and the uncertainty of the duty-situations.

By way of contrary argument to the above, one could argue that *Evans* is a natural extension of the principle in *Miller* and fills a void in the law left by drug-supply cases such as *R v Kennedy (No 2)* [2008] 1 AC 269. In *Kennedy*, the House of Lords ruled that the chain of causation on a charge of unlawful act manslaughter was broken where the victim, having been supplied with drugs, self-injected. Applying that to *Evans*, the defendant did not 'create' the dangerous situation – that was done by the victim when she self-injected. However, Evans could be (and was) liable if the court found that the dangerous situation was contributed to by the supply of drugs. This is an important step in the development of the law to ensure that drug-dealers are appropriately dealt with under the law.

Evans is a judgment of the Court of Appeal, whilst *Miller* is one of the House of Lords. It could be argued, therefore, that *Evans* was decided *per incuriam* given that Lord Judge CJ did not follow the approach adopted by Lord Diplock. Interestingly, the High Court of Australia declined to follow the approach in *Evans* in the case of *Burns v The Queen* [2012] HCA 35, when it held that the relationship of supplier of prohibited drugs and recipient did not give rise to a duty to preserve life on the part of the supplier. It does appear as though *Evans* is an accepted authority at this stage given that the Crown Court Compendium (at section 19-25) acknowledges the extension in *Evans* and includes it as part of the directions to the jury.

The second variation in the terminology is identified in **Table 2.9**.

Table 2.9 Miller and Evans continued

R v Miller	***R v Evans***
Defendant is liable if he 'becomes aware' that he has created a dangerous situation.	Defendant is liable if he 'knows or ought reasonably to know' that he has created/contributed to a dangerous situation.

In *Miller,* the defendant's duty to act only arose at the point that *he* became personally aware of the danger he had created (a subjective test). In contrast, in *Evans*, the Court of Appeal stated that the duty would arise when the defendant realises or *should have realised* that the danger was created (an objective test). Williams ('Gross Negligence Manslaughter and Duty of Care in "Drugs" Cases: *R v Evans*' [2009] Crim LR 631) makes the point that *Evans* has the result of allowing for the possibility of liability from a failure to act, even where the defendant did not realise the danger she had created, if a reasonable (objective) person would have realised such danger. Further, Ashworth ('Manslaughter by Omission and the Rule of Law' [2015] Crim LR 563) argues that the expansion of the duty into a state of mind where the defendant *ought to have known* about the danger goes 'too far' and reasons that such a ruling may offend the requirement for certainty of the criminal law in Article 7 of the ECHR. Had the case of *Lewin* (above) been decided post-*Evans*, it is likely that the defendant would have been charged with a criminal offence given that he *should* have realised that he had created a dangerous situation. In *R v Bowler* [2015] 2 Cr App R (S) 307, the victim had been asked to be mummified as part of an unusual sexual activity. The Court of Appeal noted that a duty to act arose because the victim 'was left helpless and in a situation which was obviously dangerous'. Use of 'obviously dangerous' could indicate a preference towards an *Evans* interpretation (though, do note that *Bowler* was an appeal against sentence and these words were said in *obiter*). See also *R v Bowditch* (Maidstone Crown Ct, 26 January 2017). **Figure 2.1** demonstrates this distinction in the form of a timeline.

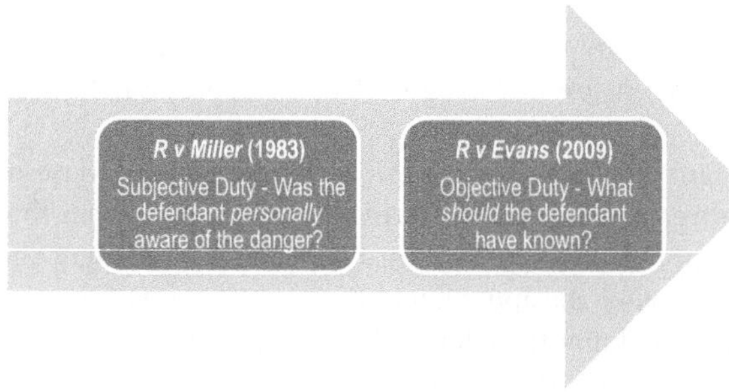

Figure 2.1 The duty to avert danger

Two further issues arise as a result of the decision in *Miller* that bear consideration.

First, the House of Lords in the above cases spoke only in terms of a physical act on the part of the defendant in setting the chain of events in motion. What, then, about an omission that creates a dangerous situation? The courts have yet to address the question of whether an omission, which creates a dangerous situation, might found liability where a further omission fails to avert the danger. One might argue that the principle of *Miller* should be extended to cover these situations.

example

Jack is cooking dinner and leaves the house to go to the local pub for a few beers. Whilst at the pub he realises that he left on the gas on the oven. Despite this, he does nothing and continues to drink in the pub. Jill comes home from work and lights a cigarette in the kitchen which causes an explosion.

In this case, there is no physical act on the part of Jack; rather, it is an omission (failure to turn off the gas) that created the dangerous situation which he then failed to avert.

Secondly, what of multiple defendants involved in the same transaction? Should one defendant be liable for a failure to avert a danger set in motion by another defendant?

example

Jack punches Andy to the floor. Jill, Jack's friend, walks past Andy and notices that he is shaking violently with white foam emerging from his mouth. Jill simply ignores this and steps over Andy without calling for assistance.

In this scenario, it is debateable whether Jill would be liable for failing to avert a dangerous situation set in motion by her friend, Jack.

in practice

There is no statement as yet that the *Miller* principle extends to cover these sorts of situations. It is questionable whether the latter scenario would contravene the 'no Good Samaritan' principle. In practice, an advocate would have to argue these points in determining whether an individual was liable for an offence.

An interesting application of the *Miller* principle can be seen in the case of *DPP v Santana-Bermudez* [2004] Crim LR 471. In this case, the victim, a police officer, undertook a lawful search of the defendant and asked him to turn out his pockets, the contents of which included some syringes. Specifically, the officer asked the defendant whether he had any 'sharps' on him; the defendant failed to answer. When asked whether he had any more needles, the defendant lied, resulting in the victim pricking her finger on a hypodermic needle. The Divisional Court ruled that the defendant had created a dangerous situation through his lie, thereby exposing the officer to a risk of injury, which he failed to rectify by informing the officer of the presence of needles. The defendant was charged with and convicted of ABH.

2.6.4.7 Are the categories 'closed'?

The list of established duties above is not a 'closed list' (*R v Khan and Khan* [1998] Crim LR 830). These are common law duties (ie judge-made duties) and the list is not exhaustive. As a result, there is the possibility that, in a future case, one of the existing duties may be extended to cover other situations, or you may argue that a new duty may be recognised. The latter is highly unlikely and rather remote but is still worth considering. It is advised, therefore, that when faced with a failure to act in a problem-based question and a recognised duty cannot be found, but it seems right that liability should be found, these possibilities should be highlighted.

in practice

An important practical point is to question who is responsible for 'extending' the various duties to act. Is that a matter for Parliament, the judiciary, or the jury on a given day?

As stated above, the general view is that, despite a few exceptions, the duties exist in the common law and thus should be modified, extended or created by the judiciary. Indeed this is the approach taken in the case of *R v Singh (Gurphal)* [1999] Crim LR 582. However, a difficulty has arisen since the case of *R v Khan v Khan* [1998] Crim LR 830, where the Court of Appeal held that whether a duty of care exists is a matter for the jury on the facts they are trying.

2.6.4.8 Who decides whether there is a duty to act?

Above, you will see that the Court of Appeal in *Khan* identified that whether a duty to act exists is a matter for the jury. Jefferson (*Criminal Law*, 12th edn (Pearson, 2015)) argues that '*Khan* is wrong. Juries cannot expand and contract the various duties to act ... juries cannot alter the outcome ... by changing the law.' Jefferson goes on to say that '... *Singh* represents the better view, because *Khan* might lead to a jury saying that because the victim is dead, there must have arisen a duty to prevent that death'. The issue has been addressed and resolved by the Court of Appeal in *Evans.* In particular, Lord Judge CJ explained that:

> In any cases where the issue is in dispute ... and assuming that the judge has found that it would be open to the jury to find that there was a duty of care, or a duty to act, the jury should be directed that if facts a + b and/or c or d are established, then in law a duty will arise, but if facts x or y or z were present, the duty would be negatived.

In essence, whether a duty to act exists is a matter for the jury once the trial judge has decided that there is evidence *capable* of establishing a duty.

2.6.4.9 Multiple duties

There may of course be circumstances where more than one duty to act arises in a given case. It will be necessary, therefore, to consider each duty to act and analyse which duty would be the strongest to take forward when considered in light of the three requirements for omission liability. It may be the case that one duty stands out, or that a combination of duties can work together to establish liability. Take the case of *Evans* as an example. The number of duties that arose in that case were quite substantial:

- duty based on a special relationship (half-sisters);
- duty based on the assumption of responsibility and care (the defendant looked after the victim); and
- duty based on the creation of a dangerous situation (Evans contributed to a dangerous situation by supplying the drugs and failed to avert it).

2.6.5 Can an individual be 'released' from his duty?

Whether an individual can be 'released' from his duty is different from that of a 'termination' of duty. In the latter case, we are concerned with a situation where the duty to act has finished as a result of the completion of a certain act or after a certain time period. For example, the statutory duty under s 1 of the Children and Young Persons Act 1933 is terminated upon the child reaching 16. Some other examples may assist with this idea of 'termination':

- During the school day, the individual teachers have a duty to act in relation to their pupils. Out of school hours, however, their duty is terminated until it recommences the following day.
- Upon Jack placing his elderly mother into a care home, his duty towards her will have terminated. If his elderly mother were to return to his care, however, the duty would naturally recommence.

The idea of termination is not concrete. One may argue that a duty never terminates but, rather, is put 'on hold'. One may also argue that there is no distinction between a 'termination' of duty and being 'released' from one's duty. In both cases, the individual is no longer under a duty to act in certain circumstances.

It is contended, however, that the distinction lies in the manner of being released from a duty. Should a duty extinguish as a result of the passage of time, eg the end of employment or the completion of an act, this would amount to the 'termination' of a duty. A 'release', on the other hand, is concerned with the circumstances where the victim, orally or by conduct, voluntarily relieves an individual of his duty to act. In theory, this is useful distinction; in practice, however, it is unlikely to have any great effect.

In relation to being 'released' from one's duty to act, we are concerned with two specific contexts.

2.6.5.1 Duty passing to another

The first circumstance to consider is whether an individual can be released from his duty upon it being passed to another.

example

Jack finds Jill unconscious in their home. Jack attempts to revive her but fails and instead calls for an ambulance.

In this example, Jack has established a duty upon attempting to revive Jill; however, upon arrival of the ambulance, surely common sense would dictate that the duty to act would transfer from Jack to the emergency services who are now responsible for the care of Jill.

2.6.5.2 Duty is absolved

The second circumstance is where the victim releases the individual from his duty to act, as opposed to the duty being passed on to another. This is a difficult concept to understand given the necessity for a rational and autonomous decision on the part of the victim who releases the individual from his duty. Some light was shed on this area by the first instance decision of *R v Smith* [1979] Crim LR 251, where the trial judge in the Crown Court suggested that if a rational decision is possible from the victim, such decision may lawfully remove the defendant from his duty to act. Specifically, Griffiths J directed the jury to consider the following:

> If [the victim] does not appear too ill it may be reasonable to abide by her wishes. On the other hand, if she appeared desperately ill then whatever she may say it may be right to override.

A number of cases in the civil courts have determined that where a rational and mentally competent adult chooses to release someone from their duty of care, this must be legally adhered to. This is so even where it would be against the best interests of the party releasing the duty (*Re T (adult: refusal of treatment)* [1993] Fam 95; *Re C (adult: refusal of treatment)* [1994] 1 All ER 819; *St George's Healthcare NHS Trust v S* [1999] Fam 26).

example

Jack is a prisoner who has spent the majority of his young life in prison. Jack is addicted to drugs and has a history of self-harm. Jack voluntarily decides to go on hunger strike and dies from starvation. A number of psychiatrists confirmed Jack to be mentally competent.

These were the facts of *Secretary of State for the Home Department v Robb* [1995] Fam 127. The Family Division of the High Court ruled that where an individual is competent to make a decision, his decision overrides all state interests, and the prison authorities were within their right to abide by his decision. In effect, the prisoner released the prison authorities from their duty to provide him with nutrition.

The cases listed above, however, are civil cases and thus not binding in criminal matters. But should a criminal case such as this come forward in the appellate criminal court, the decision would likely accord with that of the civil courts. The issue for the courts will be the whether the individual was acting in an autonomous and rational manner. Autonomy is considered in more detail in **Chapter 7**, but for an excellent discussion of autonomous decision making, see Herring, *Medical Law & Ethics*, 8th edn (OUP, 2020).

2.6.6 Act or omission?

Up to this point, we have discussed the difference between positive acts or conduct and a failure to act. One thing to note, however, is that such a distinction is not an easy one to draw. Child and Ormerod (*Smith, Hogan, & Ormerod's Essentials of Criminal Law*, 3rd edn (OUP, 2019)) provide an excellent example of the difficulty in making this distinction, which has been adapted to conform to our previous examples.

example

Jack and Jill are playing tug-of-war and Jack lets go of the rope, causing Jill to fall and hurt herself. In this instance, the question becomes whether Jack has:

- acted (ie by letting go of the rope); or
- omitted (ie by stopping pulling the rope).

One might say that we look towards Jack's intention to find whether his letting go of the rope was an act or omission; however, this results in the blurring of the elements of *actus reus* and *mens rea*. In this scenario, it is likely that Jack will have acted in letting go of the rope given that the pair were engaging in a tug-of-war and it appears nonsensical that Jack should suddenly fail to continue to pull the rope. That is but one interpretation and demonstrates that the line between a positive act and an omission is not an easy one to draw. This is especially so given that we may not be fully aware of the facts of the case. Suppose Jack let go of the rope because a bee was flying around his head, or he noticed that someone was in peril and required assistance. Those circumstances would suggest a failure to continue pulling the rope as opposed to an act of letting go of the rope.

What this example should show is that it is not always clear whether we are dealing with an act or an omission. This statement does not just apply to students studying the law, but to members of the judiciary applying/interpreting the law. Take the case of *R v Speck* [1977] 2 All ER 859 as an example.

Charge:
Gross indecency (Indecency with Children Act 1960, s 1)

Case progression:
Crown Court – Guilty

Court of Appeal – Conviction upheld

Point of law:
The definition of an act or omission varies

case example

In *R v Speck* [1977] 2 All ER 859, the victim, a young girl, placed her hand on the defendant's penis causing him to have an erection. The defendant failed to move the girl's hand. The defendant was charged with and convicted of gross indecency in the Crown Court (an offence now contained in the Sexual Offences Act 2003).

The defendant appealed to the Court of Appeal, arguing that the offence required an '*act* of gross indecency'. The Court ruled that although the defendant's failure to remove the girl's hand amounted to an omission, the inactivity on the part of the defendant was an 'invitation to the child to undertake the act'.

Speck demonstrates that although the statute required an 'act' on part of the defendant, his inactivity in preventing the girl from continuing her act could amount to an act of gross indecency. The inactivity itself amounted to an invitation for the girl to continue in her actions and thus was sufficient for the jury to find the defendant liable. On *Speck*, Herring (*Criminal Law: Text, Cases, and Materials*, 9th edn (OUP, 2020)) contends that the conduct of the defendant could 'more naturally be regarded as an omission'. Herring goes on to say that '[i]t is hard to avoid the feeling that the court understandably disapproved of the man's actions and so labelled it as an act to ensure a conviction'.

Withdrawal of life support: act or omission?

Another example worthy of consideration is that of withdrawing life support treatment and whether this amounts to an act or omission. Our authority on this point is the case of *Airedale NHS Trust v Bland* [1993] AC 789 (see also the case of *Dr Arthur* (1981) 12 BMLR 1).

case example

Charge:
n/a. Declaration sought to withdraw life-saving treatment

Case progression:
High Court – Declaration granted

Court of Appeal – Appeal dismissed

House of Lords – Appeal dismissed

Point of law:
Whether withdrawing life support treatment amounts to murder

In *Airedale NHS Trust v Bland* [1993] AC 789, Anthony Bland was injured in the Hillsborough Stadium disaster, suffering irreversible brain damage, and as a result was in a persistent vegetative state (PVS). The doctors confirmed that there was no hope of recovery or improvement in his case. The doctors, with the support of Anthony's parents, sought a declaration to withdraw life-saving treatment and to allow Anthony to die.

Stephen Brown P in the High Court granted the declaration which was appealed by the Official Solicitor to the Court of Appeal on the basis that a withdrawal of treatment would amount to murder. The Court of Appeal dismissed the appeal of the Official Solicitor, who then appealed to the House of Lords asking the question as to whether such withdrawal was a positive act or omission and whether it amounted to murder. The House of Lords dismissed the appeal and reaffirmed the declaration to allow Anthony to die.

Lord Goff answered the question as follows:

> I agree that the doctor's conduct in discontinuing life support can properly be categorised as an omission. It is true that it may be difficult to describe what the doctor actually does as an omission, for example where he takes some positive step to bring the life support to an end. But discontinuation of life support is, for present purposes, no different from not initiating life support in the first place. In each case, the doctor is simply allowing his patient to die in the sense that he is desisting from taking a step which might, in certain circumstances, prevent his patient from dying as a result of his pre-existing condition: and as a matter of general principle an omission such as this will not be unlawful unless it constitutes a breach of duty to the patient.

The removal of treatment, therefore, is considered as being an omission. One can explain the decision in *Airedale* in the following manner:

- A doctor, responsible for the patient's health, will not be considered as committing an act in circumstances where they withdraw treatment. The removal (or 'discontinuation') of treatment is to be treated in the same way as if treatment was never given in the first place. In this regard, the conduct of the doctor is to be considered an omission.
- On the other hand, should a third party turn off the life support machine (eg such as a jealous ex-partner), this is likely to be considered an act, as opposed to an omission.

This latter point was made by Lord Goff in the following terms:

> I also agree that the doctor's conduct is to be differentiated from that of, for example, an interloper who maliciously switches off a life support machine because, although the interloper may perform exactly the same act as the doctor who discontinues life support, his doing so constitutes interference with the life-prolonging treatment then being administered by the doctor. Accordingly, whereas the doctor, in discontinuing life support, is simply allowing his patient to die of his pre-existing condition, the interloper is actively intervening to stop the doctor from prolonging the patient's life, and such conduct cannot possibly be categorised as an omission.

Butler-Sloss P in *NHS Trust A v M* [2001] Fam 348 confirmed the principles in *Bland* and found that a failure to provide medical treatment will not be incompatible with Article 2 of the ECHR (the right to life) in circumstances where the continuation of life is not in the best interests of the patient.

The distinction between acts and omissions following *Bland* has been criticised by the likes of Ashworth ('The Scope of Criminal Liability for Omissions' (1989) 105 LQR 424) who argues:

> Whether we term certain events 'acts' or 'omissions' may be both flexible in practice and virtually insoluble in theory: for example, does a hospital nurse who decides not to replace an empty bag for a drip feed make an omission, whilst a nurse who switches off a ventilator commits an act? It would seem wrong that criminal liability or non-liability should turn on such fine points, which seem incapable of reflecting any substantial moral distinctions in a context where the preservation of life is generally paramount. ... The proper solution is not to warp the concepts of omission, duty, knowledge and causation, but to provide for such cases to be determined on new principles of justification. This would require the courts to be explicit about the grounds for exonerating doctors or nurses, *rather than concealing the reasons behind the act/omission distinction.* (emphasis added)

2.7 Causation

Where the defendant is charged with any result crime (ie a crime which requires a particular consequence to occur in order for liability to exist – see **2.3.2**), the prosecution must prove that his act or omission *caused* the prohibited result. Causation applies only to result crimes and has no part to play in conduct-only crimes given that the end result itself is irrelevant. **Figure 2.2** demonstrates this principle.

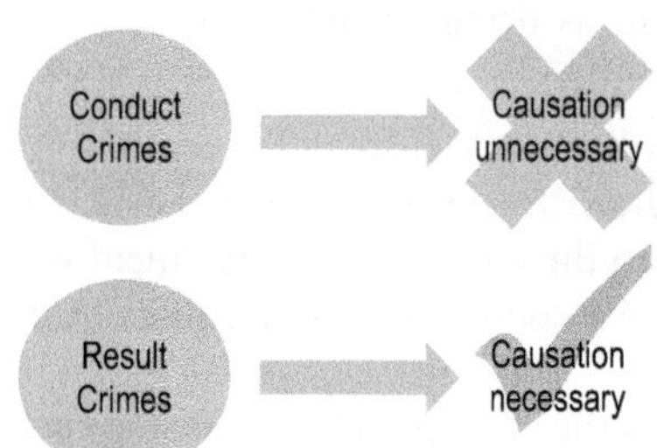

Figure 2.2 Conduct and result crimes and causation

Many students often cite causation as an element separate to that of the *actus reus* and *mens rea*. This is incorrect. Causation is an essential element of the *actus reus* of a criminal offence where an end result is necessary for liability to be present (result crimes). Therefore, ensure that when you deal with causation, you make it clear that it remains part of the *actus reus* of an offence.

in practice

In most cases, causation rarely becomes an issue. For example, in homicide cases, how the victim came to die is usually not in dispute. Often it is obvious that a victim, let us say Jack, died as a result of the act of the defendant, say Jill, in shooting him.

However, you are expected to be aware of the full remit of causation in your study of criminal law. Therefore, where there is a dispute, the question of causation is one for the jury to decide as a matter of fact. It is the duty of the trial judge to direct the jury on the legal principles relating to causation, but it is for the jury, applying those principles, to decide if the causal link between the defendant's conduct and the prohibited consequence has been established.

There are two main principles in causation:

- causation in fact (factual causation); and
- causation in law (legal/imputable causation).

The prosecution must prove both tests of causation in order for a defendant to be liable. The decision as to whether the prosecution has proven causation is a matter of fact for the jury (recently affirmed in *R v Clarke and Morabir* [2013] EWCA Crim 162). A further principle that requires discussion is that of new and intervening acts. Considered further at **2.7.3**, new and intervening acts are those that may disrupt the existence of liability against a defendant where the defendant's conduct is no longer considered the 'cause' of the end result.

In approaching an issue of causation, therefore, it is essential to follow a set plan.

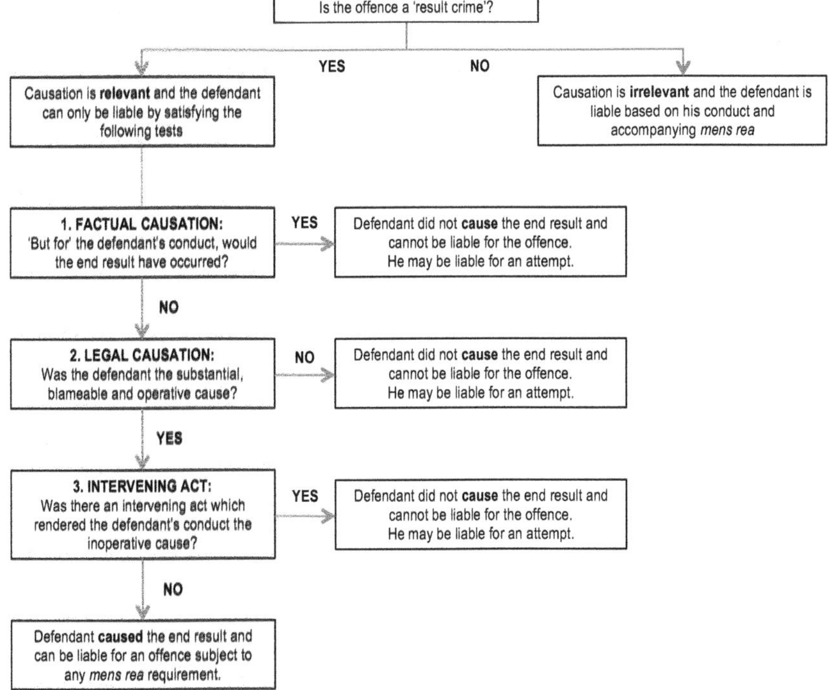

Figure 2.3 Approaching causation

We shall consider both forms of causation now and then deal with new and intervening acts.

2.7.1 Factual causation

Also known as 'causation in fact', this test requires the prosecution to establish that the consequence or end result would not have occurred as and when it did *but for* the defendant's conduct. This test is known as the 'but for' test and is one of simple fact for the arbiters of fact. Essentially, where the consequence or end result would have happened anyway, despite the act or omission on the part of the defendant, there is no liability. We call this a *causa sine qua non* (often shortened to *sine qua non*) which essentially means 'without which it could not be'. Simply, the defendant's act or omission must have caused the end result. The classic example of factual causation in operation can be seen in *R v White* [1910] 2 KB 124.

case example

Charge:
Murder

Case progression:
Crown Court –
Not guilty, but guilty of attempted murder

Court of Criminal Appeal –
Conviction upheld

Point of law:
The defendant must be the factual cause of the end result

In *R v White* [1910] 2 KB 124, the defendant attempted to poison his mother with potassium cyanide by placing the deadly substance in her lemonade. Whilst his mother did drink some of the liquid, she died having suffered from a heart attack. The medical evidence demonstrated that death resulted from the heart attack, and not from the poison. The defendant was charged with murder.

The Court of Criminal Appeal held that the defendant could not be liable for murder as there was not a *sine qua non* because his mother would have died anyway.

Note, however, that the son was convicted of attempted murder (see **Chapter 5**).

Contrast *White* with the case of *R v Dyson* [1908] 2 KB 454 in which the victim, a three-month-old child, would have likely died from meningitis. The defendant attacked the child and the Court of Criminal Appeal was satisfied that the defendant has *accelerated* the victim's death. In this regard, the defendant was the factual cause of death as a result of his acts accelerating the child's death.

Often, students struggle to grasp the concept of 'but for' and get lost in the wording. Suppose Jack wishes to kill Jill; **Figure 2.4** will assist with this matter.

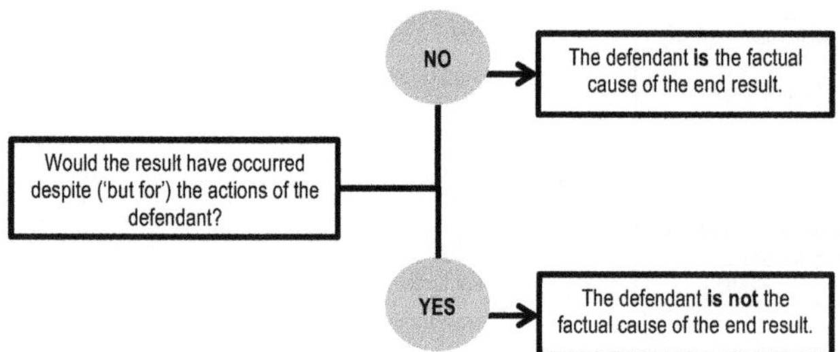

Figure 2.4 Operation of factual causation

In many cases, factual causation will be obvious, eg Jack dies from being shot in the head by Jill. In this instance, Jill is clearly the factual cause of death, but that does not mean that the principle can be ignored or brushed over; it should still be explained in full (see *R v Mitchell* [1983] QB 741).

2.7.2 Legal causation

Legal causation, also known as 'causation in law' or 'imputable causation', is a much narrower and more subjective concept than factual causation. Although both concepts use the word 'cause', the distinction between the two is of utmost importance. A significant point to remember is that 'not every cause in fact is a cause in law'.

So, factual causation looks at whether the defendant's actions caused, in a 'but for' sense, the end result. Legal causation, on the other hand, looks towards whether the defendant can be blamed for the end result that followed. Williams in his *Textbook of Criminal Law*, 2nd edn (Sweet & Maxwell, 1983) refers to this as a 'moral reaction' and helpfully summarises the position as follows:

> If the term 'cause' must be used, it can best be distinguished in this meaning as the 'imputable' or 'responsible' or 'blamable' cause, to indicate the value-judgment involved.

2.7.2.1 What is the difference between legal and factual causation?

At this moment, you may be scratching your head thinking, 'Well, what's the difference? They both deal with whether the defendant caused the end result.' Factual causation, if interpreted literally, is extremely broad, and who amounts to the 'factual' cause of harm can be extensive.

example

Jack and Jill live together. It is normal for Jack to drive Jill to work on a daily basis. The two, however, get into an argument and Jack tells Jill to take public transport. Jill does so and is injured when the bus she is riding is involved in an accident.

So, who is the factual cause of harm (ie but for their actions or conduct, Jill would not have been injured):

- the driver of the car involved in the accident ('but for' his conduct, Jill would not have been injured);
- Jack ('but for' his conduct, Jill would not have been on the bus and thus would not have been injured);
- the bus driver ('but for' his driving of the bus, Jill would not have been injured), etc?

The list, as you can see, could go on forever – it could even reach Jill's parents (ie 'but for' Jill's parents deciding to have a child, Jill would not be alive to be involved in an accident). Naturally, this is nonsensical, and if the 'but for' test is applied literally it will often lead to absurd results. Indeed, this was the view taken by the Supreme Court in *R v Hughes* [2013] UKSC 56 where Lord Hughes gave the following example:

> The law has frequently to confront the distinction between 'cause' in the sense of a sine qua non without which the consequence would not have occurred, and 'cause' in the sense of something which was a legally effective cause of that consequence. The former, which is often conveniently referred to as a 'but for' event, is not necessarily enough to be a legally effective cause. If it were, the woman who asked her neighbour to go to the station in his car to collect her husband would be held to have caused her husband's death if he perished in a fatal road accident on the way home. In the case law there is a well recognised distinction between conduct

which sets the stage for an occurrence and conduct which on a common sense view is regarded as instrumental in bringing about the occurrence

To avoid such an absurdity, legal causation steps in to narrow the scope of liability.

Legal causation requires several concepts to be met before the defendant is deemed as the legal cause of harm. These concepts are that the defendant must be:

- the substantial cause;
- the blameable cause; and
- the operative cause.

2.7.2.2 Substantial cause

The first concept provides that the defendant must be the 'substantial cause' of harm. This would appear, at first sight, to be a high threshold, requiring the defendant to be the only, or at very least the main, cause of the end result. This, however, is not the case. Rather, in English law, the defendant need only provide a contribution that is 'more than a minimal' (*R v Malcherek; R v Steel* [1981] 2 All ER 422). The phrase 'more than a minimal' has been expressed in many ways in different cases. For instance:

- In *R v Kimsey* [1996] Crim LR 35, Auld LJ upheld the trial judge's direction to the jury in which he said that the jury do not have to be sure that the defendant's conduct 'was the principal, or a substantial cause of the death, as long as you are sure that it was a cause and that there was something *more than a slight or a trifling link* between the [conduct] and the [end result]' (emphasis added).
- In *R v Cheshire* [1991] 3 All ER 670, Beldam LJ explained the requirement being that 'the defendant's acts can fairly be said to have a made a significant contribution to the victim's death'. According to Beldam LJ, 'significant contribution' means 'more than negligible'.

Both of these are simply different ways of explaining the principle that the defendant's conduct must be more than a minimal cause; any contribution that is less than a minimal will be excluded under the principle, and the defendant will not be liable for his actions.

Let us consider the following example which may assist in our understanding.

example

Jack pricks Jill's finger with a pin. The pin-prick breaks both layers of the skin (the dermis and epidermis) and causes Jill to bleed. Andy then stabs Jill in the chest. Jill is taken to hospital but dies a few hours later.

Both Jack and Andy have wounded Jill. According to *Moriarty v Brooks* (1834) 6 C & P 684, a wound is a break in both layers of the skin. Both Jack and Andy have done exactly that but on varying levels of severity. However, Jack's conduct in pricking Jill's finger will be deemed insignificant and trivial (in relation to murder) despite its status as an effective wounding. Andy's conduct is substantial whilst Jack's conduct is likely to be excluded as *de minimis*. As such, Andy will be liable for Jill's death, whereas Jack will not.

Multiple or 'concurrent' causes

There may be circumstances (as in the above example) where the defendant is not the *only* cause of harm. More often than not, multiple defendants faced with criminal liability will attempt to pass the blame (see *R v Benge* (1865) 4 F&F 504). This is often referred to as a 'cut-throat defence' and occurs when one defendant blames the other for the end result. Remember from above that the defendant, in order to be liable, need only be 'more than a minimal' cause of the end result.

What exactly does 'more than a minimal' cause mean though in such a scenario? Goff LJ in *R v Pagett* (1983) 76 Cr App R 279 reasoned that

> the accused's act need not be the sole cause, or even the main cause, of the victim's death, it being enough that his act *contributed significantly* to that result. (emphasis added)

According to the Court of Appeal in *R v Hennigan* [1971] 3 All ER 133, so long as the defendant's contribution was 'substantial', he could be liable for an offence. The Court did not wish to lay down a precise figure or limit on what conduct would be 'more than a minimal'; however, the trial judge did suggest that one-fifth of the blame was sufficient to attribute liability to the defendant. Whilst Lord Parker CJ referred to the trial judge's example of apportioning blame as 'unfortunate', the Court did not expressly reject the use of figures to assist a jury. Importantly, this does not mean that if a defendant is less than one-fifth to blame, he will not be considered a substantial cause. In all cases, the defendant must simply be more than merely a negligible or minimal cause. *Hennigan* was subsequently followed in *R v Notman* [1994] Crim LR 518 where the Court of Appeal held that anything more than a '*de minimis*' contribution will suffice. The most recent statement on contribution cases can be found in *R v Warburton and Hubbersty* [2006] EWCA Crim 627 where Hooper LJ held that:

> the test for the jury is a simple one: did the acts for which the Defendant is responsible significantly contribute to the victim's death.

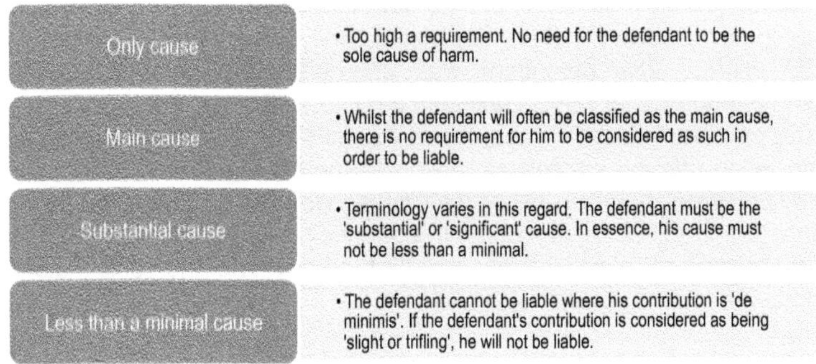

Figure 2.5 Understanding substantial cause

2.7.2.3 Blameable cause

The next concept to consider, and often the hardest for students to grasp, is that the defendant must be the 'blameworthy' cause of the end result. Naturally you may think that if the defendant caused the act, then clearly he is blameworthy. However, it is not as simple as that. When we speak of blameworthiness, we are concerned with whether the blameworthy conduct caused the end result, as opposed to whether the act or conduct was itself blameworthy.

A defendant's actions may be blameworthy in that they are unlawful or illegal; however, unless that blameworthy conduct actually *caused* the end result, the defendant is not the blameable cause for the purposes of legal causation.

Let us look at the classic example of blameworthiness in order to ascertain its meaning.

case example

Charge:
Gross negligence manslaughter

Case progression:
Assize Court – Not guilty

Point of law:
Whether a defendant's blameworthy conduct was the cause of the end result

In *R v Dalloway* (1847) 2 Cox CC 273, the defendant, whilst driving a cart and horse on a highway, allowed the reins to lie on the back of the horse, as opposed to keeping control of them. Such conduct was negligent on the part of the defendant. The victim, a small child, ran out into the road only a few yards ahead of the cart and was struck. The victim died. The defendant was charged with gross negligence manslaughter.

The court held that although the defendant's conduct was negligent, he could not have stopped the cart in time to save the victim had he had control of the reins.

Dalloway is the classic authority that the defendant is not liable for an offence unless his blameworthy conduct was the *cause* of the end result. Essentially, there must be an element of 'fault'. Emphasis is therefore best placed on whether the end result occurred *because* of the blameworthy conduct – in *Dalloway*, because of the defendant's negligent driving. Where that is not the case, the defendant cannot be said to be the blameworthy cause.

In recent years, however, the appellate courts have questioned whether this requirement for fault is necessary at all. Although the following cases all revolve around driving offences, they are entirely relevant to the broader concept of legal causation.

case example

Charge:
Aggravated vehicle taking (TA 1968, s 12A)

Case progression:
Crown Court – Guilty

Court of Appeal – Conviction upheld

Point of law:
Whether fault was necessary to convict a defendant

In *R v Marsh* [1997] 1 Cr App R 67, the defendant stole a car and was involved in an accident. The victim survived but was severely injured. The defendant was charged with and convicted of aggravated vehicle taking in the Crown Court.

On appeal, the Court of Appeal faced the question of whether fault was required in an offence worded as 'owing to the driving of the vehicle, an accident occurred by which injury was caused to any person'. The Court ruled that fault was not an element of the offence. Laws LJ held that the only relevant requirement of the offence was that the driving of the vehicle alone should have been the *cause* of the accident.

The Court of Appeal was not concerned with the *manner* of the driving. It ruled that once the basic offence of taking the vehicle had been committed, no further element of fault was required. All that was required was for the defendant to be driving the car on the road at that time. As can be appreciated, this sounds entirely contrary to *R v Dalloway*.

A similar issue arose in the case of *R v Williams* [2011] 3 All ER 969. Another driving offence, this case concerned the offence of driving when unlicensed, disqualified or uninsured, contrary to s 3ZB of the RTA 1988.

case example

Charge:
Driving when unlicensed, disqualified or uninsured (RTA 1988, s 3ZB)

Case progression:
Crown Court – Guilty

Court of Appeal – Conviction upheld

Point of law:
Whether fault was necessary to convict a defendant

In *R v Williams* [2011] 3 All ER 969, the defendant was driving through Swansea, without a licence or insurance, when a pedestrian crossed the central reservation and stepped in front of his car. The accident was entirely the fault of the pedestrian and could not have been avoided by the defendant. The defendant was charged with and convicted of driving whilst unlicensed.

On appeal, the Court of Appeal was concerned with the wording of the statute which provided that a person commits an offence if, being unlicensed, uninsured or disqualified, he '*causes the death of another person by driving a motor vehicle on a road*'. The Court of Appeal followed the decision of *Marsh* in that fault is not an element of the offence. Merely driving on the road without a licence or insurance was sufficient.

This judgment was criticised by many, including Sullivan and Simester ('Causation Without Limits: Causing Death While Driving Without a Licence, While Disqualified, or Without Insurance' [2012] Crim LR 753), who commented that *Dalloway* is the correct authority and it would be unethical to find a defendant liable for an offence where his conduct was not the blameworthy cause of the end result. Further, Hirst ('Causing Death by Driving and Other Offences: A Question of Balance' [2008] Crim LR 339), who wrote before the decision in *Williams*, contended:

> Lack of sympathy for disqualified or uninsured drivers should not however blind us to the fact that this new offence corrupts the usual principles governing causation.

See further, Crosby, 'Court of Appeal: Causing death by faultless driving' (2011) 75(2) J Crim L 111 and Ormerod at [2011] Crim LR 468.

A matter of weeks later, the Court of Appeal approached the exact same issue in *R v Hughes* [2011] EWCA Crim 1508 (also known as *R v H*). As you will see, the case eventually proceeded to the Supreme Court ([2013] UKSC 56).

case example

Charge:
Driving when unlicensed, disqualified or uninsured (RTA 1988, s 3ZB)

Case progression:
Crown Court – Guilty

Court of Appeal – Prosecution appeal upheld, defendant liable for offence

Supreme Court – Conviction quashed

Point of law:
Whether fault was necessary to convict a defendant

In *R v Hughes* [2011] EWCA Crim 1508, the defendant was driving his family's camper van without a licence or insurance, when a vehicle approached from the other direction, veering over both sides of the road. The other driver was overtired and was high on heroin. There was a collision in which other driver was killed. It was accepted that the defendant's driving was faultless and that there was nothing that he could have done to avoid the accident.

The trial judge, quite sensibly, ruled that he had not committed the offence because he had not 'caused' the death, following *Dalloway*.

The Court of Appeal overturned the ruling, once again applying *Marsh* that there was no requirement to prove fault in the manner of driving, simply that the driving of the car itself caused the end result.

Again, the Court of Appeal found liability to exist despite a lack of fault on part of the defendant. The case was, however, appealed to the Supreme Court (*R v Hughes* [2013] UKSC 56) which reversed the decision of the Court of Appeal and ruled that fault *was* an essential element of the offence.

The important passage from the Supreme Court's judgment was provided by Lord Hughes, who ruled:

> By the test of common sense, whilst the driving by Mr Hughes created the opportunity for his car to be run into by Mr Dickinson, what brought about the latter's death was his own dangerous driving under the influence of drugs. It was a matter of the merest chance that what he hit when he veered onto the wrong side of the road for the last of several times was the oncoming vehicle which Mr Hughes was driving. He might just as easily have gone off the road and hit a tree, in which case nobody would suggest that his death was caused by the planting of the tree, although that too would have been a sine qua non.

Later in his judgment, Lord Hughes concluded:

> There must be at least some act or omission in the control of the car, which involves some element of fault, whether amounting to careless/inconsiderate driving or not, and which contributes in some more than minimal way to the death.

Reviewing the Supreme Court's judgment in *Hughes*, Ormerod and Laird (*Smith, Hogan, & Ormerod's Criminal Law*, 15th edn (OUP, 2018)) comment that the decision is a 'welcome affirmation of the fundamental role played by legal causation'.

One would like to think that this was the end of the matter and that *Dalloway* had been confirmed as the correct position regarding the necessity for fault. Unfortunately it was not. In 2016, the Supreme Court was faced, yet again, with the question of whether fault was required in a driving offence. This time, the driving offence was of the same kind concerned in the *Marsh* case. This was the Supreme Court's opportunity to settle the debate once and for all.

case example

Charge:
Aggravated vehicle taking (TA 1968, s 12A)

Case progression:
Crown Court – Not guilty

Court of Appeal – Prosecution appeal upheld; defendant liable for offence

Supreme Court– Conviction quashed

Point of law:
Whether fault was necessary to convict a defendant

In *R v Taylor* [2016] UKSC 5, the defendant took a Ford Transit Tipper truck from a friend, in order to collect another friend from Exeter. The prosecution alleged that the truck was taken without the owner's consent. Having picked up the friend, the defendant was driving back home when he collided on a bend with a scooter driven by the victim. The scooter slid under the wheels of the truck, and the victim was killed. The defendant was found to be over the drink drive limit and uninsured; however, his driving was deemed faultless and open to no criticism. The defendant was acquitted of the offence which was then reversed by the Court of Appeal following *Williams*.

The Court of Appeal did, however, certify a question of public importance to the Supreme Court: 'Is an offence contrary to s 12A(1) and (2)(b) of the Theft Act 1968 committed when, following the basic offence and before recovery of the vehicle, the defendant drove the vehicle, and without fault in the manner of his driving the vehicle was involved in an accident which caused injury to a person.'

Lord Sumption, providing the unanimous judgment of a seven-member Supreme Court, allowed the appeal, answering 'no' to the certified question and ruling:

> ... the accident must have occurred 'owing to the driving of the vehicle', that there will have been something wrong with the driving ... the driving cannot be said to have caused the accident if it merely explained how the vehicle came to be in the place where the accident occurred.
>
> It follows from the admitted absence of fault in the driving of the vehicle that the driving did not cause the death of Mr Davidson-Hackett.

Lord Sumption would conclude:

> I would express the test applicable in this case in the same terms as Lord Hughes and Lord Toulson expressed it in *Hughes* at para 36. There must be 'at least some act or omission in the control of the car, which involves some element of fault, whether amounting to careless/inconsiderate driving or not, and which contributes in some more than minimal way to the death'.

It would appear that the law has now finally been clarified with *Taylor* effectively re-endorsing the decision of *Dalloway*. As a result, therefore, the defendant's blameworthy conduct must be the *cause* of the end result. There must be an element of fault in causation. Simply having conduct that is blameworthy is not sufficient; there must be fault.

Figure 2.6 should assist in understanding the position as a result of *Taylor*.

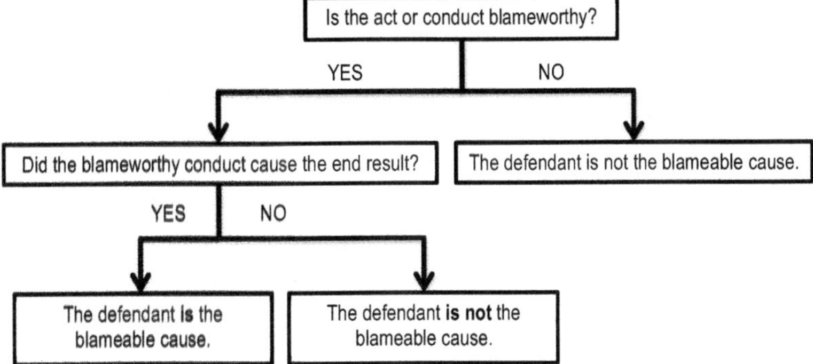

Figure 2.6 Understanding blameable conduct

2.7.2.4 Operative cause

The final factor is that the defendant must remain the 'operative' cause of harm. This means that the operation of his act or omission must remain the significant cause of the end result and must not have been superseded by another act, independent of the defendant. Indeed, a defendant may be both the factual and legal cause of the end result, but he may not be held liable if there is an intervening event (an act or an omission) which may 'break the chain of causation'. In this circumstance, the defendant will no longer be the operative cause of harm. For a detailed account of causation, see Hart and Honoré, *Causation in the Law*, 2nd edn (OUP, 1985). Intervening acts will be considered now at **2.7.3**.

2.7.3 New and intervening acts

A break in the chain of causation, also known as a *novus actus interveniens* or 'new and intervening act', will rid the defendant of liability for the consequence of his original act. Although the defendant will remain the factual cause of harm, the intervening act may supersede the blameable element of the defendant's conduct, thus ridding him of criminal liability for the end result. Remember, though, that he may still be liable for the original act or for an attempt.

The chain of causation may be broken in three distinct circumstances:

- the act of a third party (see **2.7.3.2**);
- an act of the victim (see **2.7.3.3**); or

- an unforeseeable natural event, sometimes called an 'act of God' (see **2.7.3.4**).

Lord Hoffmann in *Empress Car Co (Abertillery) Ltd v National Rivers Authority* [1999] 2 AC 22 stated:

> [I]t is of course the causal significance of acts of third parties (as in this case) or natural forces that gives rise to almost all the problems about the notion of 'causing' and drives judges to take refuge in metaphor or Latin.

Each of these three circumstances will be considered below. However, it is first essential to consider the general principles that arise when one considers new and intervening acts.

2.7.3.1 General principles

According to Goff LJ in *R v Pagett* (1983) 76 Cr App R 279, an intervening act is one that is 'so independent of the act of the accused that it should be regarded in law as the cause of the victim's death to the exclusion of the act of the accused'. **Table 2.10** details the most important principles to be aware of, and these principles will be fleshed out below.

Table 2.10 Principles of novus actus interveniens

Principle
No intervening act can break the chain of causation if it merely complements or aggravates the effects of the defendant's initial conduct.
Where the defendant's act is still the 'substantial and operating cause' of the result, the defendant may still be liable.
The intervening act must be independent of the defendant's conduct or an unforeseen event which is the immediate and sufficient cause of the end result.
The intervening act must be 'free, deliberate and informed'.

2.7.3.2 Act of a third party

A matter that has come before the courts on a number of occasions is the issue of a subsequent intervention by a third party. As you can imagine, it would be extremely unlikely (and often impossible) for a defendant to break his own chain of causation. In the event that the defendant did break his own chain of causation, he would remain liable for the offence in question, but the focus of the prosecution's case would shift from the original act to the subsequent act. This is more a matter of evidence than it is of practice or liability. As a result, this section is only concerned with the acts of third parties.

in practice

When considering whether the act of a third party broke the chain of causation, the prosecution may decide that it is appropriate to seek a charge against that third party. However, in problem questions, unless it tells you otherwise, only the liability of the defendant concerned should be considered. The actions of the third party are therefore relevant only to the liability, or lack thereof, of the defendant in question.

As a starting point, it is necessary to set out the test to be applied. According to *R v Kennedy (No 2)* [2008] 1 AC 269, the act of a third party will only break the chain of causation where:

(a) the third party's act is 'free, deliberate and informed'; and
(b) the defendant is no longer the 'substantial and operating cause'.

Development

Prior to *Kennedy (No 2)*, the law was in a state of flux with contrasting authorities and tests to be applied.

To begin with, the classic pronouncement of the *Kennedy (No 2)* test in operation today is the case of *R v Latif; R v Shahzad* [1996] 1 All ER 353. In *Latif*, the defendants intended to import heroin from Pakistan into the UK. Unbeknownst to the defendants, the drugs were flown to Britain by a British customs officer whilst the defendants were arrested in London. The House of Lords held that the actions of the customs officer broke the chain of causation as his actions of flying the drugs into the jurisdiction were 'free, deliberate and informed'. Lord Steyn commented that 'the general principle is that the free, deliberate and informed intervention of a second person, who intends to exploit the situation created by the first, but is not acting in concert with him, is held to relieve the first actor of criminal responsibility'. Importantly, although the defendants were not liable for importing the drugs, they were still liable for attempting to do so.

One can contrast the facts of this case with that of *R v Jakeman* (1982) 76 Cr App R 223, where the defendant booked suitcases containing drugs onto a series of flights to London. The defendant got cold feet and abandoned the suitcases in Paris. The cases, however, were still sent on to London where the drugs were eventually discovered. Although *novus actus interveniens* was not an issue in that case, it is clear that the actions of the defendant were still the substantial and operating cause, and no action on the part of the airport officials would break the chain of causation as their actions would not have been 'free, deliberate and informed'. *Jakeman* and the more recent case of *R v Styles* [2015] EWCA Crim 1619 will be discussed in greater detail in **Chapter 3**.

In 1999 came the controversial authority of *Empress Car Co (Abertillery) Ltd v National Rivers Authority* [1999] 2 AC 22 (*Empress Cars*), which operated in direct conflict with the decision in *Latif*.

case example

Charge:
Polluting controlled waters (Water Resources Act 1991, s 85)

Case progression:
Crown Court – Guilty

Court of Appeal – Conviction upheld

House of Lords – Conviction upheld

Point of law:
Legal causation in pollution cases

In *Empress Car Co (Abertillery) Ltd v National Rivers Authority* [1999] 2 AC 22, the defendant stored oil on its site. During the night, X (an unidentified stranger) released the oil into a watercourse as an act of vandalism. It was learned that the defendant had failed to take precautions to prevent acts of vandalism, or to restrict the subsequent release of fuel from the tap.

The issue before the House of Lords was whether the act of the third party broke the chain of causation. The third party's actions were clearly 'free, deliberate and informed'; however, the Lords held this to be the wrong principle. Rather, according to Lord Hoffmann, the question to be asked was whether the third party's act was a 'normal fact of life or something extraordinary'. Their Lordships held this case to be an example of the former and ruled that the chain of causation was not broken. The defendant company remained liable.

Justifying it on policy grounds, the Lords effectively created confusion in the law with the lower courts unsure as to which authority to follow: *Latif* or *Empress Cars*? Thankfully, the House of Lords in *R v Kennedy (No 2)* [2008] 1 AC 269 clarified the legal position of the *Empress Cars* precedent. Lord Bingham made clear that, although the House did not wish 'to throw any doubt' on the *Empress Cars* authority, it ought to be restricted to facts involving environmental offences (see *R (Natural England) v Day* [2014] EWCA Crim 2683 for an affirmation of this). As a result, therefore, in all cases, other than pollution cases, involving the act of a third party, the test to be applied is that in *Latif*. Upon the statement in *Kennedy*, Ashworth (*Principles of Criminal Law*, 6th edn (OUP, 2009)) helpfully restated the principle of *Latif*, namely that

> voluntary conduct acts as a barrier in any causal enquiry in criminal law; by and large, D's voluntary conduct will usually be regarded as the cause of an act or omission if it was the last human conduct before the result.

Therefore, we can now be settled in our minds that the act of a third party will only break the chain of causation in circumstances where it is 'free, deliberate and informed' and the defendant is no longer the 'substantial and operating' cause. However, what exactly do these phrases mean? We shall consider each in turn.

'Free, deliberate and informed'

Table 2.11 Free, deliberate and informed acts

Principle	Explanation	Example
Free	When we speak of 'free' conduct, we are concerned with circumstances where the third party is not acting in a justified or excused manner or where their actions are not a natural or foreseeable consequence of the defendant's actions.	*R v Pagett* (1983) 76 Cr App R 279
Deliberate	When we speak of 'deliberate' conduct, we are referring to 'voluntariness' and are concerned with whether the third party's actions were willed.	*Wise v Dunning* [1902] 1 KB 167
Informed	When we speak of 'informed' conduct, we often refer to so-called 'innocent agents'. Innocent agents may be *doli incapax*, insane or have no *mens rea*.	*R v Michael* (1840) 9 C & P 356

With these principles in mind, let us now look at the three cases listed in turn. First, the act must be 'free'.

case example

Charge:
Unlawful act manslaughter

Case progression:
Crown Court – Guilty

Court of Appeal – Conviction upheld

Point of law:
Whether a third party can break the chain where their actions are foreseeable as a result of the defendant's conduct

In *R v Pagett* (1983) 76 Cr App R 279, the defendant abducted the victim, his pregnant girlfriend, and used her as a 'human shield' when confronted by the police. The defendant fired at the police who then returned fire, killing the victim in the process. The defendant was charged with and convicted of constructive manslaughter, which was upheld in the Court of Appeal.

The Court of Appeal ruled that the officers had acted 'involuntarily' and in a manner that was not 'free'. The Court reasoned that the officers had acted reasonably for the purpose of 'self-preservation' and in performance of their legal duty to apprehend the defendant. The defendant remained the legal cause of death through his unlawful act.

Pagett is a demonstration that the courts take a broad interpretation of what conduct is 'free, deliberate and informed'. To this extent, the court can find that the chain of causation is broken in circumstances where they feel it is 'just' for it to be broken. Cases involving police officers performing their duties are clearly not in this bracket, which Ormerod and Laird (*Smith, Hogan, & Ormerod's Criminal Law*, 15th edn (OUP, 2018)) argue has 'compromised' the principles of legal causation. Such application of legal principles has led to many academics criticising the courts for their inconsistent and arbitrary judgments based very much on a 'desired conclusion' basis. Indeed, Williams (*Textbook of Criminal Law*, 2nd edn (Sweet & Maxwell, 1983)) describes the judiciary's use of legal causation as a 'moral reaction' whereby the courts seek certain 'desired' results.

In *Pagett*, it is clear that the officers did not intentionally or deliberately shoot the victim. Rather, they were responding to shots fired by the defendant. It is questionable whether the officers acted reasonably in firing back at the defendant; however, this point is moot given that it would make no difference to the outcome of the case. In summary, the police officers acted in a manner that was 'deliberate and informed' but was not 'free', in that their actions were a natural and foreseeable consequence of the defendant's conduct. In this regard, the police officer's conduct did not break the chain of causation.

Secondly, the act must be 'deliberate'/'voluntary'.

case example

Charge:
Breach of the peace

Case progression:
Magistrates' court – Bind over

Divisional Court – Bind over upheld

Point of law:
Whether the actions of a third party can break the chain where they 'appear' voluntary

In *Wise v Dunning* [1902] 1 KB 167, the defendant, a Protestant preacher, gave anti-Catholic speeches in Liverpool which he knew would cause the audience to react violently, which they did. The magistrates' court bound him over (ie had him agree) to keep the peace which he then breached.

The defendant appealed by way of 'case stated' to the Divisional Court, arguing that he should not be liable for any breach of the peace caused by a third party. The Divisional Court ruled that the violence arose as a 'natural consequence' of the defendant's actions.

Dunning is a complex case involving both substantive and procedural points of law. *Dunning* has been used as an example here to demonstrate that the actions of third parties (ie the members of the crowd) will not break the chain of causation where their actions are not 'voluntary'. You may think this idea sounds absurd. Herring (*Criminal Law: Text, Cases, and Materials*, 9th edn (OUP, 2020)) agrees and argues that this case stretches the meaning of 'voluntary' to its extreme. The easiest way to appreciate this decision is to break it down into a common sense understanding:

- The violence erupted as a result of the defendant's actions in making the speech.
- The defendant knew the crowd would react violently.
- The reaction to turn to violence was 'instinctive' and without thought on the part of the crowd.

Have you ever acted without thought? Become so angry or upset that you say or do something out of character? That was the position here, and although it may be considered a stretch in meaning, it is a useful demonstration of the meaning of voluntary.

Finally, the act must be 'informed'.

Charge:
Murder

Case progression:
Court for Crown Cases Reserved – Guilty

Point of law:
Whether a third party could break the chain of causation when uninformed as to their actions

case example

In *R v Michael* (1840) 9 C & P 356, the defendant desired her baby dead and handed a bottle of laudanum (poison) to a nurse, telling her that it was medicine for the baby. The nurse regarded the medicine as unnecessary and placed it on the mantelpiece unaware that it was poison. The nurse's child, aged five, picked up the poison and administered it to the baby. The baby died as a result.

The Court held that the mother remained the legal cause of death. This was despite the actions of the five-year-old who was described by the Court as 'an unconscious agent', thus not resulting in a break in the chain of causation.

The case of *Michael* is an authority on two points. The first being the so-called 'intended results' cases where a defendant is liable where they intended a result and that result occurs. This shall be discussed in greater detail in **Chapter 3**, but for now it is worth stating that despite the manner of death of the child, the end result of death was as the defendant desired. Hart and Honoré in their text, *Causation in the Law*, 2nd edn (OUP, 1985) do not take this view and argue that the 'intended result' did not occur. The true intended result was for the nurse to administer the deadly substance, not the child. Specifically, the pair state that the child was 'not in any sense an agent, conscious or unconscious, of the mother, who intended [X] alone to give the poison to the child'.

The second point is that which we are more concerned with, namely whether the act of the child was a *novus actus interveniens*. The Court was clear that the actions of the child could not amount to a new and intervening act. Hart and Honoré go on to say that 'the decision may be justified on the ground that … the act of the child of five did not negative causal connexion between the prisoner's act and the death'. Essentially, given that the child was an 'innocent agent' (as a result of her age) and being uninformed of the poisonous substance, her actions could not amount to a 'free, deliberate and informed' intervention. Should the child have drunk the substance, as opposed to administering it to the victim, the doctrine of transferred malice (see **Chapter 3**) would operate to maintain the liability of the defendant.

That is the first element for you to consider when faced with an intervention from a third party. Ensure that you are clear in any answer given whether the third party is truly acting in a 'free, deliberate and informed' manner. If they are, you may then consider the second element; namely, whether the defendant remains the 'operating and substantial' cause.

Operating and substantial cause

This principle is merely a reflection of that considered above in legal causation. Essentially, the defendant must remain the imputable, or legal, cause of the end result. In *R v Rafferty* [2007] EWCA Crim 1846, the Court of Appeal quashed a defendant's conviction for manslaughter on account that his co-defendants (who were convicted of murder) had broken the chain of causation by inflicting further injuries on the victim and leaving him in a dangerous state in the absence of the defendant. *Rafferty* is one of those few cases in which the chain of causation has been broken by an act of a third party.

A useful way to demonstrate this particular area of law, and its development, is by looking at two different examples:

(i) cases involving driving offences; and
(ii) cases involving medical intervention.

(i) Driving cases

This first sub-section is justified on account that a common feature of accidents and collisions on the road is the attempt to pass blame. By way of a simple example, Jack is driving his car at speed and tailgates a car driven by Jill. Suppose Jill applies the brakes without due cause and Jack collides into the back of Jill's car, killing Andy who was sat in the back seat. Who is responsible for Andy's death? Jill for applying the brakes without reason, or Jack for tailgating at speed and ultimately colliding with Jill?

The point to appreciate here is that, as noted above, there may be multiple causes of the same end result. We need to consider, however, what the circumstances are where one party can legitimately pass blame from themselves to another. The test to be applied in these circumstances is whether the subsequent conduct of the third party is 'reasonably foreseeable' to the defendant (*R v Girdler* [2009] EWCA Crim 2666). In *Girdler*, the defendant had driven into the back of a taxi. The collision resulted in the taxi being propelled into the fast lane leaving it broadside to the oncoming traffic. A car in the fast lane collided with the taxi, killing both the driver of the car and the taxi. The issue for the jury was:

- Who was responsible for the death of the driver of the car?
- Who was responsible for the death of the taxi driver?

The jury found no difficulty in concluding that the defendant had caused the death of the driver of the car, through his dangerous driving that propelled the taxi into the fast lane. However, the jury could not be sure that the defendant was responsible for the death of the taxi driver, given that there was a subsequent act (ie the act of the driver of the car) which caused the fatal accident. The appeal itself is not relevant for our purposes. Rather, it was the conclusion of the Court in reviewing the existing area of law. In particular, the Court departed from the 'free, deliberate and informed' test noted above on the basis that (per Hooper LJ)

> offences of causing death by dangerous and careless driving will punish the conduct of a person who has not intended or necessarily foreseen the consequences of his driving. Such a person is in a very different position to a person who has intended to kill or cause serious bodily harm or who has the *mens rea* for manslaughter.

Hooper LJ would go on to state what he believed the appropriate direction to the jury could be:

> We suggest that a jury could be told, in circumstances like the present where the immediate cause of death is a second collision, that if they were sure that the defendant drove dangerously and were sure that his dangerous driving was more than a slight or trifling link to the death(s) then:
>
> the defendant will have caused the death(s) only if you are sure that it could sensibly have been anticipated that a fatal collision might occur *in the circumstances in which the second collision did occur*.
>
> The judge should identify the relevant circumstances and remind the jury of the prosecution and defence cases. If it is thought necessary it could be made clear

> to the jury that they are not concerned with what the defendant foresaw. (emphasis added)

Girdler is therefore authority for two propositions: (a) the test is one of reasonable foreseeability; and (b) the subsequent act need not be 'free, deliberate and uninformed' to break the chain of causation; it may be an accidental or unintended intervention that breaks the chain (so long as it was not reasonably foreseeable).

A question that naturally leads on from *Girdler*, however, is this: What must be reasonably foreseen? This was the issue in the recent case of *R v A* [2020] EWCA Crim 407. In summary, the defendant had parked her car on the hard shoulder of a motorway for no legitimate purpose. The car displayed no hazard lights, or any other car lights. A lorry driven by the second defendant, who had fallen asleep behind the wheel, traversed from the outside lane of the motorway to the hard shoulder and collided with the defendant's car, killing one of the passengers.

At trial, the judge ruled that in order for the chain to be maintained, the defendant must have reasonably foreseen the particular subsequent act that could have followed (ie that a lorry would have travelled across numerous lanes of the motorway and collided with the defendant's car). The trial judge reached this conclusion on account that, in *Girdler*, Hooper LJ used the phrase 'in the circumstances in which the second collision did occur'. As such circumstances were not reasonably foreseen, the charge was withdrawn from the jury and the defendant acquitted. The prosecution successfully appealed to the Court of Appeal on the basis that the trial judge erred in his reading of *Girdler*. The Court of Appeal agreed, with Simon LJ ruling that:

> What had to be sensibly anticipated was that another vehicle might leave the carriageway and collide with the respondent's parked car. It would not be necessary for the jury to be sure that the *particular circumstances* of the collision or 'the exact form' of the subsequent act was reasonably foreseeable.
>
> It follows that, in our view, the Judge adopted too confined an interpretation of the *Girdler* formulation, and as a consequence he erred in his conclusion that there was no case to answer.
>
> If a driver leaves a car, on the hard shoulder of a motorway for 15 minutes at 4.30 am on a November morning, without displaying any lights, a jury could properly conclude that *some form of collision* could occur, and that, if it were occupied, death or serious injury could be caused. (emphasis added)

Following *R v A*, therefore, the precise details or 'exact form' of the subsequent third party action need not be reasonably foreseeable; it is merely the case that some sort of third party intervention would be foreseeable. See also *R v Wallace (Berlinah)* [2018] EWCA Crim 690 and the Canadian authority of *R v Maybin* [2012] 2 SCR 30 (both of which were relied upon by Simon LJ).

(ii) Medical intervention cases

Foreseeably, as you can expect, a victim who has suffered at the hands of the defendant is likely to require medical assistance. What may also be foreseeable, however, is that such assistance may be negligently given with potential misdiagnosis, poorly executed procedure or maltreatment. It can be made clear at the start that a failure to provide proper treatment for an initial injury seldom amounts to an independent cause of death or injury. Indeed, Beldam LJ in *R v Cheshire* [1991] 3 All ER 670 said that it is only in

> the most extraordinary and unusual case that such treatment can be said to be *so independent* of the acts of the accused that it could be regarded in law as a cause of the victim's death to the exclusion of the accused's acts. (emphasis added)

According to the editors of *Blackstone's Criminal Practice* (OUP, 2020), 'it is far more likely that such failure will merely aggravate the original injury, or that it will allow the original injury to take its natural course'.

Despite this clear statement, it remains essential to observe how the law in this area has developed and apply that to the test of 'operating and substantial' cause. We begin our discussion with a consideration of the case of *R v Jordan* (1956) 40 Cr App R 152.

case example

Charge:
Murder

Case progression:
Crown Court – Guilty

Court of Criminal Appeal – Conviction quashed

Point of law:
Medical treatment breaking the chain of causation

In *R v Jordan* (1956) 40 Cr App R 152, the defendant stabbed the victim who was taken to hospital. During treatment at the hospital, the doctor administered a drug to which the victim was allergic. The victim died as a result of an allergic reaction to the drug. In the Crown Court, the defendant was convicted; however, on appeal, the Court of Criminal Appeal quashed his conviction, ruling that the doctor had broken the chain of causation.Two key submissions were presented on appeal:

- The original wound had largely healed at the time of death.
- The doctor should have known that the victim was intolerant to the drug.

The Court ruled that the doctor's treatment was 'palpably wrong' and thus broke the chain of causation as the defendant was no longer the 'substantial and operative' cause of death.

The decision of *Jordan* has been significantly narrowed by the subsequent decisions in *R v Smith* [1959] 2 QB 35 and *R v Cheshire* [1991] 3 All ER 670.

case example

Charge:
Constructive manslaughter

Case progression:
Court-Martial – Guilty

Courts-Martial Appeal Court – Conviction upheld

Point of law:
Medical treatment breaking the chain of causation

In *R v Smith* [1959] 2 QB 35, the defendant stabbed the victim, a fellow soldier from a different regiment, with a bayonet during a fight. Upon transporting the victim to the medical centre, several other soldiers dropped the victim twice. An overworked doctor failed to notice that one of the victim's lungs had been punctured. The treatment was described by the Courts-Martial Appeal Court as 'thoroughly bad' and such that it 'might well have affected his chances of recovery'.

The defendant was convicted of constructive manslaughter in the Court-Martial and his conviction was upheld on appeal in the Courts-Martial Appeal Court, which ruled that the defendant remained the 'substantial and operating' cause of death despite the poor treatment from the doctor.

You may well wonder why *Smith* did not follow the decision in *Jordan*. According to the Courts-Martial Appeal Court, the decision in *Smith* could be distinguished from *Jordan* in that the wounds inflicted by Smith had not healed and remained the cause of death. Whereas in *Jordan*, the wounds had virtually healed and it could not be said that the defendant remained the 'substantial and operating' cause. In the end, the Courts-Martial Appeal Court in *Smith* declared that *Jordan* was a 'very particular case depending upon its exact facts'. Indeed, this was the opinion of the Court of Appeal in *R v Blaue* [1975] 1 WLR 1411 where Lawton LJ explained that *Jordan* was 'probably rightly decided on its facts' but that it should 'be regarded as a case decided on its own special facts and not as an authority relaxing the common law approach to causation'.

The *ratio* of the decision in *Smith* is as follows (per Lord Parker CJ):

> [I]f at the time of death the original wound is still an operating cause and a substantial cause, then the death can properly be said to be the result of the wound, albeit that some other cause of death is also operating. Only if it can be said that the original wounding is merely the setting in which another cause operates can it be said that the death does not result from the wound. Putting it in another way, only if the second cause is *so overwhelming as to make the original wound merely part of the history* can it be said that the death does not flow from the wound. (emphasis added)

The most authoritative decision in this area of law now is that of *R v Cheshire.*

case example

Charge:
Murder

Case progression:
Crown Court – Guilty

Court of Appeal – Conviction upheld

Point of law:
Medical treatment breaking the chain of causation

In *R v Cheshire* [1991] 3 All ER 670, the defendant shot the victim in the leg and stomach during an argument. The victim was taken to hospital and placed in intensive care, where a tracheotomy tube was inserted into his windpipe as a result of breathing difficulties. The victim died two months after the shooting as a result of complications in the tracheotomy procedure.

The defendant was convicted in the Crown Court and his conviction upheld in the Court of Appeal despite the fact that the gunshot wounds had healed at the time of death and the medical treatment was the 'immediate' cause of death. The Court of Appeal ruled that the complications were a 'natural consequence' of the defendant's actions and the chain of causation was not broken. The defendant remained the 'operating and substantial' cause of death.

Beldam LJ concluded:

> ... when the victim of a criminal act is treated for wounds or injuries by doctors or other medical staff attempting to repair the harm done, it will only be in the most extraordinary and unusual case that such treatment can be said to be so independent of the acts of the accused that it could be regarded in law as a cause of the victim's death to the exclusion of the accused's acts ...
>
> Even though negligence in the treatment of the victim was the immediate cause of his death, the jury should not regard it as excluding the responsibility of the accused unless the negligent treatment was so independent of his acts, and in itself so potent in causing death, that they regard the contribution made by his acts as insignificant.

From the above authorities, it is clear that the chain of causation is unlikely to be broken in circumstances involving poor medical treatment. The decision in *Cheshire* has been criticised as illogical and policy-driven, given that act of the defendant was not the 'immediate' cause of death but, rather, the medical intervention was. As Jefferson (*Criminal Law*, 12th edn (Pearson, 2015)) makes clear, the defendant was held to have 'significantly contributed' to the death despite the fact that the victim was shot in the leg and chest, but died as a result of the narrowing of his throat. Despite these criticisms, the decision of *Cheshire* has subsequently been followed in such cases as *R v McKechnie* (1991) 94 Cr App R 51 and *R v Mellor* [1996] 2 Cr App R 245.

in practice

Think about the justification for the decision in *Cheshire* practically. The courts do not wish to accept an argument from an accused that, as a result of poor medical treatment, he is not liable for the act that necessitated the medical intervention in the first place. Indeed, the meaning of 'so independent' and 'so potent' remains unclear, granting the courts a wide amount of discretion to deal with cases on a fact-by-fact basis. Jefferson (*Criminal Law*, 15th edn (Pearson, 2015)) argues that the ruling 'would seem to be one which protects medical staff from the consequences of their carelessness'; others such as Stannard ('Criminal Causation and the Careless Doctor' (1992) 55(4) MLR 577) argue, however, that medical treatment cannot be regarded as 'abnormal' given the pressures placed on emergency units.

Whatever the argument, one cannot deny that policy had a great impact upon this decision and demonstrates, as Ormerod and Laird (*Smith, Hogan, & Ormerod's Criminal Law*, 15th edn (OUP, 2018)) argue, that the 'status of the third party' may well affect whether the chain of causation is broken (as also seen in *Pagett* above).

The statement of law is now clear: Although a break in the chain of causation is possible, following *Jordan*, medical intervention is unlikely to break the chain and, following *Cheshire*, will only do so where the intervention is 'so independent … and in itself so potent in causing death, that [the jury] regard the contribution made by [the defendant's] acts as insignificant'.

As a final note, according to the Court of Appeal in *R v Suratan* [2004] EWCA Crim 1246, juries require careful guidance on the issues before them, especially when they are required to decide the cause of death and whether medical treatment was so 'palpably wrong' that the defendant is no longer the substantial and operating cause of death. See also *R v Dear* [1996] Crim LR 595 and *McKechnie*. Be aware, however, as with all expert evidence, the jury are entitled to ignore it (*R v Stockwell* (1993) 97 Cr App R 260).

in practice

Do not confuse the effects that *Smith* and *Cheshire* had on the decision in *Jordan*. *Jordan* remains good law and is an authority that you can use to argue that the chain of causation is broken. Use the facts of *Jordan* to assist you, and if the facts are similar (ie a wound had largely healed and the treatment so palpably wrong), use them to suggest that the chain is broken. Ensure you substantiate why you think the chain is broken and battle against the arguments that suggest the chain remains intact.

An interesting application of the rule in *Smith*, and later in *Cheshire*, is the decision in *R v Malcherek; R v Steel* [1981] 2 All ER 422, which concerned the switching off of a life support machine several days after the defendant had inflicted serious wounds upon the victim. The defendant argued that the act of the doctor in disconnecting the life support machine had broken the chain of causation and caused the death of the victim. The defendant argued that this was so despite the injuries inflicted. Lord Lane CJ in the Court of Appeal concluded:

> There may be occasions, although they will be rare, when the original injury has ceased to operate as a cause at all, but in the ordinary case if the treatment is given

> *bona fide* by competent and careful medical practitioners, then evidence will not be admissible to show that the treatment would not have been administered in the same way by other medical practitioners. In other words, the fact that the victim has died, despite or because of medical treatment for the initial injury given by careful and skilled medical practitioners, will not exonerate the original assailant from responsibility for the death.

The defendant, therefore, remained the operating and substantial cause of death, with Herring (*Criminal Law: Text, Cases, and Materials*, 9th edn (OUP, 2020)) commenting that, 'After all, what did the victim die from when the machine was switched off, if not the injuries inflicted by the defendant?' Again, it would appear as though policy and good sense dictates the flow of this area of law with Jefferson (*Criminal Law*, 12th edn (Pearson, 2015)) quite usefully summarising that the 'courts seem to be pulling the law on causation to exculpate doctors and the police in order to catch the attacker'.

An interesting point that arises here and relates back to our discussion of omission liability concerns whether the withdrawal of treatment is an act or an omission. Kennedy ('Switching Off Life Support Machines' [1977] Crim LR 443) points out that the withdrawal of treatment may be considered an act (by physically turning off the life support machine) or an omission (by failing to continue to provide treatment). The distinction in this case is essentially moot given that we are concerned with the medical intervention and whether such would break the chain of causation; however, it may be relevant when one considers whether an omission can be 'free, deliberate and informed'.

Omissions and intervening acts

The final point worthy of consideration here is whether an omission of a third party, as opposed to a positive act, can break the chain of causation. Herring, *Criminal Law: Text, Cases, and Materials*, 9th edn (OUP, 2020) suggests not and explains:

> If the defendant stabbed the victim, who was taken to hospital but died because no medical treatment was offered, then the defendant would be said to have caused the death.

Indeed, this view has particular merit on account that the defendant in this situation would still be considered the substantial and operating cause of the end result. It is debatable how far this view can go, however. Suppose Jack pushes Jill into deep water knowing that she cannot swim. Bob is the acting lifeguard on that day, notices Jill struggling and ignores her. Jill drowns. In this circumstance, can it be said that Jack will remain the cause of Jill's death (given that he pushed her into the pool), or will Bob have broken the chain of causation given that he had a duty to act (a contractual duty as a lifeguard) and failed to do so? This is especially pertinent if Jack knew that Bob was on duty: is it appropriate to make Jack liable in these circumstances? Ultimately, this would be a question of fact for the jury, but it is worthwhile to note that an omission *may* be capable of breaking the chain of causation, in the eyes of a jury, in certain circumstances.

2.7.3.3 Act of the victim

The second circumstance where the chain of causation may be broken is as a result of the victim's own act. The victim's act may break the link between the original act of the defendant and the end result. There are three key scenarios worth considering under this heading:

(1) The victim may bring about the end result in attempting to escape from the defendant. These cases are often referred to as 'fright and flight' cases and look to see whether the acts of the victim are foreseeable or unreasonable.
(2) Known as the 'drug-dealing' cases, here the court questions whether the victim's self-administration of drugs will break the chain of causation rendering the accused, the 'drug-dealer', not liable for the death or injuries that follow administration.
(3) The final circumstance is more of a mixed bag and consists of where the victim refuses medical treatment, exacerbates their injuries through neglect or self-aggravation, or ends their own life as a result of the defendant's conduct.

We shall consider each in turn.

Fright and flight

As noted above, when considering if the victim's acts broke the chain of causation, the court looks to see whether their actions were foreseeable or unreasonable. According to the Court of Appeal in *R v Roberts* (1971) 56 Cr App R 95, the court is to question whether the response of the victim was 'daft' in the circumstances.

Importantly, the court is not concerned with whether the victim acted *reasonably*, but, rather, whether the victim's reaction was *reasonably foreseeable* by the defendant (emphasised by the Court of Appeal in *R v Mackie* (1973) 57 Cr App R 453). The arbiters of fact are, therefore, concerned with whether the defendant foresaw that the victim would act in a certain matter. If it is not reasonably foreseeable, the victim's act may be considered 'daft' and thus break the chain of causation. If, however, their actions are reasonable foreseeable, the chain will remain intact and the defendant will be liable for any death or injury that follows. **Figure 2.7** below will assist on this point.

case example

Charge:
ABH (OAPA 1861, s 47)

Case progression:
Crown Court – Guilty

Court of Appeal – Conviction upheld

Point of law:
Acts of the victim must be 'daft' in order to break the chain of causation

In *R v Roberts* (1971) 56 Cr App R 95, the defendant, whilst driving the victim home from a party, began to make unwanted sexual advances towards her. The defendant also threatened her and touched her coat. The victim jumped from the moving car and suffered harm. The defendant was convicted in the Crown Court.

The Court of Appeal upheld his conviction, ruling that the acts of the victim were neither unreasonable nor unforeseeable.

Stephenson LJ commented:

> The test is: Was it the *natural result* of what the alleged assailant said and did, in the sense that it was something that could *reasonably have been foreseen* as the consequence of what he was saying or doing?

Roberts was subsequently applied and approved by the Court of Appeal in *R v Williams and Davis* [1992] 2 All ER 183. In that case, the victim, a hitchhiker, jumped from the defendant's car which was travelling at 30mph after being threatened to hand over his money. The victim died as a result of a serious head injury. The defendants were convicted of manslaughter at first instance, but their convictions were quashed on appeal on account that the trial judge had failed to give adequate directions to the jury. On appeal, the test of 'daftness' was slightly modified by Stuart-Smith LJ who stated that the jury must instead consider whether the victim's act was

> proportionate to the threat, that is to say that it was within the ambit of reasonableness and not so daft as to make it his own voluntary act which amounted to a *novus actus interveniens* and consequently broke the chain of causation.

His Lordship went on to explain the state the law:

> The jury should consider two questions: first, whether it was reasonably foreseeable that some harm, albeit not serious harm, was likely to result from the threat itself; and, secondly, whether the deceased's reaction ... was within the *range of responses* which might be expected from a victim placed in the situation which he was. The jury should bear in mind any particular characteristic of the victim and the fact that in the agony of the moment he may act without thought and deliberation.

The test of 'daftness' is still employed to this day alongside the idea of a 'range of responses'. There was, however, a conflicting of authority with *Williams*, namely that of *R v Evans* [1992] Crim LR 659, where the Court of Appeal ruled that the test to be applied is whether the flight was a 'natural consequence' of the accused's behaviour. If it was not, the chain of causation is broken. That test, however, has been dismissed by the subsequent decision of *R v Corbett* [1996] Crim LR 594. We remain, therefore, concerned with the test of 'range of responses'. The test of 'range of reasonable responses' was adopted by the Court of Appeal in *R v Tarasov* [2016] EWCA Crim 2278.

A couple of questions arise from this issue:

(1) What does the court mean by a 'range of responses' from the victim?
(2) What does the court mean by 'reasonable foreseeability' on the part of the defendant?

The first question was answered by Stuart-Smith LJ in *Williams* and later affirmed by the Court of Appeal in *Corbett*, which ruled that the jury should bear in mind any 'particular characteristic of the victim and the fact that in the agony of the moment he may act without thought and deliberation'. As a result, therefore, the range of responses will vary and fluctuate according to the victim's age, mental capacity and other internal and external circumstances. For example, where the victim is intoxicated, the jury will be required to consider if the victim's response was within the 'range of responses' of an intoxicated person. The test, therefore, is partly objective and partly subjective in that the jury are considering the individual characteristics of the victim, but from the standpoint of another individual with the same characteristics.

The second question was answered by the Court of Appeal in *R v Marjoram* [2000] Crim LR 372, which ruled that when dealing with the question of whether the victim's reaction was 'reasonably foreseeable', the jury are concerned with whether the reaction was foreseeable to an 'ordinary person' and not to a person of the defendant's age and characteristics. The defendant's own inability to foresee the reaction of the victim is, therefore, not relevant to the question of causation, but may be relevant when one considers *mens rea*. In that regard, the test is objective and not subjective. In the recent case of *R v Lewis* [2010] EWCA Crim 151, the Court of Appeal held that in cases of death during flight, there must be a causal link, with the jury asking themselves whether the victim's response 'might have been expected'. Pitchford LJ made clear that the judge did not need to use the language of *Williams* so long as the fundamental nature of the test was communicated:

> [The jury] could not have been in doubt that they were being asked to measure the nature of the threat posed by the unlawful act with the form of escape adopted by the deceased.

in practice

Ensure that you consider the specific facts of each case presented before you. For example, should there be a difference in law between jumping from a vehicle travelling at 30mph and from a vehicle travelling at 70mph? Many would argue that to jump from a vehicle travelling at high speed is daft and unreasonable. Others would argue that the victim's reaction depends upon the situation they are escaping from. Consider both of these matters carefully and reach a reasoned conclusion.

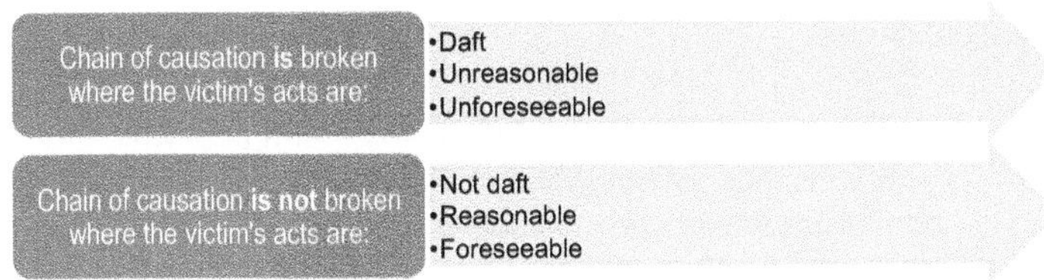

Chain of causation is broken where the victim's acts are:
•Daft
•Unreasonable
•Unforeseeable
Chain of causation is not broken where the victim's acts are:
•Not daft
•Reasonable
•Foreseeable

Figure 2.7 Fright and flight outcomes

Drug-dealing cases

A specific area of law was required to deal with the circumstance when the defendant supplied drugs to the victim who self-administered such drugs that then resulted in their death or injury.

Following the defendant's original conduct, where the end result has come about because of the victim's 'free, voluntary and informed' act, the chain of causation will be broken and the defendant is not to be regarded as the legal cause (*R v Dalby* [1982] 1 All ER 916). Similar to considering the acts of a third party, each element must be satisfied. Where the victim acts in a free and voluntary manner but is uninformed or unaware of the circumstances, they will not break the chain of causation.

The key authority in this area of law is the House of Lords decision in *R v Kennedy (No 2)* [2008] 1 AC 269.

case example

Charge:
Constructive manslaughter

Case progression:
Crown Court – Guilty

Court of Appeal – Conviction upheld

Court of Appeal (CCRC reference) – Conviction upheld

House of Lords – Conviction quashed

Point of law:
Self-administration by a free, deliberate and informed act will break the chain of causation

In *R v Kennedy (No 2)* [2008] 1 AC 269, the defendant prepared a syringe of heroin and gave it to the victim upon their request. The victim self-injected and died. The defendant was convicted in the Crown Court for constructive manslaughter (due to the supply of unlawful drugs) and his appeal was dismissed in the Court of Appeal.

The defendant returned to the Court of Appeal a second time (following a Criminal Cases Review Commission (CCRC) reference), where his conviction was again upheld.

The House of Lords allowed his appeal and quashed his conviction, ruling that where the victim acts in a 'free, voluntary and informed' manner by self-administering the drug, the chain of causation will be broken and the defendant will not be the legal cause of death despite the supply of the drugs by the defendant.

Lord Bingham concluded:

> There is, clearly, a difficult borderline between contributory acts which may properly be regarded as administering a noxious thing and acts which may not. But the crucial question is not whether the defendant facilitated or contributed to administration of the noxious thing, but whether he went further and administered it. What matters ... is whether the injection itself was the result of a voluntary and informed decision by the person injecting himself.

Effectively, Lord Bingham ruled that where the victim self-injects, the defendant can never be guilty if the victim is a fully informed adult making a free and voluntary decision. *Kennedy (No 2)*, therefore, had the effect of overruling *R v Rogers* [2003] 1 WLR 1374 and *R v Finlay* [2003] EWCA Crim 3868 and reversing the Court of Appeal's ruling in *R v Kennedy (No 2)* [2005] EWCA Crim 685. In *Rogers*, the defendant applied a tourniquet to the victim's arm, to allow the victim to self-inject. This was held not to break the chain of causation as the defendant was 'playing a part' in the mechanics of the injection which caused death. In *Finlay*, the defendant had produced the situation to allow the victim to inject herself. She did so and died. Both of these cases have now been declared as incorrect in law.

When then will the defendant be liable? As the court in *R v Evans* [2009] EWCA Crim 650 made clear, 'supply alone' is not sufficient for a conviction of unlawful act manslaughter, unless the defendant was under a specific duty to act as a result of creating a dangerous situation (refer back to *Miller* and *Evans* above in relation to omissions).

Therefore, post *Kennedy (No 2)*, for liability to be found in these circumstances, the jury would have to be sure that the defendant took part in the administration of the drug.

This means that the defendant must either:

(a) inject the victim himself (*R v Cato* [1976] 1 All ER 260); or
(b) jointly inject the victim (*R v Burgess* [2008] EWCA Crim 516).

in practice

Do not forget to consider all the possible outcomes of a case based on similar facts. If the victim dies as a result of injection by the defendant, the defendant may be liable for unlawful act manslaughter. Should the victim live, the defendant may be liable for administering a noxious substance contrary to s 23 of the OAPA 1861. The prosecution will consider all of these outcomes in its case preparation.

For commentary on these cases, see Ormerod and Fortson, 'Drug Suppliers as Manslaughterers (Again)' [2005] Crim LR 819 and Jones, 'Causation, Homicide and the Supply of Drugs' (2006) 26 LS 139.

Further acts of the victim

As detailed above, this final category is a mixed bag concerned with the numerous other acts that may or may not break the chain of causation. **Table 2.12** details these further acts.

Table 2.12 Further potential intervening acts of the victim

Act	Example	Break the chain?
Refusal to consent to medical treatment	In *R v Blaue* [1975] 1 WLR 1411, the victim refused a blood transfusion on religious grounds which would have saved her life after being wounded by the defendant. The victim died as a result of loss of blood caused by the wounds inflicted by the defendant.	No
Neglect of injuries	In *R v Wall* (1802) 28 State Tr 51, the victim died as a result of an illegal flogging which he aggravated and neglected by drinking spirits to ease the pain.	No
Aggravation of injuries	In *R v Dear* [1996] Crim LR 595, the victim aggravated his wounds so that they reopened after being repeatedly slashed by the defendant. The victim died and the defendant remained the legal cause of death despite the victim aggravating his own injuries. See also *R v Holland* (1841) 2 Mood & R 351 and the California case of *California v Lewis* (1899) 124 Cal 551 for an interesting demonstration of this area in another jurisdiction.	No
Suicide/ euthanasia	In *R v Dhaliwal* [2006] EWCA Crim 1139, the victim committed suicide as a result of the continued physical and emotional abuse she sustained from her husband, the defendant. The victim's act did not break the chain of causation, and the defendant remained liable for her death. This principle was reaffirmed in *R v Wallace (Berlinah)* [2018] EWCA Crim 690 in which the Court of Appeal concluded that the victim's own act of seeking euthanasia, following a serious acid attack by the defendant, in a different country did not break the chain of causation. The defendant remained liable given that the act of euthanasia was 'a direct response to the inflicted injuries and to the circumstances created by them for which the defendant was responsible' (per Sharp LJ). Note that the Crown Court Compendium advises (at 7-9(11)) that: 'The facts of the case, and the resulting consideration in the Court of Appeal, should be considered as being truly exceptional. It is suggested that the greatest care should be taken if seeking to apply this case to different circumstances.'	No

2.7.3.4 Act of God

The defendant will not be liable if a natural event occurs which is 'extraordinary or not reasonably foreseeable'. This is often known as 'an act of God'. According to Henry J in the Divisional Court in *Southern Water Authority v Pegrum* [1989] Crim LR 442:

> [A]n act of God is an operation of natural forces so unpredictable as to excuse a defendant all liability for its consequences.

Two case examples will help explain this principle.

case example

Charge:
Murder

Case progression:
Crown Court – Guilty

Court of Appeal – Conviction upheld

Point of law:
Whether an Act of God will break the chain of causation

In *R v Gowans* [2003] EWCA Crim 3935, the victim was placed in a coma after being attacked by the defendant. Whilst in a coma, the victim contracted septicaemia (blood poisoning) and died. The defendant was convicted of murder and his conviction was upheld on appeal.

Kay LJ in the Court of Appeal ruled that the defendant had put the victim in a state vulnerable to any infections. The defendant, therefore, was the legal (operating and substantial) cause of the death.

Gowans is an interesting authority on the point of an 'act of God'. The naturally occurring event was the risk of infection given that we are all at risk of infection at any point in our lives; it cannot be controlled. The defendant remained responsible for the death of the victim because the victim was placed in a situation where infection was much more likely and probable. This therefore meant that the 'act of God' was not unforeseeable but, rather, was a probable outcome of the defendant's actions. As it was foreseeable, it was incapable of breaking the chain of causation.

case example

Charge:
Murder

Case progression:
South Australian Full Court – Guilty

Point of law:
Whether an act of God will break the chain of causation where it arose as a natural consequence of the defendant's actions

In *The Queen v Hallett* [1969] SASR 141 (Australia), the victim, whilst drinking on a beach at night, had allegedly made a homosexual advance to the defendant. The defendant attacked the victim and left him unconscious on the beach. The tide came in and the victim drowned. The defendant's actions of knocking the man unconscious on the beach remained the substantial and operating cause of death.

What these two examples show is that the chain of causation is rarely broken by a naturally occurring event. As above, the natural act was not 'so powerful' to rid the defendant of liability.

In *Gowans*, the victim could not have acquired the serious infection without being first placed in a coma as a result of the defendant's actions. The defendant was blameable, therefore, for the death. Likewise, in *Hallett*, the defendant left the victim on the beach when the tide was low. The foreseeability that he may be drowned by the incoming tide was high, and thus the defendant was liable. In both cases, the result was a 'natural' consequence of the defendant's conduct. Thus the chain of causation was not broken.

You may ask, therefore, when an act of God will break the chain of causation. In *Empress Car Co (Abertillery) Ltd v National Rivers Authority* [1999] 2 AC 22, Lord Hoffmann explained that if an Act of God was 'abnormal and extraordinary', the chain of causation may be broken. In addition, an American academic named Perkins ('The Law of Homicide' (1946) 36 J Cr L & Cr) provides a rather useful example:

> [I]f one man knocks down another and goes away leaving his victim not seriously hurt but unconscious, on the floor of a building in which the assault occurred, and before the victim recovers consciousness he is killed in the fall of the building which is shaken down by a sudden earthquake, this is not homicide. The law attributes such a death to the 'Act of God' and not to the assault, even if it may be certain that the deceased would not have been in the building at the time of the earthquake, had he not been rendered unconscious. The blow was the occasion of the man's being there, but the blow was not the cause of the earthquake, nor was the deceased left in a position of obvious danger. On the other hand if the blow had been struck on the seashore, and the assailant had left his victim in imminent peril of an incoming tide which drowned him before consciousness returned, it would be homicide.

Another example may be where the defendant attacks the victim but leaves him in a 'safe place'. Whilst unconscious, the victim is struck by lightning. In both examples, the lightning strike and the earthquake are unforeseen and unforeseeable and will thus break the chain of causation.

in practice

Although the chain of causation is broken in relation to the 'end result', ie death, the defendant remains liable for the initial act and result, ie the initial injury. Therefore, when answering a problem question, you can discount a potential offence of murder against the defendant but you may still consider his liability for a non-fatal offence.

2.7.3.5 Summary of intervening acts

This section has included a lot of information and various different tests to apply dependent on the situation. The following figure is aimed at concentrating your understanding of the principles of *novus actus interveniens*.

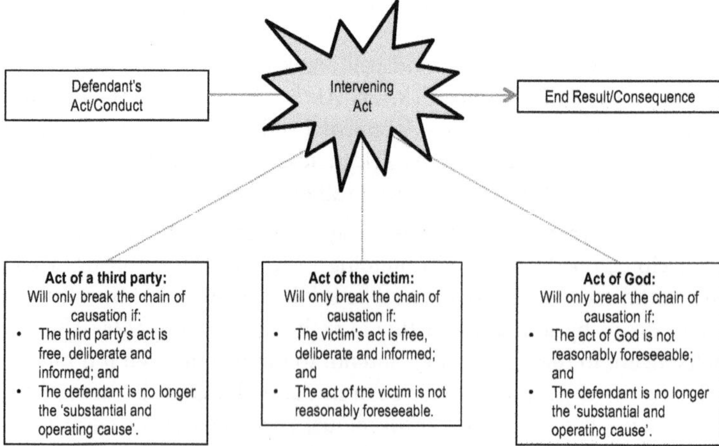

Figure 2.8 Understanding intervening acts

2.7.4 Applying causation

Consider the following example and decide whether the tests for causation are met. Use **Figure 2.8** (above) to assist you.

example

Jack stabs Jill in the leg. Whilst being transported to the hospital in an ambulance, Andy drives his truck into the side of the ambulance, killing Jill on impact. Evidence shows that Jill would not have died simply from the stab wound.

Jack most certainly is a factual cause of harm given that Jill would not have required medical attention 'but for' Jack's actions. Jack may also be considered the legal cause of harm as his actions are both substantial and blameworthy. However, the likely outcome is that Andy has broken the chain of causation through his actions, thus becoming the 'operative' cause of death. Jack, however, may still be liable for the original assault.

2.8 Thin skull rule

The defendant must 'take his victim as he finds him'. Also known as the 'egg-shell skull rule', these words have long been established as a key principle in the criminal law of England and Wales.

Most textbooks include their discussion of the thin skull rule within a section on 'acts of the victim' which break the chain of causation. Indeed, this makes a lot of sense as the question becomes whether the susceptibility of the victim is an act on their part which can break the chain of causation. For instance, Colvin (*Principles of Criminal Law*, 2nd edn (Carswell, 1991)) argues that there is no need for a 'special' rule because in all cases where the thin skull rule is used, applying the 'operating and substantial cause' test would produce the same result. It is felt, however, that given the novel area of law concerned and the fact that in many cases the 'thin skull' is not as a result of an *act* of the victim, but rather is an *integral part* of the victim, this area is best placed within its own section.

In general, the principle is concerned with the effect a defendant's act has on the victim in question.

example

Jill gives Jack a paper cut as a joke. Ordinarily, a paper cut would be of no threat to an individual. Although it may cause some discomfort, there is no likelihood of real harm or injury to the individual.

However, suppose Jill does the same thing to Andy who suffers from haemophilia (a condition where the blood does not clot). As a result of his condition, Andy is likely to suffer greater harm than an individual without such a condition. This condition, or 'susceptibility' as it is referred to in practice, is irrelevant to the liability of the defendant, as he must take his victim as he finds him. This means that the defendant will remain the factual and legal cause of the harm despite the vulnerability of the victim and regardless of whether the defendant was aware of the condition or not.

Let us take another example.

example

Jack pushes Andy off a 3ft high wall. In the majority of cases, this is unlikely to cause an individual significant harm. Andy, however, suffers from a thin skull and is severely injured upon falling. Jack remains liable for the injuries to Andy despite the fact that such an action would not have had such a great effect on another person, such as Jill.

There may be many circumstances that result in a victim's heightened vulnerability, for example:

- old age;
- young age;
- brittle bones;
- haemophilia;
- thin skull, etc.

What the examples above provide us with is a decent picture of the operation of the law (see *R v Hayward* (1908) 21 Cox CC 692 – concerning a thyroid condition). However, such examples have been intentionally restricted to 'physical' vulnerabilities to allow us to question the extent to which the principle operates. As a result of the decision in *R v Blaue* [1975] 1 WLR 1411, the principle is clearly capable of an extremely wide application.

case example

Charge:
Murder

Case progression:
Crown Court –
Not guilty of murder; guilty of manslaughter

Court of Appeal –
Conviction upheld

Point of law:
Thin skull rule applies to religious or holistic beliefs

In *R v Blaue* [1975] 1 WLR 1411, the victim was a Jehovah's Witness and refused a blood transfusion on religious grounds after being stabbed by the defendant. The victim died and Blaue was charged with and acquitted of murder. However, the defendant was found guilty of manslaughter.

The Court of Appeal upheld the conviction, ruling that the victim's susceptibilities need not be physical, but may be more holistic in character also. In particular, Lawton LJ commented:

> It has long been the policy of the law that those who use violence on other people must take their victims as they find them. This in our judgment means the whole man, not just the physical man. It does not lie in the mouth of the assailant to say that the victim's religious beliefs which inhibited him from accepting certain kinds of treatment were unreasonable.

In the older case of *R v Holland* (1841) 2 Mood & R 351, the defendant cut the victim's finger and the wound became infected. The victim refused to accept medical advice, and as a result developed lockjaw and died. The Court concluded that the original wound remained the substantial and operating cause, and the victim's conduct did not break the chain of causation. *Blaue* relied on and affirmed the decision of *Holland*.

As a result of *Blaue*, which followed *R v Holland*, it is questionable to what extent the principle now extends. The principle could now effectively cover susceptibilities of all kinds and natures. For example, vulnerabilities could now be:

- physical;
- emotional;
- psychological; or
- holistic/religious.

The case led to strong criticisms from the likes of Williams ('Criminal Law – Causation' [1976] CLJ 15), who argued that it was 'absurd' to convict an accused for murder in circumstances where the victim had unreasonably refused treatment, thus resulting in death. Williams furthers this by explaining that a defendant in most cases can be convicted of a lesser offence, such as wounding in *Blaue*, and the public interest in securing a conviction and imprisoning a wrongdoer would be served. This is furthered by Klimchuk ('Causation, thin skulls and equality' (1998) 11 Canadian Journal of Law and Jurisprudence 115), who suggests that the test should not apply 'where the outcome would offend common sense'.

So where, then, does one draw the line? Should it be the case that the defendant must take his victim as he finds him with regard to any of the above susceptibilities? Jefferson (*Criminal Law*, 12th edn (Pearson, 2015)) helpfully suggests that

> the 'take your victim' test should not apply where the outcome would offend common sense; therefore, if the victim has acted in a 'daft' manner the accused should not be guilty of the offence charged, though he may still be guilty of a lesser offence or of the attempt.

Such appears to be a logical solution and accords with the view of Child and Ormerod (*Smith, Hogan, & Ormerod's Essentials of Criminal Law*, 3rd edn (OUP, 2019)), who argue that it would be taking the thin skull rule 'too far' where the victim acts in a way which causes further harm, and 'it is better to restrict it to cases where the victim does not do anything to make their condition worse'.

2.9 Putting it all together

Consider the following issue and think how you may structure an answer to it. Then see the figure below for a sample structure to adopt.

facts

Jack is a lifeguard at the local swimming pool. Jack is employed by the local council to watch over those members of the public who frequent the pool. One day, Jack is distracted by his girlfriend, Jill, whilst a young boy, Andy, struggles to swim. Eventually Jack realises that Andy is struggling and dives into the pool to rescue him. Andy is unconscious and is not breathing. Jack calls an ambulance which arrives within a few minutes and takes Andy to hospital. Andy dies at the hospital.

Jack, upset at what happens, decides to leave work early that day and go to the local bar. On the way to the bar, Jack hits Ben with his car. Jack was driving rather erratically at the time.

Would your answer differ if:

(a) On the way to the hospital, Bill, the driver of the ambulance, crashed the ambulance as a result of his negligent driving, killing Andy before he makes it to the hospital?

(b) Jack's driving could not be faulted and in fact the car accident was entirely Ben's fault? Evidence shows that Jack would not have been able to avoid hitting Ben.

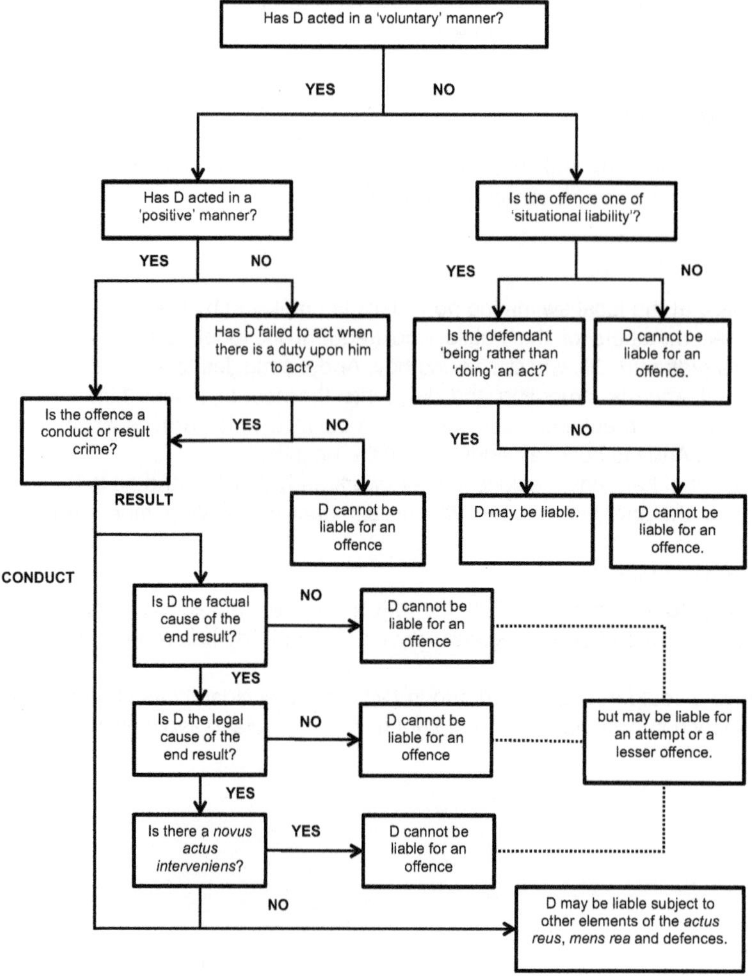

Figure 2.9 Putting together actus reus

2.10 Further reading

Actus reus **generally**

Doeggar, 'Strict Liability in Criminal Law and Larsonneur Reassessed' [1998] Crim LR 791.

Glazebrook, 'Situational Liability' in Glazebrook (ed), *Reshaping the Criminal Law* (Sweet & Maxwell, 1978).

Hart, 'Acts of Will and Responsibility' in Hart (ed), *Punishment and Responsibility: Essays in the Philosophy of Law* (OUP, 1968).

Husak, 'Does Criminal Liability Require an Act?' in Duff (ed), *Philosophy and the Criminal Law* (CUP, 1999).

Lynch, 'The Mental Element in the Actus Reus' (1982) 98 LQR 127.

Omissions

Ashworth, 'The Scope of Criminal Liability for Omissions' (1989) 105 LQR 424.

Ashworth, 'A New Generation of Omissions Offences' [2018] Crim LR 354.
Glazebrook, 'Criminal Omissions: The Duty Requirements in Offences Against the Person' (1960) 76 LQR 386.
Kennedy, 'Switching Off Life Support Machines: The Legal Implications' [1977] Crim LR 443.
Simester, 'Why Omissions are Special' (1995) 15 LS 311.
Williams, 'Criminal omissions – the conventional view' 107 LQR 86.

Causation

Laird, 'The Decline of Criminal Law Causation Without Limits' (2016) 132 LQR 566.
Nkrumah, '*R v Kennedy* Revisited' (2008) 72 J Crim L 117.
Norrie, 'A Critique of Criminal Causation' (1991) 54 MLR 685.
Padfield, 'Clean water and muddy causation: is causation a question of law or fact, or just a way of allocating blame?' [1995] Crim LR 683.
Shute, 'Causation: Foreseeability v Natural Consequences' (1992) 55 MLR 584.
Stannard, 'Criminal Causation and the Careless Doctor' (1992) 55 MLR 577.

- In order to establish criminal liability, three key elements are necessary: *actus reus, mens rea* and the lack of a defence.
- *Actus reus* (or guilty act) is concerned with the external elements of the offence and covers such matters as acts, conduct, circumstances and consequences.
- *Mens rea* (or guilty mind) is concerned with the mental element of the offence and covers such matters as intention, recklessness, foreseeability etc.
- Defences may be justificatory in nature or may provide the defendant with an excuse for a crime. Whether it justifies or excuses the defendant's conduct will determine whether the defence is an element of the offence or not.
- In general, the *actus reus* requires a voluntary and positive act.
- There are certain offences (known as state of affairs cases) where voluntary conduct is not required. In this case, the defendant is 'being', rather than 'doing' an act.
- In certain circumstances, a duty to act may impose liability on a defendant for his failure to act.
- Criminal offences can helpfully be divided into conduct and result crimes. Conduct crimes are unlawful despite the end result or consequences, whereas result crimes require the defendant's action to cause the end result.
- Causation is divided into factual and legal causation. Both must be satisfied and require the defendant to be the cause of the end result.
- The defendant may be relieved of liability where there is a new and intervening act that breaks the chain of causation. These acts take the form of the victim's own act, a free, deliberate and informed act of a third party, or an act of God.
- The defendant must 'take his victim as he finds him'. This means that the defendant cannot be relieved of liability simply because the victim is more vulnerable or susceptible to harm than another person.

test your knowledge

Problem

Jack and Jill are brother and sister. Jack suffers from a low IQ and short-term memory loss and is dependent on Jill for most activities. Whilst at the top of a hill, Jill falls down a well and is trapped at the bottom. Jack, unsure of what to do, returns home with the intention of speaking to his roommate, Andy. Upon returning home, Jack forgets the reason he wished to speak to Andy and Jill is forgotten. Jill dies at the bottom of the well.

Jill's body is later found by passers-by, a rap group called the 'Free Blind Mice'. Upon hearing the news of his sister's death, Jack suffers depression and lashes out at Andy. With a single punch, Jack knocks Andy unconscious and cracks his jaw. While Andy is being taken to the hospital, the ambulance is involved in an accident when the Free Blind Mice crash into it in a rush to get to their next rap concert. Andy dies in the ambulance.

Consider the liability of the individuals according to the above facts.

Would your answer differ if:

- Andy was found to have a very weak jaw line;
- Jill did not die in the well but died as a result of poor medical treatment at hospital;
- Andy jumped from the back of the ambulance as a result of fear of hospitals (Nosocomephobia). Andy cracks his skull and dies.

Essay

'The law of causation is in a constant state of flux. The courts are unsure how to apply both factual and legal causation to a given case, and policy reasons dictate who is, and is not, liable in any given case.'

Critically discuss this statement with regard to the operation of causation in criminal law.

chapter 3

Mens Rea: The Mental Element of Crime

After reading this chapter, you will be able to understand:

- the term *mens rea* and explain how it applies in criminal cases
- how to differentiate between the various forms of intention
- the type of offences where no *mens rea* is required
- the coincidence of *actus reus* and *mens rea*
- the contemporaneity principle
- the principle of transferred malice.

3.1 Introduction to *mens rea*

As briefly discussed in **Chapter 1**, *mens rea* (plural: *mentes reae*) loosely translates as 'guilty mind'. It is more appropriate, however, to consider the *mens rea* as the mental element of a crime. As opposed to the *actus reus*, which is concerned with the external elements of an offence, the *mens rea* is concerned with the internal elements of the offence. Importantly, *mens rea* is not concerned simply with the intention of the individual; rather the *mens rea* covers any form of state of mind on the part of the defendant. It is for this reason that the Law Commission prefers the term 'fault' over '*mens rea*'.

The most pertinent forms of *mens rea* include intention and recklessness. However, also within this topic are such matters as:

- negligence;
- knowledge;
- wilfully;
- maliciously; and
- belief.

There are some offences that do not require any form of intention or recklessness on the part of the defendant; these are known as strict liability offences and will be considered later in the chapter.

3.1.1 Classifying *mens rea*

It is technically inappropriate to refer to intention or recklessness as the *mens rea* of an offence. Indeed, these two terms – amongst the others we shall consider in this chapter – are the means by which we ascertain the guilty mind of the defendant; however, this activity will vary depending on the offence in question. This was made quite clear by Lord Hailsham in *DPP v Morgan* [1976] AC 182:

> The beginning of wisdom in all the 'mens rea' cases … is … that 'mens rea' means a number of quite different things in relation to different crimes.

It is therefore better to understand that the *mens rea* will require proof of an intention *to do something*, or proof of recklessness *about* something. Let us take a few examples:

- *Rape:* The first *mens rea* element of rape is the intention to penetrate the vagina, anus or mouth of the complainant. In this case, the defendant must have the intention to *do something*, ie penetrate the complainant.
- *Battery:* The *mens rea* of battery is the intention to apply unlawful physical force to a person or recklessness to the thought of such force being applied. In this case, the defendant must either intend to *do something*, ie apply unlawful force, or be reckless *about something*, ie the application of unlawful force.

In this regard, a helpful aide memoir is to say something along the lines of 'the defendant must have the intention *as to* …'. Simply saying that the *mens rea* of an offence is 'intention' is insufficient; 'intention *as to* …' will mitigate this problem.

It is also useful to appreciate that *mens rea* may be divided into two classes, namely subjective and objective *mens rea*.

Table 3.1 Subjective and objective mens rea

***Mens rea* term**	**Explanation**
Subjective *mens rea*	This looks internally at the thinking of the defendant at the time that the *actus reus* was committed. The jury (or magistrates) will be asked to put themselves in the defendant's shoes and ask what the defendant was thinking. Under this heading, we consider such terminology as intention and recklessness.
Objective *mens rea*	This looks externally at the thinking of the defendant at the time that the *actus reus* was committed. The jury (or magistrates) in this case will be asked to take an objective (outside-in) approach by asking whether the defendant acted in accordance with the standards expected of the reasonable person. Under this heading, we consider such terminology as negligence.

The distinction between the two classifications is based in the thinking of the defendant. The thought process of the defendant is entirely irrelevant in the context of an objective *mens rea*, which seeks to find liability based on the standards of reasonable persons. Use of correct terminology is, therefore, essential. If you are dealing with a subjective *mens rea*, for example, 'knowledge', you should be asking what the defendant *actually* knew; not what the defendant *should have* known.

3.1.2 *Mens rea* and motive

An essential point to note early on is that motive, ie the reason that the defendant committed the offence, is not generally relevant to a question of substantive law (*R v Mohan* [1976] QB 1). Nor is it generally relevant that the offence was premeditated (ie planned in advanced). We addressed this issue in **Chapter 1** and emphasised the need to distinguish matters of substantive law – which look at whether the defendant committed the offence in law – and matters of evidential law – which look at how the prosecution proves that the defendant committed the offence. Naturally, the pair go hand-in-hand, and if a defendant is found to have a motive to commit a criminal offence, a jury may be more likely to find them guilty. However, for our purposes, we are concerned just with the substantive law.

We have considered bad motives, but what about good ones? Much like bad motives, good motives are irrelevant: just because an individual acts with a good motive (eg in assisted dying cases) does not release them from potential criminal liability.

It may be useful to explain the circumstances when motive may be relevant:

- in cases involving misconduct in public office;
- in defences against offences such as theft – motive may demonstrate a lack of dishonesty;
- in matters of evidence furthering either the prosecution or defence case; and
- in matters of sentencing.

3.1.3 *Mens rea* and proof

A matter closely related to that of motive is the question of proof, namely how does the prosecution prove that the defendant held the necessary *mens rea* for the offence charged? At one point, intention was presumed. We can see this in *DPP v Smith* [1961] AC 290, which concerned an injury to a policeman who attempted to prevent the defendant from escaping with stolen goods. The House of Lords reasoned that it is to be presumed that the defendant intended or foresaw the natural consequences of his actions. This presumption, however, led to much criticism, resulting in the enactment of s 8 of the Criminal Justice Act 1967 which provides:

> A court or jury, in determining whether a person has committed an offence,—
> (a) shall not be bound in law to infer that he intended or foresaw a result of his actions by reason only of its being a natural and probable consequence of those actions; but
> (b) shall decide whether he did intend or foresee that result by reference to *all the evidence*, drawing such *inferences* from the evidence as appear proper in the circumstances. (emphasis added)

This section has the effect of enacting the law prior to that in *DPP v Smith*, namely that there is no presumption in law that a defendant intended or foresaw the natural consequences of his acts (*DPP v Majewski* [1977] AC 443).

3.1.4 Forms of *mens rea*

The remainder of this chapter will consider the various forms of *mens rea* that apply in the criminal law. Herring (*Criminal Law*, 11th edn (Macmillan Law Masters, 2019)) identifies these as a 'library of concepts'. We shall consider:

- intention (**3.2**);
- recklessness (**3.3**); and
- negligence (**3.4**).

We shall also consider other forms of *mens rea* at **3.5** and the concept of strict liability, which refers to situations in which the offence bears no respective *mens rea* element, at **3.6**.

Later in the chapter, we shall be applying these concepts and observing the necessary link that must be made between the *actus reus* and the *mens rea*.

3.2 Intention

Intention is the 'highest' form of *mens rea* that may be present in a criminal offence. As such, it is often the hardest form of *mens rea* to prove. It is concerned with the intention of *this* particular defendant on *this* particular day; it is not concerned with what he *should* have foreseen or what the reasonable man *would* have foreseen.

The present state of law can be summarised as follows:

(a) A defendant may intend for the end result to come about, ie it is his 'aim, objective and purpose' for the result to come about.
(b) Although not the defendant's 'aim, objective and purpose', a jury may nonetheless still find intention where:
    (i) the end result was a virtually certain consequence of the defendant's actions; and
    (ii) the defendant appreciated that such consequences were a virtual certainty.

3.2.1 Types of intention

'Intention' is a word that is usually used in relation to consequences. On a basic level, a defendant intends a consequence if he wishes that consequence to follow from his actions. Intention, however, is not restricted to cases where the consequence, or end result, is wanted or desired (known as 'direct intent'). Rather, intention also includes cases where the consequence is not wanted or desired but the defendant is aware that there is a virtual certainty of that consequence occurring (known as 'oblique intent').

example

Jack shoots at Jill, who is stood behind a window. Jack intends to kill Jill and realises that, in order to do so, the bullet must first break the window (and thus he will commit criminal damage).

The issue becomes: Does Jack have the direct intent to break the window, or is the window breaking merely a virtual certainty that he appreciates will happen? Norrie ('Oblique Intention and Legal Politics' [1989] Crim LR 793) would contend that 'secondary consequences' (such as breaking the window) can be regarded as being desired or intended if the consequence flows from the primary purpose (ie the consequence is part and parcel of what the defendant intended). Indeed, Lord Hailsham in *Hyam v DPP* [1975] AC 55 explained that intention includes 'the means as well as the end and the inseparable consequences of the end as well as the means'. On the other hand, Williams ('Oblique Intention' (1987) 46 CLJ 417) would contend that the breaking of the glass is merely a side effect that Jack may accept as an 'inevitable' or 'certain' accompaniment to the direct intent (to kill Jill). This should demonstrate that the classification of intention is not a simple task.

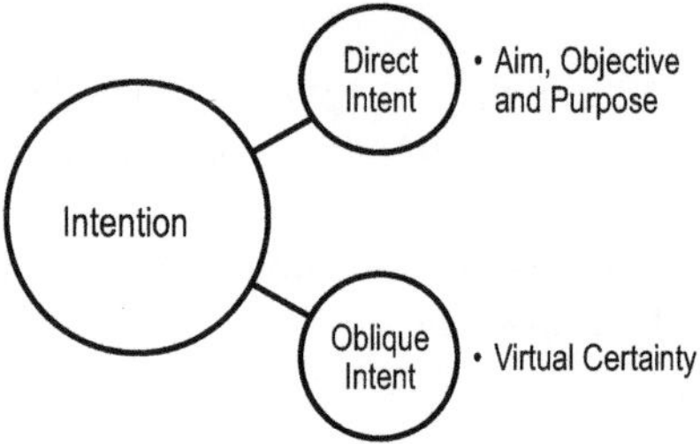

Figure 3.1 Forms of intention

There are three further forms of intention that we consider later: basic and specific intent (at **3.2.1.4**) and ulterior intent (at **3.2.1.5**).

3.2.1.1 Direct intent

This is where it is the defendant's 'aim, objective and purpose' to cause a particular result. For example, suppose Jack stabs Jill because he wants Jill to die – his direct intent to kill is clear. The House of Lords in the seminal case of *R v Moloney* [1985] AC 905 made it clear that in the majority of cases, intention will be so clear that the jury should simply be informed that intention is to be given its ordinary meaning. The judge should not try to define the term. This was evident in *R v Wright* [2000] Crim LR 928, in which Beldam LJ stated that courts should steer away 'from the chameleon-like concepts of purpose, foresight of consequence and awareness of risk'.

Duff (*Intention, Agency and Criminal Liability: Philosophy of Action and the Criminal Law* (Wiley-Blackwell, 1990)) offers an alternative explanation for the operation of direct intent. Specifically, Duff argues that direct intent must be considered as a 'test of failure', which applies where a jury are satisfied that the defendant would consider his actions a failure if the end result did not ensue. Therefore, if the defendant did consider his actions to be a failure, in circumstances where the end result did not arise, he has the requisite direct intent.

Relevance of a person's 'desire'?

Often, textbooks on this subject attempt to define direct intent as referring to the defendant's 'desire' to commit the criminal offence. However, the House of Lords in *R v Moloney* [1985] AC 905 reasoned that 'intention is something quite distinct from motive or desire' (per Lord Bridge). Indeed, this was more recently reaffirmed by the Court of Appeal in *R v Hales* [2005] EWCA Crim 1118, in which the defendant ran over a police officer with his car in an attempt to escape from an arrest. Keene LJ made it clear that 'desire' as an understanding of intention was a 'dangerous term'. The Court reasoned that the defendant was 'prepared to kill in order to escape', and therefore he had the intention to kill. Therefore, a defendant's 'aim or purpose' may be to kill, but this may not be his desire (ie you can intend a result without wanting it to happen). Take for example:

- mercy killings;
- assisted suicide; or
- survival.

In such cases, the defendant may be acting out of remorse, sympathy or pity – it is his purpose to kill but by no means his 'desire' (evident in *R v Inglis* [2011] 1 WLR 1110 concerning mercy killings). On this basis, it is advised that the term 'desire' is avoided in this context.

Direct intention is uncontroversial and in the majority of cases is quite straightforward. The difficulty associated with intention is often found when considering oblique intent.

3.2.1.2 Oblique intent

Also known as 'indirect intent', this form of intent concerns the circumstances where it was not the defendant's 'aim, objective or purpose', but the defendant did foresee that the result was likely to occur as a result of his actions and he went and did the act anyway. Williams ('Oblique Intention' (1987) 46 CLJ 417) explains the term as follows:

> Oblique intention is something you see clearly, but out of the corner of your eye. The consequence is not in the straight line of your purpose, but a side-effect that you accept as an inevitable or certain accompaniment of your direct intent … Oblique intent is, in other words, a kind of knowledge or realisation.

The present state of law is found in *R v Woollin* [1999] AC 82. The test required to be applied is to ask the jury whether (on the facts of the case):

(a) the end result was a virtual certainty as a result of the defendant's actions; and
(b) the defendant appreciated that such was the case.

Where both elements are satisfied, the jury are entitled to 'find' intention.

example

In *R v Moloney*, Lord Bridge considered the following example:

> '... the terrorist who plants a time bomb in a public building and gives timely warning to enable the public to be evacuated ... [who] knows that, following evacuation, it is virtually certain that a bomb disposal squad will attempt to defuse the bomb. In the event, the bomb explodes and kills a bomb disposal expert ...'

The issue for Lord Bridge was whether the terrorist would possess the necessary intention in this regard. We shall return to this example following our discussion of the development in the law.

Two issues remain unresolved in this area of law.

Issues involving oblique intent: (i) Status of foresight

One of the first questions to consider is the nature of the relationship between intention and foresight. In particular, it must be asked whether oblique intent (ie foresight) can amount to the same as direct intent or whether it is merely evidence to assist the jury in finding intention. Kaveny ('Inferring Intention from Foresight' (2004) 120 LQR 81) described these two approaches as follows:

- 'identity view': viewing foresight as intention itself; and
- 'inference view': viewing foresight as evidence of intention.

The distinction between these two outcomes is one of practical application. The former would amount to a question of law; the latter would amount to a question of fact. Over the years, the courts have adopted varying approaches to this question and whilst, on a practical level, the issue may have been resolved, at an academic level, the question remains as to whether foresight if synonymous with intention or whether it is merely evidence of intention.

Issues involving oblique intent: (ii) Extent of foresight

The second question to ask is as challenging as the first, namely: What is the degree/extent of foresight required to satisfy oblique intention? The most common terminology used is that foresight must be of a 'virtually certain' result. The question then becomes, however, how much foresight does that actually require? If the defendant foresees a result as *possible*, that is clearly not the same as intending it; but, what about where he foresees the result as *probable*, *highly probably* or *virtually certain*? How much foresight equals intention?

In order to answer these two issues, it will be worth looking at the development of oblique intention by the courts.

Figure 3.2 Timeline of foresight

DPP v Smith

In *DPP v* Smith [1961] AC 290, the House of Lords held that intention should be objectively assessed, approving an irrebuttable presumption of law that a man intends the natural and probable consequences of his acts. The House of Lords concluded that if the reasonable person would have foreseen death or serious injury as a 'natural and probable consequence' of his actions, then the defendant was, as a matter of law, presumed to have intended that consequence, and he would have the requisite *mens rea* for murder. This had the effect of making intention an objective concept, as opposed to a subjective one.

Criminal Justice Act 1967, s 8

As noted at **3.1.3**, this objective presumption led to a large amount of criticism and ultimately resulted in intervention by Parliament which enacted s 8 of the Criminal Justice Act 1967. This section has the effect of enacting the law prior to that in *Smith*, namely that there is no presumption in law that a man intended or foresaw the natural consequences of his acts. *Smith* is therefore no longer good authority in this regard.

Hyam v DPP

In *Hyam v DPP* [1975] AC 55, the House of Lords held that in relation to the offence of murder, the *mens rea* of that offence is established where the defendant either intended the outcome or knew that death or serious harm was 'highly probable'. In this case, the defendant set a newspaper alight and posted it through the letter-box of a woman (Mrs Booth) who was engaged to the defendant's former boyfriend. Although Mrs Booth managed to escape with her son unharmed, Mrs Booth's two daughters were unable to escape and died in the fire. The defendant claimed that she only ever intended to frighten Mrs Booth and held no intention to cause any harm to persons inside the house. At trial, the trial judge directed the jury as follows:

> If you are satisfied that when the accused set fire to the house she knew that it was *highly probable* that this would cause (death or) serious bodily harm then the prosecution *will have* established the necessary intent. (emphasis added)

The defendant was convicted and appealed all the way to the House of Lords which by a majority of 3:2 dismissed her appeal, finding that the trial judge's direction was accurate – the defendant could liable for an offence where it was 'highly probable' that her actions would cause death. Unfortunately, the three judges in the majority appeared to give different reasons for their decision:

- According to Lord Cross, mere foresight of probability was enough to allow the jury to infer intent.
- Viscount Dilhorne felt that foresight of high probability was more appropriate.

- Lord Hailsham stated that foresight of probability or high probability was too vague, and he concluded that a defendant could be said to intend death if she 'intended to create a risk of death or serious bodily harm'.

By finding that a person intends the consequence of their actions when they foresee that consequence to be a highly probable result of their actions, the House of Lords seemingly equated foresight with intention. In basic form, the House of Lords appeared to say that foresight *was* intention.

R v Moloney

The approach in *Hyam* was called into question by the House of Lords in *R v Moloney* [1985] AC 905. Lord Bridge reasoned that nothing short of an intention to kill or cause GBH was sufficient for the offence of murder; however, anything short of intention could be considered as *evidence* of intention. Lord Bridge, fearful of defining intention itself and instead leaving such a definition to the 'good sense' of the jury, provided a two-part test to assist a jury to infer intention in the hope of clarifying matters left from *Hyam*. This two-part test was as follows:

(a) Was death or really serious injury a *natural consequence* of the defendant's act?
(b) Did the defendant foresee that one or the other was a natural consequence of his act?

Lord Bridge understood natural consequence to mean 'in the ordinary course of events a certain act will lead to a certain consequence unless something unexpected supervenes to prevent it'. See Buxton, 'Some Simple Thoughts on Intention' [1988] Crim LR 484 for a discussion of Lord Bridge's explanation.

As a result, if the jury answered both questions as 'yes', they were entitled to *infer* from this evidence that death was intended. Lord Bridge confirmed that foresight is merely evidence of intention which 'belongs, not to the substantive law, but to the law of evidence'.

R v Hancock; R v Shankland

The two-stage test in *Moloney* had the advantage of removing the confusion between probability and intention left by *Hyam*, but was itself very ambiguous. What is, or is not, a natural consequence of shooting at someone? This caused a number of difficulties for juries and was later revisited by the House of Lords in *R v Hancock; R v Shankland* [1986] AC 455.

case example

Charge:
Murder

Case progression:
Crown Court – Guilty

Court of Appeal – Conviction upheld

House of Lords – Conviction quashed and replaced with manslaughter

Point of law:
Meaning of foresight in intention

In *R v Hancock; R v Shankland* [1986] AC 455, the defendants, striking miners, dropped a concrete block from the top of a bridge onto a taxi, killing the driver. Their intention was to stop the taxi as it was carrying miners who were breaking the strike.

The defendants were convicted of murder in the Crown Court after the trial judge directed the jury according to the test laid out by Lord Bridge (above).

The Court of Appeal upheld their convictions; however, the House of Lords allowed their appeal and quashed their convictions for murder, substituting them with manslaughter convictions. Their Lordships did so on account that the 'natural consequence' element of the test was too wide and lacked any reference to a degree of probability.

Lord Scarman (who gave the only speech), although agreeing with Lord Bridge that foresight is not intention, but rather, merely evidence of it, ruled that the natural consequence element of Lord Bridge's test was 'defective' as it failed to refer to a degree of probability. 'Natural consequences' were not the same, according to Lord Scarman, as 'probable consequences'. Instead Lord Scarman suggested that a jury should be directed that:...

> the *Moloney* guidelines as they stand are unsafe and misleading. They require a reference to probability. They also require an explanation that the greater the probability of a consequence the more likely it is that the consequence was foreseen and that if that consequence was foreseen the greater the probability is that that consequence was also intended. [T]he probability, however high, of a consequence is *only a factor*. But juries also need to be reminded that the *decision is theirs* to be reached upon a consideration of all the evidence. (emphasis added).

Lord Scarman's statement is a difficult one to comprehend. Reference to a greater degree of probability, meaning that the consequence was 'also intended', gives the appearance of a test of law (ie that foresight *is* intention). However, Lord Scarman then goes on to explain that the decision is one for the jury and that the probable consequence is 'only a factor... upon consideration of all the evidence'. This latter sentiment reads as a test of evidence (ie that foresight is merely *evidence* of intention, and not intention itself). A lack of a clear statement was thus evident and the issue remained unresolved.

R v Nedrick

In the same year as *Hancock*, the concept of oblique intent was clarified by the Court of Appeal in *R v Nedrick* [1986] 3 All ER 1.

case example

Charge:
Murder

Case progression:
Crown Court – Guilty

Court of Appeal – Conviction quashed

Point of law:
Meaning of foresight in intention

In *R v Nedrick* [1986] 3 All ER 1, the defendant poured paraffin through the letter box of the house of a woman with whom he held a grudge. He set the paraffin alight causing the house to set on fire, killing the woman's child inside. The defendant argued that he lacked the necessary intent for murder as he only intended to frighten the woman – not to kill or injure anyone. The defendant was convicted of murder following a direction to the jury from the judge in accordance with *Hyam v DPP*, equating foresight of consequences as highly probable with intention. (Note: The trial at first instance took place prior to the House of Lords' decision in *Moloney* – thus why the trial judge directed the jury in accordance with *Hyam*.)

The Court of Appeal, whilst acknowledging that the trial judge was in no way to blame, stated that this direction was 'plainly wrong' in light of *Moloney*. The Court quashed the defendant's conviction for murder, substituting one of manslaughter.

According to Lord Lane CJ, who gave the leading judgment of the Court, in the majority of cases where the issue is intention but the defendant's motive or desire is clear, a simple direction will be sufficient (ie intention should not be explained and the jury must pay regard to 'all the relevant circumstances, including what the defendant himself said and did' in deciding whether the defendant had the requisite intention to kill or cause serious bodily harm).

However, in cases where the defendant's desire or motive is not to cause harm, a further direction is required. Lord Lane CJ explained this as such:

> Where the charge is murder and in the rare cases where the simple direction is not enough, the jury should be directed that they are not entitled to infer the necessary intention, unless they feel sure that death or serious bodily harm was a virtual certainty (barring some unforeseen intervention) as a result of the defendant's actions and that the defendant appreciated that such was the case.

Lord Lane CJ further stated:

> When determining whether the defendant had the necessary intent, it may therefore be helpful for a jury to ask themselves two questions: [1] How probable was the consequence which resulted from the defendant's voluntary act? [2] Did he foresee that consequence?
>
> If he did not appreciate that death or really serious harm was likely to result from his act, he cannot have intended to bring it about. If he did, but thought that the risk to which he was exposing the person killed was only slight, then it may be easy for the jury to conclude that he did not intend to bring about that result. On the other hand, if the jury are satisfied that at the material time the defendant recognised that death or serious harm would be virtually certain (barring some unforeseen intervention) to result from his voluntary act, then that is a fact from which they may find it easy to infer that he intended to kill or do serious bodily harm, even though he may not have had any desire to achieve that result.

As a result of *Nedrick*, there is a clear move away from the word 'probability' and towards a greater degree of 'certainty'. The 'virtual certainty' test in *Nedrick* appears to be a much narrower test than the 'highly probable' test applied in *Hyam*. This aimed to ensure a clearer distinction between the concepts of oblique intent and recklessness. In addition, *Nedrick* clarified that a jury were entitled to *infer* intention where the end result was a virtual certainty (or 'virtually certain') as a result of the defendant's actions. Importantly, Lord Lane CJ emphasised that such virtual certainty was not *intention itself*, but rather was *evidence* from which intention may be inferred.

Williams ('Oblique Intention' (1987) 46 CLJ 417) is critical of the decision in *Nedrick* on the basis that it leaves unanswered a number of salient points and it causes confusion in certain respects.

Indeed, Buxton ('Some Simple Thoughts on Intention' [1988] Crim LR 484) referred to the position post-*Nedrick* as an 'admittedly fragile equilibrium'. Let us use an example to help explain the distinction.

example

Suppose Jack has a fight with Jill in the street. Jack pushes Jill in anger but without any intention to hurt her. Unfortunately, Jill falls backwards and severely hurts her head.

In this case, Jack lacks the necessary direct intent to found liability. However, he may be liable using oblique intent as the prosecution may be able to prove that Jack foresaw Jill's injuries as a virtual certainty of his actions. In this case, however, such foresight does not amount to intent itself. What we mean by this is that the jury are not obliged to conclude that Jack *intended* to cause Jill harm. Rather, Jack's foresight merely amounts to evidence (of which there may be much more) that the jury *may* use to conclude that the defendant intended harm. The simplicity of this lies in whether the jury *must* reach a conclusion or simply *may* reach a conclusion.

R v Woollin

The approach in *Nedrick* was later followed by the House of Lords in *R v Woollin* [1999] AC 82.

case example

Charge:
Murder

Case progression:
Crown Court – Guilty

Court of Appeal – Conviction upheld

House of Lords – Conviction quashed (manslaughter substituted)

Point of law:
Meaning of foresight in intention

In *R v Woollin* [1999] AC 82, the defendant picked up his three-month-old son, shook him and threw him towards the wall causing a fractured skull. He claimed he did so when he had 'lost his cool' when his son had choked on food. The defendant claimed that it was not his intention to kill the child, nor did he think his actions would kill the child.

The trial judge directed the jury to convict where they were satisfied that he was aware of a 'substantial risk' of death or injury to the child. The defendant was convicted of murder and appealed, arguing that the judge had misdirected the jury by use of the term 'substantial risk'.

The Court of Appeal disagreed and found that the virtual certainty test was applicable only where the *only* evidence of intention was the actions of the accused constituting the *actus reus* and their consequence on the victim. To go further than this would undermine s 8 of the Criminal Justice Act 1967 (above).

The defendant further appealed to the House of Lords which allowed his appeal on the basis that both the trial judge and the Court of Appeal had erred in law.

The House of Lords allowed the appeal, quashing the murder conviction and substituting one of manslaughter. The House held that the trial judge was correct to use the *Nedrick* direction, but that he had later misdirected the jury when he departed from *Nedrick* by using the wider phrase 'substantial risk'. Lord Steyn, giving the leading judgment of the House of Lords, stated that:

> By using the phrase 'substantial risk' the judge blurred the line between intention and recklessness, and hence between murder and manslaughter. The misdirection enlarged the scope of the mental element required for murder. It was a material misdirection.

The House of Lords confirmed that a *Nedrick* direction was required in all cases of oblique intent in order to distinguish foresight in intention cases and cases of recklessness. The two limbs of the *Nedrick* direction were approved by the House of Lords, with one slight amendment, namely that the word 'infer' in the *Nedrick* direction should be changed to 'find'. The direction now reads:

> Where the charge is murder and in the rare cases where the simple direction is not enough, the jury should be directed that they are not entitled to find the necessary intention, unless they feel sure that death or serious bodily harm was a virtual certainty (barring some unforeseen intervention) as a result of the defendant's actions and that the defendant appreciated that such was the case.

Whilst Lord Steyn did not provide a reason for this change in wording, a number of possibilities may be suggested:

- First, it could be suggested that this change came about as a result of fears that jurors were pressured into inferring intention from the facts and that the word 'find' was easier to follow, understand and apply than that of 'infer'. The Court of Appeal in *Nedrick* was clear in its opinion that foresight of a consequence was a piece of evidence from which intention could be inferred by the jury.
- Alternatively, by replacing the word 'infer' with 'find', it is unclear whether Lord Steyn elevated a rule of evidence to one of substantive law. It is likely that his Lordship simply intended to use a term which was easier for a jury to understand.
- However, it was also the case that Lord Steyn did not abandon the word 'entitled' (ie 'a jury are "entitled to find" intention where the defendant foresaw the consequence as virtually certain'). This could imply that the rule remains one of evidence.

To add additional confusion, at another point in his Lordship's judgment, Lord Steyn made a puzzling remark whilst referring to the unmodified *Nedrick* direction. His Lordship stated that, '[t]he effect of the critical direction is that a result foreseen as virtually certain *is an intended result*' (emphasis added). This statement would appear to remove a degree of discretion from the jury and elevate the direction to one of substantive law. This lack of consistency/clear statement on the part of Lord Steyn is unfortunate.

Lord Steyn, through his inconsistent remarks, has left the issue unresolved. Is intention a matter of law or one of fact? **Table 3.2** explains the distinction.

*Table 3.2 Understanding the distinction between law and evidence post-*Woollin

Term	**Explanation**
If the House of Lords defined intention as a matter of **law** ...	The jury would *not* be bound to find intention in a case where the jury were of the view that the defendant appreciated that the end result was a virtual certainty. In this regard, the jury would be obliged to conclude that the defendant held the necessary intention.
If the House of Lords defined intention as matter of **fact** ...	The jury would be *not* be bound to find intention in a case where the jury were of the view that the defendant appreciated that the end result was a virtual certainty. They could merely use such a finding as *evidence* which may go towards a finding of intention. In this regard, the jury could ignore this evidence (if they so wished) and conclude that the defendant did not have the necessary intention.

Re A

Two years later, in the civil case of *Re A (children) (conjoined twins: surgical separation)* [2001] Fam 147, the Court of Appeal (by a majority of 2:1) took favour with the approach that foresight is a question of law. The Court was tasked to consider whether a doctor intended to kill in circumstances where the separation of conjoined twins involved a foresight that the weaker twin would die. In the majority, Ward LJ stated:

> I have to ask myself whether I am satisfied that the doctors recognise that death or serious harm will be virtually certain, barring some unforeseen intervention, to result from carrying out this operation. *If so*, the doctors *intend to kill* or to do that serious harm even though they may not have any desire to achieve that result. (emphasis added)

Specific reference to foresight being an intention to kill is an indication that Ward LJ took preference with the view that foresight is the same thing as intention, and not merely evidence of such. His Lordship continued: 'Unpalatable though it may be … to stigmatise the doctors with "murderous intent", that is what *in law* they will have if they perform the operation and Mary dies as a result.' (emphasis added) Further to this, Brooke LJ (also in the majority) reasoned that 'an English court *would inevitably find* that the surgeons intended to kill Mary, however little they desired that end, because her death would be the virtually certain consequence of their acts, and they would realise that for all practical purposes her death would invariably follow …'. By way of a final example, Ward LJ identified that, following *Woollin*, a defendant must 'be taken to have intended the death which he foresaw as virtually certain'.

From the numerous examples of quotations taken from *Re A*, it is not hard to conclude that the majority were of the opinion that foresight was equivalent to intention and that proof of foresight was proof of intention; not merely evidence of such.

R v Matthews and Alleyne

This issue was addressed once more by the Court of Appeal in *R v Matthews and Alleyne* [2003] 2 Cr App R 461. In this case, the defendants robbed the victim and threw him off a bridge into a river, being aware that he could not swim. He drowned and the defendants were convicted of murder. The trial judge had directed the jury to find the necessary intent to be proved, provided they were satisfied that the defendants appreciated that death was virtually certain. The Court of Appeal held that the trial judge had misdirected the jury because he had directed them to find that intention would be proven if the defendants foresaw the end result as a virtual certainty. This elevated, according to the Court of Appeal, the *Woollin* direction from a rule of evidence to a substantive rule of law.

In the Court of Appeal, Rix LJ stated, 'we do not regard *Woollin* as yet reaching or laying down a substantive rule of law'. In addition, Rix LJ confirmed that the appropriate terminology to be used is 'find' and not 'infer'. Importantly, *Matthews and Alleyne* did not refer to *Re A*. The effect of *Matthews and Alleyne* is to clarify that *Woollin* lays down a rule of evidence – the defendant's foresight of a consequence as virtually certain to occur is evidence from which the jury could find that the defendant had the necessary intention. The jury could disregard the virtual certainty if they so wished.

Unfortunately, instead of leaving the matter as simply stated as above, Rix LJ added confusion to the mix by stating that 'there is very little to choose between a rule of evidence and one of substantive law'. In addition, the Court considered that, on the facts of the case, a finding that there was the necessary intention was 'inevitable'. This statement regarding the little difference between the two terms and reference to inevitability continues to drive confusion in this respect.

The present state of oblique intent

As a result of *Woollin*, as confirmed in *Matthews*, the jury are now able to *find* intention where:

(a) the end result was a virtual certainty as a result of the defendant's actions; and
(b) the defendant appreciated that such was the case.

Note that this is a two-part test, requiring the jury to be satisfied of both elements. Should one element be missing, the jury are not entitled to 'find' intention.

Returning to the two issues we identified earlier:

- *Is foresight the same as intention or merely evidence of intention?* Following *R v Matthews and Alleyne*, it would appear that foresight is merely evidence of intention from which the jury may go on to find intention. In this regard, oblique intention is a matter for the jury to consider – the judge cannot interfere with this fact-finding process. It is therefore better to say that a jury are 'entitled' to find intention as opposed to being 'required' to find intention. Given their ability to find intention from the virtual certainty test, the jury, if they so wish, may completely disregard the outcome of the test should it not accord with the views they hold as to the defendant's guilt. It is merely a matter of evidence; it is not a statement of law. This approach provides the jury with some 'moral elbow room' in making their decisions. According to Norrie ('After Woollin' [1999] Crim LR 532) the jury may approach the question of oblique intention using the 'moral threshold test' which essentially allows the jury to find that there is no intention (and no guilt) where the defendant foresaw the end result as a virtual certainty but was acting for a moral purpose (eg necessity).

  Whilst this clarity apparently exists from the case of *Matthews*, it is worth remembering that *Woollin* was a decision of the House of Lords whilst *Matthews* was a decision of the Court of Appeal. If it was the case that Lord Steyn intended foresight to be a question of law, *Matthews* will have been decided incorrectly. In addition, whilst the Court of Appeal in *Re A* considered the test to be one of law, their Lordships were dealing with a civil case in that regard which would not be considered binding on the criminal courts. Therefore, it remains contested whether foresight is a question of law or fact. For practical purposes, it is treated as a question of fact.
- *What degree of foresight is required?* The law has clearly developed over the years with reference to various probabilities and certainties. Following the cases of *Nedrick*, *Woollin* and *Alleyne*, the present approach appears to focus on the need for a 'virtual certainty' (ie that we are certain the end result would occur). This is a high threshold to meet.

A further issue to identify at these final stages is this: does the *Woollin* test apply only to cases of murder, or to other offences requiring proof of intention? In *Woollin*, Lord Steyn's direction specifically referred to murder, and would appear to be restricted to murder. The Crown Court Compendium, however, suggests that 'the test appears to be applied across the criminal law'. In that regard, the *Woollin* test may be applied outside of the offence of murder, to offences requiring proof of intention, eg GBH with intent, contrary to s 18 of the Offences Against the Person Act 1861.

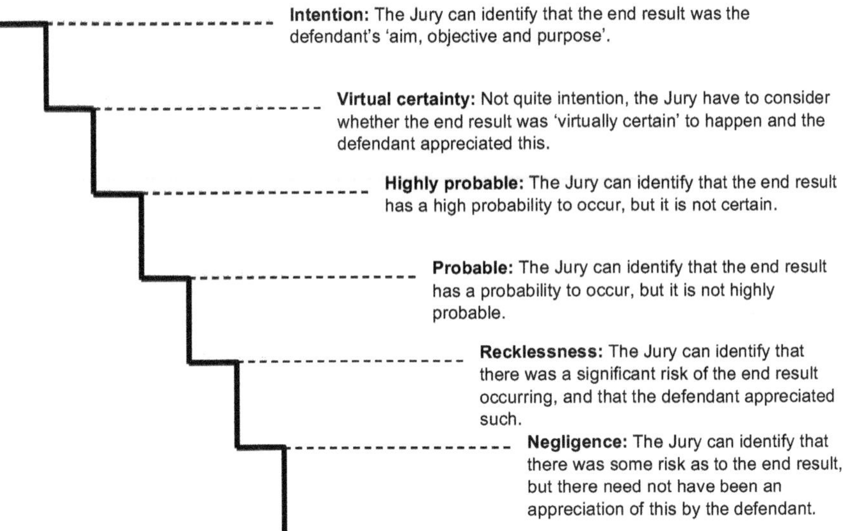

Intention: The Jury can identify that the end result was the defendant's 'aim, objective and purpose'.
Virtual certainty: Not quite intention, the Jury have to consider whether the end result was 'virtually certain' to happen and the defendant appreciated this.
Highly probable: The Jury can identify that the end result has a high probability to occur, but it is not certain.
Probable: The Jury can identify that the end result has a probability to occur, but it is not highly probable.
Recklessness: The Jury can identify that there was a significant risk of the end result occurring, and that the defendant appreciated such.
Negligence: The Jury can identify that there was some risk as to the end result, but there need not have been an appreciation of this by the defendant.

Figure 3.3 Stairway to intention

From **Figure 3.3**, you can see that at the top of the staircase sits 'intention'. This is the highest form of *mens rea* that a jury may have to deal with. You will see that, for oblique intention, a jury need not go to the highest step; they must only travel to the penultimate step towards 'virtual certainty'. In doing so, the jury will surpass such concepts as negligence, recklessness, probability, and high probability. This elevating sequence is used to demonstrate the degree to which the jury must be sure before they 'find' intention exists.

A summary of our discussion is provided in **Table 3.3**.

Table 3.3 Summary of the developments in oblique intent

Case	Legal principle
DPP v Smith (1961)	Ruled that foresight resulted in an objective irrebuttable presumption of law. A man intends the 'natural and probable consequences' of his acts.
CJA 1967, s 8	Repealed the decision in *Smith*. Subjective nature of intention restored. No jury is bound to presume intention.
Hyam v DPP (1975)	The *mens rea* for murder is satisfied if the defendant knew that death or serious harm was *highly probable*.
R v Moloney (1985)	Ruled that *Hyam* was wrongly decided. Intent could be inferred where the defendant foresaw the consequence as a *natural consequence* of his act.
R v Hancock and Shankland (1986)	The greater the probability of a consequence, the more likely it was that the consequence was foreseen and the greater the probability that that consequence was also intended.
R v Nedrick (1986)	Introduced the 'virtual certainty' test.

Case	Legal principle
R v Woollin (1999)	The jury are not entitled to *find* the necessary intention unless they are sure that death or serious bodily harm was a virtual certainty, barring some unforeseen intervention, as a result of the accused's actions and that the accused appreciated such was the case. Did not clarify whether foresight was a question of fact (only amounting to evidence of intention) or whether it was one of law (foresight is the same as intention).
Re A (2001)	A civil case in which Ward LJ identified that foresight of a virtually certainty result was equivalent to intention. Individuals are to be treated as having intended an end result that was virtually certain. Note: Only a Court of Appeal case (and a civil case).
R v Matthews & Alleyne (2003)	Reaffirmed *Woollin* and concluded that the word 'find' ought to replace 'infer' in the direction to the jury, and concluded that foresight is merely evidence of intention, not intention itself. Note: Only a Court of Appeal case, whilst *Woollin* was a House of Lords decision.

example

Let us return to our terrorist example towards the start of our discussion.

Lord Bridge was of the opinion that the terrorist would be guilty of murder, in relation to the bomb disposal expert. Following our discussion of the development in the law, it is difficult to comprehend why this is so. If the terrorist has given advanced warning of the bomb, can it really be said that he foresees death or serious injury as a virtually certain result? The terrorist may foresee as a virtual certainty that the bomb disposal expert may attempt to diffuse the bomb; but can it really be said that he foresees death or serious injury as a virtually certain result? Lord Steyn in *Woollin* considered that the terrorist would not be guilty of murder for these reasons – but would be liable for manslaughter. The example demonstrates the difficulty involved with oblique intent. For a more detailed analysis of this example, see Pedain, 'Intention and the Terrorist Example' [2003] Crim LR 579.

3.2.1.3 Directing the jury

Following our in-depth discussion of oblique intention, it will be necessary to understand the circumstances and manner in which a trial judge should direct a jury on the meaning of intention. The Crown Court Compendium (section 8-1(1)) provides that: 'The "golden rule" when directing a jury upon intent it is best to avoid any elaboration or paraphrase of what is meant by intent. It is an ordinary English word.' Reference to 'golden rule' is taken from Lord Bridge in *Moloney*, who also explained that intent should be left to the jury's 'good sense' unless 'some further explanation or elaboration is strictly necessary to avoid misunderstanding'. This approach was confirmed by the Court of Appeal in *R v McNamara and Bennett* [2009] EWCA Crim 2530.

There may be some circumstances in which a more detailed explanation is required on direct intent. In these circumstances, the Compendium states: 'the most basic proposition is that a person "intends" to cause a result if he/she acts in order to bring it about.' For cases involving oblique intention, the trial judge should direct the jury according to the test laid down in *Woollin*. According to the Court of Appeal in *R v Royle* [2013] EWCA Crim 1461, this terminology should not be deviated from. In particular, the Court expressed concerns in the use of the phrases 'high probability' and 'very high probability' as opposed to 'virtual certainty'. Importantly, the Court of Appeal in *R v*

Allen [2005] EWCA Crim 1344 emphasised that it 'is only in an exceptional case that this extended direction by reference to foresight becomes necessary'. Where the direction is required, the Court of Appeal in *R v Stringer* [2008] EWCA Crim 1222 explained that the jury must be satisfied of both elements of the *Woollin* direction; the mere fact that the end result was a virtual certainty is not sufficient on its own. The defendant must also appreciate that the end result was a virtual certainty. The Compendium helpfully provides a 'route to verdict' map for juries dealing with intention. **Figure 3.4** provides that route to verdict, amended for our purposes.

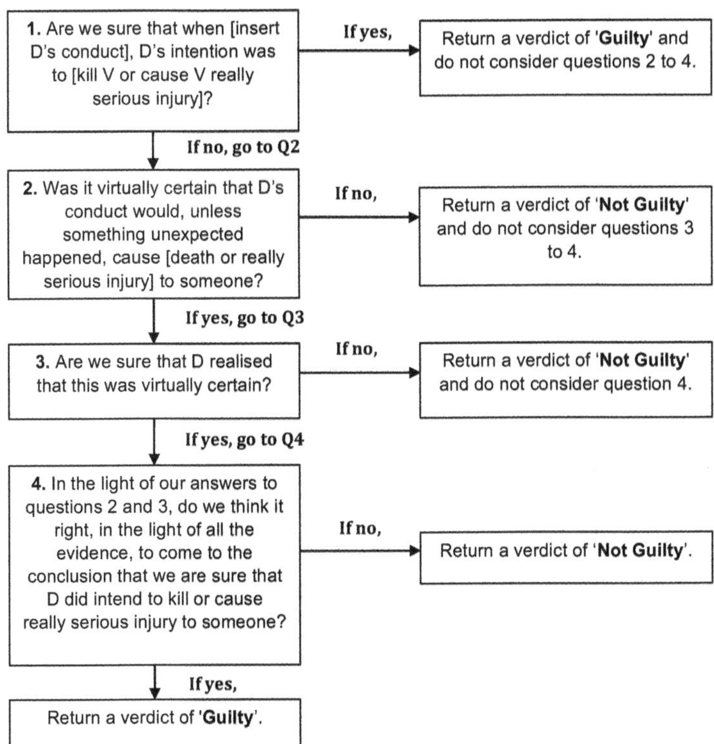

Figure 3.4 Route to verdict for intention

3.2.1.4 Basic and specific intent

In addition to understanding direct and oblique intent, it will be necessary for students to understand two further forms of intention, namely basic and specific intent. Such forms of intention are relevant in the context of defences – specifically the defence of intoxication – and will be considered in much greater detail in **Chapter 7.**

Here, however, we distinguish these two forms:

Table 3.4 Understanding basic and specific intent

Form of intent	Meaning
Basic intent	Offences which involve both intention and recklessness as an element of the offence. Voluntary intoxication is no defence to basic intent offences.
Specific intent	Offences which involve only intention as an element of the offence. Voluntary intoxication is a defence to specific intent offences.

3.2.1.5 Ulterior intent

Ulterior intent refers to an element of the *mens rea* which is additional, or 'ulterior', to the *actus reus*. It is for this reason that ulterior intent is also known as 'further intent', given that the intention must be to produce an end result which goes beyond, or further than, the *actus reus*. One example of this can be seen in the offence of theft. The *mens rea* of theft requires the prosecution to prove that the defendant had the intention to permanently deprive the owner of their property. There is no corresponding element of permanent deprivation in the *actus reus*. The defendant may fail in his intention to permanently deprive, eg he may be stopped from doing so; however, his intention alone is sufficient. In this regard, theft is an ulterior intent offence.

Other examples include the offence of burglary, contrary to s 9(1)(a) of the Theft Act 1968, causing grievous bodily harm with intent to cause grievous bodily harm or with intent to resist arrest, contrary to s 18 of the Offences Against the Person Act 1861, and aggravated criminal damage, contrary to s 1(2) of the Criminal Damage Act 1971.

As we will see in **Chapter 7**, there are many that view specific intent and ulterior intent as the same thing.

3.2.2 Duration of intention

The defendant's *mens rea* need not last any longer than the point at which he commits the *actus reus* of the offence. This means that a defendant will not be excused from liability simply because he has abandoned his venture. Suppose Jack had the intention to kill Jill and stabbed her with a knife. Upon stabbing Jill, Jack regrets his actions and attempts to save Jill's life. If Jill were to die from the stabbing, Jack would remain liable despite his change of heart.

This area of law is referred to as cases involving 'short-lived' *mens rea* and can be best demonstrated by considering the cases of *R v Jakeman* (1982) 76 Cr App R 223 and *R v Styles* [2015] EWCA Crim 1619.

case example

Charge:
Being knowingly concerned in the fraudulent evasion of the prohibition on the importation of a controlled drug (CEMA 1979, s 170(2))

Case progression:
Crown Court – Guilty

Court of Appeal – Conviction upheld

Point of law:
Short-lived *mens rea*

In *R v Jakeman* (1982) 76 Cr App R 223, the defendant booked suitcases containing drugs onto a series of flights terminating in London. The defendant later abandoned the suitcases in Paris on the basis that she, allegedly, no longer wished to import them. Despite this, the cases were sent on to London where the drugs were discovered.

The defendant was charged with and convicted of being knowingly concerned in the fraudulent evasion of the prohibition on the importation of a controlled drug, namely cannabis, contrary to s 170(2) of the Customs and Excise Management Act (CEMA) 1979.

The defendant appealed to the Court of Appeal which rejected her appeal, deciding that the defendant held the necessary *mens rea* at the time she committed the relevant *actus reus*.

Wood J in the Court of Appeal reasoned that:

> What is suggested is that she should not be convicted unless her guilty state of mind subsisted at the time of importation. We see no reason to construe the Act in this way. If a guilty mind at the time of importation is an essential, the man recruited to collect the package which has already arrived and which he knows contains prohibited drugs commits no offence.

What matters is the state of mind *at the time the relevant acts are done*, ie at the time the defendant is concerned in bringing about the importation. Although the importation takes place at one precise moment—when the aircraft lands—a person who is concerned in the importation may play his part before or after that moment. (emphasis added)

Jakeman makes it clear that so long as the *actus reus* and *mens rea* coincide at some point during the transaction of the offence (see **3.8**), it is irrelevant that the defendant has had a change of heart and no longer wishes to pursue his original conduct. This authority would seem to be a simple one without the need for further clarification; however, the principle of short-lived *mens rea* was addressed once more by the Court of Appeal in *R v Styles* [2015] EWCA Crim 1619.

case example

Charge:
Possessing a firearm with intent to commit murder (FA 1968, s 18(1))

Case progression:
Crown Court – Guilty

Court of Appeal – Conviction upheld

Point of law:
Short-lived *mens rea*

In *R v Styles* [2015] EWCA Crim 1619, the defendant left his home with the intention to murder his ex-partner's husband. At 2.45am, police stopped the defendant 300 yards from the intended victim's home carrying a loaded shotgun over his shoulder. The defendant was charged with and convicted of possession of a firearm with intent to commit murder, contrary to s 18(1) of the Firearms Act (FA) 1968.

The defendant appealed to the Court of Appeal, arguing that the trial judge had misdirected the jury regarding short-lived *mens rea*. The Court of Appeal disagreed and found his conviction to be safe.

After the jury had retired from the trial in *Styles*, they sent the judge the following question:

> Would you please let us know whether, in English law, the intent to murder, though it may be present in a person's mind for a fleeting second or more, if that person has a change of mind or begins to cool off during the course of their actions, does the intent become cancelled?

The trial judge responded:

> Intention bears its ordinary sense and its ordinary usage, it does not require any further definition than that. The intention which is referred to in these counts is his *intention at the time of committing the act*.
>
> What is the particular time? It is when he is walking down the London Road with the gun over his shoulder and he is stopped by the police. That intention may have been formed within a *very short time of that moment* I have just described, or it is an intention that may have built up over time, and the way you approach this, members of the jury, is in various ways. (emphasis added)

It was this direction that caused the defendant to appeal to the Court of Appeal. Rejecting his appeal, however, Fulford LJ stated:

> The direction the judge gave to the jury was correct in law. The offence was committed if the appellant, with the gun in his possession, intended to commit murder within the timeframe of the indictment (viz. at any stage on 5 December 2013) ... It would have been wrong for the judge to limit the circumstances in

which the jury could convict by requiring them to be sure that the appellant had held the requisite intention for the entirety of the walk between the two locations.

The result of *Styles* is to reinforce the decision in *Jakeman* and to find short-lived *mens rea* an acceptable form of internal element required for the offence charged.

3.3 Recklessness

The second form of *mens rea* relevant to our discussion in the criminal law is that of recklessness. In a general sense, recklessness simply means the taking of an 'unjustified risk'. Recklessness is most often presented as an alternative form of *mens rea* to intention and will often be considered second (in the sense that it is less blameworthy than intention). **Table 3.5** provides some examples.

Table 3.5 Examples of recklessness as an alternative element

Crime	*Mens rea*
Common assault	Intention to cause the victim to apprehend the application of unlawful physical force; or Being reckless to the thought of such apprehension occurring.
Inflicting GBH/wounding	Intention to cause 'some harm'; or Being reckless to the thought of 'some harm' occurring.
Criminal damage	Intention to damage or destroy property; or Being reckless to the thought that property would be damaged or destroyed.

However, it is also possible for this form of *mens rea* to operate independently from intention. The most obvious example being subjectively reckless manslaughter (**Chapter 8**).

The state of the law at present is found in *R v G* [2004] 1 AC 1034 (facts considered below) where the House Lords ruled that in order for a defendant to be reckless, it must be proven that:

(i) the defendant was aware of the existence of the risk; and
(ii) the defendant, nevertheless, took the risk which was unjustifiable.

We shall deal with each element in detail and consider the developments leading up to this pronouncement.

3.3.1 Element (i): appreciation of the risk

Under this first heading, it must be proven that the defendant foresaw, or appreciated, that the risk existed. By 'risk', we simply mean that as a result of the defendant's conduct, the end result could occur. This is a subjective test observing what the defendant believed the situation to be in the circumstances (*R v Cunningham* [1957] 2 QB 396). The risk need not be a large one; it must simply be the case that the defendant is subjectively aware of the risk (*R v Brady* [2006] EWCA Crim 2413).

This, however, has not always been the case, and at one point the law took an objective analysis of the situation, asking what the reasonable man would have foreseen (*Metropolitan Police Commissioner (MPC) v Caldwell* [1982] AC 341). The following sections will proceed to discuss the developments in this area of law to the point we are at now. It may be useful at first to set out our timeline.

Figure 3.5 Timeline of recklessness

3.3.1.1 The origins of recklessness: *Cunningham*

Our timeline starts with the case of *R v Cunningham* [1957] 2 QB 396.

case example

Charge:
Maliciously administering a noxious substance so as to endanger life (OAPA 1861, s 23)

Case progression:
Crown Court – Guilty

Court of Criminal Appeal – Conviction quashed

Point of law:
Meaning of recklessness

In *R v Cunningham* [1957] 2 QB 396, the defendant pulled a gas meter from the wall of an empty house in order to steal the money from it. In doing so, he left the gas pipe leading to the meter broken, causing poisonous gas to leak from it. The gas seeped through into the neighbouring house where the victim, his mother-in-law, breathed it in and suffered harm as a result.

The defendant was charged with and convicted of maliciously administering a noxious substance so as to endanger life, contrary to s 23 of the Offences Against the Person Act 1861 in the Crown Court.

The Court of Appeal quashed the defendant's conviction on the basis that he was not reckless in his actions, ie he did not appreciate that a risk of harm existed when he broke the gas meter.

The Court of Criminal Appeal established what has become known as subjective, or *Cunningham,* recklessness. Byrne J identified the accurate statement of recklessness as follows: 'the accused has foreseen that the particular kind of harm might be done and yet has gone on to take the risk of it.'

From *Cunningham*, we can say that it had to be proven that:

(a) the defendant took an unjustified risk; and
(b) the defendant was aware of the existence of the unreasonable risk.

D must personally foresee a risk

Under this form of recklessness, the defendant cannot be liable for an offence unless he personally foresaw the risk of harm occurring from his conduct. The test requires a jury to look into the mind of the defendant and ask what *this* defendant foresaw. The test is not concerned with what the defendant ought to have foreseen or what the reasonable person, in the defendant's position, foresaw. In this case, the defendant failed to appreciate that by pulling the gas meter from the wall, he would cause poisonous gas to seep into the neighbouring house. *Cunningham* was later reaffirmed in the case of *R v Stephenson* [1979] QB 695, where the Court of Appeal held that a defendant cannot be considered reckless where he did not foresee harm occurring as a result of his actions (in that case, D's schizophrenia meant that he could not appreciate the risk before him).

in practice

The language used when directing the jury on recklessness must not be overlooked. It is important that the jury appreciate that the defendant must personally foresee the risk; it is incorrect to state that the defendant 'should' or 'ought to' have foreseen the risk. The same can be said for your own answers to assessment questions.

What is not relevant to D's awareness?

As emphasised above, the defendant must personally be aware of the risk that his conduct would cause the end result. In that regard, there are a number of points to make here:

- It is not sufficient to say that the defendant could have appreciated the likely risk his actions might cause if he had stopped to think about it. The defendant must *actually* perceive the risk (see *Foster v CPS* [2013] EWHC 3885 (Admin)).
- Even if the risk is blindingly obvious to the reasonable man, if the defendant does not appreciate the risk, there is no liability.

R v Parker: an extension of *Cunningham*

Following *R v Parker* [1977] 2 All ER 37, the Court of Appeal concluded that a deliberate closing of one's eyes to the obvious risks posed by one's conduct (also known as 'wilful blindness') will be caught by the definition of recklessness. This has often been phrased as being aware of the risk but placing it to the 'back of your mind'. For arguments that *Parker* is inconsistent with *Cunningham*, see Ibbetsen, 'Recklessness Restored' [2004] 63 Camb LJ 13 and Birch, 'The Foresight Saga: The Biggest Mistake of All?' [1988] Crim LR 4.

3.3.1.2 The move towards an objective standard: *Caldwell*

Just two years after the Court of Appeal in *Stephenson* applied and reaffirmed the approach taken in *Cunningham*, the House of Lords was faced with a legal challenge to the meaning of recklessness in the case of *MPC v Caldwell* [1982] AC 341.

Charge:
Arson (CDA 1971, s 1(3))

Case progression:
Crown Court – Guilty

Court of Appeal – Conviction upheld

Point of law:
Meaning of recklessness

In *MPC v Caldwell* [1982] AC 341, the defendant, an ex-employee at a hotel, started a fire at the hotel after consuming a large amount of alcohol. The fire caused damage to the hotel but no guests were injured.

The defendant was charged with and convicted of arson contrary to s 1(3) of the Criminal Damage Act (CDA) 1971 in the Crown Court.

The defendant appealed to the Court of Appeal and subsequently the House of Lords, arguing that, following *Cunningham*, the defendant had given no thought as to the possible endangerment of life due to his intoxicated state. The House of Lords (by a majority of 3:2) rejected this submission, finding there to be requirement that his actions were not reckless in the minds of reasonable persons.

Lord Diplock in the House of Lords concluded that:

... a person charged with an offence ... is 'reckless as to whether or not any property 'would be destroyed or damaged' if (1) he does an act which in fact creates an obvious risk that property will be destroyed or damaged and (2) when he does the act he either has not given any thought to the possibility of there being any such risk or has recognised that there was some risk involved and has nonetheless gone on to do it.

That would be a proper direction to the jury; cases in the Court of Appeal which held otherwise should be regarded as overruled.

In making this statement, Lord Diplock and the majority of the House of Lords formulated what has become known as objective, or *Caldwell*, recklessness. It can be expressed (in a general sense) as follows: A person is reckless where:

(a) he does an act which in fact creates an obvious risk that the end result would occur; and

(b) when he does the act he either has not given any thought to the possibility of there being any such risk or has recognised that there was some risk involved and has nonetheless gone on to do it.

Caldwell was later applied but amended by the House of Lords in *R v Lawrence* [1982] AC 510, in relation to the offence of causing death by reckless driving, which held that in relation to part one of the test, there must not only be an 'obvious risk'; but rather there must be an 'obvious *and serious* risk'. The meaning of obvious was later explained to mean obvious to the reasonable man – thus making it an objective test.

Although the formulation of *Caldwell* recklessness by Lord Diplock above was explained in terms of criminal damage, later case law applied *Caldwell* to areas of law outside criminal damage, for example:

- causing death by reckless driving (*R v Lawrence* [1982] AC 510);
- reckless manslaughter (*R v Seymour* [1983] 2 AC 493).

Watkins LJ in the Court of Appeal in *Seymour* ((1983) 76 Cr App R 211) suggested that the *Lawrence* direction on recklessness 'is comprehensive and of general application to all offences ... and should be given to juries without in any way being diluted'. *Caldwell* recklessness was approved as the correct test by the House of Lords in *Seymour* ([1983] 2 AC 493). This approach, however, was not followed in subsequent cases, with the Court of Appeal in both *R v Spratt* [1990] 1 WLR 1073 and *R v Satnam & Kewal* (1983) 78 Cr App R 149 ruling that *Caldwell* recklessness did not apply to the relevant areas of law (assault and rape respectively). The House of Lords in *R v Adomako* [1995] 1 AC 171 drove the penultimate nail into the coffin of *Caldwell* recklessness by overruling *Seymour* and finding *Caldwell* recklessness as restricted to offences of criminal damage.

As a result of *Adomako*, the law was in a state of flux, with offences concerning criminal damage being considered using *Caldwell* recklessness, and all other offences using *Cunningham* recklessness.

3.3.1.3 Returning to the subjective standard: *G*

Caldwell amounted to a particularly harsh statement of law as it applied to the individuals subject to it. For instance, in *Elliott v C (a minor)* [1983] 2 All ER 1005 a young girl of 14 with learning difficulties was charged with and convicted of arson after having set fire to a shed by lighting white spirit. Under *Caldwell* recklessness, the Divisional Court had no option but to find the defendant guilty of an offence on the basis that the reasonable person would have foreseen the risk of damage to property. *Caldwell* thus had the effect of ignoring, or overlooking, the age and learning disabilities of the defendant, which likely meant that she *personally* was incapable of appreciating the risk.

Despite the absurdity in the application of *Caldwell*, it would not be until another 10 years after *Adomako* that the final nail was driven into its coffin with the historic decision of the House of Lords in *R v G* [2004] 1 AC 1034.

case example

Charge:
Arson (CDA 1971, s 1(3))

Case progression:
Crown Court – Guilty

Court of Appeal – Conviction upheld

House of Lords – Conviction quashed

Point of law:
Meaning of recklessness

In *R v G* [2004] 1 AC 1034, the defendants, two young boys, set light to newspapers before then throwing them under a dustbin behind a shop. The pair left the area without extinguishing the fire which caused significant damage to the shop. The defendants were charged with and convicted of arson in the Crown Court.

The defendants appealed to the Court of Appeal arguing that they had not appreciated the risk of damage to the shop – they believed that the fire would burn itself out on the concrete floor and foresaw no damage occurring as a result of their actions. The Court of Appeal dismissed their appeal following *Caldwell* as the risk of damage would have been obvious to the reasonable person.

Upon appeal, the House of Lords disagreed and overruled *Caldwell*, finding that *Cunningham* recklessness was the appropriate test to apply to all cases involving recklessness as an element.

Lord Bingham in *G* described *Caldwell* recklessness as 'neither moral nor just' and brought an end to objective recklessness in the criminal law. His Lordship stated:

> It is clearly blameworthy to take an obvious and significant risk of causing injury to another. But it is not clearly blameworthy to do something involving a risk of injury to another if … one genuinely does not perceive the risk. Such a person may fairly be accused of stupidity or lack of imagination, but neither of those failings should expose him to conviction of serious crime or the risk of punishment … It is neither moral nor just to convict a defendant (least of all a child) on the strength of what someone else would have apprehended if the defendant himself had no such apprehension.

In defining recklessness, their Lordships preferred the approach of the Law Commission in its Report on Criminal Law: A Criminal Code for England and Wales and Draft Criminal Code Bill, vol 1 (Law Com No 177, 1989), rather than that of the Court of Appeal in *Cunningham*. The draft Criminal Code provides (clause 18(c)):

> A person acts recklessly… with respect to –
> (i) a circumstance when he is aware of a risk that it exists or will exist;
> (ii) a result when he is aware of a risk that it will occur;
> and it is, in the circumstances known to him, unreasonable to take the risk.

3.3.1.4 An attempt to return to *Caldwell*?

Caldwell was a controversial judgment. By way of example, Ibbetson ('Recklessness Restored' [2004] 63 Camb LJ 13) classified *Caldwell* as 'a terrible decision' for which 'no lawyer will lament its consignment to the scrap-heap of legal history'. Despite this, however, an attempt to return to *Caldwell*-style recklessness was seen in the case of *R v Brady* [2006] EWCA Crim 2413 which concerned inflicting GBH contrary to s 20 of the OAPA 1861. In this case, the defendant had jumped from a balcony in a nightclub, landing on a person below and causing them serious injuries. The defendant was convicted of inflicting GBH in the Crown Court and appealed to the Court of Appeal on the basis that he had not foreseen the risk of harm occurring and could not be liable following *Cunningham* recklessness. The prosecution submitted that the s 20 offence required foresight of an 'obvious and significant' risk of harm. The Court rejected this submission, finding subjective recklessness to remain the state of the law for all offences, unless otherwise stated. The effect of *Brady* was to confirm the judgment in *R v G* and the position of recklessness from *Cunningham*.

Interestingly, and relatively recently, the High Court of Australia has chosen not to follow *R v G* and has made it clear that there is a requirement of unreasonableness in the risk-taking of the defendant (ie an objective standard) (*Aubrey v The Queen* [2017] HCA 18).

3.3.2 Element (ii): unjustified taking of the risk

The second element is less controversial than the first, requiring the defendant's risk-taking to be unjustifiable. The second element is objective in nature, requiring the jury to conclude whether the taking of the risk was objectively unjustifiable. Simply, this means that the jury must ask whether the reasonable man would regard the taking of the risk as unjustifiable. To determine this, the jury is likely to consider the nature of the risk itself, the severity of the risk of harm and the nature of the act done.

Importantly, the test is whether the *taking* of the risk is unjustifiable – we are not concerned with the risk itself. The most obvious situation where the defendant will have a justifiable reason to take a risk is to avoid harm to another. This is the approach taken by the Law Commission in its *Working Paper on the Mental Element in Crime* (Law Com No 89, 1978).

example

Jack is driving his car and swerves the car in order to avoid hitting a child playing in the street. By doing so, Jack hits Jill's car and causes damage.

In this case, although Jack may realise that his actions posed a risk of harm or injury, his taking of that risk would be entirely justifiable to the reasonable man.

3.4 Negligence

The third main form of *mens rea* relevant to the imposition of criminal liability is that of negligence. A defendant is considered to be 'negligent' if his conduct falls below the standard of care expected of a reasonable person. Often this is phrased as failing to appreciate a risk that the reasonable man would have; however, in many cases the elements of 'failure' and 'risk' are not always present.

3.4.1 Comparing negligence with recklessness

From the above description of negligence, it appears as though both recklessness and negligence involve an element of risk-taking. A distinction is therefore required between the two terms.

Table 3.6 Comparing negligence and recklessness

Term	Explanation
Recklessness	A defendant is reckless where they have *consciously* taken an unjustified risk. This is where the defendant is *aware* of the risk and takes it anyway.
Negligence	A defendant is negligent where they have *inadvertently* taken an unjustified risk. This is where the defendant may not be aware of the risk but the reasonable man *would have been aware* of the risk.

Indeed, Williams (*Criminal Law: The General Part*, 2nd edn (1961)) characterises the difference as follows:

> Responsibility for some crimes may be incurred by the mere neglect to exercise due caution, where the mind is not actively but negatively or passively at fault. This is inadvertent negligence. Since advertent negligence has a special name (recklessness) it is convenient to use 'negligence' generally to mean inadvertent negligence.

3.4.2 Negligence as a form of *mens rea*

The Law Commission has considered it inappropriate to refer to negligence as a form of *mens rea*. This is because negligence does not require the defendant to hold a specific state of mind – nor does it matter what state of mind the defendant held. Rather, the focus of negligence is on the conduct of the defendant and whether the defendant, through his conduct, fell below a certain standard expected of him. This was the approach taken by the Court of Appeal in *AG's Reference (No 2 of 1999)* [2000] QB 796. Despite this, negligence continues to be recognised as a form of *mens rea*.

Examples of the use of 'negligence' in the criminal law include:

- driving without due care and attention (Road Traffic Act 1988, s 3);
- dangerous driving (Road Traffic Act 1991, s 2A);
- harassment (Protection from Harassment Act 1997, s 1).

3.4.3 Culpability of negligence

You may have come across negligence in your study of the civil law, particularly the law of tort. It is more common to see negligence applied in these cases due to the harshness of the principle in its application. In the criminal law, negligence is often avoided in the more serious offences, with the exception of gross negligence manslaughter (**Chapter 8**); however, it does commonly form the basis for liability in lesser, more regulatory offences, such as driving offences. Alexander and Ferzan (*Crime and Culpability: A Theory of Criminal Law* (CUP, 2009)) are of the view that negligence is not of a sufficient culpability to justify the imposition of criminal liability. The pair argue:

> We are not morally culpable for taking risks of which we are unaware. At any point in time we are failing to notice a great many things, we have forgotten a great many things, and we are misinformed or uninformed about many things. An injunction to notice, remember, and be fully informed about anything that bears on risks to others is an injunction no human being can comply with, so violating this injunction reflects no moral defect. Even those most concerned with the well-being of others will violate this injunction constantly.

In the opinion of Alexander and Ferzan, momentary mistakes should not be punished by criminal responsibility. This view has, however, come under fire from the likes of Leipold ('A Case for Criminal Negligence' (2010) 29 Law & Phil 455) who argues:

> [N]othing in the negligence standard requires unrealistic perceptiveness or care. Nor is criminal negligence, properly defined, so widespread that everyone is routinely exceeding its limits, making it unfair to sanction the few unlucky souls who happen to get caught. Criminal negligence is explicitly relative—it only reaches those departures from the attentiveness that an ordinary person would observe. (The authors, of course, offer sharp and valid criticisms of the reasonable person standard, but that is a different point.) We know that ordinary people sometimes forget to lock up the cleaning supplies, sometimes take their eye off the road for just a moment, and do not always rotate their tires every 5,000 miles to prevent uneven tread wear that can lead to a blowout. On the other hand, those who take these behaviors to extreme degrees—taking your eye off the road for 40 seconds to send a text message—have so far departed from a reasonable standard of care that a jury can justifiably characterize it as a moral defect.

3.5 Other forms of *mens rea*

Outside the main categories of *mens rea* considered in this chapter are other forms relevant to specific offences. These forms are not of general application, such as that of intention or recklessness, but rather play a part in distinguishing specific offences and using appropriate tests to find liability. In this context, our discussion will be brief as we consider these terms more fully in their respective capacity.

3.5.1 Knowledge

The traditional understanding of 'knowledge' has borne the meaning of having information which one is absolutely sure of or feels 'virtually certain' about. More recently, however, the House of Lords in *R v Saik* [2007] 1 AC 18 has confirmed that where knowledge is required to satisfy an offence, 'knowledge means true belief' and should not be 'watered down'. In this respect, the defendant must know all the material circumstances of the offence and cannot be liable for circumstances that have yet to occur (*R v Montila* [2004] UKHL 50). Importantly, whilst intention is concerned with the state of mind of the defendant in relation to a consequence (eg D intends to kill), knowledge is concerned with the state of mind of a defendant in relation to a circumstance (eg D knows that he possesses an unlawful firearm).

Indeed, one can make a useful reference to the Canadian Supreme Court which explained in *USA v Dynar* [1997] 2 SCR 462:

> In the Western legal tradition, knowledge is defined as true belief: 'The word "know" refers exclusively to true knowledge; we are not said to 'know' something that is not so'.

See also *R v Sherif* [2008] EWCA Crim 2653.

Examples of the use of 'knowledge' in the criminal law include:

- having information knowing or believing it might be of material assistance in preventing the commission by another of an act of terrorism (Terrorism Act 2000, s 38B);

- knowingly being a passenger in a vehicle taken without consent (Theft Act 1968, s 12);
- handling stolen goods (Theft Act 1968, s 22).

An interesting application of this principle arose in the case of *R v Dunne* (1998) 162 JP 399. In this case, the defendant was convicted of being knowingly concerned in the fraudulent evasion of a prohibition on the importation of goods contrary to s 170(2) of the Customs and Excise Management Act 1979. The defendant was arrested on his arrival in the UK by customs officers who suspected that the videos in his possession were obscene. The Court of Appeal found that, given the defendant was aware of the nature of the videos, there was no basis upon which he could claim he did not have 'knowledge' as to the obscenity of those videos.

3.5.1.1 Comparing knowledge with other forms of *mens rea*

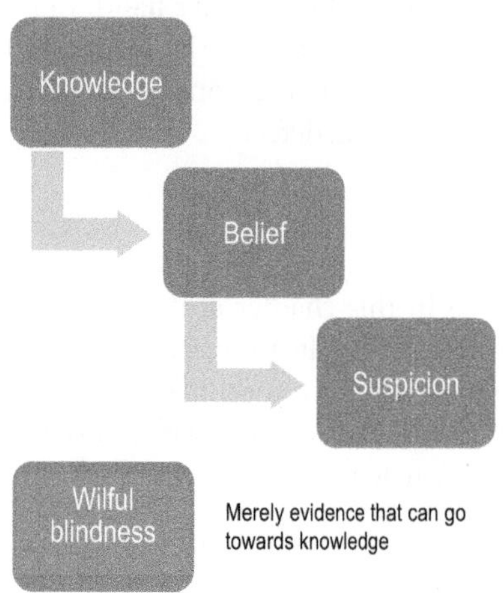

Figure 3.6 Distinguishing 'knowledge'

Knowledge as a concept in criminal liability is capable of being viewed or characterised in a certain number of lights. Often people speak of an individual's suspicion or belief when they speak of 'knowledge'; however, it is essential that a distinction is appropriately made. A clear hierarchy exists between knowledge and certain other forms of *mens rea* and this is detailed in **Figure 3.6.** Knowledge clearly being the stricter form of *mens rea.*

Knowledge vs wilful blindness

There is authority for the proposition that a defendant who is 'wilfully blind', ie he deliberately turns a blind eye and refrains from making inquiries or asking questions, has the requisite knowledge (*Warner v MPC* [1969] 2 AC 256, per Lord Reid). Williams described such wilful blindness in terms of suspicion 'plus' a deliberate omission to inquire (*Criminal Law: The General Part*, 1st edn (Stevens & Sons, 1953)).

However, the more authoritative approach is that wilful blindness is merely evidence that may be used to find knowledge and does not equate to knowledge itself. This was the view of Lord Bridge (in *obiter*) in *Westminster City Council v Croyalgrange Ltd* [1986] 1 WLR 674. His Lordship stated:

> it is always open to the tribunal of fact, when knowledge on the part of a defendant is required to be proved, to base a finding of knowledge on evidence that the defendant had deliberately shut his eyes to the obvious or refrained from inquiry because he suspected the truth but did not want to have his suspicion confirmed.

The distinction was furthered by Devlin J in *Taylor's Central Garages (Exeter) Ltd v Roper* [1951] 2 TLR 284 where his Lordship emphasised that there is

> a vast distinction between [1] a state of mind which consists of deliberately refraining from making inquiries, the result of which a person does not care to have, and [2] a state of mind which is merely neglecting to make such inquiries as a reasonable and prudent person would make.

The former amounts to wilful blindness and in many cases can be strong evidence of the defendant's knowledge – but is no more than that. The latter can be characterised as 'constructive knowledge' – essentially asking what the defendant should have known had he made reasonable inquiry. For a fuller account, see Wasik and Thompson, 'Turning a Blind Eye as Constituting Mens Rea' (1981) 32 NILQ 324.

Knowledge vs belief

Belief is somewhat different to 'knowledge' in that beliefs can often turn out to be mistaken or false, whereas knowledge imports some form of correctness in an individual's belief. This approach was confirmed by Boreham J in *R v Hall* (1985) 81 Cr App R 260:

> Belief, of course, is something short of knowledge. It may be said to be the state of mind of a person who says to himself: 'I cannot say I know for certain that these goods are stolen, but there can be no other reasonable conclusion in the light of all the circumstances, in the light of all that I have heard and seen.'

Examples of the use of 'belief' in the criminal law include:

- handling stolen goods (Theft Act 1968, s 22); and
- perjury (Perjury Act 1911, s 1(1)).

Knowledge vs suspicion

In *R v Da Silva* [2006] EWCA Crim 1654, the Court of Appeal took the opportunity to explain the term 'suspicion' (per Longmore LJ):

> [T]he essential element in the word 'suspect' and its affiliates, in this context, is that the Defendant must think that there is a possibility, which is more than fanciful, that the relevant facts exist. A vague feeling of unease would not suffice. But the statute does not require the suspicion to be 'clear' or 'firmly grounded and targeted on specific facts', or based upon 'reasonable grounds'.

In this respect, 'suspicion' imposes a subjective test, asking whether the defendant suspected, on a real possibility, that the relevant facts or circumstances existed. There is no requirement for the suspicion to be based on reasonable grounds, and the Court preferred to avoid such terms as 'fleeting thought' and 'inkling' on account that they were liable to mislead. The Court relied on the earlier authority of *Hussien v Chong Fook Kam* [1970] AC 942, where Lord Devlin in the Privy Council stated:

> Suspicion in its ordinary meaning is a state of conjecture or surmise where proof is lacking: 'I suspect but I cannot prove.' Suspicion arises at or near the starting point of an investigation of which the obtaining of prima facie proof is the end.

Examples of the use of 'suspicion' in the criminal law include:

- money laundering (Proceeds of Crime Act 2002);
- assisting another to retain the benefit of criminal conduct, knowing or suspecting that the other person was or had been engaged in criminal conduct (Criminal Justice Act 1988, s 93A).

The term 'suspicion' itself is to be distinguished from a similar, albeit slightly different, phrase of 'reasonable grounds to suspect'. The latter term has been adopted more recently in relation to money laundering offences under the Proceeds of Crime Act 2002 and offences under the Terrorism Acts. Unlike a 'mere' suspicion, the phrase 'reasonable grounds to suspect' involves a combined subjective and objective test asking whether the defendant actually suspected (subjective) and, if so, whether there were reasonable grounds for such suspicion (objective) (*R v Saik* [2007] 1 AC 18, per Lord Hope). This rule is not, however, universal, with the Supreme Court in *R v Lane and Letts (AB and CD)* [2018] UKSC 36 distinguishing *Saik* and ruling that for offences under the Terrorism Acts, the test of reasonable grounds to suspect is an objective one. Lord Hughes concluded that 'it is plain beyond argument that the expression "has reasonable grounds for suspicion" cannot mean "actually suspects"'. This approach affirmed the previous decision of the Court of Appeal in *R v AB* [2017] EWCA Crim 129. For a full discussion of this development and the case of *Lane and Letts*, see Thomas, '"Reasonable Cause to Suspect": In the Absence of Knowledge and Actual Suspicion' (2018) 82(6) J Crim L 423.

3.5.2 Maliciously

Most often found in relation to non-fatal offences against the person, 'maliciously' is an interesting feature of criminal liability. Maliciousness/malice is not to be understood as a form of 'wickedness' or 'ill-will'; rather, it is simply to be understood as requiring intention to be present, meaning both direct and oblique intent, or subjective recklessness (*R v Cunningham* [1957] 2 QB 396; *R v Savage; DPP v Parmenter* [1991] 3 WLR 914).

Examples of the use of 'maliciously' in the criminal law include:

- causing grievous bodily harm (GBH) with intent (OAPA 1861, s 18);
- inflicting GBH (OAPA 1861, s 20);
- administering poison (OAPA 1861, ss 23 and 24).

See further **Chapter 9**.

3.5.3 Wilfully

'Wilfully' may suggest that the defendant's actions must be voluntary or free-willed. Indeed, this is correct; however, it represents only a limited definition of the word. Rather, it is better to understand 'wilfully' as meaning intention or recklessness. Pill LJ, in the Court of Appeal in *AG's Reference (No 3 of 2003)* [2005] QB 73, defined the term as 'deliberately doing something which is wrong knowing it to be wrong or with reckless indifference as to whether it is wrong or not'. This was the approach taken by the Court of Appeal in *R v JD* [2008] EWCA Crim 2360, which also confirmed that trial judges should give appropriate directions as to the meaning of this term. See also the leading case of *R v Sheppard* [1981] AC 394, concerning an offence of wilful neglect of a child under s 1 of the Children and Young Persons Act 1933. In *Sheppard*, Lord Diplock stated that the proper direction to be given to a jury on such a charge is that the jury must be satisfied:

(1) that the child did in fact need medical aid at the time at which the parent is charged with failing to provide it (the *actus reus*); and
(2) either that the parent was aware at that time that the child's health might be at risk if it were not provided with medical aid, or that the parent's unawareness of this fact was due to his not caring whether his child's health were at risk or not (the *mens rea*).

Using *Sheppard*, therefore, wilfully can be understood in this respect as meaning either an awareness of a risk (akin to recklessness) or a lack of care (akin, in some respects, to intention). On a more basic level, Lord Keith in *Sheppard* explained that wilful means 'deliberate'. *Sheppard* was applied in *R v Gittins* [1982] RTR 363, and the Court of Appeal took the opportunity in *AG's Reference (No 3 of 2003)* [2005] QB 73 to explain that there is no 'material difference' between *Sheppard* and the subjectively reckless test in *R v G* (above). In *R v Turbill* [2013] EWCA Crim 1422, the Court of Appeal identified that such terms as 'carelessness' or 'negligence' when directing on wilful neglect would be inappropriate. According to Hallett LJ: 'They are not the same. ...The neglect must be "wilful" and that means something more is required than a duty and what a reasonable person would regard as a reckless breach of that duty.'

Examples of the use of 'wilfully' in the criminal law include:

- neglect of a child (Children and Young Persons Act 1933, s 1);
- misconduct in public office (common law offence);
- obstruction of a railway (Malicious Damage Act 1861, s 36).

3.5.4 Dishonestly

Most of the offences created by the Theft Acts 1968 and 1978 and the Fraud Act 2006 involve dishonesty as a specific ingredient of the *mens rea*. The test for dishonesty is applied in a uniform fashion for all such offences.

The relevant test originally came from *R v Ghosh* [1982] QB 1053 – see **Chapter 11**. In essence, the case set out a two-part test incorporating an objective and subjective test:

(a) Was the defendant's conduct dishonest according to the ordinary standards of reasonable and honest people? (objective test) If so:
(b) Did the defendant realise what he did was dishonest according to those standards (subjective test).

The Supreme Court shook the legal world in the ground-breaking case of *Ivey v Genting Casinos (UK) Ltd* [2017] UKSC 67. Here, the Supreme Court ruled that the second limb of the *Ghosh* test should be abandoned, preferring the objective test adopted by the civil law in such cases as *Royal Brunei Airlines v Tan* [1995] 2 AC 378, *Twinsectra v Yardley* [2002] 2 AC 164, *Barlow Clowes International Ltd v Eurotrust International Ltd* [2005] UKPC 37, *Abou-Rahmah v Abacha* [2006] EWCA Civ 1492 and *Starglade Properties Ltd v Nash* [2010] EWCA Civ 1314.

The effect of *Ivey* is discussed in much greater detail in **Chapter 11**.

3.6 Strict liability

Strict liability, as a term, is used to describe an offence where the *actus reus* of a criminal offence is not accompanied by a *mens rea*. This is to be contrasted with offences of 'absolute' liability, which refers to offences where there is no *mens rea* element at all and no requirement for voluntariness. You should recall that absolute liability was discussed in **Chapter 2** under the heading 'state of affairs cases'.

As emphasised in **Chapter 1**, the criminal law works on the fundamental principle of '*actus non facit reum nisi mens sit rea*'. For crimes of strict liability, however, the prosecution need not prove any form of *mens rea*, or at least not all *mentes reae*, to have the defendant found liable for an offence. This means that (dependent on the offence in question) the prosecution need not even consider whether the defendant acted:

- intentionally;
- recklessly; or
- negligently.

Although these mental elements would certainly assist the prosecution in its case, they are entirely unnecessary for the purposes of strict liability offences. Further to this, the moral blameworthiness (or lack thereof) of the defendant's conduct is also irrelevant.

For an in-depth discussion of strict liability, see Simester (ed), *Appraising Strict Liability* (OUP, 2005).

3.6.1 Need for voluntariness

If you recall from our brief discussion in **Chapter 2**, although strict liability offences include no required *mens rea* on the part of the defendant, his actions must still be voluntary, in the sense that they are willed (compared with absolute liability). Let us give an example. Section 89(1) of the Road Traffic Regulation Act 1984 provides:

> A person who drives a motor vehicle on a road at a speed exceeding a limit imposed by or under any enactment to which this section applies shall be guilty of an offence.

This is a strict liability offence in that it need not be proven that the defendant intended, or was reckless to the thought of, speeding. Rather, all that needs to be proven is that the defendant was driving the relevant car at the prescribed time and did so in excess of the speed limit. No *mens rea* is required on the part of the defendant; however, his actions must, nevertheless, still be voluntary in that he wilfully breached the speed limit. Should the defendant have suffered a heart attack behind the wheel, leading to his foot involuntarily pressing down on the accelerator, he would not be liable for an offence. Likewise, suppose the defendant was attacked by a swarm of bees whilst in his car. Involuntarily he places his foot on the accelerator; he is not liable for an offence. However, both of these circumstances would require evidence that the defendant acted involuntarily.

3.6.2 Common law strict liability offences

Strict liability at common law is rare, increasingly so in recent years. The only common law offences that remain ones of strict liability are as follows:

- public nuisance (*R v Stephens* (1866) LR 1 QB 702);
- outraging public decency; and
- criminal libel.

Blasphemous libel, which was concerned with the publication of material likely to outrage and insult the Christian religion, was also an offence of strict liability. This offence, however, was abolished by s 79 of the Criminal Justice and Immigration Act 2008. The above common law offences are rare given that the criminal conduct is covered by other offences, set out in statute. For example, the Contempt of Court Act 1981 (ss 1–7) now covers material which would have been charged as some form of criminal libel.

3.6.3 Statutory strict liability offences

Unlike the common law, there remain hundreds of statutory strict liability offences. The majority of statutory offences detail a necessary *mens rea* requirement. Take for example:

- *Theft:* The Theft Act 1968 requires the defendant to act 'dishonestly' and with the 'intention' to permanently deprive.
- *Rape:* The Sexual Offences Act 2003 requires the defendant to 'intend' to penetrate the complainant and he must lack 'reasonable belief' in consent.

Both of these offences involve an express statement as to *mens rea*; therefore, they cannot be offences of strict liability. This does not mean, however, that an offence which does not state the *mens rea* is automatically a strict liability offence. Rather, it is up to the courts, through judicial reasoning and interpretation, to decide whether the crime is one of strict liability or not. The leading authority in guiding judges in their task of 'finding' strict liability offences is that of *Gammon (Hong Kong) Ltd v Attorney-General of Hong Kong* [1985] AC 1.

case example

Charge:
Deviating in a material way from approved plans (Hong Kong Ordinance, s 40(2A)(b))

Case progression:
Court of Appeal of Hong Kong – Guilty

Privy Council – Convictions upheld

Point of law:
Finding strict liability offences

In *Gammon (Hong Kong) Ltd v Attorney-General of Hong Kong* [1985] AC 1, the defendants were involved in the construction of a building in Hong Kong. The building collapsed and the defendants were charged, contrary to Hong Kong Ordinance, with having deviated in a material way from the plans which had been submitted and approved.

The defendants appealed on the basis that *mens rea* was required in order for them to be convicted. The Privy Council agreed that *mens rea* is presumed in all cases, but concluded that, in this case, public safety could displace the requirement.

In dismissing the appeals of the defendants, the Privy Council laid out the following test to be used by judges in order to determine whether a crime imposes strict liability. The test is structured in **Figure 3.7**.

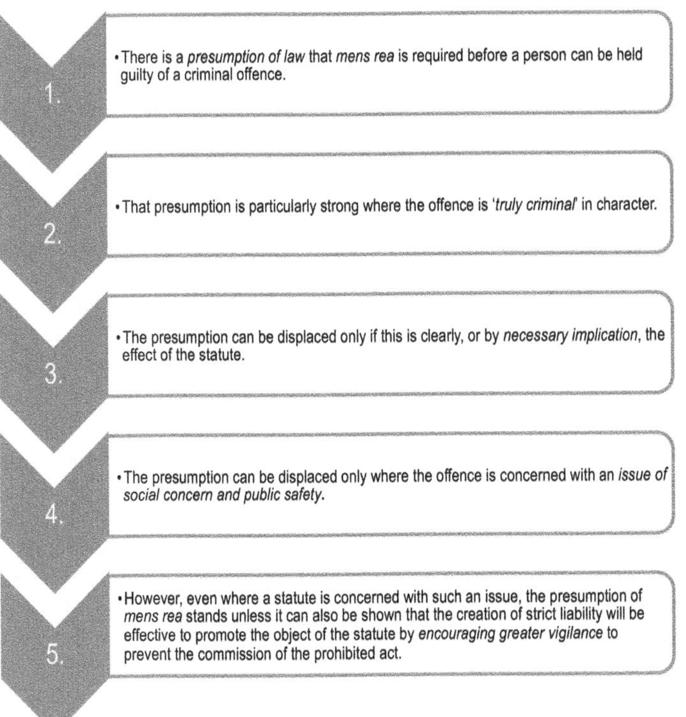

1.
• There is a *presumption of law* that *mens rea* is required before a person can be held guilty of a criminal offence.
2.
• That presumption is particularly strong where the offence is '*truly criminal*' in character.
3.
• The presumption can be displaced only if this is clearly, or by *necessary implication*, the effect of the statute.
4.
• The presumption can be displaced only where the offence is concerned with an *issue of social concern and public safety*.
5.
• However, even where a statute is concerned with such an issue, the presumption of *mens rea* stands unless it can also be shown that the creation of strict liability will be effective to promote the object of the statute by *encouraging greater vigilance* to prevent the commission of the prohibited act.

Figure 3.7 Finding strict liability offences

We shall consider each of these five steps in turn. Before we do so, it is important to emphasise that this activity is relevant only to statutory offences where the Act is silent on *mens rea*. Where the Act includes some *mens rea* term, such as intention, knowledge, recklessness etc then this exercise should not take place.

3.6.3.1 Presumption of *mens rea*

Given that strict liability involves an offence whereby the defendant is liable regardless of his intentions or motives, there remain some heavy presumptions at work in this area of law. The first, and most significant, is the presumption in favour of *mens rea*. All this simply means is that where a statutory provision is silent as to *mens rea*, it will be presumed that some form of *mens rea* is required before the defendant may be liable for an offence. A useful starting point here is the ruling of the House of Lords in *B (a minor) v DPP* [2000] 2 AC 428, where Lord Hutton provided:

> the test is not whether it is a reasonable implication that the statute rules out mens rea as a constituent part of the crime—the test is whether it is a *necessary* implication. (original emphasis)

Lord Nicholls, in the same case, explained that:

> In these circumstances the starting-point for a court is the established common law presumption that a mental element, traditionally labelled mens rea, is an essential ingredient unless Parliament has indicated a contrary intention either expressly or by necessary implication. The common law presumes that, unless Parliament has indicated otherwise, the appropriate mental element is an unexpressed ingredient of every statutory offence.

Perhaps one of the best known authorities on this point is that of *Sweet v Parsley* [1970] AC 132.

case example

Charge:
Managing premises where cannabis was used (Dangerous Drugs Act 1965, s 5(b))

Case progression:
Magistrates' court – Guilty

Divisional Court – Conviction upheld

House of Lords – Conviction quashed

Point of law:
Presumption of *mens rea*

In *Sweet v Parsley* [1970] AC 132, the defendant, a teacher, sublet a house to a number of students who, without her knowledge, were smoking cannabis. The defendant was charged with and convicted of being concerned in the management of certain premises which were used for the purpose of smoking cannabis.

The magistrates' court found this to be a crime of strict liability. The defendant appealed all the way up to the House of Lords, which allowed her appeal on the basis that the courts must apply the presumption of *mens rea*.

In the House of Lords, Lord Reid was clear:

> Our first duty is to consider the words of the Act: if they show a clear intention to create an absolute offence that is an end of the matter. But such cases are very rare. Sometimes the words of the section which creates a particular offence make it clear that mens rea is required in one form or another. Such cases are quite frequent. But in a very large number of cases there is no clear indication either way. In such cases there has for centuries been a presumption that *Parliament did not intend to make criminals of persons who were in no way blameworthy in what they did.* That means that whenever a section is silent as to mens rea there is a presumption that, in order to give effect to the will of Parliament, we must read in words appropriate to require mens rea. ... it is firmly established by a host of authorities that mens rea is an essential ingredient of every offence unless some reason can be found for holding that that is not necessary. (emphasis added)

As a result of *Sweet v Parsley*, a judge, when faced with the question of strict liability and whether it exists in a specific statutory offence, is to presume that *mens rea* is required for the offence. To do so is in order to give effect to the apparent will of Parliament. See *Pwr v DPP* [2020] EWHC 798 (Admin) for a review of the authorities and a recent example of the factors relevant to a determination of strict liability.

3.6.3.2 Truly criminal offences

The presumption in favour of *mens rea* is particularly strong where the offence in question may be categorised as 'truly criminal'. It may seem odd for the courts to classify certain crimes as 'truly criminal' and others as not – especially given that a defendant on the receiving end of a custodial sentence, or the victim on the receiving end of the crime itself, would characterise even the less serious of crimes as being 'truly criminal'. However, the phrase is simply a matter of classification by the courts, distinguishing those offences that are particularly serious in nature or with serious consequences as 'truly criminal', and the rest as not (see *B (a minor) v DPP* [2000] 2 AC 428 and *Harrow LBC v Shah* [1999] 3 All ER 302). **Figure 3.8** provides an explanation for the meaning of 'truly criminal'.

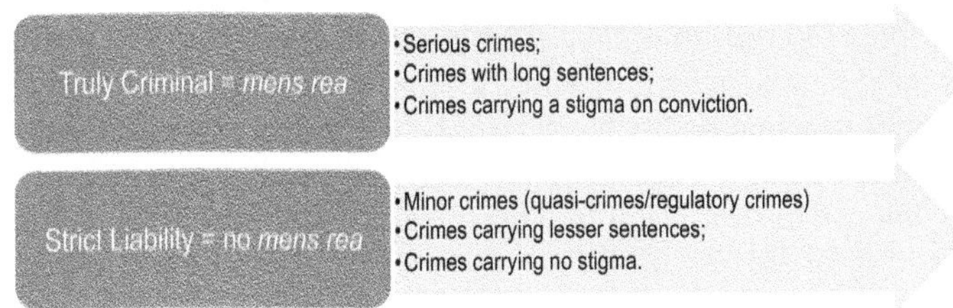

Figure 3.8 'Truly criminal' offences

On this basis, where the offence can be said not to be one of a 'truly criminal' nature, the presumption of *mens rea* may be displaced. A few examples of offences which are usually regarded as not being 'truly criminal' include:

- environmental offences;
- offences involving public health or trade descriptions; and
- driving offences.

Given the difficult task of ascertaining whether an offence is 'truly criminal' or not, some courts have tended to prefer the approach of considering the seriousness of the offence charged. In *R v Muhamad* [2003] QB 1031, the Court of Appeal signalled a slight change in the approach taken (per Dyson LJ):

> The question, whether the presumption of law that mens rea is required applies, and, if so, whether it has been displaced, can be approached in two ways. One approach is to ask whether the act is truly criminal, on the basis that, if it is not, then the presumption does not apply at all. The other approach is to recognise that any offence in respect of which a person may be punished in a criminal court is prima facie sufficiently 'criminal' for the presumption to apply. But the more serious the offence, the greater the weight to be attached to the presumption, and conversely, the less serious the offence, the less weight to be attached. It is now clear that it is this latter approach which, according to our domestic law, must be applied.

> The starting point, therefore, is to determine how serious an offence is created … and accordingly how much weight, if any, should be attached to the presumption.

3.6.3.3 Necessary implication

The presumption may only be displaced where this is *clearly* or *by necessary implication* the effect of the statute. When considering the effect, or intention, of the statute, a number of factors will bear relevance to the court's decision. We shall consider these factors now.

Words used

The use, or absence thereof, of particular words may assist the court in determining whether an offence is one of strict liability. As a starting point, should the word 'intentionally' appear in the statute, this would indicate that the offence is not one of strict liability. That is obvious. However, the difficulties arise with use of other *mens rea* terms such as knowledge, wilfully, causing, possessing etc. We shall consider two examples, namely 'causing' and 'possessing'.

For some time, 'causing' has been considered a phrase denoting strict liability. This was the outcome of the House of Lords in *Alphacell v Woodward* [1972] AC 824, which concerned the causing of polluted matter to enter a river. Likewise, the causation element of assault occasioning actual bodily harm (ABH) has been considered one of strict liability. However, it is wrong to suggest that all cases of 'causing' an end result will be considered as giving rise to strict liability. This is evident from the judgment of the Supreme Court in *R v Taylor* [2016] UKSC 5.

'Possession' is also considered an element of an offence which gives rise to strict liability. The majority of possession offences are in relation to drug and firearms offences. In *Warner v MPC* [1969] 2 AC 256, Lord Pearce concluded that the prosecution did not have to prove that the defendant knew that he was in possession of a controlled drug. The prosecution simply had to prove that the defendant knew that he was in possession of something (in this case a box with something inside it). The same applies to firearms offences, as confirmed in *R v Deyemi* [2008] 1 Cr App R 345, and possession of indecent images (see *R v Okoro (No 3)* [2018] EWCA Crim 1929) – ie the defendant need not know that the article is an offensive weapon or indecent image, but he must know that he has possession of it. In *Jenkins v DPP* [2020] EWHC 1307 (Admin), the Divisional Court found that there is no need for a conscious decision to control on the part of the defendant; having a degree of control is sufficient for possession offences.

In *R v Lane and Letts (AB and CD)* [2018] UKSC 36, the Supreme Court ruled that the words 'has reasonable grounds to suspect' found in s 17(b) of the Terrorism Act 2000 did not create an offence of strict liability. In particular, the appellants contended that because a defendant is capable of committing the offence without knowledge or actual suspicion (because he only requires a reasonable cause for suspicion to be liable), the offence was one of strict liability. Lord Hughes, who gave the judgment of the Court, concluded that:

> It is certainly true that because objectively-assessed reasonable cause for suspicion is sufficient, an accused can commit this offence without knowledge or actual suspicion that the money might be used for terrorist purposes. But the accused's state of mind is not, as it is in offences which are truly of strict liability, irrelevant. The requirement that there exist objectively assessed cause for suspicion focuses

> attention on what information the accused had. ... that requirement is satisfied when, on the information available to the accused, a reasonable person *would* (not might or could) suspect that the money might be used for terrorism. The state of mind of such a person is, whilst clearly less culpable than that of a person who knows that the money may be used for that purpose, not accurately described as in no way blameworthy. (original emphasis)

In that regard, the words used in the 2000 Act were not of the sort creating a strict liability offence. For a discussion of the meaning of possession, see Thomas and Pegg, '"Possession" in the Digital Age: The Same Old Story Applied in the Modern Day' (2019) 83(3) J Crim L 175.

In *R v Matudi* [2003] EWCA Crim 697, the Court of Appeal noted that an additional factor relevant to this determination is whether other sections of the statute include express *mens rea* requirements. For example, if the relevant statutory offence is mute on a *mens rea* requirement, whilst another section speaks of 'intention' or 'knowledge' etc, it is likely that the court will infer that the offence in question is of strict liability.

Penalty

Although not conclusive, the presence of a purely monetary penalty is likely to mean that the offence is one of strict liability (*R v Customs and Excise Commissioners, ex parte Claus* (1987) 86 Cr App R 189). This is so even though the penalty may be extremely high in monetary value. Likewise, where the offence is punishable with imprisonment, the offence is less likely to be one of strict liability. However, again, this is not conclusive – see *Pharmaceutical Society of Great Britain v Storkwain Ltd* [1986] 2 All ER 635.

Defences

Where a defence of 'due diligence' appears in the statute, the offence is likely to be one of strict liability (*Wings Ltd v Ellis* [1985] AC 272). In this case, the defendant must prove that he has taken reasonable care and has acted with due diligence in avoiding the commission of an offence. Such a defence is present in s 24(1) of the Trade Descriptions Act 1968. However, this is not conclusive and the absence of such defence does not mean that the offence is not one of strict liability (*Alphacell v Woodward* [1972] AC 824).

3.6.3.4 Social concern or public safety

The presumption of *mens rea* may only be displaced where the offence concerns an issue of social concern or a matter of public safety. For example, where a criminal offence involves the protection of public safety through offences relating to:

- food safety and preparation (*Smedleys v Breed* [1974] AC 839);
- protection of the environment (*Alphacell v Woodward* [1972] AC 824);
- road safety (*Reynolds v GH Austin & Sons Ltd* [1951] 2 KB 135); or
- access to emergency services,

the offence is likely to be one of strict liability.

An additional example can be seen in the context of under-age gambling. In *Harrow LBC v Shah* [1999] 3 All ER 302, the defendant sold a lottery ticket to a person under the age of 16. The Divisional Court, in upholding the defendant's conviction, ruled that such an offence was one of strict liability in that it was a matter of social concern to avoid under-age gambling.

3.6.3.5 Encouraging vigilance and compliance

Even where a statute is concerned with such an issue, the presumption of *mens rea* stands unless it can also be shown that the creation of strict liability will be effective to promote the object of the statute by encouraging greater vigilance to prevent the commission of the prohibited act. Lord Salmon in *Alphacell v Woodward* [1972] AC 824 reasoned:

> If this appeal succeeded and it were held to be the law that no conviction be obtained under the Act of 1951 unless the prosecution could discharge the often impossible onus of proving that the pollution was caused intentionally or negligently, a great deal of pollution would go unpunished and undeterred to the relief of many riparian factory owners. As a result many rivers which are now filthy would become filthier still and many rivers which are now clean would lose their cleanliness. The legislature no doubt recognised that as a matter of public policy this would be most unfortunate. Hence section 2(1)(a) which encourages riparian factory owners not only to take reasonable steps to prevent pollution but to do everything possible to ensure that they do not cause it.

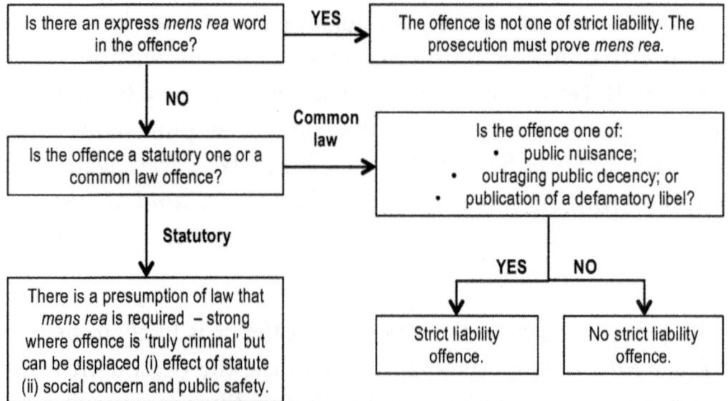

Figure 3.9 Putting together strict liability

3.6.4 Strict liability and human rights

Article 6(2) of the European Convention on Human Rights provides:

> Everyone charged with a criminal offence shall be presumed innocent until proved guilty according to law.

The presumption of innocence is in direct contrast with crimes of strict liability given that a defendant is presumed guilty upon the prosecution proving the necessary *actus reus* of the offence. This is so regardless of whether the defendant's state of mind is blameless, as such state of mind is both irrelevant and inadmissible (*R v Sandhu* [1997] Crim LR 288).

As a result of this stark contrast between the operation of strict liability crimes and the presumption of innocence, a number of cases have gone before the European Court of Human Rights (ECtHR) questioning the validity of the law in question.

In *Hansen v Denmark* (1995) 19 EHRR CD89, the ECtHR suggested that strict liability offences may breach Article 6(2) given the presumption of liability upon proof of the *actus reus*. This, however, was later questioned by the ECtHR in *Salabiaku v France* (1988) 13 EHRR 379 which ruled that the presumption of liability can operate within a legal system provided the presumption remains within reasonable limits.

Further to this, the presumption must account for the importance of what is at stake and the respect for the rights of the defendant. The Court concluded that

> the Contracting States may, under certain conditions, penalise a simple or objective fact as such, irrespective of whether it results from criminal intent or from negligence.

3.6.5 Justifying strict liability

Given that strict liability involves the criminalising of conduct despite a lack of guilty mind on the part of an individual, the arguments for and against imposing strict liability must be considered As a starting point, it is worth returning to our fundamental concept of criminal liability from **Chapter 1** – *actus non facit reum nisi mens sit rea.* Strict liability, as a principle, offends this fundamental concept.

3.6.5.1 Arguments *for* strict liability

Protection of the public

The most prominent factor justifying the imposition of strict liability is the protection of the public. In *R v Lemon* [1979] AC 617, Lord Diplock explained that the 'usual justification' for strict liability offences is the protection to 'public health, public safety, public morals or public order'. In addition, Wootton (*Crime and the Criminal Law,* 2nd edn (Stevenson & Sons 1981)) is a major proponent for the imposition of strict liability offences on the basis that the criminal law is designed to prevent harmful acts, to promote care and to protect the public. Wootton advocates:

> If the law says that certain things are not to be done, it is illogical to confine this prohibition to occasions on which they are done from malice aforethought; for at least the material consequences of an action, and the reasons for prohibiting it are the same whether it is the result of sinister malicious plotting, of negligence or of sheer accident.

Wootton goes so far as to argue that strict liability ought to become the norm or 'default' approach taken by the law in relation to *mens rea.* She justifies her approach on the basis that where such criminal harm has surfaced as a result of stupidity or accident (or where there is no fault at all), the criminal law can consider this at the sentencing stage of proceedings, but no earlier. One can further Wootton's argument here and advocate that many strict liability offences involve no deprivation of liberty given that the defendants in question are corporations (see **Chapter 6**). Further, many of the corporations in question are liable for such offences as a result of their failure to observe regulatory practices that might cost them a significant amount of money. The issuing of fines would strip a corporation of any profit made in these circumstances and would ultimately deter them from future conduct. However, Hall ('Negligent Behaviour Should be Excluded from Penal Liability' 63 CLR 632) argues that such fines are often small in amount and do not have the effect of deterring a corporation from continuing their bad practices. Rather, Hall argues that corporations treat such fines as a 'nominal tax on illegal enterprise' and furthers his argument on the basis that such companies would rather pay the fines then change their bad practices.

Deterrent value and encouraging compliance

A secondary function that strict liability achieves is to act as a clear deterrent from future crimes. For instance, Pound (*The Spirit of the Common Law* (Transaction Publishers 1962)) argues that

> statutes are not meant to punish the vicious but to put pressure upon the thoughtless and inefficient to do their whole duty in the interest of public health or safety or morals.

Indeed, such pressure may be placed by the numerous regulatory bodies responsible for ensuring these crimes are avoided, for example the Health and Safety Executive (HSE). Taylor (*Elliott and Quinn's Criminal Law*, 12th edn (Pearson, 2018)) argues that the use of such special governmental bodies to enforce regulatory breaches acts as a significant deterrent to companies and bodies regarding future conduct. Taylor refers to an apparent 'bargaining power' that the governmental bodies have over the relevant companies, and such bargaining power is used to encourage compliance. McAlhone and Wortley (*Criminal Law – The Fundamentals*, 4th edn (Sweet & Maxwell, 2016)), however, argue that there is

> no evidence to suggest that strict liability improves standards of public health and safety. [It] may even have the opposite effect to that intended in that, if liability is strict, there is no incentive to take any precautions at all.

Ease of proof and cutting court time

A further advantage to the imposition of strict liability offences is the apparent ease of proving an offence. Unlike offences that are 'truly criminal' such as murder and rape where it may be exceedingly difficult to prove the relevant *mens rea*, in strict liability offences no such difficulty arises. Indeed, the Privy Council in *Gammon (Hong Kong) Ltd v Attorney-General of Hong Kong* [1985] AC 1 suggested that the criminal justice system would reach a 'standstill' if all offences required proof of *mens rea*. Suppose, for example, Jack is charged with speeding. It would extremely hard for a prosecutor to prove that Jack knew he was speeding or that he intended to speed. On that basis, it is fair to attach strict liability.

3.6.5.2 Arguments *against* strict liability

Injustice

As emphasised above, strict liability is harsh and results in what many may perceive as an injustice to the individual concerned. Specifically, strict liability offences do not account for any reasonable errors or those errors made in good faith and without negligence. Take for example *Callow v Tillstone* (1900) 64 JP 823. In that case, the defendant unknowingly sold bad meat – indeed, he believed the meat to be 'good' meat. Frankly, there is nothing more the defendant could have done in order to comply with the law – however, strict liability remained imposed.

Human rights

Although (as discussed above) conviction of a strict liability offence does not necessarily breach the presumption of innocence, the courts may find that a challenge under Article 7, requiring certainty in the criminal law, may be well founded (*R v Muhamad* [2003] QB 1031).

Ineffectiveness

A major argument in favour of strict liability offences, as discussed above, is that they act as a deterrent. However, there are many arguments that demonstrate that strict liability crimes are ineffective. For example:

- The chance or fear of being caught is often the strongest deterrent; however, where an individual or body thinks it is unlikely that they will be caught, clearly they will not be deterred from their actions – such as a motorist who does not believe that they will be caught speeding (see Jackson, '*Storkwain*: A Case Study in Strict Liability and Self-regulation' (1991) Crim LR 892).
- Ensuring compliance is also a top priority for strict liability offences; however, concern is raised that the imposition of strict liability will have the opposite effect instead. Knowing that conviction is probable, even where no further precautions or actions can be taken, may reduce the incentive to comply.

3.7 Correspondence of *actus reus* and *mens rea*

Although *actus reus* and *mens rea* have been dealt with in two separate chapters, it is essential to remember that, in general, liability may only be found where the defendant commits the *actus reus* and possesses the *mens rea* for that offence. As we know from our discussion above, there are certain offences (strict liability) where there is no necessity for *mens rea* to accompany the *actus reus*.

The necessity for both the *actus reus* and *mens rea* to be present in a given case is non-contentious. This section is concerned with the 'correspondence' principle, which is used to describe the situation where the *actus reus* of an offence is linked, or coupled, with a corresponding *mens rea* element. This coupling of elements has often been labelled as the 'interaction between the *actus reus* and *mens rea*' or as 'constructive liability' by Macdonald (*Text, Cases and Materials on Criminal Law*, 2nd edn (Pearson, 2018). For example, the offence of murder requires the unlawful killing of a human being under the Queen's peace; this forms the *actus reus* of the offence. This element is coupled with the intention to kill or cause grievous bodily harm (GBH), which forms the *mens rea* of the offence. However, certain offences do not include a corresponding *mens rea*, one of the best examples being the offence of assault occasioning actual bodily harm (ABH) contrary to s 47 of the OAPA 1861 (dealt with in **Chapter 9**). Where such correspondence does not exist, any form of *mens rea* is considered to be one of 'ulterior intent' (considered at **3.2.1.4**).

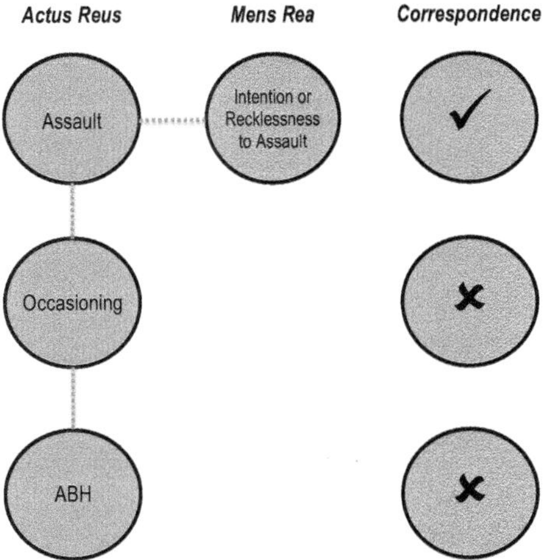

Figure 3.10 ABH and the correspondence principle

ABH is phrased as such given that it is simply as aggravated form of common assault. We shall discuss this further in **Chapter 9**.

3.8 Coincidence of *actus reus* and *mens rea*

Also known as the 'contemporaneity' principle, the fundamental requirement for liability in criminal law is that the *actus reus* coincides at a point in time with the *mens rea*. At a basic level, this simply means that the defendant must possess the *mens rea* for a criminal offence at the time of performing the act or omission in question. Further, the *mens rea* must relate to that particular *actus reus* for liability to be found.

example

Jack and Jill are husband and wife. Jill is having an extra-marital affair with Jack's best friend, Andy. Jack, upon learning of this, wishes to kill Andy. He arranges for the pair of them to go for a drive out of the city and into the countryside. Jack intends to kill Andy in the forest and bury his body there. As they are travelling out of the city, Jack and Andy are involved in a car accident that kills Andy.

In this scenario, Jack had every intention to kill Andy and he may even have been considering killing him at the time of the accident. However, his *mens rea* (his intention/desire to kill) does not coincide with his *actus reus* as no act or omission has been performed by Jack against Andy. Prima facie, the car crash was an accident. Therefore Jack is not liable for the offence of murder. This is so despite Jack's potential happiness that may ensue as a result of Andy's death; however, given that no coincidence existed, there is no unlawful killing.

If, however, Jack intended to kill Andy by crashing the car, and this car crash was no accident, Jack may be liable for murder. The difficulty would arise in proving his liability.

This rule is justified on the basis that a defendant ought not to be liable for guilty thoughts alone that failed to transpire until a later date. The rule of contemporaneity may be explained by the use of a sliding scale built on a timeline. The solid line represents the act and intention on the part of the defendant.

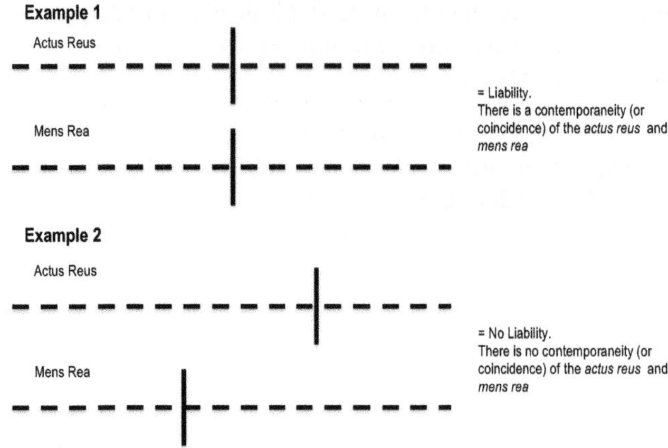

Figure 3.11 Understanding the coincidence of actus reus *and* mens rea

The need for coincidence has caused numerous problems in cases where there has been a delay between the *actus reus* and *mens rea* (ie there is no coincidence). The courts have been faced with a predicament: do they abandon the principle of contemporaneity or develop it? The courts have chosen the latter and have ruled that contemporaneity may be interpreted and construed to include:

- cases involving a continuing act; and
- cases involving a chain of events.

It is important to stress that these two circumstances are not exceptions to the contemporaneity rule. The rule is absolute and subject to no qualifications. Rather, the courts, in order to stop a defendant from 'getting away with it', have created these two concepts that will allow them to find contemporaneity in less straightforward cases. Monaghan (*Criminal Law Directions*, 6th edn (OUP, 2020)) appears to be critical of these two circumstances, providing that through use of these circumstances, the 'courts have circumvented the principle of coincidence'. With respect, it ought not be said that the courts have 'circumvented' or gone behind the doctrine of coincidence. Instead, it should merely be understood that the courts have 'found' ways to attach liability where it is right to do so, ie where there is a continuing act or where there is a chain of events.

We shall consider each in turn.

3.8.1 Continuing act

This circumstance occurs where the defendant's voluntary action that forms the *actus reus* remains 'in action' during a course of events, as opposed to being a single and instantaneous action. We refer to this as a continuing act and, for liability to follow, the *mens rea* must be formed at some point during the duration of the act.

An example of a continuing act that you will discover later in the text is present in the offence of rape. The *actus reus* of rape requires there to be a 'penetration'. Penetration is defined in s 79(2) of the Sexual Offences Act 2003 as 'a continuing act from entry to withdrawal'. As a result, where the defendant does not possess the relevant *mens rea* for rape (ie intention and lack of belief in consent), he may still be liable for an offence where he later becomes aware that consent has been withdrawn. As penetration is a continuing act until withdrawn, should the defendant not withdraw his penis after consent has been removed, he is liable for an offence under the continuing act doctrine (*Kaitamaki v The Queen* [1985] AC 147).

The key authority on continuing acts is the case of *Fagan v Metropolitan Police Commissioner (MPC)* [1969] 1 QB 439.

case example

Charge:
Battery (CJA 1988, s 39)

Case progression:
Magistrates' court – Guilty

Divisional Court – Conviction upheld

Point of law:
Meaning of continuing acts

In *Fagan v MPC* [1969] 1 QB 439, the defendant was directed by a police officer to park his car at a nearby kerb. The defendant did so and accidentally drove his car directly onto the foot of the officer. The officer requested that he move the car from his foot, to which the defendant responded 'Fuck you. You can wait.' The defendant switched off the ignition and sat in his car for two or three minutes before moving it. The defendant was charged with and convicted of battery, contrary to s 39 of the Criminal Justice Act 1988 in the magistrates' court.

He appealed to the Divisional Court, arguing that he did not drive onto the officer's foot on purpose and thus there was no contemporaneity between his *actus reus* and *mens rea*. The Divisional Court held that the refusal to move the car after the request amounted to a battery as the *mens rea* was formed at the point the defendant refused to move his car, and as the car remained on the officer's foot, the battery was 'continuing'.

In the Divisional Court, James J commented:

It is not necessary that *mens rea* should be present at the inception of the *actus reus*; it can be superimposed on an existing act. On the other hand, the subsequent inception of *mens rea* cannot convert an act which has been completed without *mens rea* into an assault.

The important point to note in this case is that the act remained in motion whilst the defendant held the car on the victim's foot. No liability would ensue where the act has been completed, but the result of the act continued to exist. For example, had the defendant moved his car from the foot of the victim from which the victim then sustained injuries not contemplated by the defendant, this result would not upgrade the battery to an offence of GBH, for example.

There is the argument that *Fagan*, and other cases of its kind, would be decided differently should they arise today. The most prominent argument is to follow the reasoning of the court in *R v Miller* [1983] 2 AC 161 (see **Chapter 2**) and the rule that the defendant's original act set in motion a chain of dangerous events that the defendant then had a duty to correct. On this basis, in *Fagan*, the defendant's original act of parking on the police officer's foot, whilst accidental, set in motion a dangerous set of events. The defendant thus held a duty to correct that situation which he failed to do by removing his car. The *Miller* principle thus operates to achieve the same result as a continuing act but without the rather 'artificial' way of doing so (Ormerod and Laird, *Smith, Hogan, & Ormerod's Criminal Law*, 15th edn (OUP, 2018)).

The difficulty that can be found in using *Miller* is in understanding the interpretation that the courts would take in finding there to be an 'omission' in the case of *Fagan*. Indeed, one could argue that *Fagan* failed or omitted to remove his car from the officer's foot (as Bridge J did in his dissenting judgment); however, it is contended that this was not a mere omission on the part of the defendant. Rather, this was a wilful and intentional *action* on the part of the defendant. By such account, *Miller* would be inapplicable given a positive act, and one would have to continue with a reference to a continuing act.

3.8.2 Chain of events

In a similar fashion to the continuing act, this circumstance occurs where the *actus reus* forms part of some larger sequence of events. In this case, the *mens rea* may be formed at some point during that sequence of events.

The key distinction to make between a continuing act and a chain of events is in the number of actions conducted by a defendant. In the former, the defendant will perform a single act that continues for a prolonged period of time. In the latter, however, the act will play a part in a sequence of other acts conducted by the defendant. Further to this, in the former circumstance, the *mens rea* comes after the *actus reus*, whilst the reverse is the case for chain of events cases.

There are three key cases used to identify a chain of events.

case example

Charge:
Murder

Case progression:
High Court of Basutoland–Guilty

Privy Council – Conviction upheld

Point of law:
Liability by way of a chain of events

In *Thabo Meli v The Queen* [1954] 1 All ER 373, the defendants hit the victim over the head, knocking him unconscious whilst intending the kill him. Believing he was dead, the defendants rolled his body off a cliff in an attempt to make his death appear accidental. The victim died from exposure at the bottom of the cliff.

The Privy Council found that the initial act was accompanied by the *mens rea* to kill, whilst the latter act contained no *mens rea* given that the defendants believed the victim to be already dead. As such, the court had to find there to be a chain of events such that the *mens rea* was present at some point in that chain.

Interpreting the series of actions as one logical transaction, Lord Reid in the Privy Council ruled that it was:

> ... impossible to divide up what was really one transaction in this way. There is no doubt that the accused set out to do all these acts in order to achieve their plan and as parts of their plan; and it is much too refined a ground of judgment to say that, because they were under a misapprehension at one stage and thought that their guilty purpose had been achieved before in fact it was achieved, therefore they are to escape the penalties of the law.

Arenson (‘*Thabo Meli* Revisited: The Pernicious Effects of Result-Driven Decisions’ (2013) 77 J Crim L 41) is critical of the decision in *Thabo Meli*, arguing that the effect of the decision has been to ‘emasculat[e] the doctrine of temporal coincidence beyond recognition’.

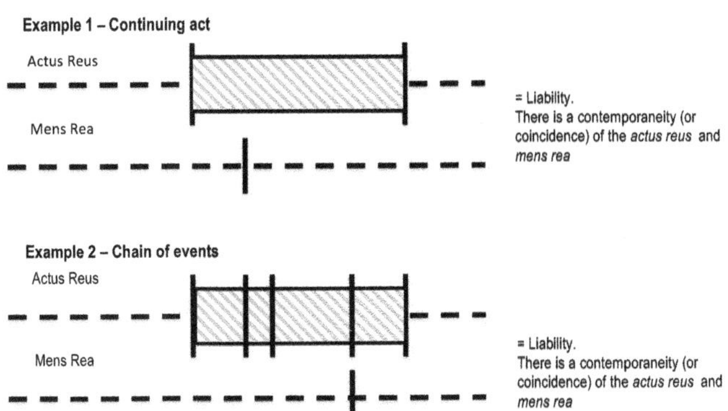

Figure 3.12 Understanding continuing acts and chain of events

case example

Charge:
Murder

Case progression:
Crown Court –
Not guilty, but guilty of manslaughter

Court of Criminal Appeal –
Conviction upheld

Point of law:
Liability by way of a chain of events

In *R v Church* [1966] 1 QB 59, the defendant struck a woman and attempted to strangle her after she had mocked him for failing to satisfy her sexually. Mistakenly believing she was dead, the defendant threw her into a river, whereby she drowned.

The defendant was charged with murder, but convicted of unlawful act manslaughter. The Court of Criminal Appeal found that although there was no pre-conceived plan to kill, the series of acts leading to the death of the victim amounted to a single *transaction.*

Edmund-Davies J, giving the judgment of the Court of Criminal Appeal, held:

> ... the defendant's behaviour from the moment he first struck her to the moment when he threw her into the river [was] a series of acts designed to cause death ... if a killing by the first act would have been manslaughter, a later destruction of the supposed corpse should also be manslaughter.

case example

Charge:
Unlawful act manslaughter

Case progression:
Crown Court –
Guilty

Court of Appeal –
Conviction upheld

Point of law:
Liability by way of a chain of events

In *R v Le Brun* [1992] QB 61, the defendant struck the victim, his wife, in the course of an argument outside their house. The blow knocked the victim unconscious. Upon attempting to drag the victim into the house, the victim's head struck the pavement, fracturing her skull and killing her.

On appeal, the defendant attempted to argue that since the fatal blow was accidental only, and there was no plan to kill, there could be no series of events making the defendant liable. The Court of Appeal dismissed this appeal, ruling that although the original strike was accidental, the fatal blow arose when the defendant was dragging the body in an attempt to conceal what he had done. The concealment was a major part of the Court's reasoning as to why there was a single transaction.

Lord Lane CJ, giving judgment of the Court, stated that:

> It seems to us that where the unlawful application of force and the eventual act causing death are parts of the same sequence of events, the same transaction, the fact that there is an appreciable interval of time between the two does not serve to exonerate the defendant from liability. That is certainly so where the appellant's subsequent actions which caused death, after the initial unlawful blow, are designed to conceal his commission of the original unlawful assault. ...In short, in circumstances such as the present...the act which causes death and the necessary mental state to constitute manslaughter need not coincide in point of time.

Herring (*Criminal Law: Text, Cases, and Materials*, 9th edn (OUP, 2020)) argues that had the defendant intended to carry his wife to the hospital, and had dropped her in transit, this might fall outside of the definition of a chain of events. Indeed, Ormerod and Laird (*Smith, Hogan, & Ormerod's Criminal Law*, 15th edn (OUP, 2018)) further this by stating that the transaction 'certainly continues while D is engaged in some kind of wrongdoing arising out of, and immediately following, the unlawful blow'. On this basis, the important point to stress is whether the later acts of the defendant remained in a state of wrongdoing.

The above cases demonstrate the circumstance where the cause of death is clear and unarguable. However, it may be more difficult for a court to find there to be a coincidence where it is not clear what act caused the end result of death. This was the predicament faced by the Court of Appeal in *AG's Reference (No 4 of 1980)* [1981] 2 All ER 617. In that case, the defendant killed a woman and cut up her body to allow for easy disposal. A number of acts took place during this transaction that might have resulted in her death. Specifically:

- the defendant slapped the victim;
- the victim fell head-first down a flight of stairs;
- the defendant tied a rope around the victim's neck and dragged her back up the stairs;
- the defendant placed the victim in a bath and slit her throat; and
- the defendant cut the victim up and disposed of the body.

In such a case, the Court of Appeal ruled that it was unnecessary to consider which action led to the death of the victim as each were equally capable of doing so. There was no requirement to use either the continuing act or chain of events principle to find liability; rather, the Court could find liability by referring to each individual act that might have been responsible for the victim's death and asking whether the defendant had the *mens rea* for at least one of those actions.

From the above, it can be seen that the essential requirement in chain of events cases is for the court to link together separate acts and construe or interpret them as a single line of events.

3.9 Transferred malice

Criminal actions need not be directed to a specific individual. A defendant may commit an offence where his actions apply indiscriminately (ie they are directed at any person or object in the relevant area). For example, an individual who wishes to detonate a bomb on a plane will understand that many individuals will die; however, his malice is 'indiscriminate' or 'general' in that he does not intend one specific person on that plane to die. In such cases, the defendant will remain liable regardless. Further to this, in circumstances where the defendant attacks one person, mistakenly believing them to be another person, he remains liable for that offence. Mistaken identity is not a defence as the *actus reus* and *mens rea* are still fulfilled (and the doctrine of transferred malice is not relevant).

However, there may be cases where the defendant intends his actions to target a specific individual. Of course, should the defendant fulfil the *actus reus* and *mens rea* of the relevant offence against that targeted individual, and succeed, he may be liable for an offence. Difficulties arise, however, where the defendant directs his actions at a particular person or object intending a set outcome, but the defendant's actions fail to connect with the intended person or object and connect with another instead.

example

Jack is annoyed at Jill and swings his fist at her, intending to punch her in the face. Jack misses because of his poor aim and strikes Andy instead.

In this case, Jack has clearly intended to cause harm to another; however, the harm was never intended to be directed at Andy. Naturally, Jack may be liable for an attempt (a very serious criminal offence in its own right); however, it would appear unfair on the *actual* victim that the defendant should 'get away' with the main offence.

The law, on this basis, has had to react and has been faced with the following question: 'Will the defendant be liable for an offence despite his lack of intention to strike the victim?'

This question can be answered in the affirmative and has been developed and understood through a doctrine known as 'transferred malice' (also known as 'transferred *mens rea*'). Herring (*Criminal Law: Text, Cases, and Materials*, 9th edn (OUP, 2020)) prefers the title transferred *mens rea* as he argues that the former is a 'misleading label as the doctrine does not apply just to malice, but to any *mens rea*'. We shall continue to use the word malice for ease, but on the understanding that the principle does not concern *only* cases involving malice.

3.9.1 The basis of the doctrine

The basis of the doctrine was explained by Lord Mustill in *AG's Reference (No 3 of 1994)* [1998] AC 245 where his Lordship stated that 'the intended victim and the actual victim are treated as if they were one'. As a result, therefore, we can characterise the parties in a case of this kind as follows:

- the defendant (D);
- the *intended* victim (IV); and
- the *actual* victim (AV).

The *intended* victim is the individual against whom the *mens rea*, or malice, was directed; however, the *actus reus* is completed against the *actual* victim. Understanding this by reference to a diagram may be easier.

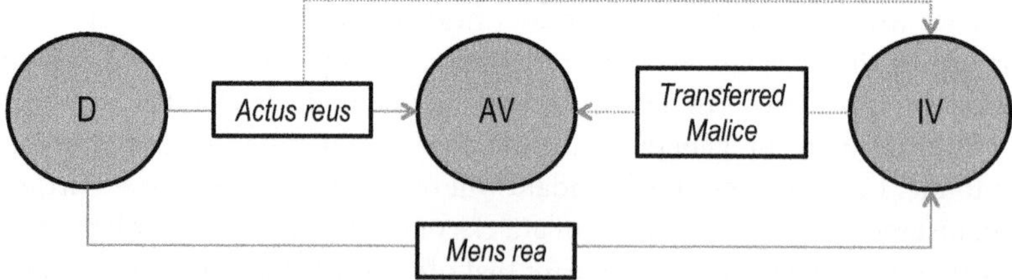

Figure 3.13 Understanding transferred malice

As can be seen from **Figure 3.13**:

- the *mens rea* is directed from the defendant to the intended victim and is completed (shown by the solid line);
- the *actus reus*, although directed to the intended victim, has not been completed (shown by the dotted line);
- the *actus reus* has been completed in relation to the actual victim (shown by the solid line); and
- malice is effectively transferred as the intended crime and the actual crime bear the same *mens rea*.

Ormerod and Laird (*Smith, Hogan, & Ormerod's Criminal Law*, 15th edn (OUP, 2018)) have usefully justified this doctrine by providing:

> It is this intuition that D deserves liability for the full offence that has given rise to the legal fiction that is transferred malice, with the court manipulating D's mens rea towards one object into a mens rea towards another.

Transferred malice can be demonstrated through a number of key cases.

case example

Charge:
Inflicting wounding (OAPA 1861, s 20)

Case progression:
Crown Court – Guilty

Court for Crown Cases Reserved – Conviction upheld

Point of law:
Transferred malice

In *R v Latimer* (1886) 17 QBD 359, the defendant swung his belt over his head in an attempt to hit the intended victim. The belt glanced off the intended victim and accidentally hit the actual victim, causing serious injury. The defendant was charged with and convicted of maliciously wounding contrary to s 20 of the OAPA 1861.

His appeal was dismissed by the Court for Crown Cases Reserved on the basis that his malice was transferred from the intended victim to the actual victim. Lord Coleridge CJ ruled that:

> It is common knowledge that a man who has an unlawful and malicious intent against another, and, in attempting to carry it out, injures a third person, is guilty of what the law deems malice against the person injured, because the offender is doing an unlawful act, and has that which the judges call general malice, and that is enough.

A more recent case on this point (well, more recent when compared to *Latimer*) is the case of *R v Mitchell* [1983] QB 741, where the defendant became involved in a scuffle with an elderly gentleman in the queue at a Post Office. The defendant pushed the elderly gentleman, who, as a result, fell onto an elderly lady causing her significant harm and resulting in her eventual death. The defendant was charged with and convicted of unlawful act manslaughter due to the transfer of malice from the elderly gentleman (the intended victim) to the elderly woman (the actual victim).

Staughton LJ in the Court of Appeal commented that: 'We can see no reason of policy for holding that an act calculated to harm A cannot be manslaughter if it in fact kills B.'

Both cases were later restricted in *AG's Reference (No 3 of 1994)* [1998] AC 245.

case example

Charge:
Murder

Case progression:
Crown Court – Not guilty (no case to answer)

Court of Appeal (by AG's Ref) – Conviction justified

House of Lords – Murder not justified; conviction of manslaughter justified

Point of law:
Double transferred malice

In *AG's Reference (No 3 of 1994)* [1998] AC 245, the defendant (known as 'B') stabbed his girlfriend ('M') in the stomach knowing that she was pregnant. The defendant was charged with and convicted of wounding in relation to the mother. When the child died, the defendant was charged with murder. However, following a submission of no case to answer on the part of the defence, the defendant was acquitted. The prosecution appealed against this ruling to the Court of Appeal.

The Court of Appeal allowed the appeal by the prosecution and concluded that a conviction in this regard would have been justified. The Court concluded that an intention to injure the mother could be transferred as an intention to injure the foetus. The defendant appealed to the House of Lords.

The House of Lords, in allowing the defendant's appeal, made it clear that malice cannot transfer from a human being to a human in-waiting (given that a foetus is not recognised as a person in law). Specifically, the House ruled that such transfer would require a *double* transfer of malice, given that the malice would transfer from the intended victim to the foetus, and then from the foetus to the developed child.

A more recent statement of transferred malice as it applied to the law of murder was made by the Supreme Court in *R v Gnango* [2011] UKSC 59 (see **Chapter 4** for a more detailed account in terms of accessorial liability).

case example

Charge:
Murder

Case progression:
Crown Court – Guilty

Court of Appeal – Conviction quashed

Supreme Court – Conviction reinstated

Point of law:
Transferred malice applies to homicide

In *R v Gnango* [2011] UKSC 59, the defendant was engaged in a shoot-out with the intended victim (known as 'Bandana man') in a public place. The victim was unfortunately caught in the cross-fire and was killed by a bullet from Bandana man's gun. Bandana man could not be found and the defendant was charged with and convicted of murder.

His appeal was allowed by the Court of Appeal on the basis that the defendant was not party to a joint enterprise (see **Chapter 4**) and could not be liable for the death of the actual victim.

On appeal by the Crown, the Supreme Court reinstated the defendant's conviction, ruling that the defendant's malice could be transferred in circumstances where he had no lawful excuse to be engaged in a shoot-out and the offence against his intended victim was the same as that against the actual victim. In this respect, their Lordships felt that the trial judge was correct to direct the jury according to the principles of transferred malice.

Horder ('Transferred Malice and the Remoteness of Unexpected Outcomes from Intentions' [2006] Crim LR 383) is critical of the present state of transferred malice, arguing that it remains too broad and encompassing. Specifically, Horder gives the following example (adapted for our purposes):

example

Jack shoots a gun at Jill intending to kill. The noise of the gun shot startles Andy who is hiding in the bushes nearby. Andy suffers a heart attack as a result and dies.

Horder argues that although the courts may accept transferred malice in this case, they ought not to, as to do so would allow a defendant to be convicted in relation to a victim who was neither intended nor *anticipated* to suffer from the defendant's actions. As a result, Horder argues that there remains a need to introduce a 'remoteness'-based test that will closely examine causation to establish whether malice can truly be transferred.

For a relatively recent application of the doctrine (and a potential extension of the doctrine), see *R v Grant* [2014] EWCA Crim 143 in which the defendant fired two shots at a rival gang member (V1), with the intention to kill. Both shots missed and instead hit two bystanders (V2 and V3), causing serious injury. The Court of Appeal upheld the defendant's conviction for GBH on account that his intention to kill could be transferred to an intent to cause GBH to V2 and V3. In the Court of Appeal, Rafferty LJ explained that '[p]roof of the mens rea for attempted murder by definition involves proof of the mens rea for causing grievous bodily harm with intent'. Her Ladyship would go on to conclude that:

> On these facts a finding of intention to kill (count 1) leads inevitably to a finding of intention to cause grievous bodily harm (counts 2 and 3) – the consequence of the hierarchy of intent, with intention to kill at the top. It is impossible to kill without causing really serious harm.

3.9.2 Limitations on transferred malice

Two further comments are necessary on the doctrine of transferred malice.

3.9.2.1 Transferred defences

Importantly, where the defendant would have a valid defence to the action against the intended victim (had the *actus reus* been completed), he will also have a valid defence to a charge against the intended victim (where malice is transferred). For example, should Jack attempt to punch Andy whilst acting in self-defence and accidentally punches Jill, Jack would still have a valid defence in relation to an offence against Jill (see *R v Gross* (1913) 23 Cox CC 455 on this point).

3.9.2.2 The rule in *Pembliton*

There remains one key exception to the rule of transferred malice. Namely, the doctrine operates only where the *actus reus* and *mens rea* of the same offence coincide. In basic form, this means that the defendant must have the *actus reus* and *mens rea* for the same offence in order for his malice to be 'transferred'. Therefore, if the defendant has the *mens rea* of one crime, but commits an act which is the *actus reus* of another crime, the malice cannot be transferred. This is demonstrated in the case of *R v Pembliton* (1874) LR 2 CCR 119.

case example

Charge:
Criminal damage

Case progression:
Crown Court – Guilty

Court for Crown Cases Reserved – Conviction quashed

Point of law:
Transferred malice and the need for the same crime to exist

In *R v Pembliton* (1874) LR 2 CCR 119, the defendant threw a stone at a group of people with whom he had been fighting. The stone missed and struck a window causing damage. The defendant was charged with criminal damage, with the prosecution alleging that the malice had transferred from the intended victims to the property.

The Court for Crown Cases Reserved ruled, however, that the defendant's intention to injure the intended victims was not of sufficient malice to be transferred to the damage of property. The *actus reus* and *mens rea* must be linked.

The crux of *Pembliton* was that the doctrine is unable to join the *actus reus* of an offence against property (the breaking of a window) with the *mens rea* of an offence against the person (the intention to injure the intended victims). The rule also works the other way round, in circumstances where the defendant throws a stone at a window intending to break it but misses and hits a person walking by the window. This is justified on the basis that an intention to injure another person is far different from an intention to damage property. As such, it would be inequitable to a defendant for such malice to be transferred when he neither intended to damage, nor was reckless to the thought of damaging, property in the first place.

Returning to *Latimer*, had the belt buckle hit the victim and then rebounded and hit a piece of property, no malice could be transferred to that property (though the defendant may still be reckless as to such damage).

However, now consider a scenario where the defendant in *Pembliton* had intended to throw the stone at the group of people, and, knowing that his aim was poor and there was a chance of the stone hitting the window, he threw the stone anyway. Where damage is caused in this case, one may find the defendant liable in two ways:

- for an offence against the intended victims – by way of an attempt;
- for a separate offence against property – using recklessness as the *mens rea*.

Here, the 'legal fiction' of transferred malice need not be considered, and the case may be understood through the ordinary course of establishing criminal liability. Indeed, this is the view taken by Ashworth ('Transferred Malice and Punishment for Unforeseen Consequences' in Glazebrook (ed), *Reshaping the Criminal Law: Essays in Honour of Glanville Williams* (Steven & Sons, 1978)).

3.10 Further reading

Intention

Buxton, 'Some Simple Thoughts on Intention' [1988] Crim LR 484.

Kaveny, 'Inferring Intention from Foresight' (2004) 120 LQR 81.

Stark, 'It's Only Words: On Meaning and Mens Rea' (2013) 72 Camb LJ 155.

Recklessness

Amirthalingam, 'Caldwell Recklessness is Dead, Long Live Mens Rea's Fecklessness' [2004] 63 MLR 491.

Keating, 'Reckless Children' [2007] Crim LR 546.

Williams, 'The Unresolved Problem of Recklessness' (1988) 8 LS 74.

Knowledge

Griew, 'Consistency, Communication and Codification—Reflections on Two Mens Rea Words' in Glazebrook (ed), *Reshaping the Criminal Law* (1978).

Shute, 'Knowledge and Belief in the Criminal Law' in Shute and Simester (eds), *Criminal Law Theory: Doctrines of the General Part* (2002).

Sullivan, 'Knowledge, Belief and Culpability' in Shute and Simester (eds), *Criminal Law Theory: Doctrines of the General Part* (2002).

Negligence

Hart, 'Negligence, Mens Rea and Criminal Responsibility' in *Punishment and Responsibility* (1968).

Simester, 'Can Negligence be Culpable?' in Horder (ed), *Oxford Essays in Jurisprudence* (OUP, 2000).

Contemporaneity

Wells, 'Goodbye to Coincidence' (1991) NLJ 1566

Sullivan, 'Cause and the Contemporaneity of Actus Reus and Mens Rea' (1993) J Crim L 487.

Strict liability

Manchester, 'Knowledge, Due Diligence and Strict Liability in Regulatory Offences' [2006] Crim LR 213.

Horder, 'Strict Liability, Statutory Construction and the Spirit of Liberty' (2002) 118 LQR 458.

Simester, 'Is Strict Liability Always Wrong?' in Simester (ed), *Appraising Strict Liability* (OUP, 2005).

Transferred malice

Bohlander, 'Transferred Malice and Transferred Defenses: A Critique of the Traditional Doctrine and Arguments for a Change in Paradigm' (2010) 13 New Criminal Law Review 555.

Horder, 'Transferred Malice and the Remoteness of Unexpected Outcomes from Intentions' (2006) Crim LR 383.

- *Mens rea* loosely translates as 'guilty mind'.
- The Law Commission prefers the term 'fault' over *mens rea*.
- *Mens rea* includes various states of mind, including intention, recklessness and negligence.
- Intention may be direct or oblique. Direct intention is where it is the defendant's aim, objective and purpose to cause the end result; oblique intention is where the consequences of the defendant's actions are a virtual certainty and the defendant is aware of this.
- Recklessness is now firmly established as a subjective test looking at what the defendant appreciated the situation to be.
- Negligence requires an objective standard and it must be demonstrated that the accused fell below this objective standard.
- Other forms of *mens rea* are applicable to specific offences, such as knowledge, belief and maliciousness.
- Some offences do not require any form of *mens rea*, known as strict liability offences.
- Criminal offences require contemporaneity between the *actus reus* and *mens rea*. There are exceptions to this rule, known as continuing act and chain of events cases.
- A criminal offence need not be directed at an individual. This allows for the concept of transferred malice to operate.

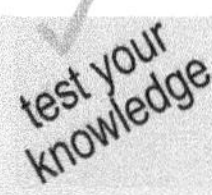

Problem

Jack and Jill, as a joke, tie a rope between two trees which are separated by a road. The rope is stretched across the road at a height of about four feet. Their intention is to unseat their friend, Andy, as he rides his motorcycle along the road. Andy travels down the road and hits the rope which decapitates him.

Consider the liability of Jack and Jill.

Would your answer differ if Andy had not died and had simply suffered minor harm?

Essay

'There is no justification for imposing strict liability in the criminal law.'

Critically discuss this statement in light of the arguments for and against imposing such liability.

chapter 4

Parties to a Crime: Principal and Secondary Offenders

After reading this chapter, you will be able to understand:

- the difference in law between a principal and secondary offender
- the legal basis of a secondary party's liability
- the concept of derivation as it applies to accessorial liability
- the respective elements for an offence of complicity
- the defences available specifically to secondary offenders.

4.1 Introduction to principal and secondary offenders

In the preceding chapters, we have discussed the necessary elements that must be established in order for an individual to be liable for an offence. We have been concerned up to now only with offences where there is one individual liable. This chapter, however, will discuss the potential liability of more than one individual for the same criminal offence. By way of illustration at this early stage: Suppose Jack burgles a house – we know that he may be liable for the offence of burglary. But what if Jill stands outside the house and acts as a 'lookout'. What offence has Jill committed?

This area of law is often referred to as the law of 'accessories' or the law of 'complicity' and concerns the liability not only of those who 'commit' a criminal offence, but also of those who are complicit in the commission of that criminal offence. Simply, in this area of law, the responsibility for a criminal offence may be incurred by:

- a principal offender; and
- a secondary offender (known as an 'accessory'/'accomplice').

Importantly, consideration of this area of law is focused on the commission of a *single* offence, but with *multiple* parties criminally responsible for it.

4.1.1 Terminology used

To fully understand this area of law, the terminology used must be made clear from the outset. In summary, we have three main (potential) parties to a crime, plus the victim of the crime. These are detailed in **Table 4.1**.

Table 4.1 Understanding terminology

Party	Definition
Principal offender	A principal offender (who is referred to throughout this text as the 'defendant') is the actual perpetrator of the offence in question, known as the 'principal offence'. It is his conduct that has satisfied the *actus reus* and *mens rea* of the particular offence concerned.

Party	Definition
Joint principal offender	A joint principal offender (referred to simply as a 'co-defendant') has engaged in a joint venture with another against the victim. Both offenders complete the necessary *actus reus* and *mens rea* of the offence.
Secondary offender	A secondary offender (referred to in law as an 'accessory') is one who aids, abets, counsels or procures the commission of the principal offence. The accessory's liability is *derivative of* or *parasitic on* the principal's conduct.
Victim	The victim is the subject of the criminal offence.

The manner in which these parties interact can be seen in **Figure 4.1**.

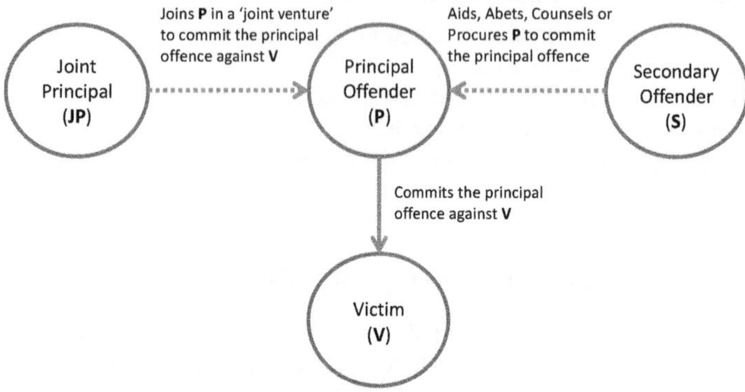

Figure 4.1 Understanding terminology in complicity

A further party worth mentioning at this stage is the 'innocent agent'. Dealt with in more detail at **4.1.1.4**, the innocent agent represents a party that commits the *actus reus* of an offence but for some reason is considered in law as being an 'innocent' participant in the criminal offence.

It is now necessary to consider the liability of these types of offenders in further detail.

4.1.1.1 Single principal offender

This scenario is concerned with the case where one person, acting alone, commits a criminal offence. In order to establish liability against this individual, one must simply consider whether the respective *actus reus* and *mens rea* of the offence are fulfilled, as will be dealt with in the remainder of this text.

The principal offender can be characterised as the individual that has 'committed' the offence. To this extent, it is the individual who pulls the trigger of the gun and kills another; or takes a tin of beans from a supermarket without paying; or attacks another with a knife causing serious wounds. Quite simply, we can identify this person as the 'perpetrator' of the offence.

4.1.1.2 Joint principal offender

This scenario concerns the case where two or more people join together in committing a *single* criminal offence. A number of examples can be used to demonstrate this.

example

Jack and Jill agree to commit a robbery against Andy. Both attack Andy, kicking and punching him, before then making off with his wallet and smartphone.

example

Jack and Jill decide that they are tired of seeing Andy succeed whilst they continue to struggle financially. The pair decide to kill Andy. One night, they attack Andy with a knife. Both Jack and Jill stab the victim multiple times. Andy dies.

example

Jack and Jill agree to commit a burglary against Bill and Ben. They break into the house and both steal items found in the house.

In all of these cases, each party has performed all the elements of the respective offences (both the *actus reus* and *mens rea*) in his and her own right. In such cases, both parties are considered liable as 'joint principal offenders' (*Macklin and Murphy's Case* (1838) 2 Lew CC 225). This means that the ordinary principles of liability (as discussed in Parts II and III of this text) are relevant and not those principles set out in this chapter.

Where, however, an individual merely persuades another to commit an offence and that individual does not take part in the commission of the offence personally, it cannot be said that they are a joint principal (but see **4.1.1.4** for a discussion of the innocent agent principle). Rather, our focus would change to either inchoate liability (see **Chapter 5**) or liability as a secondary party.

4.1.1.3 Secondary offender

This scenario concerns the case where one party assists or encourages another (the principal) to commit a single crime. A helpful summary of the position of secondary parties was provided by Lords Hughes and Toulson in *R v Jogee* [2016] UKSC 8, in which their Lordships stated:

> In the language of the criminal law a person who assists or encourages another to commit a crime is known as an accessory or secondary party. The actual perpetrator is known as a principal, even if his role may be subordinate to that of others. It is a fundamental principle of the criminal law that the accessory is guilty of the same offence as the principal. The reason is not difficult to see. He shares the physical act because even if it was not his hand which struck the blow, ransacked the house, smuggled the drugs or forged the cheque, he has encouraged or assisted those physical acts. Similarly he shares the culpability precisely because he encouraged or assisted the offence. No one doubts that if the principal and the accessory are together engaged on, for example, an armed robbery of a bank, the accessory who keeps guard outside is as guilty of the robbery as the principal who enters with a shotgun and extracts the money from the staff by threat of violence. Nor does anyone doubt that the same principle can apply where, as sometimes

> happens, the accessory is nowhere near the scene of the crime. The accessory who funded the bank robbery or provided the gun for the purpose is as guilty as those who are at the scene. ... These basic principles are long established and uncontroversial.

A number of examples (adapted from the previous examples) can be used to demonstrate this.

example

Jack and Jill agree to commit a robbery against Andy. Jill, although not present at the scene of the crime, provides Jack with a gun to use during the robbery.

example

Jack and Jill decide that they are tired of seeing Andy succeed whilst they continue to struggle financially. The pair decide to kill Andy. One night, Jack attacks Andy with a knife. Whilst Jack is stabbing Andy, Jill shouts words of encouragement to Jack. Andy dies.

example

Jack and Jill agree to commit a burglary against Bill and Ben. Jack alone enters the house and steals items found in the house. Jill acts as the lookout and drives Jack to and from the scene of the crime.

In all of these cases, Jack is liable as a principal offender as he has committed the relevant offences (both the *actus reus* and *mens rea*). However, Jill may also be liable for an offence as an accessory because she has assisted or encouraged Jack to commit the offences in question. Jill can therefore be correctly identified as an 'accessory' or 'accomplice' in these cases.

It is the liability of Jill, in cases such as these, that is the focus of this chapter.

4.1.1.4 Innocent agent

The final term that requires consideration is that of 'innocent agent'. As explained above, an innocent agent is an individual who commits the relevant *actus reus* or conduct element of the criminal offence in question but, for some reason, cannot be liable for a criminal offence. Such reasons may include that the individual lacks capacity, has a valid defence or does not satisfy the mental element of the offence. These reasons make the individual an 'innocent' participant in the offence. Prima facie, it would appear that such an individual can be classified as the 'principal offender' given that their conduct has led to the commission of the offence; however, as we shall see, such individuals are unknowing in their conduct, making them 'innocent' in their dealings. Barker (*Glanville Williams Textbook of Criminal Law*, 4th edn (Sweet & Maxwell, 2015)) describes this circumstance as follows:

> [T]he physical actor is treated as a puppet, so that the guilty actor who activates him to do the mischief becomes responsible not as an accessory but as a perpetrator acting through an innocent agent.

Such persons are thus not considered to be principal offenders in the law; they are to be considered 'innocent agents'.

example

Jack intends to kill Alice, his child, by poisoning her food. Jack delivers the poison to Andy, telling him that it is medicine and to administer it to Alice. Andy decides not to administer the medicine and leaves it on the shelf. Another child, Janice, then picks up the bottle and administers it to Alice. Alice dies.

These are, broadly, the facts of *R v Michael* (1840) 9 C & P 356, considered in more detail in **Chapter 2**. In this case, Jack is clearly the principal offender, whereas Janice is merely an innocent agent. Jack has committed the offence *through the use of* Andy/Janice. Similarly in *R v Stringer and Banks* (1991) 94 Cr App R 13, an employer used his employees to fraudulently transfer money unknowingly. An oft-cited example is that of a postman who unknowingly delivers a letter bomb. All are cases of innocent agency. We can demonstrate this concept in **Figure 4.2**.

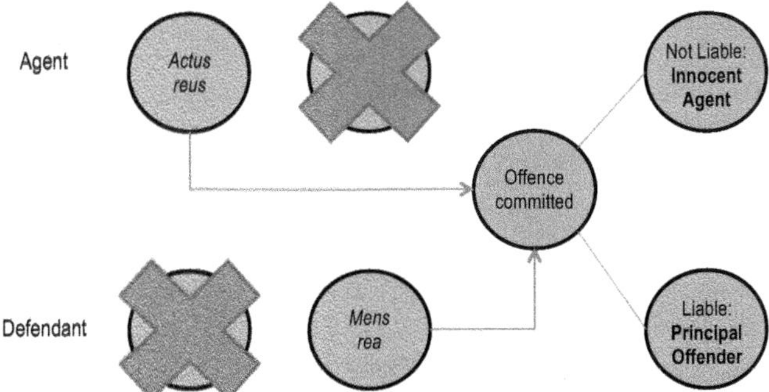

Figure 4.2 Innocent agency

In these cases, the principal is considered in law to be the person who causes the innocent agent to commit the *actus reus* of the offence. As such, although the defendant is not a true 'perpetrator', in the sense that he has not committed the *actus reus* himself, legally he is considered as such and will be liable in such circumstances.

Whether an individual is 'innocent' will ultimately depend on the facts of the case; however, there are a number of situations that can be identified at an early stage as involving innocent agents.

Table 4.2 Categories of innocent agents

Innocent agent	Explanation
Children/those who lack capacity	A child under the age of 10 years is not capable of committing a criminal offence (known as the principle of *doli incapax* – see **Chapter** 7). Given that the child is not capable of committing a criminal offence, they themselves cannot be a principal – thus meaning that any conduct they do fulfil will be in the context of innocent agency (*R v Michael* (1840) 9 C & P 356). The defence of insanity will also prevent an individual from being classified as a principal offender, given that in such circumstances they will lack capacity (*R v Tyler* (1838) 8 C & P 616).

Innocent agent	Explanation
Lacks *mens rea*	Where an individual has performed the necessary *actus reus* of the offence but does so unknowingly, or unwittingly, to such an extent that it cannot be said that they have the respective *mens rea* for that offence, it is clear that they are merely an innocent agent (*R v Millward* [1994] Crim LR 527).
Valid defence	Where an individual has performed the respective elements of the offence but has a valid defence which excuses their liability, it cannot be said that they are a principal offender in any sense. For example, a successful defence of duress will prevent an individual from being considered a principal in all offences except murder (*R v Bourne* (1952) 36 Cr App R 125).

The Law Commission in its Report, 'Participating in Crime' (Law Com No 305, 2007) proposed replacing the common law doctrine of innocent agency with a new offence defined clearly in statute. The operation of the offence, although methodical, would be quite complex in practice. In essence, a defendant would be liable in circumstances where he intentionally causes a principal offender, an 'innocent agent', to commit the conduct element of an offence but he cannot commit the mental element of the offence because he is under the age of 10 years, is insane or acts without fault.

Taylor ('Procuring, Causation, Innocent Agency and the Law Commission' [2008] Crim LR 32) contends that such a change would immerse 'within an automatic fiction of innocent agency' far too many cases that should be dealt with as cases of secondary liability. For more general comments regarding innocent agency, see Alldridge, 'The Doctrine of Innocent Agency' (1990) 2 Crim L Forum 45 and Williams, 'Innocent Agency and Causation' (1992) 3 Crim L Forum 289.

4.1.1.5 Uncertainty as to the party status

There may, of course, be a number of cases where the status of the defendant, ie whether he is a joint principal or accessory, is unclear. In the majority of cases, this uncertainty arises as a result of the factual information present before the court. Take the following as an example:

example

Jill has been found dead in her home. There is evidence to suggest that Jack either killed Jill or had his friend, Andy, kill her.

In this case, there is a clear uncertainty as to whether Jack is a principal offender or merely an accessory. There is evidence to support both possibilities, so what is the outcome?

According to the Court of Appeal in *R v Giannetto* [1997] 1 Cr App R 1, so long as the prosecution is able to prove that the defendant was involved in the commission of the criminal offence, it is not necessary for it to allege that he was either the principal offender or a secondary party (see also *R v Fitzgerald* [1992] Crim LR 660). In that case, the victim had been murdered either by the defendant (her husband) or a hired killer. The Court of Appeal concluded that where it can be proven that the defendant was either the principal or the accessory to the offence (ie the prosecution can prove the necessary *actus reus* and *mens rea* elements of the offence), it will not be contrary to law to charge a defendant with an offence alleging him to be either one of those parties. In *Giannetto*, Kennedy LJ explained this rule as follows:

> The Crown is not required to specify the means, because the legal definition of the crime does not require it; and the defendant knows perfectly well what case he has to meet. Of course, if (as will very often be so) the Crown nail their colours to a particular mast, their case will, generally, have to be established in the terms in which it is put. Our judgment should give no encouragement to prosecutors casting around for alternative possibilities where the essential evidence does not show a clear case against the defendant. But the facts of the present appeal are by no means an instance of that.

The rule is justified on the basis that both the principal and accessory are prosecuted in the same manner, and are subject to the same penalty, regardless of whether they were in fact the principal or accessory.

This statement of law must, however, be distinguished from the case where the prosecution is unable to prove that the defendant was involved in the offence in some capacity. For instance, in *R v Lane and Lane* (1985) 82 Cr App R 5, evidence demonstrated that the victim, a child, had died between 12 noon and 8.30 pm and that each of his parents had been present (ie at home) and equally absent (ie away from home, for example at work) during this time. It could not be said with certainty whether either of the defendants was the principal offender, nor could it be proven that one or the other was an accessory. In this instance, both defendants had to be acquitted. See *R v Strudwick* (1993) 99 Cr App R 326 for similar facts and outcome. The same approach was taken in the more recent case of *R v Banfield* [2013] EWCA Crim 1394. Both cases are justified on the basis that the crime could have been committed by:

- X and Y together;
- X alone;
- Y alone;
- X assisting Y; and
- Y assisting X.

Without such clarity that each defendant was involved in some capacity, however, there cannot be liability. It is noteworthy that the outcome in *Lane and Lane* has now been resolved by Parliament in enacting the Domestic Violence, Crime and Victims Act 2004, which creates an offence of causing or allowing the death of a child or vulnerable adult (s 5(1)). For an application of s 5 on very similar facts as in *Lane and Lane*, see *R v Ikram and Parveen* [2008] EWCA Crim 586.

4.1.1.6 Directing the jury

The decision to prosecute the defendant as a joint principal or as an accessory is one for the prosecution. In the majority of cases, where such uncertainty arises as identified at **4.1.1.5**, the prosecution will likely allege both. Section 7-3(4) of the Crown Court Compendium provides that:

> In such cases it is not necessary for the jury to be satisfied whether any one D was a principal or an accessory, provided that they are satisfied that he/she participated. An example would be where W suffered injuries in an attack in which several Ds took a physical part, but it is not known which D caused which injuries if any.

4.1.2 Nature of liability

Traditionally, secondary liability was predicated on the existence of a criminal offence, committed by the principal offender. Under this justification, without the existence of the criminal offence, there can be no secondary liability for a party that has assisted or encouraged the commission of the offence. In this sense, secondary liability is derivative in nature, meaning that the liability of the defendant (in our examples, Jill) 'derives' from the conduct of the principal (in our examples, Jack). It is only upon the principal committing the requisite conduct element of the offence that liability for the secondary party arises.

example

Jill provides Jack with a knife with the intention that Jack will use it to kill Andy.

In this instance, Jill can only be liable as a secondary party where Jack actually commits the murder in question. The prosecution must thus prove that Jack committed the *actus reus* and *mens rea* of murder (ie the unlawful killing of a human being under the Queen's peace with malice aforethought, express or implied) and Jill aided or abetted him in the commission of the offence.

Another way of explaining this is to say that the secondary offender's liability is 'parasitic' on the completion of the conduct of the principal offender or, in the words of Kadish ('Complicity, Cause and Blame: A Study in the Interpretation of Doctrine' (1985) 73 California Law Review 324), the defendant's liability is 'dependent' on the existence of conduct from the principal offender.

Derived from conduct, not guilt

The various expressions used to explain the nature of such liability are terms of art and can be used interchangeably when describing the principle of secondary liability. Importantly, however, secondary liability is derived from the *conduct* (ie the *actus reus*) of the principal, not *conviction* or *guilt*. By this we mean that accessories may be liable for an offence even in circumstances where no conviction of the principal takes place. This is because derivative liability is based upon the completion of certain conduct by the principal and not the finding of guilt against the principal (*R v Cogan and Leak* [1976] QB 217).

The nature of such liability is detailed in **Figure 4.3** and is evident in the decision in *R v Millward* [1994] Crim LR 527.

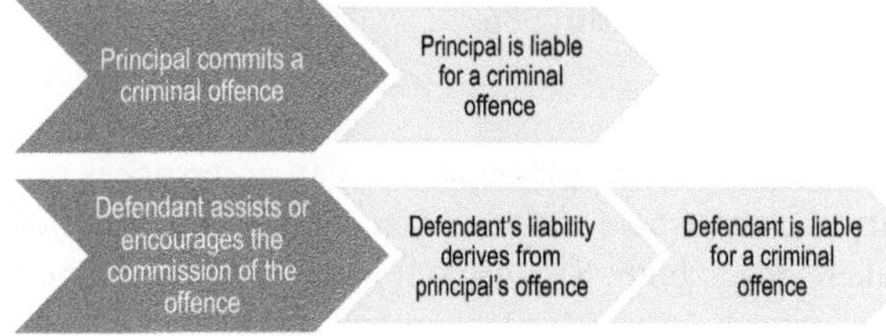

Figure 4.3 Understanding derivative/parasitic liability

Charge:
Causing death by reckless driving (Road Traffic Act 1988, s 1)

Case progression:
Crown Court – Guilty

Court of Appeal – Conviction upheld

Point of law:
Liability of accessory where the principal is not liable for an offence

case example

In *R v Millward* [1994] Crim LR 527, the defendant, an employer, instructed the principal, his employee, to drive a poorly-maintained vehicle which resulted in a car accident which killed the victim, another driver. The defendant was charged with and convicted of procuring the principal to cause death by reckless driving. The principal was found not guilty given the lack of *mens rea* on his part – ie he was not reckless as he did not know about the vehicle's dangerous condition.

The defendant appealed on the basis that he could not be convicted where the principal himself had not committed an offence. The Court of Appeal disagreed, finding that an accessory can still be liable in circumstances where the principal is not, so long as the principal has at least committed the *actus reus* of the offence and the accessory possesses the relevant *mens rea.*

Of course, where the principal is found not to have even committed the *actus reus* of an offence, the accessory cannot be liable as a secondary party (*Thornton v Mitchell* [1940] 1 All ER 339). However, he may still be liable for an inchoate offence (see **Chapter 5**).

In considering this matter, therefore, one should begin by establishing the existence of the criminal offence (or in some situations, the *actus reus* of an offence), as committed by the principal offender. Once the principal offence has been identified, it is then necessary to consider whether any liability arises *as a result* of the commission of that offence. Whether liability exists will depend on a specific identification of *actus reus* and *mens rea*, distinct from the principal offence. We shall observe these rules below at **4.2**.

4.1.3 Scope of liability

Importantly, according to the Court of Appeal in *R v Jefferson* [1994] 1 All ER 270, liability as an accessory applies to all offences, including statutory ones, unless such liability is expressly excluded by a statute. See, for example, s 78 of the Sexual Offences Act 2003 which provides a partial exclusion of the rules of complicity in certain cases relating to the commission of offences against children.

As we shall examine below (at **4.2**), liability for secondary offenders is detailed in statute. Liability for indictable offences is contained in s 8 of the Accessories and Abettors Act 1861, and liability for summary offences is set out in s 44(1) of the Magistrates' Courts Act 1980. According to Auld LJ in *Jefferson*, these statutory provisions are merely 'deeming provisions' as to how secondary parties are to be dealt with at trial; their liability remains vested in the common law. Interestingly, although ss 8 and 44 respectively are unrestricted in ambit, there remain a number of statutory offences specifically stating the liability of accessories to the commission of an offence. Such offences include:

- inciting another to commit an offence contrary to the Official Secrets Act 1920 (s 7);
- aiding or abetting another to commit an offence contrary to the Perjury Act 1911 (s 7);
- aiding or abetting another to commit suicide contrary to the Suicide Act 1961 (s 2).

4.1.4 Accessorial liability and strict liability offences

As has been discussed in **Chapter 3**, strict liability offences do not require *mens rea* on the part of the perpetrator of the offence. Despite this, in order to be liable as an accomplice, the secondary party must possess the necessary *mens rea* for the offence. This was evident in the case of *Callow v Tillstone* (1900) 64 JP 823 where the defendant, a vet, could not be liable for aiding and abetting the principal, a butcher, to expose unfit meat for sale in circumstances where they were unaware that the meat was unfit. The principal, however, was liable for an offence as it was one of strict liability. See also *R v Webster* [2006] EWCA Crim 415.

4.1.5 Distinguishing offences of complicity and inchoate offences

A matter that continuously troubles students is understanding the distinction between offences of complicity and offences of an inchoate nature.

Inchoate liability is considered in the next chapter (**Chapter 5**) and refers to cases where the liability of an individual is determined by his conduct regardless of whether the offence is actually committed. For example, a defendant may be liable for an attempt where the intended offence is not actually committed. Likewise, a defendant may be liable for assisting or encouraging crime under the Serious Crime Act (SCA) 2007 where he has assisted another to commit an offence but the offence has not been completed.

This can immediately be distinguished from liability as an accessory which is built on the commission of an offence by another – quite simply, there cannot be liability for an offence as a secondary party unless and until a substantive offence has actually been committed.

A number of examples will assist with this distinction.

example

Jack and Jill agree to commit a burglary. Jill supplies Jack with a jemmy (a small crowbar) to use in gaining access to the house. On the night of the intended burglary, Jack gets cold feet and chooses not to burgle the house.

In this case, Jack has committed no offence, ie there is no 'principal offence' or 'offender'. Jill cannot be liable as a secondary party to the burglary, given that no burglary took place. However, Jill may be liable for conspiring to commit a burglary, given the presence of a clear agreement to do so, and Jill may also be charged under s 45 of the SCA 2007 for encouraging or assisting an offence – despite it not actually taking place.

Another example where inchoate liability is relevant, as opposed to liability as an accessory, is the circumstance where an offence is committed by a principal and the defendant encouraged the principal to do so, but there is no *causal* link between the encouragement and the commission of the offence.

example

Jill posts an entry on Facebook encouraging her friends to commit public order offences. Jack, a friend of Jill on Facebook, does not read Jill's post but nevertheless commits an offence that she encouraged.

In this case, there is no causal link between Jill's conduct of encouragement and the commission of the offence by Jack. It cannot be said that Jill encouraged Jack in circumstances where Jack never read the Facebook post. As such, Jill cannot be liable as an accessory. However, Jill does perform the *actus reus* of a SCA 2007 offence by posting on Facebook. This is so regardless of whether Jack receives the communication or acts upon it.

It is therefore essential to bear in mind the distinction between the two categories of offences and understand the possibility that a defendant may still be liable for an inchoate offence in circumstances where he cannot be liable for an offence as an accessory. **Figure 4.4** demonstrates the distinction.

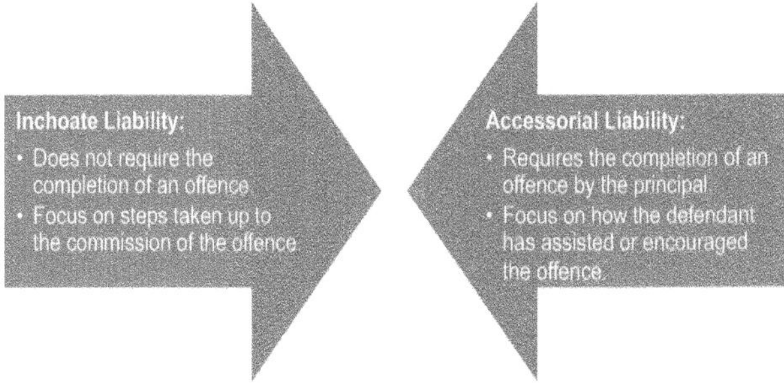

Figure 4.4 Distinguishing inchoate and accessorial liability

4.1.6 *R v Jogee*

In 2016, the law went through a major change with the delivery of the judgment of the Supreme Court in *R v Jogee* [2016] UKSC 8. The effect of this decision was to change the face of accessorial liability. The facts of *Jogee* shall be presented here but the legal principles of *Jogee* and the position pre- and post-*Jogee* will be considered at **4.3**.

case example

Charge:
Murder

Case progression:
Crown Court – Guilty

Court of Appeal – Conviction upheld

Supreme Court – Conviction quashed and retrial ordered

Point of law:
Mens rea in cases of joint enterprise

In *R v Jogee* [2016] UKSC 8, the defendant and his principal went to the house of the victim and began a fight with the victim. The principal went to the kitchen, took a knife and killed the victim with it. The principal was charged with and convicted of murder in the Crown Court. The defendant was also charged with murder in the Crown Court but as an accessory.

The defendant appealed to the Court of Appeal, unsuccessfully alleging that although he had foreseen the possibility of serious harm being caused to the victim, he did not intend such harm to be caused. The defendant further appealed to the Supreme Court which allowed his appeal and quashed his conviction on the basis that a defendant's liability requires him to intend to assist the principal and to intend for the principal to have the *mens rea* for the offence charged. Mere foresight as to the potential for the offence was no longer sufficient. Such was merely evidence that could be used by the jury.

It is important to note that *Jogee* was in fact a combined appeal case with that of *Ruddock*. *Ruddock*, on appeal from the Court of Appeal of Jamaica to the Privy Council, concerned a defendant who had, alongside his principal, robbed the victim's car. The victim had been tied up and the principal killed him. The defendant claimed that he foresaw that the principal might act with the intention to cause the victim serious harm but did not intend him to do so. Like Jogee, Ruddock's conviction was quashed.

Jogee had the effect of abolishing the concept of 'parasitic accessory liability'. This concept is best explained by way of an example:

example

Jack and Jill agree to burgle the home of Andy. Jack burgles the house whilst Jill stands as a lookout. Whilst in the home, however, Jack is confronted by Andy who threatens to telephone the police. Jack attacks Andy, killing him in the process.

In this case, Jack is liable for burglary as a principal offender and Jill is liable as an accessory. Jack is also liable for murder as a principal offender and, under the old rules of 'joint enterprise', Jill would be liable for murder as an accessory where she had foreseen the possibility that Jack might act as he did, ie in killing Andy. Under this principle, mere foresight was considered as being equal to an intention on the part of the secondary party for the principal to commit the second offence. This was clearly an unjust rule and was abolished by the Supreme Court. Now, Jill could only be liable for such an offence where she assisted or encouraged Jack and intended or conditionally intended that the murder of Andy should be committed, if the occasion arose.

4.2 Elements of complicity

Section 8 of the Accessories and Abettors Act (AAA) 1861, as amended by s 65 of the Criminal Law Act 1977, provides:

> Whosoever shall aid, abet, counsel or procure the commission of any indictable offence, whether the same be an offence at common law or by virtue of any Act passed or to be passed, shall be liable to be tried, indicted, and punished as a principal offender.

This provision applies solely to indictable-only offences and either-way offences tried on indictment. In relation to summary-only offences and either-way offences tried summarily, s 44(1) of the Magistrates' Courts Act (MCA) 1980 provides:

> A person who aids, abets, counsels or procures the commission by another person of a summary offence shall be guilty of the like offence and may be tried (whether or not he is charged as a principal) either by a court having jurisdiction to try that other person or by a court having by virtue of his own offence jurisdiction to try him.

The *actus reus* and *mens rea* of complicity are outlined in **Table 4.3**.

Table 4.3 Elements of complicity

AR/MR	Elements of the offence
Actus reus	(i) an offence; (ii) aid, abet, counsel or procure.
Mens rea	(i) knowledge of essential matters; (ii) intention.

We shall consider each element in turn.

Before we do so, it is useful to dissect the wording of s 8 a little further. Section 8 refers to the fact that the secondary party shall be 'liable to be tried, indicted, and punished *as a* principal offender' (emphasis added). Simply, this means that where an individual has acted as an accessory, they shall be charged with the same offence as that of the principal (emphasised by the Supreme Court from the outset of its judgment in *Jogee and Ruddock* [2016] UKSC 8). For example, even though Jill is an accessory to burglary, she will still be charged with the basic offence of burglary, but the particulars of the offence (ie how the offence is alleged to have been committed) will be stated differently in the charge. This is so even in circumstances where the accessory could not be tried individually for the principal offence. For example, in *DPP v K & B* [1997] Crim LR 121 the Court of Appeal found that a woman (or two girls in this case) may be liable as an accessory to rape, even though she is not capable of committing the offence herself (see **Chapter 10** for the definition of rape).

example

Jack and Jill agree to burgle Andy's house whilst he is out for the evening. Jack burgles the house, whilst Jill stands guard at the door looking out for the return of Andy or for sight of trouble, ie the police. Jill also acts as the getaway driver.

In this example, both Jack and Jill will be liable for the offence of burglary contrary to the Theft Act 1968. Jack's particulars will be that he entered a building as a trespasser and stole from within the building; whereas Jill's particulars will be that she aided and abetted Jack in the commission of the offence by acting as a lookout and getaway driver. The offence charged is the same; the difference exists in the manner in which the offence was allegedly committed.

4.2.1 *Actus reus:* (i) an offence

Often overlooked by textbooks, the first requirement needed in order for the secondary party to be liable for an offence is that the principal offender must have succeeded in the commission of the offence (*R v Kenning* [2008] EWCA Crim 1534). Without such an offence, one's attention should be drawn towards inchoate liability (see **Chapter 5**). This was evident in the case of *Thornton v Mitchell* [1940] 1 All ER 339 where the conductor of a bus was charged with aiding and abetting a bus driver to drive carelessly. The principal offender was acquitted of careless driving as the prosecution could not prove that his actions were 'careless'. Given that the prosecution was unable to prove the *actus reus* of the principal offence, the defendant could not be liable as an accessory.

As explained above at **4.1.2**, the focus of the defendant's liability is on whether the principal has committed the relevant *actus reus* of the offence, as opposed to a full completion of the offence. This is evident in the case of *R v Bourne* (1952) 36 Cr App R 125 where the defendant forced his wife, the principal, to commit buggery with a dog on two occasions. The wife in this instance was acting under duress and thus could not be liable for an offence; however, as the *actus reus* of the offence had been completed (ie the buggery), the defendant could still be liable as an accessory.

4.2.2 *Actus reus:* (ii) aid, abet, counsel or procure

There are four ways in which a person can commit the *actus reus* in order to be liable as an accessory (detailed in s 8 of the AAA 1861 (above)):

(a) *aiding* the principal in the commission of the offence;
(b) *abetting* the principal in the commission of the offence;
(c) *counselling* the principal to commit the offence; and
(d) *procuring* the commission of the offence by the principal.

Where it is alleged that the defendant has committed any four of these forms of *actus reus*, it must be proven that the defendant committed them voluntarily. Where the conduct is performed involuntarily, eg the defendant accidentally drops a tool that is then used by the principal in committing the offence, the defendant cannot be said to have 'assisted' him in the commission of the offence.

It is worth noting that a fifth manner of complicity existed in the common law, known as 'joint enterprise' (see below at **4.3**). As a result of the Supreme Court's decision in *R v Jogee*, the notion of joint enterprise as a separate way of proving a case of complicity has been expressly removed. The Court was clear that all cases must be prosecuted under the statutory principles listed above and no reference should be made to the language of 'joint enterprise'.

4.2.2.1 Defining assistance

If possible, the words 'aid, abet, counsel or procure' in the statute should be given their ordinary meaning. According to Lord Widgery CJ in the Court of Appeal in *AG's Reference (No 1 of 1975)* [1975] QB 773, the use of four words suggests that

> the probability is that there is a difference between each of those four words and the other three, because, if there were no such difference, then Parliament would be wasting time in using four words where two or three would do. Thus, in deciding whether that which is assumed to be done under our reference was a criminal offence we approach the section on the footing that each word must be given its ordinary meaning.

From this, it can be said with certainty that a defendant need only commit one of the four 'forms' to be charged as an accessory. This, however, does not mean that the charge must specifically refer to only one of these four methods of liability. Rather, according to the court in *Re Charles Smith* (1858) 3 H & N 227, the phrase 'aid, abet, counsel and procure' may be used to describe an individual's conduct 'as a whole' despite his conduct being properly described as one of those four words. This was more recently affirmed by the Court of Appeal in *R v Bryce* [2004] EWCA Crim 1231 where it was suggested by Potter LJ that:

> So far as the charging of secondary parties is concerned, it is frequently advisable (as was done in this case) to use the 'catch-all' phrase 'aid, abet, counsel or procure' because the shades of difference between them are far from clear.

This would prevent wrongful acquittals arising from any technicality in the words used.

This is evident from the Law Commission's Consultation Paper, 'Assisting and Encouraging Crime' (Law Com No 131, 1993) where it was stated that the distinction between the four forms of conduct 'partakes of a considerable element of over-elaboration and indeed artificiality'. As a result, the Law Commission preferred to refer to the physical elements of encouragement and assistance. This wording was subsequently adopted in the Commission's 2007 Report ('Participating in Crime' (Law Com No 305, 2007)). Further to this, Lord Hughes in *R v Jogee* [2016] UKSC 8 referred to the *actus reus* requirement as simply 'assisting or encouraging'.

4.2.2.2 Aid and abet

Although the terms are dealt with together under this heading, it is necessary to distinguish the two by definition.

Table 4.4 Defining aiding and abetting

Term	Definition
Aid	To 'assist', 'help' or 'support' in the commission of the offence.
Abet	To 'encourage', 'instigate' or 'incite' the commission of the offence.

Aiding may include:

- driving the principal to the scene of the crime (*DPP for Northern Ireland v Maxwell* [1978] 1 WLR 1350);
- providing the principal with information which helps him to commit the principal offence (*R v Grundy* [1977] Crim LR 543);
- providing the principal with a weapon or equipment to help him commit the principal offence (*R v Bainbridge* [1960] 1 QB 129);
- acting as a lookout (*R v Betts & Ridley* (1930) 22 Cr App R 148; *Robinson v The Queen* [2011] UKPC 3).

Abetting, on the other hand, may include:

- shouting words of encouragement during the commission of the offence (*R v Giannetto* [1997] 1 Cr App R 1);
- cheering and applauding another (*Wilcox v Jeffery* [1951] 1 All ER 464);
- engaging in a 'shoot-out' with another person (*R v Gnango* [2011] UKSC 59).

Time of the aiding or abetting

In *Ferguson v Weaving* [1951] 1 KB 814, the Divisional Court stated that the words 'aid and abet' are used to describe the conduct of an individual who is present at the time of the commission of the *actus reus* and takes some part in the commission of the offence.

example

Jack robs a local grocery store. Jill acts as the getaway driver.

In this instance, Jill has 'aided' Jack by acting as a getaway driver – by doing so, Jill has 'assisted' Jack.

However, in later authorities such as *National Coal Board v Gamble* [1959] 1 QB 11, it was ruled that the words 'aiding and abetting' are much wider and include acts and conduct committed by the secondary party prior to the commission of the *actus reus* by the principal. For instance, McCullough J in *Blakely v DPP* [1991] RTR 405 considered that the supplying of equipment and articles to be used in a robbery would more aptly be described as 'aiding and abetting' than 'counselling and procuring'. Further, in *Nedrick-Smith v DPP* [2006] EWHC 3015 (Admin), the Divisional Court, on appeal from the magistrates' court, concluded that the defendant could accurately be described as an accessory as a result of his driving the principal to the scene of the crime. Although his actions were prior to the commission of the offence, the Court held that he could still be liable for his assistance in its commission (ie the offence would not have occurred had the accessory not driven the principal to the scene). The Court of Appeal has now firmly rejected the notion that aiding and abetting can occur only at the time of the crime – assistance before the crime will be just as sufficient to found liability (*R v Stringer* [2011] EWCA Crim 1396).

It is not possible, however, for an individual to be liable as an accessory for actions committed *after* the principal has committed the offence in question. Liability for such conduct is found in ss 4 and 5 of the Criminal Law Act 1967 (see **4.4**). An important distinction, therefore, needs to be made between conduct that takes place *during* the commission of the offence and conduct arising after its commission. In *R v Fury* [2006] EWCA Crim 1258, the Court of Appeal considered the example of an accessory who restrains a police officer who would have prevented the principal from committing the offence. This conduct, although it may appear to be *post* the commission of the offence, in actual fact remains conduct capable of establishing liability as an accessory.

It is therefore essential not to think of aiding and abetting as solely involving conduct at the time of the commission of the principal offence. Presence is not a determining factor but rather acts as evidence for the jury to infer encouragement (*R v Coney* (1882) 8 QBD 534; *Bauer v DPP* [2013] 1 WLR 3617). The present state of law on this point can thus be explained as follows:

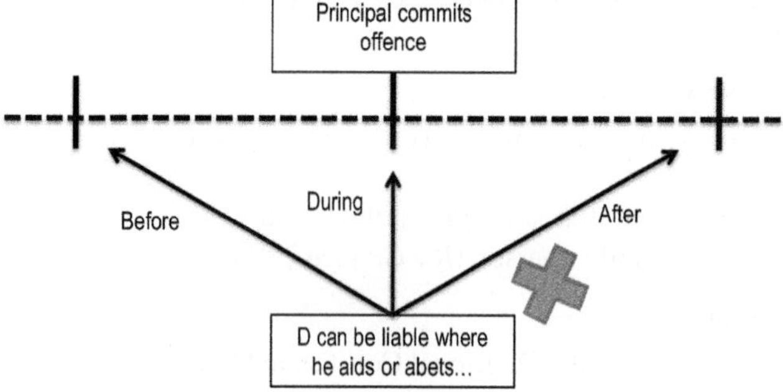

Figure 4.5 Timeline of aiding or abetting

Need for causation

In order for an individual to be liable as an accessory, it must be proven that there is some causal link between his assistance or encouragement and the offence. The extent of this causal link was explained by Toulson LJ (as he then was) in *R v Stringer* [2011] EWCA Crim 1396 in the following terms:

> It is well established that D's conduct need not cause P to commit the offence in the sense that 'but for' D's conduct P would not have committed the offence. … But it is also established … that D's conduct must have *some relevance to the commission* of the principal offence; there must, as it has been said, be *some connecting link*. The moral justification for holding D responsible for the crime is that he has involved himself in the commission of the crime by assistance or encouragement, and that presupposes some form of connection between his conduct and the crime. (emphasis added)

As such, it can be said that the defendant's causation need not be 'full' in the sense that the offence would not have happened had it not been for the actions of the defendant. Rather, the focus on causation here is on the need for 'some causal link'. Although a useful starting point, this statement from *Stringer* is not helpful in understanding what sort of conduct can be said to be sufficient to amount to a 'causal link' between the defendant's actions and the commission of the offence. It is therefore necessary to consider what conduct is capable of satisfying this test, and we can do so by explaining causation as it applies to aiding and abetting respectively.

Table 4.5 Understanding causation for aiding and abetting

Term	Causation
Aiding	This requires that the defendant's conduct has 'contributed' to the commission of the offence in some way, for example where Jack supplies Jill with a knife to kill Andy. In this scenario, where Jill uses the knife to kill Andy, Jack has contributed to the commission of the offence. There is no need, however, for the contribution to be significant or substantial. It is sufficient that the contribution is more than minimal in that it has effected the manner in which the offence is committed (see *R v Bryce* [2004] EWCA Crim 1231 where a significant time delay between the defendant's actions in assisting the principal and the actual commission of the offence was considered irrelevant – the defendant's conduct remained contributory to the end result).
Abetting	This requires that the defendant's encouragement is actually 'communicated' to the principal (*R v Calhaem* [1985] QB 808). Once it is proven that the encouragement has been communicated, it is irrelevant if that encouragement has no, or little, effect on the actions of the principal. For example, where Jill tells Jack to punch Andy and he does so, the issue is whether Jack actually heard Jill or not (ie whether the encouragement came to the attention of the principal). If not, there is no causal link between the encouragement and the commission of the offence (an example adapted from *R v Stringer* [2011] EWCA Crim 1396).

Requirement of participation

Importantly, and in line with the requirement of causation, in order to establish liability for aiding and abetting, it must be proven that the individual 'participated' in the offence. The Supreme Court in *Jogee* dealt with the issue of participation in its judgment and addressed two areas which often cause difficulty for the trial courts. These issues are:

- where the defendant is merely present at the scene of the offence; and
- where there is an association between the defendant and the principal.

The Court noted that guilt by association or guilt by simple presence has no 'proper part' in the common law. It is worth considering each issue in more detail.

Mere presence

Mere presence at the scene of a crime is not sufficient on its own to establish liability. Where an individual simply stands by and allows the offence to be committed, he cannot be considered an aider and abettor (*R v Fretwell* (1862) Le & Ca 161). There must be some 'participation' on the part of the defendant. In the words of Hawkins J in *R v Coney* (1882) 8 QBD 534:

> to constitute an aider and abettor some *active steps* must be taken by word, or action, with the intent to instigate the principal, or principals. (emphasis added)

Such 'active steps' were evident in the case of *R v Kousar* [2009] EWCA Crim 139, where the defendant's husband had stored counterfeit goods in the loft of their matrimonial home. The Court of Appeal concluded that the defendant could not be liable as an accessory for possession of such goods where she took no part (in a broad sense) in the storing of the counterfeit goods. Likewise, in *R v Bland* [1988] Crim LR 41, the Court of Appeal held that the simple matter of sharing a home with an individual who was in unlawful possession of controlled drugs was not sufficient to amount to an encouragement of the offences charged. Commenting on this decision, Horder (*Ashworth's Principles of Criminal Law*, 9th edn (OUP, 2019)) notes that such cases offer 'a vivid conflict between the individuals' rights of privacy in their personal relationships and the social interest in suppressing serious crime'.

It would, however, be naïve to consider that participation must be express or 'active' in form. Rather, a number of cases demonstrate that a mere presence is capable of being sufficient for liability where that presence can be inferred as amounting to an assistance or encouragement to the commission of the offence. For example, in *R v Coney* (1882) 8 QBD 534, the defendant's presence at an illegal prize-fight was held to be capable of 'abetting' the principal offenders. Such presence acted as encouragement to those organising the fights given that an audience meant that the fights were desired (see also *L v CPS* [2013] EWHC 4127 (Admin)). Furthering this point, in *Wilcox v Jeffery* [1951] 1 All ER 464, the defendant's presence at an illegal jazz concert was held to be sufficient to amount to an 'encouragement' for the purpose of secondary liability. Lord Goddard CJ identified the following factors which demonstrated a purpose:

> The appellant attended that concert as a spectator. He paid for his ticket. Mr Hawkins went on the stage and delighted the audience by playing the saxophone. The appellant did not get up and protest in the name of the musicians of England that Mr Hawkins ought not to be here competing with them and taking the bread out of their mouths or the wind out of their instruments. It is not found that he actually applauded, but he was there having paid to go in, and, no doubt, enjoying the performance, and then, lo and behold, out comes his magazine with a most laudatory description, fully illustrated, of this concert.

Importantly, however, the presence at the scene must be voluntary – in that the defendant has actively sought to be at the scene. Where an individual accidentally stumbles upon, or unwittingly finds themselves at, the scene of a crime, there will be no liability (*R v Kousar* [2009] EWCA Crim 139). This is evident from Cave J's statement in *R v Coney* (1882) 8 QBD 534, where his Lordship stated:

> Where presence may be entirely accidental, it is not even evidence of aiding and abetting. Where presence is *prima facie* not accidental it is evidence, but no more than evidence, for the jury.

Further to this, simple presence at the scene amounts only to potential *evidence* of assistance or encouragement – it is not a conclusive statement of 'participation' (*R v Allan and others* [1965] 1 QB 130, per Edmund Davies J). In *Allan*, the defendant's presence at an affray, in circumstances where he was totally passive, was not sufficient to find encouragement for the jury to use in reaching their decision. A secret intention to help out if needed was not sufficient and was compared in kind to guilty thoughts (for which no prosecution can be made out).

As such, all cases must be determined on a case-by-case basis. With this in mind, the prosecution will often rely on the number of spectators present at the scene of the offence. The Supreme Court in *Jogee* noted as follows (per Lord Hughes):

> Numbers often matter. Most people are bolder when supported or fortified by others than they are when alone. And something done by a group is often a good deal more effective than the same thing done by an individual alone. A great

> many crimes, especially of actual or threatened violence, are, whether planned or spontaneous, in fact encouraged or assisted by supporters present with the principal lending force to what he does.

The extent to which presence alone is capable of satisfying the requirement of abetting was taken to a logical extreme in the case of *R v Clarkson & Carroll* [1971] 3 All ER 344.

case example

Charge:
Rape (SOA 1967, s 1)

Case progression:
Court-Martial – Guilty

Courts-Martial Appeal Court– Conviction quashed

Point of law:
Mere presence amounts to abetting

In *R v Clarkson & Carroll* [1971] 3 All ER 344, the defendants, two soldiers, had entered a room in their barracks upon hearing screams, whereby they discovered a woman being raped by fellow soldiers (the principal offenders). The defendants chose not to intervene, nor to leave – the pair merely remained present during the offence. The pair were charged with and convicted of rape as accomplices in the Court-Martial.

The pair appealed to the Courts-Martial Appeal Court, arguing that their presence at the scene was insufficient to amount to encouragement for the purposes of 'abetting' the principals. The Courts-Martial Appeal Court disagreed, finding that voluntary presence at such a scene was capable of amounting to encouragement for the purpose of the *actus reus* of complicity. However, the Appeal Court allowed the appeal on the basis that there was no evidence proving that the defendants had satisfied the requisite *mens rea* of the offence, ie there was no evidence to prove that they intended their presence at the scene to encourage the principals to commit the offence.

This case demonstrates that it is possible, in some circumstances, for the defendant's presence at the scene to amount to evidence that he encouraged the offence. This is often addressed by the prosecution in explaining that the defendant did not:

- intervene to prevent the conduct from continuing;
- offer opposition to it, especially so where he had the power to do so; or at least
- express dissent to the conduct of the principal.

This statement can be reinforced by the case of *Robinson v The Queen* [2011] UKPC 3, in which Sir Anthony Hughes (reading the judgment of the Privy Council) stated:

> If D2's presence can properly be held to amount to communicating to D1 (whether expressly or by implication) that he is there to help in any way he can if the opportunity or need arises, that is perfectly capable of amounting to aiding … It is, however, important to make clear to juries that mere approval of (ie 'assent' to, or 'concurrence' in) the offence by a bystander who gives no assistance, does not without more amount to aiding

Another example may assist your understanding even further.

example

Jack and Jill are members of a gang called the 'Nursery Club'. The gang has a bitter rivalry with another gang from a different part of the country. Both gangs arrange to meet in an alleyway for a fight between the two gang leaders. Jack and Jill are present at the scene of the fight.

In this case, Jack and Jill's presence is capable of amounting to clear evidence that they are encouraging the conduct of the principal offenders (ie the gang leaders). It would not be difficult in this case to establish intention on the part of Jack and Jill.

Mere presence, therefore, is capable of amounting to sufficient evidence that the defendant 'participated' in the offence through his encouragement. Presence, however, is *no more* than mere evidence, and whether the defendant has encouraged the principal must still be determined on the facts. Further, note that simple presence alone is not enough – there must still be an intention on the part of the defendant to encourage the principal. Megaw LJ in *Clarkson* referred to this as a requirement of 'wilful' encouragement. Without this, as was the case in *Clarkson*, the defendant cannot be liable for complicity (see **4.2.4** for a discussion of the *mens rea*). See also *R v Daley* [2015] EWCA Crim 1515. In *R v N* [2019] EWCA Crim 2280, the Court of Appeal emphasised the need to direct the jury (per Green LJ)

> (i) that mere presence was not enough; (ii) that mere presence together with knowledge that others were planning an attack was also not enough; but (iii), that presence plus knowledge of what others intended to do coupled to an intention to assist in an appropriate way in the attacks to be perpetrated by those others *could* suffice to found joint enterprise. (original emphasis)

Given the potentially complex nature of cases involving 'mere presence', the Crown Court Compendium emphasises the utility of using written directions when directing the jury. In *R v N*, the Court of Appeal noted that a conviction would not be unsafe simply because of a lack of written directions (this would only occur where the oral direction was wrong or materially confusing); however, it did note the importance of ensuring such directions occur.

in practice

A discussion of an individual's presence amounting to sufficient encouragement for the offence is only required where there is no evidence present which demonstrates an active participation on the part of the defendant. Where such evidence exists, for example if, in *Clarkson*, the defendants had stood watch or locked the door, that active participation would be stronger evidence than their mere presence at the scene.

Mere association

As stated above, guilt by mere association has no part to play in the criminal justice system. This was emphasised by the Supreme Court in *Jogee*; however, it is possible in some cases for such association to amount to strong evidence that the defendant participated in the crime alleged. Ordinarily, however, such association is only strong evidence when coupled with a presence at the scene of the crime.

An example will assist here.

example

Jack and Jill are 'friends' on social media. The pair agree to meet at a local club but Jack does not explain why. Before the pair meet, Jill notices a number of posts on Jack's site stating that 'Andy's gonna get it tonight' and 'Time's up, Andy'. Once at the club, Jack begins to attack Andy and stabs him with a knife. Jill merely stands by in shock and watches it happen.

In this instance, Jill's awareness of Jack's communications and posts on social media may show that Jill is not merely a disinterested bystander but that her presence is intended to assist or encourage Jack.

Commission by omission

It is possible for a defendant to aid or abet by omission. This may seem strange given our discussion above that mere presence at the scene without active participation is normally not enough. However, liability is capable of being founded in certain omission-type cases.

Cases where omission-based liability can be found were identified in **Chapter 2**. Liability as an accessory is thus possible in circumstances where:

- there was a recognised duty on the defendant to act; or
- the defendant had the right or power to control the actions of another and chose not to.

In relation to the former, a defendant may be liable in cases where he is obligated by contract to do an act or has assumed responsibility over another and has failed to fulfil that duty. In *R v Russell and Russell* (1987) 85 Cr App R 388, one parent gave their child a fatal overdose of methadone, whilst the other parent merely stood by and watched. Similarly, in *R v Russell* [1933] VLR 59 (an Australian case) the defendant was liable as an accessory to murder when he stood back and watched his wife drown their three children in a public pool, before then drowning herself. The Australian courts found that the defendant did not owe a duty of care to his wife but did owe such a duty to his children, and in finding the defendant liable as an accessory (by abetting the wife), Cussen ACJ stated:

> I am of the opinion (1) that if a person present at the commission of a crime in the opinion of the jury on sufficient evidence shows his assent to such a commission, he is guilty as a principal, and (2) that assent may in some cases be properly found by the jury to be shown by the absence of dissent, or in the absence of what may be called an effective dissent.

In relation to the latter, the inactivity of a defendant who has either the right or the power to control the actions of the principal is capable of amounting to positive encouragement to perform an illegal act. In *Tuck v Robson* [1970] 1 All ER 1171, the defendant, a licensee of a public house, allowed a number of his customers to continue drinking outside licensed hours. The principal offence was committed by the customers in drinking alcohol outside the permitted licensed hours, and the defendant was liable for aiding and abetting such conduct by standing by and allowing them to do so. The same outcome was reached in the earlier cases of *Du Cros v Lambourne* [1907] KB 40 and *Rubie v Faulkner* [1940] 1 KB 571. In the former, the defendant allowed another person to drive his Mercedes motor car at a dangerous speed.

Du Cros v Lambourne was approved by the Court of Appeal in *R v Webster* [2006] EWCA Crim 415, where Moses LJ held that

> a defendant might be convicted of aiding and abetting dangerous driving if the driver drives dangerously in the owner's presence and *with the owner's consent and approval.* (emphasis added)

In both *Du Cros* and *Webster*, it was emphasised, however, that it must be proven that the defendant knew of those features of the principal's conduct (in this case their driving) which rendered it dangerous and failed to take action within a reasonable time. In *Webster*, Moses LJ concluded:

> [T]he prosecution had to prove that [the defendant] knew that [the principal] was, by virtue of the speed the vehicle was travelling, driving dangerously at a time when there was an opportunity to intervene. It was [the defendant's] failure

> to take that opportunity and, exercise his right as owner of the vehicle, which would lead to the inference that he was associating himself with the dangerous driving.

The Court of Appeal in *R v Martin* [2010] EWCA Crim 1450 took the opportunity to state and clarify the present situation of the law. The defendant, a driving instructor, had failed to instruct the principal, a learner driver, to slow down or be cautious as to his driving in circumstances where the principal had lost control of the car. As a result, the principal died and a passenger in the car was also killed. Due to a misdirection at trial, the defendant's conviction was quashed, but the Court did go on to explain what would have been required for the defendant to be convicted. Specifically, Hooper LJ explained that a jury

> must be sure that P committed the offence of causing death by dangerous driving and–
>
> (i) D knew that the driver, P, was driving in a manner which D knew fell far below the standard of a competent and careful driver;
> (ii) D, knowing that he had an opportunity to stop P from driving in that manner, deliberately did not take that opportunity;
> (iii) by not taking that opportunity D intended to assist or encourage P to drive in this manner and D did in fact by his presence and failure to intervene encourage P to drive dangerously;
> (iv) D foresaw that someone might be killed by P driving in this manner.

The draft Criminal Code (1989) offered the following offence in clause 27(3) to cover this circumstance. Clause 27(3) provides:

> Assistance or encouragement includes assistance or encouragement arising from a failure by a person to take reasonable steps to exercise any authority or to discharge any duty he has to control the relevant acts of the principal in order to prevent the commission of the offence.

Williams ('Letting Offences Happen' [1990] Crim LR 780) argued that such a clause was astoundingly wide, contending that under this provision, 'everyone who lets an offence happen shall be liable as though he had committed it himself'.

4.2.2.3 Counsel

Counselling is similar to abetting in the sense that it amounts to an encouragement to commit the offence in question. However, 'counsel' is understood to be a narrower concept and should be given its 'ordinary meaning, which is ... "advise", "solicit", or something of that sort' (*R v Calhaem* [1985] QB 808, per Parker LJ).

In *R v Giannetto* [1997] 1 Cr App R 1, the Court of Appeal cited an example of counselling given by the trial judge to the jury:

> Supposing somebody came up to [the defendant] and said, 'I am going to kill your wife', if he played any part, either in encouragement, as little as patting him on the back, nodding, saying, 'Oh goody', that would be sufficient to involve him in the murder, to make him guilty, because he is encouraging the murder.

Need for causation

As above with aiding and abetting, in order to be liable for counselling, there must be a causal link between the counselling and the commission of the offence (*R v Bryce* [2004] EWCA Crim 1231, per Potter LJ).

The causal link need not be substantial but, rather, is satisfied where the counselling contributed *in some part* to the commission of the offence. The principle was made clear by the Court of Appeal in *R v Calhaem* [1985] QB 808 where it concluded that any counselling, so long as it is not *de minimis*, will be sufficient to found liability. In *Calhaem*, the defendant counselled a private detective to kill a woman who had been sleeping with the defendant's solicitor. The private detective killed the victim and was convicted of her murder. Parker LJ explained that in order to find liability in such case

> there must clearly be, first, contact between the parties and, second, a connection between the counselling and the [offence committed]. Equally, the act done must ... be done within the scope of the authority or advice and not, for example, accidentally.

For similar facts, see *R v Luffman* [2008] EWCA Crim 1379. The Court of Appeal confirmed this in the earlier authority of *AG v Able* [1984] QB 795 where it held that it is irrelevant whether the principal would have the committed the offence regardless of the advice or encouragement of the accessory, so long as that advice or encouragement comes to the attention of the principal. The Supreme Court in *R v Jogee and Ruddock* [2016] UKSC 8 confirmed that the encouragement need not have any 'positive effect' on the principal's conduct.

4.2.2.4 Procure

According to Lord Widgery CJ in the Court of Appeal in *AG's Reference (No 1 of 1975)* [1975] QB 773:

> To procure means to produce by endeavour. You procure a thing by setting out to see that it happens and taking the appropriate steps to produce that happening. We think that there are plenty of instances in which a person may be said to procure the commission of a crime by another even though there is no sort of conspiracy between the two, even though there is no attempt at agreement or discussion as to the form which the offence should take ...

Essentially, this means that a defendant is liable for procurement of an offence where his conduct has caused the offence to come about. There is no requirement that the defendant assisted, or even encouraged, the commission of the offence so long as it can be proven that the offence would not have come to fruition had it not been for the actions of the defendant. It is for these reasons that, unlike abetting and counselling, procuring is not capable of commission by omission.

This principle thus applies in circumstances where the principal is unaware of the defendant's conduct in procuring an offence. The best example of this can be seen in *AG's Reference (No 1 of 1975)* [1975] QB 773, which is the leading authority in this area.

case example

Charge:
Driving with excess alcohol (RTA 1972, s 6(1))

Case progression:
Crown Court – Not guilty

Court of Appeal (by way of AG's Reference) – D should have been liable

Point of law:
Principal not aware of D's procurement

In *AG's Reference (No 1 of 1975)* [1975] QB 773, the defendant, without the principal's knowledge, laced the principal's soft drink with alcohol. The principal later drove home, which the defendant knew that he would, and was found to be driving with excess alcohol. The principal was charged with driving with excess alcohol contrary to s 6 of the Road Traffic Act (RTA) 1972 (now found in s 5 of the RTA 1988). The defendant was charged as an accessory to the offence.

The defendant was found not guilty of an offence as an accessory on the basis that the principal was unaware of the defendant's conduct, there was no shared intention between the parties, and the defendant was not present in the car at the time.

The prosecution appealed (by way of an AG's Reference), and the Court of Appeal found that the defendant ought to have been liable for an offence, despite the lack of knowledge on the part of the principal. The defendant had procured the offence and it was not necessary for the parties to share an intention. The Court found that the defendant ought to have been liable for such procurement.

In this case, the Court made it clear that it is irrelevant that the principal was unaware of the defendant's conduct, and it was equally irrelevant that the defendant did not aid or abet in the commission of the offence (ie he did not assist or encourage the principal to drive whilst over the limit). The defendant had procured the offence by placing the principal offender in a position whereby he would not have committed the offence but for the defendant's conduct.

Need for causation

As above, there must be a causal link between the procurement and the offence. On that basis, where the defendant orders or advises the principal to commit a specific offence, such as murder, and the principal commits a different crime, for example arson, the counsellor would not be liable for this offence. Similarly, where the defendant procures an offence but such an offence does not take place, the defendant cannot be liable for procurement.

Troubled cases of procurement

It is necessary at this stage, however, to identify a number of troubling scenarios where the courts have found the defendant liable for the procurement of an offence where an offence has not technically taken place. A starting point is the case of *R v Cogan and Leak* [1976] QB 217.

case example

Charge:
Rape (SOA 1967, s 1)

Case progression:
Crown Court – Guilty

Court of Appeal – Conviction upheld

Point of law:
Procurement without a criminal offence

In *R v Cogan and Leak* [1976] QB 217, the defendant (Leak) had directed his wife, the victim, to have sexual intercourse with his friend (Cogan), the principal. The victim did not consent but had sexual intercourse with Cogan anyway out of fear of her husband. The principal was unaware that the victim was not consenting but was charged with and convicted of rape in the Crown Court. The defendant was equally charged and convicted as an accessory to rape.

The defendant and principal appealed to the Court of Appeal. The Court allowed the appeal of the principal on the basis of a misdirection to the jury as to the necessary *mens rea* required for the offence. The Court, however, upheld the conviction of the defendant on the basis that his actions had procured the offence to take place. Despite the innocence of the principal, the defendant remained liable for his procurement.

Cogan and Leak is a difficult case to comprehend at first as it appears to contradict the statement made above that where no crime is committed, the defendant cannot be liable, logically speaking, for procurement. However, as discussed above, the law recognises the doctrine of innocent agency (ie where the principal commits the relevant *actus reus* of the offence but lacks the necessary *mens rea*). In such a case, the defendant will remain liable for an offence given that he has procured the *actus reus* of the offence – which, according to the Court, was sufficient. Lawton LJ was of the opinion that the act of sexual intercourse with the victim was the necessary *actus reus* as performed by the principal; however, that act 'had been procured by [the defendant] who had the appropriate *mens rea*'. In effect, so long as the defendant bears the necessary *mens rea* for the offence committed and has procured through his own actions the *actus reus* of the offence by the innocent agent, the defendant will be liable for an offence. The same reasoning was applied in the case of *R v Millward* [1994] Crim LR 527 (considered above). This principal can also be used in circumstances where the principal commits the *actus reus* and *mens rea* of the offence but has a defence to liability. In this instance, the principal will not be guilty but the defendant will (*R v Bourne* (1952) 36 Cr App R 125 – where the defendant forced his wife to commit buggery with a dog).

4.2.2.5 Summarising the *actus reus*

The four methods of satisfying the *actus reus* of secondary liability can be now summarised as follows:

Table 4.6 Summarising the actus reus *of accessorial liability*

Term	Definition	Example
Aid	To help or assist the principal with the commission of the principal offence	Acting as a lookout; supplying information; acting as a driver
Abet	To encourage the principal to commit the principal offence	Shouting encouragement; mere presence at the scene in certain circumstances
Counsel	To advise, solicit or instigate the commission of the principal offence	Hiring a hitman; providing instruction; planning the crime

Term	Definition	Example
Procure	To produce by endeavour, or to cause/contribute towards the existence of the principal offence	Forcing another person to act in a certain way; directing a person to conduct themselves in some way

4.2.3 *Mens rea:* (i) knowledge of essential matters

To date, the most authoritative statement of law on the *mens rea* of complicity is that in *R v Jogee and Ruddock* [2016] UKSC 8, where their Lordships stressed (per Lord Hughes):

> [T]he mental element in assisting or encouraging is an *intention* to assist or encourage the commission of the crime and this requires *knowledge* of any existing facts necessary for it to be criminal.
>
> If the crime requires a particular intent, D2 must intend to assist or encourage D1 to act with such intent. (emphasis added)

As such, the *mens rea* of complicity can be effectively stated as:

- having knowledge of facts; and
- intention to assist, encourage or procure.

We shall consider both knowledge (below) and intention (**4.2.4**) in turn.

4.2.3.1 Defining 'essential matters'

Prior to *Jogee*, the seminal authority on the *mens rea* for an accessory was that of Lord Goddard CJ in *Johnson v Youden* [1950] 1 KB 544, where his Lordship stated:

> Before a person can be convicted of aiding and abetting the commission of an offence he must at least know the *essential matters* which constitute that offence. He need not actually know that an offence has been committed, because he may not know that the facts constitute an offence ... If a person knows all the facts and is assisting another person to do certain things, and it turns out that the doing of those things constitutes an offence, the person who is assisting is guilty of aiding and abetting that offence. (emphasis added)

Reference to the 'essential matters' means that the defendant knew:

- the circumstances which form the *actus reus* of the principal offence that might be committed; and
- that the principal would act with the requisite *mens rea* for the principal offence.

In essence, the defendant must know that the principal will commit both the *actus reus* and *mens rea* of the principal offence. Knowledge, in this regard, is of the respective facts, as opposed to knowledge of the law (*O'Neil v Gale* [2013] EWCA Civ 1554). Importantly, the defendant need not actually know that the offence has been committed; he must simply know that the principal will act with the relevant *mens rea*.

4.2.3.2 Extent of the knowledge

The defendant's knowledge extends to a:

- belief;
- contemplation; or
- foresight,

that the essential elements might be committed.

Given the difficulty in proving the defendant's knowledge as to future events or matters, the courts have interpreted the requirement to foresee the likelihood of the essential matters. 'Foresee' in this respect means to contemplate or turn a blind eye to the type of act that might be committed by the principal offender and the circumstances that constitute the *actus reus* of the offence. This was made clear by Potter LJ in the Court of Appeal in *R v Bryce* [2004] EWCA Crim 1231, where his Lordship stated that the secondary party must foresee a 'real risk' or contemplate a 'real possibility' that the principal might commit an offence.

This statement was explained further by the Court of Appeal in *R v Webster* [2006] EWCA Crim 415, where Moses LJ held that the prosecution must prove that the defendant 'foresaw the likelihood' that the principal offender would perform the *actus reus* of the offence, in order for the secondary party to be liable. This is, according to the court, a subjective test. Specifically, Moses LJ stated:

> It is the Defendant's foresight that the principal was likely to commit the offence which must be proved and not merely that he *ought to have* foreseen that the principal was likely to commit the offence. (emphasis added)

4.2.3.3 Specificity of knowledge

In *R v Bainbridge* [1960] 1 QB 129, the defendant had supplied oxygen cutting equipment which was used to break into the Midland Band in Stoke Newington, Hackney. The defendant accepted that he held a suspicion that the principal offenders wanted the equipment to do 'something illegal' but did not accept that his suspicion extended to a belief that they would use the equipment to break into a bank. He believed it was to be used to break up stolen materials. The trial judge directed the jury that the prosecution bore the burden of proving that the defendant 'knew that a [crime] of that kind was intended'. The defendant was convicted as an accessory and appealed to the Court of Criminal Appeal. Lord Parker CJ, in upholding the conviction, found that the trial judge had provided a perfectly valid direction. Specifically, Lord Parker CJ commented that 'there must be not merely suspicion but knowledge that a crime *of the type in question* was intended' (emphasis added).

Lord Parker CJ would go on to explain that the defendant's knowledge must be more than simply knowing that the equipment was to be used for 'some illegal venture', such as the breaking up of stolen materials, but need not extend to knowing that a *particular* crime would be committed. It is also not necessary for the defendant to know when and where the crime would be committed. As a result, therefore, it was enough for the defendant in *Bainbridge* to know that the principals intended to use the equipment to commit a crime *of that type*.

Table 4.7 Understanding the extent of knowledge in Bainbridge

Extent of knowledge	Explanation
Too little ...	Knowledge of the existence of 'some illegal venture'.
More than is necessary...	Knowledge of a particular crime or knowledge of the particular victim, time or place.
Just right ...	Knowledge of the type of crime that may be committed.

The difficulty we face at this stage is the uncertainty as to the meaning of crimes of 'that type'. Does the phrase mean specific crimes, such as burglary, theft or murder? Does the phrase mean descriptions of crimes, such as dishonesty crimes or violent crimes? This uncertainty was resolved in part by the House of Lords in *DPP for Northern Ireland v Maxwell* [1978] 1 WLR 1350.

case example

Charge:
Planting a bomb and possession of a bomb (ESA 1883, s 3(a) and (b))

Case progression:
Crown Court – Guilty

Court of Appeal – Conviction upheld

House of Lords – Conviction upheld

Point of law:
Meaning of 'knowledge'

In *DPP for Northern Ireland v Maxwell* [1978] 1 WLR 1350, the defendant, a member of the UVF (a terrorist organisation in Northern Ireland), drove a car to a pub; a bomb was thrown into the pub by the principals. The bomb caused no injury or damage and the defendant was charged with and convicted of aiding and abetting the unlawful and malicious doing of an act with intent to cause an explosion likely to endanger life, contrary to s 3(a) of the Explosive Substances Act (ESA) 1883, and possession of a bomb under s 3(b).

The defendant appealed to the Court of Appeal on the basis that he did not know the nature of the job that he was carrying out, nor did he know about the presence of the bomb. The Court of Appeal found against the defendant, who subsequently appealed to the House of Lords, albeit unsuccessfully. In the House of Lords, Lord Fraser said that the 'possible extent of [the defendant's] guilt was limited to the *range of crimes* any of which he must have known were to be expected that night' (emphasis added).

Viscount Dilhorne would apply this by stating:

> [The defendant] knew that a 'military' operation was to take place. With his knowledge of the UVF's activities, he must have known that it would involve the use of a bomb or shooting or the use of incendiary devices. Knowing that he led them there and so he aided and abetted whichever of these forms the attack took. It took the form of placing a bomb.

In essence, the House of Lords concluded that the defendant had enough information in front of him that he could foresee an attack on the pub and that a bombing was one of the possible offences that could be committed. The simple fact that the defendant did not know the precise details of the offence, as in *Bainbridge*, was not fatal to a conviction. Lord Scarman would extend the principle in *Bainbridge* and explain:

> [A] man will not be convicted of aiding and abetting any offence his principal may commit, but only one which is within his contemplation. He may have in contemplation only one offence, or several: and the several which he contemplates he may see as alternatives. An accessory who leaves it to his principal to choose is liable, provided always the choice is made from the *range of offences from which the accessory contemplates the choice will be made*. Although the court's formulation of the principle goes further than the earlier cases, it is a sound development of the law and in no way inconsistent with them. I accept it as good judge-made law in a field where there is no statute to offer guidance. (emphasis added)

The extent of knowledge was confirmed by the Court of Appeal in *R v Bryce* [2004] EWCA Crim 1231 where Potter LJ concluded that 'it is thus sufficient for the accused to have knowledge of the type of crime in contemplation'. The extent of knowledge in that case required the defendant to know 'the purpose to which the equipment is to be put or realises that there is a real possibility that it will be used for that purpose and the equipment is actually used for that purpose'.

Relevance of a weapon?

An important issue to raise at this point is the question of how relevant it is that the defendant assists the principal with the knowledge that the principal has a weapon.

Prior to *Jogee*, a detailed set of rules applied in relation to this question. Now, following *Jogee*, the relevance is simply one of evidence. Lord Toulson in *Jogee* explained:

> Knowledge or ignorance that weapons generally, or a particular weapon, is carried by [the principal] will be evidence going to what the intention of [the defendant] was, and may be irresistible evidence one way or the other, but it is evidence and no more.

This was the view adopted by Williams (*Criminal Law: The General Part*, 2nd edn (Stevenson & Sons, 1961)), where he stated:

> The knowledge on the part of one criminal that his companion is carrying a weapon is strong evidence of a common intent to use violence, but is not conclusive.

This issue came to light in the case of *R v Brown* [2017] EWCA Crim 1870. In this case, the principal and defendant entered a shop where the victim (a member of a rival gang) was. The victim chased the pair out of the shop with a bottle, upon which the principal revealed a knife and stabbed him. The pair were charged with and convicted of unlawful wounding. On appeal, the defendant argued that the trial judge should have directed the jury that the defendant's knowledge of the weapon was essential to determining whether he should be liable for an offence as an accessory. The Court of Appeal disagreed. Simler J explained:

> Post-*Jogee*, knowledge of a weapon used by a principal to inflict harm is not determinative of secondary party liability. It is evidence that may inform a jury's decision as to whether a defendant who did not himself wield a weapon intended to cause harm to the victim; and if he did, the level of harm ... Thus, the judge on the facts of this case was not obliged to direct the jury that they could only convict a secondary party of either a section 18 offence or a section 20 offence if they were sure that the secondary party knew that the principal had a knife.

See recently *R v Tas* [2018] EWCA Crim 2603 and *R v Harper* [2019] EWCA Crim 343 on directing a jury regarding the presence of a weapon.

4.2.3.4 Understanding the requirement of knowledge

Following *Bainbridge* and *Maxwell*, the following can be said to be the extent of the knowledge requirement:

- The defendant need not know that the crime has been committed.
- The defendant must know more than simply that an illegal venture will be committed.
- The defendant need not know of the particular type of crime that is to be committed or of the particulars of the offence (ie time, place and victim).
- The defendant must know of the type of crime committed or the range of crimes that may be committed.

4.2.4 *Mens rea:* (ii) intention

In *National Coal Board v Gamble* [1959] 1 QB 11, Devlin J stated the necessary *mens rea* for an individual to be liable as an accessory. His Lordship provided:

> [A]iding and abetting is a crime that requires proof of *mens rea*, that is to say, of intention to aid as well as of knowledge of the circumstances, and that proof of the intent involves proof of a positive act of assistance voluntarily done.

The meaning, and extent, of intention in relation to accessories has, however, been the subject of considerable controversy and has developed significantly in recent years. The leading authority in this area is now that of the Supreme Court in *R v Jogee and Ruddock* [2016] UKSC 8 (for the facts, see **4.1.6**).

According to Lord Hughes:

> If the crime requires a particular intent, [the defendant] must intend to assist or encourage [the principal] to act with such intent. [The defendant's] intention to assist [the principal] to commit the offence, and to act with whatever mental element is required of [the principal], will often be co-extensive on the facts with an intention by [the defendant] that that offence be committed. Where that is so, it will be seen that many of the cases discuss [the defendant's] mental element simply in terms of intention to commit the offence. But there can be cases where [the defendant] gives intentional assistance or encouragement to [the principal] to commit an offence and to act with the mental element required of him, but without [the defendant] having a positive intent that the particular offence will be committed. That may be so, for example, where at the time that encouragement is given it remains uncertain what [the principal] might do; an arms supplier might be such a case.

Lord Hughes continued:

> With regard to the mental element, the intention to assist or encourage will often be specific to a particular offence. But in other cases it may not be. [The defendant] may intentionally assist or encourage [the principal] to commit one of a range of offences, such as an act of terrorism which might take various forms. If so, [the defendant] does not have to 'know' (or intend) in advance the specific form which the crime will take. It is enough that the offence committed by [the principal] is within the range of possible offences which [the defendant] intentionally assisted or encouraged him to commit ...

As such, it can be said that the defendant must possess the intention:

- to assist or encourage the principal in committing the principal offence; and
- that the principal acts with the necessary *mens rea* of the offence charged.

Child and Ormerod (*Smith, Hogan, & Ormerod's Essentials of Criminal Law*, 3rd edn (OUP, 2019)) have usefully explained this distinction as requiring the defendant to possess the intention as to his own conduct and to the principal offence.

We shall consider each in turn.

4.2.4.1 Intention to assist or encourage

Intention is a legal construct defined as including desire, belief, and foresight of consequences (see **Chapter 3**). In the context of accessorial liability, the secondary party must provide *deliberate* assistance or encouragement (ie he must intend to aid, abet, counsel or procure). In the majority of cases, where the defendant intends to assist or encourage the principal, he will also intend for the offence to be committed. However, it is not necessary for the defendant to intend for the offence to be committed; the defendant may be entirely indifferent to the end result.

example

Jill supplies Jack with a gun which she knows is to be used to kill Andy. Jill claims, however, that she is utterly indifferent as to whether Jack actually commits the offence or not.

In this instance, Jill will still be liable as an accessory in circumstances where Jack does commit the relevant offence as a result of her clear intention to aid and abet by supplying the gun.

Devlin J in *National Coal Board v Gamble* [1959] 1 QB 11 would justify this situation as follows:

> [A]n indifference to the result of the crime does not of itself negative abetting. If one man deliberately sells to another a gun to be used for murdering a third, he may be indifferent about whether the third man lives or dies and interested only in the cash profit to be made out of the sale, but he can still be an aider and abetter, To hold otherwise would be to negative the rule that *mens rea* is a matter of intent only and does not depend on desire or motive.

This area of intention is relatively simple; however, two concepts have arisen in recent times that warrant attention, namely:

- the extent to which foresight is a sufficient *mens rea*; and
- the circumstances where the defendant's intention is conditional.

Inferring intention from foresight

The Supreme Court in *Jogee* confirmed that: 'Foresight may be good evidence of intention but it is not synonymous with it.' In that regard, foresight can be used as evidence to infer intention.

example

Jill sells a gun to Jack knowing that Jack wishes to use it to kill Andy.

In this instance, Jill may not care whether Jack kills Andy or not, but the jury would be able to infer an intention from Jill's actions as going towards proving she had the intention to assist or encourage Jack.

As we know from the case of *R v Woollin* [1999] AC 82 (see **Chapter 3**), a jury is entitled to find intention in cases where the end result was a virtual certainty of the defendant's actions and the defendant appreciated this certainty (known as 'oblique intent'). In the context of accessorial liability, however, the Supreme Court did not provide any guidance as to how a jury may be directed regarding the inference of foresight. Ormerod and Laird ('*Jogee*: Not the End of a Legal Saga But the Start of One?' [2016] Crim LR 539) note as follows:

> [T]here is no explicit statement as to what threshold of foresight the defendant must possess before the jury will be entitled to infer the requisite intent—will the defendant's foresight of even the slightest possibility of the principal intentionally acting in the proscribed way be sufficient for a jury to be entitled to infer that he possessed the requisite intention? Alternatively, does there have to be a high level of foresight before the jury will be entitled to infer from this foresight that he

> possessed the requisite intention? It is the failure to specify what intention means in this context that could lead to difficulty.

The pair go on to state:

> It is unclear whether it is safe to conclude from this omission that the Supreme Court did not intend for some version of the *Woollin* direction to apply. The House of Lords in *Woollin* did expressly state that its decision applied only to murder and did not state whether it extended to accessorial liability. Indeed, Lord Steyn prefaced his judgment in *Woollin* by remarking that intention does not necessarily have the same meaning in every context of the criminal law. To the extent that the restatement of the law in *Jogee* applies in non-murder cases, a different formulation may therefore be applicable anyway. There will, we suggest, be considerable reluctance to apply the virtual certainty test, because if applied rigorously that test will mean that it will be difficult to secure convictions for murder for any participant.

The likely outcome is that foresight is capable of amounting to evidence of intention, which the jury may use in reaching their decision. Foresight, however, may only ever amount to evidence and is unlikely to have any weighty effect unless it could be said that the defendant was sure that the principal was going on to commit the offence.

Conditional intent

A notion of considerable importance at this stage is the Supreme Court's statement regarding the extent of conditional intention and its presence in accessorial liability. In *Jogee*, Lord Hughes explained:

> In cases of secondary liability arising out of a prior joint criminal venture, it will also often be necessary to draw the jury's attention to the fact that the intention to assist, and indeed the intention that the crime should be committed, may be conditional. The bank robbers who attack the bank when one or more of them is armed no doubt hope that it will not be necessary to use the guns, but it may be a perfectly proper inference that all were intending that if they met resistance the weapons should be used with the intent to do grievous bodily harm at least. The group of young men which faces down a rival group may hope that the rivals will slink quietly away, but it may well be a perfectly proper inference that all were intending that if resistance were to be met, grievous bodily harm at least should be done.

Conditional intent in this respect simply means that the defendant intends the principal to act in a certain way, with the relevant *mens rea*, should the circumstances require it. The jury are entitled to use conditional intent to find that the defendant had the relevant intention to assist the principal. An additional example to those given by Lord Hughes may be as follows:

example

Jack and Jill intend to burgle a house. Jack is to burgle the house whilst Jill acts as a lookout. Jill hands Jack a knife, telling him, 'This is for you, in case you run into trouble.' Whilst in the house, Jack is confronted by Andy, the householder. Jack stabs Andy, causing him serious bodily harm.

In this instance, Jill has intended for Jack to commit burglary with the necessary *mens rea*. In this respect, Jill is liable as an accessory for burglary. Jill may also be liable for an offence of wounding or causing grievous bodily harm with intent as an accessory given her conditional intent that Jack is to use the knife if he needs to.

This is a question of fact for the jury to consider whether they believe that conditional intent is present and is enough to say that the defendant intended to assist the principal (*R v Anwar* [2016] EWCA Crim 551).

Child and Ormerod (*Smith, Hogan, & Ormerod's Essentials of Criminal Law*, 3rd edn (OUP, 2019)) are critical of the use of the term 'conditional intent'. Specifically, the pair contend that

> the court's approach here seems faulty. Conditional intention is a concept employed to understand intention as to future conduct; a decision to act in the future if certain conditions obtain. ... Yet here, we are discussing intention to assist or encourage P through completed conduct. Thus, rather than describing D's intention as conditional, which may lead to confusion, it is more accurate to describe D's intention as simply specific in its content: to encourage P to perform specified conduct in certain circumstances only.

4.2.4.2 Intention that the principal has the requisite *mens rea*

This element of accessorial liability is potentially one of the most complex in the entire chapter. Under this requirement, the defendant must *intend* for the principal to possess the relevant *mens rea* for the crime committed. This requirement is often characterised as an element of the defendant's knowledge 'of the essential matters', ie the defendant must have 'knowledge' that the principal will act with the requisite *mens rea*. The author prefers, however, to speak of this requirement as an additional element of intention on the part of the defendant given the ease of explaining that the defendant must possess intention as to his own conduct (ie to assist) and intention that the principal acts with his own *mens rea*.

Under the law prior to *Jogee*, it was sufficient that the defendant *foresaw* the real possibility that the principal *might* commit the offence (see *R v Powell; R v English* [1999] 1 AC 1 at **4.3.2.2**). Now, however, nothing short of intention as to the principal's *mens rea* will suffice.

example

Jack is burgling a house owned by Andy. He is assisted by Bill and Ben who act as the getaway driver and lookout respectively. All three parties have the intention to burgle. Jack is disturbed, however, whilst in the house by Andy. Jack stabs him and Andy dies.

In this instance, Jack is no doubt liable for both burglary and murder (if not, at least manslaughter). Bill and Ben will also be liable for burglary but the difficulty arises as to whether they will be liable for murder (or manslaughter) also.

Until the Supreme Court's decision in *Jogee* in February 2016, Bill and Ben would have been liable for the murder of Andy as accessories in circumstances where they had *foreseen* a real possibility that the principal *might* have committed that offence, ie murder. This was the principle arising from the case of *Chan Wing-Siu v R* [1985] AC 168 where Sir Robin Cooke in the Privy Council stated:

> [A] secondary party is criminally liable for acts by the primary offender of a type which the former foresees but does not necessarily intend. That there is such a principle is not in doubt. It turns on contemplation or, putting the same idea in other words, authorisation, which may be expressed but is more usually implied. It meets the case of a crime foreseen as a possible incident of the common unlawful enterprise. The criminal culpability lies in participating in the venture with that foresight.

Chan Wing-Siu was confirmed as representing the law of England and Wales by such subsequent cases as *R v Powell; R v English* [1999] 1 AC 1, *R v Yemoh* [2009] EWCA Crim 930 and *R v Rafferty* [2007] EWCA Crim 1846.

The position in *Chan Wing-Siu* was, however, changed by the Supreme Court in *R v Jogee*. There, the Supreme Court overruled the principle in *Chan Wing-Siu* on the basis that the law had taken a 'wrong turn' and was in error, as it equated foresight with intention to assist. Lords Toulson and Hughes commented that the principle was 'based on an incomplete, and in some respects erroneous reading of the previous case law, coupled with generalised and questionable policy arguments'. The correct approach, according to the Supreme Court, is to treat foresight as *evidence* of intent to assist, not as synonymous with intention. Although foresight may sometimes be powerful evidence of intent, it is not conclusive of it, and it is for the jury to decide whether, in fact, the defendant intended that the principal would commit the offence in question. The *mens rea* element can now be stated, quite simply, as a requirement of intention.

In this respect, where the principal offence is carried out as intended, it will not be difficult to prove *mens rea* where the defendant has the requisite intention. Difficulties have arisen, however, where the offence is not carried out by the principal as agreed, and instead the principal offender commits an offence unforeseen or unintended by the defendant. Under this heading, we are concerned with:

- cases where the principal commits a more serious offence;
- cases where the principal commits a less serious offence; and
- cases where there is an overwhelming supervening event (note that this terminology was formerly known as the 'fundamentally different' rule).

We shall deal with each in turn.

Principal commits a more serious offence

The essential questions here are whether:

- the defendant can be liable for the more serious offence than the one envisaged; or
- the defendant can be liable for a less serious offence than the one charged against the principal.

example

Jill procures Jack to commit a battery against Andy. Jack, however, goes on to commit GBH.

In this instance, Jack has committed a more serious offence than the one Jill envisaged. Jack will be liable as a principal for GBH. The question becomes, will Jill be liable for GBH too, even though that was not the offence envisaged by her, or is it possible for her to be liable for the expected less serious offence of battery?

We can break down our discussion into the two possible offences:

- *The offence of GBH:* In order to be liable as an accessory to the more serious offence of GBH, Jill will have had to intend for Jack to commit the more serious offence of GBH. This is a simple matter and one which their Lordships in *Jogee* emphasised was the cornerstone of accessorial liability. Quite simply, a defendant cannot be liable for conduct or results that go beyond her desired intention. In this instance, Jill will not be liable for GBH.
- *The offence of battery:* In order to be liable as an accessory to the lesser offence of battery, Jill will either have had to intend for Jack to commit the lesser offence or may be liable where the lesser offence is included within the definition of the more serious offence. For example, the conduct of battery (ie application of unlawful force) is present in the offence of GBH. In this respect, Jill will be liable for battery. An additional example is the offence of robbery which has included within its definition the lesser offence of theft.

(See *R v Day* [2001] Crim LR 984 in which the principal was convicted of murder whilst the defendant was convicted of manslaughter.)

Principal commits a less serious offence

The essential question here is whether the defendant can be liable for a more serious offence than the one charged against the principal.

example

Jill procures Jack to commit GBH against Andy. Jack, however, only commits a battery.

In this instance, Jack has committed a less serious offence than the one Jill envisaged. Jack will be liable as a principal for battery. The question becomes, will Jill be liable for battery or is it possible for her to be liable for the expected more serious offence of GBH?

It is, of course, possible for the principal to be acquitted of the principal offence (because, for example, they have successfully pleaded a defence). In this regard, an accessory can still be liable where the principal has been acquitted. The issue here, however, is whether the principal can be liable for a lesser offence, whilst the accessory is liable for a more serious offence.

In the case of *R v Howe* [1987] AC 417, the principal shot the victim dead but claimed that he had been forced to do it by the defendant and, in any event, the gun went off accidentally and unintentionally. The Court of Appeal ([1986] QB 626) quashed the principal's conviction for murder and replaced it with one of manslaughter; however, it upheld the defendant's conviction for murder, stating that he was capable of being charged with a more serious offence than the principal in circumstances where his *mens rea* for the more serious offence was present. In the Court of Appeal, Lord Lane CJ gave the example

> where A hands a gun to D informing him that it is loaded with blank ammunition only and telling him to go and scare X by discharging it. The ammunition is in fact live, as A knows, and X is killed. D is convicted only of manslaughter, as he might be on those facts. It would seem absurd that A should thereby escape conviction for murder.

The Court of Appeal certified a question of general public importance to the House of Lords, namely:

> Can one who incites or procures by duress another to kill or be a party to a killing be convicted of murder if that other is acquitted by reason of duress?

The House of Lords answered in the affirmative and found that the accessory could be liable for a more serious offence than the principal (in doing so, the House of Lords overruled the decision of *R v Richards* [1974] QB 776). In his judgment, Lord Mackay stated:

> I would affirm [Lord Lane CJ's] view [in the Court of Appeal] that where a person has been killed and that result is the result intended by another participant, the mere fact that the actual killer may be convicted only of the reduced charge of manslaughter for some reason special to himself does not, in my opinion in any way, result in a compulsory reduction for the other participant.

In addition, the defendant would also be liable to an inchoate charge for the more serious offence.

'Overwhelming supervening event'

As discussed above, a defendant's liability arises in circumstances where the defendant intends the principal to commit the offence with the relevant *mens rea*. A concept arose under the old common law, however, that where the offence committed by the principal was so 'fundamentally different' from the one envisaged by the defendant, no liability should arise. In these circumstances, the defendant will remain liable for an inchoate offence of assisting but not for the accessorial offence charged. The lead authority under the old common law was that of *R v Powell; R v English* [1999] 1 AC 1, where the House of Lords concluded that a defendant could not be liable as an accessory to murder where the principal's action (of stabbing the victim with a knife) was so fundamentally different from that of the defendant's intentional assistance (of hitting the victim with bamboo posts).

It is questionable to what extent the fundamentally different rule continues to apply, as a result of *Jogee*. Lord Hughes in *Jogee* was of the view that

> it is possible for death to be caused by some overwhelming supervening act by the perpetrator which nobody in the defendant's shoes could have contemplated might happen and is of such a character as to relegate his acts to history; in that case the defendant will bear no criminal responsibility for the death.
>
> This type of case apart, there will normally be no occasion to consider the concept of 'fundamental departure' as derived from *English*. What matters is whether [the defendant] encouraged or assisted the crime … The tendency which has developed … to focus on what [the defendant] knew of what weapon [the principal] was carrying can and should give way to an examination of whether

> [the defendant] intended to assist in the crime charged. If that crime is murder, then the question is whether he intended to assist the intentional infliction of grievous bodily harm at least ... Very often he may intend to assist in violence using whatever weapon may come to hand. In other cases he may think that [the principal] has an iron bar whereas he turns out to have a knife, but the difference may not at all affect his intention to assist, if necessary, in the causing of grievous bodily harm at least. Knowledge or ignorance that weapons generally, or a particular weapon, is carried by [the principal] will be evidence going to what the intention of [the defendant] was, and may be irresistible evidence one way or the other, but it is evidence and no more.

The 'fundamentally different' rule appears, therefore, to no longer apply following *Jogee*. In its place, the Supreme Court made reference to circumstances where the principal's act is an 'overwhelming supervening' event/act such that any assistance or encouragement that may have been given by the defendant will have been superseded. In that case, the defendant cannot be liable.

The concept of 'overwhelming supervening event' was addressed by the Court of Appeal in *R v Tas* [2018] EWCA Crim 2603, where Sir Brian Leveson P explained that the test is whether the principal's act is such that 'nobody in the defendant's shoes could have contemplated [what] might happen and is of such a character as to relegate his acts to history'. His Lordship was clear that this test should not be 'abbreviate[d]', in the sense that it should not be broadened or diluted.

His Lordship would explain what whether there is an evidential basis for the overwhelming event is a matter for trial judge. In particular, it was said that:

> In our judgment, whether there is an evidential basis for overwhelming supervening event which is of such a character as could relegate into history matters which would otherwise be looked on as causative (or, indeed, withdrawal from a joint enterprise) rather than mere escalation which remained part of the joint enterprise is very much for the judge who has heard the evidence and is in a far better position than this court to reach a conclusion as to evidential sufficiency.

See also *R v Harper* [2019] EWCA Crim 343, where the Court rejected the argument that a failure to leave the principle of overwhelming event to the jury undermined the safety of the conviction (note: that was particularly due to the focus on the presence of a weapon which, as enunciated in *Jogee*, is evidence of intention only).

Transferred malice

What is the situation where the defendant intends for the principal to commit an offence against a particular individual (V1) but the principal goes on to commit an offence against another person (V2)? This was the issue in the very old authority of *R v Saunders and Archer* (1573) 2 Plowd 473 where the defendant wished to kill his wife. He hired the principal to kill her but the principal, accidentally, killed their child. The principal was liable for murder through the doctrine of transferred malice (see **Chapter 3**), but no liability could be found against the defendant as an accessory. This rule will hardly stand up today in light of the Supreme Court's ruling in *R v Gnango* [2011] UKSC 59. In *Gnango*, the Supreme Court reaffirmed that transferred malice applies equally to secondary parties as it does to principal parties. The doctrine does not, however, apply where the principal deliberately selects a different victim from that foreseen or intended by the defendant. In such situations, consideration should be given to a charge under the Serious Crime Act 2007, or a charge of conspiracy.

4.2.4.3 Understanding the requirement of intention

Following *Jogee*, the law of intention can be stated as follows:

- The defendant must intend to assist or encourage the principal.
- The defendant must intend for the principal to commit an offence with the necessary *mens rea*.
- The defendant may still be liable in circumstances where the principal commits a more serious, or less serious, act than the one intended or envisioned by the defendant.
- The defendant may avoid liability where the principal's conduct was an 'overwhelming supervening event' (formerly the 'fundamentally different' rule).
- Transferred malice applies equally to secondary offenders as it does to principal offenders except where the principal has deliberately chosen a different victim to the one intended or foreseen by the defendant.

4.2.5 Defences

Just as a principal offender can rely on a defence to either excuse or justify his actions, a secondary party can equally rely on such a defence to rid him of liability. These defences may be general in nature (ie those defences that are available to all) such as duress, insanity, infancy etc, and these will be considered in **Chapter 7**. However, there are also certain defences that are specifically available to secondary parties only:

- withdrawal;
- cases where the conduct is merely a thing of the past;
- the victim rule; and
- acting under a legal duty.

4.2.5.1 Withdrawal

In certain cases, an accessory may have a 'change of heart' before the completion of the offence by the principal. In circumstances where this change of heart is coupled with effective steps to withdraw himself from participation, the accessory may rid himself of liability. This is known as the defence of withdrawal.

The defence is based upon the notion that the defendant's liability as an accessory does not materialise unless and until the principal has committed the offence in question. Given this requirement for the defendant's liability to 'derive' from the principal, all cases of this kind will involve some form of interval, which may be short, between the acts of the accessory and the principal's offending conduct. This interval, or 'window of opportunity', allows for an accessory to effectively withdraw himself from the commission of the offence. Exactly what is required to effectively withdraw oneself from participation in the offence will vary and will have to be judged on a case-by-case basis.

The leading authority in this area is that of *R v Becerra and Cooper* (1975) 62 Cr App R 212.

case example

Charge:
Murder

Case progression:
Crown Court – Guilty

Court of Appeal – Leave to appeal refused

Point of law:
Extent needed for effective withdrawal

In *R v Becerra and Cooper* (1975) 62 Cr App R 212, the defendants broke into a house with the intention to steal from within the house. D1 handed D2 a knife to use in case they were disturbed during the course of the burglary. During the burglary, the defendants were disturbed by a tenant of the house, the victim. Hearing the tenant approaching, D1 called to D2, 'There's a bloke coming. Let's go', and jumped out of a window and fled. D2, however, unable to escape, stabbed and killed the victim. Both D1 and D2 were convicted of murder in the Crown Court.

D1 sought leave to appeal in the Court of Appeal which was refused. Roskill LJ, giving the judgment of the Court, ruled:

> [I]f [D1] wanted to withdraw at that stage, he would have to 'countermand', to use the word that is used in some of the cases or 'repent' to use another word so used, in some manner vastly different and vastly more effective than merely to say 'Come on, let's go' and go out through the window.

The case is authority for the proposition that an 'unequivocal notice' of withdrawal is required. However, it remains unclear what the defendant must actually do in order to effectively withdraw himself from participation in a criminal offence. This will ultimately depend on many factors, including the time of the withdrawal. For instance, where a withdrawal is made before the commission of an offence, a simple communication of the withdrawal may be sufficient. Where, however, the withdrawal is made whilst the offence is being committed, it appears that much more must be done by the defendant. The Court used the words 'countermand' and 'repent' to describe the conduct of the defendant; however, it is unclear exactly what these words mean. The Court did suggest that the further into the commission of the offence the defendant is, the more likely it is that he is required to actually intervene to prevent the crime from occurring. Specifically, Roskill LJ recounted that there may come a point in time where 'the only way in which [the defendant] could effectively withdraw ... would be physically to intervene'. Importantly, a simple absence, in circumstances where such presence is expected or planned for, will not amount to an effective withdrawal (*R v Rook* [1993] 2 All ER 955); there must be a communication of the withdrawal. The issue, however, becomes the extent to which withdrawal is effective.

The Court of Appeal in *R v Mitchell and King* [1999] Crim LR 496 noted that the defence of withdrawal will operate only in exceptional circumstances. Despite this, a number of factors may be relevant in determining the question of withdrawal, including:

- the withdrawal must be communicated unless impossible – *R v Robinson* [2000] EWCA Crim 8;
- the withdrawal must be 'unequivocal' – *R v O'Flaherty* [2004] EWCA Crim 526;
- the nature of the withdrawal itself (a mere change of mind is insufficient; there must be some physical act demonstrating disengagement) – *R v Bryce* [2004] EWCA Crim 1231;
- how imminent the completed offence is at the time of the attempted withdrawal (ie did the defendant try to withdraw too late?) – *R v Becerra* (1975) 62 Cr App R 212;
- the nature and extent of assistance or encouragement already given by the accessory (ie how substantial the defendant's actions were) – *R v Gallant* [2008] EWCA Crim 1111;

- whether the defendant had attempted to prevent the principal from committing the crime (eg by going to the police) – *R v Otway* [2011] EWCA Crim 3. This, however, is not necessary; it is merely good evidence of withdrawal. For a cross-comparison, see the judgment of McDermott J in *Eldredge v US* (1932) 62 F.2d 499.

Whether a withdrawal has been effective is a question for the jury, and in considering these factors, the jury must balance the weight of the defendant's assistance or encouragement against the action taken to 'disengage' (*R v O'Flaherty* [2004] EWCA Crim 526). **Table 4.8** details a number of key cases dealing with the principle of withdrawal.

Table 4.8 Key cases on withdrawal

Key case	Facts and principle
R v Baker [1994] Crim LR 444	Having inflicted three knife wounds, D1 passed the knife to D2 saying 'I'm not doing it'. D1 moved a few feet away and turned his back whilst D2 inflicted further wounds. D1's conduct and words were insufficient to amount to unequivocal notice that D1 was 'wholly disassociating' himself from the crime.
R v Whitefield (1984) 79 Cr App R 36	D1 and D2 had planned a burglary together. However, evidence demonstrated that D1 had served unequivocal notice on D2 that if D1 proceeded with the burglary, he would be doing so without the aid or assistance of D1. It was held that if the jury accepted this evidence, the defence of withdrawal existed.
R v Mitchell and King [1999] Crim LR 496	D1, D2 and D3 became involved in a fight at an Indian take-away. The fight involved other customers and damage had been caused to the take-away. D1 and D2 walked away but D3 returned and inflicted fatal injuries to the victim. Walking away was sufficient to demonstrate withdrawal.
R v Grundy [1977] Crim LR 543	D1 supplied D2 with information valuable to D2 in the commission of a burglary. Two weeks before the commission of the burglary, D1 tried to stop D2 from breaking into the house. This attempt was sufficient to amount to evidence of a withdrawal which should have been left to the jury.

The most recent statement regarding the extent of withdrawal comes from *R v Bryce* [2004] EWCA Crim 1231, where Potter LJ stated:

> [I]f the secondary party is to avoid liability for assistance rendered to the perpetrator in respect of steps taken by the perpetrator towards the commission of the crime, only an act taken by him which amounts to countermanding of his earlier assistance and a withdrawal from the common purpose will suffice. Repentance alone, unsupported by action taken to demonstrate withdrawal will be insufficient.

in practice

From the case law, it is apparent that the withdrawal must be communicated to the principal offender(s). A matter that has yet to be determined by the courts, however, is whether an individual can withdraw where they inform the police about the commission of the offence. It is also unclear, in circumstances where there is more than one principal, whether they must communicate their withdrawal to all principals or whether it is sufficient to communicate withdrawal simply to one person.

Distinguishing withdrawal cases

It appears from the case law that a distinction needs to be made between cases involving planned violence and those involving spontaneous violence.

Spontaneous violence

There may be circumstances where violence arises spontaneously in that it is not pre-planned or organised. Such circumstances may arise where two rival gangs accidentally meet in the street and a rumble unfolds as a result. The lead authority on this point is the case of *R v Robinson* [2000] EWCA Crim 8 in which the defendant had originally joined the principal in inflicting harm to the victim but subsequently stopped when the violence became too much. The Court of Appeal took the view that even in cases of spontaneous violence, an unequivocal communication of withdrawal will still be required.

This case is contrary to the earlier decision of *R v Mitchell and King* [1999] Crim LR 496 where the Court of Appeal found that a withdrawal could be made from spontaneous violence even in circumstances where a communication is not made. In that case, the defendant was involved in an unplanned fight alongside the principal against a restaurant owner and his two sons. The defendant had attacked one of the men with a weapon but quickly dropped his weapon and walked away. The principal then picked up the weapon and attacked the victim with it, killing him. The defendant was convicted as an accessory to murder and appealed on the basis that the dropping of his weapon and the movement away from the scene amounted to a withdrawal. The Court of Appeal agreed and quashed his conviction.

Mitchell was subsequently followed in *R v O'Flaherty* [2004] EWCA Crim 526, where the Court of Appeal held that the question of communication was the wrong one to ask. Rather, the correct question was 'whether a particular defendant disengaged before the fatal injury or injuries were caused or joined in after they had been caused' (per Mantell LJ)'. In essence, the question is whether the original joint venture was still continuing at the time of the principal's act. See also *R v Mitchell and Ballantyne* [2009] 1 Cr App R 438.

Otton LJ in the Court of Appeal in *Robinson* noted that *Mitchell and King* was an 'exceptional case' and confirmed that communication was generally required for a withdrawal to be effective. His Lordship justified this approach on the basis that it affords 'the principal offenders the opportunity to desist rather than complete the crime'. This requirement existed in all cases unless (according to Otton LJ)

> it is not practicable or reasonable so to communicate as in the exceptional circumstances pertaining in *Mitchell* where the accused threw down his weapon and moved away before the final and fatal blows were inflicted.

This element of the judgment seems evident in the decision of the Court of Appeal in *R v Stringer* [2011] EWCA Crim 1396, where the Court held that, in many cases, it will be unjust to require the defendant to effectively communicate his withdrawal where there is a spontaneous outbreak of violence. In *Stringer*, for example, the defendants had begun to chase the victim but eventually dropped back, thinking better of the situation. In this case, it would be unjust to expect them to communicate their withdrawal in circumstances where they stop in the chase but the principal continues to run. Any original encouragement provided by the defendants could be said to be spent by the time the principal commits the offence without the presence of the defendants.

Otton LJ in *Robinson* would go on to compare spontaneous violence where the defendant was present and violence which was initiated by the defendant. In the latter case, the Court held that simply moving oneself away from the scene would not be sufficient to effectively withdraw from participation. Otton LJ specifically stated:

> Indeed it would be a very curious state of our law if a person who had encouraged or incited violence by initiating the attack, could stand aside when he was aware that those who were to continue the violence might form the necessary intention to commit (and did commit) an offence of grievous bodily harm and could thereafter escape all responsibility except for assault occasioning actual bodily from the initial blow. Commonsense and the Common Law go hand in hand.

Planned violence

In *R v Rajakumar* [2013] EWCA Crim 1512, the Court of Appeal explained that what may suffice to constitute a withdrawal in spontaneous and unplanned group violence may not necessarily suffice in pre-planned group violence. In essence, the withdrawal will require a clear communication, above and beyond a mere repent, in order for the defence to exist. In *R v Becerra and Cooper* (1975) 62 Cr App R 212, Roskill LJ explained that '[t]here must be more than a mere mental change of intention and a physical change of place. There must be a timely communication of the intention to abandon the common purpose.' See also *R v Grundy* [1977] Crim LR 543 in **Table 4.8** (above).

Withdrawal and inchoate liability

It is worth noting that where the defendant is not considered as being liable as an accessory to the offence charged, by reason of withdrawal for example, he may still be liable for an inchoate offence, such as conspiracy or attempt (see **Chapter 5**).

4.2.5.2 Merely a thing of the past

The Supreme Court in *R v Jogee* did not explicitly address the issue of withdrawal, but it did deal with a separate issue where the defendant's conduct is merely a thing of the past. Specifically, Lord Hughes commented that the defendant will not be liable for the act of the principal

> where anything said or done by D2 has faded to the point of mere background by the time the offence was committed. Ultimately it is a question of fact and degree whether D2's conduct was so distanced in time, place or circumstances from the conduct of D1 that it would not be realistic to regard D1's offence as encouraged or assisted by it.

4.2.5.3 The victim rule

Not a defence, *per se*, the 'victim' rule provides that where an offence has been created or designed for the protection of a specific class of person, any person within that class cannot be liable as an accessory where they assist or encourage another to commit an offence against them. Williams identified this as the 'victim rule' ('Victims and Other Exempt Parties in Crime' (1990) 10 LS 245).

This rule has also become known as the '*Tyrrell* defence' from the case of *R v Tyrrell* [1894] 1 QB 710.

case example

Charge:
Having unlawful carnal knowledge (CLAA 1885, s 5)

Case progression:
Central Criminal Court – Guilty

Court for Crown Cases Reserved – Appeal allowed

Point of law:
Whether victims can be accessories to crimes against themselves

In *R v Tyrrell* [1894] 1 QB 710, the defendant, a young girl (between the age of 13 and 16), encouraged the principal to engage in sexual intercourse with her. The defendant was charged with and convicted of having unlawful carnal knowledge of any girl under the age of 16 in the Central Criminal Court as an accessory to the principal's offence.

The defendant appealed to the Court for Crown Cases Reserved which held that the defendant could not be liable as an accessory to an offence committed against herself. The 1885 Act had been passed to protect victims, not to criminalise them. Lord Coleridge CJ stated:

> The Criminal Law Amendment Act [CLAA], 1885, was passed for the purpose of protecting women and girls against themselves. ... With the object of protecting women and girls against themselves the Act of Parliament has made illicit connection with a girl under that age unlawful; if a man wishes to have such illicit connection he must wait until the girl is sixteen, otherwise he breaks the law; but it is impossible to say that the Act, which is absolutely silent about aiding and abetting or soliciting or inciting, can have intended that the girls for whose protection it was passed should be punishable under it for the offences committed upon themselves.

The extent to which the 'defence' applies is unclear. It has been applied subsequently in further sexual offences cases, such as *R v Whitehouse* [1977] QB 868, where the defendant, a 15-year-old girl, had been convicted or aiding and abetting her father to commit incest with her, contrary to s 11 of the SOA 1956. Her conviction was quashed following the *Tyrrell* principle. See a critique of modern pieces of legislation for failing to adopt this rule by Bohlander ('The Sexual Offences Act 2003—The *Tyrrell* Principle—Criminalising the Victim' [2005] Crim LR 701).

Two limitations, however, must be noted about the defence:

- It applies only to those offences which are designed to protect a certain sub-class of the population and not offences designed to protect the population as a whole, nor does it operate generally where a person is an actual or intended victim of the offence. In *R v Gnango* [2011] UKSC 59, for example, the Supreme Court took the opportunity to explain that the victim rule could not apply in circumstances where the defendant took part in a shoot-out with the principal. Likewise, in *R v Sockett* (1908) 1 Cr App R 101, the Court of Criminal Appeal held that the victim had aided and abetted the principal to perform an unlawful abortion upon her and the victim rule could not apply. See also *R v Brown* [1994] 1 AC 212 regarding sado-masochistic acts of violence.
- It will not apply where the defendant, a member of the particular sub-class protected, assists or encourages the principal to commit an offence against another person within that class.

The Law Commission in its Report, 'Participating in Crime' (Law Com No 305, 2007) has recommend that the *Tyrrell* principle (referred to as the 'protective principle') be codified and confined to offences specifically designed to protect particular categories of victim, eg the elderly, children and those trafficked for exploitation.

4.2.5.4 Acting under a legal duty

A rather narrow defence in scope, this particular defence operates to exclude the defendant from liability in circumstances where his conduct merely amounted to the completion of his legal duty to act. For instance, in the case of *R v Lomas* (1913) 9 Cr App R 220, the defendant had returned a jemmy that he had borrowed to the principal. The principal then went on to use the jemmy to commit a burglary. It could not be said that the defendant aided and abetted a burglary simply by returning property, ie the jemmy, to the rightful owner (ie the principal). On the other hand, in *Garrett v Arthur Churchill (Glass) Ltd* [1970] 1 QB 92, the Divisional Court held that a person who hands over goods belonging to another person (in this case a goblet), knowing that this person intends to export the goods unlawfully (in this case to the USA), cannot rely on his obligation (or duty) in civil law to deliver the goods. Parker CJ was of the view that the duty to hand over such goods gives way to the public interest in preventing such exportation. Particularly his Lordship stated:

> [A]lbeit there was a legal duty in ordinary circumstances to hand over the goblet to the owners once the agency was determined, I do not think that an action would lie for breach of that duty if the handing over would constitute the offence of being knowingly concerned in its exportation.

4.2.6 Charging accessories

Section 8 of the AAA 1861 is clear that an accessory 'shall be liable to be tried, indicted, and punished as a principal offender'. Lord Hughes in *Jogee* justified this approach on the following basis:

> It is a fundamental principle of the criminal law that the accessory is guilty of the same offence as the principal. The reason is not difficult to see. [The defendant] shares the physical act because even if it was not his hand which struck the blow, ransacked the house, smuggled the drugs or forged the cheque, he has encouraged or assisted those physical acts. Similarly he shares the culpability precisely because he encouraged or assisted the offence.

In this respect, where the principal has committed murder, and accessorial liability can be made out against the defendant, the defendant will also be liable for murder. As a result, the same rules of liability and procedure discussed in Parts II and III apply to accessories also.

4.2.6.1 Mode of trial

Given that an individual is capable of being an accessory to any offence, the rules of mode of trial will depend ultimately on the offence committed by the principal. Should the offence be one of a summary-only nature, the same rules will apply to an accessory. The same can be said for either-way and indictable-only offences.

4.2.6.2 Sentencing

Unless otherwise stated, the same sentencing principles are to be applied to the accessory as they are to the principal. Some exceptions do exist, however. For example, s 34(5) of the Road Traffic Offenders Act 1988 prescribes:

> The preceding provisions of this section shall apply in relation to a conviction of an offence committed by aiding, abetting, counselling or procuring, or inciting to

the commission of, an offence involving obligatory disqualification as if the offence were an offence involving discretionary disqualification.

In essence, where the disqualification of a principal offender is mandatory for that offence (eg in cases of driving with excess alcohol), a person convicted of aiding and abetting is only liable to a discretionary disqualification.

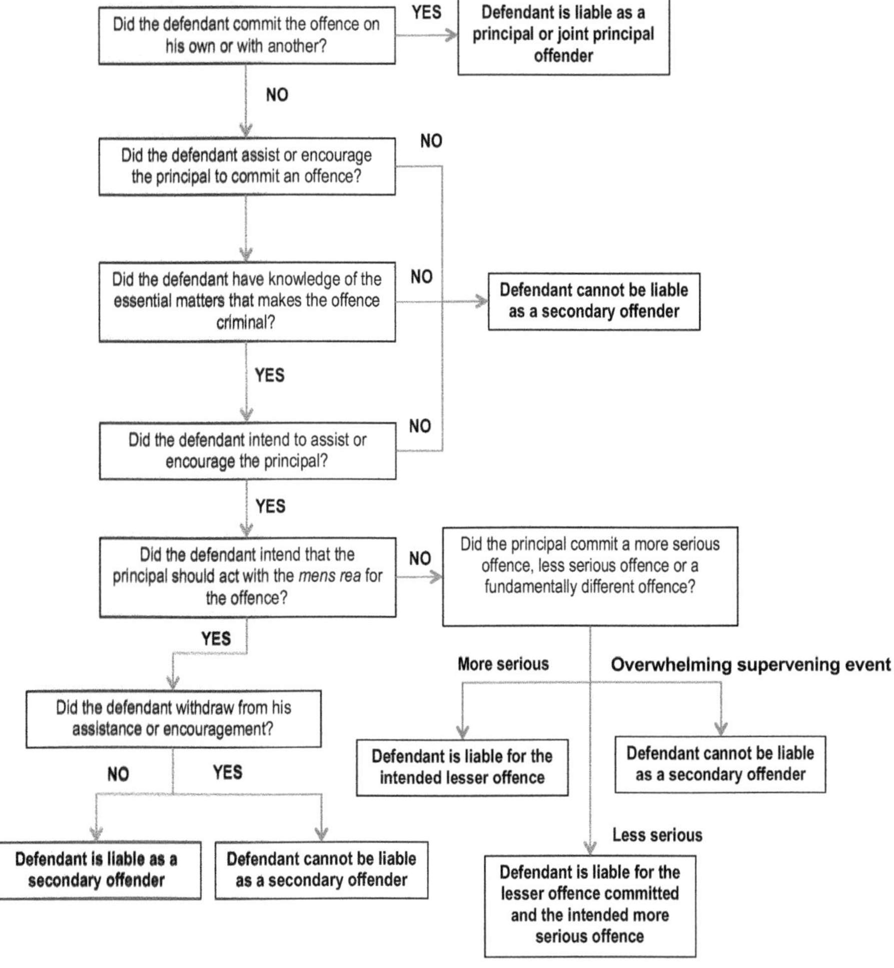

Figure 4.6 Putting together secondary liability

4.3 Joint enterprise

This section is designed to give you a brief overview of the law of 'joint enterprise' as it previously stood, the effect of the decision in *Jogee* and the situation post-*Jogee*. Note, according to the Supreme Court in *Jogee*, that the term 'joint enterprise' is not a legal term of art, and it no longer has any value as a separate form of accessorial liability.

4.3.1 Defining a case of 'joint enterprise'

The general principal of joint enterprise (also known as 'joint venture') was quite simple, ie where two or more persons embarked on a joint venture together, each was liable for the acts done in the achievement of that joint enterprise. Smith named this principle 'parasitic accessory liability' ('Criminal Liability of Accessories: Law and Law Reform' (1997) 113 LQR 453).

example

Jack and Jill agreed that they would murder Andy at 10pm that evening.

Should the pair succeed, they were, and still are, liable as joint principals given their joint participation in the commission of the offence.

The point at which the law struggled to attach liability, however, included the circumstances where the venture, for some reason, went above and beyond what was agreed between the parties to the venture. The doctrine had often been explained in these circumstances or, as the Supreme Court noted in *Jogee*, became 'understood (erroneously) by some to be a form of guilt by association or of guilt by simple presence without more'.

example

Jack and Jill agreed to attack Andy and 10pm that evening but agreed that they would go no further than hurting him. Jill decided, without consulting Jack, that she was going to murder Andy and did so.

Ordinarily, in this situation, Jack would not be liable for murder as the outcome of the events went beyond what was agreed/intended by the parties in their enterprise.

Whether, of course, the consequences arose as part of the joint enterprise or outside the scope of the agreement is a question for the jury (*R v Anderson and Morris* [1966] 2 QB 110). However, the law began to take a turn in finding a defendant liable for joint enterprise in circumstances where he foresaw that the principal might act to commit this other offence.

4.3.1.1 Legal basis for joint enterprise

It was thought at one point that joint enterprise was a form of liability separate to that of secondary liability. Indeed, Simester ('The Mental Element in Complicity' (2006) 122 LQR 578) was of the view that

> Through entering into a joint [criminal venture], [the defendant] changes her normative position. [She] becomes, by her deliberate choice, a participant in a group action to commit a crime. Moreover, her new status has moral significance: she associates herself with the conduct of the other members of the group in a way that the mere aider and abettor, who remains an independent character throughout the episode does not.

This opinion can be contrasted with the likes of Buxton ('Joint Enterprise' [2009] Crim LR 233) who considered the principle of joint enterprise to simply be a part of the general law of accessorial liability. This argument was affirmed by the Court of Appeal in *R v Mendez and Thompson* [2010] EWCA Crim 516, *R v Stringer* [2011] EWCA

Crim 1396 and *R v ABCD* [2010] EWCA Crim 1622. In each case, the Court of Appeal emphasised that no distinction was to be made between cases where those involved share a common purpose to commit a crime and cases where there is no such shared purpose. In *Jogee*, Lord Toulson reaffirmed this view and stated that 'there is no reason why ordinary principles of secondary liability should not be of general application'. As discussed above, therefore, liability in so-called cases of joint enterprise is now to be considered under the ordinary principles of complicity, ie to aid, abet etc, and the phrase 'joint enterprise' is to be avoided.

4.3.2 Development of the law

4.3.2.1 The early principle of joint enterprise

In its earliest form, joint enterprise liability was predicated on the existence of an agreement between the parties. Such agreement could be express or implied by the tactics adopted. Liability could only arise in cases where the principal acted within the remit of the agreement. In this sense, liability could not be founded where the principal acted in a manner outside of the agreement (*R v Anderson and Morris* [1966] 2 QB 110).

The focus at this point, therefore, was whether the principal was acting within the common purpose of the parties or not.

4.3.2.2 The principle in *Chan Wing-Siu*

The law as we recently knew it, however, was contained in the decision of the House of Lords in *R v Powell; R v English* [1999] 1 AC 1, where Lord Hutton explained:

> [W]here two parties embark on a joint enterprise to commit a crime, and one party *foresees that in the course of the enterprise the other party may carry out*, with the requisite *mens rea*, an act constituting another crime, the former is liable for that crime if committed by the latter in the course of the enterprise. ... the secondary party is subject to criminal liability if he contemplated the act causing the death as a possible incident of the joint venture. (emphasis added)

The focus, therefore, moved away from liability where the principal acted within the remit of the agreement to a case where the defendant is liable in circumstances where he *foresaw* a real possibility that the principal might commit this other offence. In *Powell*, the defendant and two other persons went to the victim's house in order to buy drugs. One of those persons with the defendant (the principal offender) was carrying a gun and shot the victim upon the house door being opened. The defendants knew that the principal was carrying the gun but claimed that it was not their intention for him to use it. The House of Lords had to consider whether the defendants were liable for the murder committed by the principal, a crime which fell outside the common purpose of the parties. Lord Hutton took the view, with which his fellow judges agreed, that the defendants did foresee the real possibility that the principal might kill or cause GBH to the victim given that they knew of the existence of the gun. Their Lordships in *English* relied heavily on the Privy Council decision in *Chan Wing-Siu v R* [1985] AC 168 and the Court of Criminal Appeal's decision in *R v Anderson and Morris* [1966] 2 QB 110.

Despite the continued endorsement for the *Chan Wing-Siu* principle by the appellate courts (see *R v Yemoh* [2009] EWCA Crim 930 and *R v Rafferty* [2007] EWCA Crim 1846), it remained subject to considerable controversy and criticism. The principle was most heavily criticised on the basis that an accessory could be liable for murder in circumstances where he *foresaw* the commission of the offence, whereas the principal could only be liable in circumstances where he acted with malice aforethought, ie intended to kill or cause GBH. Indeed, Spencer ('*Jogee* – the "Parasite" Excised' [2016] 3 Arch Rev 4) commented:

> [T]he extended form of accessory liability [under *Chan Wing-Siu* was] unreasonably harsh ... it resulted in people being convicted of grave crimes in respect of which, in reality, their blameworthiness was comparatively small.

This criticism was acknowledged by Lord Steyn in *English* when his Lordship recounted that 'there is substance in the argument that it is anomalous that a lesser form of culpability is required in the case of a secondary party' than of the principal. However, his Lordship would go on to justify the principle in *Chan Wing-Siu* for 'practical and policy considerations'. **Table 4.9** details Lord Steyn's justifications in more detail.

Table 4.9 Justifying Chan Wing-Sui

Consideration	Lord Steyn's justification
Practical	'[I]t would in practice almost invariably be impossible for a jury to say that the secondary party wanted death to be caused or that he regarded it as virtually certain.' In effect, Lord Steyn is saying that a test based on intention would result in too many acquittals.
Policy	'It is just that a secondary party who foresees that the primary offender might kill with the intent sufficient for murder, and assists and encourages the primary offender in the criminal enterprise on this basis, should be guilty of murder.' In effect, Lord Steyn stated that it is legitimate to find liability in cases where foresight is present.

Indeed, it was this rationale that provided the basis of the Law Commission's Report ('Participating in Crime' (Law Com No 305, 2007)) in which it recommended the preservation of joint enterprise liability with an attached element of reckless *mens rea*. Other arguments went so far as to suggest that the general law of complicity should be abolished but the wider case of joint enterprise (applying to 'coordinated criminal activity') should be retained and furthered (Sullivan, 'Doing Without Complicity' [2012] JCCL 199).

4.3.2.3 The fundamental change in *Jogee*

In *Jogee*, the Supreme Court concluded that the approach adopted by the courts in *Chan Wing-Siu* and *Powell and English* could not be supported. Their Lordships abandoned the former law and restated the principles of accessorial liability as follows:

- The secondary party must *intend* to aid, abet, counsel or procedure the principal to commit the offence.
- The secondary party must also *intend* that the principal will have the respective *mens rea* for that offence.
- *Foresight* is not intention, but may be evidence of that intent.

The Supreme Court treated its decision as a 'restatement' of the principles of accessorial liability and not as a substantive reform of the law. See Stark, 'The Demise of "Parasitic Accessorial Liability": Substantive Judicial Law Reform, Not Common Law Housekeeping' (2016) 75 CLJ 550 for a critique of this categorisation.

The decision in *Jogee* has largely been met with outright approval. Dyson ('Shorn-off Complicity' (2016) 75 CLJ 196) offers his thoughts by stating:

> [T]he law is now more principled: the test for an accomplice's liability is set at an appropriate threshold, which is no longer significantly lower than the principal's. No longer will be it be so easy for [the defendant's] involvement in a death to lead to a murder conviction.

4.3.2.4 The situation post-*Jogee*

Upon release of the judgment in *Jogee*, it was thought that all convictions under the old *Chan Wing-Siu* principle were liable to be overturned. However, the Supreme Court in *Jogee* was quick to emphasise that previous convictions under the old law were not automatically invalid. According to Lord Hughes:

> The effect of putting the law right is not to render invalid all convictions which were arrived at over many years by faithfully applying the law as laid down in *Chan Wing-Siu* and in *Powell and English*. The error identified, of equating foresight with intent to assist rather than treating the first as evidence of the second, is important as a matter of legal principle, but it does not follow that it will have been important on the facts to the outcome of the trial or to the safety of the conviction.

His Lordship went on to say:

> Moreover, where a conviction has been arrived at by faithfully applying the law as it stood at the time, it can be set aside only by seeking exceptional leave to appeal to the Court of Appeal out of time. That court has power to grant such leave, and may do so *if substantial injustice be demonstrated*, but it will not do so simply because the law applied has now been declared to have been mistaken. This principle has been consistently applied for many years. (emphasis added)

Impact on convictions pre-*Jogee*

Interestingly, decisions in the Court of Appeal post-*Jogee* have indicated that there is little, if any, impact on previous convictions as a result of the restatement of law. In *R v Johnson & Others* [2016] EWCA Crim 1613, the Court of Appeal dismissed 13 appeals against convictions for murder secured under the old law. Lord Thomas CJ gave the following guidance regarding appeals following *Jogee*:

> In determining whether that high threshold has been met, the court will primarily and ordinarily have regard to the strength of the case advanced that the change in the law would, in fact, have made a difference. If crime A is a crime of violence which the jury concluded must have involved the use of a weapon so that the inference of participation with an intention to cause really serious harm is strong, that is likely to be very difficult. At the other end of the spectrum, if crime A is a different crime, not involving intended violence or use of force, it may well be easier to demonstrate substantial injustice. The court will also have regard to other matters including whether the defendant was guilty of other, though less serious, criminal conduct. It is not, however, in our view, material to consider the length of time that has elapsed. If there was a substantial injustice, it is irrelevant whether that injustice occurred a short time or a long time ago. It is and remains an injustice.

See also *R v Noble* [2016] EWCA Crim 2219.

Many appeals against conviction are likely to fall by reason of being out of time. Section 1(2)(b) of the Criminal Appeal Act 1968 prescribes that notice of an appeal against conviction or sentence in the Crown Court must be served within 28 days of the conviction or sentence. Appeals may be brought outside this time period if it is in the interests of justice to do so. However, as noted above, the Supreme Court in *Jogee* was clear that a 'substantial injustice' must also be demonstrated. Some of the appellants in the *Johnson* case sought a certificate from the Court of Appeal that the test of 'substantial injustice' raised a point of law of general public importance to be determined by the Supreme Court. However, this certificate was ultimately refused (*R v Garwood* [2017] EWCA Crim 59). Since *Jogee*, there have been a large number of failed appeals demonstrating the high threshold for the substantial injustice test. The following are but a few examples:

- *R v Agera* [2017] EWCA Crim 740;
- *R v Varley* [2017] EWCA Crim 268;
- *R v Quinn* [2017] EWCA Crim 1071;
- *R v Grant-Murray* [2017] EWCA Crim 1228;
- *R (Davies) v Criminal Cases Review Commission* [2018] EWHC 3080 (Admin);
- *R v Towers; R v Hawkes* [2019] EWCA Crim 198;
- *R v Daley (Kyrone)* [2019] EWCA Crim 627; and
- *R v Jackson* [2019] EWCA Crim 1461.

Since *Jogee*, there has been one successful appeal overturning a conviction of joint enterprise out of time: *R v Crilly* [2018] 4 WLR 114.

Charge:
Robbery (TA 1968, s 8) and murder

Case progression:
Crown Court – Guilty

Court of Appeal – Conviction quashed

Point of law:
Overcoming the 'substantial injustice' test

case example

In *R v Crilly* [2018] 4 WLR 114, the defendant took part in a burglary with the principal offender. Whilst the defendant searched the house for money, the principal punched the victim, a 71-year-old man, in the face, killing him. The defendant and his principal were convicted of robbery and murder in the Crown Court. Following *Jogee*, the defendant appealed to the Court of Appeal, contending that his conviction for murder was unsafe given the substantial change in the law from *Jogee*. The Court of Appeal allowed the appeal, overturning his conviction.

Hallett LJ explained that:

> We derive the following principles from the judgments in *R v Jogee* and *R v Johnson* as relevant to the applications. First, to qualify for the grant of exceptional leave the applicant must establish a 'substantial injustice' would be caused if it was denied. The fact that there has been a change in the law is not in itself sufficient where a person was properly convicted on the law as it stood at the time of trial, as here. Second, the threshold for demonstrating a substantial injustice is a high one. Third, in determining whether that high threshold has been met the court will have regard to the strength of the case advanced, that a change in the law would in fact have made a difference.

Her Ladyship would then proceed to apply those principles to Crilly's case:

- 'The applicant was guilty of robbery and at the very least he foresaw that grievous bodily harm might be caused to the victim of the robbery yet continued to participate in it.'
- '[T]his was planned as a burglary of an unoccupied dwelling house. It was not planned as a robbery and no violence was initially intended.'

- '[T]he violence does not seem to have been a sustained and savage attack; it may have been solely a push and a punch.'
- 'We place the robbery between the middle to the lower end of the *R v Johnson* spectrum'.

Based on these factors (*inter alia*), Hallett LJ would conclude:

> It is in that context we consider whether *R v Jogee* compliant directions would have made a difference and whether a refusal of exceptional leave would cause a substantial injustice. We are satisfied we should grant exceptional leave. The case against the applicant was to all intents and purposes a case about his foresight. Foresight may be evidence of intent but it does not equate to intent. The evidence against him was not so strong that we can safely and fairly infer the jury would have found the requisite intent to cause really serious bodily harm had the issue been left to them by the judge.

For an appeal overturning a defendant's conviction following *Jogee* that was submitted *in time* (and thus avoiding the difficulties of s 1(2)(b) of the Criminal Appeal Act 1968 noted above), see *R v Dreszer* [2018] EWCA Crim 454.

in practice

On a practical level, there is no longer a reason, or justification, for practitioners to refer to the authorities that came before *Jogee*. For academic purposes, however, it is essential to understand the development of the law before *Jogee*.

The effect of *Jogee* has been considered in two other jurisdictions, namely Hong Kong and Australia. In *HKSAR v Chan Kam Shing* [2016] HKCFA 87, the Court of Final Appeal of Hong Kong refused to apply *Jogee*, and in *Miller v The Queen* [2016] HCA 30, the High Court of Australia held that any change to the rules governing accessorial liability, should there be a change, must come from the legislature.

4.4 Assistance after the fact

As explained above, the rules regarding accessorial liability apply only in circumstances where the assistance or encouragement is provided either before or during the commission of the offence. There is scope, in the law, however for a person to be held criminally liable for assisting an offender *after* the commission of the offence. These circumstances are provided for in ss 4 and 5 of the Criminal Law Act (CLA) 1967.

4.4.1 Impeding an arrest (CLA 1967, s 4)

Section 4(1) of the CLA 1967 provides:

> Where a person has committed a relevant offence, any other person who, knowing or believing him to be guilty of the offence or of some other relevant offence, does without lawful authority or reasonable excuse any act with intent to impede his apprehension or prosecution shall be guilty of an offence.

Reference to 'any act' in s 4 would indicate that the offence cannot be committed by omission. Further to this, there is no requirement that the act actually impedes an offence; the section is worded in such a way that a mere intention to impede arrest is sufficient. In terms of *mens rea*, the defendant must intend to impede arrest, coupled with knowledge or belief of the principal's guilt in respect of the relevant offence. This latter requirement of knowledge indicates that an actual offence must have taken place first, by the principal, before a defendant may be liable for impeding his arrest (*R v Morgan* [1972] 1 QB 436). According to the Court of Appeal in *R v Brindley* [1971] 2 QB 300, it is neither necessary for the defendant to have exact knowledge as to the offence committed (mere knowledge of the general nature of the offence will suffice), nor is it necessary for the defendant to know the principal's identity. However, it is a requirement that the defendant has 'knowledge' of the relevant offence; a mere suspicion (however well founded) will not suffice.

By s 4(4), in order to institute criminal proceedings for a s 4 offence, the consent of the Director of Public Prosecutions (DPP) must be secured first.

4.4.2 Compounding an offence (CLA 1967, s 5)

Section 5(1) of the CLA 1967 provides:

> Where a person has committed a relevant offence, any other person who, knowing or believing that the offence or some other relevant offence has been committed, and that he has information which might be of material assistance in securing the prosecution or conviction of an offender for it, accepts or agrees to accept for not disclosing that information any consideration other than the making good of loss or injury caused by the offence, or the making of reasonable compensation for that loss or injury, shall be liable on conviction on indictment to imprisonment for not more than two years.

This section essentially criminalises the acceptance of payment in return for not disclosing information which might secure the prosecution of an offender. The *actus reus* in this respect consists of accepting, or agreeing to accept, consideration for failing to provide information which may assist in the prosecution or conviction of an offender. Consideration, as in contract law, simply means an exchange in value (ie money or monies worth). The *mens rea* of the offence includes an intention to accept the consideration and knowledge that a relevant offence has been committed.

By s 5(3), in order to institute criminal proceedings for a s 5 offence, the consent of the Director of Public Prosecutions (DPP) must be secured first.

4.5 Further reading

Alldridge, 'The Doctrine of Innocent Agency' (1990) 2 Crim L Forum 45.
Buxton, 'Jogee: Upheaval in Secondary Liability for Murder' [2016] Crim LR 324.
Buxton, 'Joint Enterprise' [2009] Crim LR 233.
Crewe, Liebling, Padfield and Virgo, 'Joint Enterprise: The Implications of an Unfair and Unclear Law' [2015] Crim LR 252.
Dyson, 'Principals without Distinction' [2018] Crim LR 296.
Green and McGourlay, 'The Wolf Packs in our Midst and Other Products of Criminal Joint Enterprise Prosecutions' (2015) 79 J Crim L 280.
Krebs, 'Joint Criminal Enterprise' (2010) 73 MLR 578.
Sullivan, 'Participating in Crime: Law Com No. 305—Joint Criminal Ventures' [2008] Crim LR 19.

Taylor, 'Procuring, Causation, Innocent Agency and the Law Commission' [2008] Crim LR 32.

Virgo, 'Joint Enterprise Liability is Dead: Long Live Accessorial Liability' [2012] Crim LR 850.

Warburton, 'Supreme Court and Judicial Committee of the Privy Council: Secondary Participation in Crime' (2016) 80 J Crim L 160.

Wilson, 'A Rational Scheme of Liability for Participation in Crime' [2008] Crim LR 3.

Wilson and Ormerod, 'Simply Harsh to Fairly Simple: Joint Enterprise Reform' [2015] Crim LR 3.

- Secondary liability relates to those offenders who assist or encourage a principal offender to commit the offence.
- Secondary liability is also referred to as the law of accessories or the law of complicity.
- The *actus reus* of complicity involves circumstances where the defendant aids, abets, counsels or procures the commission of the principal offence.
- To 'aid' means to provide some assistance either before or at the time of the commission of the offence; to 'abet' means to provide some form of encouragement either before or at the time of the commission of the offence; to 'counsel' means to advise or solicit the commission of the offence; and to 'procure' means to produce by endeavour.
- The *mens rea* of complicity involves an intention on the part of the defendant to assist or encourage the principal offender, with the knowledge of the essential matters.
- Knowledge of the essential matters means that the defendant knows of the potential offence, or range of offences, committed by the principal and that the principal would act with the respective *mens rea* for the offence.
- The defendant may be liable for more serious offences than the principal in cases where the principal has a defence or fails to forms the *mens rea* for the offence.
- The defendant may also be liable for a less serious offence than the principal in cases where the principal has gone beyond the agreed plan and the defendant lacks the *mens rea* for the more serious offence. The defendant will still be liable for the lesser offence.
- The concept of joint enterprise liability has now been changed by the Supreme Court in *R v Jogee*. Now, only intention will satisfy the *mens rea* for complicity; foresight is now only evidence of intention.
- The defendant may have a number of defences available to him, including withdrawal. Such withdrawal must be clearly communicated to the principal.
- Victims are not to be treated as accessories where a statute has been designed to protect them.

Problem

Jack and Jill are activists protesting against the UK's involvement with commercial organisations notorious for animal testing and the use of cheap labour outside the UK. In an attempt to draw attention to their cause, Jack and Jill wish to blow up one of the regional headquarters of WellWorth, a beauty company that matches the above description. They ask Bill, a friend, to supply equipment to make a bomb. Bill is reluctant at first, but Jack threatens the life of Bill's brother, Ben. Bill succumbs to the threat and provides the pair with the bomb. The pair ask Andy, Jill's cousin, to drive them to and from the location. Andy believes that the pair are intending to use spray paint on the headquarters walls and agrees to drive them to their location. On the day in question, Jack and Jill make their way to the headquarters and plant the bomb. Jill says to Jack, 'Make sure we get everybody out before you detonate.' Although Jack has no intention to make sure people get out of the building safely, he agrees with Jill. Jill plants the bomb and informs Jack that she will set a 5-minute countdown when the building is clear of people. Jack lies to Jill and informs her that he has cleared the building. Jill, believing this to be the case, sets the timer and the bomb explodes. Unfortunately, a number of people are caught in the blast and die.

Advise the CPS as to offences that may be charged against Jack, Jill, Bill and Andy.

Essay

'The *mens rea* of complicity has long been the subject of considerable difficulty and criticism. With the Supreme Court's decision in *R v Jogee* [2016] UKSC 8, the law is now in a state of common sense and application.'

Critically discuss this statement with a focus on how the law has developed from the principles in *Chan Wing-Siu* to *Jogee*.

chapter 5

Inchoate Offences

After reading this chapter, you will be able to understand:

- the fundamental basis for inchoate liability
- the rationale for the existence of such offences
- the offence of attempt, its scope and elements of the offence
- the offence of conspiracy, its scope and elements of the offence
- the offence of assisting or encouraging an offence, its scope and elements of the offence
- the concept of double inchoate liability and that of substantive inchoate crimes.

5.1 Introduction to inchoate offences

The word 'inchoate' is defined in the Cambridge Dictionary as 'only recently or partly formed, or not completely developed or clear'. An inchoate offence, therefore, can be defined as the circumstance where a full offence has not yet been completed by a defendant, but the defendant has taken some steps towards the commission of the offence. His offence is often said to be 'in the works'.

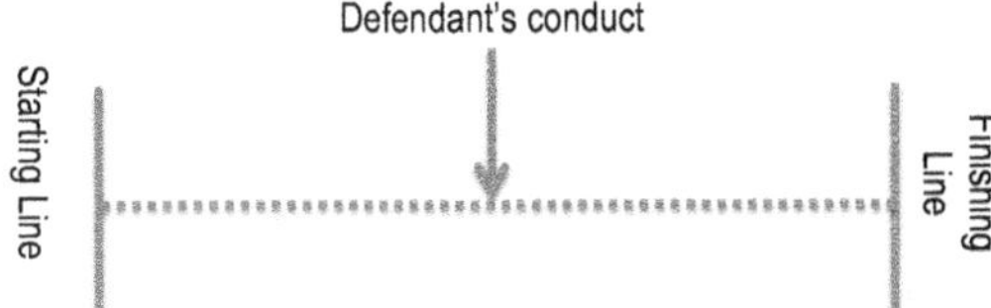

Figure 5.1 The timeline of inchoate liability

In this respect, inchoate offences can be likened to a running track for athletes. It includes a start, a middle and an end. Before the runner steps over the line, it cannot be said that he has 'taken part' in the race. The same is to be said for the criminal law, in that a defendant cannot be liable for guilty thoughts alone where there were no actual 'steps taken' towards the commission of an offence. Likewise, a runner cannot be said to have finished the race unless and until he passes the finish line. Again, the same can be said for the criminal law – a defendant cannot be liable for a full criminal offence unless and until he has completed all elements of the offence in question.

Inchoate liability, therefore, attempts to find a middle ground where a defendant may be liable for an offence, short of a full offence, as a result of his stepping over the starting line. Specifically, the law has found three means by which a defendant may be liable for an offence in circumstances where his conduct fell short of crossing the finishing line.

- *Attempts:* A defendant will be liable for an attempt in the circumstances where he intends to commit the relevant *actus reus* of the full offence but, for some reason, is unable to do so. So long as the defendant's conduct can be classed as 'more than merely preparatory', he may be liable for a criminal attempt (see **5.2**).

- *Conspiracy:* A defendant will be liable for conspiracy in the circumstances where he enters into an agreement, with at least one other person, that a criminal offence will be committed (see **5.3**).
- *Assisting or encouraging:* A defendant will be liable for assisting or encouraging in the circumstances where he either assists or encourages another party to commit an offence (see **5.4**).

We shall also have the opportunity to consider in brief the common law offence of incitement, which continues to apply to offences committed before 1 October 2008 (see **5.5**) and the circumstances where a defendant may be liable for substantive inchoate offences (see **5.7**).

5.1.1 Rationale for inchoate liability

Given that inchoate liability reflects the circumstances where the defendant's conduct falls short of a 'full' crime, it is necessary to understand the legal basis upon which punishment of such incomplete offences can be justified. For the most part, inchoate liability is designed to reflect the law's stance on participation, in whatever sense, in a criminal offence. Where such offences exist, the defendant will have revealed an intention, or willingness, on his part to be involved, to some extent, in the commission of a crime. In this respect, inchoate liability can be justified as designed to prevent harm or crime occurring. As Monaghan (*Criminal Law Directions*, 6th edn (OUP, 2020)) comments, 'Criminal law would … be farcical if it required a police officer to wait for an offender to complete the full offence before he could be arrested.' The criminal law therefore justifies such criminalisation on account of the protection of society and the prevention of harm.

An important element of the justification for such offences, however, is knowing when the appropriate point is for the law to intervene. Naturally, it would not be appropriate for the law to intervene where the defendant merely possesses a guilty mind and does not put that to use. Likewise, a defendant who plans the commission of an offence, albeit only in his own head, should not have the full weight of the law coming down on him. The law must strive, therefore, to find that appropriate balance, and it attempts to do so through the law of inchoate liability. The importance of inchoate liability cannot be denied.

example

Jill intends to shoot Jack in the head with a gun but is a bad shot and misses.

In this case, it would be absurd if the criminal law did not intervene to criminalise Jill's conduct. She has clearly demonstrated her willingness, and it is only through her poor aim, or perhaps more accurately, Jack's sheer luck, that Jill is not liable for a fuller offence. On the point of luck in inchoate liability, see Ashworth, 'Criminal Attempts and the Role of Resulting Harm' (1988) 19 Rutgers LR 725.

In light of finding the appropriate time to intervene, Child and Ormerod (*Smith, Hogan, & Ormerod's Essentials of Criminal Law*, 3rd edn (OUP, 2019)) note that 'there is a necessary and obvious balancing of legal priorities' in any given case between the fairness to the defendant and the protection of society. We addressed the latter interest above, but it is worth considering the former at this stage. As discussed in **Chapter 1**, a fundamental principle of the criminal law is the notion of fair labelling. Under this principle, the defendant should only be charged with an offence that reflects his relevant conduct and intention. In this respect, a defendant should only be liable in circumstances where his conduct is sufficient to suggest that he has committed himself to the commission of the offence. Child and Ormerod helpfully phrase the extent of this liability in the following terms: 'We want to criminalise D who would have gone on to commit the principal offence, not D who might have changed her mind if left alone.'

5.1.2 Terminology and common themes

Much of the terminology discussed in this chapter will be reflective of that considered in **Chapter 4** ('Principal and Secondary Offenders'). This is because the substantive basis for both categories of offences are roughly mirrored – both aim to criminalise a defendant who did not personally commit the full offence, but rather assisted another to commit the offence, or attempted to commit the full offence and failed. In this respect, it is useful to reconsider the terminology discussed in the previous chapter.

Table 5.1 Inchoate terminology

Term	Definition
Principal offence	Refers to the substantive offence (often referred to as the 'full offence') that the defendant attempts/conspires/assists or encourages the commission of.
Principal offender	Refers to the party who perpetrates the principal offence.
Defendant	Refers to the party who attempts to commit the principal offence, conspires to do so or assists or encourages the principal offender to commit the offence.

At this stage, it is also useful to explain two common themes that run through the course of inchoate liability:

- *No liability in the abstract:* It is incorrect to speak of a defendant being charged with an offence simply of 'attempt' or 'conspiracy', for example. Rather, the defendant must be charged in relation to a principal offence, eg 'attempted murder' or 'conspiracy to rob'. In this respect, it can be said that inchoate liability does not exist in the abstract and any potential offences committed must be understood as interrelated to a principal offence.
- *Irrelevance of commission:* Although the alleged offence must relate to a principal offence, it is unnecessary for that principal offence to have actually been completed. The focus of inchoate liability is on the conduct of the defendant leading up to the potential commission of the principal offence – not its actual commission.

In practice

Of course, should the full offence be committed, the CPS would consider whether there is a sufficient evidential basis to charge the defendant with a full offence as a principal offender (in cases where he has the relevant *actus reus* and *mens rea*) or, in circumstances where the defendant merely assisted or encouraged another to commit the offence, with an offence as an accessory (see **Chapter 4**). In the former case, a defendant cannot also be liable for an inchoate offence.

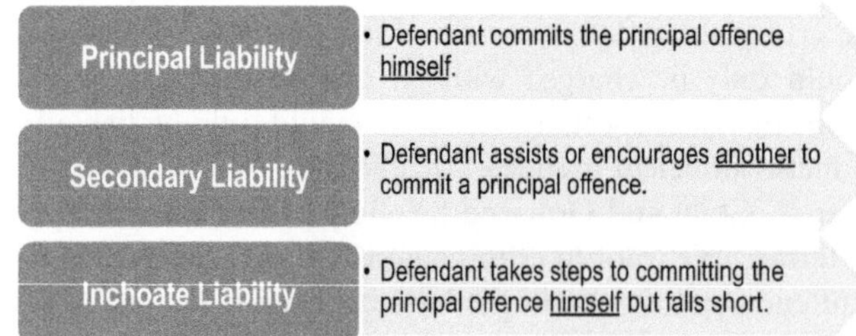

Figure 5.2 Differing cases of principal, accessorial and inchoate liability

5.2 Attempts

By s 6(1) of the Criminal Attempts Act (CAA) 1981 the offence of attempt at common law was abolished, as was any offence at common law of 'procuring materials for crime'. The CAA 1981 created a brand new offence of statutory attempts.

For a full discussion, see the rather dated but seminal text by Duff, *Criminal Attempts* (OUP, 1996) and the more recent text by Yaffe, *Attempts* (OUP, 2010).

5.2.1 Defining attempts

An attempt refers to the situation in which the defendant has, for some reason or another, failed to complete the full offence in question. This failure may have come about as a result of a change of heart or as a result of being physically prevented from acting further. The law intervenes, however, only in circumstances where the defendant has taken sufficient steps, or has made sufficient progress, towards the completion of the full offence. Take, for instance, the case of *R v White* [1910] 2 KB 124 (considered in **Chapter 2**). In *White*, the defendant placed poison in his mother's drink, intending her to take it and die as a result. The defendant's mother died that evening but from natural causes and not from the poison ingested. The defendant could not, therefore, be liable for her murder, but it would have been absurd for him to avoid liability outright. As such, the defendant was rightly convicted of attempted murder. This case is a clear demonstration as to the need for a law of attempts.

As explained above, 'attempts' is not an isolated term and must be considered 'in relation to' a principal offence. In this respect, a defendant may be liable of:

- attempted murder;
- attempted rape;
- attempted theft, etc.

5.2.2 Elements of attempt

Section 1 of the CAA 1981 provides:

> (1) If, with intent to commit an offence to which this section applies, a person does an act which is more than merely preparatory to the commission of the offence, he is guilty of attempting to commit the offence.
>
> (2) A person may be guilty of attempting to commit an offence to which this section applies even though the facts are such that the commission of the offence is impossible.

The *actus reus* and *mens rea* of an attempt are outlined in **Table 5.2**.

Table 5.2 Elements of attempt

AR/MR	Elements of the offence
Actus reus	(i) an offence which can be attempted; (ii) an act; (iii) which is more than merely preparatory.
Mens rea	intention to commit an offence

It is worth stating at this stage that some statutory provisions may create a substantive offence in the form of an attempt. Under s 3 of the CAA 1981, unless otherwise stated in that legislation, an offence of attempt of a specific offence shall be construed in the same manner as an attempt under the CAA 1981.

We shall consider each element in turn.

5.2.2.1 *Actus reus:* (i) an offence which can be attempted

The first essential element of the offence of attempt is prescribed in s 1(4) of the CAA 1981. Section 1(4) provides a circumstance element of the *actus reus* that the principal offence must be one that can be attempted.

As a general rule, under s 1(4), a defendant may be convicted of an attempt to commit any offence so long as that offence is one that is triable on indictment. From **Chapter 1**, we know that an indictable offence is an offence that:

- is triable only on indictment (ie only in the Crown Court); or
- is an either-way offence (ie it can be tried in either the Crown Court or the magistrates' court). See the Interpretation Act 1978, Sch 1.

In this respect, a defendant may not be convicted of an attempt to commit a summary-only offence (ie one that can only be tried in the magistrates' court). A defendant may be liable for an attempt in relation to a summary-only offence in circumstances where the statute prescribing the offence creates an offence of attempt specific to that crime, for example attempting to drive with excess alcohol contrary to s 4(1) of the Road Traffic Act 1988. This position has been recommended as being retained by the Law Commission ('Conspiracy and Attempts' (Law Com No 318, 2009)). For a discussion of where such offences can be tried, see **5.2.4.1**.

The statutory exceptions to the general rule in s 1(4) are set out in s 1(4)(a)–(c). These exceptions are detailed in **Table 5.3**.

Table 5.3 Offences that cannot be attempted

Section	Exception
CAA 1981, s 1(4)	A defendant cannot generally be liable for an attempt to commit a summary-only offence (eg common assault).
CAA 1981, s 1(4)(a)	A defendant cannot be liable for an attempt to conspire either at common law or under s 1 of the Criminal Law Act 1977. This avoids criminalising offences too far removed from the principal offence.
CAA 1981, s 1(4)(b)	A defendant cannot be liable for an attempt of a secondary offence, ie he cannot be liable for attempting to aid, abet, counsel or procure. Interestingly, however, a defendant can be liable for aiding and abetting an attempt (*R v Dunnington* [1984] QB 472).
CAA 1981, s 1(4)(c)	A defendant cannot be liable for attempting to impede an arrest under s 4 of the Criminal Law Act 1967 or compounding an arrest under s 5 of the 1967 Act.

5.2.2.2 *Actus reus:* (ii) an act

Section 1(1) of the CAA 1981 is clear in that an offence is committed where 'a person does an *act*' (emphasis added). Taking a literal interpretation of the statute, this would mean that attempts may only be committed by way of a positive act and not by way of omission (or a failure to act). This was one of the many issues raised in the case of *R v Nevard* [2006] EWCA Crim 2896.

case example

Charge:
Attempted murder

Case progression:
Crown Court – Guilty

Court of Appeal – Conviction upheld

Point of law:
Whether omissions are sufficient for attempt liability

In *R v Nevard* [2006] EWCA Crim 2896, the defendant attacked his wife, the victim, with an axe and a knife. When the wife attempted to call the emergency services, the defendant forced her to hang up. The emergency services returned the call, and the defendant informed them that the first call was a mistake. Despite this, the emergency services arrived and saved the victim. The defendant was charged with and convicted of attempted murder and malicious wounding with intent (he had pleaded guilty to the latter offence).

In the Court of Appeal, Richards LJ was critical of the trial judge's direction to the jury that the defendant's failure to summon emergency services was relevant as a matter of evidence to whether the defendant was liable for attempted murder. Richards LJ stated:

> The judge should have made explicit to the jury that attempting to divert the emergency services could not in itself constitute attempted murder.

This case can be used for the proposition that omissions are not capable of giving rise to an attempt. It is worth noting, however, that *Nevard* is not the strongest authority on this point given that the husband had actually committed a positive act (in telling the emergency services that the first phone call was a mistake) as opposed to an omission. In this respect, the defendant's conduct should have been relevant to the jury's considerations.

Despite the statement in *Nevard*, there remains a sense of uncertainty as to whether the *actus reus* may be performed by an omission. The Law Commission ('Conspiracy and Attempts' (Law Com No 318, 2009)) identified that it 'seems doubtful that the law currently allows for an attempt by omission'. The Commission went on to recommend:

> [S]ince the most serious offences, such as murder, can be committed in some circumstances by omission, it seems wrong not to make it clear in law that there can be an attempt to commit offences by omission.

The Commission views such an amendment as desirable to cover such cases as *R v Gibbins and Proctor* (1918) 13 Cr App R 134 (see **Chapter 2**). Indeed, this was the approach adopted by the Law Commission in its draft Criminal Code (1989), in which it was proposed that the word 'act' in this context should include 'an omission only where the offence intended is capable of being committed by an omission'.

example

Jack and Jill intentionally starve their child, Alice, wishing for her to die of starvation. Alice is rescued, provided with life-saving treatment and survives.

In this scenario, Jack and Jill would clearly be liable for murder should Alice have died, so, according to the Law Commission, there should be 'no good reason' that Jack and Jill should not be liable for attempted murder.

5.2.2.3 *Actus reus:* (iii) more than merely preparatory

The real core of an attempts offence is the final element of the *actus reus*, namely that the defendant's actions must be considered to be 'more than merely preparatory'. Using our running track, we can identify the point at which liability arises. As can be seen, liability can only arise for an attempt in circumstances where the defendant's conduct is *more than* merely preparatory. Conduct which is 'merely preparatory' is not sufficient.

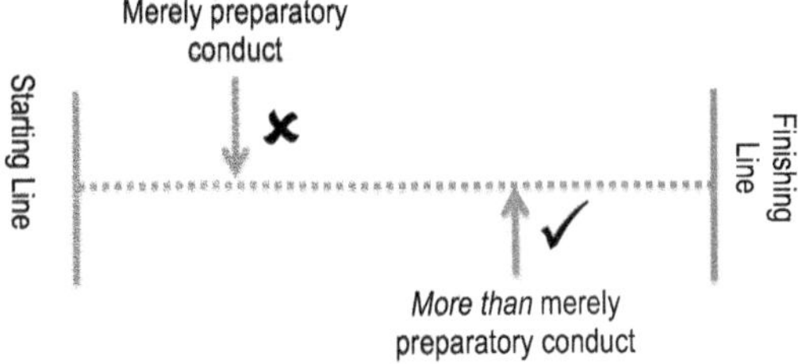

Figure 5.3 Overview of 'more than merely preparatory'

Unfortunately, no definition is provided in the statute as to the meaning of 'more than merely preparatory'. However, the Court of Appeal has stated that the term is to be given its 'ordinary meaning' (*R v Jones* [1990] 3 All ER 886). Despite the Court's resilience in maintaining that this phrase should be given its ordinary meaning, subsequent decisions have shown that the courts do not agree as to the extent to which the defendant must go in order to be liable for an attempt. Over the years, a number of approaches have been developed in order to answer this question. It will be useful for our purposes to divide these authorities between those that arose before the CAA 1981 and those that arose following the 1981 Act. It is important to note at this stage that the phrase 'more than merely preparatory' is a creation of the CAA 1981 and such wording was not present in the pre-1981 common law. Rather, prior to the introduction of the CAA 1981, the *actus reus* of the common law offence of attempt was simply that the defendant 'attempted' to commit the full offence. No further interpretation or expansion was given to that word.

Interpreting 'attempt' – pre-1981

A number of common law tests arose which were used to identify the point at which the defendant had 'attempted' to commit the offence.

Some of these tests adopted what might be called a 'hindsight' approach, in which discussion began with the completed full offence (ie the finishing line) and looked backwards from that point to identify whether the defendant's conduct could be classified as an attempt. In *R v Eagleton* (1855) 19 JP 546, the Court for Crown Cases Reserved adopted a test that looked at whether the defendant's conduct was so 'immediately connected' to the *actus reus* of the full offence that it could be justified to impose liability. This became known as the 'proximity' or 'last act' test and was explained in full by Parke B as follows:

> [S]ome act is required and we do not think that all acts towards committing a [criminal offence] are indictable. Acts remotely leading towards the commission of the offence are not to be considered as attempts to commit it, but acts immediately connected with it are.

In the 1970s, the House of Lords was again tasked with the question as to the meaning of an attempt in *DPP v Stonehouse* [1978] AC 55. Lord Diplock adopted the 'Rubicon test', which was explained in the following way:

> Acts that are merely preparatory to the commission of the offence such as, in the instant case, the taking out of insurance policies are not sufficiently proximate to constitute an attempt. They do not indicate a fixed irrevocable intention to go on to commit the complete offence unless involuntarily prevented from doing so. … In other words the [defendant] must have crossed the Rubicon and burnt his boats.

Note: The 'Rubicon' is a reference to the river at the edge of the Roman Empire which separated Italy from Cisalpine Gaul. At the point the Rubicon was crossed, Caesar was committed to war with Sicily and the Senate.

A notable statement of when conduct is more than merely preparatory comes from Stephen (*Digest of Criminal Law*, 5th edn (MacMillan, 1984)): 'an attempt to commit a crime is an act done with intent to commit that crime, and forming part of a series of acts which would constitute its actual commission if it were not interrupted'.

Table 5.4 Pre-1981 approaches to 'more than merely preparatory'

Case/authority	**Test**
R v Eagleton (1855) 19 JP 546	'Proximity test' – acts immediately connected with the *actus reus* of the full offence.
DPP v Stonehouse [1978] AC 55	'Rubicon test' – focus on the defendant's fixed irrevocable intention.
Stephen (*Digest of Criminal Law*, 5th edn (MacMillan, 1984))	'Series of acts test' – focus on a series of acts which, if not interrupted, would constitute the commission of the full offence.

Interpreting 'more than merely preparatory' – post-1981

Shortly after the introduction of the 1981 Act, courts were faced with the task of understanding what the new phrase 'more than merely preparatory' meant. At first, the courts were of the opinion that the pre-1981 authorities subsisted as the statements of law. For instance, in *R v Widdowson* (1986) 82 Cr App R 314, the Court of Appeal adopted Lord Diplock's Rubicon test, whilst a year later the Court adopted the 'series of acts' test formulated by Stephen (*R v Boyle and Boyle* [1987] Crim LR 111).

However, in later years, it appeared that the courts wished to moved away from such pre-1981 tests and apply a more modern understanding. For instance, in *R v Gullefer* [1990] 3 All ER 882, Lord Lane CJ was of the view that the provision meant that the defendant 'embarks upon the crime proper'. This would accord with the earlier authority of *R v Osborn* (1919) 84 JP 63 in which Rowlatt J phrased the question as being whether the defendant was 'on the job'. Substantially, in *R v Geddes* [1996] Crim LR 894, Lord Bingham CJ stated:

> It is, we think, an accurate paraphrase of the statutory test and not an illegitimate gloss upon it to ask whether the available evidence, if accepted, could show that a defendant has done an act which shows that he has actually tried to commit the offence in question, or whether he has only got ready or put himself in a position or equipped himself to do so.

We can now observe a number of cases (post-1981) in which the courts have attempted to explain the notion of 'more than merely preparatory'. Unfortunately, the cases lack a degree of consistency. For this reason, the most appropriate manner of dealing with such authorities may be to set them out in a chronological order. We can thus consider the conduct in question and whether the respective courts found there to be conduct that was 'more than merely preparatory', and then bring all the cases together to attempt to find the common ground.

The first of our long list of cases is that of *R v Boyle and Boyle* [1987] Crim LR 111.

case example

Charge:
Attempted burglary (CAA 1981, s 1)

Case progression:
Crown Court – Guilty

Court of Appeal – Conviction upheld

Point of law:
Meaning of 'more than merely preparatory'

In *R v Boyle and Boyle* [1987] Crim LR 111, the defendants had broken a lock and the hinges on a door of a house with a view to entering the property. Before they were able to enter the building, the defendants were apprehended by a passing policeman. The defendants were charged with and convicted of attempted burglary.

The defendants appealed against their conviction, arguing that they had not crossed the Rubicon in that they had not yet entered the building. The Court of Appeal found this to be irrelevant and held that the defendants had committed a series of acts towards the commission of the offence. The defendants' convictions were upheld.

The actions in *Boyle* can thus be explained as follows:

Table 5.5 Understanding the conduct in Boyle

Extent of conduct	Specific conduct within the case
Merely preparatory	Walking towards the door of the house; inspecting the door.
More than merely preparatory	Damaging the door, its hinges and lock.

A rather noteworthy case is that of *R v Gullefer* [1990] 3 All ER 882.

case example

Charge:
Attempted theft (CAA 1981, s 1)

Case progression:
Crown Court – Guilty

Court of Appeal – Conviction quashed

Point of law:
Meaning of 'more than merely preparatory'

In *R v Gullefer* [1990] 3 All ER 882, the accused had placed a bet on a greyhound race. Once the race had started, it was clear that the dog would most likely lose. In an attempt to disrupt the race, the defendant ran onto the track, waving his arms and hoping to distract the other dogs. The defendant did so in the hope that the race would be declared null and void and he would be entitled to his money back (£18). The dogs were not distracted, however, and the race was not called off. The defendant was charged with and convicted of attempted theft in the Crown Court.

The defendant appealed to the Court of Appeal on the ground that his actions could not be classified as 'more than merely preparatory'. The Court of Appeal agreed, finding that there was no evidence to support the contention that the defendant's conduct was more than mere preparation. The Court reasoned that the defendant had not started on the 'crime proper'. Specifically, Lord Lane CJ was of the opinion that:

> [An attempt] begins when the merely preparatory acts come to an end and the defendant embarks on the crime proper. When that is will depend of course on the facts in any particular case.

In providing this judgment, Lord Lane CJ acknowledged that the words of the 1981 Act seek to 'steer a midway course' between the approaches adopted under the pre-1981 law. The 'crime proper' in *Gullefer* was not the stopping of the race; rather, the last act necessary would have been the attempt to get his money back as a result of the disruption to the race. The defendant did not take any steps to secure his money back (because he was prevented from doing so), and on that basis his actions could not be said to be 'more than merely preparatory'. Lord Lane CJ was, however, cautious to avoid saying that it was necessary, as some earlier cases had suggested, that the defendant should have reached a 'point of no return' in respect of the full offence.

The actions in *Gullefer* can thus be explained as follows:

Table 5.6 Understanding the conduct in Gullefer

Extent of conduct	Specific conduct within the case
Merely preparatory	Running onto the track; waving arms at dogs to try to disrupt the race.
More than merely preparatory	Going to the bookmakers; asking for his money back.

Immediately following *Gullefer* came the case of *R v Jones* [1990] 3 All ER 886, where the defendant's conduct *was* found to be more than merely preparatory.

case example

Charge:
Attempted murder (CAA 1981, s. 1)

Case progression:
Crown Court – Guilty

Court of Appeal – Conviction upheld

Point of law:
Meaning of 'more than merely preparatory'

In *R v Jones* [1990] 3 All ER 886, the defendant bought a shotgun and sawed off the barrel. The defendant hid in disguise and waited for the victim (a love rival). The defendant jumped into the backseat of the victim's car and pulled the gun on him. After a struggle between the pair, the victim managed to escape unharmed and the defendant was charged with attempted murder in the Crown Court.

The defendant appealed to the Court of Appeal, arguing that his conduct could not be considered more than merely preparatory as he had not taken the 'last step' necessary to attempt murder. The Court of Appeal disagreed. For Taylor LJ, although the steps taken by the defendant building up to his confrontation with the victim could be considered merely preparatory, his conduct whilst in the victim's car was sufficient to say that he had begun the 'crime proper'.

The defendant argued that he had a number of further steps to take before he could be said to have taken the 'last act' before the commission of the offence. He contended that he would have had to have taken at least three more steps before his conduct could be considered an attempt:

- releasing the safety catch;
- putting his finger on the trigger; and
- beginning to squeeze the trigger.

The actions in *Jones* can thus be explained as follows:

Table 5.7 Understanding the conduct in Jones

Extent of conduct	Specific conduct within the case
Merely preparatory	Obtaining the gun; sawing off the barrel; loading the gun; dressing in disguise; lying in wait for the victim.
More than merely preparatory	Getting into the car; taking out the gun; pointing the loaded gun at the victim.

The next case worth considering is that of *R v Campbell* (1991) 93 Cr App R 350.

Charge:
Attempted robbery (CAA 1981, s 1)

Case progression:
Crown Court – Guilty

Court of Appeal – Conviction quashed

Point of law:
Meaning of 'more than merely preparatory'

case example

In *R v Campbell* (1991) 93 Cr App R 350, the defendant stood outside a sub-post office for around 30 minutes, wearing a motorcycle helmet and carrying a fake gun and a threatening note. The defendant was arrested a yard from the door to the post office following concerns raised by the staff of the post office. The defendant admitted that he originally intended to rob the post office but had later changed his mind. Importantly, he had never drawn the gun. The defendant claimed he was about to depart the scene at which point he was arrested. The defendant was charged with and convicted of attempted robbery in the Crown Court.

The defendant successfully appealed to the Court of Appeal, arguing that his conduct had not gotten to the stage that it could be classed as 'more than merely preparatory'. Indeed, Watkins LJ was clear in his statement that:

> If a person in circumstances such as this, had not even gained the place where he could be in a position to carry out the offence, it is extremely unlikely that it could ever be said that he had performed an act which could be properly said to be an attempt.

Watkins LJ was of the view that there was no evidence upon which a jury could 'properly and safely' have concluded that his acts were more than merely preparatory. For Watkins LJ, too many acts remained undone by the defendant, and what had been done could be characterised as 'indicative of mere preparation'.

The actions in *Campbell* can thus be explained as follows:

Table 5.8 Understanding the conduct in Campbell

Extent of conduct	Specific conduct within the case
Merely preparatory	Leaving his home to go to the post office; dismounting his bike; walking towards the entrance; loitering outside the post office for 30 minutes; possessing a threatening note and imitation firearm.
More than merely preparatory	Drawing the gun; entering the building; approaching the counter; threatening the use of force/demanding money.

The decision has been the subject of considerable criticism on the grounds that the defendant could not have done much more – other than actually commit the robbery – before he could be convicted of attempted robbery. Indeed McAlhone and Wortley (*Criminal Law – The Fundamentals*, 4th edn (Sweet & Maxwell, 2016)) are of the view that this decision

> [leaves] the police in the unsatisfactory position of having to wait until [the defendant] has entered the building and approached the counter before arresting him, with all the dangers to which this exposes people inside the building.

Further, Jefferson (*Criminal Law*, 12th edn (Pearson, 2015)) is critical of the decision in *Campbell*, arguing that it is 'not a helpful decision in the prevention of crime'. Jefferson goes on to compare *Campbell* with the authority of *R v Griffin* [1993] Crim LR 515, in which a mother was found guilty of attempting to abduct her own child. The evidence provided that the mother had purchased ferry tickets for Ireland and had informed the child's teacher that she was taking the child out of school in order to visit the dentist. The mother had not come into contact with the child or even made any headway towards the port and yet was still liable for attempted abduction. Jefferson explains that, had the issue been left to the jury in *Campbell*, a similar outcome is likely to have been reached. Herring (*Criminal Law*, 11th edn (Macmillan Law Masters, 2019)) attempts to explain the decision in *Campbell* on the basis that the courts will be reluctant to convict where 'there is a realistic possibility that the defendant will change his mind and decide not to complete the offence'.

Shortly after *Campbell*, the Court of Appeal heard the decision of *AG's Reference (No 1 of 1992)* [1993] 1 WLR 274.

case example

Charge:
Attempted rape (CAA 1981, s 1)

Case progression:
Crown Court – Guilty

Court of Appeal – Conviction upheld

Point of law:
Meaning of 'more than merely preparatory'

In *AG's Reference (No 1 of 1992)* [1993] 1 WLR 274, the defendant had attacked the victim before proceeding to drag her up some stairs. The defendant pushed the victim to the ground before then tearing off some of her clothes, exposing himself and touching the victim's private parts. The defendant was arrested before he could proceed further. The defendant was charged with and convicted of attempted rape.

The defendant appealed against his conviction on the basis that he had not taken enough steps towards the attempted commission of rape. In particular, the defendant emphasised throughout the appeal that his penis was flaccid during the entire encounter so it could not be said that he had embarked on the crime proper. The Court of Appeal disagreed and ruled that there was no obligation on the prosecution to prove that the defendant had physically attempted to penetrate the victim, so long as the jury were satisfied that his conduct was more than merely preparatory towards the commission of the offence. The defendant's conduct was sufficient for this. Lord Taylor CJ concluded that:

> It is not, in our judgment, necessary, in order to raise a prima facie case of attempted rape, to prove that the defendant … had necessarily gone as far as to attempt physical penetration of the vagina. It is sufficient if … there are proved acts which a jury could properly regard as more than merely preparatory to the commission of the offence. For example, and merely as an example, in the present case the evidence of the victim's distress, of the state of her clothing, and the position in which she was seen, together with the defendant's acts of dragging her up the steps, lowering his trousers and interfering with her private parts, and his answers to the police, left it open for a jury to conclude that the defendant had the necessary intent and had done acts which were more than merely preparatory. In short that he had embarked on committing the offence itself.

This case was interesting in that although the defendant never attempted to penetrate the victim with his penis, there was still sufficient evidence to show that his conduct was more than merely preparatory to attempted rape. In more recent times, the courts have strayed away from finding liability for attempted rape, instead choosing to find liability for the full offence of sexual assault which (in many cases) may be easier to prove (see *R v Beaney* [2010] EWCA Crim 2551; *R v Ferriter* [2012] EWCA Crim 2211).

The actions in *AG's Reference (No 1 of 1992)* can thus be explained as follows:

Table 5.9 Understanding the conduct in AG's Reference (No 1 of 1992)

Extent of conduct	Specific conduct within the case
Merely preparatory	Confronting the victim; using threatening language.
More than merely preparatory	Evidence of the victim's distress; state of the victim's clothing; position in which she was seen; dragging the victim up the stairs; lowering of his trousers; interfering with her private parts.

Some years after *Campbell* and *AG's Reference (No 1 of 1992)* came the unfortunate decision of *R v Geddes* [1996] Crim LR 894, in which the Court of Appeal cited *Campbell* with approval.

case example

Charge:
Attempted false imprisonment (CAA 1981, s 1)

Case progression:
Crown Court – Guilty

Court of Appeal – Conviction quashed

Point of law:
Meaning of 'more than merely preparatory'

In *R v Geddes* [1996] Crim LR 894, the defendant was found in the boys' toilets at a school, equipped with a rucksack containing a knife, masking tape and rope. The defendant had not come across any students and was located by a member of staff. The defendant ran from the scene, leaving behind the rucksack. The defendant was charged with and convicted of attempted false imprisonment of a person unknown in the Crown Court.

The defendant appealed against his conviction on the basis that his conduct could not be said to be 'more than merely preparatory' given that he had not actually come across any students whilst in the toilets. The Court of Appeal agreed and surprisingly ruled that the defendant could not be liable for attempted false imprisonment. Lord Bingham CJ provided the judgment of the Court, in which his Lordship stated:

> [T]he line of demarcation between acts which are merely preparatory and acts which may amount to an attempt is not always clear or easy to recognise. There is no rule of thumb test. There must always be an exercise of judgment based on the particular facts of the case. It is, we think, an accurate paraphrase of the statutory test and not an illegitimate gloss upon it to ask whether the available evidence, if accepted, could show that a defendant has done an act which shows that *he has actually tried to commit the offence in question*, or whether he has only got ready or put himself in a position or equipped himself to do so. (emphasis added)

Lord Bingham CJ appeared to set a test in law for attempts, namely 'Has the defendant actually tried to commit the offence?' Although a simple test on its face, this remains subject to the same difficulties as one would have relying on the mere statement that the conduct must be 'more than merely preparatory', ie when can it be said that a defendant has *actually tried* to commit the offence? The troubling element of this case is that the Court of Appeal was in no doubt as to the defendant's intentions. He had made this clear from his presence in the toilets with the relevant apparatus in hand. However, on the evidence provided, there was not enough (in the mind of the Court of Appeal) to say that the defendant had performed an act which was more than merely preparatory or (in the words of the Court) showed that the defendant 'actually tried to commit the offence'. The Court made particular reference to the fact that the defendant did not 'try' to make contact with any pupils. To my mind, this argument is absurd given that the defendant was clearly 'lying in wait' for a victim – ie he was waiting for the opportunity to present itself. Should he have attempted to make first contact himself, his entire plan may have been foiled. Such a requirement that he needed to have tried to make contact expects too much of the defendant. It is thankfully the case that such a defendant could now be liable for trespass with intent to commit a sexual offence (Sexual Offences Act 2003, s 63).

Despite my own view, *Geddes* has been commended by subsequent courts as a 'helpful decision [that] illustrates where and how the line should be drawn' (*R v Nash* [1999] Crim LR 308, per Otton LJ).

The actions in *Geddes* can thus be explained as follows:

Table 5.10 Understanding the conduct in Geddes

Extent of conduct	Specific conduct within the case
Merely preparatory	Entrance into the school; presence in the toilets; possession of rucksack containing tape, rope and knife.
More than merely preparatory	Trying to make contact with a child; actually coming into contact with a child; using the equipment in the rucksack on the child.

The question of whether the defendant has actually tried to commit the offence was applied by the Court of Appeal a year later in the case of *R v Tosti* [1997] Crim LR 746.

case example

Charge:
Attempted burglary (CAA 1981, s 1)

Case progression:
Crown Court – Guilty

Court of Appeal – Conviction upheld

Point of law:
Meaning of 'more than merely preparatory'

In *R v Tosti* [1997] Crim LR 746, the defendants intended to burgle a farm. The pair took oxy-acetylene (oxygen cutting) equipment with them to the farm. Upon arrival at the farm, the pair hid the equipment in a hedge whilst they went to inspect the padlock on the barn door. The pair kneeled down to inspect the padlock with a light as it was almost midnight. At this point, the defendants were disturbed by the farm owner who called the police. The defendants were charged with and convicted of attempted burglary in the Crown Court.

The defendants appealed to the Court of Appeal, alleging that their conduct could not be considered to be more than merely preparatory. The Court disagreed, finding that a jury could reasonably conclude on the facts that the defendants had 'actually tried' to commit the offence, rather than having only gotten ready to do so.

The Court in *Tosti* followed the test laid out by Lord Bingham CJ in *Geddes* with a focus on whether the defendants had actually tried to commit the offence. Particular regard was also had, however, to the meaning of the phrase 'more than merely preparatory'. Beldam LJ took the time to focus on the word 'merely' and stated that

> there may be actions which are preparatory which are not merely so and which are essentially the first steps in the commission of the offence.

Tosti is a rather difficult decision to comprehend when placed in comparison with such authorities as *Geddes*. The defendants in *Tosti* would have had to return to the hedge to collect the cutting equipment before they could embark upon the crime proper. However, the Court took the opportunity to distinguish acts which are *merely* preparatory (for which there is no attempt) and acts which are *more than merely preparatory* (for which there is an attempt). From this, Beldam LJ stated that the question to be asked is whether the defendants

> had committed acts which were preparatory, but not merely so – so that it could be said the acts of preparation amounted to acts done in the commission of the offence. Essentially the question is one of degree: how close to, and necessary for, the commission of the offences were the acts which it was proved that they had done.

The actions in *Tosti* can thus be explained as follows:

Table 5.11 Understanding the conduct in Tosti

Extent of conduct	**Specific conduct within the case**
Merely preparatory	Purchasing the oxygen cutting equipment; driving towards the farm.
More than merely preparatory	Hiding the equipment in the hedge; inspecting the padlock on the barn door.

A rather contentious case was next tested by the Court of Appeal, namely that of *R v Dagnall* [2003] EWCA Crim 2441.

case example

Charge:
Attempted rape (CAA 1981, s 1)

Case progression:
Crown Court – Guilty

Court of Appeal – Conviction upheld

Point of law:
Meaning of 'more than merely preparatory'

In *R v Dagnall* [2003] EWCA Crim 2441, the defendant engaged in conversation with the victim at a bus stop before the victim began to walk away. The defendant chased after the victim and put his arms around her whilst stating that if he wished to have sexual intercourse with her, he could and no one would hear her if he were to take her to a dark road and rape her. The victim ran away before being dragged back by her hair. The defendant held the victim in an arm lock and covered her mouth as he dragged her to another bus stop. The defendant was arrested at this point. The defendant was charged with and convicted of attempted rape in the Crown Court.

The defendant appealed to the Court of Appeal, arguing that his conduct could not be said to be more than merely preparatory. He submitted that there was no evidence to suggest that he had taken steps to attempt rape; specifically, he had not attempted to remove the victim's clothing or touched her in any sexual way. The Court of Appeal disagreed and found that the defendant's conduct could be more than merely preparatory given the facts leading up to the defendant's arrest.

From *Dagnall*, it would appear that the law is willing to intervene in cases which would appear to fall significantly short of the commission of the full offence. Rape requires, as its *actus reus*, the penile penetration of the vagina, anus or mouth – following *Dagnall*, conduct that falls rather short of this commission may give rise to liability for a criminal offence. A mere physical confrontation appears to be enough for a criminal attempt. Interestingly, the Court of Appeal appeared to place great emphasis on the belief of the victim (ie that she was convinced that she would be raped). This belief, the Court said, demonstrated that, in the mind of the victim, the defendant's conduct was sufficient to say that it was more than merely preparatory. Compare *Dagnall* with the older authority of *R v Kelly* [1992] Crim LR 181, a case also concerning attempted rape.

The actions in *Dagnall* can thus be explained as follows:

Table 5.12 Understanding the conduct in Dagnall

Extent of conduct	**Specific conduct within the case**
Merely preparatory	Following the victim from the bus stop; placing his arms around the victim; stating that he could rape the victim if he wished to; dragging the victim back by her hair.
More than merely preparatory	Placing the victim into an arm lock; covering the victim's mouth; dragging the victim to another bus stop; belief of the victim that she was going to be raped.

Our last substantive authority to consider under this heading is that of *R v K* [2009] EWCA Crim 1931.

case example

Charge:
Attempting to cause a child to watch a sexual act (SOA 2003, s 12)

Case progression:
Crown Court – Guilty

Court of Appeal – Conviction quashed

Point of law:
Meaning of 'more than merely preparatory'

In *R v K* [2009] EWCA Crim 1931, the defendant approached a 6-year-old child who was playing near the place of the defendant's work. Upon approaching the child, the defendant asked the child whether he wished to watch pornography on the laptop in his office. The defendant was charged with and convicted of attempting to cause a child to watch a sexual act (a substantive inchoate offence) in the Crown Court.

The defendant appealed to the Court of Appeal on the basis that his conduct could not be classified as more than merely preparatory. The Court of Appeal agreed, finding that the defendant's steps in approaching the child and asking the question were merely preparatory. The defendant did not embark on the crime proper by leading the child to his office.

This case is quite a difficult one to comprehend given the presence of a similar authority appealed roughly around the same time. In *R v R* [2009] 1 WLR 713, the defendant was found liable for attempting to arrange or facilitate the commission of a child sex offence contrary to s 14 of the Sexual Offences Act 2003. In this case, the defendant had sent a text message to a prostitute asking if she knew any 12-year-olds who were available for sex. According to the Court of Appeal, the text message was sufficient to amount to conduct which was more than merely preparatory.

The actions in *K* can thus be explained as follows:

Table 5.13 Understanding the conduct in K

Extent of conduct	Specific conduct within the case
Merely preparatory	Approaching the child; asking the child if he wanted to watch pornography.
More than merely preparatory	Leading the victim to his office; putting the victim in front of the laptop.

Some of the more recent authorities have been concerned with attempts to drive whilst in excess of the alcohol limit. For instance, in *Mason v DPP* [2010] RTR 120, the defendant could not have been said to have 'attempted to drive' whilst intoxicated as he was prevented from actually entering the vehicle (his car was stolen at knife point). The Divisional Court felt that his act of opening the door was merely preparatory. The defendant would have had to get into the vehicle, insert his car keys into the ignition and start the engine before his actions could be said to be more than merely preparatory. This can be contrasted with the later authority of *Moore v DPP* [2010] RTR 429, where the Divisional Court found that a defendant could be convicted of such an offence where he had started his car on private property and had travelled a few metres towards the public road. In that case, it was easy to declare that the defendant had attempted to drive on a public road. In *Moore*, Tolson LJ explained that the focus was on

> [p]reparatory conduct by D which is sufficiently close to the final act to be properly regarded as part of the execution of D's plan … In other words, it covers the steps immediately preceding the final act necessary to effect D's plan and bring about the commission of the intended offence.

Relevance of the offence charged?

In determining whether the defendant has committed an act which is more than merely preparatory, the courts have tended to focus on the essential nature of the *actus reus* of the substantive offence which is alleged to have been attempted. This was explained by the Court of Appeal in *R v Nash* [1999] Crim LR 308 as 'the essential act or transaction on which it is based and any consequence required to effect it'. Potter LJ took the opportunity in *R v Qadir* [1997] 9 Arch News 1 to explain the importance of the nature of the substantive offence. His Lordship reasoned:

> Whether or not an act crosses the threshold between preparation and embarkation on the commission of the crime will always depend on an examination of the scope or substance of the crime aimed at ... In a case of [killing], wounding or causing actual bodily harm, it would be likely that any act leading up to the commission or completion of the crime but substantially anterior to it in time will be an act merely preparatory. In a case of deception ... since the *actus reus* of the crime itself may take place over an extended period of time, the moment of embarkation upon it may be quite remote in time from the point of its anticipated successful outcome.

The relevance of the defendant's offence was obvious in *R v Toothill* [1998] Crim LR 876, in which the defendant was charged with attempted burglary with intent to rape (this offence no longer exists and was replaced by a similar offence in s 63 of the Sexual Offences Act 2003 – attempted trespass with intent to commit a sexual offence). The defendant knocked on the victim's door at night and was discovered to be masturbating. The defendant claimed to be lost but was in possession of a knife, a glove and a condom. The defendant was convicted of an offence and appealed against his conviction, arguing that there was no evidence that he had attempted to rape – which he argued was an essential element of the offence. The Court of Appeal disagreed, ruling that the *actus reus* of this offence merely required an attempt to enter as a trespasser. As the defendant attempted to gain entry by knocking on the door, his conviction for attempted burglary with intent to rape was safe.

As a result, when considering whether a defendant has done an act which is more than merely preparatory, it is always important to bear in mind the actual substantive element of the full offence attempted.

Bringing together cases on 'more than merely preparatory'

From what has been seen above, it should be obvious at this stage that there is no clear, precise or objective statement as to the meaning of 'more than merely preparatory'. Although each case has tended to understand the defendant's conduct as either satisfying the test where he has 'embarked' on the crime proper (*Gullefer*; *Jones*) or where there is evidence to say that he has 'actually tried' to commit the offence (*Geddes; Tosti*), there remains no statement as to which point the defendant must reach in order to be liable for an offence of attempt. Of course, the courts should not lay down such a rigid structure of liability, and cases ought to be determined on their own factual bases. However, the cases continue to show a stark level of inconsistency in the decisions reached. A summary of the cases is provided in **Table 5.14**.

Table 5.14 Summarising cases of more than merely preparatory conduct

Authority	Attempted offence and conduct	Attempt?
Gullefer	Theft: Jumping on a race track in the hope of disturbing the race.	✗

Authority	Attempted offence and conduct	Attempt?
Jones	Murder: Getting into a car and pointing a loaded gun at the victim.	✔
Campbell	Robbery: Loitering outside a post office entrance with an imitation gun and note.	✗
AG's Reference (No 1 of 1992)	Rape: Lying on top of the victim, lowering his trousers and interfering with the victim's private parts.	✔
Geddes	False imprisonment: Presence in school toilets with a rope, knife and tape.	✗
Tosti	Burglary: Hiding cutting equipment in a hedge and examining a padlock at night.	✔
Dagnall	Rape: Holding the victim in an arm lock and covering her mouth. Also victim's belief in rape.	✔
K	Causing a child to watch a sexual act: Approaching the child and asking him if he wanted to watch pornography.	✗
R	Arranging a sexual offence with a child: Sending a text message to another asking for sexual intercourse with any 12-year-old children.	✔
Mason v DPP	Driving whilst intoxicated: Opening the door to a car whilst intoxicated.	✗
Moore v DPP	Driving on a public road: Driving a few metres on a private road towards a public road.	✔

Smith ('Proximity in Attempt: Lord Lane's "Midway Course"' [1991] Crim LR 576) has, rightly, contended that cases such as *Gullefer* and *Jones* offer 'inadequate guidance' to the lower courts as to how the phrase is to be interpreted. Indeed, Clarkson ('Attempt: The Conduct Requirement' (2009) 29 OJLS 25) has argued that the only real consistency between the cases revolves around whether there has been a 'confrontation' between the defendant, the victim or their property. Rather interestingly, Glazebrook ('Should We Have a Law of Attempted Crime?' (1969) 85 LQR 27) went so far (back in 1969) as to argue that it was 'neither necessary nor desirable' to have a law of criminal attempts at all. Instead, substantive offences should be redesigned to cover such preparatory conduct. Williams ('Wrong Turning on the Law of Attempt' [1991] Crim LR 416) has argued that the question of whether such conduct is more than merely preparatory should be a question of law for the judge. Specifically, Williams comments that '[w]hat the judges have lost is their power to protect the public by telling the jury firmly that the defendant's act, if proved … did amount to an attempt'. I do not accord with the view of Williams. Although it is possible (and probable) that different juries will reach different decisions on the same facts, it is vital that the question remains one of fact.

Instead of removing the question for the jury, it is my submission that the jury should be able to rely on more information when reaching their decision – for example, the clear intention or motives of the defendant. Indeed, the Supreme Court of New Zealand in *Johnston v The Queen* [2016] 1 NZLR 1134 decided that in determining whether the defendant's acts were more than merely preparatory, the court is permitted to take account of the defendant's proved intentions. Specifically, the Court stated:

> Where there is clear intent to commit the full offence, the maker of the 'more than preparation' decision has available to him or her information about what the defendant's ultimate plan was, which enables him or her to assess more accurately

> whether the defendant's acts amount to an attempt to commit the planned offence. Without that information, the acts may be seen as equivocal, and the decision maker could not be confident that they amount to an attempt to commit a particular offence. This does not turn mere preparation into an attempt. Rather, it is recognising that where clear intent is shown, the decision-maker has a basis to determine whether the conduct is more than mere preparation.
>
> Even in a case of clear intent, ... a merely preparatory act ... would not be an attempt. The clear evidence of intent would not change that. But an act that is done in the context of a known plan can be classified as preparation or proximate with greater certainty than when the plan is unknown (or is excluded from consideration).

This approach could have the effect of finding a different result in cases such as *Geddes* where the Court of Appeal made specific reference to the clear intentions of the defendant. The author hopes such an approach is adopted in the English and Welsh jurisdiction. Until then (if at all), *Johnston* will be a rather persuasive authority.

Role of judge and jury

When faced with a criminal offence of attempt, it is essential to understand the roles of the trial judge and jury:

- *Trial judge:* The trial judge must first determine whether there is enough evidence to support a contention that the defendant's conduct was 'more than merely preparatory'. If the prosecution is unable to provide such evidence, the case will be withdrawn from the jury and the defendant will be acquitted.
- *Jury:* If, however, the trial judge is satisfied that the defendant's conduct is *capable* of amounting to a more than merely preparatory act, it is then for the jury to determine (without any assistance from the trial judge) whether they think the defendant's actions were enough to be considered 'more than merely preparatory'. This is a question of fact (CAA 1981, s 4(3)). See *R v Wang* [2005] UKHL 9.

5.2.2.4 *Mens rea:* intention

The *mens rea* of an attempt is clear in the statute – the defendant must intend to commit an offence. Reference to 'an offence' is to be interpreted as meaning an intention to commit a 'full offence' (ie an intention to commit all elements of the offence and not just the steps which are more than merely preparatory). This is the essential principle in *R v Pace and Rogers* [2014] EWCA Crim 186. In this sense, it can be said that the *mens rea* of an attempt goes well beyond that of the *actus reus* (*R v Wheeler* [2014] EWCA Crim 2706).

example

Jack throws stones at Jill's window, intending to get her attention but not intending to damage the window. Before Jack is about to throw a rather large stone, which would likely have smashed the window, he is stopped by a passing police officer.

In this case, although Jack could be liable for the full offence of criminal damage in circumstances where he was merely reckless as to the damage caused, in the case of an attempt, however, Jack can only be liable where he intends to damage property. In this case, Jack claims that he intended to get Jill's attention – not to damage the window.

It would be incorrect to state, therefore, that the *mens rea* of an attempt is *always* identical to that of the full ('substantive') offence. For instance, according to the Court of Criminal Appeal in *R v Whybrow* (1951) 35 Cr App R 141, the *mens rea* of attempted murder is the intention to kill; an intention to cause GBH is not sufficient. This is because the defendant's *mens rea* requirement is an intention to commit the *full offence* (ie the end result). In that case, the defendant intended for his wife to suffer an electric shock whilst in the bath as a result of his connecting the electricity mains to a soap dish in the bathroom. His conviction for attempted murder was upheld by the Court of Criminal Appeal, as, according to Lord Goddard, intent is 'the principal ingredient of the crime'. The classic statement as to this effect is from James LJ in *R v Mohan* [1976] QB 1, in which his Lordship held that the prosecution is obligated to prove the existence of

> a decision to bring about, in so far as it lies within the accused's power, the commission of the offence which it is alleged the accused attempted to commit, no matter whether the accused desired that consequence of his act or not.

The extent of this is evident in the case of *R v O'Toole* [1987] Crim LR 759, where the defendant was charged with attempted arson which required (as a full offence) that the defendant intended to cause or was reckless as to causing damage by fire. The Court of Appeal held, however, that he could only be liable in circumstances where he *intended* to cause damage by fire. The defendant's conviction was thus quashed. See also *R v Millard and Vernon* [1987] Crim LR 393.

in practice

It would appear more difficult to establish an offence of attempt than it would a full offence. In the case of murder, for example, a defendant may be liable where he either intends (directly or indirectly) to kill or to cause GBH. In the case of an attempt, however, where the focus is on the actual end result envisaged by the full offence, the defendant can only be liable if he intends to kill. The prosecution's task is, therefore, harder in cases of attempt than in cases involving the full offence.

A number of specific principles need to be addressed at this stage, namely:

- whether recklessness will suffice for an offence;
- whether conditional intention will suffice for an offence; and
- whether oblique intention will suffice for an offence.

Recklessness

It was once thought that where the full offence allows for a lower form of *mens rea* in relation to the circumstances of the case, ie recklessness, a defendant's *mens rea* requirements for attempts would be the same. This was the judgment in *R v Khan* [1990] 2 All ER 783, a case concerning attempted rape. Under the former law, the Sexual Offences Act 1967, a defendant could be liable for rape if (*inter alia*) he was reckless as to whether the complainant consented or not. This has now been changed by the Sexual Offences Act 2003 as requiring the defendant to lack reasonable belief in the complainant's consent (see **Chapter 10**). As a result of *Khan*, the phrase 'with intent to commit an offence' in s 1 of the CAA 1981 was to be interpreted as requiring an intention (and nothing less) to commit the physical parts of the full offence (ie the conduct and consequences of the offence), but it was acceptable that the defendant possessed a lower level of *mens rea* in relation to the circumstances of the offence. In this sense, the defendant could be liable for attempted rape given that he was reckless as to the complainant's consent. Russell LJ was clear that

> [T]he intent of the defendant is precisely the same in rape and in attempted rape and the mens rea is identical, namely an intention to have intercourse plus a knowledge of or recklessness as to the woman's absence of consent.

The same decision was reached, but on different facts, in *AG's Reference (No 3 of 1992)* [1994] 2 All ER 121, which concerned the offence of attempted aggravated arson contrary to s 1(2) of the Criminal Damage Act 1971. The Court of Appeal concluded that it was necessary for the prosecution to establish that the defendant intended to cause damage by fire (ie conduct and consequence), but it was not necessary to prove intention as to whether life would be thereby endangered; recklessness was sufficient (per Schiemann J). The focus, according to Schiemann J, was on the so-called 'missing element' of the full offence. Particularly, his Lordship explained that

> a defendant, in order to be guilty of an attempt, must be in one of the states of mind required for the commission of the full offence, and did his best, as far as he could, to supply what was missing from the completion of the offence. It is the policy of the law that such people should be punished notwithstanding that in fact the intentions of such a defendant have not been fulfilled.

These approaches are obviously contrary to the more recent case of *R v Pace and Rogers* [2014] EWCA Crim 186.

Charge:
Attempting to conceal, disguise or convert criminal property (CAA 1981, s 1)

Case progression:
Crown Court – Guilty

Court of Appeal – Conviction quashed

Point of law:
Meaning of 'intention' for attempts

case example

In *R v Pace and Rogers* [2014] EWCA Crim 186, the defendants worked in a scrap metal yard which police officers suspected involved dubious dealings in scrap metal. As part of an undercover operation, police officers sold metal to the defendants who believed that the metal was stolen (in fact it was not). The defendants were charged with and convicted of attempting to conceal, disguise or convert criminal property (the full offence being contrary to s 327(1)(c) of the Proceeds of Crime Act (POCA) 2002).

The defendants appealed on the ground that the trial judge had misdirected the jury that a suspicion that the metal was stolen was sufficient to found liability. The defendants contended that the Act required them to intend/know that the metal was stolen. The Court of Appeal agreed. Davis LJ stated:

> ... as a matter of ordinary language and in accordance with principle, an 'intent to commit an offence' connotes an intent to commit *all* the elements of the offence. We can see no sufficient basis, whether linguistic or purposive, for construing it otherwise. (emphasis added)

Opinion is divided as to the correct approach to take. Child and Hunt ('*Pace and Rogers* and the *mens rea* of criminal attempt: *Khan* on the scrap heap?' (2014) 78 J Crim L 220) contend that *Pace* represents the correct approach, arguing that

> an intention/knowledge based approach is the only one which properly marries the wording of the Criminal Attempts Act 1981 with the achievement of a coherent model of attempts liability.

Such a view conforms with that of Bruneau and Taylor ('In defence of Pace and Rogers' (2015) 8 Arch Rev 6) who argue that the Court of Appeal in *Pace* gave 'the most natural available meaning' to the wording of the CAA 1981. Likewise, Mirfield ('Intention and Criminal Attempts' [2015] Crim LR 142) more recently explained that *Pace* is the 'legally correct' position, with Simester ('The Mens Rea of Criminal Attempts' (2015) 131 LQR 169) affirming this view, arguing that the Court of Appeal offered 'a helpful new take' on the *mens rea* of attempts in *Pace*.

A contrasting opinion is taken by the likes of Stark ('The *mens rea* of a criminal attempt' (2014) 3 Arch Rev 7) who argues that to follow *Pace* 'risks setting a dangerous precedent'. Stark goes on to explain that attempted rape will be 'virtually impossible to prosecute' if the prosecution is required to prove both an intention to penetrate and an intention that the complainant does not consent. Stark has received support from Dyson ('Scrapping *Khan*' [2014] Crim LR 445) who appreciates that the decision in *Pace* is 'more faithful to the literal meaning' of the legislation but critiques the decision on the basis that 'as a matter of policy [it] cannot be right'. Likewise, Virgo ('Criminal Attempts—The Law of Unintended Circumstances' (2014) 73 Camb LJ 244) contends that *Pace* should be ignored as *per incuriam* (ie made in mistake). It is also worth noting that the Law Commission ('Conspiracy and Attempts' (Law Com No 318, 2009)) has endorsed the approach in *Khan* and recommended that the CAA 1981 be amended to reflect that approach. It should be noted that this endorsement came prior to the decision of *Pace* so it is questionable whether the Law Commission retains this view.

It should be noted that *Khan* was not overruled by the Court of Appeal in *Pace*. As such, it remains the unfortunate case that both *Khan* and *Pace* represent accurate statements of law. In dealing with such matters therefore, it is best advised to consider a defendant's liability under both *Khan* and *Pace*. Clarity is obviously needed on this issue, and it is hoped that the Supreme Court will deal with this situation in the near future.

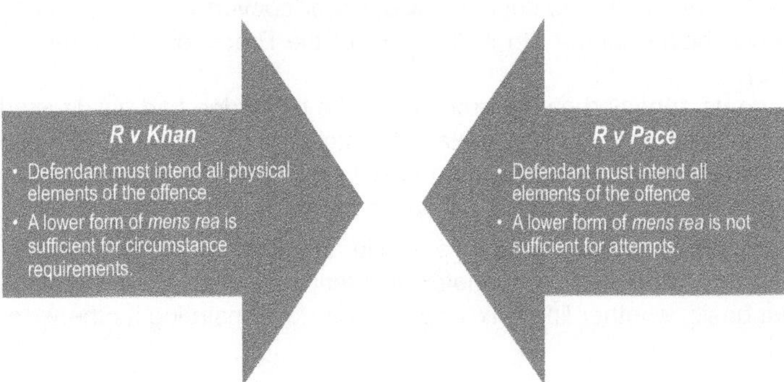

Figure 5.4 Understanding Khan *and* Pace

Conditional intention

A conditional intention reflects the circumstances where the defendant will only perform a particular act, or do some conduct, if a certain condition exists (or alternatively does not exist). This can be demonstrated by an example.

example

Jack places his hands into Jill's handbag intending to steal anything of value that he finds. Jack cannot find anything worth stealing and removes his hands from the handbag without taking anything.

In this case, Jack's intention to commit theft is conditional to the extent that he will only do so if there is something worth stealing (ie a condition). Whether Jack may be liable in such a case requires determination.

A conditional intention to commit the full offence is just as sufficient as a full intention to do so. This was illustrated in *AG's References (Nos 1 and 2 of 1979)* [1980] QB 180 where the Court of Appeal felt that a defendant should be guilty of attempted burglary in circumstances where he intended to steal anything of value without a specific item in mind. The Court was quick to note that this will require careful drafting of the indictment to indicate that the defendant attempted to steal something of value from the location in question, as opposed to a specific item. This was the issue raised in *R v Husseyn* (1977) 67 Cr App R 131, where the defendants were charged with attempted theft of sub-aqua equipment from a van. In fact, the defendants had broken into the van with the intention of stealing something of value, and upon finding the van to be full of such sub-aqua equipment, they decided to leave and not steal any of the contents. The defendants were thus incapable of being charged with attempted theft of sub-aqua equipment (as was specified in the indictment) given that they held no intention to do so. The Court of Appeal in *AG's References (Nos 1 and 2 of 1979)* made clear that had the indictment charged the defendants with attempted theft of *anything* in the van, the defendants could have been rightly convicted. The same problem arose in the earlier case of *R v Easom* [1971] 2 QB 315.

Oblique intention

In crimes requiring intention, the jury are entitled to find intention in circumstances where the end result is a virtual certainty and the defendant appreciated that such was the case (*R v Woollin* [1999] AC 82). The Court of Appeal in *R v Pearman* (1985) 80 Cr App R 259 ruled that 'intention' under the Criminal Attempts Act 1981 is to be interpreted in the same way as it is under the common law. Indeed, the Court of Appeal reaffirmed this position in *R v Walker and Hayles* (1989) 90 Cr App R 226 which applied the decision of *R v Nedrick* [1986] 3 All ER 1 to criminal attempts. It appears, therefore, that oblique intention may be used by the jury to find intention – and, like its common law counterpart, is to be treated as no more than merely evidence of intention. This has most recently been affirmed by the Court of Appeal in *R v MD* [2004] EWCA Crim 1391. In its 2009 Report, the Law Commission ('Conspiracy and Attempts' (Law Com No 318, 2009)) supported the application of the *Woollin* two-prong test to the present law of attempts.

5.2.3 Limitations

A number of limitations or exclusions can be identified at this stage, including the extent to which impossibility may extinguish a defendant's liability (**5.2.3.1**) and whether the defendant can avoid liability if he withdraws from the attempt (**5.2.3.2**).

5.2.3.1 Attempting the impossible

Section 1(2) of the CAA 1981 provides:

> A person may be guilty of attempting to commit an offence to which this section applies even though the facts are such that the commission of the offence is impossible.

It is noteworthy that s 1(2) is explicit that impossibility is of no defence on the *facts*. Where an offence is *legally* impossible, therefore, a defence will exist.

Legal impossibility

'Legal impossibility' refers to the situation in which the defendant attempts to commit a principal offence which, contrary to his own belief, is not a recognised offence in law. In this circumstance, an offence simply does not exist. Another example of legal impossibility is where an offence, though it does exist in law, is not capable of being committed as a result of a mistaken belief as to an essential element of that offence. In either circumstance, the defendant cannot be liable for an offence given that no principal offence exists in law. This principle was made clear in the case of *R v Taaffe* [1984] AC 539, where the defendant attempted to import foreign currency into England believing such importation to be a criminal offence. Given that no offence of this type existed in law, the defendant could not be liable for an attempt.

example

Jack is a foreign national and wishes to have sexual intercourse with Andy. In Jack's home country, acts of homosexuality are unlawful. Believing it to be the same in England, Jack arranges to meet with Andy to engage in such conduct, but the pair do not proceed to engage in such conduct.

In this case, it is questionable as to whether Jack has even taken such steps necessary to commit an attempt, but, in any event, Jack has attempted an act which does not give rise to criminal liability in England. Given that the *actus reus* of attempts requires the defendant to have attempted to commit a criminal offence, there can be no liability for Jack.

Taaffe has been confirmed as good law by the House of Lords in *R v Forbes* [2001] UKHL 40.

Factual impossibility

'Factual impossibility' refers to the situation in which the defendant attempts to commit a principal offence that is a recognised offence in law, but it is one that is physically impossible to perform, for one reason or another. In such circumstances, the defendant will still be liable for an attempt. By s 1(3) of the CAA 1981, the defendant is to be taken by the facts as he or she believed them to be. This means that even if an offence is physically impossible to perform, if the defendant believes that it is possible to perform (and the offence exists in law) then he will be liable for an attempt. This was confirmed to be the case in *R v Shivpuri* [1987] AC 1 (see below).

example

Jack intends to kill Jill. Unbeknownst to Jack, Jill is already dead.

In this instance, the act would be physically impossible to perform (ie the killing of Jill). With a focus on Jack's belief as to the facts, Jack may still be liable for an offence of attempted murder despite its physical impossibility.

A rather useful example is provided by Herring (*Criminal Law: Text, Cases, and Materials*, 9th edn (OUP, 2020)) where he states:

> [I]f the defendant believes he or she is dealing in illegal drugs he or she can be convicted of an attempted drug-dealing offence, even if in fact what he or she is selling is chalk. He or she will be guilty of an attempt to deal in drugs.

Inadequate means

A phrase often used in the case law is where the offence is factually impossible as a result of 'inadequate means'. This is often referred to as impossibility due to 'ineptitude'. This principle can be demonstrated by an example.

example

Jack wishes to kill Jill with a gun. He points the gun directly at Jill's head and pulls the trigger. The gun, however, is not loaded.

In this scenario, Jack has attempted to kill Jill; however, such a result is physically impossible given that Jack does not have 'adequate means' to perform the unlawful act. This will not, however, provide Jack with a defence, and he will still be liable for attempting to murder Jill by reason of the operation of s 1(2) of the CAA 1981.

The leading authority in this area is now that of *R v Shivpuri* [1987] AC 1.

case example

Charge:
Attempting to be concerned in dealing with prohibited drugs (CEMA 1979, s 170)

Case progression:
Crown Court – Guilty

Court of Appeal – Conviction upheld

House of Lords – Conviction upheld

Point of law:
Whether impossibility affords a defence

In *R v Shivpuri* [1987] AC 1, the defendant was arrested by customs officials with a suitcase which he believed contained prohibited drugs. In fact, and unbeknownst to the defendant, the suitcase merely contained a harmless vegetable substance (ie not a prohibited drug). The defendant was charged with and convicted of attempting to be knowingly concerned in dealing with and harbouring prohibited drugs contrary to s 170 of the Customs and Excise Management Act (CEMA) 1979 in the Crown Court.

The defendant appealed unsuccessfully to the Court of Appeal and eventually to the House of Lords, which also dismissed his appeal. Their Lordships took the view that a defendant may still be liable for an offence if the court focuses on the facts as the defendant believed them to be. Particularly, Lord Bridge explained:

> What turns what would otherwise, from the point of view of the criminal law, be an innocent act into a crime is the intent of the actor to commit an offence.

The effect of this decision was to overrule the previous House of Lords' decision in *Anderton v Ryan* [1985] AC 560, where the House of Lords found the defendant not to be liable for an offence of handling stolen goods in circumstances where a video recorder had been purchased in the mistaken belief that it was stolen. *Anderton,* itself, relied on the earlier authority of *Haughton v Smith* [1975] AC 476 where the House of Lords reached the same conclusion.

The status of the law is now clear – where the defendant attempts to commit an offence but that offence is not factually possible, impossibility will not afford a defence where the facts remain as the *defendant believes them to be.* The statement that the courts are to focus on the facts as the defendant believes them to be is made clear in s 1(3) of the CAA 1981. This requirement was evident in the cases of *R v S* [2005] EWCA Crim 819 and *R v Jones* [2008] QB 460. In *A*, the defendant was convicted of attempting to aid and abet a suicide, in circumstances where the victim had no actual intention to commit suicide, but the defendant believed as much. In *Jones,* the defendant engaged in text-messaging communication with an undercover police officer whom the defendant believed to be a 12-year-old girl. The defendant indicated his wish to perform sexual acts on the child and was convicted of attempting to incite a child to engage in sexual conduct. The defendant appealed on the grounds that his offence was physically impossible given that no child actually existed. The Court of Appeal dismissed his appeal on the basis that, although no child actually existed, the defendant believed the facts to be (in line with s 1(3)) that he was speaking to a child and inciting that child into sexual activities. His conviction was, therefore, rightly upheld.

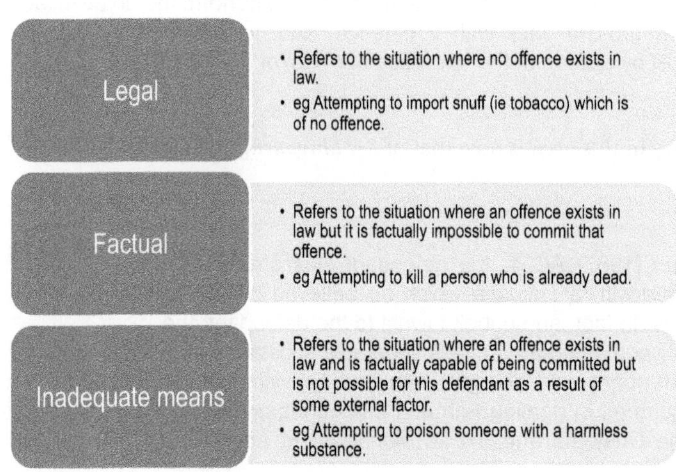

Figure 5.5 Observing impossibility in inchoate offences

5.2.3.2 A defence of withdrawal?

English law does not recognise a defence of voluntary withdrawal. In cases where the defendant's conduct has not gone beyond what is merely preparatory, the defendant cannot be liable for an attempt. Where, however, the defendant has gone beyond that stage, a withdrawal made by the defendant will be irrelevant in terms of the defendant's liability for attempt (though it may be relevant at the sentencing stage). In *R v Taylor* (1859) 1 F & F 511, for instance, the defendant remained liable for attempted criminal damage in circumstances where he approached a stack of corn with a lit match but put the match out when he realised he was being watched. Although the defendant had withdrawn from the offence, he remained liable for the offence. See also *R v Lankford* [1959] Crim LR 209.

For a detailed discussion, see Wasik 'Abandoning Criminal Intent' [1980] Crim LR 785.

5.2.4 Charging attempt

5.2.4.1 Can D be convicted of an 'attempt' if the offence has been completed?

Where the defendant is charged with an attempt but there is evidence to prove that he in fact completed the full offence, the defendant can still be liable for the attempt (CAA 1981, s 6(4)). The defendant cannot, however, be liable for both an attempt and the full offence. In circumstances, however, where the defendant is charged with the full offence but the jury return a verdict of not guilty, they may, by way of s 6(3) of the Criminal Law Act 1967, return an alternative verdict of attempt to commit the full offence (CAA 1981, s 4(2)).

5.2.4.2 Mode of trial

As discussed at **5.2.2.1**, a defendant may only be liable for an offence of attempt where the full offence is one triable on indictment. This means that the offence must either be one that is triable either way (eg theft) or triable on indictment only (eg murder). This does not mean, however, that an offence cannot be *tried* in the magistrates' court. Where the offence is one triable either way, the defendant may choose (like any either-way offence) whether to be tried in the magistrates' court or in the Crown Court (Magistrates' Courts Act 1980, Sch 1, para 34).

The following position (reflecting s 4(1) of the CAA 1981) sets out the mode of trial applicable to a defendant charged with an attempt:

- indictable-only offence: a defendant must be tried in the Crown Court;
- either-way offence: a defendant may be tried in either the magistrates' court or the Crown Court.

5.2.4.3 Procedure

According to s 4(3) of the CAA 1981, whether the defendant's conduct is sufficient to fall within s 1(1) is to be considered as a question of fact for the jury. The judge should provide the jury with careful directions in every case as to the general principle and meaning as to what acts constitute attempts (*DPP v Stonehouse* [1978] AC 55).

5.2.4.4 Jurisdictional issues

Attempts to commit an offence outside the jurisdiction

Section 1A of the CAA 1981, as inserted by the Criminal Justice Act 1993, provides that a defendant may be liable for an attempt where the defendant intends for the offence to be committed outside of England and Wales. A number of conditions exist under s 1A:

- the more than merely preparatory act must be done in the jurisdiction (ie in England and Wales);
- the offence attempted must be an indictable offence;
- the offence attempted must be an offence in that country where it is intended to take place;
- the offence must be intended to be committed outside the jurisdiction.

Attempts to commit an offence inside the jurisdiction whilst abroad

It has long been the case that a defendant may be liable for an attempt where the offence is instigated from outside the jurisdiction with the intention that the offence be committed within England and Wales (*R v Baxter* [1972] 1 QB 1; *DPP v Stonehouse* [1978] AC 55).

5.2.4.5 Sentencing

Section 4(1) of the CAA 1981 provides:

> A person guilty by virtue of section 1 above of attempting to commit an offence shall—
> (a) if the offence attempted is murder or any other offence the sentence for which is fixed by law, be liable on conviction on indictment to imprisonment for life; and
> (b) if the offence attempted is indictable but does not fall within paragraph (a) above, be liable on conviction on indictment to any penalty to which he would have been liable on conviction on indictment of that offence; and
> (c) if the offence attempted is triable either way, be liable on summary conviction to any penalty to which he would have been liable on summary conviction of that offence.

Although the statute is clear that a defendant can be sentenced in the same way as if he were convicted of the full offence, the appellate courts have repeatedly stated that an attempt should normally carry a lesser sentence than the full offence (*R v Joseph* [2001] 2 Cr App R (S) 88). Indeed, Megaw LJ in *R v Robson* (CA, 6 May 1974) noted that it would be 'at least unusual that an attempt should be visited with punishment to the maximum extent that the law permits in respect of a completed offence'. On this point, see also *R v Wolin* [2006] 1 Cr App R (S) 733 and *R v Szmyt* [2010] 1 Cr App R (S) 468.

5.2.5 Putting together attempts

Consider this issue and think of how you may structure an answer to it. Then see the figure below for a sample structure to adopt.

facts

Jack and Jill agree to commit a burglary against Andy. The pair watch Andy's actions over the next few weeks to understand his daily routine. Knowing that Andy is away from the house on Fridays at 2pm, Jack and Jill decide to commit the burglary then. On the day in question, Jack and Jill approach the house and peek through the windows. Jill acts as a lookout whilst Jack breaks a window. As Jack is beginning to climb through the window, he is caught by a passing police officer.

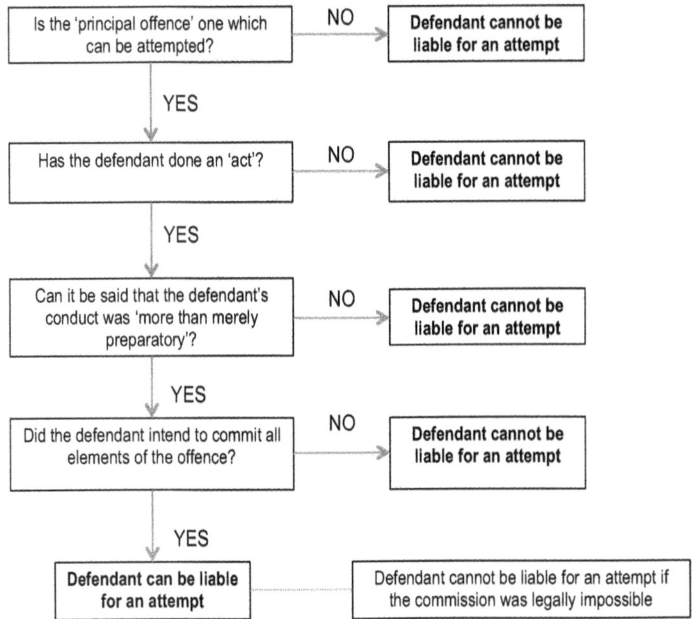

Figure 5.6 Putting together attempts

5.3 Conspiracy

5.3.1 Defining conspiracy

Conspiracy refers to the circumstances where two or more people agree to commit a criminal offence. Criminal liability arises as soon as the parties enter into such an agreement; it is irrelevant that the agreement does not actually come to fruition.

Conspiracy exists in English law as a statutory offence (considered at **5.3.2**) and as a number of separate common law offences (considered at **5.3.3**). The bulk of common law offences were abolished as a result of the Criminal Law Act (CLA) 1977 given the difficulties associated with those offences. For example, prior to the 1977 Act, a defendant was capable of being liable for a criminal offence of conspiracy in circumstances where he and another conspired to commit a tort (ie a civil wrong). An example of this can be seen in the case of *Kamara v DPP* [1974] AC 104, where the defendants were liable for conspiracy after reaching an agreement to commit the tort of trespass to land together. The position is no more, requiring conspiracies to be in relation to the commission of criminal offences.

Using our race track, we can identify the point at which liability can arise. As illustrated, liability can only arise for conspiracy in circumstances where the defendant has made an agreement as to the commission of an offence. Mere negotiations and thought processes are not sufficient.

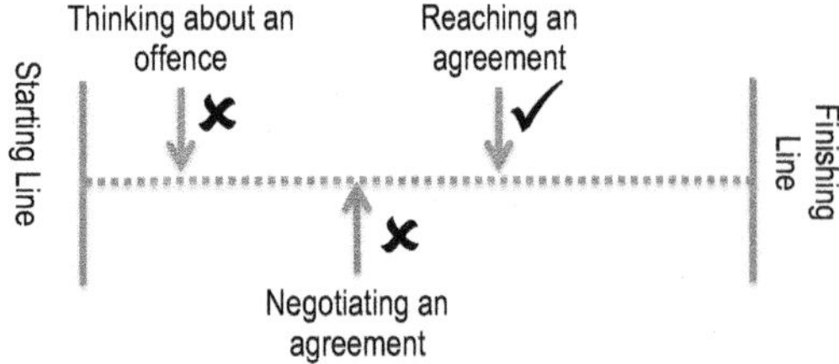

Figure 5.7 Overview of conspiracy liability

5.3.2 Elements of statutory conspiracy

Section 1(1) of the CLA 1977, as amended by s 5 of the Criminal Attempts Act 1981, provides:

> Subject to the following provisions of this Part of this Act, if a person agrees with any other person or persons that a course of conduct shall be pursued which, if the agreement is carried out in accordance with their intentions, either—
>
> (a) will necessarily amount to or involve the commission of any offence or offences by one or more of the parties to the agreement, or
>
> (b) would do so but for the existence of facts which render the commission of the offence or any of the offences impossible,
>
> he is guilty of conspiracy to commit the offence or offences in question

The *actus reus* and *mens rea* of conspiracy are outlined in **Table 5.15**.

Table 5.15 Elements of conspiracy

AR/MR	Elements of the offence
Actus reus	(i) an agreement; (ii) between two or more people; (iii) to pursue a course of conduct which amounts to a criminal offence.
Mens rea	(i) intention as to the agreement; (ii) intention as to the offence; (iii) intention or knowledge of the facts.

We shall consider each element in turn.

5.3.2.1 *Actus reus:* (i) an agreement

The first, and fundamental, element of the offence is that the parties in question (the 'co-conspirators') must come to an agreement. Although there are no formality requirements for this agreement, and the agreement does not have to be recognised as valid in civil law (ie a contract), the agreement must be one of unanimous consensus to the extent that the parties must agree to commit the same offence. This did not happen in two cases that are worth mentioning here:

- In *R v Barnard* (1979) 70 Cr App R 28, the defendant agreed to commit the offence of theft. Unbeknownst to him, the other parties involved in the conspiracy had agreed to commit robbery. The defendant could not be liable for conspiracy to commit theft on the basis that there was no agreement to commit the same offence.
- In *R v Taylor* [2002] Crim LR 203, the defendant believed the agreement with his co-conspirator to be to import Class A drugs; at the same time, his co-conspirator believed that the agreement was to import Class B drugs. In this instance, neither individual was liable for an offence of conspiracy.

Likewise, no offence is committed where the negotiations to the agreement break down and no final agreement is reached (*R v Walker* [1962] Crim LR 458). In this regard, where there is no agreement, only negotiations, there is no offence. In *R v Saik* [2007] 1 AC 18, Lord Nicholls explained: 'The offence therefore lies in making an agreement … The offence is complete at that stage.'

The Court of Appeal took the opportunity to review the law on conspiracy in *R v Mehta* [2012] EWCA Crim 2824, with Toulson LJ ruling that 'a conspiracy requires that the parties to it have a *common* unlawful purpose or design' (emphasis added). His Lordship characterised this agreement as a 'shared design'. The requirement for a 'single joint design' was emphasised by their Lordships in *R v Shillam* [2013] EWCA Crim 160 and *R v Ali* [2011] EWCA Crim 1260. For a recent case where the Court of Appeal identified the key issues in the law of conspiracies, with particular regard to the necessity for a common design between all members of the conspiracy, see *R v Johnson* [2020] EWCA Crim 482.

Can the agreement involve multiple offences?

There is no restriction on the number of offences that may be conspired to in a single offence. The Court of Appeal in *R v Roberts* [1998] 1 Cr App R 441 made it clear that the defendant may be liable for a single count of conspiracy, arising from a single agreement, but which embraces conduct involving several offences. Although in some cases it may be appropriate or 'good practice' to charge several separate counts in such cases (*R v Cooke* [1986] AC 909), it is not absolutely necessary to do so. In *Serious Fraud Office (SFO) v Papachristos* [2014] EWCA Crim 1863, Fulford LJ approved the approach taken by Toulson LJ in *R v Shillam* [2013] EWCA Crim 160 in which Toulson LJ explained:

> [T]he evidence may prove the existence of a conspiracy of narrower scope and involving fewer people than the prosecution originally alleged, in which case it is not intrinsically wrong for the jury to return guilty verdicts accordingly, but it is always necessary that for two or more persons to be convicted of a single conspiracy each of them must be proved to have shared a common purpose or design.

Whether the agreement involves a single offence or multiple offences, the indictment must be properly drafted so as to identify the individual offences in question (Indictments Act 1915, s 3(1); Criminal Procedure Rules 2015, r 10.2). In this respect, should an indictment charge a conspiracy to commit criminal damage, it must be clear on its face whether this is criminal damage in the basic sense (contrary to s 1(1) of the Criminal Damage Act 1971) or in the aggravated sense (contrary to s 1(2) of the 1971 Act). This was evident in the case of *R v Booth* [1999] Crim LR 144 regarding the offence of arson. In addition, particular care is needed where the prosecution alleged that the agreement was to commit one crime or another in the alternative (*R v Hussain* [2002] EWCA Crim 6).

Extent of the 'single design'

The need for a 'single joint design', however, need not arise from a physical meeting between the parties. In fact, it is not necessary for every party to the agreement to have communicated or met with one another. Rather, it is simply required that the defendant has communicated with *at least* one other conspirator (*R v Scott* (1978) 68 Cr App R 164). This often occurs in so-called 'chain' and 'wheel' conspiracies (see *R v Ardalan* [1972] 2 All ER 257, and recently *R v Johnson* [2020] EWCA Crim 482, for a discussion of these types of conspiracies).

Table 5.16 Forms of conspiracies

Form	Explanation
'Chain' conspiracy	Involves the situation where D1 agrees with D2, D2 agrees with D3, D3 agrees with D4, etc. Although there is no agreement (technically speaking) between D2 and D4, for example, each defendant has signed up to the same conspiracy and will each be liable in the chain. It may also be the case that D4 comes into the conspiracy much later than D1, D2 and D3. This makes no difference to the liability of D4.
'Wheel' conspiracy	Involves D1 who recruits D2, D3 and D4 to his scheme and coordinates the conduct of each party. In many conspiracies of this sort, D2, D3 and D4 will not actually meet. Rather, all defendants will be joined by a single conspiracy as led by D1. The Court of Appeal in *R v Shillam* [2013] EWCA Crim 160 emphasised the need to find a shared 'common purpose or design' (per Toulson LJ).

So long as a single design exists between the respective parties and the individual parties are aware that they are a part of a larger scheme, there will be a conspiracy (*R v D* [2009] EWCA Crim 584). This can be charged as a single conspiracy. Where, however, the agreements are separate (albeit parallel), such agreements should be charged as separate conspiracies (*R v Shillam* [2013] EWCA Crim 160 – where the defendants (D2, D3 and D4) had each engaged in a conspiracy to supply cocaine with D1 but lacked any 'grand scheme' or 'common design' between them all – they could not, therefore, be liable for the conspiracy charged). See also *R v Griffiths* [1966] 1 QB 589 in which Paull J explained that there was a requirement for the defendant to have 'knowingly attached [themselves] to a general agreement'. This distinction between single and multiple conspiracies was most recently seen in *R v Dad (Ashley Alan)* [2017] EWCA Crim 321.

case example

Charge:
Conspiracy to steal (CLA 1977, s 1)

Case progression:
Crown Court – Guilty

Court of Appeal – Conviction upheld

Point of law:
Judicial directions on the 'single design'

In *R v Dad (Ashley Alan)* [2017] EWCA Crim 321, the defendant and five others were involved in a conspiracy to steal artefacts from museums and auction houses. The defendant's role was to carry out one of those thefts but he had been aware of the larger scale of the operation. The defendant was charged with conspiracy to steal. At trial, the prosecution admitted evidence that the defendant knew of a second theft from a museum committed by his co-conspirators. The defendant was convicted of that offence in the Crown Court.

On appeal, the defendant argued that the trial judge had failed to direct the jury that, in light of the evidence presented by the prosecution, the defendant was being tried for *one* conspiracy to commit *one* burglary. The evidence presented by the prosecution, he argued, presented evidence of multiple separate conspiracies and not one common goal. The Court of Appeal dismissed his appeal, ruling that the directions were clear. Specifically, Macur LJ commented that the directions 'sufficiently alerted the jury to the requirement that they must be sure that there was only one conspiracy'. The defendant's conviction was therefore safe.

In addition, it is not necessary for the defendant to be involved in the conspiracy from the outset – he may join the conspiracy at any point prior to its fruition and be liable for an offence (*DPP v Doot* [1973] AC 807). Once the offence is committed, however (if it ever is), a defendant may not enter into the conspiracy.

5.3.2.2 *Actus reus:* (ii) between two or more people

The second element that must be proven is that the defendant made such an agreement with at least one other person. In this respect, the defendant cannot conspire to commit an offence alone – instead he may be liable for an attempt if his actions are deemed to be more than merely preparatory (see **5.2.2.3**). In the same sense, a defendant (a sole director of his own company) and that company could not be the only parties to an agreement because there can be no meeting of minds in such circumstances (even though the company and the director are two separate legal personalities) – *R v McDonnell* [1966] 1 QB 233.

Persons who cannot be conspirators

Section 2 of the CLA 1977 provides a number of exceptions where persons cannot be liable for conspiracy. Specifically, s 2 provides:

> (1) A person shall not by virtue of section 1 above be guilty of conspiracy to commit any offence if he is an intended victim of that offence.
>
> (2) A person shall not by virtue of section 1 above be guilty of conspiracy to commit any offence or offences if the only other person or persons with whom he agrees are (both initially and at all times during the currency of the agreement) persons of any one or more of the following descriptions, that is to say—
>
> (a) his spouse or civil partner;
> (b) a person under the age of criminal responsibility [10 years]; and
> (c) an intended victim of that offence or of each of those offences.

Section 2(1) is to protect the so-called 'victim' of the offence in question and essentially places on a statutory footing the rule in *R v Tyrrell* [1894] 1 QB 710, discussed in **Chapter 4**. In essence, a girl under the age of 16 could not conspire with her boyfriend to engage in under-age sex even though she planned the offence. This is because offences such as this are designed to protect victims, not punish them. Note, however, that the word 'victim' is not defined in the CLA 1977.

Under s 2(2)(a) of the CLA 1977, a husband and wife are unable to conspire together to commit an offence. This was the position at common law also (*R v Lovick* [1993] Crim LR 890). This provision is based on the principle of the sanctity of marriage and considering the husband and wife to be a single unit (*Mawji v R* [1957] AC 126). Note, however, that a husband and wife can conspire with a third party to commit an offence (*R v Chrastny* [1992] 1 All ER 189). Note also that s 2(2)(a) has been amended to include civil partnerships (Civil Partnership Act 2004) and same-sex marriages (Marriage (Same Sex Couples) Act 2013).

example

Jack and Jill are husband and wife. The pair wish to kill Andy and plan how they are going to do so.

In this instance Jack and Jill cannot be liable for conspiracy. If however, Jack and Jill were to conspire with Ben to kill Andy, the pair would be liable for conspiracy to murder. The practical effect of this is as follows:

- Jack will be liable as a co-conspirator with Ben; and
- Jill will be liable as a co-conspirator with Ben.

Where the agreement is reached before the couple are married, however, an offence of conspiracy can be made against them (*Robinson's Case* (1746) 1 Leach 37). Likewise, s 2(2)(a) has no application to so-called 'common-law' marriages (ie cohabitees – *R v Suski* [2016] EWCA Crim 24), nor does it have any application in cases where the marriage is not valid under English law (a point emphasised by Davis LJ in *R v Bala* [2016] EWCA Crim 560 (eg polygamous marriages)). This spousal exception has been described by the Law Commission ('Conspiracy and Attempts' (Law Com No 318, 2009)) as a 'conspicuous anomaly', and its abolishment was recommended in the same report. This recommendation, however, has not been adopted.

Children under the age of 10 years are incapable of committing criminal offences (under the principle of *doli incapax*). Therefore, under s 2(2)(b), they also cannot be liable as conspirators.

5.3.2.3 *Actus reus:* (iii) to pursue a course of conduct which amounts to a criminal offence

This final element of the *actus reus* is self-explanatory to the extent that it must be proven that the co-conspirators agreed to pursue a course of conduct which would *necessarily amount to or involve the commission of* a criminal offence. A mere civil wrong, therefore, is not sufficient to found an offence of conspiracy (thus reversing the decision in *Kamara v DPP* [1974] AC 104 discussed above). Note also that there is no offence of conspiracy to be an accessory to an offence (*R v Kenning* [2008] EWCA Crim 1534 – compare with *R v Dang* [2014] EWCA Crim 348).

Does the offence actually have to be committed?

The answer is no. It is irrelevant whether the criminal offence is actually committed or not (thus the use of the words 'will necessarily amount' in the legislation). The focus is on whether the agreement between the parties would amount to a criminal offence if carried out. Nor is it relevant that the parties change their mind about carrying out the offence (*R v Barnard* (1979) 70 Cr App R 28). The guilty act is therefore the agreement, and the offence is committed upon the agreement being reached (with the *mens rea* elements being present).

in practice

It will be rare for conspirators to be charged with offences where the substantive offence was not carried out as, in the majority of cases, there will be little or no evidence to support an allegation of conspiracy.

If, on the other hand, the offence is carried out, the defendant will be liable for the full offence if he took part in the offence (in alternative/addition to a charge of conspiracy). Where the offence is carried out by another, the defendant will either be liable as a conspirator or as a secondary party where there is evidence to suggest he assisted or encouraged the principal to commit the offence (see **Chapter 4**).

in practice

The Court of Appeal has noted (*R v Shillam* [2013] EWCA Crim 160, per Toulson LJ):

> [T]he prosecution should always think carefully, before making use of the law of conspiracy, how to formulate the conspiracy charge or charges and whether a substantive offence or offences would be more appropriate.

Meaning of 'necessarily'

Section 1(1)(a) uses the word 'necessarily' when setting out that the conspiracy must be to do something which 'necessarily' would be an offence. In *R v Jackson* [1985] Crim LR 442, the Court of Appeal had to decide whether it was possible for defendants to commit the offence of conspiracy if they conspired to commit an offence on the condition that an event took place (eg they conspired to commit an offence only if something else was to happen). Purchas LJ concluded that they could be so liable, ruling that:

> Planning was taking place for a contingency and if that contingency occurred the conspiracy would necessarily involve the commission of an offence. 'Necessarily' is not to be held to mean that there must inevitably be the carrying out of an offence. It means, if the agreement is carried out in accordance with the plan, there must be a commission of the offence referred to in the conspiracy count.

In this regard, 'necessarily' does not mean 'inevitably' (ie they will inevitably commit the offence in that particular circumstance), but, rather, it can include planning for contingencies.

5.3.2.4 *Mens rea:* (i) intention as to the agreement

Williams (*Textbook of Criminal Law*, 2nd edn (Stevenson & Sons, 1983)) describes the mental element of conspiracy as 'badly drafted ... succeeding only in making obscure what was almost entirely plain before'. The first requirement focuses on the agreement itself.

The defendant must, therefore, intend to enter into the agreement to pursue the course of conduct in question. There is no requirement for the defendant to have known that the proposed course of conduct would lead to the commission of a criminal offence (*Churchill v Walton* [1967] 2 AC 224). It is also irrelevant to look at the real/future motives of the conspirators. In *Yip Chiu-Cheung v The Queen* [1995] 1 AC 111, one of the conspirators was an undercover police officer who entered into the conspiracy in order to catch drug dealers. This did not, however, invalidate the conspiracy given that the officer intended (at the point of entering the agreement) that the offence would be carried out.

5.3.2.5 *Mens rea:* (ii) intention as to the offence

The second requirement of *mens rea* focuses on the offence itself and an intention for the agreement to come to fruition. The basic requirement here is that the defendant must intend for the agreement to be carried out (either by himself or a co-conspirator) and, as a result, for the full offence to be committed.

Unfortunately, this basic proposition has been thrown into turmoil as a result of the leading authority of the House of Lords in *R v Anderson* [1986] AC 27.

case example

Charge:
Conspiracy to effect the escape of a prisoner (CLA 1977, s 1)

Case progression:
Crown Court – Guilty

Court of Appeal – Conviction upheld

House of Lords – Conviction upheld

Point of law:
Requirement of intention

In *R v Anderson* [1986] AC 27, the defendant, in exchange for £20,000, agreed to supply cutting equipment to be used to break an individual out of prison. The defendant claimed that he had no intention for the offence to be carried out as he never thought the plan was capable of succeeding, and his intention was to leave the country with the money. Despite this, the defendant was charged with and convicted of conspiracy to effect the escape of a prisoner in the Crown Court.

On appeal, the defendant argued that he should not have been convicted of conspiracy given that he lacked the necessary intention. The House of Lords confirmed the view of the Court of Appeal and dismissed his appeal on the basis that there was no requirement for the defendant to have intended the agreement to be carried out; simply entering into the agreement was sufficient. Lord Bridge would explain:

> I am clearly driven by consideration of the diversity of roles which parties may agree to play in criminal conspiracies to reject any construction of the statutory language which would require the prosecution to prove an intention on the part of each conspirator that the criminal offence or offences which will necessarily be committed by one or more of the conspirators if the agreed course of conduct is fully carried out *should in fact be committed.* … Parliament cannot have intended that such parties should escape conviction of conspiracy on the basis that it cannot be proved against them that they intended that the relevant offence or offences should be committed. (emphasis added)

Rather confusingly, however, his Lordship would then go on to explain that:

> beyond the mere fact of agreement, the necessary mens rea of the crime is, in my opinion, established if, and only if, it is shown that the accused, when he entered into the agreement, intended to play some part in the agreed course of conduct in furtherance of the criminal purpose which the agreed course of conduct was intended to achieve. Nothing less will suffice; nothing more is required.

The quoted passages above from Lord Bridge are difficult to comprehend on account that they are contradictory. First, his Lordship recounts that the defendant need not intend for the offence to be carried out. His Lordship would then go on to identify, however, that the defendant must intend to play a role in the commission of the offence. We need to consider each of these notions in turn and identify the current state of law.

No need to intend for the offence to be carried out

The suggestion of Lord Bridge was that a defendant may be convicted of an offence in cases where he does not intend for the agreement to be carried out. Immediately, one can identify the conflict between Lord Bridge's statement and s 1(1). Section 1(1) is clear: a person is guilty if he 'agrees with any other person or persons that a course of conduct *shall be pursued* …' (emphasis added).

Although the case remains binding authority and has yet to be overruled, subsequent decisions have sought to move away from the decision in *Anderson*. In *R v McPhillips* [1989] NI 360, for instance, the Court of Appeal of Northern Ireland reaffirmed that it is a fundamental principle of conspiracy that the prosecution proves that the defendant intended for the agreement to be carried out. The defendant, in this case, was therefore not guilty of conspiracy to murder on the basis that he lacked the necessary intention that the offence would actually be carried out. Likewise, in the case of *Yip Chiu-Cheung v The Queen* [1995] 1 AC 111, the Privy Council confirmed that the defendant must have intended for the offence (in this case the trafficking of drugs) to actually be carried out (though do note that the Privy Council did not refer to *Anderson* in its judgment).

Unfortunately, *Anderson* remains binding authority on this point, so it is to be hoped that the Supreme Court has the opportunity to offer a restatement of the law in line with *McPhillips* and *Yip Chiu-Cheung*. In *R v Goddard* [2012] EWCA Crim 1756 (also known as *R v G; R v F*), the Court of Appeal concluded that there must be evidence from which the jury can conclude, beyond reasonable doubt, that the defendants intended to carry out the agreement. Aikens LJ explained:

> We have concluded that no reasonable jury, taking the prosecution evidence at its highest, could surely infer that the Defendants intended to carry out the agreement. The evidence is all equivocal; it is as consistent with fantasy as with an intent to carry out the plan. It is particularly striking that these men never met at any stage, either before or after the text exchange nor did they even suggest meeting to discuss the plan further. Nor is there any evidence that they took any steps to advance the plan beyond suggesting 'Friday night'. No place or time or other practical details are identified. Nothing at all happened after the exchange of text messages. We appreciate that their silence in interviews and failure to mention that this was all a fantasy can be taken into account. But that is of very little weight given the other facts or rather lack of them.

It appears, therefore, that Lord Bridge's statement in *Anderson* is to be ignored.

A need for D to 'play some part' in the agreed course of conduct

In *Anderson*, Lord Bridge was of the view (in *obiter*) that the prosecution must prove that the defendant had 'intended to play *some part* in the agreed course of conduct' (emphasis added). This statement would appear to support the proposition that the defendant must not only intend for the agreement to come to fruition (which is in direct conflict with his Lordship's earlier statement) but must also intend to have some role in carrying out the agreement. This would be a problematic reading of the judgment on account that it would mean that any individual who took part in the agreement, but who never had any intention to play a part in the carrying out of that agreement, cannot be liable for an offence. In particular, gang leaders who often organise the conspiracy, but distance themselves from its actual commission, would avoid liability.

As a result of this reading, attempts have been made by later courts to narrow the interpretation of Lord Bridge and mitigate the effects of his *obiter* statement. In *R v Siracusa* (1990) 90 Cr App R 340, for instance, O'Connor LJ in the Court of Appeal explained that Lord Bridge's *obiter* statement 'must be read in the context of that case'. His Lordship went on to say:

> We think it obvious that Lord Bridge cannot have been intending that the organiser of a crime who recruited others to carry it out would not himself be guilty of conspiracy unless it could be proved that he intended to play some active part himself thereafter.

His Lordship was of the view that '[p]articipation in a conspiracy is infinitely variable: it can be active or passive'. Specifically, his Lordship explained:

> Consent, that is the agreement or adherence to the agreement, can be inferred if it is proved that he knew what was going on and the intention to participate in the

furtherance of the criminal purpose is also established by his failure to stop the unlawful activity. Lord Bridge's *dictum* does not require anything more.

In essence, a defendant may intend to play 'some part' in the offence in remaining passive by failing to prevent the full offence from materialising. Such, the Court said, was sufficient to find an intention on the part of the defendant to participate. The effect of *Siracusa* is to reaffirm the position of Lord Bridge in *Anderson* but narrow the scope of his Lordship's *dictum*. It is thus the case that a defendant must intend to play 'some part' in the carrying out of the agreement.

5.3.2.6 *Mens rea:* (iii) intention or knowledge of the facts

The final requirement of *mens rea* focuses on the intention or knowledge of the defendant as to the facts or circumstances which constitute the *actus reus* of the offence. This requirement is explicitly provided for in s 1(2) of the CLA 1977:

> Where liability for any offence may be incurred without knowledge on the part of the person committing it of any particular fact or circumstance necessary for the commission of the offence, a person shall nevertheless not be guilty of conspiracy to commit that offence by virtue of subsection (1) above unless he and at least one other party to the agreement intend or know that that fact or circumstance shall or will exist at the time when the conduct constituting the offence is to take place.

Described by Williams (*Textbook of Criminal Law*, 2nd edn (Stevenson & Sons, 1983)) as 'mind-twisting', this provision essentially provides that where the full offence requires the existence of particular facts or circumstances as ingredients of the *actus reus* of that offence, the defendant must have knowledge of those facts or circumstances or intention of the same. The House of Lords confirmed in *R v Saik* [2007] 1 AC 18 that a mere suspicion as to the existence of such facts or circumstances is not enough; the defendant must either have known or intended those facts or circumstances.

case example

Charge:
Conspiracy to launder the proceeds of crime (CLA 1977, s 1)

Case progression:
Crown Court – Guilty

Court of Appeal – Conviction upheld

House of Lords – Conviction quashed

Point of law:
Requirement of intention/ knowledge

In *R v Saik* [2007] 1 AC 18, the defendant operated a currency exchange office in London whereby he converted a substantial amount of pounds sterling into foreign currency. The cash converted was the proceeds of drug trafficking and other criminal activity. The defendant was charged with and convicted of conspiracy to money launder in the Crown Court.

The defendant appealed to the Court of Appeal on the basis that although he suspected the money was the proceeds of crime, he had not known that fact for certain. The Court of Appeal dismissed his appeal. The defendant appealed once more to the House of Lords, which quashed his conviction, ruling that the defendant lacked a sufficient *mens rea* for the commission of the offence. Lord Nicholls ruled that the defendant must have known that the money was actually the proceeds of crime in order for him to have the intention to commit the offence.

Lord Nicholls explained:

> Section 1(2) qualifies the scope of the offence created by section 1(1). This subsection is more difficult. Its essential purpose is to ensure that strict liability and recklessness have no place in the offence of conspiracy. …

> In this respect the mental element of conspiracy is distinct from and supersedes the mental element in the substantive offence. When this is so, the lesser mental element in the substantive offence becomes otiose on a charge of conspiracy.

Saik has been followed by the Court of Appeal in *R v Tree* [2008] EWCA Crim 261, where the defendant sold a speedboat for £14,000 in cash, *suspecting* that the speedboat was criminal property (specifically, it had originally been purchased through an unlawful tax evasion scheme). The defendant was convicted of the offence in the Crown Court on the basis of his suspicion but this was overturned by the Court of Appeal, following *Saik*, which confirmed that a mere suspicion is not enough – the defendant must have known that the speedboat was criminal property. See also *R v Thomas* [2014] EWCA Crim 1958. The point to take away from *Saik* is relatively simple: in order to be liable for conspiracy, the defendant must have intention or knowledge of the relevant facts or circumstances of the offence. Anything short of intention or knowledge (eg suspicion, recklessness, negligence or strict liability) will be entirely irrelevant, even if the substantive offence itself only requires those lesser forms of *mens rea*.

example

Jack and Bob conspire to commit rape against Jill. In order to be liable for conspiracy to rape, the pair would have to *know* that Jill would not consent. This is contrary to the substantive offence of rape, in which Jack and Bob would merely require a lack of a reasonable belief that Jill was consenting.

In that respect, conspiracy is a more difficult offence to prove in many cases than the substantive offence itself. The Law Commission ('Conspiracy and Attempts' (Law Com No 318, 2009)) considers the law to be too generous to defendants in this regard.

Conditional intent

Just as conditional intention may be sufficient to give rise to an intention in cases of attempt, a defendant may be liable for conspiracy in circumstances where his (and his co-conspirators') intention is conditional. In *R v Reed* [1982] Crim LR 819, the Court of Appeal concluded that the defendants were guilty of conspiring to aid and abet suicide in circumstances where they would meet with individuals whom they knew were considering committing suicide and would either persuade them out of it or actively assist them to kill themselves. In essence, the defendants had agreed to actively assist other persons to kill themselves where the circumstances warranted it. As such, their intention was conditional and was sufficient for liability. A conditional intention was present in the case of *R v Jackson* [1985] Crim LR 442, where the defendants conspired to shoot the victim, their friend, in the leg if he was convicted of an offence (that being the condition of the offence) because they believed doing so would secure him a more lenient sentence. The defendants were liable for conspiracy to pervert the course of justice. See also *R v O'Hadhmaill* [1966] Crim LR 509 and Campbell 'Conditional Intention' (1982) 2 LS 77.

5.3.3 Common law conspiracy

Section 5(1) of the CLA 1977 provides:

> Subject to the following provisions of this section, the offence of conspiracy at common law is hereby abolished.

Two exceptions are prescribed in s 5(2) and (3) as follows:

(2) Subsection (1) above shall not affect the offence of conspiracy at common law so far as relates to conspiracy to defraud.

(3) Subsection (1) above shall not affect the offence of conspiracy at common law if and in so far as it may be committed by entering into an agreement to engage in conduct which—

(a) tends to corrupt public morals or outrages public decency; but

(b) would not amount to or involve the commission of an offence if carried out by a single person otherwise than in pursuance of an agreement.

Two offences can be identified from these sub-sections:

- conspiracy to defraud; and
- conspiracy to do acts tending to corrupt public morals or outrage public decency.

We shall consider each in turn, albeit briefly (given that these offences are exceedingly rare in practice).

5.3.3.1 Conspiracy to defraud

Section 5(2) of the CLA 1977 preserves the common law offence of conspiracy to defraud. This common law offence is designed to cover situations where a defendant dishonestly obtains someone else's property, but his conduct is not covered by the Theft Acts (considered in **Chapters 11–13**). It was thought that, upon enactment of the Fraud Act 2006, the Government would abolish this common law offence. Surprisingly, however, the Government chose not to and sought to retain the offence alongside the newly created fraud offences. In practice, the majority of offences previous charged under conspiracy to defraud are now charged as statutory conspiracy contrary to s 1(1) of the CLA 1977.

The leading authority in conspiracy to defraud cases is that of *Scott v MPC* [1975] AC 819.

case example

Charge:
Conspiracy to defraud

Case progression:
Crown Court – Guilty

Court of Appeal – Conviction upheld

House of Lords – Conviction upheld

Point of law:
Elements of conspiracy to defraud

In *Scott v MPC* [1975] AC 819, the defendant entered into an agreement with some employees of a local cinema that they would lend him the films so that he could copy them and sell the pirated copies before then returning the original films. Such conduct was performed without consent of the copyright owners. The defendant was charged with and convicted of conspiracy to defraud in the Crown Court.

The defendant appealed against his conviction on the grounds that he could not be charged with any theft offences (as there was no intention to permanently deprive the owner of the original goods), nor had there been any deception for fraud offences. The House of Lords concluded that conspiracy to defraud does not require the existence of a substantive offence. Viscount Dilhorne reasoned that:

> ... it is clearly the law that an agreement by two or more persons by dishonesty to deprive a person of something which is his or to which he is, or would be, entitled, and an agreement by two or more by dishonesty to injure some proprietary right of his, suffices to constitute the offence of conspiracy to defraud.

In essence, so long as it could be proven that there was an agreement between the parties and that agreement was to dishonestly deprive the owners of their property or injure their proprietary rights, there could be an offence of conspiracy to defraud. This formed the *actus reus* of the offence, with no requirement for the victim to actually suffer financial loss (*R v Moses and Ansbro* [1991] Crim LR 617). In *R v Evans* [2014] 1 WLR 2817, the Crown Court reasoned that as part of the *actus reus*, the dishonest agreement must also include an element of unlawfulness 'either in its object or in its means. It cannot comprise an agreement to achieve a lawful object by lawful means' (per Hickinbottom J). Reference to 'lawful object by lawful means' was dealt with by the Court of Appeal in *R v Barton; R v Booth* [2020] EWCA Crim 575, in which Lord Burnett CJ explained that 'there is no requirement of "unlawfulness" or "aggravating feature" *over and above* a dishonest agreement which includes an element of unlawfulness in its object or means' (emphasis added).

The *mens rea* of the offence required proof that the defendant intended to defraud another and that he did so dishonestly. In *R v Pabon* [2018] EWCA Crim 420 and *R v Barton; R v Booth*, the Court of Appeal confirmed that the test for dishonesty is now that in *Ivey v Genting Casinos* [2017] UKSC 67. For another recent example of a successful conviction for conspiracy to defraud, see *R v Leahu* [2018] EWCA Crim 1064.

5.3.3.2 Conspiracy to do acts tending to corrupt public morals or outrage public decency

Section 5(3)(a) of the CLA 1977 preserves the common law offence of conspiracy to corrupt public morals or outrage public decency. The offence is preserved only to the extent that the acts themselves would not amount to a criminal offence. If a conspiracy to outrage public decency, therefore, involved an agreement to commit a substantive criminal offence, the offence must be charged under s 1 of the 1977 Act.

The House of Lords in *Shaw v DPP* [1962] AC 220 held that conspiracy to corrupt public morals amounts to a substantive common law offence in its own right, as does conspiracy to outrage public decency (*Knuller v DPP* [1973] AC 435; *R v Gibson* [1990] 2 QB 619). Agreements to do acts amounting to this offence must thus now be charged as statutory conspiracies under s 1 of the 1977 Act. In effect, s 5(3) has not had the effect of preserving the existence of the offence, and, in any event, there has been no reported prosecution of this offence since the CLA 1977 came into force. No further discussion is warranted therefore.

5.3.4 Conspiring the impossible

Section 1(1)(b) of the CLA 1977 provides that a defendant can still be liable for conspiracy in circumstances where the course of conduct agreed between the parties would be impossible to carry out (eg Jack and Jill conspire to kill Bob who, unbeknownst to them, is already dead). Therefore, impossibility due to a matter of fact or ineptitude will not affect liability for statutory conspiracy.

This is contrary to the position at common law, which held that legal and factual impossibility amounted to a defence to conspiracy (*DPP v Nock* [1978] AC 979) but not impossibility by inadequate means.

example

Jack and Jill conspire with Andy to receive goods that they believe to be stolen. Unbeknownst to them, the goods are not stolen and Andy is in fact their legal owner.

In this case, Jack, Jill and Andy are all capable of being convicted of conspiring to handle stolen goods even though the actual offence itself was impossible to commit given that the goods were never stolen. Impossibility is no defence.

Given the common law position relating to impossibility, it is necessary to state that the defence of impossibility continues to apply to those common law offences of conspiracy discussed above at **5.3.3**.

5.3.5 Charging conspiracy

5.3.5.1 Mode of trial

Conspiracy is an offence triable only on indictment. This does not, however, mean that a defendant cannot conspire to commit a summary offence (see *R v Blamires Transport Services Ltd* [1964] 1 QB 278). Rather, it means that conspiracy to commit a summary offence will be triable only in the Crown Court. Note, however, that a conspiracy to commit a summary offence can only be charged against a defendant with the consent of the Director of Public Prosecutions (DPP) (CLA 1977, s 4(1)).

5.3.5.2 Procedure

Given that conspiracy involves two or more parties, it is essential to understand the effect, if any, that the outcome of the trial of one conspirator has on his co-conspirator. We can break this discussion down into two distinct situations.

Where the co-conspirator enters a guilty plea

In *R v Smith (Derk Nathan)* [2007] EWCA Crim 2105, the Court of Appeal dealt with the situation where in a closed conspiracy (ie of just two people) one co-conspirator pleads guilty whilst the other pleads not guilty. The issue being whether the guilty plea of conspirator A may be used as evidence of guilt of conspirator B. Hughes LJ would explain:

> It remains a proper approach, we are satisfied, that if there is no real question but that the offence was committed by someone and the real issue is whether the present defendant is party to it or not, evidence of pleas of guilty is likely to be perfectly fair, though of course each case depends upon its own facts. However, it also remains true that such evidence may well be unfair if the issues are such that the evidence closes off the issues that the jury has to try.

In essence, therefore, the guilty plea of X is capable of being admitted so long as the issue of whether Y was involved in the conspiracy has not been 'closed off' from the jury. This issue arose recently in the case of *R v Horne* [2020] EWCA Crim 487 in which Fulford LJ would apply *Smith* with approval, reasoning that:

> Given the fact on which the conviction was based was that [X] and the appellant conspired together—and it takes at least two conspirators to make a conspiracy—then the conviction proved just that: [X] and the appellant were both guilty of conspiracy.

Where the co-conspirator is acquitted

Section 5(8) of the CLA 1977 provides that a defendant can be convicted of conspiracy even in the circumstances where his co-conspirator has been acquitted. This was the position adopted at common law (*DPP v Shannon* [1975] AC 717).

example

Jack and Jill are on trial for conspiracy to steal Andy's watch. At trial, evidence is presented to the jury which shows that Jack appeared to exercise some sort of controlling influence on Jill. As a result, Jill is acquitted whilst Jack is convicted of the offence.

Under s 5(8), Jack has no grounds for avoiding liability from the mere fact that Jill has been acquitted. The rule is designed to ensure that guilty conspirators do not walk free simply because their co-conspirator has been acquitted by reason of evidential matters or procedural irregularities.

An exception to this rule exists, however, where such a conviction is, in all the circumstances of the case, 'inconsistent with the acquittal of the other person or persons in question' (CLA 1977, s 5(8)). Such circumstances may involve a case where D1 has a defence which should equally have been applied to D2 (see *R v Longman; R v Cribben* (1980) 72 Cr App R 121). In addition, even if there is a withdrawal from the conspiracy by the co-conspirators, this will not generally affect the defendant's own personal liability (*R v Austin* [2011] EWCA Crim 345).

5.3.5.3 Jurisdictional issues

Under the original enactment of the CLA 1977, a defendant could only be liable for conspiracy in circumstances where the agreement concerned the commission of an offence in England and Wales. Following the enactment of the Criminal Justice (Terrorism and Conspiracy) Act 1998, however, conspiracy may now be charged in circumstances where the agreement is made in England and Wales to commit an offence outside the jurisdiction. Such is now provided for in s 1A of the CLA 1977 (as introduced by the 1998 Act, and amended by the Coroners and Justice Act 2009).

example

Jack and Jill live and work in London. The pair conspire to commit a bank robbery in Paris, France.

Under s 1A of the CLA 1977, both Jack and Jill can be liable for the offence of conspiracy to rob even though the actual offence would be committed outside the jurisdiction. Note that s 4(5) of the CLA 1977 provides that no offence may be charged under s 1A without the consent of the Attorney General.

5.3.5.4 Sentencing

Given that the offence of conspiracy must relate to a full offence, an individual convicted of conspiracy is subject to the same maximum penalties as the full offence itself. For example, an offence of conspiracy to murder is subject to a maximum of life imprisonment, just as for the full offence of murder.

5.3.6 Putting together conspiracy

Consider this issue and think of how you may structure an answer to it. Then see the figure below for a sample structure to adopt.

facts

Jack and Jill, a married couple, are very unhappy with Andy who owes them a substantial amount of money. The pair agree with Paul that they will attack Andy next week in order to 'make an example' of him for not repaying the money owed. The trio agree that Paul will commit the attack.

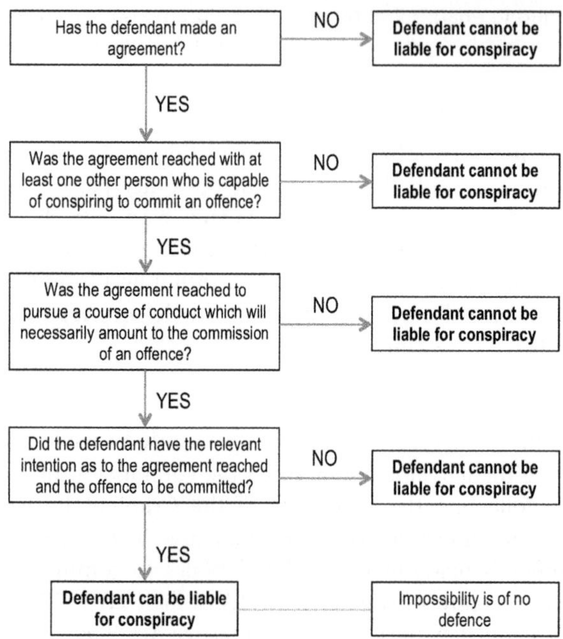

Figure 5.8 Putting together conspiracy

5.4 Assistance or encouragement

Following the publication of the Law Commission Report, 'Inchoate Liability for Assisting and Encouraging Crime' (Law Com No 300, 2006), Parliament enacted Part 2 of the Serious Crime Act (SCA) 2007. This legislation had the effect of abolishing the common law offence of incitement and creating, in its place, three new inchoate offences of assistance or encouragement. These offences are:

- intentionally encouraging or assisting an offence (**5.4.2**);
- encouraging or assisting an offence believing it will be committed (**5.4.3**); and
- encouraging or assisting offences believing one or more will be committed (**5.4.4**).

Ormerod and Fortson, 'Serious Crime Act 2007: The Part 2 Offences' [2009] Crim LR 389 identify that these offences are deceptive in their apparent simplicity and describe the offences are 'some of the most convoluted offences in decades' with 'excessive complexity' and 'unwarranted incoherence'. For a full discussion, see Fortson, *Blackstone's Guide to the Serious Crime Act 2007* (OUP, 2008).

5.4.1 Defining assisting or encouraging

A defendant may be liable for an offence under the SCA 2007 in circumstances where he assists or encourages another to commit an offence. It is irrelevant whether the offence is actually committed or not as the defendant will remain liable for an offence under the Act regardless. This is made clear in s 49(1) of the SCA 2007.

in practice

Where the offence has been committed, a defendant may not only be liable for assisting or encouraging an offence under the SCA 2007; he may also be liable as a secondary party under the Accessories and Abettors Act (AAA) 1861. In these cases, therefore, it is for the prosecution to seek the appropriate charge: either one under the SCA 2007 or one under the AAA 1861.

Prior to the introduction of the SCA 2007, a gap (or 'loophole' as the Law Commission explained it) existed in the law. It was previously not possible to convict a person of assisting another to commit an offence where the offence did not actually take place. In essence, a defendant could not be liable for assisting an inchoate offence. Liability was only possible where the full offence was committed – for which the defendant would be charged as an accessory (see **Chapter 4**). Although many offences of this sort were capable of prosecution under the common law of incitement, which covered cases of encouragement (see **5.5**), a gap in the law's ability to prosecute offenders was still present in terms of 'assisting' offences. Parliament thus took the opportunity of accepting the recommendations of the Law Commission and enacted the SCA 2007 to completely overhaul the law in this area.

The scope of these offences can be demonstrated in the case of *R v Blackshaw and Others* [2011] EWCA Crim 2312. This case was an appeal against sentence by the two defendants, but the substance of the offences committed demonstrate how the provisions of the SCA 2007 apply. We can consider the facts relating to two particular defendants, namely Blackshaw and Sutcliffe, in a case that concerned the instigation of riots across the country in 2011, having started in Tottenham, London.

Table 5.17 R v Blackshaw and Others

Defendant	Fact pattern
Blackshaw	Blackshaw had created a public event page on Facebook entitled 'Smash Down in Northwick Town'. The defendant posted a message on the group, stating that 'we'll need to get on this, kicking off all over' (referring to the riots underway elsewhere in the country). Blackshaw labelled the event as to begin behind a McDonald's restaurant at 1pm on the follow day. Blackshaw pleaded guilty to doing an act capable of encouraging the commission of riot, burglary and criminal damage, contrary to s 46 of the SCA 2007.
Sutcliffe	Sutcliffe had created a page on Facebook entitled 'The Warrington Riots'. The defendant sent a message to his 400 contacts on Facebook inviting them all to join him in the riot. Sutcliffe pleaded guilty to intentionally encouraging the commission of riot, contrary to s 44 of the SCA 2007.

With an understanding of the backdrop of the offences under the SCA 2007, we can now proceed to consider each offence in turn. Before that, however, it is worth providing some critical oversight into the rules to prepare you for what is ahead.

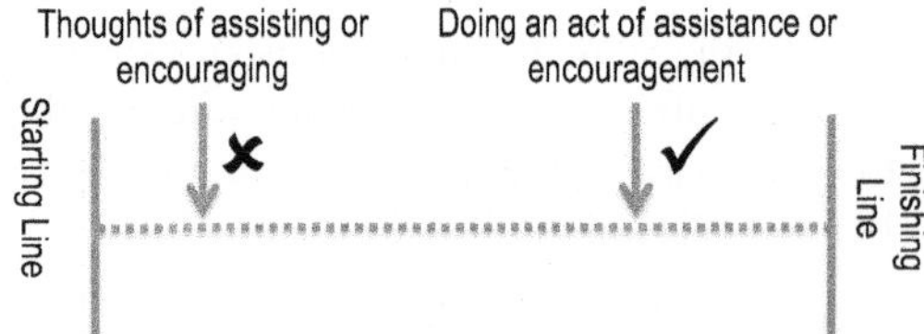

Figure 5.9 Overview of assistance or encouragement

5.4.1.1 Complexity of provisions

The statutory provisions under the SCA 2007 are ripe with confusion and complexity. Ormerod and Fortson ('Serious Crime Act 2007: The Part 2 Offences' [2009] Crim LR 389) describe the new provisions as 'complex', 'convoluted' and 'tortuously difficult'. The pair conclude that the statute contains

> some of the worst criminal provisions to fall from Parliament in recent years. … These are offences of breath-taking scope and complexity. They constitute both an interpretative nightmare and a prosecutor's dream.

Spencer and Virgo ('Encouraging and Assisting Crime: Legislate in Haste, Repent at Leisure' (2008) 9 Archbold News 7) are of the same opinion, describing the new provisions as 'complicated and unintelligible … over detailed, convoluted and unreadable'. The pair identify particular concern with s 47, defining it as an 'example of impenetrable drafting'.

5.4.2 Elements of intentionally encouraging or assisting an offence (SCA 2007, s 44)

Section 44 of the SCA 2007 provides:

> (1) A person commits an offence if—
> (a) he does an act capable of encouraging or assisting the commission of an offence; and
> (b) he intends to encourage or assist its commission.
>
> (2) But he is not to be taken to have intended to encourage or assist the commission of an offence merely because such encouragement or assistance was a foreseeable consequence of his act.

The *actus reus* and *mens rea* of intentionally encouraging or assisting an offence are outlined in **Table 5.18**.

Table 5.18 Elements of intentionally encouraging or assisting an offence

AR/MR	Elements of the offence
Actus reus	(i) an act; (ii) capable of encouraging or assisting; (iii) the commission of an offence.
Mens rea	(i) intention to encourage or assist; (ii) state of mind regarding the *mens rea*; (iii) state of mind regarding the *actus reus*.

Note that, according to s 51A of the SCA 2007, the offence under s 44 does not apply to an offence of encouraging or assisting suicide. This is because such an offence is a stand-alone 'substantive' inchoate offence contrary to s 2(1) of the Suicide Act 1961.

We shall consider each element in turn.

5.4.2.1 *Actus reus:* (i) an act

Although the legislation in s 44(1) requires the defendant to perform an 'act', this requirement has been defined rather broadly in s 47(8) as involving an omission to act. Specifically, s 47(8) provides:

> Reference in this section to the doing of an act includes reference to—
> (a) a failure to act;
> (b) the continuation of an act that has already begun;
> (c) an attempt to do an act (except an act amounting to the commission of the offence of attempting to commit another offence).

Further to this, s 65(2) provides:

> A reference in this Part to a person's doing an act that is capable of encouraging or assisting the commission of an offence includes a reference to his doing so by—
> (a) taking steps to reduce the possibility of criminal proceedings being brought in respect of that offence;
> (b) failing to take reasonable steps to discharge a duty.

Additionally, s 67 defines an 'act' as including a 'course of conduct' on the part of the defendant (ie a series of acts). No further guidance is given on this expression. From these sections, it should be identified that the words 'an act' can be interpreted as meaning:

- a single physical act;
- a continuing act;
- a failure to act, where there was a legal duty to act (ie an omission); and
- a series of acts.

5.4.2.2 *Actus reus:* (ii) capable of encouraging or assisting

Whether the defendant's acts are such to say that they are *capable* of encouraging or assisting another to commit an offence is a question of fact. This *actus reus* can helpfully be broken down into two separate limbs:

- capability; and
- encouragement or assistance.

Note that it is not necessary to prove that the encouragement or assistance actually led to the commission of a substantive offence. We can see this in s 49(1) of the SCA 2007 which reads: 'A person may commit an offence under this Part whether or not any offence capable of being encouraged or assisted by his act is committed.'

Capability

Note that the phrase used in the legislation is a mere 'capability'; this means that it is irrelevant whether the defendant's actions do *actually* assist or encourage another.

in practice

The effect of this principle (that it is irrelevant whether the offence is actually committed) can often mean that the law imposes criminal liability more strictly on those that encourage or assist an offence than on those who merely plan, or think about committing, the offence. For instance, suppose Jack says to Jill, 'I want to burn down this house', and Jill hands him a lighter. In this case, Jill is liable for an offence under s 44 as soon as she offers the lighter to Jack. Jack is only liable, however, upon taking sufficient steps that it can be said that his actions are more than merely preparatory (simply declaring his intention would not be enough) to going on to commit the offence. This is, of course, unless some other inchoate offence can be charged, such as conspiracy.

It is also irrelevant whether the third party was aware of the defendant's words or acts. For example, a defendant may shout encouragement to the third party who may never hear it. This is unlike the position at common law under *R v Ransford* (1874) 13 Cox CC 9.

Encouragement

The Law Commission in its Report, 'Inchoate Liability for Assisting and Encouraging Crime' (Law Com No 300, 2006) stated that the intention of the word 'encouraging' was to mirror the meaning of the word 'incitement' in the common law. This means that encouraging was intended to include positive acts of persuasion and instigation whilst also including negative acts of threats and coercion. Likewise, such encouragement may be express or implied. This is confirmed by the wording of s 65(1) of the SCA 2007:

> A reference in this Part to a person's doing an act that is capable of encouraging the commission of an offence includes a reference to his doing so by threatening another person or otherwise putting pressure on another person to commit the offence.

Essentially, therefore, if the defendant coerces or threatens another into committing an offence, this will satisfy the second element of the *actus reus*. This was the position under the old law of incitement (*Race Relations Board v Applin* [1973] QB 815 – see **5.5**). Though, of course, encouragement by way of coercion is merely one example of how the *actus reus* may be committed. Some other examples include:

- *Invicta Plastics v Clare* [1976] RTR 251: Placing an advert in a magazine was considered as an act of encouragement to the readers of the magazine. The Divisional Court held that the advert amounted to an implied encouragement.
- *R v Marlow* [1997] Crim LR 897: Writing a book with instructions is capable of amounting to an encouragement. The defendant wrote a book giving advice on how to grow and produce cannabis. The Court of Appeal concluded that the book 'amounted to an active and widespread encouragement of others to engage in the production and use of cannabis' (per Potter LJ).
- *R v Goldman* [2001] EWCA Crim 1684: Requesting the distribution of paedophilic materials amounted to an encouragement for the distributor to commit an offence. It was irrelevant that they were already in a position to distribute. See also *O'Shea v Coventry Magistrates' Court* [2004] Crim LR 948.

Assistance

Unfortunately, the word 'assist' is not defined in the SCA 2007. The inclusion of the word 'assistance' in the legislation is intended to fill the void left by the offence of incitement, which was specific to cases of encouragement. The Law Commission ('Inchoate Liability for Assisting and Encouraging Crime' (above)) explained that such a term was used in cases where the defendant provided some guidance or assistance to another without the presence of encouragement, *per se*. There is no requirement for such assistance to be substantive (in a similar vein to the term 'assisting' in secondary liability – see **Chapter 4**). A gap that remains, however, is that of 'procuring' an offence (ie causing it to happen). Such conduct is not covered by the offence (see Child, 'The Differences Between Attempted Complicity and Inchoate Assisting and Encouraging – A Reply to Professor Bohlander' [2010] Crim LR 924).

Indirect encouragement/assistance

In addition to this, s 66 provides that the defendant can 'indirectly' encourage or assist another by arranging for another person to do an act that is capable of encouraging or assisting the commission of an offence. In essence, where the defendant reaches an agreement with another that they will do an act capable of encouraging or assisting the commission of the offence, the defendant will be just as liable as the party committing the act of encouragement/assistance.

example

Jack gives a gun to Jill with instructions to give it to Ben with a view to killing Andy.

In this instance, Jack has indirectly done an act capable of encouraging or assisting an offence given that he has arranged for Jill to give the gun to Ben.

5.4.2.3 *Actus reus:* (iii) the commission of an offence

This section is rather self-explanatory to the extent that it must be proven that the defendant's acts are capable of assisting or encouraging the commission of an *offence*. Therefore, acts which merely encourage or assist the commission of a civil wrong will not be sufficient to find liability against the defendant.

It is possible to be liable for assisting or encouraging another to act as an accessory to a crime (ie a secondary party that we saw in **Chapter 4**). It is also possible to be liable for assisting or encouraging another to commit an inchoate offence (eg D may be liable for assisting or encouraging another to conspire to commit a criminal offence).

5.4.2.4 *Mens rea:* (i) intention to encourage or assist

This first element of the *mens rea* distinguishes a s 44 offence from offences contrary to ss 45 and 46 in that the defendant must specifically intend to encourage or assist in the commission of the full offence as a result of his conduct (SCA 2007, s 44(1)(b)). Note that this requirement is not the same thing as an intention that the offence should be committed with the relevant *mens rea* (for which see **5.4.2.3**). Rather, the focus here is whether the defendant intended for his acts or conduct to encourage or assist in the commission of the offence.

By s 47(2) of the SCA 2007, it is sufficient to prove that the defendant 'intended to encourage or assist the *doing of an act* which would amount to the commission of that offence' (emphasis added).

Intention, not foresight

The use of the words 'he intends' in s 44(1)(b) appears to be restricted to direct intention and does not include cases of oblique intention. Support for this contention would appear to be present in s 44(2), which states:

> [The defendant] is not to be taken to have intended to encourage or assist the commission of an offence merely because such encouragement or assistance was a foreseeable consequence of his act.

See also s 47(7)(b). These sections are accompanied by para 146 of the Explanatory Notes to the 2007 Act, which explains that 'foresight of consequences is not sufficient to establish intention'. There is a lack of clarity as to whether oblique intention is entirely irrelevant or whether such is only capable of amounting to evidence of intention, as opposed to intention itself (ie in line with *R v Woollin* [1999] AC 82). However, given that an offence exists under s 45 (see **5.4.3**) involving cases of foresight, it may properly be concluded that a defendant's foresight is irrelevant to cases charged under s 44.

5.4.2.5 *Mens rea:* (ii) state of mind regarding the *mens rea*

The requirements regarding the defendant's state of mind in relation to the *mens rea* elements of the offence are provided in s 47(5):

> In proving for the purposes of this section whether an act is one which, if done, would amount to the commission of an offence—
> (a) if the offence is one requiring proof of fault, it must be proved that—
> (i) D believed that, were the act to be done, it would be done with that fault;
> (ii) D was reckless as to whether or not it would be done with that fault; or
> (iii) D's state of mind was such that, were he to do it, it would be done with that fault.

Note that this is an 'or' test, requiring the prosecution to prove either that the defendant believed that the commission of the offence would be done with the relevant *mens rea* of the offence in question; the defendant was reckless as to whether or not such an offence occurred with the relevant *mens rea*; or the defendant himself would have the necessary *mens rea* elements were he to commit the criminal offence himself.

example

Jack intentionally encourages Jill to commit theft against Andy.

In order for Jack to be liable, it must be proven that Jack believed that Jill would perform the act of theft with both dishonesty and the intention to permanently deprive Andy of the property (s 47(5)(a)(i)); or that Jack was reckless as to Jill acting with such dishonesty and intention (s 47(5)(a)(ii)); or in any event that if Jack were to perform the act of theft, he himself would possess the necessary dishonesty and intention to permanently deprive.

Section 47(5)(a)(iii) is designed to reverse the common law position that a defendant could not be liable for incitement in circumstances where he used a third party merely as an innocent agent (*R v Curr* [1968] 2 QB 944). Now, it may suffice that the defendant has the relevant *mens rea* even if he knows that the incited party has not. Section 47(6) explains that where s 47(5)(a)(iii) is relied upon, the defendant 'is to be assumed to be able to do the act in question'. This essentially means that the defendant cannot avoid liability simply because he does not have the capacity/capability to commit the offence.

example

Jill encourages Jack to penetrate Alice's vagina with his penis, believing that if Jack were to do so, it would be without the consent of Alice. Jack reasonably believes that Alice is consenting.

This is an example adapted for our use from para 159 of the Explanatory Notes to the SCA 2007. In this case, Jack (the encouraged party) lacks any fault requirement in relation to s 47(5)(a). As such, a prosecutor must rely on s 47(5)(a)(iii), arguing that Jill, if she were to commit the act in question herself, would do so with the fault requirement needed. Jill (as a woman) is unable to commit the offence of rape, but she could still be liable for assisting or encouraging rape as a result of the operation of s 47(6). In essence, the impossibility of Jill being liable for the full offence herself will not prevent her from being liable for the inchoate offence of encouraging or assisting.

5.4.2.6 *Mens rea:* (iii) state of mind regarding the *actus reus*

As with the defendant's state of mind regarding the *mens rea* requirements above, s 47(5) also applies in relation to the state of mind for the *actus reus* elements. Specifically, s 47(5)(b) provides:

> ... if the offence is one requiring proof of particular circumstances or consequences (or both), it must be proved that—
> (i) D believed that, were the act to be done, it would be done in those circumstances or with those consequences; or
> (ii) D was reckless as to whether or not it would be done in those circumstances or with those consequences.

Note that this requirement only applies in cases where the anticipated offence is one which requires proof of either the existence of circumstances or consequences (ie an end result) or both. No regard is to be had to the state of mind of the defendant regarding his conduct. As is evident, it must be proven that the defendant either *believed* that an offence would be committed with those consequences or circumstances or that he was *reckless* to such circumstances or consequences.

example

Jack encourages Jill to steal Andy's smartphone.

In order for Jack to be liable, he must either believe that the property in question (ie the smartphone) belonged to another (ie the circumstances of the *actus reus* of theft) or at least was reckless as to whether the smartphone was property belonging to another.

5.4.3 Elements of encouraging or assisting an offence believing it will be committed (SCA 2007, s 45)

Section 45 of the SCA 2007 provides:

> A person commits an offence if—

(a) he does an act capable of encouraging or assisting the commission of an offence; and
(b) he believes—
  (i) that the offence will be committed; and
  (ii) that his act will encourage or assist its commission.

The *actus reus* and *mens rea* of encouraging or assisting an offence believing it will be committed are outlined in **Table 5.19**.

Table 5.19 Elements of encouraging or assisting an offence believing it will be committed

AR/MR	Elements of the offence
Actus reus	(i) an act; (ii) capable of encouraging or assisting; (iii) the commission of an offence.
Mens rea	(i) belief that the offence will be committed; (ii) belief that the act will encourage or assists its commission; (iii) state of mind regarding the *mens rea*; (iv) state of mind regarding the *actus reus*.

5.4.3.1 *Actus reus*

As you can see, the *actus reus* for s 45 is identical to that of s 44, so you are advised to reconsider the scope of the law in the discussions set out above (see **5.4.2**). Likewise, the same category of *mens rea* prescribed by s 47(5) applies to a s 45 offence – which shall not be repeated here. At this point, therefore, we shall focus solely on the *mens rea* requirements.

5.4.3.2 *Mens rea:* (i) belief that the offence will be committed

It is immediately obvious how s 45 differs from that in s 44. One can notice without any great difficulty that s 45 is broader in scope than s 44, in that the former merely requires a belief on the part of the defendant and not an intention (SCA 2007, s 45(b)). In this respect, s 45 bares a lower *mens rea* requirement than s 44. A number of points require addressing here.

The offence *will* be committed

The Court of Appeal in *R v Watling* [2012] EWCA Crim 2894 sought to emphasise that liability under s 45 depended on the defendant's belief that the offence *would* be committed, as opposed to such phrases as it 'might' or 'could' be committed. Such reasoning is logical given the choice of language in the legislation (ie belief that the offence *will* be committed – SCA 2007, s 45(b)(i)).

Belief

The concept of 'belief' was discussed in **Chapter 3** and shall only be touched upon lightly here. Belief was defined rather helpfully by Boreham J in *R v Hall* (1985) 81 Cr App R 260 as

> something short of knowledge. It may be said to be the state of mind of a person who says to himself: 'I cannot say I know for certain that these goods are stolen, but there can be no other reasonable conclusion in the light of all the circumstances, in the light of all that I have heard and seen.'

Although belief is a subjective term and can include varying degrees of belief (ranging from the 'highly probable' cases to the merely 'possible' cases), such belief must be something more than a mere suspicion (*R v Moys* (1984) 79 Cr App R 72). It is also not the case that recklessness may be sufficient for belief on the part of the defendant. As a bottom line, it must be proven that the defendant positively believed that the conduct in question would be committed.

Conditional belief

Note that, according to s 49(7), it is sufficient for the defendant to believe that the offence will be committed if certain conditions are met. In this respect, a conditional belief is sufficient to satisfy this element of the *mens rea*.

example

Jack encourages Jill to steal Andy's smartphone. He hands Jill a knife and tells her that 'if he doesn't hand over his phone, scare him with this'.

In this scenario, Jack would be liable for an offence under s 45 as he believes that a robbery will be committed if certain conditions are met (ie if Andy doesn't hand over his phone).

5.4.3.3 *Mens rea:* (ii) belief that the act will encourage or assist its commission

The same rules apply to this *mens rea* as they do to the *mens rea* under s 44 except for the fact that the defendant need only hold a *belief* that such acts *will* (not 'might') encourage or assist in the commission of the offence. Further to this, s 47 applies in a slightly different respect to s 45 than it does to s 44. Specifically, s 47(3) provides:

> If it is alleged under section 45(b) that a person (D) believed that an offence would be committed and that his act would encourage or assist its commission, it is sufficient to prove that he believed—
> (a) that an act would be done which would amount to the commission of that offence; and
> (b) that his act would encourage or assist the doing of that act.

5.4.4 Elements of encouraging or assisting offences believing one or more will be committed (SCA 2007, s 46)

Section 46(1) of the SCA 2007 provides:

> A person commits an offence if—
> (a) he does an act capable of encouraging or assisting the commission of one or more of a number of offences; and
> (b) he believes—
> (i) that one or more of those offences will be committed (but has no belief as to which); and
> (ii) that his act will encourage or assist the commission of one or more of them.

The leading authority on this offence is that of *R v Sadique* [2013] 4 All ER 924 (see below at **5.4.4.5**), where the Court of Appeal explained that s 46 provides for the 'relatively common case' where the defendant contemplates that one of a *range of offences* might be committed as a result of his encouragement or assistance. Essentially, this offence covers the circumstances where the defendant is unsure as to which offence will be committed.

The *actus reus* and *mens rea* of encouraging or assisting offences believing one or more will be committed are outlined in **Table 5.20**.

Table 5.20 Elements of encouraging or assisting offences believing one or more will be committed

AR/MR	Elements of the offence
Actus reus	(i) an act; (ii) capable of encouraging or assisting; (iii) the commission of one or more offences.
Mens rea	(i) belief that one or more of the offences will be committed; (ii) belief that the act will encourage or assist the commission of one or more of them; (iii) state of mind regarding the *mens rea*; (iv) state of mind regarding the *actus reus*.

5.4.4.1 Actus reus: (i) and (ii)

As you can see, the *actus reus* for s 46 is roughly identical to that of s 44 (in terms of elements (i) and (ii)) so you are advised to reconsider the scope of the law in the discussions above (see **5.4.2**). Below, however, we shall consider the meaning of 'one or more offences' in s 46. Likewise, the same category of *mens rea* prescribed by s 47(5) applies to a s 45 offence – which shall not be repeated here except to note that s 48(2) provides that the factors in s 47(5) need only be proven in relation to one offence. At this point, therefore, we shall focus solely on the new *actus reus* and new *mens rea* requirements.

5.4.4.2 *Actus reus:* (iii) the commission of one or more offences

Unlike ss 44 and 45, this offence is concerned with the circumstances where the defendant does an act capable of assisting or encouraging the commission of *one or more offences*. The use of 'or more' in the legislation indicates that it is not necessary for the defendant's actions to be capable of assisting or encouraging more than one offence, so long as it can be proven that at least one offence has been assisted or encouraged.

5.4.4.3 *Mens rea:* (i) belief that one or more of the offences will be committed

It is not an offence contrary to s 46 for a defendant to do an act which he merely fears or suspects may possibly encourage or assist another to commit an offence(s). The defendant is required to *positively* believe that some offence *will* (not 'might') be committed. It is irrelevant whether the offence is committed or not or whether the defendant is mistaken in his belief.

The inclusion of the words 'one or more of the offences' can often cause difficulties in understanding. It will be easier if we set out the requirement of belief in bullet-point form:

- The defendant need not *himself* believe that a particular offence would be committed. There is no requirement for him to hold such a belief – so long as he believes that one or more offences would be encouraged or assisted. This is made very clear in s 46(1)(b)(i) of the SCA 2007. Should the defendant believe that one offence in particular will be committed, he should be charged with a s 45 offence, not a s 46 offence.

example

Jack supplies Jill with a gun and positively believes that she will use it either to commit a robbery or to commit a murder, but he is unsure which one it is.

In this case, it is irrelevant that Jack does not know or believe exactly which offence Jill will commit. It is sufficient under s 47(4) for Jack to believe that one of many possible offences may be committed.

- However, a person can only be found guilty of the offence under s 46 if the offence or offences that the jury find the defendant believed would be committed are specified in the indictment. This is provided for in s 48(3) of the SCA 2007.

example

Jill hands Jack a cricket bat, telling him to 'teach Andy a lesson'.

In this case, although Jill need only hold a belief as to any relevant offence being committed, the jury are only entitled to convict her on such a belief if that offence is contained in the indictment, ie the indictment specifies (i) assault, (ii) battery and (iii) GBH, for example. The jury would not be permitted, for example, to find that Jill believed that the offence of wounding would be committed if the prosecution had not included such in the indictment itself.

Further to this, the CPS in its 'Legal Guidance on Inchoate Offences' advises:

> [W]here offences with a different maximum sentence are pleaded in a section 46 count, separate counts should be included on the indictment for each variation so the sentencing judge is clear as to the basis for conviction under section 46 …

Such guidance gives due regard to the decision of the Court of Appeal in *R v S and H* [2011] EWCA Crim 2872.

5.4.4.4 *Mens rea:* (ii) belief that the act will encourage or assist the commission of one or more of them

The statute is quite clear as to the extent of this requirement, in that the defendant must hold a belief that the act itself will encourage or assist the commission of one *or more* offences (SCA 2007, s 46(1)(b)(ii)). There is no requirement of specificity of offence in the legislation, and quite clearly s 46(2) has this in mind when it declares:

> It is immaterial for the purposes of subsection (1)(b)(ii) whether the person has any belief as to which offence will be encouraged or assisted.

By way of example, in both *R v McCaffery* [2014] EWCA Crim 2550 and *R v Duckworth* [2015] EWCA Crim 645, the defendants pleaded guilty to doing acts capable of encouraging or assisting burglary, robbery or theft. It did not matter which of the three the defendants believed in, so long as they did believe that one would be encouraged as a result of their conduct. The principles of conditional belief in s 49(7) also apply to this offence.

5.4.4.5 *Sadique* and further confusion

It cannot be denied that s 46 (like ss 44 and 45) is a complex provision. Unfortunately, the state of the law had been made even more complex as a result of the Court of Appeal's preliminary decision in *R v Sadique* [2011] EWCA Crim 2872 (also known as *R v S and H*).

R v Sadique: The first appeal

It is worth noting from the outset that this is the first appeal in *Sadique* (against a preparatory ruling); a further appeal (that time against conviction) is detailed below.

case example

Charge:
Assisting the supply of Class A or Class B drugs (SCA 2007, s 46)

Case progression:
Crown Court – n\a

Court of Appeal – Appeal dismissed (charges upheld)

Point of law:
Application of s 46

In *R v Sadique* [2011] EWCA Crim 2872, the defendants supplied chemical cutting agents on a national scale to assist the production and supply of illegal drugs. The defendants were charged with assisting the supply of Class A or Class B drugs in the Crown Court.

During a preparatory hearing, the defendants appealed to the Court of Appeal against the charges against them on the basis that they infringed Article 7 of the ECHR. The Court of Appeal ruled that a s 46 offence requires a separate charge for each offence alleged. Further, the defendant must believe that each offence listed would be committed.

It is hoped that you will have noticed that the Court of Appeal in the first appeal of *Sadique* had represented the law in a different fashion to that discussed in this section so far. Such distinctions between *Sadique* and our own discussions can be summarised here:

Table 5.21 Comparing Sadique

Sadique	**Discussions in this text**
The defendant must be charged with separate s 46 offences for each offence alleged.	The defendant is charged with one single offence under s 46 which covers an array of offences he may believe will be committed.
The defendant must believe that each of the possible offences he assisted or encouraged would be committed.	The defendant only has to believe that one of many offences will be committed. He need not specifically believe which offences will be committed.

Indeed, Virgo ('Encouraging or assisting more than one offence' [2012] Archbold Review) was blunt in his explanation as to why the Court of Appeal in *Sadique* was wrong. Virgo stated:

> For the inchoate offence involving encouragement or assistance there is no need to establish that a substantive offence has been committed, and the appropriate *mens rea* is one of belief rather than recklessness as to whether a crime will be committed, but otherwise s 46 is purporting to embody the same principle as *Maxwell* [see **Chapter 4**]: a defendant should not be acquitted of assisting or encouraging a crime simply because his act might assist or encourage a number of offences, at least where the defendant has the appropriate mens rea in respect of those offences. ... But there is a crucial difference between the application of the *Maxwell* principle where the substantive offence is committed and where no

> substantive offence is committed. … [s] 46 states that the defendant must believe that one or more of the offences which are capable of being encouraged or assisted by his act will be committed …

Virgo proceeds to ask the following question:

> But does this mean that the defendant must believe that each identified offence will be committed, or is it sufficient that the defendant contemplates that each of the offences may be committed, as long as the defendant believes that one of those offences will be committed, although he is not sure which one?

Virgo would conclude that the Court of Appeal took the former interpretation and thereby made the provision of s 46 'redundant'.

R v Sadique: The second appeal

Thankfully, a further appeal was made to the Court of Appeal – this time against the defendant's conviction for the offence in question (*R v Sadique* [2013] 4 All ER 924). In the Court of Appeal, Lord Judge CJ agreed entirely with the view of Virgo (basing a large part of its decision on Virgo's comments specifically) and reversed the decision of the prior Court. Specifically, Lord Judge CJ stated:

> As we have already explained, the 2007 Act created three distinct offences. It is not open to the court to set one or other of them aside and the legislation must be interpreted to give effect to the creation by statute of the three offences. It may well be that the common law offence of inciting someone else to commit an offence was less complex. It may equally be that the purpose of the legislation could have been achieved in less tortuous fashion. Nevertheless these three distinct offences were created by the 2007 Act, with none taking priority over the other two. S.46 creates the offence of encouraging or assisting the commission of one or more offences. Its specific ingredients and the subsequent legislative provisions underline that an indictment charging a s.46 offence of encouraging one or more offences is permissible. This has the advantage of reflecting practical reality. A defendant may very well believe that his conduct will assist in the commission of one or more of a variety of different offences by another individual without knowing or being able to identify the precise offence or offences which the person to whom he offers encouragement or assistance intends to commit, or will actually commit. As Professor Virgo explains in his most recent article, the purpose of the s.46 was 'to provide for the relatively common case where a defendant contemplates that one of a variety of offences might be committed as a result of his or her encouragement'. We entirely agree.

Now, following the second Court of Appeal decision, the law has been returned to its former understanding that a defendant may be charged with a single offence contrary to s 46 where he believed that one of many offences would be committed, and there is no requirement for the defendant to believe that each offence contemplated would be committed – one is sufficient.

5.4.4.6 Compatibility with the ECHR

Section 46 has been challenged on two occasions as being incompatible with Article 7 (and, as a result, Article 6) of the European Convention on Human Rights (ECHR). In both the first and second appeal of *Sadique*, the Court of Appeal rejected the argument that the offence created by s 46 was 'too vague and uncertain' to be compatible with Article 7 of the ECHR.

5.4.5 Limitations to liability

A number of limitations or exclusions can be identified at this stage, including the extent to which impossibility may extinguish a defendant's liability (**5.4.5.1**); whether the defendant can avoid liability if his acts of assistance or encouragement are reasonable in the circumstances (**5.4.5.2**); and whether any rule seeks to protect the victim of a full offence from being liable as a perpetrator of an inchoate offence (**5.4.5.3**).

5.4.5.1 Encouraging or assisting the impossible

Under the common law, the position was simple. A defendant could not be liable for an offence of encouraging or assisting in circumstances where the commission of an offence was impossible. This was the position according to the Court of Appeal in *R v Fitzmaurice* [1983] QB 1083. The only exception that existed under the common law was the circumstances where the impossibility was caused by inadequate means. The Divisional Court in *DPP v Armstrong* [2000] Crim LR 379 held that where the defendant encourages or assists another to commit an impossible offence, as a result of inadequate means, a defence was not capable of applying.

The position regarding impossibility is not expressly considered in the SCA 2007. The SCA 2007 requires the defendant to do an act which is 'capable' of amounting to encouragement or assistance to commit the offence in question. This requirement of capability would seem to allow impossibility to act as a defence under the SCA 2007, given that commission of an impossible offence is not 'capable' of being assisted or encouraged.

example

Jack supplies Jill with a gun with the intention of her killing Andy. Unbeknownst to Jack, the gun is not real.

In this case, Jack cannot be liable (following the reasoning above) for assisting the offence of murder given that this act of assistance was not 'capable' of causing the offence to occur. The offence was impossible based on these facts. Jack may, however, be liable for an attempt to assist or encourage if it can be said that his actions were more than merely preparatory. No defence of impossibility (except for truly legal impossibilities) applies to attempts (see **5.2.3**).

This view, however, is not one of unanimous agreement. For instance, the Law Commission ('Inchoate Liability for Assisting and Encouraging Crime' (Law Com No 300, 2006)) believed that impossibility would not act as a defence to a charge under the SCA 2007. The Commission gave the following example:

> if D … provides P with a weapon believing that P will use it to attack V1 (intending to kill V1), D is guilty of assisting murder irrespective of whether P uses the weapon to attack anyone. Were P to attack and murder V2, instead of V1, D would be equally guilty of encouraging or assisting murder. If P attacked V2 because V1 was already dead at the time that D provided the weapon, D would still be guilty of encouraging or assisting murder. It may have been impossible for V1 to be murdered but, nonetheless, D had done an act capable of encouraging or assisting the conduct element of murder, namely an attack on any human being.

Indeed, Ormerod and Fortson ('Serious Crime Act 2007: The Part 2 Offences' [2009] Crim LR 389) are of the view that no defence of impossibility exists given that s 47(6) provides that the defendant 'is to be assumed to be able to do the act in question'. This provision does, however, only apply in circumstances where s 47(5)(a)(iii) is relied upon (see **5.4.2.5**).

Herring (*Criminal Law: Text, Cases and Materials*, 9th edn (OUP, 2020)) is unsure as to the correct position to be adopted in this instance. He accepts that upon one reading of the Act, the defendant is intending to encourage the murder of *another*. Such an offence will be capable of commission. A second reading of the Act, however, may be that the defendant is intending to encourage the murder of a *specific person*. Such an offence will not be capable of commission in circumstances where that person is already dead, for example. Herring offers the following conclusion:

> It is submitted that in such a case the correct charge would be an attempt to do an act capable of assistance or encouragement.

5.4.5.2 Defence of reasonableness

Two defences of 'acting reasonably' are provided for in s 50 of the SCA 2007. These defences apply to all offences committed under Part 2 of the 2007 Act. Unfortunately, neither the Act nor the Explanatory Notes provide guidance as to what conduct falls within the relevant sections. We shall consider each in turn.

Defence under SCA 2007, s 50(1)

Section 50(1) of the SCA 2007 provides:

> A person is not guilty of an offence under this Part if he proves—
> (a) that he knew certain circumstances existed; and
> (b) that it was reasonable for him to act as he did in those circumstances.

In essence, the defendant is required to prove (ie he bears the legal burden on the balance of probabilities) that he had *knowledge* of certain circumstances that existed, and, as a result of those circumstances, it was reasonable for him to act as he did. The test is partially subjective/objective in that a jury must first consider (subjectively) what the defendant knew of the circumstances and then consider (objectively) whether it was reasonable for him to act as he did. It is not sufficient, therefore, for the defendant to prove that he *subjectively* believed that his conduct was reasonable.

example

Jill works as a typist for Jack who asks her to type a statement addressed to the solicitor acting for Jack's wife in divorce proceedings. Jill has knowledge that the statement is for divorce and ancillary financial relief proceedings but realises, in typing the statement, that it contains deliberately misleading information about Jack's assets. Jill continues to type the letter.

This example was provided by the Law Commission in its 2006 Report on the topic (adapted for our purposes). In such a case, Jill is assisting Jack to commit an offence by typing out the statement. However, the defence may apply here where the jury conclude that Jill acted reasonably because she was following her employer's instructions.

Another example provided by the Law Commission is the circumstance where the defendant locks the door to his house in order to prevent the victim seeking refuge from a gang intent on assaulting the victim. In such a case, the defendant would be assisting the gang to commit the offence, but would likely be considered reasonable in his conduct of locking the door.

In determining the extent to which this defence applies, s 50(3) provides a list of non-exhaustive factors that can be taken into account. Section 50(3) provides:

> Factors to be considered in determining whether it was reasonable for a person to act as he did include—
> (a) the seriousness of the anticipated offence (or, in the case of an offence under section 46, the offences specified in the indictment);
> (b) any purpose for which he claims to have been acting;
> (c) any authority by which he claims to have been acting.

Defence under SCA 2007, s 50(2)

Section 50(2) of the SCA 2007 provides:

> A person is not guilty of an offence under this Part if he proves—
> (a) that he believed certain circumstances to exist;
> (b) that his belief was reasonable; and
> (c) that it was reasonable for him to act as he did in the circumstances as he believed them to be.

As above, the defendant bears the legal burden of proving the existence of the defence. Compared with the defence in s 50(1), this defence operates to exclude liability in circumstances where the defendant held a *belief* as to the existence of certain factors (a subjective question), such a belief was reasonably held (an objective question), and it was reasonable for him to act as he did based on that belief (another objective question).

example

Jill is lawfully driving at 70 miles per hour in the outside lane of a motorway. Jack, driving faster, comes up behind Jill. Jill pulls over into the inside lane and allows Jack to overtake. Jack proceeds to drive at speeds in excess of 70 miles per hour.

This is another example provided by the Law Commission in its 2006 Report on the topic (adapted for our purposes). In such a case, Jill would at least believe (if not 'know') that if she moves to one side, Jack will overtake her and will commit the offence of speeding. In this sense, Jill has assisted Jack in committing an offence. The defence of reasonableness could apply in these circumstances.

The same statutory factors in s 50(3) apply to this defence also.

5.4.5.3 Victim rule

Section 51 of the SCA 2007 provides for a special rule in relation to victims who fall within a 'protected category'. Section 51 provides:

> (1) In the case of protective offences, a person does not commit an offence under this Part by reference to such an offence if—
> (a) he falls within the protected category; and

> (b) he is the person in respect of whom the protective offence was committed or would have been if it had been committed.
>
> (2) 'Protective offence' means an offence that exists (wholly or in part) for the protection of a particular category of persons ('the protected category').

A similar protection was discussed in **Chapter 4** in relation to accessorial liability with reference to the rule in *R v Tyrrell* [1894] 1 QB 710.

In essence, the rule is designed to protect victims from being liable for crimes in circumstances where the offence has been designed to protect that class of victim. The most common examples are in cases of sexual offences. Paragraph 178 of the Explanatory Notes to the 2007 Act provides that s 51 is designed to place the rule in *Tyrrell* on to a statutory footing.

example

Jill is an 11-year-old girl and actively encourages Jack, a 30-year-old man, to engage in sexual intercourse with her. Jack does not do so.

In this case, although Jill has encouraged Jack to commit an offence, the offence capable of being committed is designed to protect persons such as Jill (children under the age of 13). This means that Jill cannot be liable for assisting an offence despite her encouragement. The offence in this case would be, if committed, rape of a child under 13 contrary to s 5 of the Sexual Offences Act 2003.

5.4.6 Charging assistance or encouragement

Section 49(2) of the SCA 2007 provides:

> If a person's act is capable of encouraging or assisting the commission of a number of offences—
>
> (a) section 44 applies separately in relation to each offence that he *intends* to encourage or assist to be committed; and
>
> (b) section 45 applies separately in relation to each offence that he *believes* will be encouraged or assisted to be committed. (emphasis added)

In essence, a defendant can be charged with multiple s 44 or s 45 offences in circumstances where his conduct was capable of encouraging or assisting in more than one offence. Section 46, however, is a single offence involving the belief in the commission of a number of possible offences. There is no provision in the SCA 2007 for applying s 46 separately.

5.4.6.1 Mode of trial

The mode of trial for an offence under Part 2 of the SCA 2007 ultimately depends on which of the three offences the defendant has been charged with. This is explicit in s 55 of the SCA 2007, which provides:

> (1) An offence under section 44 or 45 is triable in the same way as the anticipated offence.
>
> (2) An offence under section 46 is triable on indictment.

As such, if the defendant is charged with a s 44 or 45 offence, mode of trial is to be determined as if the defendant had been charged with the 'full' offence. For example, if the full offence was triable summarily only, the defendant's inchoate offence would also be tried summarily only. Regardless of the type of offence anticipated in a s 46 offence, however, the defendant is to be tried on indictment.

5.4.6.2 Jurisdictional issues

This section has been included to deal with the circumstances where acts of encouragement or assistance are provided outside England and Wales. Section 52(1) of the SCA 2007 provides:

> If a person (D) knows or believes that what he anticipates might take place wholly or partly in England or Wales, he may be guilty of an offence under section 44, 45 or 46 no matter where he was at any relevant time.

This proposition is relatively simple:

example

Jack resides in Belgium and sends a number of emails to Andy in London, encouraging him to plant a bomb on the tube.

This is an example taken from para 183 of the Explanatory Notes to the SCA 2007 and adapted for our use. In this example, Jack is outside the jurisdiction but may still be liable for an offence if he has performed acts of assistance or encouragement and the offence anticipated is to take place inside the jurisdiction. This is the case here and Jack will be liable despite the fact that he is outside the jurisdiction.

A complex set of rules under s 52(2) apply in circumstances where the defendant is either 'wholly or partly' in the jurisdiction but the offence anticipated is committed abroad (ie outside of England and Wales). No further discussion is warranted on this point and readers are advised to address Sch 4 of the SCA 2007 for more information on this point.

5.4.6.3 Sentencing

Given that the defendant's offence of assisting or encouraging must relate to a full offence, a defendant convicted of an offence can be subject to the same maximum penalty as if he were charged with the full offence (SCA 2007, s 58(3)). Where the defendant is charged with assisting or encouraging murder, he is liable to a discretionary life sentence (as opposed to a mandatory one) (SCA 2007, s 58(2)).

Although there are no published sentencing guidelines applicable to these offences, the Court of Appeal in *R v Watling* [2012] EWCA Crim 2894 stated (per Parker J):

> Parliament has ... specifically provided that those who ... are guilty of offences under section 44 and 45 ... are liable to the maximum sentence available for the full anticipated offence if it had been committed ... It is therefore highly relevant to consider the potential scale of those anticipated offences.

5.4.7 Putting together assistance or encouragement

Consider this issue and think of how you may structure an answer to it. Then see the figure below for a sample structure to adopt.

facts

Jack, a keen environmentalist, intends to set fire to a research lab that experiments on animals. Jack convinces Jill that she should join him in the offence 'for the good of the animals'. Jill agrees and joins Jack on the day in question. Around the same time of convincing Jill, Jack contacts Andy over the telephone and seeks to persuade him to join in the commission of the offence. Andy says that he will 'think about it'. Jack is hopeful that Andy will join him but is unsure as to whether he will. Jack also provides gasoline to Ben, telling him to ensure that 'no persons are hurt – we want to send a message; not cause harm'. Ben has an anger-management problem, and, as a result, Jack has a suspicion that Ben will hurt a person in his venture if it becomes necessary. Jack, Jill and Ben set the building alight. In the process of pouring the gasoline, Ben attacks a number of staff members, causing serious harm, and also kills a number of staff.

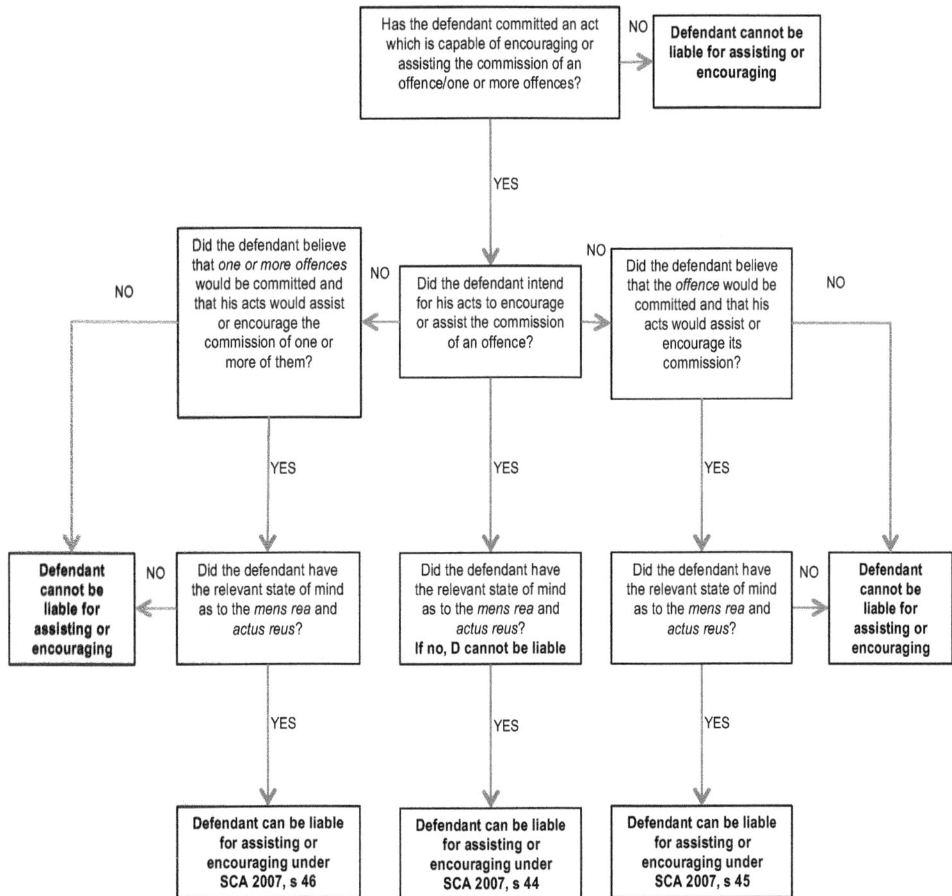

Figure 5.10 Putting together assistance and encouragement

5.5 Common law incitement

Although s 59 of the SCA 2007 abolishes the common law offence of incitement, the offence continues to apply in cases where the offence was committed before 1 October

2008 (ie when the SCA 2007 came into force). However, for this reason, we only outline the offence below.

5.5.1 Defining incitement

Lord Denning MR in *Race Relations Board v Applin* [1973] QB 815 explained:

> [It was] suggested that to 'incite' means to urge or spur on by advice, encouragement, and persuasion, and not otherwise. I do not think the word is so limited, at any rate in this context. A person may 'incite' another to do an act by threatening or by pressure, as well as by persuasion.

5.5.2 Elements of incitement

The lead authority on common law incitement is that of *R v Claydon* [2005] EWCA Crim 2827 (also known as *R v C*). Silber J explained that the offence of incitement requires the prosecution to prove that:

- the defendant incites another to do or cause to be done an act or acts which, if done, will involve the commission of an offence or offences by the other; and
- the defendant intends or believes that the other, if he acts as incited, shall or will do so with the fault required for the offence(s).

This statement forms the basis for the *actus reus* and *mens rea* of the offence and was provided by the Law Commission in its draft Criminal Code (Law Com No 177, 1989).

Although incitement is a common law offence, certain substantive statutory offences have been created, for example inciting another to commit an offence contrary to the Misuse of Drugs Act (MDA) 1971 (MDA 1971, s 19) – which remains a substantive inchoate offence (see generally **5.7** below).

5.6 Bringing together inchoate offences

The preceding text is not the easiest area of substantive criminal law to understand. We began this chapter with the finding of a lawful basis for inchoate liability, before then progressing to identify (if we can) the point at which liability can be attached, and then considering the various limitations to the offences. A stark difficulty with this area of law is the commonality that exists between the different offences. This section is justified in order to bring together our understanding and to avoid overlapping rules and principles.

5.6.1 The running track

Throughout this chapter, we have used the example of a running track to designate the stages at which a defendant may or may not be liable for an offence. In any case, where a defendant merely thinks about the commission of an offence (ie he has stepped up to the starting line but the whistle has not yet been blown), he will not be liable for an inchoate crime or, of course, a full offence. Likewise, where the defendant has completed the full offence, his liability lies there and not in the inchoate domain (ie he has stepped over the finishing line). Our focus, therefore, has been on the conduct of the defendant in the middle ground between start and finish. A summary of the point at which liability can be attached is provided below.

Table 5.22 Putting together inchoate liability

Offence	Point at which law intervenes ...	How close is this to the full offence?
Attempts	Upon the defendant's conduct being considered *more than merely preparatory* towards the commission of the offence.	Often associated as the 'last act' (though this is not always the case) before the defendant was to commit the full offence. Can be considered the closest conduct to the commission of the full offence.
Conspiracy	Upon the defendant reaching an *agreement* with at least one other person.	Can be considered quite remote from the full offence. However, given that the agreement must be for one conspirator to commit the offence, it can be identified as being within proximity to the full offence.
Assistance or encouragement	Upon the defendant offering the *assistance or encouragement* to another party or 'inciting' them to commit an offence.	Often associated as being rather distant from the offence. As with common law incitement, it is often identified as an act furthest away from the full offence itself.

Bringing together inchoate offences, one may identify a timeline of behaviour as follows:

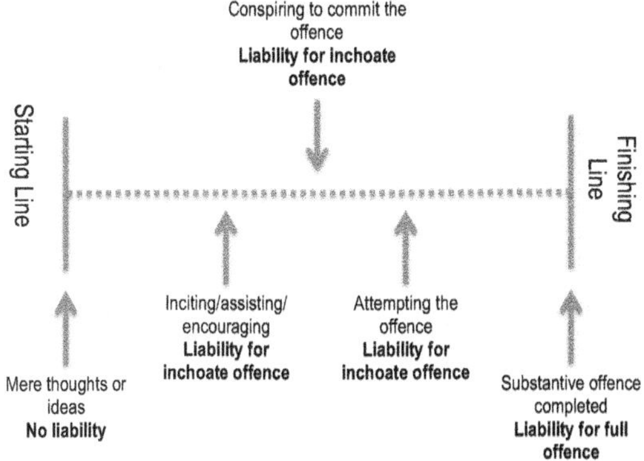

Figure 5.11 Bringing together inchoate liability

5.6.2 Impossibility and inchoate offences

Each offence considered above has been discussed in the context of possible and impossible offences. The rules vary for each offence, so it is useful to summarise them here.

Table 5.23 Putting together impossibilities

Offences and types of impossibility		Is it a defence?
Attempt	Legal	yes
	Factual	no
	Inadequate means	no
Statutory conspiracy	Legal	yes
	Factual	no
	Inadequate means	no

Offences and types of impossibility		Is it a defence?
Common law conspiracy	Legal	yes
	Factual	yes
	Inadequate means	no
Assisting or encouraging	Legal	yes
	Factual	yes
	Inadequate means	yes

5.6.3 Double inchoate liability

A point not fully touched upon in the chapter thus far is the circumstances where a defendant may be liable in a 'double inchoate' sense. 'Double inchoate' liability refers to the situation where a defendant is liable for numerous inchoate offences or is liable for an inchoate offence in relation to another inchoate offence. Given the manner in which many of the inchoate offences are drafted, it is highly possible for such double inchoate liability to be present in a given case. The following example will demonstrate the point.

example

Jill asks Jack to supply her with a gun so that she can kill Andy. Jack complies.

In this scenario, Jill has intentionally done an act capable of encouraging Jack to do an act that is capable of assisting Jill to commit an offence. In this respect, Jill has committed an offence contrary to s 44 of the SCA 2007, and Jack has committed an offence contrary to s 45.

Essentially, a defendant can be liable under s 44 for assisting a s 45 or s 46 offence. Likewise, a defendant can be liable for attempting to commit an offence under Part 2 of the SCA 2007 or engaging in a conspiracy to commit an offence under the SCA 2007. However, it is not possible for an individual to be liable for assisting or encouraging an inchoate offence under s 45 or s 46. This is made clear in s 49(4) of the SCA 2007, which provides:

> In reckoning whether—
> (a) for the purposes of section 45, an act is capable of encouraging or assisting the commission of an offence; or
> (b) for the purposes of section 46, an act is capable of encouraging or assisting the commission of one or more of a number of offences;
>
> offences under this Part and listed offences are to be disregarded.

'Listed offence' is defined in s 49(5) as 'an offence listed in Part 1, 2 or 3 of Schedule 3'. Examples of such offences listed in Sch 3 are detailed in **Table 5.24**.

Table 5.24 Inchoate offences which cannot be assisted or encouraged under s 45 or s 46 of the SCA 2007

Statutory provision	Offence
Offences Against the Person Act 1861, s 4	Soliciting to commit murder (see *R v Abu Hamza* [2006] EWCA Crim 2918)
Official Secrets Act 1920, s 7	Attempts to commit offences contrary to the 1920 Act

Statutory provision	**Offence**
Misuse of Drugs Act 1971, s 19	Attempts to commit offences contrary to the 1971 Act
Immigration Act 1971, s 25	Assisting unlawful immigration to a member state
Terrorism Act 2000, s 59	Inciting terrorism overseas

The effect of s 49(4) is that a defendant cannot be liable under s 45 or s 46 for assisting or encouraging another person to commit an inchoate offence. A defendant can only be liable under s 44 for such acts of encouragement or assistance, but (as we are aware) this offence requires intention on the part of the defendant that his acts will assist or encourage the offence in question. A useful table can be included to explain the circumstances when a defendant may be liable for a double inchoate offence.

Table 5.25 Putting together double inchoate liability

Start Here: Can D be liable for:	**Attempt**	**Conspiracy**	**SCA 2007, s 44**	**SCA 2007, s 45**	**SCA 2007, s 45**	**Secondary liability**
Attempt	No	No (CAA 1981, s 1(4)(a))	Yes	Yes	Yes	No (CAA 1981, s 1(4)(b))
Conspiracy	Yes but unlikely	Yes but unlikely	Yes	Yes but unlikely	Yes but unlikely	No
SCA 2007, s 44	Yes but unlikely	Yes but unlikely	Yes	Yes	Yes	Yes
SCA 2007, s 45	No (SCA 2007, s 49(4))	No (SCA 2007, s 49(4))	No (SCA 2007, s 49(4))	No (SCA 2007, s 49(4))	No (SCA 2007, s 49(4))	Yes
SCA 2007, s 46	No (SCA 2007, s 49(4))	No (SCA 2007, s 49(4))	No (SCA 2007, s 49(4))	No (SCA 2007, s 49(4))	No (SCA 2007, s 49(4))	Yes
Secondary liability	Yes	Yes	Yes	Yes	Yes	No

5.7 Substantive inchoate liability

This heading is used to describe a set of offences which, although inchoate in nature, are substantive to the extent that they relate to a specific offence. Two particular examples of substantive inchoate liability worth mentioning here include:

- assisting or encouraging suicide contrary to s 2 of the Suicide Act 1961; and rather more recently
- participating in organised crime contrary to s 45 of the Serious Crime Act 2015.

The reader is advised to consult a practitioner text on the subject for more detail on these offences.

5.8 Further reading

Inchoate offences generally

Bohlander, 'The Conflict between the Serious Crime Act 2007 and Section 1(4)(b) Criminal Attempts Act 1981—A Missed Repeal?' [2010] Crim LR 483.

Attempts

Glazebrook, 'Should We Have a Law of Attempted Crime?' (1969) 85 LQR 27.

Mirfield, 'Intention and Criminal Attempts' [2015] Crim LR 142.

Rogers, 'The Codification of Attempts and the Case for "Preparation"' [2008] Crim LR 937.

Simester, 'The Mens Rea of Criminal Attempts' (2015) 131 LQR 169.

Virgo, 'Criminal Attempts - The Law of Unintended Circumstances' (2014) 73 Camb LJ 244.

Williams, 'Wrong Turning on the Law of Attempt' [1991] Crim LR 416.

Conspiracy

Dennis, 'The Rationale of Criminal Conspiracy' [1997] 93 LQR 39.

Jarvis and Bisgrove, 'The Use and Abuse of Conspiracy' [2014] Crim LR 261.

Smith, 'Proving Conspiracy' [1996] Crim LR 386.

Assisting or encouraging

Child, 'Exploring the Mens Rea Requirements of the Serious Crime Act 2007 Assisting and Encouraging Offences' (2012) 76 JCL 220.

Ormerod and Fortson, 'Serious Crime Act 2007: The Part 2 Offences' [2009] Crim LR 389.

Spencer and Virgo, 'Encouraging and Assisting Crime: Legislate in Haste, Repent at Leisure' (2008) 9 Archbold News 7.

Sullivan, 'Inchoate Liability for Assisting and Encouraging Crime—The Law Commission Report' [2006] Crim LR 1047.

Stark, 'Encouraging or Assisting Clarity?' (2013) 72 Camb LJ 497.

Virgo, 'Part 2 of the Serious Crime Act 2007—Enough is Enough' (2013) 3 Archbold Review 7.

Virgo, '*R v Sadique*: Making Sense of Section 46 of the Serious Crime Act 2007' (2013) 7 Archbold Review 4.

- Inchoate offences refer to offences that are not yet complete (ie there is no commission of a 'full' substantive offence).
- Inchoate liability is justified on the basis that the defendant has taken sufficient steps towards the commission of an offence that his acts ought to be criminalised.
- A defendant is liable for an attempt where his conduct has gone far enough to say that it is more than merely preparatory and the defendant has intended to commit the full offence.
- A defendant is liable for statutory conspiracy where he has entered into an agreement with at least one other person to pursue a course of conduct that will necessarily result in the commission of a criminal offence. The defendant must intend for the agreement to be carried out and for the offence to be committed.
- A defendant may also be liable for a number of common law conspiracy offences, such as conspiracy to defraud and conspiracy to outrage public decency.
- A defendant is liable for an offence under Part 2 of the SCA 2007 where he either (i) intentionally encourages or assists another to commit a criminal offence; (ii) believes that an offence will be committed as a result of his encouragement or assistance; or (iii) believes that one or more offences will be committed as a result of his encouragement or assistance.
- A defendant may also be liable for a common law offence of incitement in circumstances where he encourages another to commit an offence prior to 1 October 2008.
- A defendant may be subject, in certain circumstances, to double inchoate liability, which refers to the situation where the defendant commits an inchoate offence in relation to another inchoate offence.
- A defendant may also be liable for a substantive inchoate offence, such as assisting or encouraging suicide.

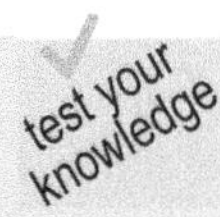

Problem question

Jack and Jill, an unmarried couple, agree to commit a robbery of a local bank. The two agree with Andy that they will observe the bank for a number of weeks before then robbing the bank. Andy is to provide handguns to be used in the robbery but will not take part in the robbery himself. On the day in question, Jack and Jill hide the guns, along with a rucksack containing face masks, in a hedge near the bank. Jack and Jill have persuaded Ben, a security guard, to leave his post at the bank whilst the robbery is to take place. Jill approaches the window of the bank whereby she notices, despite Ben's absence, an increased amount of security. Jill waits at the bank entrance for around 20 minutes before deciding to call off the robbery. Sceptical about Jill's presence at the bank for so long, security call the police and Jack and Jill are arrested. During interview, Jack and Jill reveal that they have been working with Andy and Ben.

Advise the CPS as to what offences (substantive and inchoate) have been committed by Jack, Jill, Andy and Ben.

Essay question

'The law presently struggles to pinpoint the moment that an individual's conduct can be considered such that it is more than merely preparatory. With a lack of consistency in approach, the law remains in a state of flux regarding the fixing of checkpoints relevant to a criminal attempt.'

Critically discuss this statement with regard to the state of the law of attempts.

chapter 6

Vicarious and Corporate Liability

After reading this chapter, you will be able to understand:

- the principle of vicarious liability and how it applies to the criminal law
- the principle of corporate liability and how it applies to the criminal law
- the offence of corporate manslaughter, the elements of the offence and the consequences of criminal liability.

6.1 Introduction to vicarious and corporate liability

In the preceding chapters, we have discussed the liability of natural persons, ie of human beings. Our focus in those chapters, and the chapters that will follow this one, is on the autonomy exercised by an individual in relation to the commission of a criminal offence.

In this chapter, our discussion will focus on the liability of 'artificial' legal persons, ie corporations. Such corporations cannot operate without human input; however, they remain subject to the criminal law to the same, or at least to a similar, extent as natural persons. Much debate has surrounded the liability of corporations for criminal offences. For instance, Metzger and Dalton ('Seeing the elephant: an organisational perspective on corporate moral agency' (1996) 33 Am Bus LJ 489) argue that a company is a person with the capability of moral responsibility and accountability. On this basis, it ought to be held criminally liable. Fischel and Sykes ('Corporate crime' (1996) 25 J Legal Stud 319), on the other hand, argue that corporations should never be subject to criminal prosecution. Despite arguments for and against finding liability against corporations, such an action remains a possibility in the criminal law. The manner in which the law attaches such liability is the focus of this chapter.

6.2 Vicarious liability

This principle, based in the law of tort, denotes the situation where a legal person, most often an employer, is responsible for the actions of its employees whilst they are acting within the course of their employment.

Vicarious liability can thus be explained in the following way:

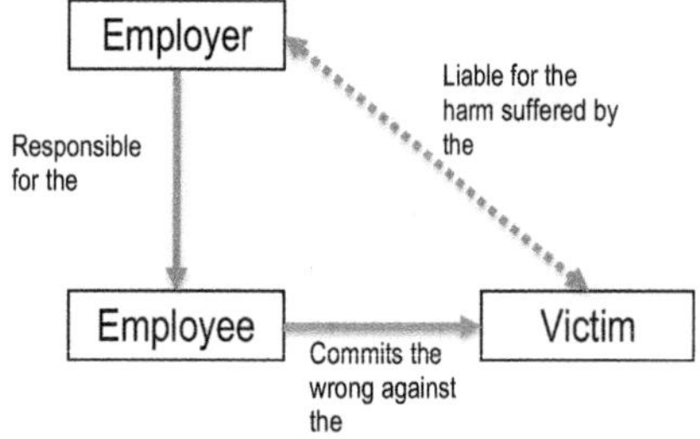

Figure 6.1 Operation of vicarious liability

It is important to note, however, that an employment relationship is not the only category of relationship where a legal person may be vicariously liable for the actions of another. Principals may be vicariously liable for the acts of their agents, and licensees, where they have delegated control, for the acts of workers.

6.2.1 Distinguishing vicarious and corporate liability

Vicarious liability is concerned with the attachment of liability to an employer (or principal) for the actions of its employee (or agent). Simply, where the employee is liable, the employer is liable.

As we shall see below, although a corporation may be liable for a criminal offence through the principle of vicarious liability, corporate liability is most commonly understood as the situation where the company itself is liable for a criminal offence. This is often a difficult concept for students to understand given that a company is artificial and not a natural person. However, given its separate legal status and ability to act as a natural person, a company is just as liable for a criminal offence as a human being. In a similar sense to vicarious liability, where liability is attached to the employer because he is responsible for the employee, corporate liability attaches to the company through the actions of its officers. In this circumstance, however, the officers are said to *be* the company, as opposed to *represent* the company.

Assistance on this point can be taken from the judgment of Bingham LJ in *R v HM Coroner for East Kent, ex p Spooner* (1987) 88 Cr App R 10, in which his Lordship stated:

> A company may be vicariously liable for the negligent acts and omissions of its servants and agents, but for a company to be criminally liable for manslaughter … requires that the *mens rea* and the *actus reus* of manslaughter should be established not against those who acted for or in the name of the company but against those who were to be identified as the embodiment of the company itself.

Bingham LJ's judgment can be expressed in the following figure.

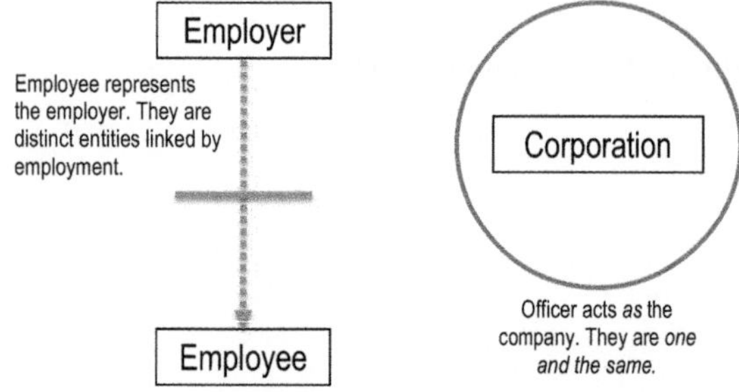

Figure 6.2 Understanding vicarious and corporate liability

It is important to distinguish the two liabilities. Although an employer may be vicariously liable for the actions of its employee, where the employer is not incorporated (ie he or she is a sole trader or it is a general partnership), there is unlikely to be any question of corporate liability.

6.2.2 Justifying vicarious liability

Vicarious liability is justified in civil law on the basis that the appropriate body to compensate a victim of a tort are those persons responsible for, and in control of, the actions of the perpetrator. Further to this, according to the 'deep pocket theory', it is appropriate for the employer to be liable to a claimant given that it has the ability to compensate the claimant for any harm suffered (through private funds or insurance); an employee may not be in as strong a position to compensate. The position of vicarious liability is firmly embedded in the civil law but has faced an uphill challenge in the criminal law.

In general, it cannot be said that an individual is liable for the actions of another, unless they have assisted or encouraged that person to act (see **Chapter 4**). As discussed in **Chapter 2**, the liability of an individual for a criminal offence is determined by their *own* actions, not by the actions of *another*. This is evident in the rather old case of *R v Huggins* (1730) 2 Stra 883 where Raymond CJ ruled:

> It is a point not to be disputed but that in criminal cases the principal is not answerable for the act of the deputy as he is in civil cases; they must each answer for their own acts and stand or fall by their own behaviour.

6.2.3 Vicarious liability in criminal law

Despite the statement of Raymond CJ in *Huggins*, the criminal law has developed to the extent that liability may be attached to an individual or body through the actions of their agents or employees. *Huggins* remains good law as the categories below are limited in application, as will be made clear.

In order to attach liability, the courts may rely on two principles, namely:

- the attribution principle; and
- the delegation principle.

Before considering these two principles, a few points are worth noting at this stage:

- Criminal vicarious liability is limited to statutory offences. In this regard, common law offences, with the exception of public nuisance (*R v Stephens* (1866) LR 1 QB 702) and (formerly) criminal libel (*R v Holbrook* (1878) 4 QBD 42), are not relevant.
- Vicarious liability rarely arises in trials on indictment; it is usually confined to summary offences.
- Although rare, some offences will be express in providing that a defendant may be vicariously liable for his agent's actions (see, for example, s 59(1) of the Licensing Act 1964 (now repealed) which concerned the sale of alcohol outside permitted hours by 'himself or by his servant or agent').
- Whether a crime is capable of commission through the principle of vicarious liability will depend on statutory construction of the respective offence. Many offences will be regulatory and strict in nature. The Court of Appeal confirmed in *R v Qureshi* [2011] EWCA Crim 1584 that an offence must be strict for the principle of attribution to apply.

6.2.3.1 Attribution

Also known as the 'extensive construction' or 'attributed act' principle, attribution works to allow the courts to attach the liability of the employee to the employer itself. It does so through the interpretation of key words and phrases within the legislation setting out the offence.

A number of points must be made regarding attribution before we consider some examples in practice:

- Attribution is only possible where the natural person would be similarly liable (*Mousell Bros Ltd v London and North-Western Railway Co* [1917] 2 KB 836).
- Attribution is only possible where the offence is one of strict liability (see **Chapter 3**).
- Attribution is only possible where the employee is carrying out an act that he is employed or authorised to do. Where the employee acts outside of his instructions or authority, the employer will not be liable (*Adams v Camfoni* [1929] 1 KB 95). Though see *Coppen v Moore (No 2)* [1898] 2 QB 306 below.

Numerous examples can be taken from the case law of the courts interpreting relevant verbs within the statute to attribute liability to the defendant corporation. **Table 6.1** details some of these examples.

Table 6.1 Examples of attribution

Authority	Word or expression attributed
Green v Burnett [1955] 1 QB 78	'using' – in relation to using a motor vehicle with a defective brake
Winter v Hinckley and District Industrial Co-operative Society Ltd [1959] 1 All ER 403	'exposing for sale' – in relation to the sale of bags of coal containing short weight
Melias Ltd v Preston [1957] 2 QB 380	'being in possession of' – in relation to stolen goods
Anderton v Rodgers [1981] Crim LR 404	'offering for sale' – in relation to the illegal sale of intoxicating liquors

The key authority on the principle of attribution in criminal liability is that of *Coppen v Moore (No 2)* [1898] 2 QB 306.

case example

Charge:
Selling goods to which a false trade description is applied (MMA 1887, s 3)

Case progression:
Magistrates' court – Guilty

Divisional Court – Conviction upheld

Point of law:
Meaning of vicarious liability under attribution

In *Coppen v Moore (No 2)* [1898] 2 QB 306, the defendant, a shop owner, gave specific instructions to his branch managers that the selling of certain American hams should be as a breakfast ham, and not according to its place of origin. A shop assistant sold the ham as 'Scotch' ham, unaware of the defendant's instructions. Selling the goods in this fashion amounted to an offence under the Merchandise Marks Act 1887 (now the Trade Descriptions Act 1968). The defendant was tried and convicted for the offence.

The Divisional Court concluded that despite the express instructions to the contrary, the defendant remained liable for the actions of his employee as he remained the owner and seller of the ham. The salesman was authorised to sell the item and acted on behalf of his employer – albeit in the wrong fashion.

Russell CJ commented:

> It cannot be doubted that the appellant [the defendant] sold the ham in question, although the transaction was carried out by his servants. In other words *he was the seller, although not the actual salesman.* (emphasis added)

Similar applications of this rule can be seen in the more recent cases of *Tesco Stores Ltd v Brent LBC* [1993] 2 All ER 718, where Tesco was found liable for *selling* an '18' certified film to persons under this age, and *Harrow LBC v Shah* [1999] 3 All ER 302, where a shop owner remained liable for their employee *selling* lottery tickets to under 16-year-olds despite express instructions to the contrary. Again, following the reasoning in *Coppen*, the employer had authorised the actions of the employee; the employee had just exercised that authority poorly.

By contrast to the above examples, such words as 'driving' or 'drives', in the context of faulty brakes, worn tyres or being over the speed limit, have been interpreted to exclude the employer from attribution. Indeed Pill J in *Richmond upon Thames Borough Council v Pinn and Wheeler Ltd* [1989] RTR 354 commented that '[t]he act of driving a lorry is a physical act which can be performed only by natural persons'. On that basis, the individual remains liable. The editors of *Archbold: Criminal Pleading, Evidence and Practice* (Sweet & Maxwell, 2020) disagree with the decision in *Pinn and Wheeler*, arguing that the decision '… overlooks the fact that all corporate activity is performed through human agency'. The editors go on to say:

> The test, it is submitted, is not whether the prohibited act can only be performed by a natural person, but whether it is one which it is possible for the agent to commit while acting as such. If it is clear that the prohibited act is one which could only be done by the actor acting in his personal capacity, then corporate liability will be excluded. Bigamy and rape would seem to be the clearest examples. If a corporation can commit manslaughter (which may be committed by an act of driving), it seems illogical that it cannot commit a regulatory offence, an ingredient of which is driving.

This opinion would appear to be in line with the conflicting authority of *James & Son v Smee* [1955] 1 QB 78 where the Divisional Court found a company liable for 'using' a motor vehicle with defective brakes. The court reasoned that the employee *used* the vehicle in the course of employment, and thus the *use* of the vehicle could be said to be that of the company's use. Given that neither authority is binding on a senior court, both will act as persuasive authority should the point arise in the Court of Appeal or Supreme Court.

6.2.3.2 Delegation

Like the attribution doctrine, which is restricted to crimes of strict liability, the delegation principle is only to be used in circumstances where the offence is one requiring *mens rea* (*R v Winson* [1969] 1 QB 371, per Lord Parker). Where the crime is one of strict liability, the defendant remains liable throughout regardless of whether there was an effective delegation of power.

The general idea of delegation concerns the situation where the employer has transferred managerial responsibility to its employee. In practice, this means that such responsibility must have been transferred from a senior manager to a junior manager or employee. The cases in this area have only concerned circumstances where the defendant has delegated his duty under a licence (as a licence-holder) to another. Importantly, the Court of Appeal in *R v St Regis Paper Co Ltd* [2011] EWCA Crim 2527 has recently confined the delegation principle to licensing cases.

One key authority to demonstrate the principle is the rather interesting case of *Allen v Whitehead* [1930] 1 KB 211.

case example

Charge:
Knowingly suffering prostitutes to meet together (Metropolitan Police Act 1839, s 44)

Case progression:
Magistrates' court – Guilty

Divisional Court – Conviction upheld

Point of law:
Whether delegated functions can impute liability to D

In *Allen v Whitehead* [1930] 1 KB 211, the defendant was charged with 'knowingly suffering prostitutes to meet together in his house and remain therein'. The defendant, a licensee of a café, delegated his powers to an employee and explicitly warned him of the rule in s 44. The employee disregarded this warning and allowed prostitutes onto the premises.

In dismissing the defendant's appeal, the Divisional Court concluded that the actions and state of mind of the employee could be imputed to the defendant. The Court found liability on the basis that the defendant had effectively transferred managerial authority to the employee. Further, the Court found liability despite the defendant being unaware of the actions of his employee, as the Court concluded that he had effectively delegated his management to the employee. The Court further justified this approach on the basis that the licence-holder could otherwise allow prostitutes to enter the café and avoid liability by simply delegating functions to the employee.

A question that has arisen, therefore, is 'how much authority must be delegated in order for an employer to be vicariously liable?' The House of Lords in *Vane v Yiannopoullos* [1965] AC 486 appeared to answer this question.

case example

Charge:
Sale of alcohol without a licence (Licensing Act 1961, s 22(1))

Case progression:
Magistrates' court – Not guilty

Divisional Court – Not guilty

House of Lords – Appeal dismissed

Point of law:
How much authority must be delegated

In *Vane v Yiannopoullos* [1965] AC 486, the defendant was the owner of a restaurant. The restaurant held a licence to sell alcohol but only to individuals who had ordered meals. The defendant warned his staff of this rule. Whilst the defendant was working on one floor of the restaurant, a waitress on another floor served alcohol to a group of individuals who had not ordered a meal.

The defendant was charged with an offence contrary to s 22 of the Licensing Act 1961, but was found not guilty by the magistrates' court and the Divisional Court on appeal by the prosecution. The Divisional Court ruled that the defendant had not delegated the management of his business to the waitress and thus her actions of unlawfully selling alcohol could not be imputed to him. The prosecution appealed to the House of Lords which found in favour, once more, of the restaurant owner.

Parker CJ, with whom Lord Evershed agreed, ruled:

> It must be shown that the licensee is not managing the business himself but has delegated the management to someone else ...

Lord Reid concurred with this approach focusing on the circumstances where the defendant is absent from the premises and has left another in charge of it. Indeed, Lord Hodson went so far as to comment that the principle:

> has never so far been extended so as to cover the case where the whole of the authority of the licensee has not been transferred to another.

By considering these *obiter* statements, it can be said that the House of Lords found there to be no delegation of powers on the following bases:

- the employer had not handed over full managerial authority – he only delegated the power to sell alcohol;
- the employer remained on the premises and in control of the restaurant;
- the waitress remained under the control of the manager at all times.

As a result, the House of Lords tightened the test for delegation in this sense, ruling that there must be an effective delegation/transfer of all, or a substantial amount of, management authority. A lack of managerial presence at the site where the offence takes place is a key indication of this. This was evident in *Bradshaw v Ewart-James* [1983] QB 671, a case concerning the delegation of a statutory duty from the ship-master to his chief officer, where the Divisional Court found there to be no full delegation of authority as the master of a ship remained on board and in full command. The Court of Appeal in *R v St Regis Paper Co Ltd* [2011] EWCA Crim 2527 recently confirmed that the delegation principle is unlikely to be extended past that expressed by the House of Lords in *Vane*.

It is also possible for vicarious liability to exist in circumstances where there has been a further delegation of managerial authority, known as a sub-delegation. Sub-delegation would work in the following way: A delegates to B who sub-delegates to C. In the circumstances where a licensee delegates to another and that individual sub-delegates, the licensee remains liable for the actions of the sub-delegated party (*Crabtree v Hole* (1879) 43 JP 799).

6.2.4 Putting together vicarious liability

The rules of vicarious liability in criminal proceedings are not as straightforward as one might like. On that basis, the following figure should make matters more clear.

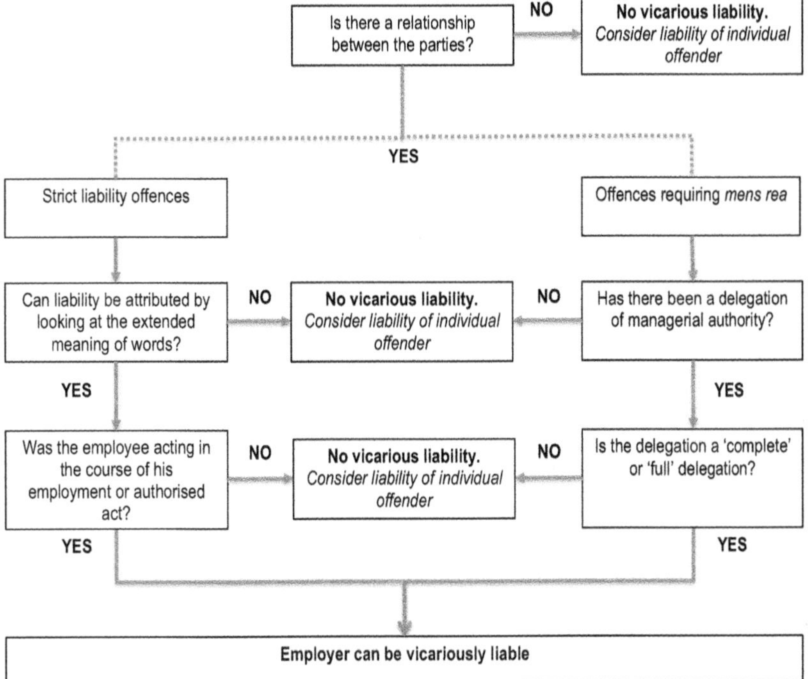

Figure 6.3 Putting together vicarious liability

6.3 Corporate liability

Corporate liability reflects the situation in which a corporation or other artificial legal entity is liable for a criminal offence. For a full discussion of the history of corporate liability, see Leigh, *The Criminal Liability of Corporations in English Law* (Weidenfeld & Nicolson, 1969).

It can be noted at this stage that the law, in developing corporate liability, has taken a multi-strand approach. In some circumstances, the law has developed to tackle the criminal liability specifically of corporations. We can see this in the introduction of the Financial Services and Markets Act 2000 and the Corporate Manslaughter and Corporate Homicide Act 2007. In other situations, however, the law has attempted to 'fit corporate liability into the existing structure' (Horder, *Ashworth's Principles of Criminal Law*, 9th edn (OUP, 2019)).

6.3.1 Defining 'corporations'

The word 'corporation' is used to target business ventures that have been successfully registered within the meaning of the Companies Act 2006 (or the Limited Liability Partnerships Act 2000), one or more of its predecessors or equivalent legislation in another jurisdiction. Upon completion of the registration process under the 2006 Act, a body is said to have become 'incorporated'. The following incorporated bodies are considered as separate legal entities:

- private limited companies (Ltd);
- public limited companies (plc);
- limited liability partnerships (LLP); and
- local authorities.

Upon incorporation, the body becomes a legal entity separate from its members (shareholders), directors and employees. This is known as the *Salomon* principle (*Salomon v Salomon & Co* [1897] AC 22). As a result of this separate legal status, a corporation is capable *(inter alia)* of:

- conducting business;
- entering into contracts;
- incurring debts;
- owning property; and
- suing and being sued.

Most importantly for our purposes, a corporation may be liable for criminal offences.

It is possible for the criminal law to attach liability to unincorporated bodies, such as sole traders, partnerships and clubs. This is provided for in s 5 and Sch 1 of the Interpretation Act 1978 which states that '"person" includes a body of persons corporate or unincorporate'. However, without the ability to 'identify' the legal personality in question, the courts often struggle and the law, as a result, is unclear (*R v L* [2008] EWCA Crim 1970).

6.3.2 Capability of criminal liability

In general, corporations are capable of committing the majority of offences contained within the criminal law in the same respect as a natural person. Indeed, the CPS in its Legal Guidance on the topic provides that '[a] company is a legal person, capable of being prosecuted, and should not be treated differently from an individual because of its artificial personality'. See Fisse and Braithwaite (*Corporations, Crime and Accountability* (CUP, 1993)) and their argument for 'reactive fault' as an alternative to having to find corporations liable for criminal offences.

6.3.2.1 Circumstances where a company cannot be liable

The first major offence for which a corporation cannot be liable is that of murder, which may only be committed by a human being or 'man of sound mind', as we shall see in **Chapter 8**. Other exceptions include treason and piracy.

These offences are excluded from the remit of corporate liability as the prescribed sentence upon conviction is imprisonment only. As it is not possible to imprison a company (for obvious reasons), the Court of Criminal Appeal in *R v ICR Haulage Ltd* [1944] KB 551 reasoned that such offences cannot be committed by corporations. On this basis, only offences for which a fine is a possible sanction can give rise to corporate liability.

Further to this, it must also be possible for an official of the company to commit the offence within the scope of their employment. Thus, offences that fall outside the scope of such employment, such as rape, cannot be committed by a corporation.

6.3.2.2 Liability of the individual

Where an individual (a human being) commits a criminal offence whilst acting in the course of their employment, or whilst they are acting on behalf of a corporation, they will be directly liable for the offence. For example, suppose Jack is the director of a company. Should Jack commit an act of dangerous driving whilst in the course of his duties to the company, he will be directly liable for the offence. In such a case, the ordinary rules of liability discussed in previous chapters will apply.

Further, where a corporation is found criminally liable, an individual within the company may also be liable as a secondary party if it can be proven that they were an accessory to the wrongdoing (Accessories and Abettors Act 1861, s 8 – see **Chapter 4**). However, the courts must avoid the potential for double punishment.

In *R v Rollco Screw & Rivet Co Ltd & Others* [1999] IRLR 439, a case concerning asbestos contamination in a factory, Lord Bingham CJ stated:

> [O]ne must avoid a risk of overlap. In a small company the directors are likely to be the shareholders, and therefore the main losers if a severe sanction is imposed on the company. We accept that the court must be alert to make sure that it is not in effect imposing double punishment.

6.3.3 Finding liability

In addition to establishing the *capability* of a corporation in committing a criminal offence, it is also necessary to understand the respective pathways to *find* liability against a corporation. These pathways are as follows:

- through offences specific to corporations;
- through the identification doctrine; and
- through vicarious liability.

Cavanagh ('Corporate Criminal Liability: An Assessment of the Models of Fault' (2011) 75 J Crim L 414) labels these pathways as the different 'modes' of corporate fault. We shall consider each pathway/mode in detail now.

6.3.3.1 Corporate offences

The first pathway in which the criminal law may find liability against a corporation is through specifically drafted offences for corporations. This pathway (also known as 'breach of a statutory duty') simply allows the prosecution to find liability against a corporation based on specifically drafted offences capable of commission only by such corporations. These offences are different from the standard offences we have come to understand, as they lack the respective *mens rea* and replace it with some other conduct-focused element. As a result, specific corporate offences are generally strict in liability. Many of these offences involve the so-called 'failure to prevent' offences, which concern circumstances where the company has failed to put into place mechanisms and procedures to avoid harm or loss.

Many of these offences, however, involve some form of 'due diligence' defence, which allows the company to escape liability where it can demonstrate that it practised due diligence and that a lack of due diligence was the fault of a person who was not a true embodiment of the company. For example in *Tesco Supermarkets Ltd v Nattrass* [1972] AC 153, the House of Lords found that a store manager acted independently of the company and was not considered the true embodiment of it.

In addition, unlike the identification doctrine that applies in the most part to incorporated bodies, eg companies, the statutory breach of duty pathway has also been identified as applying to unincorporated bodies. This is evident in the judgment of the Divisional Court in the case of *R v Clerk to the Croydon Justices, ex parte Chief Constable of Kent* [1989] Crim LR 910, where the Court held that an unincorporated body could be liable for a fine under the Transport Act 1982 where it was considered a 'registered keeper'.

Relevant offences under this heading include offences under the Corporate Manslaughter and Corporate Homicide Act 2007, the Health and Safety at Work Act 1974, the Bribery Act 2010 and the Companies Act 2006. We shall discuss the more important of these offences below at **6.4.**

6.3.3.2 Identification doctrine

Unlike the category above, which concerns offences created specifically for corporations and that lack a *mens rea* element, offences chargeable through the identification doctrine involve *mens rea* as a relevant element of the offence. The identification doctrine works to attach liability to a corporation where 'the acts and state of mind' of those who represent it are sufficient to establish liability. These individuals have become known as the 'embodiment of the company' (*Essendon Engineering Co Ltd v Maile* [1982] RTR 260). Sullivan ('The attribution of culpability to limited companies' [1996] CLJ 515) contends that this doctrine is merely a 'restricted version' of the theory of vicarious liability. Read the following sections and see if you agree.

The classic test: 'directing will and mind'

The doctrine has been examined in a number of cases over the years. The first prominent explanation of the doctrine came about in *Lennard's Carrying Co v Asiatic Petroleum Co* [1915] AC 705, where Viscount Haldane LC in the House of Lords stated:

> A corporation is an abstraction. It has no mind or will of its own any more than it has a body of its own; its active and directing will must consequently be sought in

> the person of somebody who for some purposes may be called an agent but who is really the directing mind and will of the corporation, the very ego and centre of the personality of the corporation … somebody who is not merely a servant or agent for whom the company is liable upon the footing respondent superior, but somebody for whom the company is liable because his action is the very action of the company itself.

This became known as the 'directing mind and will' test and, where proven, liability will be imputed to the company. A second, well-known explanation of the doctrine came from Denning LJ in *Bolton (Engineering) Co Ltd v TJ Graham & Sons Ltd* [1957] 1 QB 159:

> A company may in many ways be likened to a human body. It has a brain and nerve centre which controls what it does. It also has hands which hold the tools and act in accordance with directions from the centre. Some of the people in the company are mere servants and agents who are nothing more than hands … and cannot be said to represent the mind or will. Others are directors and managers who represent the directing mind and will of the company, and control what it does. The state of mind of these managers is the state of mind of the company and is treated by the law as such.

Perhaps a more straightforward expression of the identification doctrine was enunciated by Eveleigh J in *R v Andrews-Weatherfoil Ltd* [1972] 1 WLR 118, who stated that the relevant person or persons must have 'the status and authority' that makes their acts the acts of the company. Dignam and Lowry (*Company Law*, 11th edn (OUP, 2020)) characterise these explanations of the identification doctrine as 'the alter ego or organic theory of the company'; however, this view was doubted in *UBAF Ltd v European American Banking Corporation* [1984] QB 713, where the Court of Appeal found the phrase to be 'largely meaningless, save as an indication of some very wide but undefined authority' (per Ackner LJ).

As will be understood shortly, although this test appears straightforward, the law has had great difficulty in determining how to attribute liability on the basis of the 'directing mind and will' test.

The leading case in this area is that of *Tesco Supermarkets Ltd v Nattrass* [1972] AC 153.

case example

Charge:
False trade description (TDA 1968, s 24(1))

Case progression:
Crown Court – Guilty

Court of Appeal – Conviction upheld

House of Lords – Conviction quashed

Point of law:
Finding liability through identification

In *Tesco Supermarkets Ltd v Nattrass* [1972] AC 153, the defendant, Tesco, was charged with applying the wrong price to goods in its supermarket. The defendant raised a defence in s 24 of the Trade Descriptions Act (TDA) 1968 which provided that where the offence was due to the act or default of another (in this case, the branch manager), and the defendant acted in due diligence, it would not be liable.

The House of Lords had to consider whether the branch manager acted independently of the corporation, so as to allow the company to escape liability. Their Lordships concluded that he did act independently. The Court reasoned that Tesco exercised strict control over its branch managers, allowing them no power to control price fixtures. By amending the price fixture, the manager had thus acted outside of his authority and could no longer be said to be acting as the mind and will of the company. As a result, their Lordships found the identification doctrine to fail at this point.

Lord Reid in the House of Lords noted:

> A living person has a mind which can have knowledge or intention or be negligent and he has hands to carry out his intentions. A corporation has none of these; it must act through living persons, though not always one or the same person. Then the person who acts is not speaking or acting for the company. He is acting as the company and his mind which directs his acts is the mind of the company. There is no question of the company being vicariously liable. He is not acting as a servant, representative, agent or delegate. He is an embodiment of the company or, one could say, he hears and speaks through the persona of the company, within his appropriate sphere, and his mind is the mind of the company.

Who then, can be said to be the directing will and mind of the corporation? In *Tesco*, their Lordships were divided amongst themselves as to the best description of the controlling individuals. Lord Reid was of the opinion that the controllers were

> the board of directors, the managing director and perhaps other superior officers of a company [who] carry out the functions of management and speak and act as the company.

Viscount Dilhorne, on the other hand, was of the view that the controller is a person

> who is in actual control of the operations of a company or of part of them and who is not responsible to another person in the company for the manner in which he discharges his duties in the sense of being under his orders.

Lord Diplock, with whom Lord Pearson agreed, felt that the most appropriate way to characterise these controlling individuals was to look at the constitution (ie rules) of the company, known as the articles of association. Particularly, Lord Diplock felt that an answer could be reached by

> identifying those natural persons who by the memorandum and articles of association or as a result of action taken by the directors or by the company in the general meeting pursuant to the articles are entrusted with the exercise of the powers of the company.

Regardless of which opinion is taken, the House of Lords identified these persons as the 'controlling minds' of the company. As a result, the less senior officials within the company, such as sales assistants, will not act as a 'controlling mind' sufficient to find liability through the identification doctrine. To demonstrate the approach taken by the courts, **Table 6.2** gives some examples of persons who were considered not 'senior' enough to be classed as controlling minds.

Table 6.2 Controlling minds?

Case	**Individual**
John Henshall (Quarries) Ltd v Harvey [1965] 2 QB 233	Weighbridge operator
Magna Plant Ltd v Mitchell [1966] Crim LR 394	Depot engineer
Redfern v Dunlop Ltd (Aircraft Division) [1993] Crim LR 43	European sales manager

This doctrine can be justified. First, corporate officers effectively act as the embodiment of the company when acting in its business. Their acts and states of mind are effectively deemed to be those of the company. The operation of this doctrine is clear through the case of *Moore v I Bresler Ltd* [1944] 2 All ER 515, where the

Divisional Court attached liability to the corporation through the acts of its servant despite the act being done in fraud of the company itself.

in practice

In order to prosecute a corporation through this doctrine, the prosecution must first identify the 'directing mind'. To do so, the prosecution will often refer to the relevant constitution of the company (through use of the articles of association – simply the terms of how the company will run). However, such identification is often difficult for the prosecution, given the large scale of some corporations and the sheer number of potential controlling minds.

Further, the Law Commission ('Criminal Liability in Regulatory Contexts' (Law Com No 195, 2010)) has noted that

> the identification doctrine can make it easier to convict small companies of offences committed by employees. This is because the smaller the company the more likely it is that the directors played some kind of active role in the commission of the offence, for example by explicitly or implicitly authorising it.

Wells ('Corporations: Culture, Risk and Criminal Liability' [1993] Crim LR 551) criticises the decision in *Tesco*, arguing that its effect is to make the law of identification inapplicable to large, and more complex, company frameworks. In many situations a crime may be made out, but no one single individual can be segregated and identified. In *Tesco*, the company had over 800 branches; the branch manager could not be said to have controlling mind over all 800 branches, and thus he was considered to be acting as the 'hands' and not the 'mind' of the company. Dignam and Lowry (*Company Law*, 11th edn (OUP, 2020)) are equally are critical of the decision in *Tesco*, arguing that the application of the doctrine acts 'effectively as an immunity from criminal prosecution for large complex corporate organisations'. We can see examples of this in the context of manslaughter, for example the Divisional Court in *R v HM Coroner for East Kent, ex p Spooner* (1987) 88 Cr App R 10 accepted that the crime had been committed but failed to find liability when an individual could not be established at the directing mind and will of the company. The same outcome was reached in the notorious case of *R v P&O Ferries (Dover) Ltd* (1990) 93 Cr App R 72 which concerned a P&O Ferries disaster in Zeebrugge killing 193 individuals. Despite the company being '[f]rom top to bottom … infected with the disease of sloppiness' (Sheen Report), no single individual could be drawn out as the directing will and mind of the company.

Additionally, the courts are unwilling to attach liability to companies by aggregating the acts of various individuals. Devlin J was adamant on this point in the trial at first instance in *Armstrong v Strain* [1952] 1 KB 232, where he commented that '[y]ou cannot add an innocent state of mind to an innocent state of mind and get as a result a dishonest state of mind'. Ormerod and Laird (*Smith, Hogan, & Ormerod's Criminal Law*, 15th edn (OUP, 2018)) are equally critical of the aggregation principle on the basis that '[a]ny such doctrine could certainly have no application in offences requiring knowledge, intention or recklessness'. Further, Fisse and Braithwaite ('The Allocation of Responsibility for Corporate Crime: individualism, Collectivism and Accountability' (1988) 11 Sydney LR 468) contend that 'organisations are systems … not just aggregations of individuals'. Wells (*Corporations and Criminal Responsibility*,

2nd edn (OUP, 2001)), on the other hand, argues in favour of the ability to aggregate. In particular, she states:

> [A]ggregation needs to be seen as a recognition that individuals within a company contribute to the whole machine; it is the whole that is judged not the parts.

This issue has largely been resolved in the context of manslaughter as a result of the Corporate Manslaughter and Corporate Homicide Act 2007, discussed below, but problems still persist in all other areas of criminal law.

A new approach: statutory construction

The restrictive approach found in *Tesco* was challenged by the Privy Council in the case of *Meridian Global Funds Management Asia Ltd v Securities Commission* [1995] 2 AC 500. This case concerned a failure on the part of an investment manager in a company to give adequate notice of his holding in 'substantial security'. The Court of Appeal of New Zealand concluded that, generally, liability will attach as a result of the actions of the directing mind and will of the company; however, this need not be so. In fact, knowledge on the part of employees, ie the less senior company officials, could be attributed to knowledge of the corporation. The Court of Appeal found the corporation liable.

The corporation appealed unsuccessfully to the Privy Council, where Lord Hoffmann rationalised that attribution should not be taken too literally by the courts; instead the courts should focus on the language of the relevant statute, its contents and any policy underlying the provisions and the manner in which they are to apply.

Lord Hoffmann characterised this as a *special* application of the attribution principle, requiring no necessity to describe the employee as the 'directing mind and will' of the company in order to find liability. Instead, Lord Hoffmann questioned:

> Whose act (or knowledge or state of mind) was *for this purpose* intended to count as the act, etc. of the company? One finds the answer to this question by applying the usual canons of interpretation, taking into account the language of the rule (if it is a statute) and its content and policy. (original emphasis)

Given that the relevant statute, the Securities Amendment Act 1988 (New Zealand), required the immediate notice of substantial security holdings, Lord Hoffmann felt it simple to attribute that knowledge to the holders of the securities, ie the company. In that regard the company was liable.

The Law Commission in 2010 published a Consultation Paper ('Criminal Liability in Regulatory Contexts' (Law Com No 195, 2010)) where it favoured the approach adopted in *Meridian* towards liability. Specifically, proposal 13, at para 1.62, recommends:

> Legislation should include specific provisions in criminal offences to indicate the basis on which companies may be found liable, but in the absence of such provisions, the courts should treat the question of how corporate fault may be established as a matter of statutory interpretation. We encourage the courts not to presume that the identification doctrine applies when interpreting the scope of criminal offences applicable to companies.

The proposal seeks to turn the courts away from applying the identification doctrine by default and focus on the underlying purpose of a relevant statutory scheme. Although the Report has not yet been taken further, *Meridian* seems to have gained some weight in English case law. For instance, in *McNicholas Construction Co Ltd v*

Customs and Excise Commrs [2000] EWHC 357 (Admin), the Administrative Court found liability for VAT fraud from the actions of one of the company's site managers through the use of Lord Hoffmann's interpretation. Further to this, the House of Lords confirmed *Meridian* to be a part of English law in *Stone & Rolls Ltd v Moore Stephens* [2009] AC 1319. However, most recently, the Supreme Court in *Jetivia SA and Another v Bilta (UK) Ltd (in liquidation) and Others* [2015] UKSC 23 focused on the identification doctrine to determine liability, finding that the wrongdoing of the directors could not be attributed to the company without the presence of a directing mind and will.

Meridian itself has not been without its critics. Wickins and Ong ('Confusion worse confounded: the end of the directing mind theory?' [1997] JBL 524) argue that *Meridian* had the effect of diminishing the 'elegant structure' of the directing mind and will test to 'a heap of intellectual rubble'. Ormerod and Laird (*Smith, Hogan, & Ormerod's Criminal Law*, 15th edn (OUP, 2018)) comment that '[p]erhaps all that these cases demonstrate is that a statute imposes liability if that appears to be the intention of the legislature'. Quite often, however, courts are not attempting to find the true intention of Parliament in constructing statutes; rather, they are 'selecting what *they decide* is the true meaning of Parliament's words' (Cownie, Bradney, and Burton, *English Legal System in Context*, 6th edn (OUP, 2013)). Further, the Court of Appeal in *AG's Reference (No 2 of 1999)* [2000] QB 796 refused to extend the identification principle to include Lord Hoffmann's characterisation further than statutory crimes. Specifically Rose LJ ruled:

> The identification theory, attributing to the company the mind and will of senior directors and managers, was developed in order to avoid injustice: it would bring the law into disrepute if every act and state of mind of an individual employee was attributed to a company which was entirely blameless.

Rose LJ felt that any extension of the identification doctrine ought to be a matter for Parliament.

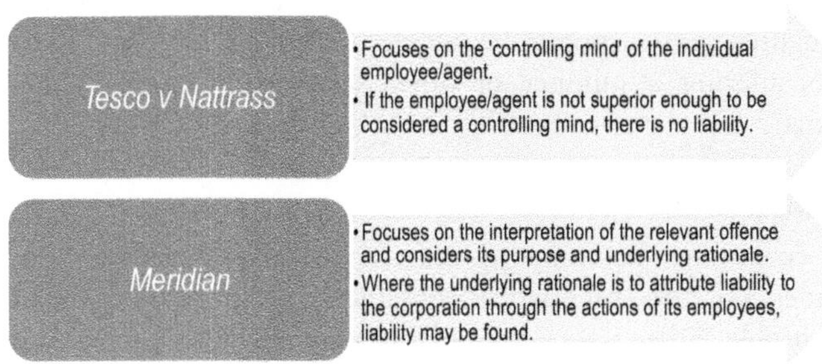

Figure 6.4 Understanding Tesco *and* Meridian

6.3.3.3 Vicarious liability

The third circumstance where the court may find liability against a corporation is through the principle of vicarious liability discussed above at **6.2**. The first recognition of this form of liability was seen in the case of *R v Great North of England Railway Co* (1846) 9 QB 315.

6.3.4 Putting together corporate liability

As with vicarious liability, the principles of corporate liability are not as clear as one might like. On that basis, the following figure should assist.

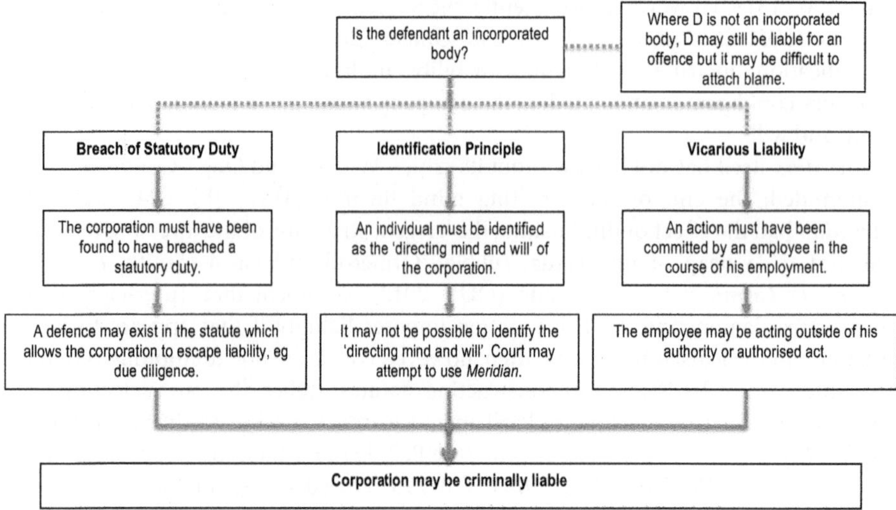

Figure 6.5 Putting together corporate liability

6.4 Corporate offences

As discussed above, Parliament has designated a number of offences as capable of commission by corporations alone. This is done to avoid the difficulties with the identification doctrine (above) and to attach liability directly to the fault of the company.

The main offence we shall be discussing is that of corporate manslaughter contained in the Corporate Manslaughter and Corporate Homicide Act 2007. Before we do so, however, it is worth considering a number of other statutory offences created specifically for corporations.

6.4.1 Offences under the Companies Act 2006

Upon becoming a body corporate, the company must act in accordance with the provisions of the Companies Act 2006. All offences contained within the 2006 Act are either summary-only or triable either way. Some of the most notable offences are detailed in **Table 6.3**.

Table 6.3 Examples of offences under the Companies Act 2006

Offence	Punishment
Failing to forward resolutions or agreements affecting the company's constitution to the registrar (CA 2006, s 30(2))	Summary-only Level 3 fine

Offence	Punishment
Failing to properly keep a register of directors containing requisite information, failing to keep it available and open for inspection, or failing to give notice to the registrar of the place where it is kept (CA 2006, s 162(6))	Summary-only Level 5 fine
Fraudulent trading (CA 2006, s 993)	Either-way: Magistrates' court: Level 5 fine Crown Court: Unlimited fine

6.4.2 Offences under the Health and Safety at Work Act 1974

The Health and Safety at Work Act (HSWA) 1974 provides for a number of offences that are capable of commission by corporations in the context of employment and work. The duty owed by an employer is contained in s 2(1), which obliges every employer to ensure, so far as is reasonably practicable, the health and safety at work of all its employees. Section 3 extends similar provisions to those persons other than employees who may be exposed to risks to their health and safety as a result of the employer's 'undertaking'. By s 33, a failure to comply with either of these duties, in addition to others contained in ss 4–7, will result in criminal liability. An infamous example of the 1974 Act in practice is that of the *British Steel* case.

Charge:
Failing to discharge duty (HWSA 1974, s 33)

Case progression:
Crown Court – Guilty

Court of Appeal – Conviction upheld

Point of law:
Liability under the 1974 Act

case example

In *R v British Steel Plc* [1995] 1 WLR 1356, the victim, a sub-contracted worker, was killed during a relocation of a steel platform whilst under the supervision of the defendant's employee.

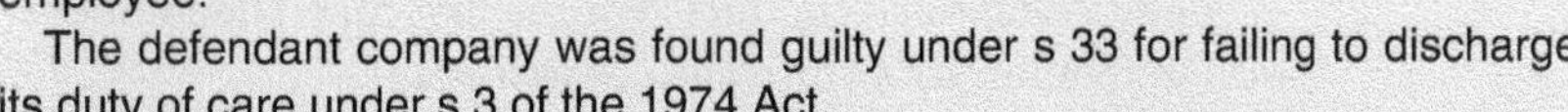

The defendant company was found guilty under s 33 for failing to discharge its duty of care under s 3 of the 1974 Act.

The Court of Appeal upheld the defendant's conviction on the basis that the duty of care was imposed on it and it had failed to discharge that duty.

A defence is available under s 40 if it can be proven, on the balance of probabilities, that it was not *reasonably practicable* to have done more than was in fact done to satisfy the duty. Section 40 does not apply to corporate manslaughter.

Breaches of health and safety legislation remain high, and the level of fines levied against such corporations can be sizeable. For example, in 1999 Great Western Trains was fined £1.5 million for a breach of s 3 of the 1974 Act in connection with the Southall train crash in 1997 where seven people died. Thames Trains was fined £2 million for its breach of health and safety law in relation to the Paddington train crash, and Network Rail was fined £3.5 million in 2005 for breach of health and safety regulations. Despite this, the sentencing of corporations for such breaches has been the focus of much criticism in recent times. In 2003, the Health and Safety Executive (HSE) reported that a total of 933 companies were convicted of health and safety offences over the year. Despite this, the Director General of the HSE at the time,

Timothy Walker, commented in a press release that the level of fines was 'disappointing' for such prosecutions. He stated:

> It is incomprehensible that fines for especially serious big company breaches in health and safety are only a small percentage of those fines handed down for breaches of financial services in similarly large firms. I understand that financial service breaches can affect people's wealth and well-being, but breaches in health and safety can, and do, result in loss of limbs, livelihoods and lives.

6.4.3 Offences under the Bribery Act 2010

The Bribery Act (BA) 2010 created a new offence under s 7 of 'failure of commercial organisations to prevent bribery'. The offence is stated in s 7(1) as follows:

> A relevant commercial organisation ('C') is guilty of an offence under this section if a person ('A') associated with C bribes another person intending—
> (a) to obtain or retain business for C, or
> (b) to obtain or retain an advantage in the conduct of business for C.

Under s 7(5), a 'relevant commercial organisation' includes a company or other body which is incorporated, or a partnership, under the law of any part of the United Kingdom and which carries on a business (whether in the United Kingdom or elsewhere). For an offence under s 7 to be committed, the bribe in question must itself be an offence under ss 1 to 6 of the BA 2010. It is irrelevant whether the bribe itself is prosecuted under ss 1 to 6 (BA 2010, s 7(3)). An 'associated person' is defined in s 8(1) of the BA 2010 as 'a person who performs services for or on behalf of C'. This means that the associated person may be C's employee, agent or subsidiary (BA 2010, s 8(3)). A defence exists under s 7(2) of the BA 2010 where the organisation can prove that it 'had in place adequate procedures designed to prevent persons associated with C from undertaking such conduct'. For the first conviction under s 7, see *R v Skansen Interiors Ltd* (Southwark Crown Ct, 7 March 2018).

By s 9 of the BA 2010, the Secretary of State must publish guidance about procedures that relevant commercial organisations can put in place to prevent persons associated with them from bribing. The Ministry of Justice published such guidance in March 2011 which is available on its website.

6.4.4 Offence under the Corporate Manslaughter and Corporate Homicide Act 2007

Prior to 6 April 2008, it was possible for an incorporated body to be liable for the common law offence of gross negligence manslaughter (*AG's Reference (No 2 of 1999)* [2000] QB 796). However, in order for the company to be guilty of the offence, it was necessary for the prosecution to establish the presence of a 'controlling mind' through the identification doctrine.

6.4.4.1 Development of the offence

A number of disasters stemming from the practices of corporations came to public attention. A few examples for you to look into are set out in **Table 6.4**:

Table 6.4 Examples of poor practice in corporations

Event	Details
Herald of Free Enterprise disaster (1987)	193 people killed

Event	Details
King's Cross fire (1987)	31 people killed
Clapham rail crash (1988)	35 people killed and around 500 people injured
Southall rail crash (1997)	7 people killed and around 150 people injured

In each case, poor practice of the relevant corporation was the underlying cause of the many deaths.

As we have explained, there was a restrictive approach to finding corporations liable and this resulted in a number of recommendations for amendment of the law. In 1994, the Law Commission opened a Consultation Paper ('Criminal Law: Involuntary Manslaughter' (Law Com No 135, 1994), in which it recommended a new corporate offence based on whether the company's conduct fell

> seriously and significantly below what could reasonably have been demanded of [it] in preventing that risk from occurring or in preventing the risk, once in being, from resulting in the prohibited harm.

In a later report ('Legislating the Criminal Code: Involuntary Manslaughter' (Law Com No 237, 1996)), the Law Commission called for a new offence of corporate killing akin to gross negligence manslaughter. The offence would focus on the quality of the company's operating systems rather than the guilt of individuals – in order to avoid the rigidity of the identification doctrine. A Corporate Homicide Bill 2000 was introduced by Andrew Dismore MP in the House of Commons but went no further. In May 2003, the then Home Secretary, David Blunkett, announced the introduction of legislation based on death caused by management failure. In 2005, the government published a White Paper based on this statement ('Corporate Manslaughter: The Government's Draft Bill for Reform' (CM6497)). In the foreword to the White Paper, the Home Secretary stated:

> The government is committed to delivering safe and secure communities, at home and in the work place, and to a criminal justice system that commands the confidence of the public. A fundamental part of this is providing offences that are clear and effective. The current laws on corporate manslaughter are neither, as a number of unsuccessful prosecutions over the years stand testament.

Based largely on the proposals in the 1996 Law Commission Report, the offence of corporate manslaughter was introduced. Consider the criticism by Glazebrook in 'A Better Way of Convicting Businesses of Avoidable Deaths and Injuries' [2002] CLJ 405.

The Corporate Manslaughter and Corporate Homicide Act (CMCHA) 2007 came into force throughout the UK on 6 April 2008. In England and Wales and Northern Ireland, the new offence was named 'corporate manslaughter', whilst in Scotland it was named 'corporate homicide'. Section 20 of the Act abolished the former offence of gross negligence manslaughter for corporations except in circumstances where an event occurred before 6 April 2008. In that case, the old rules of the common law will continue to apply (s 27) – see **Chapter 8**.

Corporate manslaughter has been placed in this chapter to distinguish it from other types of manslaughter that will be considered in **Chapter 8**. In brief, these offences of manslaughter require there to be a killing of a human being by another human being. Given that corporate manslaughter may be established by a number of acts or omissions, and is specific to corporations, it makes sense to deal with the offence here.

6.4.4.2 Defining corporate manslaughter

Corporate manslaughter reflects the situation where an individual has died as a result of a gross breach of duty by a corporation. The offence relates solely to the death of an individual and does not involve other wrongdoing, such as corporate GBH. On this point, Gobert ('The Corporate Manslaughter and Corporate Homicide Act 2007—thirteen years in the making but was it worth the wait?' [2008] MLR 414) is critical of the scope of the Act, arguing that it is

> too narrowly conceived ... Instead of addressing the generic problem of corporate wrongdoing and how to hold organisations accountable for illegality whatever form it might take, the Act ... is restricted to cases of homicide.

Describing the Act as 'limited in its vision and lacking in imagination', Gobert argues in favour of other, more general, wrongdoings such as corporate GBH – the commission of GBH through a gross breach of duty. However, our focus for this section remains on the end result of death.

Since the introduction of the Act, only a handful of prosecutions have been brought by the CPS against corporations. Some examples of convictions include:

- *R v Cotswold Geotechnical Holdings* [2011] EWCA Crim 1337;
- *R v JMW Farm Ltd* [2012] NICC 17 – guilty plea;
- *R v Lion Steel Equipment Ltd* (Manchester Crown Ct, 2 July 2012) – guilty plea;
- *R v Peter Mawson Ltd* (Preston Crown Ct, 2 December 2014) – guilty plea.

Each of these convictions was secured against small businesses that were owner-managed, meaning that the Act has not yet been properly tested in relation to large companies with multiple managerial levels. The difficulties in establishing liability against a larger company will be demonstrated in the following sections.

6.4.4.3 Elements of corporate manslaughter

Section 1 of the CMCHA 2007 provides:

> (1) An organisation to which this section applies is guilty of an offence if the way in which its activities are managed or organised—
> (a) causes a person's death, and
> (b) amounts to a gross breach of a relevant duty of care owed by the organisation to the deceased.

It should be noted that corporate manslaughter includes no *mens rea* element and, like gross negligence manslaughter, is concerned with the conduct of the defendant in causing death.

The *actus reus* of corporate manslaughter is outlined in **Table 6.5**.

Table 6.5 Elements of corporate manslaughter

AR/MR	Elements of the offence
Actus reus	(i) qualifying organisation; (ii) duty of care; (iii) breach of duty; (iv) breach is gross; (v) causes death.

Ormerod and Taylor ('The Corporate Manslaughter and Corporate Homicide Act 2007' [2008] Crim LR 589) have argued that the legislation is far from straightforward given the sheer number of issues that must be determined. The pair acknowledge that the Act succeeds 'primarily in making a symbolic statement about corporate responsibility', but state that it is unlikely to achieve that goal in practice due to the complex nature of the law. The pair conclude that '[t]he layers of technicality serve to restrict the scope of liability far more than would at first appear, and may well lead to significant difficulties in practice'. It is for these reasons that the pair denote the Act as 'disappointing'.

It is useful to note at this stage that where a breach of duty is found against someone within 'senior management', their actions giving rise to the breach will not give rise to a charge against the manager as an accessory to corporate manslaughter. This is provided for in s 18 of the CMCHA 2007:

> An individual cannot be guilty of aiding, abetting, counselling or procuring the commission of an offence of corporate manslaughter.

A charge of assisting gross negligence manslaughter against individuals who fall within the meaning of 'senior management' remains possible; however, such convictions are rare. Antrobus ('The criminal liability of directors for health and safety breaches and manslaughter' [2013] Crim LR 309) argues that this alternative is not sufficient and expresses a desire for accessorial liability to have a place in corporate manslaughter. A similar concern was raised by Gobert (above) who argues that the Act has effectively 'watered down' the responsibility of individual managers in a company.

We shall consider each element in turn.

Actus reus: (i) qualifying organisation

It must first be proven that the relevant defendant falls within the definition of 'organisation' provided for by the Act. Specifically, s 1(2) of the CMCHA 2007 defines an organisation as:

> (a) a corporation;
> (b) a department or other body listed in Schedule 1;
> (c) a police force;
> (d) a partnership, or a trade union or employers' association, that is an employer.

The bodies listed in Sch 1 include the Ministry of Defence, the Crown Prosecution Service, the Department of Transport and many others. The Secretary of State may amend or add to this list at any point. What is obvious from the above list is that a sole trader (ie an individual) cannot be liable for corporate manslaughter.

Actus reus: (ii) duty of care

Secondly, the prosecution must prove that the organisation held a duty of care to the victim. The 'relevant duty of care' is provided for in s 2(1) of the CMCHA 2007:

> A 'relevant duty of care', in relation to an organisation, means any of the following duties owed by it under the law of negligence—
> (a) a duty owed to its employees or to other persons working for the organisation or performing services for it;
> (b) a duty owed as occupier of premises;
> (c) a duty owed in connection with—
> (i) the supply by the organisation of goods or services (whether for consideration or not),
> (ii) the carrying on by the organisation of any construction or maintenance operations,
> (iii) the carrying on by the organisation of any other activity on a commercial basis, or

(iv) the use or keeping by the organisation of any plant, vehicle or other thing;

(d) a duty owed to a person who, by reason of being a person within subsection (2), is someone for whose safety the organisation is responsible.

Whether a duty of care exists in the particular case is a question of law for the trial judge (CMCHA 2007, s 2(5)). The duty of care may be excluded in a number of cases because of the operation of ss 3–7 of the Act. **Table 6.6** details these exceptions.

Table 6.6 Exceptions to the duty of care

Section	Exception
3	Any duty of care owed by a public authority in respect of a decision as to matters of public policy (including in particular the allocation of public resources or the weighing of competing public interests) is not a 'relevant duty of care'.
4	Any duty of care owed by the Ministry of Defence in respect of peacekeeping operations and operations for dealing with terrorism, civil unrest or serious public disorder, in the course of which members of the armed forces come under attack or face the threat of attack or violent resistance, is not a 'relevant duty of care'.
5	Any duty of care owed by a public authority in respect of operations for dealing with terrorism, civil unrest or serious disorder or involving the carrying on of policing or law-enforcement activities, and officers or employees of the public authority in question come under attack or face the threat of attack or violent resistance in the course of the operations, is not a 'relevant duty of care'.
6	Any duty of care owed by an organisation responding to an emergency in respect of the way in which it responds to the emergency is not a 'relevant duty of care'.
7	A duty of care owed by a local authority or other public authority in respect of the exercise by it of certain functions is not a 'relevant duty of care'.

Actus reus: (iii) breach of duty

Whether there has been a breach of duty will depend on whether the 'way in which [the organisation's] activities are managed or organised by its senior management is a *substantial element* in the breach ...' (CMCHA 2007, s 1(3)). This means that the breach of duty must be traced back to the senior management. 'Senior management' is defined in s 1(4)(c) as 'persons who play significant roles in—

(i) the making of decisions about how the whole or a substantial part of its activities are to be managed or organised, or

(ii) the actual managing or organising of the whole or a substantial part of those activities.'

Neither the words 'significant' nor 'substantial' are defined in Act. According to the CPS in its Legal Guidance on this matter:

> The former is likely to be limited to those whose involvement is influential and will not include those who simply carry out the activity.

in practice

In order to determine whether a substantial element of the breach was at senior management level, a prosecutor will rely on an organogram (an organisational hierarchy) of the company in order to identify senior management.

This test is much broader than that under the identification doctrine as it goes beyond those with a 'controlling mind' and also covers such persons who have 'substantial' control. The Act, therefore, goes beyond merely finding directors as senior controlling figures. As a result of the Act, a regional manager may hold enough power and control to be considered 'senior management'. It is important to emphasise, however, that this must be determined on a case-by-case basis and the facts of the case may present the manager in a different light. The following factors would be relevant to this discussion:

- the number of regions;
- the number of higher tiers of management;
- the diversity of the organisation's activities; and
- his or her own job description.

Focusing on the way in which the company's activities are managed or organised in determining guilt has been praised as a step away from the rigid identification doctrine. However, criticism still remains around the law's focus on persons in senior management. Specifically, Price ('Finding fault in organisations—reconceptualising the role of senior managers in corporate manslaughter' (2015) 35 LS 385) has criticised the Act for 'retaining a focus on people rather than on truly "corporate" liability').

Further to this, it is not necessary to point to the faults of a particular individual; rather, the Act allows for an 'aggregation' of senior management activities, which simply means that the arbiters of fact may take into account a selection of breaches from a group of senior managers. This ability to aggregate responsibility is not possible under the identification doctrine (*AG's Reference (No 2 of 1999)* [2000] QB 796).

***Actus reus:* (iv) breach is gross**

Once a breach of duty is established, it must then be determined by a jury whether that breach of duty was 'gross' in the circumstances. According to s 1(4)(b) of the 2007 Act:

> ... a breach of a duty of care by an organisation is a 'gross' breach if the conduct alleged to amount to a breach of that duty falls far below what can *reasonably be expected* of the organisation in the circumstances.

Section 8 of the 2007 Act provides a number of guiding factors to assist the jury in their determination of whether a breach was gross in the circumstances. Specifically, s 8 provides:

> (2) The jury must consider whether the evidence shows that the organisation failed to comply with any health and safety legislation that relates to the alleged breach, and if so—
> (a) how serious that failure was;
> (b) how much of a risk of death it posed.
> (3) The jury may also—
> (a) consider the extent to which the evidence shows that there were attitudes, policies, systems or accepted practices within the organisation that were likely to have encouraged any such failure as is mentioned in subsection (2), or to have produced tolerance of it;
> (b) have regard to any health and safety guidance that relates to the alleged breach.

You should notice from the wording of these subsections that the jury is under an obligation to consider the factors in s 8(2) and *may* consider the factors in s 8(3) if they wish to do so. Importantly, s 8(4) expressly provides jurors with the power to have 'regard to any other matters they consider relevant'. It is important to note that there is no guidance in the Act or case law at present as to how s 8 is to be read.

***Actus reus:* (v) causes death**

The standard rules of causation, namely factual and legal causation, apply here. The jury would simply be asked:

- But for the defendant's gross breach of duty, would death to the victim have occurred?
- Are the defendant's actions more than a minimal contribution to the victim's death? (*R v HM Coroner for Inner London, ex parte Douglas-Williams* [1999] 1 All ER 344).

Further to this, by s 28(1), the death must occur within the UK. Any deaths caused outside the UK will fall outside the jurisdiction of the court.

6.4.4.4 Charging corporate manslaughter

In order to prosecute an offence of corporate manslaughter in England and Wales, the consent of the Director of Public Prosecutions is required (CMCHA 2007, s 17(a)). Further, the CPS must refer the case to the Special Crime Unit in the Special Crime and Counter Terrorism Division of the CPS. This may demonstrate how seriously such matters are taken. The CPS 'Legal Guidance on Corporate Prosecutions' advises that

> prosecutors must identify the correct corporate entity from the outset. It is crucial that prosecutors ensure that the corporation is fully and accurately named in the summons/indictment. If necessary, a company search [through Companies House] should be conducted.

Mode of trial

The offence is triable on indictment only, meaning that it may only be tried in the Crown Court before a judge and jury (CMCHA 2007, s 1(6)).

Sentencing

A number of sanctions are available to the courts under the 2007 Act. Ormerod and Laird (*Smith, Hogan, & Ormerod's Criminal Law*, 15th edn (OUP, 2018)) refer to these options as 'innovative' and '[o]ne of the most welcome aspects of the 2007 Act'.

Table 6.7 demonstrates the powers available to the courts. The Sentencing Council published its definitive guideline, 'Health and safety offences, corporate manslaughter and food safety and hygiene offences', in November 2015.

Table 6.7 Sentencing options for corporate manslaughter

Sentence	Description
Fine (CMCHA 2007, s 1(6))	A corporation convicted of corporate manslaughter is liable to an unlimited fine. According to the definitive guidelines, the sentencing range for this offence if £180,000–£20 million.

Sentence	Description
Remedial order (CMCHA 2007, s 9(1))	A corporation convicted of corporate manslaughter may have a remedial order made against it, requiring the organisation to take specified steps to remedy: (a) the relevant breach in s 1(1)); (b) any matter that appears to the court to have resulted from the relevant breach and to have been a cause of the death; (c) any deficiency, as regards health and safety matters, in the organisation's policies, systems or practices of which the relevant breach appears to the court to be an indication. Failure to comply with such order is also punishable by a fine as a criminal offence (CMCHA 2007, s 9(5)).
Publicity order (CMCHA 2007, s 10(1))	A corporation convicted of corporate manslaughter may have a publicity order made against it, requiring the organisation to publicise: (a) the fact that it has been convicted of the offence; (b) specified particulars of the offence; (c) the amount of any fine imposed; (d) the terms of any remedial order made. Failure to comply with such order is also punishable by a fine as a criminal offence (CMCHA 2007, s 10(4)).

A number of comments can be identified in relation to the sentencing powers of courts for offences under the 2007 Act. For instance, Field and Jones ('The Corporate Manslaughter and Corporate Homicide Act 2007 and the sentencing guidelines for corporate manslaughter: more bark than bite?' (2015) 36 Co Law 327) comment that much further consideration is needed into the prosecution and punishment of corporate manslaughter given its 'somewhat timid prosecutorial policy' and its penalties which ultimately 'lack bite'. Further, Box (*Power, Crime and Mystification* (Routledge, 1983)) suggests that a punishment of fining a company is not sufficient to reflect the level of harm caused or to act as a valid deterrent. Box proposes a much more stringent approach to the punishment of companies, by advocating the use of, *inter alia*:

- temporary nationalisation – where the profits of the company would be held by the state;
- community service orders – requiring the company to engage in some form of social good in the community, for example by funding the building of a hospital; and
- stringent and regular training exercises performed by the HSE.

Wells ('Corporate Criminal Liability: A Ten Year Review' [2014] 12 Crim LR 849), although critical of the Act, concludes that it has achieved its purpose through the sentencing options available to the court. She states:

> With hefty fines for health and safety offences in some of these cases and with reporting often confusing corporate and director liability, it can be concluded that the Act has achieved some of its purpose, as one mechanism for flagging some of the worst examples of poor workplace safety practices.

Indeed, Wells' view has merit when one considers the sentence imposed in the case of *R v Cotswold Geotechnical Holdings* [2011] EWCA Crim 1337. In that case, the Court of Appeal upheld the fine imposed upon the company (£385,000 payable over 10 years). The Court of Appeal did so despite claims by the company that such a fine would put it out of business. Indeed, this was the outcome as, in June 2011, the company was liquidated.

6.5 Further reading

Vicarious liability

Williams, 'Mens rea and Vicarious Liability' [1956] CLP 57.

McIvor, 'The Use and Abuse of the Doctrine of Vicarious Liability' (2006) 35 CLWR 268.

Hope, 'Tailoring the Law on Vicarious Liability' (2013) 129 LQR 514.

Corporate liability

Bovens, *The Quest for Responsibility: Accountability and Citizenship in Complex Organisations* (CUP, 1998).

Lim, 'A Critique of Corporate Attribution: "Directing Mind and Will" and Corporate Objectives' [2013] JBL 333.

Sullivan, 'The Attribution of Culpability to a Limited Company' (1996) 55 CLJ 515.

Welch, 'The Criminal Liability of Corporations' (1946) 62 LQR 345.

Wells, 'Corporate Criminal Liability: A Ten Year Review' [2014] 12 Crim LR 849.

Corporate manslaughter

Ormerod and Taylor, 'The Corporate Manslaughter and Corporate Homicide Act 2007' [2008] Crim LR 589.

- Corporate liability reflects the situation where an incorporated body is criminally responsible for the actions of its senior management.
- A corporation may be liable in a number of different ways, for example through the identification doctrine or vicarious liability.
- The identification doctrine relates to cases of strict liability where the court attributes liability to the corporation based on the actions of a person who is a 'controlling mind' within the corporation.
- Vicarious liability refers to the situation where a corporation is liable for the actions of its employees when they are acting in the course of their employment.
- Vicarious liability may be established through attribution or delegation.
- Corporations may be criminally liable for statutory offences created specifically for them.
- Corporate manslaughter is a criminal offence concerned with the killing of another, where the organisation owed a relevant duty of care, grossly breached that duty and caused the death of the victim.
- The sentencing for corporate manslaughter is wide and allows the court to issue a publicity order and remedial order, both of which are intended to deter troublesome companies.

test your knowledge

Problem question

Jack is a foreman at a local construction site for a national construction company, 'The Flower Pot Men'. Whilst at the site, Jack is visited by a regional manager, Jill, who is responsible for visiting the sites and requesting updates on their progress. Jill informs Jack that they are behind schedule and demands that work be sped up. In doing so, Jill comments, 'I don't care about health and safety, just get the job done.' Jill then speedily vacates the premises. Taking on board these words, Jack orders his teams to work faster and ignore company protocol regarding who may and may not be on the site at the same time. Specifically, it is against company policy for workmen to be in a designated digging area when machines used to dig are operational. Upon ordering this, Andy, a machine operator, begins to excavate the plot. Unbeknownst to him, a fellow worker, Bill, is walking across the designated area. Andy accidentally hits Bill with the machine; Bill dies as a result of his actions.

Discuss the liability, if any, of 'The Flower Pot Men', Jack, Jill and Andy.

Essay question

'The identification doctrine is a poor attempt to attach liability to large corporations. Under the present "directing mind and will" test, large corporations are essentially immune from prosecution.'

Critically discuss and consider the scope for potential reform of this area.

chapter 7 Defences to Liability

After reading this chapter, you will be able to understand:

- the distinction between defences negating liability and defences justifying/excusing liability
- the extent to which protection is offered by the defences of infancy; private and public defence; mistake; duress; intoxication; necessity; insanity; automatism; and consent
- how these defences operate in practice and how the burden of proof applies.

7.1 Introduction to defences

In the preceding chapters we have discussed the necessary requirements to establish criminal liability against an individual. We have looked at the requirements of both *actus reus* and *mens rea* and how each operates within the criminal sphere. Further to this, we have observed the liability of principal and secondary offenders and the charging of corporations with liability. This chapter, however, is not concerned with establishing the liability of an individual, known as the 'inculpatory' elements of liability. Rather, this chapter is focused on the circumstances where a defendant may avoid criminal liability through the establishment of a 'defence', known as the 'exculpatory' element of liability. For a superb discussion of defences to criminal liability, see Reed and Bohlander, *General Defences in Criminal Law: Domestic and Comparative Perspectives* (Routledge, 2014).

Upon being faced with a criminal charge against him, a defendant must decide whether he wishes to plead guilty or not guilty. To plead guilty means that the defendant accepts the prosecution's case against him and admits liability. To plead not guilty, on the other hand, means that the defendant is denying liability and is challenging the case presented by the prosecution. The extent of the challenge, however, differs according to the remit of the defendant's case. Three situations ordinarily arise in any given case where the defendant pleads not guilty:

- The defendant claims, outright, that he had no involvement in the offence charged. In this respect, the defendant will challenge the factual basis of the alleged offence and claim that someone, other than himself, must have committed the offence. An example of such a defence is that of an alibi, ie the defendant was elsewhere (and has proof of such) when the crime occurred (see the definition of alibi in s 6A(3) of the Criminal Procedure and Investigations Act 1996).
- The defendant claims that although he may have had some involvement in the commission of an offence, one or more of the elements of liability (ie the *actus reus* and *mens rea*) have not been made out. In this respect, the defendant is claiming that the prosecution has failed to prove the elements of liability against him. In

particular, a defendant may raise a 'defence' which negates his liability, on account that it displaces the *actus reus* or *mens rea* for that offence. This is known as a defence 'negating' liability (see **7.1.1.1**).

- The defendant claims that although he may have had involvement in the commission of an offence, and he accepts that the elements of that offence have been made out, he pleads a substantive defence which justifies or excuses liability. In this respect, the defendant is arguing that there is some legal right or reason as to why he should not be liable for an offence. This is known as a defence 'justifying/excusing' liability (see **7.1.1.2**).

in practice

It is wrong to think that only the last two claims in this list amount to defences. An outright denial of involvement in the offence, to the extent that the defendant claims he is the 'wrong man', is just as much a defence as self-defence or intoxication. Indeed, Williams ('Offences and Defences' (1982) 2 LS 233) referred to the use of the term 'defences' as controversial given their potential to be used to describe all arguments raised by the defendant in his defence.

7.1.1 Nature of criminal defences

In **Chapter 1**, we discussed whether a defence amounted to an element of the offence itself (ie in order to be liable, there must be an absence of a defence) or whether it amounted to an independent part of criminal liability (ie upon proof of liability, the defendant may be excused by the operation of a defence). Both statements are true reflections of the operation of defences in the criminal law and can be characterised as defences that *negate* the offence and defences that *excuse* or *justify* the defence. A number of specific defences apply under each heading and are detailed in **Table 7.1**.

Table 7.1 Defences to criminal liability

Defences negating liability	**Defences excusing/justifying liability**
Infancy (**7.2**)	Private and public defence (**7.8**)
Mistake (**7.3**)	Duress (**7.9**)
Intoxication (**7.4**)	Necessity (**7.10**)
Insanity (**7.5**)	
Automatism (**7.6**)	
Consent (**7.7**)	

It is these defences that we shall consider in this chapter. We shall observe the individual rules of each offence, apply them to scenarios and discuss the procedural matters of each defence, including the outcome should the defence be successful.

Before we do so, let us have a deeper look into these two concepts of defences and discuss some key distinctions that must be made.

7.1.1.1 Defences negating liability

Often referred to as 'defences *per se*', this category of defence explains that the defendant cannot be liable for an offence as the essential elements of that offence, comprising both the *actus reus* and *mens rea*, have not been made out. This is because the defendant either lacks the capacity to commit an offence, has not acted (as a result of some internal or external factor) with the necessary voluntariness or *mens rea*, or has acted within a remit lawfully provided to him. For example, the defence of automatism is raised to show that defendant acted in an involuntary way – thus negating the existence of the necessary *actus reus*.

The 'defences' that we shall consider under this heading may be described as not being true defences. Rather, they demonstrate circumstances where the defendant lacks the requisite *actus reus* or *mens rea* of the offence. In this respect, the defendant has not committed an offence and is therefore in no need of a defence.

in practice

There is nothing objectionable about referring to such circumstances above as defences. I prefer to refer to them as 'technical defences' in that, although they are not substantive defences, in practice the defendant will rely on such circumstances 'in his defence' and will be required to provide evidence of the existence of such circumstances in order for his claim to be heard and decided upon. In this respect, such circumstances act, in practice at least, as defences. As a result, the term 'defences' applies equally to these cases as it does to those cases considered next.

7.1.1.2 Defences excusing/justifying liability

Often referred to as 'substantive defences', this category of defence explains that the defendant had some form of excuse or justification which required him to act in the manner that he did. The defendant is not denying in this case that he committed the offence with the requisite *actus reus* and *mens rea*. Rather, he is claiming that he acted in relation to or in response to a particular situation, and that situation provided him with a justification or excuse for the manner in which he acted.

A sub-distinction is also worth making at this stage, namely between excuse defences and justification defences. Fletcher (*Rethinking Criminal Law* (Little Brown, 1978)) provides a useful starting point:

> A justification speaks to the rightness of the act; an excuse, to whether the actor is accountable for a concededly wrongful act.

In this respect it can be said that excuses focus on the individual themselves and whether the individual can be classified as blameworthy. Justifications, on the other hand, appear to focus on the conduct of the individual and whether their conduct can be said to be blameworthy or permissible. We shall consider each heading briefly now.

Defences excusing liability

A defendant's conduct can be said to be excused in the circumstances where he is considered, by the law, not to be blameworthy for such conduct. In this respect, the defendant's conduct can be said to be innocent. An example of such a defence is that of duress, which excuses the defendant's conduct on account of threats made to him or another to perform the illegal acts in question.

Defences justifying liability

A defendant's conduct can be said to be justified in the circumstances where the law allows the conduct to take place. In this respect, the defendant's conduct can be said to be permissible. Child and Ormerod (*Smith, Hogan, & Ormerod's Essentials of Criminal*

Law, 3rd edn (OUP, 2019)) prefer to avoid describing a justification as making the defendant's conduct 'lawful' as it 'still involved the commission of a criminal mischief'. The pair prefer to say that the defendant's conduct 'should not be condemned; [it was] permissible'.

Much academic debate has been centred around this concept, specifically on the basis that such defences operate to negate the requirement of 'unlawfulness' – a circumstance found in all crimes, expressly or impliedly. If such is the case, then the defence ought to be characterised as one negating liability, as above at **7.1.1.1**. For our purposes, however, we shall continue to refer to these defences as ones justifying conduct, as opposed to negating the elements of the offence specifically. Self-defence and necessity are prime examples of defences which justify the conduct of the defendant.

Is the distinction really necessary?

Williams ('The Theory of Excuses' [1982] Crim LR 732) has suggested that whilst these distinctions between excuses and justifications have a bearing in theory, they are of no significance in practice:

> What is the difference between a justification and an excuse? Very little. They are both defences in the full sense, leading to an acquittal. However, when the act is not justified but only excused it is still regarded as being in some tenuous way wrong, for certain collateral purposes.

Indeed, Williams is correct in his summation. At a practical level, the distinction is, frankly, irrelevant – an acquittal as a result of the successful pleading of a defence remains an acquittal whether the defence is described as a justified act or an excused one. Further to this, on a practical level, no distinction is made between the existence of excuses or justifications – though judges typically direct the jury using words such as 'excuse' and 'justify' in their summations. Robinson ('Four Distinctions that Glanville Williams Did Not Make: The Practical Benefits of Examining the Interrelation Among Criminal Law Doctrines' in Baker and Horder (eds), *The Sanctity of Life and the Criminal Law: The Legacy of Glanville Williams* (OUP, 2013)), however, is critical of those who exclude or 'overlook' the distinctions in their entirety. Robinson, in particular, notes that the distinction can have an effect on what he calls 'post-acquittal collateral consequences'. In particular, Robinson states:

> For a justification defence, there ought to be none [ie post-acquittal consequences]. What the defendant did was the right thing to do, which others can do in similar situations in the future. For an excuse defence, one might want to at least ask the question whether the cause of the excusing conditions is recurring.

Robinson contends that such classifications perform an important communication function to the general public, informing them what sort of conduct is permissible and what is not. For Robinson, the general public have a right to know about the justificatory defences that exist, in order to ensure they understand their rights and what conduct is permitted. On the other hand, Robinson takes the view that excuses are not rules as such that the public need to know about, given their rather individualistic basis as a result of human frailty and behaviour. Justifications can adjust and regulate behaviour; excuses cannot.

For an example of an academic who has proceeded to define and classify defences to an even greater extent than merely as to 'justification' and 'excuse', see Simester, 'On

Justifications and Excuses' in Zedner and Roberts (eds), *Principles and Values in Criminal Law and Criminal Justice: Essays in Honour of Andrew Ashworth* (OUP, 2012).

7.1.2 Complete vs partial defences

A further distinction to make is between those defences that are 'complete' and those that are merely 'partial'. A complete defence is one that operates to exclude liability from the defendant outright. In this respect, a complete defence eradicates any blame or liability the defendant may have – simply, he is not guilty. Examples of such complete defences include self-defence, mistake and duress.

A partial defence, on the other hand, is one where the liability of the defendant is reduced. In this sense, the defendant is acquitted of the offence charged but is not entirely absolved of liability. He may still remain liable for a lesser serious offence. This is why we speak of partial defences 'reducing' liability. Examples of such partial defences include loss of self-control and diminished responsibility, which reduce a murder charge to manslaughter. The defence of intoxication has a similar effect in that it has the potential of absolving the defendant of liability for a serious crime (specifically a crime of specific intent) but it remains possible to seek conviction on a lesser charge (specifically a crime of basic intent for which the defence is not available).

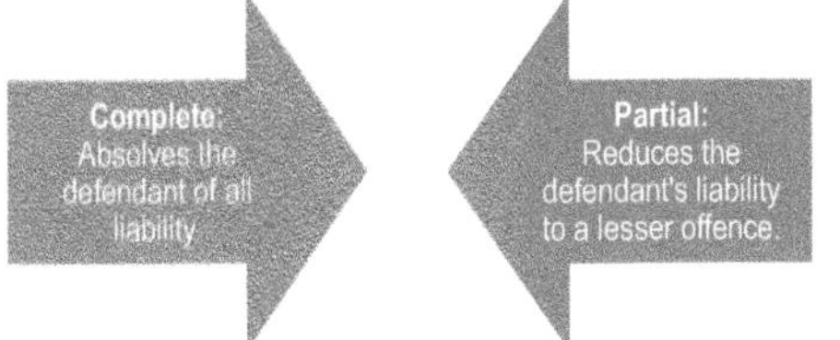

Figure 7.1 Comparing complete and partial defences

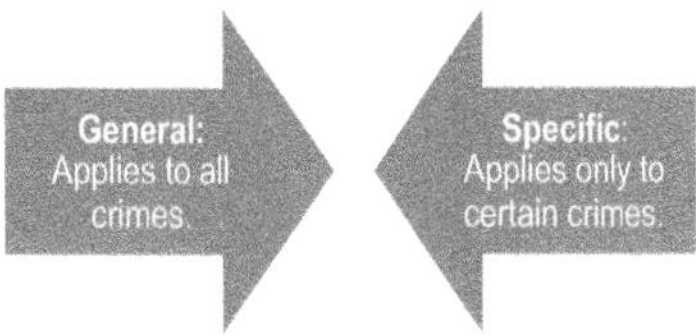

Figure 7.2 Comparing general and specific defences

7.1.3 General vs specific defences

The last important distinction to make at this stage is between the so-called 'general' and 'specific' defences. A general defence is so called as it is capable of applying to all crimes. In this respect, it can be said that the defence is of general application. All defences considered in this chapter, with the exception of duress that is no defence to a charge of murder, can be referred to as 'general defences'.

A specific defence (often known as a 'special defence'), on the other hand, is a defence that is only capable of applying to a certain crime. For example, we discuss the defences of loss of self-control and diminished responsibility in **Chapter 8**. These defences apply only to murder. In this respect, it can be said that those defences are of specific application. Likewise, the defence of withdrawal in relation to secondary participation (see **Chapter 5**) is a specific defence, as is belief in the owner's consent in relation to criminal damage (see **Chapter 14**).

7.1.4 Burden of proof

As discussed in **Chapter 1**, the burden of proving, or disproving, a fact in issue generally rests on the prosecution (*Woolmington v DPP* [1935] AC 462). This burden is known as the legal burden and must be satisfied beyond a reasonable doubt. In the majority of cases, even those involving the presence of a defence, the legal burden of proof rests on the prosecution throughout the course of trial, requiring it to prove each and every element of the offence and disprove the existence of a defence, should one exist. However, the burden of proof may, in certain cases, lie with the defence. Two applications of this are evident:

- *Where the defence bears the legal burden:* Although rare, it is possible for the legal burden of proof to be reversed onto the defendant requiring him to prove the existence of a fact in issue. In the context of defences, this would require the defendant to prove that a defence is made out. Only two defences discussed in this book are subject to such reverse burdens, namely the defences of diminished responsibility (see **Chapter 8**) and insanity (see **7.5**).
- *Where the defence bears the evidential burden:* The legal burden of proof must be distinguished from an evidential burden. The latter is merely the obligation to supply sufficient evidence capable of bringing into question a fact in issue. Such an evidential burden includes the raising of a defence. Should the defendant wish to rely upon a certain defence, he must supply enough evidence to make the issue 'live' so that it may be left before the arbiters of fact to decide upon. However, the defendant is not under an obligation to prove the existence of a defence (for that, there must be a reversed legal burden). In fact, once sufficient evidence has been raised to make the issue a live one, the prosecution retains the legal burden of disproving the existence of the defence.

The particular rules that apply to specific defences as to the burden of proof will be discussed under each heading.

7.2 Infancy

Infancy refers to the age of the defendant and may allow an individual of a certain age to escape liability. It is perhaps more accurate to refer to infancy as an element of the offence as opposed to a defence, given that a person who is below the age of criminal conduct cannot be liable for an offence. Given that no offence can be committed by such a minor, there would be no reason (practically speaking) to refer to any defences (*R v T* [2008] EWCA Crim 815).

in practice

Persons under the age of 18 are treated differently in practice. Any person under the age of 18 is considered a 'juvenile' (Criminal Justice Act 1991, s 68). Under this age, the law makes even further distinctions. They are as follows:

- offenders between the ages of 10 and 13 are described as 'children';
- offenders between the ages of 14 and 17 are described as 'young persons';
- offenders between the ages of 18 and 21 are described as 'young offenders';
- offenders aged over 21 are described as 'adults'.

These labels are relevant to how the law treats such offenders throughout the criminal process in respect of procedure and sentencing, but not criminal responsibility.

7.2.1 The conclusive presumption

Although there is no upper age restriction on liability for criminal offences, there is a lower age restriction. Specifically, s 50 of the Children and Young Persons Act 1933 provides:

> It shall be conclusively presumed that no child under the age of ten years can be guilty of any offence.

The presumption (known as *doli incapax*) is finite in that it applies even to those minors who commit some criminal wrong, even causing another's death, with intention. The justification for this is that persons of such a young and naïve age require support and protection from society – not punishment. As such, the civil law may still become involved in this situation – for example, requiring a child to go into foster care (see s 31 of the Children Act 1989). The wording of s 50 is exclusive in that it does not include persons aged 10 years – it is restricted to those aged 'under' 10, ie 9 years of age or younger. Therefore, upon their 10th birthday, a child is legally capable of committing a criminal offence (*T v UK* [2000] Crim LR 187).

7.2.2 The old rebuttable presumption

At common law, there was also a rebuttable presumption of *doli incapax* for persons aged between 10 and 13 years (inclusive). Specifically, the law presumed that a child between these ages could not commit a criminal offence where they did not know that their actions were 'seriously wrong' (ie it was presumed that they could not form the *mens rea* for the offence). This presumption could be rebutted if the prosecution could prove (beyond a reasonable doubt) that the young person knew their actions to be 'seriously wrong, and not merely naughty or mischievous' (*JM (a minor) v Runeckles* (1984) 79 Cr App R 255; *R v PF* [2017] EWCA Crim 983). Where the presumption was successfully rebutted, the young person was described as having 'mischievous discretion'. Bennion ('Mens Rea and Defendants Below the Age of Discretion' [2009] Crim LR 757) referred to this doctrine as a 'merciful concept' and it continued to receive support through the years. In *CC (a minor) v DPP* [1996] AC 1, the House of Lords was called upon to consider whether the presumption of *doli incapax* remained a part of the common law. The House of Lords found that it did, reversing the decision of the Divisional Court on that matter, and ruled that that any change in the law was a matter for Parliament alone.

With the election of a new Labour Government in May 1997, change was on the horizon. In September 1997, the Home Office produced a Consultation Paper entitled 'Tackling Youth Crime', in which the Government stated (at 7):

> The arguments for reforming the presumption of doli incapax are based on three contentions: that it is archaic, that it is illogical and that it is unfair in practice.

Subsequently, in November 1997, the Home Office produced a White Paper on the topic entitled 'No More Excuses: A New Approach to Tackling Youth crime in England and Wales' (CM 3809), in which the Government stated (at 4.4–4.5):

> The Government believes that in presuming that children of this age generally do not know the difference between naughtiness and serious wrongdoing, the notion of *doli incapax* is contrary to common sense. The practical difficulties which the presumption presents for the prosecution can stop some children who should be prosecuted and punished for their offences from being convicted or from even coming to court. This is not in the interests of justice, of victims or of the young people themselves. If children are prosecuted where appropriate, interventions can be made to help prevent any further offending.
>
> … The Government remains of the view that abolition is necessary to remove the practical difficulties prosecutors and courts face under the current law and

which they would continue to face if the presumption were reversed, rather than abolished.

Change was thereby effected by s 34 of the Crime and Disorder Act 1998, which simply provides:

> The rebuttable presumption of criminal law that a child aged 10 or over is incapable of committing an offence is hereby abolished.

Note, however, that where an offence is alleged to have been committed before the enactment of s 34 (30 September 1998), the doctrine of *doli incapax* continues to apply (*R v M (D)* [2016] EWCA Crim 674).

7.2.2.1 A special presumption

It was previously the case that boys under the age of 14 were incapable of sexual intercourse. This was a conclusive presumption and meant that boys under this age could not be convicted of any offence requiring sexual intercourse, for example rape (*R v Groombridge* (1836) 7 C & P 582) or other forms of unlawful sexual intercourse (*R v Waite* [1892] 2 QB 600; *R v Tatam* (1921) 15 Cr App R 132). This conclusive presumption was abolished by s 1 of the Sexual Offences Act 1993.

All boys over the age of 10 are now capable of committing sexual offences.

7.2.3 Confusion caused by s 34

It appeared that s 34 had made matters clear – persons aged between 10 and 13 could no longer claim *doli incapax*; the individual was either capable of committing an offence on account of their age or not. However, a number of appellate decisions and academic commentary had argued that the defence still existed. For example, Walker ('The End of an Old Song?' [1999] 149 NLJ 64) has argued that s 34 merely had the result of abolishing the '*presumption*' of *doli incapax* but not the '*defence*' of *doli incapax*. Likewise, Smith LJ in *DPP v P* [2007] EWHC 946 (Admin) reasoned (in *obiter*) that the defence continued to exist despite the abolition of the presumption. According to Smith LJ, the effect of this abolition would be to reverse the burden of proof and place it on the defendant, as opposed to the prosecution.

The situation was clarified by the House of Lords in *R v JTB* [2009] AC 1310 (also reported as *R v T*) which ruled that *both* the presumption and defence had been abolished by the enactment of s 34. Ormerod and Laird (*Smith, Hogan, & Ormerod's Criminal Law*, 15th edn (OUP, 2018)) contend that this was a 'disappointing though predictable outcome'. This furthers the view of Walsh ('Irrational Presumptions of Rationality and Comprehension' [1998] 3 Web JCLI) who contended that the presumption provided a 'benevolent safeguard' to young persons and could not be described, as it was by the Government, as illogical.

As a result, the law can now be detailed as follows:

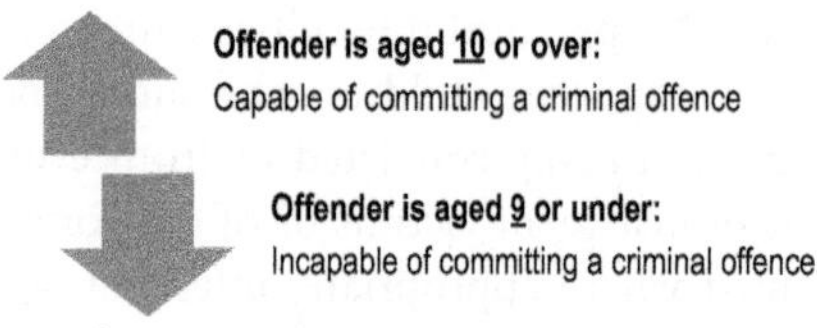
Offender is aged 10 or over:
Capable of committing a criminal offence
Offender is aged 9 or under:
Incapable of committing a criminal offence.

Figure 7.3 Criminal liability of children

in practice

None of what has been said above is to cast doubt on the relevance of an accused's age in a criminal trial. In certain cases, the defendant's age will bear weight on the assessment as to whether the defendant's conduct was reasonable (in the context of loss of self-control or self-defence), or as to whether the defendant appreciated a risk or that the end result was a virtual certainty of his conduct (in the context of subjective recklessness and oblique intent respectively).

7.3 Mistake

It is commonly said that ignorance of the law affords no defence to a criminal charge (*ignorantia juris neminem excusat*). In this respect, mistake as to the criminal law will also not afford a defence to an individual charged with an offence. Another way of explaining this is that a 'mistake of law' is not a defence (*R v Esop* (1836) 7 C&P 456).

However, a 'mistake *of fact*' may afford the defendant a defence in certain circumstances. The leading authority in cases of mistake is that of *DPP v Morgan* [1976] AC 182.

case example

Charge:
Rape (SOA 1956, s 1)

Case progression:
Crown Court – Guilty

Court of Appeal – Conviction upheld

House of Lords – Conviction upheld

Point of law:
Availability of mistake as a defence

In *DPP v Morgan* [1976] AC 182, the defendant invited three of his friends to his house to have sexual intercourse with his wife. The defendant told his friends that his wife was 'kinky' and that if she resisted, that was just a pretence and she was actually consenting. The three men had intercourse with her despite her struggling and protesting. All four men were charged with and convicted of rape in the Crown Court (Morgan was charged as an accessory).

The defendants appealed to the Court of Appeal which dismissed their appeal. The defendants appealed further to the House of Lords which held that a defendant cannot be convicted of rape if he believed, albeit mistakenly, that the victim was consenting. Such a belief would have the effect of negating the defendant's *mens rea*, as opposed to justifying his actions. Lord Hailsham stated that:

> Once one has accepted, what seems to me abundantly clear, that the prohibited act in rape is non-consensual sexual intercourse, and that the guilty state of mind is an intention to commit it, it seems to me to follow as a matter of inexorable logic that there is no room either for a 'defence' of honest belief or mistake, or of a defence of honest and reasonable belief and mistake. Either the prosecution proves that the accused had the requisite intent, or it does not. In the former case it succeeds, and in the latter it fails.

Despite this, the convictions were upheld as the House of Lords was of the opinion that no jury properly directed would have considered the belief of the defendants in the circumstances as genuine – given the clear communication of lack of consent from the victim.

As a result, the defence of mistake will only operate in circumstances where the mistake of fact negates the defendant's *mens rea*. According to the House of Lords in *B (a minor) v DPP* [2000] 2 AC 428, mistake is, therefore, not a defence *per se* but rather is a mere denial of the existence of the *mens rea*. Ormerod and Laird (*Smith, Hogan, & Ormerod's Criminal Law*, 15th edn (OUP, 2018)) explain the rule as follows:

> The rules relating to mistake are simply an application of the general principle that the prosecution must prove its case, including the mens rea or negligence which the definition of the crime requires and rebuttal of excuses raised. The so-called 'defence' is simply a denial that the prosecution has proved its case.

Another case which demonstrates this principle is that of *R v Smith* [1974] QB 354.

case example

Charge:
Criminal damage (CDA 1971, s 1)

Case progression:
Crown Court – Guilty

Court of Appeal – Conviction quashed

Point of law:
Availability of mistake as a defence

In *R v Smith* [1974] QB 354, the defendant was a tenant in a ground floor flat. With the permission of the landlord, the defendant purchased and installed, amongst other things, electrical equipment, wall panelling, flooring and roofing into the conservatory. When the tenancy came to an end, the defendant removed wiring from the property, causing damage to the wall panelling. The defendant was charged with and convicted of criminal damage in the Crown Court. The defendant claimed that he believed that the property was his to do with as he pleased (note: by installing the equipment in the property, it became the legal property of the landlord as it formed part of the flat). The judge rejected this defence and removed the defence of mistake from the jury.

The defendant appealed to the Court of Appeal on the basis that the defence of mistake had been wrongly withdrawn from the jury's consideration. The defendant had a mistaken belief as to the ownership of the goods and such mistake was sufficient to negate his *mens rea*. James LJ agreed and concluded that:

> Applying the ordinary principles of *mens rea*, the intention and recklessness and the absence of lawful excuse required to constitute the offence have reference to property belonging to another. It follows that in our judgment no offence is committed under this section if a person destroys or causes damage to property belonging to another if he does so in the honest though mistaken belief that the property is his own, and provided that the belief is honestly held it is irrelevant to consider whether or not it is a justifiable belief.

This case is often used as an example of a mistake 'of law' given that the defendant believed, legally speaking, that he owned the materials that he damaged. Indeed, the Crown Court Compendium (at section 8-7(2)) refers to this as a mistake of civil law, which is acceptable compared with a mistake as to criminal law. However, it is the author's view that this is merely another case of mistake of fact. The factual circumstance is the defendant's belief – this belief may extend to belief as to ownership or possession, but will always remain one of fact. Further, seeking to distinguish classes of mistake is apt to lead to confusion, and the focus ought to remain on whether the defendant's *mens rea* has been negated.

7.3.1 Elements of the defence

From the judgment of James LJ in *R v Smith* (above), the elements of the defence can be set out as outlined in **Table 7.2**.

Table 7.2 Elements of the defence of mistake

Elements of the defence	
(i)	the mistake must be of the 'right kind';
(ii)	the mistake must be honestly held.

7.3.1.1 Element (i): the mistake must be of the 'right kind'

In assessing whether the defence may be available, it is first necessary to consider whether the mistake is of the 'right kind'. What is meant by this is that the defendant's mistake has the effect of actually negating his *mens rea*. Where his *mens rea* still survives the mistake, he remains liable for an offence.

We can use a couple of examples to explain this principle:

example

Jack shares a room with his friend, Andy. Jack, struggling for money, takes a watch, believing it to be his own and visits a local pawn shop. Jack sells the watch. It turns out that the watch was Andy's and not Jack's.

In this case, Jack is mistaken as to the ownership of the watch – he believes it is his own. In order for the defence to operate, the mistake must negate Jack's *mens rea*. The *mens rea* for theft is dishonesty and an intention to permanently deprive. Given that Jack believes the property is his own (see s 2(1)(a) of the Theft Act 1968), it is likely that Jack's belief will negate the dishonesty requirement. This is a mistake of the right kind and Jack will therefore have a defence.

example

Jack is a member at the local hunting club. Jack intends to shoot Jill and claim that it was an accident. Jack fires his gun at a figure in the distance believing it to be Jill, but it turns out to be Andy. Andy dies from being shot.

In this case, Jack is mistaken as to the identity of his target – he believes he is shooting at Jill but in fact is shooting at Andy. As above, the mistake must negate the *mens rea* for the offence charged. The *mens rea* for murder is the intention to kill or cause grievous bodily harm. In this case, Jack has the intention to kill a person, albeit a different person. He cannot escape liability for murder using the defence of mistake as his mistake was of the 'wrong' kind.

7.3.1.2 Element (ii): the mistake must be honestly held

In *DPP v Morgan* [1976] AC 182, the House of Lords was faced with the question of whether the mistake had to be a 'reasonable' one. It answered this question in the negative. A belief needed to be honest, but it did not need to be reasonably held. *Morgan* had the effect of disapproving (not overruling) the earlier case of *R v Tolson* (1889) 23 QBD 168 which required a mistake to be both honest and reasonable. The position in *Morgan* has been confirmed by the House of Lords in *B (a minor) v DPP* [2000] 2 AC 428, where Lord Nicholls stated:

> When mens rea is ousted by a mistaken belief, it is as well ousted by an unreasonable belief as by a reasonable belief.

Lord Nicholls would go on to justify his position by stating:

> Considered as a matter of principle, the honest belief approach must be preferable. By definition the mental element in crime is concerned with a subjective state of mind such as intent or belief.

Note that *Morgan* is no longer good law in sexual offences cases as a result of the Sexual Offences Act 2003 which requires a defendant's mistaken belief in consent to be both honest and reasonable (see **Chapter 10**). In addition, the judgment in *Morgan* has no effect where the statute explicitly requires the mistake to be a reasonable one (eg a 'reasonable belief in consent' in the Sexual Offences Act 2003).

in practice

Although the defendant's belief need not be reasonable in order for the defence to operate, the more unreasonable the belief is, the less likely the jury is to accept that it was genuinely held. It is all a matter of fact for the prosecution to prove that no such belief was held.

7.3.2 Mistake in specific cases

Despite the general statement as to the application of mistake above, there are certain instances where the defence operates in a slightly different fashion. We can consider these circumstances now.

7.3.2.1 Cases of negligence

In cases where the respective *mens rea* of the offence is negligence, mistake may also act as a valid defence to a criminal charge. However, unlike the subjective approach considered above, the test for mistake is an objective one judged by the standards of a reasonable person doing the same act. Therefore, only a reasonable mistake can afford a defence; an unreasonable mistake is synonymous with a negligent one.

In **Chapter 8**, we consider the offence of gross negligence manslaughter. In such cases, the mental element of the offence is to a higher standard than mere negligence, ie it requires *gross* negligence. In this respect, a defendant may be excused from liability even in circumstances where his mistake is unreasonable, so long as it is not *grossly* unreasonable.

7.3.2.2 Cases of strict liability

Given that cases of strict liability involve a lack of *mens rea*, a mistake (even a reasonable one) is of no defence to a criminal charge.

example

Jack is driving his car on a single carriageway. He notices the speed sign indicating that the national speed limit applies. Believing that the national speed limit on a single carriageway is 70mph, Jack drives at that speed. Jack is stopped by the police for speeding and is informed that the speed limit on single carriageways is 60mph, not 70mph.

Speeding offences are strict in liability, and it is irrelevant whether the defendant intended to speed or not or was even aware that he was speeding or not. As such, although Jack honestly (and maybe reasonably) believed the speed limit was 70mph, he is still liable for an offence.

However, note that it is rare for an offence to be one for which all elements are strict (better referred to as an absolute liability offence). Most strict liability offences are strict in relation only to certain parts of the *actus reus* and not to other parts (see **Chapter 3**). In this respect, where a mistake is made which negates a part of the *mens rea* which is not strict, the defence may be available. It is therefore inappropriate to refer to mistake as being irrelevant to cases of strict liability.

For example, in a sexual offence such as sexual assault on a child under 13 where liability as to the age of the complainant is strict, it will still have to be proved that the defendant intentionally touched the complainant. Where the defendant claims that because of a mistake he had not meant intentionally to touch a person, he will be denying *mens rea*, and an honest mistake will excuse him. If he claims to have made a mistake about age, that is irrelevant because liability as to age is strict.

7.3.2.3 Cases involving a defence

A situation may arise in which the defendant's mistake relates to a particular defence they would have for the conduct committed. Whether mistake can still be claimed will depend on the defence relied upon and whether the mistake was genuinely held.

example

Jill is home alone whilst her husband, Jack, is away from home at a conference. One night, Jill hears a window being broken in the house and goes downstairs to investigate. Jill sees a dark figure in the hallway and attacks him with a cricket bat. Jill turns on the light and discovers that the dark figure was Jack who had broken the window because he forgot his key. Jack suffers grievous bodily harm.

In this instance, Jill is not mistaken as to her conduct element – she intended to attack the dark figure. The issue before the courts is whether Jill's mistake may negate any potential defence she may have.

In the above example, Jill may be able to rely on the defence of self-defence. The question for the court would be whether Jill can still rely on the defence despite her mistake. In *R v Williams (Gladstone)* [1987] 3 All ER 411, the Court of Appeal concluded that provided the mistake was an honest one, the defence is still available and reasonableness is irrelevant. Lord Lane CJ commented:

> The reasonableness or unreasonableness of the defendant's belief is material to the question of whether the belief was held by the defendant at all. If the belief was in fact held, its unreasonableness, so far as guilt or innocence is concerned, is neither here nor there.

In this respect, the defendant is to be judged on the facts as he honestly believed them to be.

The need for the mistake to merely be honest is not, however, a uniform rule. In the case of duress (see **7.9**), the courts have concluded that a mistake as to a threat or the presence of coercion will not be fatal to the operation of the defence. However, this mistake must be both honest and reasonable. This was the view of the Court of Appeal in *R v Graham* [1982] 1 All ER 801 which was approved by the House of Lords in *R v Howe* [1987] AC 417 and more recently in *R v Hasan* [2005] 2 AC 467.

Specific rules on mistake, as they apply to other defences, are considered in this chapter under their individual headings.

7.3.3 Should the law excuse mistakes of law?

As explained above, the defence of mistake does not operate in circumstances where the defendant's conduct comes about as a result of a mistake of law. Of course, where such a mistake negates the defendant's *mens rea*, for instance he lacks dishonesty in a case of theft, a defence is available. However, a simple denial of knowledge of the law is not relevant to criminal liability.

in practice

Although unlikely, should an individual mistakenly believe that they are committing a criminal offence, when in fact they are not, there is obviously no liability for such conduct. For example, a tourist from another country commits adultery, believing it be a criminal offence.

Husak and von Hirsch ('Culpability and Mistake of Law' in Shute, Gardner and Horder (eds), *Action and Value in Criminal Law* (Clarendon Press, 1996)) have argued that ignorance of the law should permit the defendant to be excused from liability in circumstances where his legal mistake is a reasonable one. In the alternative, the pair argue that where the defendant is liable for an offence, the criminal law should mitigate his punishment in circumstances where the defendant was unaware as to the illegality of his conduct.

This view holds merit in cases where the distinction between law and fact is not clear. For instance in *R v Gould* [1968] 2 QB 65, the defendant was charged with and convicted of bigamy contrary to s 57 of the OAPA 1861. At the time of his second marriage, the defendant honestly (albeit mistakenly) believed that his first marriage had been dissolved. The Court of Appeal overturned the defendant's conviction on the basis that he held a genuine and reasonable belief that his first marriage was no longer recognised in law and this mistaken belief was sufficient to negate his *mens rea*. This case is used as an example here to demonstrate the not-so-easy distinction between law and fact.

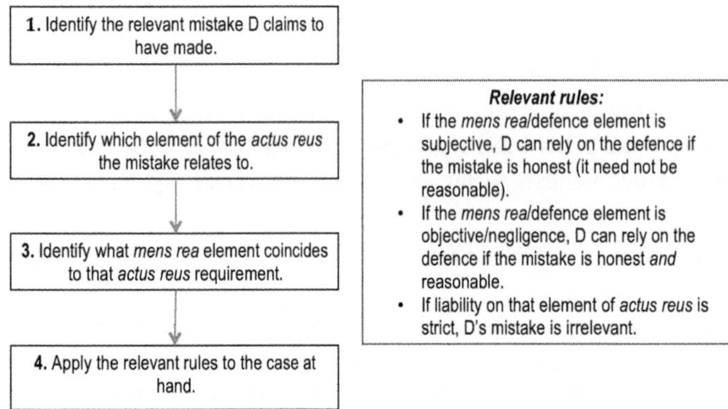

Figure 7.4 Putting together mistake of fact

7.3.4 Procedural matters and the burden of proof

7.3.4.1 Procedure

Mistake is a defence that may be pleaded in the majority of cases so long as the defendant's mistake was of the right kind, ie of fact and the mistake was an honestly held one.

7.3.4.2 Burden of proof

As discussed in **Chapter 1**, the prosecution bears the burden of proving a defendant's guilt beyond a reasonable doubt. In most cases, this applies also to disproving the existence of defences. The defendant may, however, possess an evidential burden which requires him to submit evidence of the defence before it may be properly left before the jury. According to Williams ('The Evidential Burden' (1977) 127 NLJ 156), the defendant does not bear an evidential burden in relation to cases of mistake given that it does not, technically, amount to a 'defence'. Given that mistake is merely an element of the offence itself, the defendant is under no obligation, according to Williams, to raise mistake as an issue. This view is not universally agreed upon, however, with Dickson J in *Pappajohn v R* (1980) 52 CCC (2d) 481 (Supreme Court of Canada) explaining:

> Mistake is a defence in the sense that it is raised as an issue by the accused. The Crown is rarely possessed of knowledge of the subjective factors which may have caused an accused to entertain a belief in a fallacious set of facts.

The better view, it is submitted, is that the defence of mistake is a matter which must be attested to by the defendant. Without some evidence of mistake from the defendant, the prosecution would be burdened with disproving an element that was not in contention. In this respect, Ormerod and Laird (*Smith, Hogan, & Ormerod's Criminal Law*, 15th edn (OUP, 2018)) comment:

> The judge does not have to direct the jury in every case of murder: 'You must be satisfied that D did not believe V was a turkey'; but he must give such a direction if D has testified that, when he fired, he thought V was a turkey.

7.3.5 Result of a successful plea of mistake

Should the defendant succeed in his plea of mistake, this will afford the defendant a complete defence, resulting in an acquittal, given that he is essentially demonstrating a lack of *mens rea* as a result of the mistake.

7.4 Intoxication

In a great many cases, especially cases involving non-fatal violence against another person, intoxication plays a role in the course of events. Intoxicants can affect a person's perception of their surroundings and impair their self-control, understanding and awareness of their own, and others', conduct. Intoxicants may also have the effect of reducing inhibition, increasing the likelihood of poor judgement and hindering the ability to recall events. See Dingwall, *Alcohol and Crime* (Willan Publishing, 2005).

This section will consider whether the English law affords (and should) afford a 'way out' of liability where a defendant is intoxicated. Policy reasons are addressed at **7.4.2,** and we then proceed to discuss the law itself.

There is no definition of intoxication in English law. It is generally accepted to be a broad term referring to the effect of both drink (ie alcohol) and drugs. It will be important for us to distinguish between dangerous and non-dangerous drugs a little later. Before that, however, it is worth considering the basis for the defence.

7.4.1 Basis for the defence

Continuing the theme of defences that are more 'technical' than substantive in nature, the Court of Appeal in *R v Heard* [2008] QB 43 concluded that intoxication is not a defence *per se*; rather it is an effect which may cause the defendant to lack the necessary *mens rea* of the crime charged. From *Heard*, the general idea is that where an individual is so intoxicated, through either drink or drugs, that they cannot form the necessary *mens rea* for the offence, then they cannot be liable for that offence.

Unlike other defences we shall consider, intoxication is not available as a defence to all crimes. As we shall see below, the law makes an important distinction between intoxication which is voluntary and intoxication which is involuntary. The distinction is made apparent by the different rules that apply to each. Further to this, under the banner of voluntary intoxication, the defence is only available to crimes of 'specific intent' and is not available to crimes of 'basic intent'.

A fundamental theme across the defence, however, is that the defendant must, through the intoxication, lack the relevant *mens rea* for the offence charged. Therefore, in circumstances where the defendant uses intoxication in order to commit an offence (also known as 'Dutch courage' cases) or where the defendant forms the relevant *mens rea* despite, or as a result of, the intoxication, he remains liable for the offence (see *R v Kingston* [1995] 2 AC 355 below at **7.4.5**). The latter of these circumstances has recently been seen in *R v Bunch* [2013] EWCA Crim 2498 where the defendant intentionally killed his ex-girlfriend whilst intoxicated. The defendant claimed that he would not have committed the act had he been sober; however, his actions remained intentional throughout. Using the phraseology from Geoffrey Lane LJ in *R v Sheehan* [1975] 1 WLR 739: 'A drunken intent is nevertheless an intent.'

As a result, the special rules of intoxication will only apply where the defendant, through his intoxication, lacked the necessary *mens rea*. This is often referred to as 'extreme intoxication' and involves cases where the defendant was *so intoxicated* that he could not possibly have formed the necessary *mens rea*. In all other circumstances, the defendant will remain liable despite his intoxication.

7.4.2 Rationale for the defence

The rationale behind this rule appears to be one of legal policy (*R v Kingston* [1995] 2 AC 355). Specifically, a defendant who is intoxicated to the extent that he cannot form the necessary *mens rea* ought to have available a defence for his actions to the most serious offences, such as murder or GBH with intent. At the same time, policy reasons dictate that intoxication ought not be a defence for 'lesser' offences, such as assault and battery. Indeed, this is the approach taken by the courts over time with the aim of protecting society against intoxicated individuals who commit criminal offences. Indeed, Lord Simon in *DPP v Majewski* [1977] AC 443 stated that to permit intoxication as a defence would

> leave the citizen legally unprotected from unprovoked violence where such violence was the consequence of drink or drugs having obliterated the capacity of the perpetrator to know what he was doing or what were its consequences.

A number of statements have been made by judges over the years when faced with an intoxicated defendant. For instance, Lord Birkenhead LC in *DPP v Beard* [1920] AC 479 commented:

> [A] man who by his voluntary act debauches and destroys his will power shall be no better situated in regard to criminal acts than a sober man.

This statement was relied upon by Lord Elwyn-Jones LC in *DPP v Majewski* [1977] AC 443 who stated:

> If a man of his own volition takes a substance which causes him to cast off the restraints of reason and conscience, no wrong is done to him by holding him answerable criminally for any injury he may do while in that condition. His course of conduct in reducing himself by drugs and drink to that condition in my

> view supplies the evidence of mens rea, of guilty mind certainly sufficient for crimes of basic intent. It is a reckless course of conduct and recklessness is enough to constitute the necessary mens rea in assault cases.

As a final example of the views of the appellate courts to intoxication, Griffiths LJ in *R v Bailey* [1983] 2 All ER 503 commented:

> It is common knowledge that those who take alcohol to excess or certain sorts of drugs may become aggressive or do dangerous or unpredictable things; they may be able to foresee the risks of causing harm to others but nevertheless persist in their conduct. But the same cannot be said without more of a man who fails to take food after an insulin injection.

7.4.3 Establishing the defence

When confronted with the potential defence of intoxication, it is important to hold a strong structure that will allow you to assess the situation in a step-by-step fashion. The structure recommended is that found in **Figure 7.5**. For an alternative structure, see also Brooks, 'Involuntary Intoxication: A New Six-Step Procedure' [2015] 79(2) J Crim L 138.

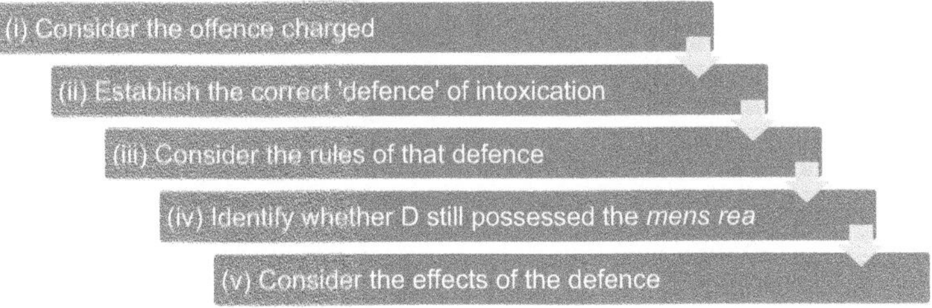

Figure 7.5 Structuring intoxication

Expanding upon the structure set out in the figure, the following points can be made:

(i) In all cases, both voluntary and involuntary, it must first be established what the potential offence is – if the defendant has not committed the relevant *actus reus* of the offence, there is no need to question whether he has a defence. Simply, there cannot be a defence without an offence. Likewise, if the offence is one not requiring proof of intention, ie a strict liability offence, then intoxication cannot avail the defendant where he alleges that his intoxication caused the relevant conduct.

(ii) Once it has been established that an offence exists, it is necessary to establish which of the relevant intoxication rules may apply, ie whether this is a case of voluntary or involuntary intoxication. In the majority of cases, the matter will be simple and clear; however, some cases are complex, involving a situation where it can be contested whether the intoxication is voluntary – for example, when considering the ingestion of prescription drugs.

(iii) Once the correct rule has been established, it is then necessary to consider the rules of the relevant intoxication in detail. If the case is one of voluntary intoxication, it will be necessary to consider whether the offence charged is one of basic or specific intent and the type of intoxicant concerned. If the case is one of involuntary intoxication, it is necessary to consider whether the defendant was aware, somehow, that he was taking an intoxicant.

(iv) Once the rules of either voluntary or involuntary intoxication, or potentially both, have been considered, it is then necessary to consider whether, despite the intoxication, the defendant still holds the necessary *mens rea* for the offence charged. In circumstances where he does, no defence exists; where he does not, a defence is available.

(v) Finally, it is necessary to understand how intoxication acts as a defence on its own and, if relevant, how it interacts with other defences present, for example mistake, self-defence and duress.

You can use **Table 7.3** when identifying the correct rule to be applied:

Table 7.3 The rules of intoxication

Type of intoxication (voluntary or involuntary)	**Type of offence (basic or specific intent)**	**Type of intoxicant (dangerous or non-dangerous)**	**Relevant rule**
Voluntary	Basic	Dangerous	Defence not available – D possesses *mens rea.*
Voluntary	Basic	Non-dangerous	Defence available so long as D lacks *mens rea*
Voluntary	Specific	Dangerous	Defence available so long as D lacks *mens rea*
Voluntary	Specific	Non-dangerous	Defence available so long as D lacks *mens rea*
Involuntary	Basic/Specific	Dangerous/ Non-dangerous	Defence available so long as D lacks *mens rea*

We shall start by examining the rules relating to voluntary intoxication (**7.4.4**) before then discussing involuntary intoxication (**7.4.5**). Remember, at all times, the defendant must lack the relevant *mens rea* for the offence.

7.4.4 Voluntary intoxication

Also known as self-induced intoxication, voluntary intoxication refers to the situation where the defendant voluntarily consumes or ingests an intoxicant, knowing that it is an intoxicant. As above, intoxicants involve both alcohol and drugs.

The leading case in the area of intoxication is that of *DPP v Majewski* [1977] AC 443.

case example

Charge:
Assault occasioning ABH (OAPA 1861, s 47)

Case progression:
Crown Court – Guilty

Court of Appeal – Conviction upheld

House of Lords – Conviction upheld

Point of law:
Meaning of basic and specific intent offences

In *DPP v Majewski* [1977] AC 443, the defendant was intoxicated as a result of taking a number of dangerous drugs and alcohol. Whilst intoxicated, the defendant became involved in a bar brawl, attacking the landlord, a number of customers and police officers who were attempting to effect an arrest. The defendant was charged with and convicted of three counts of ABH and assault of a police officer in the Crown Court.

The defendant appealed to the Court of Appeal, claiming that as a result of his intoxicated state, he could not form the necessary *mens rea* for the offence and was thus not liable for an offence. The Court of Appeal disagreed and upheld his conviction. The defendant subsequently appealed to the House of Lords on the same grounds. The House of Lords dismissed his appeal and upheld his conviction on the basis that voluntary intoxication was not a defence to basic intent offences (with which the defendant was charged). Their Lordships justified this on the basis that the act of becoming intoxicated was itself a reckless act which was capable, in basic intent offences, of replacing the *mens rea* requirement of that offence. In this respect, the *mens rea* is automatically found as a result of the voluntary intoxication.

This decision was largely based on policy reasons (as outlined above at **7.4.2**). From *Majewski*, we must consider a number of factors in order to establish whether the defence can be used. These factors are:

- whether the crime is one of basic or specific intent;
- the type of intoxicant used; and
- whether the defendant lacks the *mens rea*.

We shall consider each in turn.

7.4.4.1 Distinguishing basic and specific intent offences

Under voluntary intoxication, a distinction has been drawn by the courts between crimes of specific (or 'ulterior') and basic intent. We considered these concepts in **Chapter 3** and shall deal with them in more detail here.

Unfortunately, there is no single agreed definition of, or distinction between, basic and specific intent offences. This has been the case since the first reference was made to 'specific intent' by Lord Birkenhead LC in *DPP v Beard* [1920] AC 479. Importantly, neither term is used to describe a type of intention; rather they are used as labels of different classes of offences. There are two main opinions as to how these two types of offences can be distinguished:

- recklessness as an element of the offence; and
- purposive intention.

Interpretation (i): focus on the presence of recklessness

The former of the two is the most commonly cited and takes the greatest favour in the case law. As a general rule, crimes of specific intent require proof of knowledge or intention and nothing less, whereas crimes of basic intent allow for proof of a lower form of *mens rea*, particularly recklessness and negligence or where liability is strict. We can see this distinction in **Figure 7.6**.

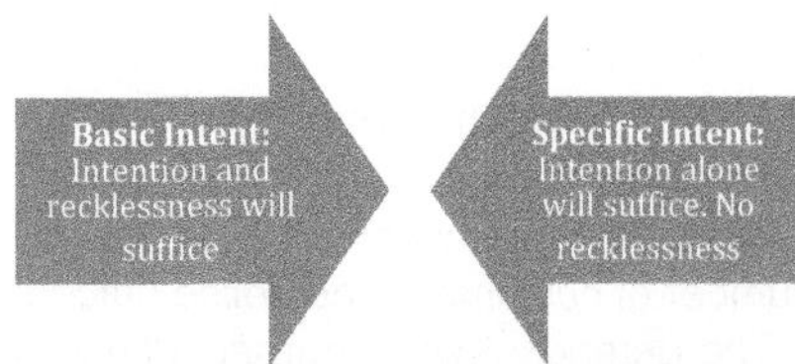

Figure 7.6 Understanding basic and specific intent offences

This was the view adopted by Lord Elwyn-Jones LC in *Majewski* and by the House of Lords in *MPC v Caldwell* [1982] AC 341. Lord Salmon had conceded in *Majewski* that this distinction between basic and specific intent offences was 'illogical'. His Lordship specifically stated:

> If voluntary intoxication by drink or drugs can … negative the special or specific intention necessary for the commission of crimes such as murder and theft, how can you justify in strict logic the view that it cannot negative a basic intention, e.g., the intention to commit offences such as assault and unlawful wounding? The answer is that in strict logic this view cannot be justified. But this is the view that has been adopted by the common law of England, which is founded on common sense and experience rather than strict logic.

Interpretation (ii): focus on the presence of a purposive intent

An alternative view has been put forward on a number of occasions which explains the distinction by looking at the so-called 'ulterior' or 'purposive' intent of the crime alleged. This second interpretation first arose from Lord Simon in *R v Morgan* [1976] AC 182. Lord Simon explained:

> By 'crimes of basic intent' I mean those crimes whose definition expresses (or, more often, implies) a *mens rea* which does not go beyond the *actus reus*. The *actus reus* generally consists of an act and some consequence. The consequence may be very closely connected with the act or more remotely connected with it: but with a crime of basic intent the *mens rea* does not extend beyond the act and its consequence, however, remote, as defined in the *actus reus*. I take assault as an example of a crime of basic intent where the consequence is very closely connected with the act. The *actus reus* of assault is an act which causes another person to apprehend immediate and unlawful violence. The *mens rea* corresponds exactly. The prosecution must prove that the accused foresaw that his act would probably cause another person to have apprehension of immediate and unlawful violence, or would possibly have that consequence, such being the purpose of the act, or that he was reckless as to whether or not his act caused such apprehension.

On this view, basic intent offences are those in which the *mens* rea of the offence 'does not go beyond' the *actus reus*.

This style of distinction was present in the case of *R v Heard* [2008] QB 43.

Charge:
Sexual assault (SOA 2003, s 3)

Case progression:
Crown Court – Guilty

Court of Appeal – Conviction upheld

Point of law:
Meaning of basic and specific intent offences

In *R v Heard* [2008] QB 43, the defendant, whilst intoxicated, exposed his penis and rubbed it up and down a police officer's thigh. The defendant was charged with and convicted of sexual assault in the Crown Court.

The defendant appealed to the Court of Appeal on the basis that he, as a result of his intoxicated state, lacked the necessary *mens rea*. The statute required an intentional touching, meaning that the offence was one of specific intent given that recklessness would not suffice. The Court of Appeal disagreed, ruling that not every offence can be classified simply as one of basic and specific intent. The offence of sexual assault contained a number of different elements (eg intentional touching – specific intent; and lack of reasonable belief in consent – basic intent). In this respect, the Court ruled that the better approach was to consider the state of mind of the defendant and, in this case, the defendant possessed the relevant *mens rea*. The defendant was thus liable for an offence.

Hughes LJ, relying upon the judgment of Lord Simon in *Majewski* rationalised that

> crimes of specific intent are those where the offence requires proof of purpose or consequence, which are not confined to, but amongst which are included, those where the purpose goes beyond the actus reus (sometimes referred to as cases of 'ulterior intent').

A good example to demonstrate the application of *Heard* is the offence of criminal damage (see **Chapter 14**).

Table 7.4 Criminal damage and intoxication

Offence	Basic or specific intent?
Basic criminal damage	Basic intent offence: The offence does not involve an ulterior *mens rea*. The defendant must destroy or damage property (*actus reus*) and must intend or be reckless as to the thought of causing such damage or destruction (*mens rea*). As you see, the *actus reus* and *mens rea* coincide; there is no 'ulterior' *mens rea*.
Aggravated criminal damage	Specific intent offence: The *actus reus* is the same as basic criminal damage. The *mens rea*, however, includes an additional requirement: that the defendant intends or is reckless as to the endangering of life. Endangerment of life is an ulterior *mens rea* and thus aggravated criminal damage is a specific intent offence, even though it can be committed recklessly. This was reaffirmed by the Court of Appeal in *R v Coley* [2013] EWCA Crim 223.

This distinction is hard to understand, however, given that Lord Elwyn-Jones LC in *Majewski* characterised murder as a specific intent crime (even though, as we will see in **Chapter 8**, the *mens rea* does not go beyond the *actus reus*).

A pragmatic approach

Given the lack of unified approach to classifying basic and specific intent offences, the courts have developed the legal jurisprudence in this area on a case-by-case basis, classifying offences accordingly. Indeed, in *R v Heard* [2008] QB 43, Hughes LJ summarised the submissions of counsel for the Crown which included that:

> There is … no universally logical test for distinguishing between crimes in which voluntary intoxication can be advanced as a defence and those in which it cannot;

> there is a large element of policy; categorisation is achieved on an *offence by offence basis*. (emphasis added)

Lord Justice Hughes would explain:

> The first thing to say is that it should not be supposed that every offence can be categorised simply as either one of specific intent or of basic intent. So to categorise an offence may conceal the truth that different elements of it may require proof of different states of mind.

In spite of this, this text attempts to demonstrate the conclusions reached by various judgments in respect of criminal offences. You will notice that many of these classifications accord with the first interpretation above (which is the author's preferred view); however, this is not always the case.

Table 7.5 Examples of basic intent offences

Basic intent	**Case authority**
Manslaughter	*R v Lipman* [1970] 1 QB 152
Rape	*R v Grout* [2011] EWCA Crim 299
Sexual assault	*R v Heard* [2008] QB 43
Wounding/GBH (s 20)	*R v Aitken* [1992] 1 WLR 1006
Assault occasioning ABH	*Bolton v Crawley* [1972] Crim LR 222
Common assault	*DPP v Majewski* [1977] AC 443
Basic criminal damage	*MPC v Caldwell* [1982] AC 341

Table 7.6 Examples of specific intent offences

Specific intent	**Case authority**
Murder	*DPP v Beard* [1920] AC 479
GBH/wounding with intent (s 18)	*R v Davies* [1991] Crim LR 469
Theft and robbery	*DPP v Majewski* [1977] AC 443
Burglary	*R v Hutchins* [1988] Crim LR 379
Attempt and complicity	*R v Clarkson & Carroll* [1971] 3 All ER 344

7.4.4.2 Type of drug

An important distinction that has been made by the courts is between categories of intoxicants, which can be classified as either 'dangerous' or 'non-dangerous'.

Table 7.7 Distinguishing intoxicants

Type of intoxicant	**Description**
Dangerous	One which is known to be dangerous in the sense that it has the commonality to cause aggressive and unpredictable behaviour.
Non-dangerous	One which is not known to cause such aggressive or unpredictable behaviour or such drugs which are medically prescribed.

These categories have been laid down by the courts in such cases as *R v Bailey* [1983] 2 All ER 503 and *R v Hardie* [1985] 1 WLR 64.

case example

Charge:
Wounding with intent (OAPA 1861, s 18)

Case progression:
Crown Court – Guilty

Court of Appeal – Conviction upheld

Point of law:
Categorisation of dangerous and non-dangerous drugs

In *R v Bailey* [1983] 2 All ER 503, the defendant attacked the victim with an iron bar. The defendant was a diabetic and had failed, early in the evening, to ingest sufficient food following his administration of insulin. The defendant claimed that he was suffering from a hypoglycaemic state and was completely unaware of what he was doing. The defendant was charged with and convicted of wounding with intent in the Crown Court.

The defendant appealed to the Court of Appeal, which concluded that whilst the defendant's consumption of insulin was not reckless, the defendant still possessed the necessary *mens rea* for the offence.

case example

Charge:
Arson (CDA 1971, s 1)

Case progression:
Crown Court – Guilty

Court of Appeal – Conviction quashed

Point of law:
Categorisation of dangerous and non-dangerous drugs

In *R v Hardie* [1985] 1 WLR 64, the defendant had taken a Valium tablet that had been prescribed to his girlfriend. He did so after feeling depressed as a result of being asked to leave the flat shared with his girlfriend. During the course of the day, the defendant consumed more of the tablets and in his intoxicated state started a fire in the wardrobe in the bedroom. The defendant was charged with and convicted of arson in the Crown Court after the judge directed the jury to ignore the effects of the Valium tablets.

The defendant appealed to the Court of Appeal arguing that, as a result of the Valium tablets, he did not know what he was doing and that the defence of intoxication should have been left to the jury. The Court of Appeal agreed, with Parker LJ ruling:

> There was no evidence that it was known to [the defendant] or even generally known that the taking of Valium in the quantity taken would be liable to render a person aggressive or incapable of appreciating risks to others or have other side effects such that its self-administration would itself have an element of recklessness. ... the drug is ... wholly different in kind from drugs which are liable to cause unpredictability or aggressiveness ... if the effect of a drug is merely soporific or sedative the taking of it, even in some excessive quantity, cannot in the ordinary way raise a conclusive presumption against the admission of proof of intoxication ... such as would be the case with alcoholic intoxication or incapacity or automatism resulting from the self-administration of dangerous drugs.

In both *Bailey* and *Hardie*, the defendants were deemed to have been involuntarily intoxicated due to a lack of reckless mind. However, whilst *Bailey* was said to still possess the *mens rea* and thus was still liable, *Hardie* did not possess such *mens rea* and his conviction was quashed.

'Dangerous' drugs

Unfortunately, there is no list of 'dangerous' or 'non-dangerous' drugs. Obvious examples of dangerous drugs include:

- LSD;
- cocaine;

- amphetamine;
- MDMA (ecstacy);
- alcohol;
- synthetic cannabis; and
- methamphetamine.

Unfortunately, the Misuse of Drugs Act 1971 (as amended by the Drugs Act 2005) is only of limited assistance, given that not all controlled drugs listed have the effect of causing aggressive and unpredictable behaviour.

The law approaches dangerous drugs as follows: knowingly taking a dangerous drug counts as voluntary intoxication. As Griffiths LJ explained in *R v Bailey* [1983] 2 All ER 503, it is 'common knowledge' that those who drink alcohol or take certain drugs can become 'aggressive or do dangerous or unpredictable things'. In this respect, in a basic intent offence, a defendant will be treated as being reckless in his consumption of dangerous drugs and a defence will not be available. In a specific intent offence, his consumption will amount to voluntary intoxication which will afford a defence only where the defendant also lacked the necessary *mens rea*.

The rule is slightly different in terms of non-dangerous drugs.

'Non-dangerous' drugs

It is likewise difficult to express what forms of intoxicant are capable of amounting to 'non-dangerous' drugs. Most certainly, the law appears to treat medically prescribed drugs as being of the non-dangerous kind (see Lord Elwyn-Jones LC's statement in *Majewski*). Unlike a dangerous drug, where it is assumed that the defendant was aware of its effects (given that it is treated as common knowledge), the effect of taking non-dangerous drugs requires an appreciation of the subjective state of mind of the accused. Specifically, Parker LJ in *Hardie* stated that the jury should have been directed that

> if they came to the conclusion that, as a result of the Valium, [the defendant] was, at the time, unable to appreciate the risks to property and persons from his actions they should consider whether the taking of the Valium was itself reckless.

In addition, Griffiths LJ in *Bailey* explained:

> The question in each case will be whether the prosecution have proved the necessary element of recklessness. ... if the accused knows that his actions or inaction are likely to make him *aggressive, unpredictable or uncontrolled* with the result that he may cause some injury to others and he persists in the action or takes no remedial action when he knows it is required, it will be open to the jury to find that he was reckless.

Essentially, the arbiters of fact must ask themselves whether the defendant was reckless in his taking of the non-dangerous substance according to his state of knowledge as to the likely effects the drug may have on him. In *Hardie*, for example, the defendant was unaware as to the potential effects that Valium (an otherwise non-dangerous drug) would have on him. Although not medically prescribed, the Court of Appeal remained satisfied that the jury were entitled to ask whether the defendant was aware of any potential effects in taking the substance. The same reasoning can be seen in the earlier case of *R v Burns* (1973) 58 Cr App R 364, concerning morphine tablets which had the effect of reducing the defendant's awareness. Where the jury conclude that the defendant was aware of the risk, he will be considered as being voluntarily intoxicated – and the same rules apply as above in relation to dangerous drugs. If, however, the jury conclude that the defendant was not aware of the effects of the drug, he will be treated as involuntarily intoxicated which, unlike voluntary intoxication, acts as a defence to both basic and specific intent offences so long as the defendant also lacks the necessary *mens rea*. The effect of this rule is that a defendant who takes prescribed medicines, being aware of the effects they may cause, will be treated as being voluntarily intoxicated.

Certainty of 'types' of drugs

As stated above, the law is not clear as to how the distinction is to be drawn between dangerous and non-dangerous drugs other than the categorisation of common knowledge regarding its effects. For example, marijuana is capable of acting as both a sedative and as a hallucinogen in certain circumstances. Likewise, heroin, although commonly understood to be dangerous, is capable of having soporific effects. Storey (*Unlocking Criminal Law*, 7th edn (Routledge, 2019)) has suggested the following factors as being relevant in determining whether a drug is dangerous or not:

> Much depends on several variables: the user himself; the amount taken; how much has been taken before; how the drug is taken (injecting generally produced more dramatic effects than smoking or eating); the surroundings in which the drug is taken; even what the user expects or hopes will happen.

7.4.4.3 Lack of *mens rea* and Dutch courage cases

As has been discussed above, in order for a defendant to succeed in his defence of voluntary intoxication to a specific intent crime, it must still be proven that he lacked the necessary *mens rea* for the offence charged. Where the defendant possesses the necessary *mens rea* despite his intoxicated state, he will still be liable for an offence (*R v Kingston* [1995] 2 AC 355). A defendant who intentionally kills whilst intoxicated will not be able to raise a defence that he only killed because he was intoxicated (*R v Bunch* [2013] EWCA Crim 2498). This was most evident in the recent case of *R v White (Lindsey)* [2017] NICA 49, where the defendant, having consumed a considerable amount of alcohol, attacked the victim and stepped on this throat, killing him. Evidence supplied by two witnesses suggested that the defendant was intoxicated, but CCTV evidence showed no sign of significant intoxication on the part of the defendant. In any event, the Northern Ireland Court of Appeal upheld the defendant's conviction for murder, ruling that intoxication is of no defence in circumstances where the defendant still possessed the necessary *mens rea* and there was no evidence to suggest that the defendant was incapable of forming the *mens rea* as a result of her intoxication (see **7.4.6.2** for a discussion of the *Sheehan* direction).

The defence is not available to individuals who use intoxicating substances in order to commit a crime, ie they use intoxication to gain the confidence, or 'courage', to commit the offence. This is known as the 'Dutch courage' rule and is demonstrated in the leading authority of *AG for Northern Ireland v Gallagher* [1963] AC 349.

case example

Charge:
Murder

Case progression:
NI Assizes – Guilty

NI Court of Appeal – Conviction quashed

House of Lords – Appeal allowed; conviction reinstated

Point of law:
Requirement for a lack of *mens rea* and presence of Dutch courage

In *AG for Northern Ireland v Gallagher* [1963] AC 349, the defendant killed his wife after drinking a large portion of a bottle of whisky. The defendant was charged with and convicted of murder in the Northern Ireland Winter Assizes.

The defendant appealed to the Northern Ireland Court of Appeal on the basis that he lacked the necessary *mens rea* for the offence as a result of his intoxication. The Court of Appeal allowed his appeal and quashed his conviction. The prosecution appealed to the House of Lords and sought guidance on this point. Their Lordships reinstated the defendant's conviction, ruling that the defendant possessed the necessary *mens rea* for the offence and this could not be discounted simply as a result of the defendant's excessive alcohol intake. As Lord Denning made clear:

> I think the law on this point should take a clear stand. If a man, whilst sane and sober, forms an intention to kill and makes preparation for it, knowing it is the wrong thing to do, and then gets himself drunk so as to give himself Dutch courage to do the killing, and whilst drunk carries out his intention, he cannot rely on this self-induced drunkenness as a defence to a charge of murder, nor even as reducing it to manslaughter. He cannot say that he got himself into such a stupid state that he was incapable of an intent to kill … The wickedness of his mind before he got drunk is enough to condemn him, coupled with the act which he intended to do and did do. A psychopath who goes out intending to kill, knowing it is wrong, and does kill, cannot escape the consequences by making himself drunk before doing it.

Following *Gallagher*, the defendant will always remain liable for the offence charged where intoxication was used in order to commit the offence. This is so whether the offence is one of specific intent or not, and regardless of whether the defendant was so intoxicated that he did not know what he was actually doing. Being frank about the rule, it lacks practical effect given that the principle is generally covered by the requirement that the defendant does not possess the *mens rea* for the offence in any event. Interestingly, the Dutch courage rule has yet to be applied in any other case.

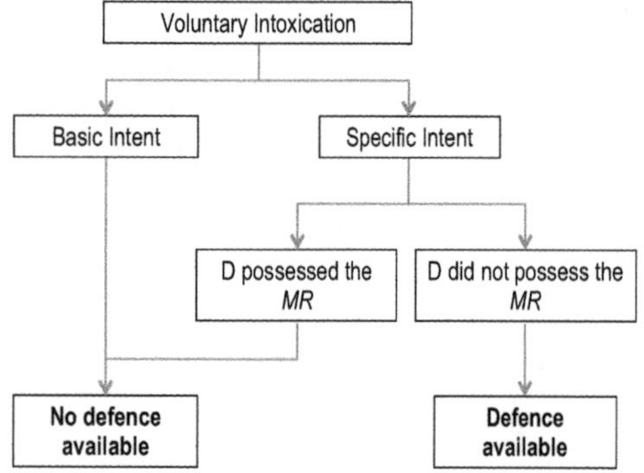

Figure 7.7 Putting together voluntary intoxication

7.4.5 Involuntary intoxication

Involuntary intoxication refers to the situation where the defendant consumes an intoxicating substance (whether alcohol or drugs) being unaware that he is doing so.

example

Jill is sat in her local bar with some friends. Jill has agreed to drive her friends to their homes at the end of the night so has chosen not to drink alcohol. Unbeknownst to Jill, Jack laces Jill's drink with an intoxicant. As a result of her intoxication, Jill attacks a barmaid.

This is the most common example of involuntary intoxication – namely where a defendant's drink is laced with some form of intoxicating substance. Jill, and other defendants in her circumstances, will not be liable for offences committed if they lacked the relevant *mens rea* to commit the offence because of the intoxicant.

Unlike voluntary intoxication which remains a defence solely to specific intent offences, where a defendant is involuntarily intoxicated, this will be a defence to both basic and specific intent offences (*R v Hardie* [1985] 1 WLR 64). In this respect, involuntary intoxication truly is a general defence and applies irrespective of whether the crime charged would ordinarily fall under the heading of a basic or specific intent offence. However, as with voluntary intoxication, the defendant must still lack the relevant *mens rea* for the offence charged. We can see the operation of this principle to involuntary intoxication through the leading House of Lords case of *R v Kingston* [1995] 2 AC 355.

case example

Charge:
Indecent assault

Case progression:
Crown Court – Guilty

Court of Appeal – Conviction quashed

House of Lords – Conviction reinstated

Point of law:
Need for absence of *mens rea* in cases of involuntary intoxication

In *R v Kingston* [1995] 2 AC 355, the defendant, a man with paedophiliac tendencies, indecently assaulted a 15-year-old boy whilst intoxicated. The defendant had been drugged by an associate of work colleagues in an attempt to blackmail the defendant with incriminating photographs of him engaging in conduct with the boy. The defendant accepted that he was attracted to young boys and at the time intended the conduct committed; however, he contended that he would not have acted in the way he did had it not been for the involuntary intoxication. The defendant was convicted in the Crown Court, with the jury being directed that drugged intent was still intent.

The defendant appealed to the Court of Appeal, which allowed his appeal and quashed his conviction on the ground that through his involuntary intoxication, the defendant was unable to control his actions – something he could do whilst sober. Lord Taylor CJ commented:

> [If a] drink or a drug, surreptitiously administered, causes a person to lose his self-control and for that reason to form an intent which he would not otherwise have formed … the law should exculpate him because the operative fault is not his.

The prosecution successfully appealed to the House of Lords, which concluded that despite the involuntary intoxication, the defendant still possessed the relevant *mens rea.* His own ability to prevent such intention materialising when sober was irrelevant.

The reasoning in *Kingston* had been previously applied by the Court of Appeal in *R v Sheehan; R v Moore* [1975] 1 WLR 739, in which the Court ruled that a drunken intent on the part of the defendant is still an intent.

in practice

Kingston is a clear example of a defendant who, though intoxicated, still possessed the relevant *mens rea* for the offence. In practice, it may be more difficult to establish that a defendant holds the relevant *mens rea*. Remember, in *Kingston*, the defendant confessed his attraction to young boys; however, in other situations it may not be so obvious.

Kingston and other cases of involuntary intoxication by drink-spiking, such as *R v Eatch* [1980] Crim LR 650, *Ross v HM Advocate* 1991 SLT 564 (Scotland) and *People v Cruz* 93 Call App 3d 308 (1978) (California), are quite straightforward examples. However, other cases may be less clear-cut, for example:

- where the defendant is ignorant of, or underestimated, the strength of the alcohol or drugs;
- in relation to the taking of non-dangerous drugs.

We consider these circumstances in turn.

7.4.5.1 Ignorance of alcohol quantity

A defendant cannot claim involuntary intoxication if he knew that he was drinking alcohol, or taking a certain drug, but underestimated or was 'ignorant' of the amount or strength of the alcohol or drug. The leading cases on this point are *R v Bailey* [1983] 2 All ER 503 and *R v Allen* [1988] Crim LR 698. For the facts of *Bailey*, see **7.4.4.2**.

case example

Charge:
Buggery and indecent assault (SOA 1956)

Case progression:
Crown Court – Guilty

Court of Appeal – Conviction upheld

Point of law:
Meaning of involuntary intoxication

In *R v Allen* [1988] Crim LR 698, the defendant had drunk a significant amount of home-made wine, believing it to be of a lower alcohol content. The defendant proceeded to commit buggery and indecent assault against X (a woman) and was charged with and convicted of these offences in the Crown Court.

The defendant appealed to the Court of Appeal arguing that he was involuntarily intoxicated on the basis that he did not know, or appreciate, the strength of the wine and as a result lacked the necessary *mens rea*. The Court of Appeal dismissed this argument, ruling that the defendant's lack of awareness as to the level of alcohol content was irrelevant. The defendant had voluntarily consumed an alcoholic drink and it was no defence to argue that he did not appreciate the strength of the drink.

Allen is a logical decision, making it clear that a defendant cannot avoid liability through involuntary intoxication simply because he did not know how strong the alcohol was. A situation not considered in *Allen*, however, is where the defendant is drinking alcohol voluntarily but his alcoholic drink is spiked, for example with a drug or shots of a highly intoxicating nature, eg vodka. In this instance, the court would have to determine whether the defendant's conduct was caused by his voluntary intoxication or by his involuntary consumption (*R v Eatch* [1980] Crim LR 650 – a case where the defendant's beer was spiked with a stronger intoxicant). Putting it another way – should the involuntary intoxication take the defendant 'over the edge' in terms of his intoxication level, this may be sufficient to persuade a court that the defendant was involuntarily intoxicated.

7.4.5.2 Non-dangerous drugs

As discussed above in relation to voluntary intoxication, the law has developed specific principles that apply in circumstances where the defendant takes a legal drug which is not commonly known to be dangerous. For example, where a defendant takes medication in *bona fide* compliance with a medical prescription but suffers serious side-effects from such medication, the law has to determine whether his taking of the medication amounts to voluntary or involuntary intoxication. Lord Elwyn-Jones LC in *Majewski* alluded to the fact that voluntary intoxication included those who take 'drugs not on medical prescription'. By implication, it would appear that medically prescribed drugs fall within the scope of involuntary intoxication. However, the law is not that simple.

The leading authority on this point is the case of *R v Hardie* [1985] 1 WLR 64 (discussed at **7.4.4.2**). In that case, the defendant had taken a number of Valium tablets which are well known to act as a sedative (a form of soporific drug). Upon being convicted of criminal damage, the Court of Appeal had to consider whether the defendant's taking of the drug amounted to voluntary or involuntary intoxication. The Court of Appeal explained that the defendant is entitled to rely on involuntary intoxication in circumstances where he is unaware of the effect the drug may have on him. The essential question is whether the defendant was reckless in taking the drug given the knowledge he has as to the effects of the drug. Given that Valium is not a dangerous drug *per se* – it is understood to be used as a sedative – and having been informed by his girlfriend that the drug was 'harmless', the Court concluded that the defence of involuntary intoxication should have been available to the defendant. This rule can also be seen in cases such as *R v Bailey* [1983] 2 All ER 503 and *R v Quick* [1973] QB 910. Importantly, the basic and specific intent distinction is not relevant to questions of involuntary intoxication.

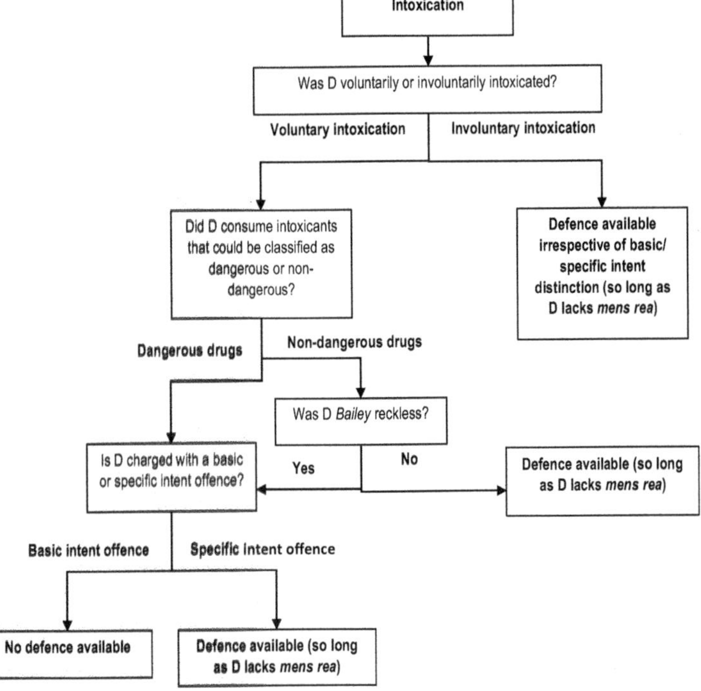

Figure 7.8 Putting together intoxication

7.4.6 Procedural matters and the burden of proof

7.4.6.1 Procedure

In the case of *R v Sheehan; R v Moore* [1975] 1 WLR 739, the Court of Appeal explained the manner in which the jury should be directed where the defendant raises the defence of intoxication. Specifically, Lane LJ (as he then was) reasoned:

> [W]e think that the proper direction to a jury is, first, to warn them that the mere fact that the defendant's mind was affected by drink so that he acted in a way in which he would not have done had he been sober does not assist him at all, provided that the necessary intention was there. A drunken intent is nevertheless an intent.
>
> Secondly, and subject to this, the jury should merely be instructed to have regard to all the evidence, including that relating to drink, to draw such inferences as they think proper from the evidence, and on that basis to ask themselves whether they feel sure that at the material time the defendant had the requisite intent.

In essence, the jury are told to consider whether the defendant was so intoxicated that he could not have formed the necessary *mens rea*. This is known as the *Sheehan* direction but can only be provided in circumstances where there is some proof that the defendant's intoxication was so far gone as to bring into question his inability to form the mental element of the offence. This point has been emphasised in recent years by the Court of Appeal time and time again. In *R v Walsh* [2015] NICA 46, the Northern Ireland Court of Appeal accepted that 'the evidence indicated that [the defendant] had consumed alcohol' but in any event he had 'stayed on the sober side of fairly'. The key element of the judgment was that (according to Morgan LCJ):

> the evidence taken at its height does not raise any case that [the defendant] was so intoxicated that it affected the issue of whether she did, in fact, form an intent.

The Northern Ireland Court of Appeal addressed a similar appeal in *R v White (Lindsey)* [2017] NICA 49, in which the Court held that the evidence in that case did not support a *Sheehan* direction to the extent that there was not enough to suggest that the defendant, as a result of her intoxication, was not capable of forming the necessary *mens rea*. In fact, she was, according to the court, perfectly capable of doing so. See also *R v Press and Thompson* [2013] EWCA Crim 1849. Recently in *R v Campeanu* [2020] EWCA Crim 362, Flaux LJ in the Court of Appeal ruled that a defendant is not entitled to a *Sheehan* direction unless the defendant has *claimed* the defence in his own evidence. His Lordship would specifically provide that:

> before such a [*Sheehan*] direction is necessary, there must be sufficient evidence of the defendant claiming not to have formed the requisite intention due to his state of intoxication. The mere facts of intoxication is not sufficient of itself. There must be a causal connection between the two.

In essence, unless the defendant specifically runs the defence of intoxication at trial, he is not entitled to a *Sheehan* direction, or for the jury to consider his late founded claims of intoxication. See also *R v Mohamadi* [2020] EWCA Crim 327.

7.4.6.2 Burden of proof

The burden of proof lies on the prosecution to prove, beyond a reasonable doubt, that the defendant, despite his intoxication, still held the necessary *mens rea* (*R v Sheehan;*

R v Moore [1975] 1 WLR 739). The prosecution need not disprove that the defendant was *incapable* of forming the *mens rea*; rather, its burden is simply to disprove that he did not form it.

7.4.7 Result of a successful plea of intoxication

Where the defendant successfully pleads intoxication to an offence alleged against him, the outcome depends on the offence.

7.4.7.1 Voluntary intoxication and specific intent crimes

In the context of voluntary intoxication, the defendant is entitled to a complete acquittal where the offence charged is one of specific intent. However, where a lesser alternative charge is placed against the defendant for a basic intent offence, the defendant may be liable for that lesser offence. Think about it this way: the jury are to be asked – did the defendant form the *mens rea* for the offence despite the intoxication?

- If no, the defendant is not guilty of the offence charged but may be liable for a lesser offence.
- If yes, the defendant is guilty of the offence charged.

7.4.7.2 Voluntary intoxication and basic intent crimes

Where, however, the crime is one of basic intent, a 'defence' is not available. Rather, the court treats evidence of the defendant's intoxication as satisfying the *mens rea* of the offence. According to the House of Lords in *DPP v Majewski* [1977] AC 443, a 'defence' of voluntary intoxication is never available to basic intent offences. Rather, the defendant is deemed to have been reckless in his consumption or ingestion of the intoxicant, regardless of the degree of intoxication. As a result, the prosecution is entitled to use the defendant's evidence of intoxication against him as the necessary *mens rea*. Because of this, the question before the jury now turns on whether the defendant would have formed the *mens rea* if sober:

- If no, the defendant is not guilty of the offence charged.
- If yes, the defendant is guilty of the offence charged; the prosecution does not have to prove that the defendant formed the *mens rea* as intoxication will be treated as a form of recklessness.

example

Jack is liable for causing GBH with intent contrary to s 18 of the OAPA 1861 (see **Chapter 9**) against Jill. Jack successfully raises voluntary intoxication as a defence. A successful plea of intoxication will render Jack not guilty for that offence; however, he may be liable for the lesser, and basic intent, offence of inflicting GBH contrary to s 20 instead, should the prosecution have placed that charge before him in the alternative.

7.4.7.3 Involuntary intoxication

In the circumstances where the defendant successfully pleads that he was involuntarily intoxicated, he is entitled to a complete acquittal. This rule is the same regardless of whether the offence charged is one of basic or specific intent.

7.4.8 Intoxication and other defences

In many cases, the defendant will not only raise the fact that he was intoxicated in an attempt to escape liability; he may also run another defence alongside his claim of intoxication. Whether the defence may be used in circumstances where the defendant was intoxicated, however, depends on the specific defence pleaded. This is dealt with for the most part under each defence but a summary of the law can be provided here. Intoxication as it applies to the partial defences of diminished responsibility and loss of self-control is considered in **Chapter 8**.

7.4.8.1 Mistake

Although an honest mistake may relieve a defendant of liability (see **7.3**), the courts have generally been reluctant to allow the defence of mistake to be raised in circumstances where the mistake has been induced as a result of the defendant's intoxicated state. See, for example, *R v Woods* (1981) 74 Cr App R 312, involving an intoxicated mistake as to consent to sexual intercourse, and *R v Hatton* [2005] EWCA Crim 2951, involving an intoxicated mistake as to the need for self-defence. The effect of these cases is usefully explained by Horder (*Ashworth's Principles of Criminal Law*, 9th edn (OUP, 2019)) in that 'where the subjective rule for mistake clashes with the objective rules for intoxication, the latter takes priority'. In essence, the rules of intoxication are to be used, not the rules of mistake.

There are occasions, however, where a statutory offence is drafted in such broad terms to allow for an intoxicated mistake to act as a defence. This was evident in the case of *Jaggard v Dickinson* [1981] QB 527 (considered in more detail in **Chapter 14**) which concerned the offence of criminal damage. Under the Criminal Damage Act 1971, the defendant may plead the special defence of 'lawful excuse'. Section 5(2)(a) provides that a defendant will have a lawful excuse for causing criminal damage

> if at the time of the act or acts alleged to constitute the offence he believed that the person or persons whom he believed to be entitled to consent to the destruction of or damage to the property in question had so consented, or would have so consented to it if he or they had known of the destruction or damage and its circumstances ...

In combination with s 5(3), which explains that 'it is immaterial whether a belief is justified or not if it is honestly held', the Divisional Court was of the opinion that the defendant was still entitled to use the defence of mistake despite having committed the offence by mistake as a result of her intoxication. The Divisional Court stated that the defence existed, despite the intoxication, in circumstances where the mistake was an honest one (see also *R v Richardson; R v Irwin* [1999] 1 Cr App R 392). Note, however, that *Jaggard* has been called into question by the Divisional Court most recently in *Magee v CPS* [2014] EWHC 4089 (Admin). In that case, the defendant (whilst intoxicated) reversed her car into another causing damage. Holding a genuine (but mistaken) belief that no damage was caused, the defendant drove away from the scene. The Divisional Court dismissed the defendant's appeal against conviction on the basis that an intoxicated mistake afforded no defence in law. Particularly, Elias LJ explained that

> the principle enunciated in *Jaggard* does not apply in the circumstances of this case. First, there is considerable doubt whether *Jaggard* is still good law in the light of such cases as *O'Connor* [1991] Crim LR 135 and *R v Hatton* [2005] EWCA

> Crim 2951. In the latter case, the Court of Appeal Criminal Division held in a murder case that an honest but mistaken belief by the defendant that he was being attacked and was entitled to use self defence was not a defence where that belief was attributable to his voluntarily being drunk. That principle is now found in the Criminal Justice and Immigration Act 2008 section 76, whenever an issue arises as to whether a defendant can rely on self defence.
>
> Second, in any event I am satisfied that *Jaggard* could, and should, be narrowly rather than widely construed. *Jaggard* turned on the construction of the specific defence in section 5 of the 1971 Act ... Here, the onus is on the defendant to negate the natural inference that once the accident has occurred she will have been aware of it. It seems to me that there is no reason why the common law should be construed so as to allow her to pray in aid her own state of drunkenness as the reason for the mistake, and there is every reason of policy why it should not be extended in that way.

7.4.8.2 Self-defence

If the defendant is voluntarily intoxicated, he cannot rely on a mistaken belief as to the need to use self-defence which is induced by intoxication. This was clear in the cases of *R v O'Grady* [1987] QB 995 and *R v O'Connor* [1991] Crim LR 135 and has been placed on a statutory footing by s 76(5) of the Criminal Justice and Immigration Act 2008. See the most recent authority on this point of *R v Taj* [2018] EWCA Crim 1743, in which the Court of Appeal ruled that a defendant may be able to rely on a genuine belief in self-defence resulting from mental illness caused by the long-term use of alcohol.

7.4.8.3 Automatism

In circumstances where the defendant's intoxication has caused or induced a state of automatism, the defence of automatism cannot be used. Instead, the ordinary rules of intoxication are said to apply (*R v Lipman* [1970] 1 QB 152). Where there is a dispute as to whether it was the intoxication, or another external factor, which caused the automatic state, the court must consider carefully which rules to apply (*R v Stripp* (1978) 69 Cr App R 318).

7.4.8.4 Insanity

See **7.5.2.3** for a discussion of how insanity and intoxication work together.

7.4.8.5 Duress

One of the key elements of the defence of duress is that the defendant has reasonable grounds to believe that there is a threat to his life or a threat of serious physical harm. If this belief has been induced by intoxication, the defence of duress is unavailable.

7.5 Insanity

A defendant may raise the 'defence' of insanity on the basis that he was insane at the time of the commission of the offence. Importantly, his insanity must be at the time of the commission of the offence and not at the time of trial. Should the latter be relevant, you ought to consider the provisions of unfitness to plead (see below at **7.5.1.2**).

In this section, insanity will be distinguished from automatism, and a summary of these differences is provided at **7.6.6**.

7.5.1 Basis for the defence

Also known as 'insane automatism', insanity is a defence available to all crimes (as recently emphasised by the Divisional Court in *Loake v CPS* [2017] EWHC 2855 (Admin)). Interestingly, insanity is not a medical term or condition concerned with madness or insane thoughts. Rather, insanity is a legal concept concerned with how the law views certain individuals. An example of this distinction is sleepwalking – the law characterises such conduct as insane; however, it is doubtful that a medical professional would characterise it in the same way in his or her field.

7.5.1.1 A 'plea' of insanity; not a defence

Before proceeding to the elements of the defence itself, it is helpful to discuss the extent to which insanity operates as a 'defence'. It is technically more appropriate to refer to insanity as a 'plea' on behalf of the defendant, as opposed to a defence. Specifically, a defendant may plead insanity which, if successful, will result in a special verdict of 'not guilty by reason of insanity'.

7.5.1.2 Insanity or unfitness to plead?

It is necessary at this stage to distinguish unfitness to plead from the defence of insanity. The former concerns the circumstances where the defendant suffers from a mental impairment *at the time of trial*, whilst the latter concerns a defendant who suffers from a mental impairment *at the time of committing the offence*. Unfitness to plead is governed by the common law and by way of the Criminal Procedure (Insanity) Act 1964, as amended by the Criminal Procedure (Insanity and Unfitness to Plead) Act 1991. Given our focus on substantive defences, our discussion of unfitness to plead will end here. In summary, where the defendant is competent at trial, but there is evidence to suggest that he lacked such competence at the time of the commission of the offence, the principles of insanity should be considered and not unfitness to plead. It is on that basis that we proceed to discuss the law on insanity.

7.5.2 Elements of the defence

The key authority on the defence of insanity is that of *M'Naghten's Case* (1843) 10 Cl & Fin 200. From this case, the law has developed what are known as the *M'Naghten* rules.

In *M'Naghten's Case*, the defendant killed the Prime Minister's (Sir Robert Peel's) secretary, believing that he was actually shooting the Prime Minister. The defendant, who was obsessed with the PM, believed that there was a plot against him. The defendant was charged with murder but was found not guilty on account that he was suffering from morbid delusions at the time of the offence, ie he was found to be insane. Due to public outrage, the case was referred to the House of Lords to decide the remit of the defence of insanity. The crucial passage in *M'Naghten* came from Tindal CJ, who ruled:

> [T]he jurors ought to be told in all cases that every man is to be presumed to be sane and to possess a sufficient degree of reason to be responsible for his crimes until the contrary be proved to their satisfaction, and that to establish a defence on the ground of insanity it must be clearly proved that, at the time of the committing of the act the party accused was labouring under such a defect of reason, from disease of the mind, as not to know the nature and quality of the act he was doing, or, if he did know it, that he did not know he was doing what was wrong.

The effect of this passage is to create a test featuring two limbs that can be considered in the alternate. From this passage, the elements of the defence are outlined in **Table 7.8**.

Table 7.8 Elements of the defence of insanity

Limb	Elements of the defence
	(i) at the time of the committing of the act; (ii) suffered from a defect of reason; (iii) caused by a disease of the mind;
First limb	(iv) not knowing the nature and quality of the act; or
Second limb	(iv) not knowing what he was doing was wrong.

As you will notice from above, the elements of the defence are the same under both limbs except for the final element. We shall consider each element in turn.

7.5.2.1 Presumption of sanity

Before we do so, however, it is essential to note that every person of the age of responsibility is presumed by law to be sane and thus remains accountable for his actions unless and until the contrary is proven. This was reemphasised by the court in *R v Layton* (1849) 4 Cox CC 149 and is relevant to the burden of proof in cases of insanity (see below **7.5.3.2**).

7.5.2.2 Element (i): at the time of the committing of the act

As stated above, the relevant insanity, or lack thereof, of the defendant is at the time of the commission of the offence and not during trial (for which see unfitness to plead at **7.5.1.2**). Further to this, it must first be proven by the prosecution that the defendant committed an act or omission. Therefore, the standard rules requiring proof of *actus reus* will continue to apply.

7.5.2.3 Element (ii): suffered from a defect of reason

The first real element of the defence itself is that the defendant must suffer from a defect of reason. This is a legal expression and not a medical term or condition and has been explained by Ackner J in *R v Clarke* [1972] 1 All ER 219 as concerning a person who is 'deprived of the power of reasoning'. Ackner J explained that this definition covers only those persons who lost the power of reasoning outright; it does not apply to persons who 'retain the power of reasoning but who in moments of confusion or absent-mindedness fail to use their powers to the full' capacity. In *Clarke*, the defendant, who was charged with theft, admitted to shoplifting but said that such taking was due to absent-mindedness and depression. The Court of Appeal concluded that a momentary failure to concentrate was not sufficient to found a defect of reason. In *Clarke*, the defendant was acquitted on account that she lacked the necessary *mens rea* for theft. Insanity was, therefore, irrelevant. Further to this, actions based on emotional impulses (as in *Sodeman v R* [1936] 2 All ER 1138) will not be sufficient to found a defence of insanity due to the lack of 'defect'.

7.5.2.4 Element (iii): caused by a disease of the mind

Meaning of 'disease of the mind'

As with the phrase 'defect of reason', a disease of the mind is a legal phrase and not one of medical terminology. This remains the case despite the necessity for medical evidence to be submitted by experts (s 1 of the Criminal Procedure (Insanity and Unfitness to Plead) Act 1991). The meaning of 'disease of the mind' was expanded on by Lord Diplock in *R v Sullivan* [1984] AC 156, where his Lordship reasoned that

> 'mind' in the *M'Naghten* Rules is used in the ordinary sense of the mental faculties of reason, memory and understanding. If the effect of a disease is to *impair these faculties so severely* as to have either of the consequences referred to in the latter part of the rules, it matters not whether the aetiology of the impairment is organic, as in epilepsy, or functional, or whether the impairment itself is permanent or is transient and intermittent, provided that it subsisted at the time of commission of the act. The purpose of the legislation relating to the defence of insanity, ever since its origin in 1800, has been to protect society against recurrence of the dangerous conduct. (emphasis added)

This focus on 'mental faculties' was relied upon from the older case of *R v Kemp* [1957] 1 QB 399 in which Devlin J held that if the defendant suffers from a condition which affects his 'mental faculties of reason, memory and understanding', he has a disease of the mind capable of founding a defence of insanity. In addition to this, the focus on 'mental faculties' demonstrates that the law is concerned with a disease or condition that affects the mind, as opposed to affecting the brain in a physical sense. Indeed, Lord Lane CJ in *R v Hennessy* [1989] 1 WLR 287 explained that disease of the mind 'does not mean any disease of the brain. It means a disease which affects the proper functioning of the mind.' In this regard, you can understand this requirement quite simply: it is a question of law, not of medicine.

Must the disease of the mind be permanent?

One final point to make here is that the disease of the mind need not be permanent. This is contrary to the judgment of Lord Denning in *Bratty v AG for Northern Ireland* [1963] AC 386, who reasoned that:

> It seems to me that any mental disorder which has manifested itself in violence and is prone to recur is a disease of the mind. At any rate it is the sort of disease for which a person should be detained in hospital rather than be given an unqualified acquittal.

Following the House of Lords in *R v Sullivan* [1984] AC 156, however, the disease of the mind need not be prone to recur, nor must it manifest itself in violence. So long as the defendant suffered from a defect of reason caused by a disease of the mind *at the time* of the offence, it is irrelevant if he *no longer suffers* from such defect of reason or disease of the mind (see also *R v Smith* [2012] EWCA Crim 2566). The distinction between temporary and permanent insanity is thus not relevant to this particular discussion, but will be relevant to the question of fitness to plead considered at **7.5.1.2.**

Requirement of an 'internal' cause

Importantly, there must be a link between the defect of reason and the disease of the mind. Specifically, the defect of reason must have been *caused* by a disease of the mind rather than by some external factor. It is this factor which distinguishes insanity and automatism. The former is concerned with an internal disease of the mind; the latter is concerned with an external cause affecting the defendant's ability to act. The distinction between *internal* or *external* factors has been considered extensively in the case law and often forms the basis of legal disputes. **Table 7.9** details this distinction, and we then proceed to discuss some of the key cases in this area and the relevant circumstances in which the arguments arise.

Table 7.9 Internal and external factors

Internal	External
Concerned with the internal workings of the defendant, specifically his mind and the manner in which the mind operates and functions.	Concerned with matters outside of the defendant's mind that may nonetheless affect the way in which he will or can act.
Relevant defence = insanity	Relevant defence = automatism

We shall now consider a number of scenarios that have come before the courts on this point. In reading the following text, consider whether you would have classified these scenarios as amounting to insanity or not. McAhlone and Wortley (*Criminal Law: The Fundamentals*, 4th edn (Sweet & Maxwell, 2016)) contend that these decisions have led to 'some bizarre distinctions' in the law.

Diabetes

In relation to the medical condition diabetes (a condition which causes the blood sugar levels of an individual to become too high), the courts have had to distinguish whether the condition arises as a result of internal or external factors. The courts do so to determine whether the defendant may plead insanity or automatism. The key authority on this point is that of *R v Quick* [1973] QB 910.

case example

Charge:
Assault occasioning ABH (OAPA 1861, s 47)

Case progression:
Crown Court – Guilty

Court of Appeal – Conviction quashed

Point of law:
Meaning of 'disease of the mind'

In *R v Quick* [1973] QB 910, the defendant, a nurse, attacked a patient. On the morning of the assault, the defendant had taken his prescribed insulin for his diabetes but then proceeded to drink alcohol and eat little food. The defendant was charged with ABH. During his trial in the Crown Court, the trial judge ruled that the appropriate defence was one of insanity and not automatism. As a result of this, the defendant changed his plea to guilty and was convicted of the offence. The defendant appealed to the Court of Appeal on the basis that the trial judge was wrong in his ruling. The Court of Appeal agreed and allowed his appeal, concluding that a failure to eat after the taking of insulin for diabetes was an external factor and not an internal one. On that basis the defendant could not rely on the defence of insanity but could rely on the defence of automatism.

Lawton LJ in the Court of Appeal ruled that:

> A malfunctioning of the mind of transitory effect caused by the application to the body of some external factor such as violence, drugs, including anaesthetics, alcohol and hypnotic influences cannot fairly be said to be due to diseases.

Lawton LJ was satisfied that the defendant's conduct in *Quick* was caused by his failure to eat after the taking of insulin. The failure to eat, coupled with the excess insulin in his blood, amounted to an external factor distinct from his condition of diabetes. As a result, the appropriate defence was one of automatism (see **7.6**). See also *R v Bingham* [1991] Crim LR 433.

The decision in *Quick* can be contrasted with the later authority of *R v Hennessy* [1989] 1 WLR 287.

case example

Charge:
Taking a conveyance without consent (TA 1968, s 12(1))

Case progression:
Crown Court – Guilty

Court of Appeal – Conviction upheld

Point of law:
Meaning of 'disease of the mind)

In *R v Hennessy* [1989] 1 WLR 287, the defendant, a diabetic, was charged with taking a conveyance without authority and driving whilst disqualified. On the day in question, the defendant had failed to take his insulin and had not eaten any food as a result of high levels of stress, anxiety and depression. This caused the defendant to suffer hyperglycaemia. The defendant attempted to plead automatism at trial, but this was refused by the trial judge who ruled that the appropriate defence was one of insanity. The defendant changed his plea to guilty (to avoid hospitalisation) and appealed to the Court of Appeal on the basis that the trial judge should have left the defence of automatism to the jury.

The Court of Appeal dismissed his appeal, distinguishing *Quick* on the basis that the defendant had failed to take his insulin. As a result of his failure to take his insulin, the conduct of the defendant was caused by his diabetes itself (ie it was an internal factor).

Lord Lane CJ stated that:

> hyperglycaemia, high blood sugar, caused by an inherent defect, and not corrected by insulin is a disease, and if, as the defendant was asserting here, it does cause a malfunction of the mind, then the case may fall within the *M'Naghten* Rules.

Although it may appear difficult to reconcile these two cases, the law on diabetes in relation to the defences of insanity and automatism can be simply explained as follows:

- Where the defendant suffers from *hypo*glycaemia (low blood sugar and excess insulin from not eating after taking insulin) as in *Quick*, this *will not* be a disease of the mind. The fault in the defendant's conduct is the failure to eat after taking insulin (ie an external factor). In such a case, the defendant cannot plead insanity but may be able to plead automatism.
- Where the defendant suffers from *hyper*glycaemia (high blood sugar from not taking insulin), as in *Hennessy*, this *will* be a disease of the mind. The fault of the defendant's conduct is the condition itself (ie an internal factor). In such a case, the defendant can plead insanity.

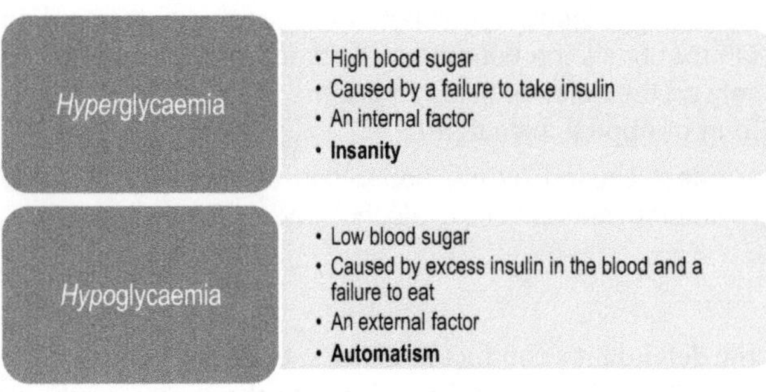

Hyperglycaemia
• High blood sugar
• Caused by a failure to take insulin
• An internal factor
• Insanity
Hypoglycaemia
• Low blood sugar
• Caused by excess insulin in the blood and a failure to eat
• An external factor
• Automatism

Figure 7.9 Characteristics of diabetes in law

You may think to yourself that it is inappropriate for the law to characterise someone as insane for a condition that is simple to prevent and treat. Indeed, the courts have adopted the same understanding, with Lawton LJ in *Quick* stating:

> [C]ommon sense is affronted by the prospect of a diabetic being sent to such a [secure mental] hospital when in most cases the disordered mental condition can be rectified quickly by pushing a lump of sugar or a teaspoonful of glucose into the patient's mouth.

Despite this statement, the law continues to distinguish between internal and external factors resulting in some diabetics being classified as legally insane. In all cases, however, it must be proven that the condition is not as a result of some prior fault on the defendant's part. For example, in *R v Clarke* [2009] EWCA Crim 921, the defendant was unable to rely on the defence of automatism having killed a child whilst driving erratically following a hypoglycaemic episode. The defendant had felt 'warning signs' of the episode (such as anxiety and sweating) and continued driving regardless. Whilst the episode was caused by an external factor, the defendant was at fault for this – he saw the warning signs and ignored them.

Epilepsy

A second example of the operation of internal and external factors is that of the medical condition of epilepsy. Epilepsy is a condition that affects the brain, and on a basic level involves sudden bursts of intense electrical activity in the brain causing a temporary disruption to its normal activity. Such disruption is referred to as an epileptic seizure.

The House of Lords held in *Bratty v AG for Northern Ireland* [1963] AC 386 and *R v Sullivan* [1984] AC 156 that a person who inadvertently assaults another, during the course of an epileptic seizure, will be regarded as legally insane. Therefore, epilepsy is considered to be an internal factor, meaning that the defence of insanity is available in such cases.

Monaghan (*Criminal Law Directions*, 6th edn (OUP, 2020)) contends that '[c]lassifying epileptic defendants as "insane" is surely improper and offensive'. Further, Mackay and Reuber ('Epilepsy and the Defence of Insanity—Time for a Change' [2007] Crim LR 782) argue that the defence of insanity requires significant reform in the context of epilepsy and contend that it is 'surely no longer acceptable to use the label "insanity" for any case of epileptic automatism or indeed for any other conditions which give rise to the special verdict'. They conclude by asking: 'Is it not time for the Law Commission to take up this challenge and to rid the law of an insanity defence which in its current form has no place in the 21st century?'

Sleepwalking

A further example of the operation of internal and external factors involves individuals who sleepwalk and commit criminal offences during this unconscious activity. The key authority on this point is that of *R v Burgess* [1991] 2 QB 92.

case example

Charge:
Inflicting GBH
(OAPA 1861, ss 18 and 20)

Case progression:
Crown Court –
Not guilty by reason of insanity

Court of Appeal –
Appeal dismissed

Point of law:
Distinguishing internal and external factors

In *R v Burgess* [1991] 2 QB 92, the defendant attacked the victim, his friend, with a bottle whilst sleepwalking. The defendant was charged with GBH in the Crown Court in which he pleaded not guilty on the grounds of automatism. The judge directed the jury to consider insanity as opposed to automatism and the defendant was found not guilty by reason of insanity. The defendant was ordered to be detained in a secure hospital causing him to appeal to the Court of Appeal.

The Court of Appeal dismissed his appeal, ruling that the defendant's sleepwalking was caused by an internal factor and treated as an 'abnormality, or disorder', and thus the appropriate and correct plea was one of insanity.

Lord Lane CJ provided the leading judgment in the Court of Appeal:

> It seems to us that ... the judge was right to conclude that this was an abnormality or disorder, albeit transitory, due to an internal factor, whether functional or organic, which had manifested itself in violence. It was a disorder or abnormality which might recur, though the possibility of it recurring in the form of serious violence was unlikely.

On 20 August 2019, a 21-year-old man named Dale Kelly was acquitted of sexual assault on account that his conduct arose whilst he was sleepwalking. The jury had found that Kelly was not in control of his actions and found him not guilty by reason of insanity. There is not, however, a consistent approach taken in this regard. A number of cases have come before the trial courts involving defendants being acquitted on account of sleepwalking by way of the defence of automatism, as opposed to insanity – notably, *R v Bilton* (2005) *The Guardian*, 20 December, concerning a charge of rape, and *R v Davies* (2006) *The Times*, 11 February, which concerned sexual assault. There remains a lack of clarity, or consistency, in the approach of the courts in this regard.

Interestingly, in October 2008, a Private Member's Bill was introduced by Harry Cohen MP entitled the Rape (Defences) Bill. The Bill was designed to amend the Sexual Offences Act 2003 to prohibit the defence of sleepwalking in cases concerning offences of rape. This Bill came about as a result of several cases which received high-profile media coverage as a result of defendants successfully raising sleepwalking (often brought about by heavy drinking) as a defence to charges of rape. These cases resulted in acquittals for defendants on the grounds of automatism, as opposed to insanity, contrary to the judgment in the court in *Burgess*. The Bill has yet to be enacted, and doubtful ever will be; however, it is obvious that the law regarding insanity and automatism in sleepwalking cases requires clarification.

Post-traumatic stress

Where violence arises as a result of post-traumatic stress, the courts have found the defendant's conduct to be caused by an external factor and not an internal one. Specifically, the Crown Court in *R v T* [1990] Crim LR 256 concluded that that 'dissociation' amounted to an external factor of witnessing or being a part of a traumatic event, and thus was automatism. In *R v T*, the defendant had been raped three days prior to the offence in question and as a result of that rape suffered from post-traumatic stress disorder. Consequently, the defendant stabbed the victim during the course of a robbery. The Crown Court concluded that she had acted in an autonomous state. This case can usefully be compared with the Canadian case of *R v*

Rabey (1977) 37 CCC (2d) 461, which involved a plea of automatism based on a dissociative state caused by the rejection by a girl with whom the defendant was infatuated. The Supreme Court of Canada said that

> the ordinary stresses and disappointments of life which are the common lot of mankind do not constitute an external cause ...

In essence, this rejection amounted to an internal factor and would fall within the *M'Naghten* rules. Naturally, rape can easily be distinguished from a mere rejection and can hardly be described as the 'ordinary stresses or disappointments of life'. In this respect, *Rabey* and *T* can easily be distinguished.

Arteriosclerosis and brain tumours

Arteriosclerosis can best be described as a hardening of the arteries which results in a congestion of blood in the brain which causes a temporary lapse of consciousness. In *R v Kemp* [1957] 1 QB 399, a case concerning an attack with a hammer on the defendant's wife by a defendant suffering from arteriosclerosis, Devlin J stated:

> The law is not concerned with the brain but with the mind, in the sense that 'mind' is ordinarily used, the mental faculties of reason, memory and understanding ... In my judgment the condition of the brain is irrelevant and so is the question of whether the condition of the mind is curable or incurable, transitory or permanent ... Temporary insanity is sufficient to satisfy them.

In *Kemp*, the defendant was charged with causing GBH to his wife, and evidence was adduced to demonstrate that, as a result of his condition, the defendant did not know what he was doing. The decision in *Kemp* was used by the House of Lords in *Bratty v AG for Northern Ireland* [1963] AC 386, in which Lord Denning took the view that a brain tumour was a disease of the mind.

Uncontrollable impulse

It was formerly the case that a defendant could rely on the defence of insanity in circumstances where he acted under an irresistible impulse (*R v Fryer* (1915) 24 Cox CC 403). This statement is, however, no longer reflective of the present law which is governed by the case of *R v Kopsch* (1925) 19 Cr App R 50, concerning a defendant who strangled his aunt with a necktie. In *Kopsch*, Lord Hewart CJ described the concept in *Fryer* as 'subversive' and identified that an impulse should not be covered by the defence of insanity as it would be too difficult to distinguish between those impulses caused by insanity and those impulses cause by greed, violence or revenge.

However, the Privy Council was quick to note in *Sodeman v R* [1936] 2 All ER 1138 that if there is medical evidence to suggest that the defendant satisfies one of the two limbs in *M'Naghten and* has an irresistible impulse, he may have a defence. In addition, the Court of Criminal Appeal in *R v Byrne* [1960] 2 QB 396 was of the opinion that an irresistible impulse may support a defence of diminished responsibility instead.

Alcohol and drugs

Where the defendant's intoxication produces a 'disease of the mind', even if such disease is temporary, the defendant may be able to rely on the defence of insanity so long as the remainder of the *M'Naghten* rules are applicable (*R v Davis* (1881) 14 Cox CC 563). However, where the defendant's intoxication does not induce a disease of the mind, the defence of insanity is unavailable and the regular rules of intoxication apply (*R v Coley; R v McGhee; R v Harris* [2013] EWCA Crim 223 – defendant had smoked cannabis). In *Coley*, Hughes LJ stated:

> Direct acute effects on the mind of intoxicants, voluntarily taken are not so classified [as a disease of the mind]. … When voluntarily taken their acute effects are not treated by the law as a disease of the mind for the purposes of the *M'Naghten* rules. Such a case is governed by the law of voluntary intoxication.

In the majority of cases, therefore, the ingestion of alcohol or drugs will be considered an 'external' factor that may be relevant to automatism as opposed to insanity (though note that self-induced automatism is not a valid defence – see **7.6.3**).

Table 7.10 Summarising internal and external factors

Internal	**External**
Hyperglycaemia (*R v Hennessy*)	Hypoglycaemia (*R v Quick*)
Arteriosclerosis (*R v Kemp*)	Reflex action (*Hill v Baxter*)
Sleepwalking (*R v Burgess*)	Post-traumatic stress disorder (*R v T*)
Epilepsy (*R v Sullivan*)	Alcohol and drugs (*R v Coley*) – unless it causes a disease of the mind

7.5.2.5 Element (iv) first limb: not knowing the nature and quality of the act

It is at this point that the first limb differs from the second. In order to fall within the first limb, the defendant must not appreciate the 'nature and quality' of his actions. According to the Court of Criminal Appeal in *R v Codère* (1916) 12 Cr App R 21, this element refers to the 'physical nature and quality' of the act and not its moral or legal quality. 'Nature' refers to the conduct itself and 'quality' refers to the consequences of the conduct. Lord Diplock explained this element in *R v Sullivan* [1984] AC 156 simply as follows:

> Addressed to an audience of jurors in the 1980s it might more aptly be expressed as 'He did not know what he was doing'.

Table 7.11 Understanding the first limb of M'Naghten

Did not know the *nature* of his acts	**Did not know the *quality* of his acts**
The defendant did not appreciate the physical nature of his acts. Another way of phrasing this is that the defendant was 'delusional' in that he did not know what he was doing.	The defendant did not appreciate the consequences of his acts. In this regard, the defendant may not realise that the consequence of his conduct will be that the victim dies, for example.

Cases under this limb may, for example, involve a person who harms another through a delusion caused by a disease of the mind. An example put forward by Lord Denning is the case of an accused believing that he was throwing a log, rather than a baby, onto a fire (*R v Codère*). Many other examples have been given across the academic literature in an attempt to explain the operation of the defence. The majority are colourful in nature and include the following:

- An insane delusion that the defendant is breaking a jar rather than hitting another person (Stephen, *Digest of the Criminal Law* (8th edn, 1947)).
- The defendant cuts the victim's throat believing it is a loaf of bread (Kenny, *Outlines of Criminal Law*, 18th edn (CUP, 2013)).
- The defendant chops off the head of a sleeping man because he feels it would be amusing to watch him look for it when he awakes (Stephen, *A History of the Criminal Law of England* (Volume III, 1883).

In these examples, the court is not questioning whether the defendant believed his actions to be wrong; rather, the court is questioning whether the defendant even knew what he was doing.

7.5.2.6 Element (iv) second limb: not knowing what he was doing was wrong

Should the defendant fail to prove that he did not know the nature and quality of his actions, he may still have a defence where he can prove that he, nonetheless, did not know what he was doing was wrong. The question that has been posed by the courts is focused on the meaning of the word 'wrong'. Specifically, are we concerned with whether the defendant believed his actions to be legally or morally wrong? **Table 7.12** explains the distinction between these two terms.

Table 7.12 Legally vs morally wrong

Legally wrong	Morally wrong
Where a defendant knows his actions are contrary to the law (*R v Windle* [1952] 2 QB 826).	If the defendant thought his actions were right but knew they were wrong to the ordinary standards of the reasonable man (*R v Codère* (1916) 12 Cr App R 21).

In *M'Naghten*, their Lordships spoke clearly of the need to prove that the defendant did not know at the time of committing the *actus reus* that he 'was acting contrary to law; by which expression we … mean the law of the land'. In this respect, our focus is on whether the defendant was aware that his conduct was criminal. Whether the defendant knew his conduct was morally wrong is therefore not the test.

This approach was confirmed by the Court of Criminal Appeal in *R v Windle* [1952] 2 QB 826, in which the defendant, having killed his wife by administering her with 100 aspirins in pursuit of a suicide pact (see **Chapter 8**), commented, upon arrest, 'I suppose they will hang me for this.' Lord Goddard CJ confirmed:

> Courts of law can only distinguish between that which is in accordance with law and that which is contrary to law … The law cannot embark on the question and it would be an unfortunate thing if it were left to juries to consider whether some particular act was morally right or wrong. The test must be whether it is contrary to law. … In the opinion of the court there is no doubt that in the McNaghten rules 'wrong' means contrary to law and not 'wrong' according to the opinion of one man or of a number of people on the question whether a particular Act might or might not be justified. In the present case, it could not be challenged that the appellant knew that what he was doing was contrary to law, and that he realized what punishment the law provided for murder.

Windle clearly knew what he was doing was wrong in law. As a result, his conviction was upheld and he was hanged for his crime.

This approach has been extensively criticised. Most notably, in 1975, the Royal Committee on Mentally Abnormal Offenders (known as the Butler Committee) considered the *Windle* definition to be 'wrong' and 'a very narrow ground of exemption since even persons who are grossly disturbed generally know that murder and arson, for instance, are crimes' ('Report of the Committee on Mentally Abnormal Offenders' (Cmnd 6244)). For additional criticism, see Mackay, 'Righting the Wrong? – Some Observations on the Second Limb of the *M'Naghten* Rules' [2009] Crim LR 80.

The key authority in this area is now that of *R v Johnson* [2007] EWCA Crim 1978.

case example

Charge:
Wounding with intent (OAPA 1861, s 18)

Case progression:
Crown Court – Guilty

Court of Appeal – Conviction upheld

Point of law:
Meaning of 'wrong'

In *R v Johnson* [2007] EWCA Crim 1978, the defendant, who suffered from delusions and auditory hallucinations, forced his way into the victim's flat and stabbed him four times with a large kitchen knife. Upon arrest, the defendant was diagnosed as suffering from paranoid schizophrenia. Both psychiatrists agreed that the defendant knew that what he was doing was against the law, but there was some evidence that the accused did not know that his act was 'wrong in the moral sense'. The defendant was charged with and convicted of wounding with intent in the Crown Court.

The defendant appealed against conviction on the basis that the trial judge had erred in law by not leaving the defence of insanity to the jury. The Court of Appeal disagreed, finding that no defence could be availed given that it was agreed between all parties that the defendant knew that his conduct was legally wrong; reference to morally wrong was irrelevant.

The Court of Appeal followed the judgment of *Windle* in finding that the defendant, although he could not grasp that his conduct was morally wrong, knew that it was legally wrong. In *Windle,* the defendant clearly knew that his conduct was unlawful despite his belief that such conduct was morally appropriate. This approach was followed by the Court in *Johnson*, which concluded that where the accused knows that his actions are legally wrong, he cannot avail a defence of insanity even though he believed his actions to be morally right according to the standards of ordinary people. Although Latham LJ in the Court of Appeal felt that the rule in *Windle* was 'strict', it did not feel comfortable to move away from the rule, citing Parliament or a higher court as being the correct body to reconsider it.

The law, therefore, is simply that the defence must prove that the defendant did not believe his actions to be legally wrong. A belief that his actions were morally wrong, without regard to his belief in law, is not sufficient to disallow the defence. Interestingly, the High Court of Australia has refused to follow *Windle*, meaning that a defendant can avail a defence of insanity in circumstances where 'through the disordered condition of the mind, [the defendant] could not reason about the matter with a moderate degree of sense and composure' (*R v Stapleton* (1952) 86 CLR 358). The Canadian courts have reached a similar conclusion (*R v Chaulk* (1991) 62 CCC (3d) 193). Mackay ('More Fact(s) about the Insanity Defence' [1999] Crim LR 715) has also contended that the narrow rule in *Windle* is rarely adopted in practice by psychiatrists who continue to speak of 'wrongness' in the sense of 'whether the defendant thought his/her actions were morally justified, and/or whether the actions were in perceived self-defence of themselves or others, in the sense of protecting their physical or spiritual well-being'.

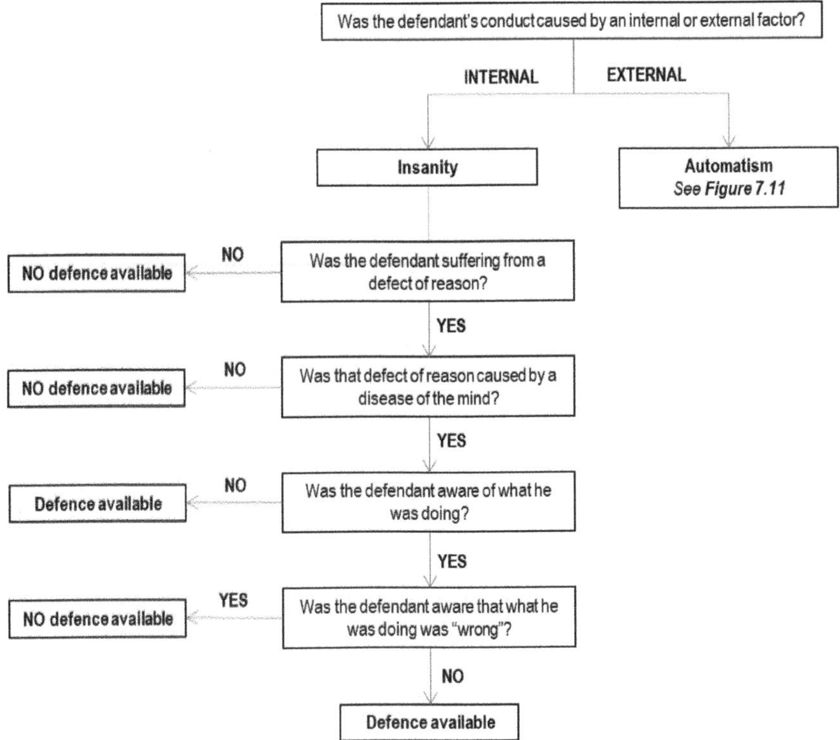

Figure 7.10 Putting together insanity

7.5.3 Procedural matters and the burden of proof

As noted above at **7.5**, insanity is a general defence that can be pleaded to all crimes (*R v Horseferry Road Magistrates' Court, ex parte K* [1997] QB 23). This has been made clear in the recent case of *Loake v CPS* [2017] EWHC 2855 (Admin), where the Divisional Court found the defence applicable in cases of harassment contrary to the Protection from Harassment Act 1997.

7.5.3.1 Procedure

By s 1 of the Criminal Procedure (Insanity and Unfitness to Plead) Act 1991, the defendant must adduce evidence from two or more registered medical practitioners in order to prove his defence. A further restriction applies to this rule, requiring at least one of those practitioners to be 'approved' to give such evidence (meaning someone who has been approved by the Home Secretary as an expert in mental disorder).

The role of judge and jury is important to note at this stage. The judge is responsible for determining whether the defendant is actually suffering with a defect of reason caused by a disease of the mind. Essentially, the judge must decide (as a matter of law) whether the defence of insanity exists in law for this defendant (*R v Dickie* [1984] 3 All ER 173). If the judge is satisfied that there is a defect of reason caused by such a disease of the mind, the defence can then be left to the jury who must decide, as a matter of fact, whether the defendant knew the nature and quality of his actions or that his conduct was wrong. This is essentially a question of fact, asking whether the defendant is actually insane (*Walton v R* [1978] AC 788).

7.5.3.2 Burden of proof

Unlike other defences, the legal burden of proving insanity is reversed and placed on the defendant (*Woolmington v DPP* [1935] AC 462). This reverse burden applies given that all persons are presumed to be sane (*M'Naghten* rules). The standard of proof is the civil standard, on the balance of probabilities. It is worth emphasising, however, that the prosecution must still prove its case, ie that the accused 'did the act or made the omission charged' (Trial of Lunatics Act 1883, s 2(1)) beyond a reasonable doubt. A failure to prove that the defendant committed the relevant *actus reus* will entitle a defendant to a complete acquittal for lack of *actus reus* despite his insanity.

Refer back to **Chapter 1** for a discussion of the burden of proof and the distinction between a legal and an evidential burden.

7.5.4 Result of a successful plea of insanity

Where the defendant's plea of insanity has been successful, the jury must return a 'special verdict' of 'not guilty by reason of insanity' as provided for in s 2 of the Trial of Lunatics Act 1883 (as amended by the Criminal Procedure (Insanity) Act (CPIA) 1964, s 1). The special verdict is not 'automatic' and must still be delivered by the jury upon effective deliberation (*R v Crown Court at Maidstone, ex parte Harrow London Borough Council* [2000] QB 719). Note, however, that the s 2 procedure applies only in the Crown Court. Where a defendant raises the defence of insanity in the magistrates' court and the plea is successful, this will result in a complete acquittal (*R v Horseferry Road Magistrates' Court, ex parte K* [1997] QB 23; *R (Singh) v Stratford Magistrates' Court* [2007] 4 All ER 407).

Under the common law, a successful plea of insanity would have a single outcome – a hospital order detaining the accused for potentially an indefinite period. This common law position was reflected in the CPIA 1964. This position would lead Lawton LJ in *R v Quick* [1973] QB 910 to describe insanity as a 'quagmire of law seldom entered nowadays save by those in desperate need for some kind of a defence'. The Criminal Procedure (Insanity and Unfitness to Plead) Act 1991 amended the 1964 Act to the extent that the court now has a range of powers and orders from which to choose where a special verdict of not guilty by reason of insanity has been returned. These options are provided for in s 5(2) of the amended 1964 Act. **Table 7.13** details these orders.

Table 7.13 Orders available upon the special verdict of insanity

Order	Description
Hospital order (CPIA 1964, s 5(2)(a))	The defendant will be detained in a hospital for the mentally ill and will be prescribed with treatment for his condition.
Supervision and treatment order (CPIA 1964, s 5(2)(b))	The defendant must be kept under the supervision of another individual, such as a social worker, and may be subject to treatment also.
Absolute discharge (CPIA 1964, s 5(2)(c))	The defendant is free to go and is subject to no restrictions.

Note, however, that s 5(3) provides that the range of available orders under s 5(2) does not apply where the offence charged is murder or any other offence for which the sentence is fixed by law. In such a case, the court must make a hospital order with a restriction order attached. The restriction order forbids the defendant from being released from hospital without the consent of the Secretary of State.

7.6 Automatism

Our next major defence available to all criminal charges is that of automatism. Automatism, also known as 'sane automatism', concerns the circumstances where a defendant lacks control over his own bodily actions as a result of some external factor. Where the defendant lacks control over his actions as a result of an internal factor, ie a disease of the mind, the more appropriate defence is that of insanity (also known as insane automatism – previously considered at **7.5**).

7.6.1 Basis for the defence

The fundamental principle in criminal liability is that the defendant is only liable for conduct that is voluntary on his part. Such conduct may be through an act or omission, but must be voluntary. For a discussion on voluntary/involuntary conduct, see **Chapter 2**.

Therefore, where the defendant's conduct, or *actus reus*, is involuntary, as a result of a state of automatism, he ought to escape liability. In this respect, automatism is a general defence available to all crimes. Given that the focus here is on whether the defendant's conduct was voluntary, it is better to refer to automatism as a denial of the commission of the offence, as opposed to a 'defence' that justifies or excuses liability.

in practice

There is no issue with the use of the word 'automatism' when directing a jury. Whilst it may be a legal term, which ordinarily should be avoided with a jury, the Crown Court Compendium (section 18–4) advises that: 'The word "automatism", despite being a legal term, is used since (a) it is likely, where this is an issue, that this word will have been mentioned at some point during the case and (b) it is useful "shorthand" to describe a complete loss of the ability to exercise control over a person's actions.'

7.6.2 Elements of the defence

The term 'automatism' refers to the situation where the defendant acts in a psychically involuntary manner. Lord Denning in *Bratty v AG for Northern Ireland* [1963] AC 386 described automatism as

> an act which is done by the muscles without any control by the mind, such as a spasm, a reflex action or a convulsion; or an act done by a person who is not conscious of what he is doing, such as an act done whilst suffering from concussion or whilst sleepwalking.

Simply, the defendant's body acts without control from his mind, ie his body is disassociated from his brain. Automatism is, however, to be distinguished from other cases where the defendant lacks voluntary control.

example

Jack and Jill are walking down the street. Jack, being a practical joker, picks up Jill and throws her onto a neighbour's car, causing a dent to the car.

In this instance, if Jill was charged with an offence of criminal damage, it cannot be said that she was acting voluntarily (because she was thrown onto the car). However, it also cannot be said that she was acting in an automatic state. In this instance, Jill can merely deny the existence of an offence on the basis that she did not act voluntarily as a result of the actions of a third party. In this instance, there is no necessity for Jill to consider raising automatism.

The elements of the defence are outlined in **Table 7.14**.

Table 7.14 Elements of the defence of automatism

Elements of the defence
(i) total loss of voluntary control; (ii) caused by an external factor.

In addition to these two elements, the defendant's automatic state must not result from voluntary intoxication. We consider so-called cases of 'self-induced automatism' at **7.6.3**. We shall consider each element from **Table 7.14** in turn.

7.6.2.1 Element (i): total loss of voluntary control

The first requirement to be proven is that the automatism caused a *total* loss (or 'destruction') of voluntary control. Impaired or reduced control is not sufficient to found a defence. The leading authority in this area is that of *AG's Reference (No 2 of 1992)* [1994] QB 91.

Charge:
Causing death by reckless driving (Road Traffic Act 1988, s 1)

Case progression:
Crown Court – Not guilty

Court of Appeal – No defence could be raised

Point of law:
Meaning of 'total destruction of voluntary control'

case example

In *AG's Reference (No 2 of 1992)* [1994] QB 91, the defendant (a lorry driver) was said to have entered a state of 'driving without awareness' after driving at night for a long period time and being subject to repeated flashing lights. In his state of unawareness, the defendant crashed his lorry whilst driving on the hard shoulder of the motorway, killing another driver who had broken down. The defendant was charged with causing death by reckless driving in the Crown Court but was found not guilty, having successfully raised the defence of automatism.

The prosecution appealed to the Court of Appeal on basis that the defence of automatism should not have been open to the defendant. The Court of Appeal agreed and found that the defendant was not entitled to raise automatism as a defence given that it could not be proven that there was a 'total loss' of awareness of what he was doing. Lord Taylor CJ concluded that:

> the defence of automatism requires that there was a total destruction of voluntary control on the defendant's part. Impaired, reduced or partial control is not enough.

The Court of Appeal relied on a previous authority of *Broome v Perkins* [1987] Crim LR 271 in which the defendant, charged with driving without due care and attention contrary to s 3 of the Road Traffic Act 1972, was found to have only been acting in an automatic state at sporadic intervals. The defendant had been seen to drive erratically, causing damage to neighbouring cars, but in any event was successfully able to drive himself home. Further, evidence was submitted to demonstrate that the defendant had, on a number of occasions, swerved to avoid other vehicles and had violently braked to avoid hitting a queue of traffic. Despite his hypoglycaemic state, the Divisional Court concluded that there was no 'total' loss of the defendant's voluntary control, merely an intermittent loss.

AG's Reference (No 2 of 1992) was followed by the Court of Appeal in *R v Coley* [2013] EWCA Crim 223, in which Hughes LJ confirmed that a defendant must have suffered a 'complete loss of voluntary control of his actions' but did go on to emphasise that a complete loss of control does not require the defendant to be unconscious. His Lordship stated:

> Automatism, if it occurs, results in a complete acquittal on the grounds that the act was not that of the Defendant at all. It has been variously described. The essence of it is that the movements or actions of the Defendant at the material time were wholly involuntary. The better expression is complete destruction of voluntary control ... Examples which have been given in the past include the driver attacked by a swarm of bees or the man under hypnosis. 'Involuntary' is not the same as 'irrational'; indeed it needs sharply to be distinguished from it.

The effect of these decisions is to rule that an individual who is prone to 'day-dreaming' will not be able to rely upon a defence of automatism, given that it cannot be said that they truly lost their ability to voluntarily control their actions. Acting irrationally, as Hughes LJ says, is not the same as acting involuntarily.

7.6.2.2 Element (ii): caused by an external factor

In our discussion of insanity, we made a key distinction between internal and external factors. For the defence of insanity to succeed, the defendant needs to prove that his conduct was caused by some internal factor. In comparison, automatism is concerned with the effects of an external factor on the defendant's conduct, such as a reflex spasm from being attacked by a swarm of bees (an example given by Lord Goddard CJ in *Hill v Baxter* [1958] 1 QB 277) or a blow to the head.

in practice

A useful distinction that is often made between internal and external factors is the possibility of reoccurrence. Internal factors are such that they will ordinarily constitute a disorder or condition which causes prohibited conduct on a basis that is susceptible to recur. External factors, on the other hand, such as muscle spasms and reflex actions, usually involve one-off incidents that are not likely to recur. This distinction has, however, been subject to cogent criticism. For instance, Lord Lane CJ in *R v Burgess* [1991] 2 QB 92 stated that

> ... if there is a danger of recurrence that may be an added reason for categorising the condition as a disease of the mind. On the other hand, the absence of the danger of recurrence is not a reason for saying that it cannot be a disease of the mind.

Although this distinction is not 'bullet-proof', it is nonetheless a useful starting point.

For a full discussion of the scenarios that may amount to internal or external factors, see above at **7.5.2.4**. What is the case, however, where the automatic state has been caused by both internal and external factors? For the answer to this question, we turn to the case of *R v Roach* [2001] EWCA Crim 2698.

case example

Charge:
Wounding with intent (OAPA 1861, s 18)

Case progression:
Crown Court – Guilty
Court of Appeal – Conviction quashed

Point of law:
Meaning of 'total destruction of voluntary control'

In *R v Roach* [2001] EWCA Crim 2698, the defendant, suffering with anti-social personality disorder and under the influence of alcohol and prescribed drugs, stabbed the victim in the hand after a trivial disagreement. The defendant was charged with and convicted of wounding with intent in the Crown Court after the jury refused to find that the defendant was insane.

The defendant appealed to the Court of Appeal on the basis that the trial judge ought to have directed the jury to consider automatism instead of insanity. The Court of Appeal agreed, ruling that the external factors could possibly have had the effect of causing the automatic state of the defendant. Potter LJ concluded that:

> the legal definition of automatism allows for the fact that, if external factors are operative upon an underlying condition which would not otherwise produce a state of automatism, then a defence of (non-insane) automatism should be left to the jury.

In essence, where an internal condition would not have otherwise produced the state of automatism, had it not been for the external factors, the defendant is able to rely on the defence of automatism. In this respect, it is said that the external factors are 'operative' upon the internal condition.

Before turning to the procedure adopted for the defence, it is worth discussing the more controversial aspect of automatism, namely that of self-induced automatism.

7.6.3 Self-induced automatism

It could be said that a third element of automatism exists, often referred to as self-induced automatism. Self-induced automatism refers to the situation in which the defendant is partly, or wholly, responsible for his automatic state. Special rules apply to defendants who, through the use of drink, drugs or other external matters, cause their automatic state. These rules are similar to those in intoxication considered at **7.4.**

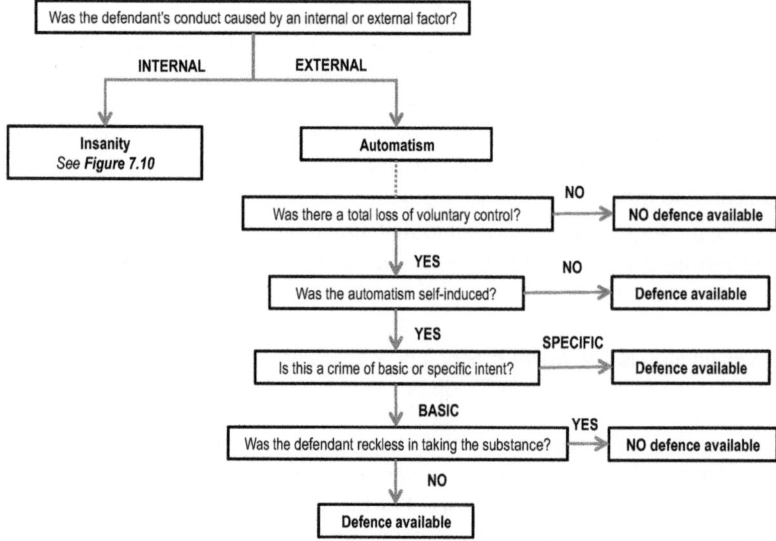

Figure 7.11 Putting together automatism

7.6.4 Procedural matters and the burden of proof

7.6.4.1 Procedure

Before the defence of automatism can be placed before the jury, a proper foundation for the defence must have been laid (*Hill v Baxter* [1958] 1 QB 277). This basically means that some evidence must have been produced to prove that the defence may have existed.

7.6.4.2 Burden of proof

Unlike the defence of insanity (where the legal burden of proving insanity is on the defence on the balance of probabilities), where the defendant raises the defence of automatism, it is for the prosecution to negative the defence beyond a reasonable doubt (*R v Burns* (1973) 58 Cr App R 364). It must be noted, however, that the defendant bears the evidential burden to provide evidence to make the issue of automatism 'live'. In *R v C* [2007] EWCA Crim 1862, Moses LJ stated:

> It is a crucial principle in cases such as this that a defendant D cannot rely on the defence of automatism without providing some evidence of it.

The Court of Appeal in *C* was quick to note that the evidence from the defendant himself will rarely be sufficient unless it is supported by some form of medical evidence. In order for the prosecution to disprove the existence of the defence, it must prove that the defendant's actions were voluntary and committed whilst he was fully conscious and aware (*R v Stripp* (1978) 69 Cr App R 318).

For a useful summation of the burden of proof in such cases, see Jones, 'Insanity, Automatism and the Burden of Proof on the Accused' (1995) 111 LQR 475.

7.6.5 Result of a successful plea of automatism

Where the defendant successfully raises a defence of automatism, he is entitled to a complete acquittal without restrictions. This is unlike the outcome in insanity cases where the defendant is found not guilty by reason of insanity but is subject to certain restrictions and orders to be determined by the court.

7.6.6 Comparing automatism with insanity

As has been discussed above, insanity and automatism are similar in some respects. Both circumstances are raised to allege that the defendant lacked an essential element of the offence allegedly committed, ie the *actus reus* or *mens rea*. However, students often struggle to distinguish the two concepts. **Table 7.15** intends to prevent this confusion.

Table 7.15 Comparing automatism with insanity

Variable	Insanity	Automatism
Element of defence	Requires proof of an internal factor (a 'disease of the mind')	Requires proof of an external factor affecting the defendant's voluntary control
Burden of proof	Legal burden is reversed onto the defendant to prove, on the balance of probabilities, that the defence is made out	Legal burden remains on the prosecution to disprove the existence of the defence. Defendant bears an evidential burden to raise the matter in issue

Variable	Insanity	Automatism
Outcome	Results in a special plea of 'not guilty by reason of insanity'	Results in a complete acquittal

For these reasons, automatism is often a more popular defence raised by defendants.

7.7 Consent

We deal with the topic of consent in considerable detail in **Chapter 9**, in the context of non-fatal offences against the person, and **Chapter 10**, in the context of sexual offences. We shall deal with consent only briefly here.

A key element of any crime is the requirement of unlawfulness. The consent of an individual who would otherwise be a victim to a crime without the presence of consent has the effect of negating the *actus reus* of an offence. In this respect, consent is not a 'defence' *per se* to a criminal charge, but rather is a denial of the essential element of unlawfulness.

In the context of common assault, consent is capable of availing a defence where the consent is effective (ie the victim possessed the necessary capacity to consent and the freedom to consent and was sufficiently informed to give consent) and the consent is given, expressly or impliedly. In a case of common assault, consent will provide a complete defence. In cases of a higher degree of seriousness, however, such as ABH, a third element is required, namely that the activity to which consent is provided must be one that is recognised in law as being in the public interest.

7.8 Private and public defence

Private and public defence is the formal title afforded to self-defence and the prevention of crime. Self-defence refers to the situation in which the defendant uses reasonable force in the defence of himself or another person. Self-defence is a common law defence which was restated, though not placed onto a statutory basis, by s 76 of the Criminal Justice and Immigration Act (CJIA) 2008. Self-defence is a 'private' defence.

Prevention of crime refers to the situation in which the defendant uses reasonable force in the prevention of the commission of a criminal offence. Prevention of crime is a statutory defence found in s 3 of the Criminal Law Act (CLA) 1967. Prevention of crime is a 'public' defence.

A further common law defence of defence of property also exists. All three defences have been restated as a result of s 76(2) of the CJIA 2008, which provides that:

> The defences are—
> (a) the common law defence of self-defence [**7.8.2**];
> (aa) the common law defence of defence of property [**7.8.3**]; and
> (b) the defences provided by section 3(1) of the CLA 1967 or section 3(1) of the Criminal Law Act (Northern Ireland) 1967 (use of force in prevention of crime or making arrest) [**7.8.4**].

For a full discussion of self-defence in the criminal law, see Leverick, *Killing in Self-Defence* (OUP, 2006) and Sangero, *Self Defence in Criminal Law* (Bloomsbury Publishing, 2006).

7.8.1 Basis for the defence

Both self-defence and prevention of crime act as justificatory defences. Where a defendant is faced with a situation where it is necessary to use force, in the defence of oneself or another, or in the prevention of crime, and that force is reasonably used, a defence justifying his conduct ought to be available. This defence has the effect of negating the unlawfulness of the defendant's conduct on account that it is considered to be justified in the circumstances. Although the phrase will be adopted in this text, it is technically misleading to refer to private and public defence as the law of 'self-defence' given that the defence operates to justify force used for the defence or protection of oneself, one's property or other persons also.

The 'classic pronouncement' as to the law relating to self-defence comes from Lord Morris in the Privy Council in *Palmer v The Queen* [1971] AC 814:

> It is both good law and good sense that a man who is attacked may defend himself. It is both good law and good sense that he may do, but may only do, what is reasonably necessary. But everything will depend upon the particular facts and circumstances. ... It may in some cases be only sensible and clearly possible to take some simple avoiding action. Some attacks may be serious and dangerous. Others may not be. If there is some relatively minor attack it would not be common sense to permit some action of retaliation which was wholly out of proportion to the necessities of the situation. If an attack is serious so that it puts someone in immediate peril then immediate defensive action may be necessary. If the moment is one of crisis for someone in immediate danger he may have to avert the danger by some instant reaction. If the attack is over and no sort of peril remains then the employment of force may be by way of revenge or punishment or by way of paying off an old score or may be pure aggression. There may be no longer any link with a necessity of defence. Of all these matters the good sense of a jury will be the arbiter. There are no prescribed words which must be employed in or adopted in a summing up. All that is needed is a clear exposition, in relation to the particular facts of the case, of the conception of necessary self-defence. If there has been no attack then clearly there will have been no need for defence. If there has been attack so that defence is reasonably necessary it will be recognised that a person defending himself cannot weigh to a nicety the exact measure of his necessary defensive action. If a jury thought that in a moment of unexpected anguish a person attacked had only done what he honestly and instinctively thought was necessary that would be the most potent evidence that only reasonable defensive action had been taken. A jury will be told that the defence of self-defence, where the evidence makes its raising possible, will only fail if the prosecution show beyond doubt that what the accused did was not by way of self-defence. ... If the jury consider that an accused acted in self-defence or if the jury are in doubt as to this then they will acquit. The defence of self-defence either succeeds so as to result in an acquittal or it is disproved in which case as a defence it is rejected.

This statement has been approved and followed by the Court of Appeal in *R v McInnes* [1971] 1 WLR 1600 and has now, effectively, been reflected in the provisions of s 76 of the CJIA 2008.

The defences considered in this section have been referred to by Padfield as 'first cousins' (*Criminal Law*, 10th edn (OUP, 2016)). This is because the rules of both private and public defence are the same. For ease and distinction, however, each defence will be considered separately.

7.8.2 Private defence: self-defence

At common law, the defence of self-defence could accurately be summed up as being divided into 'trigger' and 'response' (to use the words of Ormerod and Laird (*Smith, Hogan, & Ormerod's Criminal Law*, 15th edn (OUP, 2018)). A more common way to explain this is that there must be a 'necessity' to use force and the use of force must be 'reasonable' in the circumstances. The leading case to this date remains the seminal authority of *Palmer v The Queen* [1971] AC 814.

case example

Charge:
Murder

Case progression:
Court of Appeal of Jamaica – Guilty

Privy Council – Conviction upheld

Point of law:
The existence of self-defence to a charge of murder

In *Palmer v The Queen* [1971] AC 814, the defendant (and others) had been chased by three men, one of them being the victim, after the defendant had stolen some ganja (cannabis). The men were chasing the defendant with sticks and stones. The defendant, who was carrying a gun, fired a number of shots, one of which hit and killed the victim. The defendant was charged with and convicted of murder.

He appealed to the Jamaican Court of Appeal on the basis that an alternative charge of manslaughter should have been left to the jury alongside the defence of self-defence. The Jamaican court refused this ground and sent the case to the Privy Council, which too found the appeal to fail on account that self-defence was an all or nothing defence.

Lord Morris laid down a distinction which remains to this day the test for self-defence. The distinction can be explained as follows:

Table 7.16 Trigger and response

Phrase	Explanation
Trigger/ Necessity	Did the defendant (subjectively) believe that the use of force was necessary in the circumstances?
Response/ Reasonableness	Was the degree of force used by the defendant (objectively) reasonable in the circumstances?

This common law principle is now reflected and restated in s 76 of the CJIA 2008. Section 76 provides:

> (1) This section applies where in proceedings for an offence—
> (a) an issue arises as to whether a person charged with the offence ('D') is entitled to rely on a defence within subsection (2), and
> (b) the question arises whether the degree of force used by D against a person ('V') was reasonable in the circumstances.

The effect of s 76 is provided for in s 76(9) which states that '[t]his section, except so far as making different provision for householder cases, is intended to clarify the operation of the existing defences mentioned in subsection (2)'. This is furthered by para 532 of the Explanatory Notes to the CJIA 2008 which provides that '[s] 76 provides a gloss on the common law of self-defence [and is] intended to improve understanding of the practical application of these areas of the law'. Dennis ('Editorial'

[2008] Crim LR 507) refers to the restatement of the common law by s 76 as a 'pointless exercise'. Allen and Edwards (*Criminal Law*, 15th edn (OUP, 2019)) describe the provision as 'one of the worst examples of gesture politics resulting in pointless legislation'.

In *R v Keane; R v McGrath* [2010] EWCA Crim 2514, Hughes LJ in the Court of Appeal clarified that

> For the avoidance of doubt, it is perhaps helpful to say of s 76 three things: (a) it does not alter the law as it has been for many years; (b) it does not exhaustively state the law of self-defence but it does state the basic principles; (c) it does not require any summing-up to rehearse the whole of its contents just because they are now contained in statute.

In this respect, despite its presence in the CJIA 2008, self-defence remains a common law defence.

From this provision, and the statement of Lord Morris in *Palmer*, the elements of the defence are outlined in **Table 7.17**.

Table 7.17 Elements of the defence of self-defence

Elements of the defence
(i) trigger; (ii) response.

We now consider each element in turn in relation to the 'ordinary' defence of self-defence, and we look at the so-called 'householder' provisions at **7.8.2.3**.

7.8.2.1 Element (i): trigger

As explained above, the first requirement is for the presence of a 'trigger'. The essential question to be asked is whether the defendant believed that the use of force was *necessary* in the circumstances. This is a subjective question focusing on what the defendant believed the facts to be in the circumstances and whether, on those facts, the defendant believed in the need to use force. This has been the position of the common law from leading cases such as *R v Williams (Gladstone)* [1987] 3 All ER 411 and *Beckford v The Queen* [1988] AC 130.

example

Jill knows that she is being stalked by Jack. One night Jack grabs Jill from behind and begins to touch her breasts. Jill manages to fight back and knock Jack to the floor. Jack runs away immediately after.

In this case, Jill is clearly acting in defence of herself. It can be said that force is used to repel and ward off an attack from Jack. Suppose Jill, however, begins to chase Jack as he runs away and starts to attack him. Such conduct would more appropriately be said to be in revenge or retaliation for which the law offers no protection.

This element of the test can best be understood as a threshold test, asking whether it is necessary for the defendant to use *any* force in defence of himself or another. Questions as to the type of force, amount of force and reasonableness of such force should be left for the second element.

There are some key questions which need to be identified to fully understand this element of the defence. It may seem at first that there are a lot of questions to ask; however, this merely reflects the need to appreciate the varying circumstances that may be faced by a defendant.

(a) When is it necessary to use force?

The first point to note is that the defendant must be reacting to an unjustified threat. Importantly, the threat need not be 'unlawful' (as required by the defence of prevention of crime); the threat need only be unjustified. This first requirement is often referred to as the defendant responding to an attack or threat of an attack.

(b) How imminent must the danger be?

In order to rely on the defence, the threat posed to the defendant must be sufficiently imminent to justify the defendant's use of force. This was the reasoning of Lord MacDermott CJ in the Northern Ireland case of *Devlin v Armstrong* [1971] NI 13, who ruled that 'the anticipated attack must be imminent' and that such anticipation must be 'sufficiently specific or imminent to justify the actions [he] took as measures of self-defence'. Under this approach, the anticipation of future danger or future threats will not be sufficient unless it can be said to be in immediate apprehension of a threat. This rule has been criticised by the likes of O'Donovan ('Defences for Battered Women Who Kill' (1991) 18(2) Journal of Law & Society 219). O'Donovan contends that the requirement of immediacy ignores the fundamental basis as to whom the defence is designed to protect – those in fear of harm. In this respect, O'Donovan focuses on battered women who kill – the majority are not in imminent danger at the point in question but are acting in defence of themselves for future occasions. In particular she argues:

> With regard to the attack, the question is whether 'imminent danger' is confined to an immediate act of violence, or whether well-founded fear of a future attack, based on previous experience, suffices. Several cases concern the killing of an assailant who has gone to bed. Hitherto the courts have insisted that 'imminent danger' means that a violent attack has occurred to which there has been an immediate response in fear of personal safety. This is the rock on which many cases have foundered ...

Horder ('Redrawing the Boundaries of Self-Defence' (1995) 58 MLR 431) is of the view that the immediacy requirement detracts from the fundamental requirement of 'necessity' for the use of force. He argues:

> If 'imminent' means 'live' or 'being put into effect', the insistence on an imminent threat or attack seems more restrictive than the insistence that the use of force be necessary in meeting the threat. After all, pre-emptive strikes can be necessary and proportionate, even though the very pre-emptiveness of the strike implies that the threat being averted was not 'live'.

(c) What factors can be taken into account when considering whether force was 'necessary' in the circumstances?

When deciding whether the use of force was necessary in the circumstances, the jury must consider the circumstances as the defendant believed them to be.

In *Shaw v The Queen* [2001] 1 WLR 1519, the Privy Council explained that the subjective test of belief in necessary force should be interpreted to apply not only to the accused's belief as to the circumstances but also to his belief as to the *danger* involved in those circumstances. This view was afforded merit in *R v Oye* [2013] EWCA Crim 1725, where the Court of Appeal felt that the defendant's psychotic delusions were relevant in determining whether he genuinely held a belief in the necessity to use force. Such delusions could not be used, however, to judge the reasonableness of his response. This decision has been subsequently affirmed in *R v Harvey* [2009] EWCA Crim 469 and *R v Press and Thompson* [2013] EWCA Crim 1849.

Most recently in *R v Mohammed Ibrahim* [2014] EWCA Crim 121, the Court of Appeal explained that the physical characteristics of the defendant might be relevant to the question of his belief in the need for force but was not relevant to the question of reasonableness. For example, one would need to appreciate the difference between the necessity to use force by an elderly and frail woman, compared with a young, fit and healthy woman. In particular, the Court spoke of the fact that a physically weaker individual would genuinely hold the belief that they needed to use a weapon in defending themselves. This was a relevant factor under the trigger requirement but only amounted to 'strong evidence' under the response requirement. In *R v Robinson (Gary Lucien)* [2017] EWCA Crim 923, the defendant's action of grabbing a knife and stabbing the victim out of 'panic' was held to be relevant to the decision as to whether force was necessary in the circumstances as the defendant believed them to be.

Circumstances unknown to the accused

The emphasis on the circumstances 'as the defendant believed them to be' has been quite significant in the context of circumstances that are unknown to the accused. This principle concerns cases where the defendant is objectively justified in his actions (ie he passes the response element) but he is not actually aware of the necessity to use force for the purpose provided. In *R v Dadson* (1850) 4 Cox CC 358, the Court for Crown Cases Reserved ruled that knowledge of the circumstances justifying self-defence was essential. The defendant, a police officer, had shot the victim in the leg in order to arrest him. At the time, the law only permitted such force to be used where the individual was a felon. Although the victim here was a felon, the defendant was not aware of this. As such, according to Pollock CB, the defendant's conviction was safe as he was 'not justified in firing' at the victim.

The extent of this principle is that the defendant must be aware as to the reason that force is necessary – eg in self-defence. Where the defendant lacks knowledge as to these circumstances, no defence can be relied upon. See Christopher, 'Unknowing Justification and the Logical Necessity of the *Dadson* Principle in Self-Defence' (1995) 15 OJLS 229 for a full discussion.

(d) Who can you act in defence of?

Although commonly phrased as 'self-defence', s 76(10)(b) of the CJIA 2008 explains that 'references to self-defence include acting in defence of another person'. This has long been the common law position regarding the private defence. In *R v Rose* (1884) 15 Cox CC 540, for example, the defendant was acquitted of murder after he had shot his father whilst acting in defence of his mother. In *R v Duffy* [1967] 1 QB 63, the defendant had struck the victim with a bottle whilst acting in defence of her sister. The Court of Criminal Appeal made it clear that '[q]uite apart from any special relations between the person attacked and his rescuer, there is a general liberty even as between strangers to prevent a felony' (per Edmund Davies J). However, the Court did identify that the requirement of reasonable and necessary force must be present in the defence of another, like it is for self-defence. See also *R v Hichens* [2011] EWCA Crim 1626 and more recently the case of *Oraki v CPS* [2018] EWHC 115 (Admin), in which the defendant, in acting in defence of his mother, pulled an officer away from her. The defendant's conviction for obstructing a police officer in the performance of his duty contrary to s 89(2) of the Police Act 1996 was quashed by the Divisional Court on the basis that the defendant was acting in reasonable and lawful defence of his mother. See also *Wheeldon v CPS* [2018] EWHC 249 (Admin).

(e) May pre-emptive force be used?

In *Beckford v The Queen* [1988] AC 130, Lord Griffiths notably stated that

> a man about to be attacked does not have to wait for his assailant to strike the first blow or fire the first shot; circumstances may justify a pre-emptive strike.

This statement has the effect that a defendant may use pre-emptive force in circumstances where it is reasonably necessary to do so in self-defence (*R v Deana* (1909) 2 Cr App R 75). The extent to which the defendant may exercise a pre-emptive strike has been considered on a number of occasions by the Court of Appeal. In *R v Cousins* [1982] QB 526, the Court considered it permissible for a defendant to use threats of force, even threats of death, in order to prevent an attack on him. In *Devlin v Armstrong* [1971] NI 13, the Northern Ireland Court of Appeal held that the defence could apply where the defendant uses force to 'ward off or prevent attack'. In *DPP (Jamaica) v Bailey* [1995] 1 Cr App R 257, Lord Slynn summed up the position nicely, stating:

> Self-defence as a concept embraces not only aggressive action such as a pre-emptive strike or aggressive reaction but applies equally to a wholly defensive posture.

The extent to which the defendant may prepare himself to defend against possible threats has also come to be questioned by the courts. Most preparatory acts, for example carrying a knife in anticipation of an attack or turning-in to bed with a baseball bat in hand in anticipation of a burglary, are unlikely to be permitted. However, in *AG's Reference (No 2 of 1983)* [1984] QB 456, the Court of Appeal allowed the defence to apply in circumstances where the defendant armed himself in circumstances where he was preparing for a possible attack. In that case, the defendant, a shop-owner, had armed himself with petrol bombs in anticipation of further attacks from rioters who had damaged his store previously. Lord Lane CJ explained:

> It may be a reasonable excuse that the carrier is in anticipation of imminent attack and is carrying the weapon for his own personal defence. …
>
> In our judgment a defendant is not left in the paradoxical position of being able to justify acts carried out in self-defence but not acts immediately preparatory to it.

(f) What about 'provoked' attacks?

In *R v Rashford* [2005] EWCA Crim 3377, the Court of Appeal considered it appropriate for the defence to exist even in circumstances where the defendant seeks out the victim in order to exact revenge, but the victim then retaliates violently and the defendant believes that the use of pre-emptive force is necessary. However, in these circumstances, clear evidence is needed to prove that the defendant actually acted in pre-emptive defence and did not intentionally provoke the victim so as to retaliate and benefit from the defence (*R v Harvey* [2009] EWCA Crim 469 – the Court phrased it as the tables having been turned on the defendant).

The issue was addressed once more by the Court of Appeal in *R v Keane; R v McGrath* [2010] EWCA Crim 2514. The defendant in *Keane* believed that he was about to be punched by the victim, following an argument between the pair. The defendant claimed that he saw the victim begin to take his hand out of his pocket; the defendant punched the victim in a pre-emptive strike. The victim fell back, struck his head and suffered serious injury. Appealing against his conviction for s 20 GBH, Keane argued that he was acting in self-defence. Hughes LJ explained the situation of provoked attacks as follows:

> [S]elf-defence may arise in the case of an original aggressor but only where the violence offered by the victim was so out of proportion to what the original aggressor did that in effect the roles were reversed. …
>
> [I]t is not enough to bring self-defence into issue that a Defendant who started the fight is at some point during the fight for the time being getting the worst of it, merely because the victim is defending himself reasonably. In that event there has been no disproportionate act by the victim of the kind that Lord Hope is contemplating. The victim has not been turned into the aggressor. The tables have not been turned in that particular sense. The roles have not been reversed. …
>
> [I]t is not the law that if a Defendant sets out to provoke another to punch him and succeeds, the Defendant is then entitled to punch the other person. What that would do would be to legalise the common coin of the bully who confronts his victim with taunts which are deliberately designed to provide an excuse to hit him.

In *Marsh v DPP* [2015] EWHC 1022 (Admin), Sir Stephen Silber emphasised that the focus in these cases is not on 'who started it' (ie who the initial aggressor was) but rather on the act itself and whether it was done in self-defence.

(g) Can D rely on a mistaken belief as to the need to use force?

Section 76(4) of the CJIA 2008 has the effect of restating the common law principles relating to mistaken beliefs for the necessity of force. Section 76(4) provides:

> If D claims to have held a particular belief as regards the existence of any circumstances—
>
> (a) the reasonableness or otherwise of that belief is relevant to the question whether D genuinely held it; but
> (b) if it is determined that D did genuinely hold it, D is entitled to rely on it for the purposes of subsection (3), whether or not—
> (i) it was mistaken, or
> (ii) (if it was mistaken) the mistake was a reasonable one to have made.

In essence, provided that the defendant's belief was genuinely held, it is irrelevant whether that belief was mistaken or unreasonable. This was the approach adopted in the leading authority of *R v Williams (Gladstone)* [1987] 3 All ER 411.

case example

Charge:
ABH (OAPA 1861, s 47)

Case progression:
Crown Court – Guilty

Court of Appeal – Conviction quashed

Point of law:
Relevance of reasonableness in the belief

In *R v Williams (Gladstone)* [1987] 3 All ER 411, the defendant punched the victim whom he witnessed wrestle a youth to the ground and twist his arm behind his back. Unbeknownst to the defendant, the victim had done so in apprehension of the youth who had stolen a lady's handbag. The defendant was charged with and convicted of assault occasioning ABH in the Crown Court, after the trial judge directed the jury that a mistaken belief was only relevant if it was both genuinely and reasonably held.

The defendant appealed to the Court of Appeal on the basis that although his use of force in the defence of another was a mistaken use, that mistake should not have precluded him from being able to rely on a defence. In addition, the defendant argued that the judge had misdirected the jury. The Court of Appeal agreed, ruling that a mistaken belief will not prevent the defence from arising as long as the defendant's belief in the necessity to use force was honestly held.

Lord Lane CJ asked a pivotal question in dealing with the appeal:

> [D]oes it make any difference if the mistake of the defendant was one which, viewed objectively by a reasonable onlooker, was an unreasonable mistake? In other words should the jury be directed as follows: 'Even if the defendant may have genuinely believed that what he was doing to the victim was either with the victim's consent or in reasonable self-defence or to prevent the commission of crime, as the case may be, nevertheless if you, the jury, come to the conclusion that the mistaken belief was unreasonable, that is to say that the defendant as a reasonable man should have realised his mistake, then you should convict him.

His Lordship answered the question as follows:

> The reasonableness or unreasonableness of the defendant's belief is material to the question of whether the belief was held by the defendant at all. If the belief was in fact held, its unreasonableness, so far as guilt or innocence is concerned, is neither here nor there. It is irrelevant. Were it otherwise, the defendant would be convicted because he was negligent in failing to recognise that the victim was not consenting or that a crime was not being committed and so on.

His Lordship concluded:

> In a case of self-defence, where self-defence or the prevention of crime is concerned, if the jury come to the conclusion that the defendant believed, or may have believed, that he was being attacked or that a crime was being committed, and that force was necessary to protect himself or to prevent the crime, then the prosecution have not proved their case. If, however, the defendant's alleged belief was mistaken and if the mistake was an unreasonable one, that may be a powerful reason for coming to the conclusion that the belief was not honestly held and should be rejected.
>
> Even if the jury come to the conclusion that the mistake was an unreasonable one, if the defendant may genuinely have been labouring under it, he is entitled to rely on it.

The position in *Williams (Gladstone)* has been reaffirmed by the Court of Appeal on a number of occasions; see for example *R v Yaman* [2012] EWCA Crim 1075 and *R v Morris* [2013] EWCA Crim 436 (in both cases, the trial judge directed the jury to consider whether the mistake was a reasonable one; the Court of Appeal identifying this as a misdirection).

In practice

Whilst the reasonableness of the defendant's mistaken belief is not the relevant test to be applied, whether the mistake was a reasonable one to make will assist the jury in understanding whether the mistake was genuinely held. In this regard, should the mistake be entirely unreasonable, the jury may consider that the defendant could not have possibly held a genuine belief in that mistake. Likewise, should the mistaken belief be a reasonable one, the jury may be more persuaded that it was genuinely held by the defendant. Lord Lane CJ in *Williams* was clear on this front, and s 76(4)(a) emphasises this point also.

The position is different, however, where the defendant's mistake is induced by intoxication.

(h) Can D rely on an intoxicated mistaken belief as to the need to use force?

Where the defendant was voluntarily intoxicated and his mistaken belief in the need for force was induced by (or 'attributable to') such intoxication, the defence will be unavailable. This is the position according to s 76(5) of the CJIA 2008 and reflects the common law principle laid down by the Court of Appeal in *R v O'Grady* [1987] QB 995.

case example

Charge:
Manslaughter

Case progression:
Crown Court – Guilty

Court of Appeal – Conviction upheld

In *R v O'Grady* [1987] QB 995, the defendant hit his friend with a piece of glass after falling asleep as a result of heavy intoxication. The defendant claimed that he had been awoken by his friend who was hitting him, so in defence of himself he struck back. The victim died and the defendant was charged with manslaughter in the Crown Court. Dismissing his appeal on the basis that the defendant's mistake as to the need for force was self-induced, Lord Lane CJ ruled:

> ... where the defendant might have been labouring under a mistake as to the facts he must be judged according to that mistaken view, whether the mistake was reasonable or not. It is then for the jury to decide whether the defendant's reaction to the threat, real or imaginary, was a reasonable one. The court was not in [*Williams (Gladstone)*] considering what the situation might be where the mistake was due to voluntary intoxication by alcohol or some other drug.

His Lordship concluded:

> ... where the jury are satisfied that the defendant was mistaken in his belief that any force or the force which he in fact used was necessary to defend himself and are further satisfied that the mistake was caused by voluntarily induced intoxication, the defence must fail.

This approach was confirmed as correct by the Court of Appeal in *R v O'Connor* [1991] Crim LR 135, *R v Hatton* [2005] EWCA Crim 2951 and *R v Morris* [2013] EWCA Crim 436. In *Hatton*, the Court of Appeal ruled that the principle in *O'Grady* applies equally to basic and specific intent offences. The Court of Appeal was recently confronted with the task of considering the meaning of the phrase 'attributable to intoxication' in s 76(5) in *R v Taj* [2018] EWCA Crim 1743.

case example

Charge:
Attempted murder (CAA 1981, s 1)

Case progression:
Crown Court – Guilty

Court of Appeal – Conviction upheld

Point of law:
Meaning of 'attributable to intoxication'

In *R v Taj* [2018] EWCA Crim 1743, the defendant attacked the victim with a tyre lever, mistakenly believing him to be a terrorist. At trial, expert evidence from both the prosecution and defence agreed that the appellant suffered from 'drug induced psychosis and was suffering from a drug or alcohol induced psychotic disorder at the time of the offence'. There was no evidence, however, that the defendant had consumed drink or drug on the day in question, such to say that he was 'intoxicated'. Both experts did, however, note that the previous use of drugs and alcohol, on days leading up to the event, 'could induce a condition very similar to psychosis and that the effects could last for weeks'. The defendant was charged with and convicted of attempted murder in the Crown Court after the trial judge rejected the existence of self-defence on the basis that the defence was excluded by operation of s 76(5).

The defendant appealed to the Court of Appeal on the basis that the defence could not be excluded by s 76(5) given that he was not intoxicated at the time of committing the offence. The Court of Appeal disagreed and upheld his conviction.

Sir Brian Leveson P concluded that the defence was not available to those persons whose mistake is *attributable* to the effects of intoxication, even if the individual is not actually intoxicated at the time of the offence. In particular, his Lordship noted:

> The point is that a defendant who is suffering the immediate effects of alcohol or drugs in the system is, in truth, not in a different position to a defendant who has triggered or precipitated an immediate psychotic illness as a consequence of proximate ingestion of or drugs in the system whether or not they remain present at the time of the offence.

His Lordship identified this reasoning as 'an application of *Majewski*, rather than an extension of that decision or, at the highest, a most incremental extension'. The real crux of the Court's decision is as follows:

> In our view, the words 'attributable to intoxication' in s. 76(5) are broad enough to encompass both (a) a mistaken state of mind as a result of being drunk or intoxicated at the time and (b) a mistaken state of mind *immediately and proximately consequent upon earlier drink or drug-taking*, so that even though the person concerned is not drunk or intoxicated at the time, the short-term effects can be shown to have triggered subsequent episodes of e.g. paranoia. This is consistent with common law principles. … In the circumstances, we agree with Judge Dodgson, that the phrase 'attributable to intoxication' is not confined to cases in which alcohol or drugs are still present in a defendant's system. (emphasis added)

In summary, *Taj* is authority for the proposition that self-defence is not available where the mistaken belief in force is attributable, not only to the immediate effects of intoxication at that time, but also to the lasting effects of intoxication that are 'immediate and proximate' to the mistake. Importantly, Sir Brian was cautious to note that this decision 'does not extend to long term mental illness precipitated (perhaps over a considerable period) by alcohol or drug misuse'. As such, so long as the belief is genuinely held, if that mistake is caused by a mental illness arising from alcohol or drug abuse, the defence is still available.

(i) Is there a duty to retreat?

It has long been the common law principle that there is no requirement that the defendant should retreat if he has the ability to (*Duffy v Chief Constable of Cleveland Police* [2007] EWHC 3169 (Admin)). This principle is evident in such early cases as *R v McInnes* [1971] 1 WLR 1600 and *R v Bird* [1985] 2 All ER 513.

case example

Charge:
Malicious wounding (OAPA 1861, s 20)

Case progression:
Crown Court – Guilty

Court of Appeal – Conviction quashed

Point of law:
Whether the defendant is under a duty to retreat

In *R v Bird* [1985] 2 All ER 513, the defendant hit her ex-boyfriend in the face with a glass causing him to lose an eye. The defendant argued that she had been acting in self-defence after the pair had engaged in an argument and the victim had held her up against a wall. The defendant was charged with and convicted of malicious wounding in the Crown Court. The trial judge had directed the jury that, in order for the defence to be available, the defendant would have had to demonstrate an unwillingness to fight (ie, there was a duty to retreat on her part).

The defendant appealed to the Court of Appeal on the basis that the learned judge had misdirected the jury in regard to the duty to retreat. The Court of Appeal agreed, finding that there was no duty, on the part of the defendant, to retreat prior to the use of force.

The Court of Appeal in *McInnes* was of the view that although no duty to retreat existed, proof that the defendant either attempted to retreat or was unwilling to use force would be strong evidence in support of the proposition that the force was reasonably necessary in the circumstances. These decisions have been reiterated by s 76(6A) of the CJIA 2008, which provides:

> In deciding the question mentioned in subsection (3), a possibility that D could have retreated is to be considered (so far as relevant) as a factor to be taken into account, rather than as giving rise to a duty to retreat.

The effect of this provision, added to the 2008 Act by s 148 of the Legal Aid, Sentencing and Punishment of Offenders Act 2012, is clear – whether the accused did retreat is only one factor for the jury to consider on the question of whether the force was reasonably necessary in the circumstances (*R v Field* [1972] Crim LR 435). The section does not give rise to a duty to retreat but would seem to suggest that the defendant may be in a better position should there be evidence showing an attempt to retreat or an unwillingness to use force (*R v Bird*). Indeed, recently, the Administrative Court in *R (Aznanag) v CPS* [2015] EWHC 3017 (Admin) confirmed that although no duty to retreat exists, the defendant is still not entitled to rely on the defence where the only 'sensible option' would have been for the defendant, in those circumstances, 'to take a step backwards and walk away' (per Ouseley J). This merely reaffirms the principle that the force must be *necessary*. Indeed, in *R v Julien* [1969] 1 WLR 839, Widgery LJ explained that:

> It is not, as we understand it, the law that a person threatened must take to his heels and run … but what is necessary is that he should demonstrate by his actions that he does not want to fight. He must demonstrate that he is prepared to temporise and disengage and perhaps to make some physical withdrawal.

In that regard, if there is an ability to retreat, this may be a factor in determining whether force was actually necessary in the circumstances.

7.8.2.2 Element (ii): response

Once the jury are satisfied that a trigger existed (ie that there was a necessity to use force), they are then tasked to consider whether the defendant's reaction to the trigger was proportionate in the circumstances. Another way of explaining this is that the second limb of *Palmer* requires the jury to consider whether the degree of force used by the defendant was reasonable in the circumstances. Unlike the first element, the second limb of *Palmer* is an objective question. Although an objective test in nature, the response requirement does contain an element of subjectivity in that the jury must assess the reasonableness of the defendant's force on the facts and circumstances as the defendant believed them to be (*R v Owino* [1996] 2 Cr App R 128, per Collins J).

This common law position is now restated in s 76(3) of the CJIA 2008, which provides:

> The question whether the degree of force used by D was reasonable in the circumstances is to be decided by reference to the circumstances as D believed them to be, and subsections (4) to (8) also apply in connection with deciding that question.

In this respect, the jury are asked to 'put themselves' in the defendant's position and ask whether they would have acted in the same way. If they would, the defendant's force will be reasonable. If they would not, the defendant's conduct will not be reasonable. There are some key questions which need to be identified to fully understand this element of the defence. Note that the terms 'reasonable' and 'proportionate' in this context are interchangeable.

(a) What is the meaning of 'reasonable force'?

Section 76(6) of the CJIA 2008 provides:

> In a case other than a householder case, the degree of force used by D is not to be regarded as having been reasonable in the circumstances as D believed them to be if it was disproportionate in those circumstances.

This is a question for the jury alone as a matter of fact. Section 76(10)(c) explains that 'references to the degree of force used are to the type and amount of force used'. As a result, in deciding whether force is reasonable, the jury are to consider the situation faced by the defendant, the type of force used by the defendant and the amount of that force used. In *R v Whyte* [1987] 3 All ER 416, Lord Lane CJ in the Court of Appeal provided some guidance as to the circumstances that a defendant may be faced with. In particular, his Lordship stated:

> A man who is attacked may defend himself, but may only do what is reasonably necessary to effect such a defence. Simply avoiding action may be enough if circumstances permit. What is reasonable will depend on the nature of the attack. If there is a relatively minor attack, it is not reasonable to use a degree of force which is wholly out of proportion to the demands of the situation. But if the moment is one of crisis for someone who is in imminent danger, it may be necessary to take instant action to avert that danger.

The last point made by Lord Lane CJ is often referred to as the 'heat of the moment' and is relevant in circumstances where the defendant is faced with a situation in which he has little time to consider how he may respond.

(b) What does it mean to say that D acts 'in the heat of the moment'?

Lord Morris in *Palmer v The Queen* [1971] AC 814 was of the view that:

> If a jury thought that in a moment of unexpected anguish a person attacked had only done what he honestly and instinctively thought was necessary that would be most potent evidence that only reasonable defensive action had been taken.

In this respect, Lord Morris would go on to emphasise that in the heat of the moment, the defendant will not be expected to 'weigh to a nicety the exact measure of his necessary defensive action'. This phrasing found its way into the CJIA 2008 by s 76(7), which concerns the considerations that may be taken into account when deciding whether the force is reasonable in the circumstances. Section 76(7) provides:

> In deciding the question mentioned in subsection (3) the following considerations are to be taken into account (so far as relevant in the circumstances of the case)—
>
> (a) that a person acting for a legitimate purpose may not be able to weigh to a nicety the exact measure of any necessary action; and
>
> (b) that evidence of a person's having only done what the person honestly and instinctively thought was necessary for a legitimate purpose constitutes strong evidence that only reasonable action was taken by that person for that purpose.

'Legitimate purpose' is defined in s 76(10)(a) as meaning (i) self-defence, (ia) defence of property, and (ii) prevention of crime. Reference to not being able to weigh up the nicety of the situation means that the jury are required to consider the defendant as he was in the heat of the moment; they are not to apply reasonableness through hindsight. Section 76(7)(b) is designed to strengthen the need to focus on the heat of the moment, and essentially provides that if the defendant has done what he believed was necessary in the circumstances, that is evidence that the amount of force used was reasonable.

Section 76(7) is not an exhaustive statement as to what factors or considerations may be taken into account. Other considerations, which are relevant to determining the question of necessary and reasonable force, may also be considered (CJIA 2008, s 76(8)). These other considerations are set out below.

(c) When is force considered as being 'excessive'?

In order to decide whether force is reasonable in the circumstances, it is useful to understand the common law position regarding excessive force. As explained above, force is to be considered unreasonable if it is 'disproportionate' (CJIA 2008, s 76(6)). In this respect, the starting point will be that where the force used is excessive, it will be considered disproportionate and the defendant will not be entitled to rely on a defence.

Two starting points may be expressed at this stage to assist:

- The greater the degree of risk or harm faced by the defendant (as the defendant believed the situation to be), the greater degree of force he may use to defend himself.
- The lower the degree of risk or harm faced by the defendant (as the defendant believed the situation to be), the lower degree of force he may use to defend himself.

In any event, if the force used by the defendant is excessive, the defendant will not be able to rely on a defence. The extent to which force may be excessive/disproportionate can be seen in the leading case of *R v Clegg* [1995] 1 AC 482.

case example

Charge:
Murder

Case progression:
Crown Court – Guilty

Court of Appeal – Conviction upheld

House of Lords – Conviction upheld

Point of law:
Meaning of excessive force

In *R v Clegg* [1995] 1 AC 482, the defendant (a British soldier) was on patrol at a checkpoint in Northern Ireland. The defendant fired four shots at a car that was travelling at speed towards the checkpoint being guarded. The first three shots were fired as the car approached the checkpoint and the last shot, the fatal one, was fired after the car had passed the checkpoint. The victim was the passenger in the car. The defendant was charged with and convicted of murder in the Crown Court.

The defendant appealed to the Court of Appeal on the basis that he had acted in self-defence. The Court of Appeal disagreed, ruling his force to be excessive, and, on appeal, the House of Lords agreed. Their Lordships considered that the first three shots fired (as the car was approaching the checkpoint) were done in self-defence as the victim still posed a threat to the defendant. However, upon firing the final shot, the car had already passed the defendant, meaning that the danger had also passed the defendant. In this respect, the fourth shot fired was not in self-defence. The defence thus failed in its entirety and the defendant remained guilty of murder.

The concept of danger 'passing' the defendant appeared in the judgment of Lord Judge CJ in *R v Hussain* [2010] EWCA Crim 94. Having chased down a burglar and attacked him, the defendants were charged with causing GBH with intent. Dismissing their appeals, Lord Judge CJ remarked that '[t]he burglary was over. No one was in any danger. The purpose of the Appellants' violence was revenge.'

example

Late at night, Jack attacks Jill from behind, attempting to steal her handbag. Jill knocks Jack to the floor with her handbag. Whilst Jack is unconscious on the floor, showing no sign of movement, Jill continues to strike him with her handbag.

In this example, the danger can be said to have passed in that Jill is no longer in danger and has the ability to seek help or run away. Jill's continued attack on Jack, in circumstances where he showed no sign of posing a threat, may be treated as excessive force by the jury. However, the jury would have to view Jill's conduct from her standpoint.

A classic pronouncement of excessive force arose in the notorious case of *R v Martin (Anthony)* [2003] QB 1.

case example

Charge:
Murder

Case progression:
Crown Court – Guilty

Court of Appeal – Conviction quashed and replaced with manslaughter

Point of law:
Meaning of excessive force

In *R v Martin (Anthony)* [2003] QB 1, the defendant, a Norfolk farmer, had been the victim of burglary at his farm on a number of occasions previously. On the night in question, the victims had broken into the defendant's home whereby the defendant had armed himself with a shotgun. The defendant seriously wounded one of the victims whilst killing the other. The defendant was charged with and convicted of murder and wounding with intent in the Crown Court.

In the Court of Appeal, the defendant argued that he was acting at all times in self-defence. The Court of Appeal drew attention to the fact that the victims had both been shot in the back by the defendant as they attempted to run away. The defendant's force was considered excessive and no defence was capable of arising on the facts.

Note that the defence of diminished responsibility was held to be available to the defendant on the charge of murder, and his conviction was subsequently quashed and replaced with one of manslaughter.

(d) What factors can be taken into account when considering whether force used was 'reasonable' in the circumstances?

Section 76(8) provides that 'other matters' may be taken into account where they are relevant in deciding whether force was reasonable in the circumstances. The issue arising here is what 'other matters' are relevant:

- Are the defendant's physical characteristics (eg age, frailty) capable of being taken into account?
- Are the defendant's psychological characteristics (eg mental health issues) capable of being taken into account?

In *R v Martin* [2003] QB 1, the defendant adduced fresh evidence on appeal that he had been suffering from a paranoid personality disorder. The defence contended that such a disorder meant that the defendant perceived a much greater threat to himself than the ordinary person would have. The Court of Appeal was tasked with considering, therefore, whether a psychiatric condition such as this could be taken into account when considering the objective test of reasonableness. The Court of Appeal rejected this evidence, ruling that it should not be taken into account when considering the reasonableness of the defendant's force. Lord Woolf CJ explained:

> We would accept that the jury are entitled to take into account in relation to self-defence the physical characteristics of the defendant. However, we would not agree that it is appropriate, *except in exceptional circumstances* which would make the evidence *especially probative*, in deciding whether excessive force has been used to take into account whether the defendant is suffering from some psychiatric condition. (emphasis added)

Lord Woolf CJ was clear, therefore, that physical characteristics are relevant and can be taken into account when considering the objective test. On the other hand, psychiatric conditions are generally not relevant. However, Lord Woolf CJ did provide that such evidence could be relevant in 'exceptional circumstances' which would make the evidence 'especially probative'. This raises the question of what will count as 'exceptional circumstances' making such evidence 'especially probative'. In *R v Oye* [2013] EWCA Crim 1725 (where the defendant suffered from insane delusions that spirits of an evil nature were intent on harming him), the Court of Appeal struggled to identify the circumstances, even exceptionally, where a psychiatric condition could be relevant to the question of excessive force. Indeed, Davis LJ explained:

> Quite what Lord Woolf had in mind in his reference to 'exceptional circumstances' is unexplained. But at all events if *Martin* was not considered an exceptional case then we do not see how or why the present case should be.

Although psychiatric conditions may be relevant to whether the defendant held the necessary belief that force was required (ie the trigger requirement), Davis LJ commented that '[a]n insane person cannot set the standards of reasonableness as to the degree of force used by reference to his own insanity' (in this regard, it is not relevant to the response requirement). Further to this, the Court found it difficult to even suggest when such circumstances ought to be relevant on public policy grounds. Davis LJ concluded that if the law were different '[i]t could mean that the public is exposed to possible further violence from an individual with a propensity for suffering insane delusions'.

Indeed this was the earlier view of the Court of Appeal in *R v Canns* [2005] EWCA Crim 2264, in which it was stated that the Court found it

> impossible to identify the sort of exceptional circumstances in which it would be appropriate to take a psychiatric condition from which a defendant is suffering into account, when addressing the question of whether excessive force is used. (per Rose LJ)

Some guidance was found in the case of *R v Press and Thompson* [2013] EWCA Crim 1849 in which the defendant submitted evidence of post-traumatic stress, arising as a result of his military service in Afghanistan, which had the effect of causing the defendant to react over-sensitively to perceived threats. The trial judge had invited the jury to consider this evidence in determining whether the force was reasonable in the circumstances as the defendant believed them to be. Although the jury convicted the defendant, and the Court of Appeal upheld his conviction, the Court was quick to note that the learned trial judge was right to have left the psychiatric condition to the jury's consideration. Pitchford LJ ruled:

> A person suffering from a post-traumatic stress disorder may, by reason of its effects, hold such a belief when a reasonable person would not. ... a belief honestly held by the Defendant that he did only what was necessary in self-defence is to be treated as 'strong evidence' that the degree of force used was reasonable, but it is not conclusive evidence. The ultimate decision is entirely objective: was the force used proportionate (and therefore reasonable) in the circumstances as the Defendant believed them to be? It seems to us that the facts of the present case provide a useful example of circumstances in which the objective test was likely to resolve the ultimate question. Even if Thompson genuinely believed himself to be under threat ... the jury could assess for themselves ... whether Thompson, even upon his understanding, had gone grossly beyond what was reasonable in the circumstances.

In effect, Pitchford LJ ruled that, in resolving the questions of reasonableness, the jury could take account of the defendant's psychiatric condition when considering whether the defendant did only what he believed was necessary in the circumstances (s 76(7)(b)). This belief was merely 'strong evidence' from which the jury could consider whether his actions were therefore reasonable in the circumstances.

The law can be expressed as follows:

Table 7.18 Understanding the relevance of the defendant's condition

Trigger	Response
Any physical or psychiatric conditions of the defendant are relevant in considering whether the defendant's belief in the necessity of force was genuinely held.	Whilst physical conditions can be relevant to the question of whether the force used was reasonable in the circumstances, psychiatric conditions are not so relevant. Psychiatric conditions only amount to 'strong evidence' that reasonable action was taken by how those conditions affected D's honest and instructive belief as to what was necessary in the circumstances (s 76(7)(b)).

Recently, the Court of Appeal was faced with the issue of whether the defendant's state of panic was relevant to the question of reasonableness. Although relevant to whether the force was necessary in the circumstances, the panic of the defendant was not necessarily relevant to the reasonableness of his force (*R v Robinson (Gary Lucien)* [2017] EWCA Crim 923). In any event, the jury were sure that the defendant's 'panic' in stabbing a patron in a bar was not in self-defence, and the Court of Appeal did not interfere with this decision.

7.8.2.3 The householder provisions

The CJIA 2008 was significantly amended as a result of s 43 of the Crime and Courts Act (CCA) 2013. This section inserted a new category of self-defence, known as 'householder' cases, into s 76(5A) and (8A)–(8F). The meaning of 'householder' cases is provided for in s 76(8A) as follows:

> For the purposes of this section 'a householder case' is a case where—
> (a) the defence concerned is the common law defence of self-defence,
> (b) the force concerned is force used by D while in or partly in a building, or part of a building, that is a dwelling or is forces accommodation (or is both),
> (c) D is not a trespasser at the time the force is used, and
> (d) at that time D believed V to be in, or entering, the building or part as a trespasser.

We can use s 76(8A) to set out the conditions of the householder defence:

(a) Is D a 'householder'?

Importantly, the legislation refers to a 'householder', as opposed to an 'owner' or 'tenant'. In that respect, the defence is not strictly limited in its application. It would appear that any person who is residing at the property (whether permanently or temporarily) may be a householder (eg a friend who is having a 'sleep over' may be considered a householder for the purposes of this provision).

(b) Is force used in a 'dwelling'?

The force used must be 'in or partly in a building, or part of a building, that is a dwelling'. We need to break this criterion down into separate considerations:

- Force must be used in a 'building'. A building is defined in s 76(8F) as including 'a vehicle or vessel', meaning that people who live in caravans or houseboats can benefit from the householder provisions.
- 'Dwelling' is not defined in the statute, but must be understood as a place of residence.
- The phrase 'in or partly in' a building is used to protect householders who are confronted by an intruder at the threshold to their home, for example where the intruder is climbing in through a window or is at the doorstep of the house. This provision, however, is not capable of protecting those householders who use force wholly outside the building, for example in the garden.
- Section 76(8B) extends the operation of the householder defence to parts of a building which are used as a place of work for the defendant or another person, so long as the defendant dwells in another part of the building and the place of work is internally accessible from the part containing the dwelling. The provision has the effect of affording protection to shop keepers or pub owners who live above the shop or pub.

- Section 76(8C) makes similar provision for armed forces accommodation.

(c) Is forced used in self-defence or defence of another?

The statute makes specific reference to the common law defence of self-defence. As discussed above, the common law defence of self-defence includes the defence of oneself or others. This would provide strong reason to believe that the householder is not permitted to rely on their tailored-made provision in cases of defence of property (indeed, this is the view taken by the Crown Court Compendium – section 18-1(12)). Where the defendant is considered as defending his property, the ordinary principles of self-defence in s 76(6) apply.

(d) Was D a trespasser?

The defendant (ie the householder) must not be a trespasser at the time of using force. Section 76(8E) provides that a trespasser does not cease to be a trespasser in circumstances where they have received title or permission from another trespasser. In this respect, squatters cannot rely on the protection afforded in s 76(5A).

(e) Did D believe that V was a 'trespasser'?

The defendant must believe that the victim has entered the property as a trespasser. This belief must be genuinely, though need not be reasonably, held. The belief may also be a mistaken one. In *R v Cheeseman* [2019] EWCA Crim 149, the Court Martial Appeal Court clarified that the victim need not *actually* be a trespasser in order for the defendant to rely on the householder provision; rather, it is the defendant's *belief* that the victim is a trespasser which is the focus. Lord Burnett CJ explained that:

> In most cases where the householder defence is engaged the question whether the defendant believed the person concerned to be in the building as a trespasser will cause no difficulty. That is simply because the defence will most frequently arise in the context of an intruder. In other cases, of which this is an example, it would be unnecessary for a jury ... to wrestle with questions of property law and the niceties of whether someone who started as an invitee became a trespasser. The defence is not directly concerned with the question whether someone was or was not a trespasser but rather the defendant's belief. No doubt, the clearer it is that someone was a trespasser the more readily a jury will not be troubled by the issue whether the defendant did or did not hold the belief.

Further to this, the defence is not restricted to cases in which the householder believed the victim to have originally entered as a trespasser. The defence also includes a belief that the victim *subsequently* became a trespasser, having originally entered the building lawfully. This is in line with the 'trespasser' principles of burglary from *R v Smith; R v Jones* [1976] 1 WLR 672 (see **Chapter 11**).

For a detailed commentary on *Cheeseman*, see Thomas, 'Householders and Self-defence: Understanding a Defendant's Belief that the Victim is a Trespasser' (2019) 83(2) J Crim L 116.

(f) Was force necessary?

The 'trigger' requirement remains untouched by the CCA 2013; however, it introduced a new 'response' approach specific to householder cases.

(g) Was force reasonable?

Section 76(5A) provides:

> The degree of force used by D is not to be regarded as having been reasonable in the circumstances as D believed them to be if it was grossly disproportionate in those circumstances.

The effect of this subsection would appear to be that the householder has a greater degree of latitude in the force used than a non-householder. Indeed, I have argued (Thomas, 'Defenceless Castles: The Use of Grossly Disproportionate Force by Householders in Light of R (Collins) v Secretary of State for Justice' (2016) 80(6) J Crim L 407) that if one takes a literal interpretation of the statute, 'it can be read that householders can use reasonable force, unreasonable force, disproportionate force and excessive force, so long as it is not *grossly* disproportionate force'. One could further this with the argument that if Parliament had intended s 76(5A) to operate in accordance with the common law, it would have said so. This, however, is not the approach taken by the courts. Two major authorities require consideration here.

case example

Charge:
n/a (judicial review)

Case progression:
High Court –
No breach of Article 2

Point of law:
Meaning of 'grossly disproportionate' force

In *R (Collins) v Secretary of State for Justice* [2016] EWHC 33 (Admin), the victim (Denby Collins) entered the home of the defendant. It was unknown why Collins entered the home but he was found to be in possession of some car keys and a mobile phone. The victim was disturbed by the defendant, the householder, who struggled with the victim and forced him into a headlock on the floor. The defendant had held the victim in the headlock for six minutes until the police arrived. Upon arrival, the police noted that the victim was unconscious and not breathing.

The CPS decided not to charge the householder, and the family of the victim sought judicial review proceedings on two grounds:

(1) that s 76(5A) was incompatible with Article 2 of the ECHR; and
(2) that the CPS had erred in its decision not to prosecute the homeowner (though this ground was not proceeded with).

The High Court dismissed the application, finding that s 76(5A) was compatible with the right to life.

Although not required to do so, given that the application did not proceed on these grounds, the President of the Queen's Bench Division (Sir Brian Leveson) took the opportunity to explain the meaning of 'grossly disproportionate' force and how it applies to householder cases. For a full discussion of the judgment of Sir Leveson P, the effects of his judgment and whether the judgment accords with the will of Parliament, see Thomas, 'Defenceless Castles' (above). I will not repeat my own arguments here, so this section simply explains the approach adopted by Sir Brian Leveson P.

Sir Brian Leveson P suggests that s 76(5A) requires two questions to be put before the jury, presuming that the 'trigger' element has already been met. His Lordship phrases the questions as such:

> i) Was the degree of force the defendant used grossly disproportionate in the circumstances as he believed them to be? If the answer is 'yes', he cannot avail himself of self-defence. If 'no', then;
>
> ii) Was the degree of force the defendant used nevertheless reasonable in the circumstances he believed them to be? If it was reasonable, he has a defence. If it was unreasonable, he does not.

His Lordship would explain that a degree of force that went completely over the top *prima facie* would be grossly disproportionate and that it was not the case that 'force in a householder case is only to be regarded as unreasonable if it was grossly disproportionate'.

His Lordship concludes that s 76(5A)

> does not extend the ambit in law of the second limb of self-defence but, properly construed, provides emphasis to the requirement to consider all the circumstances permitting a degree of force to be used on an intruder in householder cases which is reasonable in all the circumstances (whether that degree of force was disproportionate or less than disproportionate). In particular, it does not alter the test to permit, in all circumstances, the use of disproportionate force ... Neither does the provision offend Article 2 of the ECHR.

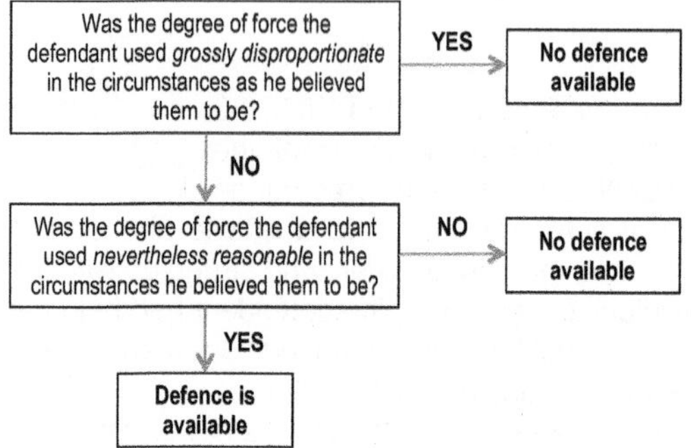

Figure 7.12 Understanding 'grossly disproportionate' force

The view of Sir Brian Leveson P was no doubt unexpected by many. The majority of academic writers, and practitioners, were of the opinion that s 76(5A) operated to grant the householder a greater degree of latitude than their non-householder counterpart. In my contention, however, Sir Brian Leveson P was correct in his interpretation of 'grossly disproportionate' force in light of the will of Parliament. Particularly, Parliament's will can be identified with ease through use of the Ministry of Justice Circular ('Use of Force in Self-defence at Place of Residence' (MoJ London, 2013/02, 2013)). At para 10 of the Circular, it is stated in no uncertain terms that

> The provision does *not* give householders free rein to use disproportionate force in every case they are confronted by an intruder. The new provision must be read in conjunction with the other elements of section 76 of the 2008 Act. The level of force used must still be reasonable in the circumstances as the householder believed them to be (section 76(3)). Section 76(7) says if people only do what they honestly and instinctively thought was necessary for a legitimate purpose, this will be strong evidence that only reasonable action was taken for that purpose. (original emphasis)

This Circular was not referred to or considered in the case of *Collins*, but Sir Brian Leveson P was still able to reach the decision that

> The effect of s. 76(5A) is not to give householders carte blanche in the degree of force they use against intruders in self-defence. A jury must ultimately determine whether the householder's action was reasonable in the circumstances as he believed them to be.

The Circular was, however, relied upon in the more recent case of *R v Ray* [2017] EWCA Crim 1391, in which the Court of Appeal reaffirmed the interpretation of self-defence in householder cases as stated by Sir Brian Leveson P above.

case example

Charge:
Murder

Case progression:
Crown Court – Guilty

Court of Appeal – Conviction upheld

Point of law:
Meaning of 'grossly disproportionate' force

In *R v Ray* [2017] EWCA Crim 1391, the defendant fatally stabbed the victim after a fight broke out between the pair. The victim was the ex-boyfriend of the defendant's girlfriend and was of a violent disposition, especially when intoxicated. On the day in question, the victim forced his way into the home of the defendant and ex-girlfriend. During the altercation between the pair, the defendant stabbed the victim. The defendant was charged with and convicted of murder in the Crown Court.

The defendant appealed to the Court of Appeal on the basis that the interpretation as to s 76(5A) as provided by Sir Brian Leveson P (above) was incorrect. A strong Court of Appeal (5 judges) disagreed, finding that the interpretation of Sir Brian Leveson P was correct. The defendant's conviction was thus upheld.

Lord Thomas CJ provided the sole judgment of the Court of Appeal and gave the following guidance on the operation of the defence:

> 25. In determining the question of whether the degree of force used is reasonable, in a householder case, the effect of s.76 (5A) is that the jury must first determine whether it was grossly disproportionate. If it was, the degree of force was not reasonable and the defence of self-defence is not made out.
>
> 26. If the degree of force was not grossly disproportionate, then the effect of s.76(5A) is that the jury must consider whether that degree of force was reasonable taking into account all the circumstances of the case as the defendant believed them to be. The use of disproportionate force which is short of grossly disproportionate is not, on the wording of the section, of itself necessarily the use of reasonable force. The jury are in such a case, where the defendant is a householder, entitled to form the view, taking into account all the other circumstances (as the defendant believed them to be), that the degree of force used was either reasonable or not reasonable.

Counsel for the appellant in *Ray* had argued that Sir Brian Leveson P's interpretation of s 76 in *Collins* had, in effect, put the position of the householder in the same position as a non-householder, something which Parliament had clearly not intended. The Court of Appeal disagreed with this view, holding that although the introduction of s 76(5A) did not have a 'wide-ranging effect' on the law, the subsection did have a slight effect on the interpretation of the response element. Specifically, the Court reasoned:

> 27. The terms of the 2013 Act have therefore, in a householder case, slightly refined the common law in that a degree of force used that is disproportionate may nevertheless be reasonable.
>
> 28. As subsection (6) makes clear, in a non-householder case the position is different; in such a case the degree of force used is not to be regarded as reasonable if it was disproportionate.

The issue would now appear to be settled – a householder may not use force which is considered to be grossly disproportionate and, in any event, must still use force that is reasonable in the circumstances. As [27] indicates, disproportionate force may nevertheless be considered reasonable in the particular circumstances faced by a householder. In directing the jury as to the application of the householder provision, Lord Thomas CJ concluded:

> It would often be helpful, for that purpose, to spell out the kind of circumstances which the jury should consider in determining whether the degree of force used by a householder was reasonable. These might, for example, include the shock of coming upon an intruder, the time of day, the presence of other help, the desire to protect the home and its occupants, the vulnerability of the occupants, particularly children, or the picking up of an object (such as a knife or stick that would lawfully be to hand in the home), the conduct of the intruder at the time (or on any relevant previous occasion if known to the defendant). Each of these might lead to the view that what was done, such as using a knife, which otherwise in a different context might be unreasonable, in the circumstances of a householder coming on an intruder might, in all the circumstances of such a case, be reasonable.

The editors of *Blackstone's Criminal Practice* (OUP, 2020) suggest that the judgment in *Ray* 'effectively supersedes' the judgment in *Collins*. The editors are of the view that 'reference to [*Ray*] will suffice if a question arises as to the application of the householder provisions'. Whilst this view has practical merit, for academic purposes, *Collins* cannot be disregarded.

7.8.3 Private defence: protection of property

The second form of private defence recognised by s 76(2) of the CJIA 2008 is that of protection of property. This recognition was not contained in the original 2008 Act, but rather was introduced as a result of an amendment in s 148 of the Legal Aid, Sentencing and Punishment of Offenders Act 2012. As a result, the ordinary principles of common law self-defence, ie trigger and response, are applicable here also.

Defence of property has long been considered a defence at common law (see *R v Hussey* (1924) 18 Cr App R 160). Defence of property was not a valid defence to murder in *R v Martin (Anthony)* [2003] QB 1 (though do note that this was because the defendant used excessive force). It was, however, a defence to battery after a householder had forcefully restrained a gas repair man, believing him to be a burglar (*R v Faraj* [2007] EWCA Crim 1033). See also *DPP v Bayer* [2003] EWHC 2567 (Admin). Importantly, the Court of Appeal in *R v Williams* [2020] EWCA Crim 193 emphasised that defence of property does not extend to 'recovery' of property. In that case, the defendant had stabbed the victim after the victim had allegedly stolen an item of jewellery from him a number of minutes prior. Flaux LJ was clear: if the law allowed for the use of force in the recovery of property, and not simply in defence of the property, 'it would be an invitation to chaos'. His Lordship reasoned that: 'If his property was stolen [the defendant] could and should have stayed in the flat and called the police. There was no necessity for him to take a knife out and pursue his alleged robber.'

Defence of one's own property has also been recognised in statute. For example, s 3 of the Criminal Law Act 1967 (see **7.8.4**) provides that a defendant has a defence of using reasonable force in the prevention of crime. As a result, if one uses force to prevent another from stealing one's property (ie a crime), then the defence is available. Further to this, a specific defence of lawful excuse applies under s 5 of the Criminal

Damage Act 1971 (see **Chapter 14**) in circumstances where the defendant damages another person's property in defence of his own.

7.8.4 Public defence: prevention of crime

Prevention of crime is treated as a 'public' defence in the sense that the defendant is acting for the self-preservation of civilised order. The defence is a statutory one contained in s 3 of the CLA 1967, but it relies heavily on common law principles.

In the majority of cases, the provisions of s 3 will come into play given that the lawful use of force will often, but not always, be done for the purpose of preventing crime. In practice, however, judges will rarely make reference to the provisions of s 3 given the application of the common law principles of self-defence (*R v Duffy* [1967] 1 QB 63). Although rarely used in practice, it is still necessary to consider s 3, which provides:

> (1) A person may use such force as is reasonable in the circumstances in the prevention of crime, or in effecting or assisting in the lawful arrest of offenders or suspected offenders or of persons unlawfully at large.
>
> (2) Subsection (1) above shall replace the rules of the common law on the question when force used for a purpose mentioned in the subsection is justified by that purpose.

From this provision, the elements of the defence are outlined in **Table 7.19**.

Table 7.19 Elements of the defence of prevention of crime

Elements of the defence
(i) reasonable force; (ii) in the prevention of crime or effecting lawful arrest.

Note that these requirements effectively reflect the 'trigger' and 'response' requirements of self-defence. Reasonable force is to be considered the response, whilst acting in the prevention of crime is to be considered the trigger. It is important to emphasise that para 534 of the Explanatory Notes to the Criminal Justice and Immigration Act 2008 explains that '[s] 76 retains a single test for self-defence and the prevention of crime (or the making of an arrest) which can be applied in each of these contexts'. The elements have only been broken down in this manner to provide discussion for specific elements of the defence, eg the meaning of crime, lawful arrest etc.

With this in mind, we shall consider each element in turn.

7.8.4.1 Element (i): reasonable force

The first requirement is that the force used must be reasonable in the circumstances. Reference to 'reasonable force' is to be judged according to the common law principles established above in such cases as *Palmer v The Queen* [1971] AC 814 (see **7.8.2**).

The Criminal Law Revision Committee (CLRC) in its 7th Report ('Felonies and Misdemeanours' (Cmnd 2659, 1965)) recommended that reasonable force be understood as taking into account

> all the circumstances, including in particular the nature and degree of force used, the seriousness of the evil to be prevented and the possibility of preventing it by other means.

In effect, the same trigger and response test is to be used in determining the force used by the defendant: (i) was the use of force necessary in the circumstances *in order to prevent a crime or effect lawful arrest*; and (ii) was the use of force reasonable in the circumstances?

What is the requirement of 'force'?

Section 3 is only capable of excusing 'force' used by a defendant in the prevention of crime. The meaning of this phrase was approached by the Divisional Court in *Blake v DPP* [1993] Crim LR 586 (see **Chapter 14**). In *Blake*, the defendant defaced a concrete pillar near the Houses of Parliament with a felt pen in protest against the Iraq war. The defendant, charged with criminal damage, claimed that his act was justified under s 3 in that it was done in the prevention of crime (ie the atrocities that would be committed in the Iraq war). The Divisional Court concluded that such conduct was 'insufficient to amount to the use of force within the section'. A similar conclusion was reached in the case of *R v Bailey (Marcus)* [2013] EWCA Crim 378.

7.8.4.2 Element (ii): prevention of a crime, etc

Section 3 is specific in its application to the prevention of crime or the effecting/ assistance in a lawful arrest.

What is a 'crime'?

In *R v Jones* [2007] 1 AC 136, the House of Lords explained that the word 'crime' referred to any 'domestic crime' (ie crimes of England and Wales) and did not cover such crimes committed under international law (in this case 'crimes of aggression'). In this respect, use of force in the prevention of a theft, robbery or even murder will justify the existence of a defence.

What does it mean to 'prevent' a crime?

Section 3 is specific in that force must be used for the prevention of crime. The meaning of 'in the prevention of' was considered by the Court of Appeal in *R v Attwater* [2011] RTR 173, which concerned a defendant who relied on s 3 when charged with dangerous driving. The defendant claimed that he acted in prevention of crime after he witnessed another driver becoming involved in an accident and failing to stop (an offence under s 170(4) of the Road Traffic Act 1988). The Court of Appeal concluded that the defence is not applicable in circumstances where the crime has already been completed at the time that the force is used. In this respect, where the defendant uses force to prevent someone from escaping after the crime has already been committed (as in *Attwater*), the defence will not be available. This is because the force was not used in the 'prevention' of crime. This statement has most recently been repeated by the Court of Appeal in *R v Williams* [2020] EWCA Crim 193, in which Flaux LJ held, rather simply, that '[t]his defence is only available in relation to *preventing crimes in progress* not in relation to *reacting to crimes* already committed' (emphasis added). See Thomas, '"Temporality": Clarifying the Extent to Which Self-Defence, Defence of Property and Prevention of Crime Operate' (2020) 84(2) J Crim L 176.

example

Jack witnesses Jill committing a robbery against an elderly lady. Jack begins to chase Jill and eventually catches her and uses force in restraining her.

In this example, it cannot be said that Jack has acted in the 'prevention' of crime. The crime (robbery) has already been committed by Jill, and she is presently attempting to escape from the scene of the already committed crime. In this respect, no defence exists on the basis of preventing crime but (as noted below) a defence may exist for effecting a lawful arrest. See *R v Bowden* [2002] EWCA Crim 1279 for a similar example.

The Court of Appeal has stressed, however, that the law should not afford a narrow view as to what it means for a crime to be 'completed'. Often the courts try to find that the crime is ongoing, as a result of the continuing act doctrine. This was evident in the case of *R v Morris (Darryl)* [2014] 1 WLR 16, in which the Court of Appeal explained that the offence of making off without payment (see **Chapter 13**) is often one where it is difficult to establish whether an offence remains in commission or not. In this respect, a liberal view should be taken as to when a crime is considered to have been completed or not. This was evident in *R v Wilkinson* [2018] EWCA Crim 2154 (another case of force used to prevent a making off without payment), in which there was no evidence to support the conclusion that the defendant's conduct (in driving the suspect back to the point at which he picked her up) could have prevented the crime from occurring. In *R v Jackson* [1985] RTR 257, the Court of Appeal considered and left open the question of whether the matter should be left to the jury to determine as a matter of fact whether the offence had been completed.

When is an arrest 'lawful'?

Should the defendant raise the defence on the basis that force was used to effect, or assist, a 'lawful arrest', the jury will often need guidance as to the meaning of such term. This aspect of the defence is likely to be raised in circumstances where the crime has already been completed and it cannot be said that the defendant acted in 'prevention' of the crime.

The relevant civil rules of arrest are contained in the Police and Criminal Evidence Act 1984. Section 24A provides for the power of arrest for non-police officers (commonly referred to as the power of citizen's arrest) and sets out four circumstances in which a citizen may lawfully effect an arrest (see **Table 7.20**).

Table 7.20 The power of citizen's arrest

Section	Circumstance
	A person other than a constable may arrest without a warrant:
s 24A(1)(a)	anyone who is in the act of committing an indictable offence
s 24A(1)(b)	anyone whom he has reasonable grounds for suspecting to be committing an indictable offence
s 24A(2)(a)	anyone who is guilty of the offence (where the offence has already been committed)
s 24A(2)(b)	anyone whom he has reasonable grounds for suspecting to be guilty of it (where the offence has already been committed)

However, an individual is not permitted to exercise a citizen's arrest simply because one of the above conditions is met. Section 24A(3) lays down two further conditions that must be met:

> … the power of summary arrest conferred by subsection (1) or (2) is exercisable only if—
> (a) the person making the arrest has reasonable grounds for believing that for any of the reasons mentioned in subsection (4) it is necessary to arrest the person in question; and
> (b) it appears to the person making the arrest that it is not reasonably practicable for a constable to make it instead.

The 'reasons' referred to in s 24A(3)(a) include the need to prevent the person in question from:

(a) causing physical injury to himself or any other person;
(b) suffering physical injury;
(c) causing loss of or damage to property; or
(d) making off before a constable can assume responsibility for him.

7.8.4.3 Which defence do I use?

As discussed above, both public and private defence operate in a similar manner – both require the existence of a reason to use force (ie the necessity element), both require that any force that is used is reasonable in the circumstances (ie the reasonableness element) and both apply in relation to the protection of persons and property. In most cases, the courts treat s 3 as synonymous with the common law principles enunciated in s 76 of the CJIA 2008, and thus it is unnecessary to consider the specific nature of s 3 and its application to crime prevention (*R v Cousins* [1982] QB 526). In this respect, as Herring (*Criminal Law: Text, Cases, and Materials*, 9th edn (OUP, 2020)) notes, 'courts and commentators usually talk about self-defence or private defence without saying whether they are talking about the statutory or common law version'.

However, a number of examples may be given where s 3 can be used in cases where s 76 is not capable of being used and vice versa. We consider two examples here:

example

Jack is a 9-year-old boy and is acting rather rowdily in the street. He approaches Jill and starts to punch and kick her. Jill, in defending herself, pushes Jack to the floor and injures him.

In this instance, Jill may be liable for an offence of battery (or potentially a more serious offence dependent on the injuries suffered). Jill will not be able to rely on the public defence of prevention of crime given that no crime is taking place – Jack is *doli incapax* and is not capable of committing a criminal wrong. In this respect, Jill will not have the defence of s 3 available to her. However, a defence under s 76 may be available if Jill used such force as was reasonable and necessary in the circumstances to defend herself. A similar outcome would be reached where a defendant is mistaken as to the commission of an offence (see *R v Morris (Darryl)* [2014] 1 WLR 16).

example

Jill catches Jack stealing from the local supermarket. She draws a police officer's attention to this who begins chase on Jack. Unable to restrain Jack on his own, Jill steps in to assist the police officer in placing the handcuffs on Jack.

In this example, Jill may be liable for battery given that she has inflicted unlawful force onto Jack. Jill will be unlikely to be able to rely upon common law private self-defence given that she personally faced no threat. However, in assisting the police officer in effecting the arrest, Jill will be able to rely on the s 3 public defence.

The scope of s 3 was seen in *R (DPP) v Stratford Magistrates Court* [2017] EWHC 1794 (Admin). Here, the Divisional Court was tasked with judicially reviewing the decision of the magistrates' court to acquit protestors who had obstructed lorries which were transporting equipment to a defence and security exhibition. The magistrates had acquitted the defendants, who alleged their actions were designed to prevent the sale or advertisement of illegal weapons or equipment, on the basis of s 3. Simon LJ concluded that the magistrates' court was wrong to acquit the protestors using s 3. His Lordship explained:

> [T]here is no finding that an apprehended crime was imminent and immediate, and no proper basis in the evidence for such a finding.
>
> There was also a lack of clarity as to what crime was being committed and how force (to the extent that it was used) was preventing it. It was effectively common ground that the DSEI exhibition was large and that most of the trade was entirely legal. Importantly in this context, there was no evidence that the vehicles that were being obstructed were involved in anything other than lawful business.

in practice

Although not impossible, it is unlikely that the Crown Prosecution Service (CPS) will seek the prosecution of an individual who has acted in the prevention of crime or to effect a lawful arrest. The CPS may decide, in considering whether to prosecute, that it is not in the 'public interest' to prosecute an individual in such a case. According to the CPS in its 'Legal Guidance on Self-Defence and the Prevention of Crime', prosecutors should have particular regard to:

- the nature of the offence being committed by the victim;
- the degree of excessiveness of the force used by the accused;
- the extent of the injuries, and the loss or damage, sustained by either or both parties to the incident;
- whether the accused was making an honest albeit over zealous attempt to uphold the law rather than taking the law into his/her own hands for the purposes of revenge or retribution.

7.8.5 The use of force and the right to life

As discussed above, so long as the defendant's force is necessary and reasonable in the circumstances, it will be a defence to all crimes, even that of murder. This, however, brings into issue whether the ability to kill another in self-defence is compliant with the European Convention on Human Rights, specifically Article 2 (the right to life).

Article 2(1) provides:

> Everyone's right to life shall be protected by law. No one shall be deprived of his life intentionally save in the execution of a sentence of a court following his conviction of a crime for which this penalty is provided by law.

Article 2(2) does go on to provide a derogation to this right, however. It provides:

> Deprivation of life shall not be regarded as inflicted in contravention of this Article when it results from the use of force which is no more than absolutely necessary:
> (a) in defence of any person from unlawful violence;
> (b) in order to effect a lawful arrest or to prevent the escape of a person lawfully detained;
> (c) in action lawfully taken for the purpose of quelling a riot or insurrection.

The requirement in Article 2(2) is focused on such force that is 'no more than absolutely necessary' in the circumstances. The validity of the law of self-defence was successfully challenged in the case of *McCann and Others v UK* (1995) 21 EHRR 97. In that case, the ECtHR ruled that lethal force may be 'justified under this provision where it is based on an honest belief which is perceived, *for good reasons*, to be valid at the time' (emphasis added). The ECtHR's inclusion of the words 'for good reasons' appears to be in direct conflict with the UK's approach that a belief in the use of force must be honestly held but need not be reasonable. Indeed Leverick ('English Self-defence Law and Article 2' [2002] Crim LR 357) is of the view that English law is incompatible with Article 2. Particularly, she claims that

> in allowing the unreasonably mistaken defendant to escape punishment ... English law fails to respect the right to life of the person who, through no fault of their own, is mistaken for an attacker. An examination of relevant case law leads to the conclusion that the substance of English law does indeed contravene Article 2 ...

This view, and the decision of the ECtHR in *McCann*, is to be contrasted with the view of the ECtHR in *Bubbins v UK* ECHR 50196/99 and the view of JC Smith ('The Use of Force in Public or Private Defence and Article 2' [2002] Crim LR 958). Smith contends that Article 2 is a provision which prohibits intentional killing done for the purpose of killing. Therefore, where an individual acts in self-defence (and not for the purpose of killing), Article 2 is not infringed. This was the view adopted in *Bubbins*.

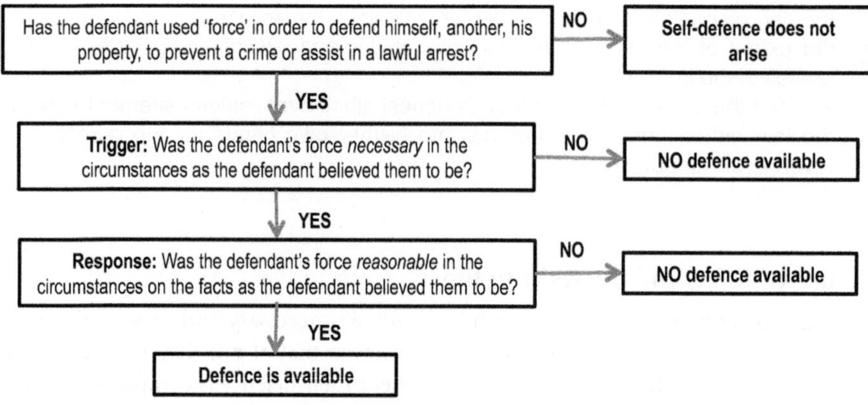

Figure 7.13 Putting together self-defence

7.8.6 Procedural matters and the burden of proof

7.8.6.1 Procedure

Self-defence can be a controversial defence. Given its operation as a complete defence resulting in an absolute acquittal, the CPS is very careful as to the prosecution of offenders pleading such a defence and will give significant attention to any potential media coverage of the process.

7.8.6.2 Burden of proof

In *R v Wheeler* [1967] 3 All ER 829, the Court of Appeal emphasised that self-defence is not a defence

> of which any onus rests upon the accused, but are matters which the prosecution must disprove as an essential part of the prosecution case before a verdict of guilty is justified. (per Wynn LJ)

In this sense, the legal burden of negating the defence rests on the prosecution (*R v O'Brien* [2004] EWCA Crim 2900).

The defendant does, however, bear an evidential burden of proof to raise a *prima facie* case of self-defence, enough that the evidence may go before the jury. This evidence may come from either the prosecution or the defence and the issue must be left to the jury, even in the odd circumstances where the defendant does not rely upon it (*R (Skelton) v CPS* [2017] EWHC 3118 (Admin); *DPP (Jamaica) v Bailey* [1995] 1 Cr App R 257; *R v Lobell* [1957] 1 QB 547). The defence will not go before the jury, however, where the evidence is such that it could be described as 'a mere fanciful and speculative matter' (*R v Johnson* [1994] Crim LR 376). See the most recent illustration of this in *Pegram v DPP* [2019] EWHC 2673 (Admin) and *R v Williams* [2020] EWCA Crim 193 – in both cases, there was insufficient evidence of a defence to justify it being considered by the magistrates (as in *Pegram*) or being left to the jury (as in *Williams*).

7.8.7 Result of a successful plea of self-defence

As discussed above, so long as the defendant's force is necessary and reasonable in the circumstances, it will be a defence to all crimes. A successful defence amounts to a complete acquittal, meaning that the defendant is not liable for any lesser offence. In circumstances where the jury conclude that the defendant's force was not necessary or reasonable, however (eg because it was excessive), no defence will be available to the accused and he will be liable for the offence charged. The defence does not operate to reduce the crime to a lesser offence, eg from murder to manslaughter (*AG's Reference for Northern Ireland (No 1 of 1975)* [1977] AC 105). In this respect, self-defence is an all or nothing defence (*R v Clegg* [1995] 1 AC 482). Note that the Law Commission in its Report, 'Murder, Manslaughter and Infanticide' (Law Com No 304, 2006) recommended that killing through the use of excessive force in self-defence should result in a conviction of second-degree murder for which a discretionary sentence can apply. This proposal has not been acted upon.

7.9 Duress

The penultimate defence in our list is that of duress. Duress has been described by the House of Lords in *R v Howe* [1987] AC 417 as a 'concession to human frailty' (per Lord Griffiths). It is concerned with the circumstances where the defendant commits both the respective *actus reus* and *mens rea* elements of an offence but only does so as a result of threats made by another person (known as 'duress by threats') or in order to avert certain consequences (known as 'duress of circumstances'). In this circumstance, the defendant is not regarded as having acted involuntarily (as Wasik, 'Duress and Criminal Responsibility' [1977] Crim LR 453, has argued); rather, the defendant has acted voluntarily (ie they had a choice as to whether to offend or not) under an extreme pressure of death or serious injury.

This section will appropriately be divided into duress by threats and duress of circumstances. Before doing so, however, it is worth considering the basis for the defence.

7.9.1 Basis for the defence

Duress is a common law defence not defined by statute. It is a complete defence in that it rids the defendant of all liability, and it is a general defence in that it applies to the majority of crimes. However, as shall be examined further below, the defence of duress cannot apply in cases of:

- murder;
- attempted murder; and
- some forms of treason.

This statement applies to both duress by threats and duress of circumstances (*R v Pommell* [1995] 2 Cr App R 607). As noted above, the defence is available where the defendant has conducted himself in a particularly criminal fashion but was forced to act as a result of the threats of another or surrounding circumstances. As Lord Parker CJ explained (reading the judgment of Widgery LJ) in *R v Hudson; R v Taylor* [1971] 2 QB 202:

> duress provides a defence in all offences … if the will of the accused has been overborne by threats of death or serious personal injury so that the commission of the alleged offence was no longer the voluntary act of the accused.

From this quotation, it is important therefore to appreciate that the defence is not concerned with negating the *actus reus* or *mens rea* of the offence in question (like intoxication); nor is it concerned with justifying the defendant's conduct (like self-defence). Rather, Lord Wilberforce in *DPP for Northern Ireland v Lynch* [1975] AC 653 clarified that duress is to be treated as an *excuse* for the defendant's conduct, stating that it is

> something which is superimposed upon the other ingredients which by themselves would make up an offence, i.e., upon act and intention. … the victim completes the act and knows that he is doing so; but the addition of the element of duress *prevents the law from treating* what he has done as a crime. (emphasis added)

This approach was confirmed by the House of Lords in *R v Hasan* [2005] 2 AC 467.

7.9.2 Distinguishing threats from circumstances

There are two types of duress that may apply:

- duress by threats; and
- duress of circumstances.

Consider the following examples:

example

Jack says to Jill, 'Steal Andy's mobile phone or else I will kill you and your family.'

Here, Jack has given an instruction to Jill, and if she does not comply, she faces a threat of death to her and her family; Jill has been mandated to act. If she does so, Jill may have a defence of *duress by threats.*

example

Jill, whilst driving home late a night, is confronted by Jack who attempts to break into her car. Jill manages to drive away but sees that she is being followed by Jack. Jill causes damage to multiple cars in her attempt to escape.

Here, however, Jill has not been given an instruction coupled with a threat should she not complete the task. Rather, Jill has acted in a way she believed was necessary in the circumstances, ie her will has been overtaken by the circumstances before her. If she feared death or serious harm as a result of Jack's conduct, Jill may have a defence of *duress of circumstances.*

This was the distinction made by the Court of Appeal in *R v Willer* (1986) 83 Cr App R 225, where the defendant had damaged property in order to 'escape' the threats of the third party. In that situation, the defence was one of duress of circumstances, not duress by threats. However, in *R v Conway* [1989] QB 290, Woolf LJ did not regard the distinction between the two as being helpful. In discussing duress of circumstance, his Lordship explained: 'What is important is that, whatever it is called, it is subject to the same limitations as to "do this or else" species of duress.'

7.9.3 Duress by threats

Lord Lane CJ in *R v Graham* [1982] 1 All ER 801 provided the test for duress as follows:

> [T]he correct approach on the facts of this case would have been as follows:
>
> (1) was the defendant, or may he have been, impelled to act as he did because, as a result of what he reasonably believed [X] had said or done, he had good cause to fear that if he did not so act [X] would kill him or (if this is to be added) cause him serious physical injury?
>
> (2) if so, have the prosecution made the jury sure that a sober person of reasonable firmness, sharing the characteristics of the defendant, would not have responded to whatever he reasonably believed [X] said or did by taking part in the killing?

Stage (1) is often referred to as the subjective limb, whilst stage (2) is known as the objective limb. This test was approved by their Lordships in *R v Howe* [1987] AC 417 and *R v Hasan* [2005] 2 AC 467. Lord Bingham in *Hasan* helpfully identified the relevant elements of the defence (outlining seven elements in total), which are set out in **Table 7.21**.

Table 7.21 Elements of the defence of duress

Elements of the defence
(i) crime is one where the defence is available. (ii) threat of death or serious injury; (iii) threat is made to the relevant person; (iv) reasonable belief in threat and response; (v) conduct is caused by threat; (vi) threat is immediate (ie no evasive action can be taken); (vii) D has not voluntarily laid himself open to the threat.

You will note immediately that the defence is subject to a significantly high number of conditions and limitations. Lord Simon in *DPP for Northern Ireland v Lynch* [1975] AC 653 has justified the approach of the courts on the basis that the defence may become 'a charter for terrorists, gang-leaders and kidnappers' should the defence become easier to prove. This approach in itself has been criticised on the basis that a narrow interpretation of each element has the effect that the defence is over-restrictive and does not apply in the cases most deserving of it (see Loveless, 'Domestic Violence, Coercion and Duress' [2010] Crim LR 93).

Although we shall consider each element in turn, it is worth noting that the test for duress remains the two conditions expressed by Lord Lane CJ in *R v Graham* [1982] 1 All ER 801. The seven elements we shall consider are merely projections (or 'limitations' as Lord Bingham in *Hasan* stated) into specific aspects of that two-part test.

7.9.3.1 Element (i): crime is one where the defence is available

As noted above, the defence of duress is available to all crimes except:

- murder (whether as a principal or as an accessory);
- attempted murder; and
- treason.

In this respect, duress is technically still a 'general defence', but one which is subject to derogations (*R v Pommell* [1995] 2 Cr App R 607). **Table 7.22** provides some examples of cases where the defence has been available. It is by no means a complete list.

Table 7.22 Offences where duress has acted as a defence

Offence accepting duress	Case authority
Causing GBH with intent	*R v Cairns* [2000] RTR 15
Criminal damage	*R v Crutchley* (1831) 5 C & P 133
Theft	*R v Gill* [1963] 2 All ER 688
Handling stolen goods	*AG v Whelan* [1934] IR 518
Obtaining property by deception	*R v Bowen* [1996] 4 All ER 837
Perjury	*R v Hudson; R v Taylor* [1971] 2 QB 202

It will be useful to consider each 'excluded offence' in detail.

Murder

In *R v Howe* [1987] AC 417, the House of Lords unequivocally held that the defence of duress is not available on a charge of murder (whether the accused be a principal or secondary offender) (relying heavily on *R v Dudley and Stephens* (1884) 14 QBD 273). Lord Griffiths explained that duress is not available to a crime of murder because:

> We face a rising tide of violence and terrorism against which the law must stand firm recognising that its highest duty is to protect the freedom and lives of those that live under it. The sanctity of human life lies at the root of this ideal and I would do nothing to undermine it, be it ever so slight.

This view has most recently been affirmed by the Court of Appeal in *R v Wilson* [2007] EWCA Crim 1251 (also known as *R v W*). This case concerned a 13-year-old boy who murdered his next-door neighbour after complying with instructions from his father whom he was too frightened to disobey. No defence existed for the child, and Lord Phillips CJ took the view that

> There may be grounds for criticising a principle of law that does not afford a 13-year-old boy any defence to a charge of murder on the ground that he was complying with his father's instructions, which he was too frightened to refuse to disobey. But our criminal law holds that a 13-year-old boy is responsible for his actions and the rule that duress provides no defence to a charge of murder applies however susceptible the Defendant may be to the duress, absent always any question of diminished responsibility, and applies whether the Defendant is a principal in the first or the second degree.

To single out murder as an offence for which no defence is available is certainly an anomaly given that the defence is open to other serious offences, including grievous bodily harm and wounding with intent contrary to s 18 of the Offences Against the Person Act 1861. This is especially so given that the *mens rea* for murder includes, alongside the intention to kill, an intention to cause grievous bodily harm (see **Chapter 8**).

example

Jill attacks Jack in the dark after threats made against her and her family by Andy. Jack suffers extreme injury and falls into a coma. Jill is charged with causing GBH with intent.

In this scenario, although it may be difficult to prove, the defence of duress by threats is available to Jill for her actions against Jack. However, should Jack die a few months later from those injuries, the defence will cease to exist.

However, the exclusion has been justified on a number of occasions. According to Lord Hailsham in *R v Howe*, it was not possible to regard

> a law as either 'just' or 'humane' which withdraws the protection of the criminal law from the innocent victim and casts the cloak of protection on the coward and the poltroon in the name of a 'concession to human frailty'.

Lord Hailsham was also of the view that the 'lesser of two evils' argument could not be applied in cases of murder on the basis that it is never the lesser of two evils to take another life. This view accorded with that of Lord Griffiths, who stated that *Dudley and Stephens* was based on 'the special sanctity that the law attached to human life and which denies to a man the right to take an innocent life even at the price of his own or another's life'.

Criticism of the rule has been levied by the likes of Arenson ('The Paradox of Disallowing Duress as a Defence to Murder' (2014) 78 J Crim L 65). Arenson is critical of the courts' 'hypocrisy and sheer folly' in permitting the defence of provocation (and now loss of self-control) to be used by a defendant, but not duress. Arenson contends that those who kill under duress are 'far less morally culpable' than those who kill as a result of a loss of self-control. In its Report, 'Murder, Manslaughter and Infanticide' (Law Com No 304, 2006), the Law Commission recommended that duress should be a defence to murder, especially in cases of young defendants who are less mature than adults, but with the legal burden on the accused. This recommendation has not been acted upon.

Attempted murder

Duress may also not be used as a defence to a charge of attempted murder (*R v Gotts* [1992] 2 AC 412). In *Gotts*, Lord Jauncey explained that he could 'see no justification in logic, morality or law in affording to an attempted murderer the defence which is withheld from a murderer'. Citing Lord Lane CJ from the decision of the Court of Appeal in *Gotts* ([1991] 1 QB 660), Lord Jauncey concluded that 'the fact that the attempt failed to kill should not make any difference'. Despite this statement, it is interesting to note that the defence is available for a charge of conspiracy to murder (*R v Ness and Awan* [2011] Crim LR 645). This latter statement is justified by the likes of Child and Ormerod (*Smith, Hogan, & Ormerod's Essentials of Criminal Law*, 3rd edn (OUP, 2019)) on the basis that 'these offences will never involve the direct application of force to [the victim] as part of their *actus reus*'.

in practice

An issue that is surely to cause confusion and complexity involves the circumstances where the defendant is charged with multiple offences, including offences that are capable of being excused by the defence of duress and offences that are not.

Suppose a defendant (in one act and under duress by threats) kills victim A but only injures victim B.

In this example, the defendant is likely to be liable for two offences – murder (victim A) and GBH (victim B). Given that the two acts happened during the same course of events, it is likely that the defendant would be tried for both offences on the same indictment. Should the defendant wish to plead duress, the jury would hear evidence of duress in relation to the GBH charge but would be expressly told not to consider evidence of duress in their determination of the murder charge. As you can appreciate, this would be a strange and troubling experience for a jury.

In such a case, the prosecution may try to sever the indictment and have the defendant tried separately for each offence or may attempt to charge the defendant with attempted murder against victim B (should the evidence provide for that).

Some offences of treason

Treason is understood to be a collective term for offences committed against the state. There appears to be no guiding principle as to whether duress is available to all crimes of treason or not. Authority in favour of duress being available to a charge of treason has been seen in cases such as *Oldcastle's Case* (1419) 1 Hale PC 50 and *R v Purdy* (1945) 10 JCL 182. However, more recent authority would seem to suggest that the more serious the treason offence, the less likely a defence will be available (see Lord Goddard CJ's comments in *R v Steane* [1947] KB 997). Judges in other cases have reserved their opinion as to whether duress may play a part in treason offences (eg Lord Brandon in *R v Howe* [1987] AC 417); however, the matter appears to remain one to be determined on a case-by-case basis.

7.9.3.2 Element (ii): threat of death or serious injury

The first, and arguably most important, element of the defence is that the threat which is relied upon must be to cause death or serious injury. According to Lord Judge CJ in *R v A* [2012] EWCA Crim 434 (in *obiter*), duress involves

> pressure which arises in extreme circumstances, the threat of death or serious injury, which for the avoidance of any misunderstanding, we have no doubt would also include rape. (note that the case involved a threat of rape against the defendant)

Mere pressure that falls short of death or serious injury, however, is not capable of founding a plea of duress. Lord Judge CJ in *R v A* justified this approach on the basis that 'the circumstances in which different individuals are subject to pressures, or perceive that they are under pressure, are virtually infinite'.

This has been the approach of the courts for a long period of time and has been recently reaffirmed by the Court of Appeal in *R v Dao; R v Nguyen* [2012] EWCA Crim 1717 (in *obiter*). The following can therefore be categorised as falling outside of the scope of the defence:

- threat of false imprisonment (*R v Joseph* [2017] EWCA Crim 36 and *R v Dao* [2012] EWCA Crim 1717, disapproving *R v Steane* [1947] KB 997);
- threat of serious levels of pain (*R v Quayle* [2005] EWCA Crim 1415 – in that case D had been charged with growing cannabis contrary to the Misuse of Drugs Act 1971. His contention that his serious level of pain was a duress of circumstance was rejected);
- threat of serious psychological injury (*R v Baker and Wilkins* [1997] Crim LR 497 – though this decision must now be questioned in light of *R v Ireland; R v Burstow* [1998] AC 147 in which the House of Lords concluded that serious psychological injury can amount to grievous bodily harm (GBH));
- in response to being trafficked (*R v N* [2013] QB 379);
- threats to damage or destroy property (*M'Growther's Case* (1746) 1 East PC 71; *DPP for Northern Ireland v Lynch* [1975] AC 653);
- threats to expose a secret sexual orientation (*Singh (Gurdev) v R* [1974] 1 All ER 26).

Where must the threat emanate?

Importantly, the threat must come from a source external to the defendant. This simply means that the defendant must not be the cause of his own conduct in committing a criminal offence. This point was made by the Court of Appeal in *R v Rodger and Rose* [1998] 1 Cr App R 143 in which the defendants relied on the defence of duress for offences relating to their escape from prison. The defendants contended that due to the poor conditions of prison, they would have committed suicide had they not escaped. Sir Patrick Russell in the Court of Appeal would reject the defence of duress, ruling:

> The feature which was causative of the defendants committing the offence was in all the authorities [cited in the appeal] *extraneous to the offender himself.* In contrast, in these appeals it was solely the suicidal tendencies, the thought

> processes and the emotions of the offenders themselves which operated as duress. That factor introduced an entirely subjective element not present in the authorities. (emphasis added)

This point was affirmed by the Court of Appeal in *R v Shayler* [2001] 1 WLR 2206 in which Lord Woolf CJ referred to the need for 'action by some external agency'. This was confirmed as the position by the Court of Appeal in *R v Quayle* [2005] EWCA Crim 1415.

Must the threat be 'directly relayed' to D?

It is the case that the threat need not be 'directly relayed' to the accused (ie the defendant may come across the threat 'second hand', or have the threat communicated to him by someone other than the duressor). In *R v Brandford* [2016] EWCA Crim 1794, the Court of Appeal disapproved of the trial judge's withdrawal of the defence from the jury on account that the threat was only indirectly relayed to the accused. In particular, the defendant had no first-hand knowledge that her partner had been threatened. Although the Court explained that there is no express requirement for the threat to be directly relayed, it did note that such may be a factor in deciding whether the threat was enough to constitute duress. Gross LJ explained:

> It is very likely that the more directly a threat is conveyed, the more it will be capable of founding a defence of duress: e.g., the telling example of the loaded pistol in the back, given by Lord Simon of Glaisdale in *DPP for Northern Ireland v Lynch* [1975] AC 653 ... Conversely, the more indirectly the threat is relayed the more, all other things being equal, a defendant will struggle to satisfy the requirements of the defence, or (put in burden of proof terms) the more readily the prosecution will disprove it.

Note, however, that the convictions in *Brandford* were upheld on account that there was no immediacy to the threat (ie the defendant had the opportunity to escape, seek protection etc).

7.9.3.3 Element (iii): threat is made to the relevant person

A question that has come before the courts on a number of occasions is whether the threat of death or serious injury has to be directed to the accused or whether threats to third parties, especially close relatives, can suffice. In *R v Ortiz* (1986) 83 Cr App R 173, the Court of Appeal appeared to find that threats to the accused's wife or family are sufficient to found a defence. This approach was confirmed and extended by Lord Bingham in *Hasan* [2005] 2 AC 467, who commented that the threat may also be directed 'if not to the defendant or a member of his immediate family, to a person for whose safety the defendant would reasonably regard himself as responsible'. Lord Bingham would go on to comment that 'if strictly applied [this would be] consistent with the rationale of the duress exception'. A number of examples can be taken from the case law:

- *R v Conway* [1989] QB 290, where the passenger in the defendant's car was threatened.
- *R v Martin* [1989] 1 All ER 652, where the defendant's wife threatened to harm herself.

example

Jack is on the run from the police, after having committed a murder in the street. Jack forces his way into Jill's car and demands that she drives, or else he will randomly kill a group of school children standing at a bus stop.

In this example, Jill may be able to plead the defence of duress by threats on the basis that she may 'reasonably feel responsible' for the lives of the school children given Jack's threats.

The meaning of 'for whose safety the defendant would reasonably regard himself as responsible' is an interesting one. Lord Woolf CJ in *R v Shayler* [2001] 1 WLR 2206 explained that 'the evil must be directed towards the defendant or a person or persons for whom he has responsibility or, we would add, persons for whom the situation makes him responsible'. His Lordship then provides an example:

> by way of example, the situation where the threat is made to set off a bomb unless the defendant performs the unlawful act. The defendant may not have had any previous connection with those who would be injured by the bomb but the threat itself creates the defendant's responsibility for those who will be at risk if he does not give way to the threat.

See also *R v GAC* [2013] EWCA Crim 1472 in respect of a pregnant defendant fearing for the safety of her unborn child.

In *R v Wright* [2000] Crim LR 510, the trial judge took the words in *Hasan* to an extreme in a case involving the defendant and her boyfriend. The judge directed the jury that the defence was only available in cases where the threat was made to the defendant herself or to a 'member of her immediate family'. The judge informed the jury that the defendant's boyfriend did not live with the defendant nor were they married. Kennedy LJ in the Court of Appeal felt that it was

> both unnecessary and undesirable for the judge to trouble the jury with the question of the [the boyfriend's] proximity. Still less to suggest, as he did, that [the boyfriend] was insufficiently proximate.

7.9.3.4 Element (iv): reasonable belief in threat and response

In *R v Graham* [1982] 1 All ER 801, Lord Lane CJ explained that the defendant's conduct must be one which the 'sober person of reasonable firmness' could not have resisted. This focus was approved by the House of Lords in *R v Howe* [1987] AC 417. It will be useful at this stage to break down the constituent parts of the test as laid down by Lane CJ.

Question (i): reasonable belief as to a good cause to fear

The first question, for the most part, is a subjective question, asking what the defendant believed the facts to be to give rise to the fear of death or serious injury. In asking this question, however, the jury must also consider whether (on an objective standard) such a view was reasonably held and provided the defendant with 'good cause' to hold such a fear (*R v Hasan* [2005] 2 AC 467). In this regard, there are two issues that need to be addressed: (i) what did the defendant *subjectively* believe?; (ii) was the defendant's belief *objectively* reasonable?

In considering whether the defendant subjectively believed that he had to perform the act as instructed, the Court of Appeal has explained that the focus is not on whether the threat actually existed *in fact* but, rather, whether the defendant *believed* that such a threat existed. In this respect, the belief held by the defendant may be mistaken, so long as it is reasonable. This was emphasised by the Court of Appeal in *R v Cairns* [2000] RTR 15 and reaffirmed in *R v Nethercott* [2001] EWCA Crim 2535 and *R v Safi* [2003] EWCA Crim 1809. In *Nethercott*, the defendant feared serious harm or death as a result of a previous incident of violence against him by the duressor (ie the duressor had stabbed him a number of months previously). The Court of Appeal ruled that this evidence was sufficient to demonstrate that the defendant subjectively believed that he had a good cause to fear serious harm or death. Any change to this rule, according to the Court of Appeal in *Safi*, would have to be made by Parliament.

As stated above, the first question is subject to two elements of objectivity.

- First, the defendant's belief must be a *reasonable* one. An honest or genuine belief, unlike in the defence of mistake, is not enough; it must also be a reasonably held belief (emphasised recently in *R v CS* [2012] EWCA Crim 389). However, a mistaken belief is permitted so long as it was reasonably held. Lord Bingham in *Hasan* [2005] 2 AC 467 confirmed the requirement of reasonableness, stating:

  > It is of course essential that the defendant should genuinely, ie actually, believe in the efficacy of the threat by which he claims to have been compelled. But there is no warrant for relaxing the requirement that the belief must be reasonable as well as genuine.

- Second, the defendant's belief must have given him 'good cause' to fear death or serious injury. A defendant's belief will lack 'good cause' to fear death or serious harm where such an event is unlikely to occur.

Question (ii): sober person of reasonable firmness

The second question is an objective one, asking whether the ordinary and sober person of 'reasonable firmness' would have submitted to the threat. Although the question is purely objective, the sober and reasonable person is to be considered as 'sharing the characteristics' of the defendant.

In *R v Graham* [1982] 1 All ER 801, Lord Lane CJ reasoned:

> As a matter of public policy, it seems to us essential to limit the defence of duress by means of an objective criterion formulated in terms of reasonableness. Consistency of approach in defences to criminal liability is obviously desirable. Provocation and duress are analogous. In provocation the words or actions of one person break the self-control of another. In duress the words or actions of one person break the will of another. The law requires a defendant to have the self-control reasonably to be expected of the ordinary citizen in his situation. It should likewise require him to have the steadfastness reasonably to be expected of the ordinary citizen in his situation.

The characteristics of the defendant which would be relevant to a determination of the second question are set out in **Table 7.23** (from criteria set out by Stuart-Smith LJ in *R v Bowen* [1996] 4 All ER 837).

Table 7.23 The relevant/irrelevant characteristics of a defendant

Characteristic	Relevant?	Why is this relevant/ irrelevant?
More pliable	No	'The mere fact the defendant is more pliable, vulnerable, timid or susceptible to threats than a normal person is not a characteristic with which it is legitimate to invest the reasonable/ordinary person for the purpose of considering this objective test.'
Age	Yes	'[A] young person may well not be so robust as a mature one'.
Sex	Yes	Women may not have as much 'courage' or firmness as a man – though the Court did, quite rightly, doubt the extent of this: 'though many women would doubtless consider that they had as much moral courage to resist pressure as men'.
Pregnancy	Yes	Those who are pregnant have the 'added fear for the [welfare of their] unborn child'.
Serious physical disability	Yes	A physical disability may 'inhibit self-protection'.
Recognised mental illness	Yes	A mental illness or some other psychiatric condition may have the effect of making people more susceptible to pressure and threats, for example 'post-traumatic stress disorder leading to learned helplessness'.
Characteristics relevant to loss of self-control, but not duress	No	For example, 'homosexuality may be relevant to [loss of self-control] if the provocative words or conduct are related to this characteristic; it cannot be relevant to duress, since there is no reason to think that homosexuals are less robust in resisting threats of the kind that are relevant in duress cases.'
Self-induced characteristics	No	'Characteristics due to self-induced abuse, such as alcohol, drugs or glue-sniffing, cannot be relevant.' Lord Lane CJ agreed with this statement, as was the case in *R v Flatt* [1996] Crim LR 576.

Buchanan and Virgo, 'Duress and Mental Abnormality' [1999] Crim LR 517 are critical of the classifications made in *Bowen*, arguing that the test is 'unworkable'. The pair contend that, practically, there can be no criteria for identifying a group of people whose ability to withstand threats is reduced. A number of cases can be used to demonstrate these relevant characteristics and those characteristics that are not relevant:

- *R v Bowen* [1996] 4 All ER 837: The defendant's low IQ could not be considered a relevant characteristic where it fell short of a mental impairment. The Court of Appeal felt that a lower IQ would not make those persons any 'less courageous and less able to withstand threats and pressure'. See *R v Antar* [2004] EWCA Crim 2708 (below) as to the importance of distinguishing mere low IQ and low IQ which amounts to mental impairment.
- *R v Hegarty* [1994] Crim LR 353: The defendant's 'grossly elevated neurotic state' (ie a high state of anxiety) was not a relevant characteristic despite the possibility that it made him more vulnerable to threats.
- *R v Horne* [1994] Crim LR 584: The defendant's pliable state (ie he was easily agreeable) was not a relevant characteristic to be used in the second question.

In *R v Antar (Kayed Kevin)* [2004] EWCA Crim 2708, the Court of Appeal held that evidence of the defendant's low IQ (being of a sufficient level to be classed as a mental impairment) should have been left to the jury. According to the Court, it is a task for the jury to determine, on all the evidence in front of them, whether the defendant 'fell into a category of persons who were less able to resist pressure than the sober person of reasonable firmness'. The Court of Appeal in *Antar* also accepted post-traumatic stress disorder as a relevant characteristic (see also *R v Sewell* [2004] EWCA Crim 2322). Furthermore, the Court of Appeal in *R v Flatt* [1996] Crim LR 576 held that the use of the word 'sober' in relation to a person of reasonable firmness makes it plain that intoxication, or any other self-induced conditions, cannot be a relevant characteristic.

7.9.3.5 Element (v): conduct is caused by threat

This requirement is simply one of causation – has the threat caused the defendant to commit the crime alleged? This question is essentially whether there is a nexus between the threat and the defence – was the defendant directed to commit a particular crime, eg robbery, theft etc? In this respect, duress is not a concept to be considered in the abstract; the crime must have been selected by the person making the threat. This was evident in the case of *R v Cole* [1994] Crim LR 582.

case example

Charge:
Robbery (TA 1968, s 8)

Case progression:
Crown Court – Guilty

Court of Appeal – Conviction upheld

Point of law:
Requirement for a nexus between the threat and the offence

In *R v Cole* [1994] Crim LR 582, the defendant had been threatened by moneylenders to whom he owed a significant amount of money. The moneylenders threatened the defendant, his girlfriend and his child, demanding return of their money. The defendant proceeded to rob two building societies in order to repay the money. The defendant was charged with and convicted of robbery in the Crown Court.

The defendant appealed to the Court of Appeal, claiming that the defence of duress by threats should have been available to him. The Court of Appeal disagreed, finding that the defendant had not been directed to commit robbery or any other offence. This was merely a case of threatening behaviour and not a case of duress.

The easiest way to understand *Cole* is to appreciate what the defendant was being asked to do by the moneylenders. He was told in no uncertain terms to get them the money; however, that was not a threat or demand to commit a particular offence, or any offence for that matter. The moneylenders demanded return of the money; there was no insistence on how the defendant did so. For example, the moneylenders would have accepted payment that the defendant could borrow from family members, friends or through some other lawful action. Essentially, the defence was not available given the lack of threat as to the commission of a certain crime. For a more recent and interesting application of this rule, see the Canadian case of *R v Ryan* [2013] 1 SCR 14.

The next question that arises is whether the defendant must be charged with the crime that was nominated for him to commit, or whether any nominated crime will suffice, even if it is not the crime charged. The former appears to be the approach taken by Brown LJ in *Cole*. His Lordship would explain:

> In our judgment, it is plain that the defence of duress by threats can only apply when the *offence charged* (the offence which the accused asserts he was constrained to commit) is the very offence which was nominated by the person making the threat, ie when the accused was required by the threat to commit the offence charged ... (emphasis added)

In *R v Ali* [1995] Crim LR 303, the Court of Appeal seemed to indicate that a defence could be available where the crime charged was nominated (robbery) but not with precision (of a particular bank).

Must the threat be the sole cause?

Importantly, the Court of Appeal in *R v Ortiz* (1986) 83 Cr App R 173 held that the requirement that the threat be of death or serious injury is merely the minimum (or 'starting point') for the defence to exist. It is therefore a misdirection to inform the jury that the threat of death or serious injury must be the *sole* cause of the defendant's conduct. This discussion is often referred to as the 'mixed motives' of the defendant.

Such mixed motives were evident in the case of *R v Valderrama-Vega* [1985] Crim LR 220, where the defendant had imported cocaine, alleging that he had done so because of threats made to his life, his need for money due to his severe debts and out of fear that his homosexuality would be revealed to his family. The judge directed the jury that a defence existed only in circumstances where the threats of death (ie the first reason listed above) were the *sole* cause of the defendant's conduct. The Court of Appeal quashed his conviction, finding that the death threats need not be the sole reason for acting, and all three matters, when taken together, were relevant in considering whether the defence was available. In this regard, the cause of action may be cumulative and the jury should simply apply the 'but for' test: but for the threat of death or serious injury, would the defendant have committed the offence?

7.9.3.6 Element (vi): threat is immediate (ie no evasive action can be taken)

It is obvious that a threat made to the defendant must have been operative on the manner in which the defendant acted at the time of the offence. This has been the position since such cases as *R v Hudson; R v Taylor* [1971] 2 QB 202 and has been affirmed by the likes of *R v Abdul-Hussain* [1999] Crim LR 570 and *R v Safi* [2003] EWCA Crim 1809. The immediacy of the threat has been confronted by the courts on a number of occasions, with various approaches taken.

'Imminent' not 'immediate'

In *Abdul-Hussain*, the Court of Appeal ruled that the threat to persons needed to be 'imminent' but not 'immediate'. The distinction was understood as being that 'immediate' meant at the point the threat was capable of being carried out, whereas 'imminent' was explained as follows by Rose LJ:

> The peril must operate on the mind of the defendant at the time when he commits the otherwise criminal act, so as to overbear his will.

In *Hudson*, for example, the defendants were charged with perjury. The pair pleaded duress on the basis that they had been threatened with injury to lie in court. The pair were convicted when the trial judge directed the jury that the defendants could not plead duress because the threat made was not a 'present immediate threat capable of being then and there carried out'. The Court of Appeal allowed their appeals against conviction on the basis that, despite the inability of the threat to be carried out immediately (because the coercer was sat in the public gallery of the courtroom in which there were police officers), the threat could have been carried out later that day, and thus it was not reasonable for the defendants to have escaped the threat. Widgery LJ explained:

> When ... there is no opportunity for delaying tactics and the person threatened must make up his mind whether he is to commit the criminal act or not, the existence at that moment of threats sufficient to destroy his will ought to provide him with a defence even though the threatened injury may not follow instantly but after an interval.

Returning to a requirement of immediacy

This issue was returned to by the House of Lords in *R v Hasan* [2005] 2 AC 467 (for the facts see **7.9.3.7**). The House of Lords in effect overruled the previous decisions, deciding that the defence applied only in cases where the threat was believed by the defendant to be 'immediate' or 'almost immediate'. Lord Bingham, providing the lead judgment, ruled:

> It should however be made clear to juries that if the retribution threatened against the defendant or his family or a person for whom he reasonably feels responsible is not such as he reasonably expects to follow *immediately or almost immediately* on his failure to comply with the threat, there may be little if any room for doubt that he could have taken evasive action, whether by going to the police or in some other way, to avoid committing the crime with which he is charged. (emphasis added)

Lord Bingham would justify his departure from cases such as *Hudson* on the basis that those decisions had 'the unfortunate effect of weakening the requirement that execution of a threat must be reasonably believed to be imminent and immediate if it is to support a plea of duress'. The law is now as stated by Lord Bingham in *Hasan* – the threat must be believed by the defendant to be 'immediate' or 'almost immediate'. This approach has been confirmed as correct by the Court of Appeal in *R v Hammond* [2013] EWCA Crim 2709 and *R v Batchelor* [2013] EWCA Crim 2638, where the Court ruled (in the latter case) that there was no evidence to support that the defendant 'could not reasonably believe that the execution of the threat was imminent and immediate' (per Elias LJ).

It is necessary to understand at this stage when a threat will be immediate or almost immediate. In order to consider this, we need to appreciate the circumstances where the defendant has the opportunity to escape or to seek police protection.

Opportunity to escape/seek police protection

The law expects a defendant to take advantage of any reasonable opportunity that he may have to escape or seek protection from the person exercising the threat (ie the 'duressor'). Where the defendant fails to take such an opportunity, the defence may not be available. This issue was evident in the cases of *R v Gill* [1963] 2 All ER 688 and *R v Pommell* [1995] 2 Cr App R 607. In the former, the defendant was threatened with violence to steal a lorry; however, evidence demonstrated that a significant period of time existed whereby the defendant could have raised the alarm and escaped harm. In the latter case, Kennedy LJ explained that

> in some cases a delay, especially if unexplained, may be such as to make it clear that any duress must have ceased to operate, in which case the judge would be entitled to conclude that ... the defence was not open.

In *R v Hudson; R v Taylor* [1971] 2 QB 202, the prosecution contended that the defendant should have sought police protection after being threatened to lie in court. Widgery LJ in the Court of Appeal rejected this argument, stating that it would

> in effect, restrict the defence of duress to cases where the person threatened had been kept in custody by the maker of the threats, or where the time interval between the making of the threats and the commission of the offence had made recourse to the police impossible.

His Lordship would go on to explain that a number of factors would be relevant in determining whether it was reasonable for the accused to seek an escape route or police protection. His Lordship explained:

> In deciding whether such [an escape] opportunity was reasonably open to the accused the jury should have regard to his age and circumstances, and to any risks to him which may be involved in the course of action relied upon.

As stated above, following *R v Hasan*, the judgment in *R v Hudson; R v Taylor* has to be called into question. Recently, in *R v Batchelor* [2013] EWCA Crim 2638, the Court of Appeal concluded that the defendant had many opportunities in which he could have approached the police, explaining that the defendant had a period of two-and-a-half years in which he could have done so. In *Batchelor*, Elias LJ also cited disapproval of *Hudson*.

7.9.3.7 Element (vii): D has not voluntarily laid himself open to the threat

The defence does not apply in circumstances where the defendant has voluntarily placed himself in a position (or 'laid himself open' to use the words of Lord Bingham in *Hasan*) where he knows or ought reasonably to know that he may be the subject of compulsion to commit a crime. Labelled as 'prior fault' by Child ('Prior Fault: Blocking Defences or Constructing Crimes' in Reed and Bohlander (eds), *General Defences in Criminal Law: Domestic and Comparative Perspectives* (Routledge, 2014)), the principle aims to exclude defendants from the scope of the defence where they have allowed themselves to become involved or associated (or remain involved or associated) with persons who are engaged in criminal activity, for example where they join a criminal organisation. One might refer to this as 'self-induced duress'.

Early developments

A number of cases came before the courts, dealing with the issue of a defendant pleading duress in circumstances where he had voluntarily joined a criminal organisation. A few can be set out here:

- *R v Fitzpatrick* [1977] NI 20 (Northern Ireland): The accused voluntarily joined the IRA and attempted to plead duress when charged with an armed robbery that was carried out on behalf of the organisation. The Northern Ireland Court of Appeal found that no defence could exist where a defendant voluntarily associates himself with persons who are in a position to compel others to commit criminal offences. Any other conclusion, the Court said, 'would surely be monstrous'.
- *R v Sharp* [1987] QB 853: The accused was a member of a gang which carried out a number of armed robberies. The defendant attempted to plead duress to a charge of manslaughter following the death of a sub-postmaster who was shot during a robbery. The defendant alleged that he had attempted to withdraw from the robbery at an early stage but was threatened with a gun pointed to his head unless he complied. Lord Lane CJ, in the Court of Appeal, notably commented that

  > where a person has voluntarily, and with knowledge of its nature, joined a criminal organisation or gang which he knew might bring pressure on him

> to commit an offence and was an active member when he was put under such pressure, he cannot avail himself of the defence of duress.

The effect of these two cases would appear to rule out the defence where the defendant engaged with a person or persons who were capable of exercising or likely to exercise compulsion or duress and the defendant was aware of this circumstance upon joining the group. This point was in contention in the case of *R v Shepherd* (1987) 86 Cr App R 47, where the defendant had joined a shoplifting gang and, upon attempting to leave the group, had been threatened with violence to himself and his family. In particular, the defendant had had a gun pointed at him. The trial judge withdrew the defence from the jury on the basis that the defendant had voluntarily joined a criminal organisation. The Court of Appeal quashed the defendant's conviction, finding that the judge was wrong to withdraw the defence *purely* on the basis of the defendant's membership of the group. Mustill LJ explained that

> the concerted shoplifting enterprise did not involve violence to the victim either in anticipation or in the way it was actually put into effect. The members of the jury have had to ask themselves whether the appellant could be said to have taken the risk of P's violence simply by joining a shoplifting gang of which he was a member.

A similar approach was seen in *R v Lewis* (1992) 96 Cr App R 412, where the defendant had been threatened not to testify against his fellow armed robbers when in prison. Both cases have been confirmed as correct in *R v Hasan* [2005] 2 AC 467.

The law, however, was not restricted to cases where the defendant joined a criminal gang or organisation. The law recognised circumstances where a defendant's voluntary *association* (as opposed to membership) to persons who have a propensity for violence would often be enough to refuse the existence of the defence. Two cases can be offered as examples at this stage:

- *R v Ali* [1995] Crim LR 303: The defendant was a drug user and committed a robbery in order to pay money to his supplier who had threatened him with violence if he did not pay. The Court of Appeal concluded that the defendant had voluntarily placed himself in a position where the threat of violence was likely.
- *R v Heath* [2000] Crim LR 109: The defendant joined a gang dealing in drugs. Knowing from his membership that drug debts are enforced through violence, the defendant could not plead the defence of duress when he was called upon to repay his own debts by committing offences. See also *R v Harmer* [2001] EWCA Crim 2930 for similar facts and reasoning.

The current approach

These cases do not, however, reflect the precise ambit of the defence and the state of the accused's knowledge. The leading case in this area is now that of *R v Hasan* [2005] 2 AC 467 (also reported as *R v Z*).

case example

Charge:
Aggravated burglary (TA 1968, s 10)

Case progression:
Crown Court – Guilty

Court of Appeal – Conviction quashed

House of Lords – Conviction reinstated

Point of law:
Scope of the defendant's knowledge

In *R v Hasan* [2005] 2 AC 467, the defendant was involved in a prostitution racket. As a result of threats made to him by another member of the racket, the defendant committed a burglary. The defendant was charged with and convicted of aggravated burglary in the Crown Court on the basis that no defence of duress could exist given that the defendant had voluntarily joined the criminal organisation and was aware that he may be subject to a compulsion to commit criminal activity.

The defendant appealed to the Court of Appeal on the basis that the defence of duress should be open to him, and the accused's participation in a prostitution racket did not open him up to the thought that he may be compelled to commit an offence such as burglary. The Court of Appeal agreed and allowed the appeal, quashing the defendant's conviction in doing so. However, the Court of Appeal did certify a question of public importance to the House of Lords for their Lordships to determine. Their Lordships found against the accused and restored the defendant's conviction.

The certified question sent by the Court of Appeal was as follows:

> Whether the defence of duress is excluded when as a result of the accused's voluntary association with others:
> (i) he foresaw (or possibly should have foreseen) the risk of being subjected to *any compulsion* by threats of violence, or
> (ii) only when he foresaw (or should have foreseen) the risk of being subjected to compulsion to commit criminal offences, and, if the latter,
> (iii) only if the offences foreseen (or which should have been foreseen) were of the same type (or possibly of the same type and gravity) as that ultimately committed.

Lord Bingham, with whom the majority agreed (Baroness Hale dissenting), answered the question by selecting option (i) from the list above. In doing so, his Lordship opted for a restrictive objective approach, requiring a jury to ask whether the risk of *any compulsion* ought to have been foreseen (ie an objective approach), as opposed to asking whether it was actually foreseen by the defendant (ie a subjective approach). Under this approach, the foresight of compulsion need not be specific in nature (thus the words 'any compulsion'), nor does it require any foresight as to the commission of offences at all. Lord Bingham specifically stated:

> The policy of the law must be to discourage association with known criminals, and it should be slow to excuse the criminal conduct of those who do so. If a person *voluntarily becomes or remains* associated with others engaged in criminal activity in a situation where he *knows or ought reasonably to know* that he may be the subject of *compulsion* by them or their associates, he cannot rely on the defence of duress to excuse any act which he is thereafter compelled to do by them. (emphasis added)

example

Jack has recently joined an activist group against the use of animals in cosmetic tests. The group wishes to break into a research lab and free the animals there before then setting fire to the lab. Jack does not wish to set the lab on fire and refuses. Jill, the leader of the group, informs him that if he does not join them in their actions, his life and his children's lives are 'at risk'. Jack submits and petrol bombs the lab.

In this example, Jack will only be able to use the defence of duress in circumstances where the jury consider that the reasonable man would not have known of the risk of compulsion on fear of death or serious injury. It remains irrelevant that Jack does not foresee a particular kind of compulsion; any risk of compulsion will suffice.

Following *Hasan*, the approach of the courts can thus be expressed as follows:

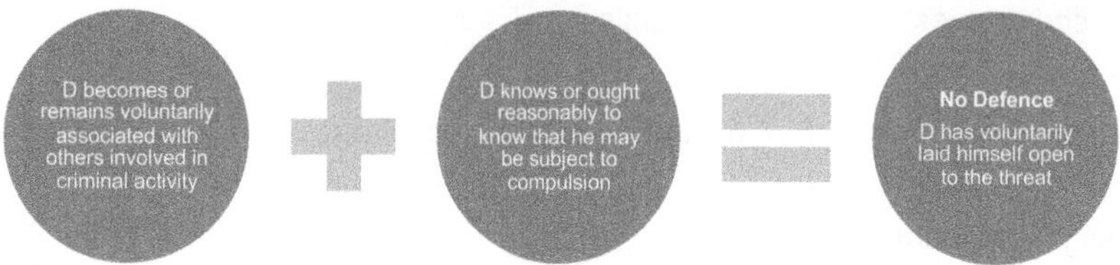

*Figure 7.14 The state of the law post-*Hasan

A number of criticisms have been levelled at the majority opinion, most notably by Baroness Hale. Although Baroness Hale agreed with Lord Bingham, and the majority, as to the decision to reinstate the conviction of the accused, her Ladyship chose to answer the certified question in a different fashion to that of Lord Bingham. Baroness Hale took favour with option (ii) listed above, taking the view that upon the defendant's membership into the criminal organisation, it must be proven that he should have foreseen (ie an objective approach) the risk of being compelled to commit criminal offences. The majority took no favour with option (iii) and in doing so overruled cases such as *R v Baker and Ward* [1999] 2 Cr App R 335.

Smith's criticisms of the decision in *Heath* (above) ('Comment on *Heath*' [2000] Crim LR 109) can be used to criticise *Hasan*, given their similar findings. Particularly, Smith argues that the requirement of objective foresight of *any* compulsion is too wide and impractical to operate:

> It is one thing ... to be aware that you are likely to be beaten up if you do not pay your debts, it is another to be aware that you may be required under threat of violence to commit other, though unspecified, crimes, if you do not.

Despite the criticism of the majority opinion, *Hasan* has been reinforced and approved on a number of occasions.

- *R v Ali* [2008] EWCA Crim 716: The defendant stole a car at knife point, claiming that he had been threatened with violence to do so. The Court of Appeal relied on evidence that the defendant was a friend of the alleged duressor, and this friendship was enough to say that the defendant either foresaw or should have foreseen the risk of being subject to compulsion.
- *R v Mullally* [2012] EWCA Crim 687: The Court of Appeal ruled that threats made in circumstances where the defendant has laid himself open to them will not only

fail to give rise to a defence of duress but will also likely have little impact on sentence.

7.9.4 Duress of circumstances

7.9.4.1 Existence of the defence

Traditionally understood as applying solely to road traffic offences, duress of circumstances is now recognised as a general defence in all cases where the defendant is not subject to any direct threat from another, but is the subject of surrounding circumstances that have a bearing on the will of the defendant (*R v Pommell* [1995] 2 Cr App R 607; *R v Backshall* [1998] 1 WLR 1506).

One of the first cases to recognise the existence of the defence was that of *R v Willer* (1986) 83 Cr App R 225, where the defendant drove his car on to the pavement and through a shopping precinct in order to escape from a violent gang attempting to attack him and his passengers (see also *R v Conway* [1989] QB 290 for similar facts). The defendant was charged with reckless driving and the trial judge refused to allow the defence of necessity to be put to the jury. The defendant was convicted and appealed to the Court of Appeal, which approved the trial judge's refusal to put forward the defence of necessity (see **7.10**) but felt that a 'very different defence', that of duress, should have been available. According to Watkins LJ, the question for the jury when confronted with a case of duress should be

> whether or not upon the outward or the return journey, or both, the appellant was wholly driven by force of circumstance into doing what he did and did not drive the car otherwise than under that form of compulsion, ie under duress.

In *R v Martin* [1989] 1 All ER 652, Brown J identified duress of circumstances as a defence applicable to the offence of driving whilst disqualified. The defendant was compelled to drive whilst disqualified in response to his wife's threats to commit suicide. Brown J was of the opinion that the offence could arise from 'objective dangers threatening the accused or others'. His Lordship did go on to say, however, that

> the defence is available only if, from an objective standpoint, the accused can be said to be acting reasonably and proportionately in order to avoid a threat of death or serious injury.

In that case, the defendant was clearly acting in response to a threat of circumstances (ie the suicide of his wife), in order to avoid that same circumstance coming to fruition (ie the death of his wife).

7.9.4.2 Elements of the defence

According to the Court of Appeal in *R v Martin* [1989] 1 All ER 652, the test for duress of circumstances would be virtually identical to that for duress by threats. As a result, you are advised to refer back to **Table 7.21** and the elements of duress. Brown J reasoned that in the context of duress of circumstances, the jury are to be directed to determine two questions:

> first, was the accused, or may he have been, impelled to act as he did because as a result of what he reasonably believed to be the situation he had good cause to fear that otherwise death or serious physical injury would result? Second, if so, may a sober person of reasonable firmness, sharing the characteristics of the accused, have responded to that situation by acting as the accused acted? If the answer to both those questions was yes, then the jury would acquit.

Table 7.24 Elements of the defence of duress of circumstance

Elements of the defence
(i) circumstances involved a threat or demand; (ii) D responded reasonably.

We shall consider each in turn, though note that these rules are largely reflective of what has been considered above. In *R v Petgrave* [2018] EWCA Crim 1397, the Court of Appeal confirmed the test in *Martin* to be an accurate statement of law.

Element (i): circumstances involved a threat or demand

The first requirement is that the defendant acted *as a result of* threatening circumstances where death or serious injury might result. Importantly, references to 'circumstances' involve only those circumstances that are external to the accused himself. Therefore, escaping prison as a result of suicidal thoughts could not amount to a relevant 'circumstance' in the case of *R v Rodger and Rose* [1998] 1 Cr App R 143. This principle is further used to demonstrate the ability for the circumstances to arise by nature, as opposed to from a person (eg causing damage as one drives away in haste from a tidal wave). The *Rodger* principle was enunciated further by the Court of Appeal in *R v Quayle* [2005] 1 All ER 988, where it was held that the possession and supply of cannabis for the purpose of pain relief was not capable of amounting to a duress of circumstance for two reasons:

(1) the additional pain suffered by the defendants from not using cannabis was not sufficient enough to amount to a threat of death or serious injury; and
(2) the use of cannabis to repress pain and seek relief was an internal and not external circumstance.

As with duress by threats, the circumstances must be such that the threat is one of death or serious injury. It is incorrect to state that the requirement is that the threat must be 'life threatening'; the only conditions are that the threat is either of death or serious injury (*Pipe v DPP* [2012] EWHC 1821 (Admin)). This condition is to be compared with the defence of necessity, which simply requires the court to consider whether the defendant's actions were the lesser of two evils. Where the threat is not one of death or serious injury, the defence must fail and the defendant may consider pleading necessity.

Element (ii): defendant responded reasonably

The second requirement is that the defendant responded to the situation in a manner that the 'sober person of reasonable firmness' would have. As with duress by threats, the reference to the sober person of reasonable firmness indicates that the focus for the jury, in determining the defence, is not whether the defendant is justified in his actions, but, rather, whether a reasonable person would have acted in the same way as a result of the circumstances before him. As with duress by threats, the defendant must have made reasonable efforts to avoid offending and must have demonstrated reasonable fortitude in resisting the threats.

The focal point of duress of circumstances is that the court must consider whether the defendant was still acting in response to the perceived threat or whether such danger had passed (in a similar vein to self-defence – see above at **7.8.2.1**). This is evident in three High Court decisions.

- *DPP v Bell* [1992] RTR 335: The defendant drove whilst intoxicated in order to escape from his pursuers. The Court took note that the defendant had not continued to drive all the way home as this demonstrated that his conduct was in response to the threat of serious harm or death and not simply as an excuse to allow him to drive home intoxicated.
- *DPP v Jones* [1990] RTR 33: In a similar vein to *Bell*, the defendant drove whilst intoxicated; however, the Court heard evidence that the defendant had driven for two miles back to his home without even checking whether he was still being pursued.
- *DPP v Mullally* [2006] EWHC 3448 (Admin): As in *Bell* and *Jones*, the defendant drove a car whilst intoxicated to escape her sister's partner who had assaulted her and threatened to throw her down some stairs. The defendant telephoned the police and, upon seeing that the partner was pursuing her, got into her car. The defendant drove past her sister's house (where the threat took place) and saw that the police had arrived. As a result of this, the defendant continued to drive home and was later stopped and breathalysed. The defendant alleged that she was acting under duress to drive whilst intoxicated. The Divisional Court concluded that the defendant was acting under duress from the point that she ran from the pursuer and drove away in her car. However, Fulford J would explain that 'from the moment she was aware that the police had attended at the premises, it ceased being necessary for her to continue to drive whilst over the limit in order to avoid a serious assault'. The focal point here was that the defendant continued to drive despite witnessing the police arriving (ie the defendant had no compulsion to continue driving).

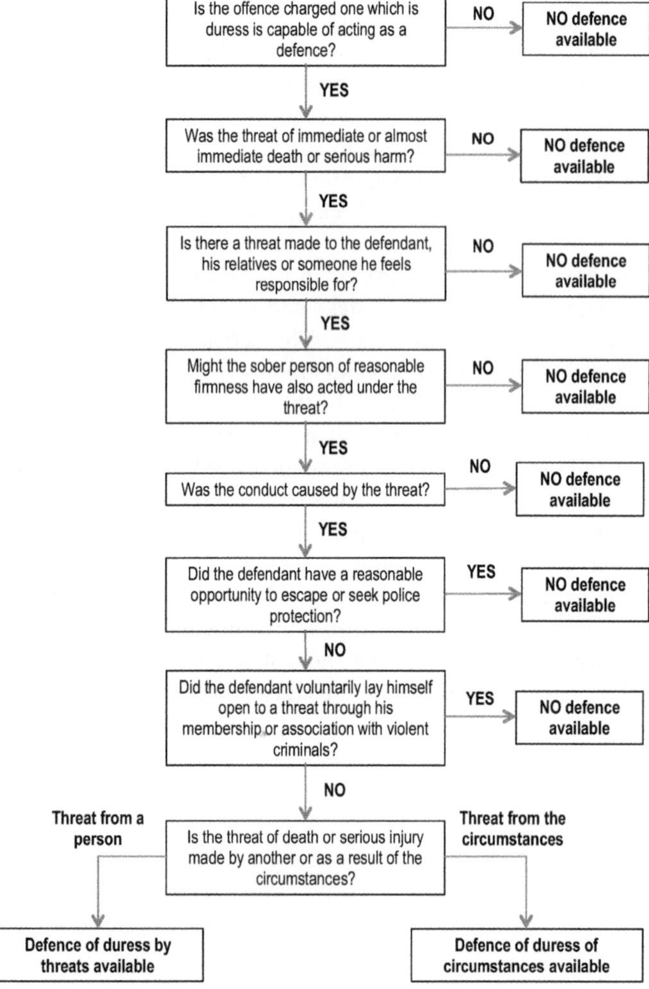

Figure 7.15 Putting together duress

7.9.5 Procedural matters and the burden of proof

7.9.5.1 Procedure

Unless the case is one of the excluded categories (ie murder, attempted murder or treason), the defence is capable of being left to the jury to determine as a matter of fact whether the defendant acted under a threat to himself or another of death or serious injury. In *R v Petgrave* [2018] EWCA Crim 1397, Holroyde LJ emphasised that whether the defence existed was a question of fact for the jury; not one of law for the judge. In this regard, his Lordship would explain:

> We accept that there may be cases in which the evidence adduced as part of the prosecution case provides a basis for a successful submission of no case to answer on the ground that that evidence in itself raised the issue of duress and was such that no reasonable jury, properly directed, could find that the defence had been disproved. But, having regard to the nature of the defence, we think that such cases will be rare. In our judgment, this case is certainly not one of them.

7.9.5.2 Burden of proof

The defendant bears an evidential burden in relation to duress in that he must adduce some evidence of duress in order to make the issue a live one. Importantly, in *R v Petgrave* [2018] EWCA Crim 1397, Holroyde LJ explained that

> a defendant who wishes to rely on the defence of duress of circumstances cannot put it in issue through his advocate. It must be put in issue by evidence.

By this, Holrodye LJ means that the defendant must give evidence at trial in order to rely on the defence. This position is contrary to other defences noted in this chapter, including self-defence (see *R (Skelton) v CPS* [2017] EWHC 3118 (Admin) above at **7.8.6.2**).

If the defence is able to do this, the legal burden of proof then rests on the prosecution to disprove duress beyond a reasonable doubt (*R v Bone* [1968] 1 WLR 983). Given the potential exploitation of the defence by gangs and criminal organisations, this reverse burden appears to go some way to ensuring that the defence is only available to those who truly act as a result of threats posed to them.

7.9.6 Result of a successful plea of duress

Duress is a defence excusing liability. Should the defendant successfully claim duress, either by threats or of circumstances, he will be entitled to a complete acquittal. Given the difficulty in establishing the defence, duress is rarely pleaded but always offers an interesting argument when such cases come before the appellate courts.

7.9.7 Other cases of coercion

Two particular defences are worth considering at this stage, albeit briefly. These defences were introduced in order to combat a particular form of coercion that was repetitive in criminal cases. These are:

- defences of marital coercion; and
- defences under the Modern Slavery Act 2015.

Table 7.25 Other cases of coercion

Cases of coercion	Brief explanation
Marital coercion	Prior to the enactment of s 177 of the Anti-social Behaviour, Crime and Policing Act 2014, marital coercion acted as a defence for a woman who committed a crime whilst in the presence of her husband and under his coercion. This defence was provided for in s 47 of the Criminal Justice Act 1925 and applied to all crimes except murder and treason. The defence was a complete defence, meaning that the wife could be acquitted of an offence in circumstances where the husband could not. The defence was abolished in May 2014, meaning that such defendants must now rely on the general defence of duress. As a result of s 177(3) of the 2014 Act, the defence is still available to married women for offences alleged to have been committed before the date when the provision came into force, ie 13 May 2014.

Cases of coercion	Brief explanation
Slavery/trafficking	In more recent times, attention has been drawn to victims of trafficking who, through coercion or compulsion, go on to commit criminal offences. At common law, no separate defence existed for such victims who had been coerced into committing an offence, though the courts did accept such coercion as being capable of founding a defence of duress (*R v O* [2008] EWCA Crim 2835, *R v N* [2013] QB 379, *R v L* [2014] 1 All ER 113 and *R v Joseph (VS)* [2017] EWCA Crim 36). In July 2015, the Modern Slavery Act 2015 came into force, granting defences to both adult and child victims of slavery and trafficking who are coerced into committing offences. The defence is provided in s 45 of the 2015 Act.

7.10 Necessity

Necessity can best be described as a defence of last resort; where all else fails, a defendant pleads that his actions were necessary in the given circumstance in order to avoid an inevitable evil from occurring. Child and Ormerod (*Smith, Hogan, & Ormerod's Essentials of Criminal Law*, 3rd edn (OUP, 2019)) label the defence as an 'imperfect safety net' applying where 'no other defence is available but it is clear that liability would be inappropriate'.

7.10.1 Basis for the defence

7.10.1.1 Does a defence of necessity actually exist?

The defence remains a difficult one to grasp within English law given the sheer uncertainty as to its existence. As discussed above (at **7.9.3**), the courts have recognised the existence of duress of circumstances as a defence; this defence appears to achieve the same results as that intended to be covered by the defence of necessity. Indeed, in many cases, the courts appear to treat necessity as synonymous with duress of circumstances. In *R v Conway* [1989] QB 290, a reckless driving case, Woolf LJ in the Court of Appeal explained that 'it is still not clear whether there is a general defence of necessity'. His Lordship went on to say that 'necessity can only be a defence to a charge of reckless driving where the facts establish "duress of circumstances"'.

However, the key distinction between necessity and duress of circumstances is that the former acts as a justification of the defendant's actions (to the extent that we can say the defendant's actions were 'right' in the circumstances), whereas the latter amounts to excusing, on the basis of human frailty and threats, the defendant's conduct. This distinction in evident in *Re F (mental patient: sterilisation)* [1990] 2 AC 1, where Lord Goff applied the doctrine of necessity to justify the doctors' actions in sterilising a patient without consent. It is clear that the doctors were under no threat in terms of the circumstances presented before them, so clearly duress of circumstances was not appropriate, but some other defence was required to justify their actions as 'right'. Therefore, if the defence of necessity does exist, it is best understood as a justificatory one.

7.10.1.2 Scope of the defence

As discussed above, the defence is a justification of the defendant's actions. It operates to justify the conduct of a defendant where his actions (or 'evil' as it has been referred to) are less serious than the evil that is to be avoided. Another way to phrase this is that the defendant's evil is outweighed by a greater evil that will occur should the defendant not act. This requires a simple balancing exercise.

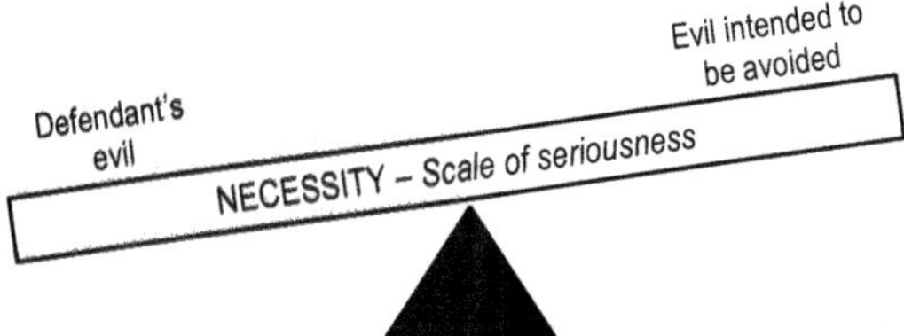

Figure 7.16 *Balancing the two evils*

As one can see from the figure above, the balancing exercise works like this:

- Should the balance tip towards the defendant's evil being of a more serious nature than the evil intended to be avoided, the defendant cannot raise the defence of necessity.
- However, should the balance tip towards the defendant's evil being the lesser of the two evils, the defendant will be able to raise the defence of necessity.

The difficulty with approaching necessity as a defence which simply balances two evils is in setting the parameters or limits on the defence. Consider the following:

example

Jack is homeless and breaks into Jill's home for shelter from a storm. Jack believes he will not survive the storm unless he finds shelter.

If we apply the simple balancing exercise in this scenario, it would appear that Jack's evil of breaking into Jill's home to shelter himself from the storm is outweighed by the evil that would occur should Jack not seek shelter, ie his potential death in the storm. Should necessity afford a defence to Jack in this instance?

Let us consider another example based on slightly different facts.

example

Jack is homeless and has not eaten any food for a number of weeks. Out of desperation for food and in fear that he may die from starvation, Jack enters a grocery store and steals a number of food items.

Again, applying the balancing exercise, it would appear that Jack's death is an evil which substantially outweighs Jack's evil of stealing food. Suppose Jack stole the food to feed his five-year-old son who was also likely to die from starvation. It would appear that the balancing exercise would be tipped even further in Jack's favour.

It would appear, *prima facie* at least, that a defence would be properly available for Jack in this instance. However, to allow a defence to exist in such circumstances may lead to an extension of the defence never anticipated by the courts that identified its existence at the outset. Indeed, this was the understanding of Lord Denning MR in *Southwark London Borough Council v Williams* [1971] Ch 734 where his Lordship reasoned that

> if hunger were once allowed to be an excuse for stealing, it would open a way through which all kind of disorder and lawlessness would pass … If homelessness

> were once admitted as a defence to trespass, no one's house could be safe. Necessity would open a door which no man could shut.

Edmund Davies LJ would add to this by saying:

> The reason for such circumspection is clear – necessity can very easily become simply a mask for anarchy.

7.10.2 The leading cases

The legal principles involving necessity have developed through the common law and through a raft of legal authorities, involving both criminal and civil matters. We shall consider some of the more important cases first, before then considering other cases on our journey to discovering whether the defence of necessity actually exists and, if it does, how far that defence extends.

7.10.2.1 *R v Dudley and Stephens*

The defence of necessity cannot be considered without reference first to the leading case of *R v Dudley and Stephens* (1884) 14 QBD 273.

case example

Charge:
Murder

Case progression:
Assize Court – Case sent to the High Court

High Court– Guilty

Point of law:
Necessity as a defence to murder

In *R v Dudley and Stephens* (1884) 14 QBD 273, the defendants, two sailors, were shipwrecked and found themselves adrift in a small boat with a third man and a young cabin boy. The group had been at sea for 20 days with virtually no food for seven days or water for five days and had been reduced to drinking their own urine. The defendants, believing that they would not survive, decided to kill and eat the cabin boy in order to survive. The third man had died before the defendants undertook this act. The defendants were rescued four days later and upon rescue were charged with murder.

The High Court, having had the case adjourned to it by the Assize Court, found the defendants guilty of murder, sentencing them to death (which would later be replaced by six months' imprisonment without hard labour).

Lord Coleridge CJ stated:

> [I]t is admitted that the deliberate killing of this unoffending and unresisting boy was clearly murder, unless the killing can be justified by some well-recognised excuse admitted by the law. It is further admitted that there was in this case no such excuse, unless the killing was justified by what has been called 'necessity'. But the temptation to the act which existed here was not what the law has ever called necessity. Nor is this to be regretted.

His Lordship would go on to say that

> the broad proposition that a man may save his life by killing, if necessary, an innocent and unoffending neighbour … certainly is not law at the present day.

One interpretation of this statement is that the defence of necessity, if it does actually exist, does not apply to murder. This is certainly the approach taken in our second case.

7.10.2.2 *R v Howe*

We came across the authority of *R v Howe* [1987] AC 417 when discussing the defence of duress, the issue in that case being whether the defence of duress was available to a charge of murder. The House of Lords concluded, unequivocally, that it could not be.

One factor which influenced their Lordships' reasoning was the decision of Lord Coleridge CJ in *Dudley and Stephens*. To be specific, Lord Mackay in *Howe* explained:

> [F]or this House now to allow the defence of duress generally in response to a charge of murder would be to effect an important and substantial change in the law. In my opinion too, it would involve a departure from the decision in the famous case of [*R*] *v Dudley and Stephens*.

This is, however, only one interpretation of Lord Coleridge CJ's ruling. There are many who contend that Lord Coleridge CJ excluded the defence of necessity to a charge of murder in all cases; there is also a collection of examples which consider that the defence of necessity may be available in some circumstances. This is particularly evident in our next authority.

7.10.2.3 *Re A*

Dudley would go on to be distinguished in the more recent case of *Re A (children) (conjoined twins: surgical separation)* [2001] Fam 147.

case example

Charge:
n/a (doctors sought declaration)

Case progression:
High Court – Declaration granted

Court of Appeal – Declaration upheld

Point of law:
Scope of necessity as a defence

In *Re A (children) (conjoined twins: surgical separation)* [2001] Fam 147, doctors applied to the High Court for a declaration that separating conjoined twins would not be unlawful. The twins (referred to as 'J' and 'M') shared a common artery as a result of which, if they remained conjoined, both twins would die within a matter of months. However, if the doctors could separate the twins, 'J' would have the chance to live a full life, but 'M' would die within minutes.

The High Court granted the declaration on the basis that necessity required that the lesser evil (ie that 'J' be given the chance of life at the expense of 'M' dying) was outweighed by the greater evil (ie that both children die).

The parents of the twins, who objected to the surgery on religious grounds, appealed to the Court of Appeal. The Court of Appeal dismissed the appeal and upheld the declaration.

Brooke LJ appeared to base his decision on the necessity defence and laid down three requirements that must exist for the defence to be present. These were taken from the famous jurist, Sir James Stephen, and are that:

(1) the act is needed to avoid inevitable and irreparable evil;
(2) no more should be done than is reasonably necessary for the purpose to be achieved; and
(3) the evil inflicted must not be disproportionate to the evil avoided.

Brooke LJ concluded:

> Given that the principles of modern family law point irresistibly to the conclusion that the interests of Jodie must be preferred to the conflicting interests of Mary, I consider that all three of these requirements are satisfied in this case.

Importantly, however, *Re A* was a civil law decision, meaning that Brooke LJ's reasoning is only of persuasive authority to the criminal courts. Despite this, Brooke LJ's judgment does suggest that the defence of necessity is capable of existing independently of the defence of duress and applying to a charge of murder. It is interesting to look at how Brooke LJ distinguished *Dudley and Stephens* from the instant case. The main distinction concerned *who* were to choose that the other should die. In *Dudley and Stephens*, the choice to kill the cabin boy was made by the defendants who chose him given his frailty and the likelihood, or lack thereof, of his survival. Whereas, in *Re A*, Brooke LJ identified that Mary (the weaker twin) was 'self-designated for a very early death'. In this regard, it was nature that had chosen Mary to die, not the doctors. The choice made by the doctors was whether both twins should die or whether Jodie should be given the chance to survive. In that regard, Brooke LJ concluded that the doctors performing the separation of the twins would not be committing murder. In effect, his Lordship distinguished *Dudley and Stephens* from *Howe*.

7.10.2.4 *Nicklinson v Ministry of Justice*

Our last authority to consider is the case of *R (Nicklinson) v Ministry of Justice* [2014] UKSC 38. In this case, necessity was found not to be available as a defence to murder or assisted suicide in cases of voluntary euthanasia or assisted dying. The Court of Appeal ([2013] EWCA Civ 961) had explained that there is no 'general defence of necessity', and although 'these considerations would bear upon the likely sentence', they do not provide a defence. Further, in relation to *Re A* and its application to the criminal law, the Court of Appeal noted that *Re A* was 'too slender a thread on which to hang such a far-reaching development of the common law'. In particular, the Court of Appeal was concerned with the distinction between killing a person in order to save a life and killing a person because they wish to die. According to the Court of Appeal, only Parliament could make those sorts of decisions regarding the status of the law.

Although, on appeal, the Supreme Court was not concerned with the defence of necessity, it agreed with this assessment. In particular, Lord Neuberger stated:

> [To] extend the defence of necessity to a charge of assisted suicide would be a revolutionary step, which would be wholly inconsistent with both recent judicial dicta of high authority, and the legislature's intentions.

7.10.3 Further cases to consider

7.10.3.1 Cases which found the defence to exist

Despite a reluctance to find that a defence of necessity exists in English law, the courts have, on a number of occasions, seemingly applied the principle with success. For instance, in *R v Bourne* [1939] 1 KB 687, the Court of Criminal Appeal construed the words 'unlawfully' in s 58 of the Offences Against the Person Act 1861, in relation to unlawful abortions, as meaning that some abortions must be capable of being 'lawful'. This case concerned the performance of an abortion on a 14-year-old girl who had become pregnant as a result of a violent rape. The doctor was charged with unlawfully procuring a miscarriage and the question for the court was whether a defence existed. The Court concluded that a 'lawful' abortion was one that was performed in good faith for the purpose of preserving the life of the mother (ie on grounds of necessity for the mother's life – though see now the Abortion Act 1967). In this respect, the defence was allowed and the doctor acquitted. This reasoning was evident in *Gillick v West Norfolk and Wisbech Area Health Authority* [1986] AC 112, a judicial review case. In this case, the applicant had challenged the legality of the Department of Health's policy which advised doctors that they would not be acting unlawfully if they prescribed contraceptive drugs to girls under the age of 16 and without parental consent so long as they were acting in good faith to protect the girl against the harmful effects of sexual intercourse. The House of Lords concluded that the *bona fide* exercise by doctors within their clinical judgment was sufficient to negate their *mens rea* for the offence. This reasoning was further observed and approved in *R (Axon) v Secretary of State for Health* [2006] EWHC 37 (Admin).

Perhaps the most vivid illustration of necessity can be seen in the case of *Re F (mental patient: sterilisation)* [1990] 2 AC 1, which concerned the sterilisation of a patient in a psychiatric hospital without her consent. The House of Lords concluded that the defence of necessity was open to the doctors who performed the treatment without consent on the basis that evidence suggested that should the patient become pregnant, the effects of her condition might be 'disastrous' for both herself and the child. In *obiter*, both Lord Brandon and Lord Goff appeared to favour the acknowledgement of necessity as a general defence. Whilst Lord Brandon phrased his discussion more around *medical* necessity, Lord Goff was broader in his approach, reasoning that

> a man who seizes another and forcibly drags him from the path of an oncoming vehicle, thereby saving him from injury or even death, commits no wrong.

7.10.3.2 Cases which found the defence not to be made out

In *R v Quayle* [2005] 1 All ER 988, the Court of Appeal was faced with the question as to whether necessity was available as a defence to possession of cannabis in circumstances where the use of cannabis was for medicinal purposes to alleviate pain. The Court concluded that no defence existed. The same reasoning was adopted by the Court of Appeal in *R v CS* [2012] EWCA Crim 389, a case concerning abduction by a parent contrary to s 1 of the Child Abduction Act 1984. The defendant had taken her child, aged 10 years, out of the UK and had moved her to Spain in breach of a court order. The Court of Appeal concluded that no defence of necessity existed within the legislative scheme of the 1984 Act. The Court did say, however, that if it was incorrect as to the existence of the defence, it would nonetheless have not been made out given the lack of fulfilment of the conditions in *Re A*.

7.10.4 Where does the law stand?

It is no secret that the Law Commission has been as unsure as to whether the defence of necessity should exist or not in English law. In its 1977 Report, the Law Commission recommended that any general defence of necessity that might exist should be abolished ('Defences of General Application' (Law Com No 83, 1977)). This recommendation was extensively criticised by the likes of Williams ('Necessity' [1978] Crim LR 128), who reasoned that such a policy would severely restrict the courts' ability to deal with exceptional cases where a defendant has acted in response to a greater evil but has no defence of duress due to the lack of threats or relevant circumstances. This is an anomaly that could not work in practice. The recommendation was quickly dropped and the Law Commission approached the topic for a second time in 1992 ('Offences Against the Person and General Principles' (Law Com No 218, 1992). In this Report, the Law Commission proposed that the defence should continue to exist but should not be codified (unlike other defences that were proposed to be reformed in the 1992 Report). Further, the Law Commission sought to limit the use of necessity by recognising the defence of duress of circumstances as one which would cover the majority of cases which could be dealt with by necessity, and one which was open to less criticism. Indeed, the Law Commission took particular favour with the judgment of Dickson J in the Canadian authority of *Perka* (1984) 13 DLR (4th) 1, where he stated that duress of circumstances

> rests on a realistic assessment of human weakness, recognising that a liberal and humane criminal law cannot hold people to the strict obedience of laws in emergency situations where normal human instincts, whether of self-preservation or of altruism, overwhelmingly impel disobedience. The objectivity of the criminal law is preserved; such acts are still wrongful, but in the circumstances they are excusable. Praise is indeed not bestowed, but pardon is, when one does a wrongful act under pressure.

It is submitted that this is the correct approach to take in relation to the use of necessity in criminal law. First, the courts should identify whether the defence of duress of circumstances is present and may be used. If it is the case that duress cannot provide a defence, in such cases as where there is no threat or relevant circumstances, then the courts may consider the defence of necessity as a last resort. Gardner ('Necessity's Newest Invention' (1991) 11 OJLS 125) regards this approach as a welcome opportunity to avoid the defence of necessity. Alternatively, it may be more appropriate to understand necessity as a defence available to specific offences, in certain exceptional circumstances, as opposed to a general defence applying to all cases. Most certainly, it must be appreciated that the courts are much more willing to excuse the defendant by reason of duress of circumstances than justify his actions as necessary.

in practice

Although the defence of necessity is haphazard and restricted to exceptional cases, the law does take a pragmatic approach to situations where the defence may be pleaded. In *Buckoke v Greater London Council* [1971] 1 Ch 655, Lord Denning MR appreciated that although a defence may be denied in law, the realities of the defence are recognised in practice through the discretion of prosecutors as to whether they should seek a prosecution and through judges in terms of sentencing. Denning MR specifically commented that a defendant '... should not be prosecuted. He should be congratulated.'

7.10.5 Procedural matters and the burden of proof

The following discussion will be brief and is predicated on the basis that a defence of necessity actually exists in law.

7.10.5.1 Procedure

Necessity exists in circumstances where the defendant is faced with two options, both of which will result in some repugnant outcome, but the act chosen by the defendant is one of a lesser of two evils.

7.10.5.2 Burden of proof

As with other defences, the burden of proof will be on the prosecution to disprove the existence of the defence beyond a reasonable doubt. The defendant will no doubt bear some evidential burden to raise the matter in issue.

7.10.6 Result of a successful plea of necessity

If the defence of necessity exists, it no doubt will apply in the same way that the defence of duress of circumstances does, ie as a complete defence resulting in an acquittal for the defendant.

7.10.7 Comparing necessity and duress

It is useful at this stage to conclude with a brief comparison to highlight the similarities and differences in the defence of duress (duress of circumstances to be exact) and the defence of necessity. We can do this by use of **Table 7.26**.

Table 7.26 Distinguishing duress and necessity

Duress	Necessity
Can never be a defence to murder.	According to *Re A*, can be a defence to murder in limited circumstances.
Limited to threats of death or serious injury.	Not limited in the same way; the conduct may be necessitated in response to a threat to property.
Limited to immediate threats.	Not limited in the same regard; though if the circumstance is 'inevitable and irreparable', it is likely also to be immediate.
A mistaken belief will afford a defence, so long as the mistake is reasonable.	Mistaken belief will not avail a defence of necessity.

7.11 Further reading

Defences in general

Dressler, 'Justifications and Excuses: A Brief Review of the Concepts and the Literature' (1987) 33 Wayne L Rev 1155.

Williams, 'The Theory of Excuses' [1982] Crim LR 732.

Wilson, 'The Structure of Defences' [2005] Crim LR 125.

Infancy

Brown, 'Reviewing the Age of Criminal Responsibility' [2018] Crim LR 904.

Bennion, 'Mens Rea and Defendants Below the Age of Discretion' [2009] Crim LR 757.

Hoyano, 'Coroners and Justice Act 2009: Special Measures Direction Take Two' [2010] Crim LR 345.

Mistake

Husak and von Hirsch, 'Culpability and Mistake of Law' in Shute, Gardner, and Horder (eds), *Action and Value in Criminal Law* (OUP, 1993).

Tur, 'Subjectivism and Objectivism: Towards Synthesis' in Shute, Gardner, and Horder (eds), *Action and Value in Criminal Law* (OUP, 1993).

Intoxication

Brooks, 'Involuntary Intoxication: A New Six-Step Procedure' (2015) 79 J Crim L 138.

Gough, 'Surviving without Majewski' [2000] Crim LR 719.

Lynch, 'The Scope of Intoxication' [1982] Crim LR 139.

Insanity

Child and Sullivan, 'When Does the Insanity Defence Apply? Some Recent Cases' [2014] 11 Crim LR 788.

Fennell, 'The Criminal Procedure (Insanity and Unfitness to Plead) Act 1991' (1992) 55 MLR 547.

Mackay, 'The Insanity Defence in Operation' (2014) 65 NILQ 153.

Automatism

Ebrahim, Wilson, Marks, Peacock and Fenwick, 'Violence, Sleepwalking and the Criminal Law: (1) The Medical Aspects' [2005] Crim LR 601.

Mackay and Mitchell, 'Sleepwalking, Automatism and Insanity' [2006] Crim LR 901.

Rumbold and Wasik, 'Diabetic Drivers, Hypoglycaemic Unawareness, and Automatism' [2011] Crim LR 863.

Public and private defence

Bleasdale-Hill, '"Our home is our haven and refuge – a place where we have every right to feel safe": Justifying the Use of Up to "Grossly Disproportionate Force" in a Place of Residence' [2015] 6 Crim LR 407.

Horder, 'Redrawing the Boundaries of Self-Defence' (1995) 58 MLR 431.

Thomas, 'Defenceless Castles: The Use of Grossly Disproportionate Force by Householders in Light of R (Collins) v Secretary of State for Justice' (2016) 80(6) J Crim L 407.

Duress

Alldridge, 'Developing the Defence of Duress' [1986] Crim LR 433.

Dennis, 'Duress, Murder and Criminal Responsibility' (1980) 106 LQR 208.

Laird, 'Evaluating the Relationship Between Section 45 of the Modern Slavery Act 2015 and the Defence of Duress: An Opportunity Missed?' [2016] Crim LR 395.

Necessity

Clarkson, 'Necessary Action: A New Defence' [2004] Crim LR 81.

Gardner, 'Necessity's Newest Invention' (1991) 11 OJLS 125.

Glazebrook, 'The Necessity Plea in English Criminal Law' (1972) 30 CLJ 87.

- Defences may operate to negate an element of an offence, excuse the defendant's conduct or justify the actions of the defendant as lawful.
- Defences may be general in that they apply to all cases, or specific in that they only apply to a select set of offences.
- Defences may be complete in that they result in an acquittal for the accused, or partial in that they result in a lesser conviction.
- The defence of infancy provides that a child under the age of 10 years cannot be liable for a criminal offence. This defence operates to prevent criminal liability existing in the first place.
- The defence of mistake of fact provides that a defendant cannot be liable in circumstances where he has made a mistake of fact which negates his *mens rea* and that mistake is a genuinely held one. The defence operates to negate the *mens rea* of the accused.
- The defence of intoxication applies in circumstances where the defendant lacks the necessary *mens rea* as a result of his intoxication. Voluntary intoxication is a defence to specific intent offences but not basic intent offences. Involuntary intoxication is a defence to all crimes. The defence operates to negate the *mens rea* of the accused.
- The defence of insanity applies in circumstances where the defendant suffers from a defect of reason caused by a disease of the mind in circumstances where the defendant does not know what he is doing or does not know what he is doing is wrong. The defence operates to negate the *mens rea* of the accused.
- The defence of automatism applies in circumstances where the defendant, as a result of some external factor, has suffered a total loss of voluntary control. Where such automatism is self-induced, no defence is available. The defence operates to negate the *actus reus* of the accused.
- The defence of consent applies in circumstances where the defendant has obtained permission to act in a certain way. Consent is only valid in cases where the consent is freely given and informed. The defence operates to negate the *actus reus* of the accused.
- The defence of self-defence applies in cases where the defendant has used force in circumstances where it is necessary to do so on the facts as the defendant believes them to be and when such force is reasonable in the circumstances. The defence applies to the protection of oneself, other persons, property and in the prevention of crime. The defence operates to justify the defendant's conduct.
- The defence of duress applies in circumstances where the defendant is faced with a threat and reacts as a reasonable man would to such a threat. The defence operates to excuse the defendant's conduct.
- The defence of necessity applies in circumstances where the defendant is faced with unavoidable outcomes and chooses the outcome which is considered to be the lesser of two evils. It is questionable where this defence exists in English law. The defence operates to excuse the defendant's conduct.

test your knowledge

Problem question

Jill is of a nervous disposition and is particularly concerned about the possibility of burglary and rape in view of recent attacks upon women in her area. One day, her husband, Jack, calls her to say that he has to go to London and will not be home that night. Jill locks and bolts the door and retires to bed with a cricket bat to hand in case there is a burglary. Shortly after midnight she is woken by the sound of breaking glass. Taking the bat she goes downstairs and sees a hand being inserted through a broken window on the door and the bolt being drawn back. A dark figure enters the hallway. Believing it to be a burglar, Jill strikes out with the bat. On switching on the light, she sees that she has struck Jack, who has lost his keys, and, as she discovers later, fractured his skull.

Jill, in a rather distraught state, visits the local public house whilst Jack is being treated for his injuries in hospital. In the space of a few minutes, Jill has already drunk three glasses of wine but would still consider herself to be sober. Unbeknownst to Jill, Andy spikes Jill's wine with an intoxicant. Upon leaving the public house, Jill attacks a passer-by, scratching and kicking him, causing serious cuts to his arms and face. The pub landlord attempts to drag Jill off the passer-by, but Jill, believing that she is being attacked by the landlord, starts to scratch and kick him also. Jill cannot remember what happened.

Advise Jill as to what defences she may rely upon if charged with:

- GBH with intent against Jack;
- wounding within intent against the passer-by; and
- GBH with intent against the landlord.

Would your answer differ for any of these offences if Jill were charged with a lesser offence instead?

Essay question

'The operation of the *M'Naghten* rules leads to absurd results. Diabetics, epileptics and sleepwalkers are all being classified in law as criminally insane. The law has taken a wrong turn here.'

Critically discuss this statement in light of the rules regarding insanity and automatism.

chapter 8

Fatal Offences

After reading this chapter, you will be able to understand:

- the meaning of homicide and have an ability to compare homicide, as a term, with specific offences under the umbrella heading of homicide
- the offence of murder, its elements and punishment upon conviction
- the partial defences to murder, namely diminished responsibility, loss of self-control and suicide pact. You will also be able to understand that these defences are open only to a charge of murder
- the offences under the heading involuntary manslaughter and the elements and punishment of these offences.

8.1 Introduction to fatal offences

The law of fatal offences, often referred to as the law of 'homicide', is a complex and challenging area of law. In this chapter, we are dealing with some of the most serious offences known in the criminal law, namely the taking of another person's life. We shall consider non-fatal offences in **Chapter 9**.

Homicide is a general term describing multiple different forms of actions that result in the killing of another. It is essential to note that homicide is not an offence in its own right; it is simply a label to describe a multitude of offences (similar to using the terms 'sexual offences' and 'property offences'). It is incorrect to say, for example, that Jack is liable for homicide. Rather, a better statement is that Jack may be liable for a homicide-related offence, namely murder or manslaughter.

Homicide can be detailed as follows:

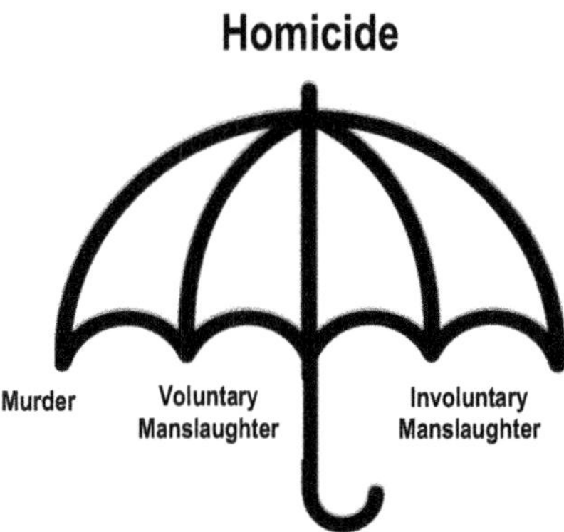

Figure 8.1 Umbrella of homicide

Other homicide offences outside the scope of this text include:

- child destruction;
- causing death by dangerous driving;
- causing death by careless driving, etc.

Unlike our American counterparts, homicide is not built upon a system of degrees (ie first and second degree murder). Instead, the law distinguishes one homicide-related offence from another by observing the intention on the part of the defendant. At a basic level, should a defendant intend to kill, he may be liable for voluntary homicide. Should a defendant not intend to kill, he may then be liable for involuntary homicide (neither of which are terms of art in English law).

8.2 Murder

Murder is a common law offence, not defined by statute. It may only be committed by a natural person (see below), and there is no offence of murder chargeable against a corporation. We considered corporate liability for the death of individuals in **Chapter 6**.

8.2.1 Defining murder

The offence was defined by Sir Edward Coke CJ in his third edition of *Coke's Institutes* (3 Inst 47) as follows:

> Murder is when a man of sound memory, and of the age of discretion, unlawfully killeth within any county of the realm any reasonable creature in *rerum natura* under the king's peace, with malice aforethought, either expressed by the party or implied by law, so as the party wounded or hurt etc die of the wound or hurt etc within a year and a day after the same.

The more modern understanding of murder can be stated as 'the unlawful killing of a human being under the Queen's peace, with malice aforethought, express or implied'.

Murder is a result crime and thus causation must also be established, as with other result crimes such as grievous bodily harm (GBH), which we shall consider in the next chapter.

8.2.2 Elements of murder

Murder is an offence that may be committed by any person 'of sound memory and of the age of discretion' (Coke CJ). Two points may be made here:

(a) 'A man of sound memory' simply means that he is sane (as opposed to insane under the M'Naghten Rules (*M'Naghten's Case* (1843) 10 Cl & Fin 200)). See the discussion of insanity in **Chapter 7**.

(b) The age of criminal liability, known as *doli capax*, begins at the age of 10 (Children and Young Persons Act 1933, s 50). Specifically, s 50 provides that '[i]t shall be conclusively presumed that no child under the age of ten years can be guilty of any offence'. (It was formerly the case that where a person under the age of 14 committed an offence, to be guilty of that offence they must have known that their actions were 'seriously wrong'. This presumption no longer applies.) As a result, where a child under the age of 10 does an action that would ordinarily be considered criminal, they will be deemed incapable (*doli incapax*) of committing a criminal offence. Please note that the phrase 'under the age of ten' is exclusive of that age, not inclusive.

Two further points can be noted from Coke CJ's definition:

(a) A murder need not be committed in England and Wales for the courts to exercise jurisdiction. By way of s 9 of the Offences Against the Person Act (OAPA) 1861 and s 3 of the British Nationality Act 1948, any murder committed outside the UK by a British citizen can be tried in England and Wales. Likewise, by s 10 of the OAPA 1861, where death occurs in another country from a fatal blow struck in England and Wales, the English courts will retain jurisdiction to try the matter. Under the Merchant Shipping Act 1995 and the Civil Aviation Act 1982, homicides on a British ship or British aircraft respectively also come within the jurisdiction of the English courts.

(b) It used to be the case that in order for an individual to be convicted of murder, the charge must have been brought within a year and a day of the victim dying. This was known as the 'year and a day' rule. With the development of medical knowledge and technology, it is now possible to establish the cause and time of a person's death with precision despite a potentially long period of time elapsing between the original injury inflicted and the end result of death. As a result of the Law Reform (Year and a Day Rule) Act 1996, in force from 17 June 1996, this rule has now been abolished. Instead, so long as causation can still be established, the defendant may now be liable for murder regardless of the delay between his original conduct and the death of the victim. Importantly, however, if the cause of death occurred more than three years before the victim died, or the defendant has already been convicted of some other offence (for example GBH) in relation to the act that caused the death, the consent of the Attorney General must be secured before a prosecution can be brought (s 2). Where a prosecution is brought, s 74(3) of the Police and Criminal Evidence Act 1984 allows for the earlier conviction to constitute admissible evidence to prove that the defendant was guilty of assaulting the victim but also potentially guilty of murder. The year and a day rule continues to apply where any act or omission causing death was committed before 17 June 1996.

The *actus reus* and *mens rea* of murder are outlined in **Table 8.1**.

Table 8.1 Elements of murder

AR/MR	Elements of the offence
Actus reus	(i) unlawful; (ii) killing; (iii) of a human being; (iv) under the Queen's peace.
Mens rea	express malice aforethought; or implied malice aforethought

We shall consider each element in turn.

8.2.2.1 *Actus reus*: (i) 'unlawful'

The first element to prove is that the killing is 'unlawful'. This may sound obvious; however, it is essential to note that not all homicides, or killings for that matter, will be unlawful. For instance, a killing will not be unlawful where it is in self-defence (*Beckford v The Queen* [1988] AC 130) or where a doctor performs a lawful act (for example, an abortion); nor was it previously unlawful for the executioner to kill an individual when sentenced to death. See generally Leverick, *Killing in Self-Defence* (OUP, 2007). Note, however, that the consent of the victim to die is not valid. The defendant will still be liable for murder even if he has the consent of the victim to kill him or her.

Withdrawal of life support – a lawful or unlawful act?

There is, however, a distinction to be made between the (lawful) withdrawal of life support treatment and (unlawful) active termination of a patient's life. In *Airedale*

NHS Trust v Bland [1993] AC 789, the House of Lords made this distinction clear by noting that a withdrawal of treatment supporting life would amount to a 'lawful killing', whilst an active step in ending the life of a patient, for example through lethal injection, would amount to 'unlawful killing'. Lord Goff explained (in *obiter*) that

> where the doctor's treatment of his patient is lawful, the patient's death will be regarded in law as exclusively caused by the injury or disease to which his condition is attributable.

In the earlier case of *R v Adams* [1957] Crim LR 365, Devlin J explained, in the Crown Court, that no special defence exists in law which justifies a doctor in giving medicine which shortens the life of a patient in severe pain. Devlin J did go on to say, however, that

> a doctor aiding the sick or dying [does not have to] calculate in minutes or hours, or perhaps in days or weeks, the effect on the patient's life of the medicines which he administers ... he is entitled to do all that is proper and necessary to relieve pain and suffering even if the measures he takes may *incidentally* shorten life. (emphasis added)

The situation appears to be this:

- Where a doctor administers medicine to ease the pain and suffering of a patient and that medicine has the 'incidental' or 'eventual' effect of ending the patient's life, the doctor will not be liable for murder so long as their intentions remained honourable throughout (*Bland*).
- Where a doctor administers medicine with the intention of shortening the life of the patient, even with good intentions, they will be liable for murder (*R v Cox* (1992) 12 BMLR 38).

This approach was reaffirmed by the Court of Appeal in *R v Inglis* [2011] 1 WLR 1110. In answering a problem question on this issue, it is best to establish the *actus reus* and *mens rea* of the offence in full, before then considering substantive defences. When you consider the defences, it will be helpful to refer back to this requirement of unlawfulness.

8.2.2.2 *Actus reus*: (ii) 'killing'

The word killing, in this context, means two things:

(a) a death must occur; and
(b) the death must be *caused* by the defendant.

Death

At **8.2.2.3** we consider when a human comes into being; when they become a person. At this point, however, we are concerned with the point when an individual is considered to no longer be in being, ie the point of death. Importantly, there is no authoritative definition in law of when life ends. As a result, the courts will often refer to medical definitions to assist them. The Code of Practice for the Diagnosis and Confirmation of Death (Academy of Medical Royal Colleges, 2008) lays down guidelines for doctors in determining the point at which a patient is dead. Section 2 specifies that:

> Death entails the irreversible loss of those essential characteristics which are necessary to the existence of a living human person and, thus, the definition of death should be regarded as the irreversible loss of the capacity for consciousness, combined with irreversible loss of the capacity to breathe.

From this definition, a number of possibilities at which point death occurs include:

- when the victim stops breathing; and
- when the victim's heart stops beating.

However, as Child and Ormerod (*Smith, Hogan, & Ormerod's Essentials of Criminal Law*, 3rd edn (OUP, 2019)) put it, these possibilities are not the most accurate to describe the occurrence when a person dies as 'as such occurrences can, if treated in good time, often be reversed'. Further to this, it must be emphasised that persons in a persistent vegetative state (PVS) who have permanently lost their capacity for consciousness will not be considered as legally dead as the capacity, or lack thereof, for consciousness must be combined with the loss of capacity to breathe.

From these definitions, the general *legal* understanding is that a person will be considered 'dead' at the point of brain death (*R v Malcherek; R v Steel* [1981] 2 All ER 422). A number of definitions were offered by the House of Lords in *Airedale NHS Trust v Bland* [1993] AC 789, each of which endorsed the idea that a person is legally dead when there is an absence of brain stem function:

- Lord Keith explained that '[i]n the eyes of the medical world and of the law a person is not clinically dead so long as the brain stem retains its function'.
- Lord Goff described death in the following manner: '[A]s a result of developments in modern medical technology, doctors no longer associate death exclusively with breathing and heartbeat, but it has come to be accepted that death occurs when the brain, and in particular the brain stem, has been destroyed.'
- Lord Browne-Wilkinson understood death as being 'brain stem death, i.e., the death of that part of the brain without which the body cannot function at all without assistance'.

There may be multiple degrees of state that fall short of death. Lord Browne-Wilkinson in *Airedale* explained that:

> Recent developments in medical science have fundamentally affected these previous certainties. In medicine, the cessation of breathing or of heartbeat is no longer death. By the use of a ventilator, lungs which in the unaided course of nature would have stopped breathing can be made to breathe, thereby sustaining the heartbeat. Those … who would previously have died through inability to swallow food can be kept alive by artificial feeding.

In such cases, therefore, the victim will still be considered a person in being who is capable of being murdered. This was emphasised by the Court of Appeal in *R v Inglis* [2011] 1 WLR 1110, where Lord Judge CJ stated that:

> the law does not recognise the concept implicit in the defence statement that [the victim] was 'already dead in all but a small physical degree'. The fact is that he was alive, a person in being. However brief the time left for him, that life could not lawfully be extinguished. Similarly, however disabled [the victim] might have been, a disabled life, even a life lived at the extremes of disability, is not one jot less precious than the life of an able-bodied person.

A reaffirmation that death means 'brain dead' can be seen in *Re A (a child) (withdrawal of life support)* [2015] EWHC 443 (Fam), *Oxford University NHS Trust v AB and others* [2019] EWHC 3516 (Fam) and recently in *Re M (Declaration of Death of Child)* [2020] EWCA Civ 164.

Causation

Murder is a result crime and therefore there must be a causative link, both factual (*R v White* [1910] 2 KB 124) and legal (*R v Cato* [1976] 1 All ER 260; *R v Smith* [1959] 2 QB 35), between the defendant's actions or omissions and the end result of death (see **Chapter 2**). As with all other forms of causation, the question of whether the defendant had caused the death of the victim remains a question for the jury to determine (*R v Clarke and Morabir* [2013] EWCA Crim 162).

What is critical in our understanding of killing, however, is that you do not simply state that the defendant 'caused death'. Dying is a natural occurrence in every person's life; therefore to say that the defendant caused another person's death is technically too broad a concept. Rather, the better phrasing is that adopted by the Lord Alverstone in the Court of Criminal Appeal in *R v Dyson* [1908] 2 KB 454 which held that the defendant's acts or omissions must have *accelerated* or *hastened* death.

example

Jack is suffering from a fatal infection that is likely to kill him in a matter of days. Jill comes into Jack's hospital bedroom and shoots him in the head, killing him.

In this case, although Jack was bound to die as a result of a serious infection, Jill has nevertheless hastened his death *even further* and is thus liable for murder.

In the majority of cases, causation will not be an issue. For example, if Jack shoots or stabs Jill and she dies from her wounds, causation is satisfied without difficulty. Where there is an issue of causation, however, expert evidence will often be adduced to assist the jury in their deliberations.

Importantly, at common law, an expert was not entitled to comment on what is known as the 'ultimate issue' in the case. In the case of murder, the ultimate issue would naturally be whether the defendant did the killing. This rule has largely become irrelevant and experts are now entitled to comment on the ultimate issue so long as the judge makes clear to the jury that they are not bound by the expert's opinion. In basic terms, the jury can ignore the expert if they so wish. This was the ruling in *R v Stockwell* (1993) 97 Cr App R 260, where the Court of Appeal stated that the rule against commentary by experts '... has long been more honoured in the breach than the observance' (per Lord Taylor CJ).

The issue of expert evidence in causation was recently addressed by the Court of Appeal in *R v Kimel* [2016] EWCA Crim 1456, where the Court noted that a lack of conclusive expert evidence on which the jury could base their decision will not be fatal to a conviction. In particular, Simler J, giving the judgment of the Court, commented:

> In many cases a pathologist can identify a clear cause of death. The fact that he was not able to do so in this case does not, however, mean that the issue of causation could not or should not be left. Here there were physical findings which were consistent with smothering: for example, the injuries consistent with the deceased being bound and having an object placed across his face. DNA from the applicant found on the deceased's mouth was as consistent with smothering as it was consistent with the defence case that the applicant tried to resuscitate the deceased. There was also independent evidence from a neighbour of the deceased screaming at the time he was attacked and robbed; that the deceased's house had been thoroughly cleaned with cleaning products found in various places around

the house; and that DNA matching the applicant was found on an aerosol can of kitchen surface polish and on a broom.

Two further facts may also be stated. First, the method of killing is unimportant. This is uncontroversial. Secondly, the defendant need not know who the victim is to be liable for murder. Lord Mustill described this random killing as 'indiscriminate malice', which he explained in *AG's Reference (No 3 of 1994)* [1998] AC 245 as follows:

> I pause to distinguish the case of indiscriminate malice from [grievous bodily harm and transferred malice rules] although even now it is sometimes confused with them. The terrorist who hides a bomb in an aircraft provides an example. This is not a case of 'general malice' where under the old law any wrongful act sufficed to prove the evil disposition which was taken to supply the necessary intent for homicide. Nor is it transferred malice, for there is no need of a transfer. The intention is already aimed directly at the class of potential victims of which the actual victim forms part. The intent and the *actus reus* completed by the explosion are joined from the start, even though the identity of the ultimate victim is not yet fixed. So also with the shots fired indiscriminately into a crowd. No ancient fictions are needed to make these cases of murder.

8.2.2.3 *Actus reus*: (iii) 'of a human being'

As discussed in **Chapter 6**, there are two forms of 'legal personality':

- natural persons, ie a human being; and
- artificial persons, ie an incorporated body, for example a company.

Murder, along with other fatal and non-fatal offences, may only be committed against a 'natural person' or, as Coke CJ put it, 'a reasonable creature in rerum natura' (*rerum natura* meaning 'in existence'). Although Article 2 of the ECHR protects the right to life, a question that has come before the courts on a number of occasions is simply: at what point does life begin?

When does life begin?

At a basic level, the ECtHR ruled in *Vo v France* (2004) 40 EHRR 259 that life begins at birth; however, it ruled that States have a certain margin of appreciation on this point. The courts, however, have struggled to find a single accepted meaning of 'birth' and, given the influence of legal, medical, ethical, philosophical and religious issues, it is of little surprise that the ECtHR has left this matter for the domestic authorities.

The English courts have taken a characteristically medical understanding of the point at which life begins. According to the Assize Court in *R v Enoch* (1833) 5 C & P 539, in order to be classed as a human being, a child must have 'an existence independent of its mother' (even if this is for only the briefest moment – *R v Crutchley* (1837) 7 C & P 814). Further, the Assize Court in *R v Poulton* (1832) 5 C & P 329 explained that the child must be 'wholly expelled' from the mother's body in order to be classed as a person in being. In *R v Brain* (1834) 6 C & P 349, Park J stated that breathing is not essential so long as the child is born alive and has the capability to breathe, and in *R v Reeves* (1839) 9 C & P 25 the Assize Court held that it is not necessary for the umbilical cord and after-birth to be expelled or severed for the child to be considered a human being.

The most recent statement as to the rights of an unborn child can be seen in the case of *Criminal Injuries Compensation Authority v First-Tier Tribunal (Social Entitlement Chamber)* [2015] QB 459. Although not concerned with the offence of murder, the

Court of Appeal was asked to consider whether a foetus was considered 'any other person' for the purposes of the offence of administering poison, contrary to s 23 of the OAPA 1861. In providing the leading judgment, Lord Dyson MR concluded that

> a foetus was an unique organism, neither a distinct person nor an adjunct of the mother and as such was not 'any other person'.

The same conclusion was reached in the older case of *R v Tait* [1990] 1 QB 290, where the Court of Appeal held that the defendant could not commit an offence of a threat to kill under s 16 of the OAPA 1861 against a foetus. Therefore, a 'human being in waiting' does not have the same rights as a 'human being'.

Is it possible to kill a foetus?

Ensure, however, that you understand the distinction between the killing of a foetus and the killing of a child once born. Where a foetus has been injured whilst in the womb and dies once it has been given birth to, this may amount to an offence of murder, dependent on the intention of the accused. According to *AG's Reference (No 3 of 1994)* [1998] AC 245, the defendant must intend to kill or cause GBH to the foetus that would then become a person in being. Do not confuse this with an intention to kill or seriously injure the foetus whilst in the womb. The intention must be for the child to die or be seriously injured upon being born alive. In this respect, the law can be quite complex.

In the absence of such an intention, or where the intention is to kill or cause GBH to the mother, the defendant may be liable instead for the offence of unlawful act manslaughter. The principle in *AG's Reference (No 3 of 1994)* is so regardless of how short that life may turn out to be as, at the point the child is expelled from the womb, it is considered a person in being for the purposes of the law.

You may feel that this means that criminals can get away with harming the foetus whilst it remains in the womb. Although this is correct in relation to the offence of murder, the law has responded to this issue by creating specific offences to tackle this behaviour, namely:

- unlawfully procuring an abortion under ss 58 and 59 of the OAPA 1861;
- child destruction under the Infant Life (Preservation) Act 1929; and
- unlawful abortion under the Abortion Act 1967.

8.2.2.4 *Actus reus*: (iv) 'under the Queen's peace'

'Under the Queen's peace' simply means that 'the killing of the Queen's enemies in the course of military operations' will not amount to murder (*R v Page* [1954] 1 QB 170, per Lord Goddard CJ). Of course, should the next Monarch be a King, this will become known, once more, as 'the King's peace' – the last time being 1952 prior to Queen Elizabeth II taking the throne.

Please note that this element of the *actus reus* is purposefully brief to demonstrate that it is now more of a formality in discussion, rather than a substantive point of law. This is so given the very specific, and arguably rare, instances where murder would not be deemed to be 'under the Queen's peace', namely when one is at war. For a discussion of the use of 'under the Queen's peace' in the definition of murder, see Hirst, 'Murder under the Queen's Peace' [2008] Crim LR 541.

Despite this, the Court of Appeal has been faced with such a legal question as to the meaning and application of the Queen's peace in the criminal law in *R v Adebolajo* [2014] EWCA Crim 2779 (the Lee Rigby murder case).

case example

Charge:
Murder

Case progression:
Crown Court – Guilty

Court of Appeal – Conviction upheld

Point of law:
Meaning of Queen's peace

In *R v Adebolajo* [2014] EWCA Crim 2779, the defendant attacked the victim, Lee Rigby, on the streets of Woolwich and attempted to decapitate him, killing him in the process. He was convicted of murder in the Woolwich Crown Court.

Adebolajo requested leave to appeal to the Court of Appeal, arguing that the trial judge erred in rejecting his submission that he had not killed under 'the Queen's peace'. His submission was based on the claim that he 'honestly believed he was a soldier fighting a war against the Queen and her forces'. The trial judge had ruled that the 'Queen's peace' element of the *actus reus* related to the victim of the offence and not to the perpetrator and his beliefs. The Court of Appeal agreed.

Lord Thomas CJ, refusing leave to appeal, stated:

> The law is now clear. An offender can generally be tried for murder wherever committed if he is a British subject, or, if not a British subject, the murder was committed within England and Wales. The reference to 'the Queen's Peace' … went essentially to jurisdiction. Although the Queen's Peace may play some part still in the elements that have to be proved for murder as regards the status of the victim (and it is not necessary to examine or define the ambit of that), *it can only go to the status of the victim; it has nothing whatsoever to do with the status of the killer.* The argument was completely hopeless. We have set out at some length why it was hopeless; it should never have been advanced. We dismiss this ground of appeal as entirely misconceived. (emphasis added)

The Queen's peace is concerned, therefore, with whether the victim was under the Queen's peace at the time of the killing, not the defendant, which is contrary to the argument raised by Hirst (above).

8.2.2.5 *Mens rea*: malice aforethought, express or implied

'Malice aforethought' simply means intention (*R v Vickers* [1957] 2 QB 664; *R v Moloney* [1985] AC 905). Although the term 'malice' is used, it is important to note that such intention does not require any form of ill will, wickedness or premeditation towards the victim; although all three of these may be useful forms of evidence during trial. Further, malice aforethought does not require any form of motive on the part of the defendant.

This has led some commentators, such as Kenny (*Outlines of Criminal Law*, 19th edn (CUP, 1966)), to argue that maliciousness is 'a mere arbitrary symbol … for the "malice" may have in it nothing really malicious; and need never be really "aforethought"'. The term remains an important one, however, to distinguish itself from cases of manslaughter which, according to Stephen J in *R v Doherty* (1887) 16 Cox CC 306, is an unlawful homicide *without* malice aforethought.

In addition to this, a person who kills out of mercy or compassion may still be guilty of murder. Despite such acts of compassion, a defendant who kills in such circumstances is just as liable as a person who kills in the 'heat of the moment'. This issue arose in the Court of Appeal case of *R v Inglis* [2011] 1 WLR 1110 where a mother killed her son, who lay seriously ill in a hospital bed, by injecting him with a large dose of heroin. The defendant treated her act as a form of mercy killing and claimed her intention was to rid her son of suffering. Lord Judge CJ ruled that all 'mercy killings' are unlawful and any change in the law is a matter for Parliament. In particular, Lord Judge CJ stated that

> we must underline that the law of murder does not distinguish between murder committed for malevolent reasons and murder motivated by familial love. Subject to well established partial defences, like provocation or diminished responsibility, *mercy killing is murder*. (emphasis added)

The same applies in cases of euthanasia where an individual assists another to die. Although suicide (and a failed attempt at suicide) was decriminalised as an offence as a result of the Suicide Act 1961, euthanasia (the act of assisting a person to bring about that person's death through a positive act) remains unlawful. In a case of euthanasia, the defendant is not to be charged with murder, but rather with assisting suicide under s 2(1) of the Suicide Act 1961. Although *Inglis* was not concerned with euthanasia, as there was no evidence of a request from the son to die, the same principles of mercy killings can be applied here. This is made clear in the famous case of *R (Nicklinson) v Ministry of Justice* [2014] UKSC 38 where the Supreme Court confirmed the position of the High Court ([2012] EWHC 2381 (Admin)) and later the Court of Appeal ([2014] 2 All ER 32) that voluntary euthanasia will amount to unlawful homicide. Specifically, Lord Neuberger in *Nicklinson* emphasised that the right to private and family life under Article 8 of the ECHR does not provide a recognisable defence to taking the life of another, whether it be in mercy or for some other reason.

If this topic is of interest to you, you may like to consider in more depth the following high-profile cases:

- *R (Pretty) v DPP* [2001] UKHL 61;
- *R (Purdy) v DPP* [2009] UKHL 45;
- *R (Nicklinson) v Ministry of Justice* [2014] UKSC 38;
- *R (Kenward) v DPP* [2015] EWHC 3508 (Admin);
- *R (Conway) v Secretary of State for Justice* [2018] EWCA Civ 1431; and
- *R (Lamb) v Secretary of State for Justice* [2019] EWHC 3606 (Admin).

Malice aforethought

For our purposes, we shall now return back to malice aforethought. In light of the points made above, the phrase has come under heavy criticism. For instance, Lord Hailsham in *Hyam v DPP* [1975] AC 55 argued that '... the sooner the phrase is consigned to the limbo of legal history the better the precision and lucidity in the interpretation of our criminal law'. Further to this, Lord Bridge in the House of Lords in *R v Moloney* [1985] AC 905 described the phrase as an 'anachronistic and now wholly inappropriate phrase which still lingers on in the definition of murder to denote the *necessary mental element*' (emphasis added).

This 'necessary mental element' can usefully be divided into:

- express malice; and
- implied malice.

Table 8.2 Malice aforethought

Malice	Meaning
Express	Intention to kill
Implied	Intention to cause grievous bodily harm (GBH) or resist lawful apprehension resulting in death

Express and implied malice can then be subdivided into direct and indirect (or oblique) intention (as discussed in **Chapter 3**). Remember that oblique intention is only evidence of intention; it is not to be equated with intention (*R v Moloney* [1985] AC 905).

Table 8.3 Direct and indirect intention

Malice	**Meaning**
Direct express	'Aim, objective and purpose' to kill (*R v Moloney* [1985] AC 905; *R v Mohan* [1976] QB 1)
Indirect express	Death was a virtual certainty as a result of the defendant's actions and the defendant appreciated that such was the case (*R v Woollin* [1999] AC 82)
Direct implied	'Aim, objective and purpose' to cause GBH (understood as meaning 'serious bodily harm') or resist lawful apprehension (*DPP v Smith* [1961] AC 290)
Indirect implied	Serious bodily harm was a virtual certainty as a result of the defendant's actions and the defendant appreciated that such was the case (*R v Cunningham* [1982] AC 566)

Prior to the Homicide Act (HA) 1957, there were three forms of malice aforethought, namely:

(a) express malice – intention to kill;
(b) implied malice – intention to cause GBH; and
(c) constructive malice – killing in the furtherance of a felony.

The HA 1957 abolished 'constructive malice', with s 1 providing that:

> (1) Where a person kills another in the course or furtherance of some other offence, the killing shall not amount to murder unless done with the same malice aforethought (express or implied) as is required for a killing to amount to murder when not done in the course or furtherance of another offence.
>
> (2) For the purposes of the foregoing subsection, a killing done in the course or for the purpose of resisting an officer of justice, or of resisting or avoiding or preventing a lawful arrest, or of effecting or assisting an escape or rescue from legal custody, shall be treated as a killing in the course or furtherance of an offence.

Now, according to the House of Lords in *R v Vickers* [1957] 2 QB 664, we simply have express and implied malice (see **Figure 8.2**).

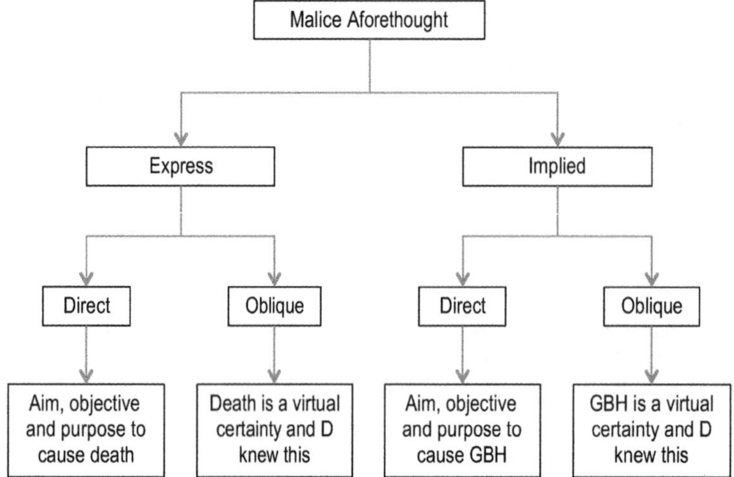

Figure 8.2 The forms of malice

Express malice

Simply meaning an intention to kill, express malice is the most commonly understood form of intention, ie you intend the eventual result. Horder (*Ashworth's Principles of Criminal Law*, 9th edn (OUP, 2019) suggests that express malice can better be understood as a 'test of failure' whereby the defendant would regard it as a failure if the victim was not killed by the defendant's conduct. See also Duff (*Intention, Agency and Criminal Liability: Philosophy of Action and the Criminal Law* (Wiley-Blackwell, 1990)).

example

Jack aims a gun point blank at Jill and shoots her in the head. Jill dies.

In this instance, the prosecution would have no difficulty in establishing that Jack held a clear intention to kill Jill. His intention would be 'direct' in the sense that it was his aim, objective and purpose to kill Jill. No other explanation could possibly be entertained. Should Jill, somehow, not die from her injuries, Jack's purpose can be said to have 'failed' – another way of understanding that direct intention is satisfied.

example

Jill wishes to kill her husband, Jack, and places a bomb on the aeroplane that Jack is taking for a business trip. The bomb explodes, killing Jack and all the other passengers on the aeroplane. Jill says that she never intended to kill any other person.

This case is a demonstration of both direct and indirect express malice in action. In this scenario, it is Jill's 'aim, objective and purpose' to kill Jack by placing the bomb on the aeroplane. Although Jill says that she did not intend to kill the other passengers, it cannot be said that Jill did not know that her actions would result in the death of the other passengers and crew. In this scenario, the jury would be asked to consider whether the end result (ie the death of the other passengers) was a virtual certainty and, if so, whether Jill appreciated that such an end result was a virtual certainty (*R v Woollin* [1999] AC 82). Should the jury find this to be the case, Jill will be just as liable for murder of the other passengers as she is for the murder of Jack.

Implied malice

Simply meaning an intention to cause GBH or resist lawful apprehension resulting in death, implied malice is not as widely understood to be a sufficient form of intention for the *mens rea* of murder. The ability to be found guilty of murder without having the intention to kill has come under a lot of criticism.

As will be discussed in **Chapter 9**, grievous bodily harm is to be interpreted as meaning 'really serious harm' (*DPP v Smith* [1961] AC 290), though the word 'really' (in some contexts) has been doubted as adding anything to the term (*R v Janjua; R v Choudhury* [1999] 1 Cr App R 91). In *R v Sidhu and others* [2019] EWCA Crim 1034, Green LJ in the Court of Appeal expressed the importance of distinguishing 'grievous', 'really serious' and 'serious' harm (all of which would suffice for murder) from merely moderate serious harm (which would not be sufficient for murder). In sentencing the defendant, the trial judge was alleged to have confused the two (thus erring in his sentencing). In the appeal on sentence, Green LJ in the Court of Appeal stated that judges must ensure that the distinction is clearly drawn. His Lordship explained:

> We accept that it might have been better if the judge had said in the relevant paragraph in his sentencing remarks that in his view the applicant intended to cause 'serious injury *but falling short of that required for murder*'. Indeed, judges might well, to avoid the risk of confusion such as has arisen in this case, be better either using the expression 'really serious' or, if they do use the expression 'serious' in a manslaughter case making it expressly clear that the intent to cause 'serious' injury was one, falling short of the intent required for murder. (original emphasis)

Sidhu is an additional authority in this regard on the point that whilst it is appropriate to refer to the *mens rea* for murder as an intention to cause 'serious harm', judges must be alert to the distinction between serious harm which is sufficient for a murder charge, and serious harm which falls short of murder (thus amounting to manslaughter).

Importantly in the context of murder, there is no requirement for the defendant to intend to cause GBH that is 'likely to endanger life'. This was the decision of the House of Lords in *R v Cunningham* [1982] AC 566.

case example

Charge:
Unlawful act manslaughter

Case progression:
Crown Court – Guilty

Court of Appeal – Conviction upheld

House of Lords – Conviction upheld

Point of law:
Implied malice

In *R v Cunningham* [1982] AC 566, the defendant killed the victim in a jealous rage.

The defendant contended that he did not intend to kill the victim and thus could not be liable for murder. The jury found him guilty of murder in that he intended to cause the victim serious bodily harm.

The Court of Appeal dismissed his appeal and this was affirmed by the House of Lords which approved its own previous decision in *Hyam v DPP* [1975] AC 55 that implied malice is sufficient *mens rea* for murder.

Lord Edmund-Davies commented that:

> I find it passing strange that a person can be convicted of murder if death results from, say, his intentional breaking of another's arm, an action which, while undoubtedly involving the infliction of 'really serious harm' and, as such, calling for severe punishment, would in most cases be unlikely to kill.

Although, Lord Edmund-Davies goes on to recognise that any change in the law must be a task for Parliament, this leads us nicely into the many criticisms laid against the rule of implied malice. In his article, 'The Mental Element in the Crime of Murder' (1988) 104 LQR 30, Goff LJ criticises the law for labelling people as murders who are not in true fact murderers. Specifically, Goff LJ provides that

> it seems very strange that a man should be called a murderer even though not only did he not intend to kill the victim, but he may even [in certain cases] have intended that he should not die.

Further, in *AG's Reference (No 3 of 1994)* [1998] AC 245, Lord Mustill described 'implied malice' as a 'conspicuous anomaly'; whilst in *R v Powell; R v English* [1999] 1 AC 1, Lord Steyn commented that it turns

> murder into a constructive crime. The fault element does not correspond to the conduct leading to the charge, i.e. the causing of death. A person is liable to conviction for a more serious crime than he foresaw or contemplated. ... The present definition of the mental element of murder results in defendants being classified as murderers who are not in truth murderers. ... It results in the imposition of mandatory life sentences when neither justice nor the needs of society require the classification of the case as murder and the imposition of a mandatory life sentence.

His Lordship went on to recommend that

> a killing should be classified as murder if there is an intention to kill or an intention to cause really serious harm coupled with awareness of the risk of death.

As above, however, his Lordship accepted that the problem was one which only Parliament could resolve.

8.2.3 Charging murder

8.2.3.1 Mode of trial

Murder is an offence triable only on indictment. Criminal procedure dictates that a defendant shall always start his criminal case in the magistrates' court. However, by s 51 of the Crime and Disorder Act 1998, upon a defendant being tried with an indictable offence, such as murder, the magistrates shall send him to the Crown Court for trial.

8.2.3.2 Sentencing

Murder was formerly an offence punishable by death. Indeed, prior the enactment of the HA 1957, all persons who were convicted of murder were automatically sentenced to death. Section 5 of the HA 1957 had the effect of singling out certain offences and labelling them as 'capital murders'. Such capital murders continued to be punishable by death, whilst those offences not deemed to be 'capital' were, instead, punishable by imprisonment for life. As a result of the Murder (Abolition of the Death Penalty) Act 1965, the penalty for murder in all cases is now a mandatory life sentence, which Wasik ('Sentencing in Homicide' in Ashworth and Mitchell (eds), *Rethinking English Homicide Law* (OUP, 2000)) argues was a 'necessary political compromise'.

8.2.4 Putting together murder

Consider the offence of murder and think of how you may structure an answer on this topic. Then see **Figure 8.15** at the end of this chapter for a sample structure to adopt.

facts

Jack is desperate for money to support his children. Jill, a wealthy neighbour, is walking down the street and is confronted by Jack. Jack approaches Jill and threatens her with a knife to hand over all of the money that she has on her person. The pair jostle with Jill's handbag before Jack stabs Jill in the stomach and escapes. Jill dies.

(There is no need for you to consider any liability for robbery.)

8.3 Manslaughter

By s 6(2) of the Criminal Law Act 1967, a person found not guilty of murder may be found guilty instead:

> (a) of manslaughter, or of causing grievous bodily harm with intent to do so; [or]
>
> ...
>
> (c) of an attempt to commit murder, or of an attempt to commit any other offence of which he might be found guilty;
>
> but may not be found guilty of any offence not included above.

This provision, along with the common law decision in *R v Coutts* [2006] 1 WLR 2154, is authority for the proposition that where a defendant is charged with murder, manslaughter ought to be present on the indictment as an alternative. Mitchell ('Distinguishing Between Murder and Manslaughter in Practice' (2007) 71 J Crim L 318) notes that difficulty will often arise in deciding on what basis the jury has reached their decision of manslaughter where the defence has claimed both a special defence and a denial of the *mens rea*. See *R v Braithwaite* [2019] EWCA Crim 597 for a recent example of manslaughter (specifically constructive manslaughter) used as an alternative verdict.

8.3.1 Distinguishing murder from manslaughter

The essential point to note is that where death has resulted from the actions of the defendant, murder should always be considered first, before then considering voluntary or involuntary manslaughter. The relevant discussion will ultimately depend on the intention of the defendant, given that the end result in all three cases (ie death) is the same (see *R v Sidhu and others* [2019] EWCA Crim 1034 above regarding the distinction between harm which is 'serious' enough for murder, and serious harm that falls short of murder).

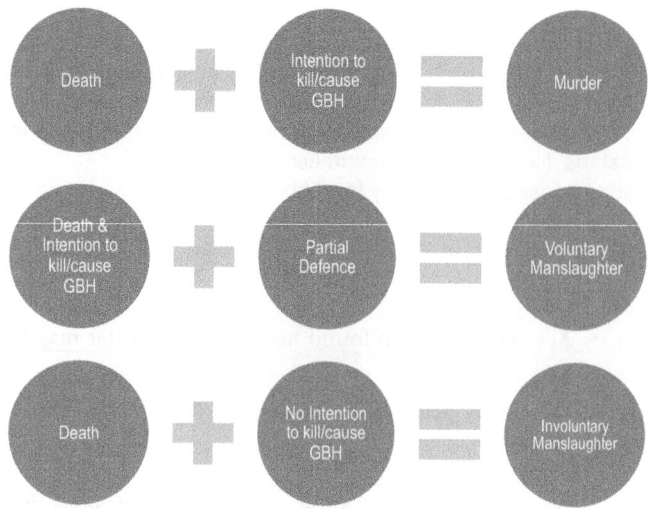

Figure 8.3 Understanding homicide

8.3.2 Distinguishing voluntary and involuntary manslaughter

Manslaughter can be conveniently divided into voluntary and involuntary manslaughter.

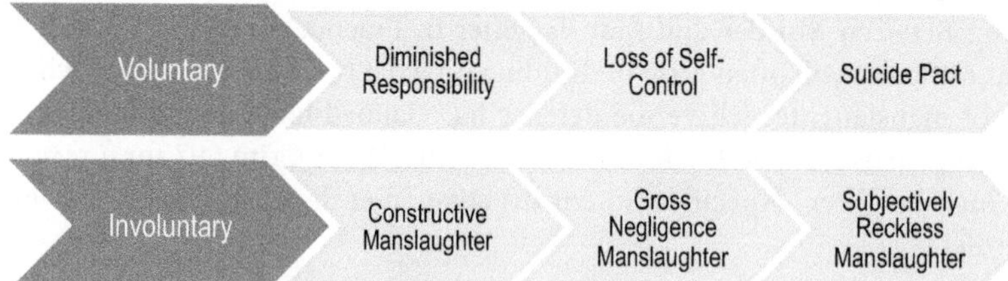

Figure 8.4 Types of manslaughter

As can be seen from **Figure 8.3** above, voluntary and involuntary manslaughter can be distinguished in the following manner:

- *Voluntary manslaughter:* These cases involve unlawful killings where the defendant possesses both the *actus reus* and *mens rea* for murder but he is capable of pleading a special defence which reduces his liability to manslaughter. As **Figure 8.4** demonstrates, voluntary manslaughter is concerned with the special defences of diminished responsibility, loss of self-control and suicide pacts.
- *Involuntary manslaughter:* These cases involve unlawful killings where the defendant possesses the *actus reus* of murder, but he lacks the *mens rea* (ie intention to kill or cause GBH). As **Figure 8.4** demonstrates, involuntary manslaughter is concerned with the offences of constructive manslaughter, gross negligence manslaughter and subjectively reckless manslaughter.

An important point to note, however, is the misleading nature of the terminology used (ie 'voluntary' and 'involuntary'). As we know from **Chapter 2**, all criminal offences require some form of voluntary conduct on the part of the accused. Unless the offence is one of 'absolute' liability, a defendant cannot be liable where his actions are considered involuntary. More so, in relation to manslaughter, the distinction between the two categories of offences has no relevance nor bearing on the voluntariness of the defendant's conduct.

We shall deal with voluntary manslaughter at **8.4** and involuntary manslaughter at **8.5**.

8.4 Voluntary manslaughter

It is essential that you appreciate that voluntary manslaughter is not an offence that is charged against a defendant. Therefore, stating that 'Jack may be liable for voluntary manslaughter' is wrong. Voluntary manslaughter is the result of a conviction (not an acquittal) arising out of the use of one of the three partial defences to murder. The defendant must still have the *actus reus* and *mens rea* for murder; however, his conduct is reduced to manslaughter by reason of one of the partial defences. Therefore, it is more appropriate to say that 'Jack may be liable for murder; however, he may instead be convicted of manslaughter if he is capable of raising one of the three special defences'.

in practice

A defendant may be convicted of manslaughter in two ways. First, where upon trial by jury he is found not guilty of murder but, in the alternative, is found guilty of voluntary manslaughter. Alternatively, the case may never reach a jury as the prosecution may offer the defendant a 'plea bargain' in that it offers him the partial defence of, eg, diminished responsibility, in return for a guilty plea of voluntary manslaughter.

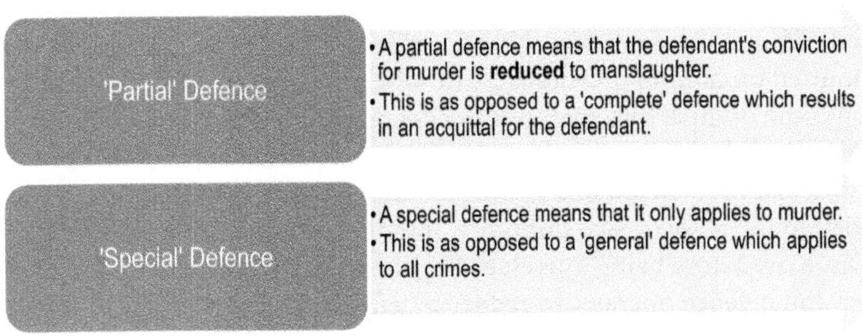

Figure 8.5 Understanding 'partial' and 'special' defences

There are three special defences to murder:

- diminished responsibility (**8.4.1**);
- loss of self-control (**8.4.2**); and
- killing in pursuance of a suicide pact (**8.4.3**).

These defences came into existence in an attempt to avoid the harshness of the law and the death penalty as prescribed for offences of murder. Upon the abolition of the death penalty, these defences now operate in order to avoid the mandatory life sentence that faces anyone convicted of murder.

Arguably, there is a fourth partial defence to murder, created by legislation, known as the act of infanticide. The CPS refers to this as a 'concealed' partial defence given that infanticide can be used as an alternative verdict to murder or charged in its own right (unlike the other partial defences, which are exactly that – defences). We shall consider infanticide alongside the other three partial defences at **8.4.4**.

It is important to emphasise that the partial defences apply only to murder. Therefore, you should not consider diminished responsibility, loss of self-control or suicide pact in relation to any other type of offence, even attempted murder (*R v Campbell* [1997] Crim LR 495). They are 'special defences' available only to the offence of murder. Should Jack slap Jill in anger because she has mocked him, he cannot argue as a defence to battery that he has lost his self-control.

in practice

Although a defendant may benefit from the use of a special defence, such as diminished responsibility or loss of self-control, lawyers for the defendant should always consider first whether there are any complete defences to the criminal charge, for example self-defence. Complete defences will excuse or justify the defendant's actions absolutely, whereas partial defences will simply reduce the conviction of murder to one of manslaughter. This is a point that students often miss – they skip directly into a discussion of partial defences and voluntary manslaughter without first considering any complete defences.

Follow this key:

Murder → Complete defences → Partial defences

8.4.1 Diminished responsibility

Section 52 of the Coroners and Justice Act (CAJA) 2009 substitutes the old partial defence of diminished responsibility under s 2 of the HA 1957 with one of the same name. The amendment of s 2 of the HA 1957, effected by the CAJA 2009, came into force on 4 October 2010 as a result of the Law Commission Report, 'Murder, Manslaughter and Infanticide' (Law Com No 304, 2006). The new defence applies to all murders committed on or after 4 October 2010, whereas murders committed prior to that date will use the original enactment of the defence. (We do not deal here with the law prior to the amendment so, should an issue arise requiring a discussion of the old law, it is advised that you consult one of the practitioner texts from that time.)

Historically viewed as a form of temporary insanity, diminished responsibility stemmed from Scots law before being introduced by the HA 1957. Much broader than insanity, however, the defence operates to reduce a defendant's conviction of murder to manslaughter which grants the trial judge a discretion in sentencing the offender. It is, in fact, quite rare for a plea of diminished responsibility to even go before a jury. Dell ('Diminished Responsibility Reconsidered' (1982) Crim LR 809) found that 80 per cent of guilty pleas based on diminished responsibility were accepted by prosecutors. Dell found that where the case goes to trial, as a result of the prosecution not accepting the guilty plea to manslaughter, there was a 60 per cent chance of a murder conviction. Overall, the failure rate of the defence was considered to be low, around 10 per cent.

in practice

Whilst the phrase 'diminished responsibility' was retained as the name for this partial defence, the Crown Court Compendium (section 19–1) notes that 'whenever it is raised the focus is on abnormality of mental functioning and the use of the words "diminished responsibility", depending on the circumstances, may not be helpful when directing the jury'.

8.4.1.1 Elements of diminished responsibility

Section 2 of the HA 1957 (as amended by s 52 of the CAJA 2009) provides:

(1) A person ('D') who kills or is a party to the killing of another is not to be convicted of murder if D was suffering from an abnormality of mental functioning which—
  (a) arose from a recognised medical condition,
  (b) substantially impaired D's ability to do one or more of the things mentioned in subsection (1A), and
  (c) provides an explanation for D's acts and omissions in doing or being a party to the killing.

(1A) Those things are—
  (a) to understand the nature of D's conduct;
  (b) to form a rational judgment;
  (c) to exercise self-control.

(1B) For the purposes of subsection (1)(c), an abnormality of mental functioning provides an explanation for D's conduct if it causes, or is a significant contributory factor in causing, D to carry out that conduct.

(2) On a charge of murder, it shall be for the defence to prove that the person charged is by virtue of this section not liable to be convicted of murder.

The elements of the defence can thus be set out as follows:

Table 8.4 Elements of diminished responsibility

Elements of the defence
An abnormality of mental functioning
A recognised medical condition
A substantial impairment of mental ability
Provides an explanation for D's acts and omissions in doing or being a party to the killing

Please note that each of these 'elements' must be proven. Should one fail, the entire defence fails.

8.4.1.2 (i) An abnormality of mental functioning (HA 1957, s 2(1))

The phrase 'abnormality of mental functioning' replaces the former concept of 'abnormality of mind' found in the original HA 1957. Neither term is defined by statute but rather they have been resolved by the common law.

The key authority on this term is that of *R v Byrne* [1960] 2 QB 396.

case example

Charge:
Murder

Case progression:
Crown Court – Guilty

Court of Criminal Appeal – Conviction quashed

Point of law:
Meaning of abnormality of the mind

In *R v Byrne* [1960] 2 QB 396, the defendant was charged with the murder of a young girl. The defendant was found guilty of strangling the girl before mutilating her dead body. The defendant introduced medical evidence to show that he suffered from abnormal sexual urges which were so strong that he could not resist them.

The defendant was found guilty in the Crown Court before appealing to the Court of Criminal Appeal. The Court allowed the appeal and substituted his conviction for murder with one of manslaughter.

The phrase abnormality of mind was defined in *Byrne* by Lord Parker CJ as

> a state of mind so different from that of ordinary human beings that the reasonable man would term it abnormal. It appears to us to be wide enough to cover the mind's activities in all its aspects, not only the perception of physical acts and matters, and the ability to form a rational judgment as to whether an act is right or wrong, but also the ability to exercise willpower to control physical acts in accordance with that rational judgment.

From 'mind' to 'mental functioning'

The change of wording from 'mind' to 'mental functioning' was not intended to change the meaning derived from *Byrne*. Rather, the legislature wished for the language of the Act to reflect a more accurate and appropriate description of the defence. The focus on mental functioning allows the courts to assess how medical and psychiatric conditions affect an individual's ability to control and understand their actions. Further, abnormality of mental functioning will continue to allow up-to-date medical evidence and knowledge to be produced at trial and avoids rather philosophical questions of the 'mind' and its nature. Indeed, this was made clear in *R v Brown* [2011] EWCA Crim 2796, where the Court of Appeal noted that 'one purpose of [the 2009 amendments] was to ensure a greater equilibrium between the law and medical science' (per Lord Judge CJ). See also the comments of the Law Commission in 'Murder, Manslaughter and Infanticide' (Law Com No 304, 2006).

Use of medical evidence

Rational judgment is, of course, a question for a jury (*Byrne*) who will rely on expert evidence to assist them. In *R v Dix* (1981) 74 Cr App R 306 (reaffirmed in *R v Bunch* [2013] EWCA Crim 2498) the Court of Appeal declared that medical evidence was 'a practical necessity if that defence is to begin to run at all' (per Shaw LJ). However, it is imperative to note that the jury are not bound to accept medical evidence (*R v Sanders* [1991] Crim LR 781). In many cases, the jury will be faced with conflicting medical evidence from both parties and will be tasked in weighing up the evidence and determining which view they prefer. It is for the jury to decide whether the defendant has a valid defence or not. This is known as the 'ultimate issue'. Wake ('Psychiatry and the New Diminished Responsibility Plea: Uneasy Bedfellows?' [2012] 76 J Crim L 122) remarks that: 'The jury are … left with the unenviable task of deciding between the competing views of reputable medical experts.'

Uncontested defence evidence

An issue that has come before the courts on a number of occasions concerns the circumstances where the defence presents medical evidence to prove diminished responsibility and such evidence goes unchallenged by the prosecution. In *R v Brennan* [2014] EWCA Crim 2387, Davis LJ explained that:

> It is therefore, in a diminished responsibility case where the expert evidence is uncontradicted, to be left to the evaluation by the trial judge of all the circumstances of the case, where an application to withdraw the case of murder is made at the close of evidence. The judge will assess the position in the light of the uncontradicted expert evidence and in the light of any other evidence. It at all events seems unprincipled in cases of this type, where an application to withdraw is made, that murder should be left to the jury simply and solely because the prosecution wants it to be. A charge of murder should not be left to the jury if the trial judge's considered view is that on the evidence taken as a whole no properly directed jury could properly convict of murder.

His Lordship had previously explained that '[w]here there simply is no rational or proper basis for departing from uncontradicted and unchallenged expert evidence then juries may not do so'. This approach was endorsed as correct by the Supreme Court in *R v Golds* [2016] UKSC 61. Whether the charge of murder is always withdrawn from the jury where the evidence goes undisputed, however, was not clear.

In *R v Blackman* [2017] EWCA Crim 190, the Court of Appeal applied *R v Golds*. Lord Thomas CJ stated:

> It is important to note the emphasis in the *Golds* judgment not only on the prosecution's right (if not duty) to assess the medical evidence and to challenge it, where there is a rational basis for so doing, but also on the primacy of the jury in determining the issue. It is clear that a judge should exercise caution before accepting the defence of diminished responsibility and removing the case from the jury ... The fact that the prosecution calls no evidence to contradict a psychiatrist called by the defence *is not in itself sufficient justification* for doing so. ... it will be a *rare case* where a judge will exercise the power to withdraw a charge of murder from the jury when the prosecution do not accept that the evidence gives rise to the defence of diminished responsibility. (emphasis added)

The following features can be extracted from the judgment in *Blackman*:

- The prosecution has the right to assess the medical evidence, and the jury have the right to determine whether they agree with the evidence.
- A murder charge should only be withdrawn from the jury in 'rare cases'.
- If the prosecution does not contradict the medical evidence, this is not synonymous with the fact that it accepts that the evidence is sufficient to prove diminished responsibility. The prosecution may not dispute the evidence that the defendant suffered from an abnormality of mental functioning, but it may still reject that the abnormality caused the killing, for example.

This approach was confirmed recently by the Court of Appeal in *R v Hussain* [2019] EWCA Crim 666 and *R v Sargeant* [2019] EWCA Crim 1088. Importantly, where the evidence does go unchallenged, and the charge is not withdrawn from the jury, the judge should issue the jury with a number of 'safety warnings' (*R v Sargeant*). These warnings come from the Supreme Court in *R v Golds*:

> Where, however, in a diminished responsibility trial the medical evidence supports the plea and is uncontradicted, the judge needs to ensure that the Crown explains the basis on which it is inviting the jury to reject that evidence. He needs

to ensure that the basis advanced is one which the jury can properly adopt. If the facts of the case give rise to it, he needs to warn the jury that brutal killings may be the product of disordered minds and that planning, whilst it may be relevant to self-control, may well be consistent with disordered thinking. While he needs to make it clear to the jury that, if there is a proper basis for rejecting the expert evidence, the decision is theirs – that trial is by jury and not by expert – it will also ordinarily be wise to advise the jury against attempting to make themselves amateur psychiatrists, and that if there is undisputed expert evidence the jury will probably wish to accept it, unless there is some identified reason for not doing so. (per Lord Hughes)

8.4.1.3 (ii) A recognised medical condition (HA 1957, s 2(1)(a))

The second requirement is that the defendant's abnormality of mental function 'arose from a recognised medical condition'. An important change made to the definition of diminished responsibility by s 52 of the CAJA 2009 is that the defence applies only if the defendant has a recognised medical condition. Formerly, no such requirement was necessary and it was sufficient to show that the abnormality arose from 'a condition of arrested or retarded development of mind or any inherent causes or induced by disease or injury'. This allowed for such conditions as a lack of sleep or heavy intoxication/ drunkenness to amount to an abnormality of the mind.

Now, medical evidence will need to be admitted to establish the existence of a recognised medical condition, which the jury will then assess. This was made clear by the Court of Appeal in *R v Bunch* [2013] EWCA Crim 2498, which stressed that such medical evidence must be capable of discharging the burden on the accused to show, on the balance of probabilities, that each ingredient of the defence is made out. As noted above, the Court referred to this as a 'practical necessity'.

To assist the jury, the courts may rely on a number of 'accepted classificatory lists', which encompass recognised physical, psychiatric and psychological medical conditions. The lists most commonly referred to are shown in **Figure 8.6**:

Figure 8.6 Classificatory lists

Both documents provide detailed and thorough lists of conditions that are to be medically recognised. However, it is important to note that the lists are not the sole or exclusive statement of law on this matter.

Specifically, in *R v Dowds* [2012] EWCA Crim 281, the Court of Appeal made clear that simply because a medical condition appears in the classificatory lists, and is 'recognised' as such, does not necessarily mean that it is capable of being relied upon to show an abnormality of mental functioning. Whether such a condition is to be 'recognised *in law*' remains a matter for the trial judge. In this case, Hughes LJ specifically made reference to the *Oxford Dictionary of Sports Science & Medicine*, which includes within it 'unhappiness', 'anger' and 'paedophilia', and made clear that such would not amount to recognised medical conditions in the eyes of the law. *Dowds* specifically was concerned with acute voluntary intoxication, which the Court of Appeal, although accepted to be medically recognised by the World Health Organization (WHO), refused to recognise as sufficient for the purposes of diminished responsibility.

On the flip side of this statement, the CPS has advised its prosecutors to consider that a condition which is not included in either list may still be deemed a 'recognised medical condition' for the purposes of this test. This open-ended nature is essential to allow for emerging conditions which, while being recognised, might not yet have been included in the accepted classificatory lists to be relied upon in court.

Examples of recognised medical conditions include the following (a combination of cases dealing with the law both before and following the 2009 amendments):

Table 8.5 Recognised medical conditions

Medical condition	**Authority**
Adjustment disorder	*R v Blackman* [2017] EWCA Crim 190 *R v Brown* [2011] EWCA Crim 2796
Autism spectrum disorder	*R v Conroy (Jason John)* [2017] EWCA Crim 81
ADHD	*R v Dietschmann* [2003] 1 AC 1209
Alcoholic dependency (but not voluntary acute intoxication)	*R v Bunch* [2013] EWCA Crim 2498 *R v Stewart (James)* [2009] EWCA Crim 593 *R v Tandy* [1989] 1 All ER 267
Asperger's syndrome	*R v Jama* [2004] EWCA Crim 960
Battered woman syndrome	*R v Ahluwalia* [1992] 4 All ER 889 *R v Hobson* [1998] 1 Cr App R 31
Dementia	*R v Beaver* [2015] EWCA Crim 653
Depression	*R v Seers* (1984) 79 Cr App R 261 *R v Swan* [2006] EWCA Crim 3378 *R v Potts* [2015] EWCA Crim 1488
Epilepsy	*R v Campbell* [1997] Crim LR 495
Othello syndrome ('morbid jealousy')	*R v Vinagre* (1979) 69 Cr App R 104 – it is questionable whether this defence would succeed under the new law
Post-traumatic stress disorder (PTSD)	*R v Janiszewski* [2012] EWCA Crim 2556
Psychopathic personality	*R v Foye* [2013] EWCA Crim 475
Schizophrenia	*R v Jenkin* [2014] EWCA Crim 1394 *R v Graciano* [2015] EWCA Crim 980 *R v Khan (Dawood)* [2009] EWCA Crim 1569
Paranoid personality disorder	*R v Squelch* [2017] EWCA Crim 204

Battered woman syndrome was added to the classification list in 1994 following the high media attention following the case of *R v Ahluwalia* [1992] 4 All ER 889.

Charge:
Murder

Case progression:
Crown Court – Guilty

Court of Appeal – Conviction quashed

Point of law:
Battered woman syndrome in diminished responsibility

case example

In *R v Ahluwalia* [1992] 4 All ER 889, the defendant poured petrol over the victim, her husband, whilst he slept and set him alight. The defendant had been subjected to domestic abuse for a number of years. The victim died from his burns a few days later. The defendant was charged with and convicted of murder.

The defendant appealed to the Court of Appeal, arguing the defence of provocation that she had suffered violence and abuse from her husband over a long period. The Court of Appeal rejected her appeal on provocation but allowed her appeal on the grounds of diminished responsibility.

Battered woman syndrome was later confirmed by the Court of Appeal in *R v Hobson* [1998] 1 Cr App R 31 as a condition capable of giving rise to the defence of diminished responsibility. We shall see later in this chapter whether the defendant in *Ahluwalia* could rely on the new defence of loss of self-control if the same facts were to arise today.

An issue closely related to that of battered woman syndrome is that of 'coercive control'. In the high-profile case of *R v Challen* [2019] EWCA Crim 916, Hallett LJ, in the Court of Appeal, explained that:

> it is important to remember that coercive control as such is not a defence to murder. The only partial defences open to the appellant were provocation and diminished responsibility, and coercive control is only relevant *in the context* of those two defences. (emphasis added)

In *Challen*, the Court of Appeal quashed the appellant's conviction on account that she suffered 'from borderline personality disorder and a severe mood disorder, probably bipolar affective disorder, and suffered from those disorders at the time of the killing. … it is in that context that the theory of coercive control may be relevant.' The important aspect of *Challen*, therefore, is that coercive control is not a defence to murder; however, it may be used as evidence to support a claim of diminished responsibility (and perhaps loss of self-control, see below).

in practice

Many appeals in this area of law concern the circumstances where fresh psychiatric evidence was unavailable at the time of trial which supported a defence of diminished responsibility and is now being submitted on appeal under s 23 of the Criminal Appeal Act 1968. This was the situation in both *Hobson* and *Challen*; however, this process is not the norm. Hallett LJ in *Challen* explained:

> As this court has observed frequently, any available defences should be advanced at trial, and if evidence, including medical evidence, is available to support a defence it should be deployed at trial. As a general rule, it is not open to a defendant to run one defence at trial and when unsuccessful, to try to run an alternative defence on appeal, relying on evidence that could have been available at trial. This court has set its face against what has been called expert shopping. Nor is it open to an appellant to develop and sometimes embellish their account to provide material upon which a fresh expert can base a new report and diagnosis.

This approach was recently affirmed by the Court of Appeal in *R v Foy* [2020] EWCA Crim 270, in which Davis LJ in the Court of Appeal distinguished between evidence that was not available at trial; evidence that was available but was overlooked; and evidence that was available, considered and rejected. In the latter circumstance, the mere fact that a different opinion as to the evidence has arisen post-conviction is not sufficient to adduce the evidence under s 23 (what Davis LJ referred to as 'expert shopping'). See Thomas, '"Expert Shopping": Appeals Adducing Fresh Evidence in Diminished Responsibility Cases' (2020) 84(3) J Crim L 249.

An interesting point arises in the context of immaturity; specifically whether the immaturity of adult defendants should be considered a recognised condition. Although such immaturity will often coincide with a recognised condition, for example autism, it is not always the case that it will do so. In its Report ('Murder, Manslaughter and Infanticide' (Law Com No 304, 2006)), the Law Commission recommended that 'developmental immaturity', as it called it, should be explicitly included as an element for diminished responsibility. As opposed to extending the meaning of a recognised medical condition, the Commission proposed that such immaturity should stand as an alternative to a recognised medical condition. This proposal was rejected by the Government, which Child and Ormerod (*Smith, Hogan, & Ormerod's Essentials of Criminal Law*, 3rd edn (OUP, 2019)) refer to as 'unfortunate'. The Government justified its actions on the basis that an 'abnormal immaturity' would already fall within the recognised categories prescribed, namely general learning disabilities and autistic-related conditions. However, the Government was adamant that simple developmental immaturity, without a subsisting condition, will not suffice for diminished responsibility. Allen and Edwards (*Criminal Law*, 15th edn (OUP, 2019)) question the validity of this response and provide the argument that

> this omission leaves the developmentally immature adult at an advantage over the normal child as a 40-year-old with the mental age of 10 may raise the defence relying on a medical condition to explain his developmental immaturity whereas a normal 10-year-old will be accorded no such opportunity even though the self-control he may be expected to exercise is no different.

This may be a point you wish to consider further.

8.4.1.4 (iii) A substantial impairment of mental ability (HA 1957, s 2(1)(b))

Interestingly, despite its name, nowhere in s 2 of the HA 1957 will the word 'diminished' be found. Rather, the law focuses on the phrase 'substantially impaired'. We shall first deal with the meaning of the word 'substantially' before we proceed to consider the various mental abilities that may be 'impaired'.

Meaning of 'substantially'

The word 'substantial' would appear intentional by the legislature to distinguish it from a 'total' or 'complete' impairment. That is not controversial. The issue becomes, though: what is the extent of 'substantially'?

In *R v Lloyd* [1967] 1 QB 175, the trial judge directed the jury on the word 'substantially' as follows:

> I am not going to try to find a parallel for the word 'substantial'. You are the judge, but your own common sense will tell you what it means. This far I will go. Substantial need not be totally impaired, so to speak, destroyed altogether. At the other end of the scale substantial does not mean trivial or minimal. It is

> something in between and Parliament has left it to you and other juries to say on the evidence, was the mental responsibility impaired, and, if so, was it substantially impaired?

On appeal in the Court of Criminal Appeal, Edmund Davies J ruled:

> The word 'substantially' obviously is inserted in the Act with a view to carrying some meaning. It does carry a meaning. This court is quite unable to see that the direction given to the jury on the meaning of this word, can validly be criticised …

More recently, the Court of Appeal in *R v Ramchurn* [2010] 2 Cr App R 18 reviewed the earlier authorities of *Lloyd, R v Egan* [1992] 4 All ER 470 and *R v Mitchell* [1995] Crim LR 506 and ruled that 'substantially' is not a word that a judge should try to define or find a synonym for, but one which the jury should approach using their own common sense and good judgement. Lord Judge CJ concluded:

> In our judgment, faced with this problem at a murder trial, it is necessary for the judge to convey to the jury the plain meaning of the statute, no more, no less. Provided in the language he uses he does not exaggerate the burden on the defendant, or improvise some extra statutory additional obligation on the defendant in relation to the meaning of 'substantially impaired', no valid ground for complaint exists.

The court's position on the word 'substantially' was reviewed by the Court of Appeal in *R v Golds* [2014] EWCA Crim 748 which held that it meant 'significant' or 'appreciable'.

Charge:
Murder

Case progression:
Crown Court – Guilty

Court of Appeal – Conviction upheld

Point of law:
Meaning of 'substantially' in diminished responsibility

case example

In *R v Golds* [2014] EWCA Crim 748, the defendant stabbed his partner. The defendant had a history of mental illness, and at trial two forensic psychiatrists and one forensic psychologist were called by the defence to give evidence. The defendant was charged with and convicted of murder in the Crown Court.

The defendant appealed to the Court of Appeal on that basis that the trial judge had refused to give a direction on the meaning of the word 'substantial'.

The Court of Appeal noted that the specimen direction in the Crown Court Bench Book was ambiguous, leading juries to be wrongly directed. The Court emphasised that a two-stage approach ought to be followed:

(i) The jury should be left to apply the word for themselves.
(ii) If a jury should ask for help, they should be given a direction based on that given in *R v Simcox* [1964] Crim LR 402.

In *R v Simcox*, the trial judge directed the jury in these words:

> Do we think, looking at it broadly as common-sense people, there was a substantial impairment of his mental responsibility in what he did?' If the answer to that is 'yes,' then you find him not guilty of murder, but guilty of manslaughter. If the answer to that is 'no', there may be some impairment, but we do not think it was substantial, we do not think it was something which really made any great difference, although it may have made it harder to control himself, to refrain from crime, then you would find him guilty …

Importantly, the case of *Golds* was appealed to the Supreme Court ([2016] UKSC 61). The appellant (Golds) asked for clarification on the following two questions which were certified by the Court of Appeal as being of general public importance:

(1) Where a defendant, being tried for murder, seeks to establish that he is not guilty of murder by reason of diminished responsibility, is the Court required to direct the jury as to the definition of the word 'substantial', as in the phrase 'substantially impaired' in section 2(1)(b) of the Homicide Act 1957 as amended by section 52 of the Coroners and Justice Act 2009?

(2) If the answer to the first question is in the affirmative, or if for some other reason the judge chooses to direct the jury on the meaning of the word 'substantial', is it to be defined as 'something more than merely trivial', or alternatively in a way that connotes more than this, such as 'something whilst short of total impairment is nevertheless significant and appreciable'?

Fully affirming the ruling of the Court of Appeal, Lord Hughes answered the two questions asked by the Court of Appeal in the following fashion:

(1) Ordinarily in a murder trial where diminished responsibility is in issue the judge *need not direct the jury* beyond the terms of the statute and should not attempt to define the meaning of 'substantially'. Experience has shown that the issue of its correct interpretation is unlikely to arise in many cases. The jury should normally be given to understand that the expression is an ordinary English word, that it imports a question of degree, and that whether in the case before it the impairment can properly be described as substantial is for it to resolve.

(2) If, however, the jury has been introduced to the question of whether *any impairment* beyond the merely trivial will suffice, or if it has been introduced to the concept of a spectrum between the greater than trivial and the total, the judge should explain that whilst the impairment must indeed pass the merely trivial before it need be considered, it is not the law that *any impairment* beyond the trivial will suffice. The judge should likewise make this clear if a risk arises that the jury might misunderstand the import of the expression; whether this risk arises or not is a judgment to be arrived at by the trial judge who is charged with overseeing the dynamics of the trial. Diminished responsibility involves an impairment of one or more of the abilities listed in the statute to an extent which the jury judges to be substantial, and which it is satisfied significantly contributed to his committing the offence. Illustrative expressions of the sense of the word may be employed so long as the jury is given clearly to understand that no single synonym is to be substituted for the statutory word. (emphasis added)

Lord Hughes laid out a number of ways in which the concept of 'substantial impairment' might be illustrated or explained. His Lordship explained that 'substantial' could be used in two senses, either:

> (1) 'present rather than illusory or fanciful, thus having some substance' or (2) 'important or weighty', as in 'a substantial meal' or 'a substantial salary'.

Lord Hughes confirmed that it is the second sense of the word that should apply when considering whether the medical condition substantially impairs the defendant's ability to understand the nature of his act, form rational judgments or exercise self-control.

Further in his judgment, his Lordship stated that

> Various phrases have been used in the cases to convey the sense in which 'substantially' is understood in this context. The words used by the Court of Appeal in the second certified question in the present case ('significant and appreciable') are one way of putting it, providing that the word 'appreciable' is treated not as being synonymous with merely recognisable but rather with the connotation of being considerable. Other phrases used have been 'a serious degree of impairment' (*Seers*), 'not total impairment but substantial' (*Ramchurn*) or 'something far wrong' (*Galbraith*). These are acceptable ways of elucidating the sense of the statutory requirement but it is neither necessary nor appropriate for this court to mandate a particular form of words in substitution for the language used by Parliament.

Lord Hughes concluded his explanation of this point by emphasising that

> The jury must understand that 'substantially' involves a matter of degree, and that it is for it to use the collective good sense of its members to say whether the condition in the case it is trying reaches that level or not.

Golds was applied in the case of *R v Squelch* [2017] EWCA Crim 204, where the Court of Appeal found that the trial judge's direction to the jury that 'substantial' meant 'less than total and more than trivial' was in line with the guidance provided in *Golds*. The Court of Appeal felt that the trial judge had not elaborated unduly beyond the principle in *Golds*, especially given that the jury were told: 'Where you, the jury, draw the line is a matter for your collective judgment.'

The judgment in *Golds* has the effect of reaffirming *R v Eifinger* [2001] EWCA Crim 1855, which held that the question of what is 'substantial' is one for the jury as a matter of fact and degree with the assistance of medical experts (*R v Khan (Dawood)* [2009] EWCA Crim 1569). In *R v Jennion* [1962] 1 WLR 317, the Court of Criminal Appeal concluded that where medical experts differ (which happens more than you may think), it is for the jury alone to resolve the issue. The Court held that although this is a matter of psychiatry, it ultimately remains a question of fact and degree for the jury. See also *R v Kimel* [2016] EWCA Crim 1456 (above).

Impairment of mental abilities

Now that we understand the meaning of the word 'substantial', it is important to note that the defendant is required to show that the abnormality of mental functioning substantially impaired his 'ability' to do one or more of the conditions set out in s 2(1A) of the HA 1957. The former wording in the original 1957 Act was of 'mental responsibility'. At the time, the word 'responsibility' was viewed favourably in that it allowed a great deal of flexibility for the courts and jury to find a just and fair outcome in the case. However, the Law Commission was less convinced by this term, arguing it to be 'chaotic' and 'grossly abused' in certain cases given its incapability of medical assessment (Law Commission, 'Partial Defences to Murder' (Law Com No 290, 2004)).

As a result of the 2009 Act, however, the word used is one of 'ability' and specifically concerns the defendant's ability to:

(a) understand the nature of his own conduct
(b) form a rational judgment;
(c) exercise self-control.

Table 8.6 Conditions of substantial impairment

Conditions of s 2(1A) of the HA 1957
(a) To understand the nature of his own conduct
(b) To form a rational judgment
(c) To exercise self-control

Given the relatively recent nature of the Act's introduction, little case law is present on the interpretation of these conditions. Instead, we have examples given by the Law Commission in its Report, 'Murder, Manslaughter and Infanticide' (Law Com No 304, 2006). A further point to note is that a defendant may fall within more than one of these circumstances, though only one needs to be proven.

To understand the nature of his own conduct (HA 1957, s 2(1A)(a))

Does the defendant have the ability to understand the nature of his own conduct? Note the key words here: 'his own conduct'. It does not encompass his ability to understand anyone else's ability or conduct.

The Law Commission ('Murder, Manslaughter and Infanticide' (Law Com No 304, 2006)) gives the following example:

> [A] boy aged 10 who has been left to play very violent video games for hours on end for much of his life, loses his temper and kills another child when the child attempts to take a game from him. When interviewed, he shows no real understanding that, when a person is killed they cannot simply be later revived [or 'regenerated' to the use the technical gaming term], as happens in the games he has been continually playing.

This example is justified on the basis that the defendant may understand the physical nature of his action, but would not understand the outcome or impact of his action. This defence is unlikely to arise in practice: it will rarely be possible for a defendant to not understand the nature of his conduct but still possess the intention to kill or cause GBH (remembering that D still has the *mens rea* for murder when alleging voluntary manslaughter).

To form a rational judgment (HA 1957, s 2(1A)(b))

This second circumstance overlaps with the former in that a person who is unable to understand the nature of his act is also likely not to be able to form a rational judgment.

The Law Commission gives the following example:

> [A] mentally sub-normal boy believes that he must follow his older brother's instructions, even when they involve taking part in a killing. He says, 'I wouldn't dream of disobeying my brother and he would never tell me to do something if it was really wrong.'

Another example may be that of a battered wife who kills her abuser, or that of a mercy killer who kills his sick son or daughter. In these cases, the Commission argues that the pressure of the circumstances may have the result of substantially impairing the defendant's ability to make rational choices. Allen and Edwards (*Criminal Law*, 15th edn (OUP, 2019)) further this by arguing that such pressure may 'distort' an individual's perception to the extent they believe the 'only way' to solve their problems is to kill. Child and Omerod (*Smith, Hogan, & Ormerod's Essentials of Criminal Law*, 3rd edn (OUP, 2019)) summarise this circumstance excellently by providing that:

> the issue [in such cases] is really about whether D was able rationally to make a choice rather than whether the choice made was a rational one.

A relatively recent case that has come before the courts concerning the interpretation of this section is that of *R v Conroy (Jason John)* [2017] EWCA Crim 81. This case concerned the strangulation by the defendant who suffered from autism of a fellow care home resident. In directing the jury at the trial proper, the judge informed the jury that they ought to focus on the 'decision making process' as opposed to the 'outcome' in order to determine the defendant's ability to form a rational judgment.

The Court of Appeal, in dismissing the appeal for the defendant, held that

> the jury may properly assess all relevant circumstances preceding, and perhaps preceding over a very long period, the killing as well as any relevant circumstances following the killing. (per Davis LJ)

In effect, the Court of Appeal ruled that it was 'over-refined to separate the decision making process from the outcome' and, in doing so, a court could lead to 'undue glossing of section 2 of the Homicide Act 1957.' For a case commentary on *Conroy*, see Storey, '"Rational" Reconstruction: Diminished Responsibility and Substantially Impaired Ability to Form a Rational Judgment' (2017) 81(3) J Crim L 247.

A second case dealing with this section is that of *R v Blackman* [2017] EWCA Crim 190. This high-profile case concerned so-called 'Marine A' and his conviction for murder of a wounded insurgent. The Court Martial Appeal Court concluded that the marine's murder conviction should be replaced with a verdict of manslaughter by reason of diminished responsibility on account of an adjustment disorder suffered by the defendant and a number of 'stresses' which exacerbated his situation. The difficulty the Court was faced with was that the defendant, despite all of this, continued to act in a 'rational' fashion. The question was whether the defendant could nonetheless avail a defence despite his rational-seeming exterior.

The Court concluded:

> [A] person with such a disorder can appear to act rationally. In this case examples include moving the body out of the sight of the camera, waiting for the helicopter to move away, stating that he was not be shot in the head and other similar comments which we have described.
>
> However, that type of planning is quite distinct from the effect of an adjustment disorder which can affect the ability to form a rational judgement about (1) the need to adhere to standards and the moral compass set by HM Armed Forces and (2) putting together the consequences to himself and others of the individual actions he is about to take. In our view, the adjustment disorder had put the appellant in the state of mind to kill, but the fact that he acted with apparent careful thought as to how to set about the killing had to be seen within the overarching framework of the disorder which had substantially impaired his ability to form a rational judgement.

What *Conroy* and *Blackman* should demonstrate is that there is no requirement for the defendant to act 'entirely' irrationally. There may be aspects of the defendant's thinking that were rational, and aspects that are entirely irrational. However, the jury are tasked with looking at the situation as a whole to determine whether there was an impairment of rationality.

To exercise self-control (HA 1957, s 2(1A)(c))

The final circumstance under s 2(1A) of the HA 1957 is that the defendant is impaired substantially from exercising self-control. This final category is similar to that of the loss of self-control defence (see **8.4.2**) in that the defendant is unable to exercise self-control.

The Law Commission gives the following example:

> [A] man says that sometimes the devil takes control of him and implants in him a desire to kill, a desire that must be acted on before the devil will go away.

The Law Commission has made clear that this circumstance is much broader than the former two and thus may provide a defence when the former would not. You could say, therefore, that this circumstance is the defence of last resort.

Given the similar terminology between this element of diminished responsibility, and the separate defence of loss of self-control, it is worth identifying the differences (so that you may identify the appropriate defence in a problem scenario):

Table 8.7 Distinguishing s 2(1A)(c) from the defence of loss of self-control

'To exercise self-control' in diminished responsibility	Loss of self-control
There must be an abnormality of mental functioning arising from a recognised medical condition	There is no such requirement for an abnormality or a medical condition
There is no restriction on the response of the defendant	The defendant must have shown a normal degree of tolerance and self-restraint

8.4.1.5 (iv) Provides an explanation for D's acts and omissions in doing or being a party to the killing (HA 1957, s 2(1)(c))

The final element of this defence is that the substantial impairment must 'explain' the defendant's acts in killing. This essentially means that there must be some causal link between the defendant's abnormality of mental functioning and the killing. For instance, if the defendant suffers from an abnormality of mental functioning, but that abnormality actually has nothing to do with the killing, then the defendant cannot avail the defence.

To assist the jury with the meaning of this element, s 2(1B) of the HA 1957 states that an abnormality of mental functioning provides an explanation for D's conduct if it 'causes, or is a significant contributory factor in causing, D to carry out that conduct'. From the wording in s 2(1B), it is clear that the abnormality need not be the sole cause of the killing; it can be a contributory cause, although this must be a significant rather than trivial contribution. A lot of the case law in this regard has concerned the effect of intoxication on the defence of diminished responsibility.

Effect of intoxication on diminished responsibility

The main authority on this point is that of *R v Dietschmann* [2003] 1 AC 1209.

Charge:
Murder

Case progression:
Crown Court –
Guilty

Court of Appeal –
Conviction upheld

House of Lords –
Appeal allowed (conviction substituted for voluntary manslaughter)

Point of law:
Multiple causes explaining the defendant's conduct

case example

In *R v Dietschmann* [2003] 1 AC 1209, the defendant, upon becoming heavily intoxicated, killed the victim.

At trial, the defendant raised the defence of diminished responsibility on account that he suffered from depression following the death of his aunt. It was this depression that led him to become heavily intoxicated.

Despite this, the Crown Court convicted the defendant of murder, which was upheld by the Court of Appeal on the ground that it was intoxication that led to the act of killing; not the depression.

In allowing his appeal, the House of Lords ruled that although the defendant's actions may have been in some way caused by his intoxication, the matter still remained open to the jury to determine whether his depression (the abnormality) remained a substantial aspect of his killing.

This case has been subsequently reaffirmed in *R v Wood* [2008] EWCA Crim 1305, *R v Hendy* [2006] EWCA Crim 819, *R v Michael Robson* [2006] EWCA Crim 2749, *R v Swan* [2006] EWCA Crim 3378 and *R v Dowds* [2012] EWCA Crim 281.

These cases were recently reviewed in detail by the Court of Appeal in *R v Kay; R v Joyce* [2017] 4 WLR 121. The Vice President of the Court of Appeal, Hallett LJ, providing the judgment of the Court, ruled that:

> The law does not debar someone suffering from schizophrenia from relying on the partial defence of diminished responsibility where voluntary intoxication has triggered the psychotic state, but he must meet the criteria in section 2(1). He must establish, on the balance of probabilities, that his abnormality of mental functioning arose from a recognised medical condition that substantially impaired his responsibility. The recognised medical condition may be schizophrenia of such severity that, *absent intoxication*, it substantially impaired his responsibility; the recognised medical condition may be schizophrenia *coupled with* drink/drugs dependency syndrome which together substantially impair responsibility. However, if an abnormality of mental functioning arose from voluntary intoxication and not from a recognised medical condition an accused cannot avail himself of the partial defence. This is for *good reason*. The law is clear and well established: as a general rule voluntary intoxication cannot relieve an offender of responsibility for murder, save where it may bear on the question of intent. (emphasis added)

Hallett LJ concluded:

> The defendant in this case, therefore, had to establish either that his intoxication was involuntary and together with the schizophrenia substantially impaired his responsibility (as the defence experts argued) or that the schizophrenia standing alone substantially impaired his responsibility.

Following *Dietschmann* and *Joyce*, the law can be stated as follows:

(1) Intoxication alone cannot provide an explanation for the defendant's actions when using the defence of diminished responsibility – it is not a legally recognised condition (*R v Fenton* (1975) 61 Cr App R 261; *R v Lindo* [2016] EWCA Crim 1940 – concerning a drug-induced psychosis).

(2) In the circumstances where the defendant is intoxicated but also has a separate recognised condition (other than alcohol dependency – see (3) below), the defendant is not debarred from raising the defence. Rather, the jury are entitled to ask whether the defendant's conduct was, nonetheless, caused by the recognised condition. In such a case, the jury should exclude the intoxicated state of the defendant from their consideration and consider whether the condition 'standing alone' was severe enough to substantially impair the defendant's responsibility (*R v Gittens* [1984] QB 698).

(3) Where the defendant has a drug or alcohol dependency, and a separate and distinct abnormality, these may be classed as two distinct abnormalities for the purpose of diminished responsibility. In such a case, the jury are entitled to take both into account when considering causation. In the case of the drug or alcohol dependency, the jury are to assess the 'nature and extent of the syndrome' before considering causation (*R v Stewart (James)* [2009] EWCA Crim 593, per Lord Judge CJ).

Miles ('A Dog's Breakfast of Homicide Reform' [2009] 6 Arch News 6) argues that causation in this context is a much more difficult concept than causation in all other aspects of criminal law. Specifically Miles comments that the causation requirement in this context looks towards the effect of the abnormality internally as opposed to the standard test of external causation. Miles notes that 'even with the help of medical experts, this is far from an exact science' and could prove difficult for the court to decide. Mackay ('The New Diminished Responsibility Plea' [2010] Crim LR 290) responded in some way to this matter and questions the need for any form of internal or external causal link when the elements in s 2(1A) of the HA 1957 must, nevertheless, be proven.

8.4.1.6 Procedure and sentencing

Diminished responsibility is a defence only to a charge of murder and results in a conviction of manslaughter. Importantly, in order to rely on the defence, the defendant must be charged with murder. Whilst he may be subsequently convicted of manslaughter, due to diminished responsibility, he cannot be charged with manslaughter. Horder (*Excusing Crime* (OUP, 2004)) justifies this defence on the basis that the defendant should not be held to the standard of a 'normal' person because of their medical condition (in contrast with the justification for loss of self-control, see below). Therefore, before one can consider the defence of diminished responsibility, the prosecution must first prove murder beyond a reasonable doubt.

Sentence

A defendant convicted of manslaughter by diminished responsibility may be sentenced to life imprisonment; however, this is at the discretion of the trial judge. In *R v Edgington* [2013] EWCA Crim 2185, the Court of Appeal made clear that the disposal powers following conviction were a matter for the trial judge, and not the jury.

Burden of proof

The burden on raising the defence is on the defendant. The trial judge has no power to raise the issue of diminished responsibility if the defence does not do so. However, note that if the trial judge identifies evidence of diminished responsibility, the judge has the right to point this evidence out to defence counsel. It will then be for defence counsel to decide whether to raise the defence or not (*R v Campbell* (1986) 84 Cr App R 255).

As with insanity, the burden of proof is on the defendant to prove diminished responsibility (HA 1957, s 2(2)). The standard of proof is the civil standard, on the balance of probabilities (*R v Dunbar* [1958] 1 QB 1). In the conjoined appeals of *R v Lambert; R v Ali; R v Jordan* [2002] QB 1112, the Court of Appeal was confronted with the question of whether the reverse burden in s 2 was compatible with the presumption of innocence in Article 6(2) of the ECHR. Lord Woolf CJ, giving the judgment of the Court, ruled that

> If the defendant is being required to prove an essential element of the offence, this will be more difficult to justify. If, however, what the defendant is required to do is establish a special defence or exception this will be less objectionable ... [I]t is important to have in mind that article 6(2) is specifically directed to the application of the presumption of innocence of the 'criminal offences' charged.

Lord Woolf CJ concluded that there was no breach of Article 6(2) by way of the reversed burden. His Lordship appears to justify his judgment on the basis that the defendant is required to 'prove a defence' as opposed to 'disprove an element of the offence'. McAlhone and Wortley (*Criminal Law: The Fundamentals*, 4th edn (Sweet & Maxwell, 2016)) are especially critical of this decision, arguing that Lord Woolf's reasoning is 'no justification at all'. The pair go on to say that

> The prosecution has the burden of disproving [loss of self-control], which is also a special defence or exception to liability, so it is nonsense to suggest that where a defence permits an exception to liability, it is ever appropriate for the defendant to have to prove it.

Despite this criticism, the Court of Appeal in *R v Foye* [2013] EWCA Crim 475, and more recently in *R v Wilcocks* [2016] EWCA Crim 2043, has confirmed that the reverse burden does not infringe the presumption of innocence under Article 6(2).

8.4.2 Loss of self-control

The second partial defence to murder is that of loss of self-control (also known simply as 'loss of control').

Loss of self-control is a special and partial defence to murder, enacted by ss 54 and 55 of the CAJA 2009. The previous common law defence of provocation was abolished by s 56(1) of the CAJA 2009, although the common law decisions under the pre-2009 defence may still be relevant to our discussion of loss of self-control.

As with diminished responsibility, the 2009 provisions apply to defendants charged with murder where the acts or omissions resulting in the death of the victim took place on or after 4 October 2010. Any murder committed prior to this date shall be conducted in accordance with the former rules of provocation. We shall discuss the former law in no further detail at this stage. In *R v Gurpinar; R v Kojo-Smith* [2015] EWCA Crim 178, Lord Thomas CJ in the Court of Appeal clarified that it 'should rarely be necessary to look at cases decided under the old law of provocation. When it is necessary, the cases must be considered in the light of the fact that the defence of loss of control is a defence different from provocation and is fully encompassed within the statutory provisions.'

8.4.2.1 Elements of loss of self-control

Section 54 of the CAJA 2009 provides:

(1) Where a person ('D') kills or is a party to the killing of another ('V'), D is not to be convicted of murder [but of manslaughter] if—
   (a) D's acts and omissions in doing or being a party to the killing resulted from D's loss of self-control,
   (b) the loss of self-control had a qualifying trigger, and
   (c) a person of D's sex and age, with a normal degree of tolerance and self-restraint and in the circumstances of D, might have reacted in the same or in a similar way to D.

(2) For the purposes of subsection (1)(a), it does not matter whether or not the loss of control was sudden.

(3) In subsection (1)(c) the reference to 'the circumstances of D' is a reference to all of D's circumstances other than those whose only relevance to D's conduct is that they bear on D's general capacity for tolerance or self-restraint.

The elements of the defence can thus be set out as follows:

Table 8.8 Elements of loss of self-control

Elements of the defence
Killing resulted from the loss of self-control
The loss of self-control had a qualifying trigger
Test of 'degree of tolerance and self-restraint'

Each component of the defence must be analysed sequentially and separately; if one is absent the defence will fail (*R v Rejmanski* [2017] EWCA Crim 2061).

8.4.2.2 Killing resulted from the loss of self-control (CAJA 2009, s 54(1)(a))

The first element that must be proven is that killing occurred as a result of a loss of self-control. Loss of self-control is not defined in the statute and thus it has been left to the courts to plug the gap.

The most appropriate understanding of loss of self-control was provided by Rafferty LJ in the Court of Appeal in *R v Jewell (Darren)* [2014] EWCA Crim 414 as involving the 'loss of the ability to act in accordance with considered judgment or a loss of normal powers of reasoning' (approved from *Smith and Hogan's Criminal Law*). Reference to acting without 'considered judgment' is emphasised through s 54(4), which explicitly states that the defence is not available where the defendant is acting with a 'considered' desire for revenge (see below for a full discussion of s 54(4)).

D must actually lose his self-control

This heading may seem redundant; however, it is important to emphasise that there may be circumstances in which the defendant acts (perhaps even with a qualifying trigger) without having lost his self-control. For example, suppose Jill calmly concludes that she must kill Jack in order to prevent an attack; there is no loss of self-control.

In that regard, where there is no evidence that the defendant has lost his self-control, the defence will not be capable of being run. In *R v Nixon* [2020] EWCA Crim 336, Irwin LJ approved the conclusions of the trial judge who found that 'there is no evidence arising from the prosecution case to show a loss of control, rather the evidence is all to the effect that there was an aggressive confrontation with the appellant *retaliating or responding to what was going on*' (emphasis added). A mere response, therefore, is insufficient; there must be an actual loss of self-control.

Subjective nature of the test

Whether there has been a loss of self-control is a subjective test for the jury. This means that the jury are required to assess whether there was a loss of self-control by placing themselves in the situation of the defendant (as opposed to asking whether the reasonable man would have lost his self-control). In doing so, the jury are entitled to take into account all relevant circumstances such as (inter alia):

- the nature of the conduct which constitutes the qualifying trigger;
- the sensitivity of the defendant (*R v Gregson* [2006] EWCA Crim 3364); and
- the time between the trigger and the killing.

in practice

It is essential to emphasise that the loss of self-control *must* be temporary. A permanent loss of self-control would mean that the defence of insanity could properly be pleaded or come into play. This is a point raised by advocates in the courts when defending their client; namely that the defendant had a 'sudden and brief' loss of control rendering his actions excusable to the extent of manslaughter.

The nature of the test requires us to consider two principles:

- Must the loss of control be 'total'?
- Must the loss of control be 'sudden'?

Must the loss of control be 'total'?

As a starting point, Lord Taylor CJ in the Court of Appeal in *R v Richens* [1993] 4 All ER 877 recommended that provocation (as the defence then was) should not be interpreted too widely so as to require a 'complete loss of control' (ie such cases where the defendant lacks full control over his body and its movement). This approach is justified on the basis that the criminal law already accommodates for such circumstances through the law of insanity and automatism. That was the position with the old law of provocation – what about the new law of loss of self-control?

In *R v Gurpinar; R v Kojo-Smith* [2015] EWCA Crim 178, Lord Thomas CJ considered it to be undesirable to answer the question whether the loss of self-control 'had to be a total loss or whether *some* loss of self-control was sufficient' (emphasis added). Such an answer was undesirable given that the question did not arise on the facts of the case. It is unlikely that the law has changed from *Richens*, and it is the author's view that the loss of control need not be total.

Must the loss of control be 'sudden'?

The previous law of provocation required the loss of control to be 'sudden and temporary' (*R v Duffy* [1949] 1 All ER 932). By s 54(2) of the CAJA 2009, however, there is no longer such a requirement. The law appreciates that an individual may lose their self-control only some time after the incident that provoked their behaviour. For example, the individual may 'mull' it over or overthink the situation, before then exploding in anger at a later stage (often referred to as a 'slow-burn' reaction). In effecting this change to the law, the Government in its Consultation Paper, 'Murder,

Manslaughter and Infanticide: Proposals for Reform of the Law' (2008) identified that this change would largely benefit the victims of domestic violence who, following a long period of abuse, kill their partner. The principle of immediacy in this area has developed substantially over time. We can demonstrate this through a timeline.

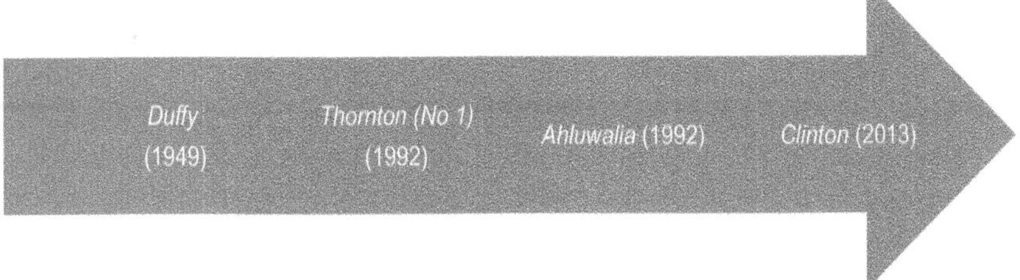

Figure 8.7 Timeline of suddenness

To begin our timeline, in *R v Duffy* [1949] 1 All ER 932, the defendant killed her violent husband following an assault and threat of violence made previously in the evening. The crux of the *Duffy* case was based on the time delay between the assault and the murder. Devlin J directed the jury as follows:

> [C]ircumstances which induce a desire for revenge are inconsistent with provocation, since the conscious formulation of a desire for revenge means that a person has had time to think, to reflect, and that would negative a sudden temporary loss of self-control which is of the essence of provocation.

Devlin J treated the delay between assault and murder as a 'cooling down' period, allowing Duffy to consciously plot her act of murder and plan her revenge. Devlin J discounted the idea of a 'slow burn' or chronic 'boiling over', preferring the argument that Duffy remained in a state of cooling down. Lord Goddard CJ in the Court of Criminal Appeal approved Devlin J's direction to the jury, referring to it as 'as good a definition of the doctrine of provocation as it has ever been my lot to read'. See below for a discussion of a 'considered desire for revenge' contained in the CAJA 2009.

Our second authority is that of *R v Thornton (No 1)* [1992] 1 All ER 306, which is another high profile case involving an abusive spouse. In this case, Sara Thornton had stabbed her husband with a carving knife after a threat made by him that he would kill her whilst she slept. The crux of the case in *Thornton* was that she had retreated to the kitchen in order to sharpen the carving knife. The Court of Appeal felt that the delay in time between the threat and the killing was too long and lacked immediacy. Further, the sharpening of the kitchen knife indicated a desire for revenge and not a loss of control. Specifically, the Court of Appeal noted that '... provocation produces a sudden or impulsive reaction leading to loss of control'. *Duffy* and *Thornton (No 1)* had the result that a defendant could only rely on provocation in circumstances where they:

- had 'snapped';
- had 'seen red'; or
- had been 'so angry'.

The question of immediacy was confronted by the Court of Appeal yet again in *R v Ahluwalia* [1992] 4 All ER 889, which we considered earlier in the context of diminished responsibility. Rejecting Ahluwalia's defence of provocation but substituting it with diminished responsibility, Lord Taylor CJ ruled:

> We accept that the subjective element in the defence of provocation would not as a matter of law be negatived simply because of the delayed reaction in such cases, provided that there was at the time of the killing a 'sudden and temporary loss of self-control' caused by the alleged provocation. However, the longer the delay and the stronger the evidence of deliberation on the part of the defendant, the more likely it will be that the prosecution will negative provocation.

In effect, Lord Taylor CJ reasoned that whilst the loss of self-control had to be 'sudden and temporary', it did not matter that the loss did not follow immediately from a provocative event. As a result of the appeal from *Ahluwalia*, *Thornton* appealed a second time to the Court of Appeal (*R v Thornton (No 2)* [1996] 2 All ER 1023), this time arguing diminished responsibility. Thornton was successful and a retrial was ordered.

It was only as a result of Parliament's intervention in the CAJA 2009 that clarity (and common sense) was imparted on the law where there is a delay between the provoking act and the end result of murder. As we know, s 54(2) now provides that the loss need not be sudden, but it is debateable whether the outcome would be different should these cases come before the courts post-2009.

Importantly, however, simply because a defendant's actions are or are not sudden will not automatically entitle them to a defence. This is made clear in para 337 of the Explanatory Notes to the CAJA 2009 which provides:

> Although subsection (2) in the new partial defence makes clear that it is not a requirement for the new partial defence that the loss of self control be sudden, it will remain open, as at present, for the judge (in deciding whether to leave the defence to the jury) and the jury (in determining whether the killing did in fact result from a loss of self-control and whether the other aspects of the partial defence are satisfied) to take into account any delay between a relevant incident and the killing.

Post-2009, the leading authority in this area is the case of *R v Clinton, Parker and Evans* [2013] QB 1.

case example

Charge:
Murder

Case progression:
Crown Court – Guilty

Court of Appeal – Conviction quashed and retrial ordered

Point of law:
Loss of self-control is available where multiple triggers are present

In *R v Clinton, Parker and Evans* [2013] QB 1, the defendant killed his wife by repeatedly beating her on the head with a wooden baton. The defendant also strangled her with his belt before then taking photographs of her dead naked body in various poses and texted them to her lover. At trial, the defence produced evidence that the defendant suffered from depression and suffered stress as a result of his separation from his wife. Before the killing, the wife had revealed to the defendant that she had been having an affair.

The defendant was convicted of murder in the Crown Court on the basis that loss of self-control was not available due to the impact of sexual infidelity. This was subsequently quashed by the Court of Appeal who ordered a retrial on the basis that the defence of loss of self-control should have been put to the jury as sexual infidelity was not the sole qualifying trigger in the case.

Following s 54(2) and as a result of the decision in *Clinton*, loss of control need not be sudden, but some form of actual loss of control must be present. Lord Judge CJ made a similar comment in the case of *R v Dawes* [2013] EWCA Crim 322, where his Lordship stated that

> Provided there was a loss of control, it does not matter whether the loss was sudden or not. A reaction to circumstances of extreme gravity may be delayed. Different individuals in different situations do not react identically, nor respond immediately. Thus for the purposes of the new defence, the loss of control may follow from the cumulative impact of earlier events.

From this, it can be said that even where there has been a delay between the trigger incident and the murder, the defence may still be put before the jury. However, the judge will have to determine, in accordance with *R v Clinton*, whether the time delay was sufficiently substantial to render the defence of loss of control untenable and therefore not sufficient to put before the jury. In *R v Clinton*, the Court of Appeal confirmed that where the defendant's actions are thought about and considered, the defendant will not be entitled to raise a defence. This element of 'considered' will lead us nicely into our discussion of cases involving revenge.

'A considered desire for revenge'

In relation to the requirement, or lack thereof, of suddenness, the courts may face difficulty in identifying appropriate defences where there is the potential argument of a considered desire for revenge. Specifically s 54(4) of the CAJA 2009 provides that the defence will not apply where there is a 'considered desire for revenge' on the part of the accused. This is so even if the defendant loses self-control as a result of one of the qualifying triggers.

Some cases may be clear-cut, as in *R v Jewell (Darren)* [2014] EWCA Crim 414, where the Court of Appeal affirmed the ruling of the trial judge not to leave the defence to the jury. In that case, referred to by Rafferty LJ as a case of 'pre-planned, cold-blooded execution', the defendant had shot the victim. Before doing so there was evidence to suggest that he went out of his way to arm himself with a gun, packed spare clothing, packed his passport and packed a substantial sum of cash. It is clear in this case that the act was for the fulfilment of some desire for revenge.

Other cases may be not so obvious, for example cases involving battered spouses who go on to kill their partners. The jury may conclude there to be a loss of self-control by the spouse; however, following *R v Duffy* (above), they may also find the defendant to have acted in a form of retaliation or revenge. Consider the following cases:

- *R v Thornton (No 1)* [1992] 1 All ER 306, where the defendant, having suffered years of abuse at the hands of her husband, went into the kitchen, took a sharpened carving knife and fatally stabbed her partner. It is to be noted that Thornton had previously stated her intention to kill her partner.
- *R v Ahluwalia* [1992] 4 All ER 889, where the defendant, also having suffered years of abuse at the hands of her husband, waited for him to fall asleep before then dousing him in petrol and setting him on fire.
- *R v Pearson* [1992] Crim LR 193, where the defendants (two brothers) had killed their father after the younger brother had revealed to his elder sibling that his father had abused him whilst the elder brother was away from home.

What these examples should show is that many cases may present an obvious case of retaliation or revenge, but the guiding line is not an easy one to draw. First, the word 'considered' is unfortunately not defined by the statute. Ordinary language would dictate that it means that the defendant acted with some form of premeditation. In *R v Clinton, Parker and Evans* [2013] QB 1, the trial judge explained in his direction to the jury that s 54(4) was concerned with

> [a]n act of retribution as a result of a deliberate and considered decision to get your own back, that is one that has been thought about. If you are sure that what the defendant did was to reflect on what happened and the circumstances in which he found himself and decided to take his revenge … that would not have been a loss of self-control as the law requires.

Lord Judge CJ in the Court of Appeal identified that the direction 'accurately encapsulated the issue to be decided by the jury, and the way they should approach to it'. His Lordship further approved the trial judge's direction that '[a] considered act of revenge, whether performed calmly or in anger, is not a loss of self control'.

Coupling this with the fact that a loss, under the new law, need not be 'sudden', a judge and jury are going to have a hard time deciding whether the defendant acted in retaliation or not. Further, in many cases, a defendant may have both lost their self-control and acted in a considered desire for revenge. The task of the jury is again a difficult one.

Imagine that a father, having learned that his son's school teacher has been sexually abusing the son, loses his control and kills the teacher. Can it be said that the death, in this case, is caused by a loss of self-control or by revenge? On this point we can look at the case of *R v Baillie* [1995] 2 Cr App R 31.

case example

Charge:
Murder

Case progression:
Crown Court – Guilty

Court of Appeal – Conviction quashed and manslaughter substituted

Point of law:
Loss of self-control may still be available even where there is evidence of a chance to cool down

In *R v Baillie* [1995] 2 Cr App R 31, the defendant became aware that the victim, a drug dealer, had been supplying drugs to his sons and had threatened to 'punish' them if they chose a different dealer. The defendant went into a rage and drove to the victim's house armed with a shotgun and a razor. The defendant seriously injured the victim with the razor. As the victim was trying to escape, the defendant shot and killed him. The defendant was charged and convicted with murder in the Crown Court.

His appeal was successful in the Court of Appeal, which found that the defendant remained out of control during the entire transaction of events and had no ability to cool down, even during the drive over to the victim's house. The defendant's conviction for murder was substituted for manslaughter in light of his provocation.

The question becomes whether Baillie, should the case arise again today, would be liable for murder or could rely on the new defence of loss of self-control. Most certainly there is a considered desire for revenge in this case, given the threats made to his sons; however, it may be the case that the defendant remained out of control of his actions, thus allowing him to plead the defence.

in practice

A jury may be sympathetic to the actions of a defendant, especially where they are acting as a result of an incident involving their child. In the example given above, in relation to the sexual abuse by a school teacher, a jury may 'support' the defendant in circumstances where they believe a just outcome occurred – ie the death of a paedophile. On this basis, you may wish to question whether the exclusion of a defence as a result of a 'considered desire for revenge' will make a difference where the jury are sympathetic (or empathetic for that matter) to the actions of the defendant.

Herring ('The Serious Wrong of Domestic Abuse and the Loss of Control Defence' in Reed and Bohlander (eds), *Loss of Control and Diminished Responsibility: Domestic, Comparative and International Perspectives* (Routledge, 2011)) argues that s 54(4) is 'superfluous' in that there can never be a loss of self-control where there is a 'considered' desire for revenge; more specifically, there can never be a loss of self-control where there is a 'considered desire for anything'. Had the legislation merely provided for a 'desire for revenge', s 54(4) may still be of some use in the circumstances where there was a loss of control, but that loss arose from the desire for revenge instead. However, with the inclusion of the term 'considered', this would have the result that no actual loss of self-control could ever arise in the circumstances. Horder (*Ashworth's Principles of Criminal Law*, 9th edn (OUP, 2019)) is particularly critical of the provision in s 54(4), stating that, although an intelligible position, it is

> based on fine distinctions that it may be very difficult to draw, not least in circumstances where it is likely that D's account of his or her own thoughts, feelings, and actions will be the only or main source of evidence of those thoughts, feelings and actions.

From the above, the law is evidently not clear. The author advises that the provision is to be used by the judge and jury to single out cases where the killing is thought-out and for a clear and single motivation of revenge. The provision will not affect situations where the defendant had lost their self-control, and revenge, although present as a motivation, is merely part of a complex multitude of emotions, feelings and motives. Although the judge will have to question whether a considered desire for revenge exists in the latter case, the inability to single out the defendant's motive as one of revenge alone may mean the task is made a little easier. A helpful way of approaching this question was considered by the Court of Appeal in *R v Clinton, Parker and Evans* [2013] QB 1 in which Lord Judge CJ explained that the greater the level of deliberation, the less likely the killing will have resulted from a loss of self-control. In particular, his Lordship stated:

> In the broad context of the legislative structure, there does not appear to be very much room for any 'considered' deliberation. In reality, the greater the level of deliberation, the less likely it will be that the killing followed a true loss of self-control.

8.4.2.3 The loss of self-control had a qualifying trigger (CAJA 2009, s 54(1)(b))

The second requirement is that the actual loss of self-control was caused by, or came by as a result of, a qualifying trigger (s 55(2)). Under the previous law, the defence of provocation simply required that the defendant lost his self-control in response to 'things said or done' (Homicide Act 1957, s 3). This was considered as being inappropriate and was replaced by the qualifying triggers in s 55(3) and (4). The qualifying triggers are listed in s 55 of the CAJA 2009 and have been characterised by Herring (*Criminal Law: Text, Cases, and Materials*, 9th edn (OUP, 2020)) as the 'fear trigger' and the 'anger trigger'.

Table 8.9 Qualifying triggers for loss of self-control

Qualifying triggers
s 55(3): Fear of serious violence ('fear trigger')
s 55(4): Things done or said ('anger trigger')
s 55(5): Combination of the matters in subsections (3) and (4)

Section 55 seeks to restrict the scope of the defence, compared to the wide triggers set out under the old law, as can be seen in *R v Doughty* (1986) 83 Cr App R 319. Further to this, the statute specifically requires the triggering factors to be 'attributable' to the loss of self-control. This simply means that the trigger must have caused the loss of self-control (compare with *R v Acott* [1997] 1 All ER 706, under the old law of provocation, in which the defendant was said to have 'just lost it' without any justification or reason). Also be aware that restrictions are placed on the sorts of things that may amount to a qualifying trigger in s 55(6). These are discussed at **8.4.2.5**.

We shall consider each trigger separately.

Fear of serious violence (CAJA 2009, s 55(3))

Section 55(3) of the CAJA 2009 provides:

> This subsection applies if D's loss of self-control was attributable to D's fear of serious violence from V against D or another identified person.

A number of points can be made at this stage from this provision:

(a) The law does not require that the defendant is actually subjected to serious violence; the law merely requires that there is a 'fear' of serious violence.

(b) The fear must be of 'serious' violence. Fear of a slap, for example, or other minor acts will not be enough.

(c) The fear must be of violence against a person (ie the defendant or another). Violence against property is thus not included.

(d) The addition of 'another identified person' allows for the defendant to claim that he feared serious violence might be taken out on a person close to him, for example his child or partner. This was evident in the case of *R v Wood* [2012] EWCA Crim 3139 in which the defendant attacked the victim with a pickaxe handle after the victim head-butted his brother. Note that in *Wood* the prosecution accepted the defendant's plea of guilty by reason of loss of self-control – the appeal to the Court of Appeal concerned matters of sentencing.

(e) The fear of serious violence must emanate from the victim (thus the use of the words 'from V'). The defence is inapplicable if Jill fears serious violence from Jack but then in response goes on to kill Andy. Note that this principle must be distinguished from the case where Jill attempts to kill Jack but misses and accidentally kills Andy. In this regard, much like transferred malice, the defence should be able to be transferred.

(f) The trigger does not arise where a person takes revenge for serious violence that he has *already* suffered (ie where the defendant is not responding to a fear of violence being used in future, but is responding to violence that has already occurred). On this point, see *R v Nixon* [2020] EWCA Crim 336.

As with self-defence (see **Chapter** 7), the test in s 55(3) requires the defendant to show that they *genuinely* feared that the victim would use serious violence against them. That fear need not be reasonable in the circumstances, but must be genuine (para 345 of the Explanatory Notes to the CAJA 2009). This subsection is designed, primarily, for women who kill their abusive partners, in circumstances where they kill in order to thwart an anticipated (but not necessarily imminent) attack; and where they overreact to what they perceive to be an imminent threat.

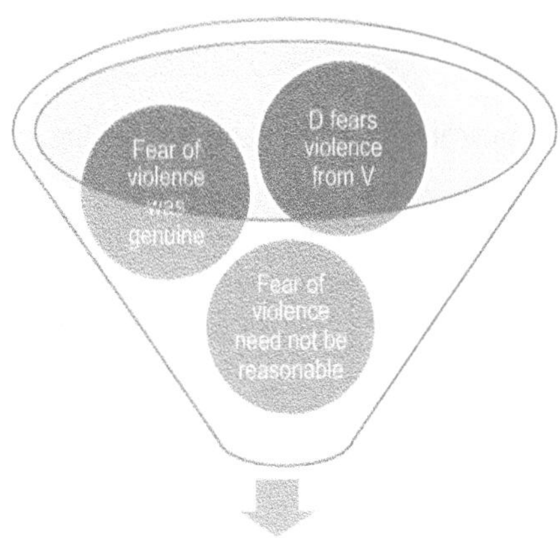

Figure 8.8 Fear of serious violence as a trigger

Where there is a history of abusive conduct from one person to their partner, and such continued prolonged abuse has led to a post-traumatic stress disorder (PTSD) or 'battered woman syndrome', a jury is able to find there to be a loss of self-control. This can be so even where the trigger is a minor incident in a long line of incidents which the defendant has endured over a long period of time. In this context, the defendant snaps and kills their abusive partner. They have had enough; this was the 'last straw'.

Distinguishing loss of self-control and self-defence

It is necessary, at this stage, to compare the loss of self-control defence (a partial defence) with self-defence (a complete defence). Where the defendant pleads both the partial and complete defence, the jury must deal with self-defence first, given that it will result in a complete acquittal, whereas the loss of self-control defence will reduce a murder charge to one of manslaughter. It will be helpful to compare the two defences now to assist you in understanding which defence is more appropriate for a defendant.

Table 8.10 Comparing self-defence to loss of self-control

Self-defence	Loss of self-control
Available on any charge	Only available to murder charge
Complete defence	Partial defence resulting in manslaughter verdict
Response can be calculated	There must be an actual loss of self-control
Threat of imminent attacks	Fear of future non-imminent attacks
Fear of any violence	Fear of serious violence
Force used must be reasonable. Excessive force will bar the use of the defence	Force can be excessive, so long as the sober and reasonable person might have acted in the same or similar way (see *R v Goodwin* [2018] EWCA Crim 2287)

As was considered in **Chapter** 7, self-defence will not be available to a defendant where:

- the threat to the defendant was not imminent; or
- the force used was unreasonably excessive.

In those circumstances, the defendant may rely on loss of self-control, so long as there was a qualifying trigger causing their actions. Child and Ormerod (*Smith, Hogan, & Ormerod's Essentials of Criminal Law*, 3rd edn (OUP, 2019)) refer to the loss of self-control defence as a 'safety net' in this regard as it will ensure the defendant will still receive some 'credit' for the state or purpose of their actions. Note, however, that in *R v Martin* [2017] EWCA Crim 1359, the Court of Appeal recently emphasised that in any murder trial where both self-defence and loss of control were advanced, a 'rigorous evaluation' of the evidence would be required before loss of control could be left to the jury (per Davis LJ).

Things said or done (CAJA 2009, s 55(4))

Section 55(4) of the CAJA 2009 provides:

> This subsection applies if D's loss of self-control was attributable to a thing or things done or said (or both) which—
>
> (a) constituted circumstances of an extremely grave character, and
> (b) caused D to have a justifiable sense of being seriously wronged.

Note that this is an 'and' test; therefore, all elements of s 55(4) must be satisfied. **Figure 8.9** allows you to consider each element in turn.

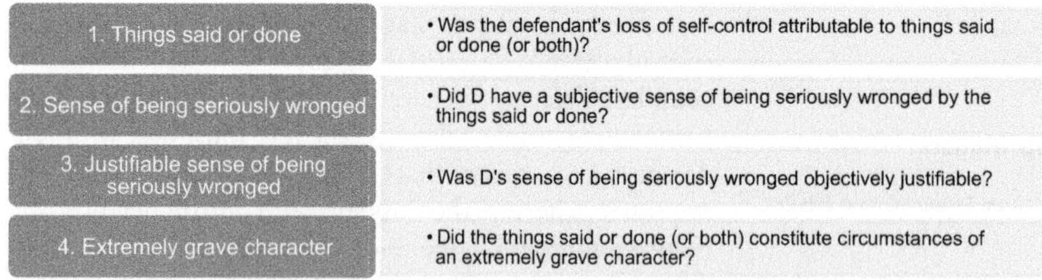

Figure 8.9 Understanding s 55(4)

Before we discuss the elements under this section, it is important to note a few points:

- Mere circumstances that do not amount to something 'said or done' cannot amount to things said or done (*R v Acott* [1997] 1 All ER 706).
- The things said or done do not need to come from the victim (*R v Davies (P)* [1975] QB 691 – the defendant was provoked by a third party, namely the victim's lover).
- The things said or done do not need to be said or done to the defendant; they may be said or done to another person (*R v Pearson* [1992] Crim LR 193).

Attributable to things said or done (s 55(4))

First, the defendant's loss of self-control must be attributable to things said or done. Reference to things said or done specifically imposes a requirement of human input (by words or conduct, for example). Being aggrieved to learn that your house has been flooded (an example used by Macdonald (*Text, Cases and Materials on Criminal Law*, 2nd edn (Pearson, 2018)) is therefore insufficient. In *R v Nixon* [2020] EWCA Crim 336, Irwin LJ identified that the trigger will not arise where the defendant is responding, in revenge, to being hit in a fight.

Extremely grave character (CAJA 2009, s 55(4)(a))

Although not defined in the statute, 'extremely grave character' has been interpreted to mean things said or done that fall outside of the normalities that a defendant may face on a daily basis. According to the Court of Appeal in *R v Clinton, Parker and Evans* [2013] QB 1, whether the things said or done constituted circumstances of an extremely grave character is to be considered objectively. Lord Judge CJ in *Clinton* explained that the defendant 'cannot invite the jury to acquit him of murder on the ground of loss of control because he personally sensed that he had been seriously wronged in circumstances which he personally regarded as extremely grave'.

Justifiable sense of being seriously wronged (CAJA 2009, s 55(4)(b))

This second element can be taken in two parts:

(a) Did the defendant, himself, have a sense of being seriously wronged? This is a subjective test based on the defendant's own perception. However, according to Lord Judge CJ in *Clinton*, 'that is not the end of it'. You must then ask:

(b) Was the defendant's sense of being seriously wronged justifiable?

The second element remains objective in that the defendant must be justified in feeling seriously wronged. This means that a defendant may feel wronged; however, unless the jury find such feelings to be justified, there can be no defence. Lord Judge CJ in *R v Dawes* [2013] EWCA Crim 322 reaffirmed the test to be objective as otherwise 'it would mean that a qualifying trigger would be present if D were to give an account to the effect that, "the circumstances were extremely grave *to* me and caused me to have what *I* believed was a justifiable sense that *I* had been seriously wronged"' (emphasis added).

His Lordship also emphasised the need for the trial judge to assess this section (as a matter of law) before then leaving it to the jury to deliberate (as a matter of fact). This was a matter in the case of *R v Meanza* [2017] EWCA Crim 445, where the defendant attacked a care worker after being asked to turn down the volume on his television following a complaint. The defendant claimed that he acted in such a way because he feared that the care home would send him back to hospital as a result of the previous complaints made against him. The Court of Appeal emphasised the need to find circumstances causing a justifiable sense of being seriously wronged, with particular focus on the word 'justifiable'. Jay J concluded that the defendant could have 'no justifiable grievance in relation to hospital and restriction orders that were lawfully imposed, nor in relation to the restrictions upon his relationship with his girlfriend'.

The objective element is designed to restrict the sort of cases, or circumstances, where the defendant may try to allege that he felt 'seriously wronged'. For example, under the pre-2009 law, the continuous noise of a crying baby could be considered a provocative act (*R v Doughty* (1986) 83 Cr App R 319 – where a father threw the child across the room because of its crying), as could the poor cooking of a steak (an example given by the Law Commission, 'Murder, Manslaughter and Infanticide' (Law Com No 304, 2006), para 1.47).

One point to note, however, is that a specific defendant may find things said or done to be of a seriously wrong nature; whereas other individuals would not. The difficulty here becomes how the jury treats this evidence. Herring (*Criminal Law: Text, Cases, and Materials*, 9th edn (OUP, 2020)) gives the example of throwing bacon at an individual. For most people, this would not cause them to feel seriously wronged; however, a Muslim may consider such actions to seriously wrong him, and a jury may find that, given his faith, a Muslim defendant would be justified in feeling such a way. A further example involves an avid football fan. Suppose the defendant is a football fanatic; football is his life, his hobby and his love. Should an individual insult the defendant's football team, ordinarily this would not be considered a case of being serious wronged that could be justified. However, looking at the characteristics of the defendant and the way he genuinely feels about football, it may be the case that the jury can find him to be justified in his feelings of being seriously wronged. This possibility of finding one defendant liable for murder and another liable for manslaughter for the same act has been labelled as gravely unpredictable by Withey ('Loss of Control, Loss of Opportunity?' [2011] Crim LR 263). Specifically, Withey notes that juries are provided with 'considerable discretion' such that there remains a high 'potential for inconsistency'.

Combination of triggers (CAJA 2009, s 55(5))

Section 55(5) of the CAJA 2009 provides:

> This subsection applies if D's loss of self-control was attributable to a combination of the matters mentioned in subsections (3) and (4).

Under this provision, a defendant may rely on both qualifying triggers under s 55 in combination. Ormerod and Laird (*Smith, Hogan, & Ormerod's Criminal Law*, 15th edn (OUP, 2018)) consider a difficulty that may arise as a result of this provision:

> One problem that may arise is whether a judge should withdraw the defence in a case if, where D who relies on both limbs, there is insufficient evidence of each limb in isolation, but in combination the evidence would satisfy s 54(5).

Given that s 55(5) refers to the loss of self-control being attributable to a 'combination of matters', there would appear to be no difficulty in finding that the defence should be left to the jury. Indeed, this was the view taken by the Court of Appeal in *R v Dawes* [2013] EWCA Crim 322, in which Lord Judge CJ stated: 'In most cases the qualifying trigger based on a fear of violence will almost inevitably include consideration of things said or done, in short, a combination of the features identified in s 55(3) and (4).' For a successful case involving use of both triggers, see *R v Lodge* [2014] EWCA Crim 446.

8.4.2.4 Degree of tolerance and self-restraint (CAJA 2009, s 54(1)(c))

The third and final requirement for a valid defence is that a person of the same sex and age as the defendant, with a normal degree of tolerance and self-restraint and in the circumstances of the defendant, might have reacted in the same or a similar way. This matter is an objective test and remains a question of fact for the jury.

There a number of key points to pick out from the section.

'A person of D's sex and age'

The statute emphasises that the focus is to be on a person of the same 'age and sex' as the defendant. This provision came about as a result of the divergence in case law between *R v Smith (Morgan)* [2001] 1 AC 146 and *AG for Jersey v Holley* [2005] UKPC 23. In *Smith*, the House of Lords ruled that a jury would be entitled to take into account all of the circumstances and characteristics that are shared by the defendant and the objective person assessing the case. This was doubted by the Privy Council in *Holley* which held that the only relevant circumstance and characteristic is the age and gender of the defendant. Rather controversially, the Court of Appeal in *R v James; R v Karimi* [2006] EWCA Crim 14 endorsed the approach of the Privy Council.

Parliament has now resolved this debate by focusing on the age and sex of the defendant through s 54(1)(c). Mitchell, Mackay and Brookbanks ('Pleading for Provoked Killers: In Defence of Morgan Smith' (2008) 124 LQR 675) believe that this debate ought to be reopened to allow the defence to operate in a wider fashion.

Hallett LJ in the Court of Appeal in *R v Rejmanski* [2017] EWCA Crim 2061 held that:

> the wording of section 54(1)(c) is clear: … the defendant is to be judged against the standard of a person with a normal degree, and not an abnormal degree, of tolerance and self-restraint. If, and in so far as, a personality disorder reduced the defendant's general capacity for tolerance or self-restraint, that would not be a relevant consideration.

Rejmaniski was approved by the Court of Appeal in *R v Sargeant* [2019] EWCA Crim 1088.

'Normal degree of tolerance and self-restraint and in the circumstances of D'

The statute makes reference to 'the circumstances of defendant'. This provision is a reference to 'all of D's circumstances other than those whose only relevance to D's conduct is that they bear on D's general capacity for tolerance or self-restraint' (CAJA 2009, s 54(3)).

The emphasis on *all* of the defendant's characteristics is crucial and allows the jury to consider a multitude of factors relevant to the case. For example, a history of abuse on the part of the victim will be relevant in determining their response, compared to an individual who has never been subject to such abuse.

Importantly, however, it does not include such circumstances that only go to a defendant's ability to control his actions, ie the degree of tolerance and self-restraint. For example, a defendant who is particularly short-tempered cannot ask the jury to consider whether another equally short-tempered individual might have acted in the same or similar way. The jury must ask whether an individual with a 'normal degree of tolerance and self-restraint' might have acted in the same or similar way.

Instead, this provision is focused on the case where the defendant's circumstances have a bearing on the trigger (*R v McGrory* [2013] EWCA Crim 2336; *R v Wilcocks* [2016] EWCA Crim 2043). Indeed, in *R v Rejmanski* [2017] EWCA Crim 2061, the Court of Appeal held that a mental disorder, for example, would be relevant to the 'gravity of the qualifying trigger'. Hallett LJ was clear that

> if a mental disorder has a relevance to the defendant's conduct other than a bearing on his general capacity for tolerance or self-restraint, it is not excluded by subsection (3), and the jury will be entitled to take it into account as one of the defendant's circumstances under section 54(1)(c).

However, a mental abnormality which only goes to the defendant's general ability to exercise tolerance and self-restraint is not to be taken into account (more likely, the defendant should be pleading diminished responsibility).

From this general discussion, there are two specific points that must be considered under this heading:

(a) the operation of intoxication on the defence; and
(b) the effect of sexual infidelity on the defence.

First, the question of degree and tolerance must be considered by the jury without regard to the voluntary intoxication of the defendant. This was recently reaffirmed by the Court of Appeal in *R v Asmelash* [2014] QB 103, which held that a finding that the defendant was intoxicated at the time of the killing does not mean that the defendant (per Lord Judge CJ) is

> deprived of any possible loss of control defence: it simply means, as the judge explained, that the loss of control defence must be approached without reference to the defendant's voluntary intoxication. If a sober individual in the defendant's circumstances, with normal levels of tolerance and self-restraint might have behaved in the same way as the defendant confronted by the relevant qualifying trigger, he would not be deprived of the loss of control defence just because he was not sober.

The Court of Appeal did, however, note that different considerations would apply where the defendant suffered from an addiction to drink or drugs. Specifically, Lord Judge CJ provided that:

> if a defendant with a severe problem with alcohol or drugs was mercilessly taunted about the condition, to the extent that it constituted a qualifying trigger, the alcohol or drug problem would then form part of the circumstances for consideration.

Secondly, although it would appear that sexual infidelity must remain irrelevant to the decision of a jury in relation to the qualifying triggers (s 55(6)(c)), the Court of Appeal in *R v Clinton* has held that, despite s 55(6)(c), the jury may still take sexual infidelity into account when determining the 'circumstances' that the defendant was faced with for the purposes of s 54(1)(c).

'Might have reacted'

The statute places emphasis on the word 'might' when considering whether the ordinary person *might* act in the same or similar way to the defendant, as opposed to whether the ordinary person *would* act in the same or similar way.

'In the same or similar way'

This reference requires the ordinary person to have not only lost self-control, but to have acted in the same or similar way in killing the victim. It is not enough if the ordinary person would have lost their self-control but would have not killed (eg they may have just seriously injured the victim). This was evident in *R v Goodwin* [2018] EWCA Crim 2287, a case in which the defendant hit an older man over the head with a hammer repeatedly. The Court of Appeal clarified that whilst the reasonable man might have lost their self-control in the same circumstances, the jury still have to be sure that the reasonable man might have reacted in the same or similar way to this loss of control (ie would the reasonable man have continued to beat the victim over the head with a hammer for five minutes?). Indeed, a similar view was taken in *R v Christian* [2018] EWCA Crim 1344, where Simon LJ stated: 'The judge was fully entitled, in our view, to conclude that such ferocious multiple stabbings with that intent could not conceivably be consistent with the notional reasonable man's possible reaction.'

8.4.2.5 Exclusions to the defence (CAJA 2009, s 55(6))

Section 55 also provides a number of exceptions (or 'exclusions') to the defences. These are detailed in s 55(6) which provides that:

> In determining whether a loss of self-control had a qualifying trigger—

(a) D's fear of serious violence is to be disregarded to the extent that it was caused by a thing which D incited to be done or said for the purpose of providing an excuse to use violence;
(b) a sense of being seriously wronged by a thing done or said is not justifiable if D incited the thing to be done or said for the purpose of providing an excuse to use violence;
(c) the fact that a thing done or said constituted sexual infidelity is to be disregarded.

Inciting the thing said or done (s 55(6)(a) and (b))

The operation of s 55(6) was considered in *R v Dawes* [2013] EWCA Crim 322, where the Court of Appeal ruled that where the defendant acts or behaves in a poor manner, and indeed is acting in a provocative or troubling manner, this will not prevent the defendant from using a defence unless it can be proven that the defendant intended his actions to provide an opportunity to use violence. This is aptly phrased by Child and Ormerod (*Smith, Hogan, & Ormerod's Essentials of Criminal Law*, 3rd edn (OUP, 2019)) as restricting the exclusions to cases where the defendant 'consciously manipulate[s] the circumstances'.

example

Jack dares Andy to punch him to prove that he is 'man enough', stating that to not punch him proves that Andy is 'a coward'. Andy punches Jack who then retaliates in anger by stabbing Andy and killing him.

In this scenario, although Jack may have accurately lost his self-control as a result of Andy punching him, that chain of events arose only because of Jack's own conduct in daring Andy. Following s 55(6)(a), Jack has incited Andy's action as an excuse for his own violence. Jack would not, therefore, be able to rely on a defence.

Let us change the facts slightly and see how the law might apply.

example

Jack dares Andy to punch him to prove that he is 'man enough', stating that to not punch him proves that Andy is 'a coward'. Instead of punching Jack, Andy punches Jack's wife, Jill, who is stood next to him. In anger, Jack stabs Andy and kills him.

In this scenario, although Jack has incited violence by daring Andy to punch him, it would appear that the incited violence was towards himself. Given that Jack never wished for Andy to punch Jill, it cannot be said that Jack has incited a fear of serious violence by his actions in daring Andy to punch him. Although it remains unlikely, Jack may have a valid claim to loss of self-control in this instance.

Sexual infidelity (s 55(6)(c))

In relation to the final exclusion under s 55(6)(c), where a defendant claims to have a justifiable sense of being seriously wronged as a result of the victim's sexual infidelity, the courts will not entertain the defence. The aim here being to prevent jealous defendants from killing their unfaithful partners.

Whilst s 55(6)(c) excludes sexual infidelity as a trigger for the defence, the Court of Appeal in *Clinton* did identify the circumstance where infidelity may nonetheless be relevant. In particular, Lord Judge CJ identified that:

> In our judgment, where sexual infidelity is integral to and forms an essential part of the context in which to make a just evaluation whether a qualifying trigger properly falls within the ambit of sub-ss 55(3) and (4), the prohibition in s 55(6)(c) does not operate to exclude it.

This simply means that where the sexual infidelity alone causes the loss of control, no defence is available. However, if the loss of self-control is caused by other factors (in addition to the sexual infidelity), the evidence of sexuality infidelity is not excluded. Rather, the evidence may be used as part of the context or circumstances of the loss of self-control.

An example of this was provided in the Ministry of Justice Circular 2010/13:

> a woman discovers her husband has raped her sister, loses her self control and goes on to kill her husband. The fact that this would amount to sexual infidelity must be disregarded. However, the defendant's actions may still meet the qualifying trigger under section 55(4). The defence could argue that discovering the rape of a family member is what amounted to circumstances of an extremely grave character, and caused the defendant to have a justifiable sense of being seriously wronged such that the partial defence could still be argued.

The decision in *Clinton* has been criticised by Baker and Zhao ('Contributory qualifying and non-qualifying triggers in the loss of control defence: a wrong turn on sexual infidelity' [2012] 76 J Crim L 254) on the basis that the courts have seemingly ignored the will of Parliament in preventing sexual infidelity from being used as a qualifying trigger (whether it merely accompanies another qualifying trigger or not). Specifically, the pair state:

> The decision seems to ignore that a core aim of reforming the law in this area was to give women greater protection. The aim was to deny angry and jealous men a concession for killing in revenge or out of jealousy. The government took a bold and commendable step in expressly excluding sexual infidelity as a qualifying trigger. The law was not changed on the basis that a person never loses control when he or she is provoked by sexual infidelity; it was changed because society no longer views a loss of control resulting from this as reasonable. Society expects a person to maintain control in such cases even though the provocation may in fact be immense for him or her. Some people will in fact lose control in such circumstances, but Parliament is no longer willing to recognise this type of loss of control as an excuse for killing.

With respect to Baker and Zhao, the will of Parliament was made clear in the introduction of the CAJA 2009 by way of Explanatory Notes. Specifically, para 349 expressly refers to the situation where sexual infidelity may still be relevant as part of the context of the situation. It provides:

> [W]here a person discovers their partner sexually abusing their young child (an act that amounts to sexual infidelity) and loses self-control and kills, [the] fact that the partner's act amounted to sexual infidelity must be discounted but that act may still potentially be claimed to amount to the qualifying trigger in section 55(4) on the basis of the other aspects of the case (namely the child abuse).

Leigh ('Two New Partial Defences to Murder' (2010) 174 CL&J 53), on the other hand, describes the provision in s 55(6)(c) as 'incoherent' on the basis that it ignores the genuine loss of control one may suffer when faced with an adulterous and unfaithful partner. Further to this, Wake ('Political Rhetoric or Principled Reform of Loss of

Control? Anglo-Australian Perspectives on the Exclusionary Conduct Model' [2013] 77(6) J Crim L 512) argues that:

> It seems perverse to continue to allow the defence for all sudden provocations other than those that touch on intimate relationships including marriage. This is unrealistic and reflects an extreme ideological, individualistic view of marriage and of personal sexual relationship.

Whether the infidelity forms part of the context or the 'cause' for loss of self-control, however, will not be an easy divide. Such was argued by Stark ('Killing the Unfaithful' (2012) 71 Camb LJ 260).

example

Jack comes home from work one day and finds his wife, Jill, engaging in sexual intercourse with Andy. As a result, Jack kills both Jill and Andy.

In this circumstance, Jack has killed as a result of sexual infidelity (ie it is the cause of the loss of control). This is expressly excluded by s 55(6)(c), and Jack would be unable to argue that this formed a necessary qualifying trigger under either s 55(3) or (4). He may still have a defence where there remains a qualifying trigger.

example

Jack comes home from work one day and finds his wife, Jill, engaging in sexual intercourse with Andy. Jack is naturally upset and asks the pair to leave the house. Instead of leaving the house, the pair shout abuse at Jack, stating that he is 'sexually inadequate', a 'waste of space" and 'boring'. As a result of these words, Jack kills both Jill and Andy.

In this circumstance, Jack has killed as a result of things said or done. The sexual infidelity does play a part in these facts; but only so when looking at the wider circumstances or context of the defendant's actions. In this case, the sexual infidelity of Jill will not be excluded by s 55(6)(c) but, rather, will be relevant to proving the necessary 'anger trigger'.

Norrie ('The Coroners and Justice Act 2009—Partial Defences to Murder: (1) Loss of Control' [2010] Crim LR 275) raises an excellent question regarding the circumstance where the sexual infidelity plays a potential part in the loss of control. He asks the following:

> [W]here a taunt of infidelity is part of a range of taunts and the taunting is systematic, should it be the case that one somehow excludes the one taunt and admits the others?'

As above with Jack and Jill, and following *Clinton*, the jury would be entitled to find a defence of loss of self-control, ignoring the sexual infidelity taunts as a *cause* for the loss, but appreciating them as part of the *context* of the loss of control. This latter point is emphasised by Herring (*Criminal Law: Text, Cases, and Materials*, 9th edn (OUP, 2020)) who contends that '[t]he distinction between sexual infidelity being a trigger itself (which is forbidden) and being the context for a permitted trigger (which is not forbidden) may escape most juries'.

8.4.2.6 Procedure and sentencing

Loss of self-control is a defence only to murder and results in a conviction of manslaughter (CAJA 2009, s 54(7)).

Sentence

A defendant convicted of manslaughter by loss of self-control may be sentenced to life imprisonment; however, this is at the discretion of the trial judge.

Burden of proof

Unlike diminished responsibility, the prosecution bears the legal burden of disproving the defence (s 54(5)). The standard of proof is beyond a reasonable doubt. However, the defence may only be put to the jury where 'sufficient evidence is adduced to raise an issue with respect to the defence' (s 54(5)). This simply means that sufficient evidence of the defence must be raised (by the defence or any other witness) before it can then be placed before the jury. A 'mere speculation' will not suffice; there must be an actual loss of self-control as a result of a qualifying trigger (see *R v Charles* [2013] EWCA Crim 120 and *R v Workman* [2014] EWCA Crim 575 where the judge removed the defence from the jury's consideration as there was simply 'no evidence' capable of satisfying s 54(5)). Similarly in *R v Jewell (Darren)* [2014] EWCA Crim 414, Rafferty LJ in the Court of Appeal noted that the trial judge had been correct to withdraw the defence from the jury on the basis there was no evidence to support that there was a qualifying trigger. Rather, her Ladyship made clear that this killing 'bore every hallmark of a pre-planned, cold-blooded execution … the evidence that this was a planned execution is best described as overwhelming'. See also *R v McDonald* [2016] EWCA Crim 1529 and *R v Martin* [2017] EWCA Crim 1359. The defence has also been withdrawn from the jury where there is no evidence on which a jury could conclude that a person of the same age and sex as the defendant in his circumstances might have acted in a similar way (*R v Christian* [2018] EWCA Crim 1344; *R v Goodwin* [2018] EWCA Crim 2287; *R v Meanza* [2017] EWCA Crim 445).

Whether the defence ought to be placed before the jury is a matter for the trial judge (s 54(6)). Where the judge is prepared to leave the defence to the jury, he is required to direct them accordingly (*R v Gurpinar; R v Kojo-Smith* [2015] EWCA Crim 178). Importantly, the legal burden never leaves the prosecution; it remains responsible for disproving the entire defence.

Where the defence has not been left to the jury, they are not entitled to speculate that the defendant may have lost his self-control (*R v Evans (John Derek)* [2010] Crim LR 491).

8.4.3 Suicide pact

The final partial defence to murder is that of a suicide pact under s 4 of the HA 1957. Section 4 operates to reduce a conviction of murder to voluntary manslaughter where the survivor (if there is one) of a joint suicide pact took part in the killing of another person in the pact or was a party to that other person being killed by a third person (eg where a husband and wife agree that they will die together).

It is important to note that the act of suicide itself is no longer a criminal offence as a result of s 1 of the Suicide Act 1961. Prior to this Act, individuals who failed in their attempt to commit suicide could be charged and convicted for an offence. Although it was impossible to attach criminal liability to an individual who successfully committed suicide, their property would be forfeited – meaning their families could be left with nothing.

8.4.3.1 Elements of suicide pact

Section 4 of the HA 1957 (as amended by the Suicide Act 1961) states:

> (1) It shall be manslaughter, and shall not be murder, for a person acting in pursuance of a suicide pact between him and another to kill the other or be a party to the other… being killed by a third person…
>
> (2) Where it is shown that a person charged with the murder of another killed the other or was a party to his … being killed, it shall be for the defence to prove that the person charged was acting in pursuance of a suicide pact between him and the other.
>
> (3) For the purposes of this section 'suicide pact' means a common agreement between two or more persons having for its object the death of all of them, whether or not each is to take his own life, but nothing done by a person who enters into a suicide pact shall be treated as done by him in pursuance of the pact unless it is done while he has the *settled intention* of dying in pursuance of the pact.

The elements of the defence can thus be set out as follows:

Table 8.11 Elements of a suicide pact

Elements of the defence
Agreement that the defendant and the victim will die together
Settled intention on the part of the defendant to die alongside the victim in line with their agreement

As with diminished responsibility, the burden of proof is on the defendant to establish the elements of the defence (HA 1957, s 4(2)). The standard of proof is the civil standard, on the balance of probabilities. For a review of the law in this area, see Wheat, 'The law's treatment of the suicidal' (2000) 8(2) Med LR 182.

example

Jack and Jill both suffer with depression and wish to end their lives together. They enter into an agreement (a 'suicide pact') so that Jack will kill Jill, before then taking his own life. Upon Jack killing Jill, he is stopped by Andy and is prevented from killing himself.

In this scenario, Jack will be liable for the offence of murder; however, he may raise the defence of a suicide pact. The same outcome would apply if Jack relented on the idea of killing himself and chose not to do so upon killing Jill. An important point to mention, however, is that if there is evidence to suggest that Jack never intended to kill himself, no defence would arise. Were Jack simply to encourage or assist Jill in killing herself, he will not have committed a homicide-related offence. Instead, he would be liable for assisting or encouraging suicide contrary to s 2 of the Suicide Act 1967 (as amended by s 9 of the CAJA 2009), which carries a maximum penalty of 14 years.

The CPS policy (2010, updated 2014) for prosecuting assisted suicide cases is provided for at <www.cps.gov.uk/publications/prosecution/assisted_suicide_policy.html>.

The Law Commission, in its Consultation Paper ('A New Homicide Act for England and Wales?' (Law Com No 177, 2005)), recommended the repeal of this defence, arguing that it was better suited within the diminished responsibility defence. However, in its 2006 Report ('Murder, Manslaughter and Infanticide' (Law Com No 304, 2006)), the Commission withdrew this recommendation and took the view that the defence should be maintained pending a review into the broader issue of mercy killings and whether a defence ought to be available in such cases.

8.4.4 Infanticide

Infanticide arises where a woman kills her child, who is under the age of 12 months, by any wilful act or omission and, at the time, the balance of her mind was disturbed due to the birth. Note that the offence applies only to biological mothers within the first 12 months of birth. Therefore, fathers, or mothers outside the 12-month period, that kill the child cannot be charged with infanticide or raise it as a defence. Instead they are to be charged with the other relevant homicide offences.

Infanticide may be charged as a separate offence of infanticide under s 1(1) of the Infanticide Act (IA) 1938 or raised as a partial defence to murder under s 1(2) of the IA 1938. Infanticide is treated like a conviction for manslaughter (though it is not considered as manslaughter), and thus carries a maximum sentence of life imprisonment.

8.4.4.1 Elements of infanticide (as an offence)

Section 1(1) of the IA 1938 (as amended by s 57 of the CAJA 2009) provides that:

> Where a woman by any wilful act or omission causes the death of her child being a child under the age of twelve months, but at the time of the act or omission the balance of her mind was disturbed by reason of her not having fully recovered from the effect of giving birth to the child or by reason of the effect of lactation consequent upon the birth of the child, then, if the circumstances were such that but for this Act the offence would have amounted to murder or manslaughter, she shall be guilty of felony, to wit of infanticide, and may for such offence be dealt with and punished as if she had been guilty of the offence of manslaughter of the child.

The elements of the offence can thus be set out as follows:

Table 8.12 Elements of infanticide

Elements of the offence/defence
A woman
Wilful act or omission
Causes the death of her child under the age of 12 months
The balance of her mind was disturbed by reason of her not having fully recovered from the effect of giving birth to the child

8.4.4.2 Elements of infanticide (as a defence)

Section 1(2) of the IA 1938 (as amended by s 57 of the CAJA 2009) provides that:

> Where upon the trial of a woman for the murder or manslaughter of her child, being a child under the age of twelve months, the jury are of opinion that she by any wilful act or omission caused its death, but that at the time of the act or omission

> the balance of her mind was disturbed by reason of her not having fully recovered from the effect of giving birth to the child or by reason of the effect of lactation consequent upon the birth of the child, then the jury may, if the circumstances were such that but for the provisions of this Act they might have returned a verdict of murder or manslaughter, return in lieu thereof a verdict of infanticide.

Section 1(2) operates to provide the jury with an alternative verdict to murder where they are satisfied that the defendant fulfilled the requirements for the defence. The requirements for the defence are the same as the elements of the offence set out above at **Table 8.12**.

In *R v Gore* [2007] EWCA Crim 2789, the Court of Appeal established that there is no requirement for all the ingredients of murder to have been proven before a defendant could be convicted of infanticide (ie there is no requirement to prove an intention to kill or cause GBH). This case indicates that the intention of Parliament was to create a new offence of infanticide. Unlike diminished responsibility, the burden of disproving this defence is on the prosecution beyond a reasonable doubt.

In *R v Kai-Whitewind* [2005] 2 Cr App R 31, Judge LJ clarified that:

> Under s.1(2) provision is made for infanticide to be an alternative verdict available to the jury trying a mother for murder of her infant child. It does however require evidence that the 'balance of her mind was disturbed' either because the mother has not recovered from giving birth to the child, or the effect of lactation on her. *No other circumstances are relevant.* (emphasis added)

The phrase 'no other circumstances' was the subject of the appeal in *R v Tunstill* [2018] EWCA Crim 1696 in which the Court of Appeal provided a detailed analysis of the law of infanticide.

case example

Charge:
Murder

Case progression:
Crown Court – Guilty

Court of Appeal – Conviction quashed; retrial ordered

Point of law:
Meaning of 'other circumstances'

In *R v Tunstill* [2018] EWCA Crim 1696, the defendant had given birth to her child in the bathroom of her home and then, shortly thereafter, had stabbed the baby 14 times with a pair of scissors. The defendant had then disposed of the baby in the kitchen bin. The defendant was tried and convicted of murder in the Crown Court. At trial, the appellant unsuccessfully pleaded the defence of diminished responsibility which was rejected by the jury. The trial judge (Davis J) had also refused to leave infanticide as an alternative verdict to murder to the jury on the basis of Judge LJ's statement in *Kai-Whitewind*. The trial judge interpreted this to mean that if a defendant's post-birth mental disorder was not *exclusively* caused by the effects of having given birth, but based on a pre-existing mental disorder, a verdict of infanticide could not be supported.

The defendant appealed to the Court of Appeal on the basis that infanticide should have been left to the jury. The Court of Appeal agreed, allowing her appeal and ordering a retrial.

Treacy LJ in the Court of Appeal concluded that:

> It would seem anomalous to us that a person who, prior to childbirth, is in a fragile mental state and whose balance of mind is disturbed as a result of a failure to recover from childbirth should be placed in a different and less favourable position from someone affected solely by the experience of childbirth. We do not see that such an approach is required by the observations of Judge LJ in *Kai-Whitewind*.

Treacy LJ provided the ratio of the Court, in which his Lordship stated:

> The phrase 'by reason of' in s.1(1) does not in our judgment necessarily need to be read as if it said 'solely by reason of'. It seems to us that as long as a failure to recover from the effects of birth is an operative or substantial cause of the disturbance of balance of mind that should be sufficient, even if there are *other underlying mental problems* (perhaps falling short of diminished responsibility) which are part of the overall picture. (emphasis added)

The effect of *Tunstill* is clear: in circumstances where a defendant to murder suffers with a pre-existing mental condition, the alternative verdict of infanticide is still capable of being left to the jury to decide upon as a matter of fact. For a detailed account of the decision of *Tunstill*, see Thomas, 'Infanticide and Pre-Existing Mental Conditions: Disentangling the Causal Factors Relevant to a Jury's Deliberations' (2018) 82(5) J Crim L 366.

8.4.5 Putting together voluntary manslaughter

Consider this issue and think of how you may structure an answer to it. Then see the figure below for a sample structure to adopt.

facts

Jill suffers from post-traumatic stress disorder following a sexual assault committed against her in 2017. As a result of this, Jill is extremely nervous when walking the streets at night. One night, Jill is walking down the street and is approached from behind by Jack, a homeless man. Jack places his hand on Jill's shoulder with the intention of begging her for money. Out of fear, Jill hits Jack with her handbag and knocks him to the floor. With Jack on the floor, Jill proceeds to hit him with a nearby brick, eventually killing him.

Bill and Ben have been married for a year. On the date of their one-year anniversary, Bill has to work late and cancels the date night the pair had planned. Bill, believing Ben to be upset, leaves work early to surprise him. Upon returning home, Bill discovers Ben in bed with Andy. In a fit of rage, Bill attacks Andy with a knife from the kitchen and kills him.

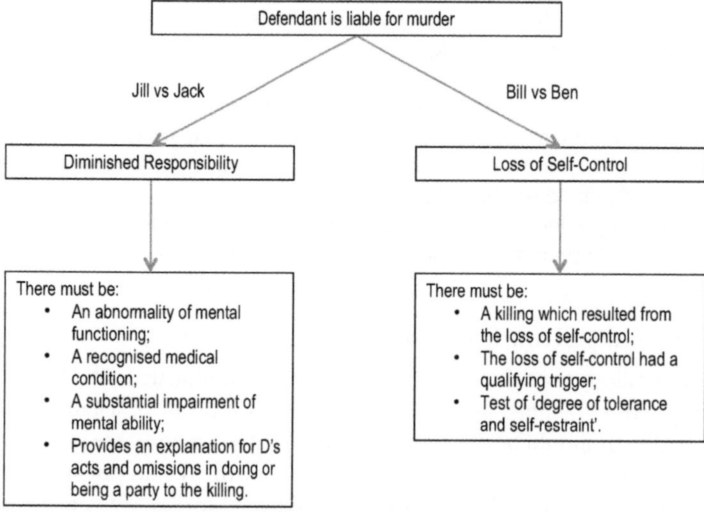

Figure 8.10 Putting together voluntary manslaughter

8.5 Involuntary manslaughter

Unlike voluntary manslaughter, which is concerned with the application of partial defences to a charge of murder where the defendant has the intention to kill or cause GBH, involuntary manslaughter is concerned with separate and distinct offences where the victim dies as a result of the defendant's conduct but there is no intention on the part of the defendant to kill or cause GBH. Breaking this down, the defendant has the *actus reus* for murder but no accompanying *mens rea*.

Despite its name, involuntary manslaughter has no relevance or bearing on the voluntariness of the defendant's actions. Rather, the term is simply used to differentiate itself from voluntary manslaughter.

There are three main types of involuntary manslaughter, namely:

- unlawful act manslaughter (also known as 'constructive manslaughter') (**8.5.1**);
- gross negligence manslaughter (**8.5.2**); and
- subjectively reckless manslaughter (**8.5.3**).

These three forms of involuntary manslaughter are based in the common law.

Technically, there is a fourth form of involuntary manslaughter, namely the offence of corporate manslaughter. However, given the key distinctions in the *actus reus* of corporate manslaughter, we considered that offence separately in **Chapter 6**.

8.5.1 Unlawful act manslaughter

Unlawful act manslaughter (also known as 'constructive manslaughter') is concerned with an unlawful and dangerous act committed by the defendant that then results in the death of the victim. The term 'constructive' is used to show that the offence is built upon the foundations of a 'base' criminal offence. Should one of the foundations be missing, the offence cannot be made out.

8.5.1.1 Defining unlawful act manslaughter

Unlawful act manslaughter is a rather broad criminal offence and is defined by Allen and Edwards (*Criminal Law*, 15th edn (OUP, 2019)) as containing 'ill-defined boundaries'. It may cover serious offences that fall short of murder by a margin; whilst at the same time covering very minor offences that, unexpectedly, result in the death of a victim. This might explain the research found by Mitchell and Mackay ('Investigating Involuntary Manslaughter: An Empirical Study of 127 Cases' (2011) 31(1) OJLS 165) that unlawful act manslaughter was the most frequently committed of the three involuntary manslaughter offences.

Consider the following examples to assist you.

example

Jack kicks Jill whilst she is lying on the ground. Although Jack does not intend to kill Jill or cause her GBH, he foresees death as a virtual certainty of his actions.

In this scenario, Jack may be liable for murder given that the end result of death was a virtual certainty as a result of Jack's conduct, and Jack appreciated this to be the case.

example

Jack kicks Jill whilst she is lying on the ground. Jack does not intend to kill Jill or cause her GBH, nor does he foresee death as a virtual certainty of his actions. However, Jack does appreciate that death is a high probability of his actions.

In this scenario, Jack has fallen short of the virtual certainty test and cannot be liable for murder. Jack may be liable for unlawful act manslaughter.

example

Jack punches Jill who falls to the ground and hits her head and dies. Jack merely intended to express his anger and had no intention to kill or cause GBH; he had no foresight that death was a virtual certainty; nor had he any foresight that it was merely a high probability.

In this final scenario, Jack cannot be liable for murder as he has fallen short of the virtual certainty test. However, he may still be liable for unlawful act manslaughter. This final scenario has been described by Mitchell ('More Thoughts About Unlawful and Dangerous Act Manslaughter and the One Punch Killer' [2009] Crim LR 502) as sheer 'bad luck'; however, this does not affect Jack's liability for unlawful act manslaughter.

8.5.1.2 Elements of unlawful act manslaughter

The leading cases in this area are:

- *DPP v Newbury; DPP v Jones* [1977] AC 500;
- *R v Goodfellow* (1986) 83 Cr App R 23; and
- *AG's Reference (No 3 of 1994)* [1998] AC 245.

In *Newbury and Jones*, Lord Salmon explained that an individual was guilty of constructive manslaughter if he 'intentionally did an act which was unlawful and dangerous and that act inadvertently caused death'. From this, we can find that the *actus reus* and *mens rea* of unlawful act manslaughter are as outlined in **Table 8.13**.

Table 8.13 Elements of unlawful act manslaughter

AR/MR	Elements of the offence
Actus reus	(i) an act (the base offence); (ii) which is unlawful; (iii) which is objectively dangerous; and (iv) the act caused the death of the victim
Mens rea	Intention to perform the unlawful act

We shall consider each element in turn.

***Actus reus*: (i) an act (base offence)**

The first requirement stated in *R v Goodfellow* (1986) 83 Cr App R 23 is that there is:

(a) an act; which is
(b) unlawful.

The first point to note is the requirement for an 'act'. In the case of *R v Senior* [1899] 1 QB 283, the Court for Crown Cases Reserved found that a defendant, who failed to summon medical help for his child, was liable for manslaughter when the child died. However, the later Court of Appeal case of *R v Lowe* [1973] QB 702 – a case concerning the wilful neglect of a child under s 1 of the Children and Young Persons Act 1933 – made clear that constructive manslaughter requires an act. In particular, Phillimore LJ ruled that:

> [If] I strike a child in a manner likely to cause harm it is right that, if the child dies, I may be charged with manslaughter. If, however, I omit to do something with the result that it suffers injury to health which results in its death, we think that a charge of manslaughter should not be an inevitable consequence, even if the omission is deliberate.

Lowe expressly disapproved *Senior*, and whilst *Lowe* was overruled in relation to its interpretation of the 1933 Act (by the House of Lords in *R v Sheppard* [1981] AC 394), it remains good law for the purposes of unlawful act manslaughter. As a result of *Lowe*, an omission, or failure to act, will not suffice for the offence.

What is most striking about this judgment is that Phillimore LJ expressly excludes wilful omissions from the scope of constructive manslaughter. As to the distinction between positive acts and *wilful* omissions, see **Chapter 2**. This case alone has been subject to widespread criticism from academics and members of the profession. Here is a selection:

- Dennis ('Manslaughter by Omission' (1980) 33 CLP 255) argues that should this matter come before the courts again, it is likely to be reversed allowing for an omission to satisfy the requirements for constructive manslaughter.
- Glazebrook ('Insufficient Child Protection' [2003] Crim LR 541) calls the decision 'irredeemably irrational and confused'.
- Child and Ormerod (*Smith, Hogan, & Ormerod's Essentials of Criminal Law*, 3rd edn (OUP, 2019)) further this by arguing that the 'act/omission distinction in this context lacks any coherent basis … and so the use of the distinction here simply adds unnecessary complexity to the law'. Child and Ormerod agree with Dennis that this rule is unlikely to survive future appellate judgments.
- Allen and Edwards (*Criminal Law*, 15th edn (OUP, 2019)) likewise throw their hats into the ring by arguing that:

  > there is a great difference between neglect which is due to a lack of thought and that which is wilful, in the sense that there is a deliberate decision not to give food or liquids or to seek medical attention. Such conduct is just as reprehensible as positive acts which are likely to cause harm. *Lowe* is a decision which clearly requires reconsideration.

Until that time, however, where the defendant has failed to act, and his failure has led to the death of the victim, he may be liable for gross negligence manslaughter or subjectively reckless manslaughter, but not unlawful act manslaughter.

Actus reus: (ii) which is unlawful

Once you have satisfied yourself that there is an act, and not an omission, on the part of the defendant, it must then be questioned whether the act is unlawful. By this, the law requires a criminal act, known as the 'base crime'. The easiest way to understand the base offence is to identify what offence the defendant would have been liable for had the victim not died.

example

Jack and Jill are engaged in an argument in the street. Jack punches Jill in the face, who then falls to the floor hitting her head on the curb. Jill survives but suffers a serious head injury.

In his scenario, Jack cannot be liable for a homicide offence (in this case constructive manslaughter) as Jill has not died. In this case, Jack is more likely to be liable for a non-fatal offence against the person, namely actual bodily harm or grievous bodily harm (see **Chapter 9**). Once it is established what criminal offence would be committed had the victim not died, the base offence can be identified.

Civil wrongs insufficient

Given the requirement for the act to be an 'unlawful one', civil wrongs committed by the defendant against the victim will fall outside the definition of an unlawful act. Only criminal offences will suffice.

The criminal law has not always been consistent in this regard, however. In *R v Fenton* (1830) 1 Lew CC 179, the defendant threw some stones down a mineshaft for sport. The stone broke some scaffolding and killed a miner. The defendant was liable for manslaughter despite the fact that his act was one involving civil liability (ie trespass to the person), and not criminal liability. In the Court for Crown Cases Reserved, Tindal CJ ruled:

> If death ensues as the consequence of a wrongful act, an act which the party who commits it can neither justify nor excuse, it is not accidental death, but manslaughter. ... In the present instance, the act was one of mere wantonness and sport, but still the act was wrongful, it was a trespass. The only question therefore is, whether the death of the party is to be fairly and reasonably considered as a consequence of such wrongful act; if it followed from such wrongful act, as an effect from a cause, the offence is manslaughter; if it is altogether unconnected with it, it is accidental death.

In that regard, the defendant was guilty of manslaughter. A number of years later, the Court for Crown Cases Reserved was faced with a second opportunity to identify the correct state of law. In *R v Franklin* (1883) 15 Cox CC 163, the defendant threw a box into the sea, killing a person bathing in the water. No criminal act was committed; instead, a civil wrong (fly-tipping) was the relevant act of the defendant. Field J ruled:

> The mere fact of a civil wrong committed by one person against another ought not to be used as an incident which is a necessary step in a criminal case.

Whilst *Fenton* is authority for the proposition that a civil wrong is sufficient for liability for constructive manslaughter, the better approach is that of *Franklin* (ie that a civil wrong is insufficient for liability in manslaughter).

Proving the base crime in full

The base crime must be 'proved in full' (*R v JF and NE* [2015] EWCA Crim 351), meaning that the defendant must satisfy both the *actus reus* and *mens rea* for the act (*R v Arobieke* [1988] Crim LR 314). Where there is no criminal act, there can be no possibility of a manslaughter conviction, regardless of how dangerous the act is. This was the ruling in *R v Lamb* [1967] 2 QB 981 where a lack of apprehension and *mens rea* in the case of an assault meant that the base offence could not be satisfied for the purposes of unlawful act manslaughter (see **Chapter 9**).

in practice

The courts must ensure that they consider the full elements of the base offence before they move on to consider whether the base offence was objectively dangerous, even though, in *DPP v Newbury; DPP v Jones* [1977] AC 500, the House of Lords failed to specify the base offence which resulted in the conviction of unlawful act manslaughter.

In your assessments, ensure that you deal with the base offence in full at this stage (as though you were answering a question solely dealing with that base offence).

An important point to note is that should any defences arise in relation to the base offence, these defences will remain pertinent when a defendant is charged with unlawful act manslaughter. For example, in *R v Scarlett* [1993] 4 All ER 629, the defendant relied on self-defence to argue that his actions were not 'unlawful'. By way of another example, where the defendant is intoxicated and his base offence is one of specific intent, he may have a defence. However, where the crime is one of basic intent allowing for both intention and recklessness to satisfy the *mens rea* of the offence, no defence will be available and liability for unlawful act manslaughter will continue to be upheld. This was the decision in the fascinating (albeit gruesome) case of *R v Lipman* [1970] 1 QB 152.

case example

Charge:
Murder

Case progression:
Crown Court – Not guilty of murder; guilty of manslaughter

Court of Appeal – Conviction upheld

Point of law:
Defence to unlawful act manslaughter

In *R v Lipman* [1970] 1 QB 152, the defendant and victim, his girlfriend, took a hallucinogenic drug (namely LSD) and experienced an LSD 'trip'. As a result of taking the LSD, the defendant believed that he was descending to the centre of the earth where he was being attacked by snakes. In fighting the snakes, the defendant killed the victim by cramming nine inches of bedsheet down her throat. The Crown Court convicted the defendant of unlawful act manslaughter on the basis that his intoxication was no defence given the basic intent nature of constructive manslaughter.

The Court of Appeal upheld his conviction, confirming the base offence to be the basic intent offence of battery.

Likewise, where there is evidence of a general defence, such as consent (*R v Slingsby* [1995] Crim LR 570) or self-defence, there shall be no unlawful base offence.

The definition of unlawful act has been broadly interpreted as:

(a) not requiring the defendant to know that the act he is committing is unlawful (*DPP v Newbury; DPP v Jones* [1977] AC 500); and
(b) not requiring the act to be directed against the victim.

The first of these interpretations merely represents the idea that ignorance of the law is no defence ('*ignorantia legis neminem excusat*'). The second has been the subject of increasing contradictory statements from the courts over the years. For instance, Waller LJ in *R v Dalby* [1982] 1 All ER 916 emphasised that unlawful acts must be directed at the victim, while the Court of Appeal in *R v Goodfellow* (1986) 83 Cr App R 23 and *R v Watson* [1989] 2 All ER 865 ruled that there is no requirement of direct actions against the victim. Instead, the focus ought to be placed on whether there is a *novus actus interveniens* (see **Chapter 2**) in the given case.

case example

Charge:
Unlawful act manslaughter

Case progression:
Crown Court – Guilty

Court of Appeal – Conviction upheld

Point of law:
Need to direct the unlawful act to the victim

In *R v Goodfellow* (1986) 83 Cr App R 23, the defendant killed his wife and child by setting fire to their council flat in an attempt to obtain alternative housing. The defendant alleged that his actions were not directed to his wife and child and thus he could not be liable for an offence. The Crown Court found the defendant guilty of constructive manslaughter on the basis that the defendant need not direct his unlawful act to a specific person. The Court of Appeal affirmed his conviction, ruling that there is no requirement for the defendant's unlawful act to be directed to the victim. The only requirement is that the act was a direct cause of death; there was no intervening act and it was objectively dangerous.

Goodfellow was approved by the House of Lords in *AG's Reference (No 3 of 1994)* [1998] AC 245. The most recent statement on this point, however, has been provided by the Court of Appeal in *R v Bristow* [2013] EWCA Crim 1540.

case example

Charge:
Unlawful act manslaughter

Case progression:
Crown Court – Guilty

Court of Appeal – Conviction upheld

Point of law:
Meaning of objectively dangerous

In *R v Bristow* [2013] EWCA Crim 1540, the defendant, along with five other individuals, raided several workshops located next to a farmhouse. The victim attempted to intervene and prevent the burglary from occurring. Evidence from the pathologist found that the victim died upon being hit by a car at speed.

The defendant, and his accomplices, were charged and convicted with constructive manslaughter on the basis that the base offence (the burglary) was obviously dangerous from the start, given that the escape from the farmhouse would necessarily have involved a risk of injury to anyone who tried to intervene.

Treacy LJ emphasised that the unlawful act need not be directed to a specific individual, rather:

> What needed to be considered was the foresight of the participants as they embarked upon the crime, and what, if anything a reasonable bystander would inevitably have recognised as a risk of physical harm to any person intervening.

Essentially, this means that where reasonable and sober persons consider the defendant's actions to be objectively dangerous to any individual who may become involved in the matter (ie the unlawful action is dangerous from the outset), that is sufficient to found a claim of manslaughter. This case is controversial to the extent that the unlawful act in this case (burglary) would not cause the risk to the victim; rather, other actions that the defendants would undertake should a person interfere would do so.

Typically, the unlawful acts will reflect the non-fatal offences against the person (considered in **Chapter 9**). However, the offence can encompass any unlawful criminal act, not just offences against the person. In this regard, the unlawful act itself need not be generally dangerous.

Examples of unlawful acts include the following:

Table 8.14 Examples of unlawful acts

Unlawful act	Authority
Assault	*R v Hayward* (1908) 21 Cox CC 692 *R v Mallett* [1972] Crim LR 260
Battery	*R v Church* [1966] 1 QB 59 *R v Mitchell* [1983] QB 741
Affray	*R v Carey* [2006] EWCA Crim 17 *R v JM and SM* [2012] EWCA Crim 2293
Criminal damage	*DPP v Newbury; DPP v Jones* [1977] AC 500 *R v JF and NE* [2015] EWCA Crim 351
Arson	*R v Goodfellow* (1986) 83 Cr App R 23 *R v Willoughby* [2005] 1 WLR 1880
Theft	*R v Willett* [2010] EWCA Crim 1620
Robbery	*R v Dawson* (1985) 81 Cr App R 150
Burglary	*R v Watson* [1989] 2 All ER 865
Administering drugs	*R v Cato* [1976] 1 All ER 260 *R v Rogers* [2003] 1 WLR 1374

Actus reus: (iii) which is objectively dangerous

The third requirement is that the unlawful act is objectively dangerous. This is a question of fact for the jury. The use of the word 'objectively' gives rise to a test concerned with what the reasonable and sober person would have been aware of.

This was the decision in the case of *R v Church* [1966] 1 QB 59:

case example

Charge:
Unlawful act manslaughter

Case progression:
Crown Court – Guilty

Court of Criminal Appeal – Conviction quashed

Point of law:
Meaning of objectively dangerous

In *R v Church* [1966] 1 QB 59, the defendant struck the victim after she mocked him during a sexual encounter. The defendant knocked the victim unconscious and, in a panic, mistakenly believing the victim to be dead, threw her body into the river. The pathology report concluded that the victim died as a result of drowning. The defendant was charged and convicted of unlawful act manslaughter in the Crown Court and appealed, arguing that his actions (throwing the body into the river) could not possibly have been *dangerous*, given that he believed the victim to already be dead.

The Court of Criminal Appeal rejected this argument.

Edmund-Davies J in *Church* justified the Court's conclusion by adopting the view of Glanville Williams in his textbook *Criminal Law: The General Part* (Stevens & Sons, 1961):

> if a killing by the first act would have been manslaughter, a later destruction of the supposed corpse should also be manslaughter.

In the context of objective danger, his Lordship went on to say that:

> the unlawful act must be such as all sober and reasonable people *would inevitably recognise* must subject the other person to, at least, the risk of some harm resulting therefrom, albeit not serious harm. (emphasis added)

Lord Salmon in *DPP v Newbury; DPP v Jones* [1977] AC 500 reaffirmed this to be an objective test.

Necessity that the risk would have been foreseen

The test must not be interpreted too broadly to allow for a mere possibility of harm. Rather, the risk of harm must be one that a reasonable and sober person *would* have foreseen, as opposed to one that they *may* have foreseen. Further, the reasonable and sober person need only be satisfied that the harm foreseen was of *some* harm and need not be *serious* harm.

What harm must be foreseen?

As is clear from *Church*, the level of harm foreseen need only be of 'some harm'. This means that death need not be foreseen, nor need serious harm. A question that has arisen is whether reference to 'some harm' is inclusive only of physical harm, or whether it extends to emotional harm (such as fear or panic). In *R v Carey* [2006] EWCA Crim 17, the Court of Appeal would make continuous reference to the need for the risk of 'physical harm'. In *R v Dawson* (1985) 81 Cr App R 150, Watkins LJ explained that directing the jury that they may find 'emotional disturbance' to be appropriate was a misdirection. According to his Lordship: 'Emotional disturbance does not occur to us as sensibly descriptive of injury or harm to the person.' However, Watkins LJ would identify that 'harm in the context of manslaughter includes injury to the person through the operation of shock emanating from fright'. The Court was therefore satisfied that shock was capable of amounting to physical harm (affirmed by the Court of Appeal in *Carey*).

A further issue faced by the Court of Appeal was whether the form of harm *actually* suffered by the victim has to be foreseen by the reasonable and sober person.

case example

Charge:
Unlawful act manslaughter

Case progression:
Crown Court – Not guilty

Court of Appeal – Appeal allowed

Point of law:
The level of harm foreseen by the bystander

In *R v JM and SM* [2012] EWCA Crim 2293, the defendants, two brothers, were involved in a scuffle with a nightclub bouncer (the victim). As a result of the scuffle, the victim suffered a ruptured aneurysm in his heart as a result of a surge in blood pressure. The prosecution alleged the base offence to be one of affray. In a pre-trial hearing, the trial judge ruled that the prosecution could not prove that a reasonable and sober bystander would have foreseen 'that kind of harm'. The trial against the defendants was stopped by the trial judge.

The prosecution appealed against this ruling in the Court of Appeal, arguing that the trial judge had applied the wrong test, focusing too much on the 'type' or 'sort' of harm the victim suffered. The Court of Appeal agreed and directed that the defendants be tried for the offence.

Lord Judge CJ ruled that

> it has never been a requirement that the defendant personally should foresee any specific harm at all, or that the reasonable bystander should recognise the precise form or 'sort' of harm which did ensue. What matters is whether reasonable and sober people would recognise that the unlawful activities of the defendant inevitably subjected the deceased to the *risk of some harm resulting from them*. (emphasis added)

JM and SM is relevant for showing that the actual form of harm that ensued in the case need not be foreseeable by the sober and reasonable person (ie the bystander need not have foreseen the 'sort' or 'type' of harm which the victim was exposed to). Rather, the sober and reasonable person need only be sure that, as a result of the defendant's unlawful actions, the victim was placed at risk of some harm occurring. That harm need not have been the harm that ensued as the end result.

Dangerousness of base offence

A point of importance to note is that the base offence need not, in general, be a particularly dangerous or serious offence. For instance, in *R v Bristow* [2013] EWCA Crim 1540, Treacy LJ stated that '[w]hilst burglary of itself is not a dangerous crime, a particular burglary may be dangerous because of the circumstances surrounding its commission'. In that case, the Court of Appeal concluded that 'foresight of the risk of intervention to prevent escape' from the burglary was sufficient to make that particular burglary objectively dangerous. The same can be said of offences such as assault and battery which, in a legal sense, are not particularly serious or dangerous; however, that does not mean that they can be automatically discounted. Rather, emphasis must be placed on the commission of the particular unlawful act in question and the circumstances surrounding its commission.

Relevance of D's state of mind and characteristics

The crux of this element is that the accused's state of mind is only relevant to establish that the act was committed intentionally and that it was an unlawful act. The Court of Appeal in *R v Ball* [1989] Crim LR 730 ruled that once these points are established, the question of whether the act was dangerous is not to be judged by the defendant's appreciation of the situation, but rather by the sober and reasonable person observing the whole course of the defendant's conduct throughout the unlawful act. In that case, the defendant shot the victim believing that the gun was loaded with blanks. His mistake did not excuse liability:

> the question whether the act is a dangerous one is to be judged not by the appellant's appreciation but by that of the sober and reasonable man, and it is impossible to impute into his appreciation the mistaken belief of the appellant that what he was doing was not dangerous because he thought he had a blank cartridge in the chamber. At that stage the appellant's intention, foresight or knowledge is irrelevant. (per Stuart-Smith LJ)

In *R v JF and NE* [2015] EWCA Crim 351, the Court of Appeal was asked to modify this test to reflect the defendants' age and mental capacity. The Law Commission in its 2006 Report ('Murder, Manslaughter and Infanticide' (Law Com No 304, 2006)) recommended reform that 'would require subjective foresight of the risk of causing some injury'. Both appeals against conviction were refused, however, on the ground that 'the law is clear and well established' and it 'must be for Parliament to determine whether the long established law needs changing in the light of the Law Commission's various recommendations or whether a further examination is needed by the Law Commission'. Such reform has yet to be introduced.

Facts available to the reasonable and sober person

One issue requiring particular attention is the question of what facts and circumstances may be taken into account by the reasonable and sober person.

case example

Charge:
Unlawful act manslaughter

Case progression:
Crown Court – Guilty

Court of Appeal – Conviction quashed

Point of law:
Knowledge of the defendant at the time of the unlawful act

In *R v Dawson* (1985) 81 Cr App R 150, the defendant and others attempted to rob a petrol station using an imitation firearm and a pickaxe. The victim, a 60-year-old petrol station attendant, suffered a heart attack and died. Unbeknownst to the defendant, the victim suffered from a heart disease. The defendant was charged and convicted of unlawful act manslaughter in the Crown Court, where the jury were directed to consider the risk of harm to the victim from the viewpoint of a reasonable and sober person knowing that the victim suffered from a heart condition.

The Court of Appeal disagreed. Lord Lane CJ explained that:

> The unlawful act in the present circumstances comprised the whole of the burglarious intrusion and did not come to an end upon the appellant's foot crossing the threshold or windowsill. That being so, the appellant (and therefore the bystander) during the course of the unlawful act must have become aware of [the victim's] frailty and approximate age, and the judge's directions were accordingly correct.

As such, the defendant's actions were confirmed as objectively dangerous.

Watkins LJ explained that the dangerousness test

> … can only be undertaken upon the basis of the knowledge gained by a sober and reasonable man as though he were present at the scene of and watched the unlawful act being performed and who knows that, as in the present case, an unloaded replica gun was in use, but that the victim may have thought it was a loaded gun in working order. In other words, he has the same knowledge as the man attempting to rob and no more. It was never suggested that any of the appellants knew that their victim had a bad heart. They knew nothing about him.

Dawson is relevant for showing that where a defendant is unaware of a particular characteristic of the victim, his acts will not be 'dangerous' if the reasonable and sober person would also have had no knowledge of such a condition. From the facts in *Dawson*, the defendant believed the victim to be:

- not elderly,
- in apparent good health, and
- protected behind bullet-proof glass.

This means that the reasonable and sober person shall be accredited with the same information before the defendant throughout the course of the unlawful act. Do not be mistaken as to the impact of this case. Dawson did cause the death of the victim, and did so through a relevant base offence (attempted robbery); however, his actions could not be characterised as objectively dangerous in the eyes of the reasonable and sober person. On that basis, although he did cause death, there was no unlawful act manslaughter due to a lack of objective danger.

case example

Charge:
Unlawful act manslaughter

Case progression:
Crown Court – Guilty

Court of Appeal – Conviction upheld

Point of law:
Knowledge of the defendant throughout the time of the unlawful act

In *R v Watson* [1989] 2 All ER 865, the defendant attempted to burgle the house of the victim, a frail 87-year-old man. The victim confronted the defendant who then proceeded to shout abuse at the victim before fleeing the scene. Upon the arrival of the police, the victim died of a heart attack caused by the distress created by the break-in.

The defendant was charged and convicted of unlawful act manslaughter in the Crown Court and appealed to the Court of Appeal, arguing that, following *Dawson*, there was no evidence that he knew the age or physical condition of the victim and therefore he could not be liable.

The Court of Appeal disagreed, holding that, during the course of a burglary, the defendant *must* have become aware of the victim's age and frailty. More so, the sober and reasonable person would also have become aware of those circumstances. As such, the defendant's actions were confirmed as objectively dangerous.

Watson is relevant for showing that where it would become apparent over the course of the unlawful act, to the reasonable and sober person, that an individual has a particular condition or susceptibility, the actions of the defendant will be deemed as dangerous. *Watson* differs from *Dawson* due to the length of time spent by the defendant committing the unlawful act. In *Dawson*, the unlawful act could best be characterised as a 'snatch and grab', meaning that the victim's vulnerabilities would not have become apparent to the defendant (and, more importantly, the sober and reasonable person). Whereas, in *Watson*, the defendant undertook a prolonged and lengthy unlawful act which gave him (and the reasonable and sober person) sufficient time to appreciate the victim's vulnerabilities.

In both cases, death was caused by the defendant, but only in *Watson* was there unlawful act manslaughter. See also *R v Carey* [2006] EWCA Crim 17 where the victim's heart disease was unknown even to her, her family and her doctors. In this respect, it was impossible for the reasonable and sober person to know of this also. As such, the act of affray could not be considered objectively dangerous.

R v Bristow	R v Dawson	R v Watson
• Information available to the R&SP before the act. • **Relevant** to the assessment.	• Information available to the R&SP after the act. • **Not** relevant to the assessment.	• Information available to the R&SP during the act. • **Relevant** to the assessment.

Figure 8.11 Understanding the facts available to the reasonable and sober person

Actus reus: (iv) the act caused the death of the victim

The final element of the *actus reus* is that the defendant's unlawful and dangerous act caused the death of the victim. The regular rules of causation, including both factual and legal causation, must be satisfied. The point to emphasise at this stage is that we are concerned with the defendant's actions that are unlawful and objectively dangerous. Therefore, should a defendant perform a number of acts, some being unlawful and objectively dangerous, and the others not being so, the jury would have to determine which of the two was the cause of death. If they reach the conclusion that the latter of the two was the cause, there is no unlawful act manslaughter.

example

Jill walks away from Jack after an argument. As Jill is walking away, Jack shouts abuse at Jill claiming that she is a 'slut' and a 'bike'. Jill continues to walk away from Jack who then begins to throw stones at Jill to get her attention. One of the stones hits Jill on the head and she then begins to run from Jack. Upon reaching her home, Jill dies of a heart attack as a result of the confrontation with Jack.

The difficulty here for the prosecution would be to prove which act by the defendant caused the death of Jill. Although shouting the words 'slut' and 'bike' at Jill are nasty and derogative comments, unless Jill apprehended any form of unlawful personal force as a result of those words, there is no unlawful act. Whereas the throwing of the stones at Jill would amount to an unlawful act of battery given the application of force to Jill's person. Two outcomes may unfold in this scenario:

- If the cause of the heart attack was the words spoken by Jack, there is no unlawful act manslaughter. Death was not caused by an unlawful and objectively dangerous act.
- If the cause of the heart attack was the throwing of the stones, there is likely to be unlawful act manslaughter. Death in this case would have been caused by an unlawful and objectively dangerous act, namely a battery.

The prosecution may choose to argue that both actions led to the death of the victim; however, unless the jury can be sure that the throwing of the stones was the cause of death (potentially coupled with the insulting words), there can be no conviction.

As with all applications of the rule of causation, it is essential that you do not forget the rules of new and intervening acts. It is advised you return to **Chapter 2** to recap your understanding of *novus actus interveniens*. Further, for a discussion of the situation involving the supply and administration of drugs where death occurs, see **Chapter 2**.

Mens rea: intention

The final element to be proven for the offence of unlawful act manslaughter is the requirement of intention. Importantly, the requirement is not for the defendant to intend the end result (ie to kill, as that would result in a charge of murder); rather, the intention required is to do the relevant act. In this respect, it must be proven that the defendant not only possessed the *mens* rea for the base offence (whatever that may be) but, in addition, intended to commit the act which formed the base offence. For example, in *R v Lamb*, whilst the defendant did not possess the *mens rea* for assault (intention or recklessness as to causing another to apprehend unlawful force), he did intentionally commit an act of pointing a gun at the victim. In this regard, it may assist, for your own understanding, to explain that the defendant must perform a 'deliberate' act, rather than an intentional one. For example, you can express the duty of the prosecution in *Newbury* as being required to prove that the defendants (on the facts) *deliberately* threw a paving stone from a railway bridge, killing a train guard (in addition to proving that they possessed the *mens rea* of the base offence).

The House of Lords addressed the issue of intention in *Andrews v DPP* [1937] AC 576.

case example

Charge:
Gross negligence manslaughter

Case progression:
Crown Court – Guilty

Court of Criminal Appeal – Conviction upheld

House of Lords – Conviction upheld

Point of law:
Distinction between gross negligence manslaughter and unlawful act manslaughter

In *Andrews v DPP* [1937] AC 576, the defendant killed the victim, a pedestrian, whilst overtaking another car.

The defendant was charged with and convicted of manslaughter in the Crown Court, which was upheld by the Court of Criminal Appeal.

The question before the House of Lords on appeal was whether the defendant was liable for gross negligence manslaughter or unlawful act manslaughter.

Lord Atkin ruled that dangerous driving is not enough to constitute an unlawful act for the purposes of unlawful act manslaughter. As a result, the focus had to be on whether his actions were so negligent that they could be considered 'gross'. The House of Lords affirmed his conviction.

Lord Atkin stated (in *obiter*) that a base offence for unlawful act manslaughter required an intrinsically criminal offence. His Lordship explained:

> There is an obvious difference in the law of manslaughter between doing an unlawful act and doing a lawful act with a degree of carelessness which the Legislature makes criminal. If it were otherwise a man who killed another while driving without due care and attention would *ex necessitate* commit manslaughter.

Although this statement may appear complex and confusing, it simply means that the base offence cannot be one:

- where the *mens rea* is satisfied by negligence, such as in the case of dangerous driving; or
- that requires no *mens rea* at all on part of the defendant (ie a strict liability offence).

It was for the first of these reasons that Andrews was convicted of gross negligence manslaughter and not unlawful act manslaughter.

More recently, in *R v Meeking* [2012] EWCA Crim 641, Toulson LJ ruled that it was wrong for the prosecution to charge the defendant with unlawful act manslaughter, rather than gross negligence manslaughter, where the behaviour was such that could merely be characterised as negligent. Although this is not a direct statement by the Court of Appeal that negligent behaviour cannot suffice for unlawful act manslaughter, it may certainly be interpreted that way given the emphasis placed on *Andrews v DPP* by the Court.

Therefore, a defendant cannot be liable for unlawful act manslaughter where the *mens rea* of the base offence may be satisfied by negligence or where the offence is one of strict liability.

8.5.2 Gross negligence manslaughter

The second type of involuntary manslaughter is that of gross negligence manslaughter. As discussed in **Chapter 2**, 'negligence' is a legal concept (or 'cause of action') taken from the civil law. Unlike in the civil law, however, liability in crime is founded upon any such negligence being gross. The actual meaning of 'gross', however, has troubled the courts for a number of years.

8.5.2.1 Defining gross negligence manslaughter

Gross negligence manslaughter is concerned with the occasions where death results from a grossly negligent act or omission on the part of the defendant. Lord Hewart CJ in *R v Bateman* (1925) 19 Cr App R 8 emphasised the need to distinguish criminal and civil understandings of negligence and stated that the criminal standard

> went beyond a mere matter of compensation between subjects and showed such disregard for the life and safety of others as to amount to a crime against the State and conduct deserving punishment.

As discussed above, the inclusion of omissions within gross negligence manslaughter is to catch any offences missed by unlawful act manslaughter, which does not recognise omissions as leading to a conviction for constructive manslaughter.

8.5.2.2 Elements of gross negligence manslaughter

The leading authority on gross negligence manslaughter is that of *R v Adomako* [1995] 1 AC 171, which provides the five-point test for establishing liability (the *Adomako* test).

case example

Charge:
Gross negligence manslaughter

Case progression:
Crown Court – Guilty

Court of Appeal – Conviction upheld

House of Lords – Conviction upheld

Point of law:
Test for gross negligence manslaughter

In *R v Adomako* [1995] 1 AC 171, the defendant (an anaesthetist) failed to notice that a tube supplying oxygen to the victim, his patient, had become detached. As a result of this, the victim died. The defendant was charged and convicted with gross negligence manslaughter in the Crown Court.

The defendant appealed against his conviction, arguing that the trial judge should have directed the jury to objective recklessness. This was refused by both the Court of Appeal and the House of Lords, which provided the test for gross negligence manslaughter.

Lord Mackay LC in *Adomako* established the test for gross negligence manslaughter as follows:

> [T]he ordinary principles of the law of negligence apply to ascertain whether or not the defendant has been in breach of a duty of care towards the victim who has died. If such breach of duty is established the next question is whether that breach of duty caused the death of the victim. If so, the jury must go on to consider whether that breach of duty should be characterised as gross negligence and therefore as a crime. This will depend on the seriousness of the breach of duty committed by the defendant in all the circumstances in which the defendant was placed when it occurred. The jury will have to consider whether the extent to which the defendant's conduct departed from the proper standard of care incumbent upon him, involving as it must have done a risk of death to the patient, was such that it should be judged criminal.

This test was reaffirmed by the Court of Appeal in *R v Misra; R v Srivastava* [2005] 1 Cr App R 328. Importantly, and rather oddly, when we speak of the elements of gross negligence manslaughter, we do not refer specifically to the *actus reus* and *mens rea* of the offence. This is because, although the *actus reus* can be easily defined, the *mens rea* is not so easy given that there is no requirement of intention or recklessness. However, this offence is also not one of strict liability. The requirement that the negligence was 'gross' is, in fact, the *mens rea* of the offence (an objective form of *mens rea* that we have yet to consider in full). On this basis, we shall simply refer to each part as an 'element' of the offence.

The elements of gross negligence manslaughter as stated by Lord Mackay LC are outlined in **Table 8.15A**.

Table 8.15A Elements of gross negligence manslaughter (in Adomako)

Elements of the offence
Duty of care owed
Duty of care negligently breached
Serious and obvious risk of death was reasonably foreseeable
Breach of duty caused death
The negligence was 'gross'

Following *R v Kuddus* [2019] EWCA Crim 837, it might be said that there is a sixth element of liability, namely that the breach of duty *actually* gave rise to a serious and obvious risk of death. This requirement is different to element 3 in the Table above in that there must actually exist a serious and obvious risk of death in fact; not merely a foreseeability of such. Indeed, the approach of the Crown Court Compendium (section 19–3(5)) is to treat gross negligence manslaughter as requiring proof of six elements, not merely five. In *Kuddus*, Sir Brian Leveson P accepted that the actual existence of such a risk will generally be 'implicit' where the breach has actually caused death. In this regard, we can amend the Table of elements of the offence as follows:

Table 8.15B Elements of gross negligence manslaughter (following Kuddus)

Elements of the offence
Duty of care owed
Duty of care negligently breached
Serious and obvious risk of death was reasonably foreseeable
An actual serious and obvious risk of death existed
Breach of duty caused death
The negligence was 'gross'

We shall consider each element in turn following *R v Kuddus* and **Table 8.15B**.

(i) Duty of care owed

The first element of this offence is that a duty of care was owed by the defendant to the victim. There is no 'general' duty of care owed by one citizen to another (ie there is no 'Good Samaritan law', as discussed in **Chapter 2**).

The phrase 'duty of care' may ring a bell in your mind if you have already studied the law of torts, specifically the neighbour principle as established in *Donoghue v Stevenson* [1932] AC 562. Lord Atkin in *Donoghue v Stevenson* recounted that

> You must take reasonable care to avoid acts or omissions which you can reasonably foresee would be likely to injure your neighbour.
>
> Who, then, in law, is my neighbour? The answer seems to be – persons who are so closely and directly affected by my act that I ought reasonably to have them in contemplation as being so affected when I am directing my mind to the acts or omissions which are called in question.

In *R v Adomako* [1995] 1 AC 171, Lord Mackay LC stated that such tortious principles are just as applicable in the criminal law as they are in tort. In this regard, to determine whether a duty of care is owed, one must apply the ordinary principles of tort law. This does not, however, mean that all the rules or technicalities of the law of tort are applicable. One example we can take in this regard is that of *ex turpi causa*, which means that a relationship between those involved in a criminal enterprise does not give rise to a duty of care owed by one participant to another. We can see this in *R v Wacker* [2003] QB 1207.

case example

Charge:
Gross negligence manslaughter

Case progression:
Crown Court – Guilty

Court of Appeal – Conviction upheld

Point of law:
Use of civil principles in gross negligence manslaughter

In *R v Wacker* [2003] QB 1207, the defendant drove a lorry carrying 60 illegal Chinese immigrants from Rotterdam to England. The immigrants were placed in a concealed compartment and, once inside, they were sealed in. The lorry had no ventilation system and contained one air vent. In order to avoid detection by officers, the defendant closed the air vent and forgot to re-open it. As a result, 58 of the immigrants suffocated. The defendant was charged with and convicted of gross negligence manslaughter in the Crown Court.

The defendant appealed to the Court of Appeal on the basis that the tortious principle of *ex turpi causa non oritur actio* applied to the gross negligence manslaughter and could negate the defendant's liability.

Kay LJ concluded that:

> the very same public policy that causes the civil courts to refuse the claim points in a quite different direction in considering a criminal offence. The criminal law has as its function the protection of citizens and gives effect to the state's duty to try those who have deprived citizens of their rights of life, limb or property. It may very well step in at the precise moment when civil courts withdraw because of this very different function. The withdrawal of a civil remedy has nothing to do with whether as a matter of public policy the criminal law applies.
>
> ...
>
> Thus, looked at as a matter of pure public policy, we can see no justification for concluding that the criminal law should decline to hold a person as criminally responsible for the death of another simply because the two were engaged in some joint unlawful activity at the time or, indeed, because there may have been an element of acceptance of a degree of risk by the victim in order to further the joint unlawful enterprise. Public policy, in our judgment, manifestly points in totally the opposite direction.

As a result of *Wacker*, the principle of *ex turpi causa* does not apply in gross negligence manslaughter to negate criminal liability (though it is does apply in corporate manslaughter – see **Chapter 6**). This was confirmed in *R v Willoughby* [2005] 1 WLR 1880. A case involving very similar facts to that of *Wacker* can be seen in *R v Robinson* (Crown Ct, 8 April 2020) involving the high-profile case of Maurice Robinson, a lorry driver, who pleaded guilty to manslaughter for the deaths of 39 people found dead in the back of a refrigerated lorry.

Examples of established duties include the following:

Table 8.16 Established duties in gross negligence manslaughter

Established duty	**Authority**
Doctor/Patient	*R v Bateman* (1925) 19 Cr App R 8 *R v Misra; R v Srivastava* [2005] 1 Cr App R 328 *R v Adomako* [1995] 1 AC 171
Driver/Passenger	*R v Litchfield* [1998] Crim LR 507 *Page v Smith* [1996] AC 155 *R v Wacker* [2003] QB 1207
Employer/Employee	*R v Pittwood* (1902) 19 TLR 37

Established duty	Authority
Electrician/Customer	*R v Prentice* [1994] QB 302
Landlord/Tenant	*R v Singh (Gurphal)* [1999] Crim LR 582
Creation of/contribution to a dangerous situation	*R v Miller* [1983] 2 AC 161 *R v Ruffell* [2003] EWCA Crim 122 *R v Evans* [2009] EWCA Crim 650

Do not think that the jury must arbitrarily place a duty of care within one of these listed examples. In fact, according to the Court of Appeal in *R v Willoughby* [2005] 1 WLR 1880, a duty of care may arise from a combination of these circumstances and may even arise where the victim and the defendant had engaged in some form of unlawful activity together (*R v Wacker* [2003] QB 1207 above). For a detailed look at the duty of care in gross negligence manslaughter cases, see Herring and Palser, 'The Duty of Care in Gross Negligence Manslaughter' [2007] Crim LR 24.

A question that has come before the courts on a number of occasions is whether it is a part of the judge's or the jury's role to find there to be a duty of care owed. In *R v Singh (Gurphal)* [1999] Crim LR 582, the Court of Appeal held that it is for the trial judge to rule if there is a duty of care. This was doubted in *R v Willoughby* [2005] 1 WLR 1880, where the Court of Appeal held that the judge is only responsible for deciding whether sufficient evidence is produced to establish a duty of care, and whether the duty actually does exist is a matter solely for the jury. Rose LJ in *Willoughby* stated that:

> Whether a duty of care exists is a matter for the jury once the judge has decided that there is evidence capable of establishing a duty.

The Court of Appeal confirmed in *R v Evans* [2009] EWCA Crim 650 that whether a duty exists is a question of law for the judge. The judge will inform the jury that if they find X, a duty will exist; whereas if they find Y, no duty will exist. Further to this, the Court of Appeal in *R v Oughton* [2010] EWCA Crim 1540 ruled that a jury do not require expert evidence to find a duty of care to have existed. Directions from the trial judge in this regard are sufficient.

in practice

A jury are unlikely to struggle to find that a duty exists where the relationship is obvious, even to the layperson (eg doctor/patient). In these circumstances, a judge may feel it appropriate to direct the jury to find that a relationship exists.

(ii) Duty of care negligently breached

Once it is established that a duty of care exists, the prosecution must then prove that the duty was breached in a negligent fashion. The breach occurs when the defendant falls below a particular standard expected and may occur by way of positive act or omission (see *R v Litchfield* [1998] Crim LR 507). In the case of an omission, for gross negligence manslaughter, not only must it be proven that the defendant owed a duty of care, but also that the defendant owed a duty to act to the victim. In **Chapter 2**, we observed the case of *R v Pittwood* (1902) 19 TLR 37. There we saw that the defendant owed a duty to act based on his contractual obligations and breached that duty by unreasonably failing to lower the gate. For gross negligence manslaughter, which

Pittwood was convicted of, it also had to be proven that he owed a duty of care. In the majority of cases, where an individual possesses a duty to act, he will also possess a duty of care (see *R v Evans* [2009] EWCA Crim 650).

When one considers a breach of duty, the ordinary law and language of negligence applies to these cases. Namely that a person who owes a duty of care to another must act as a 'reasonable person would do in their position'. The classic phrase adopted by the courts is that provided by Greer LJ in *Hall v Brooklands Auto-Racing Club* [1933] 1 KB 205, where his Lordship defined the reasonable man as 'the man on the street' or as the 'man on the Clapham omnibus'. A failure to meet this objective standard of the reasonable person will result in a breach of duty.

When determining the standard by which a defendant's behaviour should be measured, the civil courts consider several requirements (also known as 'risk factors'). These factors may be pertinent to a defendant in a criminal case who shall be compared to a person in a similar situation as the defendant.

The factors used to determine liability include the following:

Table 8.17 Civil law factors to establish the standard of care

Factors
Foreseeability of risk
Magnitude of risk
Extent of harm
Practicability of precautions
Social utility of activity

Naturally, many of these factors may not be relevant to criminal practice, as made clear by the Court of Appeal in *R v Wacker* [2003] QB 1207.

In light of these factors, if the defendant has acted within the standard expected of a reasonable person in the same circumstance as the defendant (even if the defendant's personal standard is towards the lower end of acceptable conduct), the prosecution will struggle to prove that the defendant fell below such reasonable standard expected. On this point, the respective skills (or lack thereof) of a defendant may also be relevant to their liability. The CPS, in its 'Legal Guidance on Gross Negligence Manslaughter', has provided that

> An unqualified person is not to be judged at a lower standard than a qualified person. Therefore the lack of skill will not be a defence if the conduct is deemed negligent. If however, the defendant has particular skills and knowledge of a danger that the reasonable person would not have, his actions should be judged in the light of those skills or knowledge.

From case law established in the law of tort, it would appear that amateurs are not to be treated at the same level of their skilled counterparts. For instance, in *Philips v William Whiteley Ltd* [1938] 1 All ER 566, a jeweller pierced ears using sterilized equipment; the claimant contracted a blood disorder as a result of the piercing. The King's Bench Division of the High Court held that the defendant had taken all reasonable steps in the circumstances to avoid the risk of harm and could not be fixed with the same standard of care as a person more skilled, for example a surgeon. On that basis, the defendant must be held to the standard of their reasonable counterpart – ie a person holding the same sets of skills and experience (*Bolam v Friern Hospital*

Management Committee [1957] 1 WLR 582). In this regard, should the defendant be performing a skilled activity, he will be compared to a reasonable person with that skill. In *Philips*, for example, the defendant had to be compared with another jeweller. However, this does not mean that a person with less experience can rely on that inexperience as a defence to liability (*Nettleship v Weston* [1971] QB 691 – where it was held that a learner driver was expected to meet the same standard as a reasonable qualified competent driver).

example

Jack is a qualified electrician but is understood by other electricians in the area to be very poor at his job. This is based upon his lack of experience, having qualified only two weeks ago. Jack is contracted to rewire Jill's electrics in her kitchen. Jack performs the job to a poor standard and Jill is electrocuted when she attempts to use one of her appliances. Jill dies.

In this scenario, Jack is not to be held to the standard of the man on the Clapham omnibus. This is because, as a qualified electrician, Jack has more skill and knowledge than the man on the street. On this basis, Jack is to be held to the same standard as a reasonably competent electrician. It is irrelevant, in this case, that Jack is recently qualified and lacks a significant amount of experience – he will still be held to the standard of the reasonably competent electrician.

This was the situation in *R v Adomako*. The House of Lords confirmed that Adomako had to be compared to a reasonably competent anaesthetist and not to an unexperienced and overworked anaesthetist as the defence alleged.

(iii) Serious and obvious risk of death was reasonably foreseeable

From the listed elements of the offence, you should notice that the breach of duty comes in two parts: the first being that the breach itself involved a foreseeable risk of death; and the second that the breach caused the death of the victim (and, as such, there was a serious and obvious risk of death in fact). Both tests are necessary to demonstrate that the breach was sufficiently serious that the risk was clear to the defendant before death ensued as a result.

When considering the breach of a duty of care, the jury must consider whether there was a risk to life. The degree of this risk has fluctuated over time. **Table 8.18** details this development.

Table 8.18 Development of levels of risk of death

Case authority	Degree of risk
R v Bateman (1925) 19 Cr App R 8	'Such disregard of the life and safety of others' (per Lord Hewart CJ)
R v Adomako [1995] 1 AC 171	'[A] risk of death' (per Lord Mackay LC)
R v Misra; R v Srivastava [2005] 1 Cr App R 328	'A *serious and obvious* risk of death, not merely of injury, even serious injury, but of death' (per Judge LJ)
Brown (Uriah) v The Queen (Jamaica) [2006] 1 AC 1	'[A] very high degree of risk' (per Lord Carswell)

The current accepted definition of risk is that in *R v Singh (Gurphal)* [1999] Crim LR 582, where the Court of Appeal (judgment delivered by Schiemann LJ) approved the judgment of the trial judge, namely that

> The circumstances must be such that a reasonably prudent person would have foreseen a *serious and obvious risk* not merely of injury, even serious injury, but *of death*. (emphasis added)

The CPS has made it clear, as a matter of policy, that it will not prosecute on any evidence less than 'a serious and obvious risk of death'.

Three points must be considered at this stage:

- What is the relevant time for the jury to consider whether a serious and obvious risk of death was foreseeable?
- Whose perception are we concerned with when considering the risk of death?
- Must the risk be a serious and obvious one to that particular victim?

In relation to the first question, the relevant time period when considering whether a serious and obvious risk of death was foreseeable is when the defendant is presented with the relevant information or facts from which he is to base his conduct. This means that a defendant cannot be liable as a result of 'hindsight'; his actions are determined 'there and then'. The Court of Appeal recently demonstrated this in the case of *R v Rudling* [2016] EWCA Crim 741.

case example

Charge:
Gross negligence manslaughter

Case progression:
Crown Court – Not guilty *(no case to answer)*

Court of Appeal – Appeal dismissed

Point of law:
Timing of 'serious and obvious risk' of death

In *R v Rudling* [2016] EWCA Crim 741, the defendant, a GP, failed to visit the victim, a 12-year old boy, who was, unbeknownst to the defendant, suffering with Addison's disease – an extremely rare disease that attacks the immune system. The defendant had been asked to visit the victim by the victim's mother who had described the victim's symptoms. The victim died and the defendant was charged with gross negligence manslaughter in the Crown Court.

In the Crown Court, the prosecution argued that the mother's description of the victim's symptoms was 'so alarming' that the defendant ought to have visited the victim whereupon she would have seen that he needed urgent medical care. The breach of duty arose from the defendant's failure to visit the boy immediately. The defence made a submission of no case to answer, arguing that Addison's disease was not something any GP could be expected to recognise and that, at the time of the breach, ie when speaking to the mother, there was no obvious risk of death in the case. The trial judge agreed and the case against the defendant was stopped.

The prosecution appealed to the Court of Appeal on the basis that a reasonably competent GP would have said to herself, 'I cannot eliminate the possibility that the child may be suffering from a rare risk to life without the child being seen urgently', and that this equated to an obvious and serious risk of death. The Court of Appeal disagreed and dismissed the appeal.

Sir Brian Leveson P ruled (emphasis added):

> In our judgment, that proposition simply does not follow, as is apparent when one focuses on each of the three aspects of this ingredient of the offence of gross negligence manslaughter. *At the time of the breach of duty, there must be a risk of death, not merely serious illness; the risk must be serious; and the risk must be obvious.* A GP faced with an unusual presentation which is worrying and undiagnosed may need to ensure a face to face assessment urgently in order to investigate further. That may be in order to assess whether it is something serious ... which may or may not be so serious as to be life-threatening. *A recognisable risk of something serious is not the same as a recognisable risk of death.*

> What does not follow is that if a reasonably competent GP requires an urgent assessment of a worrying and undiagnosed condition, it is necessarily reasonably foreseeable that there is a risk of death. Still less does it demonstrate a serious risk of death, which is not to be equated with an 'inability to eliminate a possibility'. There may be numerous remote possibilities of very rare conditions which cannot be eliminated but which do not present a serious risk of death. Further, and perhaps most importantly, a mere possibility that an assessment might reveal something life-threatening is not the same as an obvious risk of death. *An obvious risk is a present risk which is clear and unambiguous, not one which might become apparent on further investigation.*
>
> These distinctions are not a matter of semantics but represent real differences in the practical assessments which fall to be made by doctors …

This case shows the subtle difference between a proven case of gross negligence manslaughter and a failed case of such. The defendant chose not to visit the victim, meaning that her assessment of the situation was based on the information provided to her by the mother. That information, although it may have presented a case of serious injury or harm to the child, did not present the defendant with a situation where there was a serious and obvious risk of death. Indeed, the prosecution's own expert witness testified that the life-threatening seriousness of the victim's condition would not have been apparent to the defendant unless and until she had carried out a face-to-face examination. Had the defendant in this case visited the victim, as requested by his mother, the prosecution would have had a stronger case that there was at that time a serious and obvious risk of death before the doctor. This, however, is not conclusive as the Court of Appeal has noted that the doctor could still have concluded that there was a serious risk of injury, but not necessarily of death. In the words of Sir Brian Leveson P in the more recent case of *R v Rose (Honey)* [2017] EWCA Crim 1168, '… the court could not impute to the doctor the knowledge that would have been obtained had there not been a breach of duty …'.

The position can thus be summarised as follows:

> The question of whether there is a serious and obvious risk of death must exist at, and is to be assessed with respect to, knowledge at the time of the breach of duty. (per Sir Brian Leveson P in *R v Rose (Honey)*)

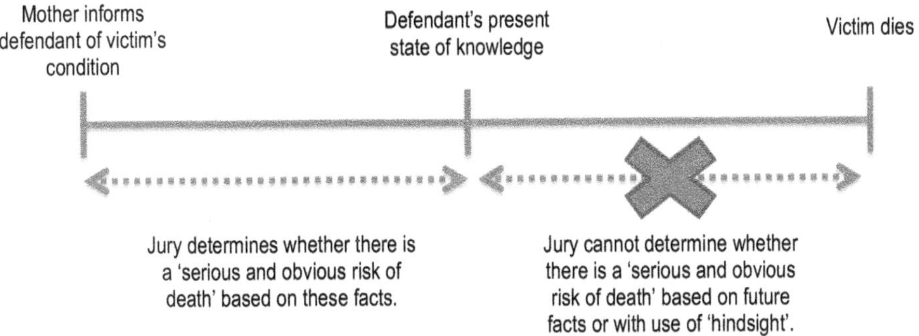
Mother informs defendant of victim's condition
Defendant's present state of knowledge
Victim dies
Jury determines whether there is a 'serious and obvious risk of death' based on these facts.
Jury cannot determine whether there is a 'serious and obvious risk of death' based on future facts or with use of 'hindsight'.

Figure 8.12 Relevant time of assessing the serious risk of death

In relation to the second question, the essential point to note is that it is irrelevant whether the defendant appreciated the serious and obvious risk of death (*R v Mark* [2004] EWCA Crim 2490). The test requires the reasonable person standing in the defendant's shoes to appreciate the risk. This was made clear by the Divisional Court in *R v DPP, ex parte Jones* [2000] IRLR 373 and the Court of Appeal in *AG's Reference (No 2 of 1999)* [2000] QB 796. This was affirmed in *R v S* [2015] EWCA Crim 558 by the Court of Appeal, where Cranston J stated:

> In our judgment, the issue for the jury ... was not based on a subjective test (what did the applicant know, believe or foresee) but rather an objective one: whether a reasonable and prudent person of the applicant's age and experience would have foreseen a serious risk of death and, if so, whether the applicant's conduct fell so far below the standard of care required that it was grossly negligent such that it constituted a crime.
>
> In answering that objective question, it was open to the jury to conclude on the evidence before it that the applicant's conduct fell below the standard of care in pointing a gun and pulling the trigger when just a short distance away from [the victim]. The judge distinguished ordinary negligence and said that whether this was gross negligence turned on the circumstances.

Despite the apparent clarity that is present in this area, the Court of Appeal was recently faced with an appeal relating to the test of foreseeability in *R v Rose (Honey)* [2017] EWCA Crim 1168.

case example

Charge:
Gross negligence manslaughter

Case progression:
Crown Court – Guilty

Court of Appeal – Conviction quashed

Point of law:
Meaning of foreseeability in gross negligence manslaughter

In *R v Rose (Honey)* [2017] EWCA Crim 1168, the defendant, an optometrist (an eye specialist) was charged with and convicted of gross negligence manslaughter in the Crown Court after the victim, a young boy, died as a result of hydrocephalus – an obstruction behind the eye causing a blockage to the brain. The defendant had examined the victim's eye and found no sign of a problem from the photographs taken. Upon further investigation by the police, the defendant acknowledged that she must have viewed the wrong photograph of the victim's eye examination as there were clearly marks on that image showing problems with the eye.

At trial, the defence made a submission of no case to answer, alleging that there was no serious and obvious risk of death at the time of the breach given that the defendant was not even aware that a problem existed.

The trial judge, Stuart-Smith J, refused the submission on the basis that the relevant test to apply concerned facts and knowledge that the defendant 'had or would have had but for the breaches of duty that are alleged'.

The defendant was convicted and appealed to the Court of Appeal on the basis that the trial judge had used the wrong test and that the jury may only consider what information the defendant had *at the time of the breach*. The Court of Appeal agreed and quashed the defendant's conviction.

Giving the judgment of the Court, Sir Brian Leveson P concluded:

> The inherently objective nature of the test of reasonable foreseeability does not turn it from a prospective into a retrospective test. The question of available knowledge and risk is always to be judged objectively and prospectively as at the moment of breach, not but for the breach. The question of reasonable foreseeability is evident from the words used, i.e. what is reasonably *fore*-seeable at the time of the breach (a prospective view). It is not what would, could or should have been known but for the breach of the identified duty of care, i.e. if the breach had not been committed (a retrospective view). (original emphasis)

Sir Brian Leveson P proceeded to explain the position in the law as follows:

> [T]he [Trial] Judge appears to have confused or elided two separate matters: (a) the actual knowledge of Ms Rose at the time of the breach and (b) the putative knowledge of the reasonably prudent optometrist in the position of Ms Rose at the time. The two are quite different concepts: the former is subjective; the latter is objective. The test of reasonable foreseeability is, of course, resolutely objective and there is no question of it being decided by reference to the subjective knowledge of the person whose conduct is under scrutiny. The test of reasonable foreseeability simply requires the *notional objective exercise of putting a reasonably prudent professional in the shoes of the person whose conduct is under scrutiny and asking whether, at the moment of breach of the duty on which the prosecution rely, that person ought reasonably (i.e. objectively) to have foreseen an obvious and serious risk of death.* (emphasis added)

In summary, the law is not concerned with what the defendant 'should have', 'would have', or 'ought to have' known. Rather, the court applies a simple test of placing a reasonably objective person into the mindset (or shoes) of the defendant at the time of the breach and asks whether, *at that time*, there was a serious and obvious risk of death. In some circumstances, as identified by the Court of Appeal in *R v Winterton* [2018] EWCA Crim 2435, the foreseeability of such a risk will actually be obvious to the defendant. In that case, the defendant, a construction manager, argued that there was no evidence that a trench had been dug in an unsafe manner. The trench had collapsed and killed the victim, a worker. The Court of Appeal considered that the trench was bound to collapse (it being more a question of *when*, and not *if*). In that regard, Macur LJ summed up:

> [For] the anaesthetist in *Adomako* and the doctors in *Misra and Strivastata*, the warning signs and serious and obvious risk of death were there for them to see. They either did see them and ignored them, or failed to do so in circumstances that would provoke an objective observer to say, 'but on the facts and in their position they should have done'.

For a recent example of this, see *R v Zaman* [2017] EWCA Crim 1783, in which the defendant, a restaurant owner, failed to take steps to ensure customers who suffered from peanut allergies were not served with food containing peanuts. The defendant was aware of his persistent failure to address the issue, with one customer having suffered a violent allergic reaction on an earlier occasion, and it could not be said that the defendant did not foresee a serious and obvious risk of death when another customer died after suffering an allergic reaction.

Zaman can be contrasted with the most recent authority on this point, namely *R v Kuddus* [2019] EWCA Crim 837. In *Kuddus*, the victim ordered a meal from the defendant's restaurant from the takeaway website. In placing her order, the words 'nuts, prawns' were inserted into the comments section of the order, given that the victim believed she had a mild allergy to these ingredients. Despite this, the food served contained peanut proteins, and the victim suffered an allergic reaction from which she died in hospital two days later. The defendant was convicted of gross negligence manslaughter. On appeal, the defendant contended that he lacked the appropriate knowledge for a duty of care to be imposed upon him, given that he had never been notified of the terms of the order and, in particular, the allergens. Indeed, it was agreed by both sides that the defendant was never made aware the listed allergens – the ticket containing the relevant allergens had been printed and read by his co-defendant, but the defendant himself had never been notified of the terms of the order. The Court of

Appeal allowed the defendant's appeal. Sir Brian Leveson P explained that the reasonable and sober person, who must foresee the serious and obvious risk of death, must do so armed with the knowledge of the relevant defendant. Given that the defendant knew nothing of the victim's allergens, neither would the reasonable and sober person. On the basis of the trial judge's direction to attribute the knowledge of the business and his co-defendant with the knowledge of the defendant, the conviction could not stand. *Kuddus*, therefore, is authority for the proposition that, given that the sober and reasonable person is infused with the knowledge of the defendant, in a case where the defendant was not aware of the situation, neither could the reasonable person be considered as being aware.

In relation to the third and final question, the Court of Appeal in *R v Kuddus* had to consider to whom the serious and obvious risk of death was posed. In particular, the defendant in *Kuddus* argued that it was 'illogical if a defendant could be convicted on the basis that a reasonable person should have foreseen a serious risk of death unless that level of risk *actually* existed' (emphasis added). To be clear, the defence submitted that the prosecution must prove that the victim him- or herself was exposed to a serious and obvious risk of death, as opposed to the general class of individuals with nut allergies being so exposed.

Sir Brian Leveson P rejected this submission, ruling that:

> In our judgment, to focus on the particular circumstances of this specific victim is to misunderstand what has to be established to prove gross negligence manslaughter. There is no requirement that there must be proved to be a serious and obvious risk of death *for the specific victim who dies.* If it is in issue, the question to be answered is whether the defendant's breach gave rise (as an objective fact) to a serious and obvious risk of death to the class of people to whom the defendant owed a duty. Thus, in the present case, where the duty was to take reasonable steps not to injure members of the class of nut allergy sufferers (of whom Megan was one), the question to be answered would be whether any proved breach by the appellant would give rise to a *serious and obvious risk of death for members of that class.* (emphasis added)

In that regard, the sober and reasonable person need not foresee a serious and obvious risk to the particular victim in question; rather, the focus is on the particular class or group of individuals who would be at risk (eg those with nut allergies ordering from a takeaway restaurant).

(iv) An actual serious and obvious risk of death

As noted towards the start of this section, there is now arguably another element that must be proven to the jury's satisfaction, namely, that the breach of duty *actually* involved a serious and obvious risk of death. In *R v Kuddus* [2019] EWCA Crim 837, Sir Brian Leveson P ruled that:

> Although the third element [of liability] is primarily concerned with foreseeability, it is implicit … that the Defendant's breach of duty must give rise to (1) a risk of death, that was (2) obvious and (3) serious. These are objective facts, which are not dependent upon the state of mind or knowledge of the Defendant.

His Lordship explained that this condition is often 'implicit' within the requirement that the breach caused death (ie element (v) below): 'In any case of gross negligence manslaughter there is, by definition, a risk of death, because it must be proved that the

Defendant's breach caused the death of the victim.' Therefore, if the element is non-contentious, it can be subsumed by the requirement of causation. However, his Lordship did appreciate that '[i]f there is a real issue as to their existence, each must be proved by relevant and admissible evidence'.

Advice on dealing with this section is as follows:

- If it is non-contentious that a serious and obvious risk of death existed, this element can be subsumed into element (v): Breach of duty caused death.
- If it is contentious that a serious and obvious risk of death existed, this element would have to be proven as a separate element.

(v) Breach of duty caused death

The fifth element of this offence is that the breach itself caused the death of the victim. For this, the ordinary test of causation applies – ie factual and legal causation (*R v Bawa-Garba* [2016] EWCA Crim 1841) (see **Chapter 2**).

In *R v HM Coroner for Inner London, ex parte Douglas-Williams* [1999] 1 All ER 344, Lord Woolf MR in the Court of Appeal ruled that:

> in relation to both types of manslaughter it is an essential ingredient that the unlawful or negligent act must have caused the death at least in the manner described. If there is a situation where, on examination of the evidence, it cannot be said that the death in question was caused by an act which was unlawful or negligent as I have described, then a critical link in the chain of causation is not established. That being so, a verdict of unlawful killing would not be appropriate and should not be left to the jury.

(vi) The negligence was 'gross'

The final element to prove is that the breach of duty was so bad (or 'sufficiently serious') that it can be classified as 'gross'. Lord Mackay LC in *R v Adomako* [1995] 1 AC 171 took the opportunity to explain the distinction between mere negligence and 'gross negligence'. His Lordship surmised:

> The essence of the matter which is supremely a jury question is whether having regard to the risk of death involved, the conduct of the defendant was so bad in all the circumstances as to amount in their judgment to a criminal act or omission.

In addition, in *R v Misra; R v Srivastava* [2005] 1 Cr App R 328, the Court of Appeal concluded that it is for a jury to decide whether the defendant's conduct was so bad/gross in all the circumstances that it can be classified as criminal. In both *Adomako* and *Misra*, the court conceded that the test is rather 'circular' in nature.

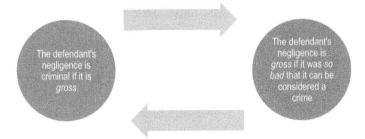

Figure 8.13 The circular test

The circularity of this test has been extensively criticised on the basis that it affords no degree of consistency or clarity to the law. In *Misra*, defence counsel contended that the circularity of the grossness test contravened Article 7 of the ECHR. Judge LJ was not persuaded by this argument and concluded that 'the element of circularity which [Lord Mackay LC] identified did not then and does not now result in uncertainty which offends against Article 7'. Further to this, the test is criticised on the ground that it leaves a question of law to the jury. Ormerod and Laird (*Smith, Hogan, & Ormerod's Criminal Law*, 15th edn (OUP, 2018)) compare the question of grossness with that of intention. The pair argue that

> The task is quite unlike that in say applying the definition of intention, which has been supplied by the judge. In such a case the jury looks at the facts and applies the legal definition of intention as provided by the judge. In gross negligence, the jury has to determine whether on their view the conduct should be called grossly negligent and if so that amounts to the crime.

Despite these criticisms, Lord Mackay LC in *Adomako* stated:

> [I]n this branch of the law I do not believe that is fatal to its being correct as a test of how far conduct must depart from accepted standards to be characterised as criminal. This is necessarily a question of degree …

The term 'reprehensible' has been accepted by the Court in *Misra* as an appropriate description for the nature of the defendant's conduct, whilst the term 'badness' was given particular weight by the Divisional Court in *R (Rowley) v DPP* [2003] EWHC 693 (Admin).

Importantly, negligence which satisfies civil liability is not necessarily enough to amount to a 'crime'; however, this remains a question for a jury. Further, in *R v Adomako* [1995] 1 AC 171, Lord Mackay LC ruled that it would be 'unwise' to categorise conduct which may fall within the meaning of 'gross' negligence. In *R v S* [2015] EWCA Crim 558, the trial judge directed the jury as follows:

> So in relation to the word 'gross', you must concentrate on whether or not the prosecution have made you sure that the defendant's conduct, considering all the circumstances you have heard about and as you find them to be, fell *so far below the standard* to be expected of a reasonable 15 year old with his experience, that it was something that, in your assessment, was *truly exceptionally bad* and which showed such an indifference to an obviously serious risk to life, and such a departure from the standard to be expected, as to amount, in your judgment, to a grossly negligent and therefore criminal act. (emphasis added)

A recent statement on the manner in which a judge should direct a jury was provided by the Court of Appeal in *R v Sellu* [2016] EWCA Crim 1716, which concerned the charging of a consultant specialising in colorectal medicine and surgery with gross negligence manslaughter. In the Court of Appeal, Sir Brian Leveson P accepted that, when directing the jury in cases of alleged gross negligence manslaughter, there is no mandatory formulation of the concept of gross negligence. Sir Brian Leveson P did add, however, that

> what is mandatory is that the jury are assisted sufficiently to understand how to approach their task of identifying the line that separates even serious or very serious mistakes or lapses, from conduct which … was '*truly exceptionally bad* and was such a departure from that standard [of a reasonably competent doctor] that it consequently amounted to being criminal'. (emphasis added)

A question arising from this discussion is: What sort of factors will the jury take in account? Whilst the decision is a matter of fact for the jury who may take many things into account when reaching their decision, the following are likely to be relevant to their assessment (note that these are just a few examples):

- The jury have to be satisfied that the defendant fell below the standard expected of him, in order to be in breach of his duty (element 2). However, the further below the standard the jury consider the defendant to be, the more likely they will consider his conduct to be criminal. On the other hand, if they consider that the defendant is only just short of the standard expected, they may consider his actions not to be criminal.
- Whilst there is no requirement for foresight of risk on the part of the defendant (the foresight is on the part of the sober and ordinary person), if there is evidence that the defendant himself perceived the existence of a risk of death, the jury are more likely to consider his conduct to be criminal (*AG's Reference (No 2 of 1999)* [2000] QB 796), and vice versa it may work in the defendant's favour (*R (Rowley) v DPP* [2003] EWHC 693 (Admin)).

A factor that is closely aligned with the two above is whether the defendant has a legitimate explanation for the reason that he acted (or failed to act) in the way that he did (eg what his motives were). For example, in *R v Singh (Gurphal)* [1999] Crim LR 582, the landlord had failed to maintain the proper repair of gas fires in his flats, resulting in the death of one of his tenants. Suppose the landlord had a good reason for this failure, the jury might consider that he had a legitimate reason for acting (or omitting) in the way that he did. What would amount to a 'good reason' would be a matter for the jury – some of whom may be sympathetic to a landlord's situation, whilst others would most certainly not be.

8.5.3 Subjectively reckless manslaughter

The final type of involuntary manslaughter is that of subjectively reckless manslaughter, also known simply as reckless manslaughter. The term 'subjectively reckless manslaughter' is preferred by the author (and by Herring (*Criminal Law: Text, Cases, and Materials*, 9th edn (OUP, 2020)) to distinguish it from any argument of objective recklessness formerly held in *MPC v Caldwell* [1982] AC 341. Child and Ormerod (*Smith, Hogan's, & Ormerod's Essentials of Criminal Law*, 3rd edn (OUP, 2019)) specifically use two other terms to describe the nature of this offence, namely 'manslaughter by advertent recklessness' and 'manslaughter by conscious risk-taking'.

This offence is rarely seen in practice; however, it has been formally recognised as a form of involuntary manslaughter by the Law Commission ('Murder, Manslaughter and Infanticide' (Law Com No 304, 2006)), and more recently by the Court of Appeal in *R v Hussain* [2012] EWCA Crim 188. But, as a result of its limited application in practice, this section will be unavoidably brief.

The main explanation as to why subjectively reckless manslaughter is not prosecuted is that the majority of offences that may be charged under this offence will also likely satisfy the elements of unlawful act manslaughter or gross negligence manslaughter. Further to this, given that neither of those offences requires a reckless *mens rea* as to death, it remains technically easier to prosecute a defendant under unlawful act and gross negligence manslaughter. However, subjectively reckless manslaughter remains necessary for a specific circumstance that is not covered by unlawful act or gross negligence manslaughter. This circumstance can be detailed as where:

(a) the defendant kills by omission or by reckless lawful act (thus meaning he cannot be liable for unlawful act manslaughter);
(b) the defendant's act or omission does not satisfy the tests of gross negligence manslaughter, namely there is no foreseeable risk of death; or
(c) his actions involve the risk of serious harm or death but fall short of the virtual certainty requirement for murder.

Case authority on this offence is limited. The main authority for our purposes is that of *R v Lidar* [2000] 4 Archbold News 3.

case example

Charge:
Subjectively reckless manslaughter

Case progression:
Crown Court – Guilty

Court of Appeal – Conviction upheld

Point of law:
Meaning of subjectively reckless manslaughter

In *R v Lidar* [2000] 4 Archbold News 3, the defendant was driving his car away from a fight. Whilst driving, the victim (one of the antagonists) was seen to be hanging from the passenger window whilst still fighting with one of the defendant's passengers who was inside the car. The defendant accelerated, resulting in the victim falling under the wheels and dying.

Lidar was convicted in the Crown Court for subjectively reckless manslaughter, and this was upheld on appeal by the Court of Appeal.

The Court of Appeal set the test for subjectively reckless manslaughter (see **Table 8.19**).

Table 8.19 Elements of subjectively reckless manslaughter

Elements of the offence
The defendant foresaw a serious (highly probable) risk that the victim would suffer serious injury and The defendant was indifferent to that risk or took the risk unjustifiably

More recently, in *R v Hussain* [2012] EWCA Crim 188, the defendant was convicted of subjectively reckless manslaughter on account that he accidentally ran over a child who thus became trapped under the car. Although not responsible for the initial accident, the defendant panicked upon releasing the child was trapped and carried on driving. The victim died and the defendant was convicted and sentenced to eight years' imprisonment (reduced to six on appeal).

The following factors, albeit brief, can be understood from the offence of subjectively reckless manslaughter:

- awareness need not be as to the risk of death (*R v Pike* [1961] Crim LR 547); but
- awareness must be as to the risk of serious injury (*R v Lidar* [2000] 4 Archbold News 3).

8.5.4 Putting together involuntary manslaughter

Consider this issue and think of how you may structure an answer to it. Then see the figure below for a sample structure to adopt.

facts

Jill and Jack are playing a game of Russian roulette with a gun. Both of them know that the gun is loaded but are not aware which chamber the bullet is in. Not believing the bullet is loaded into the chamber, Jill points the gun and Jack and pulls the trigger. Jack dies. In a panic at what has happened, Jill drives away in an attempt to escape. In doing so, Jill drives in excess of 80 mph and accidentally strikes Ben with her car. Ben dies from his injuries.

(In considering the liability of Jill, do not consider liability for causing death by dangerous driving as that remains outside the scope of this book.)

Meanwhile, Andy and Bill are playing an extreme version of tug-of-war whilst stood at the top of a cliff. Neither of them intend to hurt the other and they are merely engaging in a bit of horseplay. Andy's mind drifts and he lets go of the rope. Bill falls to his death.

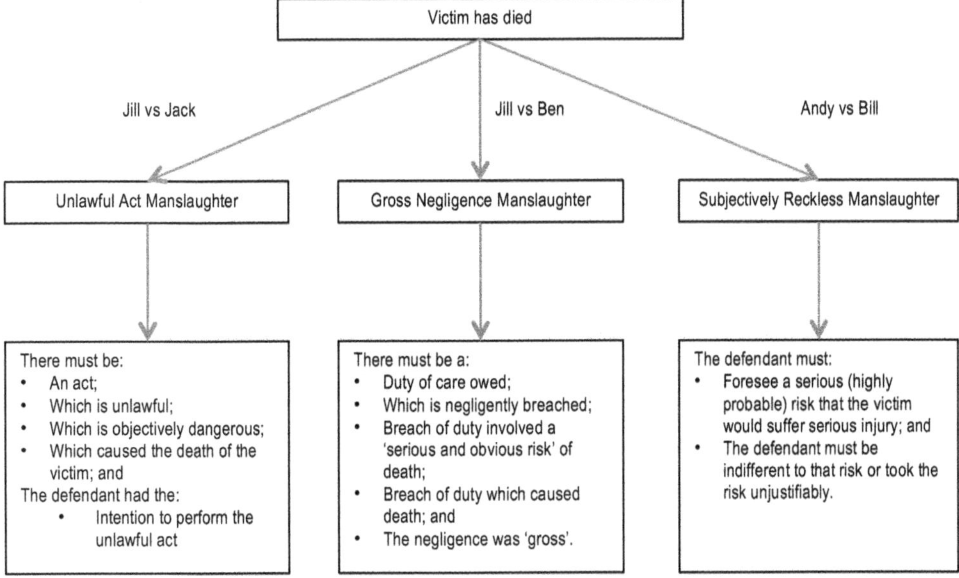

Figure 8.14 Putting together involuntary manslaughter

8.6 Putting it all together

Consider this issue and think how you may structure an answer to it. Then see the figure below for a sample structure to adopt.

facts

Jack sets out to kill his arch rival Andy who has 'stolen his woman', Jill. Jack aims a gun at Andy and shoots him in the chest. Unbeknownst to Jack, Jill is stood behind Andy and is also shot as the bullet hits both Andy and Jill. Both die as a result.

Ensure that any answer you provide considers the victims separately.

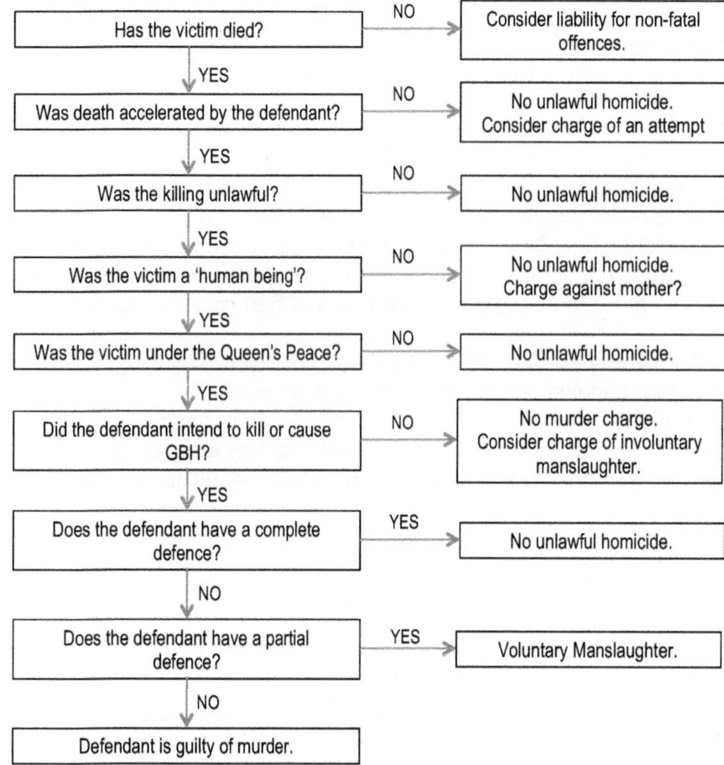

Figure 8.15 Putting together fatal offences

8.7 Further reading

Murder

Ashworth, 'Reforming the Law of Murder' [1990] Crim LR 75.

Norrie, 'Legal and Social Murder: What's the Difference?' [2018] Crim LR 531.

Williams, 'Mens Rea for Murder: Leave it Alone' (1989) 105 LQR 387.

Wilson, 'A Plea for Rationality in the Law of Murder' (1990) 10 LS 307; 'The Structure of Criminal Homicide' [2006] Crim LR 471.

Voluntary manslaughter

Allen, 'Provocation's Reasonable Man: A Plea for Self-control' (2000) 64 J Crim L 216.

Bettinson, 'Aligning Partial Defences to Murder with the Offence of Coercive or Controlling Behaviour' [2019] Crim LR 71.

Mackay, 'The Coroners and Justice Act 2009—Partial Defences to Murder (2) The New Diminished Responsibility Plea' [2010] Crim LR 290

Norrie, 'The Coroners and Justice Act 2009—Partial Defences to Murder: (1) Loss of Control' [2010] Crim LR 275.

Wake, 'Recognising Acute Intoxication as Diminished Responsibility? A Comparative Analysis?' (2012) 76 J Crim L 71

Involuntary manslaughter

Freer, 'We need to talk about Charlie: Putting the Brakes on Unlawful Act Manslaughter' [2018] Crim LR 612.

Herring and Palser, 'The Duty of Care in Gross Negligence Manslaughter' [2007] Crim LR 24.

Horder and McGowan, 'Manslaughter by Causing Another's Suicide' [2006] Crim LR 1035.

Mitchell, 'More Thoughts about Unlawful and Dangerous Act Manslaughter and the One Punch Killer' [2009] Crim LR 502.

- Homicide is a word used to describe a set of offences including murder and manslaughter.
- Murder is best defined as the unlawful killing of a human being under the Queen's peace with malice aforethought, express or implied.
- Murder is a result crime and requires proof of causation. Causation is normally non-contentious; however, it can often leave prosecutions unstable.
- Manslaughter can be divided into voluntary and involuntary manslaughter. Voluntary manslaughter is concerned with the specific and partial defences to murder, namely loss of self-control, diminished responsibility, suicide pact and infanticide.
- Voluntary manslaughter is not a chargeable offence; instead it acts a defence to a charge of murder.
- Involuntary manslaughter is a chargeable offence allowing the prosecution to charge the defendant in the circumstances where he did not hold the intention to kill.
- Involuntary manslaughter includes such offences as constructive manslaughter and gross negligence manslaughter.

test your knowledge

Problem

On 20 November 2016, Jack went to the pub for a few drinks with some friends to watch a football match. Jack's favourite team was playing that night and Jack is extremely sensitive about the success of his team. During the evening, Jack and his friends are confronted by a number of supporters of the rival team who start shouting abuse towards Jack and his friends regarding the support for their team. Jack, clearly upset by these remarks, grabs a bottle of beer from the table where he is sat, smashes it and stabs one of the rival supporters in the face. The rival supporter dies. In an attempt to escape from the pub, Jack raises the broken bottle towards the face of the pub security guard who allows him to pass by. Once Jack has left the pub, the guard suffers from a heart attack brought about by Jack's actions. In an unconscious state, the guard is loaded into an ambulance to take him to the local hospital. Unbeknownst to the ambulance crew, the guard has a severe fear of hospitals and, upon waking and finding himself in an ambulance, the guard jumps out of the back of the ambulance and falls to his death. The paramedics state that the victim was not strapped to the table and the door was not locked.

Discuss the potential liability of Jack and the paramedics for the deaths of the rival supporter and the security guard.

Essay

'Murder is one of the oldest criminal offences and yet has seen little by way of reform. It remains, to this day, out-dated, unfair and problematic.'

Critically discuss this statement in light of the law of murder, necessary reforms and the impact of voluntary manslaughter on the offence.

chapter 9

Non-Fatal Offences

After reading this chapter, you will be able to understand:

- the purpose for the existence of non-fatal offences against the person
- the offence of common assault, its elements and punishment upon conviction
- the offence of assault occasioning actual bodily harm (ABH), its elements and punishment upon conviction
- the offence of maliciously wounding or inflicting grievous bodily harm (GBH), its elements and punishment upon conviction
- the offence of maliciously wounding or causing GBH with intent, its elements and punishment upon conviction
- the basic and aggravated forms of offences against the person.

9.1 Introduction to non-fatal offences

The law of non-fatal offences is a vast and diverse topic deriving from common law and statute. The essential requirement that distinguishes this chapter from the previous chapter is the element of death. In **Chapter 8**, we were concerned with the law relating to homicide and the acceleration of death caused by the defendant. In this chapter, however, we are concerned with the circumstances where a defendant may be liable for an offence where his victim is still alive.

One point to note is that although sexual offences are classed as non-fatal offences against the person, they are treated differently given their nature and characteristics. On that basis, sexual offences shall be dealt with in **Chapter 10**. This chapter now goes on to consider some of the most common non-fatal (and non-sexual) offences to be taught at degree level.

9.1.1 Interference with autonomy

The law relating to non-fatal offences is based on the idea that our bodies should be free from unwanted violence or interference from another (as enshrined in Article 8 of the ECHR). Should such an infringement take place, our individual autonomy and right to personal integrity are compromised (*St George's Healthcare NHS Trust v S* [1999] Fam 26). Goff LJ in *Collins v Wilcock* [1984] 3 All ER 374 explains that

> every man's person [is] sacred, and no other [has] a right to meddle with it, in any the slightest manner.

The law of non-fatal offences therefore works to protect citizens from violence and compensates them, in some part, by use of the criminal justice system.

9.1.2 Coronavirus offences

This second edition of *Criminal Law* would not be complete unless some discussion was had as to the effect of coronavirus on non-fatal offences against the person. At **9.7**, we consider how the criminal law has adapted to deal with the numerous reported prosecutions of members of the public spitting and coughing on others, and the fears of coronavirus infection.

The effect of coronavirus is not limited to non-fatal offences, however. There are a number of reported prosecutions involving criminals exploiting coronavirus for their own gain, such as fraud offences targeting the elderly.

9.1.3 Charging non-fatal offences

When deciding on the appropriate charge against a defendant, prosecutors and police officers must consider the *Charging Standards* published by the Crown Prosecution Service (CPS). Under the *Charging Standards*, when considering which charge is the most appropriate in a given case, the prosecutor must base their decision on:

- the level of injuries that have resulted; and
- the likely sentence that the court will pass.

Parliament has determined that there should be separate offences reflecting three levels of injury: common assault, ABH and GBH. These are considered in our 'ladder of seriousness' below.

The process is detailed in the *Charging Standards* as follows:

- As a starting point, where there is no injury or injuries which are not serious, the offence charged should generally be common assault.
- Where there is serious injury and the likely sentence is clearly more than six months' imprisonment, the offence charged should generally be ABH.
- Where there is really serious injury, the offence charged should generally be GBH.

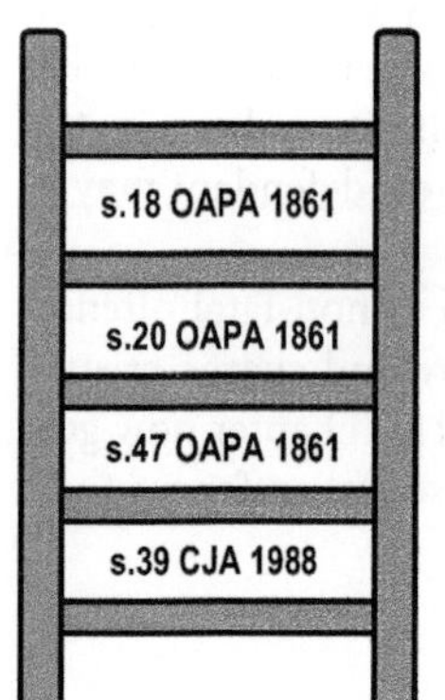

Figure 9.1 The ladder of non-fatal offences

Finally under this heading, it is important to note that all the offences considered in this chapter, with the exception of wounding or GBH contrary to s 18 of the Offences Against the Person Act (OAPA) 1861, are basic intent offences. This means that the *mens rea* of the offences may be satisfied by way of intention or recklessness, and it is no excuse for a defendant to argue that he lacked the *mens rea* as a result of his voluntarily intoxicated state (*R v Heard* [2008] QB 43– see **Chapter 7**).

9.1.4 Alternative verdicts

In a similar sense to murder, where a jury may return an alternative verdict of manslaughter as a result of finding a defendant not guilty of murder, a jury may reach an alternative verdict in the context of non-fatal offences.

According to the House of Lords in *R v Mandair* [1995] 1 AC 208, an indictment alleging GBH or wounding with intent contrary to s 18 of the OAPA 1861 will also include, as an alternative, an offence of inflicting GBH or wounding contrary to s 20 of the OAPA 1861. Equally, the House of Lords in *R v Wilson* [1984] AC 242 ruled that a charge under s 20 also involves an allegation of assault occasioning ABH contrary to s 47 of the OAPA 1861. Given that assault occasioning ABH is a constructive offence built upon the foundations of common assault, it is also possible for a tribunal of fact to find common assault as an alternate verdict to s 47. Following *R v Coutts* [2006] 1 WLR 2154 and *R v Foster* [2009] EWCA Crim 2214, if there is evidence to support an obvious alternative offence identified by a 'knowledgeable and alert criminal trial judge' (per Lord Bingham in *Coutts*), then this should to be left to the jury.

Table 9.1 Non-fatal offences and alternative verdicts

Original charge	If not, then ...	If not, then ...
Causing GBH/wounding with intent (OAPA 1861, s 18)	Inflicting GBH/wounding (OAPA 1861, s 20)	Assault occasioning ABH (OAPA 1861, s 47)
Inflicting GBH/wounding (OAPA 1861, s 20)	Assault occasioning ABH (OAPA 1861, s 47)	n/a
Assault occasioning ABH (OAPA 1861, s 47)	Common assault (Criminal Justice Act 1988, s 39)	n/a

9.2 Common assault

Common assault is the collective term used to describe the two separate offences of assault and battery. Both offences are charged under s 39 of the Criminal Justice Act (CJA) 1988 which states:

> Common assault and battery shall be summary offences and a person guilty of either of them shall be liable to a fine not exceeding level 5 on the standard scale, to imprisonment for a term not exceeding six months, or to both.

As can be noted from s 39, no definition is provided as to what elements are required to prove the offence of common assault. Rather, s 39 simply concerns the mode of trial and sentence for the offence. To seek a definition, one must turn to the common law.

9.2.1 Defining common assault

Goff LJ in *Collins v Wilcock* [1984] 3 All ER 374 defined common assault as including within its definition both an assault and a battery. His Lordship defined each as follows:

> The law draws a distinction … between an assault and a battery. An assault is an act which causes another person to apprehend the infliction of immediate, unlawful force on his person; a battery is the actual infliction of unlawful force on another person.

Williams (*Textbook of Criminal Law* (Stevens & Sons, 1978)) suggested the use of new terminology in order to effectively differentiate between these two offences. He refers to 'assault' as 'psychic assault' and 'battery' as 'physical assault'. Naturally, as times move on, definitions and phrases will change. The terminology used in this chapter is as follows:

- common assault – general umbrella term covering both offences
- technical assault – offence of assault requiring apprehension of harm
- battery – offence of battery requiring actual infliction of unlawful force.

Technical assault was formerly regarded as an attempted battery in that should the defendant's actual application of force fail, an assault would nonetheless be committed. Although many attempted batteries will involve an assault, this will not always be the case.

example

Whilst Jack is sleeping, Jill stands above him staring menacingly with a knife in her hand and whispering his name. As a result of Jack not awaking from her calls, Jill hits him on the head with the butt of the knife. Jack wakes up but is not injured.

In this instance, Jill cannot be liable for the offence of technical assault as there can be no apprehension of harm on the part of Jack as he is asleep and unaware of what Jill is doing. On the other hand, being struck by the butt of a knife amounts to an infliction of unlawful force for which Jill can be liable for a battery. Changing the facts slightly, should Jill attempt to hit the sleeping Jack and miss, it cannot be said that Jill is liable for an assault (as an attempted battery), given that Jack remains unaware of Jill's conduct.

You will note from these definitions that the language used differs from how the public naturally perceive these offences. For example, the word 'assault' is generally considered by the everyday public to be a physical violent attack and the word 'battery' to mean an extremely serious attack, whereas, in truth, the law recognises both offences as the least serious of non-fatal offences against the person. One could argue this is a problem in the law as it results in a lack of awareness or knowledge of the legal system and fails to provide effective information for the public at large. Indeed, this argument was raised in some fashion in a recent judicial review claim in *R (Ward) v Black Country Magistrates' Court* [2020] EWHC 680 (Admin).

9.2.1.1 Common law or statutory offence?

The lack of a definition in s 39 has led many to dispute whether common assault remains a common law offence or whether it is a statutory offence charged under s 39. In *DPP v Taylor; DPP v Little* [1992] QB 645, the Divisional Court made clear that both offences are based in statute. Mann LJ explained that:

> My conclusion upon the question of whether the offences of common assault and battery are statutory offences is that they are and have been such since 1861 and accordingly that they should now be charged as being 'contrary to section 39 of the Criminal Justice Act 1988'.

In *Haystead v Chief Constable of Derbyshire* [2000] 3 All ER 890, however, Laws LJ (also in the Divisional Court) explained that '[a]lthough the charge referred to s 39, in truth, common assault by beating remains a common law offence'.

There remains, therefore, a lack of clarity as to the status of common assault. The latter approach in *Haystead* appears to have been preferred by both the Court of Appeal in *Cross v DPP* (CA, 20 June 1995) and by the Law Commission in its 2015 Report, 'Offences Against the Person' (Law Com No 361, 2015). In this Report, the Law Commission noted that:

> [Assault and battery] continue to be common law offences, we conclude, even though Criminal Justice Act 1988, s 39 provides for the mode of trial and maximum penalty.

Further to this, McAlhone and Wortley (*Criminal Law: The Fundamentals*, 4th edn (Sweet & Maxwell, 2016)) note that s 39 does not prescribe that 'a person who commits an assault or a battery does so contrary to the provision'. Indeed, this is correct and raises a concern as to the validity of *DPP v Little*; however, without authority to the contrary from a more senior court, the position appears to remain one of uncertainty. Recently in *R (Ward) v Black Country Magistrates' Court* [2020] EWHC 680 (Admin),

Hickinbottom LJ in the Divisional Court chose not to answer the question of whether common assault was a common law or statutory offence, on the basis that it was not a matter of law to be determined by that court. However, in his judgment, his Lordship did state that a 'widely held claim' is that they are statutory offences. Perhaps this is an indication from Hickinbottom LJ that he believes the offences to be based in statute.

The author's view is that the offences are based in the common law, not statute.

in practice

You may feel that such a discussion is moot and simply based in theory. However, this distinction is of great importance to practitioners when they 'lay' the information/charge before the accused. They must make specific reference to the statute, should there be one. For example, Jack would be liable for assault against Jill contrary to s 39 of the Criminal Justice Act 1988.

It is also worth noting that both assault and battery are civil wrongs in the law of tort. Thus, many cases which deal with common assault in the civil context are effectively applied and referred to in criminal law.

9.2.1.2 Causation and common assault

To conclude our preliminary discussion, we need to identify the applicable rules on causation. Assault requires the defendant to *cause* apprehension. This means that assault is a result crime requiring a discussion of causation (see **Chapter 2**). Battery, on the other hand, includes no statement of causation in its definition. Rather, it simply prescribes a form of conduct (namely unlawful application of force). As a result, battery is a conduct crime requiring no proof of causation.

9.2.2 Elements of a technical assault

In *Fagan v Metropolitan Police Commissioner (MPC)* [1969] 1 QB 439, it was said by James J that

> An assault is any act which intentionally – or possibly recklessly – causes another person to apprehend immediate and unlawful personal violence.

Assault is not concerned with any form of physical contact. Rather, the offence is focused on a more 'psychic attack' (Williams (above)) and is based on what the victim 'thought' was to going to happen to them. Battery, on the other hand, is concerned with the application of force by the defendant. Think about it this way:

- *Assault:* Focus on the victim and what they thought or expected.
- *Battery:* Focus on the defendant and his conduct of applying force.

The *actus reus* and *mens rea* of technical assault are outlined in **Table 9.2**.

Table 9.2 Elements of technical assault

AR/MR	Elements of the offence
Actus reus	(i) an act; (ii) which causes another person to apprehend; (iv) immediate; (v) unlawful personal violence.
Mens rea	intention; or recklessness

We shall consider each element in turn.

9.2.2.1 *Actus reus:* (i) an act

The term 'act' has been given a very wide meaning in the context of a technical assault. The standard example can be seen by the raising of a fist in the direction of another, the waving of a weapon (suppose a knife or a gun) in the face of another, or the making of threats by words or gestures. In *R v Misalati* [2017] EWCA Crim 2226, the defendant was convicted of racially aggravated assault when he spat at (but missed) the victim. This shows the broadness of the offence.

Assault by omission

According to the Divisional Court in *Fagan v MPC* (above), technical assault cannot be committed by an omission – it requires some form of positive act or conduct on the part of the defendant. The positive act may be slight – such as picking up the telephone and calling a number before then remaining silent (as in *R v Ireland* [1998] AC 147) – but some act is required. However, see the discussion of 'Battery by omission' below (see **9.2.3.2**).

Assault by words alone

The use of words to constitute an assault is one of the main points of discussion in this area of law. Once thought and argued (by the likes of Williams, 'Assault and Words' [1957] Crim LR 219) to be not capable of amounting to an assault, mere words are now understood as sufficient to found a case of assault – see *R v Constanza* [1997] 2 Cr App R 492; *R v Ireland; R v Burstow* [1998] AC 147. In *Constanza*, the defendant (amongst other things) sent over 800 threatening letters to the victim, a woman he had been stalking; in *Ireland*, the defendant made a number of silent telephone calls to the victim. The position was summed up quite usefully by Lord Steyn in *Ireland*, where his Lordship stated:

> The proposition that a gesture may amount to an assault, but that words can never suffice, is unrealistic and indefensible. *A thing said is also a thing done.* There is no reason why something said should be incapable of causing an apprehension of immediate personal violence … I would, therefore, reject the proposition that an assault can never be committed by words. (emphasis added)

These cases had the effect of rejecting *R v Meade and Belt* (1823) 1 Lew CC 184, where Holroyd J stated that 'no words or singing are equivalent to an assault'. Following *Ireland* and *Constanza*, words contained in an email, text message, tweet, fax etc appear to be capable of amounting to an assault.

Negating an assault (a qualified threat)

It is important to note, however, that words can also have the effect of negating an assault. What this means is that a qualification of the threat undermines the possibility that it will actually be carried out.

example

Jack and Jill are involved in an argument over finances. Jack say to Jill, 'I would hit you if your mother wasn't here.'

In this example, it is clear that although Jack's words are threatening, no imminent attack will take place as a result of the presence of the mother. As a result, there can be no technical assault.

The classic authority for this point is that of *Tuberville v Savage* (1669) 1 Mod 3, where the defendant, in the course of a quarrel with Savage, placed his hand on the hilt of his sword and stated, 'If it were not assize-time, I would not take such language from you.' Assize-time refers to the period of time when the justices of assize courts (periodic courts throughout England and Wales) would visit that specific area. Ordinarily, the placing of the defendant's hand on his sword would be an act which might have been construed as an assault; however, the use of a qualification ('if it were not assize-time') results in the assault being negated.

This can be contrasted with the case of *R v Light* (1857) 21 JP 758, where the defendant raised a shovel above the victim's (his wife's) head and said, 'If it were not for the bloody policeman outside, I would split your head open.' It was held to be an assault on the part of the husband. One might say that this ought to be decided in the same way of *Tuberville*; however, the mere fact that the husband was stood over his wife with the shovel whilst making the threats meant that the threat could not have been negated by his words. Horder ('Reconsidering Psychic Assault' [1998] Crim LR 392) further justifies this by arguing that such a threat amounts to an 'implied threat' in that once the police officer has left, the attack will be carried out. The essential point is that the principle must be considered on a case-by-case basis.

Reinforcing an assault (a conditional threat)

The position in *Tuberville*, and other examples involving a qualification to the threat, can be contrasted with cases involving conditional threats. A conditional threat is based on the provision that the victim does as the defendant is told.

example

Jack says to Jill, 'Keep your mouth shut or I will slap you.'

In this scenario, Jack has issued Jill with a conditional threat, ie Jill has nothing to fear should she keep quiet.

However, such conditional threats will still be considered assaults given the infringement of the victim's autonomy in not permitting them to speak or perform an action without fear of violence. This can be observed in two cases:

- *Read v Coker* (1853) 13 CB 850 – where a threat of violence (to break the victim's neck), unless the victim left the property, was considered an assault (though note this was a civil case of assault); and
- *R (Kracher) v Leicester Magistrates' Court* [2013] EWHC 4627 (Admin) – where the words, 'If you come round the back I will beat you up', were held to be an assault, despite the condition that the threat would only be carried out if the victim came 'round the back'.

Williams ('Assault and Words' [1957] Crim LR 219) likens this area to a circumstance where a victim is told to put their hands in the air whilst stood in a darkened room. Williams argues that the use of other sensory functions is not necessary for this individual to fear imminently for their safety.

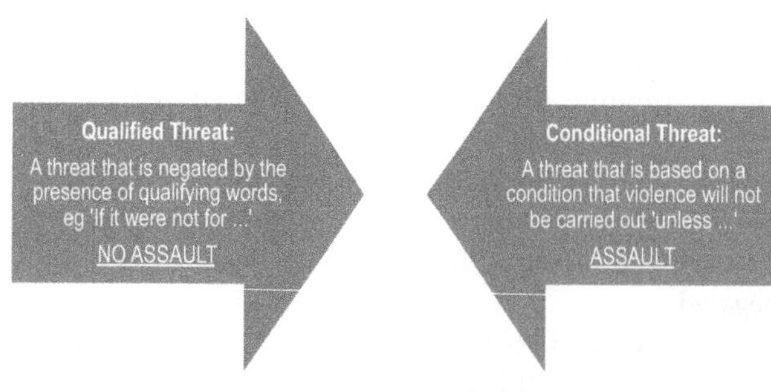

Qualified Threat:
A threat that is negated by the presence of qualifying words, eg 'If it were not for ...'
NO ASSAULT
Conditional Threat:
A threat that is based on a condition that violence will not be carried out 'unless ...'
ASSAULT

Figure 9.2 Distinguishing qualified threats from conditional threats

Threats to kill

A threat to kill is a criminal offence contrary to s 16 of the OAPA 1861. The key words in s 16 are that the victim 'fear[s] it would be carried out'. Unlike a technical assault, there is no requirement of immediacy here. For a more substantive understanding of threats to kill, see *R v Solanke* [1970] 1 WLR 1 and *R v Williams* (1986) 84 Cr App R 299.

9.2.2.2 *Actus reus:* (ii) which causes another person to apprehend

The key words in this element of the *actus reus* are 'causes' and 'apprehend'.

Causes

The word 'cause' simply requires a discussion of causation. It must be established that the defendant is both the factual and legal cause of the apprehension. In this respect, assault is a result crime. See **Chapter 2** for a discussion of causation.

Apprehend

On a basic level, no assault can be committed against an individual unless the act causes the victim to 'expect' unlawful violence to their person. The term apprehension is synonymous with 'expect' and 'anticipate'. It is important, therefore, to distinguish apprehension from mere fear. A victim may be in fear of a defendant's threat, but unless they are in apprehension that such a threat will be carried out, there is no assault. In this regard, there is no requirement for the victim to fear, or be afraid of, an assault; they must, however, expect it to happen.

So, if the victim does not 'expect' to be harmed, there is no technical assault. This is demonstrated in *R v Lamb* [1967] 2 QB 981.

case example

Charge:
Unlawful act manslaughter

Case progression:
Crown Court – Guilty

Court of Appeal – Conviction quashed

Point of law:
Meaning of 'apprehension' of unlawful force

In *R v Lamb* [1967] 2 QB 981, the defendant was playing a game of Russian roulette with his friend, the victim. The revolver in question had five chambers, two of which were loaded with live bullets. Neither the defendant nor the victim believed that the live bullets were aligned with the striking pin. In jest, the defendant pulled the trigger and killed the victim. The defendant was charged with and convicted of unlawful act manslaughter in the Crown Court.

On appeal, the Court of Appeal was faced with the question of whether an unlawful act occurred, in order for the defendant to be liable for manslaughter. Given that neither child believed the gun to be loaded, the Court of Appeal felt that there could be no assault as there was no apprehension on the part of the victim, nor did the defendant possess the necessary *mens rea* for the assault.

Often, the phrase that is adopted is that the victim must 'perceive' the threat.

example

Jack throws a stone at Jill's head. Jill, upon seeing the stone coming in her direction, dodges out of the way.

In this scenario, Jack may still be liable for assault despite Jill dodging out of the way. This is because Jill was apprehensive that the stone may hit her and as a result of that apprehension moved out of the way.

If, however, the stone was thrown past Jill and she failed even to notice that the stone was thrown, there can be no assault. This is because Jill cannot be said to have apprehended something that she did not know was happening. Similar circumstances may arise where the victim is asleep or simply does not believe that the threat will be carried out.

An excellent illustration of apprehension can be seen in the case of *Logdon v DPP* [1976] Crim LR 121.

Charge:
Assault

Case progression:
Magistrates' Court – Guilty

Divisional Court – Conviction upheld

Point of law:
Meaning of 'apprehension' of unlawful force

In *Logdon v DPP* [1976] Crim LR 121, the defendant threatened the victim with an imitation firearm (a toy gun) as a joke. The defendant was charged with and convicted of assault in the magistrates' court.

The defendant appealed to the Divisional Court on the basis that his threat, which was a joke, could not be carried out. The question for the Court was thus whether the victim could be placed in 'apprehension' of unlawful force despite the fact that the threat could not be carried out. The Divisional Court decided that the victim could and ruled that this threat did amount to an assault even though the gun could not be fired.

Lord Widgery CJ ruled that the key principle is what the victim 'thought' was going to happen. In this case, the victim thought that the gun was real and was thus placed in apprehension of unlawful force.

It is clear in this case that there was no immediate threat to the victim that could be carried out, as the gun could not have been fired. However, the focal point remains what the victim 'thought' might happen; this satisfies the test of apprehension. Naturally, had the victim known that the gun was not real, there could have been no assault unless another matter caused the victim to fear unlawful force. Lord Steyn in *Ireland* [1998] AC 147 suggested that it is sufficient for assault for the victim to perceive that the defendant *might* carry out some violence, as opposed to being certain of it.

9.2.2.3 *Actus reus:* (iii) immediate (or perhaps 'imminent')

Immediate does not mean instantaneously. That is the key point to make under this heading. In *R v Constanza* [1997] 2 Cr App R 492, the Court of Appeal ruled that the conduct in question must at least provoke a fear of violence 'at some time not excluding the immediate future' (per Schiemann LJ). A threat of violence that is expected, but only in the more distant future, cannot suffice for an assault.

example

Jack says to Jill, 'I am going to punch you in the face when I get home from work tonight.'

In this case, although Jill will naturally be apprehensive about the threat of force, such a threat cannot be said to be 'immediate' as it remains one to be carried out in the future.

Similarly, suppose Jill were to threaten to push Andy off a wall, but the wall is situated away from Jill across a body of water with no access to cross. In this case, the threat, although valid, could not be considered immediate.

Meaning of immediacy

The best demonstration of this principle of immediacy can be seen in *Smith v Chief Superintendent of Woking Police Station* (1983) 76 Cr App R 234.

case example

Charge:
Assault

Case progression:
Magistrates' Court – Guilty

Divisional Court – Conviction upheld

Point of law:
Meaning of 'immediate'

In *Smith v Chief Superintendent of Woking Police Station* (1983) 76 Cr App R 234, the defendant was outside the victim's home, looking in at her through a window. The victim feared that he may cause her harm should he enter the property. The defendant was charged and convicted with assault in the magistrates' court.

The Divisional Court was faced with the question of whether any threat of violence could be said to be 'immediate' given that the defendant was outside the property. The Court held that a threat of violence could be considered 'immediate', even though any threat could only be carried out upon forcibly entering into her property.

Kerr LJ concluded that:

> What she was frightened of, which she probably could not analyse at that moment, was some innominate terror of some potential violence. It was clearly a situation where the basis of the fear which was instilled in her was that she did not know what the defendant was going to do next, but that, whatever he might be going to do next, and sufficiently immediately for the purposes of the offence, was something of a violent nature. In effect, as it seems to me, it was wholly open to the justices to infer that her state of mind was not only that of terror, which they did find, but terror of some immediate violence.

His Lordship noted that 'there can be no assault if it is obvious to V that D is unable to carry out his threat, as where D shakes his fist at V who is safely locked inside his car'. Further, his Lordship went on to say that an assault remains possible even where the defendant has no means of carrying out the threat.

Further guidance on this was provided in *R v Horseferry Road Metropolitan Stipendiary Magistrate, ex parte Siadatan* [1991] 1 QB 260, which concerned the public order offence of fear or provocation of violence (Public Order Act 1986, s 4(1)). In this case, Watkins LJ in the Divisional Court stated that

> the word 'immediate' does not mean 'instantaneous'; that a relatively short time interval may elapse between the act which is threatening, abusive or insulting and the unlawful violence. 'Immediate' connotes proximity in time and proximity in causation; that it is likely that violence will result within a relatively short period of time and without any other intervening occurrence.

The rather arbitrary phrase adopted by the House of Lords in *R v Ireland* [1998] AC 147 is that apprehension of an attack in 'a minute or two' may be sufficient to amount to an assault. Lord Steyn in *Ireland* preferred the term 'imminent' as oppose to 'immediate'.

case example

Charge:
ABH (OAPA 1861, s 47)

Case progression:
Crown Court – Guilty

Court of Appeal – Conviction upheld

House of Lords – Conviction upheld

Point of law:
Meaning of 'immediate'

In *R v Ireland* [1998] AC 147, the defendant made 'silent' telephone calls to a number of women. These calls placed the women in extreme anxiety and apprehension that something untoward may happen to them. The defendant pleaded guilty; the issue on appeal being whether silent phone calls could amount to an assault.

The House of Lords ruled that such conduct could amount to the *actus reus* of assault if it caused the victims to fear that physical violence might be used against them in the immediate future. The phrase adopted by the Court was that a 'mere possibility of *imminent* violence' will be sufficient.

Lord Steyn in the House of Lords explained that whether harm is 'imminent':

> involves questions of fact within the province of the jury. After all, there is no reason why a telephone caller who says to a woman in a menacing way 'I will be at your door in a minute or two' may not be guilty of an assault if he causes his victim to apprehend immediate personal violence. Take now the case of the silent caller. He intends by his silence to cause fear and he is so understood. The victim is assailed by uncertainty about his intentions. Fear may dominate her emotions, and it may be the fear that the caller's arrival at her door may be imminent. She may fear the *possibility* of immediate personal violence. (original emphasis)

You may feel that *Ireland* is not justified in its approach given that the victim was unaware as to the location of the defendant and thus could not possibly be placed in apprehension. That, however, is the entire point of *Ireland*. Because the victim did not know exactly where the defendant was when making these calls, there was no way that she could rule out the possibility that the defendant could attack her in a very short period of time. The change from 'immediate' to 'imminent' would thus appear to be more than just a change of wording.

The requirement for immediacy was questioned by Horder ('Reconsidering Psychic Assault' [1998] Crim LR 392) who argued that the meaning of imminence remains far too arbitrary. What is required is

> an account of the qualitative – as opposed to the quantitative – difference between (say) a threat of violence 'in a minute or two', and a threat of violence 'later tonight', that warrants marking out the former alone as an assault … In all of these cases the nature of the conditions holding threat in suspense is different; but it is the fact that there is such a threat, inducing a fear of violence, that matters. And in this regard, the amount of time during which the threat's implementation is suspended, the degree of imminence, should be regarded as of little moral significance.

As persuasive as this argument is from Horder, it would appear to rid our understanding of an assault as a crime of immediate apprehension. To remove the need of immediacy from the scope of the offence, leaving only apprehension of force, rids the law of any form of consistency in approach. Admittedly, the system is not perfect; however, to do away with the idea of immediacy would open the offence up to a much wider scope of crimes that are both unanticipated and unintended by the law. That being said, the attempt to widen the scope of immediacy came about as a result of the judiciary's desire to provide protection to those suffering from harassment, prior to the introduction of the Protection from Harassment Act 1997, and those suffering from stalking, prior to the introduction of the Protection of Freedoms Act 2012. Given the introduction of these offences (which are not considered in this book), it appears to be the case that the law can retain its restriction on requiring assaults to be 'immediate' in the circumstances.

From *Ireland,* however, the following can be said with authority not to satisfy the meaning of immediate:

- if the victim fears only the prospect of receiving further calls;
- if it is clear to the victim that the defendant or his friends can do nothing to harm her in the immediate future.

Immediate apprehension vs apprehension of immediate force

As a final point, one needs to distinguish an immediate apprehension of unlawful force from an apprehension of immediate unlawful force. The former case refers to the apprehension itself (ie the apprehension is immediate), whereas the latter case refers to the harm (ie the harm is apprehended immediately). In the former case, the victim is not said to have been assaulted as, although their apprehension is immediate, it is not of immediate force. In the latter case, the victim is said to have been assaulted as their apprehension is of immediate force that will occur at some moment in the very near future.

Let us take two examples to explain this point:

example

Jill says to Jack, 'I am going to the supermarket to buy a knife. When I come back, I am going to cut you with it.'

In this case, there is no technical assault as, although the apprehension itself is immediate, the apprehension is not of immediate force. Rather, the apprehension is of force in the future.

example

Jill says to Jack, 'I have a knife in my hand; I am going to cut you with it.'

In this case, there is a technical assault as the apprehension is immediate and it is of immediate unlawful force. The unlawful force is perceived to take place there and then.

To further assist us with this point, let us consider *R v Arobieke* [1988] Crim LR 314.

Charge:
Unlawful act manslaughter

Case progression:
Crown Court – Guilty

Court of Appeal – Conviction quashed

Point of law:
Meaning of 'immediate'

case example

In *R v Arobieke* [1988] Crim LR 314, the defendant (colloquially known as 'Purple Aki' in the Liverpool area) went to a railway station looking for the victim. The defendant admitted that there had been animosity between the two of them. The victim had boarded a train but left the train immediately upon seeing the defendant stood on the platform looking into the carriage. The victim, in fear of serious violence, left the train and was electrocuted whilst trying to cross the tracks. The defendant was convicted of unlawful act manslaughter in the Crown Court (the unlawful act being an assault).

The Court of Appeal quashed the defendant's conviction on the basis that, although there was evidence that the victim apprehended unlawful force, there was no evidence to suggest that the defendant had issued any threats that could have been carried out 'immediately'.

The justification for this rule is that an individual may have the time to prevent the threat from actualising, for example by seeking refuge or contacting the police. In *Arobieke*, the victim was aboard a train and it remained physically impossible for the defendant to inflict immediately unlawful force. From the above, it can simply be stated that unless the threat is imminent, there can be no assault. Jefferson (*Criminal Law*, 12th edn (Pearson, 2015)) notes the lacuna in this area of law, when one compares a threat of future violence with a threat to damage property in the future. In particular, Jefferson argues that 'It is certainly anomalous that a threat to destroy or damage property is a crime but a threat to injure is not'.

9.2.2.4 *Actus reus:* (iv) unlawful personal violence

A number of key points can be raised from this element of the *actus reus.*

Unlawfulness

First, the actions cause the victim to apprehend something that is unlawful. 'Unlawful' in this sense is something that is non-consensual (consent is discussed below at **9.2.5.1**) or non-justified (for example, where D acts in self-defence). So, should a police officer threaten to handcuff a potential suspect of a criminal offence, clearly that threat will not be of unlawful conduct. Likewise, where an individual is acting in self-defence (see **Chapter 7**) and raises his fist or conducts himself in some other way that would ordinarily cause apprehension, there is no unlawful element where it can be proven that he was acting in self-defence.

Personal violence

Personal violence requires the victim to believe that unlawful force will be applied to their own person. This means that it cannot amount to an assault if the defendant were to threaten the victim's daughter instead. Unless it can be proven that the victim believed that the defendant, upon attacking the daughter, would then attack the victim, there can be no assault. However, the requirement of personal violence does not require that violence to come directly from the defendant. The defendant may threaten violence in some direct form, such as threatening that another person may attack the victim or, as in the case of *R v Dume* (1986) *The Times*, 16 October, threatening the victim with a dog.

example

Jill threatens to punch Jack's girlfriend, Alice. Jill walks towards Alice with her fist raised.

Naturally, in this case, Alice may apprehend unlawful personal force at this stage, but Jack cannot claim to have been assaulted unless Jill were then to walk towards him with fists raised.

9.2.2.5 *Mens rea:* intention or recklessness

Technical assault is a basic intent offence, thus meaning that it may be committed by way of intention or recklessness (*R v Savage; DPP v Parmenter* [1991] 3 WLR 914). Given that it is a basic intent offence, voluntary intoxication will provided no defence (see **Chapter** 7).

Intention

Under the first heading, it is necessary for the prosecution to prove that the defendant intended to cause the victim to apprehend immediate and unlawful force.

Recklessness

Under the second heading, if it cannot be proven that the defendant intended to cause apprehension of unlawful force, it is necessary to prove that he was reckless to the thought as to whether such apprehension would be caused. As detailed in **Chapter 3**, the test for recklessness is that found in *R v Cunningham* [1957] 2 QB 396 (as recently emphasised by the Divisional Court in *R (Pinkney) v DPP* [2017] EWHC 854 (Admin)).

Applying the *Cunningham* test to technical assault, it must be asked whether:

(a) the defendant foresaw the possibility that the victim would apprehend immediate and unlawful violence; and
(b) the defendant took that risk unjustifiably.

in practice

Consider the difficulty that the prosecution may have in proving that the accused intended the victim to apprehend *immediate* unlawful force. This is especially difficult when one considers the cases involving silent telephone calls and threatening letters. It is for this reason that the courts rely on *Cunningham* recklessness to catch those individuals who may not intend to cause such apprehension but are most certainly reckless to the idea of such apprehension and take the risk regardless.

Further, this difficulty has led to many prosecutions being based on offences under the Communications Act 2003 or the Protection from Harassment Act 1997, which according to *DPP v Collins* [2005] EWHC 1308 (Admin) are easier to prove.

9.2.3 Elements of battery

Formally known as 'assault by beating' (*DPP v Taylor; DPP v Little* [1992] QB 645; *R (Kracher) v Leicester Magistrates' Court* [2013] EWHC 4627 (Admin)), battery is concerned with the actual application of unlawful force to another person. Technical assault simply involves the apprehension of an attack, whereas battery concerns the actual application of unlawful force. In addition to the definition provided by Lord Goff in *Collins v Wilcock* above, we can observe two further definitions.

In *R v Williams (Gladstone)* [1987] 3 All ER 411, battery was defined by Lord Lane CJ as

> an act by which the defendant, intentionally or recklessly, applies unlawful force to the complainant.

A further useful definition can be found in Lord Lane CJ's judgment in *Faulkner v Talbot* [1981] 3 All ER 468 where his Lordship defined battery as

> any intentional touching of another person without the consent of that person and without lawful excuse.

9.2.3.1 Must the battery be preceded by apprehension?

A key point to note is that a battery does not require a preceding apprehension of unlawful force. In a standard case, the defendant may wave his fist at the victim before then striking the victim. In this case, an assault is likely to have preceded the actual infliction of force on the victim. But as Ormerod and Laird make clear in *Smith, Hogan, & Ormerod's Criminal Law*, 15th edn (OUP, 2018):

> It used to be said that every battery involves an assault; but that is plainly not so, for in battery there need be no apprehension of the impending violence. A blow from behind is not any less a battery because [the victim] was unaware that it was coming.

example

Jill creeps up behind Andy and pushes him off a wall. Prior to being pushed, Andy is unaware that Jill is behind him.

In this scenario, there is no apprehension of unlawful personal violence given that Andy is unaware that Jill is behind him. On that basis, Jill cannot be liable for a technical assault. However, Jill has still committed the offence of battery through her actual application of unlawful force to Andy. On this point, the victim need not be aware of the unlawful touching – for example, where they are asleep at the time.

The *actus reus* and *mens rea* of battery are outlined in **Table 9.3**.

Table 9.3 Elements of battery

AR/MR	Elements of the offence
Actus reus	infliction of unlawful force on another
Mens rea	intention; or recklessness

We shall consider each element in turn.

9.2.3.2 *Actus reus:* infliction of unlawful force on another

The first point to note under the definition of battery is the lack of requirement for injury. Battery simply requires the application of force and is not concerned with the result of injury that may arise as result. Where such injury does arise, the correct charge to consider is one of assault occasioning ABH or inflicting GBH/wounding.

Amount of force

Any unlawful force, or touching, may be considered a battery. According to the Court of King's Bench in *Cole v Turner* (1704) 90 ER 958, even the slightest touch in anger is sufficient to bring about a charge of battery. This was clear in *R v Thomas* (1985) 81 Cr App R 331, where a school caretaking was prosecuted for touching the hem of a pupil's skirt. The touching of the skirt was held to be sufficient, despite the victim not being able to feel the touch through her clothes. Ackner LJ concluded simply that '[t]here could be no dispute that if you touch a person's clothes whilst he is wearing them that is equivalent to touching him' (see also *R v Day* (1845) 1 Cox CC 207).

The clearest statement in this regard comes from Goff LJ in *Collins v Wilcock* [1984] 3 All ER 374: 'It has long been established that any touching of another person, however slight, may amount to a battery.' However, Goff LJ was clear that the force applied must go beyond 'generally acceptable standards of conduct'. This means that whilst force may be slight, it must not be the type of force generally accepted to occur during the ordinary course of life (eg jostling in a busy high street). In *Pegram v DPP* [2019] EWHC 2673 (Admin), the Divisional Court emphasised that the level of force used, and whether it is considered as going beyond generally acceptable standards of conduct, must be considered according to the context and circumstances of the case (ie force used in one circumstance may be acceptable, whilst in another circumstance it is not). See **9.3.1.3** for more detail.

Need for injury?

A defendant will be liable for battery, even in circumstances where no injury is caused. This is merely a reaffirmation that the slightest touch is sufficient. In *Collins v Wilcock* [1984] 3 All ER 374, Goff LJ explained that 'everybody is protected, not only against physical injury, but against any form of physical molestation'. This was reaffirmed by the Divisional Court in *Afolabi v CPS* [2017] EWHC 2960 (Admin). In *R v Misalati* [2017] EWCA Crim 2226 (a sentencing case), the defendant had spat at the victim, though the spit had missed. The defendant had been convicted of racially aggravated assault; it is likely that the defendant would have been charged with racially aggravated battery had the spit made contact with the victim.

Need for hostility?

Although it is generally accepted that hostility will be a feature of a battery, as made clear by Lord Lane CJ in *Faulkner v Talbot* [1981] 3 All ER 468, battery 'need not necessarily be hostile, or rude, or aggressive …'. This view took favour with Lord Goff in the civil case of *Re F (mental patient: sterilisation)* [1990] 2 AC 1.

However, alternative views have been raised in cases such as *Cole v Turner* (1704) 90 ER 958, *Wilson v Pringle* [1987] QB 237 and *R v Brown* [1994] 1 AC 212. In *Cole*, Lord Holt CJ explained that that the touching had to be 'in anger'. In *Wilson*, Croom-Johnson LJ in the Court of Appeal held:

> In our view, the authorities lead one to the conclusion that in a battery there must be an intentional touching or contact in one form or another of the plaintiff by the defendant. That touching must be proved to be a hostile touching. That still leaves unanswered the question 'when is a touching to be called hostile?' Hostility cannot be equated with ill-will or malevolence. It cannot be governed by the obvious intention shown in acts like punching, stabbing or shooting. It cannot be solely governed by an expressed intention, although that may be strong evidence. But the element of hostility, in the sense in which it is now to be considered, must

be a question of fact for the tribunal of fact. It may be imported from the circumstances.

In *Brown*, the majority of the House of Lords seemed to have thought that hostility was a requirement for battery. Lord Jauncey stated that '[i]f the appellants' activities in relation to the receivers [of the painful acts] were unlawful they were also hostile and a necessary ingredient of assault was present'. It is important to explain that Lord Jauncey was speaking in the context of a lack of consent, however. The better view is that expressed by Lord Lane CJ in *Faulkner*, which the Court of Appeal in *R v Braham* [2013] EWCA Crim 3 approved and suggested that any reference to hostility simply refers to 'unlawful' conduct.

The courts have continuously made clear, however, that touching must not be of an 'everyday nature' (*McMillan v CPS* [2008] EWHC 1457 (Admin)). Goff LJ in *Collins v Wilcock* [1984] 3 All ER 374 provided the classic statement on this, whereby touching must not be such that is 'generally acceptable in the ordinary conduct of daily life'.

By this, Goff LJ meant that such touching as:

- the correction of children;
- the lawful exercise of the power of arrest;
- the use of reasonable force when the necessity to act in self-defence arises;
- jostling in crowded places; and
- touching a person for the purpose of engaging his attention,

will not be classed as a battery in the basic circumstances. In addition, if another individual consents to the application of force, it will not be 'unlawful'.

Need for physical contact

Unlike its technical counterpart, physical assault (battery) must be committed by way of physical contact between the defendant and the victim. Ormerod and Gunn ('In Defence of *Ireland*' [1996] 3 Web JCLI) explain that this means that, should psychological harm be inflicted on another, without physical contact between the defendant and the victim, there will be no battery (for example, the silent telephone calls in *Ireland*). However, this does not mean that the victim needs to be aware that the touching/force has been applied. The most common example is that cited in *R v Thomas* (1985) 81 Cr App R 331 where a defendant applies unlawful force to another whilst they are asleep.

Although physical contact is a requirement for the *actus reus* of battery, the manner in which the physical contact is applied remains up for debate. In particular, our discussion now turns to the use of 'direct' and 'indirect' force.

Direct and indirect force

Most batteries are inflicted by way of *direct* force. This means that the defendant has physically used unlawful force on the victim with his own hands. This does not mean that direct force is restricted solely to touchings from the defendant's person; rather, it also extends to force inflicted by use of a weapon, or other implement, such as a car.

A battery may, however, also be committed by use of *indirect* force. Indirect force refers to the circumstances where the defendant causes force to be applied to the victim without any physical touching between the two. An example given in *R v Martin* (1881) 8 QBD 54 involves the defendant digging a pit for the victim to fall into. In this scenario, there has been no physical contact between the defendant and the victim, but as a result of the defendant's conduct, unlawful force has been inflicted upon the victim.

Let us take two examples to explain direct and indirect battery:

- Jack punches Jill in the face. This is a standard case of direct battery.
- Jack punches Jill in the face, who, as a result of the punch, drops her 2-year-old baby. This is a non-standard case of indirect battery, and similar facts are to be found in *Haystead v Chief Constable of Derbyshire* [2000] 3 All ER 890.

The essential point relating to indirect battery is that the defendant has taken some step to cause a battery. Two examples can be taken from this principle, namely the cases of *DPP v K (a minor)* [1990] 1 All ER 331, involving the pouring of acid into a hand-dryer in fear of being caught in possession of the acid by a teacher, and *R v Martin* (1881) 8 QBD 54, involving the placing of an iron bar across an exit in a theatre before then shouting 'fire!'. In *DPP v* K, Parker LJ cited with approval Stephen J's comments in *R v Clarence* (1888) 22 QBD 23:

> If a man laid a trap for another into which he fell after an interval, the man who laid it would during the interval be guilty of an attempt to assault, and of an actual assault as soon as the man fell in.

As Parker LJ would thus express: 'In the same way a defendant who pours a dangerous substance into a machine just as truly assaults the next user of the machine as if he had himself switched the machine on.'

example

Jack wishes to play a practical joke on Jill and ties fish-wire across the top of the stairs. Jill trips down the stairs and is injured.

In this case, although the force was not applied directly, Jack has committed the *actus reus* of battery against Jill. Whether he will be liable for an offence is dependent on his respective *mens rea*.

An interesting area of law in relation to the indirect application of force can be seen in relation to the use of animals to cause harm to others. In the case of *Murgatroyd v Chief Constable of West Yorkshire Police* [2000] All ER (D) 1742, concerning the use of a police dog in a raid where the dog bit the suspect, the Court of Appeal ruled that setting a dog on another undoubtedly amounts to a battery by way of indirect force. This case must, however, be read in conjunction with the earlier case of *R v Dume* (1986) *The Times*, 16 October, in which the defendant wounded a police officer by directing his dog to 'kill that man'. The dog proceeded to jump on the victim and bite him on the leg. The Court of Appeal found that a charge of malicious wounding might in principle be appropriate in such a case; however, the Court expressed the view that there remains a need to find some act of the defendant, committed with the necessary *mens rea*, that had been the proximate cause of the victim's injury.

Force applied via an object

An issue closely linked to that of whether force is applied directly/indirectly is whether force can be applied via an object. We have previously come across the case of *Fagan v MPC* [1969] 1 QB 439 in which the defendant ran over the victim's foot with his car. One issue for the Divisional Court was whether the force applied to the victim's foot could have been done through the medium of the defendant's car. According to James J:

> Where an assault involves a battery, it matters not, in our judgment, whether the battery is inflicted directly by the body of the offender or through the medium of

> some weapon or instrument controlled by the action of the offender. An assault may be committed by the laying of a hand upon another, and the action does not cease to be an assault if it is a stick held in the hand and not the hand itself which is laid on the person of the victim. So for our part we see no difference in principle between the action of stepping on to a person's toe and maintaining that position and the action of driving a car on to a person's foot and sitting in the car whilst its position on the foot is maintained.

Examples of force applied via an object include those listed above in relation to direct and indirect force.

Battery by omission

The final point on the *actus reus* concerns liability by omission. As discussed above, an omission cannot normally satisfy liability for common assault (*Fagan v MPC*). This rule would seem rather odd considering that other non-fatal offences, such as inflicting GBH and some fatal offences, such as murder and gross negligence manslaughter, allow for the offence to be committed by way of omission. The Divisional Court agreed that a battery could not be committed by omission and would only find liability in *Fagan* based on the continuing act principle (see **3.8.1**). However, doubt was shed on this point by the authority of *DPP v Santana-Bermudez* [2004] Crim LR 471.

case example

Charge:
ABH (OAPA 1861, s 47)

Case progression:
Magistrates' court – Guilty

Crown Court – Not guilty (retrial)

Divisional Court (Admin) – Conduct gave rise to liability

Point of law:
Omission liability in common assault

In *DPP v Santana-Bermudez* [2004] Crim LR 471, the defendant assured the victim, a policewoman, that he was not carrying any 'sharps' in his pockets. She asked him to confirm that he was carrying no hypodermic needles before she carried out a search. The defendant denied such objects were in his possession and the victim pricked her finger on a needle and was injured. The defendant was charged with and convicted of ABH in the magistrates' court.

The defendant appealed to the Crown Court which reheard the case as a full trial. The Crown Court found the defendant not guilty on the basis that the *actus reus* element of battery was missing given that there was no positive act. The prosecution appealed to the Divisional Court, which ruled that although the defendant's conduct amounted to an omission, omissions were sufficient to satisfy the elements for a battery.

Maurice Kay J concluded that:

> where someone (by an act or word or combination of the two) creates a danger and thereby exposes another to a reasonable foreseeable risk of injury which materialises, there is an evidential basis for the *actus reus* of an assault occasioning actual bodily harm. It remains necessary for the prosecution to prove an intention to assault or appropriate recklessness.

It must be remembered from **Chapter 2** that in order to establish omission liability, there must be three key elements:

(a) the defendant's offence must be capable of commission by omission;
(b) the defendant must have a legally recognised duty to act; and
(c) the defendant must have unreasonably failed to act on that duty.

In *Santana-Bermudez*, the duty to act arose from the creation of a dangerous situation (in line with the *Miller* principle – see **2.6.4.6**) and the assurance of the defendant that he had no needles in his possession. It would thus appear to be the case that a defendant may be liable for common assault by way of omission in the limited circumstance where the defendant has created a dangerous situation and has failed to rectify it.

in practice

Be sure to consider the operation of precedent when considering *Santana-Bermudez*. This case was concluded in the High Court which acts merely as persuasive authority to the senior courts. This means that the senior appellate courts have no obligation to follow *Santana-Bermudez* in the future should a similar question arise. Instead, they may decide to follow *Fagan*, which was also decided in the High Court.

9.2.3.3 *Mens rea:* intention or recklessness

As with technical assault, battery is a basic intent offence, meaning that the *mens rea* of battery may be satisfied where the defendant intends to inflict unlawful force on another or where he is reckless as to the thought whether force would be inflicted and unjustifiably takes such a risk regardless (*R v Venna* [1976] QB 421). In *Venna*, defence counsel contended that a battery could only be committed by way of intention; recklessness was not sufficient. This was rejected by the Court of Appeal. James LJ stated that:

> We see no reason in logic or in law why a person who recklessly applies physical force to the person of another should be outside the criminal law of assault. In many cases, the dividing line between intention and recklessness is barely distinguishable.

Recklessness as a relevant form of *mens rea* was confirmed by the Court of Appeal in *R v Spratt* [1990] 1 WLR 1073.

Is the *mens rea* of assault interchangeable with the *mens rea* of battery?

Given that assault and battery are commonly referred to as 'common assault', a point worth considering at this stage is whether the *mens* rea of those particular offences is interchangeable. In principle, the *mens rea* of assault and battery are not interchangeable. What is meant by this is that the defendant cannot be liable for an offence where he commits the *actus reus* for technical assault but possesses the *mens rea* for battery.

example

Jack intends to hit Jill over the head with a bottle as revenge for a prank she pulled on him a few days earlier. Before Jack can strike Jill, she turns around and moves to avoid the blow. Jack contends that he only held the intention to strike Jill; he was never concerned with scaring her.

In this scenario, Jack has committed the *actus reus* of technical assault – by causing Jill to apprehend the infliction of immediate unlawful force – but only possesses the *mens rea* of battery – to intend to apply unlawful force. In that circumstance, Jack cannot be liable for an offence as he does not possess the relevant *actus reus* and *mens rea* of one or the other offence. A prosecutor could argue that Jack was at least reckless to the thought that Jill would apprehend unlawful force being applied (thus amounting to a full crime of technical assault). However, the defence could dispute this on the basis that Jack at no point believed that Jill would turn around and see that he was about to strike her – meaning that he could not have been reckless as to the thought of Jill apprehending unlawful force.

No case has yet to address this point, and it remains to be seen whether the courts maintain the stark divide between these two offences, or whether they feel, as a matter of justice, that the two should share a common *mens rea*. The former appears more likely given the repetitious decisions of the courts that common assault prescribes two distinct offences, and not one (see *R v Nelson* [2013] EWCA Crim 30).

9.2.4 Charging common assault

Although the term common assault is used to cover both technical assault and battery and s 39 of the Criminal Justice Act 1988 provides sentence for both forms, technically assault and battery are two separate crimes. This was made clear in the case of *R v Nelson* [2013] EWCA Crim 30. The confusion between the two offences was clear in the recent case of *R (Kracher) v Leicester Magistrates' Court* [2013] EWHC 4627 (Admin) where the defendant was charged with and convicted of battery. On appeal, the magistrates accepted that they could not agree whether the defendant had struck the victim, but they were confident that he had threatened the victim. The Divisional Court quashed the conviction, stating that the defendant was charged with battery and thus could not be convicted of a technical assault. To do so would be 'bad for duplicity' (*DPP v Taylor; DPP v Little* [1992] QB 645).

In *R (Ward) v Black Country Magistrates' Court* [2020] EWHC 680 (Admin), the claimant had initially been charged with 'common assault'. This charge was later amended, in his presence, to 'assault by beating'. The claimant alleged that this amendment had not taken place in his presence and, as a result, he was disadvantaged at trial given that he had prepared his defence to a technical assault, not a battery. Hickinbottom LJ dismissed this claim. First, his Lordship identified that he was satisfied the charge against the claimant was amended in his presence and that amendment 'made the case against him clear: the basis of it was a battery strictly so-called'. His Lordship then proceeded, however, to deal with the situation if the charge had not been amended. His Lordship stated: 'that general description [ie "common assault"] would have incorporated the more specific "battery" or "assault by beating".' In essence, so long as the case is proceeded on either assault or battery, and a conclusion is reached on that basis, then it is non-contentious to simply use the word 'common assault' in charging a defendant.

in practice

In such circumstances, prosecutors are likely to charge a defendant with both assault and battery contrary to s 39 of the CJA 1988.

9.2.4.1 Mode of trial

Common assault is an offence triable only summarily, meaning that it may be tried only in the magistrates' court.

It is possible for a charge of common assault to be tried in the Crown Court, but only in circumstances where the charge is founded on the same facts or evidence as a count charging an indictable offence, or where it is part of a series of offences of the same or similar character as an indictable offence which is also charged (CJA 1988, s 40). This means that the charge for common assault will feature on the indictment, alongside the other offences with which the defendant is charged. Importantly, s 40 does not have the effect of making common assault an indictable offence (*R v Walton* [2011] EWCA Crim 2832).

9.2.4.2 Sentencing

Where tried in the magistrates' court, the maximum penalty for common assault is a maximum of 6 months' imprisonment and/or a fine not exceeding level 5 (£5,000).

9.2.5 Putting together common assault

Consider this issue and think how you may structure an answer to it. Then see the figure below for a sample structure to adopt.

facts

Jill comes home intoxicated one day and decides to play a joke on Jack. She hides behind the kitchen door with a toy knife in her hand and waits for Jack to come home. Jill jumps out from behind the door with the toy knife and scares Jack. Jack, in fear, runs out of the house. As Jack runs from the house, he passes his arch rival, Andy, who is sat on a wall eating an ice-cream. Jack pushes Andy from behind, and Andy falls and hurts his head.

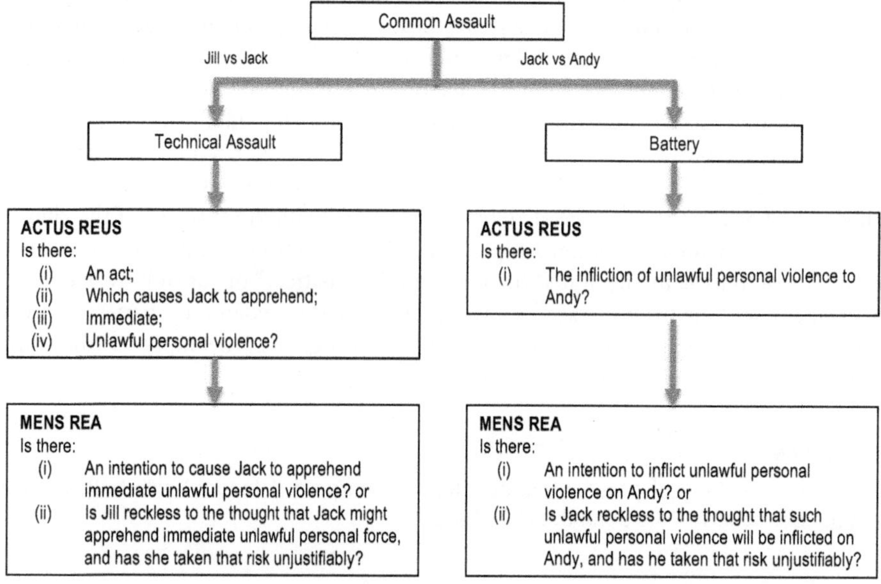

Figure 9.3 Putting together assault and battery

9.3 Defence of consent

Before we move on to our discussion of the more serious non-fatal offences, it is first necessary to consider the 'defence' of consent to common assault. For both assault and battery, the *actus reus* requires the defendant's conduct to be 'unlawful'. One reason that a defendant's conduct will not be unlawful is if he acts with consent. It is for this reason that the defence is dealt with here, and only briefly in **Chapter 7**, given its application to this form of non-fatal offence. Other defences relevant to unlawfulness, such as self-defence, are considered in **Chapter 7**.

9.3.1 Consent to common assault (and to ABH/GBH where activity 'recognised in law')

9.3.1.1 Consent and the level of harm

The 'defence' of consent is available only to a charge of common assault or battery, unless the activity involved is one recognised in law. Concisely, this means that a victim of an offence possesses the ability to consent to any activity that may give rise to a charge of assault or battery contrary to s 39 of the CJA 1988 so long as their consent is effective.

Students often incorrectly state that consent may not be given for any harm above the level of assault or battery, ie ABH, GBH or wounding (see **9.4–9.6**). It is better to say that consent may be valid to a charge of ABH or GBH, *but only if* the activity giving rise to the injury is 'recognised in law'. In essence, a *prima facie* presumption will apply against the defence of consent where the harm inflicted is greater than a common assault, but that presumption can be reversed where a recognised exceptional category can be identified. Indeed, this was made clear by Lord Lane CJ in *AG's Reference (No 6 of 1980)* [1981] QB 715:

> [I]t is not is the public interest that people should try to cause or should cause each other actual bodily harm *for no good reason*. … it is immaterial whether the act occurs in private or in public; it is an assault if actual bodily harm is intended and/or caused. (emphasis added)

We shall discuss the relevant 'categories' later in this chapter; however, for present purposes, **Figure 9.4** sets out the circumstances where consent may be given.

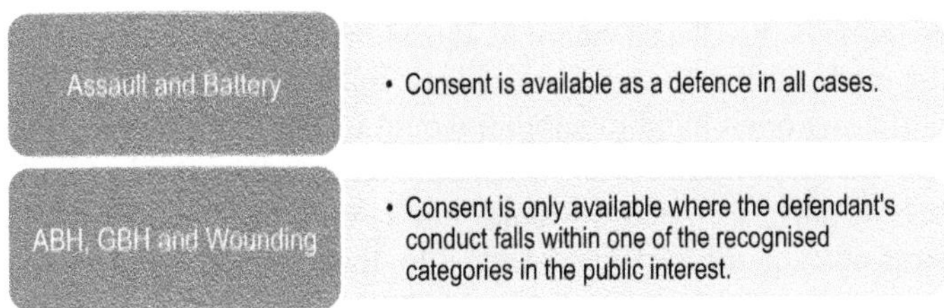

Assault and Battery
• Consent is available as a defence in all cases.
ABH, GBH and Wounding
• Consent is only available where the defendant's conduct falls within one of the recognised categories in the public interest.

Figure 9.4 When may consent be used as a defence?

9.3.1.2 Is consent truly a 'defence'?

You will have noticed above that, in the context of consent, the word defence is placed in inverted commas. We have discussed the legal bases of defences in the criminal law in **Chapter 7** and no further reference will be given here.

For the offence of common assault, the prosecution is required to prove that the defendant's conduct (whether through the *apprehension* of force or the *application* of force) was 'unlawful'. Where the defendant acts in self-defence, the conduct cannot be said to be 'unlawful'. Likewise, in the circumstances where it can be proven that the victim consented to the force, the defendant's conduct cannot, therefore, be 'unlawful'. It is thus appropriate to note that consent is not a defence, *per se*, to common assault; rather, it remains an element of the offence which, if proven, will negate any potential unlawfulness. Where unlawfulness is negated, the defendant will necessarily lack the *actus reus* for the offence.

The view that consent is an element of the offence as opposed to a stand-alone defence was recently affirmed by Lord Woolf CJ in *R v Barnes* [2005] 1 WLR 910, reaffirming the former judgments in *B (a minor) v DPP* [2000] 2 AC 428 and *R v Kimber* [1983] 1 WLR 1118. Furthering these authorities, Williams ('Consent and Public Policy' [1962] Crim LR 74) notes that it is 'inherent in the concept of assault and battery that the victim does not consent'.

An alternative view was taken by a bare majority of their Lordships in the case of *R v Brown* [1994] 1 AC 212 who ruled that consent remains a limited defence available to a non-fatal offence charge. Their Lordships considered the word 'unlawfully' to be restricted to the justifications of public and private defence (ie prevention of crime and self-defence) – not to consent.

in practice

The importance of this distinction lies more in practice than in theory, in that it affects the evidential burden of proof (see **Chapter 1**). If the absence of consent is an element of the offence, the prosecution must set out to prove it (*DPP v Shabbir* [2009] EWHC 2754 (Admin)). If, on the other hand, consent was considered as a defence to the charge, the defendant would then bear an evidential burden of proof requiring him to introduce evidence of the defence to make the issue 'live'. It is important to remember, however, that the ultimate burden of proof remains on the prosecution (*Woolmington v DPP* [1935] AC 462).

9.3.1.3 Forms of consent

Consent may be express or implied.

Express consent

Express consent simply requires the alleged victim to agree to the defendant's conduct. Such agreement may be made orally, in writing or may be made through the victim's conduct. For example, offering one's hand to another would indicate consent through conduct. The individual would consent to the defendant reciprocating and offering their hand to shake. Naturally, the victim would not consent to the defendant brandishing a knife and cutting the victim's hand – in that case, consent is not proffered by conduct.

Implied consent

Implied consent is essential to allow the everyday happenings of daily life to continue.

example

Jack meets a potential new business partner for lunch. Upon arrival Jack offers his hand to shake.

In this scenario, it would be illogical to expect Jack to state. 'I consent to you shaking my hand.' To expect so would disrupt the ordinary pattern of daily life. Instead, the law allows for consent to be implied in the circumstances where the conduct is 'generally accepted'.

Goff LJ in *Collins v Wilcock* [1984] 3 All ER 374 explained implied consent in the sense that

> most of the physical contacts of ordinary life are not actionable because they are impliedly consented to by all who move in society and so expose themselves to the risk of bodily contact. So nobody can complain of the jostling which is inevitable

> from his presence in, for example, a supermarket, an underground station or a busy street; nor can a person who attends a party complain if his hand is seized in friendship, or even if his back is (within reason) slapped … Although such cases are regarded as examples of implied consent, it is more common nowadays to treat them as falling within a general exception embracing all physical contact which is *generally acceptable in the ordinary conduct of daily life*. (emphasis added)

Goff LJ gave the following examples of 'generally acceptable' contact in daily life:

- jostling in crowded places;
- handshakes;
- back slapping;
- tapping to gain attention (as in *Wiffin v Kincard* (1807) 2 Bos & PNR 471).

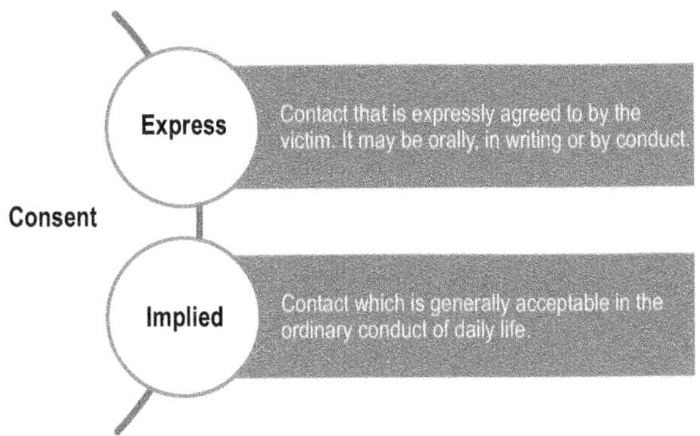
Consent
Express
Contact that is expressly agreed to by the victim. It may be orally, in writing or by conduct.
Implied
Contact which is generally acceptable in the ordinary conduct of daily life.

Figure 9.5 Forms of consent

The Divisional Court has emphasised, however, in *H v CPS* [2010] EWHC 1374 (Admin), that an exposure to violence is not synonymous with consent to violence in the context of unruly school children in a special educational needs centre. In *Pegram v DPP* [2019] EWHC 2673 (Admin), the Divisional Court identified that the context and circumstances of the case have to be considered when deciding whether the conduct was within the 'generally acceptable standards of conduct'. In particular, Kerr J explained that:

> acceptable standards of everyday conduct tolerate a higher degree of contact to attract attention in such a febrile atmosphere than might be tolerated amid calm and tranquillity; since in a tense situation it takes more to attract someone's attention than usual, especially where the person whose attention needs attracting is a cause of the commotion.

In this regard, when considering whether the force applied was within the generally acceptable standards of conduct, you must consider the context in which force was applied. For example, force applied in the hustle and bustle of a football match (eg a slap on the back in celebration) may be acceptable, but the same application of force applied in a different context (eg walking down the street) may not be so acceptable. For a discussion of *Pegram*, see Thomas, 'Atmosphere and Context: Use of Force in the Execution of Duty and Retaliatory Force' [2019] 84(1) J Crim L 94.

In *CPS v Shabbir* [2009] EWHC 2754 (Admin), Goldring LJ identified with clarity that in proving a lack of consent or in disproving the defence of consent, evidence may be obtained other than from the victim, such as a CCTV recording.

9.3.1.4 Requirements for consent

For consent to be valid in any circumstance, it must be 'effective'. By this, we mean that the victim of the alleged offence must have the requisite capacity, freedom in choice, and sufficient information, to give consent. In the context of assault and battery, there are no additional requirements given the low levels of harm. This means that the victim can validly provide consent to harm or force despite it being for an activity not generally recognised as socially acceptable. In the context of more serious offences, however, it must also be proven that the activity causing such harm comes within an accepted category recognised in law, for example consent to medical treatment. **Table 9.4** details the requirements for the defence.

Table 9.4 Elements of consent

Offence	Elements of the defence
Common assault	Consent must be effective Consent must be given expressly or impliedly
ABH/GBH/wounding	Consent must be effective Consent must be given expressly or impliedly The activity must be recognised in law

As stated earlier, for consent to be 'effective', the victim must have:

- the capacity to consent;
- the freedom to consent; and
- sufficient information to consent (known as informed consent).

Only if these three factors are present will the victim's consent be 'effective' or 'real'. We have considered express and implied consent above at **9.3.1.3**, and we shall consider here each factor in turn and then the recognised categories at **9.3.1.5**.

Capacity to consent

Capacity as a legal term is extremely broad. It encompasses mental disorders and learning difficulties. We can be assisted in our understanding of capacity through the Mental Capacity Act (MCA) 2005. Section 2(1) of the MCA 2005 states:

> ... a person lacks capacity in relation to a matter if at the material time he is unable to make a decision for himself in relation to the matter because of an impairment of, or a disturbance in the functioning of, the mind or brain.

Section 3(1) further expands on the meaning of being 'unable to make a decision':

> ... a person is unable to make a decision for himself if he is unable—
> (a) to understand the information relevant to the decision,
> (b) to retain that information,
> (c) to use or weigh that information as part of the process of making the decision, or
> (d) to communicate his decision (whether by talking, using sign language or any other means).

Impairment of mental functioning is not, however, restricted to mental disorders or conditions. Rather, capacity may also be called into question when the courts are confronted with a child victim. This was made clear by the High Court in the case of *Burrell v Harmer* [1967] Crim LR 169 where the defendant was charged with battery after tattooing the arms of two boys aged 12 and 13. The High Court ruled that the boys were incapable of consenting to the tattooing given their age. Due to their infancy, the boys could not give effective consent and the defendant remained liable for battery. Child and Ormerod (*Smith, Hogan, & Ormerod's Essentials of Criminal Law*, 3rd edn (OUP, 2019)) argue that the approach of the High Court is 'rather superficial' given the broad-brush approach taken to infancy. Indeed, the decision of *Burrell* could be called into question given s 2(3)(a) of the MCA 2005, which states that '[a] lack of capacity cannot be established merely by reference to a person's age or appearance' (though note that as a result of the Tattooing of Minors Act 1969, it is an offence to tattoo a person under the age of 18). Note that there is no statutory age of consent for piercing in England; local authorities and London boroughs establish their own licensing regulations. In *London Borough of Hounslow v Aslim* [2018] EWHC 733 (Admin), Holgate J explained that body piercing of a minor, under the London Local Authorities Act 2011, is a strict liability offence.

Further to this, in the civil case of *Gillick v West Norfolk and Wisbech Area Health Authority* [1986] AC 112, the House of Lords ruled that the appropriate test for competence was not to base the decision on age, but rather on the 'maturity, understanding and intelligence' of the individual concerned. Although the criminal courts are not bound by the MCA 2005 in the context of non-fatal offences, its provisions may still have a great deal of influence over those courts assessing consent.

It is essential to note, however, that simply because the alleged victim suffers from a mental condition or is considered a child, this is not an automatic conclusion that the individual lacks capacity. Indeed, this is made clear in s 1(2) and (3) of the MCA 2005:

> (2) A person must be assumed to have capacity unless it is established that he lacks capacity.
>
> (3) A person is not to be treated as unable to make a decision unless all practicable steps to help him to do so have been taken without success.

A further point to note on this is that the capacity of one individual may vary to that of another individual. In addition to this, there may be varying degrees of capacity in relation to the same individual. In *Re S and another (protected persons)* [2010] 1 WLR 1082, HHJ Marshall QC in the Court of Protection made it clear that

> capacity is not a blunt 'all or nothing' condition, but is more complex, and is to be treated as being issue-specific. A person may not have sufficient capacity to be able to make complex, refined or major decisions but may still have the capacity to make simpler or less momentous ones, or to hold genuine views as to what he wants to be the outcome of more complex decisions or situations.

On this basis, when confronted with a situation involving a victim who potentially lacks capacity, arguments must be weighed up on both sides and an overall opinion reached in light of the facts of the case.

Freedom to consent

The second element is that the victim must have the freedom to consent. Freedom as to choice simply means that the victim is not pressured or forced into consenting. Where the victim consents as a result of threats made to them, their consent will not be effective (often said that their consent will be 'vitiated'). A threat may be criminal, for example the threat of death should the victim not consent to a beating, or non-criminal, such as a threat of being dismissed from employment. As discussed in **Chapter** 7, where an individual acts in a certain way as a result of the threats of another, they may be acting under duress. For consent to be negated by duress, however, it must be proven that the consent given by the victim was *caused* by the defendant's threat. In circumstances where consent is given regardless of the threat, the victim's consent will remain effective so long as they have the capacity and understanding to consent.

A further situation where a victim may not have the freedom to consent is in circumstances where consent is procured by fraud. Consent may be procured by fraud on the basis of the identity of the defendant or as to the nature or purpose of the activity involved. This will be discussed in much greater detail in **Chapter 10** in relation to sexual offences; however, it is worth briefly discussing the law in relation to non-fatal offences.

First, fraud as to identity has been construed quite strictly by the courts as involving impersonation of another, but not including deception as to qualities, qualifications or characteristics. This construction was made clear by the Court of Appeal in *R v Richardson* [1999] QB 444.

case example

Charge:
ABH (OAPA 1861, s 47)

Case progression:
Crown Court – Guilty

Court of Appeal – Conviction quashed

Point of law:
Meaning of fraud by identity

In *R v Richardson* [1999] QB 444, the defendant, a dentist, was suspended from practice but continued to treat patients. The defendant was charged with and convicted of ABH in the Crown Court on the basis that the patients would not have consented had they known that the defendant was suspended from practice. On this basis, the defendant procured consent by fraud as to identity by presenting herself as a licensed dentist.

The Court of Appeal allowed the defendant's appeal and quashed her conviction on the basis that there was no fraud as to identity. The defendant did not lie about who she was; simply about her status as a licensed dentist. Her status was not an 'identity' and therefore there could be no conviction.

Otton LJ explained that:

> In all the charges brought against the defendant the complainants were fully aware of the identity of the defendant. To accede to the submission [that identity should be extended to cover qualifications or attributes] would be to strain or distort the everyday meaning of the word identity, the dictionary definition of which is 'the condition of being the same'.

The decision in *R v Richardson* may now be called into question by the Court of Appeal's decision in *R v Melin* [2019] EWCA Crim 557.

case example

Charge:
GBH (OAPA 1861, s 20)

Case progression:
Crown Court – Guilty

Court of Appeal – Conviction partly upheld

Point of law:
Deception as to qualifications

In *R v Melin* [2019] EWCA Crim 557, the defendant administered Botox injections to three women on two occasions each for cosmetic purposes. The defendant was not medically qualified and it is unknown whether the substance injected was actually Botox. The three women suffered serious bodily harm as a result of the injection. The defendant was charged with and convicted of GBH, contrary to s 20 of the OAPA 1861, in the Crown Court. The appeal concerned whether consent was vitiated by the fact that the defendant was not medically qualified.

The defendant argued, following *R v Richardson*, that deception as to qualifications or attributes will not vitiate consent (such consent may only be vitiated by fraud as to identity or the nature or purpose of the activity consented to). The Court of Appeal accepted that *Richardson* was correct and it would be 'undesirable' to extend the law. However, Simler J explained that 'it seems to us that there may be cases where a person's identity is inextricably linked to his or her professional status'. The Court of Appeal upheld the defendant's conviction in respect of one victim, on account that his representations did vitiate consent but quashed a second conviction on account that there was no reliance on the misrepresentation.

Simler J would explain:

Depending on the facts, it seems to us that deception as to a person's identity as a doctor where that is *integral* to his or her identity, can as a matter of law vitiate consent. That is different to what happened in *R v Richardson* and does not amount to including qualifications within this definition in the sense referred to in *R v Richardson.* (emphasis added)

The Court thus made a distinction between *Richardson* and the present case, in that, in *Richardson*, the fraud related to whether the dentist remained licensed by her regulatory body, as opposed to being qualified. In this case, the focus was itself on the qualifications. Indeed, Simler J explained that:

> If as a matter of fact, administration of the injection by a medically qualified practitioner was for each complainant a condition of giving her consent and without it, consent would not have been given or would have been withdrawn, it seems to us that this would go to the question of the appellant's identity and the legal validity of their consent. Accordingly, in our judgment there was at least potentially a deception as to identity rather than merely qualifications or attributes in this case. We also consider, as Mr Jones submitted, that whereas in *R v Richardson* there was a failure to inform, here there were, on the Crown's case, positive false representations that the Appellant was a doctor.

With that in mind, the Court ruled that deception as to attributes which are 'inextricably linked' to identity can vitiate consent. The appeal was allowed on Ground 1, relating to the first complainant, because there was no evidence upon which a jury could reasonably find that the complainant's consent was vitiated by this. The appeal was denied on ground 2, however, which related to the third complainant, on the basis that the complainant only consented to the treatment because of her belief that the appellant was medically qualified as a result of his representations. As such, the conviction was still safe on this ground. For a more detailed account of the effects of *Melin* on *Richardson*, see Pegg and Thomas, 'Deception and Qualifications: Revisiting the ruling in *R v Richardson*?' [2019] 83(4) J Crim L 298.

The second form of fraud is as to the nature or purpose of the act. The most common example involves situations where the defendant declares his action to be for a particular purpose, which the victim consents to, but his action is for a different purpose. This is demonstrated in the following cases, which we discuss further in **Chapter 10**:

- *R v Tabassum* [2000] 2 Cr App R 328: The defendant conducted breast examinations for his own sexual gratification. He did so on the pretence that he was collecting data for a cancer-screening programme and required participants. The Court of Appeal approved the trial judge's direction to the jury when he stated, '... consent in such cases does not exist at all, because the act consented to is not the act done. Consent to a surgical operation or examination is not consent to sexual connection or indecent behaviour.'
- *R v Green* [2002] EWCA Crim 1501: The complainants were asked to masturbate to assess their potential for impotence. The defendant was undertaking this action for sexual gratification, as opposed to for a medical test or purpose.

Informed consent

Not only must the victim have the capacity to consent, they must also have a sufficient idea of what they are consenting to. This is known as informed consent and requires the victim to have a sufficient understanding, or level of knowledge, as to what actions they are to consent to. Naturally, there is no blanket level of information that may be given to a victim at which point they will be considered as being 'informed'; rather, the level of information necessary will vary dependent on the degree of harm at risk. **Figure 9.6** explains this principle further.

The more serious the harm, the more knowledge required for the consent to be 'informed'.

The less serious the harm, the less knowledge required for the consent to be 'informed'.

Figure 9.6 Degrees of harm for informed consent

The key authority on the level of knowledge required for non-fatal offences is that of *R v Konzani* [2005] EWCA Crim 706.

case example

Charge:
Inflicting GBH
(OAPA 1861, s 20)

Case progression:
Crown Court – Guilty

Court of Appeal – Conviction upheld

Point of law:
Meaning of informed consent

In *R v Konzani* [2005] EWCA Crim 706, the defendant engaged in unprotected sexual intercourse with a number of complainants. Each complainant consented to unprotected sex and as a result contracted HIV. The defendant was aware that he had the infection but failed to inform the complainants of his status as a carrier.

The defendant was charged with and convicted of inflicting GBH in the Crown Court.

The defendant appealed to the Court of Appeal on the ground that the complainants consented to unprotected sex and thus consented to the risk of contracting HIV. The Court of Appeal disagreed and dismissed the defendant's appeal, ruling that consent to unprotected sexual intercourse was different to consent to the risk of contracting HIV.

Judge LJ in the Court of Appeal explained the court's reasoning as follows:

> If an individual who knows that he is suffering from the HIV virus conceals this stark fact from his sexual partner, the principle of her personal autonomy is not enhanced if he is exculpated when he recklessly transmits the HIV virus to her through consensual sexual intercourse. *On any view, the concealment of [the defendant's condition] from her almost inevitably means that she is deceived. Her consent is not properly informed, and she cannot give an informed consent to something of which she is ignorant.* ... Silence [of the defendant] in these circumstances is incongruous with honesty, or with a genuine belief that there is an informed consent. Accordingly, in such circumstances the issue either of informed consent or honest belief in it will only rarely arise: in reality, in most cases, the contention would be wholly artificial. (emphasis added)

Judge LJ goes on to make a key distinction that remains the essential starting point for informed consent, namely:

> There is a critical distinction between taking a risk of the various, potentially adverse and possibly problematic consequences of sexual intercourse, and giving an informed consent to the risk of infection with a fatal disease.

From this, the following accurately reflects the law in this area:

- a complainant can give effective consent to unprotected sexual intercourse where they are informed of the defendant's actions; but
- unless the complainant is informed as to the defendant's condition as a carrier of the virus, there can be no effective consent to the risk of contracting HIV on the part of the complainant.

This distinction allows the defendant to avoid liability for a sexual offence – given that appropriate consent was provided – but also allows him to be correctly prosecuted for an offence against the person by his transmission of the infection. This aspect of the decision has been extensively criticised for its over-reliance on the aspect of disclosure and non-reliance on the victim's own responsibility. Specifically, Munro ('On Responsible Relationships and Irresponsible Sex' (2007) CFLQ 112) argues that the victim must take some responsibility over their own sexual safety, and to assume that a lack of disclosure will result in a criminal offence is to ignore the victim's own responsibility to protect themselves from harm. Despite this argument, it is important to note, as shall be discussed below in relation to GBH, that a victim cannot consent in law to the intentional transmission of HIV from the defendant; consent is only valid to the *risk* of transmission.

A final point to note on the decision in *Konzani* is that the knowledge of both the defendant and the potential victim/complainant is relevant to the question of informed consent.

example

Jack is a carrier of the HIV infection but is unaware of its existence. Before engaging in unprotected sexual intercourse with Jack, Jill asks whether he is 'clean'. Jack responds in the affirmative believing that he is clear of infection. The pair engage in intercourse, as a result of which Jill contracts HIV.

In this example, Jack cannot be liable for an offence against the person given that he lacked the sufficient knowledge that he himself carried the infection. Both Jack and Jill can be described as being 'uninformed' as to the risk of HIV given that neither was aware of its existence. The question arises whether Jack should have said 'yes' to the question of whether he is 'clean', or whether he should have said 'I don't know' or 'I think so'.

Indeed, this was the approach accepted by their Lordships in *Konzani* who stated in *obiter* that in the circumstances where the defendant is unaware of his HIV status, the complainant's consent will remain *effective*. This element of the decision has been criticised for over-criminalising the offence (Ryan, 'Reckless Transmission of HIV: Knowledge and Culpability' [2006] Crim LR 981). This principle applies to all non-fatal offences and simply requires the court to question whether the defendant was aware of the risk associated with a particular action and, if so, whether that risk was communicated to the victim. This can be demonstrated in **Figure 9.17**.

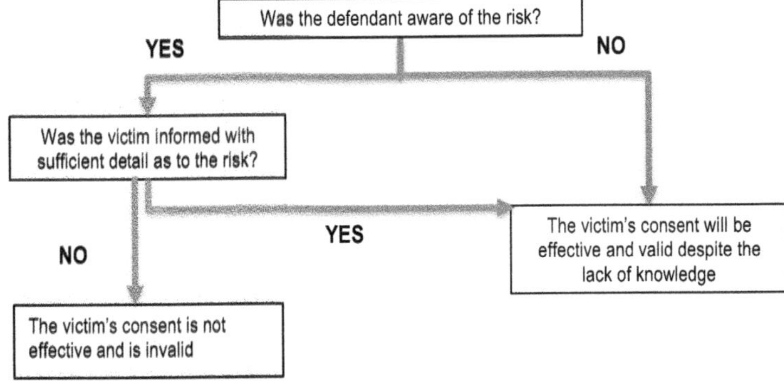

Figure 9.7 Determining informed consent

9.3.1.5 Recognised categories in law

As stated above, consent is an available defence to a charge of common assault in all cases. However, where a defendant is charged with ABH or GBH/wounding, in addition to the requirement for consent to be express or implied and to be 'effective', it must also be proven that the activity involved is one recognised in law as being in the public interest. This was the judgment of the House of Lords in the infamous case (amongst law students at least) of *R v Brown and others* [1994] 1 AC 212.

case example

Charge:
ABH (OAPA 1861, s 47) and inflicting GBH/wounding (OAPA 1861, s 20)

Case progression:
Crown Court – Guilty

Court of Appeal – Conviction upheld

House of Lords – Conviction upheld

Point of law:
The meaning of the public interest for the purpose of consent to ABH and GBH/ wounding

In *R v Brown and others* [1994] 1 AC 212, the defendants, a group of sadomasochists, engaged in the commission of acts of violence against each other for sexual pleasure. Each defendant was a willing and consenting participant and no participant required medical attention.

The defendants were convicted of causing GBH/wounding in the Crown Court. After losing their appeal in the Court of Appeal, the defendants appealed to the House of Lords.

The House of Lords (by a majority of 3:2) ruled that it was contrary to the public interest to allow an individual to intentionally cause ABH or wound another for sexual pleasure. Sexual pleasure through sadomasochism was not a 'recognised category' or 'accepted activity' that was in the public interest.

The 'public interest' argument was furthered by Lord Woolf in *R v Barnes* [2005] 1 WLR 910, where his Lordship admitted that the categories were not based on legal principle, medical knowledge or degree of harm; rather, the categories have developed as a matter of 'public policy'. The courts thus exercise control over what conduct they consider to be socially acceptable. Ormerod and Laird (*Smith, Hogan, & Ormerod's Criminal Law*, 15th edn (OUP, 2018)) argue that:

> This policy-based approach allows the courts to maintain the incoherent list of exceptions and to add or subtract from that list based on its perception of the social utility of particular conduct and the circumstances in which it occurs.

Further to this, Allen, Derry and Loveless (*Complete Criminal Law: Text, Cases, and Materials*, 7th edn (OUP, 2020)) comment that '[t]he public interest is a variable and unpredictable measure of what is regarded as lawful'.

What, then, are the 'recognised categories' in the public interest? Lord Lane CJ in *AG's Reference (No 6 of 1980)* [1981] QB 715 commented that:

> Nothing which we have said is intended to cast doubt upon the accepted legality of properly conducted games and sports, lawful chastisement or correction, reasonable surgical interference, dangerous exhibitions, etc. These apparent exceptions can be justified as involving the exercise of a legal right, in the case of chastisement or correction, or as needed in the public interest, in the other cases.

A list of 'recognised categories' is provided in **Table 9.5**. We shall consider each category separately.

Table 9.5 Recognised categories in the public interest

Recognised category
Sports
Surgery
Body modification
Religious flagellation
Horseplay
Some sexual activity

Note that one cannot consent to being killed (see **8.2.2.1**).

Sports

Consent is recognised as being present in all sporting activities on the basis of the social good that sports bring to society (eg enhancing the fitness and health of the population) and the acceptance that flows from those sports. Indeed, Lord Mustill in *Brown* commented, in relation to boxing:

> It is in my judgment best to regard this [ie boxing] as another special situation which for the time being stands outside the ordinary law of violence because society chooses to tolerate it.

However, consent will be invalidated when an individual's conduct is deemed to be 'criminal'. The principles under this heading have developed in response to the fear that violence might be exercised under the 'veil' or 'guise' of the sport. In this regard, the first point to note is that where the defendant intentionally causes actual bodily harm or worse outside the parameters of the sport, the victim's consent to the sport is irrelevant and the defendant is liable.

example

Jack is playing a rugby game for his local town's team. On the opposing team is Andy, who recently started dating Jack's former girlfriend. Furious about this, Jack has it in his mind that, upon tackling Andy, he will 'give him a knee to show him who's boss'. Jack tackles Andy to the ground and then strikes him in the head with his knee causing a concussion.

In this scenario, Jack has set out to inflict harm to Andy for reasons that are outside the parameters of the sport. It cannot be said that Andy consents to this sort of behaviour.

Secondly, the sport must be one that is properly organised or regulated. Where the sport is unlawful or the rules of the game permit an unacceptably dangerous act, the law is not obligated to find the victim's consent to be valid. The Court of Appeal in *AG's Reference (No 6 of 1980)* [1981] QB 715 gave the example of a fist fight in the street which, although consensual, would not fall within a recognised sport or game; nor would it fall under the heading of rough and undisciplined horseplay (as made clear by the Court for Crown Cases Reserved in *R v Coney* (1882) 8 QBD 534).

The third point to note is that the rules of the game may have some influence in the decision as to whether or not the victim's consent is valid. The Court of Assizes in *R v Bradshaw* (1878) Cox CC 83 held that consent is invalidated once a player of the sport goes outside the rules of the game. However, this principle was declared too simplistic by the Court of Appeal in *R v Barnes* [2005] 1 WLR 910, which held that the more appropriate approach would be to consider whether the individual has gone beyond what can be reasonably expected to occur in that game or sport by those consenting. On this basis, although fouling is against the rules of the game, a player is to expect that fouls may occur – thus penalty points or sanctions may be awarded against the fouling team or individual. The Court of Appeal noted a number of non-exhaustive factors that would demonstrate whether the conduct could amount to something 'criminal'. These factors include the:

- type of sport played and whether the conduct is 'alien' to that sport;
- level at which the sport is played (ie an amateur or professional level);
- nature of the act itself;
- degree of force used;
- extent of the risk of injury; and
- state of mind of the defendant.

The Court was, however, careful to note that the conduct must be considered in *all the circumstances* of the case. Therefore, in competitive sports, or matches of significant importance, players may expect certain conduct to occur in the 'heat of the moment'. Although such conduct is technically outside of the rules, given the importance of the match or competitiveness of the individual, a court may find that their actions were not sufficient to be 'criminal'.

Likewise, the criminal courts will not be concerned with conduct that forms part of the general nature of the game (for example harsh tackles in a game of rugby). Further to this, the court stressed the importance to note that although the rules of the sport are indications of what conduct is and is not acceptable, such rules are not binding on the criminal courts and as a result will not necessarily determine whether the defendant's actions are criminal.

example

Jack is playing football in his local county tournament. Desperate to win, Jack conducts a number of harsh tackles against other players. As a result of his conduct, Jack is warned, penalised and 'sent off' for his conduct on the football pitch.

In this example, Jack's conduct does not *automatically* equate to criminal action on his part. Although a particular sporting body may have a grievance against Jack, that does not mean that his actions are inherently criminal, capable of having liability attached.

In the *Barnes* case itself, the victim suffered a serious leg injury as a result of a late tackle from the defendant. The Court of Appeal in *Barnes* noted that the jury's task in this case is to ask whether the late tackle was a matter of misjudgement on the part of the defendant or an intentional desire to inflict harm to the victim (as in the Crown Court case of *R v Billinghurst* [1978] Crim LR 553).

Prosecution is to be reserved for the truly criminal conduct that arises in a game. Simply playing outside of the rules or in the 'heat of the moment' will not suffice for criminal liability. However, Lord Woolf CJ would explain that:

> If what occurs goes beyond what a player can reasonably be regarded as having accepted by taking part in the sport, this indicates that the conduct will not be covered by the defence.

Where no criminal liability can be found, individuals may, nonetheless, be subject to disciplinary procedures within their own sporting organisation or to civil remedies.

Surgery

Consent to surgical operations will always be valid when performed by medical professionals. It includes essential and non-essential surgery (*Corbett v Corbett* [1971] P 83 – consent to gender reassignment surgery) and also includes surgery for non-medical purposes (see below under body modifications). Importantly, where a doctor acts contrary to the wishes of a competent patient, even where those acts are for the purpose of life-saving treatment, the doctor will be liable for a criminal offence (*St George's Healthcare NHS Trust v S* [1999] Fam 26).

Body modification

Body modification may come in a number of forms, each of which constitute bodily harm capable of giving rise to a charge of ABH or above. These may include tattooing, piercing and haircutting. A rather contentious case on the topic of body modification is that of *R v Wilson* [1997] QB 47 which concerned 'DIY tattooing'.

case example

Charge:
ABH (OAPA 1861, s 47)

Case progression:
Crown Court – Guilty

Court of Appeal – Conviction quashed

Point of law:
Whether branding was considered a 'recognised category'

In *R v Wilson* [1997] QB 47, the defendant branded his initials onto the bottom of his wife, the victim. Such was done with a hot knife at her own request. The mark became infected and the victim suffered harm. The defendant was charged with and convicted of ABH in the Crown Court on the basis that the victim could not consent to harm above common assault (following *Brown*).

The Court of Appeal allowed the defendant's appeal on the basis that the defendant's conduct was akin to that of tattooing and other body modifications. As such, the defendant's activity fell within a recognised category.

Wilson can be distinguished from other cases, such as *Brown* and *Donovan* (see below), on the basis that the defendant's actions were to represent the love felt by the defendant for his wife and to bestow on her an adornment which she desired. In *Brown* and *Donovan*, the defendants' purpose was one of sexual gratification which the courts appear to condemn. In *R v BM* [2018] EWCA Crim 560 the defendant (a tattoo and body piercing artist by trade) performed certain body modification procedures on request of his clients (of particular importance for this appeal: removal of an ear, removal of a nipple and splitting a tongue to resemble a reptile) and was charged with GBH contrary to s 18 of the OAPA 1861. The Court of Appeal rejected the defence of consent to GBH, distinguishing body modification from tattooing and piercing. Lord Burnett CJ would explain that whilst tattooing and piercing are 'so deeply embedded in our law and general culture', there was no public benefit in exempting body modification from the rule that consent to ABH or GBH provides no defence. A factor relevant to the Court was that the defendant was not medically qualified and that the modifications were not for medical purposes but rather for aesthetic purposes. For a full consideration of *BM* and the law in this area, see Pegg, 'Not so clear cut: the lawfulness of body modifications' (2019) 7 Crim LR 579.

Other forms of body modification relevant to consent are those undertaken for religious purposes, for example male circumcision in the Jewish faith. Such is protected by Article 9 of the ECHR which grants protection to the freedom of religion. However, female circumcision (also known as 'genital mutilation') remains an illegal body modification in England and Wales (Female Genital Mutilation Act 2003).

Religious flagellation

Beating or whipping for religious purposes to express penitence for sins is likely to be recognised as a category in the public interest. Such was stated with confidence by Lord Mustill in *Brown*, recognising the right to religious freedom under Article 9 of the ECHR.

Horseplay

Beyond the category of sport, individuals (often children) may engage in what has been referred to by the courts as 'rough and undisciplined play'. In the circumstances where no intention to cause injury is present, consent may be valid.

The key authority on the use of horseplay as a defence is *R v Jones* (1986) 83 Cr App R 375.

case example

Charge:
Inflicting GBH (OAPA 1861, s 20)

Case progression:
Crown Court – Guilty

Court of Appeal – Conviction quashed

Point of law:
Consent to horseplay

In *R v Jones* (1986) 83 Cr App R 375, the defendant threw a school friend up into the air as a form of joke. The victim suffered serious injury as a result. The defendant was charged with and convicted of GBH in the Crown Court.

The defendant appealed to the Court of Appeal on the basis that the trial judge failed to leave the defence of consent to the jury. The Court of Appeal ruled that the defendant had the right to have the defence left to the jury who could then decide whether effective consent existed.

Jones is also good authority that a genuine belief, albeit mistaken or unreasonable, in consent may be sufficient to allow the defence to exist. Although rarely argued in practice, such genuine belief would have to exist alongside the recognised categories and strong evidence would be required on the defendant's part to prove this apparent belief.

Jones was affirmed in the later case of *R v Aitken* [1992] 1 WLR 1006 where the defendants, a number of RAF officers, set fire to the victim's (supposedly) fire-resistant suit as a practical joke. The victim suffered serious burns as a result. The Court-Martial Appeal Court ruled that the officers were engaged in some form of 'robust game' for which the victim was previously a willing participant, and his continued presence during the horseplay was sufficient to found an effective consent. *Jones* and *Aitken* were further relied upon in *R v Richardson; R v Irwin* [1999] 1 Cr App R 392 which concerned two university students who, in a drunken belief in consent, threw the victim over a balcony causing serious harm.

The courts have recognised, however, that where it is the clear that the victim is not consenting and it is not credible that the defendant believed he was, consent will not be effective in the circumstances. The law must ensure that a non-consenting individual remains protected, even in the midst of undisciplined play. This was the judgment of the Court of Appeal in *R v A* [2005] EWCA Crim 1960.

case example

Charge:
Unlawful act manslaughter

Case progression:
Crown Court – Guilty

Court of Appeal – Conviction upheld

Point of law:
Consent to horseplay

In *R v A* [2005] EWCA Crim 1960, the defendant dropped the victim off a bridge into a river. The victim could not swim and had been resisting so as not to be thrown off the bridge. The victim drowned. The defendant was charged with and convicted of unlawful act manslaughter in the Crown Court.

The defendant appealed to the Court of Appeal, alleging that the trial judge had misdirected the jury in terms of consent and when consent was valid. The Court of Appeal disagreed, finding that, in this instance, the victim was clearly not consenting and it was not credible for the defendant to believe that the victim was consenting.

Sexual activity

Under this heading, we need to consider three different scenarios, each involving sexual activity. In this section we shall consider:

- sexual activity involving a risk of sexually transmitted infection;
- non-sadomasochistic sexual activity; and
- sadomasochistic sexual activity

Sexual activity involving a risk of sexually transmitted infection

Discussed above in relation to informed consent, engaging in sexual intercourse where a risk of contracting a venereal disease is present has been held to be a lawfully recognised activity. Judge LJ, in the Court of Appeal in *R v Dica* [2004] QB 1257, took the view that

> The problems of criminalising the consensual taking of risks like these include the sheer impracticability of enforcement and the haphazard nature of its impact. The process would undermine the general understanding of the community that sexual relationships are pre-eminently private and essentially personal to the individuals involved in them. And if adults were to be liable to prosecution for the consequences of taking known risks with their health, it would seem odd that this should be confined to risks taken in the context of sexual intercourse, while they are nevertheless permitted to take the risks inherent in so many other aspects of everyday life …

This decision has naturally caused controversy when compared to the decision in *Brown* (see below).

Non-sadomasochistic sexual activity ('accidental injury')

Where injury can be said to have been caused by sexual activity, of a non-sadomasochistic type, where there is no 'aggressive intent' to cause harm, there is no liability. This was the decision of the Crown Court in *R v Slingsby* [1995] Crim LR 570.

Charge:
Unlawful act manslaughter

Case progression:
Crown Court –
Not guilty

Point of law:
Consent to sexual activity which results in harm

case example

In *R v Slingsby* [1995] Crim LR 570, the defendant and the victim engaged in what was described as 'vigorous' sexual activity. The defendant digitally penetrated the victim whilst wearing a signet ring, which had the result of cutting the victim internally causing blood poisoning and leading to her eventual death. The defendant was charged with unlawful act manslaughter in the Crown Court. At trial, the defendant argued that the victim had consented to the act of digital penetration (amounting to a battery) and there was no requirement to prove consent to injury given that it was neither anticipated nor considered by either party. The victim sustained her injuries as a result of an accidental consequence of consensual sexual activity and thus the defendant could not be liable for unlawful act manslaughter. The Crown Court agreed and the defendant was acquitted.

In the Crown Court, Judge J (as he then was) held:

> [T]he sexual activity to which both the deceased and the defendant agreed did not involve deliberate infliction of injury or harm and but for the coincidental fact that the defendant happened to be wearing a signet ring, no injury at all would have been caused or could have been contemplated. The question of consent to injury did not, in fact, arise because neither anticipated or considered it. At the time, all they were considering was this vigorous sexual activity. Therefore, the reality was that the deceased sustained her unfortunate injuries, not when she or the defendant were consenting to injury, but as an accidental consequence of the sexual activity which was taking place with her consent. It would be contrary to principle to treat as criminal activity which would not otherwise amount to assault merely because in the course of the activity an injury occurred.

In this sense, the easiest way to understand *Slingsby* is that the harm was never intended, but rather was an unfortunate effect of the vigorous sexual activities engaged in by the defendant and the victim. As a result, it appears that the law distinguishes between consent as to the deliberate infliction of injury for sexual gratification and consent to sexual activity in which injury is accidentally caused. This approach was followed in *R v Meachen* [2006] EWCA Crim 2414. The effect of *Slingsby* and *Meachen* is that if the defendant intends to commit a battery but, through accident, commits a more serious offence (such as GBH), he is entitled to rely on the defence of consent given that the level of injury involved was never intended nor foreseen. Where such foresight or risk did exist, and was appreciated, however, then the principles in *Brown* (below) would apply.

Sadomasochistic sexual activity

The word 'sadomasochism' is used to describe conduct where individuals give and receive specific and targeted pain for the purpose of sexual pleasure. The law at present tolerates injury during sexual activity of an apparent accidental nature; however, it has failed to recognise the intentional infliction of harm for sexual gratification as a valid and recognised category of consent.

The leading case in this area is that of *R v Brown* [1994] 1 AC 212, discussed above. Lord Lane CJ in the Court of Appeal ([1992] QB 491) ruled that 'the satisfying of sadomasochistic libido does not come within the category of good reason' as explained by the Court in *AG's Reference (No 6 of 1980)* [1981] QB 715. The Court of Appeal in

Brown dismissed the appeal but granted leave to appeal to the House of Lords, certifying the following question as a matter of public importance:

> Where A wounds or assaults B occasioning him actual bodily harm in the course of a sadomasochistic encounter, does the prosecution have to prove lack of consent on the part of B before they can establish A's guilt under section 20 and section 47 of the Act of 1861?

By a bare majority of 3:2, the House of Lords answered this question in the negative and found the defendants' conduct to fall outside the public interest.

Table 9.6 Majority/minority judgments in Brown

Majority	**Minority**
Lord Templeman	Lord Mustill
Lord Jauncey	Lord Slynn
Lord Lowry	

The majority reasoned that the defendants' conduct was intended to cause pain and suffering for sexual gratification; this was violent behaviour, not sexual behaviour. Such conduct was not capable, and should not be capable, of protection from the law. Public policy requires the conviction of individuals who set out to cause harm to others, and in doing so the law will protect society from a cult of violence and the danger of proselytization and corruption of young minds.

Of particular note, Lord Templeman stated:

> In some circumstances violence is not punishable under the criminal law. When no actual bodily harm is caused, the consent of the person affected precludes him from complaining. There can be no conviction for the summary offence of common assault if the victim has consented to the assault. Even when violence is intentionally inflicted and results in actual bodily harm, wounding or serious bodily harm the accused is entitled to be acquitted if the injury was a foreseeable incident of a lawful activity in which the person injured was participating. Surgery involves intentional violence resulting in actual or sometimes serious bodily harm but surgery is a lawful activity. Other activities carried on with consent by or on behalf of the injured person have been accepted as lawful notwithstanding that they involve actual bodily harm or may cause serious bodily harm. Ritual circumcision, tattooing, ear-piercing and violent sports including boxing are lawful activities.

His Lordship continued:

> In my opinion sado-masochism is not only concerned with sex. Sado-masochism is also concerned with violence. …
>
> The violence of sado-masochistic encounters involves the indulgence of cruelty by sadists and the degradation of victims. Such violence is injurious to the participants and unpredictably dangerous. I am not prepared to invent a defence of consent for sado-masochistic encounters which breed and glorify cruelty and result in offences under sections 47 and 20 of the Act of 1861.

Lord Templeman would go on to conclude:

> Society is entitled and bound to protect itself against a cult of violence. Pleasure derived from the infliction of pain is an evil thing. Cruelty is uncivilised. I would

answer the certified question in the negative and dismiss the appeals of the appellants against conviction.

The minority took the view, however, that the actions of the defendants amounted to private sexual behaviour between consenting adults for which the law should not intervene. Lord Mustill summarised his judgment as follows:

> [I]t must be emphasised that the issue before the House is not whether the appellants' conduct is morally right, but whether it is properly charged under the Act of 1861. When proposing that the conduct is not rightly so charged I do not invite your Lordships' House to endorse it as morally acceptable. Nor do I pronounce in favour of a libertarian doctrine specifically related to sexual matters. Nor in the least do I suggest that ethical pronouncements are meaningless, that there is no difference between right and wrong, that sadism is praiseworthy, or that new opinions on sexual morality are necessarily superior to the old, or anything else of the same kind. What I do say is that these are questions of *private morality*; that the standards by which they fall to be judged are not those of the criminal law; and that if these standards are to be upheld the *individual must enforce them upon himself according to his own moral standards*, or have them enforced against him by moral pressures exerted by whatever religious or other community to whose ethical ideals he responds. The point from which I invite your Lordships to depart is simply this, that the state should interfere with the rights of an individual to live his or her life as he or she may choose no more than is necessary to ensure a proper balance between the special interests of the individual and the general interests of the individuals who together comprise the populace at large. Thus, whilst acknowledging that very many people, if asked whether the appellants' conduct was wrong, would reply 'Yes, repulsively wrong,' I would at the same time assert that this does not in itself mean that the prosecution of the appellants under sections 20 and 47 of the Offences against the Person Act 1861 is well founded. (emphasis added)

The minority felt that unless strong reasons could be found as to why the conduct should not be permitted, then a defence should be available. The minority focused their judgment on the level harm caused to society, for which they concluded there was no harm caused. This view seems to have been adopted by the High Court in *Mosley v News Groups Newspaper Ltd* [2008] EWHC 1777 (QB) where the Court held that it was not in the public interest to prosecute spanking between consenting adults in private.

Brown relied on the earlier decision of *R v Donovan* [1934] 2 KB 498.

case example

Charge:
Indecent assault

Case progression:
Crown Court – Guilty

Court of Criminal Appeal – Conviction quashed

Point of law:
Consent to harm involving sexual gratification

In *R v Donovan* [1934] 2 KB 498, the defendant beat the victim, a 17-year-old girl, with a cane for purposes of sexual gratification. The young girl consented, but the defendant was charged with and convicted of indecent and common assault (pre-1988 understanding).

The defendant appealed to the Court of Criminal Appeal on the basis that the trial judge had failed to leave the defence of consent to the jury. The Court of Criminal Appeal concluded that this omission was immaterial given that consent could not be afforded to such acts. The conviction was, however, quashed for other reasons.

Swift J ruled that where a person beats another for the purpose of sexual gratification 'with such a degree of violence that the infliction of bodily harm is a probable consequence, and when such an act is proved, consent is immaterial'.

You may find *Donovan* a peculiar case given that the charge was simply one of common assault which, as we know from earlier, requires no evidence of a 'recognised category'. Lord Lowry in *Brown* was critical of the decision, reasoning that '[i]f the jury, properly directed, had found that consent was not disproved, they must have acquitted the appellant of the only charges brought against him'. Indeed, should the facts of *Donovan* come before the courts again, the result is likely to be different given the level of harm suffered. However, the principles of *Donovan* remain relevant in light of the judgment in *Brown*. You may question why a conviction was upheld in *Brown* and *Donovan* but not in the case of *Wilson*, discussed above. In *Wilson* [1997] QB 47, the Court of Appeal reasoned that the defendant's conduct of branding his wife at her request was not for sexual gratification, but rather was akin to a form of body modification. The Court held that the branding was a sign of the love and devotion the wife felt towards her husband; it was not for sexual pleasure. On this basis, the Court of Appeal felt assured that there was no contradiction in law between this decision and those in *Brown* and *Donovan*. In fact, the Court of Appeal noted that branding, and other demonstrations of love to one's partner, is not a matter for the criminal law to interfere with. In *Wilson*, Russell LJ stated that:

> Consensual activity between husband and wife, in the privacy of the matrimonial home, is not, in our judgment, normally a proper matter for criminal investigation, let alone criminal prosecution.

Brown was affirmed as good law by the ECtHR in *Laskey, Jaggard and Brown v UK* (1997) 24 EHRR 39 where the Court unanimously ruled that the prosecution, conviction and sentence of the defendants was not contrary to Article 8 of the ECHR (right to private and family life). The Court doubted whether the activities of the defendants fell within Article 8, but it did note that in any event the interference would be justified as 'necessary in a democratic society for the protection of health and the interests of others'. *Laskey* was affirmed by the ECtHR again in the later case of *KA and AD v Belgium* (App Nos 42758/98 and 45558/99) (ECtHR, 17 February 2005), where it was emphasised that national courts possess a margin or appreciation to prescribe the level of physical harm to which the law should permit an adult to consent.

In order to avoid bringing the judgment of *Brown* into question, subsequent court decisions have attempted to find a sensible distinction. This distinction has, unfortunately, been to focus on the degrees of harm suffered at the hands of the defendant. In *R v Emmett* (1999) *The Times*, 15 October, the defendant burnt the victim's breasts with lighter fluid, with consent, causing injury. In upholding the defendant's conviction, the Court of Appeal focused its attention on distinguishing *Wilson*, based on the level of harm caused. Wright J stated that the 'actual or potential damage to which the appellant's partner was exposed in this case, plainly went far beyond that which was established by the evidence in *Wilson*'.

It is unfortunate that the Court in *Emmett* felt that the appropriate direction to take was to focus on the level of harm inflicted and to compare it with the harm inflicted in *Wilson*, given that both cases involved ABH. It would be a dangerous path to take should the courts decide matters according to some unspoken measure of severity. This is especially so when one considers that, from all the cases above, it was only the victim in *Wilson* who required hospital treatment.

As a concluding comment, it remains the case that the law sits in an unpredictable and contradictory setting. There remains a distinct lack of clarity on the point of whether sexual gratification which results in bodily harm, beyond common assault, is capable of amounting to a recognised category in law. Following *Wilson*, the conduct may be acceptable where it can be related or compared to other acceptable practices, such as tattooing or piercing. On the other hand, following *Donovan*, it may be the case that the courts distinguish between conduct which is 'violent' as opposed to 'sexual', the former being something that cannot be consented to. It may be the case, following *Emmett*, that the courts undertake an evaluation of the degree or nature of the harm and determine, from that, whether the defence is available.

9.3.2 Lawful chastisement

Also known as 'corporal punishment', chastisement of children is a defence to parents or adults acting in *loco parentis* ('in the place of a parent') to a charge of common assault so long as the force used was reasonable and proportionate in the circumstances.

9.3.2.1 Position at common law

Chastisement was a lawful form of punishment under the common law, so long as the force used was reasonable. In *A v UK* (1998) 27 EHRR 611, the ECtHR ruled that this common law rule allowing parents to inflict physical chastisement on their children offended Article 3 of the ECHR which prohibits torture and inhumane or degrading treatment. Law reform was necessary, but an agreement could not be reached on the extent of the reform. In the interim, the courts continued to uphold the parental right to chastise in cases such as *R v H (Assault of Child) (Reasonable Chastisement)* [2002] 1 Cr App R 59.

9.3.2.2 Legislative reform

The resulting change came about under the Children Act 2004. Section 58 provides:

> (1) In relation to any offence specified in subsection (2), battery of a child cannot be justified on the ground that it constituted reasonable punishment.
> (2) The offences referred to in subsection (1) are—
> (a) an offence under section 18 or 20 of the Offences against the Person Act 1861 (wounding and causing grievous bodily harm);
> (b) an offence under section 47 of that Act (assault occasioning actual bodily harm);
> (c) an offence under section 1 of the Children and Young Persons Act 1933 (cruelty to persons under 16).

The result of s 58 is that chastisement remains lawful so long as it is a reasonable and proportionate punishment amounting only to an assault or battery. The defence was removed for any person charged with an offence under the OAPA 1861, ss 18, 20 or 47. Importantly, where a conflict exists between a child's freedom from torture under Article 3 and a parent's right to inflict corporate punishment for the purposes of religion, the child's rights succeed (*R (Williamson) v Secretary of State for Education and Employment* [2002] EWCA Civ 1820).

9.3.2.3 Chastisement in schools

Traditionally, *in loco parentis* applied to school teachers by virtue of their position (*Clearly v Booth* [1893] 1 QB 465). By s 549(4) of the Education Act 1996, however, 'a member of staff' will no longer benefit from the defence merely by virtue of their status. Instead, a number of provisions exist which lay out when reasonable force may be used in a school environment:

- to restrain pupils who are violent or disruptive (s 550A);
- to search a pupil for weapons (s 550AA); or
- to avert an immediate danger of personal injury or damage to property (s 548(5)).

9.4 Assault occasioning actual bodily harm

Assault occasioning actual bodily harm (ABH) is a statutory offence charged contrary to s 47 of the OAPA 1861. Commonly explained as an aggravated assault, ABH is not defined in the statute. Rather, s 47 merely provides:

> Whosoever shall be convicted upon an indictment of any assault occasioning actual bodily harm shall be liable to be kept in penal servitude.

Other forms of aggravated assault include:

- racially or religiously aggravated assaults (CADA 1998, s 29);
- assault upon a constable in the execution of his duty (Police Act 1996, s 89);
- assault on a prison officer (Police Act 1996, s 89);
- assault on an immigration officer (UK Borders Act 2007, s 22);
- assault with intent to rob (Theft Act 1968, s 8);
- administering a noxious substance (OAPA 1861, ss 23 and 24);
- assault with intent to resist arrest (OAPA 1861, s 38); and
- assault upon emergency workers and those who assist such workers (Assaults on Emergency Workers (Offences) Act 2018 – see *R v McGarrick* [2019] EWCA Crim 530 for one of the first convictions under the Act).

9.4.1 Defining ABH

Herring (*Criminal Law: Text, Cases, and Materials*, 9th edn (OUP, 2020)) refers to liability for ABH as 'constructive'; by this he means that the offence of ABH is built on the foundations of the lesser offence of assault and battery. Child and Ormerod (*Smith, Hogan, & Ormerod's Essentials of Criminal Law*, 3rd edn (OUP, 2019)) refer to assault and battery in this context as the 'base offence' which ABH is then built on top of. The only addition to the offence of common assault for the purposes of ABH is the requirement for bodily harm. As will be discussed below, no additional *mens rea* is required in respect of the bodily harm.

Ormerod and Laird (*Smith, Hogan, & Ormerod's Criminal Law*, 15th edn (OUP, 2018)) suggest that s 47 had the effect of creating two statutory offences, and not one. Specifically the pair argue that the statute created:

- assault occasioning actual bodily harm; and
- battery occasioning actual bodily harm.

Although this is a logical way to observe s 47, especially in light of the *mens rea* requirements of each offence, the author submits that it is better to understand ABH as an offence involving the commission of 'common assault' (ie a general term allowing prosecutors to choose either a technical assault or a battery) which then results in actual bodily harm. Most certainly, prosecutors will charge a defendant with 'assault occasioning actual bodily harm' despite the base offence being one of battery, and this is likely to be on the basis that the word 'assault' here refers to 'common assault'. To introduce an additional procedural element requiring the prosecution to charge the defendant with 'battery occasioning actual bodily harm' despite s 47 referring expressly to an 'assault' would, in the author's opinion, be an unnecessary constraint.

9.4.2 Elements of ABH

Although the name of the offence may be shortened to ABH, it is essential to remember that actual bodily harm merely refers to the harm or injury suffered by the victim. Before one can consider the injury part of the offence, one must first consider the assault or battery which occasions (causes) the harm.

The *actus reus* and *mens rea* of ABH are outlined in **Table 9.7**.

Table 9.7 Elements of ABH

AR/MR	Elements of the offence
Actus reus	(i) an assault or battery; (ii) which occasions; (iii) actual bodily harm.
Mens rea	intention to assault or batter; or recklessness as to assault or battery.

We shall consider each element in turn.

9.4.2.1 *Actus reus:* (i) an assault or battery

The first element that must be proven is that a defendant committed an assault or battery. It is for this reason that the phrase 'aggravated assault' is often used to describe ABH; however, this is not a legal term.

In answering a problem question concerning ABH, you would first need to consider the *actus reus* of assault or battery in full as set out in our discussion above.

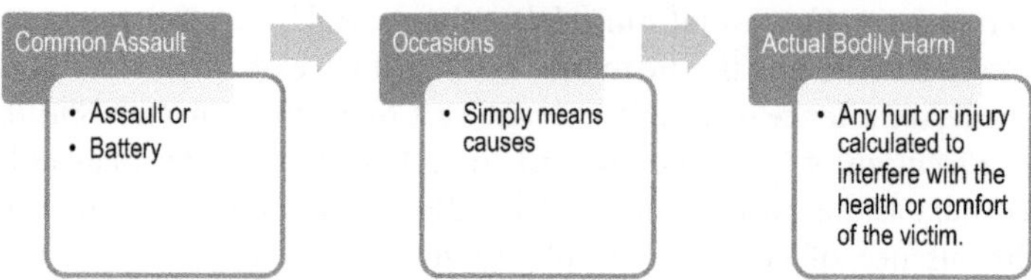

Figure 9.8 Assault or battery occasioning ABH

The assault or battery may be inflicted directly or indirectly and may give rise to liability for ABH where the omission causes actual bodily harm (*DPP v Santana-Bermudez* [2004] Crim LR 471). Although the majority of cases will involve a battery which results in actual bodily harm, many cases also involve assaults which lead to such harm – particularly in cases of psychiatric harm.

9.4.2.2 *Actus reus:* (ii) which occasions

'Occasioning' is simply synonymous with 'causing' in the given case (*R v Roberts* (1971) 56 Cr App R 95). The phrase 'assault occasioning ABH' could be changed to 'assault causing ABH' and it would have the same meaning. Consider our discussion of causation in **Chapter 2**.

In the context of an assault, it must be proven that:

- *but for* the apprehension of unlawful force, the victim would not have suffered actual bodily harm (factual causation); and
- the defendant is the substantive and operative cause of the bodily harm (legal causation).

In the context of a battery, it must be proven that:

- *but for* the force inflicted, the victim would not have suffered actual bodily harm (factual causation); and
- the defendant is the substantive and operative cause of the bodily harm (legal causation).

Given that the regular rules of causation are applied here, the chain of causation may be broken by a *novus actus interveniens*. See **Chapter 2** for a discussion of *Roberts* and the applicable causation principles as applied in cases of ABH.

9.4.2.3 *Actus reus:* (iii) actual bodily harm

Actual bodily harm was defined in *R v Miller* [1954] 2 QB 282, by Lynskey J, as

> any hurt or injury calculated to interfere with the health or comfort of the [victim].

This phrasing was also adopted in *Archbold: Criminal Pleadings and Practice* (of which Lynskey J approved) and the earlier case of *R v Donovan* [1934] 2 KB 498 by Swift J.

In *DPP v Smith (Michael)* [2006] 2 All ER 16, the Divisional Court chose to further define the key terms of ABH. Using the *Concise Oxford English Dictionary*, Sir Igor Judge P (as he then was) explained:

> It is necessary to look at definitions because there is nothing to assist us in the decided cases. In ordinary language, 'harm' is not limited to 'injury', and … extends to 'hurt' or 'damage'. According to the same dictionary, 'bodily', whether used as an adjective or an adverb, is 'concern[ed] [with] the body' … 'Actual', as defined in the authorities, means that the bodily harm should not be so trivial or trifling as to be effectively without significance.

Extent of the harm

Whether a particular injury amounts to ABH is a question of fact for the jury. Guidance may be provided to the jury by the trial judge to assist them in their decision.

According to the Court of Criminal Appeal in *R v Donovan* [1934] 2 KB 498, the hurt need not be serious, permanent or lasting, but must be 'more than merely transient *and* trifling'. This was reaffirmed by the Court of Appeal in *R v Chan-Fook* [1994] 2 All ER 552 in which Hobhouse LJ explained that 'actual bodily harm'

> … are three words of the English language which require no elaboration and in the ordinary course should not receive any. The word 'harm' is a synonym for injury. The word 'actual' indicates that the injury (although there is no need for it to be permanent) should not be *so trivial as to be wholly insignificant.* (emphasis added)

In *R (T) v DPP* [2003] Crim LR 622, Maurice Kay J focused on the wording in *Donovan* that the harm must be more than merely transient and trifling and emphasised that the test was an 'and' test, not an 'or' test, ie harm must be more than 'transient *and* trifling' as opposed to 'transient *or* trifling'. Further, his Lordship ruled that 'physical pain consequent on an assault is not a necessary ingredient of this offence' (ie there is no need to feel pain).

Types of harm covered

Whilst the 1861 Act refers to 'bodily harm', the courts have concluded that ABH is not limited to physical injuries. In *R v Ireland; R v Burstow* [1998] AC 147, Lord Steyn concluded that 'I would hold that "bodily harm" in sections 18, 20 and 47 must be interpreted so as to include recognisable psychiatric illness.' See **Table 9.8** for the meaning of 'recognisable psychiatric illness'.

An important document to be aware of when considering non-fatal offences is the *Charging Standards* produced by the Crown Prosecution Service (CPS). The *Charging Standards* suggest that ABH should be charged where 'the injuries exceed those that can suitably be reflected by a common assault'. The *Charging Standards* previously listed types of injuries which may fall within the definition of actual bodily harm. However, the most recent version of the guidance no longer lists the types of injuries which might constitute actual bodily harm; instead, it lists injuries which should be charged as common assault, and not ABH: 'Grazes; scratches; abrasions; minor bruising; swellings; reddening of the skin; superficial cuts.' It goes on to suggest that prosecutors should only charge a defendant under s 47 where the injuries are 'serious':

> Whilst the level of charge will usually be indicated by the injuries sustained, ABH may be appropriate in the circumstances of the case including where aggravating features set out below are present:
>
> - the circumstances in which the assault took place are more serious e.g. repeated threats or assaults on the same complainant or significant violence (e.g. by strangulation or repeated or prolonged ducking in a bath, particularly where it results in momentary unconsciousness)
> - there has been punching, kicking or head-butting (as distinct from pushing or slapping which would fall to be dealt with as battery)
> - a weapon has been used
> - the victim is vulnerable or intimidated ... This may include: a pattern of similar offending against the victim, either in the past or in a number of offences to be charged; relevant previous convictions; whether the victim would likely be the beneficiary of special measures.

Although the *Charging Standards* no longer provide a list of matters that would amount to actual bodily harm, we can construct our own list based on the case law.

Table 9.8 Examples of ABH from the case law

Injury	Further information
Temporary loss of sensory functions	Such as 'an injurious impairment to the victim's sensory functions', ie loss of consciousness (*R (T) v DPP* [2003] Crim LR 622 – in which the defendant kicked the victim in the head).
Cutting off a substantial part of someone's hair	*DPP v Smith (Michael)* [2006] 2 All ER 16 (a case where a woman's ponytail was cut off – no need to show pain on the part of the woman). Note that Sir Igor Judge P made reference to the cutting off of a 'substantial part' of the victim's hair. It is questionable, therefore, whether any lesser cuttings would amount to ABH (it would certainly be a battery at least). Forceable hair cutting was also considered to be ABH in *R v Stefanski* [2019] EWCA Crim 831.

Psychiatric injury Must be a recognised psychological disorder, eg depression (*R v Chan-Fook* [1994] 2 All ER 552 – in which Hobhouse LJ explained that: 'The body of the victim includes all parts of his body, including his organs, his nervous system and his brain. Bodily injury therefore may include injury to any of those parts of his body responsible for his mental and other faculties.').

Must be more than mere fear, distress or panic (*R v Dhaliwal* [2006] EWCA Crim 1139 – in which there was no evidence of a recognised illness).

The prosecution must call expert evidence to prove the alleged claim and to prove causation (*R v Morris* [1998] 1 Cr App R 386 – in which there was evidence of anxiety, fear and sleeplessness but no evidence of a recognised medical condition).

Without appropriate expert evidence, the question whether an assault had occasioned psychiatric injury should not be left with the jury (*R v Chan-Fook*).

in practice

Arguments are often raised by the defence to argue that the harm falls within the meaning of 'transient and trifling'. For example, in *DPP v Smith (Michael)* [2006] 2 All ER 16, the defendant argued that the cutting off of his girlfriend's ponytail could not amount to ABH as the hair was not part of the body as it was, technically, dead tissue. Further, there was no bruising, bleeding of scarring of the victim and thus there could be no bodily harm (in which case, one would consider charging battery). Although these arguments were rejected, it is important to note that defendants will continue to raise them in the hope that the court in question decides that the harm was not to the body or was so transient and trifling that it was insignificant.

Other relevant forms of ABH may include:

- extensive or multiple bruising and swelling;
- minor fractures;
- displaced broken nose;
- loss or breaking of tooth or teeth; and
- cuts requiring stitches.

Williams ('Force, Injury and Serious Injury' (1990) 140 NLJ 1227) has criticised the breadth of offences that may constitute actual bodily harm. In particular, Williams notes:

> What the Victorian draftsman intended by 'actual' is anyone's guess. He was evidently searching, unsuccessfully, for something between 'trivial' and 'serious'. The courts have not helped him by sensible pronouncements …
>
> The question is held to be one for the unrestricted discretion of the jury or magistrates who are allowed to find that even a bruise is enough. In the scale of harms, a bruise is trivial. The offence under s 47 is relatively serious, carrying a possible sentence of five years. If only a bruise is caused, s 47 is *an overcharge*. (emphasis added)

9.4.2.4 *Mens rea:* intention or recklessness

At a basic level, the *mens rea* of ABH is the same as the *mens rea* for assault and battery respectively. This means that ABH, like common assault, is a basic intent offence (*R v Roberts* (1971) 56 Cr App R 95).

Therefore:

- Should the offence charged be one of '*assault* occasioning actual bodily harm', the prosecution would have to prove that the defendant intended to cause the victim to apprehend immediate unlawful personal violence or be reckless to the thought of such apprehension.
- Should the offence charged be one of '*battery* occasioning actual bodily harm', the prosecution would have to prove that the defendant intended to inflict unlawful personal violence to the victim or be reckless to the thought that such violence would be inflicted (*R v Spratt* [1990] 1 WLR 1073).

Must D intend/be reckless as to ABH?

Although the *actus reus* involves an additional requirement of causing actual bodily harm, there is no such requirement in the *mens rea* of the offence for the defendant to intend or be reckless to the thought of causing ABH. This distinction has been made clear by the House of Lords in *R v Savage; DPP v Parmenter* [1991] 3 WLR 914 (for the facts, see **2.4.2.1**).

Lord Ackner reasoned:

> The verdict of assault occasioning actual bodily harm may be returned upon proof of an assault together with proof of the fact that actual bodily harm was occasioned by the assault. The prosecution are not obliged to prove that the defendant intended to cause some actual bodily harm or was reckless as to whether such harm would be caused.

A similar approach can be seen in the case of *R v Ireland* [1998] AC 147, where threats made by silent telephone calls caused the victim to apprehend violence and, as a result, suffer psychiatric injury. In this circumstance, the defendant did not need to intend or foresee the risk of causing psychiatric injury; rather, he merely needed to intend or be reckless to the thought that the victim may apprehend immediate personal violence (ie the base offence of common assault).

9.4.3 Charging ABH

9.4.3.1 Mode of trial

Assault occasioning actual bodily harm is an either-way offence, meaning that it may be tried in either the magistrates' court or the Crown Court.

9.4.3.2 Sentencing

Where tried in the magistrates' court, the maximum penalty for ABH is 6 months' imprisonment and/or a level 5 fine. In the circumstance where the defendant is charged with multiple either-way offences (whether they all be ABH or not), the magistrates then have the power to sentence the defendant to a maximum of 12 months' imprisonment.

Should a defendant be tried in the Crown Court, the maximum sentence that can be imposed by the Crown Court is 5 years' imprisonment. The power to sentence an individual to a maximum of 5 years' imprisonment has led to a great deal of criticism from academia and the legal profession. Allen and Edwards (*Criminal Law*, 15th edn (OUP, 2019)) specifically refer to this as an 'anomaly', which is reaffirmed by Ormerod and Laird (*Smith, Hogan, & Ormerod's Criminal Law*, 15th edn (OUP, 2018)) as making 'little sense'. This, however, is defended by the likes of Gardner ('Rationality and the Rule of Law in Offences Against the Person' (1994) 53 CLJ 502), who argues that the defendant has 'altered his normative position' towards the victim by choosing to assault him, and therefore must take the consequences of the further harm.

9.4.4 Putting together ABH

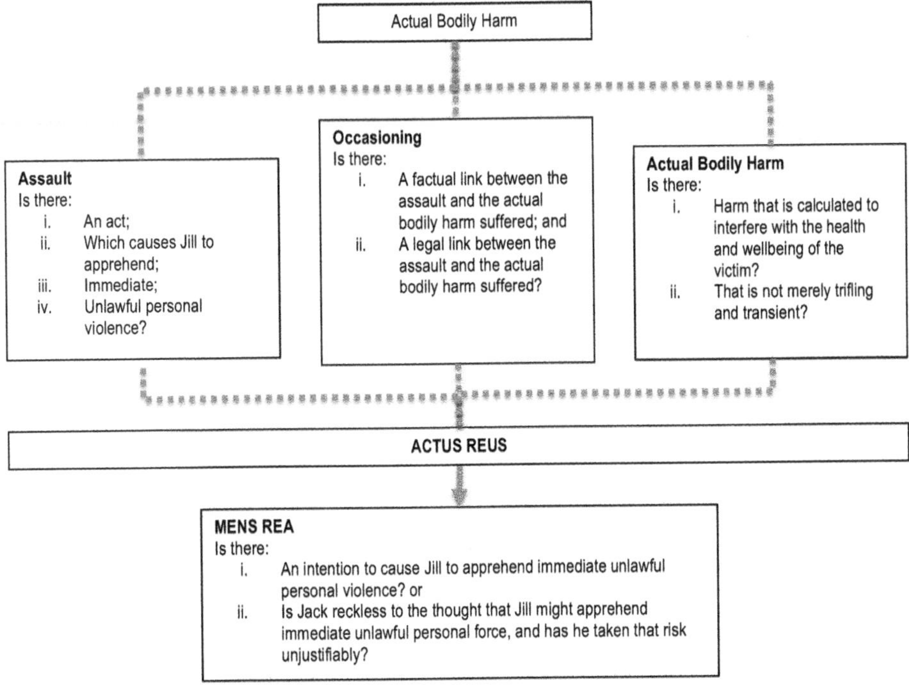

Figure 9.9 Putting together ABH

Consider the following issue and think of how you may structure an answer to it. Then see the figure above for a sample structure to adopt.

facts

Jack, angry that Jill has not prepared his dinner for him, stands at the kitchen table with a knife in his hand waiting for Jill to return from Bingo. Upon Jill entering into the kitchen, Jack waves the knife at Jill, causing her to flee from the house. Upon fleeing, Jill trips over the garden steps and suffers severe grazing to her arm and minor bruising to her face.

9.5 Malicious wounding and inflicting grievous bodily harm

This offence is committed when a person unlawfully and maliciously, either:

- wounds another person; or
- inflicts grievous bodily harm (GBH) upon another person.

Wounding/GBH is a statutory offence charged contrary to s 20 of the OAPA 1861. As with its less serious counterparts, wounding/GBH is not defined in the statute. Rather, s 20 merely provides:

> Whosoever shall unlawfully and maliciously wound or inflict any grievous bodily harm upon any other person, either with or without any weapon or instrument, shall be guilty of a misdemeanor, and being convicted thereof shall be liable to be kept in penal servitude.

9.5.1 Defining wounding and inflicting grievous bodily harm

Wounding and GBH are two separate offences, both charged under s 20 of the OAPA 1861. It is the choice of the prosecutor, following set guidelines, as to which offence he or she feels best reflects the circumstances of a given case. It is always advisable to consider wounding first (even if it is obvious that there is no wound) as the court has ruled in *R v Wood and M'Mahon* (1830) 4 C & P 381 that any injuries that fall outside the scope of wounding may instead be charged as GBH. In this respect, prosecutors must ask themselves when charging an offence: Is there evidence of a wound? If yes, they should charge wounding. If no, they should charge GBH.

Before we consider the specifics of an offence under s 20, it is worth noting a number of fundamental principles:

(a) The jury may take into account the totality of injuries (in *R v Birmingham* [2002] EWCA Crim 2608, the Court of Appeal stated that a number of individually minor injuries may collectively be considered grievous). See also *R v Grundy* [1977] Crim LR 543.

(b) Although the determination of whether the injury constitutes grievous bodily harm is to be assessed objectively, a victim's characteristics may be taken into account, including their health and age, eg a child will likely suffer more harm from a slap than a grown adult (*R v Bollom* [2004] 2 Cr App R 50 – injuries to a 17-month-old child).

(c) In determining seriousness of any wound or grievous bodily harm, account must be taken of its effect on the individual victim (in *R v Golding* [2014] EWCA Crim 889, the Court gave the example that an injury to a finger could be considered grievous bodily harm where the victim was a professional musician). We will break down our discussion into wounding and GBH.

9.5.2 Elements of wounding

The *actus reus* and *mens rea* of wounding are outlined in **Table 9.9**.

Table 9.9 Elements of wounding

AR/MR	Elements of the offence
Actus reus	unlawful wounding
Mens rea	intention to cause some harm; or recklessness as to the thought of causing some harm.

We shall consider each element in turn.

9.5.2.1 *Actus reus:* unlawful wounding

Unlawfulness

The offence includes an element of 'unlawfulness', meaning that a valid defence or excuse will render the accused not guilty of an offence. In *R v Stokes* [2003] EWCA Crim 2977, Henriques J explained that:

> A jury must *always* be directed as to the element of unlawfulness, if only by way of pointing out that the requirement of unlawfulness imports no more than that self-defence, defence of others, defence of property, force used for the prevention of crime and accident are all defences. (emphasis added)

Wounding

A wound is concerned with a break in the continuity of the whole outer skin, including both the dermis and epidermis (*Moriarty v Brooks* (1834) 6 C & P 684). Only an injury which breaks both layers of the skin can be classified as a wound. Although bleeding is not an essential requirement for a wound, it would appear (biologically speaking) to be an inherent aspect of a wound. This break in the skin is an essential requirement for a wound as demonstrated in *JCC (a minor) v Eisenhower* [1984] QB 331, where the Divisional Court ruled that internal bleeding, as a result of being shot in the eye by an air pistol – where there is no cut to the skin – is insufficient, and *R v M'Loughlin* (1838) 8 C&P 635, where the Court held that mere scratches to the skin, even those that cause blood to show and a scab to occur, are insufficient (unless both layers are broken). The exception to this was detailed in *R v Waltham* (1849) 3 Cox CC 442 which concerned a cut on the inner skin within the cheek or lip which is sufficient to amount to a wound.

Further to this, should the victim suffer broken bones as a result of an attack from the defendant, where the bones have not pierced the skin, there can be no wounding (*R v Wood and M'Mahon* (1830) 4 C & P 381, where the defendant broke the victim's collarbone; however, as the skin remained intact, there was no wound).

It was previously understood to be the case that in order for a wound to be inflicted, it had to be done so by direct physical contact from the defendant, eg the defendant stabbed or shot the victim (*R v Beasley* (1981) 73 Cr App R 44). Support for this proposition could be found by comparing the wording of s 18 to s 20. In particular, unlike s 18, s 20 does not include the phrase 'by any means whatsoever' when referring to an unlawful wound. This might be seen to indicate that the harm has to be directly inflicted. By the same token, however, s 20 does use the phraseology 'with or without any weapon or instrument'. This might indicate, however, that the harm need not be directly inflicted. In that regard, whilst a clear answer is not available, the author takes the view that a wounding contrary to s 20 is capable of being committed by way of direct or indirect force to the person.

Further, although the definition of a wound encompasses relatively minor injuries, for example a small cut or prick to a finger, as well as the more substantial cuts to the skin, the former is advised to be charged as a battery or ABH.

9.5.2.2 *Mens rea:* malice (intention or recklessness)

Both s 20 offences require the defendant to have committed the offence 'maliciously'.

Meaning of malice

Maliciously is not a part of the *actus reus* of the offence but rather forms part of the *mens rea*. Maliciousness simply refers to the necessity for intention or recklessness, and does not require any form of 'ill-will', hatred or wickedness (*R v Cunningham* [1957] 2 QB 396; *R v Savage; DPP v Parmenter* [1991] 3 WLR 914). In *R v Beeson* [1994] Crim LR 190, the Court of Appeal emphasised that it was unnecessary and unwise to direct the jury on the meaning of the word 'maliciously'. With respect to the Court of Appeal, although the phrase was unimportant on the facts of the instant case, many other cases may still require careful guidance and understanding on its meaning given that the potential liberty of a defendant is at stake.

Kind of harm intended

One might think that the *mens rea* of s 20 involves an intention or recklessness as to wounding or grievous bodily harm. However, that is not the case. The defendant merely needs to intend to cause, or be reckless to the thought of causing, 'some harm'. In *R v Mowatt* [1968] 1 QB 421, Diplock LJ concluded that

> the word 'maliciously' does import upon the part of the person who unlawfully inflicts the wound or other grievous bodily harm an awareness that his act may have the consequence of causing some physical harm to some other person. … It is quite unnecessary that the accused should have foreseen that his unlawful act might cause physical harm of the gravity described in [s 20], ie, a wound or serious physical injury. It is enough that he should have foreseen *that some physical harm to some person, albeit of a minor character, might result.* (emphasis added)

This was reaffirmed in *R v Savage; DPP v Parmenter* [1991] 3 WLR 914 by Lord Ackner.

Therefore, the *mens rea* can be stated simply as:

- the defendant intends to cause *some harm*; or
- the defendant is reckless to the thought that *some harm* might occur and unjustifiably takes the risk anyway.

A brief moment needs to be taken on the recklessness element of s 20. In *DPP v A* [2001] Crim LR 140, the Divisional Court ruled that the test of recklessness for a s 20 offence is not that the defendant foresaw a risk that some harm *would* occur, and took the risk unjustifiably. Rather, the Court made clear that the correct form of recklessness in this circumstance is that the defendant foresaw a risk that some harm *might* occur, and took the risk unjustifiably. To confuse *might* and *would* could lead to a distortion of the meaning of oblique intention (see **Chapter 3**) and would result in a 'too generous' interpretation of the phrase for the defendant (*R v Rushworth* (1992) 95 Cr App R 252).

Williams (*Textbook of Criminal Law* (Stevens, 1978)) argued that the test of s 20 'distorts the accepted meaning of statutory malice'. He further argues that a defendant should only be guilty if he foresees the *actus reus* of the offence charged and not that of a lesser offence. Importantly then, a defendant cannot be held liable in circumstances where he was unaware that his conduct might cause any injury at all (*R v Meachen* [2006] EWCA Crim 2414).

9.5.3 Elements of inflicting grievous bodily harm

The *actus reus* and *mens rea* of inflicting grievous bodily harm are outlined in **Table 9.10**.

Table 9.10 Elements of inflicting grievous bodily harm

AR/MR	Elements of the offence
Actus reus	unlawful infliction of really serious bodily harm
Mens rea	intention to cause some harm; or recklessness as to the thought of causing some harm.

We shall consider each element in turn.

9.5.3.1 *Actus reus:* unlawful infliction of really serious bodily harm

Unlawfulness

As above with wounding, the jury must be directed to consider whether the harm caused was unlawful (ie without consent or justification).

Meaning of 'really serious'

According to Viscount Kilmuir LC in the House of Lords in *DPP v Smith* [1961] AC 290:

> I can find no warrant for giving the words 'grievous bodily harm' a meaning other than that which the words convey in their ordinary and natural meaning. 'Bodily harm' needs no explanation and 'grievous' means no more and no less than 'really serious'.

However, the use (or omission) of the word 'really' in defining grievous has been an issue before the appellate courts on a number of occasions. In *R v Saunders* [1985] Crim LR 230, Lord Lane CJ in the Court of Appeal identified the omission of the word 'really' when directing a jury as 'not significant', making 'no difference at all'. In *R v Janjua; R v Choudhury* [1999] 1 Cr App R 91, Curtis J explained that in some circumstances (as in that case) 'the use of the word "really" before "serious" [is] not required on any sensible view'. In that regard, the word 'serious' alone may be sufficient when directing a jury. However, his Lordship would then proceed to explain that:

> there could be circumstances in which a judge would think it right to use the word 'really' before 'serious bodily harm'; but the proposition that it is required in every single case is not a correct representation of the law. *It is a matter for the judge* in the light of the factual situations with which he is confronted to make the decision whether or not to use the word 'really' before the word 'serious'. (emphasis added)

In other words, the use of 'really' is not required in all cases; whether it is appropriate or necessary to include that phraseology is a matter for the trial judge on the facts before him. In *Janjua*, the nature of the injuries and the weapon used (the victim had been stabbed with a knife of at least five-and-a-half inches long) was sufficient for the Court to conclude that the word 'really' was unnecessary.

Whether the harm is 'really serious' is a question of fact for the jury. Hogan ('The Fourteenth Report of the Criminal Law Revision Committee: (3) Non-Fatal offences' [1980] Crim LR 542 has posed the question, 'Who knows what considerations [the jury] may take into account when deciding what is "really serious harm"?' It is arguable, therefore, that whether injury is really serious should be a question of law for the judge, whilst the jury should be concerned with whether the defendant actually *caused* that harm, should it be considered really serious.

Importantly, according to the Court of Appeal in *R v Brown; R v Stratton* [1998] Crim LR 485 and *R v Grundy* [1977] Crim LR 543, the offence does not require one significant injury in order to be classed as 'really serious'. Rather, a collection of relatively minor injuries may amount to grievous bodily harm when considered in totality. In this case, the victim suffered a broken nose, three lost teeth and a concussion. In combination, these injuries were capable of amounting to grievous bodily harm.

'Inflict'

The word 'inflict' in s 20 has, in itself, caused problems. Traditionally it was viewed as a narrower concept than to 'cause' (found in s 18 of the OAPA 1861) and implied the necessity for a technical assault and the application to the body of direct or indirect force, ie a battery (*R v Clarence* (1888) 22 QBD 23). In *R v Wilson* [1984] AC 242, the House of Lords rejected this statement and provided that 'inflict' simply means 'force being directly applied violently to the body of the victim so that he suffers grievous bodily harm' (per Lord Roskill). This approach, however, led to the conclusion that GBH could only be caused by a 'direct application of force' and could not include indirect conduct.

It appears to have been resolved by the House of Lords in *R v Ireland; R v Burstow* [1998] AC 147. The judgment came from the appeal in relation to Burstow, which concerned (amongst other matters) the making of silent phone calls leading to the victim suffering from depression. The defendant argued on appeal that he could not be liable for a s 20 offence given that there was no 'infliction' of direct force. Lord Steyn disagreed and found that psychiatric harm is sufficient to found a case under s 20. His Lordship stated that an offence under s 20 can be committed where no physical violence is applied directly or indirectly to the body of the victim, ie no assault is needed. Lord Steyn concluded that such a distinction would be 'absurd'. An offence of inflicting GBH does not, therefore, require the application of physical force.

In addition, Lord Steyn was clear in that there is no 'radical divergence' between the meanings of the words 'cause' and 'inflict (following Lord Mackay LC in *R v Mandair* [1995] 1 AC 208)'; however, he went on to cause a level of uncertainty by stating that the terms are also not synonymous. Lord Hope developed this understanding further and provided that the word 'inflict' implies that the consequence of the act is something which the victim is likely to find unpleasant or harmful. Whilst there may remain an unclear answer in this regard, for practical purposes, it is appropriate to treat cause and inflict as synonymous as requiring proof of causation (both factual and legal).

'Bodily harm': types of harm covered

The *Charging Standards* formerly provided a list of injuries that were appropriate to be charged under s 20. These included:

- injury resulting in permanent disability, loss of sensory function or visible disfigurement;
- broken or displaced limbs or bones, including fractured skull, compound fractures, broken cheek bone, jaw, ribs, etc;
- injuries which cause substantial loss of blood, usually necessitating a transfusion or resulting in lengthy treatment or incapacity;
- serious psychiatric injury. As with assault occasioning actual bodily harm, appropriate expert evidence is essential to prove the injury.

This list of examples has now been removed (though it remains a helpful list of examples) and replaced with the following statement:

> Life-changing injuries should be charged as GBH. Just as the need for medical treatment may indicate ABH injuries, significant or sustained medical treatment (for instance, intensive care or a blood transfusion) may indicate GBH injuries, even if a full or relatively full recovery follows.

Two points require further consideration under this section, namely serious psychiatric injury, and the transfer of sexually transmitted infections (STIs), which is not listed in the *Charging Standards* above.

Serious psychiatric injury

The CPS *Charging Standards* recommend that 'serious psychiatric injury' should be charged under s 20. This is in line with the case law (*R v Ireland; R v Burstow* [1998] AC 147). In *R v Gelder* (1994) *The Times*, 25 May, the court held that 'obscene' acts, which are serious and cause psychiatric injury, may be charged under s 20.

Biological harm

Secondly, in relation to the transfer of an STI (also known as biological harm), the *Charging Standards* provide that in circumstances where the defendant is reckless to the thought that the complainant might contract the infection via unprotected sexual activity but goes on to take that risk unreasonably, the defendant should be charged under s 20 and not with a s 47 offence (*R v Dica* [2004] QB 1257; *R v Barnes* [2005] 1 WLR 910). This was evident in the more recent case of *R v Golding* [2014] EWCA Crim 889 where the defendant knew that he suffered from genital herpes and that it was a sexually transmitted disease but did not inform his girlfriend of such before they then engaged in sexual intercourse. The Court of Appeal found s 20 to be the appropriate charge given that, although the defendant did not intend to infect his girlfriend, he was reckless as to inflicting GBH, and the injury was such that it could be classified as really serious harm.

Note that it is debatable whether the Court was satisfied that genital herpes was serious enough to justify a s 20 conviction. The expert evidence adduced by the appellant doubted such. However, s 47 was not open to the Crown to prosecute given that there was no assault or battery, and the Court concluded that it was open to the jury to find that genital herpes was serious enough to be classed as grievous bodily harm.

Should a defendant intend to cause the complainant to contract an STI, this will be considered as suitable for charging as s 18 GBH with intent (see *R v Rowe (Daryll)* (Lewes Crown Court, 15 November 2017) in which the defendant was convicted of intentionally infecting 10 men with HIV (having convinced them to engage in unprotected sexual intercourse or having tampered with the condoms used)). Indeed, the Legal Guidance provided by the CPS on this matter has stated, quite plainly, that the 'appropriate' charges in a case of intentional or reckless transmission are under either s 20 or s 18, and not s 47 (CPS Legal Guidance, 'Intentional or Reckless Sexual Transmission of Infection' (London, 2013)).

For the purposes of s 20 GBH, the issue of recklessness and reasonableness is ultimately dependent on the circumstances. For instance, should the defendant have a condition which is highly infectious, his actions in engaging in unprotected sexual activity are likely to be considered reckless. Where, however, his condition is understood to be of a low risk, he may not be considered reckless through his actions. In addition, where the defendant chooses to wear a condom, the risk of infection becomes even lower. What then, is the standard of risk? It is important to note that the defendant need not be aware that he suffers from an STI, provided that he was reckless to the thought that he *might* suffer and the complainant *might* contract the same infection as a result. This view is contrary to that of some commentators, such as Weait ('Knowledge, Autonomy and Consent' [2005] Crim LR 763) who believes that the defendant will only be guilty where he *knew* that he was a carrier of the infection.

A complainant's consent may provide a defence to a charge of s 20 GBH (*R v Dica* [2004] QB 1257); however, the case of *R v Konzani* [2005] EWCA Crim 706 has held that informed consent must be given for the *risk* of infection, rather than the act of sexual intercourse.

example

Jack is a carrier of the HIV infection and is aware of this fact but fails to inform Jill of his condition. He engages in sexual intercourse with Jill, not thinking that he may transmit the infection to Jill.

In this scenario, Jack will be liable for an offence under s 20 as he has failed to seek informed consent from Jill as to the risk of infection. The facts of the case are clear that Jack knows he is HIV positive but does not believe the infection would transmit. As such, Jack would be liable for s 20 GBH but not s 18 GBH on the basis that he lacks any intention to transmit the infection.

Judge LJ in *Konzani* emphasised that not all cases need to feature a conversation between the defendant and victim about the defendant's HIV status (ie not all cases require disclosure from the defendant). Judge LJ explains:

> [We] accept that there may be circumstances in which it would be open to the jury to infer that, notwithstanding that the defendant was reckless and concealed his condition from the complainant, she may nevertheless have given an informed consent to the risk of contracting the HIV virus. By way of example, an individual with HIV may develop a sexual relationship with someone who knew him while he was in hospital, receiving treatment for the condition. ... Alternatively, he may honestly believe that his new sexual partner was told of his condition by someone known to them both.

example

Jack is a carrier of the HIV infection and is aware of this fact. Jill is best friends with Jack's former partner who informs Jill that Jack is HIV positive. Jack and Jill engage in consensual sexual intercourse.

In this case, Jack may have a defence of informed consent on the basis that Jill has been told, by a person other than the defendant, that Jack is HIV positive. Importantly, the consent must be effective and informed to be valid. Should Jill simply be informed, by Jack or another person, that Jack has 'slept with a lot of people', can it be said that Jill is fully informed? That is ultimately a question for the jury.

Further, the complainant cannot consent to the intentional transmission of an STI. We considered informed consent above in relation to common assault and we shall consider it in **Chapter 10** in relation to sexual offences.

An interesting point that will be discussed in fuller detail in **Chapter 10** is that, following the case of *R v B* [2007] 1 WLR 1567, a person who does not disclose the fact that he or she has an STI, and then has consensual sexual intercourse with another, is not liable for rape. Under the previous law in *R v Tabassum* [2000] 2 Cr App R 328, this would have been the case, ie the defendant would have been liable for rape.

9.5.3.2 *Mens rea:* intention or recklessness

As above (see **9.5.2.2**), in relation to wounding, GBH is a basic intent offence, and the *mens rea* for inflicting grievous bodily harm is simply that:

- the defendant intended to cause *some* harm; or
- the defendant was reckless to the thought that *some* harm *might* occur and unjustifiably took the risk anyway (*DPP v A* [2001] Crim LR 140).

As in wounding, the term 'maliciousness' simply means intention or recklessness in relation to GBH.

9.5.4 Charging wounding and GBH

Where both a wound and GBH have been inflicted, the CPS will use discretion to choose which one reflects the true nature of the offence (*R v McCready* [1978] 3 All ER 967). Where, however, there is evidence of a serious wound, this ought generally to be charged as wounding, rather than as inflicting grievous bodily harm.

9.5.4.1 Mode of trial

Like ABH, s 20 wounding/GBH is an either-way offence, meaning that it may be tried in either the magistrates' court or the Crown Court.

9.5.4.2 Sentencing

A s 20 offence gives rise to the same punishment as the offence of ABH contrary to s 47, namely 6 months' imprisonment and/or a level 5 fine in the magistrates' court, and a maximum of 5 years' imprisonment in the Crown Court.

9.5.5 Putting together wounding and GBH

See **9.6.4** (following the discussion of wounding/causing GBH with intent).

9.6 Wounding and causing grievous bodily harm with intent

This offence is committed when a person unlawfully and maliciously, with intent to do grievous bodily harm, or with intent to resist or prevent the lawful apprehension or detainer of any other person, either:

- wounds another person; or
- causes grievous bodily harm to another person.

Wounding/GBH with intent is a statutory offence charged contrary to s 18 of the OAPA 1861. In rather archaic terms, s 18 (as amended by the Criminal Law Act 1967) provides:

> Whosoever shall unlawfully and maliciously by any means whatsoever wound or cause any grievous bodily harm to any person with intent to do some grievous bodily harm to any person, or with intent to resist or prevent the lawful apprehension or detainer of any person, shall be guilty of felony, and being convicted thereof shall be liable to be kept in penal servitude for life.

9.6.1 Defining wounding and causing grievous bodily harm with intent

The only distinction between a s 20 offence and an offence charged under s 18 is within the *mens rea*. The *actus reus* of s 18 is identical to that of s 20. There are two elements to the *mens rea* of a s 18 offence, which must be established.

Accordingly, an offence under s 18 may take one of four different forms, namely:

(a) wounding with intent to do grievous bodily harm;

(b) maliciously wounding with intent to resist or prevent the lawful apprehension of any person;
(c) causing grievous bodily harm with intent to do so; or
(d) maliciously causing grievous bodily harm with intent to resist or prevent the lawful apprehension of any person.

9.6.2 Elements of wounding and causing grievous bodily harm with intent

The *actus reus* and *mens rea* of wounding and GBH with intent are outlined in **Table 9.11**.

Table 9.11 Elements of wounding and causing grievous bodily harm with intent

AR/MR	Elements of the offence
Actus reus (wounding)	unlawful wounding (a break in both layers of the skin)
OR	
Actus reus (GBH)	unlawfully causing really serious bodily harm
Mens rea	intention to cause GBH; or intention to resist or prevent lawful apprehension

9.6.2.1 *Actus reus:* unlawful wounding/unlawfully causing infliction of really serious bodily harm

The *actus reus* of the s 18 offence is identical to that of s 20. The defendant's conduct must have caused the victim to suffer either a wound and/or GBH. The only difference appears in the wording of s 18 in relation to GBH. Section 18 requires that the harm is 'caused' by the defendant, whereas s 20 requires that the harm is 'inflicted' by the defendant. Following *R v Constanza* (above), neither term is controversial and simply means that the defendant must be the cause of the harm by way of his actions (ie the terms are synonymous).

'Any person'

For those readers who appreciate attention to detail, there is one aspect of ss 18 and 20 which you may have missed. Specifically, s 20 makes reference to wounding or inflicting GBH on 'any other person', whilst s 18 only makes reference to wounding or causing GBH on 'any person'. A literal interpretation of this reading could be that s 18 allows for a defendant to commit an offence by harming himself, whilst s 20 requires the harm to be inflicted on a person other than the defendant. An interesting debate, but one that will likely never see the light of day in practice.

9.6.2.2 *Mens rea:* intention

Unlike s 20, a s 18 offence is one of specific intent. This means that it may only be committed with intention; recklessness is not sufficient (*Re Knight's Appeal* (1968) 12 FLR 81; *R v Belfon* [1976] 3 All ER 46). For a recent case in which the trial judge mistakenly directed the jury that recklessness was sufficient for s 18 GBH, see *R v Atta-Dankwa* [2018] EWCA Crim 320. The Court of Appeal, led by Holroyde LJ, appreciated that the misdirection arose as a result of a confusion between the charges alleged against the defendant; however, it did note that it was 'very regrettable' that a conviction should be quashed in these circumstances. Holroyde LJ emphasised that the use of written directions, in accordance with the Criminal Procedure Rules 2015, could have prevented this situation from occurring.

The *mens rea* of a s 18 offence is the same regardless of whether the defendant has committed a wound or caused GBH. In both cases, the *mens rea* for s 18 is identical, namely:

- the intention to cause GBH; or
- the intention to resist or prevent lawful apprehension.

A number of points require consideration.

Level of harm intended

First, s 18 requires the defendant to intend to cause GBH. Unlike s 20, for which it is sufficient for the defendant to intend to cause *some harm*, it must be proven in the case of s 18 that the defendant intended to cause GBH. Further to this, it is irrelevant whether the defendant would regard the harm inflicted as really serious harm.

Will an intention to wound suffice?

Secondly, it is essential to note that although s 18 creates an offence of wounding, an intention to cause a wound will not be sufficient for the purposes of s 18. This was made clear in *R v Taylor* [2009] EWCA Crim 544 where the Court of Appeal allowed the defendant's appeal on the ground that although the defendant stabbed the victim in the back during a fight, he had no intention to cause GBH. The Court of Appeal substituted a s 18 conviction with a conviction for s 20 wounding. Thomas LJ would explain that 'an intent to wound is insufficient. There must be an intent to cause really serious bodily injury.' In that regard, s 18 requires an intention to cause GBH regardless of whether the *actus reus* is GBH or wounding (see also *R v Brown* [2014] EWCA Crim 2176); an offence of 'wounding, with intent to wound', therefore, does not exist. See also *R v O'Donnell* [2010] EWCA Crim 1480.

Meaning of maliciously in s 18

A further point to note is the use of the word 'maliciously' in s 18. As we saw in s 20, maliciousness simply means the foresight of some harm. In *R v Mowatt* [1968] 1 QB 421, the Court of Appeal stated, *obiter*, that 'in section 18 the word "maliciously" adds nothing'. However, subsequent cases have ruled that the meaning of maliciously may become relevant dependent on the type of s 18 offence concerned. This was the judgment in *R v Morrison* (1988) 89 Cr App R 17.

case example

Charge:
Malicious wounding (OAPA 1861, s 18)

Case progression:
Crown Court – Guilty

Court of Appeal – Conviction quashed

Point of law:
Meaning of 'malicious' in s 18

In *R v Morrison* (1988) 89 Cr App R 17, the defendant was seized by a police officer who stated that she was arresting him. To avoid arrest, the defendant dived through a window pane, dragging the police officer with him. This caused serious facial lacerations to the police officer. The trial judge directed the jury that if he intended to resist arrest and was reckless in the *Caldwell* sense as to causing the officer harm, he was guilty of the s 18 offence. The defendant was convicted of the s 18 offence in the Crown Court.

The Court of Appeal quashed the conviction, holding that where the prosecution relies on intention to resist lawful force, it must also prove that the defendant was reckless (in the *Cunningham* subjective sense) as to some harm occurring.

Therefore:

- where the prosecution simply relies on the intention to cause GBH, there is no need to prove that defendant acted maliciously as the defendant will logically have foreseen the risk of some harm where he intends really serious harm (*R v Brown* [2005] EWCA Crim 359); but
- where the prosecution relies on the intention to resist lawful apprehension, there must also be proof of maliciousness on the part of the defendant (ie that the defendant foresaw the risk of some harm) (*R v Morrison* (1988) 89 Cr App R 17).

The *Charging Standards* provide that there are a number of factors that may indicate that the defendant has the direct intent for the offence. The *Charging Standards* state:

> Factors that may indicate specific intent include a repeated or planned attack, deliberate selection of a weapon or adaptation of an article to cause injury, such as breaking a glass before an attack, making prior threats or using an offensive weapon against, or kicking, the victim's head. The gravity of the injury may be the same for section 20 or 18 although the gravity may indicate the intention of the defendant.

9.6.3 Charging wounding and grievous bodily harm with intent

9.6.3.1 Mode of trial

Wounding/GBH with intent is an offence triable only on indictment, meaning that it may only be tried in the Crown Court.

9.6.3.2 Sentencing

The maximum sentence for an offence contrary to s 18 is life imprisonment.

9.6.4 Putting together wounding and GBH with intent

Consider this issue and think of how you may structure an answer to it. Then see the figure below for a sample structure to adopt.

facts

Jack visits his local pub with his friend, Jill. Whilst at the pub, the pair consume a large quantity of alcohol. Later into the evening, the pair get into an argument over whose turn it is to purchase the next set of drinks. Jack, who has a short temper, punches Jill in the face and kicks her as she lays on the floor defenceless. This causes Jill to suffer a broken nose and four broken ribs. Andy, a police officer, attempts to intervene and restrain Jack. Jack then smashes a bottle of beer over Andy, causing a deep cut to Andy's head.

Do not consider potential defences of intoxication in your structure.

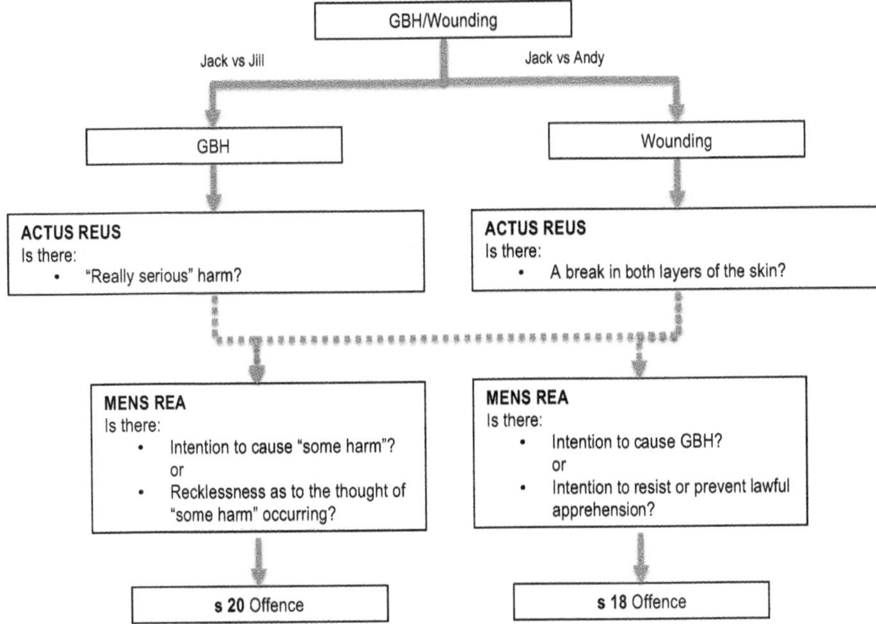

Figure 9.10 Putting together GBH/wounding

9.7 Coronavirus and non-fatal offences

Some substantive criminal offences have been specially created to deal with the coronavirus pandemic, such as the prohibition on people leaving or being outside of the place where they are living without reasonable excuse, contrary to reg 6(1) of the Health Protection (Coronavirus, Restrictions) (England) Regulations 2020 (SI 2020/350). For the purposes of non-fatal offences against the person, however, no new offences have been created. Rather, the law has adapted in part to deal with the unusual times the public face during the coronavirus pandemic. This section aims to briefly outline the apparent approach taken by prosecuting authorities in respect of coronavirus-related non-fatal offences. Our focus will remain on common assault, ABH and GBH; however, it is worth noting that an offence contrary to s 23 of the OAPA 1861 (administering a noxious substance), which is not considered in this text, may also be made out if a defendant spits at another person whilst he is infected with the virus.

9.7.1 Common assault

To spit at another person is to be charged as common assault. This is fairly straightforward given that there will be the actual application of force (spittle contacting the victim – battery) or at the very least there is the potential of an apprehension of such force (spittle missing the victim – assault). That is largely non-controversial for our purposes and the CPS has reported a number of successful prosecutions in that respect.

The more difficult issue relates to whether to cough on, at, or towards another person can amount to an offence of common assault. It would appear that cases of coughing have been dealt with, and with success, by the CPS as cases of assault. Indeed, on 26 March 2020, the DPP warned that coughing at another person would be charged as common assault. It is debatable, however, whether this is an accurate reflection of the law or a public policy-style response to the coronavirus situation. For instance, as discussed at **9.2.2.3**, the offence of assault requires the victim to apprehend *immediate* unlawful personal violence. Whilst the House of Lords in *R v Ireland; R v Burstow* [1998] AC 147 provided a rather flexible approach to the requirement of immediacy (preferring the term 'imminent' over 'immediate'), it is questionable whether the apprehension of contracting the COVID-19 strain of coronavirus would satisfy the requirement of 'imminency'. Likewise, an offence is only committed in circumstances where the victim apprehends 'force'. Could it be said that the apprehension of contracting COVID-19 is the same as an apprehension of force? This matter is certainly up for debate, and it will be interesting to see how the appellate courts respond to any appeals against conviction in this regard.

9.7.2 ABH and GBH

What of the situation where a victim has contracted the COVID-19 strain of coronavirus following them being coughed at or spat on? Could a more serious offence of ABH or GBH be made out? A number of matters require consideration here:

- *Causation:* In order to satisfy the offences of ABH and GBH, the prosecution must prove that the act of the defendant (ie the coughing or spitting) *caused* the end result of contracting COVID-19. This would mean that the prosecution would have to prove that the virus was not contracted from some person other than the defendant. In the case of emergency workers, that may be difficult to prove to the criminal standard. Dependent on how many people the victim has come into contact with prior to contracting the virus, the list of potential causes may be quite lengthy. As we appreciated in **Chapter 2**, the defendant need not be the sole or main cause of the harm inflicted; the defendant need only be more than a minimal contribution. Using this approach, a court may be more ready to find that the defendant, in coughing at, or spitting on, the victim, was the cause of the end result.
- *Harm:* In both offences, it must be proven that the victim has suffered actual harm. The issue would become, therefore, whether the virus would be classed as 'harm'. This returns us to our discussion of 'biological harm' at **9.5.3.1**. As we saw from such cases as *R v Dica* [2004] QB 1257, the transfer of an STI from the defendant to the victim is to be classed as GBH. Likewise, in *R v Golding* [2014] EWCA Crim 889 genital herpes was considered to amount to GBH. Would the causing of another to contract the virus amount to a sufficient level of harm to satisfy the offence? There does not appear to be any reason why this is not possible; the virus has proven to be deadly.
- *Mens rea:* For the offence of ABH, it must simply be proven that the defendant intended (or was reckless) to cause an assault or a battery. Should a charge of ABH be brought, there is little difficulty in proving that. However, in respect of GBH, it must be proven that the defendant intended (or was reckless) to cause *some harm.* The difficulty here would be on the knowledge state of mind of the defendant. If the defendant has tested positive for COVID-19 and intentionally sets out to infect another person, the offence can be made out (so long as evidence is available). What about a defendant who has not been tested, but who believes he has the

virus? Will he be reckless by coughing or spitting on another in those circumstances?

9.8 Aggravated forms of non-fatal offences

9.8.1 Aggravated offences

For all offences (bar the s 18 offence) considered in this chapter, the defendant may be liable for an aggravated form of the offence. By way of s 29 of the Crime and Disorder Act (CADA) 1998, as amended by the Anti-terrorism, Crime and Security Act 2001 and the Protection of Freedoms Act 2012, all crimes of violence may be racially or religiously aggravated.

Formerly, whether an offence was aggravated by race or religion remained merely a factor for sentencing. However, as a result of the CADA 1998, the defendant may now be liable for more serious versions of the offences that we deal with below.

The Law Commission in 2014 ('Hate Crime: Should the Current Offences be Extended?' (Law Com No 348, 2014)) proposed the expansion of aggravating factors to include hostility towards people on the grounds of disability, sexual orientation and gender identity (meaning 'transgender identity'). At present, such factors remain relevant only to sentencing.

The aggravated offences are provided for in ss 29 and 32 of the CADA 1998. Section 29 concerns the aggravated forms for common assault, assault occasioning ABH, and s 20 malicious wounding/GBH. Section 32 concerns the aggravated forms for harassment and stalking.

The meaning of racially or religiously aggravated offences is detailed in s 28(1) of the CADA 1998 which provides:

> An offence is racially or religiously aggravated for the purposes of sections 29 to 32 below if—
>
> (a) at the time of committing the offence, or immediately before or after doing so, the offender demonstrates towards the victim of the offence hostility based on the victim's membership (or presumed membership) of a racial or religious group; or
>
> (b) the offence is motivated (wholly or partly) by hostility towards members of a racial or religious group based on their membership of that group.

- Note that this section provides an 'or' test, meaning that the prosecution need only prove that the defendant objectively demonstrated such hostility (an *actus reus* element) under s 28(1)(a) or where the defendant's conduct was motivated by such hostility (a *mens rea* element) under s 28(1)(b).

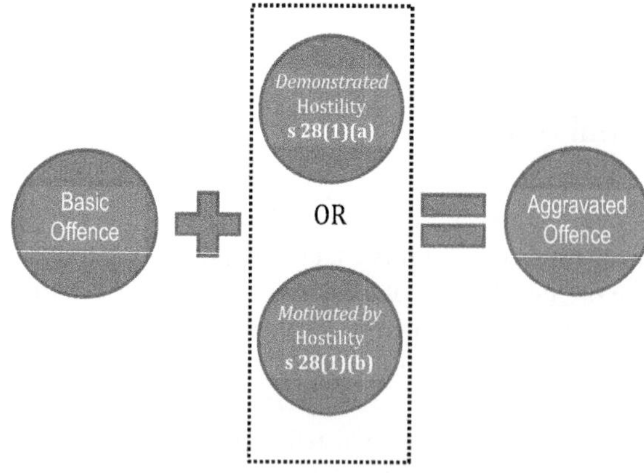

Figure 9.11 Aggravated offences

Section 28(4) and (5) of the CADA 1998 provides definitions of racial and religious groups in the following terms:

(4) In this section 'racial group' means a group of persons defined by reference to race, colour, nationality (including citizenship) or ethnic or national origins.

(5) In this section 'religious group' means a group of persons defined by reference to religious belief or lack of religious belief.

Hostility is not defined in the CADA 1998 but is understood by reference to the *Oxford English Dictionary* as simply meaning 'unfriendly'. Importantly, the relevant hostility need not be connected with the 'basic' offence, which may have been committed for reasons other than concerning race or religion. However, where in the act of committing the basic offence, the defendant demonstrates a form of hostility towards another on the grounds of race or religion, this will be sufficient for an offence under s 28. This was made clear by the Divisional Court on two occasions in *DPP v McFarlane* [2002] EWHC 485 (Admin) and *DPP v Woods* [2002] EWHC 85 (Admin), which concerned the use of racially abusive language expressed in anger and frustration. The Divisional Court was strong in emphasising that once the basic offence is proven, and it can be proven that the defendant demonstrated hostility on grounds of race or religion, the aggravated offence is proven.

example

Jack and Jill are arguing over a parking space in a shopping centre and, in a state of anger, Jill attacks Jack with her handbag and utters racial abuse in doing so.

In this case, although Jill's argument with Jack is not motivated by race (at least not expressly), she has demonstrated hostility towards him as a result of race. On that basis, Jill would be liable in accordance with s 28(1)(a).

in practice

It is often difficult for prosecutors to prove a case under s 28(1)(b). Without an express statement by the defendant that his actions were motivated by hostility towards the victim based on race or religion (for example in a confession), the prosecution is unlikely to succeed. The prosecution will thus rely on background evidence to support its case to establish a motive. For example, should the defendant be a member of, or have an association with, a racist group, or have made some express statement in the past, the prosecutor may find this evidence useful in securing a conviction.

9.9 Further reading

Offences against the person

Horder, 'Reconsidering Psychic Assault' [1998] Crim LR 392.

Ormerod and Gunn, 'In Defence of *Ireland*' [1997] 3 Web JCLI.
Stannard, 'Sticks, Stones and Words: Emotional Harm and the English Criminal Law' (2010) 74 J Crim L 533.

Consent

Allen, 'Consent and Assault' (1994) 58 J Crim L 193.
Bamforth, 'Sado-Masochism and Consent' [1994] Crim LR 661.
Cooper and James, 'Entertainment – The Painful Process of Re-thinking Consent' [2012] Crim LR 188.
Murphy, 'Flogging Live Complainants and Dead Horses: We May No Longer Need to Be in Bondage to *Brown*' [2011] Crim LR 758.
Pegg, 'Not So Clear Cut: The Lawfulness of Body Modifications' [2019] Crim LR 579.

Transmission of infection

Ryan, 'Reckless Transmission of HIV: Knowledge and Culpability' [2006] Crim LR 981.
Withey, 'Biological GBH: Overruling *Clarence*?' (2003) 153 NLJ 1698.

- Non-fatal offences against the person are concerned with offences of violence that do not result in death.
- Such offences of violence may be charged at a basic level or at an aggravated level where the violence was motivated by hostility towards the victim on the grounds of religion or ethnicity.
- Common assault is a statutory offence charged in circumstances where the defendant has caused another to fear the application of unlawful force or actually inflicts unlawful force upon them.
- Common assault may be consented to so long as the victim has the capacity to consent and the freedom to do so.
- Assault occasioning actual bodily harm (ABH) is charged in circumstances where a defendant causes an assault or battery which results in the victim suffering bodily harm that is more than merely transient or trifling.
- Grievous bodily harm (GBH) is chargeable where the defendant has caused really serious harm to another; wounding is chargeable where the defendant causes a wound to the victim (a break in both layers of the skin).
- GBH and wounding may also be charged at a more serious level where the defendant has the intention to cause GBH or resist lawful apprehension.

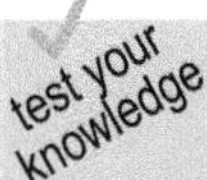

Problem

Jack visited his friend Jill at her home. Whilst there, the pair engaged in consensual sexual intercourse. Unbeknownst to Jack, he was a carrier of HIV and caused Jill to contract the same infection. Also during their exchange, Jill whipped Jack several times across the back and buttocks causing welts to his skin. Jack consented to the whipping across the back, but not across the buttocks.

Advise Jack and Jill as to their potential liability.

Essay

'The present structure of offences against the person is riddled with complexity, confusion and difficulty. The Law Commission's 2015 scoping report will eradicate these problems.'

Critically discuss this statement. In doing so, consider the current problems with the law of non-fatal offences and whether the Law Commission proposals will deal adequately with these problems.

chapter 10

Sexual Offences

After reading this chapter, you will be able to understand:

- the purpose of classifying sexual offences as distinct from non-fatal offences against the person
- the offence of rape, its elements and punishment upon conviction
- the offence of assault by penetration, its elements and punishment upon conviction
- the offence of sexual assault, its elements and punishment upon conviction
- the offence of causing a person to engage in sexual activity, its elements and punishment upon conviction.

10.1 Introduction to sexual offences

The law of sexual offences is one of the most troubling and difficult subjects for students to read and to get to grips with given its nature. Indeed, the law of sexual offences is also a challenging and stressful area in which to practise.

In this chapter, we shall consider the four most common sexual offences found on an undergraduate criminal law course. These are the offences of:

- rape (**10.2**);
- assault by penetration (**10.3**);
- sexual assault (**10.4**); and
- causing a person to engage in sexual activity without consent (**10.5**).

For a superb discussion of the key themes, historical developments and sociological influences on the law of sexual offences, see Pegg & Davies, *Sexual Offences: Law and Context* (Routledge, 2016).

10.1.1 Sexual offences, myths and stereotypes

It is unfortunate that the law of sexual offences is predicated on myths and stereotypes relating to both the defendant and complainant in a given case. These 'myths' or commonly held beliefs, ideas or explanations, although misconceived, have created false impressions around sexual offences. The Crown Prosecution Service (CPS) released a public document entitled 'Societal Myths' which it hoped would enable people to 'recognise these myths [reproduced below] and challenge them at every opportunity'.

As part of your learning, you must ensure that you remain critical and practical in your approach. Therefore, in reading through these myths, think of the sort of implications that they may present to a jury faced with such propositions. Think of how the jury may treat these implications and then consider the true facts that are present in the majority of cases.

Table 10.1 Myths of rape

Myth
Rape occurs between strangers in dark alleys
Women provoke rape by the way they dress or act
Women who drink alcohol or use drugs are asking to be raped
Rape is a crime of passion
If she didn't scream, fight or get injured, it wasn't rape
You can tell if she's 'really' been raped by how she acts
Women cry rape when they regret having sex or want revenge
Only gay men get raped/only gay men rape men
Prostitutes cannot be raped
If the victim didn't complain immediately it wasn't rape

These myths naturally raise the implications that:

- home is safe;
- rapes are randomly committed;
- the victim is to blame for being raped;
- rape is for sexual gratification;
- women who 'dress up' to attract attention are 'asking for it'.

In the real world, however, these myths have no foundation. In fact, you will find that:

- the majority of rapes are committed by persons known to the victim;
- victims are often raped in their homes;
- only the rapist is responsible for the rape;
- rape is often a demonstration of power and control, and not for sexual gratification.

It is the job of the prosecution to ensure that the jury do not take such prejudices into the jury room and acquit the defendant based on such assumptions (in *R v D* [2008] EWCA Crim 2557 the Court of Appeal accepted that a judge may give appropriate directions to the jury to mitigate the risk of stereotypes and assumptions). However, it is also essential to note that the defendant has a right to present his case. If his case is that he 'reasonably believed' that the complainant was consenting because she was not struggling or screaming, this is a valid defence and ought to be placed before a jury.

10.1.2 A brief history

Unlike other areas of law, such as homicide-related offences that have been stagnant for a number of years, the law relating to offences categorised as 'sexual offences' has seen substantial and fast-moving change in recent years.

Amendment of the former law was inevitable. Lord Falconer in the House of Lords described the previous law as 'archaic, incoherent and discriminatory' in nature (HL (2002), vol 644, col 771). This was in furtherance of the position taken by Temkin ('Getting it Right: Sexual Offences Law Reform' (2000) 150 NLJ 1169) who argued that the old law was 'cumbersome and inadequate' in its application.

The Sexual Offences Act (SOA) 2003 represented a major overhaul of the law of sexual offences. Its introduction came about as a result of an independent review by the

Home Office ('Setting the boundaries, reforming the law on sexual offences' (Vol 1, 2000)) and a White Paper on the same topic (Home Office, 'Protecting the Public: Strengthening the Protection Against Sex Offenders and Reforming the Law on Sexual Offences' (Cm 5668, 2002)). The Home Secretary at the time, David Blunkett, made it clear in the White Paper that

> Protection for children and the most vulnerable is a priority for the Government. All crime has a damaging effect on individuals and communities. But sexual crime, especially against children, can tear apart the very fabric of society. We live in a world of mass communication where access to degrading material is easily available and where common values can be undermined by the behaviour of a minority. The laws on sex offences were in desperate need of modernisation. They did not reflect today's society and attitudes or provide effective protection against today's crimes. For the past 50 years people have been reluctant to engage in these difficult issues.

The terms of the Home Office Review were stated as follows:

> To review the sex offences in the common and statute law in England and Wales, and make recommendations that will:
>
> - provide coherent and clear sex offences which protect individuals, especially children and the more vulnerable, from abuse and exploitation;
> - enable abusers to be appropriately punished; and
> - be fair and non-discriminatory in accordance with the ECHR and Human Rights Act.

From these terms of reference, the Review was founded on three key themes, which are detailed in **Table 10.2**.

Table 10.2 Themes of sexual offences reform

'Theme'	Explanation
Protection	The government wished to 'provide a framework of law that would deter and prevent sexual violence from happening, enable perpetrators to be prosecuted fairly and to provide justice to victims'. By doing so, they would enhance protection to the most vulnerable in society.
Fairness	The government wished to 'recommend a law that was self-evidently fair to all sections of society, and which made no unnecessary distinctions on the basis of gender or sexual orientation'.
Justice	The government wished to balance 'the need to increase protection for the complainant with upholding the interests of justice and fairness to defendants'. To do so, it stated that it was 'essential that the law is clear and evidently fair and just for both prosecution and defence and this is as important for sexual offences as for other crimes.

Whilst many of the previous offences were removed from the statute books, a number of new offences were created to reflect modern times and culture. The Act was brought into force by way of statutory order, namely the Sexual Offences Act 2003 (Commencement Order) 2004 (SI 2004/874). The Act came into force on 1 May 2004. **Figure 10.1** provides a brief history of sexual offences in England and Wales.

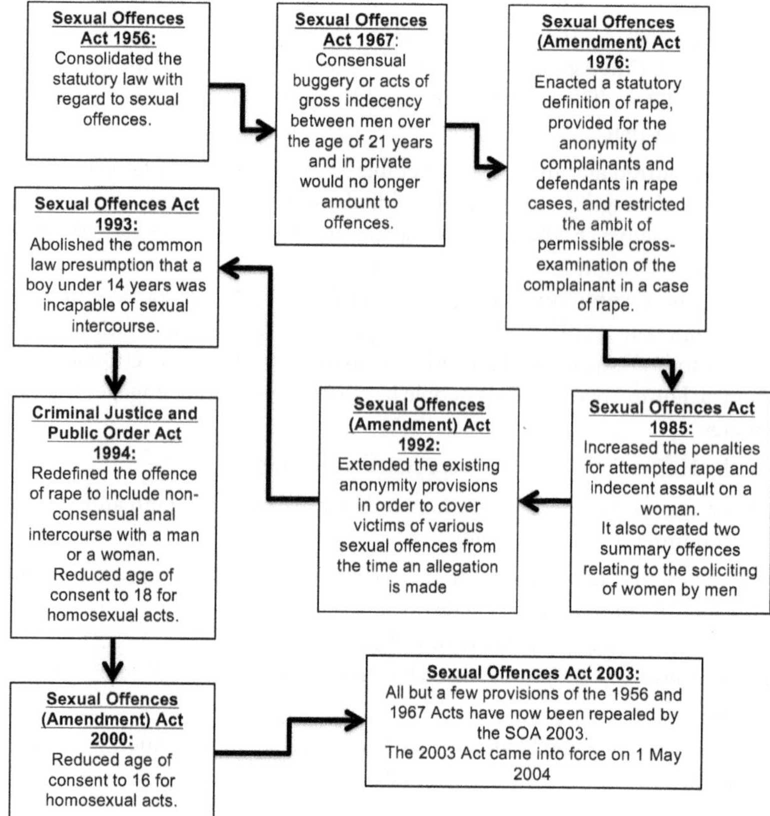

Figure 10.1 History of sexual offences legislation

10.1.3 Charging sexual offences

As with homicide, considered in **Chapter 8**, there is no single 'sexual offence'. Instead, there are a number of offences, known as 'principal' offences, contained in the SOA 2003. The SOA 2003 came into force on the 1 May 2004 and applies to all offences committed on or after that date. The effect of the SOA 2003 was to repeal all previous statute law in relation to sexual offences and restate them in the SOA 2003. Some offences were restated; other offences removed. Should an offence have been allegedly committed prior to 1 May 2004, the old rules apply. Where there is confusion or uncertainty as to which point the offence took place, see s 55 of the Violent Crime Reduction Act 2006.

There are a number of offences which are both outside of the SOA 2003 and outside the scope of this text. These include:

- offences involving prostitution, contrary to Part II of the Policing and Crime Act 2009; and
- taking, distributing or possessing indecent images of children, contrary to s 1 of the Protection of Children Act 1978 and s 160 of the Criminal Justice Act 1988.

in practice

Rape cases can be difficult to prove. This is so because the evidence is frequently limited to the victim's word against that of the defendant. In the majority of cases, the parties are not disputing that sexual intercourse took place; rather they dispute whether or not the complainant consented.

In proving or defending one's case, a number of evidential issues arise in sexual offences cases. Specifically, the defendant will often seek to rely on the sexual history of the complainant in an attempt to argue that the complainant consented because she has 'done it before'. Recall, for instance, the case of Ched Evans. In this case, the defendant (Evans) adduced evidence of the complainant's sexual history demonstrating that she had, on a number of previous occasions, had sexual intercourse with two other men in very similar circumstances. The general rule is that such evidence of sexual history/behaviours is restricted and may only be admitted where certain conditions are met (see s 41 of the Youth Justice and Criminal Evidence Act 1999). See also *R v Evans (Chedwyn)* [2012] EWCA Crim 2559 and his second appeal via the CCRC: [2016] EWCA Crim 452.

The defence may also wish to allege that the complainant has fabricated the entire story by reference to her delay in reporting the crime to the police. Delay may be justified on the grounds of fear, shame, guilt or embarrassment; however, the defence is still likely to argue that such delay means that the complaint is false. Commonly, the defence will ask the jury to consider why the complaint was delayed – it will often try to persuade the jury into thinking that the complainant used the time in order to construct a viable story against the defendant. Ultimately, if the defence can persuade the jury of this, the jury will clearly sway towards finding for the defendant.

Evidence is not a part of most criminal law modules; however, in order to understand the context of the law of sexual offences, it may be worth briefly reading around the subject.

10.1.4 Offences against children

This chapter is concerned primarily with sexual offences committed against adult complainants. However, it is useful here briefly to discuss the law relating to sexual offences against children (for these purposes, we mean persons above the age of consent, ie 16 years of age). The SOA 2003 identifies three categories of offences against children of different ages. They are:

- offences against those under 13 (SOA 2003, s 5–8);
- offences against those under 16 (SOA 2003, ss 9–15); and
- offences against those under 18.

The offences against a child under 13 largely mirror those that we shall be considering in this chapter, for example rape, assault by penetration and sexual assault; however, these offences apply specifically to children under the age of 13. In such cases, consent is irrelevant given that a child under 13 cannot be said to hold the legal capacity to consent to any form of sexual activity or conduct. During the passage of the Sexual Offences Bill, Lord Falconer said:

> A fundamental justification for the under-13 offence is the age and vulnerability of the victim. We do not think it is right that where the victim is 12 or under the question of consent should arise. There will be many cases where it would be

utterly invidious for a 12 year old or under to have to give evidence in relation to consent.

From this, the prosecution need only prove two facts:

- the intentional sexual activity (as defined in ss 5–8); and
- proof of the complainant's age (ie that they are 12 or younger).

Although the prosecution is under an obligation to prove that the defendant was intentional in his sexual activity with the child (ie it must prove his *mens rea*), the age of the complainant is strict in the sense that there is no requirement to prove that the defendant knew, or believed, that the complainant was a child under the age of 13. The House of Lords in *R v G* [2008] UKHL 37 confirmed such an interpretation to be in line with Article 6 of the ECHR. On this, see Spencer, 'The Sexual Offences Act 2003: Child and Family Offences' [2004] Crim LR 347.

For a detailed discussion of sexual offences against children, see Rook and Ward in their seminal authority, *Rook and Ward on Sexual Offences. Law & Practice*, 5th edn (Sweet & Maxwell, 2019).

10.1.5 General principles

Before we move on to discuss the substantive law of specific sexual offences, it is important to note a few general principles that apply to all sexual offences:

(a) *Naming of parties:* In a matter concerning a sexual offence, the appropriate terminology to use is that of defendant and complainant (as opposed to victim). As a matter of simplification, the Act refers to the defendant as 'A' and to the complainant as 'B'.

(b) *Type of offence:* All offences detailed in the SOA 2003 are conduct crimes, meaning that there is no requirement to prove causation, and crimes of basic intent, meaning that voluntary intoxication is of no defence (*R v Heard* [2008] QB 43).

(c) *Consent:* All sexual offences require proof of a lack of consent on the part of the complainant and a lack of reasonable belief in consent on the part of the defendant. It is essential that these two elements are not confused, nor are they mixed. They form two key and distinct elements of an offence.

(d) *Marital rape:* As a result of the landmark decision of *R v R (Rape: Marital Exemption)* [1992] 1 AC 599, the House of Lords overturned the law that a man may not be liable for the rape of his wife (a principle not formerly recognised, as Ormerod and Laird (*Smith, Hogan, & Ormerod's Criminal Law*, 15th edn (OUP, 2018)) put it, '[t]o the shame of the criminal law'). The husband in *R v R* unsuccessfully appealed to the ECtHR in *CR v UK* [1996] 1 FLR 434.

10.1.6 Practical considerations

It is worth bearing in mind that the law of sexual offences deals with some of the most challenging and upsetting cases in the law. In that regard, it may be helpful to appreciate some practical considerations relevant to sexual offences. Given that this is a text of the substantive law, and not one of procedure or evidence, our discussion shall not extend further than a simple list of issues.

Table 10.3 Practical consideration of sexual offences

Issue	Explanation
Complainant's sexual history	By s 41(3) of the Youth Justice and Criminal Evidence Act 1999, evidence may be adduced, or questions may be asked, regarding the 'sexual behaviour' of the complainant. This is only possible in narrow circumstances. It should be questioned whether the complainant's previous history is ever relevant to a trial given that consent is supposed to be 'issue and person' specific.
Anonymity	As a result of the Sexual Offences (Amendment) Act 1992, complainants in sexual offences cases are protected by the rules of anonymity (ie their name, address and image are protected). No such protection applies to defendants, however.
Cross-examination	Although s 34 of the Youth Justice and Criminal Evidence Act 1999 prescribes that a defendant may no longer personally cross-examine a complainant in a sexual case, this does not mean that complainants are protected from a form of 'secondary victimisation' suffered as a result of the style of questioning adopted by defence counsel. Ellison ('Cross-examination in Rape Trials' [1998] Crim LR 605) likens cross-examination of complainants to 'bullying and browbeating'.

10.1.7 Rationale behind sexual offences

In the previous chapter, we discussed the law relating to non-fatal offences against the person. This chapter is concerned with a specific form of non-fatal offence, ie sexual offences. It is for this reason that Horder (*Ashworth's Principles of Criminal Law*, 9th edn (OUP, 2019)) refers to this general area of law as non-fatal *violations* against the person. The fundamental principle behind the law of sexual offences is the determination to protect an individual's bodily autonomy. Lacey, Wells and Quick (*Reconstructing Criminal Law*, 4th edn (CUP, 2010)) are quick to note, however, that the term autonomy is a loose one at best. Specifically, the trio note that

> Bodily autonomy can demand protection in two senses: first, protection of one's own choices, and second, protection against interference by others.

Bodily autonomy, however, has not always been at the forefront of the rationale for a law against unwanted sexual activity. Sexual offences law was originally designed to protect the virginity of the complainant – owing to the religious principle that a female should remain a virgin unless and until she is married. Further to this, protection of a woman's virginity was often considered as protection of the proprietary right held by men over their wives, daughters and sisters (Burgess-Jackson, *Rape: A Philosophical Investigation* (Dartmouth, 1996)).

It was not until the mid-20th century that the principle of personal autonomy was recognised. However, there remains no agreed consensus on whether autonomy leads the race in providing a rationale for the law of sexual offences. For instance, Rubenfeld ('The Riddle of Rape-by-Deception and the Myth of Sexual Autonomy' (2013) 122 Yale LJ 1372) argues that to consider rape as a violation of bodily autonomy is a 'red herring'. Rather, Rubenfeld argues that sexual offences are best considered as violations of self-possession, akin to slavery and torture. This view can be furthered by Gardner and Shute ('The Wrongness of Rape' in Horder (ed), *Oxford Essays in Jurisprudence* (OUP, 2000)) who argue that sexual offences are a denial or interference with the 'personhood' of an individual given the apparent humiliation and dehumanising nature of such offences. Similarly, Childs ('Sexual Autonomy and Law' (2001) 64 MLR 309) argues that bodily autonomy is not the key; the key is the psychic and emotional autonomy that follows with it.

Regardless of the view that one takes towards the rationale of sexual offences, it is accepted by all that sexual offences are some of the worst crimes that are capable of commission.

We shall now go on to consider the substantive offences that may be charged against an individual.

10.2 Rape

Rape is not an offence created by the SOA 2003. Rather, the SOA 2003 had the effect of amending the previous common law and statute law and replacing it with a more modern and approachable definition. Under the former law, in s 1 of the SOA 1956, it was an offence for a man to rape a woman by penetration of the vagina. There was no protection against penetration of any other orifice of a woman, nor was there protection for homosexual rape. It was only in 1994 with the introduction of the Criminal Justice and Public Order Act 1994 that the law recognised rape of the anus, thus allowing for homosexual rapes.

Now, in accordance with the SOA 2003, rape is a statutory offence which may be committed by a man upon a woman or another man. The key element of rape, compared with other forms of sexual intercourse, is the lack of consent.

10.2.1 Defining rape

Rape is likely to be the most commonly understood of all the sexual offences. It remains one of the nastiest and most intrusive offences that may be committed against an individual and is largely comprehended by the majority of the public. However, rape remains a difficult and challenging offence to grasp given the focus on the victim's consent, coupled with the defendant's belief in consent. These competing claims are often present in everyday trials and give rise to the law's complexity.

Importantly, even if the complainant did not consent, the defendant can still avoid liability by proving that, at the time of the offence, he reasonably believed the complainant consented. In actual fact, therefore, trials often come down to the question of the defendant's belief.

10.2.2 Elements of rape

Section 1 of the SOA 2003 provides:

> (1) A person (A) commits an offence if—
> > (a) he intentionally penetrates the vagina, anus or mouth of another person (B) with his penis,
> > (b) B does not consent to the penetration, and
> > (c) A does not reasonably believe that B consents.
>
> (2) Whether a belief is reasonable is to be determined having regard to all the circumstances, including any steps A has taken to ascertain whether B consents.
>
> (3) Sections 75 and 76 apply to an offence under this section.

The *actus reus* and *mens rea* of rape are outlined in **Table 10.4**.

Table 10.4 Elements of rape

AR/MR	Elements of the offence
Actus reus	(i) penetration; (ii) of the vagina, anus or mouth; (iii) with a penis; (iv) without the complainant's consent.
Mens rea	(i) intentional penetration; (ii) without reasonable belief in consent.

We shall consider each element in turn.

10.2.2.1 *Actus reus:* (i) penetration

Penetration, although not specifically defined in the SOA 2003, is described in s 79(2) as a 'continuing act from entry to withdrawal'. This would suggest that penetration need not be substantial or repetitive.

According to the Court of Appeal in the pre-2003 Act case of *R v Cooper and Schaub* [1994] Crim LR 531, even the slightest penetration is sufficient and ejaculation is not relevant to liability. Although there is no express reference in the SOA 2003 that penetration is complete without ejaculation, one can refer to the previous law under s 44 of the SOA 1956 which detailed that 'it shall not be necessary to prove the completion of the intercourse by the emission of seed'. It would be absurd to suppose that the law is not the same today, and given the fact that s 2 of the SOA 2003, amongst other offences, requires 'penetration' without the use of a penis, it only makes sense that ejaculation is irrelevant.

A question that has come before the courts on a number of occasions is the circumstance where the defendant lawfully penetrates the complainant, who subsequently retracts their consent. Quite simply, according to the Privy Council in *Kaitamaki v The Queen* [1985] AC 147, if consent to penetration is no longer present, despite it first being so, the man must withdraw his penis. This was exemplified in *R v Cooper and Schaub* where the Court of Appeal provided that if the man is aware that a person has ceased to consent to penetration, he cannot claim that there was consent to its continuation (*R v Leaver* [2006] EWCA Crim 2988). These cases demonstrate the importance of s 79(2): that penetration is a continuing act from entry to withdrawal.

10.2.2.2 *Actus reus:* (ii) of the vagina, anus or mouth

At common law, rape protected only against penetration of the vagina. Therefore, it was an offence only capable of commission by a man against a woman. Temkin ('Getting it Right: Sexual Offences Law Reform' (2000) 150 NLJ 1169) states that the justification in this narrow concept arose in the historic background to rape, namely that it was an offence protecting a woman's virginity.

By 1994, the concept of anal rape was introduced by s 142 of the Criminal Justice and Public Order Act 1994 and, in 2003, the concept of oral rape was introduced by the SOA 2003. These changes were in line with more modern thinking that sexual offences should protect sexual and bodily autonomy more generally.

As of 2003, the defendant may be liable for rape where he penetrated either the:

- vagina;
- anus; or

- mouth.

As a result of the expansion in terms, a man may now also be the victim of rape.

Vaginal penetration

At common law, the vagina was to be construed in the general sense of 'female genitalia' (*R v F* [2002] EWCA Crim 2936, per Bell J). The term was further expanded upon by the SOA 2003 to include the vulva – the outer part of the vagina (s 79(9)) – and includes surgically reconstructed vaginas (s 79(3) – ie male-to-female transgender). According to the Assize Court in *R v Hughes* (1841) 9 Car & P 752, it is not necessary to show that the hymen has been ruptured, merely that there has been some penetration, however slight, of the vulva.

Penetration of the anus or mouth

Under the former law, non-consensual anal sex was not to be considered rape but, rather, was to be considered as an offence of buggery. Likewise, non-consensual oral sex was not considered to be an offence of rape but, rather, an offence of indecent assault – an offence that no longer exists. Following the SOA 2003, both are now considered rape.

Penetration of more than one orifice

Where the defendant is alleged to have committed rape by penetrating the complainant in more than one orifice, for example both the vagina and anus, the defendant is liable for multiple offences of rape. This is justified on the basis that although there is only one transaction involving the complainant, the defendant has performed multiple acts (or forms) of non-consensual penetration and thus ought to be liable for multiple acts of rape. Importantly, such multiple counts should be charged and tried separately so as not to taint the mind of the jury on the issue of penetration of a different orifice to the one charged.

example

Jack met Jill at a bar and took her back to his place to engage in sexual intercourse. Jill told Jack that he could penetrate her vagina, but not her anus. Jack intentionally penetrates Jill's anus despite her statement. Subsequent to this, Jill has now retracted consent to intercourse completely. Jack then begins to penetrate Jill's vagina.

In this case, Jack is potentially liable for two counts of rape:

- rape of the anus; and
- rape of the vagina.

Should he be liable for both, the prosecution should try the counts separately with a different jury for each count. This is to ensure that the jury do not convict the defendant on count two, because they have also convicted him on count one.

Uncertainty as to the penetrated orifice

In some cases, there may be an uncertainty as to which orifice was penetrated. Remember that rape may only be committed by penetration with a penis. Let us take a look at our example again but with different facts.

example

Jack, whilst back at his place with Jill, grabs a beer bottle and starts to penetrate Jill's vagina with it. At the same time, Jack with his penis is penetrating Jill's anus. Jill does not consent to either penetration and cannot be sure whether Jack's penis penetrated her vagina, anus or both.

In this scenario, the Court of Appeal in *R v K* [2008] EWCA Crim 1923 has ruled that where there is uncertainty as to whether penetration with a penis was of the vagina or of the anus, the prosecutor is permitted to allege penetration of 'the vagina *or* the anus'. This will entitle the jury to convict the defendant of rape if they are sure that there was non-consensual penetration of one or the other by the defendant with his penis. In *K*, the Court of Appeal confirmed that this charge would not be bad for duplicity.

Despite the relatively recent acknowledgement of penetration of the anus (1994) and of the mouth (2003) in the offence of rape, the law is clear that a defendant's sentence will not be distinguished on the orifices penetrated. This was the statement of Lord Woolf CJ in *R v Ismail* [2005] EWCA Crim 397, where his Lordship stated that 'the fact that this was oral rape does not mean that it is any less serious than vaginal or anal rape'.

10.2.2.3 *Actus reus:* (iii) with a penis

The next requirement of the *actus reus* of rape is that the penetration must be with a penis. This means that the offence of rape can only be committed by a man (as a principal offender) or transgender person (see below).

The restriction of the offence to men alone has led many to question the legitimacy of this provision. The Home Office in its Report, *Setting the Boundaries* (2000), considered the removal of this requirement in order to achieve what it called 'gender equality'. In the end, the Government concluded that the 'penis' element of the offence should remain to reflect the general characterisation and perception of rape as an action of non-consensual *sex* (thus requiring a penis) involving the risk of injury to the complainant (both physical and emotional) and the risk of pregnancy and disease transmission. Should penetration occur with any other object, or body part, the appropriate charge would be assault by penetration under s 2 of the SOA 2003 (see **10.3**).

Age of the man

Prior to the SOA 1993, it was presumed that a boy under the age of 14 was incapable of sexual intercourse. This presumption was abolished by s 1 of the SOA 1993. Now, so long as the child is above the age of criminal responsibility, he may be liable for rape.

Transgender defendants

The definition of penis does include that of a post-operative transgender person who can commit rape with his surgically constructed penis (SOA 2003, s 79(3)).

Can a woman commit rape?

At the start of this section, we qualified the statement that only a man can commit rape as a principal offender. This means that a woman cannot be a principal offender but can be an accessory (see **Chapter 4**). A woman who encourages or assists a man to penetrate another, without reasonably believing the other person is consenting, may be liable for aiding and abetting rape (*R v Cogan and Leak* [1976] QB 217). A woman who causes a man to penetrate her vagina, anus or mouth without his consent may be liable for causing a person to engage in sexual activity, contrary to s 4 of the SOA 2003 (see **10.5**).

10.2.2.4 *Actus reus:* (iv) without the complainant's consent

The final element of the *actus reus* is that there must be an absence of consent on the part of the complainant. Consent is a feature of all sexual offences under the SOA 2003. The majority of our discussion will be present in this section, and when considering other offences later in this chapter, you will be referred back to this point in an effort to avoid repetition. As a result, many of the cases we look at in this section do not relate to the offence of rape but are still applicable as establishing general principles of law.

Under the old law, the SOA 1956 contained no statutory definition of 'consent'. Instead, juries were told that the word should be given its 'ordinary meaning' (*R v Olugboja* [1982] QB 320) and that they should apply their common sense and good judgement in defining consent. The jury, in this sense, were the arbiters of both law (the definition of consent) and fact (the application of consent in the present case). Williams (*Textbook of Criminal Law* (Stevens & Sons, 1978)) appreciated the danger of this and critically stated that this was 'one more manifestation of the deplorable tendency of the criminal courts to leave important questions of legal policy to the jury'. Allowing the jury to decide a matter of law was clearly inappropriate in the law of sexual offences, which thus resulted in the enactment of a statutory definition in s 74 of the SOA 2003. For a defence of the approach in *Olugboja*, see Gardner, 'Appreciating *Olugboja*' (1996) 16 LS 275.

Consent is now detailed in statutory form in ss 74–76 of the SOA 2003.

Table 10.5 Consent and sexual offences

Section	Rule
Section 74	Provides a general definition of consent.
Section 75	Provides six specified circumstances which give rise to a rebuttable presumption that there was no consent.
Section 76	Provides two conclusive presumptions (ie not rebuttable) that no consent is present where the defendant deceives the complainant.

We shall now consider each section in detail.

in practice

In practice, the sections would be considered in descending order from s 76 to s 74. The reason for this is due to the conclusive nature of s 76 in that should the complainant have been deceived, it shall be conclusively presumed (ie not rebuttable) that no consent was present. Should s 76 fail, the prosecution would then attempt to find a circumstance in s 75 to argue a rebuttable presumption that the complainant did not consent. In the majority of cases, the prosecution will be forced to retreat to the general definition of consent in s 74, allowing both sides to argue whether consent was present in a given case. As such, although they are laid out sequentially in this text, you are advised in answering problem questions to approach them as follows (in relation to consent):

s 76 ➡ s 75 ➡ s 74

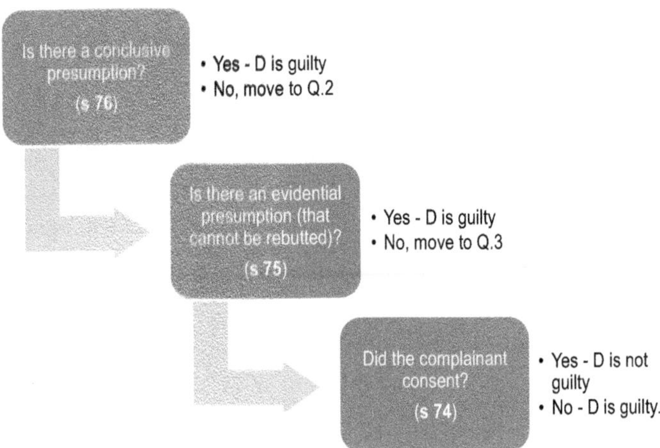

Figure 10.2 Dealing with consent

Despite its continued use in practice, the rationale for adopting this structure is admittedly unclear. Temkin and Ashworth ('Rape, Sexual Assaults and the Problems of Consent' [2004] Crim LR 328) attempt to give meaning to this tripartite construction of consent. Specifically, the pair raise the following question:

> Are the three categories intended to reflect some kind of moral hierarchy, so that the most serious cases of non-consent give rise to irrebuttable presumptions and the next most serious to rebuttable presumptions, with the remainder falling within the general definition? Or is the organising principle one of clarity and certainty, so that it is the clearest cases (not necessarily the worst) that give rise to irrebuttable presumptions and the next clearest to rebuttable presumptions, with the remainder falling within the general definition? Or is it a mixture of the two, with an added element of common law history?

Further to this, the Court of Appeal in *R v H* [2006] EWCA Crim 853 emphasised that it is not necessary to direct a jury in every case on all aspects of the law of consent. Where the ss 76 and 75 presumptions do not apply, the judge should not make reference to them and should allow the jury simply to consider the ordinary meaning of consent in s 74. This approach can be seen in the Court of Appeal's judgment in *R v Taran* [2006] All ER (D) 173. In this case, the complainant was raped at gun point. The Court of Appeal followed *R v H* and explained that there was no need to explain to the jury the intricacies of ss 75 and 76 in such a case. Here, it was obvious the complainant had not consented and there could be no basis for asserting that the defendant held a reasonable belief in consent.

Before proceeding to our discussion of consent, one brief diversion is necessary. What is the situation where the complainant cannot remember whether they had consented or not? This question was recently answered by the Court of Appeal in *R v Tambedou* [2014] EWCA Crim 954, also known as *R v T(S)*, where the Court confirmed that a lack of recollection or memory as to whether the complainant consented would not be fatal to a prosecution. Specifically, Rafferty LJ commented that '[t]he jury was entitled to consider absence of consent and to distinguish it from evidence of absence of memory'.

General meaning (SOA 2003, s 74)

Section 74 of the SOA 2003 provides that

> a person consents if he agrees by choice, and has the freedom and capacity to make that choice.

This definition is of great importance and allows the jury to focus on the autonomy of the complainant, with emphasis placed on the idea of 'free choice'. The phrase 'agrees by choice' would appear to denote a requirement for some positive sign of willingness on the part of the complainant. The Court of Appeal in *R v Malone* [1998] 2 Cr App R 447 made it clear that such agreement by choice is different to a simple absence of objection, although such objection would be clear evidence of non-consent. As a result of s 74, consent, or lack thereof, can cover a range of behaviour from enthusiastic agreement to reluctant acquiescence to violent submission, all of which the jury must determine.

As discussed above, under the old law, the jury were required to establish their own understanding of consent and then apply that understanding to the case before them. As a result of s 74, the jury merely needs to apply this definition of consent to the facts before them.

In addition to the concept of agreement through choice, the definition in s 74 also raises two issues which we must consider in further depth:

(a) Does the complainant have the *capacity* (ie the age and understanding) to make a choice about whether or not to take part in the sexual activity at the time in question?
(b) Was the complainant in a position to make that choice *freely*, and was not constrained in any way?

Assuming that the complainant had *both* the freedom and capacity to consent, the crucial question is whether the complainant agrees to the activity by *choice*.

The next section will look at the concepts of capacity and free choice in turn, before then considering the application of s 74 to cases of intoxication and cases of so-called 'conditional consent'.

Before that, it is worth noting that the jury will always be assisted in their enquiries into consent by understanding the surrounding context of the case. This was made clear by the Court of Appeal in *R v C* [2012] EWCA Crim 2034.

case example

Charge:
Rape (SOA 2003, s 1)

Case progression:
Crown Court – Guilty

Court of Appeal – Conviction upheld

Point of law:
Apparent consent is not real consent

In *R v C* [2012] EWCA Crim 2034, the defendant had sexually abused the complainant, his step-daughter, over the course of her life, starting when she was 5 years old, with the most recent offence taking place at the age of 25. The defendant was charged and convicted with 18 different sexual offences, including rape, in the Crown Court.

The defendant appealed to the Court of Appeal, arguing that the complainant had consented in the later years to such sexual activity. The Court of Appeal disagreed, ruling that the apparent consent when she was an adult was not real, given the abusive and controlling role the defendant had established in her childhood.

Lord Judge CJ observed that:

> the reality of this case cannot be understood without reference to the long years of the complainant's childhood during which, as the jury found, she was the victim of repeated sexual abuse by the appellant. ... [E]vidence of prolonged grooming and potential corruption of the complainant when she was a child provided the context in which the evidence of her apparent consent after she had grown up should be examined and assessed ...

His Lordship went on to conclude:

> Once the jury were satisfied that the sexual activity of the type alleged had occurred when the complainant was a child, and that it impacted on and reflected the appellant's dominance and control over the complainant, it was open to them to conclude that the evidence of apparent consent when the complainant was no longer a child was indeed apparent, not real, and that the appellant was well aware that in reality she was not consenting.

Capacity

Capacity is not defined in the SOA 2003. We know from para 139 of the Explanatory Notes to the SOA 2003 that capacity is concerned with age and mental disorder and whether, through such conditions, the individual *understood* what they were consenting to. 'Understanding' is the key to capacity.

According to Sir Igor Judge P in *R v Bree* [2007] 2 All ER 676, capacity is 'integral to the concept of "choice"' and, according to Lord Parker CJ in *R v Howard* [1966] 1 WLR 13, a complainant will not have had capacity to agree by choice where 'her understanding and knowledge was such that she was not in a position to decide whether to consent or resist'.

The most authoritative statement given on capacity is that given in *R v Cooper* [2009] 4 All ER 1033. Although *Cooper* dealt with an offence contrary to s 30 (sexual activity with a person with a mental disorder impeding choice), the principles of capacity remain relevant here.

case example

Charge:
Sexual activity with a person with a mental disorder impeding choice (SOA 2003, s 30)

Case progression:
Crown Court – Guilty

Court of Appeal – Conviction quashed

House of Lords – Conviction reinstated

Point of law:
Meaning of capacity

In *R v Cooper* [2009] 4 All ER 1033, the defendant befriended the complainant, offering her crack cocaine and making her perform oral sex on him and on another. The victim claimed that she had only consented out of fear for her own safety and admitted evidence of a history of mental disorders.

The defendant was charged with and convicted of a s 30 offence in the Crown Court.

The defendant appealed to the Court of Appeal which allowed his appeal on the basis that the complainant's capacity was not undermined by her mental disorders. The complainant understood what she was consenting to.

The House of Lords, on appeal, however, disagreed. Their Lordships concluded that the complainant may lack capacity in their ability to make a real choice, despite actually knowing the nature of the act they were consenting to.

Baroness Hale, in the House of Lords, ruled that to be able to make a decision, a person:

(a) must be able to understand the information relevant to making it; and
(b) must be able to weigh that information in the balance to arrive at a choice.

Further to this, Baroness Hale reasoned that '[o]ne does not consent to sex in general. One consents to this act of sex with this person at this time and in this place'. Ormerod and Laird (*Smith, Hogan, & Ormerod's Criminal Law*, 15th edn (OUP, 2018)) further this by stating that capacity is 'situation and person specific'.

A more recent statement on capacity has come from the Court of Appeal in *R v Avanzi* [2014] EWCA Crim 299 (also known as *R v A(G)*), where the Court stated that capacity to consent to sexual activities should be construed and informed by the definition and guidance relating to capacity in the Mental Capacity Act (MCA) 2005.

Section 2(1) of the MCA 2005 provides that

> a person lacks capacity in relation to a matter if at the material time he is unable to make a decision for himself in relation to the matter because of an impairment of, or a disturbance in the functioning of, the mind or brain.

Further to this, s 3(1) of the MCA 2005 provides that

> a person is unable to make a decision for himself if he is unable—
>
> (a) to understand the information relevant to the decision,
> (b) to retain that information,
> (c) to use or weigh that information as part of the process of making the decision, or
> (d) to communicate his decision (whether by talking, using sign language or any other means).

In *A Local Authority v H* [2012] EWHC 49 (COP), the Court of Protection was asked to determine whether H lacked capacity to consent to sexual relations, capacity to marry and capacity to make decisions about contraception. H was a 29-year-old woman, who suffered from mild learning difficulties and atypical autism and had an IQ of 64. On the first question asked, Hedley J explained:

> So let me turn then to s 3(1) of the 2005 Act with the question of sexual relations specifically in mind. First comes the question of understanding the relevant information, but what is that? Clearly a person must have a basic understanding of the mechanics of the physical act and clearly must have an understanding that vaginal intercourse may lead to pregnancy. Moreover it seems to me that capacity requires some grasp of issues of sexual health. However, given that that is linked to the knowledge of developments in medicine, it seems to me that the knowledge required is fairly rudimentary. In my view it should suffice if a person understands that sexual relations may lead to significant ill health and that those risks can be reduced by precautions like a condom. I do not think more can be required.

This approach would be approved by the Court of Protection in *London Borough of Southwark v KA* [2016] EWCOP 20.

The Court of Appeal in *Avanzi* emphasised that the jury would not be required to follow the strict step-by-step process that the courts must do in mental capacity proceedings; however, it would remain a useful starting point for the jury to consider the 2005 Act. In adopting the approach of the Civil Division of the Court of Appeal in the earlier case of *IM v LM* [2014] EWCA Civ 37, Macur LJ in *Avanzi* stated that:

> The question relating to the understanding of reasonable foreseeable consequences obviously should not become divorced from the actual decision-making process carried out in that regard on a daily basis by persons of full

> capacity ... [T]his process is 'largely visceral rather than cerebral, and owes more to instinct and emotion rather than to analysis'.

The Court of Appeal in *R v Hysa* [2007] EWCA Crim 2056 has reinforced that the question of capacity is one for the jury, not the judge.

Free choice (distinguishing consent from mere submission)

Where a complainant does have the capacity to consent, it must also be clear that they have the freedom to consent. As with capacity, 'freedom' is not defined in the SOA 2003, but has been developed in recent years through a number of Court of Appeal decisions. On a literal reading, 'freedom' refers to the situation where the complainant is free from external pressures or threats. Naturally, the reasons that a complainant may submit to sexual intercourse are endless. A few examples may assist in understanding why a complainant may submit to sexual activity:

- They may fear being subject to physical or emotional harm or violence.
- They may fear being subject to continuing torment or harassment.
- They may fear that they will suffer financially.
- They may fear that they will be alone without a partner or family.
- They may fear that they will be subject to a disparaging label or comment.

In this section, we shall consider the distinction between apparent consent and submission to consent.

A lack of consent can be seen where a complainant 'submits' or 'acquiesces' to sexual intercourse. Similarly, a complainant may 'freeze' with no protest, objection or resistance. In such cases of submission, it cannot be said that the complainant truly has a 'free choice' in the matter. Dunn LJ in *R v Olugboja* [1982] QB 320, a case involving submission as a result of fear of violence, stated that:

> [The jury] should be directed that consent, or the absence of it, is to be given its ordinary meaning and if need be, by way of example, that there is a difference between consent and submission; every consent involves a submission, but it by no means follows that a mere submission involves consent.

His Lordship would proceed to explain:

> [The jury] should be directed to concentrate on the state of mind of the victim immediately before the act of sexual intercourse, having regard to all the relevant circumstances; and in particular, the events leading up to the act and her reaction to them showing their impact on her mind.

In this regard, the jury are required to focus on the effect of anything said or done leading up to the relevant act to decide whether the complainant was actually consenting. The question is therefore subjective to the complainant.

Two authorities stand out at this stage. The first is that of *R v Kirk* [2008] EWCA Crim 434 which concerned a historical conviction for rape under the SOA 1956.

case example

Charge:
Rape (SOA 1956, s 1)

Case progression:
Crown Court – Guilty

Court of Appeal – Conviction upheld

Point of law:
Meaning of free choice

In *R v Kirk* [2008] EWCA Crim 434, the complainant, a homeless 14-year-old girl, agreed to sexual intercourse with the defendant for money so as to buy food (£3.25 to be exact). Evidence was admitted that the defendant had abused the complainant in the past, and the defendant was convicted of rape in the Crown Court.

The defendant appealed to the Court of Appeal on the basis that there was no evidence of pressure, threats or deception by the defendant at the time of the sexual intercourse. The Court of Appeal dismissed his appeal on the basis that the complainant had clearly submitted to sexual intercourse out of desperation due to her situation.

The second case, also under the old 1956 law, is that of *R v Robinson* [2011] EWCA Crim 916 where the Court of Appeal found that the complainant, a 12-year-old girl, had submitted to sexual intercourse. The Court took account of extensive evidence of grooming and previous accounts of mere 'acquiescence' but not 'enthusiastic consent'.

A more recent case, specifically in the context of grooming and its relevance to freedom of choice, is that of *R v Ali; R v Ashraf* [2015] EWCA Crim 1279. In this case, the defendants had allegedly groomed a number of young girls over a long period of time to such an extent that their consent had become merely compliance. In rejecting the defendants' appeal, that there was no evidence of a lack of consent, Fulford LJ concluded that compliance has the ability to 'mask true consent' on the part of a complainant. His Lordship went on to say:

> Although … grooming does not necessarily vitiate consent, it starkly raises the possibility that a vulnerable or immature individual may have been placed in a position in which he or she is led merely to acquiesce rather than to give proper or real consent. One of the consequences of grooming is that it has a tendency to limit or subvert the alleged victim's capacity to make free decisions, and it creates the risk that he or she simply submitted because of the environment of dependency created by those responsible for treating the alleged victim in this way. Indeed, the individual may have been manipulated to the extent that he or she is unaware of, or confused about, the distinction between acquiescence and genuine agreement at the time the incident occurred.

On this basis, the defendants were found liable under the SOA 2003. Fulford LJ would approve the directions of the trial judge: 'where there is evidence of exploitation of a young and immature person who may not understand the full significance of what he or she is doing, that is a factor the jury can take into account in deciding whether or not there was genuine consent.'

A more difficult case that has come before the courts is that of *R v Doyle* [2010] EWCA Crim 119 which concerned the rape of an ex-girlfriend. At first instance, evidence was admitted that the defendant and complainant had previously been involved in a volatile relationship involving significant periods of violence. However, it was also admitted that the pair on a number of occasions had settled their differences and made up. In his summing up, the trial judge made a stark distinction between 'reluctant but free exercise of choice on the one hand, especially in the context of a long term and loving relationship, and unwilling submission to demand in fear of more adverse consequences from refusal on the other'. The Court of Appeal approved the trial judge's distinction, explaining that it appropriately drew the line between the prosecution and defence case and that there was little opportunity for misunderstanding.

in practice

Although the distinction between free choice and submission looks obvious on these pages, it may not be so easy to make in practice. Consider long-term sexual relationships at one end of the spectrum and an individual losing their virginity at the other. In both cases, it may not be so easy for the jury to determine whether the actions of the individuals were free-willed or through reluctance. In such cases, a jury may require careful guidance on this point (*R v Watson* [2015] EWCA Crim 559).

Conditional consent and deception

In recent years, a number of cases have come before the courts which can best be described as cases of conditional consent. These cases involve a level of deception, outside the scope of s 76, where the complainant has given consent on the basis of a condition that has not been complied with.

Three key cases are worth discussing under this heading:

- *Assange v Swedish Prosecution Authority* [2011] EWHC 2849 (Admin);
- *R (F) v DPP* [2013] EWHC 945 (Admin); and
- *R v McNally* [2013] EWCA Crim 1051

Rogers ('The Effect of "Deception" in the Sexual Offences Act 2003' (2013) 9 Arch Rev 4) argues that there is severe inconsistency between these cases. Read the following summaries and see if you agree with him.

case example

Charge:
n/a
a case of extradition

Case progression:
High Court of Justice

Point of law:
Conditional consent

In *Assange v Swedish Prosecution Authority* [2011] EWHC 2849 (Admin), the defendant engaged in sexual intercourse with the complainant, known as 'AA', knowing that such consent was only given if the defendant wore a condom. The defendant did not wear a condom.

The High Court, in determining the defendant's extradition case, considered that such a deception (ie the wearing of a condom) fell outside the scope of the s 76 conclusive presumption, and as an 'issue of materiality' it could be determined under s 74.

Sir John Thomas P commented:

> It would plainly be open to a jury to hold that, if AA had made clear that she would only consent to sexual intercourse if Mr Assange used a condom, then there would be no consent if, without her consent, he did not use a condom, or removed or tore the condom without her consent. His conduct in having sexual intercourse without a condom in circumstances where she had made clear she would only have sexual intercourse if he used a condom would therefore amount to an offence under the Sexual Offences Act 2003, whatever the position may have been prior to that Act.

An interesting discussion at this stage may be had in comparing the decision in *Assange* with that of *R v B* [2007] 1 WLR 1567. We discussed the case of *B* briefly in **Chapter 10** when discussing the transfer of STIs. Recalling the cases of *R v Dica* [2004] QB 1257 and *R v Konzani* [2005] EWCA Crim 706, a defendant may be liable for an offence of grievous bodily harm (GBH) where they have either intentionally or recklessly caused the transmission of an STI. In such cases, the complainant requires informed consent in order for the defendant to be found not guilty. However, the question that came before the courts in *B* is whether such transmission would be enough to negate consent on part of the complainant.

example

Jack and Jill engage in sexual intercourse. Jack believes that he has contracted an STI from a previous partner but does not disclose this to Jill. Upon realising that Jack has an STI, Jill states that she would not have had sexual intercourse with him had she known of his condition.

In this example, Jill's consent is clearly conditional on the basis that Jack does not have an STI. We can say that this condition is inferred, given that no one wishes to be infected in such a way. On this basis, Jill's consent is similar to that at issue in *Assange*. However, the Court of Appeal in *B* ruled that such consent could not be vitiated by a lack of disclosure as to the STI, with Latham LJ stating that '[t]he act remains a consensual act'. Rogers ('The Effect of "Deception" in the Sexual Offences Act 2003' (2013) 9 Arch Rev 4) is highly critical of this decision, stating that it is inconsistent and without merit. Specifically he argues that

> If a man with HIV is charged for communicating it through sexual intercourse, having deceived his partner about his status, he faces a maximum penalty under s 20 of the OAPA. But following *Assange* a man who is sexually healthy and does not wear a condom which he is asked to wear can be charged for the more serious and stigmatic offence of rape.

Rogers questions whether we need to return to the state of law under *R v Tabassum* [2000] 2 Cr App R 328 or create a new offence specific to this scenario. For a reaffirmation of *R v B*, see *R v Lawrance* [2020] EWCA Crim 971 in respect of a deception as to the fertility of the defendant.

case example

Charge:
n/a
a case of judicial review

Case progression:
Divisional Court – decision of DPP should be reviewed

Point of law:
Conditional consent

In *R (F) v DPP* [2013] EWHC 945 (Admin), the defendant engaged in sexual intercourse with his partner on the clear understanding that he would not ejaculate inside her vagina. The defendant, however, failed to withdraw his penis before ejaculation.

The Divisional Court, in determining the judicial review claim against the DPP's refusal to prosecute the defendant, explained that the phrases 'choice', and 'freedom' to make such choice, must be considered in a 'broad common sense way'.

Lord Judge CJ commented that upon ejaculation into the complainant's vagina, the complainant was:

> deprived of choice relating to the crucial feature on which her original consent to sexual intercourse was based. Accordingly her consent was negated. Contrary to her wishes, and knowing that she would not have consented, and did not consent to penetration or the continuation of penetration if she had any inkling of his intention, he deliberately ejaculated within her vagina. In law, this combination of circumstances falls within the statutory definition of rape.

case example

Charge:
Assault by penetration (SOA 2003, s 2)

Case progression:
Crown Court – Guilty

Court of Appeal – Conviction upheld

Point of law:
Material deception based on gender

In *R v McNally* [2013] EWCA Crim 1051, the defendant (a female) entered into a relationship with the complainant, another female. The defendant presented herself as a man – a deception which she maintained throughout the relationship. The complainant was unaware of her true sex. The pair engaged on a number of occasions in sexual intercourse where the defendant would use a dildo to penetrate the complainant. Upon realisation of the deception, the defendant was charged and convicted with six counts of assault by penetration in the Crown Court.

The defendant appealed to the Court of Appeal, alleging that gender could not undermine the consent provided by the complainant. The Court of Appeal, however, disagreed and ruled that a deception as to gender can go towards undermining an individual's choice and freedom.

Leveson LJ reasoned that:

> Thus while, in a physical sense, the acts of assault by penetration of the vagina are the same whether perpetrated by a male or a female, the sexual nature of the acts is, on *any common sense view*, different where the complainant is deliberately deceived by a defendant into believing the latter is a male. Assuming the facts to be proved as alleged, [the complainant] chose to have sexual encounters with a boy and her preference (her freedom to choose whether or not to have a sexual encounter with a girl) was removed by the defendant's deception. (emphasis added)

As a result of *McNally*, the courts are clearly taking a wide interpretation as to what may amount to a material deception or conditional consent. Wary that such a ruling may expand the circumstances beyond reason, the court restricted such deceptions to 'active deceptions' and concluded that: 'In reality, some deceptions (such as, for example, in relation to wealth) will obviously not be sufficient to vitiate consent.'

Rogers ('The Effect of "Deception" in the Sexual Offences Act 2003' (2013) 9 Arch Rev 4) takes favour with the approach of the Court of Appeal in *McNally*. Rogers states that since the victim 'wished to experience a heterosexual encounter, the nature of the acts done by [the defendant] were thereby different'. Rogers goes on to say that the victim

> was used for the sexual gratification of another in a manner which in no way accorded with her own sexual preferences and it is right that she be regarded as the victim of a non-consensual sexual offence.

Sharpe ('Criminalising Sexual Intimacy: Transgender Defendants and the Legal Construction of Non-Consent' [2014] Crim LR 207), on the other hand, is critical of the decision in *McNally*, arguing that the rationale emphasised by Leveson LJ is contrary to transgender equality. Sharpe argues that there can be no deception where a transgender individual identifies themselves as a particular sex and then engages with another person under this identification. Specifically, Sharpe states that the defendant

> apparently identifies as female, a gender position consistent with her birth designated sex. At the time of the alleged offences, however, she appears to have identified and lived as a young man and made reference to her desire for gender reassignment surgery.

Sharpe goes on to say:

> [A]t the time of conviction and appeal there was sufficient information available to conclude that McNally identified as a male prior to and at the time of the alleged offences, and therefore that [the complainant's] apparent consent was valid consent and that McNally was not deceptive.

The decisions of *Assange*, *F*, and *McNally* are difficult to justify when one compares them with two of the more recent cases in this area, namely *R (Monica) v DPP* [2018] EWHC 3508 (QB) and *R v Lawrance* [2020] EWCA Crim 971. In *Monica*, the complainant had engaged in a sexual relationship with an undercover police officer, believing that he was an environmental protester (as the complainant was). Following discovery that he was in fact a police officer, the complainant alleged that she would never have consented to sexual intercourse had she known the truth. The DPP had refused to prosecute the police officer for rape and the complainant sought judicial review of that decision. The Divisional Court rejected the judicial review claim, finding that the deception of the police officer did not vitiate the complainant's consent. Lord Burnett and Jay J would identify that only 'deception which is closely connected with "the nature or purpose of the act", because it relates to sexual intercourse itself rather than the broad circumstances surrounding it, is capable of negating a complainant's free exercise of choice for the purposes of section 74 of the 2003 Act'. The Court of Appeal would use this quotation in *Lawrance* to establish the question to be asked, namely: 'The question is whether [the deception] is so closely connected to the nature or purpose of sexual intercourse rather than the broad circumstances surrounding it that it is capable of negating consent. Is it closely connected to the performance of the sexual act?' In *Lawrance*, the defendant had deceived the complainant into believing that he had had a vasectomy. The Court of Appeal considered that such deception was insufficient to vitiate consent. Lord Burnett CJ would conclude that 'a lie about fertility is different from a lie about whether a condom is being worn during sex [ie *Assange*], different from engaging in intercourse not intending to withdraw having promised to do so [ie *F*] and different from engaging in sexual activity having misrepresented one's gender [ie *McNally*]'. His Lordship would justify this on account that the complainant was 'deceived about the nature or quality of the ejaculate and therefore of the risks and possible consequences of unprotected intercourse ... [but not about] the physical performance of the sexual act'.

Intoxicated consent

In many instances, the complainant may be intoxicated at the time of sexual intercourse. Dependent on their level of intoxication, it may be the case that the complainant's capacity was affected to such an extent that they could not give full and true consent. We shall see below that intoxication is a circumstance relevant to the evidential presumption in s 75(2). Here, however, we consider the situation when the evidential presumption does not apply, or if the defendant has successfully rebutted the evidential presumption.

Sir Igor Judge P, as he then was, in the case of *R v Bree* [2007] 2 All ER 676 set out a number of points that may need to be addressed in a judge's summing up to the jury:

(1) Consumption of alcohol or drugs may cause someone to become disinhibited and behave differently. If she is aware of what is happening, but the consumption of alcohol or drugs has caused her to consent to activity which she would ordinarily refuse, then she has consented no matter how much she may regret it later. The fact that a person makes an unwise choice does not mean that she lacked the capacity to make it. *A drunken consent is still a consent* if a person has the capacity to make the decision whether to agree by choice.

(2) However, if a complainant becomes *so intoxicated* that she no longer has the capacity to agree, there will be no consent. Clearly she will not have the capacity to agree by choice where she is so intoxicated through drink or drugs, and her

understanding and knowledge are *so limited* that she is not in a position to decide whether or not to agree. (This relates to understanding and knowledge of what is going on, as opposed to the quality of the decision-making.)

(3) A person may reach such a state without losing consciousness. For instance, the complainant may be in a state where she knows that she does not want to take part in any sexual activity with someone, but she is *incapable of saying so*. Alternatively, she may have been affected to such a degree that, whilst having some limited awareness of what is happening, she is incapable of making any decision at all.

(4) If a person is asleep or has lost consciousness through drink or drugs, she cannot consent, and that is so even though her body responds to the accused's advances.

The approach in *Bree* has been expressly endorsed by the Court of Appeal in *R v Coates* [2008] 1 Cr App R 52 and more recently by the Court of Appeal in *R v Kamki* [2013] EWCA Crim 2335.

Figure 10.3 provides a summary of consent and intoxication following *R v Bree*.

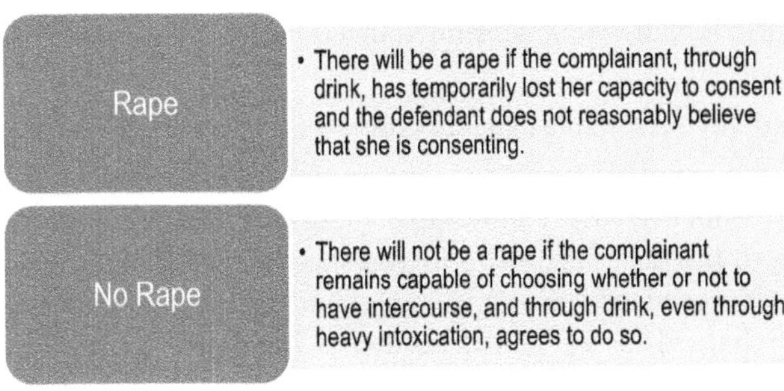

Rape
• There will be a rape if the complainant, through drink, has temporarily lost her capacity to consent and the defendant does not reasonably believe that she is consenting.
No Rape
• There will not be a rape if the complainant remains capable of choosing whether or not to have intercourse, and through drink, even through heavy intoxication, agrees to do so.

Figure 10.3 Understanding consent and intoxication

in practice

It is necessary to consider how it can be proven that the complainant was in such a state that he or she was incapable of consenting to sexual intercourse. For instance, evidence from friends, taxi drivers and forensic physicians describing the complainant's intoxicated state may support the prosecution case. Further, it may be possible to obtain expert evidence in respect of the effects of alcohol/drugs and the effects if they are taken together. On these sorts of issues, see the highly controversial case of *R v Evans (Chedwyn)* [2012] EWCA Crim 2559 (original appeal); [2016] EWCA Crim 452 (subsequent appeal).

What happens if the complainant does not remember what happened?

This question is rife with difficulty given the numerous circumstances in which it may arise. For instance, a complainant may have been asleep or unconscious when the alleged assault took place. Likewise, a complainant may have been so intoxicated that they cannot remember what happened. In these circumstances, what is the position in law? In *R v Hysa* [2007] EWCA Crim 2056 (also known as *R v H*), the defence alleged that the fact that the complainant cannot remember whether she consented or not would be 'fatal' to a prosecution. The Court of Appeal did not agree and, citing *Bree*, ruled that the question remains one for the jury.

Evidential presumptions (SOA 2003, s 75)

Section 75 of the SOA 2003 provides:

> (1) If in proceedings for an offence to which this section applies it is proved—
>
> (a) that the defendant did the relevant act (defined in section 77),
> (b) that any of the circumstances specified in subsection (2) existed, and
> (c) that the defendant knew that those circumstances existed,
>
> the complainant is to be taken not to have consented to the relevant act unless sufficient evidence is adduced to raise an issue as to whether he consented, and the defendant is to be taken not to have reasonably believed that the complainant consented unless sufficient evidence is adduced to raise an issue as to whether he reasonably believed it.

Section 75 operates to find a defendant liable for rape in the circumstances described in s 75(2). The circumstances in s 75(2) raise a presumption of no consent which may then be rebutted and challenged by the defendant. Section 75(1) is clear in this regard; should one of the circumstances in s 75(2) arise, coupled with the defendant's knowledge of that circumstance, then it will be presumed that:

- the victim did not consent (*actus reus*); and
- the defendant did not hold any reasonable belief in consent (*mens rea*).

In order for the presumption against consent to not apply, the defendant must satisfy the judge by adducing evidence which shows that there is a 'real issue' about consent that is worth putting to the jury. Section 75 imposes an evidential burden on the defendant to prove the existence of evidence capable of rebutting the presumption. Where the defendant has discharged his evidential burden, s 75 ceases to have any application and the jury should not hear of the rebuttable presumptions. The prosecution then retains the legal burden of proving beyond a reasonable doubt that the complainant did not consent in accordance with s 74 and that the defendant did not reasonably believe that the complainant consented.

in practice

In practice, the evidence produced may be from evidence that the defendant himself gives in the witness box, or from evidence given on his behalf by a defence witness, or resulting from evidence given by the complainant during cross-examination.

The Court of Appeal in *R v Ciccarelli* [2012] 1 Cr App R 190 ruled that, before the question of the defendant's reasonable belief could be left to the jury, some evidence 'beyond the fanciful or speculative' had to be adduced (per Lord Judge CJ). A mere assertion of belief in consent, therefore, is not sufficient.

In order to presume an absence of consent/a lack of reasonable belief in consent under s 75, the prosecution must prove three matters:

(a) the accused did a relevant act under s 77;
(b) any of the circumstances in s 75(2) existed; and
(c) the defendant knew those circumstances existed.

Without these three factors, the s 75 presumption must not be placed before the jury. Instead, the jury should be directed in accordance with s 74. This was the judgment of the Court of Appeal in *R v White* [2010] EWCA Crim 1929 which emphasised that a s 75 presumption will exist *unless* sufficient evidence is adduced by the defendant to raise an issue as to whether the complainant consented. Specifically, Goldring LJ ruled (citing *Blackstone's Criminal Practice*):

> There must be some foundation in the evidence and it must not be merely speculative or fanciful for there to be sufficient evidence. However, it is vital to understand that if the trial judge decides (presumably at the close of the evidence) that there is sufficient evidence to raise an issue as to whether the complainant consented and/or the accused reasonably believed that the complainant was consenting, then the judge will put the issues to the jury in accordance with the key sections (ie 74 and 1(2)), and *the section 75 route is barred.* In the relatively rare cases where the judge decides that there is not sufficient evidence on one or both of the issues, a section 75 direction must be given on that issue. (emphasis added)

This approach was justified by the Court of Appeal in *R v Kapezi* [2013] EWCA Crim 560, which ruled that an evidential presumption must not be elevated to a conclusive presumption by placing it before a jury where evidence is present to rebut.

We shall consider each factor now.

Relevant act

The reference to a relevant act in s 75(1)(a) simply means the respective *actus reus* and *mens rea* of that offence. The relevant acts are defined in s 77 as follows:

Table 10.6 Relevant acts under s 77

Offence	**Relevant act**
Rape	The defendant intentionally penetrating, with his penis, the vagina, anus or mouth of another person ('the complainant').
Assault by penetration	The defendant intentionally penetrating, with a part of his body or anything else, the vagina or anus of another person ('the complainant'), where the penetration is sexual.
Sexual assault	The defendant intentionally touching another person ('the complainant'), where the touching is sexual.
Causing a person to engage in sexual activity without consent	The defendant intentionally causing another person ('the complainant') to engage in an activity, where the activity is sexual.

The circumstances

Section 75(2) lists six exhaustive circumstances ((a)–(f)) that will raise a presumption against consent which may then be rebutted by the defence. Where a circumstance arises that falls outside the definition in s 75, this shall be dealt with under s 74. Note that the circumstances listed below are paraphrased from the statute – please refer to the statute for the full wording of s 75.

Table 10.7 Circumstances under s 75(2)

Circumstances	**Authority**
(a) Use of violence or threat of immediate violence against the complainant. *NB the violence need not come from D (it could come from his friend).*	*R v Dagnall* [2003] EWCA Crim 2441

Circumstances	**Authority**
(b) Use of violence or threat of immediate violence against *another* person. *NB the violence need not come from D.*	None yet reported
(c) The complainant was unlawfully detained (ie cases of kidnap). *NB D must not also be detained (ie a fellow kidnapee).*	*R v David T* [2005] EWCA Crim 2668
(d) The complainant was asleep or unconscious.	*R v Blacklock* [2006] EWCA Crim 1740; *R v Ciccarelli* [2012] 1 Cr App R 190. See also the pre-2003 case of *R v Larter and Castleton* [1995] Crim LR 75
(e) The complainant had a physical disability by which he was unable to communicate any consent or lack of consent to the defendant.	*R v Cooper* [2009] 4 All ER 1033
(f) The complainant was administered with a substance that was capable of stupefying or overpowering them. *NB the substance must have been administered without consent; D need not administer the substance.*	*R v Abbes* [2004] EWCA Crim 1813

The statute does not require that the existence of these circumstances *caused* the complainant to lack consent. Rather, the Act merely prescribes that where a circumstance is found to exist, the complainant's lack of consent is to be presumed.

All of the above circumstances are self-explanatory and can be understood by reading the cases cited. A number of points do have to be made in relation to circumstance (a) and (b) which are the most common evidential presumptions to arise. Specifically, the violence or threat must occur either at the time of the relevant act or immediately before it began (SOA 2003, s 75(3)). Therefore, it does not relate to future violence (which would be dealt with under s 74). Further, the violence must relate to violence to a person; it does not involve violence to property. Threats to destroy property would be relevant under s 74 of the SOA 2003.

For a critique of s 75 and the circumstances therein, see Temkin and Ashworth, 'The Sexual Offences Act 2003 – (1) Rape, Sexual Assaults and the Problems of Consent' (2004) Crim LR 328.

Defendant knew of those circumstances

This provision was inserted by the SOA 2003 to ensure that the defendant was given all reasonably opportunity to rebut a s 75 presumption. Although s 75(1)(c) provides that the defendant must know that '*those* circumstances existed', the defendant need only have knowledge of *one* circumstance.

In cases where he was unaware that such circumstances were present, there can be no s 75 presumption. However, these circumstances will still be relevant under s 74.

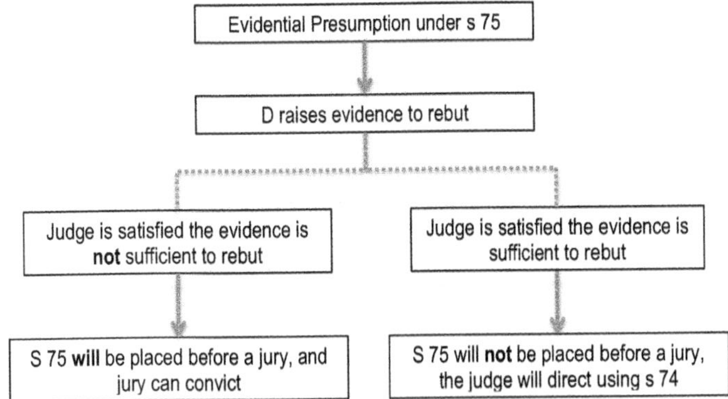

Figure 10.4 Understanding the rebuttable presumption

Conclusive presumptions (SOA 2003, s 76)

Section 76 of the SOA 2003 provides (emphasis added):

> (1) If in proceedings for an offence to which this section applies it is proved that the defendant did the relevant act and that any of the circumstances specified in subsection (2) existed, *it is to be conclusively presumed*—
> (a) that the complainant *did not consent* to the relevant act, and
> (b) that the defendant *did not believe* that the complainant consented to the relevant act.
>
> (2) The circumstances are that—
> (a) the defendant *intentionally* deceived the complainant as to the *nature or purpose* of the relevant act;
> (b) the defendant *intentionally induced* the complainant to consent to the relevant act by impersonating a *person known personally* to the complainant.

Section 76 operates to conclusively find a defendant liable for rape in the circumstances described in s 76(2). We know this because s 76(1) expressly states that should the defendant fulfil either of the circumstances, it shall be conclusively proven (ie that D cannot rebut) that the complainant did not consent (the *actus reus*) and the defendant did not reasonably believe that the complainant consented (the *mens rea*). As above in relation to s 75, a 'relevant act' must have been committed under s 77. The same rules apply to s 76 as they do under s 75.

There are a number of terms that have been emphasised in the statute that we shall now consider in greater depth.

Table 10.8 Understanding the terms in s 76

Term	Meaning
Nature	The physical action itself. Does the complainant appreciate that the act itself is of a sexual nature, for example?
Purpose	The reason for the action. Does the complainant appreciate that the purpose of the act is for a sexual reason, for example?
Deception	There must be an actual deception on part of the defendant. If the complainant is mistaken as to the nature or purpose and there is no deception on the part of the defendant, there is no conclusive presumption.

Term	Meaning
Intention	The defendant must intentionally deceive the complainant. Where the defendant inadvertently deceives the complainant without necessarily realising it, he may not be subject to a conclusive presumption.
Induce	The deception must induce or cause the complainant to consent. Where the complainant would have consented irrespective of the deception, there is no conclusive presumption. Note that this only applies to deception as to identity.

Nature or purpose (SOA 2003, s 76(2)(a))

The first circumstance under s 76(2)(a) is concerned with the 'nature or purpose' of the defendant's actions. Under this section, the complainant must have been intentionally deceived by the defendant as to the nature or purpose of his actions. The 'quality' of his actions, for example lies told as to attributes, qualities and characteristics of the defendant, are not relevant (*R v Jheeta* [2007] EWCA Crim 1699).

Please note that the statute is explicit in that the complainant need only be deceived as to the nature *or* purpose of the act. Deception need not require both.

Let us look at a few examples in the case law to understand the operation of this section:

- *R v Tabassum* [2000] 2 Cr App R 328: The defendant conducted breast examinations for his own sexual gratification. He did so on the pretence that he was collecting data for a cancer screening programme and required participants. In this case, the Court of Appeal ruled that there was clearly no genuine consent given by the complainants because they had only consented to the act believing it to be of a medical nature and for a medical purpose. See also *R v Flattery* (1877) 2 QBD 410 and *R v Kumar* [2006] EWCA Crim 1946.
- *R v Green* [2002] EWCA Crim 1501: The complainants were asked to masturbate to assess their potential for impotence. The defendant was undertaking this action for sexual gratification, as opposed to conducting a medical test or purpose as the complainant thought. Whilst not a case of rape, the principle of consent is still applicable, and *Jheeta* has confirmed that this would, today, amount to deception as to the purpose of the act.
- *R v Williams* [1923] 1 KB 340: A singing teacher convinced his pupil to engage in sexual intercourse with him in order to 'improve her singing' by creating an air passage to strengthen her breathing. Naturally, should this case have arisen today, there would be a deception as to the nature *and* purpose of the act given that the complainant believed the nature of the act to be to improve her singing and likewise in respect of the purpose of the act. The defendant's conviction for rape was upheld on appeal.

example

Jack is a doctor who has called Jill in for a medical examination. He claims that he must digitally penetrate her vagina to undertake a certain test. Jack is not undertaking a test but is deriving sexual gratification from his actions.

In this case, although Jill is aware of the nature of the action, ie digital penetration, she is not aware of the true 'purpose' of the action, namely sexual gratification. On this basis, Jill has been deceived as to the nature or purpose of the activity (see *R v Flattery* (1877) 2 QBD 410 for a case involving similar facts).

The test of 'nature or purpose' was arguably expanded in the case of *R v Devonald* [2008] EWCA Crim 527.

case example

Charge:
Causing another to engage in sexual activity (SOA 2003, s 4)

Case progression:
Crown Court – Guilty

Court of Appeal – Conviction upheld

Point of law:
Meaning of nature or purpose

In *R v Devonald* [2008] EWCA Crim 527, the defendant was the father of a girl who had recently split up with the complainant. The defendant sought revenge for the complainant breaking up with his daughter and wished to embarrass him by 'teaching him a lesson'. The defendant posed as a young woman and persuaded the complainant to masturbate in front of a webcam which he would then place online. The defendant was convicted in the Crown Court by use of the s 76 presumption and appealed, arguing that there was no deception as to the nature or purpose of the sexual activity.

The Court of Appeal agreed that there was no deception as to the nature of the act (ie sexual conduct on a webcam) but, rather, there was deception as to the purpose of the act.

Leveson LJ concluded that:

> On the facts, as we have described them, it is difficult to see how the jury could have concluded otherwise that the Complainant was deceived into believing that he was indulging in sexual acts with, and for the sexual gratification of, a 20-year-old girl with whom he was having an on line relationship. That is why he agreed to masturbate over the web cam. In fact, he was doing so for the father of his ex girlfriend who was anxious to teach him a lesson doubtless by later embarrassing him or exposing what he had done.

The defendant was thus guilty of an offence under s 4.

Devonald has caused much controversy amongst practitioners and academics as a result of the broad interpretation of 'purpose' adopted by the Court of Appeal. One could explain *Devonald* on the basis that the complainant was deceived as to the motives of the defendant. Indeed, this is the approach adopted by Miles ('Sexual Offences: Consent, Capacity and Children' (2008) 10 Archbold News 6) who explains *Devonald* as follows:

> ... wherever D's true view of the relevant act's purpose (whether sexual or non-sexual) is unknown to V—in the context of s 76, because he has intentionally induced V's participation on the basis of some other ostensible purpose—the latter's consent is vitiated. This may be the right approach. Whether Vs wrongly think they are participating in a sexual act or a non-sexual act, their sexual autonomy—their right to decide whether to engage in sexual conduct (or not)—is compromised by either type of mistake. But this justification would take us quickly towards accepting any sort of 'but for' mistake as a vitiating mistake, a position that is surely too broad.

Devonald also demonstrates that a defendant may have multiple purposes, ie to induce sexual behaviour and embarrass the complainant. In this situation, the court must ask itself what the 'dominant' purpose was that the complainant may be deceived as to. *Devonald* may have had the effect of expanding the scope of 'nature and purpose' beyond that intended by Parliament. Suppose in *R v Green* [2002] EWCA Crim 1501, the defendant was genuinely undertaking a medical examination to test impotence amongst men. During the examination, however, the defendant also received sexual gratification from the acts performed by the participants. In that case, the defendant has two purposes, and it will be for the court to consider whether the complainants were deceived by the defendant's secondary purpose – ie sexual gratification.

Allen and Edwards (*Criminal Law*, 15th edn (OUP, 2019)) argue that *Devonald* was 'wrongly decided' and reason that the case would more appropriately fall under s 76(2)(b). As convincing as this argument is, the prosecution would equally have struggled under s 76(2)(b) to convince a jury that the defendant impersonated a person known personally to the accused. Although there is evidence in *Devonald* that the defendant built a relationship with the complainant before asking him to masturbate online, there remains no evidence to suggest that the defendant was impersonating someone 'known personally' to the complainant, given that the person whom the defendant was impersonating was both random and unknown to the complainant. A more promising argument against the judgment in *Devonald* is that raised by Rogers ('*R v Devonald*: Consent and the "purpose" of the defendant' (2008) 72(4) J Crim L 280) who suggests that the Court of Appeal went too far in *Devonald* by failing to distinguish between the purpose of the *act* (as is required by the offence) and the purpose of the *actor* (not a requirement of the offence).

We can compare the outcomes in *Tabassum*, *Green* and *Devonald* with a number of other cases in this area:

- *R v Linekar* [1995] QB 250: A pre-2003 Act case, the Court of Appeal emphasised that 'fraud' is concerned only with deception as to the nature or purpose of the act itself; or the identity of the defendant. In that case, the defendant was charged with and convicted of rape. The complainant, a prostitute, consented to sexual intercourse on the basis that the defendant would pay for her time (£25 to be specific). The defendant agreed to pay but refused to pay after engaging in sexual intercourse. The complainant claimed that she would not have consented if she had known that the defendant had no intention to pay her. The Court of Appeal allowed the defendant's appeal on the basis that the complainant was deceived as to neither the nature (sexual intercourse) nor purpose (sexual gratification) of the act; nor was she deceived as to the identity of the defendant. On this basis, should this case be heard today, there would be no conclusive presumption in play as the intention to not pay would not be a deception as to the nature of the act, within the meaning of the Act. On a similar front, see *R v B* [2007] 1 WLR 1567, in which a failure to disclose HIV was not a deception as to the nature of the act. The woman had still consented to the act of sexual intercourse and there was no deception there (he could have been liable for GBH if he had been charged with that offence – see **Chapter 9**). Surely, if *Linekar* were to repeat itself in today's world, there could be a deception as to the purpose of the act; from the complainant's point of view, the purpose of sexual intercourse was to make money. Could it be said that she was deceived as to the purpose, given that the defendant never intended to pay her? (See *Jheeta* for the answer.)
- *R v Jheeta* [2007] EWCA Crim 1699: The defendant deceived and pressured the complainant into having sexual intercourse on more frequent occasions than she would have done otherwise. Specifically, the defendant sent text messages to the complainant purporting to be from the police, directing her to sleep with defendant or she would be liable for a fine. The reason it is said to be unique is that there was no evidence in this case that the complainant was deceived as to the nature or purpose of the activity. Although such conduct might be described as deceptive or persuasive, the complainant was not deceived as to the nature and

purpose of the conduct. As such, no conclusive presumption could stand. However, the defendant remained liable for rape by use of s 74. In *Jheeta*, the Court took the opportunity to consider the outcome of *Linekar* if it were to be heard today. The Court concluded that there would be no deception within the meaning of s 76(2)(a) given that reference to 'nature or purpose' relates to the penetration, not to what would happen after penetration (ie being paid). Doubt could be raised on this following *R v Devonald*.

- *R v Matt* [2015] EWCA Crim 162: The defendant, a plumber, posed as a film maker and deceived the complainant into believing that she was undergoing a casting process. In doing so, the defendant was able to convince the complainant to perform sexual acts with him. The Court of Appeal found there to be a deception under s 76(2)(a) as to the purpose of the activity. The complainant believed the purpose to be one of simulated sexual pleasure for commercial purposes, whereas the real purpose was simply one of sexual gratification on the part of the defendant.

The final case for comparison is one of the more recent authorities on this point, namely that of *R v Bingham* [2013] EWCA Crim 823 (also known as *R v B*).

case example

Charge:
Causing another to engage in sexual activity (SOA 2003, s 4)

Case progression:
Crown Court – Guilty

Court of Appeal – Conviction quashed

Point of law:
Use of s 76(2)(a)

In *R v Bingham* [2013] EWCA Crim 823, the defendant was charged with seven counts of causing the complainant to engage in sexual activity without consent. The defendant used pseudonyms to establish an online Facebook relationship with the complainant. Sometime into the relationship, the defendant persuaded and then blackmailed the complainant into providing him with photographs of her engaging in sexual activity. He was convicted in the Crown Court by use of s 76(2)(a).

The Court of Appeal held that reliance at trial upon s 76 was 'misplaced'. The nature or purpose of the act by the defendant was sexual gratification, and there was no deception as to that.

Hallett LJ ruled that:

> reliance upon section 76 in this case, on these facts and this evidence, was misplaced. The prosecution needed to look no further than the provisions of section 74. It provides that 'a person consents if he agrees by choice and has the freedom and capacity to make that choice'. If the complainant only complied because she was being blackmailed, the prosecution might argue forcefully she did not agree by choice.

In a previous paragraph, her Ladyship commented that:

> There is, therefore, a great danger in attempting any definition of the word *purpose* and in defining it too widely. A wide definition could bring within the remit of section 76 situations never contemplated by Parliament.

Bingham had the effect of casting significant doubt on the case of *Devonald*. Indeed, Hallett LJ was clear to the extent that '[i]f there is any conflict between the decisions in *Jheeta* and *Devonald*, we would unhesitatingly follow *Jheeta*'. *Devonald* was not overruled by *Bingham*, however, and remains good authority. Laird ('Rapist or rogue? Deception, consent and the Sexual Offences Act 2003' [2014] Crim LR 492) commends the approach of the court in *Bingham*. Specifically, Laird comments that 'the applicability of s 76 has been reduced to vanishing point'. He argues that more cases are likely to be determined using s 74 alone and that this practice 'is to be welcomed'.

Table 10.9 Summary of cases under s 76(2)(a)

Case	Description	Deception as to nature or purpose
R v Tabassum	Breast examination for sexual gratification and not medical purposes	✓
R v Green	Masturbation examination for sexual gratification and not medical purposes	✓
R v Williams	Sexual intercourse for sexual gratification and not to improve singing voice	✓
R v Devonald	Intention to embarrass victim and not to engage in sexual gratification	✓
R v Linekar	Refusal to pay for sexual intercourse	×
R v Jheeta	Pressuring the complainant to engage more frequently in sexual intercourse than she would otherwise have done	×
R v Matt	Convincing the complainant to engage in sexual conduct as part of a film casting process	✓
R v Bingham	Blackmailing the complainant to engage in sexual activity	×

Person known personally (SOA 2003, s 76(2)(b))

The second circumstance under s 76(2)(b) is concerned with the situation where the defendant impersonates a 'person known personally' to the complainant. This section, to the dismay of the Law Commission ('Consent in the Criminal Law' (Law Com No 139, 1995), is not concerned with deception as to specific attributes of the defendant, for example that he has a well-paid job, or that by engaging in sexual activity with him, the complainant would earn a promotion (*R v Richardson* [1999] QB 444; though see *R v Melin* [2019] EWCA Crim 557 in **Chapter 9**). Rather, this section covers situations where, for example, the defendant impersonates the complainant's partner and thereby causes the complainant to consent to the relevant sexual act. Under the former law, s 142(3) of the Criminal Justice and Public Order Act 1994 stated that it was rape where a man induces a woman to engage in sexual activities by impersonating her husband. This restriction was extended to other long-term relationships outside of marriage by the Court of Appeal in *R v Elbekkay* [1995] Crim LR 163. As a result of s 76(2)(b), the law has now been extended to 'persons known personally'. Although Ormerod and Laird (*Smith, Hogan, & Ormerod's Criminal Law*, 15th edn (OUP, 2018)) comment that 'this [provision] is a welcome extension', it is argued that the section is also clouded with difficulty.

case example

Charge:
Rape (SOA 1956, s 1)

Case progression:
Crown Court – Guilty

Court of Appeal – Conviction upheld

Point of law:
Deception as to identity

In *R v Elbekkay* [1995] Crim LR 163, the defendant at night time entered the bedroom of the complainant who believed him to be her boyfriend. The pair engaged in sexual intercourse, despite the defendant realising the complainant's mistake. Upon realising her mistake, the complainant punched the defendant and ran. The defendant was charged with and convicted of rape in the Central Criminal Court, the trial judge having directed the jury that the statutory presumption involving an impersonation of a husband should extend to impersonation of a long-term partner.

The Court of Appealed upheld the defendant's conviction. McGowan LJ explained that:

> How could we conscientiously hold that it is rape to impersonate a husband in the act of sexual intercourse, but not if the person impersonated is merely, say, the long-term, live-in lover, or in the even more modern idiom, the 'partner' of the woman concerned?
>
> The vital point about rape is that it involves the absence of consent. That absence is equally crucial whether the woman believes that the man she is having sexual intercourse with is her husband or another.

Should *Elbekkay* be heard today, it is likely that the same conclusion would be reached. A number of points are still worth considering under this section:

(1) The person impersonated must be someone 'known personally' to the complainant. This means that the complainant cannot claim to have been induced to engage in sexual intercourse with a film or sports star in circumstances where they have not met them. Arguably this is more restrictive than the approach taken in *Elbekkay* when McCowan LJ referred to the victim's mistaken belief that they were engaging in sexual intercourse with 'her husband *or another*' (emphasis added). This presumption could not, therefore, have been used in *R v Bingham* [2013] EWCA Crim 823, given that the complainant never knew the fictitious person called Grant from the USA.

(2) The impersonation must 'induce' the complainant to consent to sexual activities. This is, essentially, a test of causation. The impersonation must induce (cause) the complainant to consent. This wording allows the defence to argue that the complainant was not 'induced' as a result of the impersonation but, rather, would have consented irrespective of the impersonation (eg A sleeps with B because he looks like C, even though A knows that B is not actually C).

(3) The defendant must intend to deceive the complainant (as opposed to merely inadvertently deceiving the complainant). The point of intention then begs the question of whether the defendant can intentionally deceive by way of omission.

example

Jill is in a bar with her friends enjoying a few drinks. Jack comes through the door and Jill believes him to be a famous TV presenter that she has met on a number of previous occasions. Jill says to Jack, 'I've never been with a celebrity before.' Jack merely smiles and says nothing. Jack and Jill engage in sexual intercourse. After intercourse, Jack informs Jill that he is not the celebrity she is thinking of.

This case raises the question of whether Jack has intentionally deceived Jill by his omission to correct her mistake. If one takes a literal reading of the SOA 2003, it would seem to suggest that the defendant is not liable for rape where he simply takes knowing advantage of the complainant's own mistake. In this regard, it might be said that s 76(2)(b) is more restrictive than the approach taken in *Elbekkay*. Despite this, however, it is contended that the defendant in *Elbekkay* would still be liable for rape by the conclusive presumptions in s 76 on the following bases:

- he knew the complainant was mistaken;
- he failed to correct that mistake (thus intending to deceive);
- he engaged in sexual intercourse with the complainant as a result of that deception (ie the complainant was induced by that deception); and
- the partner, whom the complainant believed the defendant to be, was a person known to the complainant personally.

in practice

There is little case law on the operation of this section in practice; therefore, the courts are left to apply their discretion as to whether a defendant impersonated a 'person known personally' to the complainant. It is questionable, then, how far this provision extends. A number of questions can be asked:

- Is a single meeting, even if brief, enough to know a person 'personally'?
- Must there be a number of meetings? If so, how many? Of what duration?
- Are email communications sufficient to know a person 'personally'?
- What details must an individual know of another to know them 'personally'?

Section 76 operates as a conclusive presumption. This means that once it is satisfied and other elements of the offence are satisfied also (ie penile penetration of the vagina, anus or mouth) then the defendant must be convicted. There is no ability to rebut a s 76 presumption. Interestingly, Tadros ('Rape without Consent' (2006) 26 OJLS 515) argues that these cases ought not to be considered as cases where there is conclusive evidence of no consent; instead, they should be considered as cases of simply no consent. Tadros comments:

> Where the victim has been deceived as to the nature of the act this means there is no consent, not just that there is good evidence of no consent.

10.2.2.5 *Mens rea:* (i) intentional penetration

The first element of the *mens rea* of rape is that penetration must be intentional. According to the Court of Appeal in *R v Heard* [2008] QB 43, a case relating to sexual assault, intention simply means deliberate and free-willed.

example

Jack is asleep. Whilst asleep, Jill penetrates herself using Jack's penis.

In this scenario, Jack would not be liable for rape as there is no intention on his part to penetrate Jill. Jill, on the other hand, would be liable for causing a person to engage in sexual conduct without consent contrary to s 4 of the SOA 2003 (see below).

It is therefore questionable whether a defendant can 'accidentally' or 'non-deliberately' penetrate the complainant. It is submitted that in circumstances where the defendant has a reasonable belief in consent to penetrate the complainant's vagina but unintentionally and accidentally penetrates her anus, the defendant ought not to be liable for an offence (see *R v Pigg* [1983] 1 All ER 56). Should, of course, the complainant alert the defendant of his mistake and he continue to penetrate her regardless, at this point he would be liable for rape.

10.2.2.6 *Mens rea:* (ii) without reasonable belief in consent

The final element that must be proven for a conviction of rape is a lack of reasonable belief in consent held by the defendant. By s 1(2) of the SOA 2003:

> Whether a belief is reasonable is to be determined having regard to *all the circumstances*, including *any steps* the defendant has taken to ascertain whether the complainant in fact consented. (emphasis added)

in practice

In the majority of rape cases, the defendant will run one of the following defences:

(1) Admit that sexual intercourse took place and argue that the complainant consented.
(2) Admit that sexual intercourse took place and argue that the defendant reasonably believed that the complainant consented.
(3) Deny that sexual intercourse took place.

In the majority of cases, the defendant will plead defences (1) and (2) together. He will argue that the complainant consented and in the alternative that he nevertheless reasonably believed that the complainant consented.

In some circumstances, the defendant (as a form of jury psychology) will hold his hands up and say that he now knows that the complainant was not consenting but that, at the time, he did reasonably believe that she was consenting. Defence counsel may find this latter course of action to be preferable in an attempt to gain sympathy with the jury and accept that the defendant now understands that his conduct was wrong, whilst emphasising that, *at the time of the offence*, he was not aware of this circumstance.

The test of reasonable belief is a subjective test with an objective element. It can best be described as a subjective test based on reasonable standards. The easiest way of understanding and dealing with this issue is to ask two questions (see Figure **10.5**):

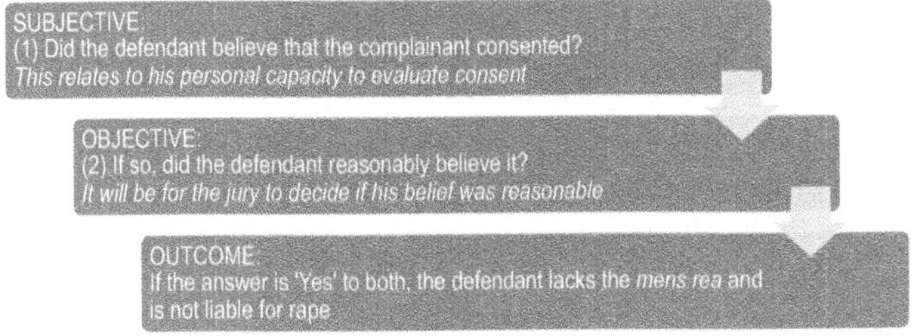

SUBJECTIVE:
(1) Did the defendant believe that the complainant consented?
This relates to his personal capacity to evaluate consent
OBJECTIVE:
(2) If so, did the defendant reasonably believe it?
It will be for the jury to decide if his belief was reasonable
OUTCOME:
If the answer is 'Yes' to both, the defendant lacks the mens rea and is not liable for rape

Figure 10.5 Understanding reasonable belief

Importantly, the presumptions in ss 75 and 76 apply to the defendant's reasonable belief in consent. In that sense, should the jury be satisfied that one of the presumptions applies, the defendant will automatically be held to lack a reasonable belief in consent. If the presumption found is that in s 76 (conclusive presumption), that is the end of the matter and the defendant has no recourse. However, if the relevant presumption is that in s 75 (evidential presumption), it will then be for the defendant to rebut its existence.

From the statement in s 1(2), there are two principles that must be considered. The first is the *circumstances* of the case, and the second is *any steps* taken by the defendant in the case to ascertain consent.

(i) The circumstances

The jury are entitled to consider 'all the circumstances' of the case to determine whether the defendant's belief was reasonable. 'All the circumstances' includes the particular characteristics of the accused – specifically his age, sexual experience and any learning disabilities, should this be relevant. Other surrounding circumstances may be relevant also, for example the defendant may attempt to argue he held a reasonable belief in consent on the basis that he was invited back to the home of the complainant; or that the complainant acted in a flirtatious and provocative manner.

Other circumstances that may be relevant include the length of time the defendant and complainant have known each other; whether they have had any sexual relations in the past; whether any discussions as to sexual relations had taken place. Importantly, however, these are only factors. They are not determinative of consent one way or another.

in practice

Members of the jury are ordinary people – some hold certain stereotypical beliefs – it is not a perfect system. As such, be aware that many sexual offences cases are difficult to win on the part of the prosecution as a result of society's understanding of rape. For example, in 2005, Amnesty International UK conducted a research poll ('Sexual Assault Research' (Amnesty International UK, 2005)) involving a participation group of 1,095 individuals. In the research, it was found that more than a quarter (26%) of those asked thought that a woman was partially or totally responsible for being raped if she was wearing sexy or revealing clothing; more than a quarter of people (30%) thought that a woman was partially or totally responsible for being raped if she was drunk; and more than a third (37%) held the same view if the woman had failed clearly to say no to the man.

(ii) Steps taken

The words 'any steps' has been given a wide interpretation to mean 'all steps taken by the defendant'. The key point to note is that there is no 'positive' requirement on the part of the defendant to take any steps. The legislation does not provide that 'A must take a number of steps …'. Instead, it shall be the responsibility of the jury to consider whether belief is reasonable in the circumstances. Where the pair are strangers, or no established relationship exists between the pair, more steps are likely to be expected from a jury. You may wish to ask yourself, when judging a particular case, how far the accused must go:

- Must the defendant go so far as to ask, 'Are you consenting?'
- Must the defendant have such consent recorded, either orally or in writing?

- Must the defendant have a third party witness the giving of consent?

Under the old law, the jury were entitled to find the defendant not guilty of rape where he held a genuine/honest but unreasonable belief in consent. This was known as the *Morgan* defence, following *DPP v Morgan* [1976] AC 182, and led to stark criticisms as a result of its operation. As a result of the 2003 Act, this defence has now been abolished.

Relevance of mental illness?

An issue faced by the Court of Appeal in *R v Braham* [2013] EWCA Crim 3 (also known as *R v B*) was whether a mental illness, which has an affect on the defendant's perception of consent, may be taken into account when determining whether the belief in consent was reasonable. In *Braham,* the defendant was a paranoid schizophrenic who believed himself to have sexual healing powers. The defendant engaged in sexual intercourse with his partner (against her will) believing that it would be good for her. This belief was confirmed as being a genuine one held by the defendant according to medical evidence. The defendant was convicted of rape and appealed unsuccessfully to the Court of Appeal. Hughes LJ in the Court of Appeal concluded that:

> If ... the defendant's delusional beliefs could have led him to believe that his partner consented when she did not, we take the clear view that such delusional beliefs cannot in law render reasonable a belief that his partner was consenting when in fact she was not. ... A delusional belief in consent, if entertained, would be by definition irrational and thus *un*reasonable, not reasonable. (original emphasis)

Hughes LJ explained that whilst the mental illness could not afford him a defence under the SOA 2003, such defendants could resort to arguing insanity.

Relevance of voluntary intoxication?

A final point to discuss in this section is the operation of intoxication on the reasonable belief in consent. Now, as we already know, intoxication cannot negate the intention of the defendant in a sexual offence case. This is because all sexual offences are deemed to be basic intent offences. This has been consistently confirmed in case law throughout the years. In particular, in both *R v Woods* (1981) 74 Cr App R 312 and *R v Fotheringham* (1988) 88 Cr App R 206, the Court of Appeal was clear that the courts shall never 'entertain the possibility' that a belief resulting from self-induced intoxication could be a 'reasonable' belief. The Court of Appeal in both cases ruled that reasonable belief is the belief of the sober person. However, the editors of Archbold (*Archbold: Criminal Pleadings, Evidence and Practice* (Sweet & Maxwell, 2020)) state:

> [I]t is a matter for the jury alone to decide whether a belief is reasonable; and that any rule to the effect that a person who is affected by alcohol or drugs could never make a 'reasonable' mistake would be an unwarranted intrusion into the province of the jury, and calculated to lead to harsh results where there are factors other than the defendant's inebriation that caused him to have the mistaken belief.

Although this view has merit in that a true drunken mistake may give rise to a question of reasonable belief, the Court of Appeal in *R v Grewal* [2010] EWCA Crim 2448 confirmed that such intoxication belief plays no part in this test.

10.2.3 Charging rape

10.2.3.1 Mode of trial

Rape is an offence triable only on indictment, meaning that the defendant may only be tried in the Crown Court.

10.2.3.2 Sentencing

The maximum sentence for rape is life imprisonment (SOA 2003, s 1(4)). The Court of Appeal in *AG's Reference (No 104 of 2004)* [2005] 1 Cr App R (S) 666 emphasised that there should be no distinction drawn between offences against a male or female complainant. This was furthered by the Court of Appeal in *R v Ismail* [2005] EWCA Crim 397, which stressed that no distinction is to be drawn between oral rape and other forms of penetration. Likewise, the Court of Appeal in *R v Millberry* [2003] 2 All ER 939 established that in terms of sentencing, all cases, regardless of whether they are 'relationship rape', 'acquaintance rape' or 'stranger rape', ought to have the same starting point. Although the actual sentence imposed may vary according to the circumstances of the case, the starting point in each case should be the same. This maintains the approach of the courts that all forms of rape are of equal seriousness.

10.2.4 Putting together rape

Consider this issue and think of how you may structure an answer to it. Then see the figure at the end of this chapter for a sample structure to adopt.

facts

Jack and Jill are 'friends with benefits'. The pair regularly engage in unprotected sexual intercourse together. Wary that her friend, Bill, has been recently diagnosed with a venereal disease and has been advised to avoid unprotected sex, Jill requests that Jack uses a condom in any future sexual encounters. Jack agrees but, during sexual intercourse with Jill, he takes the condom off without Jill knowing and continues to penetrate Jill's vagina. Jill later discovers this fact.

10.3 Assault by penetration

Introduced in response to the recommendation by the Sexual Offences Review, assault by penetration now stands alongside the offence of rape. In its Review (*Setting the Boundaries: Reforming the Law on Sex Offences* (Vol I, 2000)), the Home Office recommended the creation of a new offence of assault by penetration, originally named 'sexual assault by penetration'. The Review 'recognised that other penetrative assaults [other than with a penis] could be as serious in their impact on the victim as rape and that they should not be regarded lightly'.

10.3.1 Defining assault by penetration

In its 2000 Review, the Home Office expressed a desire to define the offence in such a way

> ... to include the non-consensual penetration of the anus, vagina and/or the external genitalia by objects or parts of the body other than the penis. This offence should also be defined in a way that would enable it to be used if there were any

doubt as to the nature of the penetration (for example when a child or mentally impaired adult is unable to furnish details of exactly what had penetrated them).

Importantly, the Home Office emphasised that this offence, unlike that of rape, is one that can be committed by both a man and a woman.

10.3.2 Elements of assault by penetration

Section 2 of the SOA 2003 provides:

(1) A person (A) commits an offence if—
   (a) he intentionally penetrates the vagina or anus of another person with a part of his body or anything else,
   (b) the penetration is sexual,
   (c) B does not consent to the penetration, and
   (d) A does not reasonably believe that B consents.

(2) Whether a belief is reasonable is to be determined having regard to all the circumstances, including any steps A has taken to ascertain whether B consents.

(3) Sections 75 and 76 apply to an offence under this section.

The *actus reus* and *mens rea* of assault by penetration are outlined in **Table 10.10**.

Table 10.10 Elements of assault by penetration

AR/MR	Elements of the offence
Actus reus	(i) penetration; (ii) of the vagina or anus; (iii) with a part of his body or anything else; (iv) the penetration is sexual; (v) without the complainant's consent.
Mens rea	(i) intentional penetration; (ii) without reasonable belief in consent.

Note that an offence of assault by penetration contrary to s 2 is applicable to any complainant who is over the age of 13. Where the complainant is under the age of 13, the defendant should instead be charged with assault by penetration of a child under 13, contrary to s 6 of the SOA 2003. As with s 5, consent is irrelevant to liability so long as all other elements are proven.

Our focus shall be the offence under s 2. Although the majority of the elements are identical to the elements of rape, we shall set out each element under its own heading to ensure you are aware of the specific requirements for the offence.

10.3.2.1 *Actus reus:* (i) penetration

Penetration holds the same meaning as rape, ie a continuing act from entry to withdrawal (s 79(2) of the SOA 2003).

See above for a discussion of penetration at **10.2.2.1**.

10.3.2.2 *Actus reus:* (ii) of the vagina or anus

See above for a discussion of vagina and anus at **10.2.2.1**. As with rape, where the defendant has penetrated both the vagina and the anus, he is liable for two counts of assault by penetration. Where, however, the prosecution alleges that the defendant penetrated the vagina *or* anus, this does not amount to an allegation of two offences (*R v P(LD)* [2010] EWCA Crim 164).

Note, however, that there is no offence committed by penetration of the mouth by a body part (other than a penis) or anything else. Such liability would lie in sexual assault contrary to s 3.

10.3.2.3 *Actus reus:* (iii) with a part of his body or anything else

Rape can only be committed by use of a penis. Therefore, only a man is capable of committing the offence of rape. Assault by penetration, on the other hand, is capable of being committed by both a man and a woman given that the requirement of penetration may be carried out by use of a 'part of his body or anything else'.

As we have already stated, should penetration occur by use of a penis, the correct charge would be rape. Technically, therefore, the statute is incomplete in that it does not make clear that penetration under s 2 cannot be with a penis. On that basis, it is better to understand the statute as meaning penetration is capable 'by a part of his body, other than a penis, or anything else'.

The use of 'a part of his body and anything else' is intentionally broad to allow all cases of penetration of the vagina or anus that are not with a penis to be included in the offence. Paragraph 11 of the Explanatory Notes to the SOA 2003 provides that

> The offence is committed where the penetration is by a part of A's body (for example, a finger) or anything else, (for example, a bottle) ...

Therefore, when observing a problem question where there has been penetration with a body part or item other than a penis, consider liability under s 2 and make it clear that the wording in s 2 is intentionally broad to encompass these sorts of cases.

10.3.2.4 *Actus reus:* (iv) the penetration is sexual

The next element of the *actus reus* is that the penetration is sexual in character. You may question why assault by penetration requires as part of its offence that the penetration must be sexual; whereas the offence of rape does not. Technically, rape does require the penetration to be sexual; however, given that penetration with a penis will *always* be sexual (unless you can find a reason that lawyers are unaware of), then it will be inferred that the penetration is always sexual.

For penetrations other than with a penis, however, it may not always be clear whether that penetration is sexual, *per se*. Section 78 of the SOA 2003 provides (emphasis added) that

> For the purposes of this Part (except sections 15A and 71), penetration, touching or any other activity is sexual if a reasonable person would consider that—
>
> (a) whatever its circumstances or any person's purpose in relation to it, it is because of its *nature* sexual, or
>
> (b) because of its nature it may be sexual and because of its *circumstances or the purpose* of any person in relation to it (or both) it is sexual.

Section 78(a) concerns activity that the reasonable person would *always* consider to be sexual because of its nature; whereas s 78(b) concerns activity that the reasonable person would consider, because of its nature, may or may not be sexual, but because of its circumstances or purpose it is sexual.

We shall consider each in turn.

Unambiguously sexual (SOA 2003, s 78(a))

There is certain conduct, such as penile penetration and oral sex, that will always be *unambiguously* sexual. By this, we mean that the conduct is sexual by its very nature in the eyes of a reasonable person irrespective of what the defendant claims. Where the reasonable person finds the conduct to be unambiguously sexual, the purpose of the defendant is also irrelevant (*R v Coomber* [2005] EWCA Crim 1113; *R v Cunliffe* [2006] EWCA Crim 1706 – the assertion of dominance as opposed to sexual gratification).

Penile penetration and oral penetration are examples of unambiguous sexual conduct by their very nature. However, other forms of conduct, such as digital penetration for medical examinations, may not be so clear.

Ambiguously sexual (SOA 2003, s 78(b))

Where the nature of the activity is ambiguous and 'may' be sexual, the correct approach was set out by the Court of Appeal in *R v H* [2005] 2 All ER 859.

According to the Court of Appeal in *R v H*, the jury must be asked two distinct questions (per Lord Woolf CJ):

> First, would they, as 12 reasonable people (as the section requires), consider that because of its nature the touching that took place in the particular case before them *could be* sexual? If the answer to that question was 'No', the jury would find the defendant not guilty. If 'Yes', they would have to go on to ask themselves (again as 12 reasonable people) whether in view of the circumstances and/or the purpose of any person in relation to the touching (or both), the touching was *in fact* sexual. If they were satisfied that it was, then they would find the defendant guilty. If they were not satisfied, they would find the defendant not guilty. (emphasis added)

example

Jack is a doctor who has invited Jill to his surgery to undertake a medical examination. In order to perform the examination, Jack has to insert his finger into Jill's vagina (known as 'digital penetration').

In this case, the jury would have to consider a number of issues before they could conclude that Jack was liable for a s 2 offence:

(a) The jury would have to consider whether the nature of the activity was sexual. In this case the activity of digital penetration is not unambiguously sexual, meaning that it may or may not be sexual.
(b) The jury would then have to consider the circumstances surrounding the activity carried out by the defendant. In this case, the conduct is carried out in a doctor's surgery which may indicate that the actions were not sexual.
(c) The jury would then have to consider the purpose of Jack in conducting the examination. If Jack's purpose is to conduct a medical examination, the conduct will not be sexual. If he has multiple purposes, and the dominant purpose is to conduct some sexual activity, he may be liable under s 2.

You may wonder: 'How can Jack ever be liable if he can simply claim that he was conducting a medical examination.' Indeed, that is a difficulty faced by the jury in their role. However, their role remains an objective one which looks at the surrounding circumstances to assist their decision. Consider the following, which may have the effect of changing the jury's mind as to the sexual nature of the conduct:

(a) In order to perform the medical examination, Jack may only need to insert one digit. If he penetrates Jill with three or more fingers, that may demonstrate sexual penetration.

(b) If the examination were to take place somewhere other than a doctor's surgery or hospital, for example in a public place, one can consider this a circumstance leading to the conclusion that the penetration is sexual.

(c) If Jack invited other persons to witness the examination for sexual gratification, this may amount to sexual penetration. These were the facts in *R v Bolduc and Bird* [1967] SCR 677 (Canada), where the accused undertook a proper and necessary medical examination but allowed his friend to be present for his own sexual gratification.

It ultimately depends on the facts and it is up to you, the lawyer, to take those facts and use them to either find liability or rid a defendant of liability. **Figure 10.6** should assist in this respect.

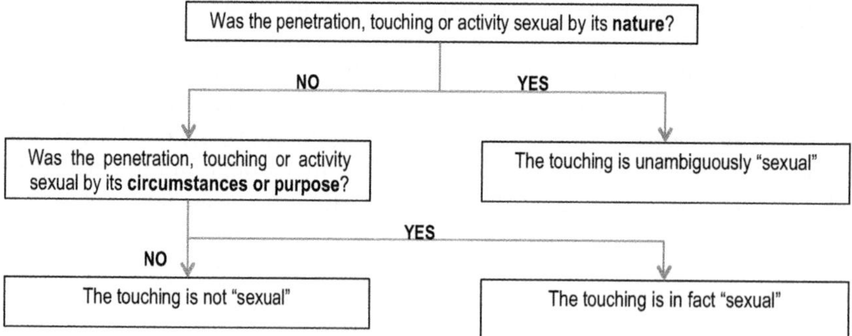

Figure 10.6 Understanding the requirement that penetration be 'sexual'

10.3.2.5 *Actus reus:* (v) without the complainant's consent

The same consensual principles found in ss 74–76 are to be used here too (s 2(3)). As with rape, ensure that you consider s 76 first, followed second by s 75 and then s 74.

See above for a full discussion of consent at **10.2.2.5.**

10.3.2.6 *Mens rea:* (i) intentional penetration

See above for a discussion of intention at **10.2.2.6.** Importantly, the penetration must be intentional; there is no offence committed where the penetration is 'reckless' (*R v Phillips* [2008] EWCA Crim 2830 where the defendant claimed to have been asleep when he digitally penetrated the complainant).

Please note from the wording of the statute that there is no requirement for the defendant to intend his penetration to be sexual. Rather, the only requirement is that the penetration itself was intentional. This means that the statute prevents a defendant from raising an argument that the penetration was never intended to be sexual, but rather it was intended to be for another purpose, eg for the purpose of inflicting harm or violence, or deriving from some unusual motive. We can observe cases on this point such as:

- *R v Hill* [2006] EWCA Crim 2575 – where the defendant digitally penetrated the complainant in a forceful manner and was charged with an offence contrary to s 8 of the OAPA 1861, in addition to assault by penetration; and
- *R v C* [2001] 1 Cr App R (S) 533 – where the defendant, unbeknownst to the complainant, inserted live maggots into her vagina.

10.3.2.7 *Mens rea:* (ii) without reasonable belief in consent

See above for a discussion of reasonable belief at **10.2.2.7**.

10.3.3 Charging assault by penetration

10.3.3.1 Mode of trial

Assault by penetration is an offence triable only on indictment, meaning that the defendant may only be tried in the Crown Court.

10.3.3.2 Sentencing

The maximum penalty for assault by penetration is life imprisonment (s 2(4) of the SOA 2003).

10.3.4 Putting together assault by penetration

Consider this issue and think of how you may structure an answer to it. Then see the figure at the end of this chapter for a sample structure to adopt.

facts

Jill finds Jack extremely attractive and wishes to have sex with him. Jack, however, is unwilling to do so as he is homosexual and is not attracted to Jill as a woman. In a club, Jill spikes Jack's drink, causing him to lose consciousness. Jill takes him back to her apartment where she proceeds to penetrate his anus with her finger, a dildo and a wine bottle.

10.4 Sexual assault

The term 'sexual assault' did not exist under the former law; rather, in its place stood the offence of 'indecent assault', which covered a broad range of offences including non-penile penetrations of the vagina, anus and mouth, indecent touchings, etc. The label of 'indecent assault' did not differentiate between the vastly different forms of conduct for which a defendant could be liable, which resulted in Temkin ('Getting it right: sexual offences law reform' (2000) 150 NLJ 1169) describing the offence as 'mindless' in operation.

As a result of the SOA 2003, these offences are now covered in various forms (eg assault by penetration, child sex offences and vulnerable adults subjected to a sexual assault). This means that the offence of sexual assault is now used to a lesser extent than its indecent assault predecessor.

10.4.1 Defining sexual assault

Sexual assault covers a wide range of potential assaults against an individual with varying levels of seriousness. In fact, the exact nature of the activity undertaken will determine the seriousness of the offence.

At the upper end of the scale of seriousness are cases where an individual uses their own naked body to 'rub, press, stroke or touch' the naked body of another individual. At the lower end of the scale of seriousness are cases where an individual touches another person through their clothing. Both cases will amount to sexual assaults causing an individual to be liable under s 3; however, the scale of seriousness will then determine the relevant sentencing of an individual.

Importantly, a case at the lower end of the scale may nevertheless be aggravated in circumstances where there has been:

- an abuse of position;
- the use of drugs or other substances;
- the use of violence/coercion;
- the use of a weapon;
- repeated offending.

Importantly, although the word 'assault' is present in the name of the offence, there is no requirement for a technical assault or battery to occur; all that is required is a touching. Where the act reflects a battery more so than a sexual assault, the better charge is one of a non-fatal offence as opposed to a sexual offence.

10.4.2 Elements of sexual assault

Section 3 of the SOA 2003 provides:

> (1) A person (A) commits an offence if—
> (a) he intentionally touches another person (B),
> (b) the touching is sexual,
> (c) B does not consent to the touching, and
> (d) A does not reasonably believe that B consents.
>
> (2) Whether a belief is reasonable is to be determined having regard to all the circumstances, including any steps A has taken to ascertain whether B consents.
>
> (3) Sections 75 and 76 apply to an offence under this section.

The *actus reus* and *mens rea* of sexual assault are outlined in **Table 10.11**.

Table 10.11 Elements of sexual assault

AR/MR	Elements of the offence
Actus reus	(i) the touching of another person; (ii) the touching is sexual; and (iii) the complainant does not consent to the touching.
Mens rea	(i) intentional touching; (ii) without reasonable belief in consent.

Note that an offence of sexual assault contrary to s 3 is applicable to any complainant who is over the age of 13. Where the complainant is under the age of 13, the defendant should instead be charged with sexual assault of a child under 13, contrary to s 7 of the SOA 2003. As with ss 5 and 6, consent is irrelevant to liability.

Our focus is the offence under s 3, and we shall consider each element in turn.

10.4.2.1 *Actus reus:* (i) the touching of another person

Sexual assault firstly requires the touching of another individual. Touching has been defined in s 79(8) of the SOA 2003 as including touching:

(a) with any part of the body,
(b) with anything else,
(c) through anything,

and in particular includes touching amounting to penetration.

There is no requirement of force, violence or hostility, and the lightest touch will be sufficient. This was demonstrated in *R v H* [2005] 2 All ER 859.

case example

Charge:
Sexual assault (SOA 2003, s 3)

Case progression:
Crown Court – Guilty

Court of Appeal – Conviction upheld

Point of law:
Meaning of touching

In *R v H* [2005] 2 All ER 859, the complainant, whilst walking her dog one evening, was grabbed by the defendant. The defendant grabbed the complainant by her track suit bottoms and dragged her towards him and asked whether she 'fancied a shag'. The complainant escaped and the defendant was charged with and convicted of sexual assault in the Crown Court.

The defendant appealed to the Court of Appeal on the basis that the touching of the complainant's track suit bottoms was not enough to constitute 'touching' under the SOA 2003. The defendant argued that touching had to be of the person's body, not just her clothes.

The Court of Appeal, however, held that the touching of an individual's clothing was sufficient to amount to 'touching' for the purposes of s 3, even where there was no touching of the actual person, eg Jack touches the hem of Jill's skirt without making physical contact with her leg through her skirt.

The use of 'with anything else' is intentionally broad to capture conduct that might not ordinarily be considered 'touching'. This can be demonstrated in *R v Bounekhla* [2006] EWCA Crim 1217, where the defendant pressed his penis against a woman and ejaculated onto her clothing whilst dancing in a nightclub. Such was done without the knowledge or consent of the complainant. The defendant appealed against sentence, whereby the Court of Appeal noted that a complainant need not be aware that they are being touched and such touching would be sufficient under s 3.

It is unclear whether this offence allows commission by omission. The word 'touching' would appear to indicate a positive act on the part of the defendant. However, given the fact that the touching may be with any part of the body, with anything else or through anything, a more generous interpretation may be afforded. In *R v Speck* [1977] 2 All ER 859 (a case concerning the old offence of gross indecency with a child), the defendant allowed a child to place her hand on his crotch and did not remove the hand. This omission was sufficient for liability, and similar reasoning could be adopted now under a charge of sexual assault.

Under the old offence of indecent assault, a defendant could be liable for an offence by causing the complainant to apprehend that she was about to be touched indecently. However, as a result of the SOA 2003, there must be an element of touching. Where no touching has taken place, no offence under s 3 has been committed; however, the defendant may be liable for an attempt.

10.4.2.2 *Actus reus:* (ii) the touching is sexual

'Sexual' in this context bears with it the same meaning as we have dealt with above in relation to assault by penetration. See **10.3.2.4** for discussion of the test in s 78.

Where touching is not automatically sexual by its nature, it is possible to ascertain whether the touching is sexual by determining whether by its nature it *might* be sexual and if so whether in the circumstances the purpose is *in fact* sexual.

Table 10.12 details a number of authorities where the touching was considered to be sexual. Please note that these cases, when heard on appeal, are largely appeals against sentence and not against conviction.

Table 10.12 Case examples of sexual touchings

Touching	Authority
Touching the complainant's breasts	*R v Burns* [2006] EWCA Crim 1451
Pressing up against the complainant's body	*R v Nika* [2005] EWCA Crim 3255
Kissing the complainant's face	*R v W* [2005] EWCA Crim 3138
Touching the complainant's private parts	*R v Forrester* [2006] EWCA Crim 1748
Kissing the complainant's private parts	*R v Turner* [2005] EWCA Crim 3436
Stroking the complainant's leg	*R v Price (David)* [2004] 1 Cr App R 145
Stroking the complainant's arm	*R v Deal* [2006] EWCA Crim 684

10.4.2.3 *Actus reus:* (iii) the complainant does not consent to the touching

The same consensual principles found in ss 74–76 are to be used here too (s 3(3) of the SOA 2003). As with rape and assault by penetration, ensure that you consider s 76 first, followed second by s 75 and then s 74.

See above for a full discussion of consent at **10.2.2.5**.

10.4.2.4 *Mens rea:* (i) intentional touching

See above for a discussion of intention at **10.2.2.6**.

In *R v Heard* [2008] QB 43, the Court of Appeal confirmed that the prosecution must simply prove that the touching was 'deliberate'. If the touching is reckless or accidental, for example by way of impairment of control over limbs, no offence under s 3 is committed. In this respect, an accident caused by the voluntary consumption of alcohol will surely excuse the defendant's conduct.

Further, note from the wording of the statute that there is no requirement for the defendant to intend his touching to be sexual. Rather, the only requirement is that the touching itself was intentional. Bantekas ('Can Touching Always be Sexual where there is no Sexual Intent' (2008) 73 J Crim L 251) argues that it is unfair to the defendant that he may be liable for an offence despite lacking the intention that his touching is sexual. This argument can be countered on the basis that the defendant's conduct must nevertheless be considered sexual by a reasonable person before he may be liable for an offence. This lack of correspondence of *actus reus* and *mens rea* remains appropriate in light of the decision of *R v H* [2005] 2 All ER 859. Despite this, a prosecutor may find it an easier task to charge a defendant with a non-sexual crime where his intention is clearly based in violence or some other non-sexual motive.

10.4.2.5 *Mens rea:* (ii) without reasonable belief in consent

See above for a discussion of reasonable belief at **10.2.2.7**.

10.4.3 Charging sexual assault

10.4.3.1 Mode of trial

Sexual assault is an offence triable either way, meaning that it may be charged in either the magistrates' court or the Crown Court.

10.4.3.2 Sentencing

Where tried in the magistrates' court, the maximum penalty for an offence is 6 months' imprisonment and/or a level 5 fine (s 3(4)(a)). Upon conviction on indictment in the Crown Court, the defendant may be sentenced to a maximum of 10 years' imprisonment (s 3(4)(b)).

10.4.4 Putting together sexual assault

Consider this issue and think of how you may structure an answer to it. Then see the figure at the end of this chapter for a sample structure to adopt.

facts

Jack is a lecturer at a university and has a particular attraction to Jill, one of his students. During a tutorial, Jack walks up to Jill, who is sat at her desk, and presses his penis up against her arm. As Jill looks at Jack, he simply smiles and then moves away.

10.5 Causing a person to engage in sexual activity without consent

It is common for laypersons to consider a sex offender as an individual who has physically forced himself onto another individual without their consent. Indeed, this is how the law has been structured above in considering the offences of rape, assault by penetration and sexual assault. However, the scope of sexual offences is much broader than that.

Formerly charged as a form of indecent assault, causing a person to engage in sexual activity without consent is now an important and useful tool for prosecutors to use where the defendant compels another person to engage in some sexual conduct.

10.5.1 Defining causing a person to engage in sexual activity without consent

The law of sexual offences encompasses within it the circumstances where a defendant does not *engage* in such typical conduct, eg rape or unwarranted touching. Instead, the defendant's liability arises through his actions in causing *another person* to engage in sexual conduct. This conduct may be extremely similar to that seen above, for example the penetration of the vagina, anus or mouth; however, it will not be the defendant in this instance penetrating the complainant. Rather, the defendant causes the complainant to penetrate themselves or a third party. Likewise, the defendant will not sexually touch another individual but may cause that individual to sexually touch the defendant.

10.5.2 Elements of causing a person to engage in sexual activity without consent

Section 4 of the SOA 2003 provides:

> (1) A person (A) commits an offence if—
> (a) he intentionally causes another person (B) to engage in an activity,

(b) the activity is sexual,
(c) B does not consent to engaging in the activity, and
(d) A does not reasonably believe that B consents.

(2) Whether a belief is reasonable is to be determined having regard to all the circumstances, including any steps A has taken to ascertain whether B consents.

(3) Sections 75 and 76 apply to an offence under this section.

It is important to note at this stage that it is irrelevant whether the defendant engages in the conduct himself. It is also irrelevant whether the defendant is actually present at the scene. His liability arises by the fact he *causes* another, by some means, to engage in such sexual conduct.

The *actus reus* and *mens rea* of causing a person to engage are outlined in **Table 10.13**.

Table 10.13 Elements of causing a person to engage in sexual activity without consent

AR/MR	Elements of the offence
Actus reus	(i) causing a person to engage in an activity; (ii) the activity is sexual; (iii) without the complainant's consent.
Mens rea	(i) intention; (ii) without reasonable belief in consent.

We shall consider each element in turn.

10.5.2.1 *Actus reus:* (i) causing a person to engage in an activity

The starting point is to note that the term 'activity' is not defined in the Act. However, as above in relation to sexual assault, the term 'activity' can be interpreted quite widely. Importantly, however, the actual activity must have occurred – there is no criminal offence under s 4 for merely hypothetical or erotic suggestions (unless such are construed by the courts to fall within the meaning of 'activity'). Paragraph 13 of the Explanatory Notes to the SOA 2003 provides three different examples of 'activity' that would come within s 4. It is useful to divide such examples into the following categories:

- activity alone;
- activity with the defendant;
- activity with a third party.

We shall see each of these in the description below:

> A may cause B to engage in sexual activity with A (for example, a woman who compels a man to penetrate her) [activity with the defendant]; on B himself (for example, where one person forces someone else to masturbate himself) [activity alone]; or with another person (for example, where one person makes someone else masturbate a third person) [activity with a third party].

Other examples outside of the Explanatory Notes could include:

- causing a person to act as a prostitute;
- causing a person to have sex with an animal;
- causing a person to watch a pornographic film (*R v Abdullahi* [2007] 1 WLR 225);

- causing a person to engage in conversation or exchange texts of a sexual nature (*R v Grout* [2011] EWCA Crim 299).

What you will have noticed from these examples is that many of them overlap with the offences previously discussed in this chapter. It is this overlapping which causes the offence to become quite complex in application. The simple way to avoid confusion is to consider what activity the *defendant* is engaging in. Let us take a few examples involving Jack and Jill:

(1) Jack penetrates Jill's vagina.
(2) Jill forces Jack to penetrate her vagina.
(3) Jill uses her hand to masturbate Jack's penis.
(4) Jill forces Jack to masturbate his penis.

Each of these examples show conduct that is broadly similar in terms of the activity involved. In example 1, Jack will be liable for the offence of rape; he has penetrated the vagina of Jill with his penis. Jack is engaged in the sexual conduct. Compare this, however, with example 2 where Jack is forced to penetrate Jill's vagina. In this instance, although Jack has penetrated the vagina of Jill with his penis, he has done so with her consent. On this basis, Jack cannot be liable for rape. However, Jill may be liable for an offence under s 4 as she has forced Jack to engage in sexual activity (see *R v Basherdost* [2009] EWCA Crim 2883 concerning a defendant who forced two individuals to engage in sexual intercourse together whilst he filmed them).

In this respect, the s 4 offence is wider than the offence of rape in that the complainant in this instance would be a man and the defendant would be a woman.

In example 3, Jill would be liable for the offence of sexual assault given that she has touched Jack in a sexual way without his consent. Section 4 would not come into play. In example 4, however, Jill has taken no part in the actual sexual conduct, ie the masturbation. Instead, Jill has procured Jack to act in a certain way. This again should demonstrate that s 4 is wider than the offences considered above, allowing the law to attach liability to an individual who, although she did not take part in the sexual activity, was the cause of such activity without the consent of the complainant. In this instance, Jill would be liable for a s 4 offence (see *R v Sargeant* [1997] Crim LR 50 and *R v Devonald* [2008] EWCA Crim 527).

In addition to proving that the conduct in question is sufficient to be labelled an 'activity' for the purposes of s 4, the prosecution must also prove that the defendant *caused* the complainant to engage in such conduct. As with 'activity', the term 'causing' is not defined in the Act but is likely to include all forms of causative conduct. Such causative conduct may include threats of violence, offer of payment or any general form of inducement or persuasion.

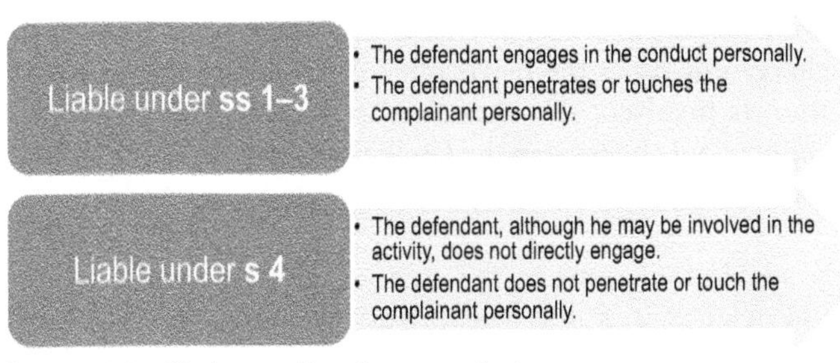

Figure 10.7 Understanding the scope of s 4

10.5.2.2 *Actus reus:* (ii) the activity is sexual

The second element that must be proven is that the activity itself is 'sexual'. As above, 'sexual' is defined, in s 78, according to the nature or circumstances of the activity. In *R v Grout* [2011] EWCA Crim 299, the Court of Appeal concluded that engaging the complainant in a conversation of a sexual nature was sufficient to amount to a sexual activity. The application of *Grout* to complainants under the age of 16 may now be called into question, however, as a result of s 67 of the Serious Crime Act 2015, which inserted s 15A into the SOA 2003. Section 15A creates a new offence of 'sexual communication with a child', and it is likely that such communications will now fall outside s 4 and within s 15A. Naturally, sexual communications with persons over 16 will still fall within s 4 where the respective conditions are met.

See above for a full discussion of 'sexual' at **10.3.2.4.**

10.5.2.3 *Actus reus:* (iii) without the complainant's consent

This element is to be read in light of all other offences considered in this chapter. By s 4(3), both the conclusive and evidential presumptions of consent apply to this offence. For an application of the presumptions to s 4, see *R v Bingham* [2013] EWCA Crim 823 and *R v Devonald* [2008] EWCA Crim 527. Likewise, the general concept of consent in s 74 also applies.

See above for a full discussion of consent at **10.2.2.5.**

10.5.2.4 *Mens rea:* (i) intention

The first element of the *mens rea* that must be proven is that the defendant intended to cause another person to enter into an activity. In this sense, the defendant's actions or conduct must be such as to deliberately cause the complainant to act in a certain way. However, as with an offence under ss 2 and 3, there is no requirement to prove that the defendant intended the activity to be 'sexual'.

See above for a full discussion of intention at **10.2.2.6.**

10.5.2.5 *Mens rea:* (ii) without reasonable belief in consent

The final element that must be proven is that the defendant did not reasonably believe that the complainant was consenting. This reasonable belief is relevant at the time the complainant actually engaged in the activity.

See above for a full discussion of consent at **10.2.2.7.**

10.5.3 Charging causing a person to engage in sexual activity without consent

10.5.3.1 Mode of trial

In general, causing a person to engage in sexual activity is an offence triable either way, meaning that it may be charged in either the magistrates' court or the Crown Court. However, where penetration is involved, the offence is triable only on indictment, meaning that the defendant may only be tried in the Crown Court.

10.5.3.2 Sentencing

The sentencing powers available to a court in this instance depend on the type of activity concerned. This is detailed in s 4(4) and (5) of the SOA 2003. Section 4 provides:

(4) A person guilty of an offence under this section, if the activity caused involved—
   (a) penetration of B's anus or vagina,
   (b) penetration of B's mouth with a person's penis,
   (c) penetration of a person's anus or vagina with a part of B's body or by B with anything else, or
   (d) penetration of a person's mouth with B's penis,

   is liable, on conviction on indictment, to imprisonment for life.

(5) Unless subsection (4) applies, a person guilty of an offence under this section is liable—
   (a) on summary conviction, to imprisonment for a term not exceeding 6 months or to a fine not exceeding the statutory maximum or both;
   (b) on conviction on indictment, to imprisonment for a term not exceeding 10 years.

Simply, where the activity involves penetration, the maximum sentence is one of life imprisonment. Any other activity is dealt with according to s 4(5). Importantly, according to the House of Lords in *R v Courtie* [1984] AC 463, where a defendant has caused the complainant to engage in conduct that would be covered in both s 4(4) and (5), this must be charged as separate criminal offences in the indictment.

10.5.4 Putting together causing a person to engage in sexual activity

Consider this issue and think of how you may structure an answer to it. Then see the figure below for a sample structure to adopt.

facts

Jack has a particular sexual fetish for watching other people react to pornographic images. He goes into his local shopping centre and stops Jill as she is moving between shops. Jack asks whether Jill would like to see some images of his dog, to which Jill replies yes. Jack, however, shows Jill an image of his penis. Jill is shocked at Jack's actions.

10.6 Putting together sexual offences

Consider this issue and think of how you may structure an answer to it. Then see the figure below for a sample structure to adopt.

facts

Jack meets his friend Jill in a nightclub. The pair agree to go back to Jack's house and engage in sexual intercourse. Jill is highly intoxicated and cannot remember the events of the night and now believes that Jack has raped her.

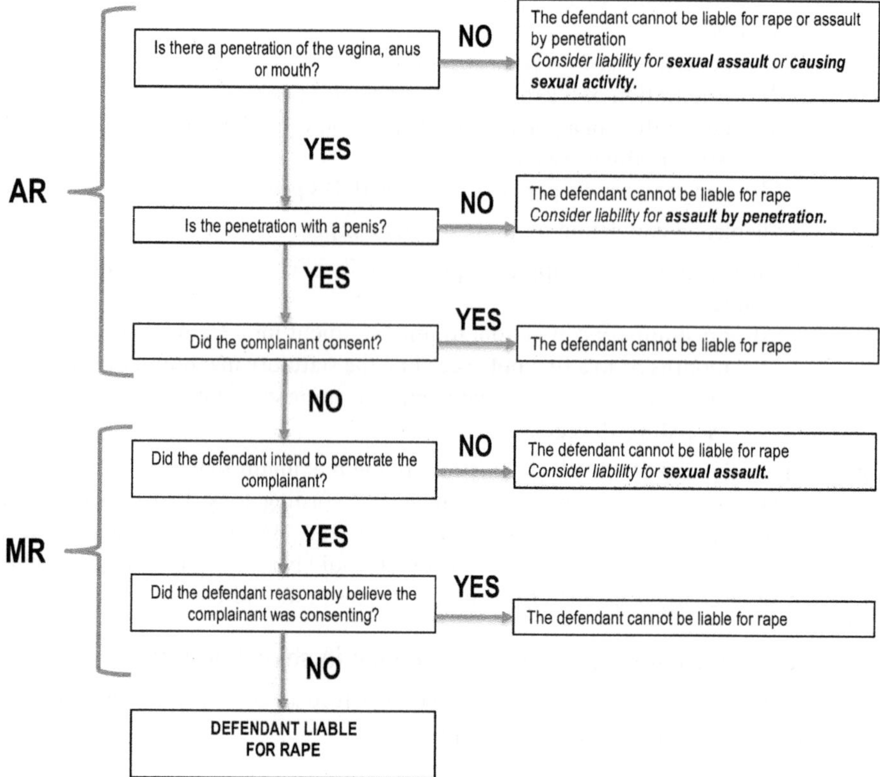

Figure 10.8 Putting together sexual offences

10.7 Further reading

De Than, 'The Case for a Rational Reconstruction of Consent in Criminal Law' (2007) 70 MLR 225.

Dempsey and Herring, 'Why Sexual Penetration Requires Justification' (2007) 27 OJLS 467.

Finch and Munro, 'Intoxicated Consent and Drug Assisted Rape Revisited' [2004] Crim LR 789.

Huigens, 'Is Strict Liability Rape Defensible?' in Duff and Green (eds), *Defining Crimes* (OUP, 2005).

Laird, 'Rapist or Rogue? Deception, Consent and the Sexual Offences Act 2003' [2014] Crim LR 492.

Power, 'Towards a Redefinition of the Mens Rea of Rape' (2003) 23 OJLS 379.

Sharpe, 'Criminalising Sexual Intimacy: Transgender Defendants and the Legal Construction of Non-Consent' [2014] Crim LR 207.

Temkin and Ashworth, 'Rape, Sexual Assaults and the Problems of Consent' [2004] Crim LR 328.

Wallerstein, '"A Drunken Consent Is Still Consent"—or Is It? A Critical Analysis of the Law on a Drunken Consent to Sex Following *Bree*' (2009) 73 J Crim L 318.

- The majority of sexual offences are contained in the SOA 2003.
- Rape is an offence which can only be committed by a man. It requires there to have been an intentional penetration of the vagina, anus or mouth with a penis. There must be no consent on the part of the complainant and no reasonable belief in consent on the part of the defendant.
- Consent is person and time specific, and the SOA 2003 prescribes three routes to which the jury can find a lack of consent: s 76 prescribes two conclusive presumptions against consent, s 75 provides a number of rebuttable presumptions, and s 74 provides the general meaning of consent.
- Assault by penetration is an offence designed to be as serious as rape but allows for the possibility of a female defendant. There is no requirement for penetration to be with a penis. However, the penetration must be 'sexual', which may be unambiguous or ambiguous.
- Assault by penetration applies, however, only to penetration of the anus and vagina. Penetration of the mouth is not sufficient and should be charged as sexual assault.
- Sexual assault requires some form of touching which is sexual. As above, there must be an intention to touch, absence of consent and absence of reasonable belief in consent.
- Causing a person to engage in sexual activity is a wide offence which covers circumstances where the defendant causes another to engage in sexual conduct either with the defendant, on their own, or with a third party.

test your knowledge

Problem

Jack is a wealthy businessman who loves to spend money on designer clothes, cars and hotels. Jack regularly makes a booking at his local 5-star hotel, which he uses to take men and women back for sexual intercourse after a night of clubbing. One evening, Jack engages in conversation with Jill, a waitress, and convinces her to come back to his hotel room later that evening. Jill agrees and later meets Jack at his hotel room. Jill agrees to engage in sexual intercourse on the basis that Jack wears a condom. Jack agrees and the pair engage in sexual intercourse. Midway through intercourse, however, Jack is displeased with using the condom and removes it. He continues to penetrate Jill without informing her of his removal of the condom. As Jill is leaving the hotel room, Jack says to her, 'See, wasn't that much better without the rubber.' Jill is shocked and goes to the police.

A few hours later, Jack requests room service from the hotel and asks his friend, Andy, the manager of the hotel whether he has a 'young and fine' guy to deliver the food to him. The manager duly sends Bill to the room with the food. Upon entering the room, Jack knocks out Bill with the serving tray. Upon awakening, Bill discovers that he has been tied to the bed. Jack goes on to penetrate Bill's anus with a champagne bottle and begins to penetrate Bill's mouth with a vibrator. Andy, who enjoys watching Jack's activities through a peephole in the wall, decides to force Bill's brother, Ben, to watch the conduct Bill is subjected to.

The police duly arrive and arrest Jack. Andy is also arrested upon the police speaking with Ben.

Advise the CPS as to the liability of Jack and Andy.

Essay

'The offences contained in the Sexual Offences Act 2003 are outdated and in need of serious reform.'

Critically consider this statement in light of the terminology used and the approach taken by the law to the offences in ss 1–4 of the 2003 Act.

chapter 11 Theft and Related Offences

After reading this chapter, you will be able to understand:

- the purpose of charging offences against property
- the meaning of property and why there is a need to protect both property and its owner
- the offence of theft, the elements of the offence and punishment for the offence
- the offence of robbery, the elements of the offence and punishment for the offence
- the offence of burglary, the elements of the offence and punishment for the offence
- the offence of going equipped, the elements of the offence and punishment for the offence.

11.1 Introduction to property offences

Up to this point, we have been concerned with the criminal law's response to offences/violations against the person. This has involved discussion of fatal offences (**Chapter 8**), non-fatal offences (**Chapter 9**) and sexual offences (**Chapter 10**). As made clear in those chapters, there is no single offence 'against the person'. Likewise, there is no single offence 'against property'. Property offences are numerous and broad, encompassing the theft of property, the possession of stolen property, the obtaining of property by fraud or deception, and the damaging of property owned by another. These offences shall be the focus of the remaining chapters.

11.1.1 Purpose of property offences

Property offences in the criminal law are designed to offer further protection to the civil law rights of individuals to their property. Child and Ormerod (*Smith, Hogan, & Ormerod's Essentials of Criminal Law*, 3rd edn (OUP, 2019)) comment that:

> Through such offences, the criminal law provides protection for the full range of civil law property rights, enabling the system of civil ownership to exist and function.

In this sense, the criminal and civil law may appear to interlink, with the aim of securing property rights for citizens of the state. However, as a result of decisions of criminal courts, there remains little harmony between the civil and criminal law understandings of property. Indeed, Lord Steyn in *R v Hinks* [2001] 2 AC 241 stated that:

> The purposes of the civil law and the criminal law are somewhat different. In theory the two systems should be in perfect harmony. In a practical world there will sometimes be some disharmony between the two systems. In any event, it would be wrong to assume on *a priori* grounds that the criminal law rather than the civil law is defective.

This is furthered by Gardener ('Property and Theft' [1998] Crim LR 35) who argues that it appropriate that the criminal law and civil law do not sit in perfect harmony. Gardener argues that the civil law is present 'to protect property rights, even if they were unsatisfactorily acquired', whereas the criminal law 'rightly concentrates on the unsatisfactory manner of acquisition'.

11.1.2 The meaning of property

The concept of what property is will vary according to the lay and legal understanding. The view of the layperson may be that property is anything that is owned or possessed by an individual. However, a more legal understanding of property has been explained by Smith (*Property Law*, 10th edn (Pearson, 2020)) who has remarked that property is not concerned with things but, rather, is concerned with the relationship between people about things. The ability for individuals to deal with a *thing* in a particular way is what characterises that thing as property. The criminal law treats property in a similar fashion; however, you are unlikely to find a jury being directed as to the legal understanding of 'property'.

11.1.3 A brief history

The former law of larceny, set out in the Larceny Act 1916, was complex, technical and wordy. In 1966, the Criminal Law Revision Committee (CLRC) published its 8th Report, *Theft and Related Offences* (Cmnd 2977, 1966). Within this Report was a draft Bill that would become the Theft Act (TA) 1968. The Act provided for a new 'face' to property offences and was designed to reduce complexity and avoid legal jargon through its provisions; whether it achieved that intention is a different matter. Old terminology, such as 'larceny', 'larceny by trick', 'false pretences' and 'embezzlement', was replaced with more modern terms of theft and fraud.

11.2 Theft

The concept of 'theft' is well understood by the layperson. They can appreciate that the taking of another person's property without that person's permission is theft. They often associate theft with pick-pockets and shoplifters. What you will quickly learn is that shoplifting plays only a small part in the law of theft.

Importantly, where a person carries with him any article for use in the course of or in connection with a theft, he may also be liable for going equipped contrary to s 25 of the TA 1968 (see **11.5**).

11.2.1 Defining theft

On a basic level, theft requires a person to take the property of another with a dishonest intention that the property will not be returned to that person. Restricting theft to the 'taking' of property is perhaps too basic when one considers the full extent to which an individual may be liable through the concept of 'appropriation'. We shall see when looking at the elements below that certain key words such as 'appropriate' and 'dishonesty' have caused the courts some difficulty in defining. Although the Act intended to simplify the manner in which a person may 'steal' another's property and make the finding of theft easier for a jury, it will be seen below that the jury are still required to grapple with concepts unusual to the layperson.

11.2.2 Elements of theft

Section 1(1) of the TA 1968 provides:

> A person is guilty of theft if he dishonestly appropriates property belonging to another, with the intention of permanently depriving the other of it; and 'thief' and 'steal' shall be construed accordingly.

From s 1(1), Megaw LJ in *R v Lawrence* [1971] 1 QB 373 (in the Court of Appeal) stated that:

> Theft, under the terms of section 1(1) involves four elements: (i) a dishonest (ii) appropriation (iii) of property belonging to another (iv) with the intention of permanently depriving the owner of it.

Whilst Viscount Dilhorne in the House of Lords in *Lawrence* ([1972] AC 626) expressly accepted this formulation, it may be more useful to consider there to be five elements of theft, and these are detailed in **Table 11.1** as the *actus reus* and *mens rea*.

Table 11.1 Elements of theft

AR/MR	Elements of the offence
Actus reus	(i) appropriation; (ii) of property; (iii) belonging to another.
Mens rea	(i) dishonesty; (ii) intention to permanently deprive.

Each of these elements is further explained in ss 2–6 of the 1968 Act. The editors of *Blackstone's Criminal Practice* (OUP, 2020) state that is incorrect to refer to those sections as providing definitions of each element of the offence. Rather, those elements are merely 'amplified' by the respective sections. It is also worth emphasising that a defendant is to be charged contrary to s 1 of the TA 1968; ss 2–7 do not provide for any criminal offences in their own right.

We shall consider each element in turn.

11.2.2.1 *Actus reus:* (i) appropriation (TA 1968, s 3)

Section 3 of the TA 1968 provides:

> (1) *Any assumption by a person of the rights of an owner* amounts to an appropriation, and this includes, where he has come by the property (innocently or not) without stealing it, any later assumption of a right to it by keeping or dealing with it as owner. (emphasis added)
>
> (2) Where property or a right or interest in property is or purports to be transferred for value to a person acting in good faith, no later assumption by him of rights which he believed himself to be acquiring shall, by reason of any defect in the transferor's title, amount to theft of the property.

Meaning of 'appropriation'

Appropriation, as a term, has been subject to stark academic criticism and debate in light of four key House of Lords' decisions, namely:

- *Lawrence v Metropolitan Police Commissioner* [1972] AC 626;
- *R v Morris* [1984] AC 320;
- *DPP v Gomez* [1993] AC 442; and
- *R v Hinks* [2001] 2 AC 241.

A key point to note is that the CLRC in its 8th Report did not provide a full definition of appropriation because it assumed that people would realise it was simply a different label for what it saw as the 'familiar concept of conversion'. Appropriation was intended to be much broader than for the previous offences of larceny, which required 'taking and carrying away'. However, most commentators would argue that these cases have extended the meaning of appropriation *beyond* understanding and beyond the intention of Parliament.

Particular academic criticism comes from the likes of Ormerod and Laird (*Smith, Hogan, & Ormerod's Criminal Law*, 15th edn (OUP, 2018)), who state that appropriation has been far too widely interpreted, so much so that the *actus reus* has been 'reduced to vanishing point'. Further to this, Smith ('Theft or Sharp Practice: Who Cares Now?' (2001) 60(1) CLJ 21) argues that, as a result of these decisions, the absence of dishonesty will be the sole factor determining whether an appropriation is lawful or not. Specifically, Smith refers to theft as a 'thought crime' with far too much emphasis placed on the *mens rea* of the offence.

We shall now look at some of the key concepts in the law of appropriation.

Appropriation of 'a' right

The key part of s 3(1) is the statement: 'Any assumption ... of the rights of an owner ...' The 'rights of an owner' are many and complex. The owner of the property has the right to, inter alia:

- touch the property;
- sell/offer for sale the property;
- hire the property out;
- give the property away (eg as a gift);
- lend the property out;
- mortgage the property; and
- destroy, damage or dispose of the property.

These rights are known as 'proprietary rights' and such rights 'bind the world' in their entirety.

A key question that has arisen in the case law on theft is this: *What number of rights must be assumed by the defendant in order to effectively 'appropriate' property.?*

Lord Roskill in *R v Morris* [1984] AC 320 stated, in *obiter*, that the assumption of rights in s 3(1) can be of 'any of the rights of the owner'. It is therefore sufficient if the defendant assumes only one right of the owner; it need not be an assumption of *all* of the rights of the owner.

case example

Charge:
Theft (TA 1968, s 1)

Case progression:
Crown Court – Guilty

Court of Appeal – Conviction upheld

House of Lords – Conviction upheld

Point of law:
Appropriation of property

In *R v Morris* [1984] AC 320, the defendant removed a price label from a joint of pork in a supermarket and attached it to a larger and more expensive joint of pork. The defendant was charged with theft of the pork and was convicted in the Crown Court with his conviction upheld in the Court of Appeal.

The House of Lords was faced with the question of whether the mere switching of price labels was sufficient to amount to appropriation. Their Lordships ruled that where the defendant adversely interferes with or usurps the rights of the owner of the goods, he would appropriate those goods.

Lord Roskill explained that:

> [I]f one reads the words 'the rights' at the opening of section 3(1) literally and in isolation from the rest of the section, [the defendant's] submission undoubtedly has force. But the later words 'any later assumption of a right' in subsection (1) and the words in subsection (2) 'no later assumption by him of rights' seem to me to militate strongly against the correctness of the submission. Moreover the provisions of section 2(1)(a) also seem to point in the same direction. It follows therefore that it is enough for the prosecution if they have proved in these cases the assumption by the respondents of *any* of the rights of the owner of the goods in question. (emphasis added)

As a result, Lord Roskill found that an assumption of one of the rights of the owner is sufficient. In that regard, his Lordship concluded:

> In cases such as the present, it is in truth a combination of these actions, the removal from the shelf and the switching of the labels, which evidences adverse interference with or usurpation of the right of the owner. Those acts, therefore, amount to an appropriation.

This was reaffirmed by the House of Lords in *DPP v Gomez* [1993] AC 442, in which Lord Keith explained that:

> In my opinion Lord Roskill was undoubtedly right when he said in the course of the passage quoted that the assumption by the defendant of any of the rights of an owner could amount to an appropriation within the meaning of section 3(1), and that the removal of an article from the shelf and the changing of the price label on it constituted the assumption of one of the rights of the owner and hence an appropriation within the meaning of the subsection.

In fact, Lord Keith went further than Lord Roskill in this regard. Lord Roskill explained that it was the switching of price labels *in combination* with removal from the shelf that resulted in an appropriation. Lord Keith expressed doubts about this:

> But there are observations in the passage which, with the greatest possible respect to my noble and learned friend Lord Roskill, I must regard as unnecessary for the decision of the case and as being incorrect. In the first place, it seems to me that the switching of price labels on the article is in itself an assumption of one of the rights of the owner, whether or not it is accompanied by some other act such as removing the article from the shelf and placing it in a basket or trolley. No one but the owner has the right to remove a price label from an article or to place a price label upon it.

One of the first major criticisms of this ruling is the lack of attention paid to the statute itself. Specifically, the statute states that there must be an assumption of the 'rights of an owner'; rights being plural. The statute intended appropriation to cover scenarios where the defendant 'assumes' ownership of the property through his appropriation. Ormerod and Laird (*Smith, Hogan, & Ormerod's Criminal Law*, 15th edn (OUP, 2018)) argue that the switching of price labels 'may be dishonest, but is hardly consistent with an assumption of ownership, and is not even the means by which he intends to deprive V of the item in question'. In addition, the pair refer to the decision in *Morris* as 'obviously wrong'. Further to this, Lord Lowry in his dissenting judgment in *Gomez* reasoned that:

> 'the rights' may mean '*all* the rights,' which would be the normal grammatical meaning, or (less probably, in my opinion) 'any rights:' … Still looking at section 3(1), I point out that 'any later assumption of a right to it' (that is, a right to the property) amounts to an appropriation of a right to it and that normally 'a right to it' means a right to the property and not a right *in* it. (original emphasis)

Despite the persuasiveness of Ormerod and Laird's arguments, and Lord Lowry's statement, I would tend to agree with Lord Keith in that the swapping of price labels is a right that can only be undertaken by the owner of the property or those with permission from the owner to do so. By taking it upon himself to change the price label, the defendant did assume ownership of the goods and thus effectively appropriated property. Such a view is supported by Melissaris ('The Concept of Appropriation and the Offence of Theft' (2007) 70 MLR 581). See *R v Darroux* [2018] EWCA Crim 1009 for a discussion of appropriation in circumstances where there is no control over the property in question.

Appropriation and consent

Under the former law of larceny, the prosecution held the burden of proving that the defendant appropriated the victim's property 'without consent of the owner' (Larceny Act 1916, s 1(1)). Therefore, if the owner had consented to the defendant taking the property, there would have been no offence. Their Lordships in *Morris* continued with this approach and provided, in *obiter*, that in order for the act to be classed as an appropriation for the purposes of theft, there must be an 'adverse interference with or usurpation of' the rights of the owner. This decision, however, was contrary to their Lordships' previous decision in *Lawrence v Metropolitan Police Commissioner* [1972] AC 626. There, the House of Lords ruled that no adverse interference with rights was necessary for appropriation.

case example

Charge:
Theft (TA 1968, s 1)

Case progression:
Crown Court – Guilty

Court of Appeal – Conviction upheld

House of Lords – Conviction upheld

Point of law:
Consent and appropriation

In *Lawrence v Metropolitan Police Commissioner* [1972] AC 626, the defendant (a London taxi driver) took £7 from the victim's wallet to pay for his fare. The victim was an Italian student with little use of English and offered the defendant the ability to take the necessary money (in this case 50p) to pay for his fare.

The defendant was convicted and his appeal dismissed in both the Court of Appeal and House of Lords, who ruled that the defendant appropriated property despite the consent given by the victim to take the necessary money.

In dismissing the defendant's appeal, Viscount Dilhorne concluded that:

> I see no ground for concluding that the omission of the words 'without the consent of the owner' [from the Theft Act] was inadvertent and not deliberate, and to read the subsection as if they were included is, in my opinion, wholly unwarranted. Parliament by omission of these words has relieved the prosecution of the burden of establishing that the taking was without the owner's consent. That is no longer an ingredient of the offence.

The problem that existed from *Morris*, however, was that there was no indication on the part of the House of Lords that *Lawrence* had been distinguished or overruled. At that point we thus had two contradictory statements from the House of Lords.

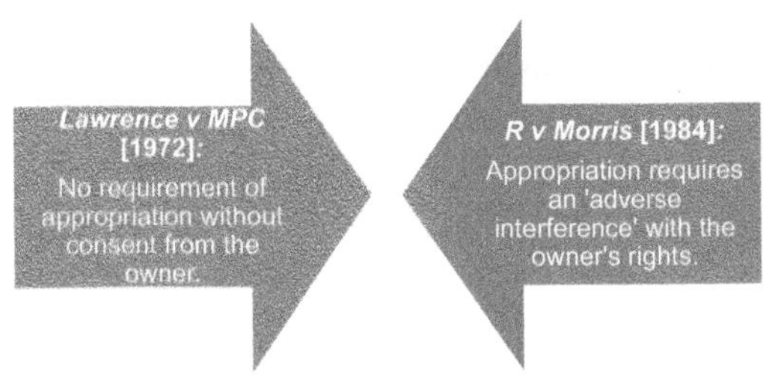

Figure 11.1 Comparing Lawrence *and* Morris

The contradiction between *Morris* and *Lawrence* was finally laid to rest by the House of Lords in *DPP v Gomez* [1993] AC 442.

case example

Charge:
Theft (TA 1968, s 1)

Case progression:
Crown Court – Guilty

Court of Appeal – Conviction quashed

House of Lords – Conviction restored

Point of law:
Consent and appropriation

In *DPP v Gomez* [1993] AC 442, the defendant, an assistant at an electrical goods shop, was asked by an acquaintance to supply goods (worth £16,000) in exchange for two building society cheques that the defendant knew had been stolen. The defendant supplied the goods after first obtaining authority to do so from the shop manager. In obtaining consent, the defendant did not inform the manager that they were stolen but in fact stated that the cheques were 'as good as cash'. The defendant was charged with and convicted of theft in the Crown Court.

The defendant appealed to the Court of Appeal which quashed his conviction on the basis that he had obtained the authority of the shop manager and could not be said to have appropriated goods without consent. The Crown appealed to the House of Lords which allowed its appeal, restoring the original conviction against the defendant. The House of Lords, by a majority of 4:1, chose *Lawrence* as the correct authority, as opposed to *Morris*, and concluded that the consent of the owner was irrelevant in deciding whether an appropriation had taken place.

Lord Keith, giving the majority decision, concluded that:

> While it is correct to say that appropriation for purposes of section 3(1) includes [an adverse interference or usurpation], it does not necessarily follow that no other act can amount to an appropriation and, in particular, that no act expressly or impliedly authorised by the owner can in any circumstances do so … an act may be an appropriation notwithstanding that it is done with the consent of the owner.

Lord Browne-Wilkinson, who agreed with Lord Keith, set out his understanding of appropriation as follows:

> I regard the word 'appropriate' in isolation as being an objective description of the act done irrespective of the mental state of either the owner or the accused. It is impossible to reconcile the decision in *Lawrence* (that the question of consent is irrelevant in considering whether there has been an appropriation) with the views expressed in *Morris*, which latter views in my judgment were incorrect.

As a result of *Lawrence* and *Gomez*, even where valid consent exists, the taking of property by the defendant will still be considered an appropriation for the purposes of theft. In his dissenting judgment in *Gomez*, Lord Lowry explained:

> The ordinary and natural meaning of 'appropriate' is to take for oneself, or to treat as one's own, property which belongs to someone else. The primary dictionary meaning is 'take possession of, take to oneself, especially without authority,' and that is in my opinion the meaning which the word bears in section 1(1). The act of appropriating property is a one-sided act, done without the consent or authority of the owner. And, if the owner consents to transfer property

> to the offender or to a third party, the offender does not appropriate the property, even if the owner's consent has been obtained by fraud.

Gomez is, without question, a controversial decision. The majority in the House of Lords had now reduced 'the *actus reus* of theft almost to vanishing point' (JC Smith, 'Commentary on *R v Gomez*' (1993) Crim LR 305). With our next case of *R v Hinks* [2001] 2 AC 241, the meaning of appropriation has been expanded even further.

Appropriation of gifts

The decisions in *Lawrence* and *Gomez* were taken to a new extreme with the House of Lords' judgment in *R v Hinks* [2001] 2 AC 241. The issue in this regard is whether it is possible for an individual with indefeasible title to the property in civil law (ie the title is technically theirs) to be guilty of theft.

case example

Charge:
Theft (TA 1968, s 1)

Case progression:
Crown Court – Guilty

Court of Appeal – Conviction upheld

House of Lords – Conviction upheld

Point of law:
Gifts and appropriation

In *R v Hinks* [2001] 2 AC 241, the victim, a middle-aged man with a low IQ, inherited a large sum of money (£60,000 to be exact) on the death of his father. The defendant, who described herself as the victim's 'carer', was gifted this money by the victim. The defendant was charged with and convicted of theft in the Crown Court.

The defendant first appealed to the Court of Appeal, which dismissed her appeal, and then to the House of Lords.

The House of Lords decided, by a majority of 3:2, that the rules of *Gomez* were just as applicable to valid gifts, meaning that the taking of a gift will still amount to an appropriation and, where coupled with dishonest intention, will amount to theft.

Lord Steyn, providing the leading judgment, concluded that:

> In other words it is immaterial whether the act was done with the owner's consent or authority. … *Gomez* therefore gives effect to section 3(1) of the Act by treating 'appropriation' as a neutral word comprehending 'any assumption by a person of the rights of an owner'.

The result of *Hinks* is that the recipient of a valid gift may be convicted of theft if the arbiters of fact are satisfied that the defendant was also dishonest in his appropriation. In the earlier case of *R v Mazo* [1996] Crim LR 435, Pill LJ stated that it is 'common ground that the receiver of a valid gift *inter vivos* could not be the subject of a conviction for theft'. This was supported by Beatson and Simester ('Stealing One's Own Property' (1999) 115 LQR 372) who argued that it was absurd that the defendant was to be liable for theft and yet 'as a matter of civil law, remain[ed] the owner of the property stolen'. Indeed, this was the view taken by the Court of Appeal in *R v Gallasso* [1992] 98 Cr App R 284 and Lords Hutton and Hobhouse in their dissenting judgments in *Hinks*. *Hinks* had the effect of overruling *Mazo*, which, in turn, has led to further criticisms of the decision in *Hinks*, most notably from JC Smith in his case commentary ('Commentary on *R v Hinks*' [2001] Crim LR 162). Smith argues that:

> The decision, with all respect, is contrary to common sense. It is absurd that a person should be guilty of stealing property which is his and in which no one else has any legal interest whatever.

As a result of *Lawrence*, *Morris*, *Gomez* and *Hinks*, appropriation of property now extends to any action taken by the defendant, whether lawful or not. Herring (*Criminal Law: Text, Cases, and Materials*, 9th edn (OUP, 2020)) notes that '[v]irtually every acquisition of property now satisfies the *actus reus* of theft …'. According to Giles and Uglow ('Appropriation and Manifest Criminality in Theft' (1992) 56 J Crim L 179), the key distinction between lawful appropriation and theft lies, therein, with the dishonesty of the defendant. The pair comment that theft is now a crime of *mens rea* lacking any 'manifest criminality' in the *actus reus*. Given the broad reading of appropriation by the House of Lords, s 3 rarely presents a problem for prosecutors to overcome.

Secondary appropriations (later assumptions)

Section 3(1) effectively deals with two situations. The first we have already considered is where the defendant first appropriates property. The second involves the circumstance where the defendant finds property 'without stealing it' (thus amounting to a primary, honest and lawful appropriation) but later decides to *keep or deal* with the property as its owner (thus amounting to a secondary, dishonest appropriation).

example

Jack comes across a watch in the middle of the street. He honestly picks up the watch before looking around and then, deciding to keep it for himself, pockets the watch.

When Jack first picks up the watch, although he appropriates property, his appropriation is honest. However, by then placing the watch in his pocket, Jack has appropriated the property for a second time, this time dishonestly.

By deciding to keep the watch, Jack has appropriated it, within the meaning of the TA 1968.

Note that any further conduct relating to the watch on Jack's part, however, will not amount to an appropriation. The property had already been stolen when it had been pocketed; it cannot be said that if he wears the watch the day after that he will appropriate it again. In this regard, an appropriation may be considered a single and instantaneous act, as multiple appropriations or as a continuing appropriation. In the majority of cases, the act of appropriation is viewed as a single and instant act. This would support the view in *R v Morris* [1984] AC 320 whereby the defendant had appropriated property the moment he laid his hands on the goods with the relevant dishonest intention.

The Court of Appeal in *R v Atakpu* [1994] QB 69 took the view, however, that appropriation can continue 'for as long as the thief can sensibly be regarded as in the act of stealing' (although this did not apply to the defendants in question). Theft may, therefore, be considered a continuing act. So long as the appropriation is said to be 'continuing' (ie the defendant is 'on the job'), the additional elements of theft may follow at any time. The main distinction to make is between that of a single appropriation, multiple single appropriations and a single continuing appropriation. Not all of these appropriations will lead to liability for theft.

Secondary appropriations, however, must be distinguished from appropriations by a *bona fide* purchaser (see below).

Appropriation by omission?

Whilst the courts have not yet dealt with the question of whether an appropriation is capable by way of omission, the author's view is that such is possible given the operation of s 3(1) above, so long as the defendant owes a duty to act (see **Chapter 2**).

Bona fide purchasers

By s 3(2) of the TA 1968, any later acquisition or dealing with stolen property which is done by a *bona fide* purchaser will not be considered as theft. A *bona fide* purchaser is simply an individual who has purchased the property in question for value (ie money or money's worth) and has done so in good faith (ie innocently). In a circumstance where a *bona fide* purchaser exists, it would be harsh and unfair for him to be liable for an offence. Indeed, this was the view taken by the CLRC which commented that 'on the whole it seems to us that, whatever view is taken of the buyer's moral duty, the law would be too strict if it made him guilty of theft'.

Note that the following conditions must be met in order for s 3(2) to apply:

- The defendant must be considered a 'purchaser'. By this, we simply mean that the defendant must have paid for the property (ie given consideration). We know this from the phrase 'transferred for value' in s 3(1). This means that if a defendant receives property as a gift (ie as a 'volunteer' in law), the s 3(2) exception does not apply.
- The defendant must be acting in 'good faith' (ie *bona fide*). In this regard, the purchaser must not know that the property is stolen. If there is knowledge that property is stolen, the defendant will be acting in bad faith (*mala fide*) and the s 3(2) exception will not apply.
- The exception only applies where the purchaser keeps the property. If the purchaser then deals with the property (eg sells it on), now knowing that it was stolen in the first place, the purchaser may be liable for fraud.

For an application of this rule, see the case of *R v Wheeler* (1990) 92 Cr App R 279 concerning the sale of stolen military antiques.

A need for 'physical appropriation'?

A question that has come before the courts on a number of occasions is whether appropriation requires the physical touching of property. The case of *R v Pitham and Hehl* (1976) 65 Cr App R 45 answers this in the negative. Specifically, the Court of Appeal ruled that an invitation from the defendant to purchase the victim's furniture whilst the victim was in prison was held to be an appropriation the moment he invited individuals to the house. See *R v Darroux* [2018] EWCA Crim 1009 for confirmation of this.

A need to gain?

Section 1(2) of the TA 1968 provides:

> It is immaterial whether the appropriation is made with a view to gain, or is made for the thief's own benefit.

The subsection simply means that where a gain was made by a person other than the defendant, the defendant can still be charged with theft. This can be seen in the case of *Pilgram v Rice-Smith* [1977] 2 All ER 658 where the defendant and his friend conducted a fraudulent scheme whereby the defendant, who worked at the meat counter in a supermarket, would sell his friend a quantity of sliced meat at a reduced price, without his employer's consent to do so. Both individuals were charged with theft despite the defendant making no gains from such agreement with his friend. Likewise in *R (A) v Snaresbrook Crown Court* (2001) *The Times*, 12 July, it was held that the defendant was liable for theft despite his actions being carried out to financially benefit the company that he worked for.

This section also operates in circumstances where the defendant intends to cause *only* a loss to the victim, as opposed to making a gain.

example

Jack is sick and tired of being bossed around by his manager at the supermarket where he works. Whilst Jack is cashing up the tills, he removes a substantial amount of money and throws it in the bin.

In this case, Jack has caused a loss to the store with no real gain for himself (other than a form of retribution for his poor treatment). Jack has appropriated property by treating the money as his own (ie he has assumed the rights of the owner), and it is irrelevant that Jack does not make a gain for himself.

11.2.2.2 *Actus reus:* (ii) of property (TA 1968, s 4)

Section 4(1) of the TA 1968 provides:

> 'Property' includes money and all other property, real or personal, including things in action and other intangible property.

Although the meaning of property would appear naturally wide by use of the phrase 'all other property', it is still necessary to consider what items can and cannot be classed as property for the purposes of s 4(1). We can take this description and break down each individual element as follows:

Table 11.2 Property in theft

Property	Meaning
Money	Coins and banknotes of any currency
Real property (*realty*)	Land and buildings
Personal property (*personalty*) (Chose in possession)	Tangible property that can be moved, such as jewellery, cars etc
Personal property (*personalty*) (Chose in action)	Intangible property such as a bank account, a cheque, intellectual property etc

Money

Coins and banknotes are property (*R v Davis* (1988) 88 Cr App R 347). Cheques or credit balances are not, however, included in the definition of 'money'. Although a cheque is a physical piece of paper, it merely represents the value of the money within a bank account. The paper itself is meaningless in terms of 'money'.

Real property

Real property, also known as 'realty', is concerned with land. Land is defined, for the purposes of civil law, in s 205(1)(ix) of the Law of Property Act 1925 as including

> ... land of any tenure, and mines and minerals, whether or not held apart from the surface, buildings or parts of buildings (whether the division is horizontal, vertical or made in any other way) ...

In basic form, land includes anything that is fixed to the ground or forms part of the foundation/realty of the estate.

Section 4(2) of the TA 1968 provides:

> A person cannot steal land, or things forming part of land and severed from it by him or by his directions, except in the following cases, that is to say—
> (a) when he is a trustee or personal representative, or is authorised by power of attorney, or as liquidator of a company, or otherwise, to sell or dispose of land belonging to another, and he appropriates the land or anything forming part of it by dealing with it in breach of the confidence reposed in him; or
> (b) when he is not in possession of the land and appropriates anything forming part of the land by severing it or causing it to be severed, or after it has been severed; or
> (c) when, being in possession of the land under a tenancy, he appropriates the whole or part of any fixture or structure let to be used with the land.
>
> For purposes of this subsection 'land' does not include incorporeal hereditaments; 'tenancy' means a tenancy for years or any less period and includes an agreement for such a tenancy, but a person who after the end of a tenancy remains in possession as statutory tenant or otherwise is to be treated as having possession under the tenancy, and 'let' shall be construed accordingly.

From this, the basic principle to understand is that land cannot be stolen *unless* one of the three circumstances is present:

Table 11.3 Exceptions to the principle that land cannot be stolen

Circumstances where land can be stolen
Appropriation by trustees/personal representatives/power of attorney: Land may be appropriated through unauthorised dispositions by persons identified in s 4(2)(a) (eg a trustee selling land belonging to the trust which he was not authorised to sell). In *R v Gimbert* [2018] EWCA Crim 2190, the Court of Appeal ruled that the exception concerning those 'authorised by power of attorney' only applied to those persons who *are* lawfully 'authorised' to act in such a way and not to those who simply *purport or hold themselves out* as acting in such a role, or where their authority is invalid for some reason. (TA 1968, s 4(2)(a))
Appropriation by persons not in possession: Appropriation only occurs when the defendant severs something from the land (eg digging up plants belonging to your neighbour). (TA 1968, s 4(2)(b))
Appropriation by tenants of fixtures: A tenant will not be guilty of theft from severance of things forming part of the land. He may be guilty, however, if he appropriates a fixture, such as a cupboard or fireplace, which is the property of the landlord. (TA 1968, s 4(2)(c))

Further, by s 4(3) of the TA 1968 (the so-called 'flora' provision):

> A person who picks mushrooms growing wild on any land, or who picks flowers, fruit or foliage from a plant growing wild on any land, does not (although not in possession of the land) steal what he picks, unless he does it *for reward or for sale or other commercial purpose*. (emphasis added)
>
> For purposes of this subsection 'mushroom' includes any fungus, and 'plant' includes any shrub or tree.

This section is designed to ensure that persons who pick wild mushrooms, flowers or berries for non-commercial purposes cannot be guilty of theft. This is so even if they trespass on private land in order to pick the mushrooms, flowers or berries. Those individuals who pick such property for commercial purposes, however, such as picking holly bushes for sale at Christmas time, may be guilty of theft. However, all other elements of the offence must also be established. Note that this rule only covers circumstances where the flora are 'picked'; if an entire plant is removed (ie uprooted), this will still amount to theft (regardless of any commercial purposes) under s 4(2)(b) above.

Should an individual pick, destroy or uproot a wild plant that is protected under the Wildlife and Countryside Act 1981, he may commit an offence under s 13 of that Act.

Personalty (chose in possession)

The word 'personalty' is interchangeable with 'personal property' and is best defined as anything other than land. Therefore, if you come across property which is not land, you know it will be personalty. Personalty itself, however, can be divided into two forms:

- choses in possession; and
- choses in action.

First, we shall deal with choses in possession. Also known as a 'thing in possession', this type of property concerns moveable and tangible goods (ie you can see them, feel them and move them). These choses in possession are most commonly referred to as 'chattels' and include such property as:

- jewellery;
- cars;
- bicycles;
- clothing, etc.

All forms of chattel amount to 'property' and are capable of being stolen.

Personalty (chose in action)

A chose, or thing, in action simply describes property that is intangible (ie it cannot be seen or felt). The rights (and value of the property) are vested in the action taken to claim the property (ie by having the ability to sue for a particular debt owed) as opposed to taking physical possession of it (*Torkington v Magee* [1902] 2 KB 427). The following are examples of choses in action:

- bank accounts;
- cheques;
- intellectual property, etc.

Reference to 'other intangible property' in s 4(1) is technically unnecessary given that choses in action cover all kinds of intangible property. It will be helpful to consider some examples where the law of theft interacts with intangible property.

Where a bank account is in credit, the relationship between the bank and customer is that of 'debtor' and 'creditor'. The victim does not have a right to the 'money in the bank' as such money remains intangible. Rather, the victim has a right to the thing in action, namely the right to payment of the money from the bank owed to him when requested. Perhaps the use of an example will help to clarify this point.

example

Jack, pretending to be Jill, contacts the bank and requests that it debits Jill's account by £1,000 and transfers the sum into his account.

In this case, Jack has not appropriated the money in the bank; he has appropriated Jill's right, or ability, to control the sum of money within the bank account through the action she may take. (Compare with *R v Darroux* [2018] EWCA Crim 1009.)

This was the point emphasised in *R v Williams (Roy)* [2001] 1 Cr App R 362 by the trial judge who directed the jury as follows:

> If you get a householder to draw a cheque on a bank or building society and cause the cheque to be presented, you cause the householder's credit balance to be diminished, and accordingly take that credit balance for your own use.

This is true even where the victim is overdrawn. If the victim still has a right to payment up to the sum allotted by the bank (ie the limit of his overdraft), this right can be appropriated (*R v Kohn* (1979) 69 Cr App R 395). In *Chan Man-sin v AG of Hong Kong* [1988] 1 WLR 196, Lord Oliver expanded on this point:

> [O]ne who draws, presents and negotiates a cheque on a particular bank account is assuming the rights of the owner of the credit in the account or (as the case may be) of the prenegotiated right to draw on the account up to the agreed figure.

For a recent comparison to *Williams (Roy)*, see *R v Darroux* [2018] EWCA Crim 1009, in which the Court of Appeal concluded that submitting falsely inflated overtime/on-call claims and claims in lieu of holiday entitlement by the defendant was not an appropriation given that there was no assumption of the rights of the owner.

Where a defendant has withdrawn funds knowing that he has no funds in his *own* account and no overdraft agreement with the bank to cover the amount withdrawn, this is likely to amount to theft of the cash withdrawn (see *Chodorek v Poland* [2017] EWHC 995 (Admin)). This must be compared with the situation where another person (ie the victim) is overdrawn and has an overdraft agreement with the bank but no overdraft facility remaining. In this instance, the defendant cannot be liable for theft should he draw a cheque on the account or transfer money, but he may be liable for attempted theft or fraud (*R v Navvabi* [1986] 3 All ER 102). The victim, in this scenario, has no contractual right to the money and thus there is no property to steal. Ormerod and Laird (*Smith, Hogan, & Ormerod's Criminal Law*, 15th edn (OUP, 2018)) liken this to 'stealing from an empty pocket'. The appropriate offence in that case is likely to be fraud.

A cheque may be stolen in three ways:

- *As a piece of paper:* If the defendant decides to keep the paper without cashing it, he will be guilty of theft of the paper (*R v Roach (Daniel)* [2011] EWCA Crim 918; though cf *R v Preddy* [1996] AC 815).
- *As a thing in action:* If the defendant presents the victim's cheque to credit his own account, he will be guilty of theft of the victim's credit balance (*R v Ngan* [1998] 1 Cr App R 331).
- *As a valuable security:* The defendant may be guilty of theft of the physical aspect of a cheque, that being the writing on the cheque (*R v Arnold* [1997] 4 All ER 1).

As a result of these three manners of stealing a cheque, Smith ('Obtaining Cheques by Deception or Theft' [1997] Crim LR 396) describes a cheque as a piece of paper which has 'special properties … it is an effective key to the drawer's bank account'.

Other forms of property

There are many other forms of 'property' which have special rules regarding their potential to be stolen under the TA 1968. Many of the types listed below *can* be stolen whilst others *cannot*. We shall deal with a few examples here:

- *Wild creatures:* By s 4(4) (the so-called 'fauna' provision), wild creatures that are tamed, for example in a zoo, are classed as property and can be stolen. However, wild creatures that are untamed cannot be stolen (*Cresswell v DPP* [2006] EWHC 3379 (Admin) – in relation to wild badgers). There must be sufficient evidence that the wild creature has been 'reduced into possession', simply meaning that the animal is deemed a 'chose in possession' (ie a pet – *R v Howlett and Howlett* [1968] Crim LR 222). On 3 July 2018, Conservative MP for Aberdeen South, Ross Thomson, introduced a Private Members' Bill in the House of Commons that would create a specific offence of theft of pets (the Pets (Theft) Bill 2017–19). The Bill has not proceeded through the House and is unlikely to do so.
- *Electricity:* Electricity is not property that can be appropriated (*Low v Blease* [1975] Crim LR 513) and thus it cannot be stolen. However, improper use or abstract of electricity can be charged under s 13 of the TA 1968. Note that whilst electricity cannot be stolen, within the meaning of s 1, gas (*R v White* (1853) 169 ER 696) and water (*Ferens v O'Brien* (1883) 11 QBD 21) that is siphoned from a container can be.
- *Quota systems:* In *AG of Hong Kong v Chan Nai-Keung* [1987] 1 WLR 1339 it was held that export quota systems are deemed as property under s 4(1) as they are things of value that can be bought and sold. Although they have not been considered as 'things in action', they are considered 'other intangible property'.
- *Intellectual property:* Many IP rights, such as patents (Patents Act 1977, s 30), copyright (Copyright, Designs and Patents Act 1988, s 1) and design rights (Copyright, Designs and Patents Act 1988, s 213) are considered as choses in action that can be stolen.
- *Confidential information:* Although confidential information can be sold and has value, it is not regarded as property under s 4(1). In *Oxford v Moss* (1978) 68 Cr App R 183, the Divisional Court concluded that the defendant could not be liable for theft for copying the questions from an examination paper he was due to sit. The exam questions amounted to mere information and could not be 'stolen'. Had the defendant taken the actual paper (as the defendant did in *R v Akbar* [2002] EWCA Crim 2241), this would be theft of the paper (so long as the other elements are satisfied – specifically, an intention to permanently deprive), but not the information contained within it. Griew (*The Theft Acts 1968 and 1978*, 7th edn (Sweet & Maxwell, 1995)) commends the approach taken by the Court in *Oxford*, stating that the TA is not the 'appropriate instrument to deal with this specialised kind of mischief'. However, *Oxford* has come under attack by the Supreme Court of New Zealand in *Dixon v The Queen* [2015] NZSC 147, which held that digital files were 'property' for the purposes of theft, given that information can be identified, has value, is capable of being transferred to others, and has a physical presence. It is unlikely that the English courts will conform to this view. Allen and Edwards (*Criminal Law*, 15th edn (OUP, 2019)) are critical of *Oxford v Moss*. They state that:

  > To read confidential information is to assume a right of an owner as it is the right of the owner to determine who should have access to it; it is arguable,

therefore, that confidential information should be regarded as property which may be appropriated.

The Law Commission in its Consultation Paper ('Legislating the Criminal Code: Misuse of Trade Secrets' (Law Com No 150, 1997)) proposed the introduction of a new offence targeting the disclosure of trade secrets without authority to do so. The new offence was an attempt to rectify the situation following *Oxford*; however, no such provision has entered into force.

- *Human bodies:* Generally, human bodies (or corpses) are not considered property, in line with the ideal of individual autonomy (*Dobson v North Tyneside HA* [1997] 1 WLR 596). However, bodies and body parts are capable of being stolen 'if they have acquired different attributes by virtue of the application of skill, such as dissection or preservation techniques, for exhibition or teaching purposes' (per Rose LJ in *R v Kelly; R v Lindsay* [1999] QB 621). *Kelly* is aimed at dealing with the theft of cadavers, or body parts used for scientific research, history or teaching purposes. Specific offences in relation to the improper and unauthorised use, storage or removal of human bodies, organs and other tissue are contained in s 5 of the Human Tissue Act 2004.
- *Other bodily matters:* Semen may be stolen (*Yearworth v North Bristol NHS Trust* [2010] QB 1 – eg from storage at an infertility clinic), as may urine (*R v Welsh* [1974] RTR 478 – eg a urine sample (evidence) stolen from police).
- *Services:* Services do not constitute property that is capable of being stolen. So, where an individual walks away from a restaurant without paying for their meal, or walks away without paying for their haircut, they cannot be liable for theft. The Theft Act 1978, s 3 attempts to correct this imbalance through the offence of making off without payment (see **Chapter 12**). Some offences of fraud may also be relevant in this regard (see **Chapter 13**).
- *Unlawful property:* In *R v Smith, Plummer and Haines* [2011] 1 Cr App R 379, the Court of Appeal ruled that unlawful property can itself be stolen (ie a defendant may steal illegal drugs from the complainant who unlawfully possesses them). Lord Judge CJ justified this decision on the basis that 'the criminal law is concerned with keeping the Queen's peace, not vindicating individual property rights' (quoting *Smith's Law of Theft*). Further to this, the defendant may be liable for theft for stealing an item from the victim that the victim had first stolen.

Given that quite a lot of property has been discussed up to this stage, it may be useful to see which property can and cannot be stolen in a concise form. This is done in **Table 11.4**.

Table 11.4 Summarising what can, and cannot, be stolen

Property	Can it be stolen?
Money	✓
Land	✓/x
Choses in possession	✓
Choses in action	✓/x
Wild creatures (tamed)	✓
Wild creatures (untamed)	x
Electricity	x

Property	Can it be stolen?
Intellectual property	✓
Quota systems	×
Confidential information	×
Human body parts	✓/×
Bodily fluids	✓
Services	×
Property that is already stolen or unlawful	✓

11.2.2.3 *Actus reus:* (iii) belonging to another (TA 1968, s 5)

Section 5(1) of the TA 1968 provides:

> Property shall be regarded as belonging to any person having possession or control of it, or having in it any proprietary right or interest (not being an equitable interest arising only from an agreement to transfer or grant an interest).

The use of 'any person', as opposed to referring to property of 'the victim' or words to that effect, indicate that the identity of the owner of the property is generally irrelevant, provided that that person, as opposed to the defendant, has a right or interest in the property in question. Therefore, a conviction of theft may be upheld even in cases where the true owner is unknown, provided that the property did belong to someone else and the defendant knew this. The emphasis, in this regard, has to be on whether another person has 'possession or control' of the property or some other proprietary right.

In *Lawrence v Metropolitan Police Commissioner* [1972] AC 626, Viscount Dilhorne stated that 'belonging to another' simply meant that the property must belong to another person at the time of the appropriation, ie there must be a coincidence in time. This may sound rather obvious, but consider the following two examples:

- Jack and Jill decide not to pay for a meal *after* they have eaten it (as in *Corcoran v Whent* [1977] Crim LR 52).
- Jack and Jill decide not to pay for the fuel in their car *after* they have refuelled the car (as in *Edwards v Ddin* [1976] 1 WLR 942).

In both of these cases, Jack and Jill have only dishonestly appropriated property *after* it belongs to them. Upon being eaten, the food no longer belongs to the restaurant, and upon entering the gas tank, the fuel no longer belongs to the petrol company. In both of these cases, Jack and Jill cannot be liable for theft as the goods do not belong to *another* at the time of the dishonest appropriation. However, the law has responded to this problem with its creation of the offence of making off without payment contrary to s 3 of the TA 1978 (see **Chapter 12**).

There are a number of concepts to be aware of when considering property belonging to another.

Table 11.5 Concepts of 'belonging to another'

Concept	Explanation	Authority
Ownership	Theft is usually committed against the *owner* of property. The owner may or may not be in possession of the property.	*R v Hancock* [1990] 2 QB 242 – theft from the Crown of 16 ancient coins found in an area which appeared to have been the site of a Romano-Celtic temple. *AG Reference (No 2 of 1982)* [1984] 2 All ER 216 – theft of company property by the directors of that company. The company is a separate legal personality from its shareholders and thus is the owner of the property.
Co-ownership	Theft may be committed by one co-owner of property against the other. Both owners have a proprietary interest that can be infringed by the other.	*R v Bonner* [1970] 2 All ER 97 – theft of scrap metal belonging to the partnership.
Possession/ control	There may be circumstances in which the owner of the property does not have possession or control of it, but another party does. Theft may be committed against the party with possession/control.	*R v Woodman* [1974] QB 754 – theft of scrap metal under the control of the former owner of the property (they had sold the scrap metal but the metal remained on site). It was irrelevant that the victim was not aware that the scrap metal remained on their site; they had restricted access and were in control of the site.
Lien	The owner of property may commit theft where he takes his property from the holder of a lien (or security).	*R v Turner (No 2)* [1971] 2 All ER 441 – theft of the defendant's own car from the victim who held a security over the car whilst it was being repaired. Compare with *R v Meredith* [1974] Crim LR 253 in which the police held no lien over a car seized which was causing an obstruction to the highway. The defendant could not be guilty of theft by surreptitiously taking the car back from the police.
Proprietary right	Where an individual or body holds a sufficient proprietary right to a property, an individual may be liable for theft of that property.	*R v Marshall* [1998] 2 Cr App R 282 – the defendant sold unused London Underground tickets and travel cards to other travellers. The tickets 'belonged to London Underground'. Although the tickets had been issued to travellers on a previous occasion, London Underground retained a *sufficient proprietary right* in the tickets.
Abandoned property	Where property has been abandoned by one party, it cannot be stolen from him by another. The owner must have relinquished all rights over the property. Where property is left by a person for the purpose that another person, or company, shall take it, it shall not be considered as abandoned.	*R v Small* (1988) 86 Cr App R 170 – the defendant took a car which had been parked at an angle on a street corner for two weeks with the doors unlocked and open and the keys in the ignition. The battery was flat, as was one of the tyres. The defendant thought it was abandoned property and so he could take it. *R (Ricketts) v Basildon Magistrates' Court* [2011] 1 Cr App R 202 – Williams J inferred that items left outside charity shops had not been abandoned as ownership was intended to be transferred to the charity shop. Whilst the charity shop could not be said to own, possess or control the items at that time, there was an intention to give and an attempt to effect delivery of the items on the part of the donor.

Concept	Explanation	Authority
	The same can be said with property that is set aside for disposal or destruction.	*Williams v Phillips* (1957) 41 Cr App R 5 – dustmen were convicted of stealing goods from dustbins collected in the course of their duties as the property was not abandoned but merely left for the dustmen to take and destroy in line with their duties.
Lost property	Property is not abandoned in circumstances where it is lost or where the owner is not currently able to recover it.	*R v Rostron* [2003] EWCA Crim 2206 – the Court of Appeal held that golf balls lying at the bottom of a lake within a golf club still belonged to the club, even where there was no immediate intention to fish them out. See also *Hibbert v McKiernan* [1948] 2 KB 142 – a case on very similar facts to *Rostron*.
Property of deceased	Property of the deceased, in circumstances when it cannot be said to belong to another, cannot be stolen.	*R v Sullivan and Ballion* [2002] Crim LR 758 – the Crown Court ruled that appropriating property from a dead body could not amount to theft, as the property did not belong to another. In the author's view, this judgment must be incorrect. The property would pass to another upon death either via a will or through the law of intestacy. This view is supported by Alan Reed ('Stealing Property from a Corpse' [2003] 67(3) J Crim L 186).
Unlawful/ stolen property	As noted above in relation to 'property', unlawful or stolen property can be stolen from another.	*R v Smith, Plummer and Haines* [2011] 1 Cr App R 379 – the defendant was convicted of stealing illegal drugs from a drug dealer. The drugs belonged to another, even if they were illegal. Likewise, if goods have already been stolen by Jack and then Jill steals them from Jack, Jill can be liable for theft.
Treasure and finder's title	Treasure, if found, is vested in the franchisee (if there is one) or, more commonly, the Crown.	Treasure Act 1996, s 4.
	Property (other than treasure) found *in* the land (ie it is buried) will generally belong to the owner of the land.	*Waverley BC v Fletcher* [1996] QB 334 – the defendant found a medieval gold brooch in a public park using a metal detector. The Council owned the park and claimed ownership of the brooch.
	Property (other than treasure) found *on* the land (ie it is not buried) will generally belong to the finder of the item.	*Parker v British Airways Board* [1982] 1 QB 1004 – the defendant, a passenger in an executive lounge at an airport, found a gold bracelet.

Trust property (TA 1968, s 5(2))

Section 5 of the TA 1968 further provides:

> (2) Where property is subject to a trust, the persons to whom it belongs shall be regarded as including any person having a right to enforce the trust, and an intention to defeat the trust shall be regarded accordingly as an intention to deprive of the property any person having that right.

Section 5(2) simply means that the two parties to a trust, ie the trustee (who holds legal title) and the beneficiary (who holds equitable title), both fall within the definition of 'belonging to another'. Therefore if the trustee appropriates the trust property, this will be considered theft under s 5(2) and vice versa.

Property received for a purpose (TA 1968, s 5(3))

Section 5 of the TA 1968 also provides:

> (3) Where a person receives property from or on account of another, and is under an obligation to the other to retain and deal with that property or its proceeds in a particular way, the property or proceeds shall be regarded (as against him) as belonging to the other.

Section 5(3) simply provides that where a person receives property to deal with it in a particular way, that property will belong to another, specifically the person who transferred the property to the defendant. It is important to note the following:

- The obligation under s 5(3) must be a legal one, as opposed to merely a moral or social one (*R v Mainwaring* (1982) 74 Cr App R 99; *R v Foster* [2011] EWCA Crim 1192). It is a matter for the judge to decide whether an obligation is a legal one or not; the beliefs of the defendant as to the nature of the obligation will not be relevant here (but may be relevant to the question of dishonesty) (*R v Dyke* [2001] EWCA Crim 2184).
- The defendant must know that he is under such an obligation (*R v Wills* (1991) 92 Cr App R 297).
- The obligation must be to deal with the particular property in a particular way. A mere contractual obligation to do something with the property is not sufficient. For example, in *R v Hall* [1973] QB 126, the defendant was a travel agent who paid client money into his general trading account. The business collapsed and the defendant had failed to use the money to pay for the holidays. The Court held that the defendant could not be liable for theft given that there was no obligation on him to deal with that particular property (eg that particular £100) and use it for the holiday payment. The defendant's obligation was to use any money that was available to the travel agency to pay for the holiday. Had the defendant deposited the money into a special client's money account (similar to a trust), the outcome may have been different (as it was in *R v Klineberg; R v Marsden* (1991) 1 Cr App R 427).

A couple of examples may assist here.

example

Jack has received an advanced payment from his flatmate, Andy, to be used specifically to pay the gas bill. Jack spends the money on Christmas presents.

In this case, there is a theft of property under s 5(3) (as in *Davidge v Bunnett* [1984] Crim LR 297).

example

Jill works for a charity, specifically dealing with sponsorship money. Jill deposits the sponsorship money in her own personal bank account as opposed to the charity account.

In this case, Jill has dealt with the money in a way other than for the benefit of the charity and as such may be liable for theft. This was the outcome in *R v Wain* [1995] 2 Cr App R 660, based on similar facts. In *Wain*, the Court of Appeal concluded that s 5(3) extends to situations where the defendant holds money 'on account for another'. Given that the sponsors in *Wain* intended that the money go to the charity, the defendant had an obligation to deal with the money in that way. A failure to pay forward the money meant that he was liable for theft.

Mistaken property (TA 1968, s 5(4))

Section 5(4) of the TA 1968 provides:

> Where a person gets property by another's mistake, and is under an obligation to make restoration (in whole or in part) of the property or its proceeds or of the value thereof, then to the extent of that obligation the property or proceeds shall be regarded (as against him) as belonging to the person entitled to restoration, and an intention not to make restoration shall be regarded accordingly as an intention to deprive that person of the property or proceeds.

In this case, where a defendant acquires property through another's mistake, he has a duty to rectify that mistake. The property is held to still 'belong to another' in such a case. Where no such restoration is made, the defendant may be liable for theft. This provision was inserted as a result of the Divisional Court's decision in *Moynes v Coopper* [1956] 1 QB 439.

Charge:
Larceny (Larceny Act 1916, s 2)

Case progression:
Magistrates' Court – Guilty

Appeal Committee – Conviction quashed

Divisional Court – Appeal dismissed

Point of law:
Keeping of property given in mistake

In *Moynes v Coopper* [1956] 1 QB 439, the defendant was overpaid in his weekly wages. The defendant failed to return this money when he discovered the mistake.

The defendant was charged with and convicted of larceny in the magistrates' court. The Appeal Committee ruled that the defendant could not be liable for larceny because he was entitled to keep the money, given his legal interest in it. The defendant's conviction was quashed. The prosecution appealed to the Divisional Court which dismissed the appeal on the same basis.

The Court of Appeal in *R v Gilks* [1972] 3 All ER 280 has recognised that, in this situation, s 5(4) would now apply to make the defendant liable for keeping the property that clearly still 'belonged' to his employer. The Court of Appeal made clear that there must be a legal obligation on the part of the defendant to restore the property; no such obligation existed in *Gilks* which concerned the overpayment of a horse-racing bet. Section 5(4) was applied in *AG's Reference (No 1 of 1983)* [1985] QB 182 where a police officer was mistakenly credited for a shift that she had not worked. The property, a chose in action, still belonged to her employer and the defendant held an obligation to make a restoration to her employer. Failure to do so amounted to theft.

Mistakes which are fraudulently induced are also covered by s 5(4) – see *R v Gresham* [2003] EWCA Crim 2070 where the defendant continued to collect the pension of his deceased mother from the Department of Education. The Court of Appeal considered that there was no authority for limiting the application of s 5(4) to transactions not influenced by a defendant's conduct.

11.2.2.4 *Mens rea:* (i) dishonesty (TA 1968, s 2)

The penultimate requirement for proof of theft is that the defendant was dishonest in his appropriation. By way of introduction, let us consider an example.

example

Suppose Jack is shopping at his local supermarket. Jack has been queuing at the checkout for a number of minutes, waiting to pay for his goods. Feeling extremely hungry and unable to wait, Jack opens up a chocolate bar and begins to eat it. He retains the wrapper and hands it to the checkout operator, Jill, who scans it. Jack pays and leaves the store.

In this example, Jack has appropriated property – by taking the product off the shelf and proceeding to eat it. In this instance, Jack may be liable for an offence of theft; however, it must be proven that Jack held a dishonest intention to permanently deprive. Despite all other elements being apparent, dishonesty is clearly not present on the facts as Jack intended to pay for the chocolate bar.

Suppose Jack ate the chocolate bar and then hid the wrapper in his jacket pocket before reaching the checkout. In this instance, Jack is dishonest in his appropriation as he intends to avoid payment. As is obvious from this example, the only element coming between Jack being found liable for theft and not is that of dishonesty.

From this, Griew ('Dishonesty: The Objections to *Feely* and *Ghosh*' [1985] Crim LR 341) makes an excellent point by stating that dishonesty is the key element of the law of theft as it 'focuses' the offence on cases where the appropriation is 'dishonest'.

Dishonesty *is not* defined by the TA 1968. Instead, s 2(1) merely provides three circumstances where a defendant will not be considered dishonest; these circumstances are known as cases of 'honest appropriations'. Section 2(2) provides a single circumstance where a defendant will be considered dishonest.

in practice

Section 2(1) should always be considered first before then moving on to the test for dishonesty contained within the *Ivey* case. Where a defendant succeeds in a claim of belief (under s 2(1)), the *Ivey* test should not left with the jury (*R v Rostron* [2003] EWCA Crim 2206 – under the *Ghosh* test but likely to apply to the *Ivey* test too).

Therefore, you should *only* consider *Ivey* where the defendant either does not raise a belief under s 2(1) or the circumstances listed cannot be met.

Honest appropriations

Section 2(1) of the TA 1968 provides:

> A person's appropriation of property belonging to another is not to be regarded as dishonest—
>
> (a) if he appropriates the property in the belief that he has in law the right to deprive the other of it, on behalf of himself or of a third person; or
>
> (b) if he appropriates the property in the belief that he would have the other's consent if the other knew of the appropriation and the circumstances of it; or
>
> (c) (except where the property came to him as trustee or personal representative) if he appropriates the property in the belief that the person to whom the property belongs cannot be discovered by taking reasonable steps.

Although the defence may raise evidence to show one of the above beliefs, the prosecution retains the burden of proving that the defendant held none of these beliefs. This is also a question of fact for the jury (*R v Hall* [2008] EWCA Crim 2086).

We shall consider each belief in turn.

Belief of right in law (TA 1968, s 2(1)(a))

First, the defendant will not be considered to be dishonest if he believes that he has a *right in law* to deprive the other person of the property. For example, in *R v Robinson* [1977] Crim LR 173, the defendant, charged with theft, successfully argued that he had a right in law to appropriate the property given that the victim, from whom the money was taken, owed him a debt.

According to the Court of Appeal in *R v Terry* [2001] EWCA Crim 2979, such belief need not be reasonable (so long as it is genuine). Whilst the belief need not be reasonable, the Court of Appeal in *R v Small* (1988) 86 Cr App R 170 identified that reasonableness is a factor to be used in determining whether the belief was genuinely held (ie the more unreasonable the belief is, the more likely the jury will consider that it was not genuinely held). It is also the case that the defendant does not have to have an accurate understanding of the law to raise such a belief (*R v Bernhard* [1938] 2 KB 264). On this latter point, it is questionable as to how far the section operates.

example

Jack is homeless and is caught stealing by a police officer. His reason for stealing is to survive as he is starving, having not eaten for a number of days. He believes that, out of sheer necessity, he has some right in law to food.

In this case, the Act does not preclude such a belief but, rather, holds it as a question of fact for the jury. The Act does specify, however, that the belief must be to a right *in law*, not a right *in morality* (though morality may be relevant to the common law test of dishonesty).

Belief of owner's consent (TA 1968, s 2(1)(b))

The second circumstance concerns the situation where the defendant holds a genuine, albeit mistaken, belief that the owner would have consented to the appropriation had he known of the appropriation and the circumstances. As we have seen in cases such as *Gomez*, whether property is appropriated with consent or not is irrelevant. The issue here, however, is whether the defendant holds a belief in consent. That belief will be relevant to the question of dishonesty, even if it is not relevant to the question of appropriation. Such cases may include a situation where a flatmate drinks their fellow housemate's milk in the belief that to do so would be okay, or where a babysitter eats food within the house whilst performing their duties. As with s 2(1)(a), the belief need not be reasonable – it merely requires a genuine belief.

example

Jack and Jill are housemates at university. Jack is making his evening meal and requires chopped tomatoes for his recipe. Jack forgot to buy chopped tomatoes when he purchased the other ingredients and uses the tin of tomatoes situated in Jill's cupboard.

In this case, Jill could allege that Jack has stolen her tin of tomatoes. Jack may contend that he held a genuine belief that Jill would consent to such taking. This contention would be easy to maintain if there was an established relationship between Jack and Jill that they share items in the flat, and more difficult if there was no such relationship.

Belief that owner cannot be found (TA 1968, s 2(1)(c))

The final circumstance is concerned with the situation where a defendant believes that the owner of the property cannot be found, even by taking reasonable steps. The defendant's belief must be genuinely held; however, the belief itself need not be reasonable. The question of reasonable steps will depend on the property in question, with larger and more expensive items requiring more steps to be taken than with regard to a smaller and cheaper item. For example, in *R v Small* (1988) 86 Cr App R 170, the Court of Appeal ruled that the defendant was not liable for theft after taking a car, believing it to be abandoned. The car had been left in the same place for two weeks with the keys in the ignition.

With regard to the type of property, the tribunal of fact may conclude that there are no reasonable steps to find the owner of a £5 note left on the floor; but that there may be reasonable steps if one finds a pearl necklace on the floor (eg take it to the local police station or to the 'lost and found' department of a shopping centre, for example).

example

Jack is walking down the high street on his way to work. During his walk, he notices a gold ring on the floor. Jack picks the ring up and looks around. He sees an elderly couple looking around and clearly distressed. Jack ignores the couple and pockets the ring.

In this case, whilst it is not conclusive that the ring belongs to the elderly couple, it cannot be said that reasonable steps could not have been taken to locate the owner. In this regard, Jack would be unlikely to be able to rely on s 2(1)(c).

Willingness to pay (TA 1968, s 2(2))

Section 2(2) of the TA 1968 provides:

> A person's appropriation of property belonging to another may be dishonest notwithstanding that he is willing to pay for the property.

This subsection has application where the defendant appropriates the property, having no right or claim to it, with the intention to permanently deprive; however, he leaves payment (either money or money's worth) in its place.

example

Jill wants to buy Jack's watch from him. She knows that the watch is worth around £300. One day Jill enters Jack's room, takes the watch and leaves £300 in its place.

In this regard, Jill's willingness to pay will not prevent her from being considered dishonest.

In *Wheatley v Commissioner of Police of the British Virgin Islands* [2006] 1 WLR 1683, Lord Bingham in the Privy Council noted that:

> It is certainly true that in most cases of theft there will be an original owner of money or goods who will be poorer because of the defendant's conduct.

In effect, this subsection operates to provide that payment will not automatically negate dishonesty; rather the question of dishonesty will remain a matter for the jury to consider in light of the payment (eg it may relate to whether the defendant believed that the owner would consent (s 2(1)(b)) or to the common law test of dishonesty).

in practice

In this circumstance, the defence is likely to ask the jury to find, from the circumstances, that he believed that the owner may have consented to selling the property if the defendant had asked. On this basis, the defendant would have an honest belief that his appropriation was lawful.

The test for dishonesty

If the defendant fails to establish an honest appropriation under s 2(1), the judge is then required to direct the jury to consider whether the defendant is nevertheless still dishonest in his appropriation.

The present state of law

The test for dishonesty has been relatively recently, and rather substantially, changed by the Supreme Court in *Ivey v Genting Casinos (UK) Ltd t/a Crockfords* [2017] UKSC 67. The present test was stated by Lord Hughes (at [74]) as follows:

> When dishonesty is in question the fact-finding tribunal must first ascertain (subjectively) the actual state of the individual's knowledge or belief as to the facts. The reasonableness or otherwise of his belief is a matter of evidence (often in practice determinative) going to whether he held the belief, but it is not an additional requirement that his belief must be reasonable; the question is whether it is genuinely held. When once his actual state of mind as to knowledge or belief as to facts is established, the question whether his conduct was honest or dishonest is to be determined by the fact-finder by applying the (objective) standards of ordinary decent people. There is no requirement that the defendant must appreciate that what he has done is, by those standards, dishonest.

This test can essentially be broken down into two elements:

(1) The jury must assess the state of the defendant's knowledge or belief as to the facts (this is a subjective question).

(2) The jury must then assess whether the defendant was dishonest according to the standards of ordinary decent people (this is an objective question).

This statement of the law was confirmed as correct by the Court of Appeal in *R v Barton; R v Booth* [2020] EWCA Crim 575. In effect, the test in *Ghosh* which stood for 35 years is no longer good law.

For completeness, it is worth considering the law prior to *Ivey* to allow for a proper understanding of the present position of the law.

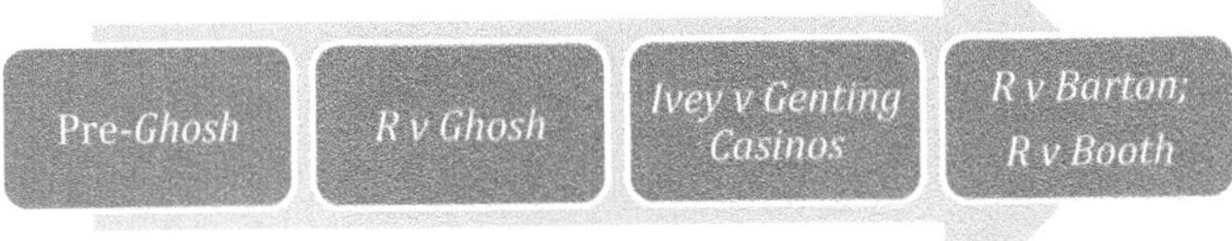

Figure 11.2 Timeline of dishonesty

(i) Pre-Ghosh: *development of the test for dishonesty*

In *Brutus v Cozens* [1973] AC 854, the House of Lords held that dishonesty was an ordinary word and was not a question of law for the judge, but a question of fact for the jury. This statement was followed by the Court of Appeal in *R v Feely* [1973] QB 530, which held that dishonesty is a question for the jury at the 'current standard of ordinary decent people'. This was obviously difficult to apply, as dishonesty may be construed differently by different people. Further to this, in *Boggeln v Williams* [1978] 2 All ER 1061, the Court of Appeal introduced a subjective element into the mix, asking the jury to consider whether the defendant believed himself to be dishonest.

Table 11.6 notes the cases pre-*Ghosh* and the side upon which they fall – ie finding the relevant standard to be objective or subjective.

*Table 11.6 Pre-*Ghosh *case law*

Objective	Subjective
R v Feely [1973] QB 530	*R v Waterfall* [1970] 1 QB 148
R v Greenstein [1975] 1 WLR 1353	*R v Royle* [1971] 1 WLR 1764
	R v Gilks [1972] 3 All ER 280
	R v Landy [1981] 1 WLR 355

(ii) A settled test in Ghosh

Given the apparent contradiction between objective and subjective tests for dishonesty, the Court of Appeal settled what would become the test for dishonesty for over 30 years in *R v Ghosh* [1982] QB 1053.

case example

Charge:
Obtaining property by deception (TA 1968, s 15)

Case progression:
Crown Court – Guilty

Court of Appeal – Conviction upheld

Point of law:
Test for dishonesty

In *R v Ghosh* [1982] QB 1053, the defendant, a surgeon, claimed fees for carrying out unnecessary operations on the victims. The defendant was charged under the old offence of obtaining property by deception and was convicted in the Crown Court.

Lord Lane CJ in the Court of Appeal stated a new test of dishonesty – what became known as the *Ghosh* test – as follows:

> In determining whether the prosecution has proved that the defendant was acting dishonestly, a jury must first of all decide whether according to the ordinary standards of reasonable and honest people what was done was dishonest. If it was not dishonest by those standards, that is the end of the matter and the prosecution fails. If it was dishonest by those standards, then the jury must consider whether the defendant himself must have realised that what he was doing was by those standards dishonest.

The *Ghosh* test was twofold, with each part having to be dealt with separately (*DPP v Gohill* [2007] EWHC 239 (Admin)).

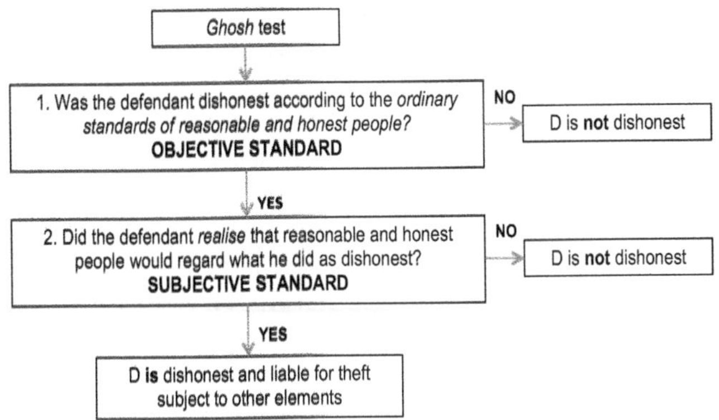

Figure 11.3 The Ghosh test

Let us look at both parts of the test in more detail.

Table 11.7 The objective and subjective limbs of Ghosh

Test	Explanation
Objective	Objective standards may change over time. The legal standard may thus change over time in line with the views of society. The Court of Appeal in *R v Hayes* [2015] EWCA Crim 1944 ruled that the appropriate test remained that of honest and ordinary persons (ie the general public). The objective standards of honesty are not to be 'set by a [relevant] market', as was submitted by the defence (eg dishonest to people in that discipline, market or industry).
Subjective	The subjective standard in this case was not concerned with whether the defendant believed her actions to be dishonest according to her own standard of honesty; rather, it was concerned with whether the defendant believed her actions to be dishonest according to the objective standard. This prevents an animal rights activist from claiming she believed her actions to be honest in line with her own views and beliefs. On this basis, it is useful to understand the second part of *Ghosh* as a subjective test based on objective foundations.

In applying the *Ghosh* test, the jury were not given a legal definition of 'dishonesty' they were required to apply; rather, they were directed to apply the common understanding of dishonesty by 'ordinary decent people'. Guest ('Law, Fact and Lay Questions' in Dennis (ed), *Criminal Law and Justice* (Sweet & Maxwell, 1987) is highly critical of the decisions in *Feely* and *Ghosh*, arguing that by requiring the jury to determine a question of law, a judge was effectively 'abdicating his constitutional responsibility'.

Further to this, the law was concerned with whether the defendant was dishonest, and whether he appreciated such according to the standards of ordinary and honest persons. McCullough J in the Court of Appeal in *R v Lightfoot* (1992) 97 Cr App R 24 emphasised that:

> There is a clear distinction between the defendant's knowledge of the law and his appreciation that he is doing something which, by the ordinary standards of reasonable and honest people, is regarded as dishonest.

In *Lightfoot*, the Court of Appeal went so far as to say that knowledge of the law is irrelevant. Indeed, although this is a persuasive argument, it ignored the subjective nature of the second test. If the defendant was not knowledgeable of the law, then surely he would not have realised or appreciated that his conduct was dishonest according to the honest and ordinary standards expected. The *dictum* in *Lightfoot* was therefore incorrect as it applied the pre-*Ghosh* test of dishonesty.

The Court of Appeal in *R v Roberts* (1986) 84 Cr App R 177 had emphasised that not every case required a *Ghosh* direction. Rather, *Ghosh* was only required where there was a dispute between the parties regarding dishonesty. For instance, suppose Jill is liable for the theft of some makeup. The prosecution alleges that Jill took the goods off the shelf and placed them in her handbag. Jill accepts that such appropriation would be dishonest, but states as her defence that she did not even perform the alleged conduct. Likewise in *R v Wood* [2002] EWCA Crim 832, the Court of Appeal emphasised that the *Ghosh* direction was only necessary where the fact-in-issue was whether the defendant was dishonest according to the ordinary person's notion of dishonesty. In *Wood*, the fact-in-issue was whether the defendant genuinely believed the property to be abandoned – this was not a question of dishonesty requiring *Ghosh*.

In applying *Ghosh*, the jury had to be directed to ensure that the respective elements were dealt with separately as objective and subjective tests. According to Campbell ('The Test of Dishonesty in *Ghosh*' (1994) 43 CLJ 349), to consider both the objective and subjective element of the test at the same time would make the latter redundant. Further to this, a mixing of the test was only likely to lead to confusion and a potential miscarriage of justice where the jury confuse the respective objective and subjective nature of acts.

The old law under *Ghosh* led to a number of cases where the jury could have struggled to reach a unanimous decision over whether the defendant was acting dishonestly, according to *Ghosh*. As a first example:

example

Jack is a foreign national from a country where public transport is free for all. Jack boards a train without payment, believing that payment is not necessary. Jack is charged with theft.

In this case, the jury would be likely to find:

- under the objective element of *Ghosh*, that the defendant's conduct was dishonest, as they (the jury) would know that public transport must be paid for;
- under the subjective element of *Ghosh*, however, that the defendant did not realise or appreciate that his conduct was dishonest according to those standards because he believes that public transport is free. Ultimately this would depend on the facts of the case, for example if there were signs on the train stating that a fare must be paid. However, in a basic sense, the defendant would not be found liable for theft.

As a second example:

example

Jill has taken it upon herself to become the Robin Hood of the 21st century. Jill travels around stealing from the rich to then give the money to the poor. Jill is charged with theft.

This case is a little harder as the view of the jury may change according to their own standards as reasonable and honest persons. In this case, the jury may have found:

- under the objective element of *Ghosh*, that the defendant's conduct was dishonest, as they (the jury) would know that, as thoughtful and caring a thought it may be, stealing from the rich to give the money to the poor remains a dishonest act;
- under the subjective element of *Ghosh*, Jill may well have understood that her actions were dishonest to those standards and may have continued to steal regardless. According to Lord Lane CJ in *Ghosh*, this was the most likely outcome and would have resulted in a conviction of theft if all other elements existed. However, Jill may have genuinely (albeit unreasonably) believed that she was not acting in a dishonest manner according to the standards of honest and reasonable people. She may have (in her own Robin Hood-style world) believed that her actions were honest and morally correct. In this case, if the jury were satisfied that Jill genuinely did not believe her actions to be dishonest by the standards of honest and reasonable people, Jill would not be found liable for theft. This is the view taken by Elliott ('Dishonesty in Theft: A Dispensable Concept' [1982] Crim LR 395).

(iii) The fundamental change in Ivey

Given the obvious difficulties that applied by use of the *Ghosh* test, the Supreme Court was prepared to fundamentally change the face of dishonesty in the case of *Ivey*.

case example

Charge:
n/a
Civil claim of breach of contract

Case progression:
High Court –
No breach of contract

Court of Appeal –
Appeal dismissed

Supreme Court –
Appeal dismissed

Point of law:
Meaning of cheating and the question of dishonesty

In *Ivey v Genting Casinos (UK) Ltd t/a Crockfords* [2017] UKSC 67, the appellant, Ivey, attended the Crockfords Club in Mayfair, London. Over two days in 2012, the appellant amassed winnings totalling £7.7 million playing a card game called 'Punto Banco'. Unknown to the casino, the defendant won the money using a tactic called 'edge-sorting'. This tactic involves the skill of being able to identify cards through memorising small differences in the patterns and edging of the playing cards. The club discovered this tactic before paying out the winnings to the appellant and then refused to pay out such winnings alleging breach of contract, specifically the implied term that neither party cheat. The appellant sued the respondent for breach of contract alleging his conduct to be 'gamesmanship' and not 'cheating', meaning that the respondent was under an obligation to pay out the winnings.

In the High Court, at first instance, Mitting J dismissed Ivey's claim and the Court of Appeal further held that the appellant had cheated and therefore breached the implied term of the contract. The appellant appealed to the Supreme Court which found his conduct to amount to cheating.

Lord Hughes identified the major problems with the operation of the *Ghosh* test. He commented:

> Thirty years on, however, it can be seen that there are a number of serious problems about the second leg of the rule adopted in *Ghosh*.
>
> (1) It has the unintended effect that the more warped the defendant's standards of honesty are, the less likely it is that he will be convicted of dishonest behaviour.
>
> (2) It was based on the premise that it was necessary in order to give proper effect to the principle that dishonesty, and especially criminal responsibility for it, must depend on the actual state of mind of the defendant, whereas the rule is not necessary to preserve this principle.

(3) It sets a test which jurors and others often find puzzling and difficult to apply.

(4) It has led to an unprincipled divergence between the test for dishonesty in criminal proceedings and the test of the same concept when it arises in the context of a civil action.

(5) It represented a significant departure from the pre-Theft Act 1968 law, when there is no indication that such a change had been intended.

(6) Moreover, it was not compelled by authority. Although the pre-*Ghosh* cases were in a state of some entanglement, the better view is that the preponderance of authority favoured the simpler rule that, once the defendant's state of knowledge and belief has been established, whether that state of mind was dishonest or not is to be determined by the application of the standards of the ordinary honest person, represented in a criminal case by the collective judgment of jurors or magistrates.

His Lordship then turned his attention to the civil standard of dishonesty. Under the law of trusts, a concept exists known as 'stranger liability', also known as 'third party liability'. Under this concept, a third party is liable in circumstances where he has knowingly received trust property in breach of trust or, more relevant to our discussion, is liable as an accessory to a breach of trust. The latter is referred to as 'dishonest assistance' and requires the defendant to have dishonestly assisted the trustee in breaching the trust. 'Dishonesty' in this respect has been interpreted on a number of occasions as an objective test. In *Barlow Clowes International Ltd v Eurotrust International Ltd* [2005] UKPC 37, the Privy Council confirmed the earlier decision of *Royal Brunei Airlines v Tan* [1995] 2 AC 378 in which Lord Nicholls stated that the test for dishonesty was an objective one based on subjective factors. In this respect, dishonesty is to be judged on an objective standard but based on the individual knowledge or state of mind of the individual concerned. This approach was confirmed by the Court of Appeal on two occasions (*Abou-Rahmah v Abacha* [2006] EWCA Civ 1492 and *Starglade Properties Ltd v Nash* [2010] EWCA Civ 1314) as an objective test based on subjective factors. The leading authority on the civil law standard is that of *Barlow Clowes* where Lord Hoffmann stated:

> Although a dishonest state of mind is a subjective mental state, the standard by which the law determines whether it is dishonest is objective. If by ordinary standards a defendant's mental state would be characterised as dishonest, it is irrelevant that the defendant judges by different standards.

For a more detailed account of the civil test for dishonest assistance, see Farran and Davies, *Equity and Trusts*, 2nd edn (Hall and Stott Publishing, 2019).

Lord Hughes in *Ivey* would reason that these cases were careful to restrict their remit to the civil law; however, he did stress that

> ... there can be no logical or principled basis for the meaning of dishonesty (as distinct from the standards of proof by which it must be established) to differ according to whether it arises in a civil action or a criminal prosecution.

Lord Hughes concluded that:

> ... the second leg of the test propounded in *Ghosh* does not correctly represent the law and that directions based upon it ought no longer to be given. The test of dishonesty is as set out by Lord Nicholls in *Royal Brunei Airlines Sdn Bhd v Tan* and by Lord Hoffmann in *Barlow Clowes*.

The present test for dishonesty (refer to the 'Present state of the law' above for the full quote from Lord Hughes) can thus be expressed as follows:

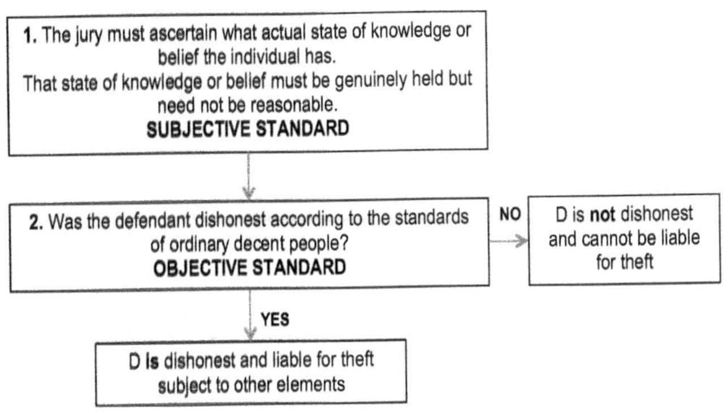

Figure 11.4 The test for dishonesty following Ivey

The first question requires the jury to take a subjective assessment as to the state of knowledge or belief of the defendant as to the facts at that time. In *R v Barton; R v Booth* [2020] EWCA Crim 575, Lord Burnett CJ explained that the phrase 'actual state of mind as to knowledge or belief *as to the facts*' refers to

> all the circumstances known to the accused and not limiting consideration to past facts. All matters that lead an accused to act as he or she did will form part of the subjective mental state, thereby forming a part of the fact-finding exercise before applying the objective standard. That will include consideration, where relevant, of the experience and intelligence of an accused.

This means that the jury must consider what *this* defendant knew or believed on *that* particular day at *that* particular time. It is essential, therefore, for the judge to direct the jury in his or her summing up to consider the case and facts put forward by the defendant. In *Barton*, for example, a relevant consideration for the jury was that Barton believed that the gifts made to him were out of gratitude and affection, those persons giving the gifts were not vulnerable and each had access to independent advice.

Furthermore, in *Ivey,* Lord Hughes was clear in his judgment that such knowledge or belief need not be reasonable in the circumstances; it merely needs to be genuinely held (though the extent of its reasonableness will go towards whether the view was genuinely held).

The second question requires the jury to take a purely objective assessment, asking themselves whether they, as the ordinary and decent people that they are, consider the defendant's conduct to be dishonest. At this stage, the defendant's subjective view of his own honesty is entirely irrelevant – the matter is entirely one for the jury as to whether *they* think the defendant was dishonest.

in practice

The securing of a conviction for dishonesty-related offences is likely to become an easier task for prosecutors. Without the ability to claim a lack of 'appreciation' for the standards of ordinary and honest persons, a defendant may struggle to convince a jury that the honest man would have acted in the same way.

Walters ('Casino ruling hands prosecutors "aces"' (2017) LS Gaz, 30 Oct, 1(1)) comments that: 'The Supreme Court's landmark decision to dismiss a 35-year-old test for determining dishonesty in criminal cases may lead to more convictions and will be an "ace in the hand of ... prosecutors".'

(iv) The effect of Ivey *and subsequent cases*

As a practical result of *Ivey*, the two-limb *Ghosh* test is no more. The twofold test laid out by Lord Hughes in *Ivey* (set out above) is now reflective of the present state of law. Upon release of the judgment in *Ivey*, the author was, and remains, sceptical as to the binding nature of the decision. First, *Ivey* was a civil case being determined by the Supreme Court. Ordinarily, a distinction is to be drawn between cases determined in the civil law and cases determined in the criminal law. The author's understanding remains that a civil case is of only persuasive authority in criminal matters – this is evident from such cases as *Re A (children) (conjoined twins: surgical separation)* [2001] Fam 147, where the Court of Appeal provided a detailed test for necessity in medical cases which, to this point, has been merely treated as persuasive authority for the criminal courts. Secondly, the *ratio* of *Ivey* is that dishonesty is not an element of the offence of cheating contrary to s 42 of the Gambling Act 2005 – that was the matter the Court had to consider in dealing with the reasoning for the decision. What was said, therefore, about *Ghosh* and the application of the dishonesty test in the criminal law can be nothing other than merely *obiter dicta*.

Soon after *Ivey*, High Court took the opportunity to review the state of dishonesty. In *DPP v Patterson* [2017] EWHC 2820 (Admin), a case concerning two counts of theft (each valued at £140), Sir Brian Leveson P discussed the statement of Lord Hughes in *Ivey*. In relation to this part of the judgment, his Lordship acknowledged that

> [t]hese observations were clearly *obiter*, and as a matter of strict precedent the court is bound by *Ghosh*, although the Court of Appeal could depart from that decision without the matter returning to the Supreme Court.

Despite accepting that *Ivey* is a decision of persuasive authority only (given that Lord Hughes was speaking in *obiter*), Sir Brian Leveson P would go on to explain that the criminal courts are not bound by the doctrine of precedent to the same extent as the civil courts. His Lordship quoted from Diplock LJ in *R v Gould* [1968] 2 QB 65, where it was stated:

> In its criminal jurisdiction, ... the Court of Appeal does not apply the doctrine of *stare decisis* with the same rigidity as in its civil jurisdiction. If upon due consideration, we were to be of opinion that the law has been either misapplied or misunderstood in an earlier decision of this court or its predecessor, the Court of Criminal Appeal, we should be entitled to depart from the view expressed in that decision ...

Sir Brian Leveson P would conclude:

> Given the terms of the unanimous observations of the Supreme Court expressed by Lord Hughes, who does not shy from asserting that *Ghosh* does not correctly represent the law, it is difficult to imagine the Court of Appeal preferring *Ghosh* to *Ivey* in the future.

In addition to *Patterson*, the Crown Court Compendium: Part 1: Jury and Trial Management and Summing Up (Judicial College, 2019) was updated to reflect the change in judicial summing-up to a jury when a matter of dishonesty is in issue. According to the Compendium, *Ghosh* is now a thing of the past. Despite the judgment in *Patterson* and the amendment in the Compendium, there remained doubt as to whether *Ghosh* or *Ivey* represented the correct state of law in respect of offences involving dishonesty.

The law was finally settled by the Court of Appeal in *R v Barton; R v Booth* [2020] EWCA Crim 575. This case concerned a number of property-related offences including theft and conspiracy to defraud. Barton, the manager of a luxury nursing home, had exploited a number of the residents at the nursing home resulting in them gifting him property; declaring him a legatee (beneficiary) in their will; and providing him with the power to make decisions in respect of their property. At trial, the learned judge directed the jury in accordance with the new test for dishonesty in *Ivey*, and the defendant was convicted on multiple counts. On appeal, Barton contended, inter alia, that the test for dishonesty was that stated in *Ghosh* and not *Ivey* on account that *Ivey* was merely *obiter dicta*. Upholding the defendant's conviction, Lord Burnett CJ opened his judgment by explaining that:

> These appeals provide the opportunity for the uncertainty which has followed the decision in *Ivey* to come to an end. We are satisfied that the decision in *Ivey* is correct, is to be preferred, and that there is no obstacle in the doctrine of *stare decisis* to its being applied as the law of England and Wales.

His Lordship would justify this position as follows:

> We conclude that where the Supreme Court itself directs that an otherwise binding decision of the Court of Appeal should no longer be followed and proposes an alternative test that it says must be adopted, the Court of Appeal is bound to follow what amounts to a direction from the Supreme Court even though it is strictly obiter. To that limited extent the ordinary rules of precedent (or stare decisis) have been modified.

Following the confirmation of the Court of Appeal that *Ivey* is the correct statement of law, the test of dishonesty from *Ghosh* is now a thing of the past.

11.2.2.5 *Mens rea:* (ii) intention to permanently deprive (TA 1968, s 6)

The final element for proof of the offence of theft is that there was an intention to permanently deprive. A number of preliminary points may be made at the outset which focus on the words used:

Table 11.8 Understanding the intention to permanently deprive

Key words	Explanation
Intention to	There must merely be an *intention* to permanently deprive; whether the defendant succeeds in permanently depriving the owner of their property is generally irrelevant. In this regard, the *mens rea* is ulterior given that there is no accompanying *actus reus* requiring actual permanent deprivation.
Permanently	An intention to *temporarily* deprive is not sufficient; it must be an intention to permanently deprive.
Deprive	The intention need only be of depriving the victim of the property; the defendant does not need to intend to make a gain for himself or another. This is evidenced in s 1(2) of the TA 1968, as explained above when considering appropriation.

in practice

Although there is no requirement for the defendant to actually deprive the owner of their property permanently, where the defendant does return the property, this is likely to be used as evidence by the defence in the criminal trial to suggest that the defendant never held the intention to permanently deprive. This is particularly relevant when you observe the idea of continuing and secondary appropriations.

For our purposes, we are concerned with whether the defendant intended to permanently deprive at the moment of appropriation.

Section 6 of the TA 1968 provides:

> (1) A person appropriating property belonging to another without meaning the other permanently to lose the thing itself is nevertheless to be regarded as having the intention of permanently depriving the other of it if his intention is to treat the thing as his own to dispose of regardless of the other's rights; and a borrowing or lending of it may amount to so treating it if, but only if, the borrowing or lending is for a period and in circumstances making it equivalent to an outright taking or disposal.
>
> (2) Without prejudice to the generality of subsection (1) above, where a person, having possession or control (lawfully or not) of property belonging to another, parts with the property under a condition as to its return which he may not be able to perform, this (if done for purposes of his own and without the other's authority) amounts to treating the property as his own to dispose of regardless of the other's rights.

Spencer ('The Metamorphosis of Section 6 of the Theft Act' [1977] Crim LR 653) has described s 6(1) as sprouting 'obscurities at every phrase'.

Intention to permanently deprive will be obvious in most cases. This means that in the majority of cases, you need *not* consider s 6 unless the case is one of a special nature. Indeed, the Court of Appeal in *R v Lloyd* [1985] QB 829 held that prosecutors should only resort to s 6 in 'exceptional circumstances', which was reinforced by the Court of Appeal in *R v Velumyl* [1989] Crim LR 299 which held that an intention to permanently deprive should be given its plain and ordinary meaning. To give it its plain and ordinary meaning avoids usage of the section outside of its intended parameters.

The special nature of s 6 involves cases where the defendant does not intend to permanently deprive the victim of their property; however, he intends to seriously compromise the owner's rights in relation to the property. We can usefully divide these 'exceptional circumstances' into two:

(a) the disposal of the property as one's own (TA 1968, s 6(1)); and
(b) parting with the property at risk of non-return (TA 1968, s 6(2)).

Disposal of the property as one's own (TA 1968, s 6(1))

The Court of Appeal in *R v Cahill* [1993] Crim LR 141 emphasised the importance of 'dispose of', meaning to deal with definitely. However, the Divisional Court in *DPP v Lavender* [1994] Crim LR 297 held that 'dispose of' in the sense of 'get rid of' was not required. In that case, the defendant removed doors in a council house and used them to replace broken doors on his girlfriend's house. Clearly, in that case, the defendant did not 'get rid of' the doors but, instead, used them for a separate purpose (ie moving them from one council house to another). Despite that, the defendant remained liable for theft (compare with *R v Mitchell* [2008] EWCA Crim 850 below). The Court of Appeal in *R v Vinall* [2011] EWCA Crim 2652 clarified that s 6(1)

> does not require that the thing has been disposed of, nor does it require that the Defendant intends to dispose of the thing in any particular way. No doubt evidence of a particular disposal or a particular intention to dispose of the thing will constitute evidence of the Defendant's state of mind but it is, in our view, for the jury to decide upon the circumstances proved whether the Defendant harboured the statutory intention. …
>
> If the prosecution is unable to establish an intent permanently to deprive at the moment of taking it may nevertheless establish that the Defendant exercised such a dominion over the property that it can be inferred that at the time of the taking he intended to treat the property as his own to dispose of regardless of the owner's rights. (per Pitchford LJ)

It is confirmed, then, that 'dispose of' simply refers to the intention to treat things as one's own, over the true owner's rights. This was evident in *R v Marshall* [1998] 2 Cr App R 282, where the defendant sold on London Underground tickets and travel cards. The Court of Appeal held that the defendant intended to treat the property as his own, in ignorance of the rights of London Underground. This is so even though the property would eventually return to London Underground when the tickets expired.

When looking at the disposal of property as one's own, it may help to consider the following examples:

Table 11.9 Examples of disposals for s 6(1)

Type of disposal	**Explanation and authority**
Ransoming property	This occurs where the defendant will only reunite the complainant with their property if they pay for it (*R v Raphael* [2008] EWCA Crim 1014, where the defendant stole the victim's car and then requested payment for its return) or on fulfilment of a condition. Compare *Raphael* with the decision of *R v Waters* [2015] EWCA Crim 402, in which the Court of Appeal explained that 'if the condition attached to the return of the item … can readily be fulfilled and may be fulfilled in the near future, the jury may well conclude that intention to deprive has not been made out'. A similar decision was reached in *R v Coffey* [1987] Crim LR 498, where the Court of Appeal held that the jury should not convict unless satisfied that the intended period of detention was of a sufficient length to amount to an outright taking. In the author's view, *Waters* (and *Coffey*) is clearly a wrong decision. Any condition imposed upon the return of the property, regardless of how quickly that condition will be satisfied, should be construed as an outright taking, and thus an intention to permanently deprive.
Replacing property	Where money or any other item is 'borrowed', the dishonest borrower has the intention to permanently deprive even though he intends to replace the money or article with another which is just as good. The defendant deprives the owner of the specific thing appropriated (*R v Velumyl* [1989] Crim LR 299, where the defendant took money from a safe intending to return it at the weekend). A common example would be where the defendant takes a £50 note and later replaces it with 5 x £10 notes. Regardless of the replacement, he may be liable for theft (he could replace it with a different £50 note and it would still be theft). In *Velumyl*, the Court accepted that an intention to provide a replacement could be relevant to the question of dishonesty.

Type of disposal	Explanation and authority
Value of the property is lost (equivalent to an 'outright taking')	The borrowing must be equivalent to an 'outright taking', meaning that the value or virtue of the property is lost or used up when the property is returned. Case law indicates that a defendant will not intend to permanently deprive unless the property has lost all (or, at least, substantially all) its 'goodness or virtue' (*R v Lloyd* [1985] QB 829, where the defendant made pirate copies of films before then returning the original copy without removing its value). Lord Lane CJ explained that 'The goodness, the virtue, the practical value of the films to the owners has not gone out of the article. ...That borrowing, it seems to us, was not for a period, or in such circumstances, as made it equivalent to an outright taking or disposal. There was still virtue in the film.' In that regard, Lloyd was not liable for theft. Compare this to a case in which a defendant borrows the victim's season ticket for his favourite rugby team and only returns the ticket once the season is over. In this regard, the ticket is useless. It is debatable whether it would be equivalent to an outright taking if the defendant returned the ticket with a few games of the season still to be played. Where the property is no longer fit to serve its purpose (it has lost its virtue), this will be theft – see *DPP v J* [2002] EWHC 291 (Admin), in which the defendant snatched the victim's headphones, snapped them and then handed them back (this would also be criminal damage – see **Chapter 14**).
Abandoning property	An intention to abandon property will amount to an intention to dispose of it. However, where the defendant leaves the property in a place that can easily be recovered by the victim, this may not be an intention to permanently deprive. In *R v Mitchell* [2008] EWCA Crim 850, the defendants carjacked the victim's car in a getaway attempt and later abandoned the victim's car undamaged on a main road a few miles away from the victim's house. Rix LJ in the Court of Appeal explained that '[t]he BMW was plainly taken for the purposes of a getaway. There was nothing about its use or subsequent abandonment to suggest otherwise.' Therefore, whilst Mitchell may have intended to treat the car as his own (by using it as a getaway car), he had no intention to treat it as his own to dispose of it. Note that s 12 of the Theft Act 1968 contains the offence of taking a motor vehicle without authority – to deal with such cases as *Mitchell*. Compare *Mitchell* with *R v Vinall* [2011] EWCA Crim 2652.

A final element to consider under the idea of disposal of the property as one's own are the cases involving 'conditional intent'. Conditional intention concerns the situation where the defendant intends to steal but only if a particular condition exists (eg a condition that the property is valuable). The issue arises: what if a defendant intends to steal but finds nothing of value or worth during his attempt? The law in this area has gone through a radical change. The original approach adopted by the Court of Appeal in *R v Easom* [1971] 2 QB 315 was that 'conditional appropriation will not do' (ie conditional intent is not sufficient for the offence of theft). In that case, the defendant picked up the victim's handbag and searched through it, looking for valuables. The defendant found nothing worth stealing and replaced the bag, having taken nothing. The Court of Appeal quashed his conviction for theft on the basis that he never intended to steal the handbag itself – he intended to steal the contents therein should they have proved to be valuable or of interest to him. This approach was confirmed in the later Court of Appeal case of *R v Husseyn* (1977) 67 Cr App R 131.

The position has now been clarified by the Court of Appeal in *AG's References (Nos 1 and 2 of 1979)* [1980] QB 180.

case example

Charge:
Burglary (TA 1968, s 9(1)(a))

Case progression:
Crown Court – Not Guilty

Court of Appeal – Guilty

Point of law:
Conditional intent

In *AG's References (Nos 1 and 2 of 1979)* [1980] QB 180, the defendants were arrested by police while attempting to break into a number of buildings. The pair were charged with burglary as there was evidence to support their intention to steal.

The Crown Court found the pair not guilty of burglary on account that a conditional intention to steal, on the basis that there was something worth stealing, is not sufficient. The Court of Appeal disagreed and found the defendants guilty on account that there is no requirement of an intention to steal any specific objects. The fact that the intention to steal was conditional on finding money in the house was sufficient.

Whilst *AG's References (Nos 1 and 2 of 1979)* concerned a burglary case, the principles are capable of applying in the law of theft. In *obiter*, Roskill LJ explained that:

> Taking as an example the facts in [*Easom*], plainly what the accused intended was to steal some or all of the contents of the handbag if and when he got them into his possession. It seems clear … that, if he had been charged with an attempt to steal *some or all of the contents of that handbag*, he could properly have been convicted, subject of course to a proper direction to the jury. (emphasis added)

In that respect, a carefully drafted indictment which describes the theft generally will allow for the possibility of a conviction based upon conditional intent. Roskill LJ explained this quite simply as follows: 'we see no reason in principle why … a more imprecise method of criminal pleading should not be adopted.'

In the alternative, according to the Criminal Attempts Act 1981, a defendant can be guilty of attempted theft, regardless of his intention as to a particular item he wished to steal (see **Chapter 5**).

Parting with the property at risk of non-return (TA 1968, s 6(2))

Section 6(2) (cited above) concerns the circumstance where the defendant intends to part with the property; however, he cannot be sure of its return. In such a case, the risk of non-return is considered an intention to permanently deprive (because the defendant is deemed as treating the property as his own (in line with s 6(1)). In *R v Fernandes* [1996] 1 Cr App R 175, the defendant, a solicitor, transferred money from his client account to a higher yielding account in an attempt to cover his personal debts. Once those debts were paid off, he would return the money. The Court of Appeal ruled that there was a clear intention to permanently deprive given the 'obviously insecure investment' and the fact that he dealt with the property 'in such a manner that he [knew] he [was] risking its loss'.

example

Jack takes Jill's gold earrings without her knowledge. He pawns them for £300 to pay off some of his personal debts. Expecting to inherit money from his aunt in a few weeks' time, Jack intends to return to the pawnbroker and buy back the earrings and return them to Jill. Unfortunately for Jack, his aunt has changed her will and Jack is entitled to no inheritance. Jack has no money to buy back the earrings.

In this case, whilst Jack did not possess the intention to permanently deprive Jill of her earrings (because he intended to give them back at a later date), Jack has fallen within the provision of s 6(2) given that he has parted with the earrings with a risk of non-return. He has thus treated the property as his own and will be considered, for legal purposes, to possess an intention to permanently deprive. Pawning goods and use of goods in gambling both fall within s 6(2).

Temporary deprivation

Unless the taking falls within s 6, an intention to temporarily deprive, for example mere borrowing, will not be sufficient to found a case of theft. Wilson (*Central Issues in Criminal Theory* (Hart Publishing, 2002)) argues that this justification lies in the approach of the criminal law in protecting property over possession. On this point, Wilson contends that cases of borrowing are better suited in the civil law. Williams ('Temporary Appropriation Should be Theft' [1981] Crim LR 129) contends that, in many cases, temporary deprivation will have similar detrimental effects on the victim's rights as permanent deprivation. On this basis, temporary deprivation is deserving of criminalisation.

The criminal law does offer some protection by way of offences dealing with temporary deprivation. One such example is taking a motor vehicle or other conveyance without authority (TA 1968, s 12) which requires no element of permanent deprivation as part of the offence.

11.2.3 Charging theft

11.2.3.1 Mode of trial

Theft is an offence triable either way, meaning that it may be charged in either the magistrates' court or the Crown Court. A special rule specifically applies to the charging of low-value shoplifting. Importantly, shoplifting is not a specific criminal offence; rather, it is simply charged as theft under s 1. These special rules were introduced by s 176 of the Anti-Social Behaviour, Crime and Policing Act 2014. Section 22A(1) of the TA 1968 now provides that low-value shoplifting is to be treated as triable only summarily. This is subject to the exception that where an accused is aged 18 or over, he may elect Crown Court trial (TA 1968, s 22A(2)). Section 22A(3) defines low-value shoplifting as where the value of the stolen goods is £200 or less (see *R v McDermott-Mullane* [2017] 4 WLR 127).

11.2.3.2 Sentencing

Where tried in the magistrates' court, the maximum penalty for an offence is 6 months and/or a level 5 fine. In the Crown Court, upon indictment, the maximum sentence is 7 years' imprisonment (TA 1968, s 7).

11.2.4 Putting together theft

Consider this issue and think of how you may structure an answer to it. Then see the figure below for a sample structure to adopt.

facts

Jack has recently been released from prison and is struggling with his life. He is invited to his friend Jill's house to stay for a few nights. Whilst at the house, Jack steals a number of pieces of jewellery from Jill's bedroom. Jack takes on a part-time job in the local MP's office. Whilst cleaning, Jack takes a number of confidential documents from the MP's office with the intention of selling them at a later date.

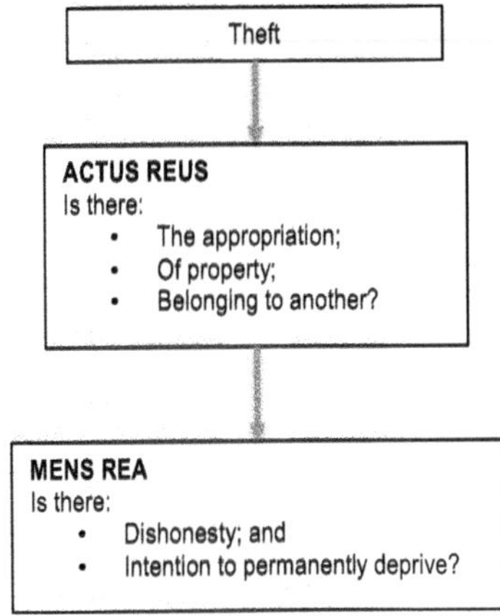

Figure 11.5 Putting together theft

11.3 Robbery

Robbery, at a very basic level, may be best described in the following terms:

Figure 11.6 Robbery at a basic level

11.3.1 Defining robbery

As robbery is simply an aggravated form of theft, the Court of Appeal in *R v Robinson* [1977] Crim LR 173 made it clear that where there is no theft, there is no robbery. There may of course be a non-fatal offence against the person committed in such a case, but there is no robbery. There may also be an assault with intent to rob under s 8(2), which we shall deal with later at **11.3.3**.

in practice

The CPS in its 'Legal Guidance on Burglary' has commented that

> Where a burglary involves theft and force is used immediately before or at the time of stealing (or attempting to steal) the defendant may have committed an offence of robbery. Prosecutors should normally charge robbery, where robbery can be made out rather than burglary (or aggravated burglary).

Consider this advice in your problem questions.

11.3.2 Elements of robbery

Section 8(1) of the TA 1968 provides:

> A person is guilty of robbery if he steals, and immediately before or at the time of doing so, and in order to do so, he uses force on any person or puts or seeks to put any person in fear of being then and there subjected to force.

The *actus reus* and *mens rea* of robbery are outlined in **Table 11.10**.

Table 11.10 Elements of robbery

AR/MR	Elements of the offence
Actus reus	(i) *actus reus* of theft; (ii) force or fear of force; (iii) on any person; (iv) in order to steal.
Mens rea	(i) *mens rea* of theft; (ii) intention to use force.

We shall consider each element in turn.

11.3.2.1 *Actus reus:* (i) *actus reus* of theft

In order for there to be a robbery, the *actus reus* of theft first needs to be fulfilled. We know this by use of the word 'steals' in s 8(1), which De Than (*Criminal Law*, 4th edn (OUP, 2014)) refers to as 'shorthand for all the ingredients of theft'. On that basis, you should consider whether there has been:

(i) an appropriation;
(ii) of property;
(iii) belonging to another.

A point to emphasise is that even if force is used, a robbery is not capable of commission where an element of theft is missing. This is aptly explained by Wilson (*Criminal Law*, 7th edn (Pearson, 2020)) who states that '[a] non-theftuous appropriation does not become robbery simply because unlawful force is used'. This was evident in *R v Skivington* [1968] 1 QB 166 in which, whilst the defendant used the fear of force to obtain money (by producing a knife), he lacked dishonesty in doing so given that he possessed a genuine belief that he had a right to the money (money was owed to his wife in her wages). In such circumstances, the more appropriate offence may be an assault with intent to rob (see **11.3.3**).

Much like with the offence of theft, robbery does not require an actual deprivation of property. There must merely be an intention to deprive. In *Corcoran v Anderton* (1980) 71 Cr App R 104, the defendants committed robbery despite the fact that they did not permanently deprive the victim of her handbag (the pair ran away without the bag when she screamed).

Once you have satisfied the *actus reus* of theft, you may then continue with the additional elements required for a robbery.

11.3.2.2 *Actus reus:* (ii) force or fear of force

The word 'force' is not defined in the TA 1968. The jury are therefore directed to give 'force' its ordinary everyday meaning (*R v Clouden* [1987] Crim LR 56). The use of force is, therefore, a question of fact for the jury.

Importantly, the statute appreciates that two 'types' of force may be present in a given case:

- actual infliction of force; and
- fear of force.

Given the presence of alternative *actus rei*, where the defendant is alleged to have actually used force in order to steal, the victim need not have apprehended the use of force (eg Jack pushes Jill to the floor from behind and steals her handbag).

Actual infliction of force

The word 'force' would appear uncontroversial. A juror would expect to see some injury, or potential injury, arising to the victim as a result of the actions of the defendant; however, there is no requirement for injury to accrue as a result of the force used by the defendant. Instead, the defendant merely needs to exert force or pressure *on* the victim. The use of the word 'on' in s 8 has been interpreted by the courts to mean 'against' the victim.

Indeed, this was the view taken by the Court of Appeal in *R v Manghan and Manghan* [2000] 1 Cr App R (S) 6, where the Court held that pickpocketing and 'jostling' ought to be charged as theft and not robbery. This is understandable given the severity of the offence of robbery and the impact it may have on an individual's long-term liberty. However, one can question the consistency of this approach when you compare *Manghan* with the previous Court of Appeal decision in *R v Dawson and James* [1976] RTR 533, where the Court of Appeal ruled that a 'nudge' (in the form of pushing and shoving causing the victim to lose their balance) is to be charged as robbery. The Court of Appeal noted that the force need not 'overpower' the victim; it must merely be directed at the property which is in the possession of the victim.

The High Court added an extra element of confusion to the mix with its decision in *P v DPP* [2013] 1 WLR 2337, where it ruled that the snatching of a cigarette without direct physical contact being made to the victim was not 'force' for the purposes of robbery. Mitting J in *P v DPP* explained that:

> This case falls squarely on the side of pickpocketing and such like, in which there is no direct physical contact between thief and victim. It cannot be said that the minimal use of force required to remove a cigarette from between the fingers of a person suffices to amount to the use of force on that person. It cannot cause any pain unless, perhaps, the person resists strongly, in which case one would expect inevitably that there would be direct physical contact between the thief and victim as well. The unexpected removal of a cigarette from between the fingers of a person is no more the use of force on that person than would be the removal of an item from her pocket. This offence is properly categorised as simple theft.

Ormerod and Laird (*Smith, Hogan, & Ormerod's Criminal Law*, 15th edn (OUP, 2018)) justify *P v DPP* on the basis that in that case there was a 'lack of sufficient force, not [that there was a] lack of direct bodily contact'. Indeed, in the author's view, the decision in *P v DPP* is to be agreed with where no force is applied to the victim whatsoever; however, it leaves open the possibility that any form of indirect force is not sufficient for robbery. As you can expect, this is hardly practicable.

It can be questioned the extent to which the outcome in *P v DPP* would have been different had the facts changed; for example if the victim had been burned by the cigarette during the snatching, that may have been sufficient for robbery. Further, consider the circumstances where Jack rips a shopping bag from Jill's hands. Jack has laid no physical direct force on Jill, but there has been force applied that is more than merely 'jostling'. In such circumstances, the CLRC in its 8th Report ('Theft and Related Offences' (Cmnd 2977, 1966)) said that it would

> ... not regard mere snatching of property, such as a handbag, from an unresisting owner as using force for the purposes of the definition [of robbery], though it might be so if the owner resisted.

The Court of Appeal, however, in *R v Clouden* [1987] Crim LR 56 ruled that the snatching of a handbasket from the victim did amount to force sufficient for robbery. In doing so, the Court of Appeal clearly disregarded the statement of the CLRC. Horder (*Ashworth's Principles of Criminal Law*, 9th edn (OUP, 2019)) is critical of the decision in *Clouden*, arguing that it has pushed the law 'well beyond its old boundaries'. Further, Horder notes that

> ... if robbery is to continue to be regarded as a serious offence, triable only on indictment and punishable with life imprisonment, surely something more than a bump, a push or a pull should be required.

Perhaps the most useful approach to understanding this difficult dividing line is to look at the categories of force enunciated by Williams (*Textbook of Criminal Law* (Sweet & Maxwell, 1978)). Williams comments that a distinction must be made between

> gentle force [used to] snatch an article by stealth or surprise ... and tugging it away when [the victim] offers resistance.

Williams offers the following examples of force sufficient for robbery. Note that any force that fell below this level would not be sufficient for robbery.

Table 11.11 Williams' examples of force sufficient for robbery

Explanation of force	Example
Force used to prevent or overcome conscious resistance	Tugging at the owner's property or applying a chloroform pad to the owner's mouth
Force used to sever an article from the possessor	Breaking the chain from a watch
Force used to cause injury	Tearing an earring from the lobe of an ear

In summary, there must be something more than an insignificant amount of force being applied. *De minimis* force will fall outside the scope of s 9 and may be charged instead as theft.

Fear of force

Importantly, the defendant need not actually use force, but may simply threaten force to the victim. This is expressly provided for in s 8(1) when it states that the victim may 'fear' force is to be inflicted. The courts have been very clear in their approach that to 'fear' force does not mean to be 'afraid' of any such force (*R v DPP; B v DPP* [2007] EWHC 739 (Admin)). Gross J in *R v DPP* justified this on the basis that 'otherwise, the bravery of the victim would determine the guilt of the assailant'. Instead, fear is simply to be understood as to 'apprehend' the infliction of force, akin, therefore, to technical assault (see **Chapter 10**).

Section 8(1) makes a distinction between cases where the defendant 'puts' the victim in fear of force and 'seeks to put' the victim in fear of force. The former concerns cases where the defendant causes the victim to apprehend force; whereas the latter concerns the circumstance where the defendant intends to put the victim in fear of force, albeit that intention fails and the victim does not actually 'fear' force (see *R v Tennant* [1976] Crim LR 133). This may be because the victim is completely oblivious to the threat (where, for example, they are deaf, blind, asleep or just generally ignorant of the defendant's presence), or where the victim knows that any threat cannot be carried out. Suppose a case came before the courts similar to that of *Logdon v DPP* [1976] Crim LR 121 that we considered in **Chapter 9**. Let us suppose that the defendant points an imitation gun at the victim and demands that she hand over her purse. The victim is aware that the gun is fake and thus is aware that any such threat cannot be carried out. In this case, the defendant is still liable for robbery as he sought to put the victim in fear that force would be applied. You may question the legitimacy of this, however. Bear in mind that the victim may believe that although the threat of using the gun cannot be carried out, another threat of force may be within the contemplation of the defendant (eg to hit the victim with the fake gun as a last resort).

In both cases, the defendant may be liable for robbery (*R v DPP; B v DPP* [2007] EWHC 739 (Admin)) as '... it is the intention of the perpetrator rather than the fortitude of the victim which is the touchstone of whether the offence is robbery or theft' (per Smith LJ in *R v DPP*). This was reaffirmed by the Court of Appeal in *R v Codsi* [2009] EWCA Crim 1618.

In addition, it must also be proven that the victim feared force 'then and there'. This is a requirement of immediacy similar, again, to that of technical assault. In *R v Bentham* [2005] UKHL 18, the defendant placed his fingers into the inside of his jacket pocket to give the appearance that he held a gun there. Coupled with a demand for money and jewellery, the House of Lords felt it obvious that the defendant used the fear of force which would be placed on the victim 'then and there'. Should the defendant make a threat of future force, this will not suffice for the offence of robbery; rather, the more appropriate charge would be that of blackmail (see **Chapter 12**).

Interestingly, Ashworth ('Robbery Reassessed' [2002] Crim LR 851) offers two potential avenues for reform of the offence. He argues as follows:

- Different levels of force ought to give rise to different levels of liability. As such, if a victim is seriously hurt by the force used by the defendant, this should give rise to a more serious charge of robbery. Ashworth's view may appear appealing at this stage; however, it would cause difficulties for a jury when directed to consider whether the actions of the defendant were not serious enough to justify robbery A, but sufficiently serious to justify robbery B. On that basis, it would make more sense to distinguish between the seriousness of force used at the point of sentencing – which is matter already covered by the Sentencing Council Guidelines.
- In the alternative, the offence of robbery should be abandoned and replaced with the charging of two separate offences, one for theft and the other for assault. Ashworth contends that such a move would 'focus the court's attention on those two elements separately and then (for sentencing purposes) in combination'. Again, although appealing, this argument lacks a focus on the sheer seriousness of the offence of robbery. The offence is understood to be one against the person and against property. Jefferson (*Criminal Law*, 12th edn (Pearson, 2015)) rightly notes that such an offence is necessary to distinguish itself as an offence to be taken seriously. Ormerod and Laird (*Smith, Hogan, & Ormerod's Criminal Law*, 15th

edn (OUP, 2018)) conclude that '[i]n short, with robbery the whole is greater than the sum of the parts'. This is to be agreed with.

11.3.2.3 *Actus reus:* (iii) on any person

In the majority of cases, force or fear of force will be used against the owner of the property. However, such force or fear of force need not be directed at the owner of the property in order to amount to robbery. This is because s 8(1) uses the words 'any person' as opposed to 'the owner'.

example

Jack threatens Jill that he will punch her in the face if she does not hand over Andy's watch. Jill is Andy's partner. In fear of the threat, Jill hands over the property.

This would be sufficient for an offence of robbery even though the force is not directed to the owner of the property, ie Andy.

11.3.2.4 *Actus reus:* (iv) in order to steal

Importantly, the use of force or fear of force must come 'immediately before or at the time of' the theft and the force must be used 'in order to' steal. Again, this is a question of fact for the jury.

'Immediately before or at the time of'

The phrase 'immediately before or at the time of' sets a temporal period within which the offence of robbery may be committed. As we know, theft is complete at the moment there is a dishonest appropriation. As a result, robbery is complete when theft is complete (*Corcoran v Anderton* (1980) 71 Cr App R 104).

'In order to steal'

In the circumstances where the appropriation takes place and there remains a gap in time before force or the fear of force is used, there is no robbery. In such a case, there may be a theft with a separate offence against the person charge instead. The courts, however, have taken a practical and common-sense approach to this issue, stating that where appropriation is a continuing act, the use of force may come slightly before or after the act of appropriation. This was made clear in the case of *R v Hale* (1978) 68 Cr App R 415.

Charge:
Robbery (TA 1968, s 8)

Case progression:
Crown Court – Guilty

Court of Appeal – Conviction upheld

Point of law:
Use of force in order to steal

case example

In *R v Hale* (1978) 68 Cr App R 415, the defendants broke into the victim's house and stole her jewellery. Whilst the first defendant stole the jewellery, the second defendant tied up the victim to prevent her from foiling the robbery. The defendants were convicted in the Crown Court and then appealed to the Court of Appeal on the basis that the judge had misdirected the jury on when and how force is to be used. The Court of Appeal dismissed the appeal, ruling that by preventing the victim from foiling the crime alleged, they used force 'in order to' steal.

Eveleigh LJ stated:

To say that the conduct is over and done with as soon as he lays hands upon the property, or when he first manifests an intention to deal with it as his, is contrary to common-sense and to the natural meaning of words...the act of appropriation does not suddenly cease. It is a continuous act and it is a matter for the jury to decide whether or not the act of appropriation has finished. Moreover, it is quite clear that the intention to deprive the owner permanently...was a continuing one at all material times. ...As a matter of common sense the appellant was in the course of committing theft; he was stealing.

The Court of Appeal in *Hale* made it clear that the key principle to this element is that the force is used to order to 'enable' the theft to take place. This principle was reaffirmed by the Court of Appeal in *R v Lockley* [1995] Crim LR 656, where the defendant stole a can of beer from an off-licence. When approached by the shopkeeper, the defendant used violence. The distinct question became whether the defendant had used force *in order to* steal. The Court of Appeal ruled that theft may be a continuing act; on which basis, the defendant was still in the 'act' of stealing when violence was used. By way of example, in *R v Vinall* [2011] EWCA Crim 2652 (discussed above in relation to theft), Pitchford LJ in the Court of Appeal approved the directions of the trial judge to the jury, in that they had to be sure that

> the purpose behind the violence or the threat [was] ... the theft of the bike. If it was just a free-standing act of violence not connected with any ulterior purpose to steal the bike, no-one could be found guilty of robbery.

A number of points must be made in relation to the requirement that the force must be used *in order to* steal. These are:

- where force is used for some other purpose and theft occurs after that other purpose;
- where force is used in order to escape, rather than in order to steal.

For some other purpose

example

Jack and Jill are bitter football rivals and are engaged in a bar fight. Suppose Jill successfully takes down Jack and knocks him unconscious. Upon rendering Jack unconscious, Jill decides to steal his wallet.

In this example, Jill has not used force on Jack *in order to steal.* In this circumstance, she has used force for the purpose of fighting – for which she may be liable for a non-fatal offence; however, it cannot be said that the force was used *in order to* steal. The theft was merely an after-thought on Jill's part.

We can see a similar outcome in the case of *R v Donaghy and Marshall* [1981] Crim LR 644, where the defendant demanded that the victim, a taxi driver, drive him to a specific location. The demands were made with threats to the victim's life. Once the victim had delivered the defendant to his location in London, the defendant stole £22 from the victim. In this case, the jury found the defendant not guilty of robbery on the basis that the threats of violence were not made in order to steal but, rather, were made in order to reach his chosen destination. Theft was, again, an after-thought.

In order to steal or escape?

As a result of the decisions in *Hale* and *Lockley*, a key distinction must also be made between cases where force is used 'in order to' *steal* and cases where force is used 'in order to' *escape*. In the former case, there will be a robbery; in the latter case, there will be no robbery. The decision as to which case is present on the facts is a matter of fact for the jury.

Figure 11.7 Use of force in robbery

This distinction, however, is not always clear. Consider this example:

example

Jack enters a jewellery store and steals a watch. In doing so, he simply grabs a watch from behind the counter when the shop assistant is distracted and runs towards the door. As he reaches the door, he is stopped by the security guard, whom Jack knocks out of the way. Jack then runs out of the store.

In this case, it is not clear whether Jack would be liable for robbery, and it ultimately depends on the view taken by the jury. The jury may view the act of stealing the watch as a continuing act and the appropriation of such watch does not come to an end until the defendant is out of the shop. On this basis, by knocking the security guard out of the way, force could be said to be used *in order* to steal. A jury may, however, take the view that the theft was complete upon taking the watch, and the force applied to the security was merely used *in order* to escape. In that case, there is no robbery.

Let us look at another example:

example

Jack enters a jewellery store and steals a watch. In doing so, he simply grabs a watch from behind the counter when the shop assistant is distracted and runs towards the door. Jack makes it out of the door but a passer-by attempts to stop him from fleeing down the street. Jack knocks the passer-by out of the way and runs away.

In this case, the jury are likely to find that the theft is complete, as Jack has left the store, and his force is merely used to effect his escape.

It can be questioned, however, why this example would clearly fall outside the offence of robbery but the previous example would not. Is this because Jack had to use force to leave the store? Is it because the force was applied to an individual working for the owner of the property stolen? Both of these questions may call into question the consistency of a jury's decision if such were to arise in a given case. Indeed, Wilson (*Criminal Law*, 7th edn (Pearson, 2020)) laments the sheer oversight of the legislature in drafting s 8 so as not to cover situations where force, or the fear of force, is exerted post-stealing. Wilson comments that '[s]uch questions would have been unnecessary if the Act had been drafted so as to encompass cases where force was used immediately after the stealing in order to effect the theft successfully'.

11.3.2.5 *Mens rea:* (i) *mens rea* of theft

In order for there to be a robbery, the *mens rea* of theft must also be fulfilled. On that basis, you should consider whether:

(a) the defendant is dishonest; and
(b) the defendant intends to permanently deprive the owner of their property.

We shall not discuss these elements any further here, except to note an example of this element in the case law. In *R v Robinson* [1977] Crim LR 173, the defendant held a belief that he had a right in law to money owed by the victim's wife. Despite taking money from the victim by force, the Court of Appeal quashed the defendant's conviction on the basis that he held a genuine belief that the money taken was his, as a matter of right. In that circumstance, no robbery was committed. See also *R v Skivington* [1968] 1 QB 166 for similar facts.

You are advised to return to our discussions at **11.2.2.4** and **11.2.2.5** respectively.

11.3.2.6 *Mens rea:* (ii) intention to use force

The defendant must intend to use force or the fear of force *in order to steal*. This means that where the defendant uses force for some other purpose (eg a purpose unconnected with theft, such as simply to inflict harm), or is accidental in his use of force, there is no robbery.

example

Jack batters Jill for having an affair with Andy. After Jack has finished the beating, he notices that Jill has a brand new smartphone which he then takes and walks away with.

In this case, the force used is for the purpose of assaulting Jill. The theft of the smartphone simply appears to be an afterthought of Jack. In this case, Jack will be liable for theft and for a non-fatal offence against the person.

11.3.3 Assault with intent to rob

Assault with intent to rob is preserved by the wording of s 8(2) of the TA 1968 which simply states:

> A person guilty of robbery, or of an assault with intent to rob, shall on conviction on indictment be liable to imprisonment for life.

As you can plainly see, the reference to assault with intent to rob is merely a fleeting statement. Quite simply, an assault with intent to rob requires the commission of an assault or battery upon a person with the intention to steal. The major difference between robbery and assault with intention to rob is in the commission of theft. In the latter offence, the defendant must have been unsuccessful in his attempt to steal the property. As we know, where there is no theft, there is no robbery. It is for this reason that assault with intent to rob is useful for prosecutors where the offence of robbery fails.

11.3.4 Aggravated/armed robbery

This heading is, admittedly, somewhat misleading. There is no such offence of aggravated robbery given that robbery itself is a form of aggravated theft. Likewise, although the term 'armed robbery' might sound familiar, there is also no chargeable offence of armed robbery. However, where a defendant carries with him an offensive weapon, in sentencing, the court will take that matter into account as an aggravating factor. Further, a defendant may also be liable for an offence under the Prevention of Crime Act 1953 for possessing an offensive weapon without justification. Likewise, where the defendant commits a robbery with use of a firearm, or imitation firearm, the prosecution is advised to seek appropriate charges under the Firearms Act 1968 in addition to the charge of robbery (*R v Murphy* [2002] Crim LR 674). In both cases, the defendant may be liable for two offences on the single indictment. See generally, O'Donnell and Morrison, 'Armed and Dangerous: The Use of Firearms in Robbery' [1997] 36(3) Howard Jnl 305.

11.3.5 Charging robbery

11.3.5.1 Mode of trial

Robbery is an offence triable only on indictment, meaning that the defendant may be tried only in the Crown Court (TA 1968, s 8(2)).

11.3.5.2 Sentencing

The maximum sentence for robbery is life imprisonment (TA 1968, s 8(2)). The Sentencing Council published its 'Definitive Guideline on Robbery' in 2016. In the Guideline, the Sentencing Council distinguish three types of robberies:

- street and less sophisticated commercial robberies;
- professionally planned commercial robberies; and
- dwelling robberies.

11.3.6 Putting together robbery

Consider this issue and think of how you may structure an answer to it. Then see the figure below for a sample structure to adopt.

facts

Jack visits his local shopping centre and enters a jewellery store. Jack threatens the customer assistant with a knife and demands money from the cash register. The assistant refuses and sounds the alarm. Jack runs from the store and pushes a number of customers out of the way to escape.

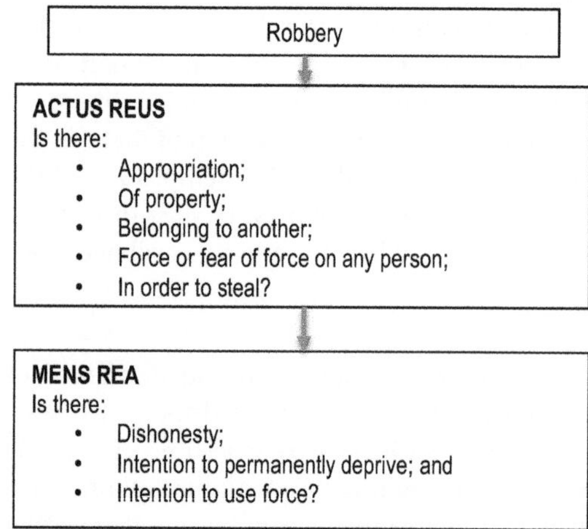

Figure 11.8 Putting together robbery

11.4 Burglary and aggravated burglary

The common image of burglary (and a 'burglar') is of breaking and entering into another person's home in order to steal. Indeed, one may have the classic image of a man dressed in black and white stripes with a mask. Burglary, however, is concerned with much wider activity than that of your simple 'cat burglar'. Importantly, where a person carries with him any article for use in the course of or in connection with a burglary, he may also be liable for going equipped contrary to s 25 of the TA 1968 (see **11.5**).

Burglary remains an offence separate to that of theft and robbery as a result of the well documented psychological effects of burglary on its victims. Specifically, Maguire and Bennett (*Burglary in a Dwelling: The Offence, the Offender and the Victim* (Heinemann, 1982)) concluded that about a quarter of victims 'are, temporarily at least, badly shaken by the experience' and that a small majority suffer long-lasting effects. Indeed, the Sentencing Council in its Definitive Guideline on 'Domestic burglary' (2012) acknowledges that the crime can cause considerable distress and fear on the basis that one no longer believes their home is safe, or that their property has been interfered with beyond reparation.

11.4.1 Defining burglary

Burglary as an offence is concerned with criminalising actions involving 'criminal trespass'. The emphasis here is placed on 'criminal'. Despite familiar signage to the contrary (eg 'Trespassers will be Prosecuted'), trespass alone (subject to a few exceptions) is not a criminal offence, although it does amount to a civil wrong. Burglary is therefore concerned with a civil trespass, but the defendant has gone one step further and has committed and intends to commit a criminal wrong whilst trespassing. It is at this stage that his trespass becomes criminal. Burglary is not concerned solely with criminal trespass in another person's home (also known as a 'dwelling burglary'); instead, burglary covers all sorts of trespass into buildings or part of buildings, whether they be domestic or commercial. We shall see also that the purpose of trespassing need not be just to steal; instead, an individual may be classed as a burglar where he assaults another person in the building, or he causes criminal damage whilst in the building.

11.4.2 Elements of burglary

Section 9 of the TA 1968 provides:

> (1) A person is guilty of burglary if—
>
> (a) he enters any building or part of a building as a trespasser and with intent to commit any such offence as is mentioned in subsection (2) below; or
>
> (b) having entered any building or part of a building as a trespasser he steals or attempts to steal anything in the building or that part of it or inflicts or attempts to inflict on any person therein any grievous bodily harm.
>
> (2) The offences referred to in subsection (1)(a) above are offences of stealing anything in the building or part of a building in question, of inflicting on any person therein any grievous bodily harm therein, and of doing unlawful damage to the building or anything therein.

Section 9(1) has the effect of creating two distinct burglary offences. As such, a defendant may be charged under either s 9(1)(a) or s 9(1)(b). The elements of the offences are virtually identical, the difference being the point at which the elements are fulfilled and the so-called 'ulterior offences' that satisfy the burglary offences. The ulterior offences under s 9(2), namely theft, grievous bodily harm (GBH) and criminal damage apply only to the offence in s 9(1)(a). Section 9(1)(b) specifically states its own ulterior offences in the form of theft or GBH. Commission of or intention to commit criminal damage is therefore not sufficient for the s 9(1)(b) offence.

It is important to emphasise that the two offences in s 9(1) are separate. The Court of Appeal in *R v Hollis* [1971] Crim LR 525 ruled that an individual charged under one section may not then be subsequently convicted under the other. In *R v Taylor* [1979] Crim LR 649, the Court of Appeal noted, however, that the same facts may give rise to both offences under s 9, and *Hollis* was eventually reversed by the Court of Appeal in *R v Whiting* [1987] Crim LR 473. As such, a defendant charged with a s 9(1) offence may be liable for both offences and charged as such.

The *actus reus* and *mens rea* of burglary are outlined in **Table 11.12.**

Table 11.12 Elements of burglary

AR/MR	Elements of the offence: s 9(1)(a)	Elements of the offence: s 9(1)(b)
Actus reus	(i) entry; (ii) any building or part of a building; (iii) as a trespasser.	(i) having entered; (ii) any building or part of a building; (iii) as a trespasser; (iv) commits or attempts to commit theft or GBH.
Mens rea	(i) intention or recklessness to enter as a trespasser; (ii) intention to commit one of the ulterior offences.	(i) intention or recklessness to enter as a trespasser; (ii) intention to commit theft or GBH.

Before we move into our discussion of the elements of burglary, under both s 9(1)(a) and 9(1)(b), it is worth explaining the difference between the two offences in greater detail.

Burglary contrary to s 9(1)(a)

Section 9(1)(a) is concerned with the actions of the defendant *prior* to his entry into the building. The law focuses on the liability of the defendant *at the point of entry* provided that he has the necessary *mens rea* for the offence. It is irrelevant whether the defendant goes on to commit or even attempt to commit one of the ulterior offences listed in s 9(2). On this basis, the prosecution is required to prove that the defendant:

- entered;
- a building or part of a building;
- as a trespasser;
- with the intention to commit an ulterior offence.

As a result of the focus of s 9(1)(a) on the intention of the defendant prior to his entry, Ormerod and Laird (*Smith, Hogan, & Ormerod's Criminal Law*, 15th edn (OUP, 2018)) have classified this offence as 'inchoate in nature' given that the actual intention need not ever be fulfilled. Indeed, Horder (*Ashworth's Principles of Criminal Law*, 9th edn (OUP, 2019)) notes that the effect of this provision is that '[w]hat ordinary people might regard as an "attempted burglary", since D has not yet stolen anything, is in fact a full offence'.

Burglary contrary to s 9(1)(b)

This can be compared with s 9(1)(b) which is concerned with the actions of a defendant *after* his entry into the building. The emphasis to be placed on s 9(1)(b) is in the wording of 'having entered ... the defendant commits or attempts to commit'. On this basis, the criminal law is concerned with the activities taken by the defendant *whilst* in the building. As opposed to s 9(1)(a), where there is no requirement for the defendant to commit or attempt to commit the ulterior offences listed, in s 9(1)(b), there is such a requirement that the defendant does commit or at least attempts to commit theft or GBH. Further, the ulterior offences referred to in s 9(1)(b) include theft and GBH only; criminal damage is thus irrelevant to the s 9(1)(b) offence. On this basis, the prosecution is required to prove that the defendant:

- entered;
- a building or part of a building;
- as a trespasser; and
- committed or attempted to commit theft or GBH.

Therefore, when confronted with a problem question concerning burglary, your focus needs to be on:

- whether the defendant is already in the building or not; and
- whether he commits or attempts to commit one of the ulterior offences.

Figure 11.9 should assist in your understanding of the operation of both s 9(1)(a) and s 9(1)(b).

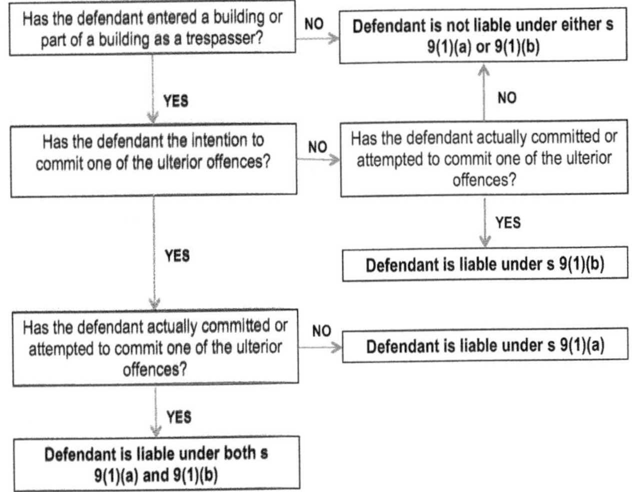

Figure 11.9 Putting together s 9(1)(a) and s 9(1)(b)

Given that the elements are, in the majority, identical, we shall consider both offences together and make the distinction where relevant or necessary.

11.4.2.1 *Actus reus:* (i) entry

Entry is not defined within s 9. Pre-1968 common law seemed to accept that the insertion of any body part, however small, into a building or part of a building was sufficient (*R v Davis* (1823) Russ & Ry 499). Over a period of time, however, post-1968 common law began to make more restrictive sense of the words 'enter' and 'entry', and a string of cases dealing with this meaning have arisen. These cases are detailed in **Figure 11.10**. In all cases, whether there has been an 'entry' is a matter of fact for the arbiters of fact.

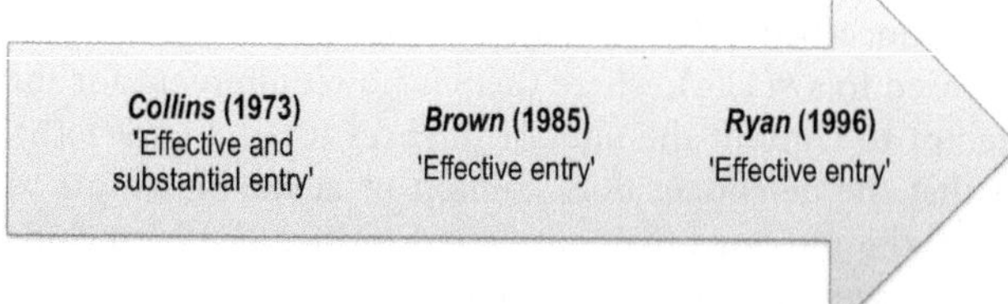

Figure 11.10 Development in the meaning of 'entry'

The first point to note throughout this development is that there is no requirement for 'breaking and entering'. This phrase, although often cited, is not of use in English law. Rather, we are merely concerned with whether the entry was *sufficient* for the purposes of s 9.

Our starting point in understanding the meaning of entry is the case of *R v Collins* [1973] QB 100.

case example

Charge:
Burglary (TA 1968, s 9)

Case progression:
Crown Court – Guilty

Court of Appeal – Conviction quashed

Point of law:
Meaning of entry

In *R v Collins* [1973] QB 100, the defendant scaled a ladder to the window of a girl's bedroom. The defendant was naked with the exception of his socks and intended to have sexual intercourse with the girl, even if he had to use force.

As the defendant was entering the window, the girl noticed him and invited him in for sexual intercourse, believing him to be her boyfriend. The defendant was charged with and convicted of burglary in the Crown Court.

The defendant appealed to the Court of Appeal, which had to decide whether the defendant was outside of the window before permission to enter was granted. The Court found that there may have been an effective entry, but found no liability on the basis that the defendant was invited into the home and the trial judge had failed to leave the jury with the question as to whether the defendant was reckless as to the mistake made by the victim.

Edmund-Davies LJ held that an entry must be 'effective and substantial'. In that case, there was uncertainty as to whether any part of Collins' body had entered the building (in particular, the question was whether his erect penis might be considered sufficient for effective entry into the building). Given that there was uncertainty in this regard, and the fact that the jury were never asked to consider this question, the defendant could not be said to have entered the building prior to being invited in. In this regard, whether the defendant's entry was *effective and substantial* in *Collins* has troubled students for some time.

The use of 'substantial' in the meaning of entry was doubted by the Court of Appeal in *R v Brown* [1985] Crim LR 212.

case example

Charge:
Burglary (TA 1968, s 9)

Case progression:
Crown Court – Guilty

Court of Appeal – Conviction upheld

Point of law:
Meaning of entry

In *R v Brown* [1985] Crim LR 212, the defendant smashed a window of an Argos shop. Upon smashing the window, the defendant leaned into the shop (so that the top half of his body was inside the building) and took certain goods.

The defendant was charged with and convicted of burglary in the Crown Court.

In the Court of Appeal, Brown argued that by the fact that his feet remained on the ground and he simply leaned into the store, his entry was not 'substantial and effective'. The Court of Appeal dismissed his appeal.

The Court of Appeal ruled that the entry need only 'effective', as the word 'substantial' did not materially assist with the definition. Rather, 'substantial' would cause confusion in suggesting that the whole of the defendant must have entered the building. The Court of Appeal noted that the defendant's entry was clearly *effective* given that he was in a position to steal.

This understanding was reaffirmed in the later case of *R v Ryan* [1996] Crim LR 320.

case example

Charge:
Burglary (TA 1968, s 9)

Case progression:
Crown Court – Guilty

Court of Appeal – Conviction upheld

Point of law:
Meaning of entry

In *R v Ryan* [1996] Crim LR 320, the defendant attempted to break into the home of the victim, an elderly man. In attempting to enter, the defendant found himself stuck in the kitchen window. Specifically, the defendant's head and right arm were stuck inside the building whilst the rest of his body was outside the building. The defendant was charged and convicted in the Crown Court.

On appeal, the Court of Appeal upheld his conviction.

The Court of Appeal held that entry need only be 'effective', and whether such entry was 'effective' was a question for the jury as a matter of fact. Further, contrary to the Court of Appeal in *Brown*, it was irrelevant that the defendant was not in a suitable position to carry out his intended offence (ie the offence could not be carried out); his entry could still be declared effective by the jury.

As a result of *Brown* and *Ryan*, the test for entry is now established as whether the entry is 'effective'. Following *Ryan*, there does not appear to be a requirement that the defendant, through his entry, is in a position to steal. This may have the effect of broadening the meaning of 'entry' and reducing the threshold to a minimal.

The judgments in *Brown* and *Ryan* have been criticised by the likes of Ormerod and Laird (*Smith, Hogan, & Ormerod's Criminal Law*, 15th edn (OUP, 2018)), who argue:

> It is unsatisfactory that such a crucial *actus reus* element of a serious offence should be left for a jury to determine; the best course would be to accept the continued existence of the common law rule: *any entry no matter how slight should suffice*. (emphasis added)

in practice

The CPS advises that '[w]hen there are any factual difficulties with the degree of entry, consideration should be given to charging another offence, for example theft'. This advice would seem to accord with Ormerod and Laird's fears that a jury should not be responsible for such an important element of the *actus reus*.

May a defendant 'enter' a building by use of an innocent agent?

Suppose Jack, an adult, sends Jill, a child, into a building to commit a burglary for him. Could Jack be liable for burglary given that he did not personally enter the building? The answer is yes. In *R v Wheelhouse* [1994] Crim LR 756, the defendant procured another (X) to enter a garage and steal a car. X was acquitted at trial on account that he was an innocent agent as he lacked *mens* rea, believing he had the right to take the property (the defendant having told him that the car was the defendant's property). The defendant's conviction for burglary was upheld on account that he satisfied the *mens rea* of the offence (see **Chapter 4**).

May a defendant 'enter' a building via an instrument?

An interesting point that has rarely come before the courts is the situation where the defendant uses an instrument to effect his entry into the building or part of the building as opposed to a part of his body. According to the Court of Appeal in *R v Horncastle* [2006] EWCA Crim 1736 – a case where the defendant used bamboo sticks with hooks on the end to hook keys in the hallway – the position at common law was as follows:

- if the instrument was inserted to effect the ulterior offence (eg by hooking a coat with a wallet inside), this amounted to an effective entry. It was considered that the instrument was an extension of the defendant and therefore that there was an effective entry; whereas
- if the instrument was inserted to facilitate access (eg to open a door or window), this did not amount to an effective entry until a part of the defendant's body was inserted into the building.

Although a case has not dealt specifically with this point, it is likely that the common law will continue to have application on this point.

11.4.2.2 *Actus reus:* (ii) any building or part of a building

The next requirement of the *actus reus* is that the entry was to a 'building or part of a building'. As with 'entry', 'building or part of a building' has not been defined in the statute to any great extent – though common sense should be used in understanding its meaning. We are assisted in part by s 9(4) which states that references to a building shall also apply to

> an inhabited vehicle or vessel, and shall apply to any such vehicle or vessel at times when the person having a habitation in it is not there as well as at times when he is.

We shall deal with the elements of building and part of a building separately.

Building

The classic statement of what amounts to a building can be found in Byles J's judgment in *Stevens v Gourley* (1859) 7 CB (NS) 99, where it was stated that a building comprised

> ... a structure of considerable size and intended to be permanent or at least to endure for a considerable time.

This matter was further alluded to by Lord Esher MR in *Moir v Williams* [1892] 1 QB 264, who stated in *obiter* that 'an ordinary building is an inclosure of brick or stonework covered in by a roof'. The necessity for 'brick or stone work', however, was recently dismissed by Lord Neuberger MR in *R (Ghai) v Newcastle City Council & Others* [2010] EWCA Civ 59, where his Lordship held that 'a significantly wider range of structures' other than stone and brick can amount to a building for the purposes of the Act.

In *Brutus v Cozens* [1973] AC 854, the House of Lords held that 'building' is an ordinary word, the meaning of which is a 'matter of fact and degree'. According to the Crown Court in *B and S v Leathley* [1979] Crim LR 314, the building in question must have 'some degree of permanence'. On that basis, a freezer container disconnected from its chassis (the underpart or frame of a motor vehicle, on which the body is mounted), that was permanently situated within a scrap yard, was considered sufficient for a 'building'. This can be compared with the later case of *Norfolk Constabulary v Seekings and Gould* [1986] Crim LR 167, where the Crown Court ruled that a freezer container on an articulated lorry, still connected to its chassis, was a non-inhabited vehicle and not a building within s 9. The Court emphasised the requirement for a degree of permanence and explained that moveable structures, such as those mounted on a chassis, which are of a temporary use only, cannot be classed as buildings.

By way of s 9(3) and (4), all dwellings are protected as buildings. 'Dwellings' are not defined in the TA 1968. The Divisional Court considered the definition of a 'dwelling' in *Hudson v CPS* [2017] EWHC 841 (Admin). The Administrative Court considered that whether the building in question is a dwelling is matter of fact, time and degree. The Court noted that, at the material time, the building:

- had residential appearance;
- had been fully furnished;
- had been let out only two days previously; and
- was ready to be reoccupied.

Despite the building being presently unoccupied, the Administrative Court found the building in question to be a dwelling. See also *R v Sticklen* [2013] EWCA Crim 615. Whether the building is a dwelling or not will not affect the defendant's liability, but will be relevant to the sentence imposed following conviction. Do note, however, that according to the Court in *R v Miller* [2010] EWCA Crim 809, where the burglary was committed in a dwelling, the defendant should be charged explicitly with burglary *of a dwelling* (this is so for the purposes of sentencing).

Further, by s 9(4), inhabited vehicles or vessels (ie they are 'lived' in) are also protected as 'buildings'. Such inhabited vehicles may include a caravan or a houseboat which may be stationary in one place for a long period of time (*R v Coleman* [2013] EWCA Crim 544 – burglary of a narrow boat used as a dwelling). However, they are unlikely to include such things as a tent, which is unlikely to be situated in one place for a long period of time. The vehicle must, however, be 'inhabited'; should an individual simply lean through a car window and steal a wallet sitting on the passenger seat, this would not be burglary (but would be theft).

We can surmise the list of most likely 'buildings' for the purpose of the Act to include the following.

Table 11.13 Meaning of building

Building
A dwelling (whether occupied or not)
Work or commercial buildings
Outhouses

Sheds

Semi-permanent containers

Part of a building

The phrase 'or part of a building' is intended to cover the situation where the defendant holds permission to be in a certain section of the building but holds no permission to be in another area of that building. The standard example is a convenience store whereby the defendant has permission to be in the building, allowing him to browse for items to purchase; however, he has no permission to go behind the counter where the public, as of a general nature, have no right of access. This was the decision of the Court of Appeal in *R v Walkington* [1979] 2 All ER 716 based on similar facts. Geoffrey Lane LJ explained the distinction between spaces open and closed to the public in the following way:

> One really gets two extremes, as it seems to us. First of all you have the part of the building which is shut off by a door so far as the general public is concerned, with a notice saying 'Staff only' or 'No admittance to customers'. At the other end of the scale you have, for example, a single table in the middle of the store, which it would be difficult for any jury to find properly was a part of the building into which the licensor prohibited customers from moving.
>
> The present situation, it seems to us, was that there was a physical partition. Whether it was sufficient to amount to an area from which the public were plainly excluded was a matter for the jury. It seems to us that there was ample evidence [on these facts] on which they could come to the conclusion (i) that the management had impliedly prohibited customers entering that area and (ii) that this particular defendant knew of that prohibition.

An interesting case dealing with this point of law is that of *R v Laing* [1995] Crim LR 395.

Charge:
Burglary (TA 1968, s 9)

Case progression:
Crown Court – Guilty

Court of Appeal – Conviction quashed

Point of law:
Meaning of 'part of a building'

In *R v Laing* [1995] Crim LR 395, the defendant had hid himself away in the stock area of a department store, intending to steal when the store was closed. Upon the store closing, the defendant was discovered.

The defendant was charged with and convicted of burglary contrary to s 9(1)(a) in the Crown Court. The trial judge directed the jury to decide whether the defendant was a trespasser at the time of being found, despite evidence that he was not a trespasser at the point of entry. The defendant appealed to the Court of Appeal which quashed his conviction on the basis that there was no evidence that the defendant was a trespasser when he entered the store.

You may think to yourself, 'Well surely he was a trespasser following the logic of *Walkington*?' However, the prosecution in *Laing* failed to argue that the defendant, although he entered the building lawfully, became a trespasser when he moved to a part of the store excluded from the public, ie the stockroom. The Court of Appeal emphasised that there must be a coincidence in time, namely that the defendant was a trespasser at the point of entry. The Court of Appeal accepted that the defendant was a trespasser at the point of being found, given that the store was closed and members of the public had no permission to be there at that time. However, there was no evidence that he was a trespasser at the point of entry. The prosecution focused on the defendant's original entry into the building and did not concern itself with the transition from the main store area to the stockroom. Had the prosecution focused on the defendant's entry into the stockroom, the defendant would likely have been convicted.

Both cases can be questioned as to their relevance as a result of the decision in *Jones and Smith* (below). It can be noted that if it can be proven that the defendant entered a building with the intention to steal, at that point, he is considered a trespasser. This eradicates the need to assert whether the defendant had permission to enter one part of the building but not another.

11.4.2.3 *Actus reus:* (iii) as a trespasser

Following the civil law on trespass, any person who intentionally, recklessly or negligently enters any building or part of a building without the permission of the owner will be a 'trespasser'. The prosecution must show that the defendant's entry was voluntary (in the sense that it was deliberate – not accidental or forced). The prosecution must also prove that the defendant knew or was reckless to the thought that he was a trespasser (this, however, is a part of the *mens rea*; here, we focus on the *actus reus*).

In the majority of cases, whether the defendant is a trespasser will not be an issue for the courts as there will often be a clear distinction between individuals with permission to enter and individuals without such permission. A list of factors which may tip the balance for or against the defendant being a trespasser are detailed below.

Should a defendant receive permission to be in the building, or part of the building, he shall not be considered a 'trespasser'. However, permission to enter will only be valid where it is given by a person with the relevant authority to do so. This may be an inhabitant of the building and need not be the owner of the building. As above, permission is often an uncontroversial matter within the criminal law; however, there remain two prime examples where the permission given by an individual can give rise to difficulties. These are:

- where permission is given in mistake; and
- where the defendant goes 'beyond' the permission given.

Mistaken permission

The main authority on permission to enter is that of *R v Collins* (see above). Mistake as to identity will vitiate permission to enter if the defendant was aware that the individual granting permission was mistaken. In *Collins* the victim mistook the defendant for her boyfriend and invited him in for sexual intercourse. Upon realising it was not her partner, the victim asked the defendant to leave (who did so speedily). Although convicted of burglary, the Court of Appeal allowed his appeal on account that the jury were not directed to consider whether the defendant was aware that the victim was mistaken. In that case, there was no evidence to suggest that he was aware of her mistake, and thus he was not a trespasser for the purposes of the Act.

In summary, a defendant's permission will be invalidated in circumstances where it was given by mistake, whether that be through fraud, deception or misinformation.

Going 'beyond' permission

Importantly, where a person goes beyond the permission granted to them by the inhabitant, they will then become trespassers from that point on. The High Court of

Australia in the case of *Barker v R* (1983) 7 ALJR 426 made this point clear by stating that, 'If a person enters for a purpose outside the scope of his authority then he stands in no better position than a person who enters with no authority at all.' An oft-cited quote comes from Scrutton LJ in *The Calgarth* [1927] P 93, where his Lordship aptly stated that

> When you invite a person into your house to use the staircase you do not invite him to slide down the banisters.

The leading case in this area is that of *R v Jones; R v Smith* [1976] 1 WLR 672 (more commonly known simply as R v *Jones and Smith*).

Charge:
Burglary (TA 1968, s 9)

Case progression:
Crown Court – Guilty

Court of Appeal – Conviction upheld

Point of law:
Meaning of trespassers

case example

In *R v Jones; R v Smith* [1976] 1 WLR 672, the defendants stole several television sets from the house of Smith's father. The defendants had a general permission to enter the house. The pair entered the house at night time with intention to steal. The defendants were charged with and convicted of burglary in the Crown Court.

The defendants appealed to the Court of Appeal, which ruled that although the defendants were lawfully in the building, they exceeded their permission upon entering the building with the intention to steal.

Smith ('Shoplifting and the Theft Acts' [1981] Crim LR 586) applies the *Jones and Smith* logic to shoplifters. Smith argues that shoplifters are liable for burglary upon entering the shop with the intention to steal. Their permission extends as far as purchasing items; it does not extend to stealing items. Smith's view can be taken further and can be applied to all circumstances where an individual enters a building with the intention to steal. Indeed, this is the view adopted by the majority of practitioners; however, the difficulty comes in enforcing this principle in practice.

in practice

The prosecution may struggle to prove all the elements of burglary in a case where the defendant does not enter an area deemed 'off limits' to the general public. In cases where the defendant does not enter a restricted area, the prosecutor is likely to charge the offence of theft as a matter of ease and logic.

A number of criticisms have arisen as a result of the decision in *Jones and Smith*. These difficulties can be identified as follows:

- The decision is inconsistent with that in *Collins* (see Williams (*Textbook of Criminal Law* (Sweet & Maxwell, 1978)).
- Burglary is now wider than was ever intended by the legislature. Horder (*Ashworth's Principles of Criminal Law*, 9th edn (OUP, 2019)) argues that the 'boundaries of burglary are being pushed wider than is necessary or appropriate'. He goes on to say that '[s]urely the proper label for what was done … is theft, and the availability of the charges of theft and attempted theft makes it unnecessary to strain the boundaries of trespass by inserting unstated reservations into general permissions given by householders'.

Ormerod and Laird (*Smith, Hogan, & Ormerod's Criminal Law*, 15th edn (OUP, 2018)) raise an interesting point on this area. Specifically, they provide:

> Interesting problems emerge where D enters with permission but the permission is then withdrawn. Where D fails to leave in a reasonable time, she becomes a trespasser. However, as she has not 'entered' as a trespasser, we would still need some kind of crossing (eg into a new area of the building) as a trespasser in order to potentially catch D within burglary.

Whilst this view would appear to have merit, a prosecutor is likely to apply the ruling in *Jones and Smith* and argue that upon the defendant having his permission withdrawn, should that defendant refuse to leave, he shall be acting outside of his original permission. On that basis, he is a trespasser for the purposes of the section following *Jones and Smith*. It is unlikely that the prosecutor will need the defendant to move into another area to consider him a trespasser.

Factors determining trespass

It is useful to identify a number of factors in determining whether the defendant was a 'trespasser' for the purposes of the Act:

- *Voluntary movements:* In the civil context, a defendant cannot be liable for trespass on land where his actions were involuntary. This was evident in the civil case of *Smith v Stone* (1647) 82 ER 533, where the Court of King's Bench held that the defendant could not be liable for trespass given that he was carried onto the land and had no control over such actions. The same principle would apply in the criminal law – though see *Gilbert v Stone* (1647) 82 ER 902 in relation to a claim of duress as a reason for trespass.
- *Use of force:* A use of force by the defendant in effecting entry will be a clear indication that the defendant is a trespasser and more importantly that he intends to be a trespasser for the purposes of the *mens rea.*
- *Banned defendants:* In many cases, the defendant may have been banned or excluded from the relevant building. Where the defendant disobeys this ban, he is considered a trespasser without any difficulty. Given that the defendant will have the respective knowledge of his ban, this would also satisfy the *mens rea* requirement.
- *Accompanying dishonest actions:* In some cases, the defendant may procure consent or permission to enter a building as a result of a false claim or persona, for example he may claim to be a local postcode lottery salesman or a gas meter reader. In such circumstances, the defendant may obtain the consent of the victim through fraud or deceit. In such circumstances, the defendant has not obtained true permission to be within the building and thus will be considered a trespasser in law.

11.4.2.4 *Actus reus:* (iv) commission of theft or GBH (TA 1968, s 9(1)(b) only)

Given that s 9(1)(b) concerns the circumstances where the defendant has already entered a building or part of a building as a trespasser, as opposed to s 9(1)(a) which concerns the future entry of the defendant, there is an extra requirement to prove that the defendant:

- committed theft
- attempted to commit theft
- committed GBH

- attempted to commit GBH.

It is worth noting that whilst s 9(1)(a) includes the offence of criminal damage within its scope, such offence is not present in s 9(1)(b).

Unlike the s 9(1)(a) offence, which refers to the 'offence' of GBH, s 9(1)(b) does not include the word 'offence' in its provision. Smith ('Burglary under the Theft Bill' [1968] Crim LR 367) contends that such omission is merely a 'legislative accident' and s 9(1)(b) ought to be interpreted in the same way as s 9(1)(a). However, the Court of Appeal in *R v Jenkins* [1983] 1 All ER 1000 held that s 9(1)(b) merely requires the infliction of GBH, as opposed to the *offence* of GBH. Ormerod and Laird (*Smith, Hogan, & Ormerod's Criminal Law*, 15th edn (OUP, 2018)) criticise this decision, arguing that the court's interpretation was a 'bad one'. The pair contend that

> When para (b) is read in the context of s 9(1) and (2), it is reasonably clear that the infliction of bodily harm required must be an offence – in effect, under s 18 or 20 ... of the Offences Against the Person Act [OAPA] 1861.

The author concurs with Ormerod and Laird and advises the reader to consider the wording 'inflicting grievous bodily harm' to mean the *offence* of GBH contrary to either s 18 or s 20 of the OAPA 1861. To make sense of the ulterior offences in s 9(1)(a) and 9(1)(b), see **Table 11.14** below.

11.4.2.5 *Mens rea:* (i) intention or recklessness to enter as a trespasser

The defendant must have known that he was a trespasser (and thus intended to trespass) or was reckless to the thought that he was a trespasser. In *Collins*, Edmund-Davies LJ explained that:

> [T]here cannot be a conviction for entering premises 'as a trespasser' ... unless the person entering does so knowing that he is a trespasser and nevertheless deliberately enters, or, at the very least, is reckless as to whether or not he is entering the premises of another without the other party's consent.

This passage was approved by the Court of Appeal in *R v Jones; R v Smith* [1976] 1 WLR 672.

In the majority of cases, this will not pose a problem for the prosecution. However, in circumstances where the defendant has raised a genuine belief that he had a right to enter, the prosecution may have a harder job of disproving such belief. This is especially so when one considers the cases involving mistaken permission (see, for example, *Collins* above).

11.4.2.6 *Mens rea:* (ii) intention to commit one of the ulterior offences

Given that the *mens rea* for a s 9(1)(a) offence is slightly different to that of a s 9(1)(b) offence, it will be useful to divide the two at this stage.

The s 9(1)(a) offence

Under s 9(1)(a), the defendant must intend (upon entering the building or part of a building as a trespasser) to commit one of the ulterior offences listed in s 9(2). The defendant must *intend*; anything short of intention, such as recklessness, is not sufficient for this element of the *mens rea*. This has the effect that an offence under s 9(1)(a) is one of specific intent (*R v Durante* [1972] 1 WLR 1612). The ulterior offences listed in s 9(2) are as follows:

- theft, contrary to s 1 of the TA 1968;

- grievous bodily harm (GBH), contrary to s 18 of the OAPA 1861; and
- criminal damage, contrary to the Criminal Damage Act (CDA) 1971.

The Divisional Court in *A v DPP* [2003] EWHC 1676 (Admin) has emphasised that the intention to commit one of these offences must exist *at the time* of entry, and it is irrelevant whether the defendant actually went on to commit the ulterior offence. To reaffirm, the full offence of burglary is committed at the point of entry with the relevant intention. Without such intention, the defendant is liable for no criminal offence (*R v Bennett* [2007] EWCA Crim 2815).

The defendant's intent may be conditional, in the sense that he may intend to steal, cause GBH or criminal damage, but there is nothing worth stealing, the owner is not at home or the property he wishes to damage is not there. This was the predicament in *AG's References (Nos 1 and 2 of 1979)* [1980] QB 180, where the defendant entered a building with the intention to steal, albeit the building was empty. The Court of Appeal ruled that the defendant remained liable for burglary under s 9(1)(a) as his intention to steal was ever-present. The Court of Appeal emphasised that the defendant need not specify any particular property as being the object of his intention given that s 9(2) states that the defendant must intend to steal 'anything in the building'. Note, however, that given that electricity cannot be stolen (see **Chapter 12**), should a defendant enter a building as a trespasser and use the electricity of the householder, by making a phone call for example, he will not be liable for an offence of burglary – although he will be liable for abstracting electricity contrary to s 13 of the TA 1968 (*Low v Blease* [1975] Crim LR 513).

in practice

Prosecutors are likely to draft an indictment broadly in order to prevent the defendant from arguing that a conditional intent will allow him to escape liability. Indeed, in *R v Husseyn* (1977) 67 Cr App R 131, a case concerning the attempted theft of sub-aqua equipment from a van, the defendants' appeals were quashed on the basis that '[i]t cannot be said that one who has it in mind to steal only if what he finds is worth stealing has a present intention to steal'. Indeed, this is the view taken in Smith's *Law of Theft*, 9th edn (OUP, 2007) where it is argued that the defendant might fall outside of this section if his intention was only to steal a specific item if, on examination, it had certain characteristics. Should a prosecutor draft an indictment stating that the defendant intended to steal the contents therein, it will avoid any argument of conditional intent, or no intent at all for that matter, from being raised.

An interesting point raised by White ('Lurkers, Draggers and Kidnappers' (1986) 150 JP 37), which has yet to come before the courts, is the statutory use of 'therein' within s 9(2). Specifically, s 9(2) states that the defendant must intend to steal, or cause GBH to any person *therein* the building or cause criminal damage to any property *therein* the building. White questions what the law would be in circumstances where the defendant takes a piece of property out of the building and then damages it (ie it is not 'therein'). Further, White questions the position where the defendant removes a person from the building and once outside the building then commits GBH (ie it is, again, not 'therein'). In the former circumstance, the defendant is likely to remain liable for burglary as his actions of removing the property from the building will be sufficient to amount to theft (the first ulterior offence) and his intention to cause criminal damage will be sufficient for an intention to steal. The latter circumstance is much more difficult to apply, and it would appear that the appellate courts would find themselves using their powers and rules of interpretation to find the true meaning of Parliament in the word 'therein'. Indeed, a battery will have been committed in the latter example, given that there will likely have been an unlawful application of force in order to remove the person from the building; however, that in itself will not be enough for a claim of really serious harm (ie GBH).

Section 9(2) previously included rape as a fourth ulterior offence capable of resulting in liability for burglary. This element of s 9(2) was removed by s 63(1) of the Sexual Offences Act 2003 which creates a much broader offence of trespassing on any premises with intent to commit a relevant sexual offence.

The s 9(1)(b) offence

Under s 9(1)(b), the defendant, having entered a building or part of a building as a trespasser, must commit, or at least attempt to commit, theft or GBH. Intention alone is insufficient if the defendant has not taken some form of action to ensure its commission.

From our discussion above, when referring to the ulterior offences in s 9(1)(b), the following is meant:

- theft, contrary to the TA 1968; and
- inflicting GBH, contrary to s 18 or s 20 of the OAPA 1861.

Further to this, commission or attempted commission of criminal damage is not sufficient to amount to burglary under s 9(1)(b). Rather, the prosecution will either have to prove an offence under s 9(1)(a) or charge the defendant separately with criminal damage.

Table 11.14 Understanding the ulterior offences

s 9(1)(a) offence	s 9(1)(b) offence
Theft – contrary to s 1 of the TA 1968	Theft – contrary to s 1 of the TA 1968
Inflicting GBH – contrary to s 18 of the OAPA 1861	Inflicting GBH – contrary to s 18 or s 20 of the OAPA 1861
Criminal damage (any offence of damage) – contrary to the CDA 1971	n/a

11.4.3 Aggravated burglary

A burglary may be aggravated into an aggravated burglary under s 10 of the TA 1968 if it is committed with the use of a listed weapon.

Section 10(1) of the TA 1968 provides:

> A person is guilty of aggravated burglary if he commits any burglary and at the time has with him any firearm or imitation firearm, any weapon of offence, or any explosive; and for this purpose—
>
> (a) 'firearm' includes an airgun or air pistol, and 'imitation firearm' means anything which has the appearance of being a firearm, whether capable of being discharged or not; and
>
> (b) 'weapon of offence' means any article made or adapted for use for causing injury to or incapacitating a person, or intended by the person having it with him for such use; and

(c) 'explosive' means any article manufactured for the purpose of producing a practical effect by explosion, or intended by the person having it with him for that purpose.

The *actus reus* and *mens rea* of aggravated burglary are outlined in **Table 11.15**.

Table 11.15 Elements of aggravated burglary

AR/MR	Elements of the offence
Actus reus	(i) *actus reus* of burglary (either s 9(1)(a) or s 9(1)(b)); (ii) at the time has with him; (iii) one of the aggravating articles.
Mens rea	*Mens rea* of burglary (either s 9(1)(a) or s 9(1)(b))

We shall consider only the second and third element of the *actus reus* given that the other elements of the offence are identical to their basic counterpart under s 9.

11.4.3.1 *Actus reus:* (ii) at the time has with him

It must be proved that the defendant had the article of aggravation at the time of the burglary. Whether the defendant has the offensive article with him *at the time* of the burglary will ultimately depend on the type of burglary charged. We can explain this principle as follows:

- where the charge is s 9(1)(a), 'at the time' must be at the time of *entry* (*R v Chevannes* [2009] EWCA Crim 2725; *R v Wiggins* [2012] EWCA Crim 885); whereas
- if the charge is s 9(1)(b), 'at the time' must be at the time of *committing or attempting to commit one of the ulterior offences* (*R v Francis* [1982] Crim LR 363; *R v Chevannes* [2009] EWCA Crim 2725).

These two circumstances were confirmed by the Court of Appeal in *R v Eletu* [2018] EWCA Crim 599. In both cases, the article must be under the defendant's control and he must be aware that such is under his control (*R v Downer* [2009] EWCA Crim 1361; *R v Russell* (1984) 81 Cr App R 315 – where the defendant forgot that he had the weapon in his possession). The Court of Appeal in *R v Klass* [1998] 1 Cr App R 453 distinguished articles that were under the defendant's control and articles that were readily accessible. The former would be sufficient for an offence, but the latter might not be.

Under the Prevention of Crime Act 1953, the defendant need not use the weapon, nor need he have the intention to use the weapon (*R v Stones* [1989] 1 WLR 156). Instead, the defendant must merely have the article under his control at the relevant time. The meaning of 'has with him' was recently considered by the Court of Appeal in *R v Henderson* [2016] EWCA Crim 965, which concerned the charge of having a bladed article contrary to s 139(1) of the Criminal Justice Act 1988. Hamblen LJ in the Court of Appeal stated as follows:

> The authorities indicate that in determining whether a person has a weapon 'with him', relevant considerations include the following: (1) Possession of a weapon is a wider concept than having it 'with him'. (2) Having a weapon 'with him' is a wider concept than carrying it. (3) The propinquity between the person and the weapon. (4) Whether the weapon is immediately available to the person. (5) The accessibility of the weapon. (6) The context of any criminal enterprise embarked upon. (7) The purpose of the applicable statute. …

Hamblen LJ concluded:

> In this case there was no close geographical, temporal or purposive link between the knife which was in a public place and the appellant who was in a private flat. Nor do we consider that it can be said that the knife was immediately available or readily accessible to the appellant.
>
> In the light of the considerations set out above we conclude that the appellant did not in law have the knife 'with him'.

Interestingly, where the defendant drops the weapon, but later rearms himself with it, this may still be sufficient for aggravated burglary (*R v O'Leary* (1986) 82 Cr App R 341). Likewise, a defendant who enters a building without a weapon but picks one up whilst inside the building, such as a kitchen knife, before committing one of the ulterior offences, may also be liable for aggravated burglary. For similar facts to these, see the case of *O'Leary*.

11.4.3.2 *Actus reus:* (iii) one of the aggravating articles

The aggravating articles are detailed in s 10(1) and are largely self-explanatory. There are, however, a number of further points that one can make on this element of the offence.

Table 11.16 Aggravating articles

Aggravating article	Explanation
Firearm	Section 10(1) does not define firearm. Instead, it merely provides airgun, air pistol or imitation firearm as examples of firearms, given that a firearm is fairly self-explanatory.
Weapon of offence	The broad nature of this section allows for seemingly innocent articles to be used as weapons where they are carried as such. For example, a DIY tool, such as a screwdriver or hammer, may be relatively innocuous unless and until it is carried as a weapon (*R v Kelly* (1992) 97 Cr App R 245 – where the defendant, having used a screwdriver to effect entry, used it to prod the householder in the stomach). Likewise, articles *made* to incapacitate a person might include a pair of handcuffs, articles *adapted* to incapacitate might include a pair of socks made into a gag, and articles *intended* to incapacitate might include sleeping pills to put in someone's tea, a rope to tie someone up, pepper to throw in someone's face, etc. For a discussion on the importance of clarity regarding the definition of a 'weapon of offence', see *R v Eletu* [2018] EWCA Crim 599, in which the trial judge failed to adequately direct the jury on the relevant terminology and the difference between any article 'made or adapted' for use for causing injury to or incapacitating a person and any article 'intended by the person having it with him for such use'.
'Explosive'	This means any article manufactured for the purpose of producing a practical effect by explosion, or intended by the person having it with him for that purpose. A box of matches would not be an explosive under the TA 1968.

11.4.4 Charging burglary

11.4.4.1 Mode of trial

Burglary is generally an offence triable either way, meaning that a defendant may be tried in either the magistrates' court or the Crown Court. This general rule may be affected, however, by the operation of a number of provisions. We shall deal with these briefly.

- *Use of violence:* Burglary becomes an offence triable *only* on indictment where it comprises the commission of, or an intention to commit, an offence triable only on indictment; or it is committed in a dwelling and any person in the dwelling is subjected to violence or the threat of violence (Magistrates' Courts Act 1980, Sch 1, para 28). In that instance, where the ulterior offence is one of GBH, contrary to s 18, the defendant's case may only be heard in the Crown Court.
- *Three strikes:* Where a defendant is charged with a third domestic burglary (the so-called 'third strike burglary'), the offence is triable *only* on indictment where:
  - a person is convicted of a domestic burglary committed after 30 November 1999;
  - at the time when that burglary was committed, he was 18 or over and had been convicted in England and Wales of two other domestic burglaries; and
  - one of those other burglaries was committed after he had been convicted of the other, and both of them were committed after 30 November 1999.

Aggravated burglary is triable only on indictment.

11.4.4.2 Sentencing

Where tried in the magistrates' court, the maximum penalty for an offence is 6 months and/or a level 5 fine. In relation to sentencing in the Crown Court, s 9(3) of the TA 1968 provides:

> A person guilty of burglary shall on conviction on indictment be liable to imprisonment for a term not exceeding—
> (a) where the offence was committed in respect of a building or part of a building which is a *dwelling*, fourteen years (emphasis added);
> (b) in any other case, ten years.

As you will notice, s 9(3) prescribes two separate offences dependent on whether the offence took place in a dwelling or a non-dwelling. The House of Lords in *R v Courtie* [1984] AC 463 ruled that the procedural effect of these two provisions has had the effect of creating two separate offences. In such circumstances, the prosecution must make clear which offence is being charged. In addition, the Court of Appeal in *R v Saw* [2009] EWCA Crim 1 made it clear that in sentencing a defendant, the court will focus on the impact of the burglary on the victim, as opposed to the cash value of the burglary itself. See the Sentencing Council's Definitive Guidelines.

By s 10(2) of the TA 1968, a person guilty of aggravated burglary shall on conviction on indictment be liable to imprisonment for life.

These two sections provide for the statutory maximum in relation to burglary. Unlike other offences, however, there is also a mandatory minimum period of sentencing in certain circumstances. Specifically, where a defendant is convicted for his 'third strike' domestic burglary, and the defendant is over the age of 18, he must be sentenced to a minimum of three years' imprisonment (Powers of Criminal Courts (Sentencing) Act 2000, s 111). This provision has been criticised by the likes of Hearnden and Magill in their Home Office Report, 'Decision-making by House Burglars: Offenders' Perspectives' (Home Office Findings 249, 2004). Hearnden and Magill found that the majority of burglaries were carried out for the purpose of finding money to buy drugs, and burglars carried out their activities in such a way that made it easier for them to commit the crimes, for example by burgling houses close to their own home. As a result of these findings, Hearnden and Magill have criticised the three-strike provision in the 2000 Act on the basis that it fails to tackle burglary offences at the very core. In order to do so effectively, the pair advocate the need to focus on prevention methods and tackling drug addictions.

11.4.5 Putting together burglary

Consider this issue and think of how you may structure an answer to it. Then see the figure below for a sample structure to adopt.

facts

Jack, whilst wandering the streets at night, notices an open window to a house at the end of the street. Jack enters the house through the open window with the intention of stealing whatever he can find of value. The house is owned by Jill, who hears a noise and goes to investigate. She discovers Jack and scares him away before he is able to take any property. Whilst Jack is running away, he breaks into another house owned by Andy, this time with the intention to hide from the police. Whilst in the house, Jack is confronted by Andy whom he attacks, causing a serious head injury. Jack continues to hide in the house and has with him a knife from the kitchen to use if necessary. The police storm the house and Jack is arrested.

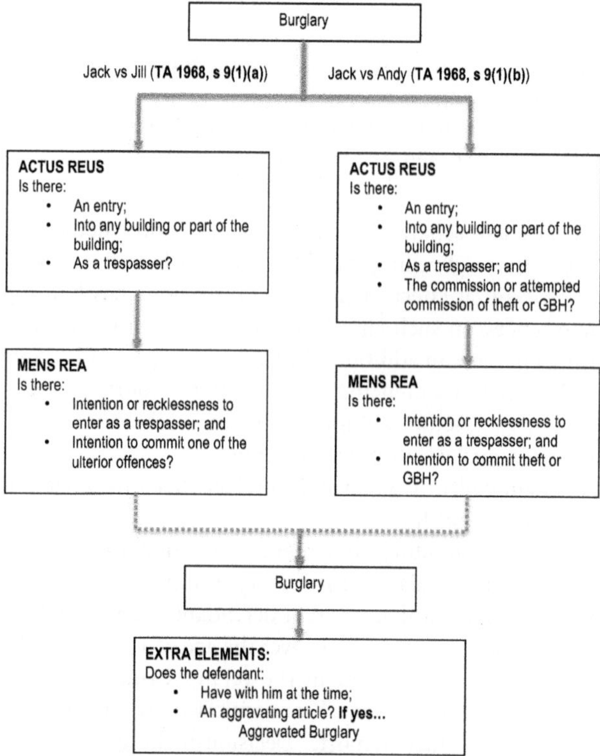

Figure 11.11 Putting together burglary

11.5 Going equipped

Section 25(1) of the TA 1968 provides:

> A person shall be guilty of an offence if, when not at his place of abode, he has with him any article for use in the course of or in connection with any burglary or theft.

It is helpful to know the offence of going equipped in case you are confronted with a problem question where a defendant has with him at any time (outside of his own home) an article that may be used in the course of or in connection with a theft or burglary.

Under s 25, a prosecutor is required to prove that:

- the defendant had a knowledge of the existence of the article; and
- the article was 'to hand and ready for use'.

Possession of an item alone, such as an empty rucksack or a pair of gloves, may be insufficient to find liability of going equipped against a defendant. However, possession of certain questionable items, such as a crowbar or bolt cutters, outside the course of work or employment may arouse suspicion on the part of the defendant (for example, in *Minor v DPP* (1988) 86 Cr App R 378 the defendants were found with two empty petrol cans and a tube as they prepared to siphon petrol from a car). The prosecution must prove intention to use the article in the course, or in connection with, theft or burglary. Importantly, the requisite possession must occur before the commission of the offence (*R v Ellames* [1974] 3 All ER 130).

Going equipped is an offence triable either way, meaning it can be tried in either the magistrates' court and the Crown Court. Where tried in the magistrates' court, the maximum penalty for an offence is 6 months and/or a level 5 fine. In the Crown Court, conviction upon indictment may give rise to a sentence of a maximum of 3 years' imprisonment and/or an unlimited fine.

11.6 Further reading

Theft

Glazebrook, 'Thief or Swindler-Who Cares?' [1991] CLJ 389.
Griew, 'Dishonesty: The Objections to Feely and Ghosh' [1985] Crim LR 34.
Halpin, 'The Test for Dishonesty' [1996] Crim LR 283.
Holroyd, 'Property and Theft' (1998) 62 J Crim L 271.
Melissaris, 'The Concept of Appropriation and the Law of Theft' (2007) 70 MLR 581.
Shute, 'Appropriation and the Law of Theft' [2002] Crim LR 445.
Smith, 'Reforming the Theft Acts' (1996) 28 Bracton LJ 27.

Robbery

Ashworth, 'Robbery Re-assessed' (2002) Crim LR 851.

Burglary

Laird, 'Conceptualising the Interpretation of "Dwelling" in Section 9 of the Theft Act 1968' [2013] Crim LR 656.
Maguire, 'The Impact of Burglary upon Victims' (1980) 20 Brit J Criminol 261.
Pace, 'Burglarious Trespass' [1985] Crim LR 716.

- Theft is concerned with the dishonest appropriation of property belonging to another with the intention to permanently deprive the other of it.
- 'Appropriate' is a broad term encompassing any form of interaction by the defendant with property (eg touching, moving, hiding etc).
- Property is also defined widely but is subject to a number of exceptions, including theft of land which, in the majority of cases, is not possible.
- 'Belonging to another' does not require the other person to be the 'owner' of property; the property may simply be in another's possession or charge.
- Dishonesty is both a subjective and an objective test for the jury. They must apply their own standards of what is dishonest to the facts of the case.
- Robbery simply means 'theft plus force'.
- The force must be used in order to steal; force in order to escape is not sufficient.
- Burglary may be of a building or part of a building and may be of a dwelling or commercial premises.
- The defendant must be a trespasser, which includes going beyond his permission to be in the building.
- The defendant must intend to commit (s 9(1)(a)), or must actually commit (s 9(1)(b)), one of the ulterior offences in order to be liable for burglary.

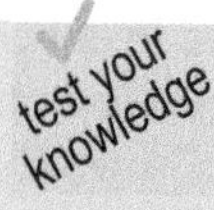

Problem

Jack and Jill have just escaped from prison and have found an old house to hide in. Believing the house to be empty, the pair break a window and climb in. Whilst in the house, the pair realise that it is not empty and are confronted by the householder, Andy. Jack attacks Andy and ties him to a chair to prevent him from alerting the police. Whilst Jack is tying Andy to the chair, Jill proceeds to search the house for anything valuable. Jill finds a number of expensive watches and takes them. The pair leave the house the following day.

Later that day, Jill is walking down the street only to spot her arch-nemesis, Alice. She notices that Alice is wearing a beautiful pearl necklace and diamond ring. Jill walks up to Alice and demands the necklace and ring. Upon Alice refusing, Jill threatens her with violence. Alice hands over the ring but shouts for help before handing over the necklace. Jill rips the necklace from Alice's neck and runs away with the jewellery.

Jack and Jill are found later by the police.

Advise Jack and Jill as to their liability for a number of property offences. (You are not expected to advise the pair on their liability for escaping from prison.)

Essay

'The *actus reus* of theft is now so wide that liability turns solely on the state of mind of the accused.'

Critically discuss.

chapter 12 Other Theft Act Offences

After reading this chapter, you will be able to understand:

- further offences contained in the Theft Acts 1968 and 1978
- the offence of blackmail, the elements of the offence and the punishment for the offence
- the offence of handing stolen goods, the elements of the offence and the punishment for the offence
- the offence of making off without payment, the elements of the offence and the punishment for the offence

12.1 Introduction to other Theft Act offences

This chapter is designed to cover some other major offences contained in the Theft Act (TA) 1968 that are not dealt with in the previous chapter. At first sight, it may appear to be an odd cumulation of offences; however, for ease, the chapter shall be devised chronologically, according to their respective section numbers within the TA 1968. This chapter shall also cover the offence of making off without payment, which is the only remaining offence under the Theft Act (TA) 1978.

The offences we shall be considering in this chapter include:

- blackmail (**12.2**);
- handling stolen goods (**12.3**); and
- making off without payment (**12.4**).

Offences that we do not deal with here include:

- removal of items from a public place open to the public, contrary to s 11 of the TA 1968;
- taking a conveyance without consent, contrary to s 12 of the TA 1968;
- aggravated vehicle taking, contrary to s 12A of the TA 1928;
- abstracting electricity, contrary to s 13 of the TA 1968.

These examples are given merely to demonstrate the breadth of property offences, and you are advised to consult a practitioner text in respect of these offences.

12.2 Blackmail

Blackmail, often referred to as 'extortion', is an offence created by the TA 1968. Prior to its introduction in 1968, no offence of 'blackmail' existed; instead, a defendant might have been charged with 'demanding with menaces' contrary to ss 29 and 30 of the Larceny Act 1916. The TA 1968 greatly simplified the law, with Hogan ('Blackmail' [1966] Crim LR 474) commenting that the 1968 Act replaced

> an ill-assorted collection of legislative bric-a-brac which the draftsman of the 1916 Act put together with scissors and paste.

Blackmail is an offence that does not fit nicely in our structure of property offences, given the combination of offence against the person and offence against property. Further to this, many would treat blackmail as a branch of fraud, given the deception and dishonesty present in a defendant. However, it is argued that blackmail is better suited within this chapter as it remains a part of the TA 1968.

12.2.1 Defining blackmail

Blackmail is an offence predicated on the use of threats by the defendant in an attempt to acquire property, and thus make a gain, or cause a loss to the victim. As stated above, the offence is often difficult to place within the criminal law, and it remains hard to find a sole rationale for its existence. Specifically, the offence of blackmail protects victims from threats involving difficult and unpleasant consequences (an offence against the person); whilst also protecting property where the defendant intends to make a gain or cause a certain loss (an offence against property). This dual protection is necessary to defend the interests of an individual from what the Court of Appeal in *R v Aziz* [2009] EWCA Crim 2337 described as an 'ugly and cruel' offence.

One argument in favour of protecting the individual is provided by Alldridge ('Attempted Murder of the Soul: Blackmail, Privacy and Secrets' (1993) 13 OJLS 368), who focuses on the protection of personal interests, such as privacy and protection from invasive demands. Alldridge took favour from the statement of the learned trial judge (HHJ Pownall QC) in sentencing in *R v Hadjou* (1989) 11 Cr App R (S) 29, where his Honour characterised blackmail in the following way:

> … in the calendar of criminal offences blackmail is one of the ugliest and it is one of the ugliest because it involves what really amounts, so often, to attempted murder of the soul.

The statement received approval from Lord Lane CJ in the Court of Appeal.

Lamond ('Coercion, Threats and the Puzzle of Blackmail' in Simester and Smith (eds), *Harm and Culpability* (Clarendon Press, 1996)), on the other hand, argues that the focus of blackmail ought to be on the property under which the demands and threats are made. It is contended that both views must be taken together in understanding the law of blackmail. Should one element exist without the other, there is unlikely to even be an offence of blackmail chargeable against a defendant.

12.2.2 Elements of blackmail

Section 21 of the TA 1968 provides that:

> (1) A person is guilty of blackmail if, with a view to gain for himself or another or with intent to cause loss to another, he makes any unwarranted demand with menaces; and for this purpose a demand with menaces is unwarranted unless the person making it does so in the belief—
>
> (a) that he has reasonable grounds for making the demand; and
>
> (b) that the use of the menaces is a proper means of reinforcing the demand.
>
> (2) The nature of the act or omission demanded is immaterial, and it is also immaterial whether the menaces relate to action to be taken by the person making the demand.

The *actus reus* and *mens rea* of blackmail are outlined in **Table 12.1**.

Table 12.1 Elements of blackmail

AR/MR	Elements of the offence
Actus reus	(i) makes a demand; (ii) with menaces.
Mens rea	(i) a view to make a gain or cause a loss; (ii) the demand is unwarranted.

Unlike other property offences, blackmail does not require any form of 'dishonesty' on the part of the defendant.

We shall consider each element in turn.

12.2.2.1 *Actus reus:* (i) makes a demand

The first element of this offence is that the defendant makes an unwarranted demand to the victim. In this section, we are concerned solely with the demand and not whether it is 'unwarranted'. This is because the nature of an 'unwarranted demand' forms part of the *mens rea* of the offence and not the *actus reus*, given that the demand is *only* warranted if it falls within s 21(1)(a) or (b) above.

There are two key points that must first be noted:

(a) There must be a demand. The word 'demand' is to be given its ordinary meaning (per Lord Diplock in *Treacy v DPP* [1971] AC 537). Where a demand is missing (eg where the defendant is *offered* property), no blackmail will exist.

(b) The demand must be made in relation to property, specifically with a view to make a gain or cause a loss. Where a demand is made in relation to something other than property, eg sexual favours, there will be no blackmail (however, a defendant may be liable for causing another to engage in sexual activities without consent – see **Chapter 10**).

Express and implied demands

The demand may be express or implied and may be made by any form of communication, whether oral or written. Further to this, although the word 'demand' may seem harsh and may imply some form of malicious wording and threatening nature, the better view is that a demand is simply a 'request' made by the defendant, regardless of whether it was said harshly or rather politely (*R v Studer* (1915) 11 Cr App R 307). This can be seen in *R v Collister; R v Warhurst* (1955) 39 Cr App R 100, where the defendants (two police officers) were convicted of the old offence of 'demanding money with menaces' contrary to s 30 of the Larceny Act 1916, after asking the victim whether he 'had anything' for them, in order to stop a prosecution arising against him. The pair were convicted and appealed to the Court of Criminal Appeal alleging that no demand was made. The Court of Criminal Appeal upheld their convictions, finding that a demand need not be express – it may be implied from conduct and circumstances – and the demand need not be hostile in any way.

Must the demand be made in England and Wales?

In the majority of cases, liability will arise where the demand with menaces is sent from a location in England, to another location in England. However, in *R v Pogmore (Nigel)* [2017] EWCA Crim 925, the Court of Appeal ruled that the criminal courts hold the jurisdiction to try blackmail cases in line with s 4(b) of the Criminal Justice Act 1993 where:

> there is a communication in England and Wales of any information, instruction, request, demand or other matter if it is sent by any means—
>
> (i) from a place in England and Wales to a place elsewhere; or
>
> (ii) from a place elsewhere to a place in England and Wales.

In *Pogmore,* the demand had been sent from Nepal to the victim, who was in England. As you can see from s 4(b), the rule works in reverse also: ie sending a demand from England to another country. Whilst *Pogmore* concerned a demand sent via email, there is no reason why this rule cannot apply to other forms of communication, eg via text messaging or through a social media platform.

Must the victim be aware of the demand?

Importantly, the demand element of the *actus reus* is satisfied upon the defendant making the demand, and it is irrelevant whether the victim was aware that a demand was made. This may include circumstances where the victim was oblivious to the demand, where a letter or message was never received or read, or where a threat over the phone was never heard. We can understand this principle by reference to the case of *Treacy v DPP* [1971] AC 537.

Charge:
Blackmail (TA 1968, s 21)

Case progression:
Crown Court – Guilty

Court of Appeal – Conviction upheld

House of Lords – Conviction upheld

Point of law:
Point at which a demand is made

case example

In *Treacy v DPP* [1971] AC 537, the defendant posted a letter to the victim who resided in Germany. The letter contained several demands with menaces attached. The defendant attempted to argue that she could not be tried for the offence in England as the demand was only 'received' upon it being read in Germany. The defendant's defence failed and she was convicted in the Crown Court of blackmail.

The House of Lords agreed with the Crown Court and the Court of Appeal and found the defendant liable for blackmail at the moment the demand was made, ie at the moment it was posted.

Important to its construction, blackmail is considered a continuing act and the demand remains in continuum until it is withdrawn. See *R v Hester* [2007] EWCA Crim 2127, in which the defendant was instructed to blackmail the victim. The demand had already been made on a previous occasion before the defendant had joined the gang. This was irrelevant and the demand was a continuing act.

12.2.2.2 *Actus reus:* (ii) with menaces

The demand must be made with menaces. In *R v Lawrence and Pomroy* (1971) 57 Cr App R 64, Cairns LJ explained that 'menaces' is 'an ordinary English word which any jury can be expected to understand'. Lord Wright in *Thorne v Motor Trade Association* [1937] AC 797 would define this term as

> to be liberally construed and not as limited to threats of violence but as including threats of any action detrimental to or unpleasant to the person addressed. It may also include a warning that in certain events such action is intended.

Blackmail is thus a much wider offence than one may initial perceive; specifically, it goes beyond the use of threat of violence to persons and property. Instead, it focuses on a threat which is 'unpleasant' to the individual concerned. This may include:

- demanding the payment of an extortionate fine to prevent prosecution (as might have been the case in *Thorne v Motor Trade Association* [1937] AC 797, with slightly different facts);
- threatening (by email) to publish material damaging to a company online (*R v Pogmore (Nigel)* [2017] EWCA Crim 925);
- threatening (and using) force against the victim's dog to induce the victim to pay for the dog's return (*R v Walker* [2010] EWCA Crim 2184);
- threatening to reveal adultery to the victim's wife (as in *R v Tomlinson* [1895] 1 QB 706).

As with demands, the menaces attached may be made expressly or impliedly. This was made clear in *R v Lawrence and Pomroy* (1971) 57 Cr App R 64, where the defendant made a statement along the lines of 'keep looking over your shoulder' to the victim, which was then accompanied with the presence of a large man requesting to speak with the victim outside his house. The Court of Appeal concluded that the menaces were present from the presence of the large man when accompanied with the previous statement to keep a look over one's shoulder. Ultimately, however, whether or not a threat was or could be carried out by the defendant (or someone else for that matter) is irrelevant. This was made clear by Moses LJ in *R v Lambert* [2009] EWCA Crim 2860, where his Lordship stated:

> It being irrelevant whether the menaces relate to action taken by the demander or somebody else, and it also being irrelevant whether the demander is in any position to effect menace. It is how the demand and menace affects the victim that matters.

Whether menaces are present within the demand is to be determined by way of an objective standard. This was made clear by the Court of Appeal in *R v Clear* [1968] 1 QB 670. Specifically, Sellers LJ stated that the menace must be

> of such a nature and extent that the mind of an ordinary person of normal stability and courage *might* be influenced or made apprehensive so as to accede unwillingly to the demand. (emphasis added)

Although the word 'might' indicates quite a low threshold, the matter remains one to be determined by a jury using their objective standards of reasonableness. For instance, in circumstances where the victim himself is not fearful or phased by the threat made, a jury may still find that they (as the objective persons) would be intimidated by the threat. On this account, the defendant remains liable for blackmail (*R v Moran* [1952] 1 All ER 803). However, in the circumstances where neither the victim nor the objective persons are phased by the threat, there shall be no blackmail. This was made clear in the case of *R v Harry* [1974] Crim LR 32, where the defendant informed the victim that if he donated to his cause, the victim would be free from 'inconveniences'. The Crown Court found that the word 'menaces' is a strong word requiring a high degree of coercion which was not present on the given facts. To demonstrate the severity of the menace, the Court of Appeal in *R v Jheeta* [2007] EWCA Crim 1699 appeared to prefer the term 'menacing pressures' to indicate the sort of conduct necessary (we considered *Jheeta* in **Chapter 10**).

What these cases show is the divergence between cases where the menacing behaviour causes the arbiter of fact to feel *influenced* and cases where it does not. In the former, there will be a menacing demand; in the latter, no such menaces will be present.

One area that has not been discussed as yet are the circumstances where the victim accedes to the demands due to a particular and unique susceptibility (or vulnerability), but the arbiters of fact would not have been so influenced, applying an objective standard. If we were to follow *Harry* above, there will be no menace where the objective persons are not influenced by the demand. However, an exception applies when one observes the decision of the Court of Appeal in *R v Garwood* [1987] 1 All ER 1032. In *Garwood*, the jury asked the trial judge whether it was relevant that the defendant appeared more menacing to the victim (who was timid) than he did to the objective reasonable man. The trial judge affirmed the jury's question, stating that the peculiarities of the victim are relevant to the jury's deliberation of menacing conduct, so long as the defendant was aware that his threat was particularly menacing to this victim. Lord Lane CJ in the Court of Appeal ruled:

> In our judgment it is only rarely that a judge will need to enter on a definition of the word 'menaces'. It is an ordinary word of which the meaning will be clear to any jury. … It seems to us that there are two possible occasions on which a further direction on the meaning of the word menaces may be required. The first is where the threats might have affected the mind of an ordinary person of normal stability but did not affect the person actually addressed. In such circumstances that would amount to a sufficient menace … The second situation is where the threats in fact affected the mind of the victim, although they would not have affected the mind of a person of normal stability. In that case, in our judgment, the existence of menaces is proved providing that the accused man was aware of the likely effect of his actions on the victim.

12.2.2.3 *Mens rea:* (i) a view to make a gain or cause a loss

The first element of the *mens rea* is that the defendant by his unwarranted demands with menaces intends to make a gain or cause a loss. The phrase 'with a view to' is synonymous with 'intention' and thus we shall adopt this phrasing for sake of ease and consistency.

We are assisted in our understanding of these terms by s 34(2), which provides:

> For purposes of this Act—
> (a) 'gain' and 'loss' are to be construed as extending only to gain or loss in money or other property, but as extending to any such gain or loss whether temporary or permanent; and—
> (i) 'gain' includes a gain by keeping what one has, as well as a gain by getting what one has not; and
> (ii) 'loss' includes a loss by not getting what one might get, as well as a loss by parting with what one has;
>
> …

Importantly, all that is required by this element is that the defendant intends to make a gain or cause a loss; there is no requirement for an actual gain or loss to occur (*R v Moran* [1952] 1 All ER 803). On this basis, blackmail is a conduct crime (*R v Pogmore (Nigel)* [2017] EWCA Crim 925). Section 34(2)(a) has the effect of refining the remit of blackmail only to demands involving property. Therefore, as stated above, where demands are made as to non-property, such as of a sexual nature, there is no blackmail.

Property

Property has been defined broadly to include 'money or other property' and the view to make a gain or cause a loss has also been described quite broadly. This can be illustrated by the case of *R v Bevans* (1988) 87 Cr App R 64.

case example

Charge:
Blackmail (TA 1968, s 21)

Case progression:
Crown Court – Guilty

Court of Appeal – Conviction upheld

Point of law:
Meaning of property

In *R v Bevans* (1988) 87 Cr App R 64, the defendant forced the victim, a doctor, at gunpoint to give him an injection of morphine for the purposes of pain relief. The defendant was charged with and convicted of blackmail in the Crown Court.

The defendant argued two grounds in the Court of Appeal: first – the morphine did not amount to property; and, secondly, the morphine was for the purpose of relief of pain – not to make a gain or cause a loss. The Court of Appeal dismissed the defendant's appeal, arguing that the morphine amounted to property and the defendant had a view to gain property by having it injected into him.

The broadness of 'property' was demonstrated by the case of *R v Read* [2018] EWCA Crim 2186 in which the defendant had demanded a payment of bitcoins (electronic currency) threatening to infect the victim's IT systems with a virus. The demand began at 15 Bitcoins and escalated to 250 Bitcoins prior to the arrest of the defendant. The defendant was charged with and convicted of blackmail. Whilst the appeal was concerned with sentence, as opposed to conviction, it must be the case that all parties to the proceedings, and potentially the Court of Appeal, accepted that Bitcoin amounted to 'property' for the purposes of s 34(2) given that no issue was raised about this on appeal.

Examples of 'gain or loss'

The view to make a gain or cause a loss can also be found in circumstances where the defendant demands money that it owed to him under a debt. This was seen in this case of *R v Parkes* [1973] Crim LR 358, where the defendant demanded money owed to him by the victim. The defendant argued at trial that his seeking of repayment was not with a 'view to make a gain or cause a loss' since he was already entitled to the money in question. Indeed, this argument is in line with the view of Hogan ('Blackmail' [1966] Crim LR 474), who argues that demanding property that an individual is legally entitled to should not fall within the offence of blackmail as there is no intention to make a gain or cause a loss. Despite this, the Crown Court considered that the demand amounted to blackmail. Although *Parkes* was only a first instance Crown Court decision, it has since been approved by the Court of Appeal in *AG's Reference (No 1 of 2001)* [2002] EWCA Crim 1768.

Therefore, following *Parkes, R v Lawrence* (1971) 57 Cr App R 64 and s 34(2)(a), 'gain' is to be interpreted as including 'getting what one has not got', even in circumstances where one has a lawful right to that property.

example

Suppose Jack threatens to reveal Jill's past exploits as a pornography star unless she does three things:

(a) sleep with him;
(b) destroy her mobile phone (which contains scandalous messages from Jack); and
(c) give him her new television.

Jill accedes to all three demands.

In this case, Jack may be liable for two counts of blackmail. The first demand cannot be blackmail as the demand is not directed with an intention to make a gain or cause a loss in relation to property. Rather, this demand may give rise to liability for a number of sexual offences, including rape and causing a person to engage in sexual activity (see **Chapter 10**). The second demand can be blackmail as Jack is intending, through his menacing demand, to cause a loss to Jill (ie of her mobile phone). The third demand can also be blackmail as Jack is intending to make a gain (ie of Jill's new television set). It is important to note that Jack need not intend to make a gain *and* cause a loss. It is sufficient for the purposes of blackmail that Jack simply intends one or the other.

12.2.2.4 *Mens rea:* (ii) the demand is unwarranted

As discussed above, the *actus reus* requires simply that a 'demand' is made. The corresponding *mens rea* element to this feature is that the demand is 'unwarranted'.

By s 21(1) of the TA 1968, a demand with menaces is 'unwarranted' unless the person making the demand believes both:

(a) that he has reasonable grounds for making the demand; and
(b) that the use of the menaces is a proper means of reinforcing the demand.

This section therefore provides a presumption *in favour* of the demand being unwarranted *unless* it can be proven that the defendant believes both of the factors laid out. It is important to note that this is an 'and' test and not an 'or' test. Both factors must be satisfied. You should therefore consider each in turn, which we shall now observe.

Table 12.2 Factors amounting to unwarranted demands

Factor	Description
Reasonable grounds for demand (s 21(1)(a))	The defendant must believe he has reasonable grounds for making the demand. It is not sufficient that the defendant believes the demand is 'correct' or 'justified', but whether the defendant believes that the objective person would find the demand to be 'correct' or 'justified'.
Proper means of reinforcing (s 21(1)(b))	If the defendant believes the objective person would find his demands to be reasonable, he must then consider whether his menaces are the proper means of reinforcing the demand. Simply, where the defendant uses menaces that would amount to criminal liability in their own regard, clearly his means will not be 'proper' (as in *R v Kewell* [2000] 2 Cr App R (S) 38 – threatening to reveal personal photographs of the victim; and *R v Harvey* (1981) 72 Cr App R 139 – threats to rape, maim and kill the victim's family).

An interesting application of the 'proper means' element was seen in *Arthur v Anker* [1997] QB 564 where it was held that car clamping may lead to a conviction for blackmail in cases where the defendant did not believe the clamping was a proper means of enforcing the demand.

Whether the defendant 'believes' either factor is present is a subjective matter to be determined by the jury. In this regard, the jury are not concerned with the nature or content of the threat or demand itself (although this will be useful evidence); but, rather, they are concerned with the subjective state of mind (or *mens rea*) on the part of the defendant. MacKenna ('Blackmail' [1966] Crim LR 467) argues that this subjective element of the offence goes 'too far … allowing the defendant's own moral standards [to] determine the rightness or wrongness of his conduct'.

Although there appears to be a presumption *in favour* of a demand being unwarranted, it remains the burden of the prosecution to disprove either of those elements if raised by a defendant (*R v Ashiq* [2015] EWCA Crim 1617).

Specifically, the prosecution is required to prove the negative elements of those factors, ie:

- that the defendant *did not* believe he had reasonable grounds to make the demands; and
- that the defendant *did not* believe that the use of menaces was a proper means of reinforcing the demand.

Given that this test is dual (ie both must be satisfied), it is enough for the prosecution to prove a lack of belief in either of these factors; it need not prove both.

in practice

Do not worry about the language used when discussing the two factors in s 21(1)(a) and (b). In practice, the courts will often vary in their phrasing of the prosecution's duty. For example, a judge may direct a jury either:

(a) that the prosecution must *prove* that the defendant either did not believe he had reasonable grounds to make the demands or that the use of menaces was a proper means of reinforcing the demand; or

(b) that the prosecution must *disprove* that the defendant either believed he had reasonable grounds to make the demands or that the use of menaces was a proper means of reinforcing the demand.

Either direction is appropriate; just do not get caught up in the variations.

In summary, in order for the defendant to be liable, there must be evidence of both factors working together to create the blackmail. This has been expressed by Lindgren ('Unravelling the Paradox of Blackmail' (1984) 84 Col L Rev 670), who attempts to explain the 'paradox' that exists in blackmail cases.

Specifically, Lindgren notes that a defendant is entitled to make demands but without menacing conduct and likewise may act in a menacing way but without the presence of a demand. It will be helpful to explain both circumstances in turn:

- In the former case, a defendant may make demands for money owed but without menacing conduct and will not be liable for an offence of blackmail. Naturally, if a debt is owed by the debtor to the defendant, the defendant has a legal right (in civil law) to demand the return of the money. Should the debtor fail to pay the debt, he may be sued under the debt.
- In the latter case, a defendant may expose a victim to his questionable activities (eg he acts menacingly by revealing a victim's sexual orientation) but without the presence of a demand; again he may not be liable for blackmail.

However, in the circumstances where the defendant uses such menacing means *in order* to make the demand, then he will be liable for blackmail.

This is known as the 'paradox' of blackmail and has led to much academic commentary throughout the years. Justifications for the offence of blackmail in light of this paradox are plentiful. One justification, provided by Lamond ('Coercion, Threats and the Puzzle of Blackmail' in Simester and Smith (eds), *Harm and Culpability* (OUP 1996)), is to think of blackmail like obtaining property by deception – both offences involve some acquisition of property through the manipulation and coercion of the victim's mind. Another justification, relying on an analogy provided by Katz ('Blackmail and Other Forms of Arm-Twisting' (1993) University of Pennsylvania Law Review 141), is that blackmail is similar to robbery in that property is taken from a victim by use of 'immoral means'.

12.2.3 Charging blackmail

12.2.3.1 Mode of trial

Blackmail is an offence chargeable only on indictment, meaning that it may only be tried in the Crown Court before a judge and jury.

12.2.3.2 Sentencing

The maximum sentence for blackmail is 14 years' imprisonment (TA 1968, s 21(3)). When sentencing the defendant, the court should consider the psychological harm done or intended to be done to the victim (*R v Ford* [2015] 2 Cr App R (S) 177).

12.2.3.3 Charging attempted blackmail

A particularly interesting topic under the offence of blackmail is whether one may be charged with attempted blackmail. It has long been thought that no such attempt offence exists, given that the offence of blackmail is in itself an attempt to make a gain or cause a loss. On that basis, Jefferson (*Criminal Law*, 12th edn (Pearson, 2015)) makes the point that '[i]t seems absurd to charge attempting to attempt to obtain property'. A justification for attempted blackmail has, however, been put forward by Griew (*The Theft Acts 1968-1978*, 7th edn (Sweet & Maxwell, 1995)) who argues that:

> If a blackmailing demand is 'made' as soon as it is spoken or dispatched beyond recall, the possibility of a case of attempted blackmail is limited to fanciful situations such as where [the accused] is affected by a stammer or interrupted in the act of posting.

Indeed, Griew's view has merit when one considers a demand that is intended to be made via telephone and, just before the demand is made, the telephone call cuts out. The problem with Griew's theoretical understanding of attempted blackmail is that, in practice, how could it be proven that the defendant was going to make a demand? Simply, it cannot. Therefore, although an attempt is possible in these circumstances, it remains unlikely to be charged for evidential reasons.

We have considered the law of attempts in **Chapter 5**.

12.2.4 Putting together blackmail

Consider this issue and think of how you may structure an answer to it. Then see the figure below for a sample structure to adopt.

facts

Jack is a bank manager in a heterosexual relationship with his wife, Jill. Unbeknownst to Jill, Jack has entered into a homosexual affair with his business colleague, Andy. A co-worker, Alice, discovers this fact and threatens to reveal Jack's affair to his wife, should Jack not provide Alice with a substantial pay rise. Jack agrees and awards the pay rise.

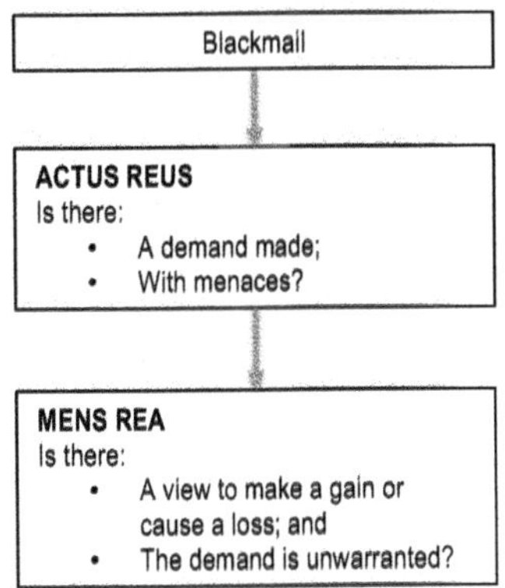

Figure 12.1 Putting together blackmail

12.3 Handling stolen goods

Handling stolen goods is a crime aimed at making theft harder to carry out. Indeed, according to the CLRC's 8th Report (*Theft and Related Offences*, 1996), the purpose of having an offence of handling is to 'combat theft by making it more difficult and less profitable to dispose of stolen property'. It is for this reason, as noted by De Than (*Criminal Law*, 4th edn (OUP, 2013)), that the 'maximum sentence is higher than for theft on the basis that handling, by facilitating disposal of the proceeds of theft, contributes to its prevalence'.

12.3.1 Defining handling

As a result of the justification noted above, Jefferson (*Criminal Law*, 12th edn (Pearson, 2015)) describes the offence as one 'secondary' to the offence of theft. By this, Jefferson means that handling does not exist unless and until some form of theft, or related offence, occurs. Further to this, Horder (*Ashworth's Principles of Criminal Law*, 9th edn (OUP, 2019)) comments that the offence of handling is drafted so widely as to 'cast a net around the main Theft Act offences'.

12.3.2 Elements of handling

Section 22(1) of the TA 1968 provides:

> A person handles stolen goods if (otherwise than in the course of the stealing) knowing or believing them to be stolen goods he dishonestly receives the goods, or dishonestly undertakes or assists in their retention, removal, disposal or realisation by or for the benefit of another person, or if he arranges to do so.

The *actus reus* and *mens rea* of handling are outlined in **Table 12.3**.

Table 12.3 Elements of handling stolen goods

AR/MR	Elements of the offence
Actus reus	(i) handles; (ii) otherwise than in the course of stealing; (iii) stolen goods.
Mens rea	(i) knows or believes them to be stolen; (ii) dishonestly deals with them.

We shall consider each element in turn.

12.3.2.1 *Actus reus:* (i) handles

From s 22(1) above, it is possible to find 18 variations of carrying out the *actus reus* of handling. Specifically, there are four broad, or basic, ways of handling goods, with more specific conduct arising under each of the four basic headings. We can see this in **Table 12.4**.

Table 12.4 Methods of 'handling' stolen goods

	Basic method of handling	Specific method of handling
1	Receiving	n/a
2	Undertaking	By retention
3	Undertaking	By removal
4	Undertaking	By disposal
5	Undertaking	By realisation
6	Assisting	By retention
7	Assisting	By removal
8	Assisting	By disposal
9	Assisting	By realisation
10	Arranging	To receive
11	Arranging	To undertake by retention
12	Arranging	To undertake by removal
13	Arranging	To undertake by disposal
14	Arranging	To undertake by realisation
15	Arranging	To assist by retention
16	Arranging	To assist by removal
17	Arranging	To assist by disposal
18	Arranging	To assist by realisation

It is important to note that although there are 18 different ways in which a person may 'handle' goods, there is only one offence (*Griffiths v Freeman* [1970] 1 All ER 1117). Although the 'type' of handling needs to be stated in an indictment, there remains only one offence chargeable, namely that under s 22 (*R v Nicklin* [1977] 2 All ER 444). However, where the defendant is charged with a specific form of handling (for example 'receiving'), he may not be convicted on the basis of a different form of handling (for example 'undertaking'). In the circumstances where there is uncertainty as to the correct form of handling, the case of *R v Sloggett* [1972] 1 QB 430 recommends the charging of separate counts on the indictment.

We shall now consider each way in which a defendant may 'handle' goods.

Receiving

The first key point to note is that this form of handling does not involve some form of qualification; namely it does not have to be 'for the benefit of another person' as required for 'undertaking', nor does the activity have to be 'by … another person', meaning that no assistance to another is required. As a result, in circumstances where the defendant is acting alone or, better yet, is not acting with or for the benefit of another, 'receiving' is the only form of handling available to prosecutors.

The receipt of goods simply requires proof that the defendant has taken physical possession or control of the stolen goods from another individual. According to the Court of Criminal Appeal in *R v Cavendish* [1961] 2 All ER 856, it must be proven that the defendant took some form of active participation in the receiving of goods. Where the defendant is simply engaged in a negotiation as to receiving the goods, he will not be liable for handling by receiving (as was the case in *R v Wiley* (1850) 2 Den 37). Likewise, where the defendant simply finds goods that are stolen, this will not be considered as receiving for the purposes of the Act (*R v Haider* (CA, 22 March 1985)).

Each act of receiving amounts to a separate offence of handling, and, thus, in the circumstances where the defendant has received stolen property from multiple individuals, each receipt will amount to a separate charge of handling (*R v Smythe* (1981) 72 Cr App R 8). In *R v Miller* (1854) 6 Cox CC 353 it was held that where the defendant's agent takes receipt of the stolen goods with his authority, this will amount to the defendant 'receiving' the stolen goods in the eyes of the law.

Receiving goods requires no form of permanence, nor does it require the defendant to receive the goods for a particular purpose, for example to keep or dispose of them. According to the Court of Assize in *R v Richardson* (1834) 6 Car & P 335, receipt of goods is complete upon the defendant taking possession or control, regardless of his purpose. In that case, the defendant took control of the goods in order to hide them for the benefit of the thief. Simply, receiving is a 'finite act', as explained by the Court of Appeal in *R v Smythe* (1981) 72 Cr App R 8.

The Divisional Court in *Hobson v Impett* (1957) 41 Cr App R 138 did, however, note that the defendant must be aware that he is in possession or control of the goods. In circumstances where the defendant was 'unaware' the goods were stolen at the point of receiving them, but later becomes aware of their stolen nature, the defendant cannot be liable for handling by receiving.

example

Jack hands over a rucksack to Jill containing a number of items of jewellery, including watches, rings and bracelets. Jack asks Jill to take possession of the items and keep them safe. Jill agrees to do so, believing them to be in the ownership of Jack. A number of weeks later, Jack informs Jill that the jewellery was stolen and that she should hide the items. Jill agrees to do so.

In this instance, Jill has not *received* the goods knowing, or believing, them to be stolen. As a result, Jill cannot be liable for handling by receiving. However, the Court of Appeal in *R v Pitchley* (1972) 57 Cr App R 30 ruled that the better charge in this circumstance would be one of 'undertaking to retain', instead of receiving.

Undertaking

The next form of handling requires the defendant to 'undertake' a certain activity for the benefit of another person. The defendant may either retain, remove, dispose of or realise the stolen goods; however, it must be emphasised that it has to be for the benefit of *another*. The meanings of these four specific forms of handling are detailed in **Table 12.5**.

Table 12.5 Understanding retention, removal, disposal and realisation

Specific form of handling	Meaning
Retention	The stolen goods are 'kept' or 'stored' for the benefit of another person, eg the thief. In *R v Pitchley* (1972) 57 Cr App R 30, the Court of Appeal coined the phrase 'keep possession of, not lose, continue to have' (per Cairns LJ).
Removal	The stolen goods must be moved or transported from one location to another (*R v Gleed* (1916) 12 Cr App R 32).
Disposal	The stolen goods must be disposed of. Disposal may include selling or exchanging the stolen property or destroying it (*R v Watson* [1916] 2 KB 385).
Realisation	The stolen goods must be exchanged for value (ie money or money's worth). This section overlaps with the previous one of 'disposal' (*R v Bloxham* [1983] 1 AC 109).

case example

Charge:
Handling stolen goods (TA 1968, s 22)

Case progression:
Crown Court – Guilty

Court of Appeal – Conviction upheld

House of Lords – Conviction quashed

Point of law:
Meaning of 'for the benefit of another'

In *R v Bloxham* [1983] 1 AC 109, the defendant bought a car from a thief, unaware that it was stolen. Almost a year later, the defendant came to believe the car had been stolen, given the lack of registration documents. As such, believing the goods to be stolen, the defendant sold the car to a third party.

The defendant was charged with and convicted of handling stolen goods on the basis that he had undertaken the realisation of the car for the benefit of another person. The trial judge directed the jury that the 'other person' was the third party purchaser. The Court of Appeal affirmed the trial judge's ruling but granted permission for appeal to the House of Lords.

The House of Lords quashed the defendant's conviction on the basis that the benefit obtained from the transaction was a benefit to the defendant and not the third party. Although the third party may have obtained a benefit by use of the car, their benefit was not what was contemplated by the wording of the section.

Lord Bridge in the House of Lords explained the Court's position in the following way:

> The critical words to be construed are 'undertakes ... their ... disposal or realisation ... for the benefit of another person'. Considering these words first in isolation, it seems to me that, if A sells his own goods to B, it is a somewhat strained use of language to describe this as a disposal or realisation of the goods for the benefit of B. True it is that B obtains a benefit from the transaction, but it is surely more natural to say that the disposal or realisation is for A's benefit than for B's.

His Lordship went on to provide the key principle we are to follow from this case, namely:

> It is the purchase, not the sale, that is for the benefit of B. It is only when A is selling *as agent for a third party* C that it would be entirely natural to describe the sale as a disposal or realisation for the benefit of another person. (emphasis added)

Griew (*The Theft Acts*, 7th edn (Sweet & Maxwell, 1995)) explains this case on the basis that

> the House of Lords effectively treats the notion of an act undertaken 'for the benefit of another person' as that of an act done on behalf of another person; it is an act that the other might do himself.

The Court of Appeal approached the question of 'benefit of another' in *R v Gingell* [2000] 1 Cr App R 88, which concerned a joint charge of handling against two defendants. The Court ruled that the phrase 'benefit of another' excludes a co-accused. 'Another' must be an individual distinct from the defendants. Despite this, where a defendant proposes to undertake a specific activity for the benefit of his co-defendant, he may be liable for conspiracy to handle (*R v Slater; R v Suddens* [1996] Crim LR 300).

Assisting

The third specific form of handling comes under the heading of 'assisting'. Under this heading, the prosecution is required to prove that the defendant assisted or encouraged another in the retention, removal, disposal or realisation of the stolen goods. Assistance or encouragement requires the defendant to be active and to be actively engaged in the handling of the goods alongside another. In *R v Kanwar* [1982] 2 All ER 528, Cantley J stated that:

> To constitute the offence, something must be done by the offender, and done intentionally and dishonestly, for the purpose of enabling the goods to be retained. Examples of such conduct are concealing or helping to conceal the goods, or doing something to make them more difficult to find or to identify. Such conduct must be done knowing or believing the goods to be stolen and done dishonestly and for the benefit of another.

As a result, the Court of Appeal in *R v Sanders* (1982) 75 Cr App R 84 ruled that merely using the items that are retained by someone else is not sufficient.

There are two cases that have caused difficulty in this area, namely *R v Kanwar* [1982] 2 All ER 528 and *R v Brown* [1970] 1 QB 105. In the former it was held that lying to the police regarding the lawful owner of stolen goods is sufficient to constitute assisting another. In the latter case, however, a failure to inform the police regarding the presence of stolen goods on the property was not capable of constituting assistance for the purposes of the Act. These two cases can be understood by reference to the actions of the defendant. In *Kanwar*, the defendant took a positive step in lying to the police officers. This step was a form of 'active' assistance to the thief. Whereas in *Brown*, the defendant merely failed to respond to police questions. The defendant was not obliged to answer such questions and there was no 'active' assistance on the part of the defendant to the thief.

Arranging

The final circumstance is where the defendant arranges to act in any of the general manners listed above (ie receiving, undertaking or assisting). If the defendant is charged with 'arranging to receive', the same rules of receiving set out above apply here. Likewise, where the defendant is charged with either 'arranging to undertake' or 'arranging to assist', the qualifications that apply to those general methods also apply here.

12.3.2.2 *Actus reus:* (ii) otherwise than in the course of stealing

As will be explained in greater detail in the next section, at the time of the respective 'handling', the goods in question must have been 'stolen'. Further to this, the offence requires the handling to be done 'otherwise than in the course of the stealing'.

This provision is a 'safety net' for original thieves who are still acting in the course of stealing. In such a case, they will not be considered as 'handling' for the purpose of s 22. We can see this in the case of *Hobson v Impett* (1957) 41 Cr App R 138, where the defendant assisted another in unloading stolen goods from a lorry. The defendant was acting 'in the course of stealing' by assisting in the removal of items from the vehicle. This does not mean that a thief cannot be liable for handling; rather, the better expression of this requirement was provided by the court in *R v Bosson* [1999] Crim LR 596, where it was said that in order to be liable for handling, the 'handling' must take place *after* the theft has been committed.

The difficulty here arises when considering whether the handling has come *after* the theft. More specifically, it is often difficult to determine that the 'course of stealing' has ended. We can demonstrate this problem through the case of *R v Pitham and Hehl* (1976) 65 Cr App R 45.

Charge:
Handling stolen goods (TA 1968, s 22)

Case progression:
Crown Court – Guilty

Court of Appeal – Conviction upheld

Point of law:
Meaning of 'in the course of stealing'

case example

In *R v Pitham and Hehl* (1976) 65 Cr App R 45, a third party offered to sell the victim's furniture to the defendants. The victim at the time was in prison and the third party held no authority to offer for sale the victim's furniture. The defendants purchased the furniture before then removing it from the house. The defendants were charged with and convicted of handling in the Crown Court.

The defendants appealed to the Court of Appeal on the basis that their actions were in the course of stealing, and thus they could be liable for theft but not handling. The Court of Appeal dismissed their appeal, ruling that the theft was complete upon the third party offering the furniture for sale. The Court reasoned that any actions taking place after this offer were 'otherwise than in the course of stealing'.

A further difficulty that arises in the case law involves the circumstance where it cannot be said with certainty that the defendant is the thief or merely a handler. The Court of Appeal in *R v Cash* [1985] QB 801 attempted to solve this problem by providing that the jury were entitled to infer that the defendant was the handler unless there was some evidence to suggest he was in fact the thief. In the case where no evidence is available, the jury should infer that the defendant is a handler without direction as to 'in the course of stealing'. Where, however, there is evidence that the defendant is the thief, the jury must be directed to consider whether his handling is 'otherwise than in the course of stealing'. If the jury conclude that his actions were within the course of stealing, he is not liable for handling (refer back to *R v Atakpu* [1994] QB 69 in **Chapter 11** and the notion of continuing acts).

12.3.2.3 *Actus reus:* (iii) stolen goods

The next element of the *actus reus* that must be proven is that the defendant handled 'goods' that were 'stolen'. We shall deal with each element individually.

Goods

Section 34(2)(b) of the TA 1968 provides:

> 'goods', except in so far as the context otherwise requires, includes money and every other description of property except land, and includes things severed from the land by stealing.

For the purposes of this offence 'goods' has been defined so widely as to almost be synonymous with the definition of 'property' under s 4 of the TA 1968. Goods can therefore include both tangible and intangible property (including choses in action – *AG's Reference (No 4 of 1979)* [1981] 1 All ER 1193); however 'goods' does not include land that has not been severed. Unlike in the law of theft and criminal damage, which allow certain non-severed fixtures to amount to property, such fixtures will not be considered as 'goods' under s 22. Further to this, under s 24(2), 'goods' includes the 'proceeds of sale'.

Stolen

In order for a defendant to be liable for handling, it must be proven that the goods were in fact 'stolen'. Now, this may appear to state the obvious; however, there may be some circumstances where the defendant believes that the goods are stolen, but in actual fact they are not (for example, the owner has given his consent for the goods to be appropriated, but the defendant is unaware of this). On this basis, where the goods are not stolen, but the defendant believes they are, the appropriate offence is not handling but, rather, attempted handling (*Haughton v Smith* [1975] AC 476).

The word 'stolen' is to be construed according to s 24(4), which provides:

> For purposes of the provisions of this Act relating to goods which have been stolen … goods obtained in England or Wales or elsewhere either by blackmail or … by fraud (within the meaning of the Fraud Act 2006) shall be regarded as stolen; and 'steal', 'theft' and 'thief' shall be construed accordingly.

As a result, goods may be stolen in the following circumstances:

- theft
- robbery
- burglary
- fraud
- blackmail.

It is not a requirement for the offence for the defendant to personally steal the goods. In a situation where the defendant does personally steal the goods, a prosecutor must charge one of the above offences as appropriate. Rather, what is required is that some person, other than the defendant, has stolen the goods by way of one of the offences above. It is not necessary that the prosecution proves who stole the goods in the first place, so long as they were in fact stolen (*R v Forsyth* [1997] 2 Cr App R 299).

The 'goods' in question are not restricted to the original goods acquired through the relevant act of theft, burglary etc. Rather, 'goods' for the purposes of s 22 also includes the proceeds of such property or the remainder. This is provided for in s 24(2):

> … references to stolen goods shall include, in addition to the goods originally stolen and parts of them (whether in their original state or not),—
>
> (a) any other goods which directly or indirectly represent or have at any time represented the stolen goods in the hands of the *thief* as being the proceeds of any disposal or realisation of the whole or part of the goods stolen or of goods so representing the stolen goods; and
>
> (b) any other goods which directly or indirectly represent or have at any time represented the stolen goods in the hands of a *handler* of the stolen goods or any part of them as being the proceeds of any disposal or realisation of the whole or part of the stolen goods handled by him or of goods so representing them. (emphasis added)

As a result of s 24(2), therefore, goods may include:

- goods or proceeds in the hands of the thief that represent the whole or part of the original stolen goods (s 24(2)(a)); and
- goods or proceeds in the hands of the handler that represent the whole or part of the original stolen goods (s 24(2)(b)).

Section 24(2) is not a simple provision. Professor Smith has described this offence as 'a source of endless fascination'. Indeed, it is hoped you will find as much enjoyment in this offence as Smith did; however, you will first need to understand the intricacies of s 24(2). The best way to do so is through a number of examples involving the theft of a single piece of property. Let us take a detailed example:

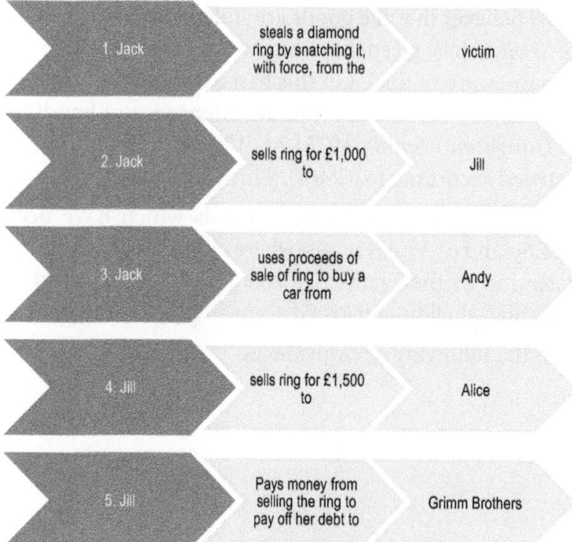

Figure 12.2 Transition of handling stolen goods

In the first instance, Jack may be liable for robbery. Our focus, however, is on the transactions that follow:

(i) *Jack sells the ring to Jill for £1,000.* If Jill is aware that the ring is stolen, she will be liable for handling stolen goods (s 24(2)(b)). Jack, by selling the ring, is also liable for handling stolen goods (s 24(2)(a)).

(ii) *Jack uses the £1,000 to buy a pre-owned car from Andy.* Jack is liable for handling stolen goods by using the £1,000 made from selling on the stolen property (it is proceeds from disposal of the stolen goods), and the car is also now 'stolen' as it 'represents' the stolen goods (s 24(2)(a)). If Andy is aware that the £1,000 is 'stolen', he will be liable for handling stolen goods (s 24(2)(b)).

(iii) *Jill then sells the ring on to Alice for £1,500.* If Alice is aware that the ring is stolen, she will be liable for handling stolen goods (s 24(2)(b)). Jill will remain liable for the selling of the ring and the money made as a result of selling the ring (s 24(2)(b)).

(iv) *Jill uses the £1,500 to settle her debt with the Grimm brothers.* Jill will be liable for disposing of stolen goods representing the original stolen goods (s 24(2)(b)). If the Grimm brothers are aware that the money is a part of the proceeds of a stolen item, they will be liable for handling stolen goods (s 24(2)(b)).

In all cases, the goods in question, and the proceeds of such goods, have moved between numerous different 'handlers' (ie they have had their hands on the goods).

A difficulty arises, therefore, in circumstances where the goods, proceeds, parts or representative goods have never been in the 'hands' of the 'handler'. In such a case, there can be no offence of handling. This is often the case where the proceeds from the sale of stolen goods is paid into the bank account of the thief who then transfers the money, or part of it, to a third party.

example

Jack is a businessman working alongside his partner, Andy. Jack is tired of working long shifts to make a profit and decides to steal money from the company safe.

At present, in this scenario, Jack is liable for theft. If Jack were to use the money to buy a car, for example, he would be liable for handling stolen goods (as the car would represent the original stolen goods). What is the case, then, if Jack pays the money into his own bank account before then transferring half the money to his wife, Jill? Clearly, the payment of monies into his own account will amount to theft but it will also amount to handling as the stolen property has become a chose in action (money in an account); but what of Jill? Under the common law (following *R v Preddy* [1996] AC 815) Jill could not be liable for handling stolen goods in circumstances where she simply retains the 'stolen' money and in circumstances where she withdraws the 'stolen' money. This is justified on the basis that the stolen property was never in the hands of the handler (in this case, Jill). This was clearly a lacuna in the law leading the Law Commission to propose ('Offences of Dishonesty: Money Transfers' (Law Com No 243, 1996)) the creation of two new offences, which came into force by way of the Theft (Amendment) Act 1996, now contained within s 24A of the TA 1968.

The two offences under s 24A are as follows:

- dishonestly retaining a wrongful credit (s 24A); and
- handling stolen goods by way of dishonest withdrawals from accounts which have been wrongfully credited (s 24A(8)).

The latter of the two is not a new offence, so to speak. Rather, it is an expansion of the current offence of handling to cover circumstances where the individual withdraws money from a wrongfully credited account.

Restored goods

Section 24(3) TA 1968 provides:

> But no goods shall be regarded as having continued to be stolen goods after they have been restored to the person from whom they were stolen or to other lawful possession or custody, or after that person and any other person claiming through him have otherwise ceased as regards those goods to have any right to restitution in respect of the theft.

In essence, this section provides that once the stolen goods have been returned to their owner, or another who is entitled to lawful possession, the goods will no longer be considered 'stolen' for the purposes of the offence of handling. This factor was vital to the conviction of the defendant in *Greater London Metropolitan Police Commissioner v Streeter* (1980) 71 Cr App R 113 and to the acquittal of the defendant in *AG's Reference (No 1 of 1974)* [1974] QB 744.

12.3.2.4 *Mens rea:* (i) knows or believes them to be stolen

The first element of the *mens rea* is that the defendant 'knows or believes' that the goods are stolen. This knowledge or belief must be present at the time the defendant 'receives' or 'handles' the goods. Knowledge or belief in this context requires the arbiters of fact to take a subjective approach and consider whether *this* defendant on *this* day knew or believed the goods to be stolen. The objective standard of a reasonable person is therefore irrelevant (*Atwal v Massey* [1971] 3 All ER 881).

Over the lifespan of this offence, the courts have consistently reinforced that the defendant must *know* or *believe* that the goods are stolen. It is therefore incorrect to ask what the defendant *ought* to have known or believed. Knowledge and belief were defined by the Court of Appeal in *R v Hall* (1985) 81 Cr App R 260, where Boreham J held:

> A man may be said to know that goods are stolen when he is told by someone with first hand knowledge (someone such as the thief or the burglar) that such is the case. Belief, of course, is something short of knowledge. It may be said to be the state of mind of a person who says to himself: 'I cannot say I know for certain that these goods are stolen, but there can be no other reasonable conclusion in the light of all the circumstances, in the light of all that I have heard and seen.' Either of those two states of mind is enough to satisfy the words of the statute.

On this basis, the Court of Appeal in *R v Forsyth* [1997] 2 Cr App R 299 ruled that 'knowledge and belief' should be given their ordinary meanings; but 'suspicion and recklessness' will not be sufficient. The Court of Appeal in *R v Reader* (1977) 66 Cr App R 33 held that foresight that goods are probably stolen cannot constitute belief either. An even more restrictive interpretation of 'knows or believes' was taken by the Court of Appeal in *R v Griffiths* (1974) 60 Cr App R 14, which held that a 'wilful blindness' to the goods being stolen will also not be sufficient to found an offence.

example

Jack buys a smartphone in his local public house from a regular patron whom he knows often deals in 'dodgy goods'.

In this circumstance, Jack's liability will ultimately depend on how he reacted to the offer of sale and eventual purchase. For example:

- where Jack avoids even considering the idea that the phone is stolen, he will not be liable for an offence; but
- where Jack *knows* or *believes* that the smartphone is stolen but thinks it is best to 'keep his mouth shut' and 'ask no questions', he may be liable for an offence.

in practice

Although a suspicion is not sufficient to find that the defendant knew or believed the goods were stolen, a prosecutor is likely to ask the jury to apply their common sense and infer knowledge to a defendant who is wilfully blind to the idea that goods are stolen. The prosecution would be wrong to suggest to the jury that a wilful blindness is sufficient but may ask them to consider whether such wilful blindness, amongst other pieces of evidence, can be used to infer knowledge on the defendant's part.

An interesting point is that the defendant need not know the nature of the goods that are stolen; he merely must know or believe that the goods are stolen, whatever they may be. For instance, in the case where Jack picks up a suitcase believing it to contain stolen necklaces but in fact it contains stolen watches, he is still liable for an offence of handling (even though he believed the goods to be something else). This was made clear by the Court of Appeal in *R v McCullum* (1973) 57 Cr App R 645.

The prosecution may be assisted in proving its case by use of two devices:

- the doctrine of 'recent possession'; and
- evidence of previous convictions.

Recent possession

The doctrine of recent possession describes the situation where the defendant is found in possession of goods that are recently stolen and offers no explanation, or no believable explanation, for his possession. In this circumstance, the jury are entitled to infer guilty knowledge on the defendant where they are satisfied beyond a reasonable doubt that he had no explanation or no 'true' explanation (*R v Abramovitch* (1914) 11 Cr App R 45). The key phrase there is that the jury are 'entitled' to infer guilty knowledge; they are not 'obliged' to infer guilty knowledge (*R v Smythe* (1981) 72 Cr App R 8).

in practice

A prosecutor must consider whether to charge the defendant with theft or burglary, as an alternative to handling, in circumstances where there is evidence to suggest that the defendant was not merely a 'receiver' of goods. The CPS advises prosecutors to look out for the following factors:

- the time and place of the theft;
- the likelihood of the property being sold on as quickly as the defendant may suggest;
- any connection the defendant has with the place where the theft occurred; and
- anything said by the defendant that may support (or conflict with) the other evidence.

Previous convictions

The prosecution may also be assisted in its task by the use of s 27(3), which permits the admission of two forms of evidence where a defendant is charged *solely* with the offence of handling.

Specifically, s 27(3) of the TA 1968 provides:

> ... the following evidence shall be admissible for the purpose of proving that he knew or believed the goods to be stolen goods:—
>
> (a) evidence that he has had in his possession, or has undertaken or assisted in the retention, removal, disposal or realisation of, stolen goods from any theft taking place not earlier than twelve months before the offence charged; and
>
> (b) (provided that seven days' notice in writing has been given to him of the intention to prove the conviction) evidence that he has within the five years preceding the date of the offence charged been convicted of theft or of handling stolen goods.

Ordinarily, if the prosecution wished to admit evidence of a previous conviction of the defendant, it would have to apply to the court for permission to admit the conviction in accordance with the 'bad character' provisions found in Part 11 of the Criminal Justice Act 2003. For the purpose of handling offences, however, s 27(3) merely requires that seven days' notice is given in writing of the intention to prove the conviction(s) and no application to the court need be made.

12.3.2.5 *Mens rea:* (ii) dishonestly deals with them

The first point to note is that the circumstances listed regarding what is *not* dishonest under s 2(1) of the TA 1968 do not apply to this offence. Instead, dishonesty remains a question of fact for the jury following the ground-breaking case of *Ivey v Genting Casinos (UK) Ltd t/a Crockfords* [2017] UKSC 67. Following *Ivey*, the jury must undertake two tasks:

(a) They must assess the state of the defendant's knowledge or belief as to the facts (this is a subjective question).
(b) They must then assess whether the defendant was dishonest according to the standards of ordinary decent people (this is an objective question).

Where the arbiter of fact finds the defendant to be dishonest according to those honest and ordinary standards, the defendant is to be considered 'dishonest' in law. In the majority of cases, even under the old *Ghosh* law, dishonesty will not be hard to prove – ie where the defendant knows or believes the goods to be stolen. The jury may find a defendant to lack dishonesty in circumstances where he knows or believes that the goods are stolen but is in the course of returning the goods to the owner or turning them over to the police. This was made clear in *R v Matthews* [1950] 1 All ER 137.

12.3.3 Charging handling

12.3.3.1 Mode of trial

Handling stolen goods is an offence triable either way, meaning it can be tried in either the magistrates' court or the Crown Court.

12.3.3.2 Sentencing

Handling stolen goods carries a maximum sentence of 14 years' imprisonment. According to the Court of Appeal in *R v Shelton* (1993) 15 Cr App R (S) 415, the offence is designed to discourage the trade in stolen goods and thus discourage theft. On that basis, the offence is to be sentenced at a much higher level of seriousness than its theft counterpart (for which the maximum is only 7 years).

in practice

In charging handling, prosecutors should consider whether to charge any of the appropriate money laundering offences under the Proceeds of Crime Act 2002 in the alternative. In *R v Rose; R v Whitwam* [2008] EWCA Crim 239, the Court of Appeal indicated a preference for the use of handling in straightforward cases (cases where the value was small). Although this text goes no further into a discussion of the Proceeds of Crime Act 2002, in a problem question, it may be worth making reference to the potential use of the 2002 Act.

Where the goods have not yet been stolen and the defendant enters into an agreement to handle the goods upon them being stolen, the defendant cannot be charged with handling. Rather, according to the Court of Appeal in *R v Park* (1987) 87 Cr App R 164, the more appropriate charge would be one of conspiracy to handle.

12.3.4 Putting together handling

Consider this issue and think of how you may structure an answer to it. Then see the figure below for a sample structure to adopt.

facts

Around Christmas time, Jack burgles the house of Andy. In the act of burgling, Jack steals a DVD recorder, a watch and a video game console. Jack takes all three goods to his local pub and attempts to sell the items to his friend, Jill. Jill asks whether the items are 'kosher', to which Jack replies with a wink. Jill purchases all three items. Jill keeps the DVD recorder for herself, gives the watch to her husband as a Christmas present, and sells the video game console to her friend for £100.

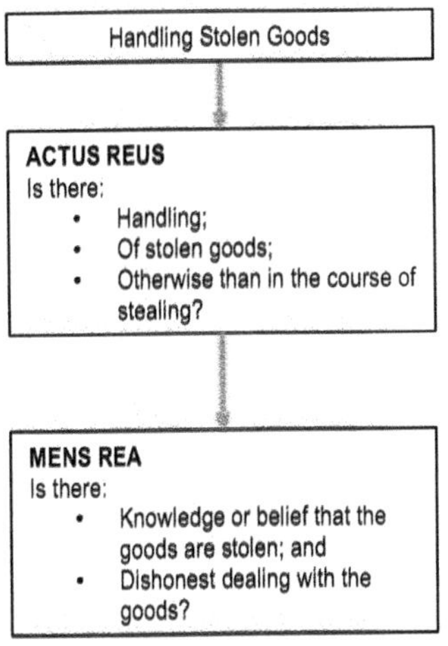

Figure 12.3 Putting together handling stolen goods

12.4 Making off without payment

Making off without payment is the last remaining offence within the TA 1978. The Fraud Act 2006 had the effect of replacing all deception offences previously found within the 1968 and 1978 Acts. Making off was unaffected by the 2006 Act, however, given that it is not a crime of deception. Instead, making off was introduced by the 1978 Act to plug the gap left by the 1968 Act. Specifically, under the 1968 Act, theft requires an individual to be dishonest and intend to permanently deprive *at the time* of the appropriation of property. This left a gap in the law where individuals only form their dishonest intent after the goods have been appropriated, at which point the goods were lawfully their own. Most notable is the case of *Edwards v Ddin* [1976] 1 WLR 942, where the Divisional Court found that the defendant could not be liable for theft of petrol where his dishonest intention was formed only after the petrol was in his tank – according to contract law, the property had already passed to the defendant at this stage (see the earlier case of *R v Greenberg* [1972] Crim LR 331 on the same issue). Smith ('R v Vincent' [2001] Crim LR 488) explains the basis for the offence as being rooted in 'a deep-seated hostility to criminalising non-payment of debts'.

The same argument can be made for the forming of dishonest intent after services were received or done. In *DPP v Ray* [1974] AC 370, the defendant ordered and consumed a meal in a restaurant with an honest intent to pay for the meal. Upon discovering he was unable to pay for the meal, the defendant ran from the restaurant when the dining area was clear. Although the House of Lords could find liability for a false representation, no offence of theft was possible as the goods had already become the property of the defendant (ie they were in his stomach) at the time he formed his dishonest intent. If the offence of making off had been available to the prosecutor, that would have been the more suitable charge. In filling this gap, the Court of Appeal in *R v Vincent* [2001] 1 WLR 1172 has noted that s 3(1) 'is indeed intended to create a simple and straightforward offence' (per Pill LJ).

12.4.1 Defining making off

As a result of s 3(1), making off now covers such activities, often referred to as 'bilking', as:

- leaving a restaurant or hotel without paying;
- not paying a taxi fare; and
- filling up with petrol and driving off.

In all of these circumstances, there is no requirement to prove any deception in the manner that the defendant made off; nor is it necessary to prove that the property in question belonged to another. Simply, the offence requires the defendant to have made off with the dishonest intent to avoid payment when expected or required.

12.4.2 Elements of making off

Section 3(1) of the TA 1978 provides:

> ... a person who, knowing that payment on the spot for any goods supplied or service done is required or expected from him, dishonestly makes off without having paid as required or expected and with intent to avoid payment of the amount due shall be guilty of an offence.

The *actus reus* and *mens rea* of making off are outlined in **Table 12.6.**

Table 12.6 Elements of making off without payment

AR/MR	Elements of the offence
Actus reus	(i) makes off; (ii) goods supplied or service done; (iii) without payment that is required or expected; (iv) on the spot.
Mens rea	(i) dishonesty; (ii) knowledge that payment on the spot is required or expected; (iii) intention to avoid payment of the amount due.

We shall consider each element in turn.

12.4.2.1 *Actus reus:* (i) makes off

The first element required to be proven is that the defendant has 'made off'. According to the Court of Appeal in *R v Brooks and Brooks* (1982) 76 Cr App R 66, the words 'making off' should be given their ordinary meaning, allowing the jury to find that the defendant merely 'departed' from the spot at which payment was required. There is no requirement for the defendant to 'leave by stealth'; he may forcibly leave the relevant spot without payment (see Bennion, 'Letter to the Editor' [1980] Crim LR 670 who gives the example of a heavyweight boxer who forces his way past a restaurant manager).

D must fully depart from the spot

The defendant must have fully exited the relevant space; anything short of that will not find liability for making off. This is often the case where the defendant is stopped before he has managed to escape from the 'spot' without payment (eg caught whilst attempting to escape via a window in a restaurant toilet). In such a case, the relevant charge is an attempt (*R v McDavitt* [1981] Crim LR 843 – though note that the defendant in that case simply went into the toilet to wait for the police to arrive).

Departing with permission

There may of course be situations where the defendant has departed from the relevant spot but has done so with the permission of the relevant authority or body to do so (for example, a restaurant manager or petrol station attendant), on the condition that he returns with payment at a later date. The Crown Court in *R v Hammond* [1982] Crim LR 611 ruled that where permission is granted, regardless as to how it was obtained, the defendant cannot be liable for making off. However, where the defendant is dishonest in his intention to leave and not return, although not liable for making off, he may be liable for a separate offence of fraud by false representation, contrary to s 1 of the Fraud Act 2006 (see **Chapter 13**). Although only a first instance decision, *Hammond* has led to stark academic debate on whether a defendant can 'make off' where permission has been granted. First, Spencer ('Making Off Without Payment' [1983] Crim LR 573) argues that the courts ought to distinguish between two cases, namely:

- where the defendant has left without a trace (ie he has walked out without communication as to how to locate him); and
- where the defendant has left whilst leaving a note of where to find him in the future (eg the note may provide his name, telephone number or address).

Spencer contends that in the latter of the scenarios, the defendant does not make off under the Act; whereas, in the former scenario, the defendant is to be liable for making off. Smith (*Organised Crime and Conspiracy Legislation* (Home Office, 2002)) refutes this argument and states that to distinguish such scenarios would be to 'read too much' into the meaning of making off. The argument of Smith is to be preferred – Spencer's claim fails to take into account the circumstances where a defendant provides details of his identity and address but, in fact, those details are false. Spencer does not state why this distinction exists. Is it the fact that a note of *some* information is left for the supplier of the goods or service, or is it the fact that a note of *true* information is left? The difficulty arises in that a supplier of goods or services will not know the truthfulness of the details until the time comes to request payment – at which point, it is too late.

12.4.2.2 *Actus reus:* (ii) goods supplied or service done

The second element requires the prosecution to prove that either:

- goods were supplied; or

- a service was done.

Goods

'Goods' are defined in s 34(2)(b) of the TA 1968, which, by s 5(2) of the TA 1978, applies to making off.

Section 34(2)(b) of the TA 1968 provides:

> 'goods', except in so far as the context otherwise requires, includes money and every other description of property except land, and includes things severed from the land by stealing.

Goods are 'supplied' when they are offered by the victim and are taken by the defendant, eg by accepting delivery. Naturally, a defendant may be liable for theft of the goods in addition to making off. Examples of supply may include:

- supply of petrol; and
- supply of goods in a supermarket.

Griew (*The Theft Acts 1968 and 1978*, 7th edn (Sweet & Maxwell, 1995)) contends that goods in a restaurant or in a self-service supermarket are not 'supplied' for the purposes of the Act. The better understanding of the word 'supply', however, is that taken from Smith ('Criminal Liability of Accessories: Law and Law Reform' (1997) LQR 113), who argues that goods are supplied if they are 'made available for sale'.

Services

Unlike 'goods', 'services' are not currently defined in either the TA 1968 or the TA 1978. Prior to the introduction of the Fraud Act 2006, s 1(2) of the TA 1978 provided that: 'It is an obtaining of services where the other is induced to confer a benefit by doing some act, or causing or permitting some act to be done, on the understanding that the benefit has been or will be paid for.' This definition was provided for the old offence of obtaining services by deception, which was abolished by Sch 1, para 1(b)(i) of the FA 2006. There is no definition of 'services' in respect of the offence of making off. Jefferson (*Criminal Law*, 12th edn (Pearson, 2015)) regards such an omission as 'inexplicable'. The *Oxford Dictionary* defines service as 'the action of helping or doing work for someone'.

A service is 'done' when the victim does a particular act or service, which need not be physical, and the defendant takes advantage of that service. Examples of a 'done' service may include:

- supplying a meal at a restaurant;
- providing a haircut;
- giving a taxi ride; and
- letting hotel accommodation.

Importantly, as noted at **12.4.2.3**, the service must have been completed before an offence can be committed.

Wilson (*Criminal Law*, 7th edn (Pearson, 2020)) notes that any services that are 'abstracted secretively' will not amount to services 'done' for the purpose of the Act. Wilson gives the example of an individual who climbs over a fence into a golf course in order to play a number of holes. In this instance, the defendant has not received the benefit of playing golf as a result of any provision of services done to him. The same view appears to have been taken by Griew (*The Theft Acts*, 7th edn (Sweet & Maxwell, 1995)).

Excluded goods and services

Importantly, by s 3(3), 'where the supply of the goods or the doing of the service is contrary to law, or where the service done is such that payment is not legally enforceable', the defendant will not be liable for an offence where he 'makes off'.

example

Jack and Jill are bank robbers. Jack is the thief and Jill is the getaway driver. The pair successfully steal £10,000; however, Jack refuses to pay Jill her share of the money.

In this scenario, Jack will not be liable for making off, given that the services offered by Jill, namely her driving skills for use in a criminal enterprise, would be unlawful and thus payment would not enforceable in the civil law (or criminal law for that matter). Similarly, suppose Jill is a prostitute. Should Jack engage in sexual intercourse with Jill on the basis of payment for services, he will not be liable where he makes off without payment as the payment is for an illegal service and is not enforceable in law.

12.4.2.3 *Actus reus:* (iii) without payment that is required or expected

This element can usefully be divided into two, namely that:

- the defendant has not paid; and
- payment is required or expected.

No payment

The first requirement of payment necessitates full payment from the defendant and the defendant has not paid. Making off after part-payment for goods or services required may still found an offence of making off given that full payment would be 'required or expected'.

Requirement or expectation of payment

The second requirement is that payment must be required or expected. Such requirement or expectation must be for payment 'on the spot'. According to the Divisional Court in *Troughton v MPC* [1987] Crim LR 138, payment is generally required immediately after goods are supplied or a service is done. Where the service is incomplete, no payment will be required.

case example

Charge:
Making off without payment (TA 1978, s 3)

Case progression:
Magistrates' Court – Guilty

Divisional Court– Conviction quashed

Point of law:
No payment required where the service is incomplete

In *Troughton v MPC* [1987] Crim LR 138, the defendant was too intoxicated to properly direct a taxi driver as to where he lived. Failing to get any information out of the defendant, and as a result of the defendant attempting to leave the taxi, the driver drove the defendant to a police station.

The defendant appealed to the Divisional Court which found that the contract between the taxi driver and the defendant was never complete. As such, the defendant was not liable for making off in circumstances where the 'spot' where payment would be required had not been reached.

The Divisional Court explained that payment was never 'legally due' given that the contract between the defendant and the taxi driver was never completed. On that basis, the defendant could not be liable for making off.

Troughton may be applied to circumstances where the defendant is provided with inedible food in a restaurant. In the circumstances where the defendant walks out of restaurant in anger without payment, he may not be liable for making off as there may not be an expectation to pay for inedible food. If the court were to accept such lack of expectation, the defendant would most certainly evade liability on the grounds of lack of dishonesty (*R v Aziz* [1993] Crim LR 708 – see below).

Further to this, where it has been agreed to postpone payment, regardless of whether it is done through fraud, it will be held to not be required or expected *at that time*. This is demonstrated by the Court of Appeal's decision in *R v Vincent* [2001] 1 WLR 1172.

case example

Charge:
Making off without payment (TA 1978, s 3)

Case progression:
Crown Court – Guilty

Court of Appeal – Conviction quashed

Point of law:
Permission to leave will void any requirement or expectation for payment on the spot

In *R v Vincent* [2001] 1 WLR 1172, the defendant stayed in two hotels for a number of weeks. He left both without payment, claiming to be suffering from financial difficulties and made arrangements to pay at a later date. The defendant claimed that he was soon about to come into money and could pay his debt. Upon failing to pay the debt, the defendant was charged with and convicted of making off without payment in the Crown Court.

The defendant appealed to the Court of Appeal, arguing that payment on the spot was no longer required or expected given that an agreement to postpone payment was reached. The Court of Appeal allowed the defendant's appeal and quashed his conviction on the grounds submitted by the defendant.

Pill LJ ruled:

> In circumstances such as these, the section does not in our view require or permit an analysis of whether the agreement actually made was obtained by deception. The wording and purpose of the section do not contemplate what could be a complex investigation of alleged fraud underlying the agreement. If the expectation is defeated by an agreement, it cannot be said to exist. The fact that the agreement was obtained dishonestly does not reinstate the expectation. While the customer would be liable to be charged with obtaining services by deception, if he continued to stay at the hotel with that dishonest intention, he would not infringe s 3.

The appropriate offence to charge in this regard would be fraud by false representation (see **Chapter 13**).

12.4.2.4 *Actus reus:* (iv) on the spot

The final requirement of the *actus* reus is that payment must be expected or required 'on the spot'. 'On the spot' is a term of art requiring no particular geographical location; instead, the court will be concerned with ascertaining where the relevant 'spot' is for the purposes of each transaction. We are provided with little assistance by s 3(2) which states that '... "payment on the spot" includes payment at the time of collecting goods on which work has been done or in respect of which service has been provided'. The 'spot' in question is where payment is required. The Divisional Court in *Moberly v Alsop* (1991) *The Times*, 13 December, ruled that there can be more than one spot where payment is due. An interesting decision on the meaning of 'spot' was provided by the Court of Appeal in *R v Aziz* [1993] Crim LR 708.

case example

Charge:
Making off without payment (TA 1978, s 3)

Case progression:
Crown Court – Guilty

Court of Appeal – Conviction upheld

Point of law:
Meaning of 'spot'

In *R v Aziz* [1993] Crim LR 708, the defendant got into a taxi and requested the driver to take him and a friend to a nightclub. The driver complied with the request and stated his fare. On arrival at the club, the defendant objected to paying the fare, which resulted in the taxi driver driving the pair to the nearest police station. The defendant was charged with and convicted of making off in the Crown Court.

He appealed to the Court of Appeal, arguing that he had not made off from the 'spot' at which payment was required (which he argued was the nightclub).

The Court of Appeal dismissed his appeal, ruling that the location of the destination is not irrelevant. The focus of the court is that payment was required on the spot, which the Court ruled, in the case of a taxi, will be at the window or in the cab itself.

See Leveson LJ's comments in *R v Morris* [2013] EWCA Crim 436, where he contended (in *obiter*) that the court's understanding of 'the spot' could be applied 'too literally [so as to] misunderstand the legislation'.

Aziz differs from *Troughton* above, in that the defendant was taken to his requested destination (thus the contract had been fulfilled and payment was thereafter required). Had the taxi driver not taken the pair to the nightclub as requested, then, as in *Troughton*, the pair would not have been liable for making off.

12.4.2.5 *Mens rea:* (i) dishonesty

The first point to note is that the circumstances listed regarding what is *not* dishonest under s 2(1) of the TA 1968 do not apply to this offence under the TA 1978. Instead, dishonesty remains a question of fact for the jury following *Ivey v Genting Casinos (UK) Ltd t/a Crockfords* [2017] UKSC 67. Following *Ivey*, the jury must undertake two tasks:

(a) They must assess the state of the defendant's knowledge or belief as to the facts (this is a subjective question).
(b) They must then assess whether the defendant was dishonest according to the standards of ordinary decent people (this is an objective question).

Where the arbiter of fact finds the defendant to be dishonest according to those honest and ordinary standards, the defendant is to be considered 'dishonest' in law.

12.4.2.6 *Mens rea:* (ii) knowledge that payment on the spot is required or expected

The second element is that the defendant knows that payment is required or expected for the goods or service received. In the majority of cases, it will be clear that the defendant is aware that he is required to pay for the goods or services on the spot. However, there may be other cases where the defendant's knowledge is not so clear as to the provision of the service.

The defendant will lack this element of the *mens rea* in circumstances where:

- he believes that payment is not required (eg it is a gift from the individual offering the goods or service);
- payment is required at a later date (ie payment is to be held on credit against the defendant, as in *R v Vincent* [2001] 1 WLR 1172); and
- payment is going to be made by another individual (as in *R v Brooks and Brooks* (1982) 76 Cr App R 66, where one defendant believed her father was to pay the bill).

There may be many more occasions where a defendant might allege that he did not believe, or know, that payment was required. The important point to emphasise is that this is a subjective test, looking at the state of mind of the defendant. The jury must ask themselves: 'Did this particular defendant, on this particular day, know that payment was required or expected for the goods or services provided to him?' If the answer is yes, the defendant may be liable subject to the other elements of the offence. If the answer is no, the defendant cannot be liable for making off.

12.4.2.7 *Mens rea:* (iii) intention to avoid payment of the amount due

The final element of the *mens rea* is that the defendant intends to avoid payment. Although the Act is silent on this point, the intention must be one of permanence, and it is not sufficient for the defendant to simply intend to defer or avoid payment for a temporary period. This was made clear by the House of Lords in *R v Allen* [1985] AC 1029.

case example

Charge:
Making off without payment (TA 1978, s 3)

Case progression:
Crown Court – Guilty

Court of Appeal – Conviction quashed

House of Lords – Appeal dismissed

Point of law:
Scope of intention to avoid payment

In *R v Allen* [1985] AC 1029, the defendant exited a hotel without settling his bill. The defendant claimed that he intended to pay the bill at a later date when he could afford to do so. The defendant returned a month later to collect his goods. The defendant was charged with and convicted of making off in the Crown Court.

The defendant successfully appealed to the Court of Appeal, which ruled that the defendant must intend to avoid payment on a permanent basis. The prosecution appealed to the House of Lords, which dismissed its appeal following the reasoning adopted by the Court of Appeal.

In the Court of Appeal ([1985] 1 WLR 50), Boreham J cited with approval the words of the trial judge, who commented:

> It follows, therefore, that the conjoined phrase 'and with intent to avoid payment of the amount due' adds a further ingredient: an intention to do more than delay or defer, an intention to evade payment altogether.

The House of Lords endorsed this view on the basis that it was consistent with the 13th Report of the CLRC ('Section 16 of the Theft Act 1968' (Cmnd 6733, 1977)), which required the intention to avoid payment to be one of permanence. Wilson (*Criminal Law*, 7th edn (Pearson, 2020)) is critical of the decision in *Allen*, arguing that '[g]iven the mischief the section was designed to counter and the absence of the word "permanently" from the definition, the decision does not appear to be a good one'. Jefferson (*Criminal Law*, 12th edn (Pearson, 2015)) is equally critical of the decision, arguing that it 'would appear to undermine the thrust of the crime'.

12.4.3 Charging making off

12.4.3.1 Mode of trial

Making off without payment is an offence triable either way, meaning it can be tried in either the magistrates' court or the Crown Court.

12.4.3.2 Sentencing

Where tried in the magistrates' court, the maximum penalty for an offence is 6 months and/or a level 5 fine. In the Crown Court, a person found guilty on conviction upon indictment may be sentenced to a maximum of 2 years' imprisonment.

12.4.4 Putting together making off

Consider this issue and think of how you may structure an answer to it. Then see the figure below for a sample structure to adopt.

facts

Jack recently went on a night out with a number of his friends. The group spent a considerable amount of money on drinks and entry into nightclubs. After closing time, Jack signalled for a taxi and requested to be taken to his home. Jack merely told the driver the area in which he lived and could not provide the street name. Upon reaching the general area, the taxi driver asked for further information from Jack without success. At that point, the driver requested his money or else he would 'take Jack to the police'. At this point, Jack ran from the cab without paying.

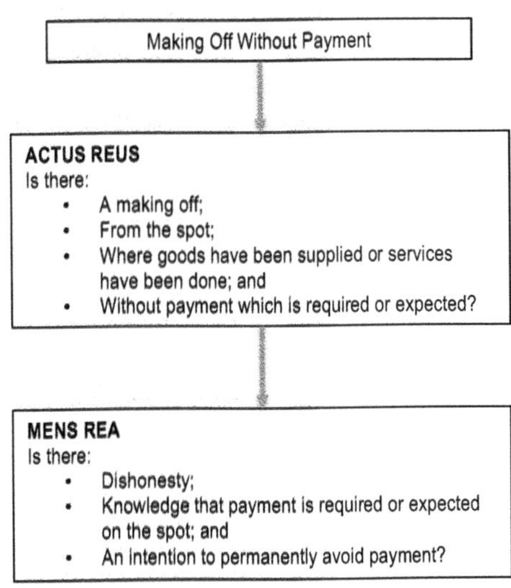

Figure 12.4 Putting together making off

12.5 Further reading

Blackmail

Alldridge, 'Attempted Murder of the Soul: Blackmail, Privacy and Secrets' (1993) OJLS 368.

Lamond, 'Coercion, threats and the puzzle of blackmail' in Simester and Smith (eds), *Harm and Culpability* (OUP, 1996).

Handling

Green, 'Thieving and Receiving: Overcriminalizing the Possession of Stolen Property' (2011) New Criminal Law Review 14.

Shute, 'Knowledge and Belief in the Criminal Law' in Shute and Simester (eds), *Criminal Law Theory* (OUP, 2002).

Spencer, 'Handling, Theft and the Mala Fide Purchaser' [1985] Crim LR 92.

Williams, 'Handling, Theft and the Purchaser who Takes a Chance' [1985] Crim LR 432.

Making off without payment

Spencer, 'Making Off Without Payment' [1983] Crim LR 573.
Spencer, 'The Theft Act 1978' [1979] Crim LR 24.

- Blackmail is concerned with the making of demands with unwarranted menaces with a view to making a gain or causing a loss.
- The gain or loss must relate to property.
- Handling stolen goods is concerned with the circumstance where the defendant is caught in possession or control of stolen goods.
- His possession or control can be interpreted broadly, but it must be otherwise than in the course of stealing.
- Making off is designed to plug the gap left by theft and other dishonesty offences.
- Making off simply requires the defendant to depart from a spot where payment is expected or required.
- The defendant must intend, when making off, to not pay for the goods or services, and this intention must be one of permanence.

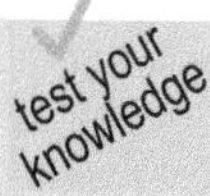

Problem

Jill has recently taken over the management of a local care home. Whilst there, Jill discovers that one of the present occupants, Tony, is a convicted paedophile. Using this to her advantage, Jill demands all of Tony's property, including a watch and a large sum of money; otherwise she will reveal this fact to the other occupants and staff members. Tony agrees and gives the property to Jill. Jill returns home that evening and hands the watch to her partner, Jack, informing him that she 'got it from an old guy at work'. When Jack enquires further as to how Jill obtained the watch, Jill informs him accordingly and Jack keeps the watch in his personal watch box. A few weeks later, Jack enters a restaurant and begins a meal. During the meal, Jack decides that he does not wish to pay for the food. He informs the manager that he has left his wallet at home and must return home to retrieve it. He writes down a fake name and address on a piece of paper and hands it to the restaurant manager. On this basis, the manager allows Jack to leave without payment.

Advise Jack and Jill as to their liability for several property-related offences.

Essay

'Despite attempting to mitigate confusion, blackmail remains a puzzle with no consistent understanding as to its purpose, operation or interaction to and in the criminal law.'

Critically discuss.

chapter

13 Fraud and Related Offences

After reading this chapter, you will be able to understand:

- the nature of fraud offences and the manner in which fraud is charged as a criminal offence
- the offences related to that of fraud, and whether a prosecutor should charge the defendant with fraud or with a related offence, such as obtaining services dishonestly
- the offence of fraud, the elements of the offence and the punishment for the offence
- the offence of obtaining services dishonestly, the elements of the offence and the punishment for the offence
- the offences of possession of and making articles for use in fraud, the elements of the offences and the punishment for the offences.

13.1 Introduction to fraud and related offences

Prior to the enactment of the Fraud Act (FA) 2006 (which came into force on 15 January 2007), there were a number of offences (eight specifically) charged under the Theft Acts of 1968 and 1978. These were generally known as crimes of deception, which were all repealed as a result of the 2006 Act (see **Table 13.1**). The Law Commission 'Report on Fraud' (Law Com No 276, 2002) was highly critical of the deception offences, arguing that, as a result of their sheer complexity and restrictive approach, change was needed. Indeed, Edmund-Davies LJ in *R v Royle* [1971] 1 WLR 1764 described the former law as 'a judicial nightmare', and Griew, in his seminal work, *The Theft Acts*, 7th edn (Sweet & Maxwell, 1990), was critical of the former law, arguing:

> No one wanting to construct a rational, efficient law of criminal fraud would choose to start from the present position. The law ... is in a very untidy and unsatisfactory condition. The various offences are not so framed and related to each other as to cover, in a clearly organised way and without doubt or strained interpretation, the range of conduct with which the law should be able to deal.

As such, a general offence of fraud came into existence with the FA 2006.

Table 13.1 Repeals made by the Fraud Act 2006

Theft Act 1968	**Theft Act 1978**
Obtaining property by deception (s 15)	Obtaining services by deception (s 1)
Obtaining a money transfer by deception (s 15A)	Securing the remission of liability (s 2(1)(a))
Obtaining a pecuniary advantage by deception (s 16)	Inducing a creditor to wait for or forgo payment (s 2(1)(b))
Procuring the execution of a valuable security by deception (s 20(2))	Obtaining an exemption from or abatement of liability (s 2(1)(c))

The offences considered in this chapter are as follows:

- fraud (**13.2**);
- obtaining services dishonestly (**13.3**); and
- preparation offences (**13.4**).

A further relevant offence not covered by the FA 2006 is that of conspiracy to defraud, which remains a common law inchoate offence. We considered this offence in **Chapter 5**.

Complexity of fraud

Fraud remains a complex and difficult area of law. Although greatly simplified by the FA 2006, fraud and related offences still test the comprehension of jurors sitting in such trials. Indeed, Wilson ('"Collaring" the Crime and the Criminal?: "Jury Psychology" and Some Criminological Perspectives on Fraud and the Criminal Law' (2006) 70(1) J Crim L 75) notes that jurors often struggle to distinguish between those individuals who are intentional in their frauds and others who are simply 'playing the system'. Lloyd-Bostock ('The Jubilee Line Jurors: Does Their Experience Strengthen the Argument for Judge-only Trials in Long and Complex Fraud Cases?' (2007) Crim LR 255), however, found that the jurors in the relevant case had a good understanding of the evidence and procedure. There have been calls over a number of years to introduce jury-less fraud trials in order to reduce the time, cost and complexity involved in such cases. Section 43 of the Criminal Justice Act 2003 sought to allow complex fraud cases to be tried by a judge alone, without a jury, but the section was never brought into force and has since been repealed by the Protection of Freedoms Act 2012. Whether that is for the best is questionable.

Fraud is not only a matter of complexity for laypersons. Legal professionals often struggle to grasp the fundamental concepts of fraud, and when presented with the various facts and figures that may be relevant in a given trial, advocates may find themselves cracking under the pressure. As a result, the Crown Prosecution Service (CPS) established its own Specialist Fraud Division which deals solely with the prosecution of serious frauds in England and Wales. Further to this, as a result of the Criminal Justice Act 1987, the Serious Fraud Office (SFO) was created as an independent investigatory and prosecuting authority.

13.2 Fraud

As a result of the FA 2006, there is now one single offence of fraud, under s 1(1) of this Act. The offence may be committed in one of three ways, listed in s 1(2) as:

(a) fraud by false representation,
(b) fraud by failing to disclose information, and
(c) fraud by abuse of position.

Unlike the old deception crimes found in the Theft Acts 1968 and 1978, fraud under the FA 2006 is a conduct crime. On a basic level, under the old law, the defendant must have caused the victim to give him something as a result of his deception (ie a result crime), whereas the new offence of fraud simply concerns the lies told by the defendant, regardless of the end result (ie a conduct crime). As we know from **Chapter 2**, given that fraud is a conduct crime, the prosecution is not required to prove causation.

13.2.1 Defining fraud

Section 1 of the FA 2006 provides:

> (1) A person is guilty of fraud if he is in breach of any of the sections listed in subsection (2) (which provide for different ways of committing the offence).
>
> (2) The sections are—
> (a) section 2 (fraud by false representation),
> (b) section 3 (fraud by failing to disclose information), and
> (c) section 4 (fraud by abuse of position).

It is best to describe fraud, therefore, as a single/general offence with three manners or ways of committing it. The phrase adopted by the FA 2006 is that of 'fraud by …'. Thus, in charging the offence of fraud, it must be clear on the indictment which 'version' of fraud has allegedly been committed. Ormerod and Laird (*Smith, Hogan, & Ormerod's Criminal Law*, 15th edn (OUP, 2018)) comment that '[t]he particularity and complexity of this scheme [is] unnecessary. Sections 2 to 4 could have been free-standing offences in their own right'.

Although it is clear what may *amount* to fraud, Ormerod and Laird contend that the *actual* meaning of fraud remains undefined. The pair go so far as to say that it is 'astonishing' that the word 'fraud' is not defined, despite its use as a label for the main offences under the FA 2006. This view can be contrasted with that of Yeo ('Bull's Eye' (2007) 157 NLJ 212) who argues that, although no definition is provided in statute, fraud has been successfully defined through its practical application. Although Ormerod and Laird are right to note the peculiar failure of Parliament to define the key term that is 'fraud', it is contended that fraud is a general term used by the public at large to denote a circumstance where an intention exists for an individual to be 'cheated' out of their property (whether money or not) by the lies told by a defendant. This understanding is reflected through the variations of fraud as listed in ss 2–4.

13.2.2 Elements of fraud by false representation

Section 2(1) of the FA 2006 provides:

> A person is in breach of this section if he—
> (a) dishonestly makes a false representation, and
> (b) intends, by making the representation—
> (i) to make a gain for himself or another, or
> (ii) to cause loss to another or to expose another to a risk of loss.

The *actus reus* and *mens rea* of false representation are outlined in **Table 13.2**.

Table 13.2 Elements of fraud by false representation

AR/MR	Elements of the offence
Actus reus	(i) making of a representation; (ii) that is false.
Mens rea	(i) knowledge that the representation was false; (ii) dishonesty; and (iii) intention to make a gain or cause a loss.

Quite simply, s 2 requires the defendant to tell a lie, that he knows is, or might be, a lie, and he does so with the intention to make a gain or cause a loss. No loss need actually occur, meaning that this offence is entirely inchoate in nature. Under the old law, a result had to be proved (ie that V was actually deceived and D actually made a gain or caused a loss). Dennis ([2007] Crim LR 2) has defined the offence as one which criminalises 'lying for economic purposes'. This was also the understanding of the law pre-2006 following *Re London and Globe Finance Corp Ltd* [1903] 1 Ch 728, where Buckley J commented that:

> To deceive is, I apprehend, to induce a man to believe that a thing is true which is false, and which the person practising the deceit knows or believes to be false. To defraud is to deprive by deceit: it is by deceit to induce a man to act to his injury. More tersely it may be put, that to deceive is by falsehood to induce a state of mind; to defraud is by deceit to induce a course of action

Ormerod ('The Fraud Act 2006—Criminalising Lying' [2007] Crim LR 193) has described the offence as 'exceptionally wide'.

We shall consider each element in turn.

13.2.2.1 *Actus reus:* (i) making of a representation

Section 2 of the FA 2006 provides:

> (3) 'Representation' means any representation as to fact or law, including a representation as to the state of mind of—
> (a) the person making the representation, or
> (b) any other person.
> (4) A representation may be express or implied.
> (5) For the purposes of this section a representation may be regarded as made if it (or anything implying it) is submitted in any form to any system or device designed to receive, convey or respond to communications (with or without human intervention).

Whether a representation has been made is a question of fact for the jury.

Meaning of representation

As a starting point, Card and Molloy (*Card, Cross & Jones Criminal Law*, 22nd edn (OUP, 2016)) explain that

> s 2(3) does not actually define what amounts to a 'representation' but defines what a 'representation' must be about.

Indeed, Card and Molloy are correct in their statement, and representation can clearly be described as a circular term in that a representation means a specific type of representation.

As explained by s 2(3), the representation may be as to:

- fact;
- law; or
- state of mind of the defendant or another person.

It will be useful to consider each briefly.

Table 13.3 Meaning of representation

Representation	Explanation
Fact	Means representations as to *present* facts, eg Jack has for a sale a genuine Rolex watch which he knows is a fake. This is opposed to representations as to the occurrence of future events or the existence of future facts.

Representation	Explanation
Law	Means representations as to the binding law of the land, whether that be in the law of contract, tort or crime, for example.
State of mind	Means representations as to the present intention of any person. If Jack were to inform Jill that he intends to pay her for her services tomorrow, this would be a representation as to his present state of mind. However, this does not include a promise as to the future (*Government of the United Arab Emirates v Allen* [2012] 1 WLR 3419).

An interesting category of statements that has exercised the brains of academics is that of the ingenious salesperson who inflates or exaggerates their sales pitch (see **13.2.2.2** for a full discussion).

Need for the representation to be conveyed to another

The representation must be *directed* at someone or something. For example, it is not sufficient for the defendant to note a dishonest representation in a private memo or diary; the representation must be conveyed. This simply means that the representation must be made to, or directed at, someone – which can include the world at large (*R v Silverlock* [1894] 2 QB 766 – fraudulent advert in a newspaper). Whether the representation is *heard or acknowledged* by the recipient, however, is irrelevant.

The word 'representation' denotes circumstances where there may, or may not be, a recipient for it to be heard. This is in contrast with the word 'communicate', which would ordinarily indicate a recipient of the message. Withey ('The Fraud Act 2006' (2007) 73(3) J Crim L 220) argues that the better approach to this offence is to understand 'representation' in the sense of 'communication'. This is unlikely given the legislature's specific choosing of the word 'representation' on the understanding that no recipient need be present for the defendant to be liable.

Timing of the representation

Given the fact that the representation must be directed at another person, though it need not be 'received', a representation will be made under the law when it is articulated. The full extent of the offence is therefore very brief: as soon as the representation is articulated (with the other elements intact), the offence is made out. The scope of an 'attempted' representation is therefore slim, covering circumstances where the defendant *prepares* to make a false statement (eg by drafting a document with such false statements) but is prevented from directing those representations to another. A second circumstance where an attempt may be charged concerns where the defendant intends to make a false representation, but the representation turns out to be true (see *R v Deller* (1952) 36 Cr App R 184 below).

Forms of representation

The use of 'express or implied' in s 2(4) allows for a wide and liberal interpretation as to what a representation is.

Express representations

In terms of an 'express' representation, the standard example would be when it is communicated in words or by conduct (*R v Hamilton* [2008] EWCA Crim 2518, where the defendants requested payment for goods , specifically fence panels, that had already been paid for). In *R v Cleps* [2009] EWCA Crim 894, the defendant used a stolen passport to open a building society account and obtained £181,950 from the true owner of the account. Use of the stolen passport, in addition to his conduct at the society, was an express representation. According to the Explanatory Notes to the FA 2006, however, there is 'no limitation on the way in which the representation must be expressed'. A concise list of representations may include those made:

- in writing;
- orally;
- by posting them in the mail or on the internet; and
- by sending via email.

Implied representations

A representation may be 'implied', on the other hand, where the defendant acts in such a manner that he knows is untruthful or misleading. In this instance, we can say that the defendant has made a representation through his conduct.

example

Jack enters a supermarket and fills his handbasket with goods. Whilst at the checkout, Jack tenders his card to Jill, the cashier, knowing that there are insufficient funds available for the transaction. Jill approves the transaction and Jack departs.

This is a classic (and rather outdated) example of a false representation. By tendering the card to a cashier, or a bank, Jack would be falsely representing that he has the authority to use it for that transaction. (This example is likely to have no application in real practice anymore given the development in technology and banking practices. Now, as opposed to Jill or another cashier 'approving' the transaction, the card payment is unlikely to have been authorised in the first place by the defendant's bank. The example serves, nonetheless, as a useful indication of the state of the law.) A second example is the drawing of a cheque. Let us suppose the same facts exist, but Jack tenders a cheque as opposed to a bank card. The Court of Appeal in *R v Gilmartin* [1983] QB 953 confirmed that, in this circumstance, a defendant will impliedly represent that:

(a) the defendant has an account on which the cheque is drawn;
(b) the defendant had authority to draw on the bank for that amount; and
(c) the cheque is a valid order for the amount stated (ie it will be honoured).

Further to this, implied representation may arise through the conduct of a defendant, for example:

- a nod of the head;
- presence in a restricted area implying the right to be there;
- taking a taxi implying that one has the money to pay for it (*R v Waterfall* [1970] 1 QB 148);
- returning an item to a shop requesting a refund implying that the item came from that shop in the first place (*R v Hoxhalli* [2016] EWCA Crim 724 – D purchased a shirt online and took another shirt, from a different retailer, back to a physical store requesting a refund);
- booking a hotel room implying the intention to pay for the room (*R v Harris* (1976) 62 Cr App R 28);
- ordering a meal in a restaurant implying the intention to pay for the meal (*DPP v Ray* [1974] AC 370); or

- being dressed or wearing identification that implies a certain status or right to be present (as in the much older case of *R v Barnard* (1837) 7 C & P 784 – wearing of university robes to obtain a discount).

Although pre-2006, the key authority in this area of law remains that of *R v Lambie* [1982] AC 449.

case example

Charge:
Obtaining property by deception (TA 1968, s 15)

Case progression:
Crown Court – Guilty

Court of Appeal – Conviction upheld

House of Lords – Conviction upheld

Point of law:
Representations by conduct

In *R v Lambie* [1982] AC 449, the defendant used a credit card in a shop to pay for certain goods knowing that she had exceeded her credit limit and having previously agreed to return the card to the bank.

The defendant was convicted of obtaining property by deception (no longer an offence) in the Crown Court.

The defendant appealed to the Court of Appeal, arguing that the shop assistant had not 'relied' on her false representation. The Court of Appeal dismissed the appeal, which was reaffirmed by the House of Lords, which held that the defendant made a representation of her authority to use the card by presenting it to the shop assistant. The shop assistant was induced by the representation as she would not have completed the transaction otherwise.

Representation by omission

Rather interestingly, a representation may also be made by omission. First, this may be where the defendant has made an initial representation and has failed to correct that misrepresentation after a change in circumstances. On this basis, the representation may be considered as a 'continuing act'. Wilson (*Criminal Law*, 7th edn (Pearson 2020)) refers to this as a 'failure to "undeceive"'. The case of *DPP v Ray* [1974] AC 370 provides an excellent example of this, where a student through his conduct in ordering a meal in a restaurant implied that he was an honest customer. Upon the defendant deciding not to pay, his representation remained the same but at that point became an untrue one. See also *R v Firth* (1990) 91 Cr App R 217 and *R v Rai* [2000] Crim LR 192.

The second circumstance is where the victim makes a mistake as to a representation made by the defendant, and the defendant fails to rectify or correct that mistake. In both cases, so long as all other elements are present, the defendant may be liable for an offence.

From the above, it is clear that what may amount to a representation is extremely broad.

Representations to machines

As made clear in s 2(5) (above), a representation can be made to a machine. For example, where a defendant enters a number into a 'Chip & PIN' machine or a bank ATM, in knowledge that they do not have the funds, or authority to do so, they may be liable for false representation (see also para 17 of the Explanatory Notes to the FA 2006, which explains that the provision is designed to deal with the situation where 'a response can be produced without any need for human involvement').

Paragraph 16 of the Explanatory Notes to the FA 2006 provides a further example of a representation in the form of a 'phishing' email. According to para 16:

> This offence would also be committed by someone who engages in 'phishing': ie where a person disseminates an email to large groups of people, falsely representing that the email has been sent by a legitimate financial institution. The

email prompts the reader to provide information, such as credit card or bank account numbers, so that the 'phisher' can gain access to others' assets.

Use of agents to make a representation

The false representation may also be made through another party. This was evidenced in the case of *Idrees v DPP* [2011] EWHC 624 (Admin), where the defendant asked a friend to impersonate him in order to pass his driving theory test, which the defendant had failed on a number of occasions. The defendant falsely represented himself (by having another impersonate him), and the representation was done in order to make a gain (to pass his theory test). As a result, the defendant was appropriately liable for an offence under s 2.

13.2.2.2 *Actus reus:* (ii) that is false

Section 2(2) of the FA 2006 provides:

> A representation is false if—
> (a) it is untrue or misleading, and
> (b) the person making it knows that it is, or might be, untrue or misleading.

Note that s 2(2)(a) is the *actus reus* requirement and will be dealt with here; s 2(2)(b) is the *mens rea* requirement and will be dealt with at **13.2.2.3**.

This provision allows not only outright lies to fall within the definition, but also statements that are merely misleading. We shall consider each in turn, but first it is important to note that the actual representation must be false. Therefore, in circumstances where the defendant makes a representation, believing it to be false but in actual fact it is true, there is no liability under s 2 (see *R v Cornelius* [2012] EWCA Crim 500).

This was the situation in the case of *R v Deller* (1952) 36 Cr App R 184.

case example

Charge:
Obtaining property by deception

Case progression:
Crown Court –
Guilty

Court of Criminal Appeal –
Conviction quashed

Point of law:
The representation must be false

In *R v Deller* (1952) 36 Cr App R 184, the defendant induced the victim to purchase his car on the basis that it was 'free of encumbrances'. The defendant made this representation in the belief that he had mortgaged the car to a finance company, which turned out to not be the case as the mortgage was void. The defendant had thus made a true statement, albeit his belief was dishonest.

The Court of Criminal Appeal quashed his conviction in the Crown Court for obtaining property by deception on the basis that he lacked the *actus reus* for the offence.

The appropriate charge in such cases would be attempted fraud (*R v Cornelius* [2012] EWCA Crim 500 – in *obiter*).

Untrue

The word 'untrue' is an ordinary English word; appropriate synonyms may include 'a lie' or 'false'. Given that it is an ordinary word, a jury should not be offered any further explanation of the word and ought to be told to apply its ordinary everyday meaning. In the context of a representation which is *wholly* untrue, there is no difficulty for a jury; however, problems may arise when jurors are asked to consider representations that are of partial truth.

It is vital to note, first, that the statute does not provide that the representation must be untrue in its entirety; it must simply be untrue. As a result, should any element or part of the representation be untrue, the defendant may still be liable for an offence (subject to satisfying the other elements of the offence). Despite this, the prosecution will face a difficult task in proving the defendant's guilt.

example

Jack enters a jeweller's and asks to look at some engagement rings for his fiancé. Jack asks Jill, the cashier, whether a particular ring he has spotted is 'made of silver'. Jill responds 'yes', knowing that the ring is made partially of silver but also partially of brass.

In this scenario, not only must the prosecution prove that the representation was untrue, albeit only partially untrue, it must also prove that Jill intended, *as a result of that representation*, that she would make a gain or Jack would suffer a loss. That may not be a difficult task to show in this situation as Jill will, as an employee of the jeweller, wish to make a sale.

Other situations may not be so easy to determine. Ormerod and Laird (*Smith, Hogan, & Ormerod's Criminal Law*, 15th edn (OUP, 2018)) accurately paint the picture in the jury room:

> Ironically, the jury may be more likely to acquit a person whose lie is a whopper of such proportions that the jury accept that, although knowingly false, no one could have intended that it would be believed.

Indeed, that is the difficulty faced by the prosecution where the untruth is either so outrageous that it could not or should not have been believed, or it is so peripheral that it should have been ignored. This question, however, remains one of fact and degree for the jury.

In the majority of circumstances, the question of whether the representation is 'untrue' is a matter of fact for the jury. However, there may be circumstances in which the question becomes one of law for the judge. In *R v Whatcott* [2019] EWCA Crim 1889, the issue for the jury at trial was whether the defendant's representation (in that case, that he could lawfully recover late payment charges from consumers) was untrue. The Court of Appeal ruled that the question of untruthfulness was one for the judge, not the jury, because there was nothing factual for the jury to consider. Whether the representation was untrue depended on an interpretation of contractual provisions and their enforceability, that interpretation being a question of law. Therefore, whether the representation was false (in that case) was a question of law not fact. It would appear that the question does remain one for the jury generally and that *Whatcott* is limited to its particular facts given the need to interpret contractual provisions.

Misleading

This alternative wording in the *actus reus* indicates the government's intention to catch as many individuals as possible within the offence. 'Misleading' is not defined in the FA 2006, but the Home Office in its paper, 'Fraud Law Reform – Government Response to Consultations' (2004) drafted the phrase rather broadly, explaining it to mean 'less than wholly true and capable of an interpretation to the detriment of the victim' (para 19). It is interesting that the Home Office sought to define the phrase in the context of it being 'less than wholly true'. This phrasing would seem to indicate that a statement is only 'untrue' if it is *wholly* false and only misleading if it is 'a bit' short of the truth. This would appear to contradict the author's interpretation of the statute (above); however, given the inherent crossover between representations which are true, partially true/false or false, it seems difficult to find that the word 'untrue' includes only *wholly* untrue statements. Unlike the former category which focuses on the falsity of the statement, however, this wording appears to focus on the likely 'interpretation' of the representation. In a sense, 'misleading' is therefore a much broader term than that of 'untrue'.

example

Jill works in a jewellery store and is approached by Jack, a customer. In trying to decide which watch to purchase, Jill informs Jack that a particular watch is 'ordinarily sold at £300 but is on sale now at £100'. What Jill means is that the watch is sold at other jewellery stores for £300 but has never been sold at that price in this store.

In this scenario, Jill's statement, although literally true and accurate – that the watch is on sale at £100 – may be misleading. Jack may interpret the representation to mean that the watch is ordinarily sold at £300 in this store and that the watch is currently discounted (ie *on sale*) at £100.

Another example may be where a haulier company uses a picture of an aeroplane to give the public the impression that it moves freight by air, when, in fact, it sends it by road unless specifically requested. In this instance, the representation is, again, technically true, in that the company can take freight by air – but only where specifically requested. As such, this representation may be misleading, given that it may cause another to interpret that their goods will be delivered by air by default.

In all circumstances, however, it must be proven that the interpretation was capable of causing a detriment to the victim. Note the key words 'capable of' in this sentence; fraud remains a conduct crime and the government continued to emphasise this through its definition of 'misleading'. Once more, in all circumstances, whether a representation is misleading is a question of fact and degree for the jury.

The breadth of this definition, however, may cause some problems in relation to the ingenious sales/tradesperson who inflates or exaggerates their sales pitches in order to induce a sale. Exaggerated sales pitches, half-truths and mere 'trade puffs' are a common factor involved in the sale of goods. Wilson (*Criminal Law*, 7th edn (Pearson, 2020)) defines these practices as salespersons simply being 'economical with the truth', and despite it being a regrettable feature of the sales pitch, such conduct is rarely punished. A fine line must be drawn, however, between a mere puff, which is so absurd that it could not possibly be believed (eg 'Red Bull gives you wings'), an exaggeration and a false representation. In most circumstances, the salesperson will assert a lack of dishonesty or a lack of intention to cause a loss – they may find this to be an easy task. However, not only are mere trade puffs and exaggerations a skill adopted by salespersons, so too may be 'white-lies' or 'half-truths'.

example

Jack asks Jill, a supermarket sales assistant, whether a particular tin of beans would remain 'on offer' for a longer period of time. Jill responds 'yes' but knows that, although the tin will remain on offer, from tomorrow, the offer will not be *as good* as it presently stands.

In such an instance, Jill's statement is factually correct (it is true) – in that the tin of beans will remain on offer for a period of time. However, Jill's representation may be viewed as misleading given the change in price.

A further example of a disreputable trade practice is that of overcharging for services rendered.

example

Jack is a builder and offers to build a conservatory for Jill. Upon completion of the work, Jack bills Jill for an amount grossly in excess of that which is reasonable in the circumstances.

In this scenario, Jack, through his overcharging, may be making a false representation. The Court of Appeal in *R v Silverman* (1987) 86 Cr App R 213 – based on similar facts – believed that this was a possibility where the defendant knows that the price is grossly excessive and the victim relies on the defendant to supply an honest bill for the work. The Court of Appeal in *R v Greig* [2010] EWCA Crim 1183 has made it clear that *Silverman* is not an authority for the proposition that overcharging does amount to a false representation, but, bearing in mind the elements of the offence detailed above, the prosecution may have little difficulty in proving such an offence. It may be the case that the prosecution seeks the jury to draw an inference that a dishonest misrepresentation as to the value of the job or product was made in these circumstances.

The phrase *caveat emptor* ('let the buyer beware') is now so widely used, it appears to denote that society will expect salespersons to attempt to 'gull' them into parting with their money. As a result, it may be questioned whether the skill of salespersons in convincing another to buy would amount to a false representation or would fall within the remit of *caveat emptor*. Likewise, *caveat auditor* ('let the listener beware') would seem to suggest that the receivers of representations should take some responsibility for their part in interpreting the message. Kyd, Elliott and Walters (*Clarkson and Keating: Criminal Law: Text and Materials*, 9th edn (Sweet & Maxwell, 2017)) comment:

> In a free market economy it is regarded as acceptable to maximise one's profits – in short, to make as big a profit as possible. Those making grossly inflated quotations had, in the past, only to contend with the risk of their quotation being rejected. Since [*Silverman*] the risk of criminal prosecution is a possibility. Again we are dealing with dubious business practices being criminalised.

The likely situation will be that most buyers will be caught by the *caveat emptor* principle unless the salesperson has gone so far beyond that of reasonable and honest business practice that their conduct is an outright lie. Vulnerable buyers, however, such as the elderly, may fall victim to the standard trade practices of these salespersons which may, on the facts, be enough to find liability against them.

13.2.2.3 *Mens rea:* (i) knowledge that the representation was false

The first requirement of the *mens rea* is detailed in s 2(2)(b), which provides that the person making the representation knows that the representation is, or might be, untrue or misleading. This is a subjective test focusing on what *this defendant* knew.

Importantly, it is irrelevant that no one believes the representation of the defendant; the requirement is merely that *he* knows the representation is or might be untrue or misleading. It can be said, therefore, that the offence is complete at the time the false representation is made.

The effect of s 2(2)(b) is to provide the prosecution with four ways in which to establish this element of the *mens rea*:

Table 13.4 Proving the defendant's knowledge

Main *mens rea* element	**Sub *mens rea* element**
The defendant *knows* the representation *is* ...	untrue or misleading
The defendant *knows* the representation *might be* ...	untrue or misleading

It is not sufficient to prove that the defendant *should* have known what they were saying was untrue (ie constructive knowledge) or that they might be *aware of a risk* that it might be untrue or misleading (*Flintshire CC v Reynolds* [2006] EWHC 195 (Admin)). Rather, it must be proven that the defendant *knew* it *was or might be* untrue or misleading (ie actual knowledge). Knowledge is a strict *mens rea* term (see **Chapter 3**) and has been interpreted by the House of Lords in *R v Montila* [2004] UKHL 50 as follows (per Lord Bingham):

> A person may have reasonable grounds to suspect that property is one thing (A) when in fact it is something different (B). But that is not so when the question is what a person knows. A person cannot know that something is A when in fact it is B. The proposition that a person knows that something is A is based on the premise that it is true that it is A. The fact that the property is A provides the starting point. Then there is the question whether the person knows that the property is A.

In a later House of Lords case, *R v Saik* [2007] 1 AC 18 – a case of conspiracy – their Lordships held that the term 'knowledge' meant 'true belief' and, as a term, must not be 'watered down'. However, it can be argued that the term has been watered down as a result of the FA 2006, given that the defendant may still be liable even where he knows the representation *might be* untrue as opposed to knowing that it *is* untrue.

The key authority on this is that of *R v Augunas* [2013] EWCA Crim 2046.

case example

Charge:
Fraud by false representation (FA 2006, s 1)

Case progression:
Crown Court – Guilty

Court of Appeal – Conviction quashed

Point of law:
Knowledge that representation is false

In *R v Augunas* [2013] EWCA Crim 2046, the defendant attempted to purchase a laptop at Harrods department store in London whilst using a false credit card. Upon arrest, the defendant was found in possession of a further counterfeit card. The defendant was charged with and convicted of fraud by false representation in the Crown Court.

The defendant appealed against his conviction, arguing that the trial judge had failed to direct the jury that the defendant must know that the representation was, or might be, untrue or misleading. The Court of Appeal agreed with the defendant and allowed his appeal on the basis that the defendant had received the false card in good faith from a third party, and he did not know that his representation by using the card would be, or might be, untrue or misleading.

In the Court of Appeal, McCombe LJ stated:

> In our judgment, it is not good enough for the prosecutor to satisfy the jury that the accused ought to have appreciated that the representation made by him was or might be untrue or misleading, nor is it enough that the circumstances must have given rise to a reasonable suspicion that the representation was, or might be, untrue or misleading.

His Lordship did go on to say, however:

> Of course, if an accused person wilfully shuts his eyes to the obvious doubts as to the genuineness of the misrepresentation that he is making, then he knows that it might be untrue or misleading and he would be guilty of the offence.

As a result of this latter statement from McCombe LJ, the offence under s 2 became even wider than previously thought. The defendant may now be liable in circumstances where he 'wilfully shuts his eyes' to the risk of the representation being false, akin to an ostrich with its head in the sand. In a similar sentiment, where an individual deliberately refrains from asking questions or making inquiries, they may hold the respective knowledge for liability (*Taylor's Central Garages (Exeter) Ltd v Roper* [1951] 2 TLR 284). From this, it is clear that the offence is dependent to an even greater extent now on the dishonesty element, which will determine the guilt or innocence of the majority who come before the courts.

13.2.2.4 *Mens rea:* (ii) dishonesty

There is no definition of 'dishonesty' in the FA 2006, nor are there any circumstances listed of what is *not* dishonest, as there are listed under s 2(1) of the TA 1968. The circumstances listed in the TA 1968 do not apply to the FA 2006. Based on the Attorney General's comments in the House of Lords (*Hansard,* HL, 19 July 2005, col 1424), the FA 2006 adopts the same test of dishonesty as we encountered in the law of theft. Paragraph 10 of the Explanatory Notes to the FA 2006 still makes reference to the *Ghosh* test (*R v Ghosh* [1982] QB 1053). However, as we now know from **Chapter 11**, the *Ghosh* test has been overruled by the Supreme Court in *Ivey v Genting Casinos (UK) Ltd t/a Crockfords* [2017] UKSC 67. Following *Ivey,* in relation to fraud by false representation, the jury must now undertake two tasks:

(1) They must assess the state of the defendant's knowledge or belief as to the facts (specifically as to the representation).
(2) They must then assess whether the defendant's false representation was dishonest according to the standards of ordinary decent people (this is an objective question).

Where the arbiter of fact finds the defendant to be dishonest according to those honest and ordinary standards, the defendant is to be considered 'dishonest' in law.

An interesting question raised by Ormerod ('Criminalising Lying' [2007] Crim LR 193) is whether 'lying is always dishonest'. Ormerod comments that if the answer to the question is 'yes' then this would render the s 2 offence as 'hopelessly wide'. Ormerod gives the examples of television adverts that are so absurd and exaggerated that no one could believe them; but provides that such would amount to a false representation if all lies were covered. Indeed, I concur with Ormerod on this point that it would be pointless to expand our understanding of false representations so widely. The law of contract operates in such cases on the idea of a mere trade puff – ie where something is so ridiculous or absurd that no one could believe it is true, it will not form a contractual term. I submit that the same should apply to the law of fraud – where a representation, albeit false, is so absurd or ridiculous that it cannot be believed, this should not amount to a false representation. The law should focus its mind on dishonest representations falling short of mere puffs.

13.2.2.5 *Mens rea:* (iii) intention to make a gain or cause a loss

The final element of the *mens rea* is that the defendant holds an intention (as a result of his representation) to:

- make a gain for himself or another; or
- cause a loss; or
- expose another to the risk of a loss,

as a result of his representation.

Given that 'loss' not only includes an actual loss, but also an intention to expose another to the *risk* of loss, the *mens rea* can be said to be much wider and less restrictive that similar provisions under the Theft Act 1968.

Intention, in this respect, refers to a specific intent to make a gain or cause a loss and also includes circumstances where such gain or loss is a 'virtual certainty' (per the Attorney General (*Hansard*, HL, 19 July 2005, col 1414)).

example

Jack contacted a number of people, including Jill, Andy and Alice, falsely informing them that they had won £100,000 on the local lottery. Jack informed each individual that, in order to claim their prize, they must pay a £500 administration fee. Jill and Andy ignore the representation, whilst Alice sends the money through accordingly.

In this scenario, Jack is liable for an offence contrary to s 2 given the clear intention on his part to make a gain and cause a loss as a result of his false representation. It makes no difference that Jill and Andy were savvy enough to not send through any money – fraud is a conduct crime and Jack is liable regardless. Alice, of course, would be a victim of fraud in this instance also. If Jack were to claim that he lacked intention to make a gain or cause a loss (on the basis that he believed no one would fall for his trick), the prosecution may still succeed on the basis of the virtual certainty test – namely that a gain or loss was a virtual certainty and Jack was aware of it.

Under this element of the *mens* rea, there are two elements that require consideration:

- meaning of gain or loss; and
- meaning of 'as a result of'.

Making a gain or causing a loss

Section 5 of the FA 2006 sets out the meaning of 'gain' and 'loss' as follows:

> (2) 'Gain' and 'loss'—
> (a) extend only to gain or loss in money or other property;
> (b) include any such gain or loss whether temporary or permanent;
> and 'property' means any property whether real or personal (including things in action and other intangible property).
> (3) 'Gain' includes a gain by keeping what one has, as well as a gain by getting what one does not have.

(4) 'Loss' includes a loss by not getting what one might get, as well as a loss by parting with what one has.

No need for an actual gain or loss

Importantly, according to para 11 of the Explanatory Notes to the FA 2006, the fact that no actual gain or loss occurs is irrelevant. This element of the *mens rea* can therefore be described as ulterior, focused on the conduct of the defendant (not the end result). The victim is, in a sense, irrelevant (as emphasised by the Court of Appeal in *R v Gilbert* [2012] EWCA Crim 2392).

in practice

To demonstrate the importance that no gain or loss need actually be made, the CPS in its 'Legal Guidance on Fraud' advises prosecutors that '[a]ny gain or loss that occurred should not appear in the charge or on the indictment'. The Guidance does go on to say that whether a gain or loss occurred will nevertheless be relevant to sentencing.

Alternative intentions

By making the intentions of the defendant alternate, the legislature has successfully made the offence even broader, encompassing the circumstances where the defendant intends to gain *or* cause a loss (see *R v Bush* [2019] EWCA Crim 29). Withey ('The Fraud Act 2006' (2007) 73(3) J Crim L 220) argues that the defendant must have both an intention to gain *and* an intent to cause loss in order to be liable. This view, however, lacks merit given the express wording of the statute – the legislature is clear that this is an 'or' test and not an 'and' test (though in many cases the pair will naturally go hand-in-hand: one person's loss is another's gain).

Money or other property

Section 5(2)(a) (above) is clear: the gain or loss must relate to money or property – it does not extend to anything other than property, such as sexual services. Property is defined very broadly, similar to that relating to theft in s 4 of the TA 1968, to account for a vast array of items. Whilst the TA 1968 provides exemptions to what can be stolen (such as land and wild animals which have not yet been 'reduced into possession'), such exemptions do not apply to fraud. Therefore, whilst you cannot steal a wild animal, you can commit fraud if you intend to make a gain of a wild animal, or cause a loss of such. In this respect, the FA 2006 is a wider offence.

The Court of Appeal in *AG's Reference (No 1 of 2001)* [2002] EWCA Crim 1768 emphasised that 'gain' should not be interpreted as simply the acquiring of profit. Gain may also include the acquisition of something that one already has or is entitled to. In that case, the defendant tricked a debtor into paying money which he was owed. However, inducing a creditor not to sue on a debt is not considered to be a gain (*R v Golechha and Choraria* [1989] 1 WLR 1050).

An example of property that need not be money was seen in *Idrees v DPP* [2011] EWHC 624 (Admin), the property in question being a valid driving licence. An example of s 5 in operation can be seen in the case of *R v Kapitenene* [2010] EWCA Crim 2061, where the defendant, an illegal immigrant, began working as a cleaner for the victim. The Court of Appeal confirmed that the gain to the defendant and loss to the victim would be the wages paid for the defendant's services.

Temporary gains or losses

Section 5(2)(b) is clear that the gain or loss may be temporary or permanent. This is clearly broader than an offence of theft, which requires an intention to *permanently* deprive. In this respect, an offence could be made out if one makes a dishonest false representation with the intention of causing X to lend his property to Y.

'As a result of'

This final point simply requires there to be a causal connection between the defendant's intention and his false representation. Specifically, the defendant must intend to gain or cause a loss *as a result of* his representation. Another way of phrasing this is that the defendant must intend to gain or cause a loss *because of* his representation. This was emphasised in the recent case of *R v Gilbert* [2012] EWCA Crim 2392.

Charge:
Fraud by false representation (FA 2006, s 1(2)(a))

Case progression:
Crown Court – Guilty

Court of Appeal – Conviction quashed

Point of law:
The gain/loss must be as a result of D's representation

In *R v Gilbert* [2012] EWCA Crim 2392, the defendant, when setting up a bank account, falsely represented his financial position in order to be eligible for the account.

The defendant was charged with and convicted of fraud by false representation. The Court of Appeal accepted that the representation was false, but quashed the defendant's conviction on the ground that the defendant did not intend to make a gain or cause a loss *as a result of* his representation.

in practice

When charged with a s 2 offence, the defence is more likely than not to argue that the defendant did not intend by his representation to *cause* a gain or a loss in the circumstances. Often, the defence will argue that the representation was simply phrased in a way as a form of persuasive advertising, or as an anecdotal statement to accompany the defendant's representation. It will strive to argue that there is no causal link.

13.2.3 Elements of fraud by failing to disclose information

Section 3 of the FA 2006 provides:

> A person is in breach of this section if he—
> (a) dishonestly fails to disclose to another person information which he is under a legal duty to disclose, and
> (b) intends, by failing to disclose the information—
> (i) to make a gain for himself or another, or
> (ii) to cause loss to another or to expose another to a risk of loss.

The *actus reus* and *mens rea* of fraud by failing to disclose are outlined in **Table 13.5**.

Table 13.5 Elements of fraud by failing to disclose information

AR/MR	Elements of the offence
Actus reus	(i) failure to disclose information; (ii) legal duty to disclose.
Mens rea	(i) dishonesty; and (ii) intention to make a gain or cause a loss.

Quite simply, s 3 criminalises lying by omission or, as Herring (*Criminal Law: Text, Cases, and Materials*, 9th edn (OUP, 2020)) provides, 'deception by silence'. Like s 2, it is irrelevant whether a defendant actually makes a gain or causes a loss. The offence is complete upon the defendant failing to disclose information that he is under a duty to disclose with the necessary dishonest intent. Wilson (*Criminal Law*, 7th edn (Pearson, 2020)) criticises the provision, arguing that it is 'unnecessary … as it is clear that a failure to disclose information which one has a duty to disclose … counts as a representation for the purpose of section 2'. It is submitted that s 3 remains a necessary offence given the particular, and more appropriate, set of facts that it would apply to.

We shall consider each element in turn.

13.2.3.1 *Actus reus:* (i) failure to disclose information

The disclosure of information is quite straightforward, ie an individual provides another with the relevant and sought-after information in a certain medium or fashion, eg company books. At this stage, however, it will be useful to separate out two key elements of this *actus reus*:

- failure to disclose; and
- information.

Failure to disclose

A *failure* to disclose information may, however, arise in a number of ways. The three most prominent ways a defendant may 'fail' to disclose information include:

- where the defendant says nothing;
- where the defendant says something, but says that there is nothing to disclose; and
- where the defendant partially discloses information.

The last of these circumstances is not expressly provided for in the statute; however, from the Explanatory Notes, we can take that a failure to disclose may also include cases where the defendant has disclosed some information as required under his legal duty but has withheld other information. The court would therefore question whether the defendant's disclosure was sufficient in the circumstances (see *R v Ali* [2006] EWCA Crim 1937, where the defendant failed to disclose a change in benefit entitlement).

An example of a failure to disclose can be seen in the case of *R v Firth* (1990) 91 Cr App R 217. In this case, the defendant, a consultant gynaecologist, treated a number of his patients using the facilities and equipment of a National Health Service (NHS) hospital. The defendant failed to inform the hospital that his patients were private, which resulted in the hospital not charging either the defendant or the patients for use of the hospital. Although committed under the old law of evading liability by deception contrary to s 2 of the TA 1978, the facts of this case, if dealt with today, would likely fall under s 3 of the FA 2006.

Information

'Information' is not defined in the FA 2006. 'Information' is an ordinary word and ought to be treated as such by the jury. The CPS in its 'Legal Guidance on Fraud' is clear that '[t]here is no requirement that the failure to disclose must relate to "material" or "relevant" information, nor is there any *de minimis* provision'. From this, it can be inferred that information may relate to any information, no matter how trivial, so long as the defendant holds a legal duty to disclose it.

13.2.3.2 *Actus reus:* (ii) legal duty to disclose

This is a legal question for the judge who must ask themselves whether a legal duty, or obligation, between the two parties arose at the time of the failure to disclose. It is important to emphasise that the defendant need not be aware that he is under a legal duty to disclose (see **13.2.3.4**).

A legal duty may be found under oral contracts as well as written contracts. Unhelpfully, however, there is no statutory definition of 'legal duty'. Assistance can be taken from the Explanatory Notes to the FA 2006, specifically paras 18 and 19. Paragraph 18 provides:

> The concept of 'legal duty' is explained in the Law Commission's 'Report on Fraud' [(No. 276, 2002)], which said at paragraphs 7.28 and 7.29:
>
> > '7.28 ... Such a duty may derive from statute (such as the provisions governing company prospectuses), from the fact that the transaction in question is one of the utmost good faith (such as a contract of insurance), from the express or implied terms of a contract, from the custom of a particular trade or market, or from the existence of a fiduciary relationship between the parties (such as that of agent and principal).
> >
> > 7.29. For this purpose there is a legal duty to disclose information not only if the defendant's failure to disclose it gives the victim a cause of action for damages, but also if the law gives the victim a right to set aside any change in his or her legal position to which he or she may consent as a result of the non-disclosure. For example, a person in a fiduciary position has a duty to disclose material information when entering into a contract with his or her beneficiary, in the sense that a failure to make such disclosure will entitle the beneficiary to rescind the contract and to reclaim any property transferred under it.'

Paragraph 7.29 above can be broken down simply to mean that a legal duty arises in circumstances where a contract between the defendant and another would either be void (right to set aside the contract) or voidable (cause of action for damages). From the above, we can take the following to be examples of legal duties to disclose information:

- duty of a solicitor to share vital information with a client (example taken from para 19 of the Explanatory Notes to the FA 2006);
- duty to disclose criminal convictions when applying for work;
- duty to disclose information relating to a heart condition when applying for life insurance (example taken from para 19 of the Explanatory Notes to the FA 2006);
- duty to disclose other financial benefits that were being received, when applying for a new financial benefit scheme (*R v Waas* [2015] EWCA Crim 1259);

- duty to disclose suspension from practice when seeking employment elsewhere (as in *R v Razoq* [2012] EWCA Crim 674); and
- duty to reveal a change in financial circumstances when receiving state benefits (as in *R v Mashta* [2010] EWCA Crim 2595 and *R v Quinn* [2015] EWCA Crim 428, in which the defendant continued to claim his mother's pension payments even after her death – totalling £4,800 in a 12-month period).

Interestingly, in *R v White* [2014] EWCA Crim 714, the Court of Appeal concluded that the defendant was under no legal duty to inform a mortgage lender that he was unemployed when the defendant had, in completing his mortgage application, falsely claimed to be employed (in order to secure the loan). Likewise, in *R v D* [2019] EWCA Crim 209, no duty existed on the defendant to inform the local government that she was liable to pay council tax. Interestingly, Davis LJ justified this on account that '[a] local authority is in a good position to get the information which it needs'.

example

Jill entered a claim with her insurance company for the theft of a diamond ring. The ring was insured as part of her home insurance, and she received over £1,000 in an insurance pay-out. A number of weeks after the insurance claim succeeded, Jill found the ring in her freezer. Jill did not inform the insurance company of this discovery.

In this instance, Jill was under a legal duty to inform the insurance company that the ring was not stolen but was, in fact, simply misplaced. As a result, the insurance company had incorrectly compensated Jill for the ring through her insurance. This scenario is useful to show that Jill, originally, had made a lawful claim on her insurance as she believed the ring to be stolen. However, upon discovering the ring's location and the fact that it had not been stolen, Jill was then under a legal obligation to disclose this information to the insurance company.

It is important to emphasise that the courts will only be looking to find a 'legal' duty and not a 'moral' duty. Such moral duties were proposed by the Law Commission ('Fraud', Law Com No 276, 2002) and would be predicated on a position of trust between the parties and a reasonable expectation of disclosure. Despite the potential of such wider-reaching duties, the recommendations were rejected by the Home Office ('Fraud Law Reform' (Consultation, 2004)) on the basis that it would create inconsistency between the criminal and civil law (ie a defendant may be liable for a criminal offence in circumstances where there is no civil duty expected of him). Green ('Lying, Misleading, and Falsely Denying: How Moral Concepts Inform the Law of Perjury, Fraud, and False Statements' (2001) 53 HLJ 157) argues that in our understanding of fraud, it will be natural to consider the morality behind a particular offence. Specifically, Green argues that there is a notable distinction in moral terms between lying and misleading and argues that this distinction ought to be reflected in the fraud offences. This is furthered by the arguments raised by Ormerod ('Criminalising Lying' [2007] Crim LR 193) who argues that the offence is one 'centred on the wrong of lying'.

in practice

There remains a close link between ss 2 and 3. In the circumstances where a defendant states that there is nothing to disclose, he has wilfully made a statement that would fall within s 2. Section 3 covers the situations where the defendant fails, outright, to disclose when a legal duty to do so exists. A slight twist of the facts may persuade a prosecutor to choose a s 3 charge over that of s 2, and vice versa.

13.2.3.3 *Mens rea:* (i) dishonesty

Dishonesty is to be interpreted in the exact same way as s 2, by reference to the test in *Ivey* (overruling *Ghosh*). Following *Ivey*, in the context of failure to disclose information, the jury must now undertake two tasks:

(1) They must assess the state of the defendant's knowledge or belief as to the facts (specifically as to his knowledge regarding his requirement to disclose information).
(2) They must then assess whether the defendant's failure to disclose information was dishonest according to the standards of ordinary decent people (this is an objective question).

Where the arbiter of fact finds the defendant to be dishonest according to those honest and ordinary standards, the defendant is to be considered 'dishonest' in law.

13.2.3.4 *Mens rea:* (ii) intention to make a gain or cause a loss

As with dishonesty, this element of the *mens rea* should be interpreted in the exact same way as s 2, namely that an intention is sufficient and no actual gain or loss need to occur.

No requirement of knowledge

One point of importance to note is that there is no corresponding *mens rea* element requiring knowledge of a legal duty. In its draft Bill, the Law Commission explicitly included such a requirement (Law Commission, *Fraud* (Law Com No 276, 2002). This proposal was clearly not followed, however. As such, it is irrelevant that the defendant was unaware that a legal duty existed if, in the circumstances, he is still dishonest and holds an intention to make a gain or cause a loss. Liability in this respect can be considered strict. However, note that in circumstances where the defendant *is* unaware of the existence of a legal duty, he is also likely not to be dishonest under the *Ivey* test, given that he may not have had the requisite knowledge to make his actions dishonest according to the ordinary standards of decent people. Under the old *Ghosh* test, he would also have avoided liability given that he may not have appreciated that his withholding of information was dishonest.

13.2.4 Elements of fraud by abuse of position

Section 4 of the FA 2006 provides:

> (1) A person is in breach of this section if he—
> (a) occupies a position in which he is expected to safeguard, or not to act against, the financial interests of another person,
> (b) dishonestly abuses that position, and

(c) intends, by means of the abuse of that position—
   (i) to make a gain for himself or another, or
   (ii) to cause loss to another or to expose another to a risk of loss.

(2) A person may be regarded as having abused his position even though his conduct consisted of an omission rather than an act.

Like ss 2 and 3, it is irrelevant whether a defendant actually makes a gain or causes a loss. The offence is complete upon the defendant abusing his position with the relevant dishonest intent.

The *actus reus* and *mens rea* of fraud by abuse of position are outlined in **Table 13.6**.

Table 13.6 Elements of fraud by abuse of position

AR/MR	Elements of the offence
Actus reus	(i) occupation of a position; (ii) expectation to safeguard; (iii) abuse of position.
Mens rea	(i) dishonesty; (ii) intention to make a gain or cause a loss.

Herring (*Criminal Law: Text, Cases, and Materials*, 9th edn (OUP, 2020)) describes this offence as 'worryingly broad' given the vast number of defendants it may potentially cover. Wilson (*Criminal Law*, 7th edn (Pearson, 2020)) is critical of this provision, arguing that as a result of its broad reading, 'fraud is cast adrift from a clearly identifiable fraudulent context'. Collins ('Fraud by Abuse of Position: Theorising Section 4 of the Fraud Act 2006' [2011] Crim LR 513), on the other hand, approves the focus of the s 4 offence being on the 'disloyalty' involved. Specifically, Collins argues:

> Disloyalty, on this account, is criminalised because it has a corrosive effect on an important basic value held by society: the importance of trust relationships where an individual is entrusted with the oversight of financial affairs of another. The risk of harm to these trust relationships (in themselves a public good) passes the threshold for criminalisation. It is desirable that as citizens we can trust those who are entrusted with our financial affairs if the relevant expectation has arisen.

We shall consider each element in turn.

13.2.4.1 *Actus reus:* (i) occupation of a position

The word 'position' is intentionally not defined in the statute; however, the Explanatory Notes to the FA 2006 describe the relevant position as a 'privileged' one (para 20). Paragraph 20 goes on to say:

> The Law Commission explain the meaning of 'position' at paragraph 7.38:
>
> > '7.38 The necessary relationship will be present between trustee and beneficiary, director and company, professional person and client, agent and principal, employee and employer, or between partners. It may arise otherwise, for example within a family, or in the context of voluntary work, or in any context where the parties are not at arm's length. In nearly all cases where it arises, it will be recognised by the civil law as importing fiduciary duties, and any relationship that is so recognised will suffice. We see no reason, however, why the existence of such duties should be essential.'

The Court of Appeal in *R v Valujevs* [2015] QB 745 has held that s 4 is not restricted to situations in which the defendant owes a fiduciary duty to the victim. Specifically, Fulford LJ states:

> To establish an abuse of position for the purposes of section 4 of the 2006 Act it is necessary for the prosecution to demonstrate a breach of a fiduciary duty, or a breach of an obligation that is akin to a fiduciary duty.

Although not the sole position that may be occupied by the defendant, a fiduciary position is the most commonly seen position in the case law. Holding a fiduciary position is a civil law term, referring to a position of responsibility to act in the best interests of a party. This was made clear in *Bristol and West Building Society v Mothew* [1998] Ch 1, where Millett LJ explained:

> A fiduciary is someone who has undertaken to act for or on behalf of another in a particular matter in circumstances which give rise to a relationship of trust and confidence. The distinguishing obligation of a fiduciary is the obligation of loyalty.

Where, for example, an individual has agreed to act as trustee over a trust for the benefit of another, they will be in a fiduciary position. Likewise, where the individual is an employee, they will hold a similar duty to act in the best interests of their employer (as seen in both *R v Ousey* [2015] EWCA Crim 984 and *R v Choi* [2015] EWCA Crim 1089). In *R v Gale* [2008] EWCA Crim 1344, the defendant, an employee of DHL at Heathrow airport, falsified documents to show that he had inspected incoming goods when, in fact, he had not. The Court of Appeal commented that a 'high level of probity and trust' is present in employment situations and it is important that such persons demonstrate this high level of trust (per Hughes LJ).

Whether the defendant occupies a certain position will, first, be a question of law for the judge. Should the judge consider that there is sufficient evidence to find that the defendant occupies a position, the judge will then leave this matter for the jury as a question of fact. This is explained in the remainder of para 20 which provides:

> This does not of course mean that it would be entirely a matter for the fact-finders whether the necessary relationship exists. The question whether the particular facts alleged can properly be described as giving rise to that relationship will be an issue capable of being ruled upon by the judge and, if the case goes to the jury, of being the subject of directions.

Examples of 'privileged' positions can be taken from the following Court of Appeal judgments:

- *R v Marshall* [2009] EWCA Crim 2076: The defendant, a manager of a residential care home, held control over the residents' finances and unlawfully withdrew over £7,000 from their accounts to be used for his own benefit. Similar facts appear in the more recent case of *R v Rouse* [2014] EWCA Crim 1128.
- *R v Rahman* [2009] EWCA Crim 2073: The defendant, a shop employee, used customers' credit card details to make purchases.
- *R v Woods* [2011] EWCA Crim 1305: The defendant, a deputy manager of a betting shop, altered a punter's bet from £1 to £100. The effect being that when the bet won (at 9-1 odds), the defendant claimed £990 whilst the punter received their £10 win.

13.2.4.2 *Actus reus:* (ii) expectation to safeguard

The second element of the *actus reus* is that the defendant is 'expected' to safeguard, or not to act against, the financial interests of the victim. The FA 2006 does not inform us, however, as to whose expectations are relevant. Indeed, Collins ('Fraud by Abuse of Position: Theorising Section 4 of the Fraud Act 2006' [2011] Crim LR 513) notes this uncertainty and questions whether we are dealing with the expectation of:

- the defendant;
- the victim; or
- the reasonable person.

Guidance on this matter has been provided by the Court of Appeal in *R v Valujevs* [2015] QB 745.

case example

Charge:
Fraud by abuse of position (FA 2006, s 4)

Case progression:
Crown Court – Guilty

Court of Appeal – Conviction upheld

Point of law:
Interpretation of 'expectation'

In *R v Valujevs* [2015] QB 745, the defendants operated as unlicensed gangmasters (persons responsible for the regulation of workers in the agricultural setting). In holding this unlicensed position, the defendants took illegal deductions from workers' earnings, charged disproportionate rental payments, and imposed unjustified fines. The defendants were charged with and convicted of fraud by abuse of position in the Crown Court. The pair appealed to the Court of Appeal, arguing that they were not in a 'position' of expectation. The Court of Appeal dismissed their appeal, deciding that the defendants placed themselves in a position which they then abused.

Fulford LJ, in the Court of Appeal, ruled that the 'expectation' in question is that of the reasonable man. In particular, his Lordship stated:

Although the statute does not provide any assistance on the issue, in our view the 'expectation' in section 4 of the 2006 Act is an objective one. It is for the judge to assess whether the position held by the individual is capable of being one 'in which he is expected to safeguard, or not to act against, the financial interests of another person'. If it is so capable, it will be for the jury thereafter to determine whether or not they are sure that was the case. It would be untenable to suggest that the expectation should be that of either the potential victim (the test would, in all likelihood, be too low) or the defendant (the test is likely to be set too high). Therefore, this is an objective test based on the position of the reasonable person.

His Lordship took authority from the previous case of *R v Pennock and Pennock* [2014] EWCA Crim 598, where it was stated by Aikens J that the relevant expectations are those of 'the reasonable member of the public as personified by the jury'.

in practice

It could be argued that the defendant is put at a major disadvantage in circumstances where he has unknowingly put himself in a position of authority, where the objective person would hold an expectation that he protects the interests of another. In practice, however, a defendant still requires the dishonesty element of the *mens rea* in order to be liable. On that basis, the defendant's perceived disadvantage is outweighed by the necessity for dishonesty.

13.2.4.3 *Actus reus:* (iii) abuse of position

The term 'abuse' is not defined in the legislation. This, however, appears intentional on the part of the legislature, given that para 21 of the Explanatory Notes to the FA 2006 provides that '[t]he term "abuse" is not limited by a definition, because it is intended to cover a wide range of conduct'. This statement can be justified by the types of position that may be occupied by a defendant in relation to an individual. For instance, where the defendant holds a fiduciary position in relation to the victim, the jury will have to be directed as to the civil law rules regarding breaches of fiduciary roles. However, not all positions may be based in a fiduciary role and thus the meaning of 'abuse' of that position must remain flexible.

As a guiding principle, the editors of *Archbold: Criminal Pleading, Evidence and Practice* (Sweet & Maxwell, 2020) submit that 'abuse' should be understood as

> acting contrary to the expectation by which the position is defined (viz. to safeguard, or not to act against, the financial interests of another person) and in a way which is made possible because of the position.

A demonstration of the wide-ranging nature of the offence can be gauged from s 4(2), which makes clear that an offence can be committed by omission as well as by a positive act.

Whether a position was abused is a question of fact for the jury. The key authority on 'abuse' in the context of s 4 is that of *R v Pennock and Pennock* [2014] EWCA Crim 598.

case example

Charge:
Fraud by abuse of position (FA 2006, s 4)

Case progression:
Crown Court – Guilty

Court of Appeal – Conviction quashed

Point of law:
Interpretation of 'abuse'

In *R v Pennock and Pennock* [2014] EWCA Crim 598, the defendants, husband and wife, opened a joint bank account with the victim, an uncle of the husband. £100,000 of the victim's money was transferred into the account and was used to purchase a house for the defendants' daughter. The victim claimed to have no knowledge of this transfer or purchase.

The defendants were charged with and convicted of fraud by abuse of position in the Crown Court and appealed to the Court of Appeal, arguing that the trial judge failed to properly direct the jury on the meaning of 'abuse'.

The Court of Appeal allowed the defendants' appeal on the basis that the trial judge failed to explain to the jury the right of the defendants to make use of funds from the joint account that remains free from securities or restrictions. In allowing the appeal on the basis that the trial judge misdirected the jury as to the meaning of 'abuse', Aikens LJ stated that abuse means:

> 'uses incorrectly' or 'puts to improper use' the position held in a manner that is contrary to the expectation that arises because of that position.

Paragraphs 21–23 of the Explanatory Notes to the FA 2006 provide three further examples of abuse of a position:

> 21. … an employee who fails to take up the chance of a crucial contract in order that an associate or rival company can take it up instead at the expense of the employer, commits an offence under this section.
>
> 22. An employee of a software company who uses his position to clone software products with the intention of selling the products on would commit an offence under this section.

23. … where a person who is employed to care for an elderly or disabled person has access to that person's bank account and abuses his position by transferring funds to invest in a high-risk business venture of his own.

example

Jack, a checkout operator at a supermarket, spots Jill, his friend, in the queue waiting to be served. Jack duly scans through Jill's items and tallies them up on the till. Jill is surprised at the amount charged, believing she was to pay more money. When asked whether this was correct, Jack winked and stated 'it's on the house', whilst brandishing his staff discount card. The supermarket that Jack works for is clear in its instructions that the staff discount must not be used for any person not considered staff.

In this instance, Jack may be liable for an offence under s 4 as he has abused his position as an employee of the supermarket, which he was expected to safeguard, by allowing Jill to benefit (thus making a gain) from his staff discount card. His use of the card for a non-staff member is clearly an abuse of his position.

An example from the case law which may be of use is that of *R v Doukas* [1978] 1 All ER 1061, where the defendant, a waiter at a hotel, sold his own wine to restaurant users and pocketed the money for himself. Should this case arise today, the defendant would clearly be liable under s 4 for abusing his position as an employee.

13.2.4.4 *Mens rea:* (i) dishonesty

Dishonesty is to be interpreted in the exact same way as under ss 2 and 3, by reference to the test in *Ivey* (overruling *Ghosh*). Following *Ivey,* in the context of an abuse of position, the jury must now undertake two tasks:

(1) They must assess the state of the defendant's knowledge or belief as to the facts (specifically as to his knowledge of the position he holds and the expectation to safeguard or not act against the victim's financial interests).
(2) They must then assess whether the defendant's abuse of that position was dishonest according to the standards of ordinary decent people (this is an objective question).

Where the arbiter of fact finds the defendant to be dishonest according to those honest and ordinary standards, the defendant is to be considered 'dishonest' in law.

Under the original Law Commission draft Bill, s 4(1)(b) read that the defendant must 'dishonestly and secretly' abuse his position. The use of the word 'secretly' did not make it into the final Bill and thus the offence may be committed where the victim knows exactly what is going on.

13.2.4.5 *Mens rea:* (ii) intention to make a gain or cause a loss

As with dishonesty, this element of the *mens rea* should be interpreted in the exact same way as under ss 2 and 3. Importantly, however, there remains a requirement for a causal link between the abuse of position and the intention to make a gain or cause a loss. Specifically, the statute provides that the defendant must intend to make such a gain or loss *by means* of the abuse of power. This causal link must be present in order for an offence to be found.

As with s 3, there is no corresponding *mens rea* element requiring knowledge of occupation of a position (see **13.2.3.4**).

13.2.5 Charging fraud

Remember from the start of this chapter that fraud is a single offence under s 1 of the FA 2006, capable of commission in a number of ways detailed in ss 2–4. This means that when charged with an offence, a defendant is charged 'contrary to s 1' of the FA 2006. It is therefore inappropriate to state that the defendant is liable under ss 2, 3 or 4.

13.2.5.1 Mode of trial

Fraud, whether committed by breach of ss 2, 3 or 4, is an offence triable either way, meaning it can be tried in the magistrates' court or the Crown Court.

13.2.5.2 Sentencing

Where tried in the magistrates' court, the maximum penalty for the offence is 6 months' imprisonment and/or a level 5 fine (FA 2006, s 1(3)(a)). Note that the statute specifically states that the maximum sentence is '12 months'; however, until s 154(1) of the Criminal Justice Act 2003 is brought into force, the magistrates' maximum sentencing power remains at 6 months.

In the Crown Court, a person convicted upon indictment may be sentenced to a maximum of 10 years' imprisonment and/or an unlimited fine (FA 2006, s 1(3)(b)). The Sentencing Council published its definitive guideline on fraud ('Fraud, Bribery and Money Laundering Offences') in 2014.

13.2.6 Putting together fraud

Consider this issue and think of how you may structure an answer to it. Then see the figure below for a sample structure to adopt.

facts

Jack visits his local Italian restaurant and is served by the waitress, Jill. Jack has no intention of paying for the food but orders the most expensive dish on the menu. When informed of the price of the dish, Jack exclaims 'Money is no issue'. Jill serves Jack his food. Upon Jill clearing the table, Jack runs from the restaurant. The following day, Jack, who works in a bank, is approached by his two friends, Bill and Ben, who wish to withdraw cash from the bank. In handing over the requested amount, Jack also hands over the counter an extra sum of money, winking at the pair as he does so. Jack is arrested by the police the following day. It has also come to light that Jack has previous convictions for theft and fraud that he failed to reveal to the bank upon beginning employment.

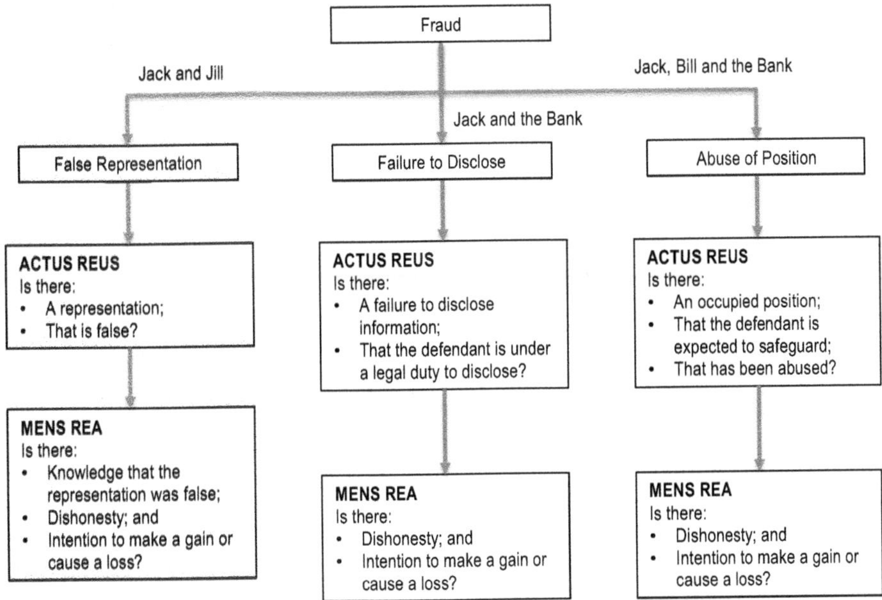

Figure 13.1 Putting together fraud

13.3 Obtaining services dishonestly

This offence replaces the old offence of obtaining services by deception, formerly contained in s 1 of the TA 1978. That offence was repealed by the FA 2006 and replaced with the offence of obtaining services dishonestly contrary to s 11.

13.3.1 Defining obtaining services dishonestly

Obtaining services dishonestly overlaps with other property offences we have considered in this text so far. In many cases, where a defendant is liable for an offence under s 11, it is likely he may also be liable for an offence under s 2 (fraud by false representation).

in practice

Prosecutors must therefore decide which offence better reflects the criminality involved. Given the need to prove causation in s 11, a prosecutor may find it easier to prove an offence under s 2 instead.

For a full account of the distinction between the old offence in s 1 of the TA 1978 and the new offence in s 11 of the FA 2006, see Withey, 'The Fraud Act 2006 – Some Early Observations and Comparisons with the Former Law' (2007) 73(3) J Crim L 220.

The Law Commission ('Fraud', Law Com No 276, 2002), on the other hand, argues that '[t]his offence would be more analogous to theft than to deception, because it could be committed by "helping oneself" to the service rather than dishonestly inducing another person to provide it'. Indeed, although this offence is closely linked, and is 'parallel' (as Herring (*Criminal Law: Text, Cases, and Materials*, 9th edn (OUP, 2020) describes it) to theft, a s 11 offence is concerned with the obtaining of services as opposed to the appropriation of property. This is a key distinction between the two offences.

13.3.2 Elements of obtaining services dishonestly

Section 11 of the FA 2006 provides:

> (1) A person is guilty of an offence under this section if he obtains services for himself or another—
> (a) by a dishonest act, and
> (b) in breach of subsection (2).
>
> (2) A person obtains services in breach of this subsection if—
> (a) they are made available on the basis that payment has been, is being or will be made for or in respect of them,
> (b) he obtains them without any payment having been made for or in respect of them or without payment having been made in full, and
> (c) when he obtains them, he knows—
> (i) that they are being made available on the basis described in paragraph (a), or
> (ii) that they might be,
>
> but intends that payment will not be made, or will not be made in full.

The *actus reus* and *mens rea* of obtaining services dishonestly are outlined in **Table 13.7.**

Table 13.7 Elements of obtaining services dishonestly

AR/MR	Elements of the offence
Actus reus	(i) by an act obtains for himself or another; (ii) services; (iii) without payment when payment is expected.
Mens rea	(i) dishonesty; (ii) knowledge that the services are provided on the basis of payment; (iii) intention to avoid payment in full or in part.

Unlike fraud by false representation, obtaining services dishonestly is a result crime requiring proof that the defendant's act *caused* services to be obtained.

We shall consider each element in turn.

13.3.2.1 *Actus reus:* (i) by an act obtains for himself or another

The first element of the *actus reus* involves the defendant committing a certain act which causes him or another to obtain services.

An act

Paragraph 34 of the Explanatory Notes to the FA 2006 provides that the defendant must obtain the services by way of an 'act'. Specifically, it provides that 'it is not possible to commit the offence by omission alone'.

in practice

Be aware that the distinction between an act and an omission is not always an easy one to make. Suppose Jack is sat in a restaurant and, whilst consuming his food, decides that he will not be paying for his food. As a matter of luck, the waiter clears the table and thanks Jack for his custom (mistakenly believing him to have paid). Jack merely sits in silence and does not respond. Arguably, this would amount to an omission as Jack has failed to make any form of statement to the waiter, whether orally or through conduct. On the other hand, one could consider this to be a positive act on Jack's behalf in positively ensuring he did not acknowledge the waiter.

The line is a fine one to draw and, if you remain unsure of this, return to **Chapter 2** for a full discussion.

The CPS offers a number of examples of 'acts' that may allow the defendant to obtain services. These include where the defendant:

- obtains chargeable data or software over the internet;
- orders a meal in a restaurant;
- attaches a decoder to his TV to enable him to access chargeable satellite services;
- uses the services of a members' club without being a member.

A further example is given in para 35 of the Explanatory Notes, which provides:

> The section would also cover a situation where a person climbs over a wall and watches a football match without paying the entrance fee – such a person is not deceiving the provider of the service directly, but is obtaining a service which is provided on the basis that people will pay for it.

Obtains

The use of the word 'obtains' demonstrates the need for a causal link between the defendant's dishonest actions and the end result of obtaining services. This offence can therefore be described as a 'result crime'. Applying our understanding of causation from **Chapter 2**, it must be proven that *but for* the defendant's dishonest actions, services would not have been obtained. This is unlike the offence of fraud by false representation, considered above, which is a conduct crime.

The prosecutor must prove that the defendant had the necessary intention at the time that the services were obtained. The offence is not inchoate; a failure to prove causation will mean the defendant cannot be liable for an offence.

example

Jack and Jill pay a visit to their local Italian restaurant. Whilst at the restaurant, Jack has every intention to pay for his food, whereas Jill has no such intention, planning instead to escape through the bathroom window mid-meal. Once Jill has finished eating, she escapes through the bathroom window as planned. Jack at this point decides also to escape without paying.

Jack cannot be liable for the offence of obtaining services dishonestly as the necessary causal link cannot be proven (ie Jack does not have the dishonest intention *at the time* the services are obtained through the defendant's actions). The correct charge for Jack would be that of making off without payment contrary to s 3 of the TA 1978 (discussed in **Chapter 11**). Jill, on the other hand, can be charged with an offence contrary to s 11 as her dishonest intention was formed before, and at the time of, obtaining the services from the restaurant.

Using the example given in the Explanatory Notes, should a defendant climb over the wall and watch a football match, he is committing an 'act'. Should the defendant watch any length of the football match, he will have 'obtained' services. Should the defendant be caught after climbing the wall but before having the chance to watch any part of the football match, he will not have 'obtained' services.

For himself or another

The final aspect of this element is that the benefit has to be for the defendant himself, or it may be for another person.

13.3.2.2 *Actus reus:* (ii) services

The second requirement is that the defendant must obtain 'services'. Services are not defined in the Act, but are understood to be wider than the definition of property in s 4 of the TA 1968. Logically, therefore, 'services' can be interpreted as including *all* services, even those that are unlawful, eg payment for prostitution (which can be compared with the offence of making off without payment – see **Chapter 12**). The single restriction placed on the definition of service is that it must be one for which payment is required.

A point of contention that has arisen in relation to the meaning of services is whether the obtaining of a credit card or the opening of a bank account was a 'service' for the purpose of s 11. The Court of Appeal in *R v Sofroniou* [2004] QB 1218 has held that such would not amount to a service, but the provisions that underlie a card or account may amount to a service. Where a credit card is obtained or a bank account opened as a result of a false representation, the card or account does not, itself, amount to a service, but rather provides access to a range of facilities that underlie the card or account.

case example

Charge:
Obtaining services by deception (TA 1978, s 1)

Case progression:
Crown Court – Guilty

Court of Appeal – Conviction upheld

Point of law:
Meaning of 'services'

In *R v Sofroniou* [2004] QB 1218, the defendant used a false identity in an attempt to deceive a number of banks into providing him with services and credit cards. The defendant overdrew one account and exceeded the limit on a credit card.

The defendant was charged with and convicted of obtaining services by deception (now abolished). The defendant appealed to the Court of Appeal, arguing that the services were not 'paid for'. The Court of Appeal dismissed his appeal, ruling that payment was required in the defendant's case given that he had exceeded the relevant account limits.

In particular, May LJ in the Court of Appeal stated:

> [T]here should no longer be any doubt but that dishonestly inducing a bank or building society to provide banking or credit card services is also within the section, provided the requirement as to payment is also satisfied.

The Divisional Court in *Mikolajczak v Poland* [2013] EWHC 432 (Admin) has recently ruled that the 'topping up' of a mobile telephone with credit by charging the credit cost to other users is not a 'service' within s 11; rather, it is the obtaining of credit (for which the defendant may be liable for dishonestly obtaining electronic communication services, contrary to s 125 of the Communications Act 2003).

Where payment is not required or is unexpected, a defendant will commit no offence if he dishonestly obtains that particular service. Examples can be taken from gratuitous services offered to certain classes of individual, eg the elderly, the young, the disabled or the homeless. Other examples include gratuitous services based on the circumstances of the defendant. For example, where the defendant falsely informs a taxi driver that he cannot pay for the fare because he has been robbed, and the taxi driver offers him a free fare home, the defendant will not be liable for an offence under s 11 as no payment was required or expected. The defendant may, however, be liable for fraud by false representation.

13.3.2.3 *Actus reus:* (iii) without payment when payment is expected

As we know, the services must be provided on the basis that 'payment has been, is being or will be made for or in respect of them'. The final element of the *actus reus* requires the defendant to obtain the said service without paying for it or without paying for it in full (ie partial payment), in circumstances where full payment is expected. As a result, even if the defendant has made a false statement but still pays the full price for the service, he will not be liable for the offence. Likewise, if the defendant has made a false statement and receives services, but there was no expectation of payment, then there is no offence.

13.3.2.4 *Mens rea:* (i) dishonesty

Despite the word 'dishonesty' being featured in the name of the offence, the word was not defined in the Act. Further, the word was not defined in the Explanatory Notes, unlike false representation. Despite this, it is likely that the dishonesty test in *Ivey* (overruling *Ghosh*) will apply. Following *Ivey,* in the context of obtaining services dishonestly, the jury must now undertake two tasks:

(1) They must assess the state of the defendant's knowledge or belief as to the facts (specifically as to his knowledge regarding the services he was obtaining).
(2) They must then assess whether the defendant's obtaining of such services without payment was dishonest according to the standards of ordinary decent people (this is an objective question).

Where the arbiter of fact finds the defendant to be dishonest according to those honest and ordinary standards, the defendant is to be considered 'dishonest' in law.

13.3.2.5 *Mens rea:* (ii) knowledge that the services are provided on the basis of payment

The defendant must know that the services are provided on the basis that payment is required or might be required (FA 2006, s 11(2)(c)). Phrased in another manner, the defendant must be aware that the services are 'chargeable'.

example

Jack visits his local theatre to watch his favourite musical. Unable to purchase a ticket, Jack accesses the building via a fire exit and watches the musical from the wings. Upon the finale of the show, Jack departs through the same fire exit.

In this instance, Jack has clearly obtained a service, ie the performance of the musical. Given that he has entered the building via a fire exit, it is clear that he is aware that payment for the service is required – given that he has been unable to purchase a ticket and has chosen to use a fire exit to gain access. A jury would no doubt find Jack dishonest in his conduct. This is a simple case of obtaining services dishonestly.

13.3.2.6 *Mens rea:* (iii) intention to avoid payment in full or in part

The final requirement is that the defendant must intend to avoid payment in full or in part (FA 2006, s 11(2)(c)). This intention must exist at the point that the defendant obtains the service dishonestly. Where the defendant has the dishonest intention to avoid payment but later changes his mind before obtaining the services, he will not be liable for a s 11 offence. However, he may be liable for an attempt. On this point, it remains unclear whether the intention to avoid payment in full or in part must be an intention to *never* pay the required amount or simply not to pay at this point in time. Following the principle in *R v Allen* [1985] AC 1029 in relation to making off without payment, the first of these statements appears more likely to be correct.

The Law Commission gave the following example of an intention that would fall outside s 11. It provided that where a parent 'lies about a child's religious upbringing in order to obtain a place at a fee-paying school, with every intention of paying the fee', they will not be liable under s 11. Indeed, this is correct given that the parents, although they are making a false statement, could not be liable under s 11 as they have the intention to pay. Amending the facts slightly, had the parents lied about their child's upbringing in order to gain a discount on school fees, it is submitted that this would fall within s 11. Specifically, where the defendant intends to pay, but that payment is of a reduced fee brought about by the defendant's dishonest actions, he will still remain liable for an offence under s 11 so long as he has obtained such reduced fee dishonestly.

13.3.3 Charging obtaining services dishonestly

13.3.3.1 Mode of trial

Obtaining services dishonestly is an offence triable either way, meaning it may be tried in either the magistrates' court or the Crown Court (FA 2006, s 11(3)).

13.3.3.2 Sentencing

Where tried in the magistrates' court, the maximum penalty for an offence is 6 months' imprisonment and/or a level 5 fine (FA 2006, s 11(3)(a)).

In the Crown Court, a person convicted upon indictment may be sentenced to a maximum of 5 years' imprisonment and/or an unlimited fine (FA 2006, s 11(3)(b)).

13.3.4 Putting together obtaining services dishonestly

Consider this issue and think of how you may structure an answer to it. Then see the figure below for a sample structure to adopt.

facts

Jack is a wealthy individual but enjoys finding ways in which he does not have to pay for goods or services. One day, Jack decides to visit his favourite French restaurant with the intention of not paying; he is accompanied by his friend, Jill, who has no idea of Jack's intentions. Upon finishing their meal, Jack goes to the toilet whereby he escapes through an open window, leaving Jill in the restaurant alone. Jill cannot afford to pay the bill and the police are called.

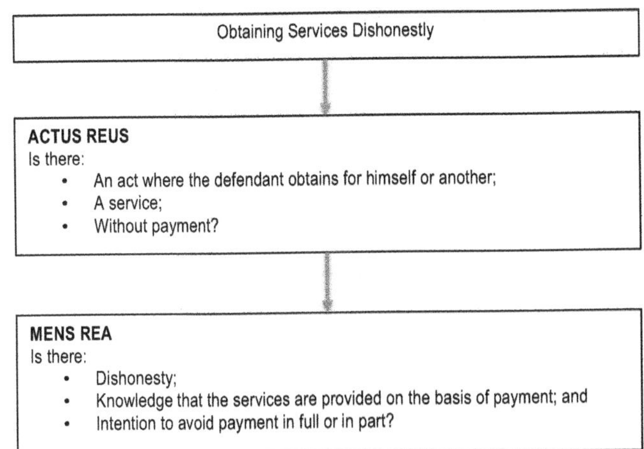

Figure 13.2 Putting together obtaining services dishonesty

13.4 Preparation offences

As can be expected, the commission of fraud can range from a complex arrangement involving a substantial number of misrepresentations and moving of large financial sums, to a more simple arrangement involving a simple act of misrepresentation on the part of the defendant. In both cases, however, a defendant may be liable before the fraud even occurs. We know these as the 'preparation offences', and they are designed to combat fraud before it even takes place.

There are two main preparatory offences contained in the FA 2006, namely:

- possession of articles for use in frauds, contrary to s 6 (replacing the offence of 'going equipped to cheat' under s 25 of the TA 1968); and
- making or supplying articles for use in frauds, contrary to s 7.

The offence contrary to s 6 is designed to deal with cases in which the defendant possesses or has under his control any article for use in the course of, or in connection with, any fraud. The phrase 'article' is broad to allow for a whole range of items to fall within the definition (eg *R v Ciorba* [2009] EWCA Crim 1800, in which the possession of a memory stick used to download data from ATM machines was considered an 'article'). Furthermore, the words 'in connection with' any fraud have been held to include articles used to commit the fraud, and articles used to 'cover up' the fraud (see the latest case of *R v Smith* [2020] EWCA Crim 38, considering *R v Sakalauskas* [2013] EWCA Crim 2278).

Section 7 is concerned with the broad offence of 'making' articles for use in fraud. The s 7 offence is extremely wide in that it catches numerous variations of conduct, namely: making, adapting, supplying, and offering. Each one of those variations forms its own offence, meaning that a defendant may be liable for two offences where, for example, he both makes an article for use in fraud and then supplies it to another.

For a more detailed discussion of these offences, see Farrell, Yeo and Ladenburg, *Blackstone's Guide to the Fraud Act 2006* (OUP, 2007).

13.5 Further reading

Collins, 'Fraud by Abuse of Position: Theorising Section 4 of the Fraud Act 2006' [2011] Crim LR 513.

Collins, 'Fraud by Abuse of Position and Unlicensed Gangmasters' (2016) 79 MLR 354.

Green, *Lying, Cheating and Stealing* (OUP, 2007).

Monaghan, 'School Application Forms and the Criminal Law' [2015] Crim LR 270.

Ormerod, 'The Fraud Act 2006—Criminalising Lying?' [2007] Crim LR 193.

Salter, 'It's Criminal Not to Disclose' (2007) 37 Fam L 432.

Sarker, 'Fighting Fraud—A Missed Opportunity' (2007) 28 Comp Law 243.

Spencer, 'The Drafting of Criminal Legislation: Need It Be So Impenetrable?' (2008) 67 CLJ 585.

Sullivan, 'Fraud—The Latest Law Commission Proposals' (2003) 67 J Crim L 139.

Withey, 'The Fraud Act 2006—Some Early Observations and Comparisons with the Former Law' (2007) 73(3) J Crim L 220.

- Offences of deception were removed and replaced with the introduction of the FA 2006.
- Fraud is a single offence which may be committed in a number of different ways.
- Fraud is not concerned with the end result, but is more focused on the conduct and state of mind of the defendant.
- Fraud by false representation is committed where the defendant makes a representation which is false with the dishonest intention to make a gain or cause a loss to another.
- Fraud by failure to disclose information is committed where the defendant owes a legal duty to disclose certain information to the victim, and fails to do so with the dishonest intention to make a gain or cause a loss to another.
- Fraud by abuse of position is committed where the defendant occupies a position which he is expected to safeguard and abuses that position with the dishonest intention to make a gain or cause a loss to another.
- Obtaining services dishonesty is committed where the defendant obtains for himself or another services for which payment is expected, the defendant knows that payment is expected and dishonestly intends to avoid such payment in full or in part.
- A number of preparation offences also exist under the FA 2006, namely the possession of, or making, adapting, supplying or offering for supply, any article for use in connection with fraud.

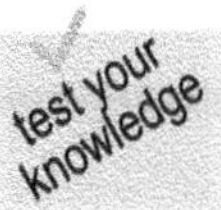

Problem question

Jack enters a supermarket and purchases a large television set with use of his credit card. Jack believed there to be no credit remaining on the card and hoped that he could get the TV for free. Jack presented the card at the checkout which was authorised by the cashier. Unbeknownst to Jack, there were sufficient funds to pay for the television set.

Jack's housemate, Jill, has recently taken on the role as a carer in the community. As part of her role, Jill visits the houses of several patients to ensure they are well and healthy. On one particular day, Jill notices one of her patient's wallets left on the side counter in the kitchen. Jill opens the wallet and steals £30 from it. Jill claims she intended to give the money back when she was paid her monthly wage.

Consider Jack and Jill's potential liability under the Fraud Act 2006.

Essay question

'The Fraud Act 2006 is unacceptably wide. The legislature has now successfully criminalised lying.'

Critically discuss.

chapter 14

Damage to Property

After reading this chapter, you will be able to understand:

- why criminal damage is dealt with separately from other property offences, such as theft
- the basic offence of criminal damage and the requirements for a defendant to be liable for the basic offence
- the aggravated forms of criminal damage, including arson, and the extra requirements necessary to find liability against a defendant.

14.1 Introduction to damaging property

In the previous chapters, we have been concerned with interferences of proprietary rights through the law of theft, theft-related offences and fraud. This chapter is designed to focus on a particular interference with proprietary rights, namely the right to not have one's property damaged. It is worth questioning whether we need to segregate property offences out in this way. Would it not be more sensible to have a single criminal offence concerned with wrongful interference with property and proprietary interests? Simester and Sullivan ('Accessories and Principals after Gnango' in Reed and Bohlander (eds), *Participation in Crime* (Routledge, 2013)) argue that criminal damage ought to remain a crime of its own for two reasons:

- Criminal damage, especially aggravated criminal damage and arson, is often linked with offences against the person. Indeed, the pair write that 'many typical instances of criminal damage involve forms of vandalism employing percussive force, fire or explosions, conduct that may well cause alarm and concern even to bystanders lacking any proprietary interest in the property being damaged'.
- Criminal damage may be a sign or statement to the general public of the individual's views or contempt for society or the victim specifically. The pair explain this second justification by reference to vandalism and graffiti.

In the author's view, criminal damage is a special form of interference with both proprietary and personal rights and interests, given that if property is damaged or destroyed, it may become irrecoverable; whereas property stolen under the Theft Act 1968 may eventually see a return to the owner.

14.2 Criminal damage

Criminal damage is a term that covers a range of property offences in the criminal law. In particular, criminal damage is concerned with four key offences against property:

- basic (also known as simple) criminal damage;
- aggravated criminal damage;

- arson; and
- aggravated arson.

Each of these four offences are charged under s 1 of the Criminal Damage Act (CDA) 1971 but as a separate and specific offence (ie not simply 'criminal damage'). Further to this, each offence of criminal damage may be racially or religiously aggravated under s 30 of the Crime and Disorder Act 1998.

There are many more offences relating to the damage of property that are outside the scope of this work, most notably:

- threats to destroy or damage property (CDA 1971, s 2);
- possessing anything with intent to destroy or damage property (CDA 1971, s 3); and
- damage caused by explosives (Explosives Act 1875; Explosive Substances Act 1883).

14.2.1 Defining criminal damage

The CDA 1971 had the effect of repealing the common law and statutory offences relating to criminal damage. In particular, the CDA 1971 repealed and replaced the majority of the Malicious Damage Act 1861, with only a few offences remaining. Wilson (*Criminal Law*, 7th edn (Pearson, 2020)) argues that the CDA 1971 had the effect of replacing a 'cumbersome and antiquated set of provisions with a new and comprehensive reforming code'. The CDA 1971 is now the primary source of offences of damaging property, compared with the Theft Act 1968 which is the primary source of offences of appropriating property.

We shall consider each offence in turn, under the umbrella of criminal damage.

14.2.2 Elements of basic criminal damage

Section 1(1) of the CDA 1971 provides:

> A person who without lawful excuse destroys or damages any property belonging to another intending to destroy or damage any such property or being reckless as to whether any such property would be destroyed or damaged shall be guilty of an offence.

The *actus reus* and *mens rea* of basic criminal damage are outlined in **Table 14.1**.

Table 14.1 Elements of basic criminal damage

AR/MR	Elements of the offence
Actus reus	(i) destroys or damages; (ii) property; (iii) belonging to another; (iv) without lawful excuse.
Mens rea	(i) intention or recklessness as to damage/destruction; (ii) knowledge or belief that property belonged to another.

We shall consider each element in turn. Note that if the elements of this offence are committed by fire, then the correct offence is one of arson (CDA 1971, s 1(3)).

14.2.2.1 *Actus reus:* (i) destroys or damages

The first element to prove is that the defendant 'destroyed or damaged property'. Since there is no legal definition of 'destroy' or 'damage' in the CDA 1971, the courts have applied liberal and common-sense definitions (*Roe v Kingerlee* [1986] Crim LR 735). It is clear by the use of destroy 'or' damage that the two words are not synonymous. Indeed, Jefferson (*Criminal Law*, 12th edn (Pearson, 2015)) notes that:

> [Destroy] does not add anything to 'damage'. If one destroys property, one damages it. It may have been included to forestall the argument that 'damage' does not cover 'destroy'.

According to the Divisional Court in *Morphitis v Salmon* [1990] Crim LR 48, both words ('destroy' and 'damage') remain a question of fact and degree for the arbiters of fact. In the earlier case of *Roe v Kingerlee*, Woolf LJ commented that

> what constitutes criminal damage is a matter of fact and degree and it is for the justices, applying their common sense, to look at what occurs and decide whether it is damage or not.

This has been doubted by the likes of Wilson (*Criminal Law*, 7th edn (Pearson, 2020)), who argues:

> While judgments of degree will be involved in determining whether a given harm counts as criminal damage, this judgment will be made by the *judge* rather than the *tribunal of fact*. (original emphasis)

Table 14.2 explains the difference between the two terms:

Table 14.2 Destroying vs damaging property

Term	Meaning	Examples
Destroy	Property is destroyed if it is useless from that point on (ie there is an element of 'finality and totality about it' – *Barnet LBC v Eastern Electricity Board* [1973] 2 All ER 319 per May J).	Demolishing a building; incinerating books.
Damage	Property is damaged if it is made 'imperfect' or 'inoperative' and the value or utility of the property has been impaired. There is no requirement for finality; damage to property can be either temporary or permanent.	Smashing the glass face of a watch; scratching the paintwork on a car.

Importantly, whilst the Act is silent in this regard, the words 'destroy or damage' are to be read as allowing for either an act or an omission to cause the said destruction or damage. This is evident from *R v Miller* [1983] 2 AC 61 (a case involving arson).

'Destroy'

As noted in **Table 14.2**, the word 'destroy' involves an element of finality. 'Destroy' is to be read as synonymous with 'destruction'. Unlike the word 'damage', which may involve a reduction in the value or usefulness of property, destruction is not, as Ormerod and Laird put it, concerned with 'half measures' (*Smith, Hogan, & Ormerod's Criminal Law*, 15th edn (OUP 2018)). A unique example of destruction, in addition to the above examples, is the killing of an animal.

'Damage'

The destruction of property is uncontroversial and subject to few difficulties, given that if property is 'destroyed', it is naturally also going to be 'damaged'. However, the courts have been pressed for a definition of the word 'damage' and whether certain actions can be deemed sufficient to amount to 'damage'.

Two interpretations of the word 'damage' have arisen in the common law; these are:

- time, expense and effort to rectify; and
- impairment of value or usefulness.

Time, expense and effort to rectify

The leading authority on this interpretation of damage is that of *Hardman v Chief Constable of Avon and Somerset Constabulary* [1986] Crim LR 330 in the Crown Court.

Charge:
Criminal damage (CDA 1971, s 1)

Case progression:
Crown Court – Guilty

Point of law:
Meaning of 'damage'

case example

In *Hardman v Chief Constable of Avon and Somerset Constabulary* [1986] Crim LR 330, the defendant painted the pavement with water-based paint. The paint would have washed away with the rain in a matter of days quite easily, but the council chose to pay for a jet wash to remove it. The defendant was charged with and convicted of criminal damage in the Crown Court.

The Crown Court held that there was sufficient damage to the pavement as it took time and expense to remove the paint.

The focus in *Hardman*, therefore, is not necessarily that the property has been physical harmed, but rather the focus is on the time, expense and effort involved in returning the property to the state it was in before the 'damage' was caused. This is visible in the case of *R v Henderson and Battley* (CA, 24 November 1984) where the defendants dumped rubbish on the victim's land. Although no physical damage or harm was caused to the land itself, the Court of Appeal found that the time and expense taken to remove the rubbish from the land was sufficient for a case of criminal damage. Of course, this does not mean that the court will ignore cases where actual damage is done to the property, as seen *Gayford v Choulder* [1898] 1 QB 316 where the Divisional Court held that the trampling of grass by the defendant was capable of being criminal damage.

Criminal damage as a result of time, expense and effort was not found, however, in the case of *A (a juvenile) v R* [1978] Crim LR 689. In this case, the defendant spat on a police officer's coat. Streeter J in the Crown Court ruled that this could not amount to 'damage' as there was no expense or effort in 'removing the damage, nor was the value or utility of the coat impaired'. In basic form, the coat was 'restored' to its original form by simply wiping away the remnants of the spittle. This case can, however, be compared with the Australian case of *Samuels v Stubbs* (1972) 4 SASR 200, where a police officer's cap was considered as having been damaged by being stamped on. This was so despite the fact that the cap could simply be pushed back into shape. Walters J reasoned:

> It seems to me that it is difficult to lay down any very general and, at the same time, precise and absolute rule as to what constitutes 'damage'. One must be guided in a great degree by the circumstances of each case, the nature of the article and the mode in which it is affected or treated. ... It is my view, however, that the word... is sufficiently wide in its meaning to embrace injury, mischief or harm done to property, and that in order to constitute 'damage' it is unnecessary to establish such definite or actual damage as renders the property useless, or prevents it from serving its normal function ...

One could question whether the painting in *Hardman* would amount to 'damage' had the council not paid for the jet wash and allowed the rain to wash the paint away. Likewise, one could question whether the spittle would amount to 'damage' where the police officer's coat required dry cleaning. In *A v R*, Streeter J was clear that if someone were to spit on a wedding dress, that would likely amount to 'damage', whilst the raincoat in that case was 'a service raincoat designed to resist the elements'.

in practice

An interesting point that you may wish to consider is whether the victim of criminal damage would wish to use the property again, despite the lack of damage or the ease in removing the damage. Let us take, for example, a defendant who urinates on a victim's mobile phone. Unless damage is caused to the inner workings of the phone, it is likely, similarly to *A (a juvenile) v R*, that the urine could easily be cleaned from the phone. However, that particular victim may never wish to use that phone again on the basis that it has been urinated on. In this regard, do you think the court would find there to be criminal damage?

Impairment of value or usefulness

An additional explanation of the meaning of 'damage' has been seen in cases such as *Morphitis v Salmon* [1990] Crim LR 48 and *R v Fiak* [2005] EWCA Crim 2381. In both cases, the courts referred to the impairment, either permanent or temporary, of the value or usefulness of the property. You will note the phraseology is 'value *or* usefulness' – either one of these is sufficient and in many cases only one will be proven. For example, suppose Jack scratches Jill's car bonnet. In this case, the value of the car has been impaired but its usefulness has not (a scratch on the bonnet will not ordinarily make a difference to how the car is used).

case example

Charge:
Criminal damage (CDA 1971, s 1)

Case progression:
Crown Court – Guilty

Court of Appeal – Conviction upheld

Point of law:
Meaning of 'damage'

In *R v Fiak* [2005] EWCA Crim 2381, the defendant, a prisoner, stuffed his blanket into the toilet of a police station and flushed repeatedly. This caused a flood in his and two adjoining cells.

The defendant was charged with and convicted of criminal damage in the Crown Court.

The defendant appealed to the Court of Appeal on the basis that the flood did not constitute 'damage'. The Court of Appeal disagreed, finding that not only was time and expense required to put the property back into the position it was before, but also the property was temporarily useless and had lost its value.

Specifically, the Court of Appeal found there to be damage in the following ways:

- to the blanket – it was unusable until it had been cleaned and dried out;
- to the cells – they were unusable until they were cleaned out.

The Court of Appeal confirmed that it is not necessary to find both an impairment of usefulness *and* value.

A common example given of impairing usefulness is the removal of parts from a machine or structure. By removal of those parts, the machine cannot function/the structure cannot be used and thus its value or usefulness has been impaired. This was the issue in *Morphitis* in which the defendant dismantled a scaffold pole by removing a clip and a bar. Neither the clip nor the bar had been damaged. The Divisional Court ruled that the removal of a part could constitute damage if it impaired the value of the article as a whole. Auld J would explain:

> where the owner is left, albeit temporarily, with an incomplete article which does not fully serve the purpose that it did before the removal of the part, there has clearly been damage to the article as a whole.

Other examples demonstrating this point can be identified here:

- *R v Tacey* (1821) Russ & Ry 452: stocking frame (on a sewing machine) damaged by removal of essential part rendering it inoperative;
- *R v Fisher* (1865) LR 1 CCR 7: disabling a steam engine by tampering with a key part of it, though no part was removed or broken;
- *Getty v Antrim County Council* (1950) NIR 114: dismantling a plough (and with no damage to any of the dismantled parts) was damage to the plough.

in practice

Care must be taken when drafting a charge of criminal damage in these cases. In *Mortiphis*, the Divisional Court quashed the defendant's conviction on account that he had been charged with damage to the individual parts he had removed. Auld J explained that had he been charged with damage to the entire unit (through an impairment of its use), the defendant could have been properly convicted. In that regard, one must be clear: is the prosecution alleging damage to the parts removed, or damage to the 'larger object'? See *R v Woodcock* [1977] Crim LR 104.

A third category – denial of use?

An interesting string of cases in this area is in relation to the wheel-clamping of a car. In both *Lloyd v DPP* [1992] 1 All ER 982 and *Drake v DPP* [1994] RTR 411, it was held that the placing of a wheel clamp on a car did not constitute criminal damage as it did not impair the integrity of the car (nor did the affixing of a large yellow sticker to the windscreen in *Lloyd*). Indeed, the Divisional Court in *Drake* was clear that clamping the car did not constitute damage as it did not involve 'intrusion into the integrity of the object'. Ormerod and Laird (*Smith, Hogan, & Ormerod's Criminal Law*, 15th edn (OUP, 2018)) justify these decisions on the basis that a mere denial of use is not sufficient to found a case for criminal damage. This argument runs contrary to the views of Smith and Wilson. Smith, in his commentary on *Lloyd v DPP*, argues that

> if a car can be damaged by removing something, it seems logical that it can damaged by adding something. The effect of attaching the clamp is no less drastic than removing the rotor arm.

Further, Wilson (*Criminal Law*, 7th edn (Pearson, 2020)) argues that 'such a denial of use should always amount to criminal damage where normal use cannot be restored without significant remedial attention …'. Should one follow Smith and Wilson's view, it would be necessary to ensure that lawful interferences such as wheel-clamping, for example in a situation where an individual has failed to pay their road tax, are considered as giving rise to a lawful excuse in s 5.

Naturally, had the wheel clamp been attached negligently, such that it caused some form of damage to the tyre or wheel arch, then there will be sufficient damage for the purposes of the Act. Likewise, should a defendant try to remove a wheel clamp and damage it in the process, he may be liable for criminal damage to the clamp.

example

Suppose Jack stole Jill's house keys. By stealing these keys, Jill is unable to access her house. Given that Jill is deprived of access to her home, could this be considered 'damage'? This would certainly not be a natural reading of the word 'damage'. Following *R v Fiak* [2005] EWCA Crim 2381 though, this example could be arguable.

So, what is 'damage'?

From the above, it can be concluded that neither interpretation of 'damage' trumps the other. Rather, it is best to understand damage in the following way:

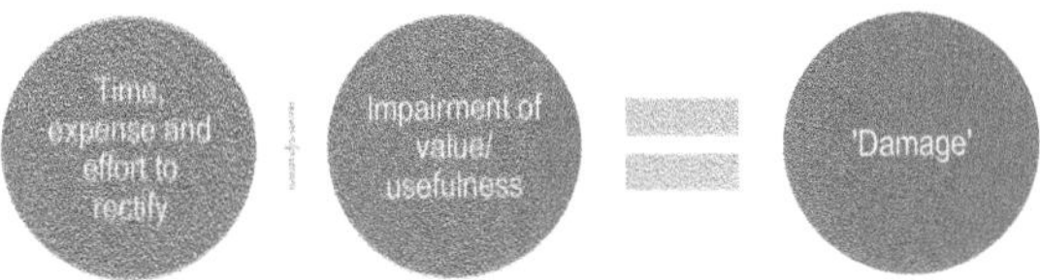

Figure 14.1 Understanding 'damage'

example

Jack, a traffic warden, places a large sticker on Jill's windscreen to inform her that she has parked illegally. Jill struggles to remove the sticker from the windscreen, taking a number of minutes to do so. Upon removing the sticker, a large opaque, sticky residue is left on the windscreen.

Jack in this instance has clearly caused 'damage' in accordance with the above definition, given that:

- Jill had to exercise time, expense and effort in removing the sticker; and
- the sticky residue left on the windscreen will result in an impairment of value or usefulness of the car should the residue not be possible to remove.

With the interpretation of 'damage' now in mind, have a look at some of the cases listed below and assess whether there was 'damage' to the property:

- *Roper v Knott* [1898] 1 QB 868: milk contaminated with water;
- *Roe v Kingerlee* [1986] Crim LR 735: smearing mud on the walls of a police cell; and
- *Blake v DPP* [1993] Crim LR 586: writing a biblical quotation on a concrete pillar.

Damaging computer programs

A number of cases have arisen concerning damage to computer programs. First, in *Cox v Riley* (1986) 83 Cr App R 54, the Divisional Court found that a plastic circuit card for controlling a computerised saw had been damaged by the erasure of the programs written on it (despite the fact that the programs were intangible). Further to this, in *R v Whiteley* (1991) 93 Cr App R 25, the Court of Appeal found that a computer disk had been 'damaged' as a result of the addition and deletion of files. The defendant in *Whiteley* argued that he could not have 'damaged' the computer disks given that any damage could only be said to have been done to the intangible files (which would fall outside of the definition of 'property' in s 10). Lord Lane CJ disagreed, however, finding that:

> It seems to us that that contention contains a basic fallacy. What the Act requires to be proved is that tangible property has been damaged, not necessarily that the damage itself should be tangible.

Although these cases remain useful in understanding the definition of 'damage', they are largely irrelevant to the law under discussion as such offences are now covered by s 3 of the Computer Misuse Act 1990 (see s 3(6)).

Relevance of the type of property

It is also pertinent to note that the question of damage must be considered in light of the type of property affected. For example, in *Morphitis v Salmon* [1990] Crim LR 48, the Divisional Court ruled that a scratch to a scaffold bar did not constitute damage given that it involved no impairment as to its value or usefulness. The Divisional Court particularly emphasised that scratching and other basic scuffs were 'an ordinary incident of its existence' and could not be considered damage (per Auld J). Helpfully, this case could be compared with the scratching of a car bonnet, which naturally would result in a reduction of value should the individual wish to sell the car on in the future, and any work to fix the problem may cost a substantial sum of money.

Damage or improvement?

An interesting case to come before the courts was that of *R v Fancy* [1980] Crim LR 171.

case example

Charge:
Possessing an article with intent (CDA 1971, s 3)

Case progression:
Crown Court –
Not guilty

Point of law:
Improvements to property capable of amounting to 'damage'

In *R v Fancy* [1980] Crim LR 171, the defendant was found in possession of a bucket of paint and a paint roller. The defendant had admitted that he had painted over (whitewashed) National Front slogans on walls. At trial, the Crown Court found there to be no case to answer against the defendant, on the basis that it was not satisfied that applying white paint over 'mindless National Front graffiti could constitute damage to a wall *per se*'.

McNair J appeared to be of the opinion that where the defendant's actions would amount to an 'improvement' to the property, then there would be no criminal damage. The improvement in this case would be the removal of National Front graffiti.

Ormerod and Laird (*Smith, Hogan, & Ormerod's Criminal Law*, 15th edn (OUP, 2018)) are critical of the decision in *Fancy*, arguing:

> The defendant's opinion that what he did was not damage is irrelevant if damage is caused in law and fact. V's wall is damaged by D's graffiti irrespective of whether D regards it as an improvement.

On this understanding, the application of white paint would amount to criminal damage on top of the existing criminal damage caused by the National Front graffiti. In both instances, a significant amount of time and effort would have to be exercised in order to remove the white paint, and the graffiti. Jefferson (*Criminal Law*, 12th edn (Pearson, 2015)) raises an excellent point in this respect, arguing that '[t]he wall was already white and it is arguable that there was no intent to cause criminal damage'. Jefferson's view is rather interesting here, as it could be asked whether the defendant was in fact *damaging* the wall, or whether he was *restoring* it to its original state. Ultimately, this would turn on a question as to whether the defendant's actions can be considered as 'damaging' the wall. I would submit that, although it might be said that the defendant is *restoring* the wall to its original state, it is not *his* wall to restore (ie it is not his property). Therefore, any application of paint – whether it be for graffiti purposes or restoration – should be considered as 'damage'.

in practice

Whether a prosecutor takes the view that the defendant's actions were an improvement or not, the likely outcome is that the defendant will be liable for criminal damage. However, it is very unlikely for the CPS to consider the charging of a defendant with an offence in such circumstances as being within the public interest.

With these cases in mind, a number of academics have questioned the extent to which the courts will go when finding there to be 'damage'. Alldridge ('Incontinent Dogs and the Law' (1990) 140 NLJ 1067) questions whether dog droppings would be considered 'damage' under the law in circumstances where money is spent to clean up such mess. Further to this, Edwards ('Banksy's Graffiti: A Not So Simple Case' (2009) 73 J Crim L 345) questions whether graffiti in the form of art may be classed as 'damage' also. Gomez ('The Writing on Our Walls: Finding Solutions through Distinguishing Graffiti Art from Graffiti Vandalism' (1993) 26 University of Michigan Journal of Law Reform 633) discusses this point in great detail and argues that 'all graffiti is vandalism regardless of a piece's artistic value' but questions whether the terms 'vandalism' and 'damage' are synonymous. A further example is that of chewing gum. The disposal of chewing gum on the pavement may be considered littering, dependent on the byelaw in place in that local government area; however, where the chewing gum requires time, effort and money to remove, surely this too ought to amount to 'damage'?

in practice

Ensure that you consider criminal damage practically. Although it is a very common offence, it is hard to regulate and enforce unless evidence is submitted to suggest it was the defendant who damaged the property. Specifically, in relation to chewing gum on the floor, how would the prosecution prove that a particular piece of gum on the floor is that of the defendant, amongst the hundreds of other pieces on the floor? This lack of certainty may give rise to evidential difficulty for the prosecution.

14.2.2.2 *Actus reus:* (ii) property

Section 10 of the CDA 1971 provides:

> (1) In this Act 'property' means property of a tangible nature, whether real or personal, including money and—
> (a) including wild creatures which have been tamed or are ordinarily kept in captivity, and any other wild creatures or their carcasses if, but only if, they have been reduced into possession which has not been lost or abandoned or are in the course of being reduced into possession; but
> (b) not including mushrooms growing wild on any land or flowers, fruit or foliage of a plant growing wild on any land.
>
> For the purposes of this subsection 'mushroom' includes any fungus and 'plant' includes any shrub or tree.

This terminology is similar to that under the law of theft, considered in **Chapter 11**, with three major exceptions, namely:

- Section 10 is wider than the Theft Act definition in that it includes land. Therefore, whilst land cannot ordinarily be stolen under the TA 1968, it can be damaged, for example, by dumping chemicals on it (see *Gayford v Choulder* [1898] 1 QB 316 where D trampled grass).

- Section 10 is narrower than the Theft Act definition in that wild plants/fungi will not be property for the purposes of criminal damage (s 10(1)(b)).
- Section 10 is also narrower than the Theft Act definition in that property does not include intangibles or choses in action. Therefore, copyright cannot be damaged, for example, by infringing it. This has led some commentators, such as Lacey and Wells (*Reconstructing Criminal Law*, 4th edn (CUP 2010)), to comment that 'the image of criminal damage which the Act reproduces is the image of the destruction of tangible goods – the smashed bus shelter, the indelible inner city graffiti, the vandalised car …'.

For an interesting case dealing with the concept of 'property', we can observe *Cresswell v DPP* [2006] EWHC 3379 (Admin) in which the defendants destroyed four badger traps that had been placed by the Department for Environment, Food and Rural Affairs (DEFRA). The defendants contended that they were acting with lawful excuse (see below) in the protection of the badgers. In order to rely on lawful excuse, however, the badgers would have to amount to 'property' in need of immediate protection (see s 5(2)(b) below). On this point, Keene LJ would conclude:

> The Crown Court was in my judgment right to hold that one has to be able to identify with some degree of precision which animal or animals are in the course of being reduced into possession. One has to be able to distinguish those which are in that state from those which are not. In the present case, matters had not reached the stage where that could be done. The evidence was that one could not tell whether the badgers ultimately caught had already visited the trap for food or not. Some, it seems, would have done but others not. In that situation, one cannot identify which badgers were in the course of being reduced into possession until the stage is reached where a badger or badgers are at least in the process of entering a set trap. I therefore conclude that the Crown Court was right to hold that the badgers in this field could not be regarded as 'property' within the meaning of s 10.

14.2.2.3 *Actus reus:* (iii) belonging to another

Section 10 of the CDA 1971 also provides:

> (2) Property shall be treated for the purposes of this Act as belonging to any person—
> (a) having the custody or control of it;
> (b) having in it any proprietary right or interest (not being an equitable interest arising only from an agreement to transfer or grant an interest); or
> (c) having a charge on it.
>
> (3) Where property is subject to a trust, the persons to whom it belongs shall be so treated as including any person having a right to enforce the trust.
>
> (4) Property of a corporation sole shall be so treated as belonging to the corporation notwithstanding a vacancy in the corporation.
>
> (5) For the purposes of this Act a modification of the contents of a computer shall not be regarded as damaging any computer or computer storage medium unless its effect on that computer or computer storage medium impairs its physical condition.

Property must belong 'to another'

By the operation of s 10, a defendant cannot be liable for basic criminal damage in cases where he destroys or damages his own property. Should Jack knock down his own garden shed or destroy his phone by throwing it against a wall, he will not be liable for criminal damage. However, where this property belongs to another, such as his neighbour Jill, Jack may be liable.

Extent of belonging to another

Section 10(2) has the effect that the owner of property may be guilty of criminal damage to his own property if at the time it also belongs to someone else within the extended meaning of s 10. The victim need not, therefore, be the owner of the property. Rather, they may simply have some sort of proprietary interest in the property (eg having custody or control of it – s 10(2)).

The Divisional Court ruled, in *Seray-Wurie v DPP* [2012] EWHC 208 (Admin), that a defendant is capable of destroying his own property, so long as some other person has physical custody over the item, holds a proprietary interest in it, for example where there is joint ownership of an asset, or holds a charge over it. The CPS offers the following example in its 'Legal Guidance on Criminal Damage':

> [I]f a person sets fire to his own house which is subject to a mortgage, he can still be charged under Section 1(1) and (3) as the mortgagor will have a proprietary right or interest in the property.

example

Jack lends his car to his friend, Jill, so that she can drive her friend to the airport. Whilst in her possession, Jack removes the wing mirror from the car as a practical joke.

In this instance, although Jack may not be liable for an offence given the clear lack of *mens rea*, Jack has nonetheless damaged property belonging to another. At the time of the damage, the property was in the possession of Jill, and she can be considered as holding a proprietary right (a bailment) over the car at the time.

14.2.2.4 *Actus reus:* (iv) without lawful excuse

The final element of the *actus reus* is a surrounding circumstance that must be present in all cases, ie the defendant acted without lawful excuse. In essence, the defendant must act unlawfully and without a defence to the charge against him. In that respect, s 5 of the CDA 1971 provides two defences, specific to basic criminal damage.

It is important to note at this stage that s 5(1) makes clear that the defence applies only to basic criminal damage and offences under ss 2 and 3 (threatening to destroy or damage property and possessing anything with intent to destroy or damage property respectively); these defences do not apply to the aggravated forms of criminal damage under s 1(2) and (3).

Section 5(2) provides that:

> A person charged with an offence to which this section applies, shall, whether or not he would be treated for the purposes of this Act as having a lawful excuse apart from this subsection, be treated for those purposes as having a lawful excuse—

(a) if at the time of the act or acts alleged to constitute the offence he believed that the person or persons whom he believed to be entitled to consent to the destruction of or damage to the property in question had so consented, or would have so consented to it if he or they had known of the destruction or damage and its circumstances; or

(b) if he destroyed or damaged or threatened to destroy or damage the property in question or, in the case of a charge of an offence under section 3 above, intended to use or cause or permit the use of something to destroy or damage it, in order to protect property belonging to himself or another or a right or interest in property which was or which he believed to be vested in himself or another, and at the time of the act or acts alleged to constitute the offence he believed—

(i) that the property, right or interest was in immediate need of protection; and

(ii) that the means of protection adopted or proposed to be adopted were or would be reasonable having regard to all the circumstances.

These lawful excuses can be simply set out as follows:

Figure 14.2 Lawful excuse to basic criminal damage

The prosecution bears the legal burden of proving beyond a reasonable doubt that the defendant did *not* have a lawful excuse to damage property. However, the defendant has an evidential burden of adducing some evidence to raise the issue before the arbiters of fact. In this respect, the Court of Appeal in *R v Cairns* [2013] EWCA Crim 172 emphasised that the offence is *not* one of 'destroying or damaging property without the consent of the owner'. King J would explain:

> What the prosecution had to prove was that the applicant had no lawful excuse for what he did if such unlawful excuse were raised by him or were raised on the evidence before the jury.

We shall consider the two excuses in more detail now.

Honest belief in consent (CDA 1971, s 5(2)(a))

The defence in s 5(2)(a) is subjective in that it looks towards the honest belief held by the defendant. This 'honest belief in consent' may manifest itself in a number of different ways:

- D honestly believes that he *has* been given consent to damage or destroy property by the owner of the property;
- D honestly believes that he has been given consent to damage or destroy property by someone whom he honestly, but mistakenly, believes is the owner of the property (or who is able to give consent);
- D honestly believes that he *would have* been given consent to damage or destroy property by the owner of the property (or someone he genuinely believed to be the

owner) had the owner known of the circumstances in which the property was destroyed or damaged.

Importantly, s 5(3) provides that 'it is immaterial whether a belief is justified or not if it is honestly held'. Therefore, the belief need not be reasonable or justified, so long as it is genuinely and honestly held.

The key authority on s 5(2)(a) is that of *Jaggard v Dickinson* [1981] QB 527.

case example

Charge:
Criminal damage (CDA 1971, s 1)

Case progression:
Magistrates' Court – Guilty

Divisional Court – Conviction quashed

Point of law:
Honest belief in consent

In *Jaggard v Dickinson* [1981] QB 527, the defendant broke two windows and damaged a curtain in the victim's home. The defendant was intoxicated and mistakenly believed she was damaging the property of her friend (not the victim). The defendant was charged with and convicted of criminal damage in the magistrates' court. This was so despite her belief that her friend would have consented to her damaging property.

The Divisional Court allowed the appeal, ruling that the defendant genuinely and honestly held this belief in consent, despite it being directed at the wrong property and that it was clearly an unreasonable belief.

In the Divisional Court, Mustill J commented that:

> the court is required by section 5(3) to focus on the existence of the belief, not its intellectual soundness; and a belief can be just as much honestly held if it is induced by intoxication, as if it stems from stupidity, forgetfulness or inattention.

This was reaffirmed in *R v Denton* [1982] 1 All ER 65, where the Court of Appeal held that the defendant was not liable for criminal damage where he honestly believed that the owner of a mill had encouraged him to burn the mill down. *Denton* is authority for the point that the reason for the provision of consent (eg to perpetrate a fraud as in *Denton*) is irrelevant (see Lord Lane CJ's comments on this in *Denton*). Note, however, that a defendant is unable to claim that God commanded him to damage property, given that God is not a 'person' capable of giving consent under s 5(2)(a) (*Blake v DPP* [1993] Crim LR 586 – the better defence there may be to claim insanity).

Jaggard is a useful (and controversial) authority to observe that intoxication will not prevent a defendant from claiming a lawful excuse. Importantly, his intoxication will not prevent him from relying upon a defence; however, it cannot be used to argue that he lacked *mens rea* given that reckless criminal damage is a basic intent offence (see below). On this point, *Jaggard* has been doubted by the Divisional Court in *Magee v CPS* [2014] EWHC 4089 (Admin). See **7.4.8.1** for a fuller discussion.

Other property in need of protection (CDA 1971, s 5(2)(b))

Section 5(2)(b) is concerned with the imminent protection of property (the imminent protection of a person is therefore not sufficient – *R v Baker and Wilkins* [1997] Crim LR 497).

The Divisional Court in *Johnson v DPP* [1994] Crim LR 673 ruled that the test under s 5(2)(b) requires a two-stage approach to be laid out before the arbiters of fact, namely:

(i) whether the act of damage was done in order to protect property (objective); and
(ii) whether the defendant believed that the property was in need of immediate protection and that the means of protection were reasonable (subjective).

Section 5(2)(b) therefore requires both a subjective and objective test to be applied by the arbiters of fact.

The objective test

First, the act must be done *in order to* protect property. The use of the words 'in order to' were emphasised by the Court of Appeal in *R v Hunt* (1977) 66 Cr App R 105 as importing an objective test. In *Hunt*, the defendant set fire to some bedding in a care home in order to demonstrate that the fire alarms were not working. The Court of Appeal made it clear that the damaging of property had to be *in order to* protect property. According to Roskill LJ, as he then was:

> The question whether or not a particular act of destruction or damage or threat of destruction or damage was done or made in order to protect property belonging to another must be, on the true construction of the statute, an objective test. Therefore we have to ask ourselves whether, whatever the state of this man's mind and assuming an honest belief, that which he admittedly did was done in order to protect this particular property, namely the old people's home in Hertfordshire? . . .
>
> [The defendant's act] was not done in order to protect property; it was done in order to draw attention to the defective state of the fire alarm. It was not an act which in itself did protect or was capable of protecting property.

This objective approach was endorsed by the Court of Appeal in *R v Ashford* [1988] Crim LR 682 and *R v Hall; R v Hill* (1989) 89 Cr App R 74.

Charge:
Possessing an article with intent to damage property (CDA 1971, s 3)

Case progression:
Crown Court – Guilty

Court of Appeal – Conviction upheld

Point of law:
Other property in need of protection

In *R v Hall; R v Hill* (1989) 89 Cr App R 74, the defendants damaged the fence of a US naval base in England, believing that to do so would protect their own property from nuclear war.

The defendants were charged with and convicted in the Crown Court of possessing an article with intent to damage property. Their convictions were upheld in the Court of Appeal on the basis that the defendants' acts were too remote from the eventual harm they were protecting the property from to fall within a lawful excuse.

For an interesting comparison with *Hall and Hill*, see *R v Kelleher* [2003] EWCA Crim 2846, where the defendant decapitated a statute of Margaret Thatcher in protest at her policies, which he believed were taking the world to its eventual doom. The Court of Appeal upheld his conviction on the grounds that he was not protecting property in his actions. For a persuasive argument that this first limb ought to be considered subjectively, see Ormerod and Laird, *Smith, Hogan, & Ormerod's Criminal Law*, 15th edn (OUP 2018).

In *R v Jones* [2005] QB 259, one matter put before the Court of Appeal was whether the defendants' acts were necessary to prevent *unlawful* damage to property. In that case, the defendants had entered an airbase and caused damage therein in an attempt to prevent that base from being used to support the war in Iraq. Counsel for the Crown contended that the jury had to be sure, as a second objective matter, that the act was done to prevent unlawful damage in order for the defence to apply (the war being a legal act). Finding against this, Latham LJ ruled:

> Whilst there are clearly strong policy arguments for imposing such a further restriction on the availability of the defence, the fact is that the statute does not so provide. Subject to the one objective element to which we have referred, the court and the jury are concerned simply with the question of a defendant's honestly held beliefs. It follows that no issue can arise in relation to this defence which involves consideration of the legality of the war in Iraq.

This matter did not arise when *Jones* was appealed to the House of Lords ([2006] UKHL 16).

The subjective test

Once the arbiters of fact are satisfied that the first objective element of the defence has been made out, they are then to turn their attention to the subjective question which asks whether the defendant believed that property was in imminent need of protection, and that he believed the means adopted to defend that property in immediate peril were 'reasonable in all the circumstances'. The means adopted need not actually be reasonable; the question is whether the defendant *believed* the means adopted to be reasonable. As with s 5(2)(a), therefore, the belief need not be reasonably held; it must, however, be genuinely held (s 5(3)).

Cresswell v DPP

A difficult case, and one ripe with controversy, is that of *Cresswell v DPP* [2006] EWHC 3379 (Admin). This case was considered above in the context of 'property' (see **14.2.2.2**).

This case is worthy of a separate section in the text given the Divisional Court's approach to the issue of lawful excuse. As noted above, the Divisional Court concluded that the badgers could not be classed as 'property' for the purposes of the 1971 Act. In addition, however, Keene LJ ruled that the defence of lawful excuse could not be used to destroy or damage another person's property in order to prevent the owner of that property from damaging or destroying it himself. Specifically, Keene LJ reasoned:

> It is not the purpose of s 5(2), as I see it, to prevent the owner of property from destroying it or damaging it if he wishes to do so, unless that in itself is an unlawful act (in which case another defence will arise) or someone in addition has some interest in the property in question.

The defence does not apply, therefore, where the damage or destruction is done to X's property to prevent X from damaging or destroying that property (ie the defence does not apply when the damaged property, and the property being protected, belongs to the same person). Walker LJ, in his judgment in *Cresswell v DPP*, would express some disagreement with this conclusion but did not wish to rule on the matter.

Operation of general defences

It is important to note that the defences under s 5 operate without prejudice to any of the general defences we have discussed in **Chapter 7** (CDA 1971, s 5(5)). As a result of s 5(5), a person cannot be liable for criminal damage where their actions arose out of (for example):

- duress;
- necessity; or

- public/private defence.

example

Jill was kidnapped by Jack, who was holding her hostage in the cellar of his house. While Jack was away, Jill managed to escape but only by breaking a number of windows in Jack's house.

Although unlikely to ever reach a trial court, Jill has technically committed criminal damage through her destruction of Jack's windows. However, Jill would have no difficultly in arguing that her actions were *necessary* in the circumstances, the necessity being her own preservation.

14.2.2.5 *Mens rea:* (i) intention or recklessness as to damage/destruction

It is important to note that the *mens rea* is not simply 'intention or recklessness' in doing an act. Instead, the *mens rea* contains two vital elements. First, the intention or recklessness as to the damage or destruction of property, and, secondly, that the defendant knew or believed the property to belong to someone else.

Intention and recklessness have both been discussed in **Chapter 3**. Intention simply requires the defendant to intend (by way of 'aim, objective and purpose') to destroy or damage property. Recklessness is now to be understood as *Cunningham* recklessness following the case of *R v G* [2004] 1 AC 1034. According to Lord Bingham in the House of Lords (adopting the meaning of recklessness given in the Law Commission's Draft Criminal Code (Law Com No 177, 1989)) in *R v G*, the test for recklessness is as follows:

> A person acts recklessly within the meaning of section 1 of the Criminal Damage Act 1971 with respect to:
> (i) A circumstance when he is aware of a risk that it exists or will exist;
> (ii) A result when he/she is aware of a risk that it will occur; and
> (iii) It is, in the circumstances known to him, unreasonable to take the risk.

It is important to appreciate the limits of the *mens rea* in this instance. The *mens rea* only involves intention that the defendant's actions will cause damage; it does not include intention to do an act which incidentally caused damage – though, of course, the defendant may be reckless in this instance.

example

Jack is furious with Jill after an argument the pair had. Jack goes outside to cool down but in his anger kicks the door of Jill's car. He does not do so with the intention to cause damage; he does so merely out of frustration.

In this case, Jack would not have the intention to cause damage to Jill's car. His actions were purely out of rage and involved no intention (ie 'aim, objective and purpose') to damage the car. A court would not struggle, however, to find that Jack was reckless in his actions – thus fulfilling the first *mens rea* element regardless.

An important point to note is that it is irrelevant that the defendant does not believe what he is doing is causing criminal damage. So long as the defendant intends the end result, he is liable for criminal damage. This was evident in the case of *Seray-Wurie v DPP* [2012] EWHC 208 (Admin) where the defendant wrote on two parking notices with black marker pens. The defendant accepted that he did the act but did not realise that such an action constituted 'damage'. On appeal, the Divisional Court ruled that the defendant was liable for criminal damage given that he held a clear intention to do the writing which caused the damage. It was irrelevant that he did not believe that such actions constituted 'damage'. Lloyd Jones J concluded that:

> I am entirely satisfied that there is ample evidence from which the Crown Court could infer that the appellant foresaw a risk of damaging the signs by writing on them. Not only was this an obvious risk in itself, but the appellant having done the same thing before was aware that the cleaning up operation on that earlier occasion had failed to erase all traces of the pen.

14.2.2.6 *Mens rea:* (ii) knowledge or belief that property belonged to another

This final element is included to allow for the defendant to avoid liability where he was mistaken as to the ownership of the property in question. This was the key principle arising out of *R v Smith* [1974] QB 354.

case example

Charge:
Criminal damage (CDA 1971, s 1)

Case progression:
Crown Court – Guilty

Court of Appeal – Conviction quashed

Point of law:
Need to know that property belonged to another

In *R v Smith* [1974] QB 354, the defendant, a tenant, removed a long piece of wiring from the property causing £130 worth of damage. The defendant had installed the wiring and thus believed it to be his. Unbeknownst to him, under civil law, the wiring once installed then belonged to the landlord.

The defendant was charged with and convicted of criminal damage in the Crown Court. His conviction was quashed in the Court of Appeal given that the defendant neither knew nor believed the property to belong to anyone but him. As a result, the defendant lacked the *mens rea.*

James LJ held:

> Applying the ordinary principles of mens rea, the intention and recklessness and the absence of lawful excuse required to constitute the offence have reference to property belonging to another. It follows that in our judgment no offence is committed under this section if a person destroys or causes damage to property belonging to another if he does so in the honest though mistaken belief that the property is his own, and provided that the belief is honestly held it is irrelevant to consider whether or not it is a justifiable belief.

As a result of *Smith*, a mistaken belief that an individual is damaging his own property, not subject to further ownership under s 10, will negate liability on the basis that he lacks the necessary *mens rea.*

in practice

An interesting point to consider is to return to our example of the graffiti artist. Although the 'artwork' will be considered 'damage' where it causes time, effort and expense to put right, do you think the graffiti artist would have the necessary *mens rea* for the offence? Can it be said that in creating the art, they *intended* to cause damage? If not, could it be said that they were *reckless* in doing so?

In practice, the court would be required to make a fine distinction between cases of intention and non-intention in order to avoid inconsistency in approach.

14.2.3 Elements of aggravated criminal damage

Section 1(2) of the CDA 1971 provides:

> A person who without lawful excuse destroys or damages any property, whether belonging to himself or another—
> (a) intending to destroy or damage any property or being reckless as to whether any property would be destroyed or damaged; and
> (b) intending by the destruction or damage to endanger the life of another or being reckless as to whether the life of another would be thereby endangered;
>
> shall be guilty of an offence.

The *actus reus* and *mens rea* of aggravated criminal damage are outlined in **Table 14.3**.

Table 14.3 Elements of aggravated criminal damage

AR/MR	Elements of the offence
Actus reus	(i) destroys or damages; (ii) property; (iii) without lawful excuse.
Mens rea	(i) intention or recklessness as to damage/destruction; and (ii) intention or recklessness as to endangering life.

14.2.3.1 *Actus reus* elements

The *actus reus* elements of aggravated criminal damage are identical to basic criminal damage, as is the first requirement of the *mens rea*. The key distinction between the basic and aggravated form can be noted as follows:

- the property need not belong to another in a case of aggravated criminal damage (the defendant may destroy or damage his own property – see *R v Maitland-Thomas* [2013] EWCA Crim 1063);
- the lawful excuse defence under s 5(2) does not apply to aggravated criminal damage (see *R v Merrick* [1996] 1 Cr App R 130). Reference to 'without lawful excuse' in s 1(2) simply means that the defendant may rely on general defences – see **Chapter 7**); and
- there is a need for the defendant to intend to endanger life, or be reckless as to endangering life, in order to be liable for aggravated criminal damage.

It is the last of these three points that we shall now consider in further detail.

14.2.3.2 *Mens rea:* (ii) intention or recklessness as to endangering life

Under s 1(2), a defendant may be liable for an offence in four circumstances:

(i) where he intends to destroy or damage property *and* intends to endanger the life of another;

(ii) where he intends to destroy or damage property *and* is reckless as to the thought of endangering the life of another;

(iii) where he is reckless to the destruction or damage of property *and* intends to endanger the life of another;

(iv) where he is reckless to the destruction or damage of property *and* is reckless as to the thought of endangering the life of another.

No need for *actual* harm to be caused

It is imperative to note that the requirement of intention or recklessness under the *mens rea* is ulterior, in that it is not met by a corresponding *actus reus*. Therefore, it is irrelevant whether any lives were *actually* placed in danger (*R v Parker* [1993] Crim LR 856) so long as the defendant *intended* to endanger life or was *reckless* as to endangering life.

Endangering life of *another*

What should be clear from the above list is that the defendant must intend to endanger or be reckless as to endangering the life of another. Whether the defendant intends to endanger his own life is irrelevant. This was confirmed by the Court of Appeal in *R v Thakar* [2010] EWCA Crim 2136 where the defendant, in a state of depression following divorce, set fire to his own car with him inside. The defendant appreciated the danger to his own life but was ignorant of the danger to any other lives. Therefore, the defendant was not liable for an offence.

in practice

The CPS in its 'Legal Guidance on Criminal Damage' advises:

> Where the defendant's intention or recklessness is obvious, just one offence may be charged. Where, as is common, the position is less clear, both offences should be charged in the alternative. If the defendant is convicted of the more serious offence (involving intent) the jury should be discharged from giving a verdict on the lesser charge.

Endangering life *by the damage or destruction*

The key authority on endangering life is that of *R v Steer* [1988] AC 111.

Charge:
Criminal Damage (CDA 1971, s 1)

Case progression:
Crown Court – Guilty

Court of Appeal – Conviction quashed

House of Lords – Appeal dismissed

Point of law:
Nexus between intention to destroy/damage and endangering life

In *R v Steer* [1988] AC 111, the defendant shot a rifle at the window of the victim's house, with whom he held a grudge.

The defendant was charged with and convicted in the Crown Court of aggravated criminal damage on the basis that he intended to break the windows and foresaw endangerment of life to the victim.

His conviction was quashed by the Court of Appeal which held that, although the defendant was reckless as to endangering the victim's life, he was only reckless as to his actions in shooting the rifle. The defendant was not reckless as to the victim's life 'by the destruction or damage of property' (ie the broken glass). The Crown appealed to the House of Lords, which dismissed the appeal following the reasoning of the Court of Appeal.

Lord Bridge concluded:

> Upon the true construction of section 1(2)(b) of the Criminal Damage Act 1971 the prosecution are required to prove that the danger to life resulted from the destruction of or damage to property; it is not sufficient for the prosecution to prove that it resulted from the act of the defendant which caused the destruction or damage.

This case may, at first, appear difficult to get one's head around. Essentially, the House of Lords, in reaffirming the decision of the Court of Appeal, held that for an offence under s 1(2), the prosecution must prove that the danger to life resulted from the *actual* destruction of, or damage to, property. This is essentially a question of causation, asking whether the defendant intended to endanger or was reckless as to endangering life, *as a result of* the damage or destruction of property (eg the broken window in *Steer*). It is not sufficient that the danger resulted from another act which caused the destruction or damage (eg the shot fired in *Steer*).

Steer was distinguished by the Court of Appeal in *R v Dudley* [1989] Crim LR 57, where the defendant was found guilty under s 1(2) in circumstances where he threw a fire-bomb at a house. Thankfully, the occupants were able to extinguish the fire before it caused more than the minor damage it had caused up to that point. Distinguishing *Steer*, the Court of Appeal held that the words 'destruction or damage' in s 1(2)(b) mean the intended or reckless destruction or damage of property as referred to in s 1(2)(a), not the actual damage caused.

This distinction is a fine one, and often difficult to make. The best way to understand it is to think of the danger to life being *caused by* the damaged property as opposed to *the way in which* it is damaged. We can see this in **Figure 14.3**.

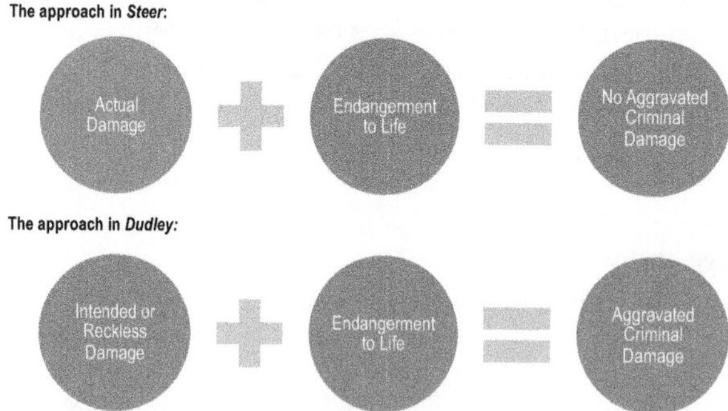

Figure 14.3 Understanding Steer *and* Dudley

This issue was clarified by the Court of Appeal in *R v Webster; R v Warwick* [1995] 2 All ER 168 (also known as *R v Asquith*), where the Court approved the approach in *Dudley* and stated that the 'true construction' of s 1(2) is that the defendant is liable where he intends to endanger or is reckless as to endangering life by the damage that he *intended to cause or was reckless as to the thought of causing* (ie what he envisioned); liability is not to be founded on the *actual* damage caused.

In concluding the Court's judgment, Lord Taylor CJ stated:

> Otherwise, the gravamen of an offence involving damage by a missile would depend not on the defendant's intention but on whether he was a good shot in seeking to carry it out. Thus, if a defendant throws a brick at the windscreen of a moving vehicle, given that he causes *some* damage to the vehicle, whether he is guilty under s 1(2) does not depend on whether the brick hits or misses the windscreen, but whether he intended to hit it and intended that the damage therefrom should endanger life or whether he was reckless as to that outcome.

Lord Taylor CJ refers to this as 'a dismal distinction'; however, such distinction remains necessary in the construction of the Act. The most recent application of this rule was seen in *R v Wenton* [2010] EWCA Crim 2361. In this case, the defendant smashed a window of a house by throwing a brick, before then throwing a petrol cannister in through the window with a lit piece of paper in it. The petrol, however, did not ignite and the occupants of the house were unharmed. The defendant successfully appealed against his conviction for aggravated criminal damage. The Court of Appeal concluded that the damage and intention to endanger life must be of the same act.

Using *Wenton*, this can be explained in the following way. The defendant could only have been liable in *Wenton* if he:

(a) intended or foresaw the endangerment to life caused by smashing the window, *or*
(b) caused damage by throwing in the canister which he intended or foresaw would endanger life.

14.2.4 Elements of basic arson/aggravated arson

Section 1(3) of the CDA 1971 provides:

> An offence committed under this section by destroying or damaging property by fire shall be charged as arson.

Arson was formally an offence charged under the Malicious Damage Act 1861, with ss 1 to 8 concerned with 'injuries by fire to buildings, and goods therein'. Arson, as an offence separate from criminal damage, is preserved as a result of s 1(3) above. The need to charge criminal damage by fire as arson was doubted by the Court of Appeal in *R v Drayton* [2005] EWCA Crim 2013, despite the mandatory wording in s 1(3). However, more recently the Court of Appeal in *R v Wenton* [2010] EWCA Crim 2361 has reminded prosecutors that when property is destroyed or damaged by fire, it must be charged as arson. In *R v Drayton*, a charge alleging 'damage by fire' was held to be acceptable, though Hedley J explained that use of the word 'arson' would have been 'desirable'. Hedley J would justify the importance of charging 'arson' on account that

> the essence of section 1(3), the mischief which it is designed to address, is that the defendant shall know that he is facing an allegation of damage by fire, because by section 1(4) the penalties in relation to damage by fire are different and significantly potentially more severe than those of simple criminal damage by other means.

In its 1970 Report ('Offences of Damage to Property' (Law Com No 29, 1970)), the Law Commission recommended the abolition of the offence of arson as a separate offence. The Law Commission felt there to be no need in maintaining such distinction between damage caused by fire and damage caused otherwise than by fire. This recommendation was not taken forward by the Government, which viewed arson as a special category of offence, stigmatising a defendant who set light to property. Further, the allocation of the maximum penalty for damage by fire remains a prominent argument for keeping the offence.

The *actus reus* and *mens rea* of arson are outlined in **Table 14.4**.

Table 14.4 Elements of arson

AR/MR	Elements of basic arson	Elements of aggravated arson
Actus reus	(i) destroys or damages; (ii) property; (iii) by fire; (iv) without lawful excuse.	(i) destroys or damages; (ii) property; (iii) by fire; (iv) without lawful excuse.

AR/MR	Elements of basic arson	Elements of aggravated arson
Mens rea	(i) intention or recklessness as to damage/destruction by fire; (ii) knowledge or belief that property belonged to another.	(i) intention or recklessness as to damage/destruction by fire; and (ii) intention or recklessness as to endangering life.

Basic arson simply requires all of the elements of s 1(1) to be present; whilst aggravated arson requires all of the elements of s 1(2) to be present. Alongside this, the property must be:

- destroyed or damaged by fire; and
- the defendant must intend or be reckless as to the thought that property would be destroyed or damaged by fire.

14.2.4.1 Destroy or damage by fire

In relation to damage, any sort of damage by fire will be sufficient – this is so whether the damage is caused by a roaring inferno or by a simple flame. A charred piece of wood will be considered as damaged but a blackened piece of wood, caused by smoke, will not be (on this, see *R v Parker* (1839) 9 C & P 45 and *R v Stallion* (1833) 1 Mood CC 398). See *R v Sangha* [1988] 2 All ER 385 for a case concerning aggravated arson.

14.2.4.2 Intention or recklessness regarding the fire

An interesting authority on intention or recklessness is that of *R v Drayton* [2005] EWCA Crim 2013, where the Court of Appeal held that no liability could be held against a defendant where he neither intended nor was reckless as to property being destroyed or damaged by fire where the damage was caused by other actions, which then unexpectedly resulted in fire. Similarly, this principle applies to an individual who aids another to cause damage but is not aware that the damage to be caused is by fire (*R v Cooper (G) and Cooper (Y)* [1991] Crim LR 524). In these cases, liability for criminal damage may still be present, however. In this regard, Williams ('Convictions and Fair Labelling' (1983) 42 CLJ 85) is correct to suggest that the rules of transferred malice would not apply where the defendant intended to damage or destroy property by means other than fire and without foresight of the risk of fire and accidentally starts a fire. Horder ('A Critique of the Correspondence Principle in Criminal Law' [1995] Crim LR 759) furthers this by arguing that it is essential to bear the correspondence principle (discussed in **Chapter 3**) in mind at all times and ask the question, 'Is it right to label D as an arsonist if he did not intend to start a fire ...?'.

As you will remember, the *Miller* ([1983] 2 AC 161) principle (see **Chapter 2**) applies to the same extent to non-fatal offences against the person as it does to damage to property (ie should a defendant create a dangerous situation, such as setting a fire, he has an obligation to put that situation right).

14.2.4.3 Lawful excuse and arson

The lawful excuses provided in s 5 apply to the basic offence of arson, as with basic criminal damage. However, these excuses do not apply to aggravated arson given the endangerment to another's life. General defences do, however, apply to both basic and aggravated arson.

14.2.5 Charging criminal damage

Each offence under the umbrella of criminal damage is to be charged separately. The aggravated and basic forms may be charged in the alternative; however, it is essential that the prosecutor does not charge an offence that is bad for duplicity. According to the Court of Appeal in *R v Booth* [1999] Crim LR 144, where mixed charges are made against a defendant, for example two counts of simple criminal damage and one count of arson, the jury should be directed individually on each charge. Likewise, the jury should return an individual verdict on each charge.

Interestingly, as with the prosecution of theft, should damage be caused to the property of the defendant's spouse or civil partner, no prosecution may be brought without the consent of the Director of Public Prosecutions (TA 1968, s 30(4)).

14.2.5.1 Mode of trial

Whether a case for criminal damage will be heard in the magistrates' court or the Crown Court is dependent on two factors:

- the type of offence; and
- the value of the damage caused.

Figure 14.4 details this on a basic level.

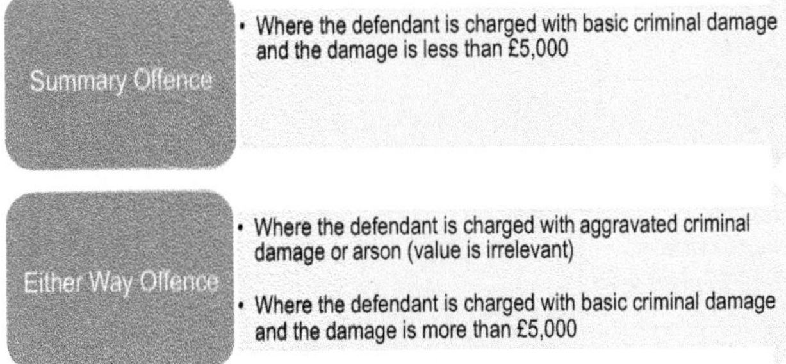

Summary Offence
• Where the defendant is charged with basic criminal damage and the damage is less than £5,000
Either Way Offence
• Where the defendant is charged with aggravated criminal damage or arson (value is irrelevant)
• Where the defendant is charged with basic criminal damage and the damage is more than £5,000

Figure 14.4 Charging criminal damage

The value of £5,000 is taken from s 22 of the Magistrates' Courts Act 1980. The Mode of Trial Guidelines (which applies to a value over £5,000) state that, in general, cases should be tried summarily unless one or more of the following features are present, and the court's sentencing powers are insufficient:

- deliberate fire-raising;
- committed by a group;
- damage of a high value; and
- the offence has a clear racial motive.

14.2.5.2 Sentencing

The sentencing for criminal damage depends ultimately on the type of criminal damage with which the defendant is charged. **Table 14.5** details the punishment for each offence.

Table 14.5 Sentencing criminal damage

Offence	Punishment
Basic criminal damage	Summarily: Maximum 6 months' imprisonment On indictment: Maximum 10 years' imprisonment (CDA 1971, s 4(2))
Aggravated criminal damage Basic arson Aggravated arson	Summarily: Maximum 6 months' imprisonment On indictment: Maximum life imprisonment (CDA 1971, s 4(1))

14.2.6 Putting together criminal damage

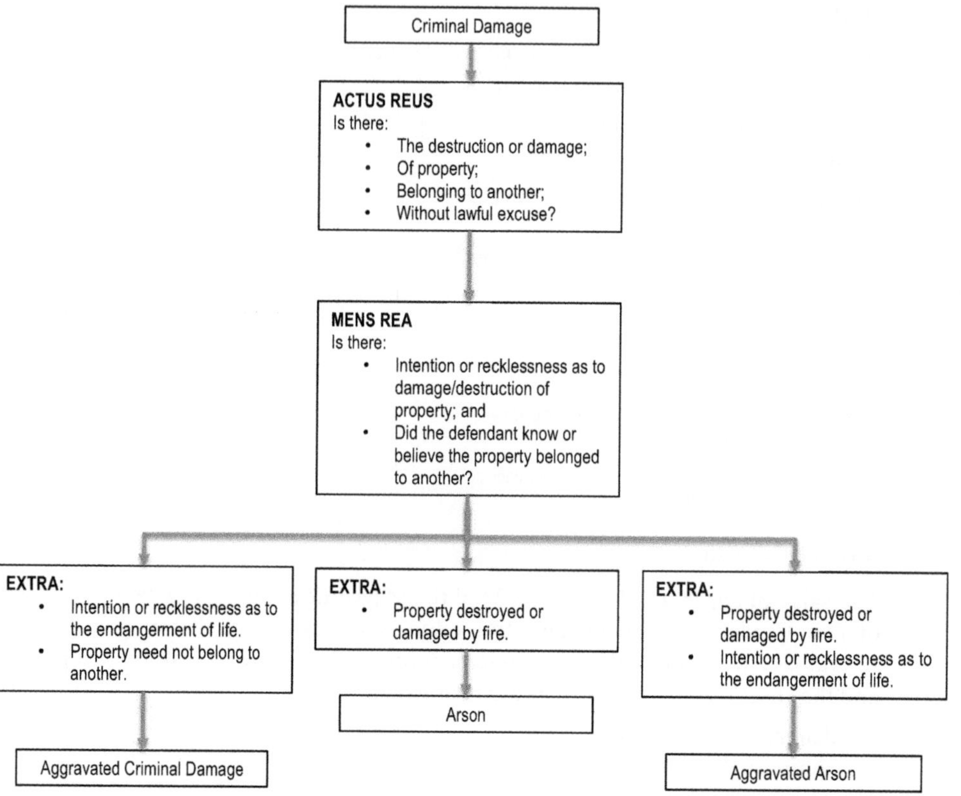

Figure 14.5 Putting together criminal damage

Consider this issue and think of how you may structure an answer to it. Then see the figure above for a sample structure to adopt.

facts

Jill, upset that her husband, Jack, has left her for another woman, visits Jack at his new home. Whilst there, Jill begins to claim certain items in the house including a digital radio, a computer console and a number of books. Jill says to Jack, 'I bought these for you, so they're mine.' Having collected all of the items, Jill begins to destroy them by kicking and stomping on them. In doing so, Jill causes the computer console to spark and then set on fire. Jill runs from the house, leaving Jack to attempt to extinguish the fire.

14.3 Further reading

Basic criminal damage

Alldridge, 'Incontinent Dogs and the Law' (1990) 140 NLJ 1067.

Edwards, 'Banksy's Graffiti: A Not-so-simple Case of Criminal Damage?' [2009] 73 J Crim L 345.

Elliott, 'Criminal Damage' [1988] Crim LR 403.

Stallworthy, 'Damage to Crops' (2000) 150 NLJ 728.

Wasik, 'Criminal Damage/Criminal Mischief' [1988] 17 A-ALR 37.

Watson, 'Graffiti—Popular Art, Anti-Social Behaviour or Criminal Damage' (2004) 168 JP 668.

Williams, 'Two Nocturnal Blunders' [1990] 140 NLJ 1564.

Aggravated criminal damage

Duff, 'Criminalising Endangerment' (2005) 65 La L Rev 941.

Elliott, 'Endangering Life by Destroying or Damaging Property' [1997] Crim LR 382.

- Damage to property is a separate and distinct offence from theft and related offences.
- Criminal damage is an umbrella term to encompass four different offences.
- Criminal damage may be basic or aggravated and, if committed by fire, is to be charged as arson.
- A specific defence of 'lawful excuse' is available to a charge of basic criminal damage and basic arson. For the aggravated forms of these offences, the defendant may only rely on the general defences.

test your knowledge

Problem question

Jack is angry at his wife, Jill, for committing adultery. In a fit of rage, Jack smashes the television set bought by Jill and throws her mobile telephone out of the window, causing a cracked screen. Jack further urinates on Jill's laptop, which, however, causes no damage to the laptop in any sense. Further to this, Jack starts a small fire using some old newspaper. The fire fails to spread and is easily extinguished by Jill.

The police arrive and arrest Jack. Advise Jack as to his potential liability for damage to property.

Essay question

Critically discuss the offence of criminal damage, both in its basic and aggravated forms, and assess whether the offence requires reform and, if so, in what areas.

INDEX